ROUTLEDGE HANDBOOK OF INTOXICANTS AND INTOXICATION

Bringing together scholars from different disciplines in the humanities and social sciences, this multidisciplinary Handbook offers a comprehensive critical overview of intoxicants and intoxication.

The Handbook is divided into 34 chapters across eight thematic sections covering a wide range of issues, including the meanings of intoxicants; the social life of intoxicants; intoxication settings; intoxication practices; alternative approaches to the study of intoxication; scapegoated intoxicants; discourses shaping intoxication; and changing notions of excess. It explores a range of different intoxicants, including alcohol, tobacco, coffee, tea, and legal and illicit drugs, including amphetamine, cannabis, ecstasy, khat, methadone, and opiates. Chapter length case studies explore these intoxicants in a variety of countries, including the USA, the UK, Australia, Bosnia & Herzegovina, Brazil, Denmark, Ireland, Japan, Kyrgyzstan, Nigeria, Singapore, and Sweden, across a broad timespan covering the nineteenth century to the present day.

This wide-ranging Handbook will be of great interest to researchers, students, and instructors within the humanities and social sciences with an interest in a wide range of different intoxicants and different intoxication practices.

Geoffrey Hunt is a Professor at the Centre for Alcohol and Drugs Research at Aarhus University, Denmark, and Director of the Institute for Scientific Analysis in San Francisco, USA.

Tamar M.J. Antin is the Founder and Director of the Center for Critical Public Health and a Senior Research Scientist at the Institute for Scientific Analysis in San Francisco, USA.

Vibeke Asmussen Frank is a Professor at the Centre for Alcohol and Drug Research at Aarhus University, Denmark.

ROUTLEDGE HANDBOOK OF INTOXICANTS AND INTOXICATION

Edited by
Geoffrey Hunt, Tamar M.J. Antin
and Vibeke Asmussen Frank

Routledge
Taylor & Francis Group
LONDON AND NEW YORK

Cover image: Christopher G Schultz, Adelaide, South Australia, Australia

First published 2023
by Routledge
4 Park Square, Milton Park, Abingdon, Oxon OX14 4RN

and by Routledge
605 Third Avenue, New York, NY 10158

Routledge is an imprint of the Taylor & Francis Group, an Informa business

British Library Cataloguing-in-Publication Data
A catalogue record for this book is available from the British Library

ISBN: 978-0-367-17870-3 (hbk)
ISBN: 978-1-032-32148-6 (pbk)
ISBN: 978-0-429-05814-1 (ebk)

DOI: 10.4324/9780429058141

Typeset in Bembo
by codeMantra

The Open Access version of chapter 15 was funded by
a grant from the Faculty of International and Political Studies under the Strategic Programme Excellence Initiative at Jagiellonian University.

The Open Access version of chapter 31 was funded by
University College Dublin.

CONTENTS

List of figures *x*
List of tables *xi*
List of contributors *xii*
Acknowledgements *xxii*

Introduction 1
Geoffrey Hunt, Tamar Antin and Vibeke Asmussen Frank

PART I
The Terrain of Intoxication **17**

1 Intoxications and their meanings 19
Craig Reinarman

2 Nic'd up: a practice theory approach to understanding vaping nicotine as intoxication 33
Ruth Lewis, Emily Kaner and Tamar M.J. Antin

3 Recreational drug use as everyday life: explorations of young adults' gendered motivations for taking drugs in Nigeria 51
Emeka W. Dumbili, MaryJane Nnajiofor and Emmanuel C. Ezekwe

4 When the clock takes over: hangovers in twentieth-century British and American fiction and poetry 69
Jonathon Shears

PART II
Social life of intoxicants **87**

5 Intoxicating consumption: Capitalism and the commodification of pleasure 89
Gerda Reith

6 Producing planned hedonism among opiate users in an online drug market 101
Angus Bancroft

7 Craft drinks, connoisseurship and intoxication 113
Thomas Thurnell-Read

8 Ecstasy: A synthetic history of MDMA 127
Peder Clark

PART III
Intoxicating Settings **141**

9 The social work of coffee: coffee consumption in bosnia and herzegovina and the bosnian diaspora 143
Ana Croegaert

10 Expanding intoxication: what can drinking places (c. 1850–1950) tell us about other intoxicants and other sites? 159
James Kneale

11 Join us for drinks: intoxication, work and academic conferences 178
Helen Keane

12 Exploring the motivations and social organisation of intoxication in prison settings 191
Torsten Kolind and Karen Duke

13 How methadone becomes an intoxicant: the making of methadone within prisons in the Kyrgyz Republic 203
Lyu Azbel and Frederick L. Altice

14 Trade-offs between intoxication, safety, and sociability within a drug-consumption facility 221
Esben Houborg and Siv Schjøll Berge

15 Intoxicants in warfare 239
Łukasz Kamieński

PART IV
Intoxication Practices **259**

16 Engaging with drug, set, and setting to understand nicotine use experiences and practices 261
Julia McQuoid

17 'Uninhibited play': the political and pragmatic dimensions of intoxication within queer cultures 272
Kane Race, Kiran Pienaar, Dean Murphy and Toby Lea

18 Ritual to reflexivity – from promotion and problematisation of intoxication to proportionality 290
John O'Brien

PART V
Alternative Approaches for Studying Intoxication **307**

19 Intoxication made visible: the sober sciences of intoxication, euphoria, and overdose in the laboratory 309
Nancy D. Campbell

20 Trip reports: exploring the experience of psychedelic intoxication 328
Jonas Bååth and Johan Nordgren

21 Passion, reason and the politics of intoxication: ontopolitically-oriented approaches to alcohol and other drug intoxication 342
Suzanne Fraser, David Moore, Adrian Farrugia and Renae Fomiatti

PART VI
Scapegoated Substances **359**

22 Alcohol, slavery and race in Brazil during the long nineteenth century 361
Lucas Brunozi Avelar and Deborah Toner

23 Street-level policing, structural violence and habitus: accounts of street-involved cannabis users in Nigeria 382
Ediomo-Ubong E. Nelson

24 Ethnified intoxication – khat use and the Somali community in Sweden 400
Johan Nordgren

25 Symbolic meaning of the amphetamine-type stimulant problem throughout the restoration of Japanese society after WWII: drug control and the construction of the other 412
Akihiko Sato

PART VII
Discourses shaping intoxication and people who use intoxicants 435

26 Risk, intoxication and death: contemporary media framing of drug-related deaths 437
Susanne MacGregor and Betsy Thom

27 Clearing the air: Toxic healthism and cigarette(s) (smoke) as (in)toxicant(s) 457
Qian Hui Tan

28 Fighting intoxication and addiction: international drug control as a self-perpetuating social system 468
Axel Klein

29 Handling complexity: constituting the relationship between intoxication and violence in Australian alcohol policy discourse 484
David Moore, Helen Keane, Duane Duncan and Emily Lenton

PART VIII
Notions of Excess 499

30 Altered states: changing conditions of excess in European drinking cultures 501
Dorota Dias-Lewandowska, Laura Fenton, Sam Goodman and Beat Kümin

31 From 'Pledge' to 'Public Health': medical Responses to Ireland's Drinking Culture, c. 1890–2018 523
Alice Mauger

32 'Drinking Himself to Death': the Chronic Drunkard in British Mid-Victorian Fiction and Culture 542
Pam Lock

33 Tea, addiction and late Victorian narratives of degeneration, c. 1860–1900 564
Ian Miller

34 Conceiving addiction: historical constructions of chronic intoxicant use 581
David Clemis

Index *601*

FIGURES

8.1 Central Office of Information 'Drugs: sometimes the after effects never wear off', 1990 128
9.1 Ismeta Buffet Display Qur'an Bosnian landscape painting džezva fildžan šešerluk 144
9.2 Tatjana and Mahira interview 148
9.3 Mostar market stall with džezve, mlinovi, and souvenirs 149
9.4 ŠTO TE NEMA Chicago installation 2017 154
22.1 Carte du Brésil 363
22.2 HARRO-HARING, Paul. Scene at a tavern: sailors trade with black women. Tropical sketches of Brazil, 1840. Available in: Paul Harro-Harring - Instituto Moreira Salles (ims.com.br) 368
22.3 Brahma Bull-Bock Advertisement 375
22.4 Brahma-Porter Advertisement 376
22.5 Companhia Cervejaria Brahma Advertisement 376
22.6 Bock-Ale Teutonia Advertisement 377
25.1 Number of arrests for violation of drug laws in Japan 1951–2019 414
27.1 Interior of a designated smoking point in Yishun, Singapore 460
27.2 A designated smoking point in Yishun, Singapore 461
27.3 Inside a designated smoking point in Yishun, Singapore 462
30.1 Extract from Barthel Beham, 'Country Fair' (woodcut, *c.* 1530) 505
30.2 Aleksander Orłowski, 'Uczta u Radziwiłłów', first half of the nineteenth century 507
30.3 Aleksander Orłowski, 'Zabawa w karczmie', 1800 509

TABLES

2.1 Pathways of nicotine product use among participants in each study 36
2.2 Practice elements identified within young adults' accounts of vaping nicotine via second- and third-generation devices (i.e. pre-pod-based systems) in California in 2016–2017 38
3.1 Sociodemographic data of the participants 54
23.1 Cannabis seizure and arrest of traffickers by the NDLEA (2010–2015) 384
23.2 Socio-demographic characteristics of the participants (n = 97) 388
25.1 Rate of prosecution (The White Paper on Crime 1960: 110) 425
25.2 Number of violent and crime syndicates 1963–1972 (made by the author based on The White Paper on Police 1973) 427
26.1 Examples of estimated DRDs by country and date 439
26.2 Themes and evidence sources in UK newspapers 448
26.3 Illustrations of coverage in national newspapers 449
26.4 Illustrations of coverage in local newspapers 451

CONTRIBUTORS

Frederick L. Altice is a Professor of Medicine, Epidemiology and Public Health at Yale University where he serves as the Director of Clinical and Community Research, the Community Health Care Van and the HIV in Prisons Program. His research training is in implementation science, decision science, behavioral interventions with expertise on intervention adaptation implementation science, including development and adaption of HIV prevention and treatment interventions and expanding evidence-based practices into real-world community settings. He is interested in the creation of novel prevention and treatment programs for the treatment of HIV, viral hepatitis, tuberculosis, and substance use disorders in vulnerable populations, including people who inject drugs, criminal justice populations, men who have sex with men and both female and transgender sex workers. Dr. Altice has spent considerable time devoted to developing and studying integrated systems of care, including integrating medication-assisted therapies such as methadone, buprenorphine, and extended-release naltrexone into managing co-morbid conditions, including people living with or at risk for HIV, HCV, tuberculosis, and mental illness. As the time from evidence to dissemination often exceeds 17 years, his recent interests have been on how to work with individuals and systems to shorten this gap. Dr. Altice is currently leading studies in Ukraine, Eastern Europe, Central Asia, Malaysia, Indonesia, Peru, and the United States.

Tamar M.J. Antin is the Founder and Director of the Center for Critical Public Health and a Senior Research Scientist at the Institute for Scientific Analysis in San Francisco, USA. An applied anthropologist, her research focuses on the social and cultural meanings of alcohol, tobacco, and other drug use for groups of people typically left at the margins in mainstream public health research, including youth of color, LGBTQ+ adults, and people living in rural communities. Her work explores the role of stigma in public health practice and policy-making and draws attention to the structures within which health practices are embedded and highlights the social processes that lead to inequities in health. She conducts primarily large-scale qualitative research studies and has received funding from the National Institutes of Health, the California Tobacco-Related Disease Research Program, and the Substance Abuse and Mental Health Services Administration.

Lucas Brunozi Avelar is a Social and Cultural Historian of alcohol, drugs and taverns in the Americas. His current research examines the origins and development of tavern culture in Brazil, and the history of cachaça in a global perspective. His recent publication is 'Bebidas: conceitos fundamentais' (Senac, 2020).

Lyu Azbel is a Public Health Sociologist exploring how medical interventions translate into new settings. As a postdoctoral fellow at Yale University, they use qualitative methods to unpack the social relations of treatment, especially where drug use, infectious diseases, and incarceration intersect. Their work tackles some of the most stubborn impasses to implementing harm reduction interventions at the heart of the world's fastest growing HIV epidemic in Eastern Europe and Central Asia. The theoretical takeaways from their research generate a space where new forms of treatment are possible.

Jonas Bååth is an assistant professor at the Department of People and Society at SLU Alnarp and a researcher affiliated to the Department of Service Studies and CIRCLE – Center for Innovation Research, both at Lund University. He holds a doctorate in sociology from Uppsala University. His research draws on qualitative methods to connect economic sociology with agri-food and intoxicants research. Current projects study the role of alcohol policy in everyday service work on licensed premises and how customers and suppliers co-create alternative markets. His work has appeared in journals such as *Journal of Rural Studies, Food Culture & Society,* and *Socio-Economic Review.*

Angus Bancroft is a Lecturer in Sociology at the University of Edinburgh. He teaches on illicit markets, intoxication and criminology. He blogs about teaching and research at https://blogs.ed.ac.uk/darkmatters/. His most recent book is Angus Bancroft, *The Darknet and Smarter Crime: Methods for Investigating Criminal Entrepreneurs and the Illicit Drug Economy* (2020), Palgrave Macmillan and he also published a novel of sociological ideas with Ralph Fevre: Angus Bancroft and Ralph Fevre (2016) *Dead White Men and Other Important People*, 2nd edition.

Siv Schjøll Berge has an MA in cross cultural studies from the University of Copenhagen, Denmark. Her area of interest lies within the fields of social processes and identity, especially what constitutes possible roles for individuals, but also organizations. Through her previous work at the Center for Alcohol and Drug Research, she focused at the area of drug treatment and harm reduction. A knowledge she has brought into her current job as a development consultant in The Coordinating Unit in Drug Treatment Copenhagen in The Municipality of Copenhagen.

Nancy D. Campbell is a Professor and Department Head of Science and Technology Studies at Rensselaer Polytechnic Institute in Troy, New York, where she has taught for over two decades. Her most recent book is *OD: Naloxone and the Politics of Overdose Prevention* (MIT Press, 2020). She was a FRIAS Senior Fellow and Marie Curie Fellow of the European Union at the Freiburg Institute for Advanced Studies (FRIAS) in 2017–2018. She is one of three editors of the *Journal of the Social History of Alcohol and Drugs*. Her books include *Discovering Addiction: The Science and Politics of Substance Abuse Research* (University of Michigan Press, 2007); *Gendering Addiction: The Politics of Drug Treatment in a Neurochemical World* (co-authored with Elizabeth Ettorre; Palgrave, 2011); *The Narcotic Farm: The Rise and Fall of America's First Prison for Drug Addicts* (co-authored with JP Olsen and Luke Walden; Abrams, 2008); and *Using Women: Gender, Drug Policy, and Social Justice* (Routledge, 2000).

Peder Clark is a Historian of health and drugs in modern Britain, based at the University of Strathclyde, Glasgow. He started his Wellcome Trust funded Research Fellowship "'The Effects Can Last Forever': Ecstasy's Risks and Pleasures in Britain, 1985–2000" in October 2021.

David Clemis is an Associate Professor of history at Mount Royal University, Calgary, Canada. His research focuses on understandings of alcohol intoxication and conceptions of craving, habit and addiction in the seventeenth and eighteenth centuries. He is the author of "'Great Annoyance to Their Mindes': the Humours, Intoxication, and Addiction in English Medical and Moral Discourses, 1550–1730," in Kaara L. Peterson and Amy Kenny, eds., *Humorality in Early Modern Art, Material Culture, and Performance* (London: Palgrave/Macmillan, 2021); "Medical Expertise and the Understandings of Intoxication in Britain, 1660 to 1830," in Jonathan Herring, Ciaran Regan, Darin Weinberg, and Phil Withington, eds., *Intoxication and Society: Problematic Pleasures*, (London: Palgrave, 2013); and "The History and Culture of Alcohol and Drinking: 18th Century" and "The History of Addiction and Alcoholism" in Scott C. Martin, ed., *"Alcohol: Social, Cultural, and Historical Perspectives"* (Thousand Oaks, CA: SAGE, 2015).

Ana Croegaert received her PhD in Cultural Anthropology from Northwestern University and conducts research focused on gender, material and expressive culture, and inequality. She has published on a range of topics, including refugee migration, coffee rituals, contested public space, street parades, monuments and memorials, and racism in Chicago, New Orleans, and Bosnia-Herzegovina. Croegaert is a research affiliate with the Field Museum of Natural History in Chicago.

Dorota Dias-Lewandowska is an Anthropologist and Historian, Assistant Professor at the Institute of Archaeology and Anthropology, Polish Academy of Science in Warsaw. Her research interest evolved from the early modern history of alcohol and Polish culinary recipes to drinking cultures, and discourses concerning sobriety and drunkenness among women in the 19th century.

Karen Duke is a Professor of Criminology and Co-Director of the Drug and Alcohol Research Centre at Middlesex University, UK. She is a Criminologist and Policy Analyst, specialising in research on drugs policy and the interfaces with the criminal justice system. She has conducted research and consultancy for the European Commission, UNODC, Home Office, Department of Health, the former Central Drugs Co-ordination Unit (Cabinet Office) and the Royal Society for the Arts. She is one of the Editors-in-Chief of the journal, *Drugs: Education, Prevention and Policy.*

Emeka W. Dumbili is a Lecturer in Sociology working at the Nnamdi Azikiwe University. Emeka is currently an Alexander von Humboldt Research Fellow at the Institute for Therapy and Health Research, Kiel, Germany. His research focuses on the sociology of drug use, gender and sexuality, social theory, qualitative methodology, and public health.

Duane Duncan is a Lecturer in Sociology at the University of New England. His research interests include gender, sexuality and men's health, including a recent role as a Research Fellow at the Australian Research Centre in Sex, Health and Society at La Trobe University on an Australian Research Council-funded project analysing the handling of gender in alcohol research and policy.

Emmanuel C. Ezekwe is currently a Research Assistant at the Department of Sociology and Anthropology, Nnamdi Azikiwe University, Awka, Nigeria. His research interests are in the areas of Alcohol, Drugs, Health Policies and Development.

Adrian Farrugia is a Research Fellow in the Drugs, Gender and Sexuality (DruGS) program at the Australian Research Centre in Sex, Health and Society at La Trobe University. He specialises in the sociological analysis of health initiatives such as hepatitis C treatment uptake, health education for young people and take-home naloxone for people who consume opioids.

Laura Fenton is a Sociologist. Her PhD investigated the drinking biographies of three generations of British women against the backdrop of changes in the role of alcohol in women's lives. She is currently working as a Research Associate at the Universities of Sheffield and Manchester. Her research interests include youth, gender, alcohol, the life course, and biographical methods.

Renae Fomiatti is a Research Officer in the Drugs, Gender and Sexuality (DruGS) program at the Australian Research Centre in Sex, Health and Society at La Trobe University. She conducts qualitative research on alcohol and other drug consumption and recovery, health and gender. Her research is informed by contemporary feminist theory and Science and Technology Studies. She previously held an appointment at the National Drug Research Institute, Curtin University.

Vibeke Asmussen Frank is a Professor at the Centre for Alcohol and Drug Research at Aarhus University, Denmark. She has been working within the social science drug and alcohol research field for over 20 years. Her main areas of research include user perspectives on different kinds of drug consumption, policy processes related to drug control, drug-reducing interventions and harm reduction initiatives, and young people's alcohol intoxication as well as use of N_2O for intoxication. She is the author of numerous articles and co-editor of *Drug Policy: History, Theory & Consequences* (Aarhus University Press, 2009) and *Markets, Methods and Messages: Dynamics in European Drug Research* (Pabst, 2011).

Suzanne Fraser is a Professor and Director of the Australian Research Centre in Sex, Health and Society, at La Trobe University. She has published widely on drug use and related issues, and is currently working on research projects on hepatitis C treatment and stigma in healthcare.

Sam Goodman is an Associate Professor in English & Communications at Bournemouth University, UK. His research interests centre around productions of Britishness and identity across literature, culture and society, the relationship between alcohol and medicine, and the medical humanities.

Esben Houborg is an Associate Professor at the Centre for Alcohol and Drug Research, School of Business and Social Sciences, Aarhus University, Denmark. His main areas of research include drug policy in a historical and contemporary perspective, criminological research particularly concerning law enforcement, sociological research in the areas of drug treatment and harm reduction and urban studies of drug-related issues.

Geoffrey Hunt is a Professor at the Centre for Alcohol and Drugs Research at Aarhus University, Denmark, and Director of the Institute for Scientific Analysis in San Francisco, USA. He is also the Principal Investigator on a US National Institute of Health-funded project on rural drinking and intoxication amongst young adults as well as two research projects in Denmark. A social and cultural anthropologist, he has published extensively on substance abuse, especially alcohol and drug use and evaluating community prevention and intervention programs. He is the co-author of *Youth, Drugs, and Nightlife* (Routledge, 2010) and the co-editor of *Drugs and Culture: Knowledge, Consumption and Policy* (Routledge, 2011) and *Handbook of Drug and Alcohol Studies* (Sage, 2016).

Łukasz Kamieński is a Professor at the Faculty of International and Political Studies, Jagiellonian University, Kraków, Poland. His work concentrates on military technology and military transformation, the history and the future of war, the military profession, and biotechnology and military human enhancement. He is an author of *Shooting Up. A Short History of Drugs and War* (OUP, 2016).

Emily Kaner is a Research Associate at the Center for Critical for Public Health and an MPH/MCP candidate at the University of California, Berkeley. Her research explores the meanings and social environmental contexts of substance use with adolescents and young adults. She is interested in the structural determinants of health, the intersection of health and place and the use of mixed methods in research.

Helen Keane is a Professor in the School of Sociology at the Australian National University in Canberra, Australia. She works on critical and qualitative approaches to drug use, with a current focus on tobacco and alcohol. She has a particular interest in concepts of addiction and critical addiction studies, with additional expertise in feminist theory. She is the co-author *of Habits: Remaking Addiction* (Palgrave Macmillan, 2014) with Suzanne Fraser and David Moore. This book builds on her earlier work *What's Wrong with Addiction?* (New York University Press, 2002).

Torsten Kolind is trained as an anthropologist. He is a Professor in drug and alcohol research and also the Director of Centre of Alcohol and Drug Research, Aarhus University, Denmark. He has a long experience in planning, conducting and managing research within the drug and alcohol field. He has published widely in the fields of criminal justice, prisons, ethnicity, young people, drug treatment, alcohol and drugs. He is one of the Editors-in-Chief of the journal *Drug: Education, Prevention and Policy.* He is the editor of The SAGE Handbook of Drug and Alcohol Studies from 2017.

Axel Klein is a Social Anthropologist with a longstanding interest in altered states and institutional efforts to gain benefit in some shape and form. Successive studies of 'drug complexes', be this cannabis in the Caribbean (Caribbean Drugs, 2004) or khat in Eastern Africa (The khat Controversy, 2007), have confirmed his viewpoint that altered states perform critical socio-cultural functions, and that prohibition is a policy perversity pursued solely for institutional and professional benefit (Drugs and the World, 2009; Collapse of the Global Order on Drugs, 2018). He is currently working in West Africa and a Fellow of the Global Drug Policy Observatory at the University of Swansea, UK.

James Kneale is a Cultural and Historical Geographer at UCL. He has longstanding interests in histories and geographies of drinking and temperance, and is currently working on the connections between life assurance, temperance, and medicine in Britain between 1840 and 1918. He is a co-editor of *Journal of Victorian Studies*.

Beat Kümin is a Professor of Early Modern European History at the University of Warwick, UK. His research interests focus on social, religious and political exchange in local communities, particularly in the German lands. Publications include the monograph *Drinking Matters: Public Houses and Social Exchange in Early Modern Central Europe* (2007) and the edited collection *A Cultural History of Food in the Early Modern Age* (2012). Alongside, he leads the 'Food & Drink Cultures' theme of Warwick's research priority on 'Food' and co-edits the book series 'Cultures of Early Modern Europe' for Bloomsbury.

Toby Lea is an Adjunct Lecturer in the Centre for Social Research in Health, the University of New South Wales (UNSW) Sydney, Australia. He is an applied social health researcher focused on the use of psychedelics as novel therapies for mental health, and substance use and harm reduction among sexual and gender minority people.

Emily Lenton is a Research and Project Officer at the Australian Research Centre in Sex, Health and Society, La Trobe University. She works on projects in both the Gender, Law and Drugs, and Drugs, Gender and Sexuality research programs, and the BBV Sector Development Program.

Ruth Lewis is a public health sociologist based at the MRC/CSO Social and Public Health Sciences Unit, at the University of Glasgow. Her research aims to explore how social relationships and identities shape health and wellbeing, and how to translate these understandings into interventions to improve population health. Much of her work focuses on young people, often using qualitative methodologies and participatory approaches to co-produce knowledge and expertise. Ruth holds degrees from the University of Leeds (BA Hons, Geography) and the University of Edinburgh (MSc Social Research; PhD Sociology). Prior to joining the University of Glasgow, Ruth worked at the University of Edinburgh, the London School of Hygiene and Tropical Medicine, and the University of the Pacific.

Pam Lock is a Lecturer at the University of Bristol. She has published a number of articles and chapters on the representation of drinking in British Victorian fiction and her monograph entitled *The Drunkard in Victorian Fiction and Culture* will be out with Edinburgh University Press in 2023. Pam is a co-Director of the Drinking Studies Network, co-lead with Dorota Dias-Lewandowska on the NCN-funded project 'Hidden Representations of Women's Drinking in Polish and British Public Discourses in the second half of the 19th Century', and Associate Editor for the ADHS Journal, *The Social History of Alcohol and Drugs*.

Alice Mauger is a UCD Wellcome Trust Postdoctoral Fellow at the Centre for the History of Medicine in Ireland, School of History, University College Dublin. Her current research explores "Patient Narratives of Alcohol Addiction in Ireland, c. 1960–2020". Prior to this, she completed a Wellcome Trust funded postdoctoral project entitled "Alcohol, Medicine and Irish Society, 1890–1970". She has published and taught on the history of medicine, psychiatry and alcohol(ism). Her first monograph, *The Cost of Insanity: Public, Voluntary and Private Asylum Care in Nineteenth-Century Ireland*, was published by Palgrave Macmillan in

2018. She completed a PhD at the UCD Centre for the History of Medicine in Ireland on this topic.

Susanne MacGregor is a Fellow of the Academy of Social Sciences. She is an Honorary Professor at the London School of Hygiene and Tropical Medicine, University of London, attached to the Centre for History in Public Health. She is also a Professor Emerita at Middlesex University London, attached to the Drug and Alcohol Research Centre. Her first degree was in Social Anthropology and her second in Politics, both from the University of Edinburgh. She has researched and taught in humanities and social sciences in Departments of Social Anthropology, Politics, Social Psychiatry, Sociology, Social Policy and Public Health. Her research has focused on social issues and political and policy responses, especially poverty, homelessness, unemployment, drug and alcohol use, and urban change. Her recent publications include *The Politics of Drugs: Perceptions, Power and Policies* Palgrave Macmillan 2017 and *Risk and Substance Use: Framing Dangerous People and Dangerous Places* (edited with Betsy Thom) Routledge Studies in the Sociology of Health and Illness 2020. She is currently researching drug-related deaths in English prisons.

Julia McQuoid is an Assistant Professor at the TSET Health Promotion Research Center and the Department of Family and Preventive Medicine at the University of Oklahoma Health Sciences Center (OUHSC). She is a health geographer interested in creative approaches to understanding relationships between people's everyday environments and health behaviors. Her research examines the everyday patterns, contexts, and motivations linked to tobacco and other substance use for priority groups. Her work has contributed to understanding and explaining sexual and gender minority tobacco use disparities. She recently received an American Cancer Society Institutional Research Grant to integrate mobile health and qualitative mapping methods to study multiple substance use in rural Oklahoma. Julia was a California Tobacco-Related Disease Research Program Fellow while completing her postdoctoral fellowship at the University of California, San Francisco. She co-founded and co-directs the OUHSC Qualitative Methods Community of Practice.

Ian Miller is a Lecturer in Medical History at Ulster University and PI on the project www.epidemic-belfast.com. He has published a medical history textbook with Palgrave Macmillan. Earlier books include *A Modern History of the Stomach: Medicine, Gastric Illness and British Society, c. 1800–1945* (2011), *Reforming Food in Post-Famine Ireland: Medicine, Science and Improvement* (2014) and *Water: A Global History* (2015). He has been awarded the Distinguished Research Fellowship at Ulster University and is a book review editor for *Social History of Medicine* journal.

David Moore is a Professorial Research Fellow in the Australian Research Centre in Sex, Health and Society at La Trobe University. He has published extensively in key sociological and health journals on youth, gender, alcohol and other drug use, addiction concepts and drug policy. David is the author of *The Lads in Action: Social Process in an Urban Youth Subculture* (Arena, 1994), and (with Suzanne Fraser and Helen Keane) *Habits: Remaking Addiction* (Palgrave, 2014). He also edited (with Paul Dietze) *Drugs and Public Health: Australian Perspectives on Policy and Practice* (Oxford University Press, 2008) and (with Suzanne Fraser) *The Drug Effect: Health, Crime and Society* (Cambridge University Press, 2011).

Dean Murphy is a Research Fellow at The Kirby Institute UNSW, and the Department of Infectious Diseases, Alfred Hospital. His work focuses on biomedical HIV prevention technologies, stigma, HIV diagnosis, experiences of sexual health and well-being, and the meanings of drug consumption. His book, *Gay Men Pursuing Parenthood through Surrogacy: Reconfiguring Kinship*, was published in 2015.

Ediomo-Ubong E. Nelson, trained as a health sociologist, is the African research project lead for the Global Drug Policy Observatory, based at Swansea University, United Kingdom. He is also an associate researcher with the Centre for Research and Information on Substance Abuse in Nigeria. His research explores how criminal justice and public health intersects, with a focus on socially marginalized populations (e.g. sex workers and people who use drugs). His latest research investigates the structural and health system drivers of prescription opioid misuse among socially marginalized women with chronic pain. Besides research, he is actively involved in advocacy for evidence-based, public health-centered drug policies in Africa. In this capacity, he currently serves as the alcohol and other drug policy advisor to the International Blue Cross, based in Bern, Switzerland.

MaryJane Nnajiofor is a Sociologist with interests in alcohol and other drug use, gender, and sexuality. She served as a Research Assistant at the Centre for Alcohol and Other Drug Research (CfADR), Department of Sociology/Anthropology, Nnamdi Azikiwe University, Awka, Nigeria, in 2018–2019.

Johan Nordgren is a Senior Lecturer at the Department of Social Work, Malmö University, Sweden. He has conducted research about khat use, synthetic cannabinoids, codependency, drug law enforcement and online drug dealing. His current research project concerns urban drug scenes in Malmö, Sweden and how people who use drugs experience everyday life and how social work- and health care professionals and the police may affect marginalization. He teaches social work practice and theories in the field of problematic drug use.

John O'Brien is a Lecturer in Sociology at Waterford Institute of Technology. He received his PhD from the Department of Sociology in University College Cork. His research interests focus on historical sociology, the use and regulation of alcohol, alcohol and crime, sociability, and classical and contemporary sociological theory. His recent research has looked at the role of alcohol in the construction of public problems and how the Covid-19 Pandemic has affected sociability and drinking culture. He is the author of 'States of Intoxication' (Routledge), which looks at the role of alcohol in state formation processes. He is the President of the Sociological Association of Ireland.

Kiran Pienaar is a Lecturer in Sociology at Deakin University, Melbourne, Australia. Kiran's research explores connections between health, gender, sexuality and the body, with a particular interest in drug consumption and sexual cultures, and the sociopolitical dimensions of health. She has published on topics related to drugs, addiction and the self; the biopolitics of disease; public health and drug policy; and drug experiences in LGBTQ cultures. Her first book *Politics in the Making of HIV/AIDS in South Africa* was published with Palgrave Macmillan.

Kane Race is a Professor of Gender and Cultural Studies at the University of Sydney. His work has explored embodied engagements with medicine in the context of sexual stigma, as well as changing forms of sexual sociability in the digital context. He is the author of *The Gay Science: Intimate Experiments with the Problem of HIV* (Routledge, 2018); *Plastic Water: The*

Social and Material Life of Bottled Water (MIT Press, 2015), co-authored with Gay Hawkins and Emily Potter, and *Pleasure Consuming Medicine: The Queer Politics of Drugs* (Duke University Press, 2009).

Craig Reinarman is a Professor Emeritus of Sociology and Legal Studies at the University of California, Santa Cruz. He was a Post-Doctoral Fellow at the Alcohol Research Group in the School of Public Health at the University of California, Berkeley. He has been a visiting professor at the University of Amsterdam and the University of Utrecht, a visiting scholar at the Center for Drug Research at the University of Amsterdam, and a principal investigator on research grants from the National Institute of Drug Abuse and the National Institute of Justice. He has also been a consultant to the World Health Organization's Substance Abuse Program and a member of the Board of Directors of the College on Problems of Drug Dependence. Dr. Reinarman is the author of *American States of Mind* (Yale University Press, 1987) and co-author of *Cocaine Changes* (Temple University Press, 1991) and *Crack in America* (University of California Press, 1997). His most recent book is a co-edited anthology of critical addiction studies called *Expanding Addiction* (Routledge 2015).

Gerda Reith is a Professor of Social Science at the University of Glasgow. She conducts research and writes on issues relating to addiction, risk and excess, and their relation to wider issues of behaviour and governance in global consumer societies. Gerda is particularly interested in the factors influencing gambling behaviour and its regulation, and has carried out numerous projects exploring the ways that behaviour changes over time, and the role of the social, physical and commercial environment on those changes. Gerda's research has been funded by a variety of academic, governmental and charitable organisations, including the Economic and Social Research Council, the Medical Research Council, the Australian Research Council, the British Academy and the National Institute for Health Research (NIHR). She has published extensively on these topics, and her work has been translated into a number of languages, including Korean, Chinese, Spanish and Hungarian. Her book, *The Age of Chance: Gambling in Western Culture*, won the Philip Abrams Prize in 2000. Her latest book is *Addictive Consumption: Capitalism, Modernity and Excess*, and is published by Routledge.

Akihiko Sato is a Professor of Sociology, School of Sociology at Kwansei Gakuin University, Japan. He has been studying both legal and illegal drug problems for thirty years. He is the author of *Drug and Discourse: Methamphetamine in Japan* (*Kakuseizai no Shakaishi, Toshindo, Tokyo, Japan*, published in Japanese, Japanese Association of Social Problems Academic Promotion Award (2007) and 7th Japanese Association of Sociological Criminology Promotion Award (2008)), and *Sociology of Drugs: Psychoactive substances and social order* (*Drug no Shakaigaku, Sekaishisosha, Kyoto, Japan*, published in Japanese). He has published many articles and book chapters on drug problems and drug policies, including "Methamphetamine use in Japan after the Second World War: Transformation of narratives", *Contemporary Drug Problems*, 35/Winter 2008, 717–746, 2009, and "Methamphetamine users and the process of condemnation in Japan: framing and influence" in S. MacGregor and B. Thom eds., *Risk and Substance Use: Framing Dangerous Places and Dangerous People*, Routledge, 2020. He is a member of the editorial board of Japanese Sociological Review.

Jonathon Shears is a Senior Lecturer in English Literature at Keele University, UK. He is the author of *The Hangover: A Literary and Cultural History* (Liverpool University Press,

2020). Besides the representation of alcohol and drinking cultures, he has research interests in poetic influence, ageing in literature, and material culture in the nineteenth century. He specialises in literature of the Romantic period and has published books and many essays on the Romantic poets, especially Lord Byron. From 2012 to 2019, he was the Editor of *The Byron Journal*.

Qian Hui Tan is a PhD student at the Department of Geography, National University of Singapore. Her MA thesis attended to the complexities of smoking spaces and subjectivities in Singapore.

Betsy Thom is a Professor of Health Policy and Co-Director of the Drug and Alcohol Research Centre at Middlesex University. She is also an honorary professor in the Department of Psychology and Behavioural Sciences, Aarhus University, Denmark. She has degrees in modern languages and sociology and has completed certificates in education and in public health. Her doctorate, from the London School of Hygiene and Tropical Medicine, was on the history of alcohol treatment. Her research includes drug and alcohol policy and practice, with current focus on young people, drug-related deaths and co-production approaches to research. She has managed European, national and local research projects and led the development of a cross-national master's programme on drug and alcohol studies. Recent publications include *Risk and Substance Use: Framing Dangerous People and Dangerous Places* (edited with Susanne MacGregor) (2020), Routledge; and *Alcohol, Power and Public Health: A Comparative Study of Alcohol Policy* (co-authored with Butler, Elmeland, Nicholls) (2017), Routledge.

Thomas Thurnell-Read is a Senior Lecturer in Sociology in the School of Social Sciences and Humanities, Loughborough University, UK. His research focuses on the social and cultural aspects of alcohol, drinking and drunkenness. He is the editor of *Drinking Dilemmas: Space, culture and identity* (Routledge, 2015) and co-editor (with Dr Laura Fenton) of *Alcohol, Age, Generation and the Life Course* (Palgrave, 2022).

Deborah Toner is a Social and Cultural Historian of alcohol, food and identity in the Americas. Her current research examines the development and interaction of racial stereotypes about drinking in the United States and Mexico, and the history of substance use disorders in Guyana. She has been the Co-Director of the Drinking Studies Network since 2010, an interdisciplinary research community exploring alcohol and drinking cultures across different societies and time periods.

ACKNOWLEDGEMENTS

The completion of this Handbook would not have been possible without all of the contributors who volunteered their time and expertise to put together a great collection of works that expand our understanding of intoxication and intoxicants. The papers in the Handbook are written by a wide-range of well-known scholars in the field of intoxicant research, and we are delighted to present the insights and data from so many expert scholars. We especially appreciate their patience during the rather long process of completing this Handbook.

We would also like to thank the generosity and commitment of the 67 peer reviewers, who reviewed the 34 chapters. These reviewers donated their valuable time and critical reflections on each chapter within this Handbook in order to help the authors produce their best work. Without their expertise, guidance, and hard work, we would have been unable to produce a Handbook that integrates the critical component of critique in the production of knowledge on intoxication and intoxicants. We would like to thank the following distinguished reviewers for their invaluable contributions to our Handbook:

Angus Bancroft, David Beckingham, Kirsten Bell, Virgina Berridge, David Bewley-Taylor, Mie Birk Haller, Alexandra Bogren, Marie Bræmer, Martin Bruegel, Nancy Campbell, Nate Chapman, Yuet-wah Cheung, Jakob Demant, Fay Dennis, Molly Doane, Tristan Duncan, Erika Dyck, Steve Earnshaw, Bryce Evans, Laura Fenton, Simon Flacks, Joao Florencio, Vibeke Frank, Suzanne Fraser, Pekka Hakkarainen, Marie Jauffret Roustide, Helen Keane, Axel Klein, Philip Lalander, Chris Land, Susanne MacGregor, Sarah MacLean, Elisabeth Malcolm, Scott Martin, Annemarie McAllister, Julia McQuoid, Brett Millier, Tamar M.J. Antin, Kristian Mjåland, Alex Mold, David Moore, Maddy Novich, John O'Brien, Aileen O'Gormann, Jennifer Patico, Craig Reinarman, Lucy Robinson, Sara Rolando, Thomas Søgaard, Bill Sanders, Robert Shaw, Blaine Stohard, Scott Taylor, Lorne Tepperman, Betsy Thom, Thomas Thurnell-Read, Tobias Kammersgaard, Debora Toner, Jukka Törrönen, Torsten Kolind, Birgitte Tylstrup, Marie Van Hout, Jennifer Wallis, Takuya Watanabe, Darin Weinberg, Bernd Werse, and Lisa Williams.

Other people we wish to thank include K.C. McNaughton, our research assistant, who had the task of ensuring that the final manuscript was complete and fitted the requirements of our publisher Routledge, and Gerhard Boomgaarden who, as a commissioning editor, initially approved the Handbook proposal. When Gerhard left Routledge, his position was filled by Rebecca Brennan, who has been both supportive and patient in waiting for us to complete the manuscript. Finally, we would like to acknowledge our families and friends, who have been tremendously supportive during the many months that it took to complete the Handbook. They have all been both sources of support and balance in our lives.

INTRODUCTION

Geoffrey Hunt, Tamar Antin and Vibeke Asmussen Frank

While the topic of intoxication continues today to be a contentious issue between researchers, who trace its endemic and often positive qualities and those, who emphasize its transgressive and pathological nature, an increasing number of scholars have begun to situate contemporary debates on intoxication within a broader context that considers "the longer, more variegated, encompassing and ambiguous history" of intoxications (Withington 2014:20), as well as the contemporary social, cultural, political and economic elements that influence intoxication and the use and practices of intoxicants. Given growing interest in intoxicants and intoxication, it is not surprising that since 2017, when we initially decided to produce this Handbook, new and important contributions have appeared. For example, in 2020 and 2021, the following have been published: *Cultures of Intoxication* (Hutton 2020), *Alcohol and Humans* (Hockings and Dunbar 2020), *Drunk* (Slingerland 2021) and the *Hangover* (Shears 2020; see also Chapter 4). This continuing flow of books on intoxication and related topics does not lessen the importance of our Handbook. Instead, collectively, these contributions highlight one important aim of our Handbook, which is to illustrate the extensive interest in intoxicants and intoxication and similarities in approaches that exist across multiple disciplines, but that so often fail to speak to one another.

The Handbook on intoxicants and intoxication emphasizes the wide-ranging nature of intoxication, providing a perspective that challenges the "silo" approach to the study of intoxicants and intoxication – an aim inspired by the work of Goodman et al. (2005), Bancroft (2009) and Withington and McShane (2014). As a result, we have intentionally avoided concentrating solely on alcohol and illicit drugs – the focus of many previous works – and instead sought to incorporate chapters which highlight various intoxicants, including coffee, tea and prescription drugs, that all, despite their various intoxicants of focus, nevertheless emphasize common themes related to the socio-cultural, contextual, situated, historical and comparative nature of intoxicants and intoxication.

In addition to providing an alternative to the silo approach, we also sought to bring together contributions that avoided a problem perspective, instead examining the multiplicity of intoxicant use among people of different ages, from totally different social backgrounds, in many different cultures, and at so many different times in history. As Rudgley (1993) has documented, people since prehistoric times have sought not only to achieve the happiness, freedom and/or euphoria from psychoactive drugs, but also, like the romantic

DOI: 10.4324/9780429058141-1

writers – Coleridge, De Quincy, Byron and Walter Scott – sought to open up new avenues of poetic inspiration offering "dreams that money can buy" and allowing the transportation "to the realms of imagination" (Boon 2002:37). Hence, our goal was to encourage contributions that adopted a more universal approach which, instead of viewing intoxication as inherently problematic, attempted to map out why the authorities have too often viewed intoxication as "the most harmful of …behaviors with a significant negative impact on individual and community safety and well-being" (Keane 2009:135), or had adopted an approach, which viewed "the goal of artificially inducing a change in one's consciousness" as immoral (Becker, 1967:164), viewing intoxication, from whatever substances, as "at best tolerated … often stigmatized or even criminalized" (Yardley 2012:1). Therefore, the overall purpose of the Handbook was to produce a compendium in which the contributions would locate an understanding of intoxication within the relationships between culture, consumption, politics and society (Sherratt 1995).

With this in mind, we began to contact a number of researchers and scholars, from a wide-range of different social science disciplines, to examine both the historical and contemporary theoretical paradigms and provide an overview of the key elements that social science researchers have identified as important for our understanding of intoxicants and intoxication. In bringing together these researchers from different social science disciplines to discuss a range of different intoxicants, from different parts of the globe, in different historical periods, our aim was to provide the reader with a critical and comprehensive sense of the range of issues, both established and emerging, that scholars have explored. We also hoped that in mapping out this arena, within an international and multi-social science approach, students, junior researchers, as well as established scholars would be encouraged and inspired to explore and develop new research interests.

Finding Contributors

Recruiting a wide-range of contributors conducting research on different intoxicants in different parts of the globe proved to be more challenging than we had initially expected. Having identified and contacted potential contributors, we discovered that while our attempts to recruit alcohol, illicit drugs and tobacco researchers proved to be very successful, finding scholars to write about coffee, tea and other ingested intoxicants was less successful, and we are grateful for those few contributors to our Handbook. The reasons for this may partly be because the three editors themselves are involved in alcohol, illicit drugs and tobacco research and hence less connected with other research arenas looking at other intoxicants. Or it could be that while research funding has been somewhat more plentiful for those of us in drug, alcohol and tobacco research, funding to study other intoxicants is less available. One final additional aim had been to ensure that scholars from different countries, other than the U.S., Europe or Australia, were fully represented in the pages of the Handbook to ensure that "northern theorizing" did not dominate (Connell 2007). While more chapters from the Global South would have been welcome, we nevertheless were able to recruit six excellent contributions focusing on Brazil, Japan, the Kyrgyz Republic, Nigeria and Singapore.

Having identified our contributors, and accepted their initial abstracts, we then waited for the papers to start rolling in. This process always takes much longer than initially planned, in spite of target dates and deadlines being specified. However, we did not expect that the process would be further derailed by the COVID-19 pandemic. As news of the pandemic began to filter in, and as universities and research centers started to close down, we and our contributors began to face new challenges. Many of our potential contributors found themselves, not only needing to learn how to teach their students online while working at home, but also balancing the pressures of their professional lives with the needs of their personal lives, such as managing children while finding time to write. Some of our contributors also fell ill from COVID-19 and then dealt with the slow process of recovery. While some were able to keep the initial deadlines, others fell behind. Consequently, we, as editors, had to adopt a much more flexible and encouraging approach to help all our contributors handle their personal/professional needs, while completing their chapters. Being in contact with our contributors, also meant that we began to learn more about their personal and professional journeys and the various and often competing duties that they were attempting to juggle. During that time, one or two e-mails struck us as accurately portraying the situation that many of our contributors were confronting and the difficulties they faced on a daily basis. For example, one contributor writing to us at the start of pandemic, in explaining their situation, noted:

> I was already behind with my schedule, when the epidemic broke out and for more than two weeks now it has not been possible for me to work on my chapter. I have been confined at home for a week and with my two year old boy around, I am not able to focus on the many things I have to do.

At the end of this e-mail, the contributor forecasts somewhat pessimistically, the future, a prediction which we all discovered was far too optimistic. "It is also clear this situation will last for several weeks and when this period is over, we will have to deal with many complicated issues." As the pandemic continued, and the situation got increasingly dire, this contributor, like many others, began to tell us that their ability to handle their work commitments had worsened, and yet at the same time also expressed the fact that they should not complain:

> we can't really complain, our place is pleasant and not small. However, working is very complicated though, our kid is two and a half years old, it is not easy for him and he requires a lot of attention of course. It is clear he is feeling out of sorts.... Overall, the general atmosphere is uncomfortable, the epidemic is an obsession, the only topic you hear about and the fact that we don't know how long it will last and how violent will the consequences be. That is a gloomy atmosphere.

Another contributor, having asked for a short extension to our latest deadline for the chapter, described their daily lives in the following ways:

> Sorry, for not being in touch...but as you can imagine, things are weird, stressful, uncertain and chaotic, in about equal measure. The University is closed, so it is very strange trying to work at home, often with 3 anxious and demanding kids. Even as I type this e-mail, they're arguing and running around the kitchen, where I work.

This was followed a few months later with another e-mail which again described their situation at home:

> We're deep into another lock-down. The schools are closed again, so it is back to herding the kids. I gave up on home-schooling almost immediately. It's just impossible with the 3 of them all at very different stages, and trying to work at the same time. It is a real challenge trying to balance everything. I try to work early morning and late evening, the rest is just treading water. Hoping things will eventually get back to normal.

Other contributors faced other obstacles in completing their papers. For example, one of them, while completing their chapter, had to deal with helping his aged parents, whose house had been struck by a typhoon and was covered in mud. Visiting his parents every week to restore their house and ensure that his parents were safe and comfortable was certainly more important than a Handbook chapter and eventually the house was restored. Given an extension to the deadline, our contributor completed the chapter, even while dealing with this catastrophe. Nevertheless, instead of receiving the chapters all around one deadline date, they drifted in slowly but always one or two every couple of weeks. Having then received the papers, we faced the next problem: finding two and sometimes three reviewers. Again, given the turmoil brought about by the pandemic, we searched for fellow academics and specialists in specific areas, who were willing to devote some time to reading and commenting on the individual papers, while handling their already burdensome workload. At times, finding willing reviewers was difficult, many either refusing or in some cases never replying to our requests. In fact, one potential reviewer, while expressing her willingness to review, told us that unfortunately she was locked down in a hotel in Southern China without her laptop computer and did not know how long the situation would continue. Nevertheless, the majority of researchers we approached were more than willing to review the papers and offered us their best wishes in completing the Handbook. These reviewers (a list of all the reviewers can be found in Section??) played an important role in the production of this Handbook. Their insightful comments guided the authors' revisions, enabling them to produce a high standard of chapters. This is the background and the momentous historical period in which this Handbook was produced.

The Field of Intoxicants and Intoxication Research

The available published research on intoxicants and intoxication, in addition to its wide-ranging nature, is quite fragmented, and only a few of the available books or collected editions on intoxication are comprehensive in terms of the social sciences, examining different intoxicants, or covering different historical periods. For example, Hutton's recent "Cultures of Intoxication" (2020) provides an excellent overview of the main intoxicants: alcohol, illicit drugs and tobacco, as well as considering important social science issues such as the impact of sexuality, gender and ethnicity on intoxicant use. While her book is intentionally focused on contemporary issues, our own Handbook sought to include both contemporary accounts and historical discussions. Bancroft's stimulating book *Drugs, Intoxication and Society* (2000) is an exemplar of a wide-ranging approach, which includes coffee, tea, prescription drugs and a short section on nicotine as well as alcohol and illegal drugs. Other compendiums, such as Davenport-Hines (2002), have also produced wonderful global histories of narcotics, unfortunately however, given both the specificity of the topic and the use of the word "narcotics," his coverage is somewhat limited. Finally, Withington and McShane's supplement to *Past and Present* (2014), based on the proceedings of a conference on the "Cultures of Intoxication" at Cambridge University in 2010, is also a good example of the wide-ranging approach to the field, an approach we sought to emulate. It covers both a wide-range of intoxicants not only in different historical periods, including, for example, ancient Greece and contemporary Hong Kong, but also in different parts of the globe, including Taiwan, South and West Africa and the Middle East.

These books are just a few examples of the available works that have examined intoxicants and intoxication against a broad backcloth. There are of course many, many other examples that we could have mentioned, including, to name but a few, Jay (2010), Siegal (2005), Grob

(2002), Dobkin de Rios (1990), Rudgley (1993), Walton (2001) and MacAndrew and Edgerton (1969). All of these books and compendiums, and many that we have not mentioned, have added to our overall knowledge about different intoxicants and intoxication in many different societies, in different historical periods, and you will see these important contributions cited throughout the subsequent pages of this Handbook.

Although our aim in producing the Handbook was to correct some of the shortcomings of contemporary compendiums, contributions within the Handbook owe an enormous debt to all these studies, which have enriched our appreciation of these topics and have provided to those of us, who conduct research within these areas, a rich and detailed reference literature.

Outline of the Handbook

Having briefly outlined the background to our Handbook, and the processes by which we assembled all the contributions, what is it that the reader can expect to find in its???? pages. One aspect, that is largely absent from the Handbook, is an opening section that sets out to accurately define either different intoxicants or different forms of intoxication. Other works have begun their examination of the topic by defining their use of intoxication or intoxicants. For example, Slingerland (2021) informs his readers that in using the term intoxication, he intends to include both "dramatic states of inebriation" (p. 6) and the mellow and happy buzz that one feels after "the first couple of sips of wine." Others, for example Hutton (2020), adopt Mary Douglas' (1987) definition in which intoxication is "viewed as a set of social and cultural practices, norms and values" (2020:3). Some writers, instead of attempting to define or precisely specify either intoxication or intoxicants, have detailed why they have adopted the term intoxication. For example, Withington (2014) in his introduction to "Cultures of Intoxication" argues that the vocabulary of intoxication "is etymologically and semantically precise" (p. 12) and is relatively "neutral… without the ideological connotations of drugs" (ibid.). He argues "that it depicts a cognitive and social condition (intoxication) as well as the substances that induces it (intoxicants)" (ibid.). We have implicitly followed Withington's lead, using similar terms as he does, hence the title of the Handbook, and decided not to specifically define the precise terrain for our contributors, thereby avoiding any attempt to pre-determine how they should approach the topic. Instead, we allowed them to determine themselves what constituted intoxication and which intoxicants they wished to focus on. We assumed, in general, given our choice of contributors, that their focus would be broad and wide-ranging and would cover issues they believed were significant, whether that be examining different conceptions of addiction across a wide-range of historical periods (for example, Chapter 34), investigating societal-level discourses about Ireland's drinking cultures (Chapter 31), exploring the interplay between the definition, regulation and practices of excess (Chapter 30) or examining the symbolic role of coffee and coffee shops among Bosnian refugees (Chapter 9).

However, while we as editors refrained from specifically defining either intoxication or intoxicants, this is not to say that some of our individual contributors have done likewise. For example, Craig Reinarman (Chapter 1), having traced the lexicographical origins of the term intoxication in Greek and Latin, argues, somewhat in opposition to Withington (2014), that the term intoxication, as referring to a "state of being poisoned," narrows the potential range of possible meanings. Instead, he suggests that, "we need a lexicon with a wider aperture so that the phenomena we refer to, with the term intoxication, do not imply a false binary, drunk or sober, but rather capture the broad array of altered states in between." In Chapter 21, Suzanne Fraser and colleagues begin their chapter by noting the extent to which intoxication is a "multivalent term" "that invokes a range of experiences – from joy and pleasure to chaos and impairment – and applies differently across different drugs and different settings of drug consumption." These characteristics, they argue, "can carry highly variable political implications and effects, entailing varying governance measures and practices." Finally, John O'Brien (Chapter 18) suggests that intoxication is a "compromised term" because of its roots in nineteenth-century medical science.

Having stayed away from pre-determining the ways in which our contributors should handle their discussion of individual intoxicants and types of intoxication, we nevertheless have had to organize all the disparate chapters into sections. In designing the Handbook initially, we had decided on possible themes under which the different contributions could potentially be grouped. However, as the papers trickled in, it became clear that some of them did not fit our initial thematic plan and hence a revised thematic plan was required. Yet, this process was not entirely clear due to the broad-ranging nature of each of the chapters, which easily fitted into more than one theme. Nevertheless, we have grouped the 34 chapters into eight different headings, which can operate as a road map to guide you, the reader, through the Handbook. Keep in mind, however, that in classifying chapters under one particular section, it became all too clear that certain chapters could easily have been listed under a different section. We believe, however, that the reality of this challenge only further provides evidence of the remarkable overlap among studies of various intoxicants and intoxication which focus on disparate settings, countries, cultures, age groups and historical periods and which are considered through the lens of different social science disciplines.

Theme 1: The Terrain of Intoxication

The aim of this initial theme is to bring together those chapters, which have examined the different social meanings of individual intoxicants and the way in which different social and cultural influences have worked to construct those different meanings. Under this heading, we have grouped four papers that we feel specifically highlight this theme. The opening chapter by Craig Reinarman seeks to explore the different meanings of intoxication and examine why not only certain forms of intoxication are "socially approved and unproblematic," while others are "feared and punished," but also why these forms change over time. Reinarman argues that intoxication as a category of behavior "warrants" further investigation, arguing that it cannot be the simple fact of producing an altered consciousness that solely influences why certain forms of intoxication are acceptable or unacceptable at different times. Instead, he suggests that we must examine "the conditions under which intoxication gets defined as troubling or not troubling, which often depends on *who* is intoxicated, by what means, when, and where." In this opening chapter, Reinarman sets the scene for other contributors to question and examine what all the different circumstances and factors are that influence how the authorities define, judge and control different intoxicants and different states of intoxication.

The second chapter by Ruth Lewis and colleagues, while unlike the broad nature of the first chapter, examines the different meanings ascribed to nicotine vaping by young adults. Using practice theory, they explore the shared meanings and processes that young people attach to vaping nicotine, emphasizing the extent to which these meanings are influenced by social inequities, based on race, class, gender and sexuality. In the third chapter, Emeka Dumbili and colleagues present a very different situation than described by the previous chapter. Instead of vaping in California, this chapter examines the intoxication practices among young adults in South-Eastern Nigeria. In tracing the meanings of drug use and specifically, cannabis and tramadol, among these young adults, clear gendered differences emerge where notions of masculinity and femininity play a significant role in the ways in which intoxication practices take place. The final chapter by Jonathon Shears, which we have grouped under this initial heading, is an unusual chapter in the sense that it does not discuss a specific form of intoxication but instead explores the consequences of intoxication. While many researchers have produced studies of intoxication, few have explored the somewhat forgotten topic of the hangover, as Shears has done in his contribution. Our reason for placing this chapter here is because the author examines how the symptoms of the hangover arise not solely as a result of imbibing too much alcohol but instead from the different psychosocial consequences of using alcohol. In other words, the meanings of the hangover are far more complex than the pharmacological properties of alcohol itself.

Theme 2: Social Life of Intoxicants

As Appadurai noted many years ago, intoxicants can be viewed primarily as commodities operating and circulating in specific spheres of different value. The values ascribed to each intoxicant are based not upon any intrinsic properties but instead depend upon "judgements made about them by subjects" (Appadurai 1986:3). Given the fact that substances circulate in specific cultural and historical milieus where they are produced, exchanged and consumed, they acquire different values as they pass from one sphere to another. Consequently, in examining the social and cultural life of individual substances, he suggests that we examine the social history of things, in order to trace the ways in which intoxicants move through different historical periods and "through different hands, contexts and uses" (Appadurai 1986:34).

Influenced by this approach, we have grouped together four papers, which examine the social life of different intoxicants. In Chapter 5, Gerda Reith examines two contemporary trends: first, the "commodification of intoxicants" and, second, the expansion of the "concept of intoxication." In examining these trends, she considers three different types of intoxicating consumption – drugs, food and gambling. By examining the discourses that operate around them, she argues, that until recently, drugs were viewed as the "paradigmatic example of intoxicating consumption." However, today, an increasingly "wide range of both substances and experiences" have been described in terms similar to those previously confined to descriptions of drug use and addiction. Moreover, it is not merely the case that new substances and experiences have become defined as intoxicating, but also that the commercial potential of these substances has become increasingly realized. Examining the ways in which corporate interests have adopted many of the scientific discoveries on how the brain operates when exposed to stimulating pleasurable experiences, such as heroin and cocaine, she highlights how these corporations have used these discoveries in marketing other commodities and experiences.

The second chapter by Angus Bancroft again examines the social life of drugs by showing how drugs become different substances in different "consumption regimes." More specifically, he explores notions of potency within drug distribution markets and the ways that these markets influence both "intoxication subjectivities" and drugs as specific types "of object[s] with tangible characteristics." Drugs as useable commodities are shaped by "the relationship between dealer, user, market and consumption context." Within these settings, drugs become interchangeable commodities, and users become consumers. In the third chapter, intoxicants as commodities take on a different shape, this time in the form of craft drinks and craft drinks culture. Thurnell-Reed examines the changing discourses and practices that have framed the consumption of craft drinks. Unlike many other alcoholic beverages, he argues that discussions surrounding craft drinks rarely deal with notions of drunkenness and disorder and instead focus on notions of cultural capital, including "discernment, taste and studied cultural appreciation." Within this context, consumers can drink "as an expression of pride and community" rather than simply drinking to intoxication. By showing the fluctuations in the cultural values and social status of individual intoxicants, he highlights the extent to which craft drinks and the discussions around them have successfully distanced themselves from being viewed as an intoxicant capable of producing intoxication.

The final chapter in this section is by Peder Clark, who examines the different meanings of ecstasy in different cultural, temporal and spatial settings. In tracing the history of ecstasy from its beginnings in 1912, with its discovery by the Merck company; its re-discovery in California by Alexander Shulgin in the mid-1960s; through its use in the 1970s and 1980s becoming an important commodity associated with the club scene, he highlights the "tension at the heart of many cultures of intoxication" between the costs to health versus the escape from the mundane. However, while noting this tension, Clark also encourages historians and other researchers "to look beyond these binaries of harm and hedonism to develop more nuanced perspectives on ecstasy."

Theme 3: Intoxicating Settings

In 1989, Ray Oldenburg wrote a book called "the Great Good Place" where he extolled the virtues of informal public gathering places. These places included the pub, the café, the tavern, beer gardens and the coffee house. While these sociable meeting places are important to examine in terms of their relationship to specific intoxicants, our aim was to broaden our approach and include settings, not normally examined under the heading of intoxicating geographies. Included under this heading are chapters that have examined intoxication settings not as static, peripheral or an "impassive backdrop to situated human activity" (Thrift 1996:3) but instead specific settings which contribute their "own constitutive and active rhythms, forces and energies" (Duff 2007:506). With this in mind, we have included discussions of coffee bars and drinking places, as well as chapters, which have examined the impact of informal drinking settings, such as drinking at academic conferences, as well as the impact of institutionalized settings, in this case prisons, on the use of intoxicants. Finally, we consider how intoxicants are used in warfare.

In Chapter 9, Ana Croegaert examines the practices and culture of Bosnian coffee drinking and specifically the role of coffee houses. However, her aim is not merely to trace the role of coffee or coffee houses in different historical periods within Bosnian society, but also to examine the "spatial elements associated with coffee drinking" and to explore what these elements might tell us about human relations. She shows how the practices of drinking coffee play an important symbolic role in connecting globally dispersed Bosnians with their homeland. In the next chapter, James Kneale seeks to highlight the extent to which drinking places, such as public houses in England, were not only sites for consuming alcohol, but important places for the consumption of other intoxicants and especially tobacco. Furthermore, in a similar way to that suggested by Duff and Thrift above, Kneale examines intoxication, within these drinking places, not solely as something resulting from the physiological and neurological effects of specific beverages, but instead "something that emerges out of the interaction of consumers, intoxicants, songs, light and visual spectacles, and a wider affective atmosphere." In so doing, he suggests that adopting a broader examination of drinking places "may well generate entirely new questions for researchers interested in intoxication."

The importance of setting in examining the practices and cultures of individual intoxicants is further developed by Helen Keane (Chapter 11), who examines drinking and networking practices at academic conferences. She argues that minor intoxication can itself be viewed not as a symbolic marker between work and play (Gusfield 2003) but instead as a form of work. Drinking and intoxication "can be interpreted as an intensification and extension of expected attachments to work." In general, psychoactive substances, alcohol and coffee (coffee at regular points during the day and alcohol in the evening) are "normalized" features of the conference schedule. However, given the fact that drinking in nighttime venues results in individuals loosening social constraints and conventions, drinking at a conference involves people still inhabiting their "professional identities." These potentially conflicting situations and norms may result in experiences of ambiguity and tension. The fourth chapter in this section, by Torsten Kolind and Karen Duke, examines the issue of intoxication in prison settings, considering both how intoxication is experienced and organized within the prison environment and the relationship between intoxication and pleasure among those who are imprisoned. More specifically, they argue that the prison context creates an environment that is different than the outside world in that it determines the kind of drug use that is possible and also how intoxication is experienced and socially organized.

Following on the theme of custodial institutions, Lyuba Azbel and Frederick Altice examine the case of methadone in prisons in the Kyrgyz Republic comparing its use with that of heroin. While noting the extent to which the medical and clinical literatures distinguish methadone from other illicit drugs, they show how the use of these substances, by the prisoners, turns this distinction on its head. Instead of methadone being viewed as a substance to be used to reduce harm, the prisoners view methadone as a "compulsive drug of addiction." In contrast to this, they view heroin, often portrayed within addiction literature as the epitome of an addictive substance, as a beneficial substance that can be used for harm reduction. In highlighting this case, the authors show the extent to which an intoxicant, previously defined in one way within public health writing, can under different circumstances be viewed in a totally different way, even producing beneficial health outcomes.

Continuing the theme of setting and intoxicant use, Houborg and Berge explore how drug users in a drug consumption room (DCR) in Copenhagen, Denmark, narrate both "modes of use" and "trade-offs" in relation to intoxication experiences. Using narrative data from in-depth interviews with drug users, they show how users consider benefits and drawbacks when using drugs in the DCR. The narratives include how to get a desired intoxicating effect of a drug and how the particular setting inside or outside DCRs can promote these effects. These "trade-offs," promoted by different settings, are also analyzed in relation to modes of use which can include intoxication, self-medication or removal of withdrawal symptoms. Houborg and Berge's study show that drug users have a variety of reasons for using or not using DCRs, compared to the overall purpose of DCRs, which are intended as ways of preventing overdose deaths and securing healthy drug taking.

Finally, in this section on intoxicated settings, we have included a chapter by Lukasz Kamienski, who examines a much broader intoxicated setting than the other papers, by considering what he calls the "weaponization of intoxicants." By considering intoxicants in different historical periods, in different societies, he shows how intoxicants and warfare are intertwined. He also, in passing, highlights the irony that while much literature has been spent on examining the "war on drugs," the analysis and examination of the use of intoxicants in armed conflict have been neglected, especially by military historians. In correcting this oversight, he shows how intoxicants are not only used to inspire courage and enhance performance by counteracting fatigue, but are also used to mitigate the long-term effects of battle experience after soldiers have been removed from the field. This last example is particularly relevant, given the very recent debate on the use of psychedelics for the treatment of PTSD, especially for soldiers.

Theme 4: Intoxication Practices

In the last section, we discussed the importance of considering the wider setting in understanding the importance of the socio-cultural context for understanding the role and culture of intoxicants. In the fourth thematic section, following on from this previous theme, we examine those chapters that have focused more specifically on the practices that have been adopted in using particular substances. In Chapter 16, Julia McQuoid argues that in considering nicotine use practices, it is important that the social context be examined to understand these practices. To do this, she suggests that building upon Zinberg's (1984) model of drug set and setting, a model used extensively in the drug field, could be fruitful when examining nicotine use practices and experiences. Furthermore, she argues that research which examines the day-to-day and lived practices of those who use nicotine is sparse "when compared to the large body of literature examining trends in prevalence of and 'risk factors' for tobacco use." Highlighting the available qualitative research studies and also exploring more contemporary theories beyond Zinberg's important work, she examines how "smoking experience" is not an isolated relationship between the individual and the substance, but instead a dynamic practice that operates within specific settings and contexts. Following the notion of practices, Kane Race and colleagues examine in Chapter 17 the practices of intoxication for LGBTQ users. Historically, research on LGBTQ drinking, drug use and intoxication have tended to view their use of intoxicants primarily from a problem perspective. Consequently, their drinking, drug using practices and intoxication were viewed as a response to the social and health problems they confront, including stigma and minority stress. In contrast to this perspective, Kane and colleagues ask the unusual question: What if intoxication were viewed not "as a plaster [band-aid] for the wound of sexual stigmatization," but instead as a "pragmatic means of carrying out certain discredited activities." By reverting the focus, the authors are able to portray their research participants not as "damaged and static identities" or submissive actors involved in pathological self-medication, driven by societal forces, but instead as active agents. Using narrative data, they show how their participants "reject the concept of intoxication" as inadequate because of its negative connotations, such as notions of toxicity. Instead, their own practices of psychoactive consumption are viewed as pleasurable and transformative and as a "practical strategy that grapples" with the situation they find themselves in.

Finally, in this thematic section, Chapter 18 by John O'Brien considers the practice of drinking proportionately. Examining the schizoid quality of the discourse on alcohol intoxication, which, on the one hand, viewed alcohol consumption as an element of modernity encompassing freedom, choice and involvement in the public sphere. On the other hand, drinking is the subject of "problematisation" and a practice that must be governed. Within this discourse, O'Brien asks the question: how do people learn to drink proportionately, a feature of every drinking culture? How do they learn the rules of the game and how do they learn what constitutes excess and the ideal forms of "drunken comportment?" In answering these questions, he argues that a process of deritualization is a major aspect of modernization. Unlike more traditional societies, in which ritual plays a central role in determining the difference between moderation and excess, control today in the context of deritualization "comes less from *ritual* as an aspect of the social structure and more from *reflexivity*, involving a more individualised navigating of risk," and it is these practices of the self that shape consumption.

Theme 5: Alternative Approaches for Studying Intoxication

Critical studies of intoxicants and intoxication have long challenged mainstream, positivistic approaches that search for a singular, unyielding truth about intoxicants and their effects. They critique the tendency to produce a single pharmacological explanation for the effects of drugs on the body and brain, while ignoring either the different modes of administration or the social and cultural contexts within which intoxicant use takes place. These studies also investigate how particular scientific methods are themselves social and cultural constructs built on particular assumptions that shape drugs in particular ways, which change over time. This approach can be seen in Nancy Campbell's chapter, in which she delineates how, over time, intoxicants and their effects have been defined and operationalized by "experimental, clinical, and behavioral scientists" as singular static entities that are considered easily observable in the laboratory. Her account critiques the ability of such positivistic and "sober" approaches to studies of intoxicants and intoxication to fully attend to the "pleasure and desire [that] stubbornly reside within intoxication," and she not only makes room for, but champions the need for post-positivistic social scientific approaches that "disrupt" mainstream studies of intoxicants and intoxication. Campbell's chapter is nicely followed by a chapter by Jonas Bååth and Johan Nordgren which provides a counter approach to neuropsychological studies of drug intoxication. They assert that conventional scientific methods, especially those employed in pharmacological and neurological research, cannot sufficiently grasp a person's experiences with intoxication and, therefore, they argue for the use of online trip reports for understanding the subjectivities of people who use intoxicants. Finally, this section concludes with a chapter by Susanne Fraser and colleagues who draw upon an "onto-politically-oriented" approach to research, further developed in Fraser (2020), that acknowledges that drug consumption realities emerge from different "contexts and discourses… [which] co-produce culturally and politically specific intoxication experiences and effects" (p#). Using two separate research projects as case studies, they illustrate the ways in which intoxication is a political designation reliant on a range of assumptions about drug-consuming subjects and practices. In making this case, the chapter sets out methodological resources for new approaches to researching politically multiple concepts such as intoxication.

Theme 6: Scapegoated Substances

As Craig Reinarman succinctly states in Chapter 1,

> whether a form of intoxication is seen as problematic is contingent on many things, not least whose consciousness is being altered and in front of whom. Narratives of 'irresponsibility' and 'danger' stick to some groups more easily than others; certain groups are depicted as prone to drug abuse, others to abstinence.
>
> *(p.6)*

The history of intoxicants and intoxication has been intimately intertwined with certain groups at the margins within many different societies. This section in the Handbook illustrates the ways in which the association of particular intoxicants with particular groups around the world ultimately shapes the meaning of the intoxicant use and of intoxication, not to mention stigmatizes the people who use. The first chapter, by Lucas Brunozi Avelar and Deborah Toner, highlights the ways in which meanings of drunkenness shifted overtime through the racialization of drinking behaviors from colonial Brazil to the twentieth century. In particular, they argue that racial discrimination in Brazil was enacted, in part, through the stigmatization of alcohol use, specifically cachaça (i.e., Brazilian rum), and the alcohol practices there were associated with Africans, who were enslaved. In the next chapter by Ediomo-Ubong E. Nelson, we are introduced to the experiences of street-involved youths in Nigeria who use cannabis and the ways in which cannabis serves as a scapegoat for police surveillance and violence. Through a large-scale qualitative data collection effort, Nelson examines the context in which cannabis use emerges among these youth and describes youths' unjust and inhumane encounters with the police, illustrating the structural violence and harmful consequences that can result in zero-tolerance approaches to drugs.

In the following chapter, Johan Nordgren takes us to Sweden describing how khat use became "ethnified" through its association with Somali communities in Malmö, thus rendering, in societal-level discourse, khat use a "Somali problem." However, his study emphasizes that there are multiple constructions of ethnicity and argues that an excessive reliance on ethnicity as it relates to drugs ends up obscuring other, and arguably far more relevant, structural conditions that contribute to the use of intoxicants. From Sweden, the reader is then taken to Japan, where Akihiko Sato presents a final chapter on the history of the control of amphetamine-type stimulants (ATSs) in post-war Japan. He challenges the conventional narrative in Japan that ATS control was solely due to its addictive properties and psychological harms, and instead suggests that the symbolic meaning of ATS has changed drastically overtime, first as a symbol to establish political and ethnic boundaries, then as an economic marker establishing what constitutes legitimate business activity, and finally as a way to draw the psychological and social boundaries of Japanese society. In all of these moments in time, Sato argues that ATS sets up boundaries between deserving citizens and scapegoated *others*.

Theme 7: Discourses Shaping Intoxication and Intoxicant Users

In the first chapter, in this section, Susanne MacGregor and Betsy Thom consider changes in how the issues of death from drug intoxication/drug overdoses have changed in recent years. Drug overdoses have increased in many countries, and become a concern for a range of actors, including policy makers and health professionals. However, as MacGregor and Thom show, the framing of the problem has altered along with associated proposed solutions, and the media's role in these shifts in framing was significant. They emphasize how the framing of drug-related deaths is underpinned by implicit assumptions and values, such as what constitutes acceptable or risky behavior; who is a "worthy" person; the nature of responsibility and blame for negative consequences. The media provide a key means through which the understanding of risk, the links between risk and behavior and the adoption of "appropriate" responses to drug intoxication are reflected and disseminated.

In the next chapter by Qian Hui Tan, we are introduced to discourses on cigarette intoxication. Tan shows how cigarette smoking is constructed as a(n) (in)toxic(ating) practice that resists spatial containment. Because of the "airy" character of cigarette smoking, smoking is not confined to the smoker, but also to non-smokers, who can become second/third-hand smokers. The toxicity and risks of cigarette smoking are thus not only related to the smoker, but is reported to be potentially even more toxic to non-smokers. Taking as her point of departure the situation in Singapore, Tan examines how the ever-extending geographical reach of public smoking bans, "fueled by paternalistic public health institutions," de-normalizes smoking. Her chapter critically investigates what she calls the "medicalization of smoking" and "healthist" discourses and advocates instead for a diversity of "not-so-toxic" or "not-so-healthist" discourses on smoking, thereby taking into account the complexities of smoking, such that smoking can be both life-enhancing and detrimental to health.

Continuing the critical tone of this section in the analysis of discourses, Axel Klein in Chapter 28, using Niklas Luhmann's systemic theory, discusses the international drug control system, arguing that it is "run as a social system, the primary concern [of which] is not resolving the world drug problem, but to perpetuate itself." As such, this self-perpetuating drug control system is argued to perpetuate the very risks that they purport to attempt to alleviate. Consequently, this configuration of the drug control system leaves the development of alternative and practice-based solutions, like measures to reduce harm or redefining the problem as "social" or "medical" instead of "criminal," to "heretics" outside the system. Klein concludes by arguing that the system needs to be "defunded, deconstructed and dismantled" in order to change to allow for different problematizations and less harmful solutions to the "drug problem" to flourish.

The last chapter in this section by David Moore and colleagues introduces us to the notion of intoxication in alcohol policy discourse and practices in Australia. They argue that intoxication, generally in alcohol and other drugs policies, is presented as a universal and singular state and is constituted as a threat to health and social order. Taking as their point of departure different Australian alcohol policy documents, the authors show how the relationship between alcohol intoxication and violence is linked in a simplistic way whereby (excessive) alcohol intoxication is considered to cause violence. However, when interviewing alcohol policy stakeholders, they identified various modes of explanations in which discussions of the alcohol intoxication and violence nexus became much more complex, yet nevertheless conclude with simplistic causal explanations. Drawing on the work of Annemarie Mol and John Law (2002), the authors provide an analysis of the relationship between alcohol intoxication and violence that takes into account both the interview participants' insistence on the complexity and multitude factors that make up both the problem and the solution, as well as their tendency to provide more simplistic explanations of alcohol intoxication and violence.

Theme 8: Notions of Excess

This section explores intoxication and the changing boundaries of excess for different intoxicants, while considering the continual interplay between the definition, regulation and practice of excess in a range of contexts. In this way, the papers in this section identify how definitions, regulations and practices of excess exist in a state of changing reciprocation, and re-inscription over time; how notions of excess associated with intoxicants have been represented over time, and how the boundaries between "acceptable" and "excessive" constantly change. In the first chapter, Dias-Lewandowska and colleagues "provide a historically and culturally comparative perspective on the socially contested boundary between excess and moderation in relation to alcohol by drawing on four distinct, yet complementary, cases." The four cases include late medieval and early modern Western Europe; sixteenth- to nineteenth-century Poland; twentieth-century Britain and finally contemporary Britain. By exploring these four cases, the chapter explores "how various religious, state and cultural authorities have sought to define excessive and moderate drinking, and how a diverse set of actors has negotiated their drinking in relation to these textual and visual discourses." By drawing on such different cases in different times and in different places, the authors show how definitions of excessive and moderate drinking are not constant, but fluctuating.

In the next chapter, Alice Mauger explores shifting representations of Ireland's drinking culture and how competing discourses have influenced changes in the perception of Irish (excessive) drinking. Her analysis examines the period from 1890 to 2018 and is based on the author's own research on medico-scientific and state responses to (excessive) alcohol consumption and addiction combined with a historiographical survey of existing work. In the chapter, she traces three distinct phases in which medico-scientific, voluntary and state responses have converged. She shows how the disease concept is accepted in Ireland in an era when, among other things, Irish nationalism and a temperance association were gaining a foothold; how in the 1960s, the interest in alcoholism intersects with attempts to reinvent Ireland's international profile; and how most recently Ireland adopts a public health approach to alcohol, including an alcohol policy on pricing, health warnings and restriction on marketing and advertising. While this chapter focuses on Ireland and gives us insights into changes in responses to the Irish alcohol culture, it also provides an important example of how it is possible to examine changes in national (policy) as possible responses to (excessive) alcohol consumption.

The alcohol theme is continued in the next chapter by Pamela Lock, who introduces us to the figure of the "chronic drunkard" in nineteenth-century British literature. Lock examines a particular figure, the "chronic drunkard," and relates the representation and understanding of this figure to broader societal and cultural discourses. The chapter gives an overview of the most influential representations of the drunkard in literary, popular and temperance fiction. These representations, despite the differences in genres, are related to anxieties, while at the same time having a didactic purpose. Lock writes:

> The fictional drunkard, usually broken and repulsive, not only warns its nineteenth-century audience to drink 'well' or not at all for their own bodily and mental health, but reminds the reader of their duties to family, community, and country by demonstrating 'Victorian' values such as moral rectitude and industry.

The chapter, however, not only explores how the representations of the fictional "chronic drunkard" relates to norms and values in an era where social hierarchies and gender roles are in a process of change, but also how it relates to medical developments; theories of how alcohol affects body and mind; and new ideas on how to treat the "chronic drunkard." Lock thus highlights the way a fictional figure relates to societal, cultural and scientific norms and values that are present, and yet changing, in nineteenth-century Britain.

While concerns about excess of alcohol have often been examined, the issue of excessive tea consumption has rarely been explored. However, in the chapter by Ian Miller, he examines the issue of tea intoxication from 1860 to 1900. In this period, tea began to be consumed at all levels of society, including the working class both in Britain and in Ireland. The chapter explores how tea drinking became viewed as excessive, addictive and intoxicating, especially for the working class and specifically working-class mothers. Miller shows how "excessive" tea drinking was considered a trigger for severe mental illness such as hysteria and concerns about "excessive tea drinking" ultimately became class- and gender-based. "Working-class mothers were accused of over-consuming strong concoctions of tea (with white bread) at the expense of more nutritious food items." Yet rather than recognizing "excessive tea drinking" as a symptom of poverty and food insecurity for working-class families, tea drinking becomes viewed solely as addictive, transgressive and pathological. The "moral panic" (Cohen 2002) that Miller describes in this period in relation to "excessive tea drinking" can also be seen in more recent times with other intoxicants, thereby emphasizing the importance of historical research and discussion.

In the final chapter, both in this section and in the Handbook, David Clemis introduces us to the different ways in which "chronic intoxicant use" – an extreme form of excess – has been framed across history. He explores how chronic use, particularly of alcohol, has been understood throughout history, chronologically considering particular eras as points of impact related to the Western world, including "The ancient West," "Early Modern Galenism," "Seventeenth Century Empiricism and Eighteenth Century Neurology," "The Nineteenth Century: Disease and Alcoholism" and "The Twentieth Century: The Meanings of Disease." By choosing different points of impact, Clemis is able to explore how particular factors have been instrumental in changing ideas about chronic intoxicant use and highlight how understandings of the self are both consistent yet varying and contested throughout history. This chapter reminds us that concepts and understandings of chronic intoxicant use or addiction as the preferred term are not constant, but changing, and rely on broader societal, cultural and medical understandings of intoxication.

Conclusion

This Handbook, and the chapters within, was crafted over many hours, days, weeks and months by so many scholars around the world, including the authors and editors themselves, as well as the 73 reviewers, who provided excellent peer-reviewed support to assist each contributor to produce their highest quality of work. We, the editors, are grateful to each contribution made by every person, who put their labor into this Handbook. The result, we believe, is a book that explores the contributions of critical studies of intoxication across disciplines, intoxicants and places. Such critical contributions so often elude the mainstream literature and yet arguably pave the way for creativity in knowledge production, innovation in research and practice and challenges to mainstream approaches in the field of public health. Using Klein's label (Chapter 29), it is left to the "*heretics*," those who are willing to dig deeper into innovative theory, methods and analysis, to challenge the status quo in an effort to shed light on the complexity of the human experience, the structures that constrain and disenfranchise certain groups of people, and the role of power and privilege in shaping social and cultural meanings, the production of knowledge and precedents of policy. We hope that the readers will find our "*heretical*" accounts as challenging and as stimulating as we do.

References

Appadurai, A. 1986. Introduction: Commodities and the politics of value. In A. Appadurai (Ed.), *The Social Life of Things: Commodities in Cultural Perspective* (pp. 3–63). Cambridge: Cambridge University Press.

Bancroft, A. 2009. *Drugs, Intoxication and Society*. Cambridge: Polity Press.

Becker, H. S. 1967. Becoming a marijuana user. *American Journal of Sociology*, 59:3235–242.

Boon, M. 2002. *The Road of Excess: A History of Writers on Drugs*. Cambridge, MA: Harvard University Press.

Cohen, S. 2002. *Folk Devils and Moral Panics*. London: Routledge.

Connell, R. 2007. *Southern Theory: The Global Dynamics of Knowledge in Social Science*. London: Allen and Unwin.

Davenport-Hines, R. 2002. *The Pursuit of Oblivion: A Global History of Narcotics*. London: Weidenfeld.

Dobkin de Rios, M. 1990. *Hallucinogens: Cross-Cultural Perspectives*. Prospect Heights, IL: Waveland Press.

Douglas, M. (Ed.) 1987. *Constructive Drinking: Perspectives on Drink from Anthropology*. Cambridge: Cambridge University Press.

Duff, C. 2007. Towards a theory of drug use contexts: Space, embodiment and practice. *Addiction Research & Theory*, 15(5):503–519.
Fraser, S. 2020. Doing ontopolitically-oriented research: Synthesising concepts from the ontological turn for alcohol and other drug research and other social sciences. *International Journal of Drug Policy*, 82:102610. doi: 10.1016/j.drugpo.2019.102610.
Goodman, J., Lovejoy, P., and Sherratt, A. (Eds.) 1995. *Consuming Habits: Drugs in History and Anthropology*. London: Routledge.
Grob, C. S. (Ed.) (2002). *Hallucinogens: A Reader*. New York: Jeremy P. Tarcher/Putnam.
Gusfield, J. R. 2003. Passage to play: Rituals of drinking time in American society. In Mary Douglas (Ed.) *Constructive Drinking: Perspectives on Drink from Anthropology* (pp. 73–90). Cambridge: Cambridge University Press.
Hockings, K. and Dunbar, R. (Eds.) 2020. *Alcohol and Humans: A Long and Social Affair*. Oxford: Oxford University Press.
Hutton, F. (Ed.) 2020. *Cultures of Intoxication: Key Issues and Debates*. Cham: Palgrave.
Jay, M. 2010. *High Society: The Central Role of Mind-Altering Drugs in History, Science and Culture*. Rochester, VT: Park Street Press.
Keane, H. 2009. Intoxication, harm and pleasure: An analysis of the Australian National alcohol strategy. *Critical Public Health*, 19(2):135–142.
MacAndrew, C. and Edgerton, R. 1969. *Drunken Comportment: A Social Explanation*. New York: Aldine De Gruyter.
Mol, A. and Law, J. 2002. Complexities: An introduction. In J. Law and A. Mol (Eds.), *Complexities: Social Studies of Knowledge Practices* (pp. 1–22). Durham, NC: Duke University Press.
Oldenburg, R. 1989. *The Great Good Place*. New York: Paragon.
Rudgley, R. 1993. *Essential Substances: A Cultural History of Intoxicants in Society*. New York: Kodansha International.
Shears, J. 2020. *The Hangover: A Literary and Cultural History*. Liverpool: Liverpool University Press.
Sherratt, A. 1995. Introduction: Peculiar substances. In J. Goodman, P. E. Lovejoy and A. Sherratt (Eds.), *Consuming Habits: Drugs in History and Anthropology* (pp. 1–10). London: Routledge.
Siegal, R. K. 1989. *Intoxication: Life in Pursuit of Artificial Paradise*. New York: E.P. Dutton.
Siegal, R. K. 2005. *Intoxication: The Universal Drive for Mind Altering Substances*. Rochester, VT: Park Street Press.
Slingerland, E. 2021. *Drunk: How We Sipped, Danced and Stumbled Our Way to Civilization*. New York: Little Brown Spark.
Thrift, N. 1996. *Spatial Formations*. Thousand Oaks, CA: Sage Publications.
Walton, S. 2001. *Out of It*. New York: Harmony Books.
Withington, P. 2014. Introduction: Cultures of intoxication. In P. Withington and A. McShane (Eds.) *Cultures of Intoxication. Past and Present*, Supplement 9 (pp. 9–34). Oxford: Oxford University Press.
Yardley, T. 2014. *Why We Take Drugs: Seeking Excess and Communion in the Modern World*. London: Routledge.
Zinberg, N. 1984. *Drug, Set, and Setting: The Basis for Controlled Intoxicant Use*. New Haven, CT: Yale University Press.

PART I

The Terrain of Intoxication

1

INTOXICATIONS AND THEIR MEANINGS[1]

Craig Reinarman

Intoxication was not born in sin. Animals apparently got high before human civilization (Siegel 1989; Rudgley 1993; Lenson 1995; Slingerland 2021). Humans fermented grapes and grain as soon as they figured out settled agriculture, perhaps before. History is strewn with luminaries who saw great value in periodically "drowning Apollonian reason in Dionysian abandon" (Lescaze 2021). Drunkenness was a normal pleasure in popular celebrations from antiquity through the Middle Ages.

And yet, in much of the Western world since the end of the eighteenth century, intoxication has carried the presumption of guilt. If something bad happens and alcohol or other drugs are found in the vicinity, a "malevolence assumption" tends to kick in and a causal connection gets implied (Hamilton and Collins 1981:261; Gusfield 1996). Blaming booze, recurring drug scares and drug wars, and a lurking "tyranny of abstinence" (Jamison 2018:452) are all common in cultures that fear intoxication. The wellsprings and consequences of such fears are vital parts of the puzzle of intoxication's complex history.

I begin this chapter by making the case that the concept of intoxication is too pinched to do justice to the multitude of altered states that are typically lumped under it. Intoxications vary far more widely than we think; some don't even involve ingesting a toxin at all. I argue that intoxication is an unstable category with blurred boundaries. I then trace the fluctuating moral careers of common intoxicants to show how such boundaries have been drawn and redrawn. Based on these cases, I outline some tentative propositions about the characteristics and conditions that inform the cultural and legal status of intoxicants. The chapter closes with a Coda on the relationship between intoxicants and social change.

A Troubled Category

The idea of "intoxication" is haunted by its genealogy. The root of "intoxication" is the Greek word "toxon," for bow, the adjectival form meaning "of or for the bow," which refers to the poison in which arrows were dipped during antiquity (as in the Latin "toxicum").[2] The *Oxford English Dictionary* (*OED*) defines the noun "intoxication" as "1. the action of poisoning; administration of poison; killing by poison; the state of being poisoned." The verb "intoxicate" means "to poison." All variations of the term have poison in the first meaning. I suggest that the denotation of intoxication as a state of being poisoned constricts the

DOI: 10.4324/9780429058141-3

connotations available to us, unnecessarily narrowing the range of meanings of intoxication. This results in a shortage of names that conceptualize the much more prevalent altered states of consciousness that fall short of the extreme of poisoning, names that are not made to carry the baggage of intoxication's semantic history.

We need a lexicon with a wider aperture so that the phenomena we refer to with the term intoxication do not imply a false binary, drunk or sober, but rather capture the broad array of altered states in between. After all, milder varieties of intoxication are a quotidian cultural practice, with cocktails or cannabis commonly deployed as a means of shifting one's psychic gears, signaling the end of the workday and the beginning of leisure time (Walker 2017).

As alcohol was the earliest and most common means of achieving an altered state, the word "drunk" stood as the initial template for subsequent intoxications, literal and figurative ("drunk on power"). In 1981, Levine compiled the rich "vocabulary of drunkenness." He reported that Benjamin Franklin found 228 terms for drunk in 1737, and that the *Dictionary of American Slang* listed 353 such terms, noting that "the concept having the most slang synonyms is 'drunk'" (1981:1038). Curiously, most such terms connote the destruction of ordinary consciousness – bombed, blitzed, hammered, shit-faced, wrecked – without implying there's anything wrong with that. For most of Western history, the term "drunk" did not necessarily carry a negative connotation. Early ascetic Protestants helped link drunkenness to poison by using the term "intoxication" to stigmatize drinking as transgressive. Since then, the word intoxication has come to cover a multitude of sins.

Marking off the territory of intoxication as a province of meaning is a tricky endeavor; its boundaries are a good deal more blurry than we usually imagine. Intoxications vary along numerous continua: in their duration, their intensity, and their degree of transgressivity. There are distinct types, depths, registers, and shades of altered state, to say nothing of the diverse meanings attached to these by different groups at different times. There is a wide expanse of terrain between a beer after work and an alcoholic blackout, or between "a little buzz" and "totally wasted." Intoxications or high states are context-specific. The same quantum of drink yields different behavioral effects at a wake than at a wedding. The experience of MDMA or ecstasy is different at a dance club than during a couple's romantic evening at home by the fire.

Other contributors to this handbook ably document culturally specific repertoires of intoxication. Such repertoires become thinkable and articulable within specific conjunctures of time/space/culture (MacAndrew and Edgerton 1969; Alasuutari 1992; Withington 2014). Learning more of their histories will enrich our understanding of the phenomena we refer to as intoxication. What structural forces and historical exigencies have shaped the systems of thought and genres of discourse that have produced and reproduced "intoxication" as a recognizable realm of meaning? For all the ink that has been spilled on intoxication over the centuries, its topography remains sketchy, perhaps rightly so.

"Intoxication," then, is a category that invites interrogation. The World Health Organization defines it as "a condition that follows the administration of a psychoactive substance and results in disturbances in consciousness, cognition perception, judgment, affect, or behavior" (2020). If we leave aside the pejorative term "disturbances," the core idea in this definition is an altered state of consciousness. But *altered compared to what*? Compared to ordinary waking consciousness without having ingested a psychoactive drug, the WHO implies. This definition has some limitations.

The distinction between altered/not-altered consciousness is most legible at opposite ends of a continuum. In many places for much of history, ordinary waking consciousness did not necessarily mean "drug-free." In parts of medieval Europe, beer-laden porridge was consumed for breakfast. A petition against brandy submitted to the English Parliament in 1673 argued that "all labor[ing] people (the greater part of the Kingdom)" need, deserve, and indeed benefit from "a pot of ale or a flagon of strong beer," which they drank "every morning and evening" (Schivelbusch 1992:159). Contrary to the mythical imagery of abstemious Puritans, colonial Americans carried rum, hard cider, and whiskey into their fields and shops for work breaks (Levine 2014) and consumed far more alcohol per capita than modern Americans (Levine and Reinarman 1991:468). Frederick the Great of Prussia felt that coffee drinking among his soldiers "must be prevented" because beer was so superior for purposes of bonding and morale (Slingerland 2021:135). In past centuries, widespread diseases, fevers, injuries, backaches, and tooth decay routinely put people in pain, in response to which they invented consciousness-altering potions containing alcohol or opium for pain relief. If a substantial proportion of the population was in some sort of altered state for a substantial proportion of the time, then at least moderate varieties of what is called intoxication were not considered aberrant.

The tobacco industry worked tirelessly to normalize smoking so that it was until recently considered just part of everyday life. Recall the ash trays that once graced all restaurant tables and were built into every automobile and airplane seat. By taking a 100 or more drags across their day, smokers alter their consciousness by mobilizing neurotransmitters to "fine-tune their arousal and mood state" to fit their situations (Krogh 1991:51). True, smoking tobacco does not lead to the crazed abandon conventionally associated with the term intoxication, but this does not change the fact that it is a drug-induced alteration of consciousness – a difference of degree, not of kind.

The same may be said for the tens of millions who take Prozac and other serotonin-based anti-depressants. Millions more (mostly Americans) ingest amphetamine-type drugs such as Ritalin to soothe attention deficit disorders and improve their ability to focus and function. These practices are considered medical treatment rather than intoxication, but they, too, entail the use of psychoactive drugs to alter consciousness and thus occupy a point on the same continuum as more extreme and obvious forms of intoxication. So, by asking "altered compared to what?," I am suggesting that the category of intoxication itself, as well as the comparative states of consciousness against which it is defined, are moving targets – variegated, permeable, and ultimately unstable.

The word intoxication is misleading in a second sense: there are common varieties of experience and behavior that bear the marks of intoxication and yet involve no "toxin" at all. Years ago on a visit to the Van Gogh Museum in Amsterdam, I saw his early masterpiece, "The Potato Eaters." Unlike the blazing colors of his more well-known work, this is a dark portrait of peasants huddled around a small table over a pot of potatoes in their low-ceiling shack. A few days later, I visited Delft and stopped at the fourteenth-century church in which the great Golden Age painter Johannes Vermeer is buried. As I sat in a back pew taking it all in, it occurred to me that medieval ancestors of Van Gogh's potato eaters could have been congregants in that church, and I tried to imagine what such people must have felt entering it for the first time:

The grand tower lofting high above graceful stone arches; sunlight streaming kaleidoscopically through stained-glass windows, colors cascading across the stone floor. Alter boys carrying candles in a solemn procession of costumed clergy spraying drops of holy water onto the bowed heads of the faithful. The air tinged with incense. Reverent silence broken only by the choir sending hymns and Gregorian chants wafting through the nave and by the priest's Latin incantations. Listening to tales from the Bible, kneeling with others to pray, ingesting the body and blood of Christ from implements of gold. All of it concocting a majesty unlike anything else in the peasant world, inducing a state of awe. All their senses mobilized to bring alive the divine, to glimpse God, I'd wager those early potato eaters found themselves in an altered state, intoxicated by the sights and sounds of the spiritual sublime. Compared to their lives of trudging labor in turbulent times,[3] they needed no drug for it all to feel positively psychedelic, *avant la lettre*.[4]

Moving from the sacred to the profane, consider the pandemonium surrounding the arrival of The Beatles in the USA in the 1960s. Thousands of teenagers screamed and jumped in uncontrollable spasms, some to the point of passing out, before a single song was played. News reports framed this as a worrying new form of mass hysteria, but before The Beatles, there was similar mania around Elvis Presley and before him among fans of Frank Sinatra. Neither alcohol nor other drugs were necessary for these altered states. Subsequent rock concerts famously involved plenty of drug use, but anyone who has attended a live concert of a favorite band can attest to the contagious eruption of an altered state of pleasure in being with thousands of others moved by the same music, with or without intoxicants.[5] When Dizzy Gillespie and Louis Armstrong brought American jazz to Africa for the first time in the 1950s, audiences were literally ecstatic. When, after decades in exile and Soviet suppression, Vladimir Horowitz returned to the USSR to play Rachmaninoff and Tchaikovsky, he was mobbed by admirers. His concerts sold out in minutes. Hundreds stood in silence squeezed together in the back of the concert hall, some in tears, overwhelmed to be in the presence of such beauty, such genius. The Cold War context added an extra measure of meaning, but the intoxicant producing those altered states was music.

Gambling casinos are designed without windows to ensure their patrons focus on the flashing lights, the flying dice, the whirring roulette wheels, the quick clicking of the cards, and the drama of big money won and lost in a blink. Hard-core gamblers describe ups and downs of adrenaline in a language of addiction that is similar to the accounts of crack cocaine users (cf. Waldorf et al. 1991:103–126; DeCaria et al. 1998). Commodities markets and stock exchanges from "Tulipmania" in seventeenth-century Holland to contemporary Wall Street also flicker with the speculative possibility of fast riches and often produce the same sort of affective roller coaster of risk, rush, and ruin. Computer games and virtual reality devices are engineered to maintain their grip on participants with their own genre of attentional intoxication.

Beyond religious rituals, rock concerts, casinos, whirling Dervishes and other dance-induced trances,[6] there is the frenzied elation found in ordinary sporting spectacles. American and global versions of football have in common tens of thousands of fans screaming in fevered states of ecstasy (or agony) about moves on the field barely visible from most stadium seats. Certainly, beer is often involved, but I submit that no drug is necessary for the intense intoxications sparked by a goal, a touchdown, a 9th-inning home run, a game-winning 3-point basket at the buzzer, or any hard-fought home team victory. And like some other intoxications, sporting events, too, are occasionally followed by violence.

I offer these examples to suggest that there are many modes of intoxication in which the "toxin" involved is not a drug ingested but rather one produced internally by the alchemical-cultural interaction of self and situation. If, therefore, it is neither a psychoactive substance nor the mere fact of altered consciousness that define the meaning province of intoxication, then what does? If intoxications are so varied and common, and may not even entail intoxicants, then how is it that the use of certain consciousness-altering chemicals has come to define what we mean by "intoxication," and to carry such moral freight? More than molecules are involved.

The Undulating Moral Careers of Intoxicants

As regards drink, I can only say that in Dublin, during the Depression when I was growing up, drunkenness was not regarded as a social disgrace. To get enough to eat was regarded as an accomplishment. To get drunk was a victory.

– Brendan Behan

While intoxication in one form or another has been ubiquitous across time and space, different intoxicants have had distinct moral careers, including some vertiginous shifts in how they are perceived by various publics and defined by governments. Certain intoxicants have been feared and punished, others accepted or even esteemed. Most interesting are those that have moved from one status to the other and sometimes back again, for these make visible the brushstrokes of their social construction.

Writing of the sixteenth-century Mediterranean world, historian Fernand Braudel found "lands of wine and vineyards" (1972:236) where wine was understood more as food than intoxicant and considered an intrinsic part of family meals. He noted that for centuries, wine had been an essential "provision," stored in cellars for the winter along with firewood and grains. "Throughout the Mediterranean the grape harvest was an occasion for merrymaking and license, a time of madness," he wrote. This form of intoxication entailed "various abuses" and some authorities tried stern measures to suppress such "pagan customs," but Braudel offered no evidence these ever succeeded. "Is there any way of fighting the combination of summer and new wine, of preventing collective revelry?" (1972:256–259).

Yet, preventing just that sort of revelry was what American anti-alcohol activists set out to do in the early nineteenth century. Their self-proclaimed temperance crusade was then the largest and longest social movement in the USA and culminated in national alcohol Prohibition in 1919. The crusaders blamed booze for a long list of personal and public problems, as if immediate intoxication and eventual ruin were inevitable consequences of drinking. Troubles associated with drink came to be defined as more threatening in a context of wrenching social change – the transformation of an agrarian to an industrial market economy, a civil war over slavery, large-scale immigration, urbanization, and class conflict (Sellers 1991). Gusfield (1963) described the "status politics" around alcohol in the nineteenth- and early twentieth-century USA as a battle between native-born, middle-class Protestants, mostly from small towns, and immigrant, working-class Catholics who lived mostly in cities. On the surface, it was "dry" vs. "wet," but the broader question animating the conflict was which groups would be dominant and whose values would stand as the law of the land.

Tobacco was the largest export in early colonial America, but its spread in England was initially greeted with royal condemnation. At the start of the seventeenth century, King James demonized this genre of intoxication as religiously offensive, casting tobacco users as immoral "fume suckers." But despite attempts to ban its use, tobacco was vindicated, largely on financial grounds. The King discovered to his chagrin that his continued reign was dependent on tobacco tax revenues, and the commercial interests whose support he needed were keen to protect their profits from the European tobacco trade (Best 1979). Modern tobacco merchants marketed their wares relentlessly, expanding the spaces in which tobacco could be smoked. By inventing cigarettes and later providing free matchbooks with each pack, they made smoking easy to do almost anywhere.

But following the 1964 U.S. Surgeon General's report documenting the deleterious health effects of smoking, a powerful anti-smoking movement began to reverse the tobacco industry's strategy. Anti-smoking activists argued forcefully on public health grounds for restricting the spheres in which smoking is allowed. They won various partial prohibitions and huge lawsuits. In the USA and increasingly other Western countries, the movement has de-normalized and re-stigmatized smoking, cutting its prevalence in half.

The moral career of cannabis provides a contrasting case. Cannabis was consumed and used as a medicine for centuries in parts of Asia and Africa. In the nineteenth and early twentieth centuries, it was commonly prescribed in medicines in the USA, listed in the *Pharmacopoeia* and the *United States Dispensatory* (Grinspoon and Bakalar 1997). But in the 1930s it was condemned as immoral and dangerous by the Bureau of Narcotics. In a report to the League of Nations, for example, the Bureau's director, Harry Anslinger, claimed that marijuana had "toxic effects," including "willful violence" and "complete loss of judgment and restraint." "Cannabis acts quickly and effectively to cut off inhibitions," which he took as a self-evident evil. He invoked racist fears, citing unsourced "estimates" that "fifty percent of the violent crimes committed in districts occupied by Mexicans, Turks, Filipinos, Greeks, Spaniards, Latin-Americans and Negroes, may be traced to the abuse of marijuana." Anslinger quoted a narcotics officer: "Marihuana has a worse effect than heroin. It gives men the lust to kill, unreasonably, without motive – for the sheer sake of murder itself" (League of Nations 1934; cited in Bonnie and Whitebread 1974:146–147).

The result of Anslinger's moral entrepreneurship was the "Reefer Madness" era in which the Marijuana Tax Act of 1937 first criminalized cannabis under federal law (Becker 1963). As marijuana use spread across U.S. college campuses in the 1960s, however, the argument against it shape-shifted. Earlier claims that marijuana caused crime and violence proved false, and for users, cutting off inhibitions and loss of restraint was the point. So then anti-drug forces claimed that marijuana caused an "a-motivational syndrome" that sapped users of ambition (Himmelstein 1983).

Marijuana remained a potent political symbol, associated with the counterculture and the anti-war movement and attacked by conservatives for that reason (Baum 2016, 1996). In 1970, President Nixon signed the Comprehensive Drug Control Act, which classified marijuana as a Schedule I narcotic, defined as a drug having "no currently accepted medical use and a high potential for abuse," neither of which turned out to be true. He soon declared "drugs" to be "public enemy #1," formally launching the War on Drugs. Lifetime prevalence of cannabis consumption, however, continued to spread from small subcultures like Beatniks and jazz musicians c. 1950 to nearly half the adult population by 2000 (SAMHSA 2012). But with the rise of the New Right and the election of Reagan in 1980, the War on Drugs expanded exponentially (Reinarman and Levine 1997:36–46), including the arrest of millions of Americans for marijuana possession, disproportionately people of color (see, e.g., King and Mauer 2005; Levine and Small 2008; Alexander 2010).

This repression, along with growing scientific evidence of the relative safety and medical utility of cannabis, sparked a growing drug policy reform movement. Between 1996 and 2020, the movement succeeded in getting 36 states to pass medical marijuana laws and 18 states and the District of Columbia to legalize adult use. There is now a burgeoning cannabis industry in many states, providing tens of thousands of jobs and millions in tax revenues (Yakowicz 2021). For the first time, the U.S. Congress is considering re-scheduling and even legalization (Edmondson 2020), moving the USA toward the Netherlands, Portugal, Switzerland, Uruguay, Canada, and other nations in the moral vindication of cannabis (*The Economist* 2021).

Troy Duster describes a "remarkable transformation in the moral interpretation of narcotics usage." In the late nineteenth century, opiate addiction was roughly eight times more prevalent than now. The addicted population was predominantly white middle-class women, most remaining unnoticed or considered patients. These included "the most respectable citizens ... pillars of middle-class morality." Opiate use was a matter between patients and their doctors. As Duster notes, "It was acknowledged in medical journals that a morphine addict would not be detected as an addict so long as he maintained his supply" (1970:9). But that supply began to dry up after the Harrison Narcotic Act of 1914, the first federal law against opiates. As the addict population began to shift, from mostly "respectable" middle-aged, middle-class women in 1900 to more "disreputable" young, working-class males in 1920, opiate addiction was reinterpreted. Medical journals wrote of two classes of addicts: "physical, mental and moral defectives, the tramps, hoboes, idlers, irresponsibles, criminals ... These are the drug fiends" in whom "morphine addiction is a vice." Others were "good citizens who have become addicted ... innocently," who were "victims" (Swaine 1918:611, in Duster 1970:11).

Armed with the Harrison Act, agents from the new Bureau of Narcotics pursued a policy of criminalization. They prosecuted a series of cases that resulted in Supreme Court decisions interpreting the Harrison Act narrowly, so that "legitimate medical use" could no longer mean maintaining opiate-dependent patients. They forced the closure of 44 morphine maintenance clinics and began arresting physicians who prescribed opiates for their patients (see, e.g., Waldorf et al. 1974). This choked off legal supplies and set up a self-fulfilling prophecy in which "drug fiends" were pushed into a growing criminal underworld (Duster 1970; Musto 1987). Opiates were criminalized not on the basis of pharmacology or addictive liability but rather on who was seen as their primary consumers.

At the same time in England, the spread of cocaine use stoked a moral panic on similar logic. British cultural historian Marek Kohn summarized it this way:

> Strongly associated with women – prostitutes, actresses, nightclub dancers, 'flappers' – [cocaine] was at the center of a discourse that used anxiety about delinquent drug use as a means of articulating deeper fears about the transformations Britain was undergoing; particularly those involving female emancipation, pleasure, morality, and perceived threats from the outside world, symbolized by drug-dealing 'men of color.' The drug panic was a spasm of reaction, as Britain struggled to come to terms with modernity... [p]art of a moral sea change, which embraced the pursuit of pleasure for its own sake.

As with alcohol, cannabis, and opiates in the USA, Kohn notes that in England, "cocaine was damned by the company it kept." The Dangerous Drugs Act of 1920 was animated by anxieties about "the jazz craze ... This, the British apprehensively realized, was the sound of the new world; chaotic, Dionysian, American, African, and altogether Other" (1999:105–106; 118–119).

Lastly, the class of intoxicants known as psychedelics has had its own checkered career. Some psychedelic substances like peyote, psilocybin mushrooms, and ayahuasca have been part of longstanding indigenous rituals in Central and South America (Rudgley 1995). LSD was discovered in the course of pharmaceutical research and initially thought to have potential in psychotherapy. The CIA soon explored its potential as a chemical weapon. But LSD, too, was damned by the company it kept. It was criminalized after being linked to Timothy Leary, Aldous Huxley, and other counterculture figures who advocated psychedelic intoxications for pleasure and exploration of the mind (Stevens 1987).

Under official stigma, scientific research on the therapeutic potential of LSD and other psychedelics ground to a halt for decades, but is now having a renaissance. Giffort (2020) documents how scientists "performed" their expertise so as to construct "boundaries of credibility" to distance their research on the therapeutic potentials of LSD from the "messianic" approach of Leary et al. Drug policy reformers pushed for new studies which eventually showed what was suspected long ago: psychedelics hold real promise in the treatment of PTSD, depression, trauma, addiction, and in end-of-life care (Tullis 2021). Scientific and public opinions are shifting (Pollan 2018). Johns Hopkins University has established the Center for Psychedelic and Consciousness Research where controlled trials have shown favorable results. The Netherlands allows the sale of psilocybin mushrooms. In 2020, Washington, DC, voters passed a law to de-criminalize them and Oregon voters legalized their medical use (Chang 2020; Smith 2021). Pharmaceutical companies are busy planning.

Controlling Intoxicants: Common Themes

Intoxicants have seen shifts in their moral-legal status under different political, economic, and cultural conditions. It follows that there is nothing natural or inevitable about the label attached to an intoxicant at any point, a historical fact that should confer some humility about drug controls. Beyond this, however, the examples above all have unique features that make generalization difficult. In each case, such shifts seem to be the result of a contingent conjuncture of actors, institutions, and contexts, so it seems best to speak a language of likelihoods and tendencies. Mark Twain famously quipped that "history doesn't repeat itself but it does often rhyme." Are there at least "rhymes" to be found across the histories of intoxicants, themes that are marbled through these cases?

Let me suggest five recurring themes. First, intoxicants and forms of intoxication are usually bound up with symbolic and identity interests that shape their uses, effects, and meanings. For example, Alasuutari's case studies of working-class drinking in Finnish taverns identify a "cultural grammar" in which drunkenness is a purposively transgressive expression of desire for personal freedom, beyond all self- or social control (1992:5). Rosenzweig makes a related case for the centrality of drinking and saloons in creating autonomous spaces in American working-class culture (1983). The use of cannabis and other illicit drugs was embraced as a badge of honor among members of the 1960s counterculture, a symbol of resistance to the established order that was central to their identity. That such intoxications had an *oppositional valence* is an important part of why defenders of the social order feared and tried to suppress them, which, in turn, often helped suffuse them with still greater transgressive value for their adherents.

Second, whether a form of intoxication is seen as problematic is contingent on many things, not least whose consciousness is being altered and in front of whom. Narratives of "irresponsibility" and "danger" stick to some groups more easily than others; certain groups are depicted as prone to drug abuse, others to abstinence. The more disreputable the users of an intoxicant in terms of class, ethnicity, status, and power, the more likely that form of intoxication is to be defined as dangerous by the state. Conversely, the higher the status of the intoxicated – the more cultural capital they have, the greater their ability to conceal or recover from problematic use and resist stigma – the lower the likelihood that their intoxication will be deemed dangerous. In some cases, there is a tendency toward *reciprocal demonization*: an intoxicant is thought dangerous in part because it is associated with a "dangerous class," and that class is thought dangerous in part because they ingest a "dangerous drug" (Himmelstein 1978).

Third, and corollary to the above, altered states or intoxications that help people transgress or loosen the grip of social control are more likely to be feared and defined as deviant or criminal. Conversely, intoxications that help people adapt to or function more smoothly within the existing social order are less likely to be defined as deviant or criminal. High states that cut against the dominant cultural grain tend to invite sanctions. Guardians of that culture worry that under the influence, the structure of social control and social order will break down, and that intoxicated individuals will slip beyond customary constraints. Slaves might cast off their chains. Workers could break the bounds of their class position to confront their "betters." Youth might rebel against their parents' world. Sober citizens in the public square can't predict what an intoxicated person will say or do, disrupting what Goffman (1983) called the interaction order. By contrast, chemically managing one's troubles with Valium, Prozac, Ritalin, or methadone tends to be supported by organized medicine and the state.

Fourth, the moral vindication of a stigmatized intoxicant is more likely if there is a constellation of businesses, an "industry," to claim that the production and distribution of the intoxicant are legitimate forms of commerce. The histories of alcohol, tobacco, cannabis, and pharmaceutical drugs suggest that industries that create jobs, profits, and taxes are better able to mitigate evidence of health harms associated with their products. Industry lobbyists have always found ways to get their views across to policy makers so as to prevent, forestall, or weaken laws to eliminate or regulate their products. This seems most obvious with the tobacco and pharmaceutical industries, but the theme has broader salience. In the Netherlands, for example, representatives from the retail cannabis industry are treated like any other business group and invited to testify in Parliament regarding regulations that affect them. The same is increasingly true in many states in the USA.

Finally, laws and policies designed to control intoxicants are inextricably part of the matrix of problems associated with their use. Drug laws and policies influence both the social settings in which intoxicants are ingested and the psychology of those ingesting them (Zinberg 1984). These, in turn, bear upon the patterns of use and the behavioral consequences thought to flow from them. Alcohol prohibition was designed to eliminate drinking but gave rise to bathtub gin, speakeasies, increased consumption of liquor, organized crime, and so many other negative consequences that some key prohibitionists soon reversed course and pushed for its repeal (McGirr 2016). Elimination of legal supplies of opiates after 1914 helped create the black market and criminal drug subculture.

It is still taken as common sense that certain intoxicants cause crime, disease, and overdose deaths, but such claims are partly self-fulfilling. A substantial portion of "drug-related crime" is caused as much by the dehumanizing "funnel" of narrowing options (Rosenbaum 1981) shaped by prohibition as by addiction *per se*. The spread of HIV/AIDS and Hepatitis C among people who inject drugs stems from syringe sharing, which has more to do with the criminalized context of use than with drugs themselves. Overdose deaths are largely a function of the lack of potency labeling and quality controls in illicit markets. In short, the dangers citizens have been led to fear most about illicit intoxicants are as much the predictable effects of drug *policy* as the effects of drugs. In this sense, punishment-based prohibitions tend to be self-ontologizing; they helped create the conditions under which intoxicant use is more likely to be problematic, and thus helped create the consequences that appear to confirm the need for prohibition.

CODA: Politics and Pleasures

The way we think about intoxicants and intoxication is evolving. Pleasure is a central goal of intoxicant use and a core reason for its persistence as a cultural practice. But all types of nation states have found it functional to draw *cordons sanitaires* around certain intoxicants

(Levine 2003) – as if to say "these forms of pleasure are just too dangerous to our health to allow." The case histories summarized above suggest, however, that the *cordons* keep getting re-drawn. Such state actions have their own genealogies and logics, but they are *always* more than mere governmental responses to health risks (see, e.g., McGirr (2016) on the importance of state building in the war on alcohol; Frydl (2013) on the influence of foreign policy in drug wars; and Reinarman and Levine (1997) on the political functions of drug scares).

In his book about state formation in early modern Europe, Philip Gorski argues that the Protestant Reformation, Calvinism in particular, "unleashed a profound and far-reaching process of disciplining – a disciplinary revolution – that greatly enhanced the power of early modern states." This led to "new mechanisms for the production of social and political order." He shows how "the technology of observation – self-observation, mutual observation, hierarchical observation" created an "infrastructure of governance" whose object was the "control of behavior and the shaping of subjectivity." This slowly resulted in "a more disciplined polity" with "more obedient and industrious subjects" (2003:x–xvi; cf. Elias 1978).

This disciplinary revolution began, however, in what historians call the "early modern" period (see, e.g., Burke 1978), and therein lies the rub; for modernity has turned out to be the cultural Big Bang in the universe of pleasure. New modes of discipline and governmentality notwithstanding, across centuries and continents Western modernity valorized pleasure seeking, legitimated the pursuit of pleasure as a basic right, and multiplied the means of pleasure. Colonialism combined with the industrial revolution spread, intensified, and accelerated this (Schivelbusch 1992; Walker 2017; Courtwright 2019). There have been ups and downs and tensions, but the general trend has been an erosion of norms against pleasure and an accumulation of norms allowing and even promoting it. This makes for a rough road for drug controls.

Historian David Courtwright shows that the trade in sugar, alcohol, opiates, tobacco, cocaine, cannabis, and other intoxicants that has been so central to modern market economies has a dark side he calls *limbic capitalism*:

> Limbic capitalism refers to a technologically advanced but socially regressive business system in which global industries, often with the help of complicit governments and criminal organizations, encourage excessive consumption and addiction. They do so by targeting the limbic system, the part of the brain responsible for feeling and for quick reaction, as distinct from dispassionate thinking. … It was a late development in a long historical process that saw the accelerating spread of novel pleasures and their twinned companions of vice and addiction. The pleasures, vices, and addictions most conspicuously associated with limbic capitalism were those of intoxication.
>
> *(2019:6)*

The mass consumption culture that came into full flower after World War II and the extraordinary economic boom it helped spawn were rooted in the notion that human needs and wants could and should be met through the consumption of commodities – not saving and scrimping, making things and making do, as most people had to do during the Great Depression, but indulging the pleasures of consumption (Ewen 1976). The notion that intoxicants could somehow be kept separate from all this seems naïve.

In not much more than a single generation, the USA experienced the repeal of alcohol prohibition, the end of the Depression, victory in World War II, the invention of television, the rise of mass marketing, a pharmaceutical revolution which established the idea that ingesting a pill could change consciousness and alleviate suffering, and the subsequent spread of recreational drug use. The production and consumption of various pleasures became fundamental to postwar America and beyond. Citizens *as workers* are still encouraged to keep their noses to the grindstone and marshal self-control as disciplined neoliberal subjects, but the modern economy has come to depend on citizens *as consumers* loosening the grip of self-control and seeking pleasure (see Bell 1976; Lenson 1995; Reinarman and Levine 1997:334–344; Alexander 2008).

Alexander (2008) argues that capitalist globalization entails accelerating forms of social and cultural *dislocation* – from families of origin, from conventional work roles, from communities, traditions, and life-ways that orient us and give us a stable conception of self. Such anomie or normative disorientation loosens the bonds that anchor the self and thereby makes obsessive behaviors more likely and more destructive. Ironically, neoliberal societies then call for individuals to "take responsibility" for their own actions by means of the self-control that these same societies tend to undermine (Bell 1976). With rising precarity and cascading diasporas, Alexander shows, the regulation of the self and its desires has grown increasingly difficult for an increasing proportion of the population. This puts governments in the difficult position of constantly having to problematize and police one or another intoxicant.

It seems unlikely that the genies of consciousness alteration can be put back in their bottles. Intoxicants of various types have become technologies of the modern self. More people now see at least *periodic* intoxication as normative – not that literally everybody is getting high all the time but rather that the majority of people have enjoyed doing so and expect to again in the future, as do many people they know (Parker et al. 1998; Eisenbach-Stangel et al. 2009;Walker 2017).

These people are no counterculture, no deviant demimonde of beatniks, hippies, junkies or marginalized others. They are ordinary neighbors, workers, and parents – educated, employed, engaged citizens. They have the demographic bulk and the social capital to resist stigma. They are the constituency who have voted repeatedly for drug policy reform, i.e., for new ways of thinking about intoxicants and intoxication.

In his study of the 1960s counterculture, Bennett Berger observed that while they did not succeed in a revolutionary sense of upending the existing social order, they did have a significant impact on Western culture. He noticed a shift in sensibility he called "consciousness of induced consciousness": "[O]ne of the basic achievements of the [Sixties] 'generation' may be a mind-set *aware* of the *induced* character of its own dissatisfied consciousness," which left them "ready to reject those inductions for more promising ones deliberately chosen" (1981:197–210, original emphasis). As Berger knew, earlier strands of this awareness ran along crooked paths from the Renaissance, the Enlightenment, and the scientific revolution. But I think he was right that in the half-century since The Sixties, consciousness of the induced character of human consciousness has seeped from the counterculture out into the broader culture.

More people are now more aware that there are discoverable reasons why we feel as we do, that it is possible to feel otherwise, that our present consciousness is but one state of consciousness among many. As consciousness-altering technologies, intoxicants have been and remain an essential element in this shift in sensibility.

Notes

1 The author gratefully acknowledges the helpful comments of Karen Bassi, Troy Duster, Harry Levine, Sheigla Murphy, Marsha Rosenbaum, Cathy Soussloff, and anonymous peer reviewers. All remaining flaws are the author's doing.

2 I am grateful to Prof. Karen Bassi for this point.
3 Lawrence Weschler (2004:18) observed that the striking thing about Vermeer's paintings is that they portrayed an intimate, interior peace in the century when the European world outside was convulsed in religious and nationalist conflict. It is impossible to know the specific consequences of religious or spiritual intoxication as we imagine we do in the case of a barroom brawl. But people walked out of such churches into a world where bloody religious wars were fought for decades by people certain they had God on their side.
4 There are, of course, strong religious traditions in our own time in which this sort of altered state is common. Many church services in African-American communities include music, singing, swaying, the call-and-response and passionate preaching that kindle in participants a joyous altered state (Gates 2021). And millions have felt a transcendent exhilaration hearing the speech-sermons of Martin Luther King, Jr.
5 My example is positive, but Walter Benjamin (1936) among others called attention to the similar process by which politics was aestheticized in service of nationalistic war in fascist regimes. Mussolini and Hitler staged mass rallies in majestic settings designed to create awe and instill the rousing, empowering feeling of being part of something larger than oneself.
6 The reference is to the 1952 documentary film, "Trance and Dance in Bali," by Margaret Mead and Gregory Bateson, depicting Balinese achieving ecstatic altered states by means of dance.

References

Alasuutari, Pertti, *Desire and Craving: A Cultural Theory of Alcoholism* (Albany: State University of New York Press, 1992).

Alexander, Bruce, *The Globalization of Addiction: A Study in Poverty of the Spirit* (New York: Oxford University Press, 2008).

Alexander, Michelle, *The New Jim Crow: Mass Incarceration in the Age of Colorblindness* (New York: The New Press, 2010).

Baum, Dan, *Smoke and Mirrors: The War on Drugs and the Politics of Failure* (Boston, MA: Little Brown, 1996).

Baum, Dan, "Legalize It All: How to Win the War on Drugs," *Harper's*, April 2016.

Becker, Howard S., *Outsiders: Studies in the Sociology of Deviance* (New York: Free Press, 1963).

Bell, Daniel, *The Cultural Contradictions of Capitalism* (New York: Basic Books, 1976).

Benjamin, Walter, "The Work of Art in the Age of Mechanical Reproduction," pp. 217–251 in Hannah Arendt, ed., *Illuminations* (Frankfurt a.M., Germany: Suhrkamp Verlag, 1968 [1936]).

Berger, Bennett, *Survival of a Counterculture: Ideological Work and Everyday Life among Rural Communards* (Berkeley: University of California Press, 1981).

Best, Joel, "Economic Interests and the Vindication of Deviance: Tobacco in 17th Century Europe," *The Sociological Quarterly* 20/2:171–182 (1979).

Bonnie, Richard J., and Charles H. Whitebread II, *The Marijuana Conviction: A History of Marijuana Prohibition in the United States* (Charlottesville: University of Virginia Press, 1974).

Braudel, Fernand, *The Mediterranean and the Mediterranean World in the Age of Philip II, Volume I* (New York: Harper and Row, 1972).

Burke, Peter, *Popular Culture in Early Modern Europe* (New York: Harper, 1978).

Chang, Ellen, "Why Investing in Psychedelic Medicine Could Be Better Than Cannabis," *U.S. News and World Report*, Sept. 11, 2020.

Courtwright, David, *The Age of Addiction: How Bad Habits Became Big Business* (Cambridge, MA: Harvard University Press, 2019).

DeCaria, Concetta M., Tomer Bergaz, and Eric Hollander, "Serotonegenic and Noradrenegenic Function in Pathological Gambling," *CNS Spectrums* 3/6:38–47 (1998).

The Economist, "Mexico Is On Track to Become the Latest Country to Legalise Cannabis," Mar. 26, 2021.

Edmondson, Catie, "House Passes Landmark Bill Decriminalizing Marijuana," *New York Times*, Dec. 6, 2020.

Eisenbach-Stangl, Irmgard, Jacek Moskalewicz, and Betsy Thom, Eds., *Two Worlds of Drug Consumption in Late Modern Societies* (Surry, UK: Ashgate, 2009).

Elias, Norbert, *The Civilizing Process* (Oxford, UK: Blackwell, 1978).

Ewen, Stuart, *Captains of Consciousness: Advertising and the Social Roots of Consumer Culture* (New York: McGraw Hill, 1976).
Frydl, Kathleen J., *The Drug Wars in America, 1940–1973* (New York: Cambridge University Press, 2013).
Gates, Henry Louis Jr., *The Black Church* (New York: Penguin, 2021).
Giffort, Danielle, *Acid Revival: The Psychedelic Renaissance and the Quest for Medical Legitimacy* (Minneapolis: University of Minnesota Press, 2020).
Goffman, Erving, "The Interaction Order," *American Sociological Review* 48:1–17 (1983).
Gorski, Philip S., *The Disciplinary Revolution: Calvinism and the Rise of the State in Early Modern Europe* (Chicago, IL: University of Chicago Press, 2003).
Grinspoon, Lester, and James Bakalar, *Marijuana, the Forbidden Medicine* (New Haven, CT: Yale University Press, 1997).
Gusfield, Joseph R., *Symbolic Crusade: Status Politics and the American Temperance Movement* (Urbana: University of Illinois Press, 1963).
Gusfield, Joseph R., "No More Cakes and Ale: The Rhetoric and Politics of Drinking Research," pp. 31–54 in his *Contested Meanings: The Construction of Alcohol Problems* (Madison: University of Wisconsin Press, 1996).
Hamilton, Claire, and James J. Collins, Jr., "The Role of Alcohol in Wife Beating and Child Abuse," pp. 255–266 in J.J. Collins, Jr., ed., *Drinking and Crime* (New York: Tavistock, 1981).
Himmelstein, Jerome L., "Drug Politics Theory," *Journal of Drug Issues* 8/1:37–52, 1978.
Himmelstein, Jerome L., *The Strange Career of Marihuana: Politics and Ideology of Drug Control in America* (Westport, CT: Greenwood Press, 1983).
Jamison, Leslie, *The Recovering: Intoxication and Its Aftermath* (Boston: Little Brown, 2018).
King, Ryan, and Marc Mauer, *The War on Marijuana: The Transformation of the War on Drugs in the 1990s* (New York: The Sentencing Project, 2005).
Kohn, Marek, "Cocaine Girls: Sex, Drugs, and Modernity in London during and After the First World War," pp. 105–122 in Paul Gootenberg, ed., *Cocaine: Global Histories* (London: Routledge, 1999).
Krogh, David, *Smoking: The Artificial Passion* (New York: W.H. Freeman, 1991).
League of Nations, Advisory Committee on Traffic in Opium and Other Dangerous Drugs, *The Abuse of Cannabis in the United States (Add.)*, Nov. 10, 1934.
Lenson, David, *On Drugs* (Minneapolis: University of Minnesota Press, 1995).
Lescaze, Zoe, "A History of Getting Hammered, and Why Some of Us Should Keep Doing It," *New York Times*, June 19, 2021.
Levine, Harry G., "Discovering Addiction: Enduring Conceptions of Habitual Drunkenness in America," pp. 25–42 in R. Granfield and C. Reinarman, Eds., *Expanding Addiction: Critical Essays* (New York: Routledge, 2014).
Levine, Harry G., "The Vocabulary of Drunkenness," *Journal of Studies on Alcohol* 42/11:1038–1051, 1981.
Levine, Harry G., "Global Drug Prohibition: Its Uses and Crises," *International Journal of Drug Policy* 14:145–153 (2003).
Levine, Harry, and Craig Reinarman, "From Prohibition to Regulation: Lessons from Alcohol Policy for Drug Policy," *Milbank Quarterly* 69/3:461–494 (1991).
Levine, Harry G., and Deborah Peterson Small, *Marijuana Arrest Crusade: Racial Bias and Police Policy in New York City, 1997–2007* (New York: New York Civil Liberties Union, 2008).
MacAndrew, Craig, and Robert Edgerton, *Drunken Comportment: A Social Explanation* (Chicago, IL: Aldine, 1969).
McGirr, Lisa, *The War on Alcohol: Prohibition and the Rise of the American State* (New York: W.W. Norton, 2016).
Musto, David, *The American Disease: Origins of Narcotic Control* (New York: Oxford University Press, 1987).
Parker, Howard, Judith Aldridge, Fiona Meacham, *Illegal Leisure: The Normalization of Adolescent Recreational Drug Use* (London: Routledge, 1998).
Pollan, Michael, *How to Change Your Mind: What the New Science of Psychedelics Teaches Us About Consciousness, Dying, Addiction, Depression, and Transcendence* (New York: Penguin, 2018).
Reinarman, Craig, and Harry G. Levine, eds., *Crack in America: Demon Drugs and Social Justice* (Berkeley: University of California Press, 1997).
Rosenbaum, Marsha, *Women on Heroin* (New Brunswick, NJ: Rutgers University Press, 1981).

Rosenzweig, Roy, *Eight Hours for What We Will: Workers and Leisure in an Industrial City, 1870–1920* (Cambridge, UK: Cambridge University Press, 1983).
Rudgley, Richard, *Essential Substances: A Cultural History of Intoxicants in Society* (New York: Kodansha, 1993).
SAMHSA (Substance Abuse and Mental Health Services Administration), *Results from the 2010 National Survey on Drug Use and Health* (Washington, DC: U.S. Department of Health and Human Services, 2012).
Schivelbusch, Wolfgang, *Tastes of Paradise: A Social History of Spices, Stimulants, and Intoxicants* (New York: Vintage, 1992).
Sellers, Charles, *The Market Revolution: Jacksonian America, 1815–1846* (New York: Oxford University Press, 1991).
Siegel, Ronald K., *Intoxication: Life In Pursuit of Artificial Paradise* (New York: E.P. Dutton, 1989).
Slingerland, Edward, *Drunk: How We Sipped, Danced, and Stumbled Our Way to Civilization* (New York: Little, Brown Spark, 2021).
Smith, Jen Rose, "Will Psychedelic Mushroom Vacations Come to the U.S.?," *Washington Post*, January 6, 2021.
Stevens, Jay, *Storming Heaven: LSD and the American Dream* ((New York: Grove Press, 1987).
Swaine, George D., "Regarding the Luminal Treatment of Morphine Addiction," *American Journal of Clinical Medicine*, 25:611 (1918).
Tullis, Paul, "How Ecstasy and Psilocybin Are Shaking Up Psychiatry," *Nature* 589:506–509 (2021).
Waldorf, Dan, Craig Reinarman, and Sheigla Murphy, *Cocaine Changes* (Philadelphia, PA: Temple University Press, 1991).
Waldorf, Dan, Martin Orlick, and Craig Reinarman, *Morphine Maintenance: The Shreveport Clinic, 1919–1923* (Washington, DC: The Drug Abuse Council, 1974).
Walker, Ingrid, *High: Drugs, Desire, and a Nation of Users* (Seattle: University of Washington Press, 2017).
Weschler, Lawrence, *Vermeer in Bosnia* (New York: Vintage, 2004).
Withington, Phil, "Introduction: Cultures of Intoxication," *Past and Present* Supplement 9:9–33 (2014).
World Health Organization, 2020. https://www.who.int/substance_abuse/terminology/acute_intox/en/. Accessed Dec. 20, 2020.
Yakowicz, Will, "U.S. Cannabis Sales Hit Record $17.5 Billion," *Forbes*, March 3, 2021.
Zinberg, Norman E., *Drug, Set, and Setting: The Basis for Controlled Intoxicant Use* (New Haven, CT: Yale University Press, 1984).

2

NIC'D UP

A practice theory approach to understanding vaping nicotine as intoxication

Ruth Lewis, Emily Kaner and Tamar M.J. Antin

Introduction

Concerns about the popularity of vaping nicotine among young people have garnered much attention in recent years, particularly within the United States where fears about the long-term health consequences associated with vaping, as well as concerns about vaping as a potential gateway into smoking, are widespread (Al-Hamdani et al. 2019). In an effort to curb the appeal of vaping among youth, major public health bodies in the United States, including the Department of Health and Human Services and the Office of the Surgeon General, have emphasized addiction in their framing of youth vaping as a health and social problem, asserting that "*America faces an epidemic of youth e-cigarette use, which threatens to engulf a new generation in nicotine addiction*" (Health and Human Services Secretary, 2018) and "*Nicotine is a highly addictive substance, and many of today's youth who are using e-cigarettes could become tomorrow's cigarette smokers*" (Office of the Surgeon General, 2016). These problem-based framings continue to define the mainstream US public health efforts, generating extensive media coverage yet telling us little about how and why young people might be drawn to vaping in the first place. Indeed, amidst the cacophony of voices debating appropriate responses to the so-called "youth vaping epidemic" (Office of the Surgeon General, 2019), the voices and perspectives of young people who vape have been largely overlooked.

Within the rapidly expanding scientific literature on vaping among youth, a dominant focus has been describing patterns in vaping behavior – who vapes, how often, how much, and so on. Driven by disciplinary concern for understanding the distribution and control of disease, epidemiological studies often seek to identify risk factors and "propensities" for vaping among youth at an individual level, often with a view to informing efforts to modify behavior. Yet, while the patterning of vaping behavior across a population is important to establish, these studies reveal little about how vaping is actually integrated within daily lives, nor how it has been able to quickly become embedded within youth cultures across the globe. This gap speaks to broader critiques of public health efforts focused on individual-level behavior change – efforts argued to have delivered only limited public health gains (Blue et al., 2016; Meier et al., 2018). As articulated by Meier et al. (2018, p. 207), "the large-scale household or health surveys that so often underpin our epidemiological and evaluation research rarely contain data on the location, purpose, paraphernalia, sociality, symbolism,

DOI: 10.4324/9780429058141-4

skills and temporalities" of the practices they purportedly describe, thus producing explanatory models that are overly individualized, and potentially limited in their scope to provide the contextual understandings necessary to effect change.

By contrast, other scholars have argued that practice theories offer an alternative paradigm with the capacity to transform efforts to improve public health by shifting focus beyond the individual as the unit of analysis, instead centering the practices themselves (Blue et al., 2016; Cohn, 2014; Hennell et al., 2020; Keane et al., 2017; Meier et al., 2018). Rather than view actions such as vaping as single behaviors, practice approaches instead conceptualize these as routinized or patterned domains of activities that involve the active integration of three key elements (Shove et al., 2012):

- *Materials* – which encompass the objects, technologies, resources, and infrastructures necessary to engage in the practice.
- *Competences* – which encompass forms of skill, practical know-how, and technique required to perform the practice.
- *Meanings* – which include shared understandings of the social significance and symbolic meanings of the practice.

Within this framework, a focus on the life of a social practice, like vaping, elucidates the elements involved in the practice, how the practice emerges, exists or dissipates, how it "recruits" practitioners, how it is performed and transformed by those who "carry" it, how it appears to change over time and by context, and how it interacts with other practices (Shove et al., 2012). A key premise of practice theories is that emergence, persistence, and change in practices are explained by the connections between elements being made, sustained, or broken (Shove et al., 2012). To illustrate this, Blue et al. (2016, p. 42) offer the example of smoking: engaging in smoking on a regular basis depends on the integration of *materials* (e.g. cigarettes, lighters, tobacco crops, transport systems, and retail infrastructures); *competences* (e.g. knowing how to light a cigarette and inhale and understanding social conventions about how to smoke in different social situations); and *meanings* (e.g. understanding smoking as associated with relaxation, sociability, glamour, masculinity, and so on). As with all practices, smoking is inherently unstable as these elements change over time: new products come in the market, necessary forms of competence evolve, meanings shift. Furthermore, social practices do not exist in isolation, but rather interact with other practices, creating "bundles" of practices which may be characterized as either in harmony or in conflict (Blue et al., 2016, p. 43). From a practice-informed perspective, declines in smoking can in part be understood as a result of tobacco control measures which have unraveled the bundling of smoking with practices such as working, eating, and socializing, by placing them in conflict and thus promoting "defection" from smoking (Keane et al., 2017).

Practice theories have recently been utilized productively in analyses of vaping, including work by Keane et al. (2017) who argue that approaching vaping as a social practice reveals "some of the less immediately apparent reasons why vaping has been able to establish itself as part of the pattern of everyday life for many vapers" (p. 466). In their analysis of written accounts from vapers in Australia, Keane et al. (2017) elucidate how vaping is easily integrated with other routinized practices, such as driving, watching television and smoking, thus opening up possibilities for nicotine consumption across space (e.g. where one can do it) and time (e.g. when one can do it). Similarly, drawing on accounts generated with poly-tobacco users in the USA, McQuoid et al. (2018) attend to the socio-temporal organization of vaping compared to the use of cigarettes and smokeless tobacco, emphasizing the "spatial flexibility" afforded by vaping. While these rich insights into the integration of practice elements help explain movement between smoking and vaping among some, elements relating to intoxication have received less focus within practice-informed analyses of vaping to date.

Intoxication is not generally a lens through which nicotine use is viewed, including within the field of drug and alcohol research. In a recent chapter, Keane (2020) argues that this may be due to the dominance of medical models, which present intoxication as a pathological state defined by impairment, harm, and loss of control. Building on broader conceptualizations of intoxication which emphasize the use of substances – both legal and illegal – to in some way alter consciousness (Bancroft, 2009; Hunt & Frank, 2016), Keane presents a compelling case for a more "expanded and de-pathologised framework of intoxication," which can attend to "small and brief shifts in mood and perception" (p. 48), and where "altered states of consciousness are not necessarily disruptive and dramatic" (p. 61), or discernible to others. From this view, the "mild and transient pleasures" experienced when people ingest nicotine – be that through smoking, vaping, or otherwise – can be encompassed within these broader understandings of intoxication.

Inspired by early work of Becker (1953), studies of intoxication have elucidated the social processes by which users of a substance learn to give meaning to the intoxicating effects of their substance of choice (Bancroft, 2009). In "In Becoming a Marijuana User," Becker emphasized that individuals' desire to use marijuana is not because of some psychological predisposition, but rather "is the result of a sequence of social experiences during which the person acquires a conception of the meaning of the behavior, and perceptions and judgements of objects and situations, all of which make the activity possible and desirable" and "lead to the use of marijuana for pleasure" (p. 235). Here, Becker highlights how identifying processes that are essentially made up of elements of a social practice – that is, the materials, competences, and meanings – leads to an understanding of why marijuana is a desirable form of intoxication for some. Though vaping has not generally been analyzed from a lens of intoxication, with some exceptions (e.g. see Keane, 2020), taking such an approach can highlight how young people who vape learn to desire and experience (or reject and refuse) the pleasurable effects of vaping nicotine, ascribe meaning to the experience of consuming nicotine without combusted tobacco, navigate the boundaries of nicotine intoxication, and derive pleasure from mastering the skills associated with vaping. Research directed toward elucidating the pleasures of intoxication is generally considered taboo in health-related research (Hunt & Evans, 2008; Hunt et al., 2007; Moore & Valverde, 2000) – it is "the great unmentionable," in Moore and Valverde's terms. Yet, pleasure is arguably a crucially important part of the process that makes drug use desirable in the first place (Reith, 2005). As such, public health efforts that fail to understand how youth learn to desire and negotiate the intoxicating effects of nicotine and instead fall back on conventional frames of addiction will ultimately result in poorly designed prevention programs and interventions that are incongruent with the experiences of young people who vape.

A tale of two studies

Below, we present a practice-focused analysis that brings together empirical accounts of vaping from two studies conducted in 2016 and 2017 with young people who vaped nicotine. Both studies were based in urban areas in Northern California – Study 1 involved in-depth interviews with 49 young people aged 15–25 in the San Francisco Bay Area, and Study 2 involved seven small group discussions with 26 young people aged 18–24 in a mid-sized city in San Joaquin county. Methodological details of each study are provided more fully elsewhere (Antin, Hess, et al., 2019; Antin, Hunt, et al., 2019; Lewis, in preparation). Here, we draw attention to a key feature of the samples of young people we spoke to: across both studies, participants were *predominantly smoking-experienced*, with the majority (59 out of 75) noting that they had smoked cigarettes prior to ever trying vaping (see Table 2.1). We highlight this shared characteristic of our samples to emphasize that these included very few of the "never-smoking" youth that have become centered within acrimonious debate about whether vaping represents a potential gateway to youth smoking (Levy et al., 2019). Rather, these were mainly current or formerly smoking youth who described being drawn to vaping as a strategy to help them reduce or stop their cigarette smoking. This common pathway from smoking to vaping among participants in Study 1 is described more fully elsewhere (Antin, Hess, et al., 2019). Given the intensifying social gradient in smoking, it is perhaps unsurprising that many of the youth in our studies were economically disadvantaged.

The landscape of vaping developed rapidly over the course of the 2016–2017 fieldwork period, in terms of both devices available in the market and their regulation. Both studies were conducted at a time *prior* to the proliferation on the market of pod-based vaping systems, such as Juul – the so-called "fourth-generation" of vaping devices. Rather, young people in our studies were using second- and third-generation devices, respectively, vape pens and tank-based systems (sometimes referred to as "mods" due to their amenability to modification). A further shared feature of the context within which these data were generated was that this was during a period of intensifying nicotine denormalization, including the introduction of the Tobacco 21 law in June 2016, which increased the minimum age for sale of both e-cigarettes and cigarettes to 21. Shortly before the studies commenced, billboards appeared across California picturing a young woman surrounded by vapor from a pen-style e-cigarette, with the tagline: "*It's the next generation cigarette, for the next generation of addicts.*" This anti-vaping campaign ad – one of a series funded by the Californian Department of Public Health in 2015 – reflected the evolution of public health messaging within a long-standing tobacco control program explicitly aiming to reduce the social acceptability of tobacco and nicotine use. Through focus on the integration between elements – material products, regulatory environments, forms of knowledge, social meanings, and so on – practice theories offer the ability to consider how practices change as these different elements evolve and are reconfigured. Our aim for this chapter has been to *work across* data from these two studies, paying particularly close attention to accounts of vaping as an intoxicating practice at a key point in the history of vaping (i.e. the immediate pre-Juul era).

Informed by an understanding of practices as dependent on the integration of materials, competences, and meanings (Shove et al., 2012), we used these three elements as a conceptual framework against which we mapped our data. We worked in parallel at first, conducting an independent thematic analysis of each dataset (Bernard & Ryan, 2010), and then integrated data from the two studies to identify shared practice elements and key differences.

Table 2.1 Pathways of nicotine product use among participants in each study

Nicotine pathway	*Study 1*	*Study 2*	*Total*
Smoking before vaping	36	23	59
Vaping before smoking	8	0	8
Vaping only (never smoked)	5	3	8
Total	**49**	**26**	**75**

An overview of key practice elements is provided in Table 2.2. Across the two studies, practice elements evident within young adults' talk about vaping nicotine were strikingly similar, indicating shared meanings that transcended the specific localities in which participants lived. The rare cases where an element only featured in accounts within one or other study are indicated in the table.

As Table 2.2 demonstrates, an overarching feature of young people's talk across studies was an understanding that the practice of vaping is intimately tied to the practice of smoking – young people made sense of vaping devices in relation to cigarettes, they talked about the forms of knowledge and skill required to vape in relation to those required for smoking, and the meanings attributed to vaping were very often relationally produced through understandings of smoking. In the context of this handbook's focus on intoxication, we turn our attention now to the practice elements within participants' narratives which are most salient to thinking about vaping nicotine as a form of intoxication.

Intoxicating elements of vaping nicotine as practice

Analysis of the practice elements associated with vaping nicotine that emerged from participants in our studies highlights the ways in which vaping nicotine is understood by these young adults as an intoxicating social practice. In particular, we emphasize three themes cutting across young adults' accounts of vaping nicotine in both studies: vaping as functional intoxication; controlling and calibrating intoxication; and forging social connection and community through intoxication.

It's not like a real high? Functional intoxication to cope with the everyday

Intoxication – simply conceptualized as the use of substances to change the mind – was a widespread goal of vaping nicotine across both studies. Indeed, getting a "nicotine fix" and achieving "a head change" (also sometimes referred to as getting "nic'd up") was widely constructed as the "point" of vaping. Yet, these head changes were not understood as a "high" in the same way as the effects of other psychoactive substances, such as alcohol, marijuana, or ecstasy – a distinction expressed explicitly by some, for example:

> …it's not like a real high. But it does give you a little bit of a head rush, and so that was cool. But it's not like a drug. It doesn't feel like a drug when you do it, because it has – because you still feel sober. You just feel kind of lightheaded and sober (laughs). So it's kind of nice. It's not like psychedelics or anything.
>
> *(Interview with 17-year-old woman)*

Here, we see a playing out of the complexities of defining what it means to be intoxicated, and which substances are considered to "count" as "drugs." Despite describing a stimulant effect (e.g. a head rush and lightheadedness), this young woman conveys an understanding that nicotine is *not* a drug because – in her view – "you still feel sober." Yet, although not expected to provide a "high," vaping nicotine was nevertheless constructed as serving a variety of mind-altering functions: to calm the mind, relax, take a break, focus, concentrate, let go, and so on. Collectively, then, vaping nicotine was articulated as a useful practice to *transform* the everyday, resonating with Bancroft's (2009) concept of "functional intoxication," where intoxication becomes fundamentally about using substances to "change the self in the world, to alter, manage and enhance an individual's efficacy in the social world" (p. 147). Although

Table 2.2 Practice elements identified within young adults' accounts of vaping nicotine via second- and third-generation devices (i.e. pre-pod-based systems) in California in 2016–2017

MATERIALS	*COMPETENCES*	*MEANINGS*
(e.g. objects, resources, and infrastructures)	*(e.g. practical know-how and skills)*	*(e.g. shared symbolic understandings)*
Vaping devices and juices • set-ups (starter kits vs sophisticated) • "authentics" vs generics/clones/fakes • product range constantly evolving and expanding • personalization/customization • fragility of devices / easily breakable • sharable (mods, juices) • portable • easily concealable • no lighter, trash or ash+ • no lasting bad smell • variable settings enable different experiences (e.g. size of clouds) • variable nicotine levels (vs fixed in cigarettes) • less satisfying throat hit than cigarettes • juices ("premium" seen as "safer") Vapor: a material facilitating the performative and sociable aspects of vaping (e.g. vape clouds) Cigarettes: a material intimately tied to the initiation and practice of vaping via aesthetic and sensory similarities and differences to vaping devices, and a necessary comparative object to describe practice elements (materials, competences and meanings) of vaping Money • Vaping as expensive, especially start-up costs – costs sometimes shared with others • Can earn money for vaping if sponsored*	Achieving desired level of intoxication • knowing how to achieve desired effects from vaping (e.g. "a head change," "nicotine fix," and "nicotine buzz") • controlling nicotine levels to avoid getting "nic sick" • vaping to moderate effects of other substances (e.g. marijuana) Learning and displaying technical know-how, e.g. • using, modifying and fixing devices (e.g. knowing which buttons to press and how to refill juice, fix coils) • about juice (e.g. understanding PG/VG ratios, how to preserve flavor, and maximize clouds) • setting and regulating nicotine levels • performing and mastering "tricks" • graduating to "higher end" devices • identifying "authentic" vs "fake" devices • recognizing nicotine levels on someone else's device (e.g. knowing what a "6" feels like) • charging and storing equipment safely* Navigating vape shop environments • as sites to experiment (e.g. with new flavors, nicotine levels, and set-ups), get help with fixing equipment, and build knowledge about vaping and harm reduction • demonstrating legitimate levels of knowledge to be seen as "worthy" of more sophisticated set-ups • involves navigating male-dominated "macho/bro" culture to get help (women's accounts)* • getting "in" with vape shop workers to get discounts	Relief from Everyday Stress • vaping to reduce and manage stress and anxiety • "time out" and momentary escapism from "real life" • enduring significance of inhalation and exhalation (as stress-relieving, pleasurable) Social Connection & Community • forging new connection with others • delineating in- and out-groups • heightening sociability • vape culture as a supportive community • sense of localism in vape culture (vs Big Tobacco as global) Reducing Harm • vaping as "healthier" alternative to smoking • easier to control than smoking • "life changing" in stopping/reducing smoking • substitute to smoking vs supplementary • reducing smoking harm by vaping as precarious practice that is easily disrupted (e.g. if device is lost or broken, costs increase, and regulations change)

Electricity: Need to charge devices Time: Required to invest in fixing equipment Commercial environments • "brick and mortar" vape shops as local sites that facilitate building of social and cultural capital for vaping • online shops and advertising • possibilities of sponsorship★ • vaping community events (e.g. mixers and conferences) Regulatory environments • (dis)parity between bans on vaping and smoking (e.g. university campuses and hospitality venues) • regulations on advertising vaping products • state laws (e.g. Tobacco 21 laws) • state taxation on e-cigarettes vs cigarettes Digital environments, e.g. social media platforms as a resource and infrastructure that facilitates: • advertising of products and practice • information sharing (e.g. videos of tricks and how to fix device) • mobilization of vaping-related activism (e.g. about upcoming changes in regulation)★	Engaging with health-related evidence, e.g. • recognizing evidence environment on vaping and health as contested • critiquing anti-vaping discourse (e.g. due to lack of long-term evidence on harms of vaping and glossing over of reduced relative risk to smoking) • knowing how to integrate vaping to minimize risk and promote smoking cessation (or at least smoking reduction) • diffusion of tobacco harm reduction practice between smoking peers (e.g. encouraging switch to vaping, sharing links to online information, loaning equipment to try, and accompanying to vape stores) Demonstrating social responsibility • by minimizing others exposure to second-hand smoke (vs smoking) • understanding and adhering to "common sense" codes of conduct (e.g. not vaping in restaurants and around children) • distancing self from "vaping others" who are irresponsible • privileging other people's comfort over vaper's desire to vape Avoiding vaping-related stigma, e.g. • not posting about vaping on public social media • not telling certain friends about vaping practice • not vaping in certain places • concealing vaping equipment from disapprovers	"Differently Stigmatised" to smoking [McQuoid et al., 2018] • situational stigma (i.e. in some contexts, by some people) • acceptability of men vaping as less contested than acceptability of women vaping "Spatially Flexible" [McQuoid et al., 2018] • vaping easily bundled with other solitary and group-based practices (e.g. walking, driving, studying, hanging out, and playing videogames) "Hardcore vapers" vs "just a hobby" • variable salience of vaping to self-identity, ranging from vaping as a core way to perform identities among "hardcore vapers," to an activity articulated as peripheral to self-identity

[+] Indicates only discussed within young adults' accounts within San Francisco Bay Area study.
★ Indicates only discussed within young adults' accounts within San Joaquin County study.

Bancroft's analysis focused on pharmaceutical drugs, the notion of functional intoxication is useful for illustrating the meanings of vaping-as-intoxication among participants in our studies. In particular, his articulation of "dispassionate drugs" used to "moderate the self into the rhythms of modern life and to blunt the edge of stresses and strains caused by its conflicting demands on the individual" (ibid) resonates strongly with young people's accounts of vaping nicotine to cope with the everyday demands of regular life.

Coping with stress was a prominent theme across our studies, with many young people describing their daily lives as stressful. In both studies, the majority of participants were growing up in social contexts characterized by multiple community-level stressors, including high levels of incarceration, poverty, violence, and substance use. Stresses relating to pressures within education settings were also commonly expressed by the young people we spoke to – both within interpersonal interactions (e.g. with other students, or teachers) and also arising from the intensity of educational cultures focused on attainment. In these contexts, vaping was commonly articulated as providing momentary relief; for example, one young man recounted how vaping during break-time enabled him to get through the school day:

> And before like second blah [*class period*], I'd just chief on [*inhale*] like someone's e-cig in the stall. So I'd (laughs) get out, like wow, I feel really good for this next class. So yeah, that's why I used it back then. Because you know, you're in school for eight hours a day, and dealing with fuckin' bullshit. So that would be my instant stress reliever. It would be like kids, yeah let's go to the bathroom.
>
> *(Interview with 19-year-old man)*

Others talked about turning to vaping to cope with more generalized forms of stress, and often as part of a concerted effort to not smoke, such as this young woman:

> ...Stress that I feel like I can't control because it's dependent upon another person, or another situation that is larger than what I have in my control. [...] Because if I can't control it, I shouldn't stress about it. But sometimes, that just makes me really tense. Because while I know that I can't control it, I still desire to have answers, or to be able to control it. And I know that's one thing that makes me want the enjoyment that comes from smoking. I know, at least temporarily relieves that feeling, at least that's what I associate it with. But since I don't like, or I really, really try hard not to smoke regular cigarettes, when I have my e-cigarette around, that's what I'll go to over it, if that makes sense.
>
> *(Interview with 24-year-old woman)*

Smoking cigarettes to cope with stress is a long-documented strategy; for example, Graham (1993) documented how mothers describe cigarette breaks as both a symbolic and literal "time out" from the mundane realities of caring for young children, which enabled them to re-establish their capacity to cope. As seen above, a sense of vaping providing a temporary "time out" from daily stress was also clearly reflected in young people's accounts. Yet, a point of contrast between vaping and smoking articulated by young people is the ability to *customize* the stress-relieving experience (i.e. via choice of nicotine level in juice), depending on self-assessed stress levels:

MAN 1: I just think it's dependent on the day, like what kind of day you're having. Sometimes when I have more of a stressful day, I need something that's higher nicotine to calm me down and relax me. If it's a regular day I might go for lower ones [*i.e. lower nicotine content juices*], so I can inhale more without feeling a nicotine head change. [...]

MAN 2: It's definitely more customizable too... Which is one of the reasons why I started to, yeah. I can control how much I inhale, or what I inhale [...] how much I want to taste the juice, or how much I just want to chug a cloud.

(*Small group discussion*)

While the stress relief of vaping was partially constructed as caused by the *amount* of nicotine consumed, the *modality* of consumption also mattered to some, with the affordances of inhaling nicotine *without* combusted tobacco enabling a different sensory experience to that of smoking. Indeed, the affective experiences of both inhalation and exhalation were constructed by some as key to the process of calming the mind, with accounts calling to mind the notion of "flow," where attention is paid to being in the moment. Among those who vaped to reduce or quit smoking, noticing and giving meaning to these contrasting affective experiences involved balancing the common complaint of vaping's diminished "throat hit" and "lung feel" against the pleasures of exhaling a greater quantity of vapor and capitalizing on its pliability. For example, one young woman identified the soothing effect derived from vapor as underpinning her success switching from smoking to vaping for health reasons:

> ...it also was kind of fun to try and do different tricks. Because with a cigarette, you (laughs) really can't do that. You get one puff in your mouth, and it's like you either swallow it, or just right back out. You can't really keep that in your mouth. It tastes terrible and it's also like the amount of smoke that you get is just, is not enough to do anything fun with. But with e-cigarettes, I liked it because <u>with other types of techniques of quitting, it's not really as intense. And it also doesn't really satisfy you in the same way</u>. But with an e-cigarette, you still kind of feel – for me, the reason that I've kept smoking so long is because I have really bad anxiety and depression. And so, to have that little thing that you can hold in your mouth and <u>kind of pay attention to with, it's almost like a tick kind of. It's more of the motion itself</u> [...].
>
> (*Interview with 18-year-old woman*)

Controlling and calibrating nicotine intoxication

Concepts of control and calibration consistently arise across cultures as themes within accounts of intoxication (Bancroft, 2009; Fry, 2011; Hunt & Frank, 2016; Measham, 2004; Measham et al., 2016). Evidence suggests that characterizations of control are contested among people with experience of both vaping and smoking; some studies have found that vaping is commonly understood by smokers as a way to control and reduce nicotine consumption (Keane et al., 2017; McQuoid et al., 2018), whereas others document a construction among some smokers of vaping as *less* controllable and more addictive than smoking (Lucherini et al., 2017). Our participants – mostly either current or former smokers – commonly articulated a sense of greater control over the frequency and extent of nicotine consumption when they contrasted vaping to smoking:

> I have more control of my smoking habits [...] Because with vaping, I don't have like a pack to myself. If I have a pack, then it's kind of an influence. Like oh, I have this much of a pack. I have to finish it, right? [...] And with vaping, I feel a little more healthier. I don't feel groggy. I don't smell bad. My tongue or my throat doesn't taste bad [...]

> because … when you smoke a cigarette, sort of like you have to finish it. Once you light it up, you have to finish it and throw it away. With vape, you can just like one or two, and okay, I'll put it down.
>
> *(Interview with 22-year-old man)*

> I prefer to smoke a regular cigarette […] I like the taste better. I like the buzz better. I enjoy it better. But there also becomes a time when all the other things, I guess stress me out about cigarettes in general. And while I don't feel like e-cigarettes are healthy, I do feel that they are marginally less harmful […] like it's easier to not chain smoke, yeah […] I think I always end up smoking more, when I have an actual cigarette. So, having the e-cigarette and being able to just take like a quick puff.
>
> *(Interview with 24-year-old woman)*

The temporalities of control over vaping compared to smoking are imbued within these accounts in more than one sense. First, there is the notion that it is easier to control one's nicotine intake *in the moment* as the compulsion to finish an entire cigarette is removed. Second, as vaping was widely constructed as less harmful to health than smoking, there is a sense of taking control over one's health, thus protecting *future time*. Indeed, some young people emphatically described experiencing the stress relief of ingesting nicotine without smoking a cigarette as "life changing" and a "game changer." For those seeking to either quit or reduce their smoking, noticing and giving meaning to the embodied experience of consuming nicotine *without* tobacco appear to be an important cognitive step supporting a shift between these practices. Yet, as illustrated above, this plays out differently between individuals. While the young man in the first extract actively values the absence of certain sensory experiences from smoking (e.g. feeling groggy, smelling bad, and tasting bad), the young woman in the second extract indicates that she has to balance the immediacy of pleasure derived from these sensations (e.g. better taste and better buzz) against her desire to reduce harm to her health.

In addition to controlling the mode and frequency of nicotine consumption, a further manifestation of control relates to decisions about how intoxicated to get, and attempts to moderate intake of a substance accordingly. Within our studies, achieving a head change from vaping nicotine was usually desired, but the threshold between being "nic'd up" and "nic'd out" was important:

> MAN 1: After a good meal you get that nicotine buzz, man. It feels hella [i.e. *very*] good. It's almost as similar as smoking a cigarette, but to me I feel that if you're rocking 6s [i.e. *using juice with 6mg nicotine content*], I feel like it's more than a pack of cigarettes. The nicotine buzz from a 6 compared to a regular cigarette is intensified by 3. A 6 can get you like, "Oh I gotta go to sleep. I feel hella heavy in my legs." A cigarette, I don't know, it doesn't feel as heavy as a 6 to me.
>
> MAN 2: That's where the term nic'd out comes from. If you've vaped so much you'll get nic'd out, and it's kind of just like, "Yo dude I'm nic'd out, take this vape out of my hands."
>
> *(Small group discussion)*

Identifying and managing this boundary between being nic'd up and nic'd out is one example of integration between material and symbolic elements of vaping as a social practice. Knowing how to avoid getting nic'd out (also sometimes referred to as "nic sick") is an important skill – or *competence* – that requires knowledge about the effects of different nicotine levels, asking others about nicotine levels in their juice when sharing devices, and learning to recognize what different levels of nicotine feel like when vaped; as one young man commented: "*with the mod when you take a hit from the vape it, like, hits you, like a ton of bricks so you, obviously you can't do 24 milligrams. It's usually, I run about like six to three milligrams now*" (small group discussion). Among those with prior smoking experience, the need to develop these new forms of practical know-how, and their articulation as forms of control relative to smoking is tied up with the material reality of vaping devices which allow users to regulate the number of puffs, as compared to the constant burn of a cigarette containing a pre-determined amount of nicotine (although of course, smokers retain a degree of choice over how many drags they take from a cigarette, and at what point they stub it out).

Finally, in addition to controlling intake of nicotine-via-vape, young people also talked about using vaping to moderate the intensity of intoxication from other substances, particularly marijuana. Vaping was commonly described as a way to be able to maintain a repetitive hand-to-mouth action and inhale *something*, without getting too high from continuous joint smoking or bong hits. For example, this young woman described how integral vaping is to moderating her intake of not only marijuana, but also cigarettes:

WOMAN 1: I just really like the feeling (laughs), like, the activity-
WOMAN 2: Like inhaling.
WOMAN 1: -yeah. The ritual of smoking.
WOMAN 2: Yeah.
WOMAN 1: Um, but it's not like I could just sit and smoke weed (laughs) for like an hour
WOMAN 2: Yeah.
WOMAN 1: The next thing you get, like, kind of high, and then you just vape after…
INTERVIEWER: Oh okay.
WOMAN 1: That's what I do.
INTERVIEWER: So you can continue doing the action?
WOMAN 1: Mm-hmm (affirmative). Because it's, like, soothing to me. Which is... I hate that, because it's so bad for you. I feel like even though I don't even like cigarettes anymore, I feel like nor do I like the taste of it, nor does it really affect me, um, unless, like, it's, like, a really strong tobacco or something. I think I'm mostly... I'm not gonna say addicted, but I do crave mostly, just, like, the action of smoking.
WOMAN 2: Yeah.
WOMAN 1: That's, like, what I'm more used to, and it just... Even though it's not- it's like a placebo effect. It calms me down.

(*Small group discussion*)

Here, we see another clear example of youth using vaping as a way to reduce tobacco-related harm. The desire to experience the pleasures of the hand-to-mouth action of cigarette smoking is balanced against an understanding of its effects ("it's so bad for you"), with a choice then made to satisfy this craving via vaping. Interestingly, this young woman locates the calming effect of vaping not in the nicotine itself, but rather in the ritual.

More than "just" a nicotine fix? Building connection and navigating community

Intoxicants have long been recognized as operating as a "medium of sociability" (Hunt & Frank, 2016; Partanen, 1991), and our participants' accounts indicate that vaping nicotine is no exception. Young people conveyed how vaping opened up possibilities for sociability, by offering a tool through which to both strengthen connection with known others and forge interaction with unknown others, as this young man explained:

> If you're standing outside vaping, I might walk up to you and say "Hi", and just talk to you because you're vaping. You're a fellow vaper. I don't really care why you're vaping, you know. But in my eyes, you're vaping so you're a vaper. That's all. There's no cool card you have to have, or and you don't have to be using a certain expensive mech mod or anything, or mod or anything. Just vaping, and not smoking (laughs) […] it's just like vaping isn't as big as smoking. So when you see someone else that's vaping, you're like 'hey, you vape? I vape', you know, like 'hey, we both vape. That's cool, man'. And sometimes, like my mod might be different than someone else's, and you just want, out of curiosity, 'what do you got in there? You build it yourself? How many wraps you got in there? What's your build look like?' Because people have these builds that are like, it's literally art. The way they wrap these things and wrap it around each other […] So it's kind of cool, just to see people's different styles. It's like art or music, and you're just like, oh cool. Just appreciative.
>
> *(Interview with 24-year-old man)*

In this extract, we grasp a sense by which vaping can diminish perceived social distance between otherwise strangers by instantly delineating an in- and out-group boundary. Due to the increasingly deviant status of smoking within mainstream Californian culture, seeing other people who vape may (at least at the time of our fieldwork in 2016–2017) signify a person's valuing of health; as another young man expressed, switching from smoking to vaping is "*a sign that you want to look after yourself*" (small group discussion). For the young man above, partaking in the practice of vaping automatically defines someone as a "vaper" – an identity that (in his view) stands separate from, and in positive contrast to, that of a smoker. On that basis, conversation with a stranger becomes possible; sharing in this practice indicates a sense that they will have things to talk about – as one young woman summarized, "*it's a conversation starter, like, it's something that a lot of guys can relate to with each other*" (small group discussion). As in the account above, these interactions are further facilitated by the customization of vaping devices, which provide a way to express oneself, and demonstrate appreciation for others. Characterization of vaping as a medium for sociability was echoed by this dual user of cigarettes and vape devices, who also contrasted vaping with a construction of smoking as less socially satisfying:

> Say if you smoke a cigarette, you can see people just standing there. Pretty much what they get from smoking cigarettes is the nicotine, which is a biological satisfaction. But say if you vape, the amount of vapor it produces is also a little fun thing to do. That you can do a lot of things with that vapor. Say people do tricks […] So that's one thing, pretty much just switching the focus from just getting that nicotine satisfaction to something else that you can actually practice. That you can actually um, show off, in front of other people. It's like something that is fun to do. Not just because, oh, you feel like nervous or something and you just want to smoke a cigarette to relax a little bit. There's something more about it than that […] it's still kind of a new thing. So, when you have a bunch of people doing it at the same time it's like uh, a kind of an icebreaker to start a conversation.
>
> *(Small group discussion)*

This account of vaping as going beyond "just" experiencing the intoxicating effects of nicotine is underpinned by a feature commonly commented on across both studies: the possibility of using vapor to do "tricks." Although disparaged by some who instead emphasized their use of vaping for smoking cessation, nevertheless, "tricks" appear to be a fundamental aspect of the sociability of vaping culture for some youth, as also described elsewhere (Cooper et al., 2016; Hilton et al., 2016; Measham et al., 2016). By capitalizing on the material features of vape devices (e.g. "softer" vapor and customizable voltage), practitioners are able to develop and display a repertoire of tricks that can, at least within certain venues and groups, create points of connection and camaraderie. For example, when asked to elaborate on how vaping helped to get closer to friends, one young man said:

> Oh yeah, like I said, the whole community, just like with the smoke, it's like when you smoke a cigarette, there's not too much. Or in a way, it's so powerful that you just want to get it out of your lungs as fast as possible. Like you'll smoke it and go (makes sound), and just spit it out. But with a vape, it can be different, because you can turn it down a notch and make it softer, so it's something you can hold in for a while, such as even a whole minute. And then, you can control when to spew it out, and like doing tricks. So that could be cool with your friends, because you could do a competition in a way. And then you'd get a little competitive with each other [...] like you can make a smoke jellyfish [...] Or even if they get super skilled at it, they can make a little caterpillar. So that was always fun to have a competition like that. It's like another type of partying.
>
> *(Interview with 18-year-old man)*

An ethos of exchange and reciprocity is recognized as a key element which can socially ease interactions between individuals within cultures of intoxication (Bancroft, 2009; Douglas & Isherwood, 1996; Heath, 2000; McQuoid et al., 2018). However, manifestations of these values vary not only by intoxicant, but also modality. McQuoid et al. (2018) argue that cigarettes and related paraphernalia (such as lighters and rolling papers) are "discrete units that can be more easily offered and received between strangers or acquaintances" compared to vape devices. Across our studies, accounts suggested that the acceptability of sharing vape devices was certainly contested; while some young people described vape pens and mods being routinely passed around multiple people at social gatherings, others expressed concerns about hygiene, noting that they would not personally use someone else's device. In lieu of ubiquitous norms governing sharing of these *material* artifacts, the sharing of *practical know-how* appeared to be the major medium of exchange between people who vape, including knowledge about how to use devices, perform tricks, fix and modify equipment, make homegrown e-juices, and so on. The very need for these exchanges of information was tied up with the material complexities of vaping technologies. In contrast to combustible cigarettes, where the innovations perceivable to smokers are few and far between, the rapid evolution of vape devices and a dizzying array of flavored juices enables a seemingly "ceaseless consumption of novelty" (see also Campbell, 1989, cited in Hunt and Frank, 2016). As argued by Keane et al. (2017, p. 473), vaping thus becomes "a site for the exercise of discernment, in which choosing becomes an expression of individual taste and distinction." The ability to exercise choice over juice and device, and to then customize "builds" appears – at least for some – to be key to "why vaping 'works' as a practice" (ibid). Ironically, however, the complexity of second- and third-generation devices was off-putting for some, presenting risks for the long-term integration of the practice as a way to stop smoking:

> Like vaping at first, I was just like over it. I was like this is so much work. Like I don't know what coils are, or I didn't even know how to change the coil. And I don't even know what it really is still, like I just know it's something that makes the vape work. But I was just struggling for a while, to figure out how to work everything on it. So at first, I was like dude, this is so ridiculous! I'm just about to go buy a pack of cigarettes, because that's so much easier.
>
> *(Interview with 21-year-old woman)*

> *[describing why he initially saw vaping as "a hassle"]* Just all the components that go into actually working it, you know. You have to unscrew the tank and clean it out and shit, and load more juices in there. It just seemed – I guess it just seemed easier to smoke cigarettes or something.
>
> *(Interview with 21-year-old man)*

In the context of this material complexity, resources providing information and support – both online and in-person – were key, and the characterization of vaping culture as a "supportive community" was common across studies. Central to this were brick-and-mortar vape shops, which were identified as important sites for accumulating knowledge about smoking cessation, trying new set-ups, finding the right level of nicotine, sampling new flavors, and learning how to fix and modify equipment. While many young people described supplementing these inputs via information online and on social media (e.g. YouTube, Instagram, and Snapchat), a striking feature of accounts was the enduring significance of face-to-face interactions within vape shops and lounges among a generation often characterized as "digital natives." Indeed, among some young people, there was a sense that they actively valued opportunities to experience and partake in local communities within an increasingly globalized world:

> This is what makes it [vaping] a community, because we know the people who make the juices. We know who owns the shops, that's what brings us closer. We talk to each other. Whereas cigarettes, I don't know anyone in Big Tobacco. I don't know the guy who makes it. With cigarettes it's like one common interest – oh, the nicotine buzz. With vaping you get, "Oh you use that? Yeah I use that too", or it's, "Oh you tasted that juice? Yeah I tasted that too", and it just keeps on coming. Everyone starts talking about it. [...] Vaping really is just small business owners, it's not like these big corporations.
>
> *(Small group discussion)*

Despite the high value placed on vape shops as sources of information and support, some young women described these venues as "macho" and "male-dominated," meaning that they did not always feel equally supported or respected compared to male customers, for instance:

> Woman 1: I've definitely only seen guys that work in smoke shops [...] They just automatically assume that they have the upper hand [...] like, they would assume that I don't know what I'm looking for, like what exactly I want or like what the price range of it should be, and so because I'm a girl, like they can take advantage of that and they're like, "Oh, like, she doesn't know what she's doing. We'll just, like, upcharge her and she'll have no clue." And I'm just like, no, like, that's actually super expensive and never mind.
>
> *(Small group discussion)*

While this young woman was assertive in taking or leaving the advice she received within vape stores, others talked about avoiding going into these venues in the first place, even noting that they had temporarily reverted to smoking when their vaping device had broken as they were reluctant to access help in a vape store due to fear of being ridiculed or patronized for not knowing how to fix their equipment. Thus, the combination of practice elements here – the fragility of devices, the requirement to possess and display a degree of knowledge in order to access help, and the coding of some venues as unwelcoming to women – is suggestive of the precarity of vaping as *harm reduction practice,* and opens up the question of what might be done to address potential gendered inequalities in access to tobacco harm reduction resources.

Concluding comments: the ever-shifting terrain of vaping as a social practice

Examining vaping nicotine as an intoxicating practice reveals elements that are central for understanding why young people are attracted to vaping in the first place and what encourages or discourages them to sustain or change their vaping practices. Unless they attend to this deeply embedded meaning of vaping nicotine, public health bodies in the United States arguably have little hope of developing approaches that are responsive to and inclusive of the experiences of youth and young adults. Participants in our studies drew attention to what is so often missing in not just the mainstream tobacco literature but also the mainstream literature in the alcohol and drugs fields – that is, that the "transient euphoria characteristic of the drug is explicitly constituted as a key element" that sustains the practice of drug use (Keane 2020, p. 58). Accounts in our studies emphasized how the intoxicating effects of nicotine were distinct from other forms of intoxication and used strategically as a functional (and less harmful) way to cope with the stresses of everyday life. Moreover, vaping appeared to be experienced as a *capacity-enhancing practice,* with participants appearing to derive pleasure from mastering the skills of vaping and describing appreciation for their greater sense of control while vaping, in terms of both the ability to control the intoxicating effects of nicotine and a notion of regaining control over their health. In this sense, vaping nicotine was positioned in opposition to smoking cigarettes – the latter being a practice that afforded a less customized experience and was seen as a far greater threat to health. These young adults' perspectives on vaping sit in stark contrast to mainstream public health campaigns in the United States that frame vaping as robbing young people of control over themselves and their behavior. Finally, participants highlighted how vaping facilitated the cultivation of social connections and enhanced sociability. Sociability has long been acknowledged as an important contribution of intoxicants; Partanen (1991) argued in his studies of alcohol-related intoxication that "drinks delineate and articulate a world in which the expression of sociability becomes possible" (p. 27), and, it appears, that vaping nicotine afforded similar experiences among the youth to whom we spoke.

Having explored some key practice elements relating to intoxication within young adults' accounts of vaping nicotine in California in 2016–2017, we end this chapter with some brief reflections on the contemporary situation as we write in 2020 – less than four years since these interviews, but a time in which the landscape of vaping and understandings about nicotine are continuing to rapidly evolve, both in the USA and globally. As the material and symbolic elements that constitute vaping shift, what might this mean for the persistence of vaping as an intoxicating practice?

Perhaps most fundamentally, the material context of vaping has changed dramatically in ways that likely impact the recruitment of new practitioners, and the defection of others.

At the time we conducted our studies, sustaining a vaping habit using second- and third-generation devices required a degree of amateur expertise, with relevant knowledge on how to fill tanks, fix coils, and so on acquired and exchanged through interactions with vaping friends, in vape stores, and via online resources. While participating in these exchanges appeared to be part of the appeal for some, for others it was not, meaning that the risk of returning to smoking was ever-present. This might in part explain the apparent popularity of the next generation of vaping devices – smaller, pod-based systems with pre-filled cartridges, such as Juul – which began to proliferate in the market later in 2017. This fourth generation of devices offers an alternative to the complexity, size and fragility of earlier tank-based systems ("mods"); they require less technical know-how to operate, are easier to conceal (both because they are smaller, and they produce less vapor); and, anecdotally at least, appear less susceptible to breaking. At the same time, however, the concentration of nicotine within salts used in pod systems is higher than the juices used in earlier devices. Given that our participants emphasized their ability and desire to control the intoxicating effects of nicotine – getting nic'd up as opposed to nic'd out – this new generation of devices may present both obstacles and opportunities to the recruitment of new vaping practitioners, and their ongoing commitment to the practice. On the one hand, the relative ease of use may convince young people who smoke that there are fewer barriers to becoming a competent practitioner and by vaping they may be able to more easily exert control over their health while simultaneously enjoying nicotine's intoxicating effects. Yet, on the other, these new devices may reduce opportunities to experience mastery and inhibit desired customization, potentially reducing (or, at least, changing) the possibilities for identity work that come with commodity consumption, and the ways in which vaping operates as a medium of sociability.

These changes in the material design of vaping technologies also raise important considerations for thinking about *connections between smoking and vaping* as practices – in particular, the tensions created as actors with divergent motives simultaneously work to tighten and loosen these relationships. Back in 2017, Keane et al. commented on the evolution in the material form of e-cigarettes; while the first-generation "cig-a-likes" were designed to closely resemble cigarettes (e.g. in size, shape, and glowing tip), the second- and third-generation devices were larger and less aesthetically similar (p. 466). Since then, the boxy, sleek, pod-based systems that now dominate the market have moved even further from the aesthetic of a cigarette, and closer to the design of popular data storage devices and health surveillance technologies (e.g. USBs and FitBits). From a practice theory perspective, these design innovations might be interpreted as efforts by the tobacco and e-cigarette industry to *loosen* associations between vaping and smoking – efforts which mainstream authorities in the USA might be understood as working to counter through public health messaging aiming to *tighten* connections between smoking and vaping within the public imagination.

Within this landscape, young people who vape nicotine as a way to reduce or quit smoking appear to be caught in the middle. As noted earlier, the widely expressed view among our smoking-experienced participants in 2016–2017 was that vaping was significantly less harmful to health than smoking, and reducing harm was central to how vaping was viewed as a practice (Antin, Hees et al., 2019; Antin, Hunt 2019; Lewis, in preparation). Yet, while these vaping youth and young adults were clear in differentiating vaping from smoking, a growing proportion of US adults perceive e-cigarettes to be as harmful or even more so than smoking combustible cigarettes (Huang et al., 2019). It is possible that public confusion about reduced relative harm may be further exacerbated by intensification of anti-vaping sentiment in the USA, which has included prominently reported stories that mislead the public about the cause of "vaping-related deaths," and an FDA-funded national campaign targeted at youth which used graphic imagery and emotive language to identify nicotine itself as the "ultimate threat" (Fairchild et al., 2019, p. 1000). If public understandings about nicotine continue to shift, might this loosen the meaning of vaping as harm reduction among smoking youth? If so, what might be the unintended consequences for smoking youth? As nicotine delivery devices will inevitably continue to evolve, greater attention to the ways in which related practices are experienced as forms intoxication may provide a more nuanced lens through which to understand how and why young people are drawn to them.

Acknowledgements

This work was supported, in part, by funds from the Tobacco-Related Disease Research Program (TRDRP), grant number 24RT-0019. The content provided here is solely the responsibility of the authors and does not necessarily reflect the opinions of TRDRP. Dr. Lewis is supported by the United Kingdom Medical Research Council [grant codes MC_UU_12017/11 and MC_UU_00022/3] and the Scottish Government Chief Scientist Office [grant code SPHSU11 and SPHSU18]. Finally, sincere appreciation is due to all of the volunteers who participated in both studies; without them, our work would not be possible.

References

Al-Hamdani, M., Hopkins, D. B., & Park, T. (2019). Vaping among youth and young adults: A "red alert" state. *Journal of Public Health Policy*. doi:10.1057/s41271-019-00193-2

Antin, T., Hess, C., Kaner, E., Lipperman-Kreda, S., Annechino, R., & Hunt, G. (2020). Pathways of nicotine product use: A qualitative study of youth and young adults in California. *Nicotine & Tobacco Research, 22*(5), 722–727.

Antin, T., Hunt, G., Kaner, E., & Lipperman-Kreda, S. (2019). Youth perspectives on concurrent smoking and vaping: Implications for tobacco control. *International Journal of Drug Policy, 66*, 57–63.

Bancroft, A. (2009). *Drugs, Intoxication & Society*. Cambridge: Polity Press.

Becker, H. S. (1953). Becoming a Marihuana user. *American Journal of Sociology, 59*(3), 235–242.

Bernard, H. R., & Ryan, G. W. (2010). *Analyzing Qualitative Data: Systematic Approaches*. Thousand Oaks, CA: Sage Publications Ltd.

Blue, S., Shove, E., Carmona, C., & Kelly, M. P. (2016). Theories of practice and public health: Understanding (un)healthy practices. *Critical Public Health, 26*(1), 36–50.

Campbell, C. (1989). *The Romantic Ethic and the Spirit of Modern Consumerism*. Oxford: Basil Blackwell Ltd.

Cohn, S. (2014). From health behaviours to health practices: An introduction. *Sociology of Health & Illness, 36*(2), 157–162.

Cooper, M., Harrell, M. B., & Perry, C. L. (2016). Comparing young adults to older adults in e-cigarette perceptions and motivations for use: Implications for health communication. *Health Education Research, 31*(4), 429–438.

Douglas, M., & Isherwood, B. C. (1996). *The World of Goods: Towards an Anthropology of Consumption : With a New Introduction*. London: Routledge.

Fairchild, A. L., Bayer, R., & Lee, J. S. (2019). The e-cigarette debate: What counts as evidence? *American Journal of Public Health, 109*(7), 1000–1006.

Fry, M.-L. (2011). Seeking the pleasure zone: Understanding young adult's intoxication culture. *Australasian Marketing Journal (AMJ), 19*(1), 65–70.

Graham, H. (1993). *When Life's a Drag: Women, Smoking and Disadvantage*. London: H.M. Stationery Office.

Health and Human Services Secretary. (2018). Results from 2018 National Youth Tobacco Survey show dramatic increase in e-cigarette use among youth over past year. Retrieved from https://www.fda.gov/news-events/press-announcements/results-2018-national-youth-tobacco-survey-show-dramatic-increase-e-cigarette-use-among-youth-over

Heath, D. B. (2000). *Drinking occasions: Comparative Perspectives on Alcohol and Culture*. New York: Routledge.

Hennell, K., Piacentini, M., & Limmer, M. (2020). Exploring health behaviours: Understanding drinking practice using the lens of practice theory. *Sociology of Health & Illness*, *42*(3), 627–642.

Hilton, S., Weishaar, H., Sweeting, H., Trevisan, F., & Katikireddi, S. V. (2016). E-cigarettes, a safer alternative for teenagers? A UK focus group study of teenagers' views. *BMJ Open*, *6*(11), e013271.

Huang, J., Feng, B., Weaver, S. R., Pechacek, T. F., Slovic, P., & Eriksen, M. P. (2019). Changing perceptions of harm of e-cigarette vs cigarette use among adults in 2 US National surveys from 2012 to 2017. *JAMA Network Open*, *2*(3), e191047.

Hunt, G., & Evans, K. (2008). "The Great Unmentionable": Exploring the pleasures and benefits of ecstasy from the perspectives of drug users. *Drugs (Abingdon, England)*, *15*(4), 329–349.

Hunt, G., & Frank, V. A. (2016). Reflecting on intoxication. In T. Kolind, B. Thom, & G. Hunt (Eds.), *The Sage Handbook of Drug & Alcohol Studies: Social Science Approaches*. London: Sage. pp. 322–336.

Hunt, G. P., Evans, K., & Kares, F. (2007). Drug use and meanings of risk and pleasure. *Journal of Youth Studies*, *10*(1), 73–96.

Keane, H., Weier, M., Fraser, D., & Gartner, C. (2017). 'Anytime, anywhere': Vaping as social practice. *Critical Public Health*, *27*(4), 465–476.

Keane, H. (2020). Smoking and intoxication: From control to the Buzz. In F. Hutton (Ed.), *Cultures of Intoxication: Key Issues and Debates* (1st ed., p. 343). London: Palgrave MacMillan.

Levy, D. T., Warner, K. E., Cummings, K. M., Hammond, D., Kuo, C., Fong, G. T., . . . Borland, R. (2019). Examining the relationship of vaping to smoking initiation among US youth and young adults: A reality check. *Tobacco Control*, *28*(6), 629.

Lewis, R. (in preparation). Vapers like you make us look bad! Managing vaping-related stigma in the context of nicotine denormalisation.

Lucherini, M., Rooke, C., & Amos, A. (2017). "They're thinking, well it's not as bad, I probably won't get addicted to that. But it's still got the nicotine in it, so…": Maturity, control, and socializing: Negotiating identities in relation to smoking and vaping—A qualitative study of young adults in Scotland. *Nicotine & Tobacco Research*, *21*(1), 81–87.

McQuoid, J., Keamy-Minor, E., & Ling, P. M. (2018). A practice theory approach to understanding poly-tobacco use in the United States. *Critical Public Health*, *30*(2), 204–219.

Measham, F. (2004). The decline of ecstasy, the rise of 'binge' drinking and the persistence of pleasure. *Probation Journal*, *51*(4), 309–326.

Measham, F., O'Brien, K., & Turnbull, G. (2016). "Skittles & Red Bull is my favourite flavour": E-cigarettes, smoking, vaping and the changing landscape of nicotine consumption amongst British teenagers – Implications for the normalisation debate. *Drugs: Education, Prevention and Policy*, *23*(3), 224–237.

Meier, P. S., Warde, A., & Holmes, J. (2018). All drinking is not equal: How a social practice theory lens could enhance public health research on alcohol and other health behaviours. *Addiction*, *113*(2), 206–213.

Moore, D., & Valverde, M. (2000). Maidens at risk: 'Date rape drugs' and the formation of hybrid risk knowledges. *Economy and Society*, *29*(4), 514–531.

Office of the Surgeon General. (2016). *E-Cigarette Use among Youth and Young Adults: A Report of the Surgeon General*. Retrieved from Atlanta.

Office of the Surgeon General. (2019). *Surgeon General's Advisory on E-cigarette Use among Youth*.

Partanen, J. (1991). *Alcohol and Drinking in Kenya, Africa and the Modern World*. Helsinki: Finnish Foundation for Alcohol Studies.

Reith, G. (2005). On the edge: Drugs and the consumption of risk in late modernity. In S. Lyng (Ed.), *Edgework: The Sociology of Risk-Taking*. New York: Routledge. pp. 227–245.

Shove, E., Pantzar, M., & Watson, M. (2012). *The Dynamics of Social Practice: Everyday Life and How It Changes*. London: Sage.

3

RECREATIONAL DRUG USE AS EVERYDAY LIFE

Explorations of young adults' gendered motivations for taking drugs in Nigeria

Emeka W. Dumbili, MaryJane Nnajiofor and Emmanuel C. Ezekwe

Introduction

Most research on gender and drugs mainly focuses on Western societies (Carliner *et al.*, 2017; Ettorre, 2016). Given that *gender* is a global phenomenon, there is a need to study how it affects drug use in non-Western contexts, and this is an important reason for the research discussed in this chapter. Studies of non-Western settings will also provide novel insights into the diverse ways in which gender shapes drug use attitudes and behaviours. The chapter aims to explore recreational drug consumption in a Nigerian city, focusing on the factors that motivate drug use and how social relations of gender are implicated in this. The chapter is divided into four sections. First, we review studies concerning drug use in Nigeria before exploring the gendering of drug use. Next, the methodology used in collecting and analysing data is presented. The subsequent section then presents the results before the chapter closes with a discussion of the results.

Drug Use in Nigeria

Recreational drug use[1] is a growing public health concern in Africa. Studies from Egypt (Bassiony *et al.*, 2015), Ghana (Appiah *et al.*, 2018), and South Africa (Brook *et al.*, 2006) indicate that amphetamine, cannabis, and non-medical use of tramadol are popular. In Nigeria, the dominant discourse surrounding recreational drug use has been problem-oriented, and this is mirrored in the ways the media reported drug use in Northern Nigeria (Bamigbola, 2019; BBC News, 2018). The government also uses a repressive (*war on drugs*) approach in regulating intoxicants in Nigeria (Nelson, 2018). Yet, licit and illicit drugs availability and consumption appear to be growing (Dumbili, 2020; Dumbili *et al.*, 2021).

Although some epidemiological studies have been conducted, especially in the North, there is a paucity of research on recreational drug use in the country. Additionally, existing literature fails to show the motives for drug use clearly or how gender impacts substance use. Research conducted among the adult population in Plateau State, North-central region, shows that among other drugs, participants took cannabis, opioids, sedatives, and amphetamine (Okonoda *et al.*, 2017). In the same region, the misuse of tramadol was reported

DOI: 10.4324/9780429058141-5

among patients attending an addiction clinic (Ibrahim *et al.*, 2017). In Lagos state, Dirisu *et al.* (2019) reveal that young people use cannabis for recreational purposes. Further, Dirisu and colleagues note that the criminalization of cannabis consumption in Nigeria did not deter the users.

The widely held notion, especially among adults in Nigeria, is that illicit drug use is a deviant behaviour, and thus, users are stigmatized (Dirisu *et al.*, 2019; Dumbili, 2020). But despite the social stigma attached to substance use, evidence shows that male and female students in Nigerian secondary schools use diverse drugs, including cannabis and cocaine (Obi *et al.*, 2017; Oye-Adeniran *et al.*, 2014). In a study that examined the frequency of drug use among 10–19-year old students in Ilorin, North-central Nigeria, Abdulkarim *et al.* (2005) found a 40.1% prevalence rate of drug use. In another study of 620 senior secondary school students in Abakaliki, Anyanwu *et al.* (2016) reported that among other substances of abuse, cannabis and cocaine were common. Among university students, Johnson *et al.* (2017, p. 11) reported that the use of various psychoactive drugs was widespread. The study revealed that the most used drugs are codeine, tramadol, and cannabis. The reasons for drug use include coping with depression or family problems (Johnson *et al.*, 2017). In another study involving undergraduates, Adekeye *et al.* (2017) indicated that codeine, cannabis, tramadol, and Rohypnol were the most used drugs.

In Nigeria, substance use is gendered and male-dominated. In the past, men occupied leisure sites and drank alcohol (the most common drug) (Heap, 1998) because 'drinking has never been part of the acceptable image of *Nigerian* women' (Ikuesan, 1994, p. 942). Recent alcohol research shows that, although women are beginning to drink, men expect them to drink what they call 'women's alcohol' (e.g., flavoured/sweetened beverages) (Dumbili and Williams, 2020). Relatedly, while men may drink and get intoxicated, women who ever get inebriated suffer heightened social stigma (Dumbili, 2015; Ikuesan, 1994), and this is related to the notion of maintaining traditional/respectable femininity (Dumbili, 2015). Although there is limited evidence on how illicit drug users are perceived in Nigeria, available research shows that women are stigmatized more than men (Dumbili, 2020). Given that gender often shapes drug use patterns and practices (Hunt *et al.*, 2016), exploring how it motivates intoxicants use in Nigeria becomes imperative.

Gendering of Drug Use

The psychological literature suggests a number of motivations (e.g., coping, conformity, enhancement, and social) for intoxicant use among young people worldwide (Cooper, 1994; Litt *et al.*, 2019; Thurnell-Read, 2016). Increasingly, scholars are looking towards more nuanced, socially, and culturally shaped meanings of drug use. With respect to gender, bourgeoning literature shows that adherence to traditional masculine and feminine gender roles and expectations influence intoxicant use in different ways (Carliner *et al.*, 2017; Ettorre, 2016; Hunt *et al.*, 2016).

According to West and Zimmerman (1987), gender is performative and enacted through specifically repetitive actions, and its performance is in interaction with real and imagined 'others'. '*Doing* gender' requires actions and resources, and one available resource is psychoactive substances (Darcy, 2020; Measham, 2002). For example, while men perform and (re) produce traditional masculinity through (il)licit drug use (Darcy, 2020; Carliner *et al.*, 2017), women are challenging traditional/respectable femininity norms with intoxicants (Ettorre, 2004; Hunt *et al.*, 2002). This is why Measham (2002, p.335) argued, 'that gender does not just influence doing drugs, *but* drug use itself can be seen as a way of doing gender'.

In most parts of the world, boys and men are more likely to use drugs and to report more drug-related problems than girls and women, and this is related to adherence to masculine norms of risk-taking (Hemsing and Greaves, 2020; UNODC, 2017). Darcy (2020), for instance, notes that illicit recreational drug use is one of the ways Irish men 'do' masculinity, to the extent that some engage in drug-taking games. Some men even construct masculinity in drug treatment settings. As Ezzell's (2012) study of two US drug treatment settings shows, male residents demonstrated their masculinity through aggression, the subordination of women and other men, and they also 'managed' their emotion to show that they were in control. Given the high rates of drug use and related problems among men, Wilton *et al.* (2014, p.291) suggested the need to show 'men how to practice an alternative model of healthy masculinity'. Research has also identified that the gaps between men and women who use illicit drugs are beginning to narrow down (Legleye *et al.*, 2014), and this is because many women are delving into drug subcultures that were hitherto occupied by men (Brady *et al.*, 2016; Hunt *et al.*, 2002).

In most communities, acceptable or unacceptable leisure behaviour is determined by cultural norms guiding gender roles and expectations (Hunt and Antin, 2019). Given that gender performance is often contextual and fluid, individuals may enact diverse femininities and masculinities in different settings (Sallee and Harris, 2011). This underpins the importance of studying masculinities and femininities of drug use trajectories geographically (Connell and Messerschmidt, 2005; Pease and Pringle, 2001). Our study begins to fill the knowledge gap in gender and drug use in Nigeria.

Methods

Study Site, Participants, and Interviews

This exploratory study was conducted in a metropolitan city located in Anambra State, South-eastern Nigeria. The city is made up of two Local Government Areas, and its population is estimated at 399,300 (City Population, 2020). The city is located on a major highway connecting two other cities and thus exposed to abundant and continuous supplies of psychoactive substances (Dumbili, 2020). Also, one of the neighbouring cities whose residents visit the study site daily for higher education, work, and other businesses is known for drug use and related violent crimes and armed robbery (Baker, 2002). The study involved semi-structured interviews with 23 (19 males; 4 females) young adults (aged 23–29) who were current substance users.[2] Nineteen of the participants were undergraduate students of a public university, while the rest were university graduates. Only one of the non-students among the participants had a fulltime job. Our study did not aim at a particular class, especially because '(illicit) recreational drug use is not restricted to particular social classes and not attributable to marginalization or disadvantage' (Darcy, 2020. p. 422). Given that women who take intoxicants suffer a higher social discrimination than men (Dumbili, 2015, 2020), many of them are reluctant to participate in intoxicant-related research (Dumbili, 2015). This was a primary barrier to the recruitment of additional women in this study, and we acknowledge this as a major limitation, especially because the study focuses on gender.

The sample selection involved a snowball sampling method, and this was aimed at gathering preliminary data on recreational drug use in Nigeria. Qualitative interviews were used to facilitate the detailed understanding of the interviewees' beliefs and perspectives on drugs and how they make meaning (Roulston and Choi, 2018) of their everyday leisure lives using drugs (Maher and Dertadian, 2018). Ethical approval was granted by Brunel University

London Ethics Board (Reference: 16853-MHR), and all the names used in this chapter are pseudonyms. Recruitment followed word-of-mouth and (convenience) snowball sampling methods (Noy, 2008), and it started with the researchers visiting drugs hotspots and students' off-campus leisure sites and asking around the city for interested individuals.

Interviews ranged between 30 and 85 minutes and were performed in the English language. We probed the participants to unpack how their drug career started, the type of drugs they use and the factors that motivate their drug use. At the end of the interview, interviewees were asked to put the researchers in contact with other drug users who would be willing to share their experiences of drug use with them. This proved to be particularly successful methods of recruitment, especially concerning out-of-school participants. Drawing on social constructionism (Burr, 2015), and following Becker's (1953) guidelines, we employed the language/jargon (drug slangs) of users, especially where and when such was deemed necessary or appropriate. Some of the popular drug slangs include *gutter-water* (a mixture of codeine, cannabis, tramadol, Rohypnol and spirit or juice), Ruchy (Rohypnol), and TM/Trams (tramadol). This allowed us to capture the nuances of meaning participants attribute to drugs they use and to put them at ease. Oral consent was obtained and interviews were recorded with a digital recorder with the permission of the participants.

Table 3.1 Sociodemographic data of the participants

Name	*Gender*	*Age student/non-student*
Adaora	Female	27 Non-student
Alex	Male	25 Student
Angela	Female	24 Student
Charles	Male	24 Student
Chibu	Male	25 Student
Chiedu	Male	25 Student
Chichi	Female	25 Student
Chuka	Male	26 Student
David	Male	24 Student
Ebuka	Male	26 Student
Eze	Male	24 Student
Harry	Male	25 Student
Ike	Male	24 Student
Ikenna	Male	24 Student
Katie	Female	26 Student
Kingsley	Male	24 Student
Nonso	Male	26 Student
Okey	Male	24 Non-student
Paul	Male	26 Student
Sam	Male	28 Non-student
Uche	Male	25 Student
Vincent	Male	23 Student
Willy	Male	29 Non-student

Source: Fieldwork.

Data Analysis

Following Braun and Clarke's (2019) suggestions, we conducted a thematic analysis of the data elicited using a mix of deductive and inductive procedures. The tape-recordings were transcribed verbatim, anonymized, and then read repeatedly. Having familiarized with, and immersed in the data, a manual inductive coding was initiated, and codes were developed (e.g., sourcing drug and smoking to cope) directly from the data using the participants' own words, terms, and phrases (Linneberg and Korsgaard, 2019). This was aimed at increasing transparency, and analytical rigor (Gioia *et al.*, 2013), mainly because our study drew on theoretical concepts ab initio. The next stage involved importing the transcripts to NVivo 12 software, which was used to manage the remainder of the analysis (Jackson and Bazeley, 2019).

After generating the first round of initial codes (e.g., pleasure and boosting sex), they were compared with those generated manually (Maher *et al.*, 2018). Following this, the coding of the remaining transcripts was completed before searching for and identifying themes (Braun and Clarke, 2019). This was achieved by reading through the codes and collating them together to develop themes. Subsequently, the themes developed were reviewed through repeated and thorough reading of the nodes. Through this process, we identified extracts that were more suitable to other nodes, and these were moved to the existing nodes, or new nodes were created for them. Subsequently, the themes (and associated subthemes) were named (Braun and Clarke, 2019). While the theoretical concepts (e.g., doing gender) facilitated in developing and naming of some key themes, some of the subthemes were identified inductively.

Findings

The data presented here described the nuanced experiences of young adults who use psychoactive substances in a Nigerian city to manage and alter their emotions and bodily feeling and experiences. In this chapter, we present findings regarding the gendering of drug use and the motivations behind it. Drug use narratives included personal and/or group experiences, and young adults highlighted how taking drugs has become a part of their everyday life.

Coping with Diverse Negative Emotions

Some of the reasons for drug use among the majority of men and all the women in this study were to cope with work and study-related stress that often resulted in insomnia, depression, anger, and negative emotion. As some of them explained, the use of cannabis to mitigate stress and sleeplessness was common:

ALEX: The thing is that marijuana actually reduces stress… After doing the day's job, you come home and after taking it, you're relieved. It makes you sleep for a very long time.

CHICHI: I was having issues with insomnia; so it was in my '300 Level' [third year of university] that I got to know that [drug can ameliorate sleeplessness] … And then, I noticed that whenever I just smoke SK [Skunk cannabis], I sleep better. It helps me sleep, and if I don't take it, I can't sleep.

Chichi, a female participant, further sheds light on the discussion she had with four of her friends who also use drugs like sleeping pills. Although she did not mention the drugs her friends used to induce sleep, the excerpt below aptly captures their reactions (suggesting a sigh of relief), when they realized that there were other people using cannabis to mitigate sleeplessness:

CHICHI: ...They were like, 'ah, so it happens to you too?' One of them was like; if she doesn't smoke, she can't sleep...

These accounts reflected the experiences of many participants. Although polydrug use was a common phenomenon, they used cannabis specifically to mitigate stress-related sleeplessness, and this is in consonance with research elsewhere on cannabis use motives (Boys *et al.*, 2001; Glodosky and Cuttler, 2020).

The participants also shared some nuanced accounts which cast light on how their drug career started and how they discovered that drugs could mitigate stress and sleeplessness. For example, Katie recounted that she was facing some family and financial problems, and thus, could not sleep. In search of solace, she placed a call to a friend, expecting some money but instead, was introduced to cannabis use as a relief measure:

KATIE: I called her and was like babe, what's up? I'm having some issues and can't even sleep. Can you help me? She was like, come over to my house. I went, hoping that she would give me [some money]... On getting to her house, she was smoking and was like, babe just 'high up'; if you high up, you will get yourself back... She was like, 'if I start to tell you my problems, you won't believe it, but see how fine I'm because I'm high'. ...I just took like two *drags*, and it really caught me. I slept like a baby in her house without thinking of anything... I really enjoyed it because it just made me forget my problem.

From this singular experience, her drug career started, and as she explained, she later learned that smoking cannabis not only induces sleep but can also relieve sorrow. In a related circumstance, Chichi narrated how she started using Rohypnol to mitigate stress, negative mood, and frustration:

CHICHI: It was my friend that actually gave it to me. She came to my house. I was just feeling so bad because of serious financial issues... So there was a lot of stress on me. She was like she wants to get my mind off the issues so that I can forget about everything... So she gave me two of the drugs and I took them, and I just felt so good. I just felt like dancing; I felt happy... So it helps with my frustration.

One of the dominant features of traditional femininity is expressing emotion (Brady *et al.*, 2016), and all the women in this study revealed how they seek help during emotional distress.

Another common practice among all the women and some men was the use of drugs when they were angry and want to induce happy moods. Adaora, a 27-year old female university graduate, who often uses cannabis to mitigate anger, stressed that 'whenever I am annoyed, I tend to smoke weed', and similar accounts were shared among other participants. As some explained, they use large quantities of cannabis in quick succession to achieve faster relief from anger:

CHARLES: I smoke out of anger... I do it whenever I am pissed off. 'I'll smoke till blood comes out of my eye'. I smoke and get *fucking* high, and will keep on smoking... I know I'm too high, but I'll still be smoking *until I no go dey see person again*; [until I will not see humans anymore].

Aside from taking drugs to cope with anger, sleeplessness, and other stress-related problems, the interviewees also used intoxicants specifically to alleviate depression (general feelings of low mood, negativity, etc.). Indeed, the incidence of depression permeated our data, and the majority attributed this to the poor state of the Nigerian economy, and lack of social support from the government. Adaora, who uses cannabis, Crystal-meth (methamphetamine), and codeine, explained that drugs keep her 'company'. She further narrated some pitiable life events that put much pressure on her and how these happenings induce depression. In her words, so *you got to pot* [you have to smoke cannabis] to alleviate such depressive mood:

ADAORA: ...Actually, it [cannabis use] is something you do because of depression from many angles. Everybody is putting pressure on you, and the next thing is drug use. Because when you take drugs, everything the government or parents said, you have forgotten.

In this cultural setting, displaying emotions (openly) by men is taboo because it contradicts the dominant discourses of masculinity, and this notion of masculinity is resilient (Uchendu, 2007). For example, young people, who participated in Uchendu's (2007, p.283) study, noted that 'absence of smiles' and being unemotional are markers of masculinity in Eastern Nigeria. All the male interviewees reproduced such traditional masculinity, in the sense that none ever mentioned telling a friend about his emotional problems (although many of them shared explicit stories of using drugs for coping reasons). Some of them even disclosed the peculiarity of such behaviours among women, who share their emotional and other problems with their girl- or boyfriends. As the account below shows, one of them recounted how he uses cannabis to *raise his spirit* and alleviate depression:

EBUKA: What I like about weed is that it gives you this kind of motivation. As in, it brings your spirit up; it raises your spirit. Like if you're depressed..., and you take weed, it will accelerate [alleviate] it.

The fact that some men associate emotional distress with weakness is not particular to our study because it is part of masculinity norms (Hemsing and Greaves, 2020). But evidence has shown that men either engage in heavy drinking or use illicit drugs in a bid to ameliorate emotional vulnerability instead of seeking help from others (Cleary, 2012).

Given these negative emotions, participants used cannabis to evoke pleasure, fun, and happiness. Interviewees noted that they use diverse strains of cannabis. Among them is Charles, who had used different varieties (Skunk and Arizona, i.e., imported). As his nuanced account reveals, each type produces different effects and has a specific perceived function, but what he called the 'normal' (locally produced) weed evokes pleasurable mood and 'makes you laugh and laugh out your mind'. Other participants corroborated his account:

CHICHI: Actually, marijuana can give pleasure... and a lot of joy and happiness in you because you feel different; you feel free. You'll feel like a big burden has just been lifted off your shoulder.

ALEX: It [weed] gives this pleasure that you might not actually explain. You just feel that all your problems are solved, [and] there is no problem again.

ANGELA: Ok... when I take weed, I feel happy... it gives excitement.

In this study, only Adaora reported solidary cannabis use. Other participants used the drug among friendship networks. Also, cannabis was used in drug hotspots and other social contexts such as students' parties, and drug users' homes/rooms. Despite the social use of cannabis, our analysis shows that when they are angry or depressed, they mostly smoked alone.

Together, these accounts reveal the gendered experiences of young adults with drugs and how they use intoxicants for recreational and therapeutic purposes. Their views suggest that anger encouraged the use of large quantities of drugs. As noted earlier, the general perceptions of drugs and their regulations have been problem-oriented and paternalistic in Nigeria (Nelson, 2018). Our data have demonstrated that young adults in contemporary Nigeria are *doing* drugs for fun and pleasure, and thus legitimizing recreational intoxicant use (Askew, 2016).

Managing Heartbreaks

Additional accounts that appeared to be gendered show how women used cannabis due to its perceived effects to soothe emotional distress resulting from heartbreaks. Three of the participants recounted how they use marijuana to manage broken relationships with their boyfriends. For example:

> CHICHI: At a point, my relationship became abusive; I was no longer [enjoying it]. I didn't want to continue, but I couldn't leave. So the only thing that kept me going was taking marijuana... That was the only thing that just made me forget the person I was dealing with and be happy within myself... I actually started taking it when I had my first breakup with my fiancé. So it helped me get my mind off everything...

A common occurrence among these young women was that because of the heartbreak and relationship trauma and abuse they experienced, the quantities of cannabis they used increased. Adaora narrated that she was already pregnant before her fiancé jilted her. Therefore, she aborted the baby and began to use more quantity of cannabis to 'manage' her sorrow. The following excerpt further explicated how women heightened cannabis use due to relationship problems:

> KATIE: I found out that my boyfriend was sleeping with my friend. So that day, I smoked and smoked and smoked, so that I can forget everything...

Many young Nigerian women experience increasingly gender-based sexual violence daily, and most of these incidences are unreported (Dumbili and Williams, 2020; Fawole *et al.*, 2002). One main reason why most women do not report sexual violence is because of the culture of silence, but this encourages a rape culture in Nigeria (Dumbili and Williams, 2020). Given that some emotions are experienced more intensely and frequently by women than men (Barrett *et al.*, 1998), this may be the reason why only women reported using drugs to heal emotional turmoil caused by the end of romantic relationships or by living with problematic and harmful relationships.

Enhancing Sexual Performance and Pleasure

Tramadol Elongates Sex

Our analysis reveals some culturally specific nuances under the enhancement motives. All the participants knew about using drugs to stimulate sexual urges and enhance performance. Relatedly, nearly all of them have used one or more drugs, specifically for sex-related purposes.

Although the participants particularly mentioned five drugs (cannabis, tramadol, codeine, Crystal-meth, and Rohypnol), our analysis shows that tramadol – an opioid – was the most used substance for sexual purposes, and the essence was to prolong sex. The awareness that men mainly use it more than women was widespread even among the female participants:

CHICHI: I have this neighbour; whenever he brings in 'heavy-duty' [fat] girls, he tends to take tramadol… to give him energy so that he will be able to satisfy them… That is just what tramadol does; it enhances their power… They use it a lot; especially those men who are weak and cannot just go on for a long time.

Men's accounts also show that they possessed a high-level knowledge of the fact that sexual uses of tramadol were widespread among Nigerian youths. Consequently, they discussed that this practice was not peculiar to the city where the study was conducted:

CHUKA: There was this friend of mine (…) he came back from [name of place] with dozens of tramadol, and I asked him the benefits he derives from using it. He laughed, and was like; tramadol helps him whenever he wants to make love with a woman. [He said] that he is not good in bed, so whenever he takes it, he lasts very long.

From personal experiences, those who use this drug stated that one of the reasons was because it helps sexually inactive men, by enhancing their energy for better sexual performance:

DAVID: Let me tell you, everybody has different reasons why they take tramadol, but in my case, the reason was that I was sexually inactive. Someone advised me to take it, and I would perform well. I took it, and it quite helped.

Interestingly, there was a consensus on another perceived function tramadol performed for men: it elongates the time they last during sex:

DAVID: Instead of you like 'coming' [ejaculating] that time [at the natural time/limit], you'll usually 'come' like… 15 minutes later. Tramadol prolongs it.

Because of the high premium placed on prolonged sexual intercourse, the use of tramadol to facilitate protracted sexual episodes was normalized among interviewees (i.e., men who used it to prolong sexual intercourse held masculine view that *longer sex is always better*). As they explained, the essence is not to enjoy pleasurable sex per se but to last long. For instance:

CHARLES: Ok, without TM, you'll enjoy sex more, but with TM, you 'strafe' longer. You won't get the whole feeling on TM, but when you 'come' [ejaculate], the strength is still there; so you make love longer...

Some of them engaged with metaphors while describing the reasons for using tramadol before sexual intercourse. First, they stated the need to satisfy their sexual partners, and most importantly, to 'defeat women in bed' because such will boost masculine ego and guarantee loyalty:

CHIBU: They normally take all these drugs to add to their [natural] energy to stay long with a woman in bed. It is common among youths nowadays, not only students. Men want to feel that they are 'strong' guys. Like, 'I am a strong guy that defeated this particular girl in bed'.

These accounts have shown that men have a good grasp of the two main functions they believe tramadol performs. The accounts also aligned with a growing popular subcultural practice in contemporary Nigeria, where young men and women engage in 'sex competition'. Media reports show that young people boast of winning sex bouts, to the extent of placing a bet before such contests start (Okpara, 2018). The accounts also reflected some nuances on how common the use of this tramadol for non-prescription purposes was in this city, and how the reproduction of dominant masculinity played out.

In contrast to the common positive features men attributed to tramadol, a few also expressed some reservations. They stressed that, although the use of tramadol to enhance sexual performance is widespread, users must urge caution. Drawing on their experiences and their friends, they note that failing to use the *required dosage* will backfire:

EZE: I took tramadol just to be at my peak, and then, I noticed that when the girl came, I was just sleeping. She even woke me up and was like 'let's start', and I was like, 'please, I want to sleep'.

Interestingly, when they were probed to unpack the 'required dosage' to use, they noted that it is through trial and error, in that what works for Mr 'A' may not work for Mr 'B'. Indeed, their accounts align with Becker's (1963) view of learning to perceive and negotiate the effects of certain drugs.

Enhancing Pleasurable Sex

The participants shared their reason for taking cannabis for sexual purposes. Unlike the reason above for using tramadol, cannabis was used to facilitate sexual fun and pleasure:

CHARLES: When you're on weed, you enjoy sex. It doesn't make you last longer, but you'll enjoy it more. As I said, it excites you, so you derive joy…

Some men explained that to maximize pleasure, both sexual partners should use cannabis because 'if it is just one-sided, it's normally somehow because the [other] person will not be able to meet up with your capacity'.

Narrating how cannabis enhances sexual pleasure, a woman noted that men often talk and behave more romantically when they use cannabis before sex than when they are sober. As she notes, this enhances foreplay, making sex more fun. She then drew on her experience with her boyfriend to describe her narratives:

CHICHI: Let me use my boyfriend as an example. Whenever he is not smoking, he seems to be a bit dull, but when he's under the influence, I find out that he's much more sexually romantic and he does a lot of romantic things than when he is clear-headed.

Charles, who had earlier noted that sex under the influence of cannabis is enjoyable, narrated how he smokes with his ex-girlfriend before sex. He added that she enjoyed sex more when he was highly intoxicated, to the extent that she encouraged him to smoke more quantity of cannabis before sex. From these accounts, it is clear that pleasure-seeking is one of the reasons why women encouraged their boyfriends to use drugs before sex.

Women's Power in Negotiating Sex

Another culturally unique aspect of our findings is that some females introduced their boyfriends to sexual uses of drugs. Narrating his experience, one man stressed that if one is not performing to his girlfriend's expectation, she will ask you: 'don't you think that you need help?' 'Why not try what others are doing?' While the following accounts supported his view, they further reveal how, according to some of the male interviewees, women use what can be called *subtle coercion* to negotiate and achieve drug-enhanced sex:

ALEX: I had a girlfriend that takes weed. She was the first person that actually got me into it... I discovered that our [sexual] capacity was not the same. So she told me that she takes drugs… So that was the first time I actually had to 'do it' with drugs so I could [perform well and satisfy her]… I now discovered that weed actually improves sexual performance.

The analysis highlights men's motivation to use drugs in an attempt to enhance their sexual prowess. One unique reason is that they believe that young women do not like what they called 'five minutes men'. That is, according to some of the men we interviewed, the demand for prolonged sex beyond the usually perceived limit among young women is very high. Therefore, to not 'disappoint' these women, which, in turn, will cast doubt on men's masculinity and virility, they use drugs. Uche recounted a related, but more nuanced experience below:

UCHE: I met a girl, and she came around, and we spent a few times [having sexual intercourse]. We were having a discussion, and she was like, how do I feel [with the way I performed?]… Like how many minutes can I last in bed? I said a maximum of five minutes because that is normal. She was like, that is abnormal. I was shocked… She said that some guys last for one hour… She said that they have this drug that facilitates longer sex… and maybe, I should try it out. She said that she doesn't like sleeping with guys who just do it ordinarily without any form of inducement.

Men stressed that if they are unable to provide prolonged sex to their girlfriend's satisfaction, two things will most likely happen. First, as we illustrated above, she would become angry and leave their house (i.e., leave the relationship). Next, men contended that the man would become an object of ridicule among her friends because when young women come together, they discuss such issues. Therefore, to avoid name-calling and shaming, some men strategically deploy drugs to enhance sexual stamina.

Sexual Arousal

Another dimension of the sexual uses of drugs, which also appeared to be gendered, is that only the women reported using substances to stimulate sexual urge. Aside from citing the use of drugs to enhance sexual stamina by prostitutes in this city, all the participants unanimously agreed that the main reason women use drugs is to activate sexual feelings and to improve pleasure:

KATIE: Sometimes, when I am high like that, I will be like guy, I want to 'fuck'. I just want to have sex and be okay…

ANGELA: When you smoke, you will feel like having sex. It will give you a sexual urge. It will even make you want to have sex with someone you never planned to have sex with…

An element of their accounts reveals what can be called spontaneity of drug-induced sexual stimulation. Still, the analysis also shows that most women intentionally use drugs to activate sexual urges. Chichi narrated that most young women smoke after having their make-up because 'smoking helps them feel sexy'. Earlier, she recounted several relationship problems, which made her boyfriend unattractive to her. As she stated, things usually turned around when she takes Rohypnol or cannabis:

CHICHI: I noticed that whenever I take the substance or I smoke, I find him more attracting… Whenever I smoke, I feel like I want to engage in sexual activity [with him], and I don't feel as irritated as I used to be when I'm clear-headed.

These accounts show how women use intoxication to achieve heightened pleasure through sex. As we also demonstrated above (i.e., under women's power in negotiating sex), our analysis has shown that women are active participants in their own experiences, and not always victims like the much extant literatures suggest (Sandal, 2020).

Smoking Competition among Men

Constructing and Reinforcing Masculinity

Our analysis also shows that masculinized drug use, in the form of a 'smoking competition', where men compete for superior masculinity is becoming a commonplace among subgroup male drug users in this city. Although we acknowledge the unequal number of male and female participants in this study, no women reported playing smoking competition. Men's performance of traditional masculinity was a significant predictor of what we called *smoking games*. To exemplify how 'smoking game' is played, we will largely draw on Alex's account. This is because it is an insightful exemplar of how drug competition starts in masculinized social contexts:

ALEX: I've witnessed a competition where two guys were arguing about who takes more [cannabis]. One said that he could take 40 sticks of weed, the other guy was like; it's not possible for somebody to take 40 sticks… So they placed a bet of 5,000 Naira [$14]… We were looking at them; so we became the judge. They brought out weed and fired it up, but the guy did not actually get to 40. I think he was getting to 30 before he could not actually go again...

INTERVIEWER: So, what is the benefit to whoever wins?

ALEX: It gives this high status among the 'drug people'… It is either they call you 'lord' or they find one name to give you for actually accomplishing that particular task. And you are actually recognized [respected] in that particular setting…

The dominant masculinity discourse in Nigeria is that men should be risk-takers (Dumbili and Williams, 2020; Uchendu, 2007). As our data reveal, smoking contexts appear to provide spaces for men to perform 'appropriate' gender because failing to do so suggests weakness. One participant shared a personal experience of how the reproduction of masculinity is implicated in drug use. He highlighted that instead of backing out of the competitive drug-taking, and then mocked by other men, he would keep smoking:

IKENNA: Sometimes you plan to smoke just one rap but because you are with friends and then, they just keep rolling up weed, especially when they are passing it around [and everyone is taking their turn]. You will not want to be the first person to leave. So, you'll just collect it and smoke...

Our data highlighted that winning a smoking contest confers superior masculine status to the winner and also facilitates the extension of his social networks among admirers, and this is in line with the competitive and hierarchical view of gender, which has been explored in Western literature (Connell and Messerschmidt, 2005; West and Zimmerman, 1987).

Discussion

The study has highlighted the contemporary drug cultures in Nigeria and the diversity of reasons for intoxicant use among young adults. To our knowledge, this is the first study exploring the gendered motivations for recreational drug use in Nigeria. We found that young adults take cannabis, tramadol, and Rohypnol to cope with diverse negative emotions, enhance sexual performance and pleasure, and construct gender identity.

We found that cannabis was used primarily to soothe anger and activate pleasure and fun, and this fits neatly with previous research (Eftekhari *et al.*, 2004). Findings also show that young adults used drugs to alleviate depression, and this corroborates a study conducted in Northern Nigeria (Johnson *et al.*, 2017). Interviewees equally used cannabis, particularly to attenuate stress and induce sleep, and this practice was widely reported. That interviewees used drugs to alleviate stress and for recreational purposes confirms Osborne and Fogel's (2008) research. Of particular note is the way our participants normalized cannabis use. We found that cannabis, an illicit drug, is becoming legitimized, and as research elsewhere (Kiepek and Beagan, 2018) shows, its social accommodation is becoming high in Nigeria. This finding raises serious concern about the government's war on drugs. Given the roles drug use play in the everyday leisure lives of Nigerian youths, it is obvious that drug use is becoming normalized despite prohibition (see Dumbili, 2020; Dumbili *et al.*, 2020). Therefore, there is a need for policymakers to reconsider the extant policies to facilitate harm reduction.

Following Becker (1963), Maher and Dertadian (2018, p.169) note that drug career is an 'interactive learning process whereby experienced drug users taught novice users how to interpret the effects and meanings of drugs'. In this study, we found that some interviewees were taught how to use drugs by their friends. While the females were introduced to cannabis and Rohypnol use for coping and pleasure motives, some of their male counterparts were initiated and/or 'coerced' into drugs for sexual purposes and also for competing with other men. The socio-cultural implication of these findings is serious because as noted earlier, drug use is highly gendered in Nigeria (Dumbili, 2015; Dumbili *et al.*, 2021). As the findings show that women even used cannabis with their boyfriends to ensure they accepted drugs, it can be said that, as part of intimate heterosexual negotiations, women are *doing* gender with drugs. Therefore, Hunt *et al.'s* (2002) assertion that women are developing subcultures within previously male-dominated drug terrain is corroborated.

Further, the findings revealed how young adult interviewees used drugs for sex enhancement purposes. While women's sexual enhancement motive for taking drugs was mostly to activate sexual urges, men's reasons are complex, although this may be in part due to differences in sample size. Our findings showcase men's predominance in taking tramadol before sex and how their reasons converge with masculinities. In what appears to be competitions in sexual contexts, men used tramadol-assisted sexual prowess to 'defeat' women and showcase masculinity. Although studies have not been conducted to determine the motivations for sex competition, it can be inferred that proving masculine sexual prowess is implicated. As we argue, this is directly related to the fact that men take pride in *defeating* their sexual partners. Unfortunately, such contests have not always ended well. For instance, a male contestant died during sex bouts (Okpara, 2018). Again, media reports show that three Nigerian students died during drug-facilitated sex, and the police recovered codeine, tramadol, cannabis and vodka from the sex scene (Awford, 2019). With these in mind, it can be concluded that what occurs among young people in other states in Nigeria is being replicated in the context where our study was conducted.

Intoxicant use is socially constructed (Hunt and Antin, 2019). As such, the socio-cultural expectations regarding masculinity in Nigeria (Uchendu, 2007) appear to encourage men to use drugs to fulfil such expectations. The implications of this finding are multifaceted. First, as the result shows that men used tramadol solely to prolong sexual intercourse, satisfy their girlfriends, and assert their masculinity, it confirms 'the traditional male sexual script in which sexual activity is goal-oriented' (Wiederman, 2005, p. 498). The result is also in line with previous research on sexual uses of alcohol in the same context, which revealed that men drink specifically to become more aggressive and demonstrate their masculinity to their girlfriends (Dumbili, 2016).

Another implication is that the performance of masculinity is facilitating the use of prescription drugs non-medically in Nigeria, and this confirms media reports on the rising rates of drug use in Nigeria (Bamigbola, 2019). Although the use of drugs to enhance elongated sex among men was popular, men's accounts have shown that women influenced this practice by demanding sex that lasts beyond the natural limit. This reveals that some young women in Nigeria are no longer doing passive femininity. Previous research shows that sex outside of marriage is taboo, and women are supposed to be sexual gatekeepers in this part of Nigeria (Izugbara, 2001). Based on the current study, it is clear that drug-facilitated sexual intercourse among unmarried youths is common, despite that drug use increases the risks of unprotected sex and sexually transmitted diseases (Bellis *et al.*, 2008).

Our findings also demonstrated another important aspect of gendering of drug use, in that only men engaged in cannabis smoking competition, and their reasons supported the dominant discourses of masculinities. That is, smoking games were played by men, and drug champions emerged after taking the highest number of cannabis joints/rolls. Again, not playing this game was associated with weakness, which attracted ridicule. Therefore, men played smoking games to protect their masculinity. The result is in line with a recent Irish study (Darcy, 2020). However, it also shows some culturally unique aspects, in that gambling partly motivated such games, and there were non-smoking umpires.

Conclusions

Our study has provided some novel insights into gender and drug use motives. Nevertheless, it has some limitations. First, only four females were included due to the sensitive nature of the research. As noted earlier, women who use intoxicants are stigmatized in Nigeria. Therefore, women mostly reject invitations to be involved in drug-related research (Dumbili, 2015). Again, we collected data from one city and region. Thus, the findings may not be representative of other areas of Nigeria. Despite these limitations, the study has cast light on some gender-related reasons for young adults' drug use in Nigeria. While drug use exposes interviewees to risks, some of them normalized these risks through drug-facilitated pleasure and fun-seeking. These results have opened the pathways for understanding the underlying gendered motives for drug use and how substance use motives could heighten drug-related problems in Nigeria.

Funding

Emeka W. Dumbili is currently receiving funding from Alexander von Humboldt Foundation through Georg Forster Research Fellowship.

Acknowledgements

We wish to thank the participants for their time and for sharing their drug use experiences with us. We also thank Drs Laura Fenton and Thomas Thurnell-Read for the comments we received on the chapter drafts.

Notes

1 Recreational drug use in this study is defined as taking drugs like cannabis and the non-medical use of pharmaceuticals for 'pleasure', 'fun', and other functional purposes.
2 This was defined as having consumed any psychoactive substance other than alcohol, at least once in the last 30 days.

References

Abdulkarim, A., Mokuolu, O. and Adeniyi, A. (2005) 'Drug use among adolescents in Ilorin, Nigeria', *Tropical Doctor,* 35(4), pp. 225–228.

Adekeye, O.A., Odukoya, J.A., Chenube, O., Igbokwe, D.O., Igbinoba, A.O. and Olowookere, E.I. (2017) 'Subjective experiences and meaning associated with drug use and addiction in Nigeria: a mixed method approach', *Global Journal of Health Science,* 9(8), pp. 57–65.

Anyanwu, O.U., Ibekwe, R.C. and Ojinnaka, N.C. (2016) 'Pattern of substance abuse among adolescent secondary school students in Abakaliki', *Cogent Medicine,* 3(1), p. 1272160.

Appiah, R., Boakye, K.E., Ndaa, P. and Aziato, L. (2018) '"Tougher than ever": an exploration of relapse prevention strategies among patients recovering from poly-substance use disorders in Ghana', *Drugs: Education, Prevention and Policy,* 25(6), pp. 467–474.

Askew, R. (2016) 'Functional fun: legitimising adult recreational drug use', *International Journal of Drug Policy,* 36, pp. 112–119.

Awford, J. (2019) *FATAL ORGY: Three Naked Men Die after Having 'Foursome with Female Student' at Hostel.* Available at: https://www.thesun.co.uk/news/8808741/three-naked-men-die-after-having-foursome-with-female-student-at-hostel/ (Accessed: September 18 2019).

Baker, B. (2002) 'When the Bakassi boys came: eastern Nigeria confronts vigilantism', *Journal of Contemporary African Studies,* 20(2), pp. 223–244.

Bamigbola, B. (2019) 'Students dominate Nigeria's drug abuse population – Bowen VC', *Punch Newspaper Online,* May 14. Available at: https://punchng.com/students-dominate-nigerias-drug-abuse-population-bowen-vc/ (Accessed: July 27).

Barrett, L.F., Robin, L., Pietromonaco, P.R. and Eyssell, K.M. (1998) 'Are women the "more emotional" sex? Evidence from emotional experiences in social context', *Cognition & Emotion,* 12(4), pp. 555–578.

Bassiony, M.M., Salah El-Deen, G.M., Yousef, U., Raya, Y., Abdel-Ghani, M.M., El-Gohari, H. and Atwa, S.A. (2015) 'Adolescent tramadol use and abuse in Egypt', *The American Journal of Drug and Alcohol Abuse,* 41(3), pp. 206–211.

BBC News (2018) *Nigeria's deadly codeine cough syrup epidemic.* Available at: https://www.bbc.com/news/av/world-africa-43944309/nigeria-s-deadly-codeine-cough-syrup-epidemic (Accessed: July 27 2019).

Becker, H.S. (1963) *Outsiders: Studies in the Sociology of Deviance.* New York: The Free Press.

Becker, H.S. (1953) 'Becoming a marihuana user', *American Journal of Sociology,* 59(3), pp. 235–242.

Bellis, M.A., Hughes, K., Calafat, A., Juan, M., Ramon, A., Rodriguez, J.A., Mendes, F., Schnitzer, S. and Phillips-Howard, P. (2008) 'Sexual uses of alcohol and drugs and the associated health risks: a cross sectional study of young people in nine European cities', *BMC Public Health,* 8(1), p. 155.

Boys, A., Marsden, J. and Strang, J. (2001) 'Understanding reasons for drug use amongst young people: a functional perspective', *Health Education Research,* 16(4), pp. 457–469.

Brady, J., Iwamoto, D.K., Grivel, M., Kaya, A. and Clinton, L. (2016) 'A systematic review of the salient role of feminine norms on substance use among women', *Addictive Behaviors,* 62, pp. 83–90.

Braun, V. and Clarke, V. (2019) 'Reflecting on reflexive thematic analysis', *Qualitative Research in Sport, Exercise and Health,* 11(4), pp. 589–597.

Brook, J.S., Morojele, N.K., Pahl, K. and Brook, D.W. (2006) 'Predictors of drug use among South African adolescents', *Journal of Adolescent Health,* 38(1), pp. 26–34.

Burr, V. (2015) *Social Constructionism.* London: Routledge.

Carliner, H., Mauro, P.M., Brown, Q.L., Shmulewitz, D., Rahim-Juwel, R., Sarvet, A.L., Wall, M.M., Martins, S.S., Carliner, G. and Hasin, D.S. (2017) 'The widening gender gap in marijuana use prevalence in the US during a period of economic change, 2002–2014', *Drug and Alcohol Dependence,* 170, pp. 51–58.

City Population (2020) Awka, Anambra. Retrieved from https://www.citypopulation.de/php/nigeria-admin.php?adm1id=NGA004

Cleary, A. (2012) 'Suicidal action, emotional expression, and the performance of masculinities', *Social Science & Medicine,* 74(4), pp. 498–505.

Connell, R.W. and Messerschmidt, J.W. (2005) 'Hegemonic masculinity: rethinking the concept', *Gender & Society,* 19(6), pp. 829–859.

Cooper, M.L. (1994) 'Motivations for alcohol use among adolescents: development and validation of a four-factor model', *Psychological Assessment,* 6(2), pp. 117–128.

Darcy, C. (2020) 'A psychoactive paradox of masculinities: cohesive and competitive relations between drug taking Irish men', *Gender, Place & Culture,* 27(2), pp. 175–195.

Darcy, C. (2020) 'Men and the drug Buzz: Masculinity and men's motivations for illicit recreational drug use', *Sociological Research Online,* 25(3), pp. 421–437.

Dirisu, O., Shickle, D. and Elsey, H. (2019) 'Perspectives of young cannabis users within the Nigerian policy context: the paradox of criminalization as a deterrence strategy', *Journal of Substance Use,* 24(1), pp. 73–78.

Dumbili, E.W. (2016) 'Gendered sexual uses of alcohol and associated risks: a qualitative study of Nigerian University students', *BMC Public Health,* 16(1), p. 1.

Dumbili, E.W. (2015) '"What a man can do, a woman can do better": gendered alcohol consumption and (de) construction of social identity among young Nigerians', *BMC Public Health,* 15(1), p. 167.

Dumbili, E.W. (2020) 'Cannabis normalization among young adults in a Nigerian City', *Journal of Drug Issues,* 50(3): 286–302.

Dumbili, E.W., Ezekwe, E. and Odeigah O.W. (2020). 'From "Codeine Diet" to "Gutter Water": Polydrug use among Nigerian young adults', *Drugs and Alcohol Today,* 20(2):95–107.

Dumbili, E.W., Gardner, J., Degge, H., & Hanewinkel, R. (2021). 'Enhancement motivations for using prescription drugs among young adults in Nigeria', *International Journal of Drug Policy,* 95: 1–8.

Dumbili, E.W. and Williams, C. (2020) '"If She Refuses to Have Sex with You, Just Make Her Tipsy": a qualitative study exploring alcohol-facilitated sexual violence against Nigerian female students', *Journal of Interpersonal Violence,* 35(17–18): 3355–3378.

Eftekhari, A., Turner, A.P. and Larimer, M.E. (2004) 'Anger expression, coping, and substance use in adolescent offenders', *Addictive Behaviors,* 29(5), pp. 1001–1008.

Ettorre, E. (2016) *Revisioning Women and Drug Use.* London: Palgrave Macmillan.

Ettorre, E. (2004) 'Revisioning women and drug use: gender sensitivity, embodiment and reducing harm', *International Journal of Drug Policy,* 15(5–6), pp. 327–335.

Ezzell, M.B. (2012) '"I'm in Control" compensatory manhood in a therapeutic community', *Gender & Society,* 26(2), pp. 190–215.

Fawole, O.I., Ajuwon, A.J., Osungbade, K.O. and Faweya, O.C. (2002) 'Prevalence and nature of violence among young female hawkers in motor-parks in south-western Nigeria', *Health Education,* 102(5), pp. 230–238.

Gioia, D.A., Corley, K.G. and Hamilton, A.L. (2013) 'Seeking qualitative rigor in inductive research: notes on the Gioia methodology', *Organizational Research Methods,* 16(1), pp. 15–31.

Glodosky, N.C. and Cuttler, C. (2020) 'Motives matter: cannabis use motives moderate the associations between stress and negative affect', *Addictive Behaviors,* 102, p. 106188.

Heap, S. (1998) '"We think prohibition is a farce": drinking in the alcohol-prohibited zone of colonial northern Nigeria', *The International Journal of African Historical Studies,* 31(1), pp. 23–51.

Hemsing, N. and Greaves, L. (2020) 'Gender norms, roles and relations and cannabis-use patterns: a scoping review', *International Journal of Environmental Research and Public Health,* 17(3), p. 947.

Hunt, G. and Antin, T. (2019) 'Gender and intoxication: from masculinity to intersectionality', *Drugs: Education, Prevention and Policy,* 26(1), pp. 70–78.

Hunt, G., Antin, T., Bjønness, J. and Ettorre, E. (2016) 'The increasing visibility of gender in the alcohol and drug fields', in Kolind, T., Thom, B. and Hunt, G. (eds.), *The SAGE Handbook of Drug & Alcohol Studies: Social Science Approaches.* London: Sage, pp. 396–417.

Hunt, G.P., Joe-Laidler, K. and Evans, K. (2002) 'The meaning and gendered culture of getting high: Gang girls and drug use issues', *Contemporary Drug Problems,* 29(2), pp. 375–415.

Ibrahim, A. W., Yerima, M. M., Pindar, S. K., Onyencho, V. C., Ahmed, H. K., Machina, B. K., ... & Wakil, M. A. (2017). Tramadol abuse among patients attending an addiction clinic in North-Eastern Nigeria: outcome of a four year retrospective study. *Advances in Psychology and Neuroscience, 2*(1–2), pp. 31–37.

Ikuesan, B.A. (1994) 'Drinking problems and the position of women in Nigeria', *Addiction,* 89(8), pp. 941–944.

Izugbara, C.O. (2001) 'Tasting the forbidden fruit: the social context of debut sexual encounters among young persons in a rural Nigerian community', *African Anthropologist,* 8(1), pp. 96–107.

Jackson, K. and Bazeley, P. (2019) *Qualitative data analysis with Nvivo.* 3rd edn. London: SAGE Publications Limited.

Johnson, O., Akpanekpo, E., Okonna, E., Adeboye, S. and Udoh, A. (2017) 'The prevalence and factors affecting psychoactive substance use among undergraduate students in University of Uyo, Nigeria', *Journal of Community Medicine and Primary Health Care,* 29(2), pp. 11–22.

Kiepek, N. and Beagan, B. (2018) 'Substance use and professional identity', *Contemporary Drug Problems,* 45(1), pp. 47–66.

Legleye, S., Piontek, D., Pampel, F., Goffette, C., Khlat, M. and Kraus, L. (2014) 'Is there a cannabis epidemic model? Evidence from France, Germany and USA', *International Journal of Drug Policy,* 25(6), pp. 1103–1112.

Linneberg, M.S. and Korsgaard, S. (2019) 'Coding qualitative data: a synthesis guiding the novice', *Qualitative Research Journal,* 19(3), pp. 259–270.

Litt, D.M., Kilmer, J.R., Tapert, S.F. and Lee, C.M. (2019) 'Marijuana use and abuse in adolescence', in Zucker, R. and Brown, S. (eds.) *Oxford Handbook of Adolescent Substance Use.* New York: Oxford University Press, USA, pp. 169–188.

Maher, C., Hadfield, M., Hutchings, M. and de Eyto, A. (2018) 'Ensuring rigor in qualitative data analysis: a design research approach to coding combining NVivo with traditional material methods', *International Journal of Qualitative Methods,* 17(1), pp. 1–13.

Maher, L. and Dertadian, G. (2018) 'Qualitative research', *Addiction,* 113(1), pp. 167–172.

Measham, F. (2002) '"Doing gender"—"doing drugs": conceptualizing the gendering of drugs cultures', *Contemporary Drug Problems,* 29(2), pp. 335–373.

Nelson, E. (2018) 'Police crackdowns, structural violence and impact on the well-being of street cannabis users in a Nigerian city', *International Journal of Drug Policy,* 54, pp. 114–122.

Noy, C. (2008) 'Sampling knowledge: the hermeneutics of snowball sampling in qualitative research', *International Journal of Social Research Methodology,* 11(4), pp. 327–344.

Obi, A.I., Adayonfo, E.O., Iwueze, O. and Ekwe, J. (2017) 'Cannabis and tobacco use among undergraduate students of a private university in Edo State, Nigeria', *IFE PsychologIA: An International Journal,* 25(1), pp. 318–333.

Okonoda, K.M., Mwoltu, G.N., Arigbede, O.O. and Yakubu, K. (2017) 'Psychoactive substance use in a sample of community outreach participants; prevalence, correlates and ease of incorporating care', *International Journal of Research in Medical Sciences,* 5(7), pp. 2845–2853.

Okpara, K., Keneth (2018) *Man dies after seventh round in sex competition*. Available at: https://guardian.ng/news/man-dies-after-seventh-round-in-sex-competition/ (Accessed: September 18 2019).

Osborne, G.B. and Fogel, C. (2008) 'Understanding the motivations for recreational marijuana use among adult Canadians', *Substance Use & Misuse,* 43(3–4), pp. 539–572.

Oye-Adeniran, B., Aina, O., Gbadegesin, A. and Ekanem, E. (2014) 'Substance use and sexual behaviour among female students in Nigerian universities', *International Quarterly of Community Health Education,* 35(1), pp. 73–83.

Pease, B. and Pringle, K. (eds.) (2001) *A Man's World? Changing Men's Practices in a Globalized World*. London: Zed Books.

Roulston, K. and Choi, M. (2018) 'Qualitative interviews', in Flick, U. (ed.) *The SAGE Handbook of Qualitative Data Collection*. Thousand Oaks, CA: SAGE, pp. 233–249.

Sallee, M.W. and Harris, F. (2011) 'Gender performance in qualitative studies of masculinities', *Qualitative Research,* 11(4), pp. 409–429.

Sandal, C. (2020) 'Drug-facilitated sexual assault', *Workplace Health & Safety,* 68(3), p. 155.

Thurnell-Read, T. (2016). 'Identity, friendship and sociality', In T. Kolind, B. Thom and G. Hunt (eds.), *The Sage Handbook of Drug & Alcohol Studies: Social Science Approaches*. London: Sage, pp. 337–351.

Uchendu, E. (2007) 'Masculinity and Nigerian youths', *Nordic Journal of African Studies,* 16(2), pp. 279–297.

United Nations Office on Drugs and Crime. (2017) *World Drug Report 2017*. New York: United Nations Publications.

West, C. and Zimmerman, D.H. (1987) 'Doing gender', *Gender & Society,* 1(2), pp. 125–151.

Wiederman, M.W. (2005) 'The gendered nature of sexual scripts', *The Family Journal,* 13(4), pp. 496–502.

Wilton, R., DeVerteuil, G. and Evans, J. (2014) '"No more of this macho bullshit": drug treatment, place and the reworking of masculinity', *Transactions of the Institute of British Geographers,* 39(2), pp. 291–303.

4

WHEN THE CLOCK TAKES OVER

Hangovers in twentieth-century British and American fiction and poetry

Jonathon Shears

Introduction

Everyone recognises the figure of the incoherent drunk, propping up the bar, slurring his words. Similarly, everyone recognises the figure of the hangover victim; the man or woman, shaky, headachy, with bloodshot eyes, who would rather pull the duvet back over their head than face the world, perhaps reaching for the paracetamol, black coffee or something stronger. They are stereotypes. They are images of a loss of control due to alcoholic intoxication, although the latter has received less attention than the former in the field of drinking studies. This may be explained by the fact that hangovers are usually separated from the period of intoxication proper – the sciences measure them only from the point at which blood-alcohol level returns to zero – but this chapter will argue that they tell us as much, if not more, than drunkenness about the ways societies and individuals manage and shape attitudes to alcohol consumption.

The hangover is often a period to reappraise one's alcohol intake. As Muraven, Collins and Neinhaus have argued, 'the ability to restrain one's drinking is critical to sticking to self-imposed drinking limits' (2002, 113) and the hangover, associated as it is with resolutions to cut down or even pledges to abstain, is heavily implicated in such decision making. However, the desire to consume more alcohol to overcome the hangover – often referred to in British and American cultures as taking a 'hair of the dog that bit you' (a reference to a folk cure for rabies) – provides an example of what they call the moment 'when the impulse to drink is stronger than the individual's capacity to override that impulse' (2002, 113). The hangover may well lower what Muraven *et al.* call 'self-control strength' (2005, 140) and it has been argued that such a response to a hangover can be predictive of problem drinking. Absence of resolve is captured neatly in the American novelist John Cheever's ironic journal entry: 'Awake before dawn, feeling tired and full of resolutions. Do not drink. Do not et cetera, et cetera' (1991, 5). The consequent use of remedies to offset the hangover has been characterised as the 'withdrawal-relief' recovery method by Sherry Span and Mitchell Earleywine (1999). In contrast, they label the abstention model a 'traditional-punishment' response, whereby 'individuals who experience the punishing effects of hangover will reduce their drinking' (1999, 121).

DOI: 10.4324/9780429058141-6

It is natural to want to overcome the physical symptoms of a hangover as quickly as possible, which explains the fascination with remedies, and feeling sick and jittery may make the average drinker more likely to lay off for a while. Yet, there are other factors in play than physiological ones in understanding an individual's reaction, and decisions in response, to the hangover. It is now well known that the hangover results from the way that the body metabolises ethanol to create toxins such as acetaldehyde and formaldehyde, that the contraction of blood vessels causes headaches and that alcohol is a diuretic, explaining dehydration. Nevertheless, the corrective aspect implied by the 'traditional-punishment' tag suggests not just physical consequences, but also emotional, spiritual and socio-cultural ones, particularly concerning moral judgement and the conscience. It is worth noting that the social function of punishment, according to Émile Durkheim, exists to express a society's moral outrage and to reemphasise acceptable standards of behaviour and social interaction (1997). Even if the hungover drinker is not generally openly punished, a negative emotional state is often the result of 'internal attributions for negative events' during the period of intoxication, as Matt Treeby and Raimondo Bruno put it, where a negative event involves 'the production of a transgressive behavior that breaches an internalized moral principle' (2012, 613), which might prompt an individual to make amends for fear of social judgement or even exclusion. In other words, the sufferer develops their own punitive mechanisms, or, as Al Young puts it in his poem 'Hangover', first published in the collection *Sea Level* (1986–1990), drunkenness, 'The preferred pain of the Western World/... might be crime & punishment, both' (1992, ll.1–2).

It is in this context that the present chapter reconsiders the significance of the hangover for discussions of drinking studies. If it is often anecdotally claimed that the hangover is nature's corrective for drinking, I take it that this is because physical symptoms have usually been given priority ahead of those more complex emotional ones that are equally unsettling to the drinker's constitution and show that the hangover is a socio-cultural corrective to drinking too. I argue that the symptoms of a hangover become meaningful when their intersections with social values and behavioural norms are identified and considered. In the process, the hungover man or woman is rendered less of a stereotype and more of an individuated subject. The chapter will argue that the period of the hangover is one when an individual's drinking is most likely to bring to light the psychosocial consequences of alcohol use. It will focus on the hangover not just as a time to reappraise alcohol intake but also as a period of recovery through reflection upon and repair of the self, a process which often involves, even as it cannot be confined wholly to, the recovery methods proposed by Span and Earleywine, just as it means giving attention to moral status as well as physical restitution.

To do this, the chapter will make British and American hangover literature – fiction and poetry in this case – its central focus. In *The Information* (1995), Martin Amis suggests that literature has an affinity with hangovers because, to some extent, every hangover is a 'whodunit' (2008, 271). That is, every hangover involves a reconstruction of past events. More importantly, as Jon Elster puts it, imaginative literature is 'the closest thing to a controlled experiment involving high-stakes human emotions' (1999, 108). There is a rich tradition of hangover description in transatlantic drinking literature of the twentieth century, which represents the intersections between social judgement and the subject, giving space to consider the messiness of the hangover's physical and emotional impacts, but also the variation in response. Analysis of this literature demonstrates that the hangover offers a unique route to understand the consciousness and, perhaps, the conscience of the drinker. It also offers an opportunity to explore the manner in which 'cultural beliefs and social practices', which Herring *et al.* (2012, 2) believe control drinking, form and are experienced and interpreted, accepted or opposed. This kind of social scrutiny and self-appraisal directly concerns alcohol use, but it is generally accompanied by larger questions about the status of the self. There is more than one way to combat a hangover, but each one tells us something about how the nature of our attitudes to alcoholic intoxication develops.

The Traditional-Punishment Model: From Myth to History

The clue is in the name to a certain extent. The word 'hangover' implies something remaining or left over from an earlier time. The first recorded use of the word in relation to alcohol comes in 1904 in a dictionary of American slang terms by the pseudonymous Gideon Wurdz where it features under the definition of 'Brain', 'usually occupied by the Intellect Bros., – Thoughts and Ideas – as an Intelligence Office, but sometimes sub-let to Jag, Hang-Over & Co' (*Oxford English Dictionary*). The more general meaning of 'A thing or person remaining or left over; a remainder or survival, an after-effect' (*Oxford English Dictionary*) is attributed to the magazine *Outing* in 1894. Naturally, this does not mean that there were no earlier documented hangovers but, for reasons that will become clear, in this chapter I am particularly concerned with the representation of the after-effects of alcohol consumption from when the term enters common use. Hangovers are also implicated in the word 'intoxication', which, as Michael G. Cooke observes, includes the word 'toxic' (1974, 27). In fact, intoxication has a longer history of meaning poisoning body and mind than the feeling of inebriation and euphoria, suggesting the hangover's implication in drunkenness from the outset.

A new word that indicates a connection to old times, hangover therefore signifies the physiological leftovers of intoxication as it also incorporates an individual's response to the events of their immediate and potentially longer past. This is underlined by the very fact of Span and Earleywine's identification of a 'traditional' response. Tradition implicates a broader relationship with a cultural past than an individual with their prior actions and the coinage of the term at the opening of the twentieth century seems significant in suggesting a transition to modernity that can't quite shake off the values of an earlier age.

Those earlier values are Victorian in part. They can be located in the warnings about the effects of alcohol on health and moral values made by temperance advocates such as Joseph Priestley, and are prominent in literary contexts, including the hangover of Charles Dickens's shame-prone David Copperfield (1849), Anne Brontë's tale of the dissolute and sadistic Arthur Huntingdon in *The Tenant of Wildfell Hall* (1848), and, most spectacularly, in Thomas Hardy's *The Mayor of Casterbridge* (1886), which follows the penitence of Michael Henchard, the hay-trusser who sells his wife to a sailor during a night of intoxication at a country fair. However, as I have argued elsewhere (Shears, 2020), this inheritance goes back at least as far as the period of the emergence of Protestantism in the sixteenth century, when drunkenness became particularly associated with transgression and the hangover with sinfulness and penance. The biblical injunction to consume alcohol in moderation deploys the hangover as a spiritual deterrent through recognisable physical symptoms. As it is put in Proverbs 23:29: 'To whom is woe? To whom is sorrow: To whom strife: To whom is mourning?; To whom wounds without cause? And to whom is the rednesse of the eyes?' In each case, the answer is the man with what we now call a hangover. In this context, the appropriate response to overindulgence is to feel remorse and seek forgiveness, which involves reconnecting with, or acquiescing to, acceptable standards of behaviour. The sinful drinker is the sort that the Puritan John Bunyan captures in *The Life and Death of Mr. Badman* (1680), composed between the two parts of *The Pilgrim's Progress* (1678; 1684), in which Mr Wiseman tells the tale of Badman's wickedness, much of which involves drunken carousing that leads him to gamble, consort with prostitutes and abuse his wife. Badman's domestic negligence is nothing compared to the dereliction of his soul and his debauchery is only curbed when he breaks his leg while reeling home from the alehouse. Attempts at amendment are quickly forgotten: 'his conscience was choked before his leg was healed' (1953, 269). Badman is irredeemable because he disregards the checks and balances of the hangover. They are the same kind of moral restraints to which Hardy's Henchard responds with repentance and regret.

It is true that literary hangovers come in different forms and guises and we should not miss the way genre directs us to variety in human experience. In *The Information*, Amis adds to the 'whodunit' a comic version of 'epic', 'thrillers' and 'tragicomedy' (2008, 271) – taking each, in turn, examples include P. G. Wodehouse's *Carry on Jeeves* (1925), Raymond Chandler's *The Long Goodbye* (1953) and Charles Jackson's *The Lost Weekend* (1944). Hangovers also offer a creative, ecstatic space of personal insight for some poets, including Robert Burns, Lord Byron and John Berryman, who in *Dream Songs* (1969) treats the hangover with an alternating jokey dismissiveness – 'Man, I been thirsty' ('Song 96', l.6) – and tranquil acquiescence that speaks of regeneration – 'out for a sit/now in the emptiest freshest park, one sober fling/before correspondence and breakfast' (ll.18–20). Nevertheless, the penitential, traditional hangover looms large over drinking literature of the twentieth century, even when the main mode is not serious.

The title of Elizabeth Bishop's hangover poem, 'The Unbeliever' (1946), which presents a poet-speaker who initially seems insulated from reprisals, indicates the strong current of religious thoughts and associated moral values that moves through drinking literature. Notably, she begins with an epigraph taken from *The Pilgrim's Progress*, itself a reference to drunkenness in the Book of Proverbs, which is also the first line of her poem: 'He sleeps on the top of a mast' (2014, l.1). In Bunyan's narrative, the character of Christian warns the allegorical figures Simple, Sloth and Presumption, each fettered by a chain representing their chief sin, that they

> are like them that sleep on the top of a Mast for the dead Sea is under you, a Gulf that hath no bottom: Awake therefore, and come away; be willing also, and I will help you off with your Irons.
>
> *(2003, 39)*

Bishop's drinker is likewise in a position of sinfulness, discovered in bed 'with his eyes fast closed' (l.2), evocative less of sleep than denial, the bedsheets discarded, 'leaving out in the air of the night the sleeper's head' (l.5), suggesting equally jeopardy and vulnerability while not ruling out a residual self-awareness. Sleep cocoons the speaker from both physical suffering and moral responsibility, but, as he dreams over a cryptic seascape, this is labelled 'introspection' (l.14). Herein he encounters only the rhyme word 'reflection' (l.15), a sign of egotism. In the final stanza, the threat of the hangover, which is a punitive hangover, rehearses the moral lesson: 'I must not fall./ The spangled sea .../... is hard as diamonds; it wants to destroy us all' (ll.24–26). Bishop's imagery indicates that the hangover is a type of fall, but it is also a submersion; it is more than suggested that the liquid sea below is an alcoholic one that might provide respite if taken as 'the hair of the dog', but which will reveal the hard threat behind its sparkle. The conclusion chimes with the lesson of the proverbial drunkard who, like Mr Badman, ignores the hangover to seek only further intoxication:

> And thou shalt bee as one that sleepeth in the middes of the sea, and as he that sleepeth in the top of the mast. They have stricken me, shalt thou say, but I was not sicke: they have beaten me, but I knew not, when I awoke: therefore will I seeke it yet still.
>
> *(Proverbs, 23: 34–35)*

The word unbeliever suggests less an absence of faith, as in *The Pilgrim's Progress*, than an inability to face up to, and accept, reality and the weaknesses of the self-involved subject.

'The Unbeliever' is indebted to a traditional narrative of punishment and remorse (although its drinker exists in a state of denial), even as it reinscribes it for a new age, in-keeping with my observation that hangover is a word that signals both new and old contexts. Hangovers are always about inheritance in some way – the relation of past to present – but similarities in form reveal differences in content, just as hangovers always have generic and individuated elements. These tensions are noticeable when literature operates close to religion, myth and allegory, as we find in early twentieth-century drinking tales such as Jack London's *John Barleycorn: Alcoholic Memoirs* (1913) where his self-styled 'alcoholic' is set in similar terms to Bishop's unbeliever, viewing hangovers as a test of character that enable him to live a life of hard, masculine excess amongst the Oyster Pirates of Oakland, California. Here, alcohol is something to be conquered in the manner of Herman Melville's Moby Dick. Similarly, in John Steinbeck's *Tortilla Flat* (1935), heavy drinking is associated, in fairly primitive ways, with the conflicting dyad of joyful exuberance and painful remorse. The tale of Danny and his friends is one of camaraderie and the strains alcohol puts on male bonding. When Danny's friends forget to extinguish a candle and burn down his house, they decide that they must 'confess ... like little children to a father', and 'the three penitents' (1958, 61) are eventually forgiven. Danny's disinclination to the responsibility of owning property means losing the house actually comes as a relief to him. Amends are made by Danny's forgiveness, which he proves by sharing a bottle of grappa. It is noticeable that the Catholic background to the novel is emphasised by a greater focus on shame and forgiveness than on the guilty introspection that we find in fiction that exhibits a Protestant front.

Nevertheless, the novels are united in the way they demonstrate that as the hangovers of the central protagonists worsen, they become less able to evade or cheat the repercussions for drinking. A change descends, which involves the depiction of the self-policing individual in breach of Treeby and Bruno's 'internalized moral principle'. For Steven Earnshaw, London's alcoholic is an early example of the 'existential' drinker, 'an ongoing project', who confronts 'what it is to exist by making a commitment to drink large amounts of alcohol' (2018, 1). That existential aspect becomes more insistent as the action progresses and the alcoholic narrator develops what he calls a 'Nietzsche sickness' (London, 2009, 189). This is a terrible depression that marks his hangovers; it manifests itself in an inability to reconcile his drinking with his earlier self-image of the adventurous alpha-male as he acquires a professional status and takes on the personal responsibilities of marriage and fatherhood. The novel plays with the movement from myth to history, where the causes of negative affect – guilt, shame, embarrassment, humiliation and self-pity – appear more deeply internalised and harder to fathom.

Precisely the same thing occurs to Steinbeck's Danny, who undertakes a week-long bender during which he flees from his responsibilities to roam the woods and the town, stealing, fighting and seducing married women. As his friends await his return, they contemplate his punishment – 'If he is not crazy he will be punished' – a reflection on their own inebriated lifestyle: '"Where is our happiness gone?" Pablo mourned. "Somewhere we have sinned. It is a judgement. We should go to confession"' (1958, 189). But when Danny eventually returns, enfeebled by his drinking, 'he was not conscience stricken, but ... [t]he rough fingers of violent experience had harped upon his soul' (200). The hangover marks a shift in the novel's action, which leads to Danny dying after falling over a cliff edge while drunk, but more noticeably a change of key, as he is first overwhelmed by an inexpressible sadness that cannot be articulated, let alone confessed; 'a heavy black thought', or his own Nietzsche sickness.

In 'Hangover', Young ponders, 'Where does it say you have to poison yourself/to have what passes for a good time' (ll.13–14), attributing this to a sort of human tendency to self-flagellation, 'the protestant ethic/of Christian churchkey indulgences' (ll.8–9). Bishop, London and Steinbeck attempt to capture an abiding quality to the hangover, crystallised out of a deeply embedded set of Western cultural attitudes to alcohol, which actually incorporate, rather than oppose, the 'withdrawal-relief' recovery method or 'the hair of the dog'. The fact that their characters drink in defiance of such norms only emphasises their existence. It is only when London's alcoholic and Steinbeck's Danny stop pushing back that they appear less as operatives in a common narrative and more as individualised subjects.

Cheever's evocative allegory of addiction, 'The Swimmer' (1964), plays around with the same kind of cultural archetypes that yield to the complexity of individual experience. On the morning following a party at the house of his friends, the Westerhazys, Neddy Merrill decides that instead of walking home with his family, he will attempt to swim back through the swimming pools that line the back gardens of the well-to-do neighbourhood. This is presented as a feat of endurance. The swimmer is, like Bunyan's Christian, on a journey of self-discovery, each pool representing a figurative drinking bout. He grandiosely labels himself 'a pilgrim, an explorer, a man with a destiny' (1964, 63). However, the idea that his is a quick route home rapidly evaporates, representing the problem drinker's delusion and denial as he is demonstrably more akin to the Simples, Sloths and Presumptions of Bunyan's allegory than to Christian, the swim representing his departure from the straight and narrow path.

Neddy's eccentric decision is contextualised by the hangover: while each of the partygoers acknowledges, 'I *drank* too much' (61), Neddy begins the tale in high spirits, sat by the Westerhazys' pool, 'one hand in it, one around a glass of gin' (61–62), the link between water and alcohol being firmly established. Cheever emphasises Neddy's carefree nature: we are told, 'he had slid down his banister that morning' and 'jogged toward the smell of coffee in his dining room' (62). Yet, the ominous green colour of the water, the fact that Neddy is 'far from young' and that '[h]e had been swimming and now he was breathing deeply, stertorously' (62), foreshadows the struggles that Neddy is to encounter on his epic swim. Each pool becomes harder to cross, as the summer takes on a strange autumnal and then wintry quality, and the increased difficulty to climb from each pool suggests the worsening of hangovers and diminishment of 'self-control strength'. Neddy's loss of status is narrated as he is mocked by passing motorists and shunned by the respectable owners of the pools. Cheever gradually reveals Neddy's character through his encounters on the swim, sketching in a story of social snobbishness, adultery, domestic negligence and betrayal of friends. Doubts creep into the earlier impervious confidence as Neddy is shocked to learn from a neighbour that he has in fact sold his house, his children are in trouble and his brother-in-law has been seriously ill. 'Was he losing his memory, had his gift for concealing painful facts let him forget'? (72): Cheever is unambiguous that 'the hair of the dog' is the choice of his own 'unbeliever', a respite from punishment that results in its intensification.

Cheever connects, rather than differentiates, the 'traditional-punishment' and 'withdrawal-relief' hangover responses. Allegory takes on the tones of tragedy in Neddy's moments of self-awareness that conflict with his persistent sense of pride in his act of endurance. This is something he cannot relinquish, even as he completes his swim to discover 'he was so stupefied with exhaustion that his triumph seemed vague' (76). Cheever jokes about memory loss here, but the drunkard's amnesia is not so much a forgetting of particular events as a symbol of his evasion of truth and inability to reconnect with the orthodox values of middle-class, mid-century America. His increased absentmindedness indicates both a physiological and socio-cultural disconnection:

> At what point had this prank, this joke, this piece of horseplay become serious? He could not go back, he could not even recall with any clearness the green water at the Westerhazys', the sense of inhaling the day's components, the friendly and relaxed voices saying that they had *drunk* too much. In the space of an hour, more or less, he had covered a distance that made his return impossible.
>
> *(69)*

Cheever suggests that the metaphoric journey back must mean all the way back to the beginning, an unpicking of the drinker's life that is all but impossible.

Cheever's drinker is an alcoholic, and it must be noted that the examples I have cited so far are of problem drinkers, but they are generally most significant in drinking literature for the ways they concern themselves first with the 'lessons' of the hangover at what I am calling its mythic, certainly its biblical, level; that is the level that draws heavily on generic dimensions and establishes paradigms and patterns. However, each in its own way departs from the inherited models to consider the drinker as a self-identifying subject. Hence, Cheever explores the quandary of Bishop's unbeliever-as-abnegator in a character who has sufficient self-awareness to recognise even amongst the apparent self-satisfaction that 'he had no freedom of choice about his means of travel' (72–73).

Social and Personal Control Mechanisms

The hangover is made painful because it is not only a physical torment but also frequently a moral and ethical one. The examples of hangover literature that I have discussed indicate that the approaches outlined by Span and Earleywine are accurate to the extent that they are starting points to thinking about socio-cultural attitudes to alcohol use, but they are only that. If Cheever's Neddy Merrill swims free of context at an allegorical level, the tragic psychodrama of the story imposes a self-present subject grappling with 'internal attributions for negative events'. Ingbar *et al.* argue that 'the view that transgressions must be balanced by pain inflicted on the transgressor has remained a major tenet of Western moral thought' (2013, 14). As far as the hangover is concerned, the infliction of such pain has a cultural – perhaps we could even go so far as to now say textual – heritage or superstructure, which I have outlined, that cannot be overlooked. Its subjective expression is, however, determined by a drinker's attitude to their specific environment and the standards to which they are held or hold themselves. Joachim Gerich argues that this is manifested in deterrents or what he terms 'control mechanisms', akin to Muraven's 'self-control strength', that take the form of either self-control, 'embedded in the person' or, 'in the social environment', social control (Gerich, 2014, 120). The internalisation of the latter, expressed during the hangover, means that they tend to demonstrate ways in which these categories are interdependent rather than independent.

Their interdependence is affirmed in Ingbar's further assertion that belief and investment in punishment 'is strong enough that people may sometimes inflict pain on themselves in order to balance their misdeeds' (2013, 14), developing the notion of personal punitive mechanisms that I earlier established. As we will now see, it is possible to identify within the broader Western mythologies of conscience and shame, set out by Ingbar *et al.*, more precise interpersonal and social control mechanisms at work in reactions to alcohol consumption.

These involve aspects of identity formation such as class, sexuality and gender – masculinity and femininity need distinguishing in this regard – and intergenerational conflicts, each generally presenting as a superstructure of values relating to status and social control.

Central to the tradition of gritty, twentieth-century drinking narratives is Patrick Hamilton's 1941 novel *Hangover Square*, a story about an underclass of drifters in the late 1930s in London, including the masochistic George Harvey Bone, whose heavy drinking exacerbates the peculiar dissociative episodes from which he suffers. If Bone is a masochist, he is perfectly matched against his love interest, the sadistically inclined Netta Longdon, who manipulates the male characters who orbit around her in dingy Earl's Court, driving Bone into spirals of self-doubt, pessimism and, finally, murder. Hamilton is an acute observer of the deprivations deriving from class consciousness, which leads to resentment in Netta and the fascistic figure of Peter, but to an overwhelming sense of diminishment in Bone who pathetically jostles for some kind of standing in the drinking circle.

Circle is the appropriate word. The group's shared joke is that each morning they collectively take 'a little stroll round Hangover Square' (2001, 29) (a pun on Hanover Square), but it is really the motif of the circle, rather than square, that exemplifies Bone's predicament, expressed through his desire, but failure, to rise 'from this sad circle in hell in which he had been condemned to wander so long' (119), as he characterises West London's drinking culture. The hangover as Dantesque circle of hell symbolically adjoins Bone to the long-historical, biblical tradition of the drinker whose self-inflicted punishment foreshadows damnation, but his particular control mechanisms are evocatively captured by the self-involving wheels of narration that frame his damaged identity in Chapter 5.

At this point in the novel, Bone's fragile self-esteem has been given a momentary boost by a chance encounter with an old school friend who represents a theatrical agency for whom Netta hopes to work. In Bone's fantasies, Johnnie Littlejohn becomes a route to higher status and romantic success with Netta, especially during a drunken night in which they plan a trip to Brighton together. Characteristically, Bone is the low-status drunk, mocked by other members of the group; treated as an 'errand boy', he is '[s]nubbed, isolated, yet obedient' (114) as he pays for drinks, fetches sandwiches or undertakes other small tasks for Netta, 'the dumb butt of their unfriendly wit' (121). The repeated, small humiliations at the hands of Netta mean that, waking hungover the following morning, Bone immediately loses faith that she will really accompany him to Brighton. The hangover is a time for painful reassessment not merely of the night before, but of Bone's larger anxieties as he lies 'grinding out the problems of his life, delving into the night before to see where he had got to exactly, where he had left off' (113).

Regret turns into the greater feeling of remorse, driven by Bone's personal dissatisfaction that is a product of his awareness of social inadequacy; even as he proclaims the desire to reconnect with a more wholesome life, and renounce the heavy episodic drinking that sets him against acceptable social norms, he knows that his devotion to Netta will draw him back to a subservient position, playing the part of the oft-ridiculed 'big drinking man' (113). Bone's trap is sprung by his own conscience as he turns over the memories of the occasion he caught Netta and Peter having sex at a party. Recalling how the scales fell from his eyes, the next morning his 'hangover was not as predicted' (117) as, rather than misery and loss, he experiences 'a sense of release from Netta' (118) through newly acquired feelings of disgust: 'He was through now' (116). But that break is not as decisive as it ought to be. Bone's restored pride is based on Netta's corresponding diminishment in his eyes because she is 'brought down to the sordid level of Peter' (118). Ties of status are inescapable. As such, it is a precarious victory that is undermined the moment Netta offers the olive branch of the Brighton trip, and she is restored to her previous, untarnished position in Bone's psychodrama.

The hangover subsequent to the mortifying discovery of Netta and Peter's relationship that destroys Bone's hopes, which brought with it a 'funny feeling of calm, of release' (117), leads him to resolve to reduce his drinking and smarten up his act, but that decision is ironically framed by the despair of Bone's current hangover, emphasising the hellish circularity of his position, where he finds that it is the hope that kills: 'He had thought, last night in drink, that all his troubles were as good as over' (123). Bone accuses himself of being 'a fool and a weakling' (115), which derives from the fact that he has breached his pledge not to be deceived again by Netta. More generally, Bone's hangovers disclose the superstructure of a class system in which his lowly status generates a sense of inferiority he cannot overcome, loading onto the derision of Netta reprisals of his own. Recalling the dual physiological and socio-cultural disconnection that characterises the hangover of Cheever's Neddy Merrill, it is noticeable that, while Bone laments his lot, his reflections are punctuated by 'the mysterious gurglings in pipes, the running of h. & c. in the bedrooms of his sober, God-fearing fellow-guests' (123), symbolising the conventional life and middle-class values from which he finds himself estranged through drink. Bone discovers that he is less 'modern' than he would wish as age-old warnings about drunkenness provide a background accompaniment to the sound of the hotel plumbing.

George Harvey Bone's hangovers play host to a conflicting set of values that can be unpacked but that he cannot personally resolve. Emotional discomfort or negative affect is a response to loss of control. Bone wrestles with a hangover of ideas and values as much as the after-effects of intoxication. In that sense, Bone's predicament is equally a crisis in masculinity. His old-fashioned ideas of romance are made to appear quaint amidst the ruthless, uncaring masculinity of the likes of Peter, who is established as the representative of a hard-faced generation of new men, secretly in thrall to the brutalism of Hitler and Mussolini. 'Couldn't he be a man, and pull himself together, and get her?' (121) Bone asks himself. But the hangover works in its familiar way, erecting a bridge between past and present, in both local and general senses, and Bone's beliefs, which mark him out as the 'interloper' in Netta's 'alien and scornful mob' (121), are the leftovers of an earlier, allegedly simpler time, that prove to be insurmountable.

Bone's hangovers are anxious affairs, and he presents differently from other, noteworthy working-class drinkers of fiction such as Alan Sillitoe's Arthur Seaton (*Saturday Night and Sunday Morning*, 1958) or Charles Bukowski's Henry Chinaski (*Post Office*, 1971 and *Factotum*, 1975), the angry young men who, as Earnshaw puts it, 'define an authentic self in the process of being repeatedly or continuously drunk' (2015, 206). For these figures, hangovers are part of the collateral damage of heavy drinking that is more distinctively ideological, undertaken in line with Seaton's motto, 'don't let the bastards grind you down' (1995, 76), where pedantic bosses and toadying workmates are to be mocked and resisted. At least that is until the social reprisals become too much to bear, as in the case of Seaton, who swaps the hedonism of Saturday nights for the correction of acceptable working-class, married life, symbolised by Sunday morning. Despite aiming to evade responsibility by being continuously drunk in defiance of orthodox values, both Seaton and Chinaski suffer humiliations that bite the most during hangovers.

Less openly rebellious, prone to bouts of self-flagellation, Hamilton's Bone shares more in common with a character at the other end of the social spectrum, the wealthy, Princeton-educated Amory Blaine of F. Scott Fitzgerald's *This Side of Paradise* (1920), who also learns, in drink, that the hangover means that his sense of masculine autonomy is inescapably tied to inherited values. Hangovers are emotionally crushing to those who invest in the kind of dreams of success that are most vivid at moments of intoxication. Blaine, like

Bone, has a code of values that, in his own estimation, set him aside from the other undergraduates, but that, when breached, prompt melodramatic outbursts of self-recrimination.

Fitzgerald styles him as the egotist *par excellence* – the vanity and pride of youth as yet unchallenged by the harder realities of life. But Blaine is also a figure of conscience. In the most extraordinary and disturbing sequence of the novel, the prideful Blaine loses control of both body and mind, but more importantly self-image, during a drunken night that concludes in a hedonistic party at the house of a young woman picked up in a nightclub by Blaine and the inebriated Fred Sloane. About to neck a glass of brandy, which he knows would commit him to a drunken night and meaningless sexual encounter with Phoebe, Blaine is stunned to notice a man in the corner of the room who had been watching him in a café earlier in the day. In a rush of paranoia, Blaine believes him to be the devil: Fitzgerald's description of the man's 'virile pallor' and hands of 'versatility' and 'tenuous strength' are offset by an incongruous pair of pointed shoes with 'the little ends curling up' (2011, 130). The near-psychedelic iconography indicates something of a moment of troubled, sexual awakening for the idealist; the conflicting messages about masculinity embodied in the 'devil' combine to function like a warning sign against sinful excess and Blaine charges out of the party.

The following morning's hangover is a personal crisis for Blaine:

> How much or how little Sloane remembered Amory did not care to know; he apparently had none of the nervous tension that was gripping Amory and forcing his mind back and forth like a shrieking saw.
>
> *(133)*

Sloane is able to put the event in perspective: 'What's the matter with you? Old remorse getting you? You'd be in a fine state if you'd gone through with our little party' (133). Walking down Fifth Avenue, Blaine has a sudden, irrational desire to get off the street: 'it's filthy, and if you can't see it, you're filthy too' (133). The filthy New York street is a projection of Blaine's self-disgust, just as, it might be argued, the 'sudden sickness' (133) he feels is both physical and metaphysical. Most remarkable is the manner in which Fitzgerald plays fast and loose with genre as Blaine's day proceeds first as psychological realism, then as horror story: 'He could feel the little hot veins on his forehead standing out, and his terror had hardened on him like plaster. He felt he was passing up again through the thin crust of horror' (134). Travelling back to college, he encounters a 'painted woman' on the train who fills him with a 'fresh burst of sickness' (134) linked to the night before. The chapter then flips into the mode of magic realism as Blaine returns to his lodgings, where both he and his flatmate, Tom, see the 'devil' looking in through the window. Like all good horror stories, there is a foreboding thunderstorm outside. Like all good horror stories, the symbolism is hard to miss: the abject monster stalking Blaine in his hungover paranoia is himself. The devil outside is really the threat that lies within; the horror at his propinquity to a world of vulgarity that threatens his own ideals of romantic love but also a fragile ego that cannot admit to strictly bodily desires.

In his hangover, Blaine must come to terms with the relationship of his own principles to, and the fact they may diverge from, a larger social context. Like Bone, there is a streak of conservatism that fights past his claims to alterity. Where the values at stake are most personal, the hangover is at its worst. The terms that apply to Blaine are not, however, the same terms that we find in women's drinking literature of the twentieth century. As Rolfe, Orford and Dalton note, women's drinking through much of Western history has been associated with 'unfeminine, immoral, unrespectable behaviour' (2009, 327) and that women receive more judgements about things like sexual impropriety, sexual availability and lack of self-control. This has been attributed to the persistence of the 'iconic position' of wife, mother and homemaker as fundamental to 'family sustainability' (Staddon, 2013, 5–6), around which accrues a set of moral norms or social control mechanisms against which women are measured and which form the superstructure of many women's experience of the 'traditional-punishment' hangover response.

In the first half of the twentieth century, the novel showcases female characters who negotiate moral judgement in different ways, including Ernest Hemingway's Lady Brett Ashley in *Fiesta: The Sun Also Rises* (1926) and Christopher Isherwood's Sally Bowles of *Goodbye to Berlin* (1939). These are stylish, cosmopolitan women or 'modern girls' who drink heavily in public, and make no attempt to conceal their sexual desires. Nevertheless, both are condemned as much as celebrated, tarnished by their association with traditionally male habits of excessive alcohol consumption. In *Good Morning, Midnight* (1939), Jean Rhys presents the more psychologically vulnerable Sasha Jansen who drinks to cope with the loss of her child and breakdown of her marriage. Jansen notably develops a habit of compulsive self-monitoring as she attempts to control, rather than deal with, her emotions through the use of alcohol and sedatives.

Bishop's poetry is foundational in establishing the lineaments of women's drinking experience in the twentieth century. According to Renée Curry, '[t]he intersection that occurs among alcohol, despair, and liminal space provides a trembling ground to peruse for insight into the imagination of' (1999) the problem drinker. If conspicuous drunkenness tends to establish 'stigmatizing subject positions' (Rolfe, 2009, 329) for women, then Bishop's drinking poems show the emotional consequences. Generally, Bishop deflects specific attention from the female subject by using male speakers, emphasising the inadmissible nature of women's drinking. However, her choice of imagery articulates her true attention. In 'Crusoe in England' (1976), for example, her speaker fantasises a new version of Daniel Defoe's tale of a castaway. His is not a story of self-reliance, but one of weakness, as the newly discovered volcanic island – combinations of images of fire and water often symbolise alcohol in Bishop's verse (Millier, 1998, 70) – on which he finds himself adrift from civilisation sees him enisled by self-pity. Independence is ironically affirmed not through the survival mechanisms undertaken by Defoe's Crusoe, but by the dreamer's inventiveness in turning the island's natural abundance into alcohol:

> There was one kind of berry, a dark red.
> I tried it, one by one, and hours apart.
> Sub-acid, and not bad, no ill effects;
> and so I made home-brew. I'd drink
> the awful, fizzy, stinging stuff
> that went straight to my head
> and play my home-made flute
> (I think it had the weirdest scale on earth)
> and, dizzy, whoop and dance among the goats.
> Home-made, home-made! But aren't we all?
>
> (2014, ll.76–85)

The effect of intoxication leads to momentary abandon, but the pride in ingenuity is likened to drunken delusion, undermined as the verse moves away from the speaker's claim to suffer 'no ill effects'. There may be no physical indisposition, but there is a moral judgement in the transferral of 'home-made' from the flute to the speaker. Geographically separated from civilisation, the island remains tied to recognisably inherited attitudes to women's alcohol use. As Brett C. Millier argues, in life 'Bishop never acquired the knack of homemaking – that is, of finding a permanent place to call home' (1998, 56) and alienation from home, literally and figuratively, is a recurring theme of her verse (1998, 64). 'Home-made' becomes an accusation directed at the female drinker: the values associated with women's drinking are fashioned in and reflect upon their relationship to domesticity.

'Crusoe in England' increasingly turns upon violated images of motherhood as the speaker's dreams of a splendid isolation – sustained by intoxicants – turn sour: 'But then I'd dream of things/like slitting a baby's throat, mistaking it/for a baby goat. I'd have/nightmares of other islands/stretching away from mine' (ll.131–133). Alcohol is associated with further haunting images of mother-child separation:

> One day I dyed a baby goat bright red
> with my red berries, just to see
> something a little different.
> And then his mother wouldn't recognize him.
>
> (ll.125–128)

Bishop's message takes the symbolism of Defoe, but sets the drinker against herself rather than the hostile environment. In each case, alcohol consumption leads to self-inflicted punishment driven by inherited notions of acceptable femininity.

'Home-made, home-made! But aren't we all?' is the theme that haunts most iconic women drinkers in fiction, including the aforementioned Sally Bowles and Sasha Jensen. The hangovers of Helen Fielding's Bridget Jones in *Bridget Jones's Diary* (1996) are often comically messy affairs, most notably in the case of the hangover buffet she consumes, which consists of Emmenthal cheese slices, a litre of orange juice, a cold jacket potato, two slices of cheesecake, a Milky Way, a 'chocolate Viennoise dessert thing', broccoli and four Frankfurter sausages, to recover after one night of particularly heavy drinking (2001, 115–116). Fielding's point here, as elsewhere, is, however, generally less about Bridget's physical discomfort than the reasons for her self-destructive drinking and associated behaviour such as comfort eating of this sort. Hangovers lead Bridget into uncomfortable confrontations with her own 'stigmatizing subject position' and a superstructure of feminine values, despite her assertions of autonomy as a self-identifying independent woman.

Although her self-assertive friend, Shazzer, proclaims that the pair represent a 'pioneer' generation of women 'daring to refuse to compromise in love and relying on our own economic power' (21), Bridget feels the pressure from her overbearing mother to marry and have children and so conform to the 'iconic position' of motherhood. Alcohol helps Bridget surmount social embarrassment and silence her inner critic and she resists the prospect of becoming what she calls a 'Smug Married', but her hangovers are full of self-recrimination – 'Oh why am I so unattractive? Why?' (16) – based around negative evaluation of body-image and personality that she attributes to contemporary representation of women in the media:

> Wise people will say Daniel should like me just as I am, but I am a child of Cosmopolitan culture, have been traumatized by super-models and too many quizzes and know that neither my personality nor my body is up to it if left to its own devices.
>
> *(68)*

Bridget's mother reminds her, '[t]here's nothing worse than a woman drunk, darling' (34). In contrast, Shazzer asserts, '[e]ven the most outrageous minxes lose their nerve, wrestling with the first twinges of existential angst: fears of dying alone … Stereotypical notions of shelves, spinning wheels and sexual scrapheaps' (20). The twinges of conscience are felt most painfully during Bridget's hangovers. In that sense, while gender is a primary focus, these hangovers are also always an intergenerational crisis as Bridget confronts her mother's values.

Bridget Jones's nerves are put under most stress during hangovers, but that is a product of the conflict of values under which she labours rather than a physiological response to drinking – of the clash between old and new that we have repeatedly seen signified by the word hangover in this chapter. The diary format is the perfect medium to communicate the episodic nature of Bridget's drinking: the abrupt relationship between the highs of intoxication and the lows of hangovers. Bridget's success or failure is measured against her level of self-control around food and alcohol, every entry famously recording the number of calories and alcoholic units she has consumed each day. Through this method, Fielding strikingly represents the diurnal presence of self-control mechanisms.

Yet, it is notable that the confessional-style technique, in-keeping with the broader pattern of the historical development of confessional literature, concerns itself at least as much with the limits placed upon the drinking subject's attempt 'to set out a personal identity' (Levin, 1998, 3) as it does with the true 'traditional-punishment' model of reconnection with moral norms. The 'existential angst' identified by Shazzer, recalling the 'Nietzsche-sickness' of London's alcoholic but also the inability to confront and resolve the problems of the self that we find in Bishop's 'The Unbeliever', is frustrating and troubling regardless of regret for specific drunken events. Unexpectedly, and despite the fact that her levels of consumption are relatively low in comparison, Bridget Jones directs us back towards the residual problem with an inexpressible sense of personal dissatisfaction or failure that we have seen in earlier drinkers of fiction and poetry. The issue is captured by Charles Jackson's Don Birnam who, in *The Lost Weekend*, cannot quite fathom why he drinks or what it is he has done wrong: 'you lived always in a state of mortal apprehension of some dreadful deed committed for which, though you were called to account, you could never bear witness' (1989, 162).

The Kafkaesque notion of being unable to wholly 'bear witness' to one's own crimes and therefore fully recognise and accept the drinker's traditional narrative of crime and punishment, and adopt effective control mechanisms in response, emphasises that the hangover problematises, even as it generates the conditions for, the individual's confession of their misdeeds. There is an element of ego in the likes of Cheever's Merrill and Fitzgerald's Blaine that makes the idea that their problems can be explained away on the terms of the hangover's traditional emotional superstructure anathema to them. Hence, the reader is often suspended from making judgements on the hangover victim even as the materials for making such a judgement appear to lie readily to hand. This is never truer than in the case of my final example of hangover literature, A. L. Kennedy's *Paradise* (2004).

Kennedy recounts the self-destructive drinking behaviour of Hannah Luckraft, a young woman who aims to defy, through being repeatedly and continuously drunk, the acceptable standards of femininity represented by her mother. The story begins with a hangover as Hannah, who suffers from alcohol-induced blackouts, attempts to piece together her sexual encounter of the previous night with a married man in a London hotel. Her possession of a credit card belonging to a Hungarian she cannot recall meeting is her only clue as to what she has done. Over breakfast where she is forced to share a table with a middle-class family, Hannah is disgusted to recall that the prim, anxious father was her sexual partner and she rushes back to her room to shower, a process she describes as 'healing' (2015, 31). Hannah cleanses herself of sexual impropriety, not because she feels guilty for this *per se*, but because she feels contaminated by the hypocrisy that she identifies with the heart of middle-class life: marriage.

The 'whodunnit' aspect of a hangover is manifestly only a jumping off point for the characteristic 'who am I?' storyline. The main plot backfills both the events that led to Hannah's arrival at the hotel – including her feelings of inferiority and resentment towards her brother who had sent her to a Canadian sanitorium to dry out – and her general attitude to life which is defined by heavy drinking, sexual promiscuity and a complete disregard for alcohol's impact on her physical and mental health. The tragic element of Hannah's story is that 'the undiluted flavour of paradise' (187) – the perfect state of intoxication is described in customary religious terms – exists only in her dreams. Her hungover proclamation that '[t]here is no current cause for gloom, or maudlin recollections of the family home and how handy my mother might have been' (30) appears to be a level of denial much greater than that expressed by Bridget Jones. Hannah is eventually forced to confront the fact that 'I do feel remorse for every sin. Inside, I am mostly built out of remorse' (217). Like Bishop's hungover women, it is the spectre of domesticity that troubles most; Hannah declares 'with home in my head I can't bear to be awake' (146). This penitent's rhetoric chimes with the 'traditional-punishment' hangover reaction as I have outlined it.

Even so, Hannah does not correct her drinking habits, nor make amends as she repeatedly promises. Her hungover pledges to reform are rapidly forgotten amidst the blackouts which become, in a postmodern fashion, a way to avoid bearing witness to the real reasons why she drinks and so she remains, in the final analysis, unfathomable to herself. Something indecipherable it is claimed is left over: an impulse towards self-destruction. As much as Luckraft's drunkenness can be read as her defiance of conventional values – a subject on which she is candid almost to the point of shamelessness – her hangovers also pose a postmodern question about the fragmentation of the self which cannot be successfully examined due to the fogginess of near-continual intoxication. Hence, the hangover is embraced by Hannah as a release from memory, an uncoupling of the present from the past:

> Because once you've begun to have blackouts, you'll never stop and so before and after don't exist – you've mastered the art of escaping from linear time. The jumps and jolts take a bit of getting used to – driving is particularly tricky, guessing what gear you're in, or if you're trying to overtake – but this keeps you bright and springy, alert. And there is nothing unnatural about it, nothing dreadful: some level of blacking out is what lets people survive.
>
> *(18–19)*

Counterintuitively, here the hangover signifies forgetting in personal but also cultural terms. Unable to remember what you have done the night before means not having to account for one's 'dreadful' deeds. It is a kind of functional amnesia, which Hannah claims disconnects her not only from the events of the previous night but from the links that bind her to the conventional narrative of crime and punishment I have charted that frames the hangover in British and American fiction and poetry.

Naturally, as a narrator whose reliability is repeatedly thrown into question by her drinking, Hannah's survival mechanism is only sustainable insofar as she is able to consume more alcohol. Her claim to have escaped linear time is also one utterance amongst many others that suggest the contrary. There always exists the threat that the unaccounted or unaccountable elements of the self that allegedly allow the postmodern drinker to cheat time, and with it social reprisals, may only temporarily be lost. Even so, inhabiting the first-person narrative plane of Hannah means that there are no objective criteria from which to judge and the reader is forced to grant that she is both fully comprehensible subject and insoluble riddle. Hannah finds that the underlying reasons she feels so bad resist final articulation, although if her 'paradise' is intoxication without the socio-cultural repercussions of a hangover, Kennedy hints that the wish is father of the thought.

Conclusion

In 'The Drunkard' (1946), Louis MacNeice describes a drinker's train journey home after a heavy night, which becomes a larger story about the repeated 'spiral back into time and down towards Hell' (2007, l.2), where Hell is both the hangover and the absence of the heavenly feelings of intoxication. In some senses, MacNeice may be more accurate when he also calls the journey, 'Purgatory in reverse' (l.1), which captures the sense of the drinker not irredeemably damned, but rather awaiting judgement for his drunken actions. I have presented similar motifs in a variety of hangover literature, partly to emphasise that the hangover is so much more than just a physical experience at the withdrawal of alcohol from the body. In this chapter, what we have seen is that the hangover is actually a complex emotional and socio-cultural phenomenon that discloses the values that individuals attach to and express through their alcohol use. The literature I have analysed shows that the sense of being judged for one's drinking habits is frequently felt most strongly during the period of the hangover. My argument is that the hangover distils many of a culture's attitudes to alcohol, particularly judgements that are associated with the way drunkenness is perceived to threaten moral norms, which are often tied to issues of class and status, gender and sexuality or the family.

I have confined my attention to examples of British and American hangover literatures in this chapter, but now we have seen that the hangover is not universal but emerges from within a culture, its potential value in appraising the attitudes to alcohol use in other alco-literary traditions, such as those in Asian and Nordic societies, should be apparent. Because what we have seen through the hangover literature I have analysed in this chapter is that the hangover has a history. That is to say emotional responses are usually attached to our ideas about ourselves and the way we are judged that belong to both our own time and earlier eras. Hence, it seems to me that MacNeice is quite right to stress the movement 'into time', in the sense that while intoxication is often seen as a temporary liberation from social and personal inhibitions, the hangover witnesses their return, made most visible at times when longstanding values and stories encounter new subject positions.

For MacNeice, the descent into the hangover as depicted in 'The Drunkard' means an 'absolute moment' (l.19), or the consequence-free timelessness of drunkenness, is 'displaced/By moments' (ll.19–20), which is another way of describing the social control mechanisms that police alcohol use, whereby values otherwise located in the environment are transformed into personal codes of value. At this point in the train journey of 'The Drunkard', 'the clock takes over – time to descend/Where Time will brief us, briefed himself to oppress/The man …/whose tongue feels around and around but cannot taste/That hour-gone sacrament of drunkenness' (ll.20–24). Here, coming down from the high of intoxication involves a process very similar to what I earlier described as a movement from myth to history. My focus in this chapter has been on that equivalent movement, which demonstrates that the hangover is, as the word indicates, a time in which alcohol use, along with many other personal issues, is framed by the way in which the present encounters the recent and remote past. Hangover literature reminds us of the personal and larger cultural reasons that explain why we so often feel bad when the aftermath of intoxication kicks in and the clock takes over.

References

Primary Texts

Amis, Martin (2008). *The Information*. [1995] New York: Vintage.
Bishop, Elizabeth (2014). *Poems: The Centenary Edition*. New York: Vintage.
Bunyan, John (1953). *Grace Abounding & The Life and Death of Mr. Badman*. [1680] London: J. M. Dent & Sons Ltd.
Bunyan, John (2003). *The Pilgrim's Progress*, ed. W. R. Owens. [1678] Oxford: World's Classics.
Cheever, John (1964). *The Brigadier and the Golf Widow*. New Work, Evanston and London: Harper & Row.
Cheever, John (1991). *The Journals of John Cheever*. New York: Vintage.
Fielding, Helen (2001). *Bridget Jones's Diary*. [1996] London: Picador.
Fitzgerald, F. Scott (2011). *This Side of Paradise*. [1920] Ware: Wordsworth.
Hamilton, Patrick (2001). *Hangover Square*. [1941] London: Penguin.
Jackson, Charles (1989). *The Lost Weekend*. [1944] London: Penguin.
Kennedy, A. L. (2015). *Paradise*. [2004] London: Vintage.
London, Jack (2009). *John Barleycorn: Alcoholic Memoirs*, ed. John Sutherland. [1941] Oxford: World's Classics.
MacNeice, Louis (2007). *Collected Poems*, ed. Peter McDonald. London: Faber & Faber.
Sillitoe, Alan (1995). *Saturday Night and Sunday Morning*. [1958] London: Harper Collins.
Steinbeck, John (1958). *Tortilla Flat*. [1935] Harmondsworth: Penguin.
Young, Al (1992). *Heaven: Collected Poems, 1956–1990*. Berkeley: Creative Arts Books.

Secondary Texts

Cooke, Michael G. (1974). 'De Quincey, Coleridge, and the Formal Uses of Intoxication'. *Yale French Studies*. 50: 26–40.
Curry, Renée (1999). 'A Thirst for Reverie: Alcohol, Despair, and Dream Space in Elizabeth Bishop's Poetry'. *Literature and Medicine*. 18.1: (100–113).
Durkheim, Émile (1997). *The Division of Labour in Society*. [1893] New York: The Free Press.
Earnshaw, Steven (2015). 'Drink, Dissolution, Antibiography: The Existential Drinker'. *Biographies of Drink: A Case Study Approach to our Historical Relationship with Alcohol*, eds. Mark Hailwood and Deborah Toner. Newcastle-upon-Tyne: Cambridge Scholars: pp. 204–222.
Earnshaw, Steven (2018). *The Existential Drinker*. Manchester: Manchester University Press.
Elster, Jon (1999). *Alchemies of the Mind: Rationality and the Emotions*. Cambridge: Cambridge University Press.
Gerich, Joachim (2014). 'The Inhibiting Function of Self-Control and Social Control on Alcohol Consumption'. *Journal of Drug Issues*. 44.2: 120–131.
Herring, Jonathan, Ciaran Regan, Darin Weinberg and Phil Withington (eds) (2012). *Intoxication and Society: Problematic Pleasures of Drugs and Alcohol*. London: Palgrave Macmillan.
Ingbar, Yoel, David A. Pizarro, Thomas Gilovich and Dan Ariely (2013). 'Moral Masochism: On the Connection between Guilt and Self-Punishment'. *Emotion*. 13.1: 14–18.
Levin, Susan M. (1998). *The Romantic Art of Confession: De Quincey, Musset, Sand, Lamb, Hogg, Frémy, Soulié, Janin*. Columbia: Camden House.
Millier, Brett C. (1998). 'The Prodigal: Elizabeth Bishop and Alcohol'. *Contemporary Literature*. 39.1: 54–76.
Muraven, Mark, R., Lorraine Collins and Kristen Neinhaus (2002). 'Self-Control and Alcohol Restraint: An Initial Application of the Self-Control Strength Model'. *Psychology of Addictive Behaviors*. 16.2: 113–120.
Muraven, Mark, R., Lorraine Collins, Saul Shiffman and Jean A. Paty (2005). 'Daily Fluctuations in Self-Control Demands and Alcohol Intake'. *Psychology of Addictive Behaviors*. 19.2: 140–147.
(2021). *Oxford English Dictionary*. Oxford: Oxford University Press.
Rolfe, Alison, Jim Orford and Sue Dalton (2009). 'Women, Alcohol and Femininity: A Discourse Analysis of Women Heavy Drinkers' Accounts'. *Journal of Health Psychology*. 14.2: 326–335.
Shears, Jonathon (2020). *The Hangover: A Literary and Cultural History*. Liverpool: Liverpool University Press.

Span, Sherry A. and Mitchell Earleywine (1999). 'Familial Risk for Alcoholism and Hangover Symptoms'. *Addictive Behavior*. 24.1: 121–125.

Staddon, Patsy (2013). 'Improving Support for Women with Alcohol Issues'. Folk.us-PenCLAHRC Awarded Study.

Treeby, Matt and Raimondo Bruno (2012). 'Shame and Guilt-Proneness: Divergent Implications for Problematic Alcohol Use and Drinking to Cope with Anxiety and Depression Symptomatology'. *Personal and Individual Differences*. 53.4: 613–617.

PART II

Social life of intoxicants

5

INTOXICATING CONSUMPTION

Capitalism and the commodification of pleasure

Gerda Reith

Introduction

Intoxication has long been regarded as problematic for the order of societies. This is especially so when it is associated with particular social groups of 'outsiders' such as ethnic minorities, women and the poor. Historically, the consumption of psychoactive or intoxicating substances has been subject to moral panics and attempts at governance (exemplified in the example of the twentieth century's 'War on Drugs'), and can be seen as an attempt to impose the values of sobriety and productivity on unruly populations of consumers.

Deliberate intoxication stands as a counter to the hegemony of sobriety. It also challenges ideals of rational, autonomous subjectivity. As Stuart Walton (2003) has noted in *Out of It*, intoxicated subjects are also unproductive subjects, whose capacity to work, plan or even consume in a rational manner is compromised. Intoxication undermines liberal and neoliberal ideals of productivity, inviting instead unruly pleasure, excess and idleness. The contemporary vernacular of intoxication – 'wasted', 'annihilated', 'obliterated', 'smashed' – reflects the insult to the values of reason and purposive action, and the overwhelming of the 'civilized' body by irrational disorder.

However, psychoactive substances can also be a source of pleasure. Their consumption has long been an important form of individual self-expression as well as an integral feature of social, collective life. Jacques Derrida (1981) noted that the concept of the *pharmakon* was founded on a contradiction: being both a remedy and a poison; a source of pleasure as well as pain. This is a dualism that continues to inform responses to intoxicating substances today.

In his general critique of classical political economy, George Bataille argued that intoxication through intense forms of consumption was a means of transcending what he described as the 'bourgeois' values of restrained expenditure and reason, writing of: 'these moments of intoxication, when we defy everything...those moments when consumption accelerates...' (1991, 20). Here, intoxicating consumption is framed as a hedonistic escape from 'straight' society, and a deliberate rejection of the values of sober, autonomous subjectivity.

Its value as a form of self-expression has also run as a countercurrent throughout history, especially in bohemian and literary circles. In the nineteenth century, for example, William James described the power of drugs to stimulate those capacities 'usually crushed... by the cold facts and dry criticisms of the sober hour. Sobriety diminishes, discriminates, says

DOI: 10.4324/9780429058141-8

no. Drunkenness expands, unites and says yes' (James 1902 [2012], 387). These contrasting framings of intoxication and intoxicants as poison vs cure, and as pleasure vs pain also possess a social gradient. While the consumption of psychoactive commodities, or 'drug foods' (Mintz 1985) such as spirit alcohols, tobacco, sugar, tea and coffee by elite social groups was regarded as a mark of status during the colonial era, popular consumption of the same substances by the wider population was frequently subject to critical opprobrium and censure. At a time when the consumption of opiates was being gradually condemned and prohibited among the urban poor, in elite circles of Victorian society, it was simultaneously regarded as an outlet for the artistic temperament, and expressed in literary offerings such as Samuel Coleridge's *Kublai Khan*, and Thomas deQuincey's *Confessions of an English Opium Eater* (Berridge and Edwards 1987).

Today, the Romantic association of drugs with self-actualisation continues to be, for many, one of the most meaningful aspects of drug use. Here, it stands in opposition to the demands of rational subjectivity which, as Walton (2003) has pointed out, is above all a sober subjectivity. For many, 'the zone' of drug consumption is an area which offers escape from the routines of everyday life in 'straight' society. It can be a space of creativity and authenticity where people feel free to explore aspects of themselves and bond with others in ways that are unconstrained by the rules of everyday life. Indeed, Walton argues, intoxication makes us question the very values of sobriety and rationality, and is the one area, he says, that 'allows us radically to question the point of moderation as a desirable goal in itself' (2003, 205).

This ongoing contradiction – between pleasure and control; intoxication and sobriety – is a theme that has run throughout history, linking various intoxicants in cycles of acceptance and prohibition that ebb and flow according to a range of social, economic and geo-political forces. Understanding these patterns has been the subject of a larger project described in the book *Addictive Consumption: Capitalism, Modernity and Excess* (Reith 2018). However, the focus in this chapter is on a more particular, but related, aspect. It is concerned with a recent trend that involves the commodification of intoxicants, as well as the expansion of the very concept of intoxication itself. This takes us beyond traditionally recognisable intoxicants such as drugs, alcohol and tobacco, to a wider range of substances and experiences, from processed foods loaded with fat, sugar and salt, to activities like gambling and gaming, the impacts of which are described as intensely pleasurable, exhilarating or addictive.

Here, the argument is that our current landscape of intoxicating consumption has been shaped by the wider political-economic climate of neoliberalism and the structural drivers of intensified consumption within it. These have produced an expansion of both the spaces and opportunities to consume intoxicating commodities as well as an expansion of the commercial possibilities of intoxication itself.

Commodification

From around the 1980s, many governments in the Global North adopted political and fiscal policies of neoliberalism. These involved scaling back state involvement in public life, reducing the regulation of commercial activity and encouraging privatisation and competition in 'free' markets. The result was that powerful corporations took advantage of loosely regulated markets and invested in technology, communications and marketing in an effort to give them an edge in such a competitive economic climate.

This economic system has driven the global expansion of mass consumer and leisure markets. Within them, the trend is towards increasingly intensified forms of consumption (Reith 2018) as well as what has been described as 'the experience economy' (Pine and Gilmore 1999):

dematerialised forms of consumption that provide experiential, rather than simply material, rewards. In this commercial landscape, the quest for excitement, thrills, pleasure and immediate gratification is valorised as legitimate forms of self-realisation. Such a dynamic has long been a driver of the growth of capitalism and has been described by Colin Campbell as a 'Romantic ethic'. In *The Romantic Ethic and the Spirit of Modern Consumerism* (1987), Campbell outlined how the manipulation of commodities could be seen as a creative practice with a crucial role in the realisation of selfhood. This perspective on consumption is particularly relevant in terms of the historical shift to neoliberalism in which sovereign individuals are tasked with using consumption to create what Giddens (1991) describes as 'a narrative of the self'. However, the dynamic described by Campbell is a distinctive one, and is one in which consumer capitalism does not actually aim to satisfy. Rather, its goal is to maintain a continual state of longing that is projected onto an ever-changing stream of new commodities and experiences. He described the most distinctive feature of modern consumption as an unlimited hunger for an apparently endless list of desires, writing that: 'the modern consumer is characterised by an insatiability which arises out of a basic inexhaustibility of wants themselves, which forever arise, phoenix like, from the ashes of their predecessors' (1987, 37).

In a highly competitive marketplace, producers measure success by the ability to monetise this dynamic: in other words, to commodify the cycle of longing, excitement and pleasure. This is the backdrop against which corporate entities such as, for example, Nestle, Apple, Diagao and SkyBet utilise all the commercial tools at their disposal, from consumer research and personalised forms of marketing to new technologies and Big Data, in order to design increasingly intensive commodities. Producers compete for profits by designing the most exhilarating experiences, the most irresistible foods, the most alluring products. As the title of the recent book, *Hooked: How to Build Habit-Forming Products* (Eyal 2014), suggests, such a quest is now framed as a legitimate business aim. Nir Eyal uses his book as a manual for the creation of 'hooks': manufactured experiences that result in 'peak experiences' that demand repetition – and so increased consumption. Ultimately, the author writes, the drive to intensify consumer experience means 'we are faced with a future where everything becomes potentially more habit forming' (Eyal 2014, 18). This process has created a landscape of 'hyper consumption': of fast foods and mobile gambling; of instant highs and extended 'happy hours', where immediate gratification is only a mouse-click away.

The effect of these political-economic and commercial processes can be illustrated by looking more closely at three different forms of intoxicating consumption: drugs, food and gambling. These are the subject of the remainder of this chapter.

Drugs: intoxicating consumption

The psychoactive substances generally described in penal-medical terms as 'drugs' are perhaps the paradigmatic instance of intoxicants. Although long regarded as problematic, they are also pleasurable, as well as highly profitable, commodities. This contradiction was not lost on William Burroughs, who wrote:

> 'Junk is the ideal product. The ultimate merchandise. No sales talk necessary. The client will crawl through a sewer and beg to buy'.
>
> *(William Burroughs 1953, vii)*

As Burroughs' quote suggests, drugs can be regarded as exemplary products of consumer capitalism. They can provide intense pleasure and exhilaration as well as offering release from stress and escape from boredom. Their effects are transient; their pleasures fleeing and sometimes habit forming. All require repeat purchase, as Burroughs was aware. The latter point means that their lucrative potential is particularly salient in a system of consumer capitalism. It is a feature that Robin Room highlighted in his description of alcohol as 'a quintessential habit-forming commodity [which] along with other psychoactive substances, is [ ] ideal for building and sustaining markets' (2015, 141).

It is undoubtedly the case that a range of such commodities, from sugar, tobacco and caffeinated drinks, to a whole variety of pharmaceutical products, are central to the profits of multinational corporations like Big Pharma and Big Sugar, Big Alcohol and Big Tobacco. All of them are descended from the 'drug foods' of the colonial era which, as a number of writers have pointed out, were integral to the creation of the international system of trade that imperial power rested on (Courtwright 2001; Bancroft 2009). Carl Trocki made clear the significance of psychoactive commerce for the development of capitalism, writing that 'the entire rise of the West from 1500–1900 depended on a series of drug trades' (1999, xii).

From roughly the 1990s, a range of commercial, political-economic and ideological features associated with neoliberalism converged to produce an expansion of the spaces and opportunities to consume psychoactive substances in what can be described as 'intoxicating environments' (Reith 2018). During this period, a range of 'soft' drugs were joined by new types, such as 'legal highs', 'smart drugs' and designer drugs, and these merged with the consumption of licit substances such as alcohol and tobacco. This psychoactive cornucopia increasingly came to feature in the leisure patterns of young people, and was described as a shift towards 'normalisation' whereby the recreational consumption of drugs moved from the margins to the centre of youth culture (Parker et al. 1998).

In Britain in particular, the liberalising agenda of the New Labour government in the late 1990s and early 2000s relaxed licencing and regulatory requirements around alcohol, creating a situation in which alcohol became cheaper, stronger and more readily available than ever before. The alcohol industry capitalised on their new freedoms, developing new types of products, as well as benefiting from increased numbers of licenced premises from which to sell them. As well as dominating the night time economy, the industry also expanded into digital space by marketing products on social networks such as Facebook and Twitter, so generating the creation of what Griffiths and Casswell have described as 'intoxigenic digital spaces' (2010). Unsurprisingly, the result of all this commercial activity was the encouragement of what Measham and Brain (2005) call 'determined drunkenness': quite simply, the act of drinking to get drunk.

During the same period, the trajectory of cannabis moved away from long-standing associations with deviance and groups of 'outsiders' and towards the commercial mainstream. The legal cannabis is predicted to be worth $91.5 billion by 2028 (Bloomberg 2021). The industry is organised along conventional business lines, with regulations around product quality and packaging, and the development of luxury products and specialist stores. This commodification has been fuelled by a range of factors, including regulatory realignment as well as the shifting status of the groups who consume it. As Joseph Gusfield pointed out in 1963, definitions of acceptable or unacceptable behaviour are partly formed by the power and status of those social groups doing the defining. This kind of 'status politics' has been at work in the case of cannabis. Away from the dropouts and hippies of the counterculture, many advocates for the drug are now drawn from the 'respectable' middle class: medical professionals, academics and law enforcement agencies. Alongside this association with more powerful mainstream groups is the linking of cannabis with medicinal benefits. Its role in alleviating pain and sickness rather than simply generating pleasure conferred legitimacy by redefining intoxication and paving the way for commodification.

This process can also work in the opposite direction, when psychoactive commodities intended solely to alleviate suffering, such as medical forms of opiates, tranquilisers and barbiturates, are repurposed for pleasure and bought and sold in the black market (Inciardi and Cicero 2009). Although this kind of cross boundary slippage is not new, the advent of technologies such as the internet, websites like the Silk Road and the manufacture of new kinds of 'legal highs' have made it much more streamlined and have fuelled the expansion of the trade in intoxicating commerce in cyberspace (Power 2013).

Status politics also influenced the normalisation of the drug Ecstasy (MDMA). Consumption by middle-class young people helped undermine long-standing associations of 'drugs' as a generic class of intoxicants with urban deprivation and social dislocation, and paved the way for the growth of commercial subcultures based on music and fashion. Ecstasy tablets themselves came to symbolise the commodification of intoxication, with pills stamped with the brand logos of corporate capitalism, such as the distinctive emblems of McDonalds, Nike and Versace.

With the imagery of drugs like Ecstasy adopted by the mainstream, with cannabis increasingly reconfigured as respectable, with 'legal highs' available online and with the increasing variety and availability of strong, cheap alcohol, the boundaries between legal and illegal; between drug and commodity and between forbidden and licit pleasures become increasingly blurred. In a situation in which, as Parker et al. put it, 'illegal drugs have become products which are grown, manufactured, packaged and marketed through an enterprise culture whereby the legitimate and illicit markets have merged' (Parker et al. 1998, 25), intoxicants have become commodified as the ultimate consumer experience.

The expanding landscape of intoxication

The broad category of 'drugs' can be seen as the paradigmatic example of intoxicating consumption. But recently an increasingly wide range of substances and experiences have come to be described in similar terms. From fast foods to the kinds of human-machine interactions with technology involved in internet and smartphone use, and activities like gambling and gaming, the concept of intoxication (along with its close semantic ally, addiction) has expanded. This expansion has been driven by a number of factors within neoliberalism more generally. In particular, by corporate efforts to commodify, and so profit from, an expanded understanding of intoxication, as well as new ways of thinking about the concept of intoxication itself that were produced by neuroscientific forms of knowledge.

Towards the end of the twentieth century, neuroscience came to attain scientific and cultural hegemony in understandings of intoxication, initially with respect to narcotic drugs, but later gradually expanding to encompass a wide range of commodities and experiences. This perspective was spearheaded by the influential U.S.-based National Institute on Drug Abuse (NIDA), and, from the outset, was tied up with understandings of addiction. Powerful brain scanning and imaging technologies were utilised to look into the 'black box' of the human brain to see what happened when individuals were exposed to stimulating, pleasurable experiences: initially, those derived from the consumption of substances like heroin and cocaine. From this vantage point, scientists produced new understandings of subjective states, based on what was described as a 'common pathway' in the brain's pleasure centre that was 'lit up' by powerful pleasurable stimulation. Ultimately, this mechanism was regarded as responsible for the generation of intoxicating – and also addictive – states. So, from the outset, understandings of intoxication were entwined with ideas about addiction – a state to be controlled and medicated, or otherwise removed from orderly society.

The application of these forms of knowledge was not limited to the effects of illegal drugs for long. As the insights from neuroscience were drawn on to explain a wide range of human behaviours, so its potential for probing the material 'source' of intoxication in consumers came to be of immense interest for the corporate realm. So, at the very point at which the mass leisure, entertainment and fast food industries were growing, these forms of scientific understanding were also expanding to a wide range of commercial applications in an effort to better understand – and so monetise – consumer desire. Fortuitously, in the lab at least, it appeared that the 'common pathways model' did not distinguish between the kinds of substances or activities that could generate pleasure. Not only heroin, but also Coca Cola, fast food, shopping and gambling could all 'light up' the zone. Such understandings opened the way for the commercial application of scientific forms of knowledge, and was mobilised by Big Business, particularly in fields such as neuromarketing, in efforts to understand, and so profit from, the pleasure centres of their customers.

Alongside a range of other commercial strategies, these insights have been utilised, particularly by the food and gambling industries as part of their aim to manufacture more intensive, more alluring, more habit-forming products. These are the subject of the next section.

'Big Food': craving and 'the bliss point'

The global food industry – 'Big Food' – has mined neuroscientific knowledge to commodify the intoxicating potential of their products. In the pursuit of their over-arching goal, neatly summed up by Marion Nestle (2002), as persuading people to 'eat more', they have adopted a number of strategies. These include tactics such as supersizing, discounting and product placement, as well as lobbying, sponsorship and heavy investment in marketing and public relations. All of this is made possible, of course, within a political-economic climate in which the state has relaxed regulatory restrictions of the industry, while encouraging commercial competition and supporting key sectors (such as the sugar industry) with protectionist economic policies. As a result, the convenience and fast food industry has generated an environment in which cheap, energy-dense foods are available in greater varieties, in more places and larger quantities than ever before.

But one of the industry's most notable tactics, from the point of view of a study of intoxication, has been its scientific engineering of foods in the quest for the key properties of taste, known in industry circles as 'the bliss point'. This is the point at which combinations of sugar, fat and salt, along with optimal consistency, are synthesised to create ultra-processed foods. The bliss point has been described as 'the defining facet of consumer craving' (Moss 2014, 30). The elusive qualities of this ultimate 'hook' are the key drivers of industry attempts to generate intense sensations of pleasure (that, naturally, require repeating) in new, ever more appealing food products. It is a quest which has led a number of the largest companies to invest heavily in brain imaging technologies and research in attempts to examine how customers react to foods. In such experiments, fMRI scanners reveal that the sight, taste and smell of foods high in fat, sugar and salt – described as 'hyper palatable' – 'lights up' the same regions of the brain as those of conventional narcotics, travelling along the same neurological pathways to reach the brain's pleasure zone, where they generate intense feelings of euphoria. Once there, the chemistry of these processed foods continues to act like a drug, generating feedback loops of reward and withdrawal (Fraser et al. 2014, 204); pleasure and pain, which require repeated consumption to satiate. As the popular brand, *Lays*, once boasted in promotions for its potato chips, 'Betcha can't just eat one!'.

The result of all this commercial activity has been a proliferation of cheap, processed, energy-dense foods. Their distribution has a social and geographical gradient, with both food outlets and marketing concentrated amongst low-income and ethnic minority groups. As with the conditions for the spread of 'intoxicating environments', such a system also contributes to an expansion of whole environments that have been characterised as 'obesogenic' (Swinburn et al. 1999). The health consequences have a similarly social gradient, with low-income population groups suffering disproportionally from a range of conditions related to obesity.

Products that are packed with sugar, fat, caffeine and salt, and scientifically engineered to deliver maximum pleasure make them akin to mildly psychoactive substances. Tellingly, the derogatory shorthand 'junk' that is often used to describe them is also slang for heroin, an association that draws attention to their psychoactive and experiential aspects. And, like drugs, these foods provide an experience that is typical of consumer culture itself: pleasurable and yet transient; consumed quickly and so requiring constant repetition. In this, today's 'junk foods' have some similarities with their historical predecessors: the psychoactive commodities or 'drug foods' of the colonial era.

'Big Gambling': into 'the zone'

The gambling industry – or what Markham and Young (2015) call the 'state-industrial complex of "Big Gambling"' – shares similar features with Big Food, both in its commodification of experience and in its commercial strategies. Gambling companies have benefited from the neoliberal trend towards greater deregulation of markets, often as a result of political lobbying and sponsorship which has provided them with unparalleled opportunities for expansion. They also benefit from globalised financial systems, communications and IT platforms and from sophisticated forms of technology, all of which have allowed them to produce faster and more intensive products. The Big Data harvested from these technological systems is used to generate aggressive and often targeted marketing of their products in ways that normalise and promote them further (Reith 2014). The expansion of the products and images of commercial gambling throughout the spaces of everyday life has generated what I have elsewhere described as 'aleatory environments' – from the Latin word *alea* to gamble – where devices like smartphones and widespread internet access make games available at the click of a button.

The gambling industry exemplifies the promotion of experiences based on risk taking and thrills rather than tangible commodities, making it a prime example of both the experience economy (Pine and Gilmore 1999) and a quintessential type of dematerialised consumption (Reith 2014). It has harnessed technological and financial systems to generate games that are increasingly fast and repetitive, and that circulate money, often dematerialised as credit and other cashless technologies, in cycles of loss.

These trends are particularly encapsulated by electronic gaming machines (EGMs), as well as by the recent ascendance of digital and mobile forms of gambling. The anthropologist Natasha Dow Schüll (2012) has documented the tactics used by industry to create machines that are manufactured for the extraction of profit, or what she describes as 'addiction by design'. In this respect, Big Gambling, like Big Food, mobilises marketing, design and technology in an effort to intensify consumption and produce particular subjective states. For example, every aspect of casino architecture, ergonomics and ambience is crafted to keep people gambling for as long as possible in order to maximise what is known in industry circles as 'time on device'. Low ceilings and an absence of clocks along with optimal levels of sound, lighting, colour, temperature and even odour are calibrated to generate an ambient climate that encourages individuals to lose track of time and money. Products, in terms of both games themselves, as well as the devices they are played on, from electronic machines to smartphones and consoles are carefully designed to produce an optimal experience. The trend is for games that are more immersive, with sophisticated graphics, customised interaction, feedback loops and cashless technologies that produce a seamless experience. As well as making financial loss invisible, these kinds of features accelerate play and generate hypnotic states in which, for players, the outside world ceases to exist (Schüll 2012, 64).

These strategies work to produce distinctive subjective states that have been described by players and researchers alike as the experience of 'the zone' (Reith 1999, Livingstone 2005, Schüll 2012): an affective, trance-like condition in which gamblers' surroundings, the passage of time, the value of money and even their sense of self are dissolved by the immersion in intensive play. Like the kind of peak experience described by Csikszentmihályi (1990) as 'flow', gamblers in the zone are fully focused on the here and now, in hypnotic rhythms of play.

As is the case in other industries, neuroscientific knowledge has been invoked to explain, and also accelerate, the impact of these commercial features on customers' brains. The application of fMRI technologies has again been used to suggest that gambling activates the reward system in much the same way that a drug does, with brains 'lighting up' in fMRI scanners when exposed to images – usually via a video screen – of gambling wins (Potenza et al. 2003). Biological markers and cognitive deficits have also been proposed as explanations for the highs, euphoria and cravings induced by gambling (van Holst et al. 2010).

Across a wide range of commercial activity, particularly the three areas of drugs, food and gambling discussed here, the result of these political-economic and scientific processes has been both an intensification and an expansion of consumption. Psychoactive commodities, cheap, energy-dense foods and commercial gambling are increasingly available and pervasive throughout everyday life, in environments that can be described, respectively, as, intoxicating, obesogenic and aleatory.

These processes also produce particular forms of subjectivity. So, for example, the engineering of foods to encourage people to 'eat more' generates the experience of the 'bliss point', while the design of gambling machines to encourage players to extend 'time on device' creates 'the zone'. In this, we can see the convergence between commercial understandings of the 'bottom line' and medicalised understandings of intoxication and addiction. The 'bliss point' has its counterpart in 'the zone': the neurological basis of pleasure, as well as the location of profit. What makes fast food taste so good is similar to what makes machine gambling so appealing, and both underscore the ability of intoxicating consumption to undermine self-control and sobriety.

Governance

This system of modern consumerism rests on a contradiction. The same political-economic drivers that commodify and encourage intoxicating consumption also produce another demand: namely, for individuals to exercise restraint. This means that, even as they are persuaded to engage in the intoxicating pleasures of the market, consumers are exhorted to control their desires and maintain a sober responsibility for their own well-being.

This tension is the latest manifestation of a long-running dualism in Western societies that has been described by writers from Aristotle and J.S. Mill to Freud and Max Weber. In various ways, they talk in terms about the taming of the unruly appetites of the body by the civilising effects of society. More recently, Daniel Bell (1976) described what he termed 'the cultural contradictions of capitalism' as the requirement to balance a production-centred ethic based on self-discipline and control with a consumerist one based on instant gratification and pleasure. All of these accounts, in one way or another, have been concerned with the wider theme of control and its necessity for the orderly functioning of society.

Today, this enduring requirement for control is deployed largely through neoliberal ideals of responsibility and is set against the supposed excesses of intoxicating consumption. The ideology of responsibility is a cornerstone of neoliberal systems of governance. It rests on the key normative values of autonomy and rationality and is an aspect of what Foucault (1991) described as 'governmentality'. This is a key feature of power in neoliberal societies. As the state has reduced its presence in the regulation of public life, individuals are increasingly tasked with governing their conduct through various forms of self-control. In this way, the state is able to govern 'at a distance', often without exerting direct disciplinary power, but rather through shaping the subjectivities and behaviour of individuals who then act as willing participants in their own control.

These kinds of governance are an aspect of what Pat O'Malley (1996) describes as a 'new prudentialism' in which the ongoing management of consumption becomes a primary means of self-realisation, health and well-being. In it, the seductions of the market are to be countered by self-governing individuals, who manage desire and restrain excess in culturally appropriate ways. Here, responsible consumption becomes evidence of the 'right' way to live; the 'right' way to be. As a corollary of this individualising and normative project, the individual is also regarded as the site of blame when things go wrong. So, problems of uncontrolled consumption – intoxication and addiction, overeating and obesity, binge drinking and gambling – tend to be framed as failures of individual behaviour, rather than as side-effects of the system of consumer capitalism itself.

These tensions run through the three examples discussed in this chapter, where exhortations to 'drink responsibly' are matched with reminders to 'gamble responsibly' and 'eat healthily'. Even consumption of the most archetypal type of intoxicant – drugs – is permitted, albeit within the shibboleths of 'controlled', 'informed' or 'responsible' behaviour, and guided by the principles informed choice and harm reduction.

In the case of the latter, governance is based less around disciplinary forms of control and binary distinctions between legal/illegal, and more around ideals of controlled/uncontrolled consumption that is enforced and monitored by individuals themselves. Ultimately, it works to produce what Angus Bancroft (2009) has described as a 'carefully managed hedonism' as a counterpoint to the expansion of psychoactive consumer culture. Researchers of illicit drug consumption have described this in various ways, with Johanna Jarvinnen (2012) writing of drug users as 'rational risk managers' and Fiona Measham (2004) describing a loss of control that is at the same time 'controlled'. Pat O'Malley's statement on the issue, which once would have read as an oxymoron, now sums up the contradictory nature of consumption under conditions of neoliberalism. As he puts it, 'as rational, calculating risk-takers, [consumers] enter the sphere of "responsible drug use"' (1999, 205).

Similar trends are in play around alcohol. At the same time that the alcohol industry promotes cheaper and stronger drinks, it warns its customers to 'drink responsibly': a tag line that accompanies every advertisement and cut-price promotion. The economic and political processes that saw the expansion of a culture of heavy drinking in British culture also produced a contradictory trend in which 'excessive' drinking came to be defined as a counterpoint to neoliberal ideals of responsible consumption. The social gradient of criticisms of intoxication was apparent here in the framing of the 'binge drinker'. This figure, which was heavily classed and gendered, was a focus for widespread disapproval over the ostentatious drinking of mainly white working-class women, whose public displays of intoxication were framed as a flouting of ideals of 'feminine' behaviour and a signifier of more general irresponsibility and promiscuity (Skeggs 1997, 967).

Meanwhile, the corollary of a global food system that promotes fat- and sugar-laden foods that are scientifically designed to induce craving is what has been described as an 'epidemic of obesity'. Such a state is framed as one that threatens both individual health and national efficiency (Schrecker and Bambra 2015) resulting in a climate in which tensions around food are consistently articulated in concerns about self-control and productivity. Here, the key message of the system of Big Food – 'eat more!' – is countered by the equally strident demands of healthy – and therefore responsible – eating: 'eat less!' It is accompanied by exhortations to eat healthily, to exercise willpower, to control appetite and to engage in ongoing care of the self. And so, monitoring diet, counting calories and rejecting 'junk' are counterposed to a commercial landscape of supersized soda and Big Macs.

It is in this context that writers such as Susan Bordo (1993) have described how the consumption of food is invested with wider metaphorical meanings, with ideas about obesity representing more general cultural fears about loss of control, unmanaged desire and unproductive bodies. On the one hand, the fit and – crucially – productive bodies that are assumed to result from healthy eating are framed as visible signs of willpower, and so markers of responsible citizenship. On the other, overweight bodies are taken as evidence of a failure to tame appetite and so a burden on healthcare and society more generally. In such a framing, we can see the 'destructive' nature of consumption counterposed to the rational and orderly values of production in a manner that recalls long-standing historical dualisms. The tension between self-control and abandon are made visible on the human body in very literal ways where the overweight frame is a physical representation of consumption that is out of control (Reith 2018).

Gamblers are faced with similar normative demands to act 'responsibly'. As the gambling industry produces ever more intensive games intended to produce maximum 'time on device', and promotes and makes them widely available throughout aleatory environments, gamblers are exhorted to resist. Their task is to inform themselves about risk, manage their money responsibly, control their impulses to avoid slipping into 'the zone' and – as if it were that simple – 'when the fun stops, stop' as the U.K.'s industry-body's Senet Group strap-line tells them. In recent years, gambling corporations have embraced this 'responsibility agenda' and have made much of their commitment to a range of measures, all of which are based on warning individual players about the potential risks of gambling and offering them similarly individualised solutions should they develop problems. These measures generally amount to supporting awareness raising campaigns and offering voluntary limit-setting schemes, of questionable efficacy, that put the onus of for example, setting limits on expenditure and banning themselves from venues, on to gamblers themselves.

End points

The celebratory, but also destructive, aspects of a range of intoxicating commodities represent the dualism of the *pharmakon*. Various substances have long embodied this contradiction but today, their place in a system of consumer capitalism brings about new dimensions. The commercial potential of a range of substances, activities and experiences has been embraced by companies who, operating in relatively unrestricted and highly competitive markets, have endeavoured to produce the most pleasurable and habit-forming products and services. In short, they have commodified intoxication.

In so doing, they have encouraged the production of what Scott Vrecko has elsewhere described as a 'landscape of temptation and excess' (2010, 559). At the same time however, action within this system is subject to contradictory pressures. The same political-economic system that produces temptation and excess also demands that individual consumers resist it. It is in this sense that Guthman and Du Pois's claim about the conflicting aspects of the modern food system has wider resonance. Just as, as they put it, neoliberalism 'encourages (over) eating at the same time that neoliberal notions of discipline vilify it' (2006: 437), so the neoliberal system encourages the consumption of intoxicating commodities and experiences at the same time that neoliberal notions of responsibility demand self-control and sobriety. Ironically, at the very point that the state rolls back its regulation of markets and consumerism proliferates on a global scale, responsibility for its control has become overwhelmingly an individualised concern.

And, because all of this is a normative venture, those who fail to control their behaviour are presented as flawed consumers, an unproductive minority who are lacking self-control or personal responsibility, and are, therefore, also blameworthy. In different ways, and at different times, those who have succumbed to the pleasures of intoxicating consumption have been regarded as outsiders, as deviants, and been subject to critical discourses based on normative-medical concerns about health and productivity.

The individualising focus of ideas about responsible, controlled, sober and productive consumption ultimately acts as a discursive sleight of hand. The emphasis on the shortcomings of individual consumers, rather than the wider political, commercial and regulatory environment, shifts the focus of the problems of intoxicating consumption away from those who enable and produce it and towards those who consume it in a way that supports the corporate status quo. All of this is part of a long-running concern in Western thought about the need to subjugate the unruly pleasures of the body to the civilising force of society. Today, the enduring historical tension between control and restraint is realised in the pairing of intoxication with responsibility: the latest in a long line of the many contradictions of capitalism.

References

Arcview (2016) *The State of Legal Marijuana Markets*, 4th Edition. Executive Summary. At: https://arcviewgroup.com/research/#.Yr3ojnbMKUk

Bancroft, A (2009) *Drugs, Intoxication and Society*. London: Polity.

Bell, D (1976) *The Cultural Contradictions of Capitalism*. London: Heinemann.

Berridge, V and Edwards, G (1987) *Opium and the People: Opiate Use in Nineteenth Century England*. London: Allen Lane.

Bloomberg UK 2021. 'Legal cannabis market size worth $91.7 billion by 2028'. Available at: https://www.bloomberg.com/press-releases/2021-07-27/legal-cannabis-market-size-worth-91-5-billion-by-2028-cagr-26-3-grand-view-research-inc

Bordo, S (1993) *Unbearable Weight: Feminism, Western Culture and the Body*. Berkeley: University of California Press.

Burroughs, W (1953) *Junky*. New York: Penguin.

Campbell, C (1987) *The Romantic Ethic and the Spirit of Modern Consumerism*. Oxford: Basil Blackwell.

Courtwright, D.T (2001) *Forces of Habit: Drugs and the Making of the Modern World*. Cambridge, MA: Harvard University Press.

Csikszentmihályi, M (1990). *Flow: The Psychology of Optimal Experience*. New York: Harper & Row.

Derrida, J (1981) 'Plato's pharmacy', in *Dissemination* (pp. 429–450) Trans B. Johnson. London: Athlone Press.

Eyal, N (2014) *Hooked: How to Build Habit-Forming Products*. London: Penguin.

Forbes (2020) Iris Dorbian 'For legal pot industry in 2021, expect to see national brands and $24 billion in sales says top researcher'. *Forbes*. Editors Pick. Dec 15 2020. Available at: https://www.forbes.com/sites/irisdorbian/2020/12/15/for-us-legal-pot-industry-in-2021-expect-to-see-national-brands-and-24-billion-in-sales-says-top-researcher/?sh=30a6cdd0443e

Foucault, M (1991) 'Governmentality', in Burchill, G, Gordon, C and Miller, P (eds) *The Foucault Effect: Studies in Governmentality* (pp. 87–105) Chicago: Chicago University Press.

Fraser, S, Moore, D and Keane, H (2014) *Habits: Re-Making Addiction*. London: Palgrave Macmillan.
Giddens, A (1991) *Modernity and Self-identity: Self and Society in the Late Modern Age*. Stanford: Stanford University Press.
Gusfield, J (1963) *Symbolic Crusade. Status Politics and the American Temperance Movement*. Urbana: University of Illinois Press.
Guthman, J and DuPois, M (2006) 'Embodying neoliberalism: economy, culture and the politics of fat'. *Environment and Planning D: Society and Space* 24, 427–448.
Inciardi, J and Cicero, T (2009) 'Black beauties, Gorilla Pills, footballs, and hillbilly heroin: some reflections on prescription drug abuse and diversion research over the past 40 years' *Journal of Drug Issues* 39, 101–114.
James, W (1902 [2012]) *The Varieties of Religious Experience: A Study in Human Experience*. Oxford: Oxford's World Classics.
Jarvinnen, J (2012) 'A will to health? Drinking, risk and social class' *Health, Risk and Society* 14(3), 241–256.
Livingstone, C. (2005) 'Desire and the consumption of danger: electronic gaming machines and the commodification of interiority' *Addiction Research and Theory* 13(6), 523–534.
Markham, F and Young, M (2015) 'Big Gambling: the rise of the global state-industrial gambling complex' *Addiction Research and Theory* 23(1), 1–4.
Measham, F (2004) 'Play space: historical and socio-cultural reflections on drugs, licensed leisure locations, commercialization and control' *International Journal of Drug Policy* 15, 337–345.
Measham, F and Brain, K (2005) 'Binge drinking, British alcohol policy and the new culture of intoxication'. *Crime, Media, Culture* 1(3), 262–283.
Mintz, S (1985) *Sweetness and Power: The Place of Sugar in World History*. New York: Viking.
Moss, M (2014) *Salt, Sugar, Fat: How the Food Giants Hooked Us*. London: WH Allen.
Nestle, M (2002) *Food Politics: How the Food Industry Influences Nutrition and Health*. Berkeley: University of California Press.
O'Malley, P (1999) Consuming risks: Harm minimization and the government of "Drug Users", in R. Smandych (ed.) *Governable Places: Readings in Governmentality and Crime Control*. (pp. 46–66). Ashgate: Dartsmouth.
Parker, H; Aldridge, J and Measham, F (1998) *Illegal Leisure: The Normalisation of Adolescent Recreational Drug Use*. London: Routledge.
Pine, J and Gilmore, J (1999) *The Experience Economy*. Boston, MA: Harvard Business School Press.
Potenza, M; Steinberg, M; Skudlarsky, P; Fulbright, R; Lacadie, C; Wilbur, C; Rounsaville, B; Gore, J and Wexler, B (2003) 'Gambling urges in pathological gambling: a functional magnetic resonance imaging study' *Archive of General Psychiatry* 60(8), 828–836.
Power, M (2013) *Drugs 2: The Web Revolution That's Changing How the World Gets High*. London: Portobello Books.
Reith, G (1999) *The Age of Chance: Gambling in Western Culture*. London: Routledge.
Reith, G (2018) *Addictive Consumption: Capitalism, Modernity and Excess*. London: Routledge.
Reith, G (2014) 'Techno economic systems and excessive consumption: a political economy of "pathological" gambling' *British Journal of Sociology* 64(4), 717–738.
Room, R (2015) 'Addiction and personal responsibility as solutions to the contradictions of neoliberal consumerism', in Bell, K; McNaughton, D and Salmon, A (eds) *Alcohol, Tobacco and Obesity: Morality, Mortality and the New Public Health* (pp. 141–151). London: Routledge.
Schrecker, T and Bambra, C (2015) *How Politics Makes us Sick: Neoliberal Epidemics*. London: Palgrave MacMillan.
Schüll, N.D (2012). *Addiction by Design: Machine Gambling in Las Vegas*. Princeton, NJ: Princeton University Press.
Skeggs, B (1997) *Formations of Class and Gender: Becoming Respectable*. London: SAGE.
Swinburn, B; Eggar, G and Raza, F. (1999) 'Dissecting obesogenic environments; the development and application of a framework for identifying and prioritizing environmental interventions for obesity' *Preventive Medicine* 29(6), 563–570.
Trocki, C (1999) *Opium, Empire and the Global Political Economy*. London: Routledge.
Van Holst, R; van der Brink, W; Veltman, D and Goudriaan, A (2010) 'Brain imaging studies in pathological gambling' *Current Psychatiry Reports* 12(5), 418–425.
Vrecko, S (2010) 'Global and everyday matters of consumption: on the productive assemblage of pharmaceuticals and obesity' *Theory and Society* 39, 555–573.
Walton, S (2003) *Out of It: A Cultural History of Intoxication*. London: Three Rivers Press (CA); Reprint edition.

6

PRODUCING PLANNED HEDONISM AMONG OPIATE USERS IN AN ONLINE DRUG MARKET

Angus Bancroft

Introduction: markets embed a specific formation of illicit drug culture

The purpose of this chapter is to outline how a specific type of online drug-focused marketplace produces drug dealer and user subjectivities. Typically, illicit drug distribution can be characterised as taking place between three different distribution modes. In one corner, there is social supply with principles of mutuality, reciprocity and a flat network distributing arrangement (Coomber and Turnbull, 2007). In another, there is distribution through market exchange which prioritises the cash nexus, profit/value incentives and relationships mediated by consumption (Felstead, 2018). Finally, there is a third mode, that of ideologically driven, altruistic supply that emphasises the drug and its use in a political, ideological or spiritual relationship (Tupper, 2008). That broad brush typology is then complicated by many nuances and subtleties in practice (Hammersvik et al., 2012). The distribution modes may involve varying degrees of exploitation and obligation, they may promote practices of care or generate harm and they may expand drug distribution or keep it within a tightly bound social and cultural context (Belackova and Vaccaro, 2013; Coomber and Moyle, 2014). Different distribution modes and self-representations may occupy the same technical infrastructure and market space (Bakken, 2020; Demant et al., 2018).

The generalisation of market exchange as a mode for illicit distribution and organisation has had wide-ranging effects on how drug users obtain and consume drugs. As has happened more broadly in capitalist societies, we have seen an expansion in the conscious use of market forms for identity formation, self-creation and expression (Dijck et al., 2018). Market principles validate certain qualities in products, sellers and users: professionalism, the capacity to make objective judgements, to act as self-directed, accountable agents, and they invite drug users to express themselves as instrumental, reflexively hedonistic consumers (Turner, 2018). Like markets, which they increasingly are integrated with and identified with, digital technologies are both disruptive and confirmatory. They transform opportunities for illicit drug exchange, the formation of cultural collectives of drug users and the capacity for self-creation. They also confirm and reproduce some existing hierarchies, especially those between self-identified recreational and dependent users. They create new spaces for trade and discussion, define new attributes and foreground the experimental and the competitive (Martin et al., 2019). That has implications for how we understand drug use normalisation as

DOI: 10.4324/9780429058141-9

happening through markets. The drug distribution mode affects the parameters of normalisation. Social supply contributes to normalising particular use patterns and destigmatising their use (Coomber et al., 2015). Self-organising digital markets can broaden that to promote and embed norms of destigmatisation and harm reduction. However, foregrounding a market-focused engagement with drug distribution can produce unwanted effects for use communities. The process may concentrate market power, promote bulk purchase over retail, create supply chain risks and ultimately increase dealer power. It can and does alter the nature of the products being sold, altering characteristics such as potency.

Cryptomarkets are one such example of market innovation forming the focus of this chapter. They are hidden, anonymous marketplaces which mostly deal in illicit drugs along with some other illicit goods and services. They are hosted on the Tor ('The Onion Router') darknet. Tor is developed and operated by a network supported by The Tor Project foundation. It emphasises benefits of privacy and security. The system uses encryption and signal routing to hide participants' digital identities. The markets are hosted by administrators who connect their servers to the Tor system. This is called 'onion hosting'. Along with the use of a distributed cryptocurrency, typically bitcoin, cryptomarkets allow transactions to take place in relative anonymity. Drugs are bought and sold, and then delivered to the buyer using couriers, the postal system or dead drops. Mostly, they handle the 'last mile' of the drug trafficking system. Their social profile varies. Many sellers, buyers and market hosters are based in more affluent countries, and within that they represent a more connected and affluent fraction of users (Dittus et al., 2017). However this mode of distribution is widely used in Russia along with the Telegram encrypted messaging app (Davitadze et al., 2020). Users are a specific demographic – not necessarily more affluent but digitally skilled and adept at operating with this kind of market. Cryptomarkets function as a drug distribution ecosystem and forum for drug users and sellers to meet virtually and examine the drugs being sold, the reliability of sellers and the desirability of particular drug effects. They also provide sites of contestation of the illegality and stigmatising of illicit drugs (Barratt et al., 2016; Hübschle, 2017).

I am focusing on market modes of distribution and the effect they have as it provides an opportunity to examine how the process of drug distribution shape intoxication subjectivities and the drug as a specific type of object with tangible characteristics. Market-based drug distribution embeds some basic principles about drugs as objects: that they are commodities, they are interchangeable, that they are consistent in form and predictable in quality. It also frames drug users as specific types of subjects: they are consumers, they are focused on product qualities such as purity and they expect and reward customer service by dealers. It emphasises competition between drug dealers and between consumers. Just to pause here: not every market really does that in practice, and as we will see, apparently open and consumer-led markets can in fact concentrate power among a small number of providers who can set the terms of trade. In this way, the illicit drug markets function much like capitalism everywhere. An apparently open, free and voluntary relationship really depends on the consumer adapting themselves to the terms of trade offered. It narrows the drug *users*' self-perception to that of a drug *consumer* focused on calculated, planned hedonism, meaning an expectation of pleasure along with a risk-reflexive subjectivity (Bilgrei, 2019). That is a powerful ideological effect of a market society and culture. The focus of this chapter will be a specific element of that, how drug buyers in cryptomarkets construct, assess and reward potency as a tangible quality of the drugs they are buying and using.

In capitalist societies markets are often presented as naturally occurring creations, places where people with something to sell and others with a need to fulfil meet in mutual exchange. This is a powerful view in understanding some qualities of illicit markets, and moving away from pathologising the actions of drug dealers and users within them. Markets are places of competitive exchange and they come into being to address problems of stability, predictability and reliable valuation (Beckert and Wehinger, 2012). Markets are also inventions, social constructs which institutionalise, design in and reward specific ways of being. Players in illegal markets face various problems. They have to succeed in making their activities work together despite relations being disparate, remote, and fleetingly interacting. There is a problem of ordering interaction in ways that will lead to the expected outcome. Market actors want to exchange but they want to do it at a price that suits them. That can be tricky to agree; hence, formal pricing mechanisms are handy. Every participant is risking something, and this is more the case in illicit markets. Therefore, participants use heuristics to reduce that risk – platform loyalty, brand loyalty, vendor loyalty and markers of quality and reliability which of course may not be that reliable. Markets can only solve these problems if they are culturally, socially and institutionally supported (Beckert, 2009). Drug markets are institutionalised whether in the street (Coomber and Maher, 2006), social media (Moyle et al., 2019) or the darknet (Aldridge and Décary-Hétu, 2016).

Digital illicit markets and cryptocurrencies promise greater transparency, democracy and accountability but this is not necessarily borne out in reality (Bratspies, 2018; van der Gouwe et al., 2017). To the extent to which these qualities do come about, they are due to the efforts of participants and sometimes involve circumventing or resisting the centralising, profit-driven logic of the markets themselves. I argue that the cryptomarkets discipline users towards a specific set of stances and towards the drugs they purchase: that the drugs they buy are 'good' drugs – both in the sense of legitimated and also being of the most suitable quality and effect, and that drugs are or should be informationalised and commodified as consumer products. Users adopt a tendency to reify, quantify and engage in cost benefit analysis and rational use discourse about their drug consumption. They show willingness to accept harm as a necessary and sometimes welcome risk as long as it allows for users' agency. There are some partial exceptions to the focus on drugs as products, particularly in the field of psychedelic use where user communities often resist commodification. Those precepts foreground a market effect in our analysis in that the supply chain matters in shaping what is being bought and consumed, and how it is consumed. The buying and distribution infrastructure places users squarely in the hyper-modern category of risk-reflexive, hedonistic consumers.

Research

The chapter draws on research from a drug cryptomarket. Discussion forum data were collected from a leading cryptomarket, Agora, from 2014 to 2015. Agora was dominant in the cryptomarket ecosystem before voluntary closing after succumbing to technical and organisational problems. Launched in 2013, it survived the coordinated takedown of cryptomarkets in Operation Onymous in 2014 and thrived afterwards (Décary-Hétu and Giommoni, 2017). For this paper 3,500 posts were coded from the whole dataset to understand the relationship between market use and the self-orientations of opiate/opioid users. The focus of my analysis of Agora was on opiate users' threads, as after reviewing the dataset potency was a theme to the fore in opiate buyers' and sellers' discussions. It was critical to their understanding of the cryptomarket as a useful mode of drug distribution. Discussions of psychedelic and other drug use were included for comparison. The threads discussed a variety of drugs as users consumed many different drugs alongside opiates. Their drug repertoires included Xanax, benzodiazepines, cocaine and amphetamines.

Making the drug

Intoxicants are valuable commodities (Reuter and Greenfield, 2001), risky objects generative of human subjectivity (Fraser and Valentine, 2008; Vitellone, 2004), totemic and productive cultural entities (Fitzgerald, 2015), effective technologies of governance (Seddon, 2009) and facilitators of social life which articulate and affirm social order (Fraser and Moore, 2011). Drugs as objects carry all of these elements which shape their effects in the world. They go into defining whether a drug is a good or bad object and in what terms. I examine potency as a biochemical matrix composed of different elements – predictability, purity, consistency, lasting effect and pharmacokinetics. The relationship between the substance and the body is critical: the pharmaceutical lasts in the body, metabolises and leaves traces and memories (Dennis, 2016). This effect is a material and social product, a human and non-human assemblage (Dennis, 2019). Power is composed of chemical potency and potency is a political quality. The two compose the intoxication consumption regime, the ontological politics of the drug (Fraser, 2020).

There is a recurring pharmaceutical myth that differences in drug effect are largely produced by differences in chemical purity and stability. To move away from that, the triptych of drug, set and setting was identified by Zinberg (1986). Outcomes are a result of the interaction between these three points, the chemical substance, the user's psychology and expectations and the consumption environment. Going slightly further, drugs themselves become different substances in different consumption regimes. Medical diamorphine and street heroin are qualitatively and quantitatively different, in composition, consumption and effect (Strang and King, 1997). This has a real world effect in the attributes applied to the drug and in decisions about regulation that directly affect the market (Moeller et al., 2021).

Cryptomarkets are notable in shaping potency because the markets are designed to expose drug purity as a factor in the purchasing decisions made by buyers. Both buyers and sellers value the market's ability to help informationalise the product and introduce explicit discussions of purity. The link between drug content and potency is one that can be examined critically. Many assumptions are made about what purity means for the user and these are picked apart in the cryptomarket user forums. Users were concerned to demonstrate that the drugs they used were 'good' drugs. In the case of psychedelic users, this meant that drugs were effective in the world. They wanted the psychedelics they shared to transmit spiritual psychedelic culture, to heal and to disrupt harmful ways of thought and life. Opiate users wanted the drugs they consumed to be effective on themselves, to be potent.

The starting point for discussions of potency was the pharmaceutical quality of the drug, which became known in several ways: as an embodied experience, through a visual and chemical assay of the drug, and through user reports of it. The qualities of the drug were viewed in terms of the way it fitted best with the context and purpose of use. Users advised caution and told others to approach stronger drugs with a degree of care. Less experienced users were thought to be more at risk and with more potent drugs it was harder to establish an effective dose-response relationship. There is a danger of the drug becoming unwanted, a bad drug that induces overdose or other unwanted effects. For opiate users, potency was a tricky feature, both desired and dangerous, as greater purity typically meant more adverse, unwanted effects. Warnings from the drug vendor could be a badge of quality and risk, as in this quote from a heroin buyer:

> *When [vendor] mentions that this is of comparable strength to Diamorphine, I undoubtedly agree. Those without a tolerance must take extreme caution with this product, the infrequent user will most probably get a very strong effect at 5mg, with a full blown nod at 10 mg.*

Users and vendors posited statements about the likely purity of each batch expressed as a percentage. However, they were also aware that purity is a slippery and subjective construct and the percentage 'purity' given was used as a rule of thumb or guide to the drug's relative effectiveness. Users expressed potency in terms of strength and the challenges the drug presented when being used, stronger batches being 'hard to come to grips with' and 'not to be trifled with'. Side effects were accepted by some heroin users as indicators of good potency. Users personified the drug as an animal, strong but dangerous as with this heroin user:

> *I got [vendor's] stuff back when he was still sending out 'good' quality, but I still rank him at the bottom. It seemed potent, but I'm pretty sure that it seemed so potent because it was cut with some antihistamine or other sedative. Didn't really make me itchy or nauseous, which good dope* [heroin] *always does.*

An unexpectedly strong effect like the heroin 'nod' could be reassuring to users. Users of this thread are often self-defined as addicted. The nod told them that they were still able to feel pleasure, to experience risk and that their drug use was not wholly defined by addiction. The unexpected pleasure that came with using a particularly effective batch was reassuring to those that experienced it. It signified that they still retained the ability to shape their drug use and experience a range of effects from it. In contrast, users of ecstasy/MDMA in the same market tended not to see those drugs in this way. Side effects were largely characterised as 'dirty', wholly unwanted contaminants. In contrast, evidence of contamination of heroin was literally rejected, such as residue in the spoon after cooking heroin. In contrast to unpleasant side effects which could be taken to be dirty or as desirable and indicating high potency, residues were always dirty, always unwanted. They signalled unused contaminants that had been introduced into the drug. In terms of potency, the remnants from cooking were a final clue before consumption as to the true nature of the drug being consumed. The residue may act as a cue and primer for consumption. A complete burn of the drug indicates purity and so prepares the user for a more exciting ride.

As Mary Douglas theorised, dirt is a matter out of place – an environmental but also primarily a moral and social contaminant (Douglas, 2013). The drugs' pharmaceutical potency mediated its moral purity. The relationship between heroin users and side effects was a complex one. Where ecstasy users sought a clear dividing line between desired effects and 'dirty' side effects, for heroin users dangerous side effects were too closely bound up with desired effects to be separable.

Commodifying the drug and introducing supply chain effects

Moving on from the drug as a good or bad object, this section is about the terms in which the drug is defined as desirable/undesirable as a market commodity. Drug users' subjective reports often are able to distinguish whether the drug is desirable, for example, distinguishing MDMA from undesired analogues by noting particular adverse effects or the lack of effect in tablets sold as ecstasy (Brunt et al., 2012). Online markets and discussion forums promote information sharing and a consumerist rationale around which users shape a drug user identity (Bilgrei, 2019).

Vendors' reputation depended on a consistent, potent product, delivered as expected. Stability was expected between testing and consumption, and the vendor's capacity to provide a consistent stream of the product. Assay data was a useful go-to for buyers. Vendors and users would post drug test results on the forum. Independent harm reduction services would also do the same. Users also assessed the methodological qualities of the testing methods being used. They discussed sampling problems and the construct validity of test results. The use of drug testing was incorporated into the narrative of the good vendor who supplied a predictable, potent product. The use of tests was not wholly reliably as an independent measure.

Agora combined many of these information sources into an understanding of the drug as a commodity. Some qualities that matter here are consistency between different batches of the same product, consistency within the same batch, and whether it is in a form that can easily be separated into smaller doses. Commodification promotes an understanding of the drug as an instrumental object. From the vendor's point of view, the ability to price different batches according to their characteristics and for that to mean something to drug users is key to their business. Selling heroin in grades according to different potencies allows them to sell batches of different purity and present this as a business choice rather than a necessity caused by variation in the supply chain.

A critical effect of commodification was the way in which changes in potency and the drugs being sold were driven by supply chain needs rather than necessarily consumer demand. Discussions of changing drug potency often make an assumption of a consistent potency-risk curve (ElSohly et al., 2016). The higher the dose, the higher the risk from each intoxication event. However, there is at most a weak long-term correlation (Desmond et al., 1978; Risser et al., 2007; Schifano and Corkery, 2008). Localised market fluctuations create short-term risks depending on the quality of shared intelligence about purity and dose (Mars et al., 2018a). Confounding factors such as disruption to local markets and injecting sites are more significant in terms of negative outcomes (Maher and Dixon, 1999).

Therefore, the vendor may not know what they are selling. Even if the vendor has a good sense of the purity of the drug – which is not a given (Coomber, 1997) – any individual package made for retail sale will vary from the total purity of the dealer's supply. The user will also introduce another degree of variation when choosing an amount from that package to use. The potent quality of fentanyl introduces challenges when it comes to dose titration (Lamy et al., 2020; Lokala et al., 2019). One of the challenges of fentanyl is framed as the drug being so potent that it is very easy to get the mix wrong. That may be a product of how it is sold. When cut to supplement heroin, it becomes difficult to manage the dose properly. Small variations in a sample will mean significant differences in the effect, and it is unlikely for a street sample to have the drug spread evenly throughout.

These challenges are not insurmountable – many users manage well and are able to titrate their dose with confidence. However, it places more demands on the dealer and user in order to achieve the expected and desired dose (Broadhurst et al., 2020). Potency mattered for heroin users in particular who elaborated on a strong link between potency and pleasure. Potency meant a combination of material qualities, including purity, lack of unnecessary adulteration and the right mix of constituents. A critical distinction was drawn between unwanted 'cutting' where the dealer padded out the drug for their own profit and necessary mixing where the dealer added to the drug either during or after production to produce particular intoxicant qualities. This required an understanding of pharmacokinetics and pharmacological effects. For example, one heroin type could be preferred because it produced a longer lasting high, or another because it staved off cravings for a longer period of time.

Users as hyper-modern and risk-reflexive consumers

Consumption begins with contemplating the drug's qualities, creating or selecting the time and place of consumption (Duff, 2014). Rationality is an orientation to a specific kind of cultural valuation that is produced by technical mechanisms and shared culture (Childs et al., 2020). The cryptomarkets are geared towards a rational actor subjectivity and cue up and reward this kind of behaviour and presentation by their users. Elements of this subjectivity were value as defined by potency; quality as reflected in price; a focus on pharmaceutical makeup and potency; and embodying drug use practice as planned hedonism. Users show a tendency to reify, quantify and engage in cost benefit analysis and rational use theory. They resist some of the implications about what being an opiate user means. Self-identified addicts in the Agora forums employed an addiction repertoire, using different types of drugs in different ways depending on the context.

This is not straightforward as users had varying degrees of control over their consumption context. Some had to hide their use from family members while still consuming or maintaining a working life. Stigma and structural harm became manifest as part of that. Use of a potent drug could be a way of affirming agency in the users' self-perception, as one heroin user argued:

> *Opiates are fairly easy to control as long as you keep a strict schedule (no longer then 3 days in a row/no using during a workweek). I have been doing heroin for about 2 months now almost every weekend and I actually decreased my initial dose.... Still gives you a pretty nice rush and a good baseline euphoria while maintaining enough wits/awareness to watch tv, play video games or what have you.*

The combination of maintaining daily life along with regular heroin consumption domesticated potency in their view. Markets may reward participants who are better placed to present themselves as instrumentally motivated rational actors mediated by a process of social embedding (Moeller, 2018). Heroin became an everyday drug rather than a problem drug. Users recognised that market information would only tell them so much and that at some point they would have to use experiential methods to assess the likely interaction with the drug such as using low solution testers and observing others (Mars et al., 2018b).

The market infrastructure reflects and reproduces that subjectivity

Key decisions taken in designing and maintaining the buying and distribution infrastructure are designed with this subjectivity in mind through a combination of the technical affordances and features of the marketplace, with the organisation and market power of both the cryptomarket administration and the vendor, and the Tor infrastructure (Collier, 2020). The listing system, the discussion forums, the reputation scoring system, the dispute resolution system, messaging, platform encryption and favoured cryptocurrency services are all part of this. Platforms present themselves as technically effective, socially neutral systems. However, they are designed to promote kinds of engagement and behaviour which are beneficial to the platform owners. For example, Finalise Early (FE) was a practice where interests diverged between vendors and buyers (Moeller et al., 2017). The practice of FE means that payment is released immediately. FE is largely in the interest of the seller. Initially, discounts were provided for using FE; over time, some vendors simply required it as a part of doing business. FE is a technical affordance of the platform. The platform concept draws on critical digital studies of integrated digital economies (Pasquale, 2017). Platforms envelop users in a system which binds them economically, culturally and personally. They promote particular kinds of performance and action such as that of being a rational participant (Childs et al., 2020).

As platforms, cryptomarkets value the vendors' ability to provide a range of product. Variety was valued as much as purity. Some users especially appreciated vendors who acted as a one stop shop for substances ranging from opium to fentanyl and counterfeit Xanax.

Platform users had to develop both their technical and cultural competence in dealing with the cryptomarket as a platform which has technical affordances and economic dynamics that they could find difficult. The cryptomarkets tend to centralise and reward bigger players – both buyers and sellers. While often beginning as fairly open retail ventures, they morph into systems that reward the more professional and well-resourced players through economies of scale and the ability of larger vendors to arrange sweetheart deals with the market administrators. These larger and more successful players can set the terms of involvement of others, for example, by only selling to better established customers. New users expressed this in terms of having to adopt the right online persona that would adapt to the norms of the platforms. In several discussions, the drug buyers expected themselves to be evaluated as a good or bad customer depending on their engagement with the vendor.

The community shared principles of adaptability to the norms of the platform. Users were encouraged to leave reviews of the drugs they bought. Most vendors had very high scores, typically at least 4.5 out of 5. This led to some suspicion that the system was easily gamed by the vendor or corrupted by the administrator. While that was likely to happen, in part the review system was normalised and supported by the community of buyers in order to make it more effective. Users admonished disgruntled customers to express their sentiments to the vendor directly or in the discussion forum rather than dropping a negative review score.

A result of the platform's qualities was account 'stickiness'. Vendors and buyers were reluctant to create new accounts despite the potential security advantage. Having to start a new account 'clean' without their established reputation and without the existing relationships with market administrators and key customers would be far too disruptive. The platform design imposes security costs on its users. This helps keep them in the walled garden.

Discussion and conclusion

Illicit markets shape subjectivities and drugs as commodities. Planned hedonism pulls opiate users who engage through the cryptomarket into that orientation. Cryptomarkets are a social-technical matrix that users must become savvy in when they use them. It involves a combination of cultural knowledge, technical and material qualities, and personal and organisational capacities. There is an overlayered network of infrastructures which are involved, from the market's technical and administrative infrastructures to at-home drug testing methods. The drug as a usable substance is shaped in the relationship between dealer, user, market and consumption context. Potency is a quality users and dealers bring into being (Moeller, 2018). Potency was a quality often referred to by users but was not a universal quality. The talk around opiates in the market was a struggle between the specificity of the particular batch that was being sold and consumed and the immutable characteristics of the drug. Producing a predictable effect involved assembling several supports – material, environmental, psychological, cultural and experiential.

Potency was desired, dangerous and elusive in the eyes of users. It was a quality they felt was acted upon them and was acted on by them. Potency was examined as a community construct that involved concepts of pharmaceutical purity, best fit to purpose and the user's set. Theorising the pharmaceutical qualities in these terms allowed me to account for its material stabilities and instabilities across different domains. The various opiates being discussed possessed relevant material qualities which were enacted in their presentation, purchase and consumption. As a political economy, it applies to other systems such as the commodification of alcohol and performance-enhancing drugs where risks and pleasures are similarly produced, distributed and enacted in consumption.

Cryptomarkets advertise their capacity for introducing predictability. As the experiences of users showed, however, markets could be vehicles for introducing risk and limiting knowledge. Users learnt and taught each other how their own experiences and judgements were ultimately the only ones that could be relied on. They are systems which embed the political economy of the digital drug market, its focus on competition, consumer identity and principles of agorism. Agorism is the principle that societies should organise around voluntary anarchic exchange. The ideological emphasis on agorism in the markets tended to obfuscate some of the political economy aspects such as supply chain effects and the dominance of better established players (Lokala et al., 2019).

Problems arose when the supply chain was seen to introduce invasive substances (Mars et al., 2019) of which fentanyl was one. Discussion around substances like that would draw on a range of data from users' trip reports to public health warnings in order to resolve the substance as unwanted or as one that, while risky, could be absorbed into the user's drug repertoire (Bilgrei, 2016). The drug was then defined as dirty or clean depending on its acceptance within the community (Douglas, 2013). Adulterants were treated in a similar way. Some could be desired as changing the form and experience of the high, others as unwanted or dangerous.

The markets presented themselves as offering tools to make the drug buying and consumption process transparent. User ratings and tests were intended to support a rational approach to drug consumption. The ability of users to manage their use effectively was both supported and limited by this. The relative transparency about the products' pharmaceutical qualities exposed the limits of users' and vendors' abilities to manage and limit pharmaceutical risks. Adulteration could be introduced further up the supply chain so it became impossible to avoid consuming unwanted adulterants. Although the markets were designed to get around supply chain risks, they often highlighted and reproduced them. These factors illustrated how markets can increase transparency and obfuscate power relationships at the same time. The markets were relatively open and supportive of users, so this was in many ways a positive harm reduction environment. Users placed a lot of store by their ability to engage in effective harm reduction practice. Alongside that it was apparent what risks could not be mitigated. Users would use the information provided to seek out some risks, associating higher potency, higher risk heroin with a better experience. Though that might sound negative, it was a useful counterpoint in that it shows users' desire to enact their agency and not reduce their experience to a balance of risk and benefit.

References

Aldridge J and Décary-Hétu D (2016) Hidden wholesale: The drug diffusing capacity of online drug cryptomarkets. *International Journal of Drug Policy* 35: 7–15. DOI: 10.1016/j.drugpo.2016.04.020.

Bakken SA (2020) Drug dealers gone digital: using signalling theory to analyse criminal online personas and trust. *Global Crime* 0(0). Routledge: 1–23. DOI: 10.1080/17440572.2020.1806826.

Barratt MJ, Ferris JA and Winstock AR (2016) Safer scoring? Cryptomarkets, social supply and drug market violence. *International Journal of Drug Policy* 35: 24–31. DOI: 10.1016/j.drugpo.2016.04.019.

Beckert J (2009) The social order of markets. *Theory and Society* 38(3): 245–269. DOI: 10.1007/s11186-008-9082-0.

Beckert J and Wehinger F (2012) In the shadow: illegal markets and economic sociology. *Socio-Economic Review* 11: 5–30.

Belackova V and Vaccaro CA (2013) "A Friend with Weed Is a Friend Indeed": Understanding the relationship between friendship identity and market relations among Marijuana users. *Journal of Drug Issues* 43(3): 289–313. DOI: 10.1177/0022042613475589.

Bilgrei OR (2016) From "herbal highs" to the "heroin of cannabis": Exploring the evolving discourse on synthetic cannabinoid use in a Norwegian Internet drug forum. *International Journal of Drug Policy* 29: 1–8. DOI: 10.1016/j.drugpo.2016.01.011.

Bilgrei OR (2019) Community-consumerism: Negotiating risk in online drug communities. *Sociology of Health & Illness* 41(5): 852–866. DOI: 10.1111/1467–9566.12864.

Bratspies RM (2018) *Cryptocurrency and the Myth of the Trustless Transaction*. ID 3141605, SSRN Scholarly Paper, 10 March. Rochester, NY: Social Science Research Network. Available at: https://papers.ssrn.com/abstract=3141605 (accessed 16 May 2018).

Broadhurst R, Ball M, Trivedi H, et al. (2020) *Fentanyl Availability on Darknet Markets*. Available at: https://nla.gov.au/nla.obj-2478366826 (accessed 10 March 2020).

Brunt TM, Koeter MW, Niesink RJM, et al. (2012) Linking the pharmacological content of ecstasy tablets to the subjective experiences of drug users. *Psychopharmacology* 220(4): 751–762. DOI: 10.1007/s00213-011-2529-4.

Childs A, Coomber R and Bull M (2020) Do online illicit drug market exchanges Afford rationality? *Contemporary Drug Problems*. Los Angeles, CA: Sage Publications. DOI: 10.1177/0091450920934186.

Collier B (2021) Infrastructural Power: Dealing with Abuse, Crime, and Control in the Tor Anonymity Network. In: Weulen Kranenbarg M and Leukfeldt R (eds.) *Cybercrime in Context: The Human Factor in Victimization, Offending, and Policing*. Crime and Justice in Digital Society. Cham: Springer International Publishing, pp. 283–301. DOI: 10.1007/978-3-030-60527-8_16.

Coomber R (1997) The adulteration of drugs: What dealers do to illicit drugs, and what they think is done to them. *Addiction Research & Theory* 5(4): 297–306.

Coomber R and Maher L (2006) Street-level drug market activity in Sydney's primary heroin markets: Organization, adulteration practices, pricing, marketing and violence. *Journal of Drug Issues* 36(3): 719–753. DOI: 10.1177/002204260603600310.

Coomber R and Moyle L (2014) Beyond drug dealing: Developing and extending the concept of 'social supply' of illicit drugs to 'minimally commercial supply.' *Drugs: Education, Prevention and Policy* 21(2). Taylor & Francis: 157–164. DOI: 10.3109/09687637.2013.798265.

Coomber R, Moyle L and South N (2015) The normalisation of drug supply: The social supply of drugs as the "other side" of the history of normalisation. *Drugs: Education, Prevention and Policy* 23(3): 255–263. DOI: 10.3109/09687637.2015.1110565.

Coomber R and Turnbull P (2007) Arenas of drug transactions: Adolescent cannabis transactions in England—Social supply. *Journal of Drug Issues* 37(4): 845–865. DOI: 10.1177/002204260703700406.

Davitadze, A, Meylakhs, P, Lakhov, A and King, EJ (2020) Harm reduction via online platforms for people who use drugs in Russia: A qualitative analysis of web outreach work. *Harm Reduction Journal* 17(1): 98. DOI: 10.1186/s12954-020-00452-6.

Décary-Hétu D and Giommoni L (2017) Do police crackdowns disrupt drug cryptomarkets? A longitudinal analysis of the effects of Operation Onymous. *Crime, Law and Social Change* 67(1): 55–75. DOI: 10.1007/s10611-016-9644-4.

Demant J, Munksgaard R and Houborg E (2018) Personal use, social supply or redistribution? Cryptomarket demand on Silk Road 2 and Agora. *Trends in Organized Crime* 21(1): 42–61. DOI: 10.1007/s12117-016-9281-4.

Dennis F (2016) Encountering "Triggers": Drug–body–world entanglements of injecting drug use. *Contemporary Drug Problems* 43(2): 126–141. DOI: 10.1177/0091450916636379.

Dennis F (2019) *Injecting Bodies in More-than-Human Worlds*. Routledge. DOI: 10.4324/9780429466137.

Desmond DP, Maddux JF and Trevino A (1978) Street heroin potency and deaths from overdose in San Antonio. *The American Journal of Drug and Alcohol Abuse* 5(1). Taylor & Francis: 39–49. DOI: 10.3109/00952997809029259.

Dijck J van, Poell T and Waal M de (2018) *The Platform Society*. Oxford: Oxford University Press. Available at: https://oxford-universitypressscholarship-com.ezproxy.is.ed.ac.uk/view/10.1093/oso/9780190889760.001.0001/oso-9780190889760 (accessed 29 March 2021).

Dittus M, Wright J and Graham M (2017) Platform criminalism: The "Last-Mile" geography of the Darknet market supply chain. *arXiv:1712.10068 [cs]*. Available at: http://arxiv.org/abs/1712.10068.

Douglas M (2013) *Risk and Blame*. London: Routledge.

Duff C (2014) The place and time of drugs. *International Journal of Drug Policy* 25(3): 633–639. DOI: 10.1016/j.drugpo.2013.10.014.

ElSohly MA, Mehmedic Z, Foster S, et al. (2016) Changes in cannabis potency over the last 2 decades (1995–2014): Analysis of current data in the United States. *Biological Psychiatry* 79(7). Cannabinoids and Psychotic Disorders: 613–619. DOI: 10.1016/j.biopsych.2016.01.004.

Felstead M (2018) Identifying factors that influence the use of dark web cryptomarkets: Qualitative interviews with cryptomarket users. *The Plymouth Law & Criminal Justice Review*. Available at: https://pearl.plymouth.ac.uk/handle/10026.1/14322 (accessed 19 September 2019).

Fitzgerald J (2015) *Framing Drug Use: Bodies, Space, Economy and Crime*. Houndmills Springer.

Fraser S (2020) Doing ontopolitically-oriented research: Synthesising concepts from the ontological turn for alcohol and other drug research and other social sciences. *International Journal of Drug Policy*: 102610. DOI: 10.1016/j.drugpo.2019.102610.

Fraser S and Moore D (2011) Governing through problems: The formulation of policy on amphetamine-type stimulants (ATS) in Australia. *International Journal of Drug Policy* 22(6): 498–506. DOI: 10.1016/j.drugpo.2011.09.004.

Fraser S and Valentine K (2008) *Substance and Substitution: Methadone Subjects in Liberal Society*. 1st ed. Houndmills Palgrave Macmillan.

Hammersvik E, Sandberg S and Pedersen W (2012) Why small-scale cannabis growers stay small: Five mechanisms that prevent small-scale growers from going large scale. *International Journal of Drug Policy* 23(6). Special Focus Issue: Drug Production and Drug Markets: 458–464. DOI: 10.1016/j.drugpo.2012.08.001.

Hübschle A (2017) Contested illegality: Processing the trade prohibition of Rhino horn. In: Beckert J and Dewey M (eds.) *The Architecture of Illegal Markets Towards an Economic Sociology of Illegality in the Economy*. Oxford: Oxford University Press. Available at: https://oxford-universitypressscholarship-com.ezproxy.is.ed.ac.uk/view/10.1093/oso/9780198794974.001.0001/oso-9780198794974-chapter-10 (accessed 1 April 2021).

Lamy FR, Daniulaityte R, Barratt MJ, et al. (2020) Listed for sale: analyzing data on fentanyl, fentanyl analogs and other novel synthetic opioids on one cryptomarket. *Drug and Alcohol Dependence*: 108115. DOI: 10.1016/j.drugalcdep.2020.108115.

Lokala U, Lamy F, Daniulaityte R, et al. (2019) Global trends, local harms: Availability of Fentanyl-type drugs on the dark web and accidental overdoses in Ohio. *Computational and Mathematical Organization Theory* 25: 48–59.

Maher L and Dixon D (1999) Policing and public health: Law enforcement and harm minimization in a street-level drug market. *The British Journal of Criminology* 39(4): 488–512. DOI: 10.1093/bjc/39.4.488.

Mars SG, Ondocsin J and Ciccarone D (2018a) Sold as heroin: Perceptions and use of an evolving drug in Baltimore, MD. *Journal of Psychoactive Drugs* 50(2): 167–176. DOI: 10.1080/02791072.2017.1394508.

Mars SG, Ondocsin J and Ciccarone D (2018b) Toots, tastes and tester shots: User accounts of drug sampling methods for gauging heroin potency. *Harm Reduction Journal* 15(1): 26. DOI: 10.1186/s12954-018-0232-z.

Mars SG, Rosenblum D and Ciccarone D (2019) Illicit fentanyls in the opioid street market: Desired or imposed? *Addiction* 114(5): 774–780. DOI: 10.1111/add.14474.

Martin J, Cunliffe J and Munksgaard R (2019) *Cryptomarkets: A Research Companion*. Bingley, UK: Emerald Publishing Limited. Available at: http://ebookcentral.proquest.com/lib/ed/detail.action?docID=5942788 (accessed 11 January 2021).

Moeller K (2018) Drug market criminology: Combining economic and criminological research on illicit drug markets. *International Criminal Justice Review* 28(3): 191–205. DOI: 10.1177/1057567717746215.

Moeller K, Munksgaard R and Demant J (2017) Flow My FE the vendor said: Exploring violent and fraudulent resource Exchanges on cryptomarkets for illicit drugs. *American Behavioral Scientist*. Early Online(v). DOI: 10.1177/0002764217734269.

Moeller K, Svensson B and Munksgaard R (2021) Fentanyl analogs on the Swedish webforum flashback: Interest and impact of scheduling. *International Journal of Drug Policy* 87: 103013. DOI: 10.1016/j.drugpo.2020.103013.

Moyle L, Childs A, Coomber R, et al. (2019) #Drugsforsale: An exploration of the use of social media and encrypted messaging apps to supply and access drugs. *International Journal of Drug Policy* 63: 101–110. DOI: 10.1016/j.drugpo.2018.08.005.

Pasquale F (2017) Two Narratives of platform capitalism. *Yale Law & Policy Review* 35(1): 11.

Reuter P and Greenfield V (2001) Measuring global drug markets. *World Economics* 2(4): 159–173.

Risser D, Uhl A, Oberndorfer F, et al. (2007) Is There a relationship between street heroin purity and drug-related emergencies and/or drug-related deaths? An analysis from Vienna, Austria*. *Journal of Forensic Sciences* 52(5): 1171–1176. DOI: 10.1111/j.1556-4029.2007.00507.x.

Schifano F and Corkery J (2008) Cocaine/crack cocaine consumption, treatment demand, seizures, related offences, prices, average purity levels and deaths in the UK (1990–2004). *Journal of Psychopharmacology* 22(1). SAGE Publications Ltd STM: 71–79. DOI: 10.1177/0269881107079170.

Seddon T (2009) *A History of Drugs: Drugs and Freedom in the Liberal Age*. Routledge is published in Abingdon, Oxfordshire.

Strang J and King L (1997) Heroin is more than just Diamorphine. *Addiction Research* 5(1). Taylor & Francis: iii–vii. DOI: 10.3109/16066359709005576.

Tupper KW (2008) The globalization of ayahuasca: Harm reduction or benefit maximization? *International Journal of Drug Policy* 19(4): 297–303. DOI: 10.1016/j.drugpo.2006.11.001.

Turner T (2018) Disneyization: A framework for understanding illicit drug use in bounded play spaces. *International Journal of Drug Policy* 58: 37–45. DOI: 10.1016/j.drugpo.2018.04.018.

van der Gouwe D, Brunt TM, van Laar M, et al. (2017) Purity, adulteration and price of drugs bought on-line versus off-line in the Netherlands. *Addiction* 112(4): 640–648. DOI: 10.1111/add.13720.

Vitellone N (2004) Habitus and social suffering: Culture, addiction and the syringe. *Sociological Review* 52(Supplement 2): 130–147.

Zinberg NE (1986) *Drug, Set, and Setting: The Basis for Controlled Intoxicant Use*. New Haven, CT: Yale University Press.

7

CRAFT DRINKS, CONNOISSEURSHIP AND INTOXICATION

Thomas Thurnell-Read

Introduction

The emergence of 'craft' drinks over recent decades has been a prominent trend in the drinking cultures of many countries. Most visibly, craft breweries play a small but growing role in the global beer industry (Danson et al., 2015), and are perceived as being at the forefront of a number of consumer trends. Craft beer has spread widely, and academic research has analysed developments in diverse contexts, including Sweden (Sjölander-Lindqvist, Skoglund & Laven, 2020), Greece (Melewar & Skinner, 2018), Ireland (Drakopoulou et al., 2018), Mexico (Gómez-Corona et al., 2017), Italy (Fastigi & Cavanaugh, 2017), Canada (Eberts, 2014), New Zealand/Aotearoa (Kuehn & Parker, 2021), Australia (Holden, 2011; Argent, 2018), the UK (Thurnell-Read, 2014; Wallace, 2019) and, most noticeably, the USA (Reid, McLaughlin & Moore, 2014, Chapman, Lellock & Lippard, 2017). However, with only a few exceptions (Thurnell-Read, 2017a; Land, Sutherland and Taylor, 2018), the fact that craft beer involves the production of an intoxicant, and its consumption explicitly gives rise to situations in which alcohol is imbibed and intoxication occurs, remains unexamined in this body of literature. As a corrective to this, the chapter observes the way in which the rise of a craft drinks culture based around ideas of taste and connoisseurship shapes understandings of intoxication. It examines changing discourses and practices that frame the consumption of intoxicants, as well as shifts in the ways in which those intoxicants are perceived and experienced. Thus, it has been shown that craft beer and, for that matter, artisan gin, 'natural' wine and craft cider (Smith Maguire, 2018a; Abbotts, 2019; Thurnell-Read, 2019a), are widely seen in a positive light and rarely, if ever, as intoxicants leading to drunkenness and disorder.

A culture of connoisseurship involving a commitment to developing knowledge and preferences within a particular category of drinks has a seemingly long history in regard to wine (Inglis, 2015; Smith Maguire, 2018a, 2018b) and whisky (Spracklen, 2013), but is a relatively new phenomenon in relation to beer (Thurnell-Read, 2018). It is only recently, with the emergence of craft beer, that beer drinkers of such products may be seen as more 'sophisticated' and as having more 'prestige' than those who drink mass-produced mainstream beer brands (Reid, McLaughlin & Moore, 2014). This shift away from mainstream, or 'macro', lager produced on an industrial scale and marketed globally under widely recognised names such as *Budweiser* and *Carlsberg* has important implications for how intoxication and

DOI: 10.4324/9780429058141-10

intoxicants are understood. Rather than being seen as 'problem' drinking, framed by notions of excess and transgression, the drinking of so-called connoisseurs tends to invoke images of discernment, taste and studied cultural appreciation. Significantly, beer consumption is increasingly seen as an activity through which beer consumers can perform their cultural capital by consuming particular beers in a culturally approved manner which is used to leverage status and respect from other consumers (Thurnell-Read, 2018). Further, there has been an increasing diversity of spaces in which this cultural capital can be performed, including specialist craft beer bars, at real ale festivals and on web-based applications such as *Untapped*. Whether or not intoxication is desired or achieved, the image of the connoisseur as a *bon vivant* who mobilises their cultural capital and good taste in the appreciation of fine wines, rare single malt whiskies and inventive artisan beers goes some considerable way to justify and legitimate what may often be substantial levels of alcohol consumption.

A striking feature of the growing corpus of academic literature on craft drinks has been the absence of discussion of drunkenness and intoxication. The real and perceived negative outcomes of intoxication – antisocial behaviour, public disorder and violence, sickness and personal injury – have been vigorously contested in policy, media and academic debates (Hadfield, Lister and Traynor, 2009; Plant and Plant, 2009); yet, they tend not to be readily associated with craft drinks consumption even when such *does* involve considerable intake, in terms of both volume and frequency. Indeed, a common refrain associated with craft drinks is that it involves a 'better' type of drinking where the emphasis on enjoyment of flavour and an appreciation of the drink itself and the context of its production, in terms of locality, ingredients and process (Thurnell-Read, 2019a), supplants the emphasis on intoxication, or 'determined drunkenness', characteristic of the 'new cultures of intoxication' that have dominated public debates in recent decades (Measham and Brain, 2005). Rather, nested into the origin stories of the craft beer movement is the idea that real ale and craft beer consumer cultures are not overtly concerned with intoxication. Indeed, Charles Papazian, the founder of the American Homebrewers Association who is considered to be one of the most influential figures in the growth of craft beer in the USA, is famed for observing that drinkers of craft beer 'got happy, not stupid' (Elzinga, Tremblay & Tremblay, 2015). The implication of this, which will be explored in greater detail in the course of this chapter, is that craft beer drinkers are not disposed to many of the problems associated with intoxication and are, instead, beneficiaries of a cultural discourse of moderation.

That so much recent research has explored an emergent social phenomenon which involves the production and consumption of alcoholic products without ever mentioning intoxication, drunkenness or, indeed, addiction is telling. This chapter goes some way in addressing this but also explains why craft drinks consumers appear to be able to successfully distance themselves and their beer consumption being associated with the more widespread negative implications of intoxication and alcohol harms. This chapter explores the ways in which the production and consumption of a specific intoxicant, alcohol, are framed by a discourse and practice of 'craft' that foregrounds notions of quality, taste and connoisseurship that result in intoxication being downplayed or legitimated. The following section outlines the emergence of craft drinks in recent decades and examines how the craft beer 'subculture', which values quality, innovation and authenticity, has produced novel spaces and practice in and through which alcohol is being consumed. Then, more specifically, the next section will examine the ways in which the rise of craft drinks has been associated with an elevation of cultural prestige associated with such drinks and increasing social status for those who consume them. Importantly, here, the sociology of culture and consumption has lent a conceptual framework with which to understand how the specific act of purchasing and drinking alcohol is part of wider social processes that reflect stratification of society in terms of social class and status. Finally, in addressing intoxication specifically, the final substantive section of the chapter will set out the central theme already alluded to in this introduction that the culture of connoisseurship that has emerged around craft drinks is invoked to legitimate and justify intoxication in a way that is not seen in relation to most other alcoholic drinks specifically and intoxicants in general.

The Craft Drinks 'Revolution'

The emergence of craft beer, and craft drinks more generally, has been described as a 'revolution' involving radical upheavals in business practices and significant changes in consumer tastes (O'Brien, 2011). This movement is now widely understood to have emerged in response to a protracted period of market rationalisation that saw the beer industry in many Western countries monopolised by a small group of large corporations specialising in increasingly centralised production and distribution of standardised products. The growth of a craft beer industry has therefore been explained as, at least in part, stemming from 'the desire of people to break away from the smothering homogeneity of popular, national culture, and re-establish connections with local communities, settings, and economies' (Schnell and Reece, 2003: 46). In a heroic response to this encroachment by big business, the now often told story goes, a small cohort of pioneers resisted this 'McDonaldisation of beer' (Thurnell-Read, 2020) by establishing small but ambitious and fiercely independent breweries producing beers that valued quality and tradition over profits. In the UK, this development was closely associated with the Campaign for Real Ale (CAMRA), a consumer group founded in 1971 with the specific remit of campaigning to promote and protect 'cask conditioned' beer, while in the USA, developments were led by key organisations and events such as the American Homebrewers Association and its flagship Great American Beer Festival (O'Brien, 2011; Acitelli & Magee, 2017).

These decades of market disruption and change have resulted in a number of outcomes. Most notably, there are a vastly increased number of breweries operating in many countries, with the meteoric rise of craft beer in the USA providing the most obvious and well-studied example (see Tremblay & Tremblay, 2005). The Brewers Association, which defines craft breweries as having an annual production of fewer than six million barrels of beer and having less than 25% of ownership or control in the hands of non-craft beverage industry companies, counted 7,450 craft breweries in the USA in 2018 with California (841), Colorado (396) and Washington (394) hosting the most craft breweries by state. Meanwhile in the UK, the number of breweries passed 2,000 in 2017 and has only recently experienced some slowing in what have been many years of continuous expansion (Featherstone, 2017). A large part of this growth is therefore accounted for in the vast array of independent quality-led breweries opening over recent decades (SIBA, 2019), as well as new sites of production and consumption such as brewpubs which have flourished in the UK and the USA in particular since the 1990s (Elzinga, Tremblay & Tremblay, 2015). Further still, as craft beer tends to distinguish itself by its diversity in terms of styles, flavours and strengths available (Reid, McLaughlin & Moore, 2014), there is now a range and variety of beers widely available that perhaps a previous generation of beer drinkers could barely dream of. Beyond the beer itself, one of the most striking trends is the proliferation of information and the means by which knowledge about drinks is communicated. Thus, there is now an increased abundance of beer guides, tasting notes, tutored tastings, 'Meet the Brewer' and 'Tap Takeover' events, brewery tours, while an increasingly diverse range of online platforms and fora all provide dynamic cultural spaces for communicating new tastes and practices. As will be examined below, consuming craft beer has become an 'intellectualised' activity with drinkers honing their knowledge about beer styles and breweries and demonstrating their cultural capital in being able to perform the selection, consumption and evaluation of different beers from a vast and changing range of options in a culturally approved manner (Thurnell-Read, 2018).

Beyond these changes to the beer itself, real ale and craft beer breweries, retailers and consumers can be attributed with numerous innovations in methods of sale and forms of consumption. Craft beer has given rise to new sites of consumption such as beer festivals (Thurnell-Read, 2017b), micropubs (Hubbard, 2019; Robinson & Spracklen, 2019), ale or brewery trails (Fletchall, 2016; Thurnell-Read et al., 2021), brewpubs and brewery taps (Wallace, 2019) and specialist retailers or 'bottle shops'. In many such venues, beers are served in smaller glasses to allow patrons to sample a wider range of beers. In addition to being new places in which alcohol is purchased or consumed, all these spaces carry with them innovations or, at least, palpable changes in the associated ethos or drinking culture that goes with the consumption of craft beer. Thus, as Schnell and Reese (2003: 46) observe, 'many brewpubs have also catered to our craving for uniqueness by providing one-of-a-kind social settings, commonly decorated with local historical photos, maps, and other artefacts of a place's personality'. Hubbard (2019), for example, identifies the emerging micropub movement in the UK as aiming to offer a sociable space in which enthusiastic landlords communicate their passion for real ale and a small but dedicated clientele of regular customers prioritise a 'friendly atmosphere and a place for convivial chat' accompanying a slow and appreciative drinking which is in contrast to the scale and pace found in main stream commercial drinking venues. While intoxication does invariably occur in these drinking spaces, a discourse of moderation is widely invoked as justifying alcohol consumption as being sociable and focused on the enjoyment of the act of drinking itself rather than the outcome of drinking in terms of drunkenness and inebriation. While it is possible that the lower alcohol content of many beers ensures a favourable impression in comparisons to 'stronger' drinks such as wines, spirits and cocktails, the ongoing trend for high strength craft beers suggests that there is a wider cultural association linking beer with sociability, conviviality and moderation which the craft beer scene readily benefits from.

A further key trend is that the real ale and craft beer movements have invested heavily in what Flack (1997) first identified as the connection between beer and an increasingly prominent trend for 'neolocalism'. To be able to draw a distinctive contrast with the placelessness of generic national and global brands 'craft breweries often attempt to ingrain themselves into their local community and represent the history and landscapes of the area through the label design, logo design, and beer names' (Murray & Kline, 2015: 1204). Thus, beers which are 'carefully named to reflect a sense of place' evoke connections with, and sense of pride in, specific localities (Melewar & Skinner, 2018: 6), while microbreweries work to build 'strong connection' to local economies and communities, thereby providing 'a means to identify and promote distinctive qualities of place' (Paulsen and Tuller, 2017: 105). In so doing, we might deduce, craft beer engenders a goodwill from consumers and, potentially, policy makers, that is far wider and more positive than many scale producers of alcoholic beverages. Craft breweries develop and deploy narratives which lay claim to an 'authenticity' which roots the beer, the brewery and the brewers themselves in the cultural and economic lives of local communities (Koontz & Chapman, 2019). Further, in the context of this chapter, it is also pertinent to speculate that because craft breweries go to such great lengths to project an image built on 'place and locality, cooperation and commitment' (Sjölander-Lindqvist, Skoglund and Laven, 2020: 10), the association of the alcoholic product with the state of intoxication is not as straightforward or automatic. Consumers can drink as an expression of pride and community rather than what might, in other settings, be seen more simply as drinking to achieve intoxication.

The implication of these changes, which shall be explored more in the sections below, is that the kinds of drinking that take place in these new types of venues is attentive to a wider range of motivations and values than simply sustained drinking for the purpose of achieving drunkenness. Rather, beer festivals, brewpubs and speciality craft beer bars invoke a range of values relating to locality, community and commitment, meaning that craft beer benefits from 'a cadre of passionate and well-informed consumers who communicate and network through brewpubs, tap houses and participation in beer clubs and festivals' (Drakopoulou et al., 2018: 641). Further still, craft drinks makers and consumers invest in ideas of 'authenticity' which are communicated via packaging, branding and the narratives told and heard by both producers and consumers (Thurnell-Read, 2019a). The discourse of 'craft' therefore goes a long way to create an aura of respectability around alcohol consumption. Indeed, craft breweries have regularly been described in positive terms as 'contributors to rural development' (Murray & Kline, 2015: 1201). Further still, drinking beer at craft breweries, which commonly draw on place-specific imagery and pursue functional collaborations with other local businesses and community organisations to display their embeddedness in locality (Argent, 2018), involves 'a very effective form of place-making' which tends to generate beneficial goodwill for breweries which are seen as hubs or focal points of their community (Fletchall, 2016: 540). As the following sections will examine, these discourses that foreground localism, taste and studied appreciation – rather than intoxication, drunkenness and social disorder – are central to images of respectability and social status embedded in craft drinks consumption.

Raising the Glass: Craft Drinks, Taste and Status

The brief summary offered by the preceding section raises several themes which help to illustrate the trend towards cultural legitimacy and status of craft beer. First, by foregrounding choice, knowledge and an emphasis on appreciation of flavour over the intoxicating effects of the beverage, craft drinks and those who consume them are distanced from mainstream products and brands that are produced and consumed *en masse* and associated with drinking for the primary or sole purpose of achieving intoxication. Second, in having given rise to numerous innovations in the mode and style of production, sale and consumption, craft drinks are often seen as progressive and inventive. Positive values associated with independence, community and locality may work to legitimate drinking craft drinks as an activity undertaken by trend setters and passionate consumers. Third, the craft drinks sector can be characterised by a great deal of symbolic labour carried out both by producers and by committed consumers to frame craft beer products as being 'authentic'. This abundance of communication about the taste and value of craft products helps inform consumers but also ensures the ongoing positive framing of products. Fourth, and related to these second and third points, the production of craft beer is seen to contribute to local economies and foster positive social interactions emphasising a community of likeminded consumers in close contact and collaboration with producers who value principles such as sustainability and innovation as well as profit. Taken together, these and other characteristics of the craft beer sector and consumer culture go some way to giving this particular intoxicant a greater cultural legitimacy than other forms, such as the consumption of mass-produced beers or branded spirits with the sole intention of getting drunk. Further, it establishes social class as an influential constituent in craft drinks consumption and whether or not it is viewed positively in wider society.

The connections between alcoholic drinks and social class can be complex and varied. Being a drinker of wine, beer, spirits or, for that matter, a consummate 'omnivore' of different drinks for different occasions (Järvinen, Ellergaard & Larsen, 2014) is significant because alcoholic drinks are consumed in social contexts and cultural values are attached to particular drinks styles and brands, the places they are bought and the people who buy and consume them. The role played by social class and social status is more overt with some forms of alcohol, and in some contexts, than with others. Thus, as Mary Douglas (1987: 9) observes, 'connoisseurship in the matter of wines is in itself a field for competition' where connoisseurship 'has its own power for social domination' marking those who do not possess the 'correct' taste and knowledge as being in an inferior position to those who do. The romance of wine and wine-making inspires 'wine tourists' motivated by the desire for learning about wine and the regions in which it is produced (Hall et al., 2004), while newly rich consumers may purchase and consume vintage wines in a conspicuous manner to impress others (Overton and Murray, 2013). We must be aware, then, that certain drinks can carry and bestow status.

The processes by which some alcoholic drinks have gained favourable status make for interesting reading. Champagne, for instance, has benefited greatly from a lengthy history of myth making that has imbued this particular variety of one intoxicant as symbolic of glamour, celebration and national identity (Guy, 2007; Rokka, 2017). More recently, the process has been observed in relation to a number of other alcoholic drinks categories. For example, as Delmestri and Greenwood (2016) explain, in Italy grappa has since the 1970s gone through a period of 'status recategorization' whereby it went from a low-status product to a desired and desirable commodity emblematic of Italian culture, taste and style. Meanwhile, the emerging terminology of artisanal and 'ultra-premium' spirits has provided telling examples of the linking of social class, taste and alcohol market segmentation activities. Both tequila in North America (Gaytán, 2017) and gin in the UK (Thurnell-Read, 2019b) have been subject to significant changes in how they are produced, marketed, sold and consumed as a product with far higher status than previously thought possible. We can even see this trend in intoxicants more widely, with Roseberry (1996) accounting for the rise of 'yuppie coffee' in the USA where efforts are made by a range of actors within the coffee trade to elevate the status of coffee following its dispersal as a mass-produced and consumed commodity.

Such developments can also be observed in the beer sector which has undergone a steady process of 'intellectualisation' over recent decades (Thurnell-Read, 2018). While producers and suppliers work to increase understanding amongst consumers by communicating increasingly more complex designations, styles and terminology, consumers, in turn, respond with a willingness to pay a higher price for beer but also their own greater commitment to increasing their knowledge by learning new modes of beer appreciation. This trend is also supported by various institutions and organisations. In the UK, the most notable example of this is the CAMRA. Founded in 1971 to protect and promote traditional cask conditioned beer, the organisation has a long history of campaigning which, in various ways, promotes beer as a culturally and economically valuable commodity rather than merely a means to intoxication. Thus, over five decades, CAMRA and its members have sought to champion traditional cask conditioned beer through activities, including publishing the *Good Beer Guide* and an annual *Great British Beer Festival*. Other organisations, although less widely recognised, have also played an influential role in either maintaining or increasing the status and value of beer. For example, *The Beer Academy* has, since 2003, run training courses such as its one-day course 'How to Judge Beer' and accredited 'Beer Sommeliers' to enhance the knowledge and appreciation of beer within the industry. These and other developments have helped a new language and aesthetic of beer appreciation become established meaning that certain beers are now accepted as high status commodities which consumers are required to learn about in order to fully appreciate in a mode which was perhaps previously reserved exclusively for wine.

As an outcome of many of these processes identified above, beer is now seen as a commodity that consumers can invest time and effort in getting to know. Using the terminology of French Sociologist Pierre Bourdieu, whose work on consumption, distinction and cultural value has become influential in recent years (Bourdieu, 1984), what we see is the establishment of a 'distance from necessity'. This is where the drink is consumed because of higher level motivations such as taste and appreciation of style, with these replacing hitherto low status more basic motivations, principally the desire to quench thirst or achieve intoxication (Bourdieu & Nice, 1980). Rather than a subsistence product, beer has become a cultural field into which people can become absorbed and, for those who choose to, the possibilities to commit to long-term pursuit of knowledge about beer and varied experiences of consuming the 'right' beers in the 'right' places as a form of 'serious leisure' (Thurnell-Read, 2016). Being familiar with a range of breweries, being able to identify varied beer styles and, importantly, being able to communicate and perform conspicuous personal preferences means some consumers are now engaged in an ongoing and complex performance of taste in selecting, consuming and evaluating craft beer which, to do well, often requires tutoring or learning (Thurnell-Read, 2018).

In many ways, these developments can be celebrated as the results of years of dedicated labours by passionate brewers who commit to ongoing improvements of the quality of their products (Fastigi & Cavanaugh, 2017). However, while the increasing glamorisation of the craft beer industry means that many craft brewers benefit from increased cultural cache that align craft brewing with creative industries, working conditions for many remain precarious (Miller, 2019; Wallace, 2019). Numerous studies have now raised concerns about persistent inequalities in the sector by outlining how both the production and consumption of craft beer tend to be dominated by white, middle-class men (Reid, McLaughlin & Moore, 2014; Darwin, 2018; Kuehn & Parker, 2021; Land, Sutherland and Taylor, 2018; Wallace, 2019). Indeed, once a particular cultural terrain becomes valued and valorised, it may also become defended by 'gatekeeping' activities which mean that new entrants face increasing barriers and resistance. The cultural politics of craft beer is, therefore, increasingly fraught with divisions and inequalities in relation to social class, gender and ethnicity.

Drink Less, Drink Better?: Connoisseurship and the Legitimation of Intoxication

Because craft intoxicants hold higher cultural status than their mass-produced equivalents, the consumer can derive social status from being seen to consume such beverages and having that consumption and their associated position as a 'knowledgeable' and 'tasteful' consumer acknowledged by others. Much of this emphasises a sense of middle-class respectability and refinement, where a studied appreciation of style, taste and flavour over consumption orientated towards inebriation and drunkenness, and means discourses of craft and connoisseurship often obscure or neutralise the physical, psychological and social harms associated with intoxication. Such concerns, which see public debates lament the errant 'binge drinking' of the working class while readily overlooking the often equally prolific alcohol consumption of the middle and upper classes, have dominated wider debates about alcohol and its place in many societies (Plant & Plant, 2009). Yet, here we see that the way in which craft beers are selected, consumed, evaluated and discussed by self-confessed 'beer geeks' raises pertinent questions to how intoxication is understood when it is, at least ostensibly, no longer the sole or even primary motivation for the consumption of intoxicants. Connoisseurs of real ale are associated with a slow, steady and studied pace of drinking unlikely to result in extremes of drunkenness and disorder (Hubbard, 2019) and in framing their own drinking practices draw on what 'discourses of moderation' to justify their alcohol intake as safe, sociable and respectable (Thurnell-Read, 2017). An emphasis on control appears to be central to this. Thus, Wallace (2019: 957–958) notes that in his research a South London brewer positioned craft beer as offering meaningful connections between customers and producers in a manner cast in contrast to hedonistic drinking, while another explained his customers approach to alcohol to be one of 'three pints of something not too strong and then home' drawing on an image of a bourgeois suburban drinking based on moderation and self-control.

As Smith Maguire (2018b) and Thurnell-Read (2018) illustrate in relation to wine and beer, respectively, high status consumption draws on a demarcation of qualities to establish that some drinks carry far greater cultural validity than others and require of the consumer an educated and intellectual disposition. Koch and Sauerbronn's (2019) study of the meanings and values of craft beer consumers in Brazil is illustrative here, as they show that craft beer consumption is informed by a 'drink less, drink better' ethos focused on taste and appreciation and an associated rejection of the perceived excesses of mass-produced beer consumed on mass. They suggest that:

> …members of the craft beer subculture of consumption do not want to be seen as drunks, troublemakers, or anything negative. They enjoy beer and try to understand it more deeply, not as merchandise, but as a combination of special ingredients made by praised brewers.
>
> *(Koch & Sauerbronn, 2019: 9)*

This 'drink less, drink better' ethos, which favours quality over quantity (Arthur, 2018) involving drinking which is 'sociable' rather than disorderly, is a framing identified across a number of recent studies as well as in wider public discourses about craft drinks and intoxication.

In the UK, where many CAMRA members spend considerable amounts of time and money pursuing their interest in beer by learning about new breweries (Thurnell-Read, 2016, 2018), the bourgeois language of connoisseurship and taste (Bourdieu, 1984) is frequently used to distinguish the respectable ale drinker from other drinkers. In contrast to stereotypical representations of hardcore drinking in the media and in youth culture (Lyons, Dalton & Hoy, 2006), craft discourse is therefore normative in that it can position the knowing and tasteful consumer of craft beer or artisanal gin as legitimate while marginalising 'other' consumers and 'other' intoxicants as illegitimate and harmful. These 'others' are often either explicitly or implicitly labelled as belonging to a working-class habitus. Robinson and Spracklen (2019), in their study of real ale micropubs in the Yorkshire town of Skipton, note the widespread use of a ready contrast between real ale drinkers and lager drinkers[1] where the latter are 'louts' and 'idiots' who drink to get drunk in contrast to the former who appreciate good beer and the convivial atmosphere of a well-run drinking venue. Similarly, Spracklen (2013) analyses the discourses that inform the drinking of Scottish whisky enthusiasts to demonstrate that, while alcohol may be consumed in large quantities, the social codes and rituals of the community ensure that misbehaviour and extreme intoxication are rarely encountered or tolerated; yet, the norms of the particular habitus ensure that such drinking rarely leads to misbehaviour. Under this emphasis on drinking for a range of intrinsic and extrinsic rewards, two drinkers consuming similar amounts of alcohol could be discursively rendered either 'sensible' or 'risky' drinkers by virtue of their alcohol being consumed in the sociable context of the local community pub or the high-volume vertical drinking of commercial drinking venues, respectively.

Rather than a singular focus on drinking for intoxication (Measham & Brain, 2005), real ale and craft beer drinking spaces have tended to develop associated events and activities such as music (Robinson and Spracklen, 2019), food, traditional games and charity events (Thurnell-Read, 2017b), meaning that the symbolism and discourses which surround craft beer production and consumption benefit from linkages to wider cultural activities. Thus, for many breweries and in many beer consumption settings, an aesthetic prevails which foreground local or national culture and readily draws on either symbolic themes of tradition, heritage and nostalgia or of contemporary urban cool and sophistication. Drinkers of real ale and craft beer can be said, in Bourdieusian terms, to be performing their cultural taste and distinction by distancing themselves from more unruly, and therefore lower-class, drinkers (Spracklen, Laurencic & Kenyon, 2013; Thurnell-Read, 2017a). Hence, associating beer more closely with food, music and other cultural fields – for example, as happened when CAMRA began hosting a stall at the BBC Good Food Show from 2005 onwards – has served to improve the image of real ale, in particular, and craft beer more recently by making the consumption of the actual alcoholic drink part of a wider grouping of pleasurable activities and leisure pursuits. Indeed, many craft beer breweries have been keen to position their products as part of new urban and suburban lifestyles based around fashions and cultural tastes (Zukin, 2008; Ocejo, 2014, 2017).

There are, however, a number of contradictions in this logic. Darwin (2018), for instance, notes that the prevailing and highly gendered ethos of craft beer consumers in the USA is to see strong beers, in terms of both alcohol content and bitterness due to higher hop flavours, as being more legitimate and more masculine. Likewise, Chapman et al. (2018: 310) identify 'beer's continued dissociation from femininity' as influencing the shape and development of craft beer communities where a supposedly manly drinking style prevails over others. Strong beer is consumed, at least in part, to signal a perpetuation of earlier images of manly drinkers 'holding' their drink as a way of displaying their masculinity (Peralta, 2007). Similarly, while contemporary craft beer sectors are notable for their striking diversity of beer styles, flavour profiles and strengths (Reid, McLaughlin & Moore, 2014), an 'ethos of continual experimental' (Drakopoulou et al., 2018) and a 'spirit of diversity, variety and novelty' (Danson et al., 2015) could all be seen as encouraging regular excessive consumption of alcohol, albeit cloaked in a justificatory rationale of wanting to 'keep up' with the latest brewery openings and beer style innovations. As such, a committed craft beer connoisseur could drink several new beers every day for many years and still not exhaust the supply of new beers to try. Likewise, a tightly knit community of real ale enthusiasts and craft beer 'geeks' means that there is rarely a shortage of opportunities to consume alcohol nor of sociable occasions, such as beer festivals and beer launch events, on which to do so. Therefore, the 'beer geek' descriptor, often knowingly or ironically invoked, potentially masks unhealthy levels of alcohol consumption whereby the desire to remain conversant with the latest developments in a rapidly changing craft beer subculture that values innovation and novelty could plausibly give rise to pressures to stay up-to-date with new brewery openings and beer launches that result in the volume and frequency of alcohol consumption being sustained or increased by such 'committed' craft beer aficionados. While, as noted at the outset, this issue has barely been considered in academic writing relating to the emergence of craft drinks sector, some actors in the industry itself have attempted to instigate a conversation about these issues.

For example, the acclaimed British beer writer Pete Brown (2018) has written about excess, alcohol and mental health issues in the craft beer sector, indicating that a wider discussion is needed about the physical and mental health of those working in, or in other ways active in, the craft beer community.

Conclusion Thoughts and Future Developments

A central concern of the chapter is the thinking through the ways in which the aesthetics, symbolism and narratives that pervade the emergent craft drinks sector function to provide a discursive and actual distance from intoxication. For craft beer drinkers, an ethos that 'the taste, quality and beer selection trumps all' (Fletchall, 2016: 554) provides a handy contrast to long-established images of alcohol consumed solely for the pursuit of intoxication. Thus, while craft beer has benefited from various forms of positive public relations, it has largely avoided any sustained criticism from public health and public order perspectives. As the chapter has shown, the assumed craft beer drinkers are middle-class, educated, probably male and likely white, and appear to be given the benefit of the doubt in terms of whether their alcohol consumption, couched as it is in a discourse of connoisseurship, leads to any negative outcomes in terms of personal physical and mental or wider social harms. It is possible to widen this conclusion by drawing some speculative connections between the rise of craft drinks and two further areas of concern where current rapid social, cultural and economic changes raise interesting tensions between intoxicants, intoxication and wider social contexts and cultural discourses by which they are consumed: first, the increasingly common legalisation of cannabis and, second, the recent growth in demand for low and no alcohol drinks.

In its legalisation in many US states and, recently, in Canada, there has been a seismic upheaval in the discourses, meanings and practice around the sale, purchase and consumption of cannabis (Barcott, 2015). This has rapidly led to a rush to establish brands which associate the formerly prohibited intoxicant with a range of positive associations such as pleasure, luxury and, in a development echoing the evolution of craft beer outlined above, taste (Shapiro, 2018). While academic study of the social and cultural conventions and meanings of the newly legalised cannabis industry remains nascent, there are perhaps some early indications that similar trends to those identified above are and will continue to take place as cannabis consumption rapidly normalises and differentiates. Discourses of connoisseurship and processes of intellectualisation are evidently already at work in this field. With its emphasis on authenticity, innovation and variety that appeal to an increasingly intellectualised consumer base, craft beer offers a range of readymade examples of market strategy which many cannabis producers and retailers may draw on as they rush to either corner a growing market or gain a foothold in an already congested sector. As these trends develop, and more countries follow suit in legalising cannabis for recreational use, the emergence of cannabis connoisseurs, and an array of products, services and spaces catering to their needs, will be a notable avenue of academic research over the coming years.

A further trend with some notable connections to the case of craft drinks outlined in this chapter is the recent rise of low and no-alcohol beers (Smale, 2019). The Society of Independent Brewers reported seeing a strong increase attributed to increasingly 'health conscious' consumers and to a generational shift away from tolerating drunkenness in public and on social media (SIBA, 2019). Recent developments have seen an increasing number of low and no-alcohol beers produced by established craft breweries or specifically low and no-alcohol beer enterprises partnering with established craft breweries in 'collaboration' brews (Gilbert, 2019). Although a very recent trend, many craft brewers now see brewing a non-alcoholic but still good tasting and stylistically 'interesting' beer as a challenge to demonstrate their skill. Likewise, certain groups of consumers seem to be exhibiting levels of commitment, passion and taste akin to the wider craft beer geek subculture but in relation to beers with 0.5% alcohol or less. Social media appears to be playing a key role here with both corporate actors and consumers using platforms such as Twitter and, in particular, Instagram to communicate about new products. The potential, indeed probable, situation where non-alcoholic versions of beer, cider, wine and spirits become widespread and culturally valued brings with it the possibility of consumers of craft drinks choosing to have the taste but without the intoxication.

Taken together, this chapter and these final speculations about future directions illustrate the importance of considering the fluctuations in cultural value and social status attached to different intoxicants. As beer has gone from being solely a widely consumed yet always relatively low-status product to a more diversified field inclusive of a subculture of craft 'connoisseurs', the discourses and practices that link it to intoxication have also undergone remarkable change. Only in recent decades has it become socially acceptable to spend significant amounts of time, effort and money in honing one's capacity to judge and appreciate beer. The research drawn on here, although notable for an ongoing absence of discussion of the intoxicating effects of craft drinks consumption, serves to foreground the importance of cultural contexts in which intoxicants are consumed, meaning that new narratives and discourses are propagated which are able to cast one form of intoxicant consumption as superior to others and, in so doing, working to justify the consumption of certain intoxicants by certain people as acceptable and, even, as desirable.

Note

1 The term Real Ale used in the UK and beyond to describe a beer brewed from traditional ingredients and matured by secondary fermentation in the container from which it is dispensed, and served without the use of extraneous carbon dioxide. The term lager originally describes German beers that were conditioned through extended storage at cool temperatures before service. In modern usage, the term lager is used more widely and is often associated with the most common and widely commercial beer brands which tend to be characterised as light, clear and having a lower flavour profile compared to traditional beer styles.

References

Abbots, E. J. (2019). "Good People Make Good Cider": Crafting Culinary Heritage in Wales and the Welsh Marches. *Food and History, 17*(2), 19–39.

Acitelli, T., & Magee, T. (2017). *Audacity of Hops: The History of America's Craft Beer Revolution*. Chicago, IL: Chicago Review Press.

Argent, N. (2018). Heading down to the local? Australian rural development and the evolving spatiality of the craft beer sector. *Journal of Rural Studies, 61*, 84–99.

Arthur, R. (2018). The key trend in the global beer industry? 'Drinking less, but drinking better'. *BeverageDaily.Com*, 5 June 2018. Access at: https://www.beveragedaily.com/Article/2018/06/05/Drinking-less-but-drinking-better-Key-trends-in-the-global-beer-industry

Barcott, B. (2015). *Weed the People: The Future of Legal Marijuana in America*. Birmingham: Time Home Entertainment.

Bourdieu, P. (1984). *Distinction: A Social Critique of the Judgement of Taste*. London: Routledge and Kegan Paul.

Bourdieu, P., & Nice, R. (1980). The aristocracy of culture. *Media, Culture and Society, 2*, 225–254.

Brown, P. (2018). The power of talking. 27 March 2018. Access at: https://www.petebrown.net/2018/03/27/the-power-of-talking/

Chapman, N. G., Lellock, S., & Lippard, C. (eds) (2017). *Untapped: Exploring the Cultural Dimensions of Craft Beer.* Mogantown: West Virginia University Press.

Chapman, N. G., Nanney, M., Slade Lellock, J., & Mikles-Schluterman, J. (2018). Bottling gender: Accomplishing gender through craft beer consumption. *Food, Culture & Society, 21*(3), 296–313.

Danson, M., Galloway, L., Cabras, I., & Beatty, T. (2015). Microbrewing and entrepreneurship: The origins, development and integration of real ale breweries in the UK. *The International Journal of Entrepreneurship and Innovation, 16*(2), 135–144.

Darwin, H. (2018). Omnivorous masculinity: Gender capital and cultural legitimacy in craft beer culture. *Social Currents, 5*(3), 301–316.

Delmestri, G., & Greenwood, R. (2016). How Cinderella became a queen: Theorizing radical status change. *Administrative Science Quarterly, 61*(4), 507–550.

Douglas, M. (1987). *Constructive Drinking: Perspectives on Drinking from Anthropology.* New York: Cambridge University Press.

Drakopoulou Dodd, S., Wilson, J., Bhaird, C. M. A., & Bisignano, A. P. (2018). Habitus emerging: The development of hybrid logics and collaborative business models in the Irish craft beer sector. *International Small Business Journal, 36*(6), 637–661.

Eberts, D. (2014). Neolocalism and the branding and marketing of place by Canadian microbreweries. In Patterson, M. W., & Hoalst-Pullen, N. (eds) *The Geography of Beer: Regions, Environments, and Societies.* London: Springer, pp. 189–199.

Elzinga, K. G., Tremblay, C. H., & Tremblay, V. J. (2015). Craft beer in the United States: History, numbers, and geography. *Journal of Wine Economics, 10*(3), 242–274.

Fastigi, M., & Cavanaugh, J. R. (2017). Turning passion into profession: A history of craft beer in Italy. *Gastronomica: The Journal of Critical Food Studies, 17*(2), 39–50.

Featherstone, E. (2017). Number of UK breweries rises 64% in five years. *The Independent*, 23 October 2017. Accessed at: https://www.independent.co.uk/news/business/news/uk-breweries-number-rise-craft-beer-over-half-four-years-start-ups-a8011641.html

Flack, W. 1997. American microbreweries and neolocalism: "Ale-ing" for a sense of place. *Journal of Cultural Geography, 16*(2), 37.

Fletchall, A. M. (2016). Place-making through Beer-drinking: A case study of Montana's craft breweries. *Geographical Review, 106*(4), 539–566.

Gaytán, M. S. (2017). The transformation of tequila: From hangover to highbrow. *Journal of Consumer Culture, 17*(1), 62–84.

Gilbert, H. (2019). Big drop to launch low-alcohol collaborative beer series. *The Grocer*, 30 October 2019. Accessed at: https://www.thegrocer.co.uk/new-product-development/big-drop-to-launch-low-alcohol-collaborative-beer-series/598989.article?utm_source=Low2NoBev_Newsletter&utm_medium=email&utm_campaign=6_Nov_2019

Gómez-Corona, C., Valentin, D., Escalona-Buendía, H. B., & Chollet, S. (2017). The role of gender and product consumption in the mental representation of industrial and craft beers: An exploratory study with Mexican consumers. *Food quality and preference, 60*, 31–39.

Guy, K. M. (2007). *When Champagne Became French: Wine and the Making of a National Identity.* Baltimore, MD: Johns Hopkins University Press.

Hadfield, P., Lister, S., & Traynor, P. (2009). 'This town's a different town today': Policing and regulating the night-time economy. *Criminology & Criminal Justice, 9*(4), 465–485.

Hall, C. M., Sharples, L., Mitchell, R., Macionis, N., & Cambourne, B. (Eds.). (2004). *Food Tourism around the World.* Abingdon: Routledge.

Holden, S. (2011). Three cheers for new beers: Marketing insights from the birth of boutique brewing in Australia. In *Australia & New Zealand Marketing Academy Conference Proceedings.* Perth: Western Australia.

Hubbard, P. (2019). Enthusiasm, craft and authenticity on the high street: Micropubs as 'community fixers'. *Social & Cultural Geography, 20*(6), 763–784.

Inglis, D. (2015). On oenological authenticity: Making wine real and making real wine. *M/C Journal, 18*(1).

Järvinen, M, Ellergaard, C.H., & Larsen, A.G. (2014). Drinking successfully: Alcohol consumption, taste and social status. *Journal of Consumer Culture, 14*(3):384–405.

Koch, E. S., & Sauerbronn, J. F. R. (2019). "To love beer above all things": An analysis of Brazilian craft beer subculture of consumption. *Journal of Food Products Marketing, 25*(1), 1–25.

Koontz, A., & Chapman, N. G. (2019). About us: Authenticating identity claims in the craft beer industry. *The Journal of Popular Culture, 52*(2), 351–372.

Kuehn, K. M., & Parker, S. (2021). One of the blokes: Brewsters, branding and gender (in) visibility in New Zealand's craft beer industry. *Journal of Consumer Culture, 21*(3), 519–538.

Land, C., Sutherland, N., & Taylor, S. (2018). Back to the Brewster: Craft brewing, gender and the dialectical interplay of retraditionalisation and innovation. In Bell, E., Mangia, G., Taylor, S., & Toraldo, M. L. (eds) *The Organization of Craft Work: Identities, Meanings, and Materialities*. Abingdon: Routledge, pp. 150–168.

Lyons, A. C., Dalton, S. I., & Hoy, A. (2006). 'Hardcore Drinking' portrayals of alcohol consumption in young women's and men's magazines. *Journal of Health Psychology, 11*(2), 223–232.

Measham, F., & Brain, K. (2005). 'Binge' Drinking, British Alcohol Policy and the New Culture of Intoxication. *Crime, Media, Culture, 1*(3), 262–283.

Melewar, T. C., & Skinner, H. (2018). Territorial brand management: Beer, authenticity, and sense of place. *Journal of Business Research*, 116, 680–689.

Miller, C. F. (2019). 'Glorified Janitors': Creativity, cachet, and everyday experiences of work in Portland, Oregon's craft brewing sector. *Geoforum, 106*, 78–86.

Murray, A., & Kline, C. (2015). Rural tourism and the craft beer experience: Factors influencing brand loyalty in rural North Carolina, USA. *Journal of Sustainable Tourism, 23*(8–9), 1198–1216.

O'Brien, C. (2011). *Fermenting Revolution: How to Drink Beer and Save the World*. Gabriola: New Society Publishers.

Ocejo, R. E. (2014). *Upscaling Downtown: From Bowery Saloons to Cocktail Bars in New York City*. Princeton: Princeton University Press.

Ocejo, R. E. (2017). *Masters of Craft: Old Jobs in the New Urban Economy*. Princeton: Princeton University Press.

Overton, J., & Murray, W. E. (2013). Class in a glass: Capital, neoliberalism and social space in the global wine industry. *Antipode, 45*(3), 702–718.

Paulsen, K. E., & Tuller, H. E. (2017). Crafting place: Craft beer and authenticity in Jacksonville, Florida. In Chapman, N., Lellock, J., & Lippard, C. (eds) *Untapped: Exploring the Cultural Dimensions of the Craft Beer Revolution*. Morgantown: West Virginia University Press, pp. 105–23.

Peralta, R. L. (2007). College alcohol use and the embodiment of hegemonic masculinity among European American men. *Sex Roles, 56*(11–12), 741–756.

Plant, M. and Plant, M. (2006). *Binge Britain: Alcohol and the National Response*. Oxford: Oxford University Press.

Reid, N., McLaughlin, R. B., & Moore, M. S. (2014). From yellow fizz to big biz: American craft beer comes of age. *Focus on Geography, 57*(3), 114–125.

Robinson, D., & Spracklen, K. (2019). Music, beer and performativity in new local leisure spaces: Case study of a Yorkshire dales market town. *International Journal of the Sociology of Leisure*, 2(4), 329–346.

Rokka, J. (2017). Champagne: Marketplace icon. *Consumption Markets & Culture, 20*(3), 275–283.

Roseberry, W. (1996). The rise of yuppie coffees and the reimagination of class in the United States. *American Anthropologist, 98*(4), 762–775.

Schnell, S. M., & Reese, J. F. (2003). Microbreweries as tools of local identity. *Journal of Cultural Geography, 21*(1), 45–69.

Shapiro, K. (2018). 8 Luxury Canadian cannabis brands to know about as legalization arrives. *Forbes*, 15 October 2018. Accessed at: https://www.forbes.com/sites/katieshapiro/2018/10/15/8-luxury-canadian-cannabis-brands-to-know-about-as-legalization-arrives/#84feda55f5ee

SIBA. (2019). *SIBA British Craft Beer Report 2019*. Rippon: SIBA: The Society of Independent Brewers.

Sjölander-Lindqvist, A., Skoglund, W., & Laven, D. (2020). Craft beer–building social terroir through connecting people, place and business. *Journal of Place Management and Development, 13*(2), 149–162.

Smale, W. (2019). Young drinkers lead the trend for alcohol-free beer. *BBC News*, 20 June 2019. Access at: https://www.bbc.co.uk/news/business-48676943

Smith Maguire, J. (2018a). Taste as market practice: The example of "Natural" wine. In *Consumer Culture Theory*. Cross, S.N.N., Ruvalcaba, C., Venkatesh, A. and Belk, R.W. (Eds). Bingley: Emerald, pp. 71–92.

Smith Maguire, J. (2018b). The taste for the particular: A logic of discernment in an age of omnivorousness. *Journal of Consumer Culture, 18*(1), 3–20.

Spracklen, K. (2013). Respectable drinkers, sensible drinking, serious leisure: Single-malt whisky enthusiasts and the moral panic of irresponsible Others. *Contemporary Social Science, 8*(1), 46–57.

Spracklen, K., Laurencic, J., & Kenyon, A. (2013). 'Mine's a Pint of Bitter': Performativity, gender, class and representations of authenticity in real-ale tourism. *Tourist Studies, 13*(3), 304–321.

Thurnell-Read, T. (2014). Craft, tangibility and affect at work in the microbrewery. *Emotion, Space and Society, 13*, 46–54.

Thurnell-Read, T. (2016). 'Real Ale' Enthusiasts, serious leisure and the costs of getting 'too serious' About Beer. *Leisure Sciences, 38*(1), 68–84.

Thurnell-Read, T. (2017a). 'Did you ever hear of police being called to a beer festival?' Discourses of merriment, moderation and 'civilized' drinking amongst real ale enthusiasts. *The Sociological Review, 65*(1), 83–99.

Thurnell-Read, T. (2017b). Atmosphere and activism at the Great British Beer festival. In Chapman, N., Lellock, S., & Lippard, C. (eds) *Untapped: Exploring the Cultural Dimensions of Craft Beer.* Morgantown: West Virginia University Press, pp. 222–235.

Thurnell-Read, T. (2018). The embourgeoisement of beer: Changing practices of 'Real Ale' consumption. *Journal of Consumer Culture, 18*(4), 539–557.

Thurnell-Read, T. (2019a). A thirst for the authentic: Craft drinks producers and the narration of authenticity. *The British Journal of Sociology*, 70(4), 1448–1468.

Thurnell-Read, T. P. (2019b). 'You won't see anyone promoting a Bronze': Awards and ambivalence amongst craft gin producers. *Journal of Cultural Analysis and Social Change*, 4(2), 1–14.

Thurnell-Read, T. (2020). Beer consumption, embodied distaste and anti-corporate consumer identities. In Falconer, E. (ed.) *Space, Taste and Affect: Atmospheres That Shape the Way We Eat*. Abingdon: Routledge, pp. 19–29.

Thurnell-Read, T., Robinson, D., Herbst, J. P., & Spracklen, P. K. (2021). Rhythm and booze: Contesting leisure mobilities on the Transpennine Real Ale Trail. *Mobilities, 16*(3), 322–338.

Tremblay, V. J., & Tremblay, C. H. (2005).*The U.S Brewing Industry: Data and Economic Analysis*. Cambridge: MIT Press.

Wallace, A. (2019). 'Brewing the Truth': Craft beer, class and place in contemporary London. *Sociology, 53*(5), 951–966.

Zukin, S. (2008). Consuming authenticity: From outposts of difference to means of exclusion. *Cultural Studies, 22*(5), 724–748.

8
ECSTASY
A synthetic history of MDMA

Peder Clark

Introduction

In 1990, posters which delivered a stark warning about drugs started appearing across England. A black and white photo depicted a ghostly pale young man, attended by health professionals and laid prostrate on a hospital bed, while white text on a red background cautioned potential users that 'sometimes the after effects never wear off' (Figure 8.1).[1] While its message and appearance were very much of a piece with the 'scaremongering approach' (Wibberly and Whitelaw, 1990) employed by mid-1980s campaigns on heroin and crack cocaine, the intoxicant that the government-backed anti-drugs campaign was primarily concerned with was relatively new: 3,4-Methylene-dioxy-meth-amphetamine, MDMA, or more commonly, 'ecstasy'.

First patented by Merck in the early twentieth century, and reinvented by the Californian chemist Alexander Shulgin (amongst others) in the 1960s and 1970s, MDMA had, from the summer of 1988 onwards, become inextricably linked with the nascent 'rave' scene in the UK. As author Sarah Champion has suggested, 'Chicago's house music and the drug ecstasy became a double-act like fish and chips' (Champion, 1997: xiii). The psychoactive properties of the substance, which include reports of euphoria, mild hallucinogenic effects and increased energy, were seemingly a perfect foil for the new house and techno music sweeping through British nightlife. Capitalising on this preference for North American dance music, a travelling New York DJ, Leonardo Didesiderio aka Lenny Dee, was struck by the lurid imagery of the billboard campaign:

> I was in a very strange place, experiencing ecstasy for the first time … This poster and billboard was all over the United Kingdom. Needless to say, I thought it was fuckin' great, as I was totally into X [ecstasy].
>
> *(Major Problems, nd)*

Didesiderio was in fact so taken by the poster that he decided to appropriate it wholesale for the label art of his next 12-inch under the moniker Major Problems. With track titles such as 'Flashback' and 'Overdose (The Final Trip)', the record gleefully parodied the

DOI: 10.4324/9780429058141-11

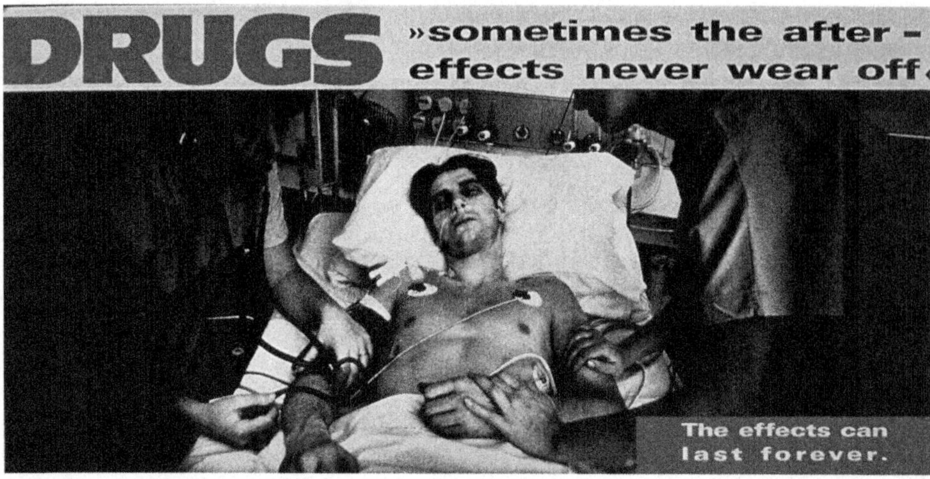

Figure 8.1 Central Office of Information 'Drugs: sometimes the after effects never wear off', 1990.
Source: Licenced under Crown copyright, image courtesy of US National Library of Medicine http://resource.nlm.nih.gov/101449661

shroud-waving tendencies of the government-sponsored *The Effects Can Last Forever* campaign in pursuit of hedonistic abandon.

The poster then, and its transatlantic response, are illustrative of the tension at the heart of many 'cultures of intoxication' (Withington, 2014) in the modern era; the possible cost to one's health balanced with the escape from the mundane. At one extremity, the puritanical tendencies of the medical establishment, warning ecstasy users that they were engaging in a 'dance of death' (Henry, 1992); at the other, the user whose lifetime consumption reportedly exceeded 40,000 pills (Kouimtsidis et al., 2006). These poles, illustrated in broader culture on the one hand by widely recirculated tabloid headlines in the *Sun* newspaper, and on the other by the nostalgic, celebratory film of *Fiorucci Made Me Hardcore* by Turner Prize winner Mark Leckey and Jeremy Deller's more recent *Everybody In the Place*, have been understood using Stanley Cohen's pliable phrase 'moral panic' (Clark, 2019; Speed, 2019).[2] Originally applied to the 'mods and rockers' subcultures of 1960s Britain, Cohen's sociological classic explained how something new and fashionable from youth culture can be deemed dangerous and a threat to wider society, a 'folk devil' that attracts widespread criticism and censorship from 'respectable' society (Cohen, 1972). Cohen's typology has offered a convenient analytical framework to explain first ecstasy and raves' appeal to youth culture, and second its condemnation by the establishment and older generations (Redhead, 1993; Thornton, 1995: 119–120). This criticism was in part predicated on colourful accounts of the handful of deaths attributed to the novel psychoactive substance, and the uncertainty around ecstasy's short- and long-term effects. But it was also ecstasy's associated cultural trappings – the repetitive, insistent music, the baggy clothes distinct from the buttoned-up power-dressing of the 1980s, and the huge raves deemed a threat to public order – that made it disruptive to the prevailing culture. The flipside of this 'moral panic' is the transgression and deviancy of the 'folk devil' in the first place, whose insurgent allure helps to explain rave's continuing attraction as a topic for contemporary art practice, amongst other audiences.

This chapter suggests that historians and other critical drugs researchers might look beyond these binaries of harm and hedonism to develop more nuanced perspectives on ecstasy.

Ecstasy has too easily been characterised as a good-time party drug with a dark side, connected in contemporary parlance with EDM (Electronic Dance Music) mega-raves and the sometimes lethal consequences of over-consumption. In doing so, this chapter also provides an intervention on academic discourses that have echoed the rhetoric of house music (such as lyrics that reference 'the House Nation' or 'Peace Love Unity and Respect') and popular histories – such as Simon Reynolds' *Energy Flash* or Matthew Collin's *Altered State* – in highlighting ecstasy's universalising affect, and that of club drugs more generally (Reynolds, 1998; Collin, 1997).[3] For example, in their article in the *Past & Present* special issue on 'cultures of intoxication', Karen Joe-Laidler and colleagues compare the experiences of users of MDMA and ketamine in disparate global cities in the early 2000s. They argue that

> the pleasure derived from intoxication involves not only a physiological reaction but also an opportunity to transcend normal everyday routines. In this process of stepping outside of oneself, one may develop a spiritual awareness—a heightened sense of self, of others, and of oneness with the collective … [this] spirituality lies at the core of the experiences of young people in both San Francisco and Hong Kong.
>
> *(Joe-Laidler et al., 2014: 66)*

Joe-Laidler et al. therefore make the case for a sort of chemically assisted 'glocalisation', in which cultural specificities are acknowledged but ultimately downplayed in order to highlight their interviewees' transcendent and semi-mystical experiences of MDMA. Clearly, these processes were to a certain extent evident in the early years of rave, with American DJ Lenny Dee's delighted reaction to British anti-drug billboards. Furthermore, such contentions are supported by ecstasy's contemporary position as an intoxicant of global popularity, a quotidian adjunct to young people's nightlife. But while the collective joy apparently provided by ecstasy should be taken seriously – and Joe-Laider and colleagues rightly assert that 'this pleasure imperative has received relatively little attention from academics' (Joe-Laidler et al., 2014: 62) – I want to instead follow musician, artist and queer theorist Terre Thaemlitz's lead, and in her words 'keep sight of the things that we are trying to escape from' (Thaemlitz, 2008).[4] As Thaemlitz argues in his consideration of New York Deep House and drag ball culture in the early 1990s:

> The House Nation likes to pretend clubs are an oasis from suffering, but suffering is in here with us … House is not universal. House is hyper-specific.
>
> *(Thaemlitz, 2008)*

Although Thaemlitz's personal position could probably be crudely characterised as anti-drugs, her approach is instructive (Saulwick, 2015). Ecstasy emerged into widespread popularity from very specific subcultures, and in highlighting the supposed universalising affect of ecstasy, there is a danger in neglecting the principles that have more readily been applied to other psychoactive substances. In common with other intoxicants, ecstasy can mean very different things in different temporal and spatial settings, and in different cultural contexts. As Thaemlitz suggests, '[h]ouse isn't so much a sound as a situation' (Thaemlitz, 2008), and similar principles should apply to our consideration of house music's most commonly accompanying intoxicant. In short, this chapter argues that ecstasy, like other psychedelic substances, needs to be considered in terms of 'set and setting' (Zinberg, 1984).

Ecstasy has meant different things to different people at different points in different locations. This chapter moves beyond existing work which focuses either on the moral panics periodically associated with ecstasy or on the apparently universalising affect that its consumers report. This brief, synthetic and inevitably partial history of the drug and its consumption, following its first synthesis in Germany to its widespread use in Britain, will illustrate this argument.

'Adam': ecstasy before the rave, 1912–1985

MDMA was first synthesised in the laboratories of Merck, the Darmstadt, Germany-based pharmaceutical corporation in 1912, not as an appetite suppressant as some accounts suggest, but as a haemostatic agent (i.e. to aid blood-clotting and prevent bleeding). Initially referred to as 'Methylsafrylamin', it was patented that same year, but only mentioned occasionally in internal company documents up until the 1950s (Freudenmann et al., 2006). Despite these inauspicious beginnings, the patent also contained a clue to one of its further usages, with an allusion to its potential use 'as an intermediate in the production of therapeutic compounds' (Pentney, 2001: 214). The chemically similar and historically linked substance MDA (3,4 methylenedioxyamphetamine) had been used by the US military as a potential 'truth serum' in the 1950s, as well as for selected medical indications by pharmaceutical companies, including as a cough remedy and appetite suppressant (Pentney, 2001: 214). Its hallucinogenic properties had been noted, and it started to find its way into recreational uses, 'quickly develop[ing] a reputation for producing a sensual, easily manageable euphoria, thus its nick-name "The Love Drug"' (Naranjo, 1983; Passie and Benzenhöfer, 2016: 68).

MDMA was synthesised around the same time – the Californian chemist Alexander Shulgin claimed to do so in the mid-1960s – and some histories suggest that it was considered less toxic than MDA (Pentney, 2001: 214; Benzenhöfer and Passie, 2010: 1357). Although Shulgin was unlikely to be the first to do so, he is widely accepted as being responsible for its introduction into clinical usage, via his friendship with psychologist and psychotherapist Leo Zeff. Zeff had been tipped off about MDMA by a chemist friend, and almost immediately became an enthusiastic proponent, postponing his retirement to proselytise about a substance that he viewed as potentially transformative for many of his patients. Zeff was also insistent that those dispensing MDMA should also have personal experience, to ensure that they 'know the effects of any such drugs in themselves, before giving them to anyone else' (Stolaroff, 2004: 18). MDMA was used in 'hundreds of [psychotherapeutic] sessions' by Zeff and other associates, but it was also beginning to be recognised for its potential as an intoxicant (Pentney, 2001: 214–215; Richert, 2019: 142–146). Indeed, Shulgin himself would refer to MDMA as his 'low-calorie martini', an understated description which belied the bacchanalian reputation it would later attain (Shulgin and Shulgin, 1991: 73).[5]

The emergence of MDMA from an object of laboratory experimentation and biomedical enquiry can therefore be traced to the mid-1970s, with unconfirmed reports of its first usage as an intoxicant in the late 1960s (Siegel, 1986). Street drug samples were seized by the Drug Enforcement Administration (DEA) in various locations across the US, but most particularly in the mid-West, between 1970 and 1974 (Passie and Benzenhöfer, 2016: 71). By the mid-1980s, the DEA estimated that MDMA was available in 21 states across the US and Canada. This availability was concentrated on the east and west coasts – New York, California, Florida – with one significant exception: the southern state of Texas (Siegel, 1986: 349). According to some accounts of ecstasy lore, it was the nightspots of Dallas that would be the making of ecstasy's reputation as a drug perfect for dancing in nightclubs – but also its unmaking as a still legal high in the US.

But before attending to this legend, it is important to stop and note the shape-shifting that MDMA had already taken in its early years. Far from being the party drug of contemporary lore, MDMA held at this stage a much more sedate and cerebral reputation. Praised by psychotherapists for its ability to evoke 'honesty' and lucidity from its patient-users, it was also, perhaps inevitably, being sampled by curious psychonauts who had previously experimented extensively with mescaline and lysergic acid diethylamide (LSD) (Richert, 2019: 144). For example, Timothy Leary first tried MDMA in 1978, and became an enthusiastic, if initially private, advocate (Leary, 1985). Indeed, in *Storming Heaven*, Jay Stevens' classic history of LSD, MDMA was discussed, alongside other 'new psychedelics' such as 2-CB, as a more sophisticated successor to acid. Stevens related an afternoon spent with 'an octogenarian former professor' who insisted that 'Adam' (a common name for MDMA at this point) was a 'very intriguing drug … extremely useful' (Stevens, 1987: 287). Upon sampling the drug himself, Stevens stated that ecstasy

> didn't create insights so much as remove barriers and eliminate the native fear of appearing emotionally clumsy and foolish. You were high, but you weren't high. There was none of LSD's powerful rush into the unconscious, no hallucinations or cosmic apercus; just a pleasant but emotionally draining communion.
>
> *(Stevens, 1987: 289)*

Indeed, researchers were at pains to distinguish MDMA from existing psychedelics, instead coining new descriptors. MDMA was an 'entactogen', or even an 'empathogen' although some researchers rejected the latter, suggesting that it might be unattractive to putative psychiatric patients, and that anyway, 'MDMA do[es] more than simply generate empathy' (Adamson, 1985; Nichols, 1986: 307).

Writing in 1986, Jerome Beck and Patricia Morgan confirmed its multiple uses in the Lone Star State; '[o]ne reason for its popularity in Texas was undoubtedly the open sales of MDMA in well-patronized, mostly student-oriented bars and in gay bars' (Beck and Morgan, 1986: 291). Consumers continued to ascribe MDMA a number of different properties; *Newsweek* reported that MDMA 'has become popular over the last two years on college campuses, where it is considered an aphrodisiac', while others 'described it as a "yuppie psychedelic" whose popularity was spreading rapidly among educated professionals in their thirties and forties' (Beck and Morgan, 1986: 292). Indeed, Beck and Morgan concluded that MDMA 'seems to possess a multiple personality' (Beck and Morgan, 1986: 290). And despite its growing popularity, not everyone in Texas was having a wholly enjoyable time on it either. The late musician and poet David Berman, a man not unaccustomed to a variety of intoxicants, recounted his experiences in Austin the summer before ecstasy's criminalisation in 1985:

> I can honestly say I'm glad it was outlawed. After three months of its use I had lost all discretion and was prepared to trust just about anyone. Worse yet, it was turning me into a joiner. That's not who I am.
>
> *(Berman, 2002)*

Beck and Morgan pointed out that, even at this juncture in the mid-1980s, '[a]lthough MDMA has been described occasionally as a "party drug," that is not its most common use pattern' (Beck and Morgan, 1986: 293). They allowed however that Dallas was an exception, and its nightclubs, most especially the one designed by architect Phillip Starck, would anticipate ecstasy's primary use over the coming decades. The Starck Club was notable not just for its chic design and high-profile guests, such as Grace Jones and Annie Lennox, but because the intoxicant of choice amongst its clientele was overwhelmingly ecstasy. 'X' was available at the bar, in common with many other clubs in Dallas where '[y]ou would order a couple of cocktails and two hits of X and put it on your Master Card' (Beck and Rosenbaum, 1994: 45). But at the Starck Club, the musical soundtrack was also significant, with the DJ's selections of synth-pop and electro foreshadowing the close association that MDMA would develop with electronic music later in the decade (West, 1989; Gonsher, 2016).

But MDMA's surging popularity in Texas was fast bringing it to the attention of the DEA and local politicians. Senator Lloyd Bentsen petitioned the DEA in 1984 to make ecstasy a Schedule 1 drug under the Controlled Substances Act, meaning that MDMA was now considered a drug that 'has high abuse potential, no accepted medical use and no accepted safety for use'. The purported reason for this move was that MDA – MDMA's close chemical analogue discussed earlier – had reportedly been shown to cause brain damage, and the DEA declared that '[a]ll of the evidence … received shows that MDMA abuse has become a nationwide problem and that it poses a serious health threat' (Associated Press, 1985). An emergency ban of MDMA took effect in June of 1985, and was made permanent the following year.

The criminalisation of MDMA had a number of ripple effects, some immediate, and some longer-lasting. For the Starck Club, this meant a raid from the DEA on 7 August 1986, and a temporary revoking of its dance licence (Gonsher, 2016). In Dallas more widely, according to Beck and Rosenbaum, 'Ecstasy had become "last year's fad"' (Beck and Rosenbaum, 1994: 46). But perhaps more significantly, an unintentional and long-term effect of the Schedule 1 designation was to push ecstasy firmly into the category of an intoxicant, now that medical and therapeutic research on the drug was no longer possible. No longer were psychiatrists able to use it as an adjunct to psychotherapy, and its reputation as a recreational drug was secured. While its criminalisation may have temporarily suppressed its use in Dallas, elsewhere it was only just taking off. Indeed, the pre-criminalisation scenes of hedonism at the Starck Club had set a blueprint for ecstasy's use globally.

'E is for England': ecstasy and dance culture in the UK, 1986–2009

Ecstasy's first major coverage in the British press was in style magazine *The* Face with two articles over the space of year, which provide an insight into how its recent arrival in the UK was greeted. The first article, in October 1985, reported on its popularity in Texas, but sounded a sceptical note about its effects, drawing unfavourable parallels with LSD in the 1960s:

> Whatever it tells us of the times, its users generally agree MDMA is not "ecstasy". It can make you feel very close and empathetic – you might feel like hugging your friends – but the affection it inspires is unlikely to send anyone into the frenzied raptures common in the Haight/Ashbury district [of San Francisco] in 1967. Ecstasy is a misleading name; the drug is so-called more for reasons of promotion than revolution.
>
> *(Naysmyth, 1985: 91)*

Journalist Peter Naysmyth's lukewarm tone was underlined by a DEA-affiliated chemist Ronald Siegel's affirmation that he had 'heard a report of someone locked in a foetal position for three days', although Siegel also conceded that other 'people [have] loving, harmonious experiences'. There seemed little evidence of ecstasy successfully transitioning to British nightlife; Naysmyth quoted an 'anonymous member of [London's] Soho club-land' saying '[p]ersonally I find it boring ... I used to do it when it first came out a few years ago, but now I find cocaine a better buzz... and it's cheaper'. Ecstasy's future in the UK seemed to be more likely to be in the clinic than club-land; radical psychiatrist R.D. Laing complained, 'it's a shame it's been criminalised because it could have taken its place in the pharmacopoeia ... It made me feel how all of us would like to think we are anyway' (Naysmyth, 1985: 91–92). However, there was as little chance of MDMA being a therapeutic adjunct in the UK as there was in the US. Ecstasy had been a Class A drug in the UK since 1977, covered by an amendment to the generic provisions of the Misuse of Drugs Act 1971 for 'other ring-substituted phenylethylamines' (Advisory Council on the Misuse of Drugs, 2009: 7).

Use in the UK was therefore very much set up to be on an illicit recreational basis, a theme that Peter Naysmyth would return to in *The Face* in October 1986, precisely a year after his original article. In this intervening period, 'use of the drug Ecstasy has increased tenfold'. Seemingly popular amongst the young and the fashionable, one 'X-head' interviewed estimated that 'of the main pop groups probably ten have tried it: five have liked it'. This ambivalence revealed a more complex picture than the unbridled enthusiasm that would seemingly later sweep Britain. For this same interviewee, who had tried it first in New York, it was 'simply the most brilliant thing I had ever taken ... [but] the emphasis had shifted from the experience of the drug to the circumstances of its use'. In other words, set and setting were highly important; for Naysmyth, this provoked an unanswered question: 'what about the other five [pop] groups? If it's so magical why didn't they swallow it too?' (Naysmyth, 1986: 53–54).

Naysmyth's second article also addressed a persistent aspect of ecstasy's early coverage in Britain; its reputation as an aphrodisiac. A female 'model in her early twenties' was equivocal about her experiences on ecstasy in general, but stated that 'I think I only felt genuinely Ecstatic on it alone with my boyfriend ... but it's better for touching than for actual sex' before Naysmyth reminded readers that '[i]t's a recognised medical fact that MDMA inhibits male orgasm' (Naysmyth, 1986: 54). This 'fact' would not prevent ecstasy being reported as a 'sex drug' in many later newspaper stories about ecstasy and raves, as they traded on a classic tabloid combination of prurience and moral censoriousness. The most-quoted example of this tendency is The Sun's headline of 24 November 1988, 'Acid Fiends Spike Page Three Girl's Drink' but ecstasy was also described as a 'sexual stimulant' in early reporting by broadsheet newspapers (Anon, 1987; Redhead, 1990: 4; Rietveld, 1993: 46). Such lurid headlines were still very much in the future however, as Naysmyth concluded his article by noting that, '[a] fter a year of Ecstasy in the UK, cynicism – that most persistent of British habits – still held the day' (Naysmyth, 1986: 55).

Nonetheless, this traditional British reserve was soon to be swept away, seemingly by a visit to foreign shores and an imported Balearic culture. This, at least, is the creation myth of raves and acid house, a holiday in Ibiza, a transformative experience with a potent mixture of electronic music and powerful pills, and a desire to recreate some of that magic in London, at clubs such as Shoom, Future and Clink Street (Collin, 1997: 47–74; Garratt, 1998: 87–117; Reynolds, 1998: 58–66; Melville, 2020: 145–152). This metropole-centric tale has of course been disputed by other accounts, which draw attention to the nascent house music scenes in Manchester, Leeds or Sheffield (Anniss, 2020), but regardless of these origins, 'the histories of British House music and Ecstasy are inseparable' (Metcalfe, 1997: 166). Indeed, it was this pairing that took ecstasy from being a drug dabbled with by a fashionable minority to the globalised mass intoxicant that it is today. A hitherto unremarked aspect of ecstasy was the energy that it gave users over a trip of between four and six hours. This drive, and the apparently pleasurable combination of its euphoric effects with repetitive electronic music such as 'acid house', made it an intoxicant highly conducive to dancing.[6]

What started at small clubs in major cities was soon spilling out into rural and suburban areas, bringing acid house and its attendant intoxicant firmly into the public eye. Restrictive licencing laws meant that most clubs closed at 3 AM or earlier, and given how long it took for ecstasy's effects to wear off, this meant that alternative, unlicenced venues for parties without curfew needed to be found. In places like Blackburn, proximal to the clubs of Manchester, this meant the disused factories left by post-industrial decline (Hemment, 1998). Near London meanwhile, it meant improvised spaces off the M25, a major road that formed an 'orbital' around the capital:

> Over the course of 1989, promoters such as World Dance, Genesis, Helter Skelter, and Energy succeeded in setting acid house nights free of the urban core's constrictions, staging ever more elaborate Orbital parties in borrowed and rented fields, the odd warehouse, or some other similarly vacant megastructure.
>
> *(Clover, 2009: 64)*

Such megastructures famously included White Waltham airfield, near Maidenhead, where '11,000 youngsters [went] drug crazy at Britain's biggest-ever Acid party' in an 'Ecstasy Airport', according to the front page of *The Sun* newspaper (Kellaway and Hughes, 1989). The same tabloid had the previous year warned its readers of 'the evil of ecstasy' and 'the danger drug that is sweeping discos and ruining lives' (Evison and Willis, 1988), while questions in the House of Commons were being raised about how the government aimed to respond to this 'acid house cult' (Written Answers (Commons): Home Department 'Acid House Cult', HC Deb 14 November 1988 vol. 140 c392W).

A 'moral panic' similar to that which had greeted previous subcultures was therefore underway, with ecstasy and acid house as 'folk devils' in the minds of the British establishment and media (Cohen, 1972). But while, no doubt, much of the tabloid hysteria was confected, ecstasy had by the end of 1989 been implicated in the deaths of several young people, providing hard evidence of its dangers for those that sought it.[7] Governmental campaigns, such as *The Effects Can Last Forever* posters mentioned in the introduction of this chapter, therefore played up the potential lethality of ecstasy, while legislation introduced in 1990 by Conservative MP Graham Bright, 'commonly known as the acid house party Bill', attempted to curb the spread of illegal raves (Graham Bright, 'Increase of Penalties: England and Wales' HC Deb, 27 April 1990, c652).

But as the introduction also detailed, such actions did little to curtail enthusiasm for ecstasy consumption or raves. Popular culture was saturated with winking reference to the drug. The techno-pop group The Shamen mischievously sneaked a song with a chorus that sounded a lot like 'Es are good' onto *Top of the Pops* on BBC television (Garratt, 1998: 256), while comedian Keith Allen attempted to include the lines 'E is for England/England starts with an E' in New Order's 'World in Motion', their official song for the English football [soccer] team at the 1990 World Cup (Russell, 2018). Organisers of raves would later assert that 'Ecstasy united black, white, yellow, and brown people as one … an across-the-board mixture of races holding hands and giving out total love and respect for one another' (Anthony, 2002: 50). Further bold claims for the universalising affect and transformative effects of ecstasy included its role in ending football hooliganism, as members of rival 'firms' apparently abandoned hostilities after dancing together in clubs (Saunders, 1993: 35–38; Collin, 1997:

129–137). Even more improbably, some journalists suggested that ecstasy could play a part in halting sectarian violence in Northern Ireland (Hollywood, 1997; Gilbert and Pearson, 1999: 4). Others believed that the changes brought by ecstasy were on a more personal level:

> The freedom to behave as you want may not seem like a real revolution to fussy old Marxist men … To have the opportunity to forget classification by race, class or gender allows a close examination of what unites us rather than our differences.
>
> *(Wright, 1998: 240)*

The former comment by Mary Anna Wright might be read as a mild rebuke to her editor George McKay, who had elsewhere sceptically suggested that many of the freedoms attributed to rave and ecstasy were weak echoes of the sixties counterculture and just as likely to be co-opted and nullified by contemporary capitalism (McKay, 1996: 103–126). More recently, media scholar Caspar Melville has contended that 'we should treat such claims for the world-changing nature of acid house and rave with caution. They can burden club culture with a political and social significance that they are not able to support' (Melville, 2020: 140). This slippage between 'ecstasy' and 'acid house and rave' reveals how intimately the two are intertwined in accounts of the period, but it is also important to note that contemporary observers also questioned both the cultural diversity and supposed radical nature of raves. Keir Starmer, at this time a young lawyer, would defend party organisers as part of his role with the National Council for Civil Liberties, but also argued that the notion 'that the "acid house" phenomenon should be seen as subversive is particularly bizarre. A car, a telephone and a fairly healthy bank account are essentials for the party-goer' (Rose, 1989; Starmer, 1990: 4).

But even if pills were priced at an average of £18, a reported 500,000 people were continuing to take ecstasy in Britain in 1993 (Anon, 1993). Subversive or not, ecstasy was now firmly established in British nightlife; in 1995, *The Guardian* newspaper would comment that 'drug-taking has become an integral part of youth culture' (Anon, 1995). While clubs were still important venues for consumption, the Criminal Justice and Public Order Act of 1994 had, despite the efforts of a coalition of resistance and protests, effectively eradicated large-scale outdoor raves (Huq, 1999; Alwakeel, 2010). The highly publicised death of Leah Betts after celebrating her eighteenth birthday with a house party at which her parents were present in the village of Latchingdon, near Basildon, Essex in late 1995 brought home how quotidian ecstasy use had become, and how it had been decoupled from the dance culture in which it emerged. This tragic incident of course also marked a revival of the moral panic around ecstasy, with widespread news coverage and billboards, echoing those used in *The Effects Can Last Forever* campaign, that warned '[j]ust one ecstasy tablet took Leah Betts' (Martin, 2005).

While highly visible at the time and much referenced since, it is questionable how much longer-term impact Betts' death had on public attitudes or private sensibilities (Anon, 1996; Gilbert and Pearson, 1999: 2). In 2000, four years after providing expert witness for Betts' inquest, and eight years after penning the article that warned users were engaged in a 'dance of death', leading toxicologist John Henry would state, on comedian Sacha Baron Cohen's *Da Ali G Show*, that 'some people can take two or three Es and [have] no problems' (Baron Cohen, 2000). Partly, this was due to the declining MDMA content of pills (Cole, 2014: 47), but it was also an admission that the vast majority of users could do so relatively unproblematically.[8] A decline in MDMA content was also accompanied by a dramatic fall in street price, such that pills could be bought for under £3 in most parts of Britain (Measham, 2004:

314). Ecstasy by the latter half of the 1990s was therefore a cheap and accessible intoxicant that was widely used by a variety of people, many of whom were not at all connected with dance subcultures. Indeed, as this chapter has maintained, a focus on both the extreme harms of ecstasy and its role in the so-called Second Summer of Love of 1988 has obscured the varied contexts and experiences of its use as an intoxicant.

One of the more unusual users and most vociferous advocates of ecstasy during the 1990s was a man in his fifties who had a strong distaste for raves and dance music, but who nevertheless became a cult figure for many young people. Nicholas Saunders, described as the 'Buddha of euphoria', was up until this point best-known as the author of countercultural guide *Alternative London*, and the hippie entrepreneur of Neal's Yard in Covent Garden, London (Bellos, 1995). After his first experience with ecstasy in 1988, in which he felt that the drug had cured his 'mild depression' and made him feel 'more positive and healthy', Saunders began to research the drug intensively (Saunders, 1993: 9). Dismayed at what he perceived to be the lack of accurate or balanced information on ecstasy, he self-published three books on ecstasy from 1993 onwards until his untimely death in a car accident in 1998. These books, including the first *E is for Ecstasy* which sold in the tens of thousands, were an eclectic mix of the latest scientific evidence, ethnographic and sociological observations, information on safe usage and harm reduction, and advice on the potential physical and mental health impacts (Albery, 1998). Saunders' books also provided an indication of the wide range of users, exploring the personal experiences of people who had used it for 'problem solving', 'improving relationships', a 'mini vacation', 'artistic expression' and even spiritual purposes, citing a Benedictine monk who noted that it had facilitated his meditation (Saunders, 1993: 20, 88–93).

But while there were clearly a range of users, not all of whom were connected to dance cultures, clubbers remained ecstasy's primary consumer group. And although, as we can see from Henry's unguarded comments, the drug began to be seen as relatively safe even by those most initially alarmed by its popularity, it also began to decline in usage around the turn of the millennium. Moral panics shifted to other psychoactive substances used in clubs such as ketamine or 2-CB, and older intoxicants such as cocaine and alcohol returned to, or continued to rise in popularity (Measham, 2004). Indeed, supply problems, the result of seizures of safrole or sassafras oil (a chemical precursor commonly used in MDMA production) in Cambodia, brought an effective 'ecstasy drought' across Europe between 2008 and 2009 (Power, 2013; Kemprai et al., 2020). 'Legal highs' such as mephedrone (4-methylmethcathinone) were used as alternative intoxicants, once again prompting tabloid newspapers to express alarm at another apparently new drug harming young lives (Fleming, 2010).

Conclusion

The first half of this chapter concentrated on the birth and reinvention of MDMA in Germany and the US, while the second half has considered its arrival in Britain and entwinement with the 'rave' scene. But while raves were most visible in late 1980s Britain, comparable music and drug subcultures also developed in the two countries that might be considered MDMA's parents. In the US, ecstasy's surging popularity was addressed in 2001 by then Senator Joe Biden's Reducing Americans' Vulnerability to Ecstasy (RAVE) Act, which, while not entering the legislature, paved the way for 2003s Illicit Drug Anti-Proliferation Act (Anderson, 2014, 2009). In Germany meanwhile, ecstasy played its part in the vibrant techno culture which greeted the fall of the Wall in 1989, and the yearly Love Parade organised by DJ Dr Motte, which attracted up to a million attendees at its height (Borneman and Senders, 2000; Denk and von Thülen, 2012). Berlin's clubs remain an international destination for techno tourists (Rapp, 2009). These are of course just two examples of the global spread of dance cultures. As Matthew Collin states, 'from the nineties onwards, it became possible to find DJs playing almost any style in any major city – dubstep in Istanbul, psytrance in Shanghai, foot-work in Belgrade' (Collin, 2018: 6).

As Karen Joe-Laidler et al. point out, accompanying these globalised dance cultures are globalised intoxicants; primarily ecstasy, but also ketamine, speed and other novel substances clustered under the umbrella term of 'club drugs'. And as they also suggest, the language that young people use to express their feelings about their drug experiences is disarmingly similar across disparate locales (Joe-Laidler et al., 2014). The apparently universalising affect of ecstasy encourages a discourse that highlights this imagined connectivity, accentuating the similarities between ecstasy consumers while neglecting their (important) differences. As sociologist Maria Pini has argued, there is a tendency to 'write about ravers in terms of sexless, ageless, raceless and otherwise non-specific or unsituated generals' (Pini, 2001: 7). This chapter has however insisted that such impulses are resisted. It has argued, after Thaemlitz, that ecstasy is in fact 'hyper-specific'. As well as highlighting some of the different contexts in which ecstasy has been used, it has demonstrated that until the drug became so intimately associated with the early rave scene, the drug was described in many different ways by its consumers, even as 'boring'. Between the unfortunate fatalities and life-changing experiences of 'ecstasy evangelists' lay the vast majority of users, most of whom enjoyed the intoxicant, while some didn't (Shewan et al., 2000). Indeed, the point that this chapter has made is quite a simple one: that is, for ecstasy to be considered just like any other intoxicant, where historical, geographical, cultural and social contexts are important factors in its consumption.

This need for nuanced and critical historical research on ecstasy has arguably gained in urgency over the last few years, as ecstasy has returned to public consciousness and popular use in many countries in the Global North. In many ways, ecstasy users are better informed than ever before, with home testing kits for pills available to order online, dedicated charities such as The Loop in the UK providing harm reduction advice, and qualitative and quantitative reviews of pills accessible from websites such as pillreports.com and at point of sale on the darkweb (Power, 2013). Nevertheless, there have been rising numbers of deaths associated with the so-called 'super strength pills'; those that contain between 200 mg and 300 mg of MDMA, which provide a massive high but also increase the risk of overdose (Coldwell, 2017). While these pills are of palpable concern to public health authorities and harm reduction charities, their existence also invites historical reflection on the nature of intoxicants. It makes plain and obvious the point that this chapter has strived to explain; that taking a pill at a festival in 2019 was not the same as taking a pill in 1989 at a rave, or in 1999 at a 'super-club', or even resorting to mephedrone during the 'ecstasy drought' of 2009. Even within the relatively culturally homogenous British context, these are all radically different historically and temporally contingent moments of intoxication. More histories exploring these complex and specific histories need to be written. 'Set' and 'setting' are as applicable to ecstasy as they have been to other intoxicants.

Notes

1 While in this chapter I use the terms MDMA and ecstasy more or less interchangeably, there is a literature that disputes their conflation (Edland-Gryta, Sandberg and Pedersen, 2017).

2 Leckey's video artwork, which traces a continuity from the amphetamine-fuelled Northern Soul parties of the 1970s to the illegal raves of the late 1980s, is from 1999. Deller's film, originally produced for Frieze in 2018, received wider screening on BBC4 in 2019. Whil placing rave in its cultural and political context, it was significant for its underplaying of the role of ecstasy.

3 Reynolds' book was published under the title *Generation Ecstasy* for the US market.
4 Thaemlitz's preferred pronouns are alternating 'she/he' and 'her/his'.
5 *PiHKAL* also contains a fictionalised account of Shulgin's rediscovery of MDMA, as well as detailed information on the chemical composition and tasting notes of many other synthetic psychoactive substances.
6 Acid house was so named because of the lysergic, trippy qualities of music made using the Roland TB-303 bass synthesi, most notably Phuture's Acid Trax, but also because LSD was the drug of choice at the gay, Black clubs of Chicago where house music originated (Salkind, 2019). 'Chicago house went hand in hand with stimulants and hallucinogens' (Reynolds, 1998: 26).
7 The deaths of two young–women Janet Mayes, in October 1988, and Claire Leighton in July 1989–received widespread media coverage, although they were in fact preceded by that of Ian Larcombe, 'who had swallowed a bag of eighteen tablets and suffered a fatal heart attack after being stopped by police on the way to a club in June [1988]' (Collin, 1997: 80).
8 Mean MDMA content of ecstasy pills fell from 103 mg in 1991 to 74 mg in 2000.

References

Adamson S (ed.) (1985) *Through the Gateway of the Heart: Accounts of Experiences with MDMA and Other Empathogenic Substances*. San Francisco, CA: Four Trees.

Advisory Council on the Misuse of Drugs (2009) *MDMA ('ecstasy'): A Review of Its Harms and Classification under the Misuse of Drugs Act 1971*. London: Central Office of Information.

Albery N (1998) Obituary: Nicholas Saunders: Putting ecstasy on the internet. *The Guardian* 5 February 1998: 14.

Alwakeel R (2010) The aesthetics of protest in UK Rave. *Dancecult: Journal of Electronic Dance Music Culture* 1(2): 50–62.

Anderson TL (2009) *Rave Culture: The Alteration and Decline of a Philadelphia Music Scene*. Philadelphia, PA: Temple University Press.

Anderson TL (2014) Molly deaths and the failed war on drugs. *Contexts* 20 November 2014. https://contexts.org/articles/molly-deaths-and-the-failed-war-on-drugs/ Last accessed 13 November 2020.

Anniss M (2020) *Join the Future: Bleep Techno and the Birth of British Bass Music*. London: Velocity Press.

Anon (1987) Six held after drug seizure. *The Times* 14 May 1987: 2.

Anon (1993) Ecstasy: Market update. *The Economist* 329(7837): 68.

Anon (1995) An infantile political debate: Why can't we have a sensible discussion about drug-taking? *The Guardian* 15 August 1995: 10.

Anon (1996) The effects of E on harm reduction. *DrugLink* January/February 1996: 4.

Anthony W (2002) *Class of 88: The True Acid House Experience*. London: Virgin Books.

Associated Press (1985) U.S. will Ban 'Ecstasy,' A Hallucinogenic drug. *New York Times* 1 June 1985: 6.

Baron Cohen S (2000) *Da Ali G Show: Series 1, Episode 4: Mohamed Al Fayed*. Broadcast 21 April 2000, Channel 4.

Benzenhöfer U and Passie T (2010) Rediscovering MDMA (ecstasy): The role of the American chemist Alexander T. Shulgin. *Addiction* 105(8): 1355–1361. DOI: 10.1111/j.1360-0443.2010.02948.x.

Beck J and Morgan PA (1986) Designer drug confusion: A focus on MDMA. *Journal of Drug Education* 16(3): 287–302. DOI: 10.2190/TW2B-2P4A-KGUM-6102.

Beck J and Rosenbaum M (1994) *Pursuit of Ecstasy: The MDMA Experience*. New York: SUNY.

Bellos A (1995) The Buddha of Euphoria. *The Guardian* 6 April 1995: 4.

Berman D (2002) The summer before the night ecstasy became Illegal in the State of Texas. *Arthur* 29 March 2002. https://arthurmag.com/2002/03/29/david-bermanon-ecstasy/ Last accessed 12 November 2020.

Borneman J and Senders S (2000) Politics without a head: Is the 'Love Parade' a new form of political identification? *Cultural Anthropology* 15(2): 294–317. DOI: 10.1525/CAN.2000.15.2.294.

Champion S (ed.) (1997) *Disco Biscuits: New Fiction from the Chemical Generation*. London: Sceptre.

Clark P (2019) Legacies of Rave in Britain. *History Workshop Online* 7 November 2019. https://www.historyworkshop.org.uk/legacies-of-rave-in-britain/ Last accessed 10 November 2020.

Clover J (2009) *1989: Bob Dylan Didn't Have to Sing About This*. Berkeley: University of California Press.

Cohen S (1972) *Folk Devils and Moral Panics: The Creation of the Mods and Rockers*. London: Routledge.

Coldwell W (2017) 'Five friends go out and take ecstasy, one doesn't come home': The rise of super-strength pills. *The Guardian* 22 July 2017 https://www.theguardian.com/society/2017/jul/22/friends-out-ecstasy-deaths-highest-level-pills Last accessed 13 November 2020.

Cole JC (2014) MDMA and the 'Ecstasy Paradigm'. *Journal of Psychoactive Drugs* 46(1): 44–56. DOI: 10.1080/02791072.2014.878148.

Collin M (1997) *Altered State: The Story of Ecstasy Culture and Acid House*. London: Serpents Tail.

Collin M (2018) *Rave On: Global Adventures in Electronic Dance Music*. Chicago: University of Chicago Press.

Denk F and von Thülen S (2012) *Der Klang der Familie: Berlin, Techno und die Wende*. Frankfurt am Main: Suhrkamp.

Edland-Gryta M, Sandberg S and Pedersen W (2017) From ecstasy to MDMA: Recreational drug use, symbolic boundaries, and drug trends. *International Journal of Drug Policy* 50: 1–8. DOI: 10.1016/j.drugpo.2017.07.030

Evison S and Willis P (1988) Evil of ecstasy. *The Sun* 19 October 1988: 16–17.

Fleming N (2010) Miaow-miaow on trial: Truth or trumped-up charges? *New Scientist* 29 March 2010. https://www.newscientist.com/article/dn18712-miaow-miaow-on-trial-truth-or-trumped-up-charges/ Last accessed 10 November 2020.

Freudenmann RW, Öxler F and Bernschneider-Reif S (2006) The origin of MDMA (ecstasy) revisited: The true story reconstructed from the original documents. *Addiction* 101(9): 1241–1245. DOI: 10.1111/j.1360–0443.2006.01511.x

Garratt S (1998) *Adventures in Wonderland: A Decade of Club Culture*. London: Headline.

Gilbert J and Pearson E (1999) *Discographies: Dance Music, Culture and the Politics of Sound*. London: Routledge.

Gonsher A (2016) Nightclubbing: Starck club. *Red Bull Music Academy* 29 February 2016. https://daily.redbullmusicacademy.com/2016/02/nightclubbing-starck-club Last accessed 10 November 2020.

Hemment D (1998) Dangerous dancing and disco riots: The Northern Warehouse parties, 208–227 in McKay G (ed.) *DiY Culture: Party & Protest in Nineties Britain*. London: Verso.

Henry JA (1992) Ecstasy and the dance of death. *British Medical Journal* 305: 5–6. DOI: 10.1136/bmj.305.6844.5.

Hollywood B (1997) Dancing in the dark: Ecstasy, the dance culture, and moral panic in post ceasefire Northern Ireland. *Critical Criminology* 8: 62–77. DOI: 10.1007/BF02461136.

Huq R (1999) The right to rave: Opposition to the criminal justice and Public Order Act 1994 15–33 in Jordan T and Lent A (eds) *Storming the Millennium: The New Politics of Change*. London: Lawrence & Wishart.

Joe-Laidler K, Hunt G and Moloney M (2014) 'Tuned Out or Tuned In': Spirituality and youth drug use in global times. *Past & Present* 222 Suppl 9: 61–80. DOI: 10.1093/pastj/gtt029.

Kellaway R and Hughes S (1989) Spaced out! *The Sun* 26 June 1989: 1.

Kemprai P, Protim Mahanta B, Sut D et al. (2020) Review on safrole: Identity shift of the 'candy shop' aroma to a carcinogen and deforester. *Flavour and Fragrance Journal* 35: 5–23. DOI: 10.1002/ffj.3521.

Kouimtsidis C, Schifano F, Sharp T et al. (2006) Neurological and psychopathological sequelae associated with a lifetime intake of 40,000 ecstasy tablets. *Psychosomatics* 47(1): 86–87. DOI: 10.1176/appi.psy.47.1.86.

Leary T (1985) XTC: The drug of the 80s. *DOPE Magazine*, July 1985: 75–76.

Major Problems "The Effects Can Last Forever" Discogs.com user comment by Alain_Patrick. https://www.discogs.com/release/4571-The-Effects-Can-Last-Forever/reviews#c55445 Last accessed 10 November 2020.

Martin L. 'Ten years have passed – Yet I'm still haunted by Leah's death'. *The Observer* 30 October 2005 https://www.theguardian.com/society/2005/oct/30/drugsandalcohol.drugs Last accessed 10 November 2020.

McKay G (1996) *Senseless Acts of Beauty: Cultures of Resistance since the Sixties*. London: Verso.

Measham F (2004). The decline of ecstasy, the rise of 'binge' drinking and the persistence of pleasure. *Probation Journal* 51(4): 309–326. DOI: 10.1177/0264550504048220.

Melville C (2020) *It's a London Thing: How Rare Groove, Acid House and Jungle Remapped the City*. Manchester: Manchester University Press.

Metcalfe S (1997) Ecstasy evangelists and psychedelic warriors, in Melechi A (ed.) *Psychedelia Britannica: Hallucinogenic Drugs in Britain* (pp. 166–184). London: Turnaround.

Naranjo C (1983) *The Healing Journey*. New York: Random House.
Naysmyth P (1985) Ecstasy: A Yuppie way of knowledge. *The Face* October 1985: 88–92.
Naysmyth P (1986) The agony and the ecstasy. *The Face* October 1986: 52–55.
Nichols DE (1986) Differences between the mechanism of action of MDMA, MBDB, and the classic Hallucinogens. Identification of a new therapeutic class: Entactogens. *Journal of Psychoactive Drugs* 18(4): 305–313. DOI: 10.1080/02791072.1986.10472362.
Passie T and Benzenhöfer U (2016) The history of MDMA as an underground drug in the United States, 1960–1979. *Journal of Psychoactive Drugs* 48(2): 67–75. DOI: 10.1080/02791072.2015.1128580.
Pentney AR (2001) An exploration of the history and controversies surrounding MDMA and MDA. *Journal of Psychoactive Drugs* 33(3): 213–221. DOI: 10.1080/02791072.2001.10400568.
Pini M (2001) *Club Cultures and Female Subjectivity: The Move from Home to House*. Basingstoke: Palgrave.
Power M (2013) *Drugs 2.0: The Web Revolution That's Changing How the World Gets High*. London: Portobello.
Rapp T (2009) *Lost and Sound: Berlin, Techno und der Easyjetset*. Frankfurt am Main: Suhrkamp.
Redhead S (1990) *The End-of-the-Century Party: Youth Pop and the Rise of the Madchester*. Manchester: Manchester University Press.
Redhead S (ed.) (1993) *Rave Off: Politics and Deviance in Contemporary Youth Culture*. Aldershot: Avebury.
Reynolds S (1998) *Energy Flash: A Journey through Rave Music and Dance Culture*. London: Faber and Faber.
Richert, L (2019) *Break On Through: Radical Psychiatry and the American Counterculture*. Cambridge: MIT Press, 2019.
Rietveld H (1993) Living the dream, 41–78 in Redhead S (ed.) *Rave Off: Politics and Deviance in Contemporary Youth Culture*. Aldershot: Avebury.
Rose D (1989) Acid house party hosts to Sue police. *The Guardian* 24 August 1989: 3.
Russell M (2018) World in motion: The making of the greatest World Cup song. *GQ* 15 June 2018 https://www.gq-magazine.co.uk/article/world-in-motion-the-making-of-the-greatest-world-cup-song Last accessed 17 November 2020.
Salkind ME (2019) *Do You Remember House?: Chicago's Queer of Color Undergrounds*. New York: Oxford University Press.
Saulwick A (ed.) (2015) *Terre Thaemlitz/DJ Sprinkles: The Arrogance of Optimism*. Berlin: mono.kultur.
Saunders N (1993) *E is for Ecstasy*. London: Nicholas Saunders.
Shewan D, Dalgarno P and Reith G (2000) Perceived risk and risk reduction among ecstasy users: The role of drug, set, and setting. *International Journal of Drug Policy* 10(6): 431–453. DOI: 10.1016/S0955-3959(99)00038-9.
Shulgin AT and Shulgin A (1991) *PiHKAL: A Chemical Love Story*. Berkeley, CA: Transform Press.
Siegel RK (1986) MDMA: Nonmedical use and intoxication. *Journal of Psychoactive Drugs* 18(4):349–354. DOI: 10.1080/02791072.1986.10472368.
Speed M (2019) *Mark Leckey: Fiorucci Made Me Hardcore*. London: Afterall.
Starmer K (1990) The party's over – Acid house and the law. *Socialist Lawyer* 10 Winter/Spring 1990: 4–5.
Stevens J (1987) *Storming Heaven: LSD and the American Dream*. New York: Grove Press.
Stolaroff MJ (2004) *The Secret Chief Revealed: Conversations with a Pioneer of the Underground Psychedelic Therapy Movement*. Sarasota, FL: MAPS.
Thaemlitz T [DJ Sprinkles] (2008) *Midtown 120 Blues*, released by Mule Musiq. Available at https://www.comatonse.com/writings/2008_midtown120blues.html Last accessed 9 November 2020.
Thornton S (1995) *Club Cultures: Music, Media and Subcultural Capital*. Cambridge: Polity Press.
West R (1989) Ecstasy & Agony at the Starck club. *D Magazine* October 1989 https://www.dmagazine.com/publications/d-magazine/1989/october/ecstasy-agony/ Last accessed 10 November 2020.
Wibberly C and Whitelaw S (1990) Health promotion, drugs and the moral high ground. *International Journal of Drug Policy* 2(3): 11–14.
Withington P (2014) Introduction: Cultures of intoxication. *Past & Present Past & Present* 222(Suppl 9): 9–33. DOI: 10.1093/pastj/gtt027.
Wright MA (1998) The Great British Ecstasy revolution, 228–242 in McKay G (ed.) *DiY Culture: Party & Protest in Nineties Britain*. London: Verso.
Zinberg NE (1984) *Drug, Set, and Setting: The Basis for Controlled Intoxicant Use*. New Haven, CT: Yale University Press.

PART III

Intoxicating Settings

9

THE SOCIAL WORK OF COFFEE

Coffee consumption in bosnia and herzegovina and the bosnian diaspora

Ana Croegaert

Introduction

When I began to explore what it was like for refugees of the 1990s political violence in former Yugoslavia to be relocated to the United States, I didn't anticipate how much I would learn about the centrality of coffee drinking practices to those in this wartime diaspora. Refugees who had been forced to leave their homes under the threat of violence had little time to pack and prepare, and had to be selective about what to bring with them—only as much as one could carry—and people often tried to include their traditional stove-top coffee pots, *džezve*, and handmills, *mlinovi*, in their hastily packed suitcases. If these belongings were lost, "disappeared," or stolen during people's escape, they were among the first objects people sought to replace once they had achieved a threshold of stability in their new home.

People preferred to purchase the finely ground powder-like imported Yugoslav coffee brands at the "ethnic" groceries in their new home towns (when available) rather than the less expensive mass-produced American brands, or the much more expensive small-batch locally roasted artisanal coffee beans. Refugees who opened small cafes and eateries catering to the diaspora distinguished their "American" coffee brewed with automated drip machines, from "Bosnian" stove-top coffee, sometimes also glossed as "Turkish" coffee on their menus (Croegaert 2011: 472). The elder generation used coffee invitations to establish and maintain friendships, and reprimanded the younger generation for ordering coffees to-go rather than sitting and savoring their coffee and conversation. In homes where Bosnian coffee was rarely prepared, coffee service objects such as džezve, mlinovi, and *fildžani*—small porcelain cups traditionally used to drink the coffee—were displayed along with other valued tableware and family photographs in hutches and atop buffets. Coffee drinking rituals and associated objects permeated everyday life and emerged as a major theme during the course of my research (Figure 9.1).

Four of the six former Yugoslav republics appear in a list of the top 15 coffee-consuming countries: Slovenia (4), Serbia (6), Bosnia-Herzegovina (11), and Croatia (14).[1] Along with Brazil and the Dominican Republic, the western Balkan countries are unique in this coffee-consuming cohort as not belonging to the so-called "first world" capitalist democracies to emerge during the Cold War.[2] Yugoslavia was sometimes considered "third world" in the language of Cold War geopolitics, and, along with Egypt, Ghana, and Indonesia, was

DOI: 10.4324/9780429058141-13

Figure 9.1 Ismeta Buffet Display Qur'an Bosnian landscape painting džezva fildžan šešerluk

a founding member of the Non-Aligned Movement comprising the countries allied neither with NATO, nor with the Soviet Union. However, unlike Brazil, the largest coffee producer in the world, and the coffee-growing Dominican Republic, there is no domestic production in the western Balkans. The region's longstanding coffee culture relies on coffee imports. Thus, as with the majority of the world's top coffee-consuming countries, consumers in the former Yugoslavia are separated from coffee producers along the commodity chain (Doane 2010, West 2012).

In this chapter, I explore the coffee-consuming cultures of one of these countries, Bosnia-Herzegovina, including that of Bosnia's refugee diaspora.[3] Scholars looking to understand consumption practices attend to how people understand the relationship between objects—including food—of consumption to their consumers. This leads to insights as to the dynamic relational processes by which meanings are attributed to both objects and people in acts of consumption, and during times of social and material changes these meanings may take on increased significance as people seek to give shape and meaning to such society-wide shifts (Caldwell 2009, Miller 1998, Patico 2009). Bosnia's coffee cultures are shaped by its histories as an Ottoman province from the late fifteenth to the late nineteenth centuries, and a Habsburg province from 1878 to 1918. During the twentieth century, Bosnia was a part of two countries that arose from the former Ottoman and then Habsburg states: the Kingdom of Yugoslavia (1918–1941), and the former Socialist Federal Republic of Yugoslavia (1945–1990s). In the political violence that erupted during conflicts over post-Cold War governance (1992–1995), fully half of the small country's population of 4.4 million was forcibly displaced, and some became part of a globally dispersed diaspora estimated at more than one million people (Halilovich et al. 2018).[4] These refugees brought their coffee drinking traditions with them.

This chapter focuses on the social practices and material culture of Bosnian coffee drinking to explore connections between coffee drinking and power. Coffee scholarship shows that consumption practices and patterns related to the beverage provide insight into politics of class formations and status distinctions that are often expressed in frictions over social norms. From the 1990s flourishing of gourmet coffee products in North America following free trade deregulation of the international market that made the consumption of "small-batch locally roasted" coffee a sign of "yuppie" status (Roseberry 1996), coincident "fair trade" projects linked to Central and South American producers (Doane 2010), efforts to forecast Turkey's entry to the European Union (Gursel 2009), to Melanesian producers' endeavors to expand and intensify their exchange relations throughout a coffee commodity chain originating in Papua New Guinea extending to markets in Europe and Australia (West 2012), coffee drinking is embedded in systems of social inequality and saturated in notions of morality. Looking at Bosnian coffee drinking practices offers a view to the beverage's role as a critical symbolic place-maker in diasporic and culturally dynamic contexts (Low and Lawrence-Zuñiga 2003).

I begin with a brief history of coffee and coffeehouses in the region and show that tracing Bosnian coffee traditions delineates longstanding connections between Muslim and Christian Europeans and highlights shifting regional social norms. I then describe and discuss the coffee memories shared by Mahira, who fled Bosnia's capital city, Sarajevo, during the 1990s siege when she was in her late sixties. Mahira's recollections of coffee drinking show how the practice is key to establishing and defining public space. Next, I look at the youth street cafe coffee culture in a small town outside of post-conflict Mostar, in the Herzegovina region, in the late aughts. After the war in this small town, coffeehouses had emerged as ethnically segregated spaces; yet, because the coffeehouses were spatially proximate, such separation was undercut by routine visiting of friends from tables at the coffeehouse nearby. Finally, I reflect on the uses of coffee in a "nomadic monument" in Chicago, 2017, commemorating the wartime genocide against Bosnian Muslims (Bosniaks). Here, Bosnian diaspora artist Aida Šehović and her volunteer partners claim public space through an annual one-day installation of Bosnian coffee service.

Coffee as a Social Stimulant

Coffee's capacity to stimulate the senses and sociality is remarked upon in accounts of coffee drinking in the early modern era. During the sixteenth century across the Ottoman Empire, for example, Yemeni Sufi mystics used a coffee beverage understood to inspire the soul during evening praise ceremonies (Hattox 1985, 24–25, 69). In these prayer rituals, called dhikir/zikir among Muslim subjects in the Empire's Balkan provinces, men gathered together and passed a communal bowl of coffee among their circle, each drinking in order to generate collective stamina for engaging with divine energy—an intoxicating force. Similar to the Eucharist practiced by Ottoman Christian subjects, dhikir coffee was understood as a material, figural conduit among participants, and between divine and human (Bynum 1987, Hattox 1985).

During this same period, coffeehouses were established in cities across the empire. Cairo, Mecca, Damascus, Istanbul and Sarajevo, for example, had coffeehouses where learned men could gather and socialize outside of either the mosque or the tavern—where wine was served. The association of coffee with intoxication among some Sufi mystics, and the similarity of the coffeehouse to the tavern as a non-religious social space led some local religious Muslim authorities to declare coffee and coffeehouses as haram, to be avoided because it was seen to violate interpretations of Islamic conduct that addressed intoxication. Ralph Hattox describes how, in a series of episodic regional decrees issued at the beginning of the sixteenth century, educated religious men (ulema) deemed to have the ability to interpret Islamic texts and teachings proclaimed coffee drinking to be illegal and engaged in efforts to sanction its social uses (Hattox 1985). Yet, prohibition did not prevail; coffee was regarded as an acceptable social stimulant for observant Muslims, and gathering in the coffeehouse would not automatically compromise one's moral standing. The coffeehouse was established extensively across the region with elaborately decorated leisure spaces for wealthy drinkers and more modest structures for laborers.

Coffee drinking spread rapidly in cities throughout the empire and by the late seventeenth century, the Ottomans had introduced coffee drinking to Central Europe (Kafadar 2014). Coffeehouses subsequently arose in cities such as Venice and Vienna and initially were also known as social spaces of consumption primarily reserved for men of the emerging bourgeoisie. During the nineteenth century, political unrest led both Ottoman and Habsburg empires to enact administrative social reforms in efforts to demonstrate tolerance to their subjects and the institution of the coffeehouse expanded, sometimes admitting women of similar status backgrounds as patrons. Prior to this, women would have only been present as audience members when a coffeehouse hosted a performance for families, often during Ramadan (Kafadar 2014, 261). Coffee drinking and coffeehouses, then, were both signs of status and power as well as sources with the potential to ignite resistance to authority. They were seen to demonstrate the social order as well as material with which to rework the social order, a phenomenon that continues today.

Hapsburg coffeehouses, for example, have been admired for their romantic aesthetics, and the Viennese coffeehouse in 2011 was awarded the prized status of being recognized as a U.N.E.S.C.O cultural heritage site deserving of protection, bringing international prestige as well as resources to maintain the actual coffeehouses and ostensibly Viennese cultures of coffee consumption.[5] In her reflections on the role of the Habsburg coffeehouse in various urban heritage and tourist attractions in the city of Trieste, Giulia Caribelli demonstrates that the cafes are a focal point projecting nostalgia both for a cosmopolitan Hapsburg imperial past and for an irredentist Italian nationalist one. In the latter, the imperial origins of the cafes are downplayed and domesticated in tourist guides' explanations, such as one who offers that Trieste's cafes are influenced by the imperial era, but are Italian because they are "'public living rooms,' where one sits and chitchats (dove si va per ciacolare)" (Carabelli 2019, 384). Edin Hajdarpašić points to this processual and permeable potential of the built environment in relation to meaning-making in his discussion of South-eastern Europe's Ottoman and Habsburg past. He includes coffeehouses among other sites such as, "mosques, churches, synagogues, taverns, tombstones, gravesites," whose meanings are not fixed in time; rather, as enduring sites of social encounter and interaction, they are layered with shifting and heterogeneous meanings and perspectives (Hajdarpašić 2008, 721).

Coffee drinking's polysemous qualities have stimulated social belonging and wide-ranging place-making practices throughout the region. In the aftermath of the 1990s wars in former Yugoslavia, including among its diaspora, Bosnian coffee drinking was a way to create space and claim time for pre-war memories of a Yugoslav past. The political conflict over post-Yugoslav governance was increasingly expressed through the language of "ethnicity," and during the 1990s erupted in violent campaigns of "ethnic cleansing" or "un-mixing" that in Bosnia was primarily organized by an ethno-nationalist Bosnian Serb military with assistance from Serbia (Hayden 1996). In addition, some Bosnian Croat militias organized similar campaigns in western Bosnia, including the southern Herzegovina region. As Bosnian Muslims and Bosnians in mixed families were the primary targets of these campaigns, and, with no "national" homeland to which they could flee, these Bosnians also make up the majority of the wartime diaspora.[6] In the coffee stories that follow, I center the lives and the experiences of Bosnian women from diverse age, regional, and ethnic backgrounds, offering what Maria Todorova has called "counterperceptions" to the ethnicity/conflict/harmony rubric that often guides representations of the Balkans (Todorova 2009). Coffee's historic connection to place-making emerges as a prominent theme in pre-war memories and a dynamic practice in people's post-war lives.

"It Was in Sarajevo, on the Hill"

In the late 1800s, ethnographer and folklorist Antun Hangi traversed Bosnia to document the "life and customs" of the country's Muslim citizens. Hangi, a Croatia-born Catholic who lived in Bosnia, published his observations first as a series of essays (1900, Mostar) and soon thereafter compiled in a single text (1906, Sarajevo) featuring numerous sketches and photographs depicting scenes of everyday life. At the time, both Croatia and Bosnia-Herzegovina were Habsburg provinces and Hangi's accounts were meant to appeal to the curiosity of administrators in the provincial capitals and in the imperial capital of Vienna regarding the newly acquired former Ottoman province and its sizable Muslim population.

A grainy photograph on page 54 illustrates that coffee preparation and consumption is a theme in Hangi's book. The photo captures a scene on a historic embankment at a bend in the Miljacka River called Bentbaša in the province's capital city, Sarajevo. A two-story square building with a porch and wooden fence provides the backdrop to a woman standing in the water, bent over as she launders linens in the river, while others appear to be seated on the enclosed porch, drinking coffee. The photograph's caption reads: "coffee and Muslim houses on Bendbaša [sic] above the Miljacka in Sarajevo," and, in a parenthetical caption beneath this, the reader is told how to interpret the significance of these activities and their emplacement: "See how our Muslims are able to choose convenient places for their apartments and parties" (Hangi 1906, 54). While Bentbaša is among the historic sites of Sarajevo's first sixteenth-century coffeehouses, Mahira, born in Sarajevo 26 years after Hangi first published his account, shared a memory of drinking coffee in one of the city's other famed coffeehouses.

On a hazy spring afternoon in 2015 in New Orleans, Louisiana, Mahira sat in a comfortable armchair in her daughter's living room. A soft-hued painting of a wooded meadow hung on the wall above the chair and a platter of colorful fresh fruits sat atop a coffee table stationed in front of the sofa to Mahira's left, upon which sat her daughter's friend, Tatjana, who was reading aloud a question from a paper she'd placed on the table top near my voice recorder. Both women had emigrated to the United States from the former Yugoslavia: Tatjana as a student from Croatia during the 1980s, and Mahira as a refugee fleeing the 1990s political violence (Figure 9.2).

When the violence began, Mahira was a widow of a mixed Muslim-Christian marriage, in her sixties, and her adult daughter had emigrated to the United States in the 1980s. This enabled Mahira to join her daughter at the beginning of the war and escape the four-year siege of Sarajevo. Mahira and Tatjana were participants in a collaborative project that was an outgrowth of my previous research on Bosnian refugees' post-war lives in Chicago. The "Gathering Grounds" project connects members of the 1990s diaspora across generations through interviews about the traditional stove-top coffee drinking practices and aforementioned associated objects: *džezve*—stove-top carafes, *fildžani*—small porcelain cups, and *mlinovi*—handmills (Figure 9.3).[7]

Figure 9.2 Tatjana and Mahira interview

Near the end of the interview, Tatjana asked one of the final questions from the prompts on the interview guide:

TATJANA: Would you share one of your memories about Bosnian coffee?

MAHIRA: There is nothing special that I remember. Only that we all enjoyed coffee—some more, some less. I can recall one coffee I enjoyed and that I remember. It was in Sarajevo, on the hill, there was an old café: Babića Baščа. And here, with my husband, I once drank coffee. But it was before we were engaged. And that coffee, I remember.

TATJANA: Because it was connected to love?

MAHIRA: Perhaps it was tied to love, but also ambience. It was a garden, on a hill, and down below, you could see Sarajevo. That coffee, I remember.

Mahira's coffee memory places the drink in time and space, locating the coffee experience in relation to the topographical and toponymic rather than human elements in the scene. When Tatjana follows up on the reference to Mahira's husband, surmising that it is the suggestion of romantic love that makes this memory stay with Mahira, the elder woman further emphasizes the significance of location in her explanation: "Perhaps," she responds, giving a nod to the potential of love's significance, but then repeats, "it was a garden, on a hill, and down below, you could see Sarajevo," providing a multi-sensory account, not based on the coffee's taste, appearance, smell—we learn nothing of this—rather, she directs us to the consumption site's aura, its sensations, and how she experienced this. Coffee drinking is part of an environmental ensemble here and it becomes a meaningful, lasting memory because it

Figure 9.3 Mostar market stall with džezve, mlinovi, and souvenirs

belongs to this temporal assemblage that creates an ambient space in her former city: "That coffee, I remember."

This emplacement of her coffee memory gains significance when situated within her forced migration. Earlier in the interview, Tatjana asks a question about handmills. Mlinovi, džezve, and fildžani were family possessions, passed down from generations, often as a part of wedding celebrations to help establish a new couple's future kitchen and demonstrate their capacity to host others in their own apartment (Bringa 1995). When Tatjana asks if Mahira had a handmill, the elder woman remarks that she had a beautiful one that she wishes she could have brought with her to the United States. "Did it get lost?" Asks Tatjana, and Mahira replies that "It disappeared in the war." As objects of material and symbolic wealth, džezve and mlinovi were among the items refugees sought to bring with them, but they were also stolen or appropriated by those who sought to force Bosnian Muslims and Bosnians in mixed families to leave. While Mahira had been able to recover her Sarajevo apartment, making repairs and return visits after the siege had ended, she had not been able to age there as she had desired. When Mahira died two years later, her daughter carried out Mahira's wish to be returned to Bosnia, and arranged for her mother's body to be flown back to Sarajevo for burial. Mahira's coffee interview incites memories of the pleasures of being in a particular place prior to the social dislocations of the 1990s political violence. Outside of Mostar, a two-hour drive southwest of Sarajevo, coffee was part of a different sort of place-making among young people grappling with stalled post-war reconstruction.

Coffee on the Street: Cafe Visits

During the late aughts in Stolac, a small historic town nestled in the Dinaric Alps, outdoor street cafes, *kafići (s. kafić)*, were popular sites for young adults to socialize with one another. At the time, things were quite difficult for this generation, many of whom had been children or teenagers during the 1990s wars. After defending the city against attacks by the Serb ethno-nationalist military, fighting broke out between Bosniaks and Croats. The Croat ethno-nationalist militia sought to create a mono-ethnic territory for Bosnian Croats. The people of Stolac, a Muslim-majority town before the war, had suffered greatly; in 1993, the Croat nationalist militia forced thousands of Muslims from the town and looted and destroyed their homes and neighborhoods (Kolind 2007). The work of rebuilding the region's social and material infrastructure began after the 1995 Dayton Peace Agreement (DPA), but had stalled a decade later in part due to the ethnic consociational governance structure established by the DPA that re-emphasized ethno-national divisions through an intra-country "entity" border that corresponded with areas seized by the Serb nationalist military during the war, and by stipulating that many government positions must be filled according to the proportions of Bosnia's three majority ethnic groups: Bosnian Croats, Bosnian Serbs, and Bosnian Muslims.[8] As Azra Hromadžić notes, this post-war consociational democracy institutionalized ethnic separation and resulted in a loss of spaces for ethnic groups to socially intermingle, in the local vernacular, "miješanje" (mixing). Not surprisingly, coffee drinking figures prominently in the lack of spaces for ethnic intermingling—which would have been common, for example, at worksites and social home visits prior to the war—as when a high school student remarked to Hromadžić, "How can we build long-lasting friendships when we do not even have a space to drink coffee together?" (Hromadžić 2011, 278).

By the time I arrived in Stolac in summer 2009, the majority of municipal operations and services in the region were segregated by ethnicity, often with Bosnian Catholics receiving superior services. (During my time there, people used the terms "Catholic," "Christian" [meaning Orthodox], and "Muslim"; I rarely heard people use "Croat" "Serb," or "Bosniak"). The two largest ethnic groups in the canton, Bosnian Catholics and Bosnian Muslims, were directed to different medical facilities, and Bosnian Croat children entered the schools' front doors, while Bosnian Muslim children entered the back door. Catholic kids attended school in the morning; Muslim kids attended in the afternoon.[9] Further complicating matters was the failed municipal election the previous year in Mostar, the canton's capitol. The city council was unable to pass a budget or elect a mayor, and had stopped paying city workers: teachers, municipal workers, and construction workers and staff at publicly owned companies had not been paid since March. As a whole, youth unemployment figures (aged 15–24) in Bosnia were recorded at a staggering 48.72%.[10] Individual households often relied on remittances from those abroad to get by; yet, the global recession of 2008 made it increasingly difficult for the diaspora to remit portions of their income to those who remained in Bosnia. Despite these fraught political and economic circumstances, young people managed to find ways to socialize, including across ethnic belonging.

I had come to Stolac to learn more about the transnational ties maintained by Bosnians in the diaspora and those who remained in Bosnia and Ajla (Eye-la) was my primary guide in Stolac. Ajla was the 23-year-old cousin of my friend Edin; Edin's father was her mother's brother. Ajla's and Edin's families were among those forced to leave Stolac during the war, and Edin's family had emigrated as refugees to Chicago, while Ajla's family had returned to Stolac. She was a civil engineering student at the University of Mostar, a full-time caregiver for her mother who was suffering from a rare and severely debilitating auto-immune disease, and enjoyed socializing at local kafići.

In Stolac, several kafići were located on the same small street near the town's center, and were open during the afternoons and into the evening when one could find multiple groupings of three to four people sitting at outdoor tabletops covered with umbrellas advertising German beer and Bosnian mineral water. The small cafes provided socially acceptable places for young men and women to gather together, typically in same-gender groups rather than in mixed groups or in male/female pairs; thus, the scene generally included several all-women groupings, and several all-men groupings with perhaps one or two groupings that included both. Tables were set apart by only a few feet and American pop music from the 1990s played in the background creating a sense of conviviality among those present. While gender-mixing did occur in the space, women and men consumed different beverages.

A typical Stolac kafić did not sell food and the menu consisted of mineral water and a set of stimulant-based beverages: coffee (traditional, espresso, or sweetened Nescafe packets), sugar-sweetened fruit drinks, cedavita (a sweetened Vitamin C packet dissolved in water), coca cola, and beer. Men tended to drink beer and I never saw a man drink a cedavita or one of the fruit juices. However, women tended to drink cedavita, or fruit juice; I never saw a woman customer drinking beer. Mineral water, coffee, and coca cola were ordered by both men and women customers. Despite the political stalemate and the economic situation, it was still summer at the height of Mostar's tourism season, also the time of year when those in the diaspora who could afford to might return for an extended visit: the kafići in Stolac were full on the evenings when Ajla and I occasioned them.

While I was attuned to the gendered differences at the kafić, I had initially missed the ways in which the town's kafići reflected the post-war spatial ethnic separations. One evening, we were sitting at a kafić that was operated by one of Ajla's friend's brothers and drinking cedavita when a young man at a different kafić across the street said Ajla's name and waved at her. "Tino!" she exclaimed, waving back, "he's a funny guy," she said to me, "I know him from before, from school." Tino was walking across the street toward us. He came and stood near Ajla's chair and the two of them chatted for a bit. He invited us to a party later that week. As he walked away, I asked, "Did you want him to join us? He could have sat down." "He is Catholic...that kafić is where the Catholics go," she replied, "So he didn't want to sit down?" I asked. Ajla paused, then said, "He could sit, but some people might say things. He doesn't care, and I don't care; we are friends with everyone. But some people are stupid." I had originally assumed that Ajla took me to this kafić instead of the one across the street because she knew the owner. But it was also because our kafić was known as a Muslim space, and the other kafić was Catholic-operated. It occurred to me that I had observed a number of these social exchanges—what I came to label "cafe visits"—over the previous weeks (Croegaert 2020). I thought it had just been friends happening upon one another, but then, why didn't they just choose one of the kafić and sit there together? The visitor always returned to their original seat after they'd conducted the social encounter.

These street-kafić social visits can be understood as a form of "trans-ethnic" social practices in the region (Hromadžić 2013). In these sorts of encounters, ethnic difference is not ignored or glossed over, nor is ethnic difference celebrated or politicized. Rather, it is acknowledged and then minimized through social exchange. These street visits were similar to the practices of high school students with whom Hromadžić worked in Mostar. While Hromadžić's students grappled with post-war ethnic spatial restrictions by seeking out alternative places wherein they could socialize such as the school bathrooms, Ajla and her peers used the interstitial zone of the street to cross over to the side of the ethnic "other," entering their kafić space and remaining standing rather than sitting. This meant that they would not drink their coffee together—a loss remarked upon by Hromadžić's student, and alluded to in Ajla's explanation to me that many people might disapprove or gossip about her and Tino's inter-ethnic exchange but that they don't care because "we are friends with everyone." These efforts to socialize across ethnic social boundaries point to the younger generation's desire for connection and collective belonging even as the war and the post-war governance structure eliminated many of the places that had previously fostered such social relations.

With Mahira and Tatjana, we have visited Bosnian coffee practices in the home, and through the Stolac outdoor kafić, we have observed Bosnian coffee practices along the street. In the final section, I look to Bosnian American artist Aida Šehović's annual nomadic monument, ŠTO TE NEMA, an artwork that brings Bosnian coffee's symbolic associations with the home into the public square in order to commemorate the genocide of Bosnian Muslims during the 1990s wars.

Coffee as Mourning: Honoring the Dead

Food is often integral to practices that mark death and honor the dead. The Jewish tradition of sitting shiva involves mourners bringing food to share with the bereaved as they commemorate the passing of life (Slochower 1993). Certain Catholic and Voudou mourning rites involve imbibing or symbolically offering alcohol to saints, spirits, and the newly deceased in honor of their life and to acknowledge that they have joined those who passed generations ago—the ancestors (Hurston 1931, 397, McCarthy-Brown 1991, 198). In the tradition of New Orleans Jazz funerals, those following the band's walking parade in the "Second Line" take food and drink during "stops" along the parade route in order to sustain their embodied performances of mourning and celebration of life (Ehrenfeucht and Croegaert 2017). In Bosnia, Muslims traditionally bury their dead within 24 hours, and, during the next day or more will receive visits from neighbors who pay respects by bringing gifts of valued foods, including coffee (Bringa 1995). Purposefully preventing members of a group from participating in their rites of mourning, in how they attribute meaning to the death of their community members, may be understood as a form of social violence that aims to sever ties between the dead and the living, and between generations.

Thus, rituals of mourning gain particular significance in the aftermath of political violence involving genocide as in the case of the 1990s wars in Bosnia when Bosnian Muslims were targeted for "ethnic cleansing" campaigns and killed by the VRS and affiliated militia, then callously denied burial rites and dumped in mass graves. The individuals who died in mass killings at Srebrenica and Prijedor regions, among other sites, were purposefully mixed together with other bodies in order to make it more difficult for survivors to identify their loved ones. Their bodies, and, by extension, their families and communities, were often further degraded by efforts to cover up the atrocities such as bulldozing grave sites, or moving body parts to secondary and even tertiary mass graves. Survivors have been presented with partial remains of their loved ones' bodies, of which only bones and perhaps remnants of the person's clothing have endured. In some cases, human remains will never be found, or, if found, may not be able to be identified via a DNA match with the living (Wagner 2008). This material fragmenting threatens the body's integrity which under normal conditions would be upheld by ritualistic washing and preparation for burial within 24 hours of death. Artist Aida Šehović's work challenges this type of dead-body violence, or "necroviolence" that conducts violence against the living in acts intended to desecrate the dead, by offering intimacy, community, and ceremony to survivors through incorporating Bosnian coffee rituals in what she describes as a "participatory public monument."[11]

Every year since 2006, Šehović has worked with survivors to mount a one-day public art sculpture on the date commemorating the beginning of the killings that took place in a United Nations "safe area" in the Srebrenica region, the largest documented massacre in the wartime genocide. On July 11, ŠTO TE NEMA is assembled and disassembled by the artist and a group of volunteers in a public square in a major city in Europe or North America. Although not from the Srebrenica region, Šehović and her family were forced to flee their homes in the city of Banja Luka, and her public social sculpture is meant to offer a space to mourn to all of those who have lost family, friends, and community members during the war. The artwork draws on an enormous amount of volunteer labor that centers on the practice of brewing and serving coffee for the war-dead, those who may never again drink it among the living.

When I took part in the 2017 installation in Chicago's Daley Plaza, there were more than forty of us in the volunteer trainings that preceded the installation and during which we were assigned roles such as setup, brewer, runner, greeter, and clean-up. In addition to those of us who would be on-site for the day of assembly and disassembly were hundreds of members of the diaspora who had throughout the previous year donated fildžani, džezve, and coffee grounds as well as food and water to sustain the volunteers for our day's work under the hot July sun. The sculpture takes shape as greeters invite passersby to pour coffee from a džezva of hot Bosnian coffee brewed in a work station located several yards away into a fildžan and place it near the center of the plaza. A greeter provides the passerby with a fildžan and tells them that each coffee cup is placed in memory of a person among the 8,372 men killed at Srebrenica, and that the coffee cup might also be placed in memory of someone whose death the passerby would like to mark. This invitation both offers a framework for mourning collective victimization by providing a conduit to link the lives lost at Srebrenica to grief participants may experience in relation to friends and family they lost to the political violence in other parts of Bosnia, and disrupts the ethno-nationalist framing of victimization by providing an opening for loss that may resonate for passersby who want to remember a loved one who has died. Šehović's installations have occasionally included participants of Croatian and Serbian background, and her permitting applications specify that no national emblems or signage may be used by participants, thereby delimiting efforts to weaponize the dead for political gain (Croegaert and Kulašić 2016, Halilovich 2012, 170). As the day progresses, the small porcelain cups are placed one next to another creating a sphere that expands outward from where the first cup is placed (Figure 9.4).

The collection of cups grows until a fildžan has been placed for every one of the 8,372 who have been identified to date. In 2017, this number was 7,500.

The monument's conceptual architecture draws on principles of hospitality and social intimacy in which coffee figures prominently. For example, in our volunteer training, Šehović reminded us that it was like we were "welcoming people into our home" when we invited them to pour a coffee. In Bosnia, social visits between homes in a village or urban neighborhood often involve women, including women of different ethnic backgrounds. Scholars have written about this as an integral component of the Bosnian principle of komšije/neighbors, or being neighborly that establishes familiarity through coffee service (Helms 2010, Sorabji 2008). Coffee drinking in this context may involve sharing information, opinions, or offering emotional support.

The majority of volunteers in Chicago were Bosnian American young adults, those who were children when their families arrived in the United States as refugees and often found it difficult to connect with their parents' generation, whose lives the political violence had dramatically altered. Due to language barriers and different accreditation systems, many adult

Figure 9.4 ŠTO TE NEMA Chicago installation 2017

refugees were unable to work in their previous professions. Further, they had arrived in the midst of 1990s neoliberal reforms to social welfare programs that severely reduced education, language, and emotional supports for refugees, pushing them into low-wage employment in the service sector within months of their arrival (Croegaert 2020, Franz 2003). Many worked more than one job and some were severely depressed as a result of their wartime and migration experiences and economic struggles in the United States. Being involved in the public monument provided a space for the younger generation to interact with one another and to engage in a ritual that was familiar and meaningful to their parents' and grandparents' generations among whom the monument also resonates. Not only did they connect with one another over the course of the 2017 installation, but through their participation they were also joining a growing community of volunteers from across the diaspora among whom were those who participated in previous installations in the Hague, Toronto, Istanbul, and future installations in Venice, and in its final iteration in this nomadic form, returning to the Mothers of Srebrenica through the memorial center at Potočari in 2020.

Šehović gives her monument the title, "ŠTO TE NEMA," a Bosnian phrase that translates literally as "Why aren't you here?" but is better understood in this context as the desire for a loved one's return, "Where have you been? Why haven't you returned?" The phrase is also the title of a well-known song in the Bosnian musical form, *sevdah/sevdalinka* which incorporates many genres, including songs that focus on melancholy sensibilities such as longing for a loved one (Imamović 2013). The lyrics are attributed to a poem published by Aleksa Šantić in 1897 and one of the most popular versions of the song among the last Yugoslav generation is Jadranka Stojaković's 1980s recording. By pairing this phrase with the practice of brewing and serving Bosnian coffee, "the real coffee," Šehović's monument indexes Bosnian histories that pre-date the modern nation-state: the region's positioning within Ottoman and Habsburg imperial regimes. This mnemonic feature of Bosnian coffee service and the phrase from Santić's poem within the sevdah song create what Kathleen Adams describes as artworks' potential "affecting presence" whereby objects are imbued with meaning that resonates within individual and group identities—art, then, may be seen as an important site through which people seek to shape and contest aspects of intra- and inter-group identity formations (Adams 2006, 11, 26).[12] For Šehović Bosnian coffee, and its adjacent objects, fildžani, džezve, serves as a way to return some care and dignity to those who were killed at Srebrenica and to enact a sense of social belonging that extends to others of varied proximity to that particular genocidal act.

Conclusion

From stimulating religious rites and reactionary prohibition to establishing coffee houses that incubated political and intellectual solidarities, coffee served as an intoxicating force for social movements in both Ottoman and Habsburg Europe. In Bosnia and Herzegovina, an administrative region in both empires and members of their twentieth-century successor states, coffee and the material culture central to Bosnian coffee service is a spatializing practice that the diaspora can draw on to share memories and imbue them with meaning by locating themselves in a particular time and place. In the fraught social landscape brought about by the aftermath of war and the structure of the DPA, young people seeking interactions across lines of ethnic difference note the absence of spaces to drink coffee together and creatively cultivate an in-between space by sending and receiving impromptu invitations to cross the street and visit at another's cafe. By serving—but not drinking—Bosnian coffee in a European or North American urban public square, Aida Šehović makes coffee into an artwork that insists on the humanity of victims of genocide, restores dignity to those who survived war, and extends hospitality and kinship to those who want to prevent future genocide.

What to make of these rememberings, minglings, and paying respects? How to understand coffee's centrality across time, in diverse spatial domains and sites of social practice—in religious spaces, cafes, homes, the sidewalk cafe, the public square, and enacting devotion, sensorially experiencing memory, extending sociality, and rites of mourning? Coffee's capacity to stimulate bodies and incite sociality renders its consumption as key to establishing sites of meaning-making, crucial to the production of social relations, and thus critical to the study of everyday encounters wherein people evaluate their past and present circumstances and envision their futures. In social conditions where it is difficult to directly challenge authority or hegemonic forms of power, the consumption of beverages with symbolic resonance such as coffee offers a way to indirectly critique such systems. Attending to who may sip coffee together, or not, offers an alternative way to listen and to hear across lines of difference.

Notes

1 Macedonia and Montenegro were the two other republics in the Socialist Federal Republic of Yugoslavia (SFRY).

2 Measured by the amount of coffee consumed per capita according to market research data from Euromonitor International. From first to fifteenth, the top 15 are listed as Finland, Norway, Netherlands, Slovenia, Austria, Serbia, Denmark, Germany, Belgium, Brazil, Bosnia-Herzegovina, Estonia, Switzerland, Croatia, and Dominican Republic. Reported in https://www.caffeineinformer.com/caffeine-what-the-world-drinks Last accessed 3.25.2021.

3 I use "Bosnia" and "Bosnia-Herzegovina" interchangeably in this chapter to refer to the medieval and modern Bosnian state.

4 The report outlines some of the limitations with quantifying this diaspora. It also notes that while the 1990s diaspora is the largest Bosnian diaspora to date, this diaspora joins earlier diasporas arising from the Ottoman-Austrian transfer (1878) and from the Yugoslav Kingdom.

5 UNESCO, "Viennese Coffee House Culture: Social Practices in Vienna, inscribed 2011" https://www.unesco.at/en/culture/intangible-cultural-heritage/austrian-inventory/detail-1/article/viennese-coffee-house-culture Last accessed November 5, 2020.

6 Officially Bosnian Croats could find refuge in Croatia, and Bosnian Serbs in Serbia, although many such refugees did not find themselves welcomed in their respective national "home" lands. I use "Bosnian Muslim" and "Bosniak" interchangeably and according to people's uses. For an extensive discussion of the uses and meanings of "Bosniak," see Edin Hajdarpašić *Whose Bosnia?: Nationalism and Political Imagination in the Balkans 1840–1914*. Ithaca: Cornell University Press, 2015.

7 Project background and full interviews can be accessed at the Gathering Grounds project website, dzezvacoffee.com.

8 The European Court of Human Rights ruled in 2009 that Bosnia's Constitution violates the rights of Bosnians who do not belong to one of the three majority-prioritized ethnicities: Serb, Croat, or Bosniak (Bosnian Muslim) by prohibiting "Others," such as Jewish and Romany Bosnians, from holding public office. As of this writing, the constitution has not been revised to address this discrimination.

9 For an in-depth study of Mostar's segregated school system, see Hromadžić 2015.

10 Official unemployment figures do not capture work in the informal economy, upon which many at the time relied.

11 Building on Achille Mbembe's discussion of "necropolitics" as an instrument of modern sovereignty, Jason De León describes "necroviolence" as "violence performed and produced through the specific treatment of corpses that is perceived to be offensive, sacrilegious, or inhumane by the perpetrator, the victim (and her or his cultural group), or both" (De León 2015: 69).

12 Adams is building here on Robert Plant Armstrong's earlier work (1971).

References

Adams, Kathleen. *Art as Politics: Re-Crafting Identities, Tourism, and Power in Tana Toraja, Indonesia*. Honolulu: University of Hawaii Press, 2006.

Bringa, Tone. *Being Muslim the Bosnian Way: Identity and Community in a Central Bosnian Village*. Princeton: Princeton University Press, 1995.

Bynum, Caroline Walker. *Holy Feast and Holy Fast: The Religious Significance of Food to Medieval Women*. Berkeley: University of California Press, 1987.

"Caffeine (Coffee) Consumption By Country," *Euromonitor International Market Research*, 2013. https://www.caffeineinformer.com/caffeine-what-the-world-drinks.

Caldwell, Melissa. "Tempest in a Coffee Pot: Brewing Incivility in Russia's Public Sphere," in *Food and Everyday Life in the Post-Socialist World*. Melissa Caldwell, Ed. pp. 101–129. Bloomington: Indiana University Press, 2009.

Carabelli, Giulia. "Habsburg Coffeehouses in the Shadow of the Empire: Revisiting Nostalgia in Trieste," *History and Anthropology* 30(4): 382–392, 2019.

Coffee Futures (documentary film). Zeynep Devrim Gürsel, director, 2009.

Croegaert, Ana. "Who Has Time For Ćejf? Postsocialist Migration and Slow Coffee in Neoliberal Chicago," *American Anthropologist*, 113(3): 463–477, 2011.

———*Bosnian Refugees in Chicago: Gender, Performance, and Post-War Economies*. Lexington: Books, Rowman & Littlefield, 2020.

Croegaert, Ana and Elmina Kulašić. "The Politics of Memory among Child Survivors of the Bosnian War Diaspora," in *Youth Circulations*, June 11, 2016. *http://www.youthcirculations.com/blog/2016/6/9/the-politics-of-memory-among-child-survivors-of-the-bosnian-war-diaspora*

De León, Jason. *Land of Open Graves*. Berkeley: University of California Press, 2015.

Doane, Molly. "Relationship Coffees: Structure and Agency in the Fair Trade System," in *Fair Trade and Social Justice: Global Ethnographies*, Sarah Lyon and Mark Moberg, Eds, pp. 229–257. New York: New York University Press, 2010.

Ehrenfeucht, Renia and Ana Croegaert. "Learning From the Streets of New Orleans: Will Revising or Relaxing Public Space Ordinances Create a Just Environment for Street Commerce?," in *Food Trucks, Cultural Identity, and Social Justice: From Loncheras to Lobsta Love*, Julian Agyeman, Caitlin Matthews, and Hannah Sobel, Eds, pp. 109–128. Cambridge: MIT Press, 2017.

Franz, Barbara. "Bosnian Refugees and Socio-Economic Realities: Changes in Refugee Resettlement Policies in Austria and the United States," *Journal of Ethnic and Migration Studies*, 29(1): 5–21, 2003.

Hajdarpašić, Edin. "Out of the Ruins of the Ottoman Empire: Reflections on the Ottoman Legacy in South-Eastern Europe," *Middle Eastern Studies* 44(5):715–734, 2008.

Halilovich, Hariz. "Trans-Local Communities in the Age of Transnationalism: Bosnians in Diaspora," *International Migration* 50(1): 162–178, 2012.

Halilovich, Hariz, Jasmin Hasić, Dženeta Karabegović, Ajlina Karamehić-Muratović, and Nermin Oruč. "Mapping the Bosnian-Herzegovinian Diaspora: Utilizing the Socio-Economic Potential of the Diaspora for Development of BiH," (Report, Development For Diaspora (D4D) Project) Sarajevo, Bosnia and Herzegovina, 2018.

Hangi, Antun. *Život I Običaji Muslimana u Bosni I Hercegovini*. Danijela A. Kajona, ed. Sarajevo, Bosnia and Herzegovina, 1906.

Hattox, Ralph. *Coffee and Coffeehouses: The Origins of a Social Beverage in the Medieval Near East*. Seattle: University of Washington Press, 1985.

Hayden, Robert. "Imagined Communities and Real Victims: Self-Determination and Ethnic Cleansing in Yugoslavia," *American Ethnologist* 23: 383–801, 1996.

Helms, Elissa. "The Gender of Coffee: Women and Reconciliation Initiatives in Post-War Bosnia and Herzegovina," *Focaal Journal of Global and Historical Anthropology* 57: 17–32, 2010.

Hromadžić, Azra. "Bathroom Mixing: Youth Negotiate Democratization in Postconflict Bosnia and Herzegovina," *PoLAR Political and Legal Anthropology Review*, 34(2): 268–289, 2011.

Hromadžić, Azra. "Discourses of Trans-ethnic Narod in Postwar Bosnia and Herzegovina," *Nationalities Papers* 41(2): 259–275, 2013.

Hromadžić, Azra. *Citizens of an Empty Nation: Youth and State-making in Postwar Bosnia and Herzegovina*. University of Pennsylvania Press, 2015.

Hurston, Zora. "Hoodoo in America," *The Journal of American Folklore*, 44(174): 317–417, 1931.

Imamović, Damir. "Deset najčešćih zabluda o sevdahu (Ten Common Misconceptions About Sevdah)," *Vaša(r) Ideja* Public Lecture Series. Kamerni Teatar, Sarajevo Bosnia-Herzegovina, November 4, 2013. https://youtu.be/rgN0dnWETjA.

International Coffee Organization, cited in Smith, Oliver "Mapped: The Countries That Drink the Most Coffee," *The Telegraph*. October 1, 2017. Last accessed October 19, 2020. https://www.telegraph.co.uk/travel/maps-and-graphics/countries-that-drink-the-most-coffee/

Kolind, Torsten. "In search of 'Decent People': Resistance to the Ethnicization of everyday life among the Muslims of Stolac," in *The New Bosnian Mosaic: Identities, Memories, and Moral Claims in a Post-War Society*, Xavier Bougarel, Elissa Helms, Ger Duizings, Eds, pp. 123–140. Burlington, VT: Ashgate, 2007.

Kafadar, Cemal. "How Dark is the History of the Night, How Black the Story of Coffee, How Bitter the Tale of Love: the Changing Measure of Leisure and Pleasure in Early Modern Istanbul," in *Medieval and Early Modern Performance in the Eastern Mediterranean*, Arzu Öztürkmen and Evelyn Birge Vitz, Eds, pp. 243–269. Turnhout: Brepols, 2014.

Low, Setha M. and Denise Lawrence-Zúñiga. "Locating Culture," in *The Anthropology of Space and Place*, Low, Setha M. and Denise Lawrence-Zúñiga. Eds, pp. 1–49. Oxford: Blackwell Publishing, 2003.

McCarthy Brown, Karen. *A Voudou Priestess in Brooklyn*. Berkeley: University of California Press, 2001 [1991].

Miller, Daniel. "Why Some Things Matter," in *Material Cultures: Why Some Things Matter*, Daniel Miller, ed. pp. 3–24 Chicago: University of Chicago Press, 1998.

Patico, Jennifer. *Consumption and Social Change in a Post-Soviet Middle Class*. Washington, DC: Woodrow Wilson Center, 2009.

Roseberry, William. "The Rise of Yuppie Coffee and the Reimagination of Class in the United States," *American Anthropologist* 98(4): 762–775, 1996.

Slochower, Joyce. "The Therapeutic Function of Shiva," *Tikkun* 8(3): 51, 1993.

Šehović, Aida, ŠTO TE NEMA project website. https://stotenema.com/en/about.

Sorabji, Cornelia. "Bosnian Neighborhoods Revisited: Tolerance, Commitment and Komšiluk in Sarajevo," in *On the Margins of Religion*, Joao de Piña Cabral, and Frances Pine, Eds, pp. 97–112. Oxford: Berghahn Books, 2008.

Todorova, Maria. *Imagining the Balkans*. Oxford: Oxford University Press, 2009 [1996].

UNESCO, "Viennese Coffee House Culture: Social Practices in Vienna, Inscribed 2011," https://www.unesco.at/en/culture/intangible-cultural-heritage/austrian-inventory/detail-1/article/viennese-coffee-house-culture. Last accessed November 5, 2020.

West, Paige. *From Modern Production to Imagined Primitive: The Social World of Coffee from Papua New Guinea*. Durham, NC: Duke University Press, 2012.

10

EXPANDING INTOXICATION

What can drinking places (c. 1850–1950) tell us about other intoxicants and other sites?

James Kneale

Introduction: expansive intoxication, unbounded drinking places

This chapter considers drinking places—sites primarily dedicated to the sale and public consumption of alcoholic drinks—between about 1850 and 1950. It can be argued that this period saw their increasing specialisation around the world, as commercial, regulatory and social developments encouraged the separation of the production, retail and consumption of alcohol from other sites like homes and workplaces (Kneale, 2021). In the process, drinking places became more distinctive as a particular kind of site. At the same time, though, they were rarely *just* places to drink alcohol; they were often also sites for the consumption of other intoxicants like tobacco and caffeine, and of course for sociable interaction.

The journalist George Sala's description of an anonymous East London beer-shop in the 1850s offers us a useful example. This beer-shop is one of many pubs Sala shows his readers on an imagined tour of 'London's Publics', but it has surprisingly little to tell us about alcohol.

> Here is a beer-shop—a little, blinking, wall-eyed edifice, with red curtains in the window, and a bar squeezed up in one corner, as though it were ashamed of itself. From the door of the tap-room which we open, comes forth a thick, compact body of smoke. There are, perhaps, twenty people in the room, and they are all smoking like limekilns. From a kiln at the upper extremity, comes forth the well-remembered notes of the old *trink-lied*, 'Am Rhein, am Rhein.' We are in Vaterland at once. All these are Teutons—German sugarbakers.
>
> *(Sala, 1859: 266)*

Here, the bar is almost 'ashamed of itself', while the most obvious intoxicant is probably tobacco consumed in clay pipes, given the description of these smokers as 'kilns'. Sala reminds us that drinking places were not exclusively focused on drinking; they also fostered other kinds of intoxication as well as a valuable sociability. How might we expand our idea of drinking places without losing sight of what it is that makes them distinctive from other sociable, and sometimes intoxicating, spaces like cafes, street corners and lidos?

DOI: 10.4324/9780429058141-14

The chapter seeks to explore these questions, expanding our understandings of drinking places in three ways. First, it considers them as sites for the consumption of other intoxicants besides alcohol. Studies of individual intoxicants can give the impression that sites of consumption were reserved for one substance alone; discussions of the regulation of alcohol often ignore nicotine and caffeine. Second, it follows recent calls for a broader understanding of intoxication. If drinking places are public, social sites, intoxication may be something more than the collision of intoxicant and consumer, "not merely the physiological and neurological effects of plants, beverages, and chemicals but also religious ecstasy, hypnotic trance, musical reverie, intense collective joy" (Withington, 2014: 12). The collective consumption of Sala's sugarbakers was visible in the 'body of smoke' they produced, for example, and their singing might have intoxicated singers and listeners alike. This broader understanding of intoxication draws connections between intoxicants and some of the social characteristics of drinking places: publicness, sociability, commensality and hospitality. We will look at these in turn. Finally, the chapter will suggest expanding our engagement with these sites beyond our usual focus on drink and drinkers, while at the same time extending the limits of drinking places themselves.

In considering these possibilities, the chapter engages with recent work in the fields of material culture and 'new materialisms'. Orthodox approaches to 'consumption' tend, via a particular reading of Veblen (1915), to analyse objects for clues about their consumers' identities (for a good example of work of this kind, see Holt, 2018). Sala's journalism follows a similar logic, as his tour of London's pubs becomes a series of sketches of social 'types'. The sugarbakers' beer-shop stands in for Whitechapel's German quarter, for example, and the description fits what one British author saw as the 'three national characteristics' of German immigrants: 'smoking, singing, and Sabbath-breaking' (Apperson, 1914: 161). Elsewhere in Whitechapel, Sala visited Jewish pubs where "Smoking is universal—cigars the rule, pipes the exception", which to Sala's racialising eye marked these smokers out as "peculiar in their amusements, as in everything else" (1859: 267).

This chapter takes a different approach. Rather than reading intoxicants as markers of pre-existing identities, this engagement with intoxicating sites sees them as places where new things might emerge. Through the sharing of intoxicants, other material things, and social practices, hospitality and generosity can be produced through commensal consumption. Examined through the lens of the new materialisms, intoxication becomes something that emerges out of the interaction of consumers, intoxicants, songs, light and visual spectacles, and a wider affective atmosphere, which expands to fill much larger and more heterogeneous spaces than Sala's beer-shop. How did intoxicants, collective social practices of consumption and their associated meanings, and material environments come together to make these sites so important to their patrons?

The value of these ideas for our understanding of drinking places is explored across six sections. The chapter begins by considering other intoxicants besides alcohol that were consumed in some drinking places in this period, concentrating on tobacco. The second section considers the relationship between intoxicants and the public sphere, opening up a discussion of the qualities and social character of these sites. The third asks an important question, developing this investigation of the character of drinking places: if pubs, cafes and bookshops can all be 'good places', as Ray Oldenburg described these vital sites of sociability (1989), how important are intoxicants? What difference did alcohol, tobacco, coffee and tea make? To answer this, we will consider the importance of sociability, commensality and hospitality in Oldenburg's good places.

The fourth section of the chapter suggests that examining the *material cultures* of intoxication might show us how social relations between consumers are actively made, so that cultural values like commensality, hospitality and generosity are materialised or objectified. Concentrating on those practices that involve *gifting* (Mauss, 1990), it's clear that not only is this more strongly associated with alcohol and tobacco than other intoxicants but may also be a central part of what makes these places 'good'. The fifth section re-thinks drinking places, intoxicants and intoxication by drawing upon expanded senses of place, materiality and meaning, and the sixth further expands our sense of the limits of drinking places, before the chapter concludes.

We begin by looking at the intoxicants consumed in these sites over this period.

Drinking places and intoxicants, 1850–1950

By 1850, much of the world was already accustomed to David Courtwright's 'big three' intoxicants: alcohol, caffeine and tobacco (2001). While Courtwright's 'little three' (opium, cannabis and coca) were consumed alongside alcohol, they are not as prominent in the historiography of drinking places. By contrast, alcohol and tobacco were often taken together, and were understood as everyday luxuries, part of 'a community of goods' (Withington, 2020a: 387) until the twentieth century. The relationship between caffeine and alcohol was more complicated; they could be posed as alternatives—or even rivals—to one another, but could also be consumed together, particularly as part of a meal. In consequence, cafés might or might not be 'alcoholized social spaces' (Toner, 2015: 28), depending on where you were. In Paris, Mexico City and Copenhagen, cafés offered wine and spirits as part of a wider range of beverages (Eriksen, 1999; Haine, 2003; Toner, 2015). British coffee- and tea-rooms tended not to be licenced for the sale of alcoholic drinks in this period, however (Burnett, 1999, 2004). Some of these places were provided as alternatives to the pub, of course (Davison, 2006), and the 'improved' pub of the first half of the twentieth century also emphasised the sale of tea, coffee and food (Greenaway, 1998; Gutzke, 2005). Restaurants, inns and hotels offered caffeinated drinks along with meals, alcoholic drinks and other services, much as they had done in the eighteenth century, when "in most provincial towns, among its many other functions, the inn was the coffee house" (Maudlin, 2019: 28), or indeed in the late seventeenth century, when "provincial coffee rooms were hidden in alehouses and inns" (Withington, 2020b: 74). Concentrating on tobacco, this section sets out to demonstrate the close relationship between smoking and alcoholic drinking places.

In 1850, the British per capita consumption of tobacco stood at 2lbs per adult, a figure unchanged for two centuries; by 1950, this figure had risen to 7lbs per adult, with the machine-rolled cigarette dominating the market following its introduction in the 1880s (Hilton, 2000: 2). Matthew Hilton's focus on what he calls the 'bourgeois-liberal context of smoking' (3), the product of 'a minority smoking culture' of gentlemanly smokers (22), reflects the difficulty of finding alternative accounts of the smoking habits of the majority of British consumers. Despite this, "a more communal pleasure and use of smoking can be discerned in the public houses frequented by the labouring classes in which the free issue of clay pipes … suggested a certain traditional ritual of hospitality" (4). This is an important insight, and one we will return to.

For many Victorian writers, though, the clay pipe served as a simple marker of class, and smoking an index of the character of smokers and their drinking place. Charles Dickens' description of a public house in Scotland Yard provides an early example, with its "lusty coalheavers, quaffing large draughts of Barclay's best, and puffing forth volumes of smoke, which wreathed heavily above their heads, and involved the room in a thick dark cloud" (1875: 407). This prodigious pipe-smoking matches their heavy drinking, both signs of masculine physicality. The close connection between smoking and drinking was noted by many British observers, often—but not always—by critics of one or both of these habits. A pamphlet produced by the Anti-Narcotic League quoted a Dr. James Hamilton on the topic, for example: "Extinguish the pipes of London, and you will go far to shut up the public-houses" (Hind Smith, undated: 6). The social investigator and journalist J. Ewing Ritchie described a London pub patronised by "the most wretched men and women possible to imagine", noting, "They are drinking gin and smoking, and all have the appearance of confirmed sots" (1858: 202). From this perspective, working-class use of these intoxicants suggested a helpless, incontinent, consumption.

In other non-fiction sources, the ordinary pipe is often simply described as 'short', as it is in the American Temperance lecturer John B. Gough's description of a Saturday night in Whitechapel: "a combination of commerce, fun, frolic, cheating, begging, thieving, deviltry, short pipes, thick sticks, mouldy umbrellas, dirty faces, and ragged coats. Here are gin palaces in profusion" (1880: 101). Salvation Army co-founder William Booth's *In Darkest England And The Way Out* quoted another description of Whitechapel, where a woman "horribly bloated with drink" argued with "Two dirty tramp-like men … smoking their short cutty pipes"; giving up, she "took herself off, her mouth full of oaths and cursing, to the public-house" (1890: 164–165).

However, the close association between pipe-smoking and drinking was also observed in the case of higher-status smokers, as this humorous entry in the dictionary of Victorian slang collected by novelist and playwright J. Redding Ware suggests:

> *Colour the meerschaum, To.* Drinking to the extent of reddening the nose. … The phrase arises from an association of ideas—those in the first place of darkening the colour of a meerschaum pipe by steady smoking, and in the second, intensifying the hue of the nose by steady drinking.
>
> *(1909: 86).*

Ware's *Dictionary* is far less critical of drinking than these other sources, suggesting that the close association between drinking and pipe-smoking could be viewed in a more even-handed way.

The machine-rolled cigarette, which replaced the pipe as the dominant form of smoking in Britain after the First World War (Hilton, 2000: 83–85), may have been associated with the fall in alcohol consumption in Britain between the 1890s and the end of the Second World War, as the cigarette offered working-class smokers something to spend their income on besides drink (Dingle, 1972). At the end of our period, the social research organisation Mass Observation estimated that 81% of British men and 39% of women smoked (1949: 95). While this meant that cigarettes and pipes could be found everywhere, "All smokers are more likely to be pubgoers than non-smokers, and heavy smokers are more than twice as likely to be so" (98). Bolton's pubs were smoky places, with 46% of their patrons smoking at any one time (Mass Observation, 1943: 203).

Where it was a new intoxicant, tobacco's relation with existing social spaces varied around the world. In Europe, smoking was stimulated by new sites like the coffeehouse, but where the public consumption of tea and coffee was already well-established, tobacco fitted into existing patterns of use. Coffee "whetted the appetites of Middle Eastern consumers for new tastes and recreations" like smoking (Grehan, 2006: 1358), with tobacco pipes in use from the late seventeenth century (Bouzigard and Saidel, 2012). The water pipe or hookah suited coffeehouses and bath houses because its bulkiness demanded 'stationary leisure' (Grehan, 2006: 1357, 1358). During the British occupation of Egypt, "observers of Cairene café culture reported the popularity of smoking the water pipe, drinking coffee, listening to Arabic music" and gambling, and beer, wine and cocktails were also available in beerhalls, hotels and bars (Fonder, 2013: 240, 40, 216). The bars and coffeehouses of early twentieth-century Ottoman ports also served beer (Fuhrmann, 2009; Georgeon, 2002). In Qing China, tobacco and alcohol were already closely linked by the seventeenth century, and in many urban areas, "pipe tobacco was simply added to the tea, alcohol, and snacks already ingested in … semi-public arenas" like teahouses, theatres, courtesan houses and restaurants (Benedict 2011: 67–68, 69). In similar sites in different parts of the world, alcohol, tobacco and caffeine mingled.

In the next section, we begin to investigate the arguments that have been made about the connection between the character of these public spaces and the intoxicants consumed in them. Is publicness a quality exclusively associated with coffee, for example?

Public places and intoxication

Alcoholic drinking places have long been associated with a cluster of ideas concerning publicness, democracy and hospitality. In nineteenth-century Russia, the urban tavern shared some of the character of the village commune (Transchel, 2006); the nineteenth-century French café was the 'church of the working class', a 'proletarian public sphere' (Haine, 1994: 16; 2006). Drinking places were also the most important sites of working-class sociability in Germany (Roberts, 1984, 1991), and a significant rival to the church in Wales and England (Harrison, 1973, Lambert, 1983). They provided newspapers, hosted political discussions and radical meetings, literary and scientific societies, friendly societies and other manifestations of civil society (Kneale, 2021). In the 1930s, Mass Observation argued that pubs represented "a temporally and spatially liberated public sphere" (Hubble, 2006: 211).

Jurgen Habermas's account of the emergence of a public sphere in the seventeenth and eighteenth centuries describes English coffeehouses, French *salons* and German literary societies as the centres of this new public culture (1991). Concentrating on the connections between print, literary and political criticism, and a growing consciousness of a wider public, Habermas had little to say about the intoxicants that shared these spaces with the men and women who constituted this new world. It has been left to others to suggest that—in the English case—it might have been significant that it was coffee, and not alcohol, that characterised these sites. Wolfgang Schivelbusch's account of coffee as the 'great soberer' sees it as the Protestant work ethic in liquid form (1993: 18), for example, enrolled in a post-Reformation campaign to drive alcohol from public life. This account of 'the tavern dethroned', as Michelet put it (cited 35), strengthens the links between coffee, sobriety and an emerging bourgeois subject. A similar reading of coffee as the solution to the problems posed by alcohol is set out in Stallybrass and White's *The politics and poetics of transgression* (1986, and see Withington, 2020b for a wider survey).

Considering work on these European sites, Matthee concludes that "Coffeehouses in the Middle East played a similar 'modernizing' role in the sense that they contributed to the creation of a cultural public sphere separate from the mosque" (Matthee, 2014: 113, and see Kömeçoğlu, 2005). However, while the elite might drink alcohol in private,

> alcohol in a Muslim environment could never become fully integrated into the idea of good living... never become the subject of a public discourse, just as the tavern, operating in the shadows, could never become part of a quasi-public sphere, unlike the often open and airy coffee house, a communal extension of the private home and the basis for political action.
>
> *(Matthee, 2014: 104)*

However, and as Matthee suggests, it is hard to map different intoxicants onto public and private spaces and spheres. Phil Withington's recent work suggests that coffee was far less important to British coffeehouses than has been assumed (2020b). Following the commodity rather than the institution, Withington concludes that coffee was relatively scarce in Britain before the eighteenth century, which meant that what was consumed in the new coffeehouses was just as likely to be another non-alcoholic or alcoholic drink; that coffeehouse sociability covered just as many activities—and could be as rowdy—as tavern sociability; and that some coffeehouses, particularly in the provinces, were simply rooms in alehouses. Withington concludes, "Rather than a transformative drug ... coffee emerges as a force and feature of hybridity—of the mixed economies of coffeehouse, alehouse, and, latterly, household, and of the range of practices, meanings, and tastes attendant to its consumption in those places" (74).

It is also difficult to map intoxicants onto different senses of the public because part of the appeal of many drinking places was their *combination* of characteristics usually associated with either the home or public space. Perry Duis described the US saloons as 'semi-public city spaces' (1983: 3), and W. Scott Haine suggested that patrons sought a 'communal privacy' in French cafés (1996: 55, and see Clement, 2020); British clubs offered both elite and ordinary men a private place in the city (Milne-Smith, 2006, 2011; Tremlett, 1987), while pubs could be 'sites of surrogate domesticity' (Booth, 2018: 290). Similarly, in Istanbul, "the coffeehouse was indeed an extension of home, the street and the market, resisting the easy and convenient distinction between the 'public' and the 'private' that has proved a pivotal ingredient of the debate on the emergence of the public sphere in early modern Europe" (Kirli, 2016: 172).

It's also worth emphasising Withington's point that coffeehouses were not necessarily orderly spaces either. In mid-Victorian Britain, a Select Committee considering places of public entertainment heard complaints from the Metropolitan Police that London's coffeeshops—unregulated, unlike pubs—witnessed "scenes of very great disorder and great mischief" (1852–1853: 13). The coffeehouses of Ottoman Istanbul were also closely surveilled (Kirli, 2016), and the Turkish Republic saw village coffeehouses as threats to rural productivity and civil society (Öztürk, 2008). Alcoholised spaces were not straightforwardly 'public', and coffee was not always associated with a sober, wakeful and rational activity.

If their appeal was not a consequence of their facilitation of public life, then perhaps drinking places were valued for their welcoming character and association with hospitality? We consider this in the next section.

Good places? Sociability, commensality and hospitality

While there might not be a straightforward relationship between intoxication and publicness, another influential characterisation of these sites, from Ray Oldenburg's *The Great Good Place* (1989), can help us consider a cluster of social theoretical ideas sometimes associated with discussions of drinking places: sociability, commensality and hospitality.

Arguing that America needed to revitalise its 'third places'—sites between home and work, which are "the core settings of informal public life" (16)—Oldenburg combined sociology, history and folksy anecdote to set out the things that make these sites 'good places'. He emphasised their openness, their nature as 'neutral ground' for all, dominated by conversation and playful interaction, with a crowd of regulars helping to set the tone. Intoxication is not essential, though, as bookshops and other urban spaces can also be good places. This wider genre of spaces has more recently been described by the sociologist Eric Klinenberg as 'social infrastructure' (2018), defined by Alan Latham and Jack Layton as "networks of spaces, facilities, institutions, and groups that create affordances for social connection" (2019: 3). From this perspective, drinking places and cafés are just one kind of commercial social infrastructure.

Georg Simmel seems to have been one of Oldenburg's inspirations, so we might imagine that in these places, we interact with others in ways that go beyond instrumental calculation, where sociability is 'the play form of association' (Simmel, 1997: 122). This is very different from Thorstein Veblen's discussion of the habits of American journeymen printers, who were well known for their "dram-drinking, 'treating,' *[round-buying]* and smoking in public places" (1915: 90). For Veblen, this was not a moral failing but a form of conspicuous consumption, a demonstration of the printer's wealth, implying secure employment and skilled labour. A printer who only socialised in order to advertise their own success and hear about employment possibilities would be a poor drinking companion, however. For Simmel, sociability must avoid both objective reality—drinking as a way of looking for work—and 'the absolutely personal and subjective', as it might if the printer treated the bartender as his personal therapist (Simmel, 1997: 123). While we have still not established the importance of intoxication in these sites, this note about sociability suggests that it might be worth examining two closely associated concepts: commensality and hospitality.

Commensality emphasises the importance of sharing a table, sharing food and drink with others. Drawing again on Simmel, Claude Fischler reminds us that while eating is inevitably individual—no one can eat what we are eating—we can at least share the *act* of consumption; "it counteracts the essential, basic, biological, 'exclusive selfishness of eating' and turns it into, at the very least, a collective, social experience" (2011: 531). While it can create exclusion and hierarchy as well as inclusion and equality, commensality may well be one of the things that gives drinking places their association with conviviality and openness. These sites also offer hospitality, where the instrumental calculations of the hospitality industry meet the kinds of 'light-touch' sociability that make us feel welcome in otherwise anonymous urban environments (Bell, 2007). While unconditional hospitality may not be possible, the work of Derrida and others indicates ways in which drinking places might provide 'hybrid' forms of hospitality to the stranger, even in 'staged' encounters with the 'affable barman' who has been trained to provide a service (Bell, 2007: 17).

Returning to temperance efforts to create 'alternatives to the pub', for example, it is clear that reformers sought alcohol-free commensality and hospitality. Temperance banquets brought hundreds of men and women of different classes together in orderly feasts to consume tea and cakes, for example (Rappaport, 2013). While tea had widely varying meanings for its consumers, these commensal events created both hierarchy and conviviality, as banquets were often chaired by local worthies or representatives of temperance societies, and friends and strangers ate and drank together.

Sociability, commensality and hospitality are found in other sites and do not depend on intoxication, so this can only explain part of the link between drinking places and the welcoming publicness of the 'great good place'. To understand the relationship between intoxicants and hospitality, we need to examine their shared material culture and the idea of the gift.

'With Beer One Thanks': intoxicants and the gift

While publicness, sociability, commensality and hospitality were often associated with drinking places, they are not dependent on the intoxicants consumed in these sites. Turning to insights developed in material culture studies allows us to find closer links between intoxicants and these social practices. In this section, we return to publicness, sociability, commensality and hospitality to argue that while they are not unique to drinking places, their strong association with these sites is the result of specific social practices and material cultures.

The importance of the gift in experiences of intoxication has not had as much attention as it deserves. Building upon a saying from 1872, however—"With beer one thanks, but with money one pays" (cited in Harrison, 1971: 55)—Mariana Adler has suggested that, "Through the giving and exchange of drinks social ties of obligation and reciprocity were established" (1991: 382). Money converted sociability into purely instrumental action, but the gift of a drink meant something more. As Marcel Mauss noted, "the thing received is not inactive. Even when it has been abandoned by the giver, it still possesses something of him" (1990: 15). A gifted drink creates the obligation to respond in kind, adding "a moral or ethical dimension to gift exchange that is fundamentally irreducible to economic calculation" (Pawlett, 2011: 659). A gift does more than express the relationship between giver and receiver; it *produces* that relationship. And as gifts create not only relationships between individuals, but also relations with wider cultural ideas like charity or generosity, the gift of a drink connects giver and receiver to a broader ethic of hospitality. In other words, the gift of a drink helps create the character of drinking places.

In Britain and the US in this period, buying drinks for others was called 'treating'. Sometimes, a treat was reciprocated, often through the buying of rounds of drinks, suggesting an equal relationship. Mass Observation noted that men sometimes completed a round, each member of a group buying their share, even though they did not want to drink that much or could not really afford to (1943). Elsewhere, some drinkers bought more than others, though. Dennis *et al.*'s study of a West Yorkshire mining community found that higher earners bought other workers drinks, suggesting that this was a form of 'capital destruction' which narrowed differences in income and status between different groups of men (1956). As this suggests, of course, this gift might create hierarchy as well as conviviality. As Dietler notes, "commensal hospitality … like the exchange of gifts, serves to establish and reproduce social relations", and these relations can be antagonistic just as gift exchanges can be (2001: 74). Skilled workers in Soviet Russia demanded vodka as 'pay' for the informal apprenticeship of new factory workers, and as this 'booty' was shared with their superiors, it flowed upwards like a tithe, creating bonds with the managers above them rather than the workers below them (Transchel, 2006: 134–135). Gifts of drink created both egalitarian and hierarchical environments.

What Mauss called 'the obligation to reciprocate' can be seen in Mass Observation's description of round-buying: "the strong social compulsion for its observance, the stigma attached to those who do not carry it out, and the resentment expressed by anyone accused of doing so" (1943: 177). Bolton's drinkers were judged on their generosity, their adoption of an ethic of hospitality. These practices created a connection between drinking places and intoxicants, and trust, sociability, hospitality and commensality. According to his biographer, Mass Observation's Tom Harrisson agreed with this understanding of drinking: "It was, he felt, the only way to know a man or to learn if you could trust him" (Heimann, 2003: 22). A similar 'code' was observed in saloons in the United States at the turn of the century: "men who did each other the honor of drinking together also were expected to celebrate and reinforce their special bond through the swapping of drinks, favors, small loans, and other gestures of mutual assistance and friendship" (Powers, 1994: 1). The saloon 'regular' was loyal to the rules that bound the group—"constancy, conformity, conviviality, commonality"—guiding the ways in which drinkers interacted with one another (Powers, 1998: 21). The 'good' qualities of drinking places were actively produced in these exchanges of material things, and the sites in which they happened took on those characteristics.

Less attention has been paid to the commensal consumption of other intoxicants. One English tobacco trade publication estimated that each publican gave away 80–100 gross of clay pipes to their customers every year, which "further suggests the importance of hospitality in the smoking ritual" (Hilton, 2000: 49). This gift from the publican might have been at small cost to them at one or two shillings per gross (British Weekly, 1889: 70), but it still suggests something more than canny marketing. Against the tendency of smokers to describe their consumption as a solitary, contemplative, pleasure, there are many indications that these gifted pipes could be commensally smoked, like the 'body of smoke' created by Sala's sugarbakers or the smoking of Dickens' coalheavers. This description of a 'smoking parliament' in London in the 1850s presents another example: "pipes were always placed on the table after dinner, together with screws of shag tobacco, and a smoking parliament moistened with hot or cold punch according to the seasons, was generally held during the following hour" (Apperson, 1914: 163).

This commensality could also be a gift between smokers. In the twentieth century, one German critic of the cigarette nonetheless recognised its value "as the symbol of a hospitable home when time does not permit that anything else be offered" (cited in Schivelbusch, 1993: 116). Mass Observation recorded cigarette 'rounds' in pubs and other drinking places; this "helped define the group, it enclosed a community to the exclusion of non-smokers and continued the public, communal mode of consumption" (Hilton, 2000: 130). Mass Observers estimated that only half of the groups they observed in ordinary post-war cafés offered cigarettes around, which they thought was actually a sign of 'cigarette close-fistedness'; "it takes the more relaxed and social atmosphere of the pub to persuade the smoker to regard his cigarettes with a less possessive eye; in the pubs packets are more freely offered round" (1949: 128–129). This identification of 'close-fistedness' echoed criticism of the 'slow-motion people' who were last to offer to buy a round of drinks (1943: 178), again indicating the obligation to reciprocate. Victorian smokers made similar complaints about 'tobacco-cadgers' who exploited the custom of sharing tobacco by taking more than one pipe's 'charge' when it was offered, or not reciprocating (Wright, 1867: 93–94). In one of W. W. Jacobs' short stories, an unpopular Londoner is described as "The sort of man that 'ad always left his baccy-box at 'ome, but always 'ad a big pipe in 'is pocket" (1919: 84). Treating might also have prompted greater consumption, as smokers reported smoking more in company; "smoking in the social relaxation of the pub is about three times as frequent as smoking in lunch-time cafes, buses, dance halls, queues or the street" (Mass Observation, 1949: 145). However, Observers saw pub smoking as "a way of underlining and embellishing enjoyment that is already there" (145). Either way, smoking was strongly associated with sociability.

This association with gifting and sharing was visible elsewhere too. In interwar Egypt, cigarette advertising "expressed the same sense of social familiarity earlier associated with the habit of the water-pipe", showing the cigarette as "a means to keep company, to connect, rather than as a way to portray individualism… In ads, smokers offered a cigarette to a friend, or lit a cigarette for a companion as a token of camaraderie and respect" (Shecter, 2005: 488). In China, tobacco was already part of the hospitality hosts were obliged to offer, "join[ing] tea as the quintessential expression of hospitality when receiving guests ... Cordially offering visitors a pipe along with tea, snacks, or alcohol signaled one's generosity, good manners, and refinement" (Benedict, 2011: 68). In twentieth-century Chengdu teahouses supplied patrons with tobacco, pipes and cigarettes, much as British pubs did (Wang, 2008: 127). Wu Zuxiang's 1944 essay 'Yan' (Tobacco) considers the changing importance of sharing tobacco; "there are no rituals one can engage in to replicate the kind of intimate sharing implied by passing along the hookah. Instead, all one can do is open a pack and offer a mass-produced stick to the other" (Benedict, 2011: 192). However even as a degraded form of hospitality, cigarette sharing was still important for masculine social networks at the end of the twentieth century (247).

Approaching the consumption of alcohol and tobacco as a form of material culture allows us to locate some of the characteristics of drinking places in particular practices and material things, rather than seeing them as part of a more nebulous association of ideas and specific places. In pre-industrial Russia, for example, a gift of vodka could create symbolic capital in different ways: for the parents of the bride at village weddings; as payment for contributors to *pomochi* (work parties for road building or harvesting); or as a fine or compensation for wrongdoing (Transchel, 2006: 17–19). Communal generosity, collective labour and justice were associated with village life, rather than drinking places, but once these practices became established in urban taverns, they took on some of the positively valued character of the commune. Drinking place sociability *produced* commensality, hospitality and generosity, just as contemporary home decoration actively *makes* homes, genders and classes (Gullestad, 1993). A gifted drink or cigarette materialises or objectifies these qualities. But does it matter that these practices and things intoxicate?

Material engagements, intoxicating atmospheres

What role does alcohol play within 'social infrastructure'? Mass Observation saw something like drunkenness without alcohol in football and holiday crowds and other contemporary forms of excitement: "the hysterical forms of revivalism and mass enthusiasm produce substantially the same effects as drink in an industrialized culture, and tend to replace altogether the need for alcohol in the individuals concerned" (1943: 252–253). Do we need to privilege sociability over intoxication, though? Bruno Latour suggested that social scientists tend to see objects as "mere receptacles for human categories" (1993: 52); from that perspective, alcohol and tobacco simply *represent* hospitality or intoxication. On the other side of the divide, natural scientists assume that intoxicants are strong and society is weak, turning "humans into so many puppets manipulated by objective forces" (53).

To get beyond the stale dichotomy Latour identified, we might turn to recent work in what is sometimes described as the 'new materialism'. A useful demonstration of the value of these ideas comes from Alan Latham and Derek McCormack's discussion of the 'psychoactive socialities' intoxicants help create in cities (2004). Drawing on Deleuze and others, they consider bodies, alcohol and other elements of city life as assemblages rather than 'solid' and singular objects. Rather than a powerful, external force acting upon us, "the fluid and volatile liquidity of alcohol confronts us with the difficulty of apprehending its materiality as an object" (715). This is because things do not have innate properties but develop capacities through their interactions with other things. Alcohol is one thing in a bottle and another in the bloodstream, but it remains lively, possessing the capacity to change, to become new things. It could be very difficult to make alcohol-free temperance drinks in the nineteenth century, for example. A British report on ginger, herb and botanic beers of this kind conducted in 1906 found that 37% of them contained more than 2% alcohol by volume (ABV), the level at which the law defined them as alcoholic drinks; around 13% of the total contained 4–6% ABV, and the strongest 3% ranged between 6 and 9.5% ABV. While some may have been misleadingly labelled by unscrupulous producers, it is more likely that their strength was the result of accidental fermentation caused by poor storage or the use of very strong alcohol to make the essences that gave them their flavour (Pratt, 1907: 223–224). The 'Bishop's Beer' sold in Bishop Fallows's temperance 'Home Salon' in Chicago was non-alcoholic only for the first two weeks after brewing, at which point fermentation (and disqualification as a temperance drink) became a real possibility (Calkins, 1901: 226).

These lively concoctions seem to fit Jane Bennett's idea of 'vital materialism', which considers "the capacity of things—edibles, commodities, storms, metals—not only to impede or block the will and design of humans but also to act as quasi agents or forces with trajectories, propensities, or tendencies of their own" (2010: xiii). Alcohol has the capacity to do different things as it forms relations with us, acting as an antiseptic bactericide in hand sanitiser gel, or intoxicating us when consumed, much as Bennett considers eating as the addition of food to a 'non-linear' assemblage (our bodies) with unpredictable and emergent effects (2010: 42). As Courtwright noted, the arrival of new substances—sugar (and the spirits made from it), tobacco, coffee, tea—from Europe's colonies triggered a 'psychoactive revolution' that changed not only tastes but also bodies, feelings and thoughts (2001). Sugar made new relations possible in the eighteenth century, quickly joining tea and coffee in British cups and encouraging rituals of gentlemanly sociability around the punchbowl (Harvey, 2012). In late nineteenth-century France, the availability of cheap sugar made from beets just as *phylloxera* was destroying the nation's vineyards encouraged a new taste for brandies and spirit drinks like absinthe, and a new commensal ritual, the *aperitif* (Prestwich, 1988). Fittingly, one of Latham and McCormack's examples of "the active, affective role played by the nonhuman (or inhuman) in shaping emergent materialities" is the sweetness of that 1990s folk devil, the 'alcopop' (2004: 717). Sugar and alcohol turn out to be lively substances, good mixers, entering into highly productive relationships with all kinds of other assemblages, including our bodies and social spaces.

But if we are looking for assemblages, for collections of things, people and affect, why stop with intoxicants, when we might see drinking places themselves as intoxicating? The material form of drinking places and the objects they contain have been thought to encourage alcohol consumption, like the 'perpendicular drinking' associated with nineteenth-century bars without seats in both London and Mexico City, or the encouragement that open, undivided bars apparently gave to drinking, as acquaintances saw and treated one another (Kneale, 1999, 2012; Toner, 2011). We might also think of the affective 'atmospheres' of intoxication, with atmospheres understood as "aesthetic and affective spaces", "spaces not so much as three-dimensional containers for activity, but as shifting configurations of bodies, materials, and ideas taking place with different degrees of affective intensity and duration" (McCormack 2013: 59, 60). The intoxicating atmospheres of drinking places emerge from the interaction of humans and non-humans, including less apparently material things like light and shadow, or the intensity and rhythm of sound (Duff, 2012; Wilton and Moreno, 2012; Shaw, 2014; Wilkinson, 2017).

Thinking historically, Dickens' famous description of an early London gin palace, originally published in 1835 (Jackson, 2019: 6), is often read for the contrast it draws between the opulence of this site and the poverty of its patrons, but it also suggests an intoxicating atmosphere:

> All is light and brilliancy. The hum of many voices issues from that splendid gin-shop … the gay building with the fantastically ornamented parapet, the illuminated clock, the

> plate-glass windows surrounded by stucco rosettes, and its profusion of gas-lights in richly-gilt burners, is perfectly dazzling when contrasted with the darkness and dirt we have just left… A bar of French-polished mahogany, elegantly carved, extends the whole width of the place; and there are two side-aisles of great casks, painted green and gold, enclosed within a light brass rail…
>
> *(1875: 166)*

Not all drinking places could offer the etched and coloured glass, mirrors, polished metal and wood, marble, tiles, gas lights, and shining bottles and glasses that were found in gin palaces or cabarets, but they would all have some kind of atmosphere: smoke and other smells, fragrant and otherwise; talk, laughter, music, contemplative or hostile silences. Different spaces might have their own specific atmospheres like the snug (private, cosy) and the open bar (public, lively); Stella Moss reads Mass Observation's study of types of rooms in Bolton's pubs as productive of different masculinities in a similar fashion (2016). Clearly, alcohol played an important part in these assemblages, and so did human bodies, but the intoxicating atmosphere of these venues belongs to the assemblage, not to those two elements alone. Cameron Duff's description of a rather different example makes a similar point. "The young man about to consume a tablet of ecstasy in a downtown warehouse party is not the only agent involved in this consumption", Duff suggests; we should also consider the text messages that connect him to friends and others; the music, the equipment that provides it and the skills of the DJ in creating and playing his set; the furniture and carefully calibrated design of spaces within the club; even the new trainers he is looking forward to testing on the dance floor (2012: 150). For Duff, this approach offers another way of thinking about the contexts of consumption: "What if one were to prioritise analysis of the *event of consumption* rather than the drug user?" (2014: 636, emphasis in original). The task of the researcher who is also part of this event is then to reflect on the shared experience of it, or the 'common-sense' of this intoxication as Thomas Thurnell-Read puts it (2011: 46), a collective sensory engagement with laughter, music or the smells of vodka and vomit.

This consideration of the event of consumption goes beyond the idea of 'drunken deportment' (MacAndrew and Edgerton, 1969) because it refuses to divide intoxication into 'physiological' and 'cultural' elements, while decentring drunkenness and the 'effects' of consumption. Sala's description of the sugarbakers' beer-shop takes in the smoke, the smokers and their song—the atmosphere as he encountered it—and alcohol is just another element. Other forms of intoxication emerge from these environments. Perhaps the short pipes that marked out working-class smokers were short for a reason, for example. While "Smoking was a mobile activity that might be combined with working as well as leisure and sociability" (Owens *et al.*, 2010: 220), the long-stemmed 'churchwarden's pipe' was, for G. L. Apperson, intended for smokers "of what I might call a sedentary nature. You could not even walk while holding a long churchwarden in your mouth… Labourers smoked short clays when out of doors, and churchwardens when they rested from their labours and took their ease in their inn in the evenings" (1914: 164–165). While the origins of its name remain obscure, there are suggestions that the churchwarden's long stem also made it the best pipe to smoke while reading, so it could be a solitary pipe as well as a sociable one. Seen as an event of consumption, as a coming together of practice, mobility and materiality, the churchwarden required a seat or at least somewhere to stand still, while the short pipe, like the cigarette that replaced it, needed fewer accessories.

Expanded sites, mobile objects

As a final consideration, we might explode these drinking places even further, following their material and affective components away from the sites themselves. British drinkers circulated from pub to pub, weaving connections between drinking places, homes, workplaces and other sites. Objects travelled with them: the clay pipes publicans gave away, the bottles, buckets, jugs or 'growlers' that carried pub-poured beer into homes, the drinking and smoking paraphernalia deliberately or absent-mindedly taken from the bar. We know that the flow of alcohol out of drinking places worried British reformers because the Child Messenger Act of 1901 restricted children to carrying beer home to their parents in containers sealed or corked after filling; after the 1908 Children's Act, only premises with a dedicated off-sales or 'jug-and-bottle' counter could sell beer to children (Moss, 2009; Jennings, 2016). Alcohol spilling out of pubs contaminated surrounding spaces (Croll, 1999; Kneale, 1999; Kneale, 2001), affecting even those charged with protecting society against it, as Richard Robinson's account of Brighton's drunken policemen shows (2016). In the US, the women and children who 'rushed the growler', carrying pails of beer from the salon, blurred the distinction between supposedly public and private spaces, but drink was also highly mobile throughout the city as beer peddlers sold bottles from wagons (Duis, 1983).

We can follow these objects, tracing their biographies and trajectories (Appadurai, 1986, and see Cook, 2004). Archaeologists, historians and historical geographers have suggested that the material culture of intoxicant consumption is ubiquitous in many urban sites. We would expect the remains of clay pipes and drinking vessels to make up a significant part of eighteenth- and early nineteenth-century American and British drinking place assemblages (Pearce, 2000), but it is more interesting when they turn up in rubbish left by households in Victorian Limehouse:

> Discarded household objects, often marked by years of wear and tear, draw attention to the minutiae of daily domestic routines: the preparation of food and drink and the coming together of people at different times of the day for their consumption; the grind of household chores; the care of children; or the moments of sociability, pleasure and release offered by alcohol and tobacco.
>
> *(Owens et al., 2010: 214).*

These objects included a pewter vessel engraved with the name of the nearby Spread Eagle pub (Owens and Jefferies, 2016), and many well-smoked pipes, possibly given away in this or another local drinking place. Elsewhere in London, this team found 'moralising china' dinner services, some with temperance connotations, alongside large numbers of wine bottles (Jeffries *et al.*, 2009). The contradictory nature of these assemblages emphasises the fluidity and complexity of these mobile material worlds. Tavern flasks, jugs, tankards and mugs are found in other domestic assemblages in Lambeth, alongside pipes (Tyler, 2004) and in the Kent village of Guston discarded jugs were probably used to carry beer from the Plough to labourers' cottages (Licence, 2015). If we can 'follow' these objects—like the Spread Eagle's pewter (Owens and Jefferies, 2016), the glass bottles the Biucchi brothers sold in Clerkenwell (Jeffries, 2009), the beer bottles thrown away by a Shropshire postman (Licence, 2015) and the bottles that evaded Prohibition restrictions at six sites in California (Mosher and Wilkie, 2010)—we can connect homes, workplaces and drinking places.

Archaeological work of this kind, coupled with a historical attention to traces of material things in archives, allows us to expand our sense of these sites, in much the same way that Ruth Slatter has approached London's Methodist chapels. The material spaces of these chapels expanded and shifted as cups, saucers, cutlery, tables and chairs travelled up and down the steep hill of Archway Road, or as a communion service was given from one East London chapel to another (2019b). These mobile, material things and spaces were as much a part of Methodist religious experience (Slatter, 2019a) as seats and gas-lights were part of the intoxicating atmosphere of the gin palace. Seeing sites as 'becoming', on the verge of turning into something else or held together by practices of care, restoration and co-habitation (Edensor, 2011), extends our apprehension of them in both time and space.

Conclusions

This chapter has suggested that we might expand our understanding of drinking places, chiefly by extending our understanding of intoxication to include other substances as well as the wider contexts, sites and meanings of consumption, and by more closely examining the relationship between intoxication and the associations drinking places have with sociability, commensality and hospitality. As mobile and expansive assemblages of affects, bodies and objects, these sites turn out to be much more diffuse places than we might have expected them to be, and much less dominated by drinking and alcohol as opposed to other practices and materials.

However, it is worth considering some of the new questions that might emerge from the synthesis of these perspectives on intoxication and place. One of the key problems here is the tension between the human-centred approach of material culture studies and the post-humanist arguments of many forms of new materialism. If a cigarette offered to a fellow smoker simply signifies hospitality, for example, does it matter that it is a cigarette and not something else? Powers notes that saloon bartenders were not allowed to accept a customer's offer of a drink; asking for cash instead was thought to be 'baldly mercenary' but it was acceptable to take a cigar, because both had the same money value and "treating with tobacco was regarded as a sociable and roughly comparable gesture to treating with alcohol" (1994: 5). From this perspective, the intoxicating capacities of beer and cigarettes are less important than their equivalence as gifts.

However, we might see intoxication as a key part of this sociability, as an affective outcome closely bound up with feelings of commensality and hospitality. Dietler sees intoxication as a special form of commensality precisely *because* these materials form new relations with their consumers:

> Alcoholic beverages frequently have a privileged role in the feasting context because they are essentially food with certain psychoactive properties resulting from an alternative means of preparation that tend to amplify their significance in the important dramaturgical aspects of ritual... Moreover, this property of fermentation as a quasi-magical transformation of food into a substance that, in turn, transforms human consciousness augments the symbolic value of alcohol in the common liminal aspects of rituals.
>
> *(2001: 72–73).*

The transformation of food into alcohol is not simply a change in meaning but a change in food's capacities. Working on the ways in which these approaches contradict and complement each other might help to draw out the importance that the special charge of intoxication, as a more-than-human outcome, has for what we tend to think of as purely human forms of sociability.

The second issue concerns critical insights that have not been explored in this chapter, but which remain of utmost importance. Much of the work on drinking places drawn upon here is concerned with social difference—class, gender, sexuality, race, age and more. Practices and substances of commensality and generosity can exclude or dominate just as easily as they bring equals together, and a consumption event or assemblage can create outcomes that divide and exclude. For Valerie Hey, masculine pub sociability was driven by a 'taboo against unbonding', for example, where men's commensal, hospitable experience is threatened by women (1986). Similarly, Mass Observation's discussion of British smoking noted that "Post-war wage increases have gone for the most part to the man of the house rather than to the housewife, and have been used by him largely to balance the extra cost of tobacco" (Mass Observation, 1949: 3).

Pub smoking, like the drinking discussed by Moss (2016), clearly created very different kinds of experiences. It also shaped other kinds of relationships. The nineteenth-century pipes bought so cheaply by the publican and freely given away to customers, the majority of them men, were made by women working at home; "Clay pipes are difficult to make, and require a great deal of practice. Sixteen must be made to the dozen, for many break, and many are imperfect. … And after all this, the pipes are sold *[to the publican]* at less than a farthing each!" (British Weekly, 1889: 70–71). In this way, masculine enjoyment of commensal smoking in 'great good places' depended in part on free pipes produced by women's poorly paid domestic labour.

Still, tracing these contradictions and connections is entirely in keeping with the argument that we should be looking at these and other spaces with a new eye for the things that emerge from them, often unexpectedly. A broader examination of drinking places may well generate entirely new questions for researchers interested in intoxication.

References

Adler, M. (1991) 'From symbolic exchange to commodity consumption: Anthropological notes on drinking as a symbolic practice', in Barrows, S., and Room, R., (Eds.), *Drinking: Behaviour and Belief in Modern History.* Berkeley: University of California Press, 376–389.

Appadurai, A. (1986) 'Introduction: commodities and the politics of value', in Appadurai (ed.), *The Social Life of Things: Commodities in Cultural Perspective.* Cambridge: Cambridge University Press, 3–63.

Apperson, G. L. (1914) *The Social History of Smoking.* London: M. Secker.

Bell, D. (2007) 'The hospitable city: Social relations in commercial spaces', *Progress in Human Geography* 31(1), 7–22.

Benedict, C. (2011) *Golden-Silk Smoke: A History of Tobacco in China, 1550–2010.* Berkeley: University of California Press.

Bennett, J. (2010) *Vibrant Matter: A Political Ecology of Things.* Durham, NC: Duke University Press.

Booth, N. (2018) 'Drinking and domesticity: The materiality of the mid-nineteenth-century provincial pub', *Journal of Victorian Culture*, 23, 289–309.

Booth, W. (1890) *In Darkest London and the Way Out.* London: The Salvation Army.

Bouzigard, A. C. and Saidel, B. A. (2012) 'A note on the dating of the clay smoking pipes collected in the course of two archaeological surveys conducted in Saudi Arabia: The Comprehensive Survey of Saudi Arabia (1976–1981) and Michael Gilmore's survey of the Darb al-Hajj', *Arabian Archaeology and Epigraphy*, 23, 116–124.

British Weekly (1889) *Toilers in London or, Inquiries Concerning Female Labour in the Metropolis.* London: Hodder and Stoughton.

Burnett, J. (1999) *Liquid Pleasures: A Social History of Drinks in Modern Britain.* London: Routledge.

Burnett, J. (2004) *England Eats Out: A Social History of Eating Out in England from 1830 to the Present.* Harlow: Pearson Education.

Calkins, R. (1901) *Substitutes for the Saloon. An Investigation Made for the Committee of Fifty*. Boston and New York: Houghton, Mifflin and Company.

Clement, W. (2020) 'The Christ in the Cabaret: Putting a Blasphemous Bar Crawl on Trial in Third Republic France.' *Cultural and Social History*, 17, 189–205.

Cook, I. (2004) 'Follow the thing: Papaya', *Antipode*, 36, 642–664.

Courtwright, D. T. (2001) *Forces of Habit: Drugs and the Making of the Modern World*. Cambridge, MA: Harvard University Press.

Croll, A. (1999) 'Street disorder, surveillance and shame: Regulating behaviour in the public spaces of the late Victorian British town', *Social History*, 24(3), 250–268.

Davison, A. (2006) 'Try the alternative', *Journal of the Brewery History Society*, 123, 92–109.

Dennis, N., Henriques, F., and Slaughter, C. (1956) *Coal is Our Life: An Analysis of a Yorkshire Mining Community*. London: Eyre & Spottiswoode.

Dickens, C. (1875) *Sketches By Boz. Illustrative of Every-Day Life, and Every-Day People*. Wakefield: William Nicholson and Sons.

Dietler, M. (2001) 'Theorizing the Feast: Rituals of consumption, commensal politics, and power in African contexts', in Dietler, M., and Brian, H. (Eds.), *Feasts: Archaeological and Ethnographic Perspectives on Food, Politics, and Power*. Washington, DC: Smithsonian, 65–114.

Dingle, A. E. (1972) 'Drink and working-class living standards in Britain, 1870–1914', *Economic History Review Second Series*, 25: 608–622.

Duff, C. (2012) 'Accounting for context: Exploring the role of objects and spaces in the consumption of alcohol and other drugs', *Social & Cultural Geography*, 13(2), 145–159.

Duff, C. (2014) 'The place and time of drugs', *International Journal of Drug Policy*, 25: 633–639.

Duis, P. (1983) *The Saloon: Public Drinking in Chicago and Boston 1880–1920*. Urbana: University of Illinois Press.

Edensor, T. (2011) 'Entangled agencies, material networks and repair in a building assemblage: The mutable stone of St Ann's Church, Manchester', *Transactions of the Institute of British Geographers*, 36: 238–252.

Eriksen, S. (1999) 'Alcohol as a gender symbol', *Scandinavian Journal of History*, 24(1), 45–73.

Fischler, C. (2011) 'Commensality, society and culture', *Social Science Information*, 50(3–4), 528–548.

Fonder, N. L. (2013) 'Pleasure, leisure, or vice? Public morality in imperial Cairo, 1882–1949', Ph.D. thesis, Harvard University.

Fuhrmann, M. (2009) 'Down and out on the quays of İzmir: "European" musicians, innkeepers, and prostitutes in the Ottoman port-cities', *Mediterranean Historical Review*, 24(2), 169–185.

Georgeon, F. (2002) 'Ottomans and drinkers: The consumption of alcohol in Istanbul in the nineteenth century', in Eugene, R. (Ed.), *Outside In: On the Margins of the Modern Middle East*. London: I. B. Tauris, 31–52.

Gough, J. B. (1880) *Sunlight and Shadow*. Hartford, CO: A. D. Worthington & Company.

Greenaway, J. (1998) 'The "Improved" public house, 1870–1950: The key to civilised drinking or the primrose path to drunkenness?', *Addiction*, 93: 173–181.

Grehan, J. (2006) 'Smoking and "Early Modern" sociability: The great tobacco debate in the Ottoman middle east (Seventeenth and Eighteenth centuries)', *American Historical Review*, 111, 1375.

Gullestad, M. (1993) 'Home decoration as popular culture: Constructing homes, genders and classes in Norway', in Del Valle, T. (Ed.), *Gendered Anthropology*. London: Routledge, 128–161.

Gutzke, D. W. (2005) *Pubs and Progressives: Reinventing the Public House in England, 1896–1960*. Dekalb: Northern Illinois University Press.

Habermas, J. (1991) *The Structural Transformation of the Public Sphere: An Inquiry into a Category of Bourgeois Society*. Burger, T. with Lawrence, F. (trans.). Cambridge: MIT Press.

Haine, W. S. (1994) 'The priest of the proletarians: Parisian Café owners and the working class, 1820–1914', *International Labor and Working-Class History*, 45, 16–28.

Haine, W. S. (1996) *The World of the Paris Café: Sociability among the French Working Class, 1789–1914*. Baltimore, MD: Johns Hopkins University Press.

Haine, W. S. (2003) 'Drinking Establishments (France)', in Blocker, Jr., J. S., Fahey, D. M., and Tyrrell, I. R. (Eds.), *Alcohol and Temperance in Modern History An International Encyclopedia*, Vol. I. Santa Barbara: ABC-CLIO, 203–206.

Harrison, B. (1971). *Drink and the Victorians: The Temperance Question in England 1815–1872*. London: Faber and Faber.

Harrison, B. (1973). 'Pubs', in Dyos, H. J., and Wolff, M. (Eds.), *The Victorian City*, Vol. I. London: Routledge and Kegan Paul, 161–190.

Harvey, K., (2012) 'Ritual encounters: Punch parties and masculinity in the eighteenth century', *Past & Present*, 214, 165–203.

Heimann, J. (2003) *The Most Offending Soul Alive: Tom Harrisson and His Remarkable Life*. London: Aurum Press.

Hey, V. (1986). *Patriarchy and Pub Culture*. London: Tavistock.

Hilton, M. (2000) *Smoking in British Popular Culture 1800–2000*. Manchester and New York: Manchester University Press.

Hind Smith, R. (undated). *The Other Narcotic: Addressed Especially and Earnestly to Abstainers from Intoxicants*. Manchester: Anti-Narcotic League. Wellcome Collection.

Holt, D. B. (2018) 'Whiskey: Marketplace Icon', *Consumption Markets & Culture*, 21: 1, 76–81.

Report from the Select Committee on Regulation of Public Houses, Hotels, Beer-Shops, Dancing Saloons, Coffee-Houses, Theatres and Places of Public EntertainmentTogether with the proceedings of the Committee, minutes of evidence, appendix, and index.

Hubble, N. (2006). *Mass-Observation and Everyday Life: Culture, History, Theory*. Basingstoke: Palgrave Macmillan.

Jacobs, W. W. (1919). 'Sam's ghost,' in *Deep Waters*. London and New York: Hodder & Stoughton, 83–104.

Jackson, L. (2019) *Palaces of Pleasure: From Music Halls to the Seaside to Football, How the Victorians Invented Mass Entertainment*. New Haven and London: Yale University Press.

Jeffries, N. (2009) 'A biography of a stoneware ginger beer bottle: The Biucchi brothers and the Ticinese community in nineteenth-century London', in White C. L. (Ed.), *The Materiality of Individuality: Archaeological Studies of Individual Lives*. New York: Springer, 57–74.

Jeffries, N., Owens, A., Hicks, D., Featherby, R., and Wehner, K. (2009). 'Rematerialising metropolitan histories? People, places and things in modern London', in Horning, A., and Palmer, M. (Eds.), *Crossing Paths or Sharing Tracks? Future Directions in the Archaeological Study of Post-1550 Britain and Ireland*. Woodbridge, Suffolk; Rochester, NY: Boydell & Brewer, 23–350.

Jennings, P. (2016). *A History of Drink and the English, 1500–2000*. Abingdon and New York: Routledge.

Kirli, C. (2016) 'Coffeehouses: Leisure and Sociability in Ottoman Istanbul', in Borsay, P. and Furnée, J. H. (Eds.), *Leisure Cultures in Urban Europe, c.1700–1870: A Transnational Perspective*. Manchester: Manchester University Press, 161–181.

Kneale, J. (1999). '"A problem of supervision": Moral geographies of the nineteenth-century British public house', *Journal of Historical Geography*, 25, 333–334.

Kneale, J. (2001). 'The place of drink: Temperance and the public, 1856–1914', *Social and Cultural Geography*, 2, 43–59.

Kneale, J. (2012). 'Surveying pubs, cities and unfit lives: Governmentality, drink and space in nineteenth- and early twentieth-century Britain.' *Journal for the Study of British Cultures*, 19, 45–60.

Kneale, J. (2021) 'Good, homely, troublesome or improving? Historical geographies of drinking places, c.1850–1950', *Geography Compass*, 15, e12557. https://doi.org/10.1111/gec3.12557

Kömeçoğlu, U. (2005) 'The publicness and sociabilities of the Ottoman coffeehouse', *Javnost – The Public*, 12(2), 5–22.

Lambert, W. R. (1983) *Drink and Sobriety in Victorian Wales, c. 1820–c.1895*. Cardiff: University of Wales Press.

Latham, A., and Layton, J. (2019) 'Social infrastructure and the public life of cities: Studying urban sociality and public spaces', *Geography Compass*, 13, e12444.

Latham, A., and McCormack, D. (2004) 'Moving cities', *Progress in Human Geography*, 28(6), 701–724.

Latour, B. (1993) *We Have Never Been Modern*. Hemel Hempstead: Harvester Wheatsheaf.

Licence, T. (2015) *What the Victorians Threw Away*. Oxford and Philadelphia: Oxbow Books.

MacAndrew, C., and Edgerton, R. (1969) *Drunken Comportment: A Social Explanation*. Chicago: Aldine.

Mass Observation. (1949) 'Man and his cigarette', *FR* 3192 (Dec 1949).

Mass Observation. (1943) *The Pub and the People*. London: Gollancz.

Matthee, R. (2014) 'Alcohol in the Islamic Middle East: Ambivalence and ambiguity', *Past and Present*, 222 (Supplement 9), 100–125.

Maudlin, D. (2019) 'The urban inn: Gathering space, hierarchy and material culture in the eighteenth-century British town', *Urban History*, 46(4), 617–648.

Mauss, M. (1990). *The Gift: The Form and Reason for Exchange in Archaic Societies*. London and New York: Routledge.
McCormack, D. (2013) *Refrains for Moving Bodies: Experience and Experiment in Affective Spaces*. Durham NC: Duke University Press.
Milne-Smith, A. (2011). *London Clubland: A Cultural History of Gender and Class in Late-Victorian Britain*. New York: Palgrave Macmillan.
Mosher, A. E., and Wilkie, L. A. (2010) 'Historical Archaeo-Geographies of Scaled Statehood: American Federalism and Material Practices of National Prohibition in California, 1917–1933', *Archaeologies*, 6, 82–114.
Moss, S. (2009) 'A grave question': The Children Act and public house regulation, c.1908–1939', *Crimes and Misdemeanors*, 3, 98–117.
Moss, S. (2016) 'Manly drinkers: Masculinity and material culture in the interwar public house', In Greig, H., Hamlett, J., and Hannan, L. (Eds.), *Gender and Material Culture in Britain Since 1600*. London: Palgrave, 138–151.
Oldenburg, R. (1989). *The Great Good Place*, second edition. New York: Paragon House.
Owens, A., and Jeffries, N. (2016). 'People and things on the move: Domestic material culture, poverty and mobility in Victorian London', *International Journal of Historical Archaeology*, 20, 804–827.
Owens, A., Jeffries, N., Wehner, K., and Featherby, R. (2010). 'Fragments of the modern city: Material culture and the rhythms of everyday life in Victorian London', *Journal of Victorian Culture*, 15, 212–225.
Öztürk, S. (2008) 'The struggle over Turkish village Coffeehouses (1923–45)', *Middle Eastern Studies*, 44(3), 435–454.
Pawlett, W. (2011). 'Gifts and reciprocity', in Dale, S. (Ed.), *Encyclopedia of Consumer Culture*. Thousand Oaks, CA: SAGE Publications, 658–661.
Pearce, J. (2000) 'A late 18th-century inn clearance assemblage from Uxbridge, Middlesex', *Post-Medieval Archaeology*, 34(1), 144–186.
Powers, M. (1994) 'The "Poor Man's Friend": Saloonkeepers, workers, and the code of reciprocity in U.S. barrooms, 1870–1920', *International Labor and Working-Class History*, 45, Drinking and the Working Class (Spring, 1994), 1–15.
Powers, M. (1998) *Faces along the Bar: Lore and Order in the Workingman's Saloon, 1870–1920*. Chicago: University of Chicago Press.
Pratt, E. A (1907) *The Licensed Trade: An Independent Survey*. London: John Murray.
Prestwich, P. E. (1988) *Drink and the Politics of Social Reform: Antialcoholism in France Since 1870*. Palo Alto: Society for the Promotion of Science and Scholarship.
Rappaport, E. (2013) 'Sacred and useful pleasures: The temperance tea party and the creation of a Sober consumer culture in early industrial Britain', *Journal of British Studies* 52(October 2013), 990–1016.
Reinarman, C. (2013) 'On the cultural domestication of intoxicants', in Weinberg, D., Herring, J., and Regan, C. (Eds.), *Intoxication and Society: Problematic Pleasures of Drugs and Alcohol*. United Kingdom: Palgrave Macmillan, 153–171.
Report from the Select Committee on Regulation of Public Houses, Hotels, Beer-Shops, Dancing Saloons, Coffee-Houses, Theatres and Places of Public Entertainment. Together with the Proceedings of the Committee, Minutes of Evidence, Appendix, and Index. HC 1852–1853 (855), XXXVII.
Ritchie, J. E. (1858) *The Night Side of London*. London: William Tweedie.
Roberts, J. S. (1984). *Drink, Temperance and the Working Class in Nineteenth-Century Germany*. Boston: Allen and Unwin.
Roberts, J. S. (1991). 'The Tavern and politics in the German labor movement, c.1870–1914', in S. Barrows, and R. Room Drinking (Eds.), *Behavior and Belief in Modern History*. Berkeley: University of California Press, 98–111.
Robinson, R. (2016) 'Off beat and in drink: Impropriety and insobriety in Brighton's police, 1880–1921', *Social History of Alcohol and Drugs*, 30, 4–30.
Sala, G. A. (1859). *Gaslight and Daylight, with Some London Scenes they Shine Upon*. London: Chapman and Hall.
Shaw, R. (2014) 'Beyond night-time economy: Affective atmospheres of the urban night', *Geoforum*, 51, 87–95.
Shechter, R. (2005) 'Reading advertisements in a colonial/development context: Cigarette advertising and identity politics in Egypt, c1919–1939', *Journal of Social History*, 39(2), 483–503.

Schivelbusch, W. (1993). *Tastes of Paradise*, translated by David Jacobson. Vintage: New York.

Simmel, G. (1997) *Simmel on Culture: Selected Writings*. London: SAGE Publications.

Slatter, R. (2019a) 'Material "becomings" and a historical geography of religious experience: Metropolitan Methodism, 1851–1932', *Area*, 51, 14–24.

Slatter, R. (2019b) 'Materiality and the extended geographies of religion: The institutional design and everyday experiences of London's Wesleyan Methodist circuits, 1851–1932', *Journal of Historical Geography* 64, 60–71.

Stallybrass, P., and White, A. (1986) *The Politics and Poetics of Transgression*. Ithaca, NY: Cornell University Press.

Thurnell-Read, T. (2011) '"Common-sense" research: Senses, emotions and embodiment in researching stag tourism in Eastern Europe', *Methodological Innovations Online*, 6(3), 39–49.

Toner, D. (2011). "Everything in its right place? Drinking places and social spaces in Mexico city, c. 1780–1900,' *The Social History of Alcohol and Drugs*, 25(1–2), 26–48.

Toner, D. (2015) *Alcohol and Nationhood in Nineteenth-Century*. Mexico: University of Nebraska Press.

Transchel, K. (2006). *Under the Influence: Working-Class Drinking, Temperance, and Cultural Revolution in Russia, 1895–1932*. Pittsburgh: University of Pittsburgh Press.

Tremlett, G. (1987) *Clubmen: The History of the Working Men's Club and Institute Union*. London: Secker and Warburg.

Tyler, K. (2004). 'Two centuries of rubbish: Excavations at an 18th- and 19th-century site at 12–18 Albert Embankment, Lambeth', *Surrey Archaeological Collections*, 91: 105–136.

Veblen, T. (1915) *The Theory of The Leisure Class: An Economic Study of Institutions*, second edition. New York and London: Macmillan.

Wang, D. (2008) *The Teahouse: Small Business, Everyday Culture, and Public Politics in Chengdu, 1900–1950*. Stanford, CA: Stanford University Press.

Ware, J. R. (1909) *Passing English of the Victorian Era: A Dictionary of Heterodox English, Slang, and Phrase*. London: Routledge.

Wilkinson, S. (2017) 'Drinking in the dark: Shedding light on young people's alcohol consumption experiences', *Social & Cultural Geography*, 18(6), 739–757.

Wilton, R., and Moreno, C. M. (2012) 'Critical geographies of drugs and alcohol', *Social & Cultural Geography*, 13(2), 99–108.

Withington, P. (2014) "Introduction: Cultures of intoxication', *Cultures of Intoxication*, *Past & Present*, 222 (Supplement 9), 9–33.

Withington, P. (2020a) 'Intoxicants and the invention of "consumption"', *The Economic History Review*, 73: 384–408.

Withington, P. (2020b) 'Where was the coffee in early modern England?', *The Journal of Modern History* 92 (March 2020), 40–75.

Wright, T. (1867). *Some Habits and Customs of the Working Classes*. London: Tinsley Brothers.

11
JOIN US FOR DRINKS
Intoxication, work and academic conferences

Helen Keane

Introduction

In medical and public health discourse, intoxication is viewed as a pathological state that is both physically harmful and morally suspect (Hunt & Frank, 2017; Keane, 2009). Drunkenness is the iconic state of pathological and risky intoxication, marked by disinhibition, mood lability, impaired judgement, inappropriate behaviour and other signs of diminished physical or mental control (American Psychiatric Association, 2013, pp. 485, 497). This version of intoxication is visible and easily observable. Legal definitions reflect medical definitions in their focus on the obviously disorderly, as operationalised in laws related to the 'responsible service of alcohol'. Bar staff are expected to identify intoxication in patrons through signs such as 'becoming bad-tempered or aggressive', 'swaying and staggering' and 'rambling or unintelligible conversation' (Pennay, 2014).

However, there is a broader and less medicalised understanding of intoxication which incorporates more subtle changes in consciousness and comportment than obvious drunkenness. For example, Sociologist Angus Bancroft states that, 'Whether smoking cigarettes, drinking alcohol and coffee, or taking illicit drugs, for the majority of society's members, some kind of intoxication is a regular, often daily practice' (2009, p. 5). By expanding the category to include substance-related changes in the relationship between the self and the world, whatever their intensity, Bancroft (2009) normalises the experience of, and the desire for, intoxication. As he states, intoxication in this mode is a regular and routine practice, rather than an event outside of normal life. Another expansive definition of intoxication is the use of substances to alter consciousness (Hunt & Frank, 2017, p. 323). 'Altered consciousness' is usually interpreted to entail the experience of a level of awareness significantly divergent from an ordinary or normal state. However, consciousness can be shifted in relatively mild and transient ways, such as a few minutes daydreaming at one's desk.

As I have argued elsewhere, smoking (and nicotine consumption in general) is an example of an intoxicating practice that induces relatively subtle but nevertheless highly rewarding alterations in mood and attention (Keane, 2020). In the words of the National Institute on Drug Abuse, 'A transient surge of endorphins in the reward circuits of the brain causes a slight, brief euphoria when nicotine is administered' (NIDA, 2018, p. 7). The notion of a

DOI: 10.4324/9780429058141-15

'slight' euphoria seems oxymoronic at first glance, but it captures the particular capacity of cigarettes to create a brief opening in the smoker's day which is a minor, but sustaining enhancement of routine.

This form of slight or minor intoxication, combined with the convenience and portability of the cigarette, enabled smoking to become a tool of productivity, self-regulation and self-control in the twentieth century (Hughes, 2003). In this context, 'substance dependence' became an ally of the virtues and disciplined forms of conduct that it is usually regarded as undermining. In particular, smoking as a practice was coordinated with work for many, as a method of coping with boredom and fatigue, and enhancing concentration, until tobacco control regulation rendered indoor spaces smoke-free.

In this chapter, my aim is to examine the experience and effects of such forms of minor and productive intoxication in relation to alcohol consumed at work or at work-related events. These forms of intoxication disrupt the conventional opposition between moderation and intoxication as they incorporate forms of alcohol consumption that are intoxicating but also socially accepted as sensible and moderate (Yeomans, 2013). This is not to deny that alcohol intoxication as it is addressed in medicine, public health and the law can be harmful to the self and others. Rather, it is to highlight common and normalised social practices in which an intoxicating drug effect is valued and sought out, yet almost taken for granted.

My focus in the second part of the chapter is academic conferences. These events involve frequent temporal and spatial transitions between sessions and breaks, with attendant shifts in atmosphere that are in part produced through the provision of food and drink (Mair & Frew, 2018). Conferences are sites of demanding and high stakes identity management. They require the simultaneous performance of collegiality and competition within a context of strong cultural norms and social hierarchies (Lipton, 2020). In this chapter, I am particularly interested in the way conferences bring together two elements that are usually understood as oppositional in contemporary neoliberal organisations: intoxication and the responsibilities and goals of the enterprising professional subject. I suggest that in the networking practices of academic conferences, we can see minor intoxication as itself a form of work. This raises important questions about the inclusivity of such events, given increasing awareness of non-drinking as a cultural and religious practice and an individual choice (Pennay et al., 2019; Savic et al., 2016; Valentine et al., 2010).

Drinking at work, drinking as work

Social scientific research on alcohol use in the workplace developed in the 1980s and 1990s. The early work in this subfield tended to focus on drinking among men in blue-collar occupations such as construction and factory work, with an emphasis on the problems, risks and harms of workplace drinking (Ames & Janes, 1992). 'Problem drinking among workers' was conceptualised as a response to powerlessness and alienation, as well as being shaped by workplace cultures and subcultures (Ames & Janes, 1992; Seeman et al., 1988).

More recently, research from an organisational perspective has investigated alcohol as an element of food and drink rituals in the workplace (Flores-Pereira et al., 2008; Plester, 2015; Walker & Bridgman, 2013). In contrast to the literature that addresses drinking as a form of employee resistance to workplace regulations, this research draws attention to the use of alcohol by organisations to encourage positive feelings and a sense of belonging among workers. As Plester argues, food and drink practices have powerful social and symbolic meanings. They provide insights into organisational culture and climate, especially since ingesting 'treats' supplied by the workplace 'is a potent way to bodily interact with and actually embody organizational culture' (2015, p. 265). Regularly occurring rituals such as after-work drinks create affective relations not only between workers, but also between workers and the organisation.

Plester's study of food/drink rituals in four organisations from different industries highlights the value employees placed on opportunities for 'bonding', 'unwinding' and 'relaxing' with colleagues at events, both with and without alcohol (p. 260). However, the intoxicating and mood altering effects of alcohol were identified by participants as part of the warmth and pleasure of memorable events. One participant, a lawyer working at a prestigious law firm, explained that

> There is always lots of fun to be had. This is going to sound really bad but lots of the funny stuff that happens around here is when we're drinking socially and someone gets a bit drunk and does silly things.
>
> *(2015, p. 262)*

This comment demonstrates the ambiguity of such rituals, in that 'a bit drunk' and 'silly things' can be light-hearted and fun, or risky and harmful, or indeed both simultaneously. As Plester notes, some individuals resisted workplace drinking rituals, and identified them as a source of potential discomfort. Plester also identifies an interplay between control and freedom in these practices: the rituals may be relaxed and even raucous, but they are also controlled and managed by the organisation, and employees can be coerced into drinking (p. 264). And as in all rituals of belonging, inclusion depends on the exclusion of those who cannot or will not participate (Buvik, 2020).

Thus, from a critical perspective, organisationally endorsed and sponsored drinking can be interpreted as an intensification and extension of expected attachments to work, one of the characteristic features of post-Fordist capitalism (Adkins & Dever, 2016). Melissa Gregg argues that the contemporary professional workplace permits only a limited range of affective states and subjectivities and yet also demands 'appropriate collegial connection' through obligatory social events (Gregg, 2010, p. 253). In her incisive analysis of workplace affects, such forms of compulsory sociality and affection mask the reality of capitalist labour relations (including long hours and precarity) while also undermining other less alienated connections between workers.

Such accounts of workplace and work-related drinking add an important dimension to the extensive research on socialising and intoxication in night-time and leisure contexts. Night-time economies are frequently identified as spaces where individuals seek the loosening of the social constraints, conventions and expectations associated with daytime roles, such as 'professional' or 'responsible student' (Bianchini, 1995; Brain et al., 2000). While workplace drinking rituals do entail the alteration of behavioural norms and notable shifts in feelings, mood and atmosphere, participants are still inhabiting their professional identities and are still 'at work'. This can result in experiences of ambiguity and tension (Flores-Perera et al., 2008; Gusfield, 2003; Walker & Bridgman, 2013).

According to recent research with Norwegian employees and employers, situations such as Christmas parties, work celebrations, work-related travel and drinking with colleagues after work produce challenges and dilemmas related to obligatory participation, pressure to drink, the balancing of work and personal time, and the management of formal and informal drinking rules (Sagvaag et al., 2019). Sagvaag et al. conceptualise these issues as the navigation of a 'grey zone' between leisure and work. They argue that the 'grey zone' is in fact a continuum, from voluntary events primarily driven by leisure, to those that are effectively compulsory, experienced as 'drinking while working' (p. 79).

Investigating the grey zone between leisure and work demonstrates that intoxication, especially in its minor or subtle forms, can readily co-exist with expectations of responsibility, productivity and the maintenance of control (at least in cultures where 'moderate' and 'social' drinking is normalised). Indeed, in accounts of workplace drinking, the ability to manifest a suitably informal, light-hearted and mildly intoxicated self at appropriate times and places is part of being an ideal worker and organisational citizen (Gregg, 2010). The boundaries of 'proper' drinking at work will vary according to situation and professional and local cultures, but individuals are expected to avoid excess and loss of control, in whatever way these states are characterised (Rolando et al., 2014).

As well as an embodiment of organisational culture, alcohol consumption can be a more direct feature of successful work performance, for example, in relation to networking and the development of positive relationships with clients (Walker & Bridgman, 2013). Walker and Bridgman's study of young employees in a professional services firm illustrates the way organisations can 'prompt' drinking by workers (2013, p. 603). One of their participants is explicit about the training she received from the company on how to use alcohol as a prop:

> You actually get taught to use, drink in the left hand shake with your right. So there's etiquette around it. If we were to be networking in a room and I just met you, and we were having a conversation, and I noticed your drink was low, and we'd been having a conversation, and there were a couple of other people in the room that I wanted to talk to, I might say, 'oh I see you're out of a drink' or 'do you want a top up can I get you one?', bring it back and say 'here you go, it's been really lovely talking with you but I'm just going to take the opportunity to go and talk to others'...
>
> *(p. 602)*

I quote this response at length, first because it describes an unremarkable exchange in which alcohol (as an object, not just its effects) is used to 'ease the process of speaking to unfamiliar individuals' in a work context (Walker & Bridgeman, p. 602). As well as the actions of the respondent, the excerpt reveals how the recipient of the drink is also tied into a work-related drinking exchange. In addition, the response is specifically related to the practice of 'networking', which is central to the following discussion of the normative intoxication of academic conferences.

As I outline in the next section, the ubiquity of drinking at academic conferences is recognised in research and popular literature, but is not usually considered in relation to the concept and experience of intoxication. The exception is the small but growing literature on bad conference behaviour (and how to reduce it) but here my concern is primarily with the accepted use of alcohol rather than its role in producing misconduct (Foxx et al., 2019). I argue that academic conferences are fruitful sites for the study of work-related drinking because they combine work, the hope of future work and escape from work in a particularly intense, and many would say, exhausting and anxiety-producing way. In addition, one of the key practices of conferences, networking, is routinely enabled by alcohol consumption and its intoxicating effects.

Academic conferences as drinking sites[1]

Academic conferences are temporally and spatially intense events in which work, professional development, career building, knowledge exchange, socialising and leisure are combined. Conferences are diverse in terms of size, structure, formality and location, but they are inevitably sites where individuals develop and perform their academic identities, and attempt to build reputation and status in their field while also exercising judgement over others' professional performance (Henderson, 2015; Walters, 2018). Attendees are usually removed from their normal workplace; however, they are on 'university business', fulfilling performance objectives and representing their institutions. As Bell and King state, academic conferences can be usefully studied as 'inter-corporeal' and pedagogic spaces where 'techniques, skills and dispositions' are acquired and academic power relations are constructed and enacted (2010, p. 429). Crucially, conferences provide the opportunity for novices to demonstrate confidence and proficiency in both the formal and informal elements of 'being an academic'.

Conferences are sites where structures of inequality within academia are readily reinforced (Biggs, 2018). Attendance costs money and time (often substantial amounts of both). Inequities of access have been increasingly highlighted, especially for those with caring responsibilities or without secure employment (Black et al., 2020; Lipton, 2019). Access is not just a matter of getting to the conference, but also relates to different levels and experiences of participation. For instance, while some conference attendees experience a sense of freedom from routine demands and roles, attendees with caring responsibilities at home are often managing a difficult state of being 'in two places at once' (Henderson, 2019).

The activities, practices, encounters and atmospheres that make up a typical academic conference range from the banal to the sublime and/or devastating. Henderson's account emphasises the embodied experience of the conference attendee: '…we eat snatched meals, sandwiches with unnameable fillings balanced on paper plates; we navigate more or less boozy dinners, drink endless coffee and tea to combat the drowsiness provoked by excessive heating or the chill of air conditioning…' (2015, p. 914). Spicer's sketch of the 'reality' of conferences combines bodily discomfort with the nastiness of academic politics: 'Indifferent food. Petty controversy of the latest theory. Many glasses of the local liquor. Extra-marital affairs. Verbal violence. Arrogant grunts. Closed circles. Dashed hopes. Petty promotionalism. Scholastic policing. Grinding headaches. Boredom. Body pain' (2005, p. 21). As these descriptions suggest, the consumption of psychoactive substances is an expected and normalised feature of the conference schedule – coffee at regular points during the day and alcohol in the evening. In addition, international participants who have travelled over many time zones often resort to prescription drugs or alternative remedies to manage their sleep/wake cycle. This is not to say that all delegates consume these substances, but that the provision of coffee/caffeine and drinks/alcohol is part of the organisation, structure and diverse atmospheres of the conference.

As well as the 'more or less boozy dinner', the reception with beer, wine and finger food is a key transition point in the conference day. At the conferences I have recently attended, I have been struck by the shift in atmosphere, mood and bodily comportment signalled by the announcement 'time for drinks!'. By 4 p.m., delegates are tired and struggling to pay attention to the last presentations of the day; at 5.30 p.m., they are enlivened, seemingly keen to chat and laugh, move around and socialise. The successful conference drinks session prompts this transition in comportment by bringing into being a lively, light-hearted and hopeful affective atmosphere, experienced as tangibly different from the earlier conference schedule, even if it takes place in the same building or room.

The concept of affective atmosphere helps us attend to intoxication as a varied and collective experience which emerges in a shared space and time (Jayne et al., 2010). As recent geographical research has emphasised, atmospheres are generated by bodies gathered in space but their corporeal, sensorial and emotional effects exceed the bodies they emerge from

(Anderson, 2009; Bissell, 2010). This insight has produced accounts of night-time and night-out socialising that highlight the 'priming' effects of different atmospheres on the actions and conduct of individuals (Duff & Moore, 2015; Shaw, 2014). Conference drinks events have their own atmospheric priming effects on participants, enhancing individuals' inclination to be open, polite and friendly to others beyond their friends and colleagues. The limited choice of food and drink, provided without direct payment, masks differences in income and taste in favour of commensality and togetherness. The circulation of wait staff with trays of mainly alcoholic drinks and food around a space with limited seating encourages mild intoxication, conversation and mingling.

However, personal experiences of the collective atmosphere of the drinks event vary according to embodied identities (such as gender, ethnicity, age, sexuality and disability) and embodied states (such as tiredness, hunger and anxiety) (Jayne et al., 2010). In addition, the socialising that occurs in these events involves particular challenges of etiquette and affective self-management because of the need to transition more or less smoothly between interactions with old friends, colleagues we see every day and people we hardly know or have never met (Thompson, 2012). Despite the convivial atmosphere, hierarchies of power and status remain salient. The negotiation of the drinks reception requires specific forms of professionalism and competence, with the attendant affective labour of managing the feelings of oneself and others.

Much of this socialising incorporates networking, which in the context of academic conferences is a form of labour which is commonly entangled with intoxication. Networking is generally understood as social interaction related to the development of beneficial professional relationships, contacts and opportunities. Notions of networking range from the ruthlessly instrumental process of 'working the room' to a more organic building of supportive and meaningful relationships over time (Petre & Rugg, 2010). Whether targeted or organic, networking is about the accrual and demonstration of social and cultural capital (de Janasz & Sullivan, 2004). The burgeoning advice literature aimed at doctoral students and early career researchers emphasises the vital role of effective network building to career success in the competitive and uncertain higher education market (Matthiesen & Binder, 2009).

In the academic advice literature, doctoral students and junior academics are exhorted to attend conferences because of the unique range of in-person networking opportunities they provide. In a recent *Chronicle of Higher Education* advice column on conference attendance, Manya Whitaker writes that 'networking is the whole point', and that maximising your networking opportunities means 'positioning yourself to meet people'. In her words,

> Early-career academics at conferences should be primarily focused on networking. Rather than attend four sessions a day where you sit quietly and then rush out, seek opportunities to genuinely talk with other scholars. Most of those opportunities are embedded in preconference events and in gatherings after the day's sessions are over.

These gatherings include the cocktail party/reception where 'you get the chance to chat with faculty members you may never have met, meet alumni, and, in general, build your social capital'.

Initiating and performing this style of complex social interaction, often with high status strangers, can be daunting and stressful, especially for newcomers and those who are marginalised or feel like outsiders (Matthiesen & Binder, 2009). It entails managing encounters that are ostensibly informal, spontaneous and reciprocal (in a space that is supposedly dedicated to relaxation and having a good time) while maintaining an entrepreneurial focus on professional goals and demonstrating one's employability. For the precariously employed, under-employed or yet to be employed, networking is one of the many forms of 'unpaid hope labour' or 'unpaid work-for-labour' that proliferate in contemporary academia (Mauri, 2019). This is work 'undertaken in the present for a better position down the road' and in the case of networking, it is usually invisible as work, as well as often being carried out for free during periods of supposed 'time-out' or leisure (Mauri 2019, p. 197). To return to Savaag et al.'s conceptualisation, these encounters take place in a grey zone between leisure and work, with no guarantee that the participants have a common understanding of where they are located in that zone (2019). A networking conversation can be both a relaxing time out from work for a senior scholar and crucial career-building labour for an early career academic.

Given these demands and tensions, it is not surprising that mildly intoxicating alcohol effects are commonly involved in conference networking. As qualitative research on social drinking demonstrates, alcohol can facilitate feelings of togetherness, closeness and sharing among both friends and strangers, thereby blurring social boundaries (Jayne et al., 2010). The positive experience of nightlife drinking includes 'friendships that emerge for just a few minutes' (p. 546). While the context is obviously different, the transmission and circulation of positive affects between bodies allow networking to feel authentic and joyful rather than cold and effortful. In her *Inside Higher Education* essay on networking, Rebekah Layton advises readers that the aim is to connect with your interlocutor 'as a person rather than as an accomplished professional' (Layton, 2019). The ideal is 'two connected human beings building a relationship' rather than a 'transactional process of trying to prove your immediate value to someone of greater experience or stature' (Layton, 2019). The time constraints of the typical conference networking encounter further increase the usefulness of alcohol as a tool which speeds up intimacy and produces short-lived feelings of connection.

Stepney's research on drinking among British women's friendship groups provides another insight into the value of alcohol effects in constructing and managing networking encounters. Among her young participants, she found that rather than straightforwardly producing closeness, drinking alcohol was a means of achieving both proximity and distance in relation to others (2014). In particular, her respondents valued alcohol because it enhanced their ability to do 'small talk', sustaining a 'superficial form of cooperation and "getting along"' (2014, p. 108). This balancing of proximity and distance resonates with the work of networking, which requires connections that are experienced as genuine but remain work-focused rather than personal or confessional. While the person desiring the networking connection may well be anxious, resentful and envious of the higher status other, any sense of confrontation or hostility must be avoided, and negative affects kept at bay.

Mild intoxication is readily incorporated into events which combine socialising and work. In fact, the case of networking demonstrates how intoxication can become work because of its potentially vitalising effect on transpersonal relations. Intoxication can recruit conference participants into networks which promote professional and institutional ends. This is not just a matter of material effects, but also engages the symbolic meaning of alcohol as a sign of conviviality and celebration. However, as mentioned earlier, intoxication must remain within the bounds of the proper and the normal in order to augment professional identity and performance (Mair & Frew, 2018). As Mair and Frew note, there are definite risks to 'over-indulging' at conference social events (2018, p. 2164).

Challenging and changing intoxication practices

As historians and sociologists have argued, the boundaries of moderate drinking, and the line between acceptable and unacceptable intoxication at work vary over time and space

(Gusfield, 2003; Yeomans, 2013). Anecdotal evidence supports the view that norms and practices of drinking in academic life have become more restrictive over recent decades, although published research on this specific topic is sparse (Donald, 2016). A US article on 'chemical dependency' among faculty published 30 years ago provides evidence of a significant change in relevant conditions of academic labour (Donovan, 1990). The article argues that a workplace culture of freedom and privacy, and the self-paced nature of academic work, allows obvious substance use problems to flourish. It states that 'remarkable tolerance often greets the boozy or pot-smoking professor whose drug use, dull or threatening in other contexts, exalts *this* eccentric as a campus character and folk hero' (Donovan, 1990, p. 21, emphasis in original).

While this account of laissez-faire tolerance of the 'colorfully alcoholic colleague' may be an overstatement (Donovan, 1990, p. 21), the professorial freedom it describes is a striking contrast to the working environment of academics in the twenty-first century. Academic work has been transformed by the rise of the corporatised and managerial university (Gill, 2009; Lipton, 2020). The regulated forms of academic subjectivity produced by performance measurement and the demand for ever-increasing productivity and entrepreneurship are a long way from the autonomous, self-directed and securely tenured professors invoked in Donovan's 1990 article (Morrissey, 2015). Performance and conduct expectations are now explicit and substance misuse at work (including alcohol consumption) is regulated by work, health and safety policies and staff codes of conduct.

Alongside institutional efforts to limit the risks produced by substance-using staff, academic drinking culture has also become a topic of critical discussion in public discourse. *The Chronicle of Higher Education* and *Inside Higher Education* have featured career advice essays on how to manage the 'omnipresence of alcohol' at professional events (Kreuter, 2011; Lundsteen, 2019). On social media, especially twitter, non-drinking academics have highlighted the challenges of navigating academic life while sober and called for a change to the routine centring of alcohol at work and social events. This critical discourse has also highlighted the exclusionary effects of normative expectations of alcohol consumption and their risks in terms of health and safety, especially in relation to sexual harassment and violence (Cohen, 2017; Jaschik, 2018; Pettit, 2019). More broadly, socially obligatory drinking has been undermined by the rise of discourses of individual choice related to consumption, diet and health (Caluzzi et al., 2020; Yeomans, 2019). Although abstinence from alcohol may remain deviant in some social contexts, the decision to abstain, whether temporarily or permanently, is increasingly understood as an element of positive self-formation, especially among young people (Paton-Simpson, 2001; Törrönen et al., 2019).

Increasing recognition of the prevalence and impact of sexual harassment and violence in academia and the growing prominence of gender equity as a strategic organisational goal has also promoted critical reflection on the role of alcohol consumption at academic events. Drunkenness is increasingly constituted as a health and safety issue, not just for the individual but also in terms of harms to others. In STEM fields in particular, conference codes of conduct are advocated as a tool for promoting a safe environment for all (Foxx et al., 2019). While conference codes of conduct may not explicitly mention alcohol consumption, the targeting of unwelcome sexual behaviour, incivility and 'unacceptable' conduct problematises intoxication as a risk. In setting out the need for codes of conduct, Foxx et al. highlight the risks to women of evening networking conversations involving alcohol, 'Women have reported instances of men distorting after-hours networking events for predatory purposes to lodge unwanted sexual advances, druggings, and sexual assault' (2019; p. 14932).

The risk of gendered and sexual harm is not the only equity issue faced by conference organisers. The assumption that attendees are more or less homogenous in their requirements and desires tends to reproduce and reinforce existing academic hierarchies (Mair & Frew, 2018; Walters, 2018). As Briony Lipton observes, conferences labelled 'international' and 'global' still tend to have a homogenising effect in their unquestioned centring and celebration of Anglo-American, English-speaking academic culture (2020). The belief that everyone enjoys the standard conference reception and feels at home within its culturally specific consumption rituals is part of this dominant culture.

It is uncertain to what extent these concerns about harm, equity and inclusion will reshape the typical conference drinks event, but it is clear that the aim of making all participants feel welcome at a conference requires abandoning the assumption that comfort, fun and pleasure are the same for everyone. While I have argued that the provision of alcohol and the effects of mild intoxication are central to the atmosphere of the drinks event, the embodied and affective experiences of non-drinking participants deserve more attention (Buvik, 2020; Kreuter, 2011).

Conclusion

Dominant medical and legal accounts of intoxication tend to focus on the pathological, dramatic and florid, such as the physical and emotional manifestations of drunkenness. While the field of drug and alcohol studies has produced an extensive literature on more diverse experiences of intoxication, there is still a tendency to think of intoxicating effects as naturally linked to 'time out' and leisure. This chapter has instead discussed the place of normative drinking and mild intoxication in work-related events and places.

My focus has been on drinking that is incorporated into the demands of work and the performance of workplace identities. Organisational research reveals the significance of food and drink rituals in creating affective ties between workers, and between workers and the organisation (Plester, 2015). But while these rituals are experienced positively by many, they can also produce discomfort and exclusion. Workers may appreciate the conviviality and fun of social events, but the obligation to drink and to conform to a model of sociable subjectivity can represent an unwelcome encroachment of work into personal space and time (Sagvaag et al., 2019). In the contemporary landscape of post-Fordist labour, appropriately timed, sociable intoxication (such as at after-work drinks) can become an obligation as well as a reward. Although intoxication is usually understood as the opposite of ideals of moderation and discipline, mild intoxication is readily incorporated into expectations of productivity, flexibility and affective attachment to work (Gregg, 2010).

To explore a specific form of work-related drinking, the second part of the chapter examined academic conferences. The provision of alcohol is an expected and taken-for-granted feature of the typical conference schedule. Drinking contributes to the varied embodied experiences of conference attendance, including the sense of belonging or being out of place. I have discussed professional networking in particular as a practice that is routinely entangled with drinking. Both the individual effects of mild intoxication and the shared affective atmosphere invoked by the drinks session promote the quick production of feelings of connection which aligns with the goals of networking. The example of networking demonstrates how intoxication can itself become work in contexts where expectations of informal spontaneity are combined with the pursuit of professional goals.

Like all cultural norms of consumption, the boundaries of acceptable work-related drinking are subject to change over time. It does seem that we are in an era of increasing restraint in relation to the expected workplace conduct of 'white collar' professionals. In 2017, the insurance market Lloyd's of London banned alcohol consumption during working hours, following an analysis of grievance and disciplinary procedures which found that many incidents involved alcohol (Addley, 2017). The Lloyd's drinking ban was widely reported as a blow to the City of London's culture of 'boozy' business lunches, which was already on the wane (Ralph, 2017).

In academia, there is also increasing awareness of the negative effects of obligatory and routinised work-related drinking, especially in relation to equity and inclusiveness. The blurring of work and leisure has differential effects and consequences depending on individual circumstances. For many, having a few drinks at the end of the day is an enlivening antidote to the emotional, social and physical demands of conference attendance (Mair & Frew, 2018). But atmospheres of conviviality and hospitality can obscure the demanding forms of 'unpaid work for labour' that continue at events that are categorised as 'time-out'. The assumption that everyone drinks and enjoys alcohol can also act as a barrier to equal participation.

Conference organisers should be encouraged to think more creatively about how positive and light-hearted affective atmospheres in collective spaces can be (and are) fostered without reliance on alcohol. However, rather than making recommendations about conference organisation, the main aim of this chapter is to contribute to an expansion in understandings of everyday intoxication and its range of effects, intensities and functions. In particular, more empirical research is needed on experiences of intoxication in different work settings. As Bancroft and others have argued, psychoactive substances are used in targeted ways to 'change the self in the world'; they fulfil a range of functions, including increased productivity and social efficacy (2009, p. 147; Hunt & Frank, 2017). But as well as investigating why and how individuals seek intoxication, we should also examine the way organisations and institutions use the shared embodied experience of intoxication to create atmospheres and produce affective bonds.

Note

1 This chapter was written in 2019, before the global coronavirus pandemic and its impact on academic conferences (and on work in general). The rise of the online conference is likely to alter future conference formats and experiences.

References

Addley, E. (2017). Lloyd's alcohol ban challenges City of London's drinking culture. *The Guardian*. 18 February 2017. Retrieved from https://www.theguardian.com/business/2017/feb/17/lloyds-alcohol-ban-challenges-city-of-londons-drinking-culture#img-1.

Adkins, L. & Dever, M. (Eds.). (2016). *The Post-Fordist Sexual Contract: Working and Living in Contingency*, Basingstoke: Palgrave Macmillan.

American Psychiatric Association. (2013). *Diagnostic and Statistical Manual of Mental Disorders (DSM-5)*, Washington: American Psychiatric Press.

Ames, G. M., & Janes, C. (1992). A cultural approach to conceptualizing alcohol and the workplace. *Alcohol, Health and Research World*, *16*(2): 112–119.

Anderson, B. (2009). Affective atmospheres. *Emotion, Space and Society*, *2*(2): 77–81.

Bancroft, A. (2009). *Drugs, Intoxication and Society*, Cambridge: Polity.

Bell, E., & King, D. (2010). The elephant in the room: Critical management studies conferences as a site of body pedagogics. *Management Learning*, *41*(4): 429–442.

Bianchini, F. (1995). Night culture, night economies. *Planning, Practice & Research in Nursing & Health*, *10*: 121–126.

Biggs, J., Hawley, P. H., & Biernat, M. (2018). The academic conference as a chilly climate for women: Effects of gender representation on experiences of sexism, coping responses, and career intentions. *Sex Roles, 78*(5–6): 394–408.

Bissell, D. (2010). Passenger mobilities: Affective atmospheres and the sociality of public transport. *Environment and Planning D: Society & Space, 28*: 270–289.

Black, A. L., Crimmins, G., Dwyer, R., & Lister, V. (2020). Engendering belonging: Thoughtful gatherings with/in online and virtual spaces. *Gender and Education, 32*(1): 115–129.

Brain, K., Parker, H., & Carnwath, T. (2000). Drinking with design: Young drinkers as psychoactive consumers. *Drugs: Education, Prevention and Policy, 7*(1): 5–20.

Buvik, K. (2020). It's time for a drink! Alcohol as an investment in the work environment. *Drugs: Education, Prevention and Policy, 27*(1): 86–91.

Caluzzi, G., Pennay, A., & MacLean, S. (2020). Reflexive habitus and the new obligation of choice: Understanding young people's light drinking and alcohol abstinence. *Journal of Youth Studies*. DOI: 10.1080/13676261.2020.1778658.

Cohen, J. (2017) Drinking and conferencing. *The Chronicle of Higher Education*, June 4 2017. Retrieved from https://www.chronicle.com/article/drinking-and-conferencing/.

De Janasz, S. C., & Sullivan, S. E. (2004). Multiple mentoring in academe: Developing the professorial network. *Journal of Vocational Behavior, 64*(2): 263–283.

Donald, A. (2016). Is alcohol still part of everyday academic life, or is it just the students? *Times Higher Education*, February 25 2016. Retrieved from https://www.timeshighereducation.com/blog/alcohol-still-part-everyday-academic-life-or-it-just-students.

Donovan, B. (1990). Chemical dependency, denial, and the academic lifestyle. *Academe, 76*(1): 20–24.

Duff, C. & Moore, D. (2015). Going out, getting about: Atmospheres of mobility in Melbourne's night-time economy. *Social & Cultural Geography, 16*(3): 299–314.

Flores-Pereira, M. T., Davel, E., & Cavedon, N. R. (2008). Drinking beer and understanding organizational culture embodiment. *Human Relations, 61*(7): 1007–1026.

Foxx, A. J., Barak, R. S., Lichtenberger, T. M., Richardson, L. K., Rodgers, A. J., & Williams, E. W. (2019). Evaluating the prevalence and quality of conference codes of conduct. *Proceedings of the National Academy of Sciences, 116*(30): 14931–14936.

Gill, R. (2009). Breaking the silence: The hidden injuries of neo-liberal academia. In R. Ryan-Flood & R. Gill (Eds) *Secrecy and Silence in the Research Process: Feminist Reflections*, Abingdon: Routledge. pp. 228–244.

Gregg, M. (2010). On Friday night drinks. In M. Gregg & G. Seigworth (Eds) *The Affect Theory Reader*, Durham: Duke University Press. pp. 250–268.

Gusfield, J. R. (2003). Passage to play: Rituals of drinking time in American society. In M. Douglas (Ed) *Constructive Drinking: Perspectives on Drink from Anthropology*, Abingdon: Routledge. pp. 73–90.

Henderson, E. F. (2015). Academic conferences: Representative and resistant sites for higher education research. *Higher Education Research & Development, 34*(5): 914–925.

———. (2019). Academics in two places at once: (Not) managing caring responsibilities at conferences. In R. Finkel et al. (Eds) *Accessibility, Inclusion, and Diversity in Critical Event Studies*, London: Routledge. pp. 2018–2229.

Hughes, J. (2003) *Learning to Smoke: Tobacco Use in the West*, Chicago: Chicago University Press.

Hunt, G. & Frank, V. (2017). Reflecting on intoxication. In T. Kolind, B. Thom & G. Hunt (Eds) *The Sage Handbook for Drug and Alcohol Studies*, London: Sage. pp. 322–336.

Jaschik, S. (2018). Dark side of a scholarly meeting. *Inside Higher Education*. June 25 2018. Retrieved from https://www.insidehighered.com/news/2018/06/25/twitter-thread-reveals-how-woman-academic-conference-was-nearly-sexually-assaulted.

Jayne, M., Valentine, G., & Holloway, S. L. (2010). Emotional, embodied and affective geographies of alcohol, drinking and drunkenness. *Transactions of the Institute of British Geographers, 35*(4): 540–554.

Keane, H. (2009). Intoxication, harm and pleasure: An analysis of the Australian National Alcohol strategy. *Critical Public Health, 19*(2): 135–142.

———. (2020). Smoking and intoxication: From control to the buzz. In F. Hutton (Ed) *Cultures of Intoxication: Key Issues and Debates*, Cham: Palgrave Macmillan. pp. 45–66.

Kreuter, N. (2011). Essay on how academics deal with booze. *Inside Higher Ed*, December 5 2011. Retrieved from https://www.insidehighered.com/advice/2011/12/05/essay-how-academics-deal-booze.

Layton, R. (2019). Advice for expanding your job network over the holiday season (opinion). *Inside Higher Ed*, December 16 2019. Retrieved from https://www.insidehighered.com/advice/2019/12/16/advice-expanding-your-job-network-over-holiday-season-opinion.

Lipton, B. (2019). Conference baby: Gendered bodies, knowledge, and re/turning to academia. *Qualitative Inquiry, 25*(2): 160–162.

———. (2020). *Academic Women in Neoliberal Times*, Cham: Palgrave Macmillan.

Lundsteen, N. (2019). Knowing when to drink alcohol, and how much, at professional events (opinion). *Inside Higher Ed*, February 25 2019. Retrieved from https://www.insidehighered.com/advice/2019/02/25/knowing-when-drink-alcohol-and-how-much-professional-events-opinion.

Mair, J. & Frew, E. (2018). Academic conferences: A female duo-ethnography. *Current Issues in Tourism, 21*(18): 2152–2172.

Matthiesen, J. & Binder, M. (2009). *How to Survive Your Doctorate: What others Don't Tell You*, Maidenhead: Open University Press.

Mauri, C. (2019). Formulating the academic precariat. In F. Cannizzo & N. Osbaldiston (Eds) *The Social Structures of Global Academia*, London: Routledge. pp. 185–204.

Morrissey, J. (2015). Regimes of performance: Practices of the normalised self in the neoliberal university. *British Journal of Sociology of Education, 36*(4): 614–634.

National Institute on Drug Abuse. (2018). *Tobacco, Nicotine, and E-Cigarettes*. Retrieved from https://www.drugabuse.gov/publications/research-reports/tobacco-nicotine-e-cigarettes.

Paton-Simpson, G. (2001). Socially obligatory drinking: A sociological analysis of norms governing minimum drinking levels. *Contemporary Drug Problems, 28*(1): 133–177.

Pennay, A. (2014). Identifying intoxication: Challenges and complexities. In E. Manton, R. Room, C. Giorgi, & M. Thorn (Eds), *Stemming the Tide of Alcohol: Liquor Licensing and the Public Interest*. Canberra: Foundation for Alcohol Research and Education. pp. 109–121.

Pennay, A., Callinan, S., Livingston, M., Lubman, D. I., Holmes, J., MacLean, S., ... Dietze, P. (2019). Patterns in reduction or cessation of drinking in Australia (2001–2013) and motivation for change. *Alcohol and Alcoholism, 54*(1): 79–86.

Petre, M. & Rugg, G. (2010). *The Unwritten Rules of PhD Research*, 2nd edn., Maidenhead: Open University Press.

Pettit, E. (2019). 'A Minefield': How scholars who don't drink navigate the conference social scene. *The Chronicle of Higher Education*, January 9 2019. Retrieved from https://www.chronicle.com/article/a-minefield-how-scholars-who-dont-drink-navigate-the-conference-social-scene/.

Plester, B. (2015). Ingesting the organization: The embodiment of organizational food rituals. *Culture and Organization, 21*(3): 251–268.

Ralph, O. (2017). Lloyd's of London bans alcohol during work hours. *The Financial Times*, February 15 2017. Retrieved from https://www.ft.com/content/8de154aa-f2d9-11e6-95ee-f14e55513608.

Rolando, S., Törrönen, J., & Beccaria, F. (2014). Boundaries between adult and youth drinking as expressed by young people in Italy and Finland. *Young, 22*(3): 227–252.

Sagvaag, H., Rimstad, S. L., Kinn, L. G., & Aas, R. W. (2019). Six shades of grey: Identifying drinking culture and potentially risky drinking behaviour in the grey zone between work and leisure. The WIRUS culture study. *Journal of Public Health Research, 8*(1585): 75–81.

Savic, M., Room, R., Mugavin, J., Pennay, A., & Livingston, M. (2016). Defining "drinking culture": A critical review of its meaning and connotation in social research on alcohol problems. *Drugs: Education, Prevention and Policy, 23*(4): 270–282.

Seeman, M., Seeman, A. Z., & Budros, A. (1988). Powerlessness, work, and community: A longitudinal study of alienation and alcohol use. *Journal of Health and Social Behavior, 29*: 185–198.

Shaw, R. (2014). Beyond night-time economy: Affective atmospheres of the urban night. *Geoforum, 51*: 87–95.

Spicer, A. (2005). Conferences. In C. Jones & D. O' Doherty (Eds) *Manifestos for the Business School of Tomorrow*, Turku: Dvalin Books. pp. 21–27.

Stepney, M. (2014). British women's experiences of drinking alcohol: Dynamics of emotional proximity and distance. *Emotion, Space and Society, 10*: 105–112.

Thompson, A., Brookins-Fisher, J., Kerr, D., & O'Boyle, I. (2012). Ethical issues in professional development: Case studies regarding behaviour at conferences. *Health Education Journal, 71*(5): 539–545.

Törrönen, J., Roumeliotis, F., Samuelsson, E., Kraus, L., & Room, R. (2019). Why are young people drinking less than earlier? Identifying and specifying social mechanisms with a pragmatist approach. *International Journal of Drug Policy, 64*: 13–20.

Valentine, G., Holloway, S. L., & Jayne, M. (2010). Contemporary cultures of abstinence and the nighttime economy: Muslim attitudes towards alcohol and the implications for social cohesion. *Environment and Planning A*, *42*(1): 8–22.

Walker, B., & Bridgman, T. (2013). Organisational identity and alcohol use among young employees: A case study of a professional services firm. *International Journal of Drug Policy*, *24*(6): 597–604.

Walters, T. (2018). A tripartite approach to accessibility, diversity, and inclusion in academic conferences. In R. Finkel et al. (Eds) *Accessibility, Inclusion, and Diversity in Critical Event Studies*, London: Routledge. Pp. 230–241.

Whitaker, M. (2018). How to get the most out of a conference. *The Chronicle of Higher Education*, March 26 2018. Retrieved from https://www.chronicle.com/article/how-to-get-the-most-out-of-a-conference/.

Yeomans, H. (2013). Blurred visions: Experts, evidence and the promotion of moderate drinking. *The Sociological Review*, *61*: 58–78.

———. (2019). New year, new you: A qualitative study of Dry January, self-formation and positive regulation. *Drugs: Education, Prevention and Policy*, *26*(6): 460–468.

12

EXPLORING THE MOTIVATIONS AND SOCIAL ORGANISATION OF INTOXICATION IN PRISON SETTINGS

Torsten Kolind and Karen Duke

Introduction

Within the existing literature on substance use and prisons, the topic of 'intoxication' in prison settings has rarely been explored. For example, how is intoxication different in prisons? What are the motivations for intoxication in prisons? How does the prison setting shape the choice of substance and intoxication? How is intoxication experienced and organised in prison environments? Is there a relationship between intoxication and pleasure within prisons?

Based on the existing literature and an application of theoretical perspectives from penology and drug studies, we aim to explore these questions.[1] First, we will investigate prisoners' motivations for drug use and intoxication in prisons, looking especially at the impact of the 'pains of imprisonment' on drug use. Second, the chapter will investigate the role that drugs play as part of the social organisation of people in prisons. In particular, we will argue that the prison context differs from outside life in many different ways and thereby determines not only what kind of drug use is possible in prisons, but also how intoxication is experienced and socially organised. Finally, we discuss the possible relationship between intoxication and pleasure in a prison context. However, before we look into prisoners' motivations for drug use and the role drugs play in prison contexts, we will offer an overview of prevalence rates of drug use before, during and after prison to set the context for our analysis. Due to the paucity of research on alcohol use in prison settings, this chapter mainly focuses on illicit substances.

Prevalence of drug use before, during and after imprisonment

In 2020, there were 1.5 million people imprisoned in the penal institutions of the Council of Europe member states, which corresponds to a prison population rate of 103.2 inmates per 100,000 inhabitants (Aebi and Tiago, 2021). The median age of this population is 36 years and the vast majority (95%) are men. Twenty-two per cent (22%) are not serving a final sentence, but are pre-trial detainees. The rest are mainly serving sentences from one to less than three years (22%), from three to less than five years (19%) and from five to less than ten years (20%). Drug-related crime is an important category of offence with 18% sentenced European

DOI: 10.4324/9780429058141-16

prisoners convicted for drug offences. In several countries, including Turkey, Estonia, Georgia, Cyprus, Albania, Azerbaijan and Greece, prisoners sentenced for drug offences represent more than one quarter of the prison population (Aebi and Tiago, 2021).

Prison populations are overrepresented by people who have been adversely affected by deprivation, trauma, poor physical and mental health, unemployment, low education levels and homelessness (de Andrade, 2018; EMCDDA, 2012). People in prison are much more likely to have used drugs, to use drugs on a regular basis and to have problems with drug use than people in the community and they are also more likely to have an alcohol use disorder (Fazel et al., 2017). Due to the disadvantages and deprivation that they have experienced, people in prison suffer from a number of complex health and social care needs. Their needs are further exacerbated by overcrowding, insanitary conditions and inadequate healthcare in some European prisons (Aebi and Tiago, 2021; EMCDDA, 2012; Sturup-Toft et al., 2018; WHO, 2014).

In general, there is a lack of data on the prevalence of substance use before, during and after imprisonment in Europe. Van de Baan et al.'s (2021) review of studies on the prevalence of illicit drug use *prior to* imprisonment in European countries found high rates of lifetime prevalence before imprisonment (60.6% pooled average estimate); last year prevalence (57.4% pooled average estimate) and last six month prevalence (43.3%). The highest rates of use were reported for cannabis, cocaine and amphetamines and to a lesser extent heroin and other drugs. Prevalence *prior to* imprisonment was particularly high among women in prison. In relation to injecting drug use *before* imprisonment, lifetime prevalence rates are higher in prison populations than the general population in most countries (Azbel and Altice, 2018). Higher rates of alcohol use and dependence are also observed in justice-involved populations across the globe (Seal et al., 2018).

Available data on substance use *in* prison has substantial heterogeneity in the methods of assessment both within and between countries, which hinder comparability (Carpentier et al., 2018; EMCDDA, 2012; 2021). A comprehensive review of 59 studies across the globe conducted by Carpentier et al. (2018) reveals high levels of drug consumption *within prisons*. The proportion of people having ever used an illicit drug *in* prison lies between 20% and 45% in most studies and cannabis was the drug used most frequently, followed by cocaine, heroin and amphetamines. The review found that those reporting having used an illicit drug *in* prison in the past year represent 2–67% of the surveyed prison population. Those using drugs in the past month *in* prison ranged from 0.7% to 65%. Regular use on a daily basis *in* prison was around 10% in the few European studies measuring frequency of use in prison. People who report injecting *in* prison represent around 10% or less of the prison population (Carpentier et al., 2018). Milloy's international review of retrospective surveys of once-incarcerated drug users in community settings revealed a substantial proportion of individuals report injecting while incarcerated and this increased risk factors of BBV transmission in prison due to increases in the likelihood of syringe sharing and injecting in an unsafe manner (Milloy, 2018). In relation to alcohol use *in* prisons, there has been limited research and wide variability in prevalence rates in the studies that do exist (Carpentier et al., 2018).

There have been very few studies of substance use on release from prison. Larney et al. (2018) reviewed the research on post-release substance use and found numerous design and methodological limitations, including sampling problems, low follow-up rates, biased attrition and variations around how substance use on release is measured. However, the available evidence suggests that many people return very quickly to harmful substance use on release (Larney et al., 2018). The use of substances may change due to increased access and availability of different substances. Release from prison can be a risky time due to lower tolerance levels and increased use of substances heightens the risk of overdose and drug-related death (Farrell and Marsden, 2008). Qualitative research conducted by Lloyd et al. (2017, 2019) examined the transition from prison to the community for those who had been in treatment in prisons. It showed how the aspirations and goals for their recovery on release which they had set in prison were quickly abandoned on release due to lack of resettlement support. At follow-up, few had entirely given up drinking and drug use, a substantial group had reduced or moderated their drug use and a large group had made few changes to their pre-imprisonment levels.

Following this overview of drug use before, during and after imprisonment, we will examine prisoners' motives for drug use in prisons, their experiences of intoxication and the social organisation of drug use and drug sale in prison in the remainder of the chapter.

Motivations for drug use: the pains of imprisonment

As Zinberg (1984) powerfully argued, not only the pharmacological properties of a drug and the psychology of the person who uses drugs, but also the social setting of drug use plays an important role in determining users' reasons for engaging in drug use and for the subjective experiences of intoxication (see also Gossop, 2000). Zinberg's insight is also highly relevant for understanding intoxication in prison settings. Often, a person's choice of drug changes when they are incarcerated as different effects are sought in a prison setting compared to the outside community (Tompkins and Wright, 2012). In addition, the individual psychology of the individual can play a central role in the way intoxication is experienced in prisons and also for the choice of drugs. Their previous experiences with drugs over a life course and the different positive and negative associations (through learning about drugs; Becker, 1953) with this use play a role for what the individual expects, aims for and experiences (Gossop, 2000). Finally, the prison setting, which in many ways can be framed as a 'risk environment'[2] (Rhodes, 2009; see also Duke and Kolind, 2020; Wilson et al., 2007), influences individual's motives for starting, continuing or discontinuing drug use (Frank et al., 2015). Although prison settings may differ considerably both between countries and in countries, they can affect individual's motives and experiences greatly. In this section, different motivations for drug use in a prison context will be considered. In particular, we will consider the pains of imprisonment experienced by prisoners.

Not all that takes place within a prison setting can be explained by intra-institutional processes and influences. Individuals' pre-prison lives, their personalities and their social networks outside the walls play important roles in how incarceration is experienced (Cohen and Taylor, 1972; Irwin, 1970; Jacobs, 1983). Nevertheless, research has convincingly showed that prison environments have some intrinsic characteristics influencing the experiences of incarceration. A generic process of institutionalisation takes place (Goffman, 1961), a range of deprivations are experienced by most people imprisoned (Sykes, 1958; Toch, 1977) and individuals' acts of both prisonisation (Clemmer, 1940) and resistance (Mathiesen, 1965) are often more or less determined by the institutional logic of the prison.

Among the most common prison deprivations documented are loss of liberty, loss of social relations, loss of personal autonomy due to a heavily controlled setting, loss of privacy, (fear of) violence and boredom (Goffman, 1961; Sykes, 1958; Toch, 1977). Moreover, some deprivations may be culturally specific as has been documented in the 'exceptional' and 'soft' Nordic prisons (Shammas, 2014; Ugelvik 2014). Crewe (2011) revisited Sykes's (1958) original pains of imprisonment and argues that contemporary penal practices in the UK have created new deprivations for people in prison, including the pains of uncertainty and indeterminacy, pains of psychological assessment and pains of self-government. The pains of indeterminacy relate to the insecurities stemming from a discretionary and inconsistent style of governance. For example, those serving indeterminate sentences have uncertainty about how long they will be inside which creates frustration as they cannot make plans and experience changing goalposts regarding what is required for their release. The pains of psychological assessment relate to the increasing emphasis on risk management where prisoners are placed in aggregate risk categories with little control over the process. In this case, use of drugs, drug dependence and drug dealing are considered 'risks' which must be managed and controlled within the prison setting through increased security and surveillance measures to detect and disrupt the supply of drugs, mandatory drug testing procedures and referrals into drug treatment. Contemporary imprisonment also creates pains of self-government where prisoners are subjected to more levers of compliance and regulation. A key example of this is mandatory drug testing which is a tool to deter and discipline those who take drugs in prisons. Those prisoners who come up positive on a mandatory drug test are sanctioned with penalties and this process was designed to act as a deterrent to drug use (see also Kolind et al., 2013). Crewe (2011: 524) concludes that penal power in the UK prisons is exercised more softly and the 'carceral experience is less directly oppressive, but more gripping – lighter but tighter'. The experience of a tighter prison may have a number of unintended consequences whereby those who have problems with drug use are reluctant to seek treatment and drug-related harms are increased due to fears of increased surveillance and punishments. For example, those who inject drugs may do so in an unsafe manner or there may be a reluctance to seek help for suspected overdoses due to fear of additional sanctions.

Looking at individuals' (strategic) practices of intoxication in prisons, these can then to a certain extent be explained by or related to these deprivations experienced as a result of incarceration. That is, prison drug use can be understood as the individual's way of coping with the emotional stress of being in prison (Keene, 1997). In fact, one can see illegal drug use as a way of self-medicating (Bullock, 2003; Crewe 2005; Mjåland, 2016; Ritter et al., 2013). In this way, drugs, which in outside settings may be used and experienced as pleasurable intoxicants, can in prison ontologically change into a substitute medicine (Kolind et al., 2016). Prisons, then, can be seen as risky environments encouraging individuals to use drugs or take up drug use after being incarcerated (Boys et al., 2002; Swann and James, 1998). Again, the individuals' pre-prison lives, their pre-prison pattern of drug use and their psychology also play a part in explaining prison drug use (Strang et al., 2006), as does research which shows that a history of drug dependence is likely to increase the risk of being imprisoned (Liebling, 1999; Stöver and Michels, 2010). As Wheatley precisely sums up: 'Inmates' outside vulnerabilities such as drug and alcohol misuse, psychosocial problems, and poor coping skills combined with a detrimental prison environment can promote drug misuse in prisons' (Wheatley, 2007: 403).

As an example of individuals' strategic use of intoxication in prison as self-medication in a high-risk environment, we see how they use drugs to manage and even manipulate time. In order to counter the feeling that time in prisons is void of content and meaning, Cope (2003) found that drugs were used deliberately in order to manipulate time. By using sedating drugs, especially cannabis, the feelings and illusions were created that prison time goes faster. More correctly, perhaps, intoxication was intentionally sought in order to create a kind of time vacuum for the individuals so that their lives and identities outside prisons were not influenced and contaminated by time inside, as time inside was associated with a degraded self-identity and meaninglessness. Intoxication, in this way, helped them to create an illusion of life that is not their real identity. This also relates to Toch's central insight about the experience of being incarcerated:

> What appears to be totally unacceptable is the idea that one's life is experienced in prison. One may be serving life, but one is not serving 'my life'.
>
> *(1972: 93)*

Since 2015, there has been growing concern about the use of NPS (new psychoactive substances) in European prisons, particularly around the increasing use of synthetic cannabinoid receptor agonists (SCRAs) in some countries (Duke, 2020; EMCDDA, 2018; 2021; Grace et al., 2020; Ralphs et al., 2017). For example, 30% of prisoners reported last month use of SCRAs (known as 'Spice' or 'Mamba') in some UK prisons (User Voice, 2016). Accordingly, SCRA use has grown popular in prisons because it, like cannabis, can help in escaping the realities and boredom of prison life and they are often used for self-medication for mental health problems or due to lack of prescribed medication (Blackman and Bradley, 2017; Grace, Lloyd et al., 2020; Reuter and Pardo, 2017). Moreover, its popularity also relates to the fact that the use of SCRAs was not initially picked up by urine testing regimes or by sniffer dogs, it does not smell like normal cannabis and is therefore more difficult to detect, they are perceived to be legal substances and, finally, they are easy to smuggle into prisons (for instance, it can be impregnated on to clothes or on a letter and then later dissolved by the use of acetone) (EMCDDA, 2018). In sum, these features contribute to making SCRAs a 'perfect' 'prison drug'. Grace and colleagues (2020) found that fewer of their respondents used SCRAs before custody or after release; hence, synthetic cannabinoids serve specific prison-related functions that might not necessarily relate to life in the community.

In the same way, some prisoners may strategically switch from cannabis to heroin while imprisoned as heroin is less detectable than cannabis in mandatory urine testing (Singleton et al., 2005, 2008; Stöver and Kastelic, 2014). Studies have also argued that the reasons for seeking intoxication change in prison context. That is, the pharmacological properties of the individual drug interact with the prison setting so that prisoners when incarcerated, for instance, often prefer drugs with calming and sedative effects compared to stimulants (Bullock, 2003; Ritter et al., 2013). Hence, drugs like cannabis, heroin and, recently, SCRAs are more popular than stimulants like, for instance, amphetamine and cocaine (Boys et al., 2002; Tompkins and Wright, 2012). In fact, in some European countries, the estimated level of cannabis use among inmates is relatively high and, moreover, is clearly a part of the daily life in prisons as it helps to relieve stress, facilitate sleep, prevent violence (i.e. social pacifier) and, ultimately, to relieve imprisonment (Keene, 1997; Kolind, 2015; Ritter et al., 2013). In addition, as cannabis use tends to help keep people calm and quiet, upholding institutional order is made easier for prison officers, and, hence, officers may turn a blind eye to inmates' cannabis use (Carlin, 2005; Duke, 2003; Kolind, 2015; Ritter et al., 2013). It should also be noted that price and availability can also be important considerations in the choice of substances in prison settings, rather than personal preferences (EMCDDA, 2018). Moreover, the level and effectiveness of drugs control shape the availability of different types of substances in prison. The prison environment – the setting – then, plays a central role in making some drugs and some kinds of intoxication popular inside the walls. Hence, prison can, in a broader sense, be seen as merely another context in which people develop their drug problems (Keene, 1997; see also Gillespie, 2005: 226).

Although the prison setting can cause individuals to start using drugs, increase their drug use or adjust their choice of drugs while incarcerated, some people will also cease to use drugs during imprisonment (Bullock, 2003; Dillon, 2001; Stöver et al., 2008; Swann and James, 1998; Turnbull et al., 2000). For some individuals, the time inside is a welcome relief from the drugs scene on the outside. The period of imprisonment may be restorative and stabilising in the sense that their physical and mental health can improve and social relationships can be repaired (Crewe, 2005). In addition, Tompkins (2013) reported how prisoners' cessation of injecting drugs when in prisons was multi-factorial and influenced by, for instance, limited availability of sterile needles and equipment, a concern with one's reputation, and the idea that prison could be used as 'an opportunity' for discontinuation. Moreover, a prison sentence can present an opportunity for assessment, referral and treatment of substance use problems. Individuals may then start drug treatment programmes inside prisons because they want to discontinue their drug use. However, their motives may also be more pragmatic. For instance, individuals may 'escape' to drug treatment wings because they are experienced as less violent and safer than regular wings, they may be seen as offering better terms of incarceration, or starting in drug treatment while incarcerated may look good in one's 'papers' for parole (Frank et al., 2015). Nevertheless, even if individuals manage to terminate their drug use while imprisoned, after release they may resume drug use as drugs can be key components of people's social lives and connected with sociability, pleasure and celebration. For instance, Lloyd et al. (2017) found that for those who did not identify as alcohol dependent, alcohol consumption was part of post-release celebrations and part of their social lives. Similarly, for some prisoners, cannabis played important functions in their post-release lives in terms of regulating emotions and a key activity in their social networks (Ibid).

Social organisation and drugs: the prisoner society

Intoxication in prisons then is heavily related to the risk environment and the pains of imprisonment produced by prisons. As part of the risk environment is also the so-called 'prisoner society'. This section will focus on how intoxication relates to the prisoner society and the values and codes produced by this community. Stated otherwise, the section overviews the role drugs play as part of the social organisation of the prisoners.

Several older classic prison ethnographies found that people in prison tended to produce some common moral values and a culture of its own related to their common experiences of imprisonment and deprivation. These moral values informed and steered the conduct of those in prison by emphasising, among other things, honesty, autonomy, solidarity and oppositional attitudes to the prison officers – the so-called 'inmate culture' (see e.g. Clemmer, 1940; Irwin and Cressey, 1962). With the increase of drugs in prisons, studies, especially from the US, documented an erosion of these moral values and the inmate culture. Instead, the importance of oppositional prison gangs grew, gangs that were linked with subcultures outside the prison. Hence, the culture and organisation of prison and street life became inextricably intertwined (Hunt et al., 1993; Trammell, 2009; see also Slade and Azbel, 2020: 3). Moreover, as Skarbek (2014) has demonstrated, in prisons where the official governance is weak, gangs tend to develop prisoner-led systems of governance often with clear links to the outside criminal world.

Similarly, recent studies from the UK have illustrated how the increase of drugs in prisons has affected and eroded the prisoner's society (Crewe, 2005, 2006). Moreover, partly due to the strengthening of prison drug policy measures, increasingly framing drug problems as crime problems and installing a zero-tolerance policy (Duke, 2003; Duke and Kolind, 2019), a profitable prison drug economy has been created. Although a strict sanctioning prison drug policy does not in itself create the drug markets in prisons, people in prison react strategically to and may exploit such policy initiatives for their own benefit (Bögelein and Meier, 2018). In consequence, some individuals gain economically by engaging with drug selling and smuggling in a highly controlled environment. Importantly however, not only do they profit economically, they also exploit the drug situation in prisons to create prestigious social identities as drug selling is becoming increasingly bound up with masculinity, self-identity, emotions and internal hierarchies (Crewe, 2005, 2006). Crewe's study on drug dealing in the UK prisons shows that although the financial power of drugs is important, drug dealing in prisons must be understood as more than simply an economic activity. Drug dealing can enhance the dealers' status and symbolic capital, for instance, by being able to bring drugs into prisons, making connections to outside drug and criminal networks, and displaying courage. Moreover, engaging in the prison drug economy can add to the feeling among inmates that they are part of a larger social group. Finally, drug dealing is, as depicted in the study by Crewe, and contrary to the US studies cited above, for everyone regardless of prior status (e.g. gang affiliation) as long as they can gain access to drugs. As Slade and Azbel (2020: 3) sum up the situation in the UK prisons: '...drugs acted as a social equalizer'. This is not to say that these drug markets were not violent and threatening. As Tompkins found in her study (2016), also from the UK, some people who were not traditionally involved in the drug market reacted to the prison environment and their present situation by (slowly) drifting into drug selling or drug supply seeing this as an opportunity within the prison.

Besides being linked to individual entrepreneurship, intoxication and drug selling can also carry subversive meanings for those in a highly controlled and stigmatised environment (Mjåland, 2016). That is, intoxication or drug selling by those imprisoned can be reinterpreted as symbolic acts of resistance towards a highly controlling system. In this way, we see how intoxication in prisons once again derives meaning from the prison context in which it takes place.

Even though the drug economy in the UK is not completely enmeshed in gang or ethnically based networks linked to outside social groups, as indicated in the above studies, drug use and drug selling – and even drug abstinence – can in prisons still be strongly linked to ethnicity. A study from Denmark shows how on a daily basis people in prison reinforce and essentialise ethnic differences by, for instance, linking a prestigious hyper-masculinity and an entrepreneurial approach related to drug selling in prisons to ethnicity (Haller and Kolind, 2018).

Summing up so far, alongside the increasing importance of the drug economy in prisons, we see an increasingly fragmented prison where the role of common prisoner values has diminished and where individual drug enterprises based on ad hoc (ethnic) social groupings dominate. Such development is also documented in Germany (Bögelein and Meier, 2018), and in several post-Soviet countries in which the drug economy has led to a commercialisation of prison social life and has disrupted existing traditional prisoner hierarchies and values (Slade and Azbel, 2020: 3–4).

However, the effect of drug use and drug selling should not be seen as only disrupting the prisoner society. Intoxication and the drug economy in prison are not only related to individual identity or to selfish profit-seeking behaviour, nor to resistance. Intoxication and drug selling can also be linked to communitarianism, solidarity and can at times produce stable social systems. This is demonstrated in a study from Kyrgyzstan prisons in which Slade and Azbel (2020) document how heroin was distributed through mutual aid funds according to need, work and social status within the prisoner society. The aid funds were managed by the 'highest caste' of prisoners (in budgetary units, a legacy of the Gulag) and built on a traditional thieves fund using a ritualised form of distribution of heroin in which pay-outs (heroin) from this fund were not necessarily commensurate to the amount paid in. In this way, the authors conclude, distribution, sale and use of heroin were not primarily governed by the logic of the market, but more by a logic of redistribution (ibid. 9). Moreover, the prisoner hierarchy was able to ban drug dealing and to establish gangs based on ethnicity or geographic origin. As a consequence of the importance, dominance and working of this system of redistribution, those in treatment also rejected formal methadone treatment as they preferred the heroin handouts of the prisoner society. That is, they opted for the socially embodied positions of power and agency which heroin distribution represented (Rhodes et al., 2019).

Similarly, in a study from Norway, Mjåland (2014) finds the existence of a 'culture of sharing' in prisons in which doses of buprenorphine (i.e. opioid substitution treatment) was illegally shared in a 'gift economy' built on reciprocity (cf. Mauss, 1990) rather than through a market logic. In this way, drug use and drug sharing in prisons contributed to building and maintaining friendships and relationships (Mjåland, 2016; see also Sandøy, 2015). Moreover, Mjåland's study documents how the prisoner society was effective in creating intra-institutional codes and moral values. It should be noted that the culture of sharing was backed up by system of sanctions such as humiliations, exclusion or, at times, violence. Although the 'culture of sharing' was built on values like compassion and solidarity, the gift economy still allowed for self-interest. That is, the more one gives away, the more drugs one can expect in return and the more often one can expect to get intoxicated. Finally, it should be noted that despite the functioning of such extra-legal systems of governance and that these prisoner societies are not built on the logic of the market, they can still be highly violent and brutal (see e.g. Symkovych, 2018).

Discussion – and the role of pleasure?

As Vasilou (2020) has pointed out, research has neglected any examination of pleasure in prison to avoid the risk of romanticising punishment. This is also the case for research on drug use in prisons. Most research depicts the prison as a site of pain, hardship and struggle and highlights how imprisonment exacerbates physical and mental health problems, including drug use, self-harm and suicide. Drug use in prison is problematised as a response to the pains of imprisonment, a means to escape the brutal reality of the prison space, a mechanism to suspend time and a part of the social organisation of people in prison. However, could those imprisoned derive pleasure from the use of drugs and involvement in the drugs market? Could drugs in prison acquire different meanings? Drawing on queer theory, Vasilou (2020) argues that prison life may produce feelings of pleasure. In relation to drugs, strategies of resistance can take the form of pleasure. For example, Crewe's study of drug dealing points to the excitement and pleasure of drug dealing as a form of resistance. The enormous difficulties getting illicit drugs into prison mean that pleasure and satisfaction are derived from obtaining something which is banned and getting around the measures to detect and intercept drugs put in place by the authorities in prison (see also Mjåland, 2016). Being involved in this game of 'cat and mouse' provides excitement and thrills helping to pass the time and boredom of the sentence. Moreover, the ability to sell and trade drugs in prison brings material benefits and pleasures to those in position of power in the prison hierarchy (Crewe, 2006). Furthermore, if one compares the motivations offered by individuals for engaging in intoxication while imprisoned, some of these motives may resemble those that, for instance, club goers highlight when accounting for their drug use. Hunt (2008) found that club goers narrated their ecstasy use in relation to the drug's ability to change the ordinary and mundane into something that was extraordinary. In this way, part of the pleasure in taking drugs derived from its ability to 'break the routine' of life, remove the ecstasy user from normal times and spaces and transform mundane activities and interactions into ones that were deeply pleasurable, satisfying and exciting. Even though there are many important differences in the lives of club goers and prisoners, as well as in their motivations for drug use, we also find similarities in their desire for escaping the everyday and 'normal', and the mundane routines of their lives (Cohen and Taylor, 1976).

Finally, when discussing the possible aspects of pleasure related to drug use in prison, it is relevant to notice that with the exception of a few qualitative studies (Lloyd et al., 2017, 2019), there has been little in-depth exploration of the motivations and meanings for use *prior* to imprisonment and *after* imprisonment. For example, we do not know if people are using drugs mainly for recreational or pleasurable purposes or in more problematic ways before they are imprisoned. We know that they often switch to more sedating drugs like cannabis and heroin in prison, but on the outside, we have little information about if they were using drugs to mainly enhance pleasure and recreational experiences in clubs or pubs, for example, or if they were using drugs due to dependence and/or wanting to escape from their lives. Similarly, there is a paucity of research on the ways in which substance use changes on release from prison and the motivations and meanings given for use. In general, there is a clear need for more qualitative research on individuals' trajectories of substance use over time, in different places and institutions, and throughout the life course. For people who are imprisoned, we especially need more examination of the key phases of drug use before prison, during imprisonment and after release and the meanings and motivations given to use (for inspiration on addiction trajectories, see Raikhel and Garriott, 2013). Not only could such knowledge aid our theoretical understandings of, for instance, the relation between different kinds of drug use and prisoners lives inside/outside prisons. It could also help addressing more holistically the different problems experienced by prisoners who use drugs and the help they might need in different phases of their lives and across institutional contexts. Demographic differences relating to age, gender, sexuality, ethnicity, religion and other variables such as employment, housing and recovery capital (i.e. social networks and family support) also need to be explored in greater depth.

Notes

1 The chapter is based on both authors' long-term engagement with prison studies and drug research. While we do not claim to have included all existing literature on the subject, we do believe that the literature referred to covers the most relevant topics within the field of prison and drug research to address the key questions set out in this chapter.

2 The term 'risk environment' focuses on the drug harms produced by social and political institutions in the interaction with the individual. In this way, the responsibility for drug harms is shifted from the individual alone to also include the social context (Rhodes, 2009).

References

Aebi, M. F. and Tiago, M. M. (2021). *Prisons and Prisoners in Europe 2020: Key Findings of the SPACE I Report*. Strasbourg: Council of Europe.

Azbel, M. F. and Altice, F. L. (2018). Drug use, HIV, and the high-risk environment of prisons. In: Kinner, S.A. and Rich, J.D. (eds.) *Drug Use in Prisoners: Epidemiology, Implications and Policy Responses*. Oxford: Oxford University Press, pp. 99–115.

Becker, H. (1953). Becoming a Marihuana user. *The American Journal of Sociology*, 59(3): 235–242.

Blackman, S. and Bradley, R. (2017). From niche to stigma – Headshops to prison: Exploring the rise and fall of synthetic cannabinoid use among young adults. *International Journal of Drug Policy*, 40: 70–77.

Boys, A., Farrell, M., Bebbington, P., Brugha, T., Coid, J., Jenkins, R., . . . Taylor, C. (2002). Drug use and initiation in prison: Results from a national prison survey in England and Wales. *Addiction, 97*(12): 1551–1560.

Bögelein, N. and Meier, J. (2018). Drogenhandel – Typologie einer illegalen Ökonomie. *Soziale Probleme,* 29: 15–43.

Bullock, T. (2003). Changing levels of drug use before, during and after imprisonment. In: Ramsay, M. (ed.) *Prisoners' Drug Use and Treatment: Seven Research Studies*. London: Home Office Research, Development & Statistics Directorate, pp. 23–48.

Carlin, T. (2005). An exploration of prisoners' and prison staff's perception of the methadone maintenance programme in Mountjoy Male Prison, Dublin, Republic of Ireland. *Drugs: Education, Prevention and Policy, 12*(5): 405–416.

Carpentier, C., Royuela, L., Montanari, L., and Davis, P. (2018). The global epidemiology of drug use in prisons. In: Kinner, S. A. and Rich, J.D. (eds.) *Drug Use in Prisoners: Epidemiology, Implications and Policy Responses*. Oxford: Oxford University Press, pp. 17–42.

Clemmer, D. (1940). *The Prison Community*. Boston, MA: The Christopher Publishing House.

Cohen, S. and Taylor, L. (1972). *Psychological Survival: The Experience of Long-Term Imprisonment*. Harmondsworth: Penguin Books.

Cohen, S. and Taylor, L. (1976). *Escape Attempts: The Theory and Practise of Resistance to Everyday Life*. London: Routledge.

Cope, N. (2003). 'It's No Time or High Time': Young offenders' experiences of time and drug use in prison. *The Howard Journal of Criminal Justice, 42*(2): 158–175.

Crewe, B. (2005). Prisoner society in the era of hard drugs. *Punishment & Society*, 7(4): 457–481.

Crewe, B. (2009). *The Prisoner Society: Power, Adaptation, and Social Life in an English Prison*. Oxford: Oxford University Press.

Crewe, B. (2011). Depth, weight, tightness: Revisiting the pains of imprisonment. *Punishment and Society*, 13(5): 509–529.

de Andrade, D. (2018). The drugs-crime nexus. In: Kinner, S. A. and Rich, J. D. (eds.) *Drug Use in Prisoners: Epidemiology, Implications and Policy Responses*. Oxford: Oxford University Press, pp. 1–16.

Duke, K. (2003). *Drugs, Prisons and Policy-Making*. New York: Palgrave Macmillan.

Duke, K. (2020). Producing the 'Problem' of New Psychoactive Substances (NPS) in English Prisons. *International Journal of Drug Policy*, 80, https://doi.org/10.1016/j.drugpo.2019.05.022

Duke, K. and Kolind, T. (2020). Framing and reframing drug 'problems' in prison spaces and populations. In: MacGregor, S. and Thom, B. (eds.) *Risk and Substance Use: Framing Dangerous People and Dangerous Places*. London: Routledge, pp. 162–182.

EMCDDA (2012). *Prisons and Drug Use in Europe: The Problem and Responses*. Luxembourg: EMCDDA.

EMCDDA (2018). *New Psychoactive Substances in Prison: Results from an EMCDDA Trendspotter Study*. Lisbon: EMCDDA.

EMCDDA (2021). *Prisons and Drugs in Europe: Current and Future Challenges*. Lisbon: EMCDDA.

Fazel, S., Yoon, I. A., and Hayes, A. J. (2017). Substance use disorders in prisoners: An updated systematic review and meta-regression analysis in recently incarcerated men and women. *Addiction*, 112(10): 1725–1739.

Frank, V. A., Dahl, H., Holm, K., and Kolind, T. (2015). Inmates' perspectives on prison drug treatment: A qualitative study from three prisons in Denmark. *Probation Journal*, 62(2): 156–171.

Gillespie, W. (2005). A multilevel model of drug abuse inside prison. *The Prison Journal*, 85(2): 223–246.

Goffman, E. (1961). *Asylums. Essays on the Social Situation of Mental Patients and Other Inmates*. New York: Anchor Books.

Gossop, M (2000). *Living with Drugs*. Aldershot: Ashgate.

Grace, S., Lloyd, C., and Perry, A. (2020). The spice trail: Transitions in synthetic cannabis receptor agonists (SCRAs) use in English prisons and on release. *Drugs: Education, Prevention and Policy, 27*(4): 271–281.

Haller, M. B. and Kolind, T. (2018). Space and ethnic identification in a Danish prison. *Punishment & Society*, 20(5): 580–598.

Hunt, G. Riegel, S., Morales, T., and Waldorf, D. (1993). Changes in prison culture: Prison gangs and the case of the "Pepsi Generation". *Social Problems*, 40(3): 298–409.

Hunt, G. P. and Evans, K. (2008). 'The great unmentionable': Exploring the pleasures and benefits of ecstasy from the perspectives of drug users. *Drugs: Education, Prevention & Policy*, 15(4), 329–349.

Irwin, J. (1970). *The Felon*. Englewood Cliffs, NJ: Prentice-Hall.

Irwin, J. and Cressey, D. R. (1962). Thieves, convicts and the inmate culture. *Social Problems, 10*(2): 142–155.

Jacobs, J. (1983). *New Perspectives on Prison and Imprisonment.* Ithaca, NY: Cornell University Press.

Keene, J. (1997). Drug misuse in prison: Views from inside: A qualitative study of prison staff and inmates. *The Howard Journal of Criminal Justice, 36*(1): 28–41.

Kolind, T. (2015). Drugs and discretionary power in prisons: The officer's perspective. *International Journal of Drug Policy, 26*(9), 799–807.

Kolind, T., Frank, V. A., Lindberg, O., and Tourunen, J. (2013). Prison-based drug treatment in Nordic political discourse: An elastic discursive construct. *European Journal of Criminology, 10*(6): 659–674.

Kolind, T., Holm, K., Duff, C., and Frank, V. A. (2016). Three enactments of drugs in Danish prison drug treatment: Illegal drugs, medicine and constrainers. *Drugs: Education, Prevention and Policy, 23*(2), 135–143.

Larney, S., Stoove, M., and Kinner, S. A. (2018). Substance use after release from prison. In: Kinner, S. A. and Rich, J. D. (eds.) *Drug Use in Prisoners: Epidemiology, Implications and Policy Responses.* Oxford: Oxford University Press, pp. 85–98.

Liebling, A. (1999). Prison suicide and prisoner coping. In: Tonry, M. and Petersilia, J. (eds.) *Prison, Crime and Justice Review of Research* (Vol. 26). Chicago: University of Chicago Press, pp. 283–359.

Lloyd, C., Page, G., McKeganey, N., and Liebling, A. (2017). *The Evaluation of Drug Recovery Wings Pilots: Final Report.* York: University of York.

Lloyd, C., Page, G., McKeganey, N., and Russell, C. (2019). Capital depreciation: The lack of recovery capital and post-release support for prisoners leaving the Drug Recovery Wings in England and Wales. *International Journal of Drug Policy*, 70: 107–116.

Mathiesen, T. (1965). *The Defence of the Weak: A Sociological Study of a Norwegian Correctional Institution.* London: Tavistock Publications.

Mauss, M. (1990). *The Gift. The Form and Reason for Exchange in Archaic Societies.* Oxon: Routledge.

Milloy, M. J. (2018). Injecting while incarcerated. In: Kinner, S. A. and Rich, J. D. (eds.) *Drug Use in Prisoners: Epidemiology, Implications and Policy Responses.* Oxford: Oxford University Press, pp. 43–56.

Mjåland, K. (2014). 'A culture of sharing': Drug exchange in a Norwegian prison. *Punishment & Society, 16*(3): 336–352.

Mjåland, K. (2016). Exploring prison drug use in the context of prison-based drug rehabilitation. *Drugs: Education, Prevention and Policy, 23*(2): 154–162.

Raikhel, E. and Garriott, W. (Eds.) (2013). *Addiction Trajectories.* Durham: Duke University Press.

Ralphs, R., Williams, L., Askew, R., and Norton, A. (2017). Adding spice to the Porridge: The development of a synthetic cannabinoid market in an English prison. *International Journal of Drug Policy, 40*: 57–69.

Reuter, P. and Pardo, B. (2017). Can new psychoactive substances be regulated effectively? An assessment of the British Psychoactive substances bill. *Addiction, 112*(1): 25–31.

Rhodes, T. (2009). Risk environments and drug harms: A social science for harm reduction approach. *International Journal of Drug Policy,* 20(3): 193–201.

Rhodes, T., Azbel, L., Lancaster, K., and Meyer, J. (2019). The becoming-methadone-body: On the onto-politics of health intervention translations. *Sociology of Health & Illness, 41*(8): 1618–1636.

Ritter, C., Broers, B., and Elger, B. S. (2013). Cannabis use in a Swiss male prison: Qualitative study exploring detainees' and staffs' perspectives. *International Journal of Drug Policy, 24*(6), 573–578.

Sandøy, T. A. (2015). Group solidarity in a hostile milieu: Immigrant experiences in a street-based drug scene. *Drugs: Education, Prevention and Policy, 22*(3): 232–238.

Seal, D. W. Vancey, S., Reddy, M., and Kinner, S. (2018). Alcohol use among incarcerated individuals. In: Kinner, S. A. and Rich, J. D. (eds.) *Drug Use in Prisoners: Epidemiology, Implications and Policy Responses.* Oxford: Oxford University Press, pp. 57–70.

Singleton, N. (2008). The role of drug testing in the criminal justice system. *Drugs and Alcohol Today,* 8(3): 4–8.

Singleton, N., Pendry, E., Taylor, C., Farrell, M., and Marsden, J. (2005). *The Impact of Mandatory Drug Testing in Prisons.* Home Office Online Report 03/05. London: Home Office.

Skarbek, D. (2014). *The Social Order of the Underworld: How Prison Gangs Govern the American Penal System.* Oxford: Oxford University Press.

Slade, G. and L. Azbel (2020). Managing drugs in the prisoner society: Heroin and social order in Kyrgyzstan's prisons. *Punishment & Society*, https://doi.org/10.1177/1462474520956280

Strang, J., Gossop, M., Heuston, J., Green, J., Whiteley, C., and Maden, A. (2006). Persistence of drug use during imprisonment: Relationship of drug type, recency of use and severity of dependence to use of heroin, cocaine and amphetamine in prison. *Addiction, 101*(8): 1125–1132.

Stöver, H. and Kastelic, A. (2014). *Drug treatment and Harm Reduction in Prisons.* Geneva: World Health Organisation.

Stöver, H. and Michels, I. (2010). Drug use and opioid substitution treatment for prisoners. *Harm Reduction Journal,* 7: 17.

Stöver, H., Weidlandt, C., Zurhold, H., Hartwig, C., and Thane, C. (2008). *Final Report on Prevention, Treatment and Harm Reduction Services in Prison on Reintegration Services on Release from Prison and Methods to Monitor/Analyse Drug Use among Prisoners.* (SANCO/2006/C4/02). Brussels: Directorate General for Health and Consumer Affairs.

Sturup-Toft, S., O'Moore, E. J., and Plugge, E. H. (2018). Looking behind bars: emerging health issues for people in prisons. *British Medical Bulletin, 125*(1): 15–23.

Swann, R. and James, P. (1998). The effect of the prison environment upon inmate drug taking behaviour. *The Howard Journal of Criminal Justice, 37*(3): 252–265.

Sykes, G. (1958). *The Society of Captives: A Study of a Maximum Security Prison* (Third Printing ed.). Princeton: Princeton University Press.

Symkovych, A. (2018). The 'inmate code' in flux: A normative system and extralegal governance in a Ukrainian prison. *Current Sociology,* 66(7): 1087–1105.

Toch, H. (1977). *Living in Prison: The Ecology of Survival.* New York: The Free Press.

Tompkins, C. (2013). Exploring motivations to stop injecting in English prisons: Qualitative research with former male prisoners. *International Journal of Prisoner Health, 9*(2): 68–81.

Tompkins, C. (2016). "There's that many people selling it": Exploring the nature, organisation and maintenance of prison drug markets in England. *Drugs: Education, Prevention and Policy, 23*(2): 144–153.

Tompkins, C. and Wright, N. (2012). "I wanted a head change" – Motivations and influences on men's illicit drug-using practices in prison. In Wouters, M., Fountain, J., and Korf, D. J. (eds.) *The Meaning of High: Variations According to Drug, Set, Setting and Time* (pp. 149–163). Lengerich: Pabst Science Publishers.

Trammell, R. (2009). Values, rules, and keeping the peace: How men describe order and the inmate code in California prisons. *Deviant Behavior, 30*(8): 746–771.

Turnbull, P. (2000). The effect of prison on drug use. In Muscat, R. (ed.) *Drug Use in Prison.* Strasbourg: Council of Europe Publishing, pp. 133–144.

Ugelvik, T. (2014). Paternal pains of imprisonment: Incarcerated fathers, ethnic minority masculinity and resistance narratives. *Punishment & Society, 16*(2): 152–168.

User Voice (2016). *Spice: The Bird Killer. What Prisoners Think about the Use Spice and Other Legal Highs in Prison.* https://www.uservoice.org/wp-content/uploads/2020/07/User-Voice-Spice-The-Bird-Killer-Report-compressed.pdf

Van de Baan, F. C., Montanari, L., Royuela, L., and Lemmens, P. (2021). Prevalence of illicit drug use before imprisonment in Europe: results from a comprehensive literature review. *Drugs: Education, Prevention and Policy,* forthcoming.

Vasilou, E. (2020). Penitentiary pleasures: Queer understanding of prison paradoxes. *Criminology and Criminal Justice,* 20(5): 577–589.

Wilson, G. B., Galloway, J., Shewan, D., Marshall, L., Vojt, G., and Marley, C. (2007). "Phewww, bingoed!": Motivations and variations of methods for using heroin in Scottish prisons. *Addiction Research & Theory,* 15(2): 205–224.

World Health Organization (WHO) (2014). *Prisons and Health.* Copenhagen: WHO Regional Office for Europe.

Zinberg, N. (1984). *Drug, Set, and Setting. The Basis for Controlled Intoxicant Use.* New Haven: Yale University Press.

13

HOW METHADONE BECOMES AN INTOXICANT

The making of methadone within prisons in the Kyrgyz Republic

Lyu Azbel and Frederick L. Altice

Introduction

Methadone maintenance treatment—prolonged treatment with an opioid agonist—is promoted within evidence-based research as an effective way to treat patients diagnosed with opioid use disorder and prevent the transmission of blood-borne infections such as hepatitis C and HIV among people who inject drugs (MacArthur et al., 2012, Platt et al., 2017). People who inject drugs in prison, and who are infected with HIV or Hepatitis C, may transmit these infections to others by sharing non-sterile injection equipment. But transmission can be prevented with the increased uptake of needle and syringe programs and opioid agonist treatment in the community as well as in prisons and after release and hence decreased injection (Altice, 2015).

The promotion of opioid agonist treatment has been the primary policy adopted by international health agencies, such as the World Health Organization, to combat the twin epidemics of addiction and associated HIV concentrated in prisons (World Health Organization, 2012). Methadone treatment within prisons, similar to community settings, has been evidenced to have the potential to treat addiction and prevent HIV and hepatitis C transmission (Boucher, 2003). The implementation of methadone treatment is therefore part and parcel of the worldwide response to HIV. Randomized controlled trials from prisons evidence the effectiveness of methadone treatment in reducing opioid injection, especially when initiated before release from prison (Kinlock et al., 2009, 2007).

Methadone's global promise hinges on sufficient coverage among people who inject opioids to significantly reduce HIV transmission on a population level (Larney et al., 2017). Yet, methadone treatment is unavailable in most prison systems worldwide due to its political unpopularity; when available, coverage among prisoners who use opioids is low (Altice et al., 2016, LaMonaca et al., 2019).

From the time the Kyrgyz government introduced methadone treatment into prisons with the support of international donors in 2008, the program has retained few patients and remained largely unpopular (Azbel et al., 2016a, 2016b, 2018). Nationally, following initial growth in methadone treatment uptake, the number of methadone patients has remained stable over the past five years (This amounts to 476 people in 6 of 11 prisons) (Borisova,

DOI: 10.4324/9780429058141-17

2018). To reach the standards of coverage the World Health Organization deems necessary to significantly reduce the number of new HIV infections, 1,224 prisoners in Kyrgyz Republic would have to receive methadone (Azbel, 2020).

Given the challenge that implementation of methadone treatment into prisons presents, the unique availability of methadone treatment in prisons in the Kyrgyz Republic (hereafter Kyrgyzstan) presents an important case study. The methadone treatment program, launched in the community in 2002 and in prisons in 2008, marks an exception in the region—making Kyrgyzstan the only country in Central Asia and one of a handful in the world to offer methadone treatment in prisons (Bielen et al., 2018). This policy move is celebrated within global health networks, which highlight Kyrgyzstan as yielding particular promise in implementing evidence-based interventions (Ancker and Rechel, 2015, Latypov, 2011). Despite championing methadone treatment in Kyrgyzstan as an outstanding achievement, researchers and international policymakers are concerned that performance indicators (e.g. coverage) are not being met by local implementers (Larney et al., 2017).

Studies of drug use and addiction treatment among prisoners in Eastern Europe and Central Asia have been dominated by quantitative analyses (Altice et al, 2016, Azbel et al., 2016a, 2016b). Qualitative studies addressing methadone implementation in Eastern Europe and Central Asia are sparse, mostly adapting an evidence-based medicine framework, and none have been carried out in prisons (Bojko et al., 2016, Marcus et al., 2018, Mazhnaya et al., 2016). While qualitative studies addressing methadone implementation in Eastern Europe and Central Asia are sparse, mostly adapting an evidence-based medicine framework, none have been conducted in prisons (Bojko et al., 2016, Marcus et al., 2018, Mazhnaya et al., 2016). And where studies have been done in prisons, for example, studying implementation with prisoners in Moldova (Polonsky, Azbel, et al., 2016a, 2016b) and with both prisoners (Polonsky, Rozanova, et al., 2016) and prison personnel (Polonsky et al., 2015) in Ukraine, none have been qualitative nor focused on Central Asia.

In this chapter, we adopt a critical social science approach which looks to the ontology of objects in translation to illustrate their different effects in different times and places. This approach moves beyond the evidence-based framework, to open up space for a critical analysis of how medical technologies travel (i.e., adoption), here with methadone treatment as an example, without taking for granted that the evidencing of intervention is fixed and transportable to the same effect potential across contexts (Rhodes and Abdool, 2016). To understand drug effects, researchers within this tradition move away from studying substances as self-evident objects with inherent properties whose representations are affected by discourse. Rather, they emphasize the way that material, social, cultural, and discursive elements—such as the instruments used to administer drugs and the processes of drug administration—come together to *produce* substances and their effects (Dennis, 2016, Duff, 2013, Keane, 2018, Lancaster et al., 2017, Moore, 2018).

Studies in this tradition have examined different ways that intoxicants have been evidenced, and why they can produce unexpected effects. Research has lent scrutiny to the way drug-objects and -subjects are constituted by—rather than pre-exist—the way that we, as researchers and policymakers, intervene to address drug problems (Bacchi, 2017, Lancaster et al., 2017). In her seminal study of the object of methadone within clinical trials, Gomart provides an account of how different methadones are produced through the inscriptions of these trials (Gomart, 2002). Through the processes of two different clinical trials, the same apparent substance produces fundamentally different material effects. She observes that methadone is a series of "effects in search of a substance" (Gomart, 2002). The performance of a substance does not precede but is *made through* its implementation events. Also Rhodes' studies of methadone in Kenya draw attention to how the methadone-in-practice, a methadone of recovery hope, is distinct from the methadone-in-policy (Rhodes, 2018), a solution to HIV-linked drug injection. This methadone is evidenced as enabling normalcy through its dynamics of delivery, including the witnessing of bodily material change among its users toward a recovered-body. Rhodes concludes, "Methadone treatment is far from a singular evidence-based intervention translated into multiple settings, but a local practice of emergent 'evidence-making' interventions" (Rhodes, 2018). Other social studies of methadone have also brought methadone objects into view that are different from those traditionally evidenced in literature: methadones of pain relief (Keane, 2013), addiction recovery (Berridge, 2012), and, in Ukraine, a means of disciplining the subject (Carroll, 2016).

We begin to see that we cannot take the effects of a substance for granted. Given different practices surrounding the implementation of medical interventions, the effects on the body can vary widely. This lens opens up new avenues of questioning that are productive for illuminating a methadone with different effect potential from the one evidenced in public health research. Indeed, the evidencing of methadone in the biomedical sciences has been characterized by a move to tease it apart from illicit opioids as a way of drawing out the therapeutic qualities of the former (Acker, 2004). Such discourses commonly draw a distinction between a drug of addiction, characterized by compulsive use, and a treatment, characterized by stabilizing effects (Keane, 2013). In this chapter, we analyze methadone's practices of use to bring a different methadone into view. While medical literature and clinical guidelines work to separate methadone from illicit drugs, we will show how its practices of use in Kyrgyz prisons produce methadone as a compulsive drug of addiction, while heroin, administered by prisoners in line with practices of harm reduction, produces health.

Theoretical approach

To understand why methadone treatment administered in Kyrgyz prisons suffers from low uptake, we, in the tradition of the aforementioned studies, do not take a singular methadone for granted (in this case, the methadone of public health: a treatment for the chronic and relapsing brain disease of addiction). Rather, we allow ourselves to consider that other methadones with differing effects may be present in Kyrgyz prisons, methadones which are not separate from but made *within* the practices of implementation. To do this, we look at methadone as an *effect* of the practices of its use.

To carry out this analysis, we turn to an analytical tool within critical drug studies—actor-network theory (Deleuze and Guattari, 1987, Latour, 2005). This tool is conceptually useful for understanding the way that objects we assume are stable are actually *multiple*, or, in other words, producing different effects in different places and times. This multiplicity can be referred to as multiple "objectivizations." As Paul Veyne (1997, cited in Bacchi and Goodwin, 2016) writes, "there are no natural objects...there are only multiple 'objectivizations.'" Accordingly, in this chapter, we discuss multiple methadone objects—the umbrella term—which can take the form of a methadone treatment or a methadone drug. Actor-network theory is therefore particularly well-suited for attending to how substances, including those unexpected, come about. It rests on the supposition that new objects, including intoxicants, are *made* through a multitude of relations, including the relations between humans, animals, things, and matter, which are in and of themselves never stable but shifting (Bennett, 2010).

Actor takes the practices of implementation as the unit of analysis to observe what kinds of objects emerge from implementation events. This can involve any practice of implementation, including the space where methadone is implemented, what tools are used to administer it, the way that users talk about its effects, or merely the act of observing bodies that have imbibed methadone. For example, in their study of the daily experience of accessing methadone treatment in Australia, Fraser and valentine (2008) draw attention to the human and non-human actors that constitute the methadone subject. They redirect inquiry, rather, to the relations and practices that make objects and subjects. They argue that relations between human and non-human actors work to materialize a particular kind of subject. In their example, the arrangement of the methadone dosing site, which necessitates the line of clients to wait outside of it, creates a "methadone client" who is most commonly "considered undesirable in modern liberal societies" (Fraser and valentine, 2008: 92).

Important here is that attention is drawn not to attitudes about a substance or other such human behaviors but, also, the non-human elements such as the material spaces where medicines are administered. Indeed, actor-network theory focuses our attention to how human and non-human actors come together differently at different times to produce different interventions (DeLanda, 2006, Deleuze and Guattari, 1987, Latour, 2005, Law and Hassard, 1999). In our fieldwork in Kyrgyz prisons where our research team was tackling the challenges to methadone implementation from a biomedical perspective, we began to notice that something else was at play, beyond the methadone proffered in evidence-based research. We repeatedly came up against the way that methadone was used differently than prescribed, particularly alongside other substances. Methadone's relations with other substances made it something different than the "evidence-based" methadone we expected (i.e., how methadone's unexpected effects were a product of its use alongside some substances as well as its non-use with other substances).

Methods

In what follows, we utilize actor-network theory to ask, what kind of methadone object is produced through the relations of different drugs within the Kyrgyz prison environment? To do this, we draw on qualitative data from two studies supported by the U.S. National Institute on Drug Abuse, which explored how prison environments shape opioid addiction treatment. Interviews were conducted after written consent from October 2016 to September 2018 with prisoners who inject drugs before (n = 24) and after (n = 20) release from prison in two male high-security prisons in Kyrgyzstan. Our team at the Yale University School of Medicine had been carrying out qualitative and quantitative studies in Kyrgyz prisons for five years and had developed a relationship with the Prison Department that allowed us access to potential participants within prison. The Prison Department provided us with a list of all prisoners with a release date within six months so that we could follow up with prisoners after release in case we had further questions. Initially, we chose randomly from the list and a representative from the prison administration called the participants on the loudspeaker in the prison yard (this is a common practice in the prison and the times when the speaker is off are less common than when it is on). Participant recruitment into the study, or "sampling,"[1] for this study was purposive (Corbin & Strauss, 1998), with attention to diverse incarceration experience, age, status within the prisoner hierarchy, drug treatment history, and ethnicity.

We met privately with potential participants, described the purpose of the study, emphasized that our work was unrelated to that of the prison administration, that interviews were voluntary and anonymous, and informed potential participants that they would face no consequences for non-participation. Participants interested in the study received an information sheet about the study and the consent form, requiring a signature. We asked participants to read the information sheet and inform us if they were interested in participating. If they agreed to take part, they signed the consent form. Interviews were recorded using an Olympus digital voice recorder and lasted 58 minutes on average. The interviews were in-depth and followed the lead of the participant to discuss issues such as drug use, health, prisoner society, and practices of methadone and drug administration. After completion, participants were reimbursed for their time with a package of hygienic goods (containing toothpaste, soap, shampoo, etc.), totaling eight dollars, commensurate with other studies in public health carried out by non-governmental organizations in Kyrgyzstan. They were also provided with a list of organizations working with released prisoners in need of housing, medical services, and bureaucratic services such as passport and housing registration.

Interviews were redacted to remove any potential identifying information and stored on a secure server (Yale File Transfer), transcribed and translated by an agency in Kyiv, Ukraine. Using Dedoose (SocioCultural Research Consultants, 2018), the research team (three people) coded 22 interviews (all of which the first author reviewed), and the first author coded the remaining 61 interviews to shape the analytic frame that "generates the bones" of our analysis (Charmaz, 2006: 46). The first author, who speaks Russian fluently, opted for coding the Russian language transcripts to stay closer to the original.

The data generation, coding, and analyses were simultaneous processes throughout the course of the study that were driven by a focus on *material practices*. That is, rather than focusing on the symbolic value of human behavior in constructing the meaning of methadone, we instead drew the interviewing and analysis deeper into the minutiae of the relations between the body, intoxicants, and methods of drug administration. We were interested in how material relationships with and within the prison space were formed (Alaimo and Hekman, 2008). The material relationships we were particularly interested in included the bodily practices surrounding heroin and methadone distribution as well as governing rituals, such as how methadone and heroin are distributed among prisoners, including the utensils used and the location of the paths in the prison yard that lead to the distribution points. In the interviews, the first author questioned the "pervasive and mundane acts" (Mol, 2002: 39) of everyday life, including which path prisoners followed through the prison yard to obtain methadone and heroin, how methadone and heroin were administered, what it looked like when punishments or rewards were meted out, how their bodies felt and looked after taking the substances, among others.

To code the interview transcripts, L.A. carried out a "Poststructural Interview Analysis" (Bonham et al., 2015). Drawing on Foucauldian concepts of governmentality (Foucault, 1991), this methodology is useful for considering the production of subjects and objects through practices. The relations between things in interview texts are treated as practices with governing potential. Take, for example, the relations between the length of a substance's withdrawal symptoms, the mode of its administration, the high (i.e., euphoria), and the punitive consequences of its use. These elements in an interview text interact (i.e., the longer the withdrawal symptoms, the stronger the punitive response) to make a substance into a particular kind of substance. In this case: an illicit drug. Following this approach, we were not interested in arriving at a participant's access to an "inner truth" about their intentions or experiences with drugs. We were, rather, interested in the politics of *what* is said, meaning, how things said establish normative *ways to be*. This is because, in paying attention to what is said, rather than the intentions of the speaker, we can start to unpack what understandings were in place to make those things *sayable*. For example, "madness" emerged as an object of thought in accordance with what criteria the authorities used to define it (Bacchi and Goodwin, 2016: 33). Accordingly, the first author used the coding framework as a form of analysis to map the entangled web of relations that set limits on the kinds of methadones and methadone subjects were possible in the Kyrgyz prison.

With a view of what "things said" *do*, the first author traced how normative implications of what participants said generated ways to be. Put differently, this form of analysis treats "things said" as productive since it is through the relations within discursive practices that subjects and objects are continually formed (Bacchi and Goodwin, 2016: 118). As Bacchi and Goodwin emphasize, "hence, they [discursive practices] need to be studied in terms of what they produce, or constitute, rather than in terms of what they 'mean'" (Bacchi and Goodwin, 2016: 118). The first author examined the effects of the way that prisoners talked about the use of intoxicants in their communal drug use rituals. Rather than treating their words as "attitudes" toward drugs that generate meaning, we looked at what was said in terms of how it affected what objects can *be* and *do*. The first author coded for objects and subjects that fell within the confines of prisoners' communal property versus objects and subjects that fell outside of it. For example, methadone was excluded from prisoners' communal distribution practices whereas heroin was included. L.A. coded for the normative assumptions that made what was said "sayable" (Foucault, 1991: 59). In other words, "what meanings need to be in place for particular 'things said' to be intelligible" (Bacchi and Goodwin, 2016: 117)? The normative assumption here was that the materials owned and distributed collectively by prisoners to prisoners confer health. The subject position that emerged was clear: the physically fit prisoner was someone who received heroin treatment while the ailing prisoner took methadone. In this way, "Poststructural Interview Analysis" allowed me to harness "*what* is said" to examine the processes through which heroin and methadone are differentiated.

Analysis

Leveraging science and technology studies into how medical technologies are produced through local practices (Mol, 2002), we will in the following analysis describe how methadone is inextricably tangled up with local drug use practices. We will show how the methadone produced within local practices of the Kyrgyz prison is an intoxicant—a substance different to the one evidenced as harm-reducing in public health research. To do this, we focus on methadone's relations with two substances in particular: heroin and Dimedrol (generic name: diphenhydramine, known as Benadryl® in the United States), an antihistamine used sometimes for allergies and occasionally sleep as it can be sedating. First, we describe how prisoners relate methadone to heroin: prisoners' accounts make up methadone as a substance inferior in terms of its health-producing and pleasurable effects. Second, we focus on methadone's use alongside Dimedrol as a way to re-enact the experience of heroin. Lastly, we delineate how these three substances entangle to produce ill health in terms of their effects on the prisoner body and in its perception by others.

Methadone: the anti-heroin object

In opposition to the notion that methadone is health-producing as can be seen within global health accounts (World Health Organization, 2012), local methadone disrupts the well-being of the body in multiple distinct ways, with effects extending to the moral character of individuals and entire social groups. Methadone's harms are made in relation to a local manifestation of heroin-as-harm-reduction, with the most pronounced effects of methadone being a dependence on a "drug" and, correspondingly, withdrawal, stronger than induced by heroin. In what follows, we outline these local manifestations of methadone as they relate to heroin in Kyrgyz prisons.

Methadone in relation to heroin: an overpowering force

Within participants' accounts, methadone is made relationally to heroin; the two substances perform related work on the body. This "work"—these material effects—are emergent from the relations within a "drug assemblage," in which heroin is a key actor. Global health discourse presents methadone as distinct from heroin. Heroin is a drug while methadone is a medical treatment because the latter reduces the ability to perceive intoxication, normalizes conduct, and fosters recovery from addiction (Berridge, 2012, Fraser and valentine, 2008, Keane, 2013). Users of methadone, in turn, are re-fashioned as more normal, healthy, and productive than those who use heroin (Bourgois, 2000).

Participants' accounts too make up the substance and effects of methadone relationally to heroin, but in the opposite direction: heroin is a necessary "treatment," enacting stability, normalcy, and health, whereas methadone is a toxic drug, leading to a breakdown of the body. Key to these relations is methadone's "neutralizing" effect on heroin: methadone messes with heroin's materialization as treatment. Through participant's accounts, we see that methadone and heroin are linked in their materialization, the former working to erase the latter. Below, we unpack the relations of the methadone-heroin assemblage.

Within participants' accounts, there is an acute sense that methadone is a more potent substance than heroin, as Victor, for example, says: "Methadone has stronger cravings, it is stronger." Methadone is constituted as a drug that, once started, is nearly impossible to discontinue, engendering a stronger dependency than heroin, as Bashir and Zheenbek say:

> It is possible to give up heroin, but methadone addiction is much stronger, much worse.
>
> *[Bashir]*

> It creates stronger dependency than heroin...When you're taking heroin, if you quit, you're recovering for a month. Whereas with methadone, it took me six months to recover.
>
> *[Zheenbek]*

And stronger dependence goes hand in hand with a more physically and psychologically intense, or "stronger," withdrawal, a point emphasized by Umar in the following quote:

> Last time I managed to stay away [from methadone] for seven days. But could not stand it anymore. The longer you stay away, the worse the withdrawals. When methadone is washed out of the system, I experimented, to see how long I would be able to stand it. It turned out, after heroin it gets better with every passing day, but after methadone...After methadone, ten days is not enough to fight physical withdrawals. Even with medicine. They gave me a drip here. They gave me Relanium. It was as useless as an udder on a bull.

The fear elicited by even the thought of withdrawal is palpable. There is a strong sense of helplessness, with users succumbing to the power of the drug. The body is talked of as being overburdened by methadone, its capacity overextended, caving into the lethal power of the substance, as Sergei, for example, explains:

> Withdrawal from methadone, a person can't get through it. If I was to just quit it cold turkey right now...as I quit heroin, where I'm sick for a week and that's it. With this, it won't work. I'll die. My body won't be able to take it...the methadone withdrawal.
>
> *[Sergei]*

Again, heroin is the point of comparison—albeit a point that is also shifting. Heroin can be overcome, if needed, bringing one closer to healing. Methadone, in contrast, is an impossible obstacle, further degrading the body.

Methadone's strength is materialized through the "overtaking" of heroin; there is a sense that methadone, through its power of acting, diminishes heroin. Repeatedly, participants recount the "blocking" effects of methadone: those taking methadone are no longer able to experience heroin, as Sergey and Anton, for example, say:

> They cannot understand heroin, even when they use it, they cannot understand it... There is no effect. Methadone neutralizes, counter-balances it.
>
> Everybody knows full well that methadone knocks down the heroin concentration, you drink a sip and then you shoot up, useless, well useless.

What, then, are the effects on the body when methadone pushes heroin out of the way? In other words, what work does methadone accomplish in taking the place of heroin?

Methadone as taking over the body

The relationship of methadone and heroin is one of incorporation, with methadone swallowing heroin so that its effects are masked. We saw that heroin is enacted as a treatment. Methadone's effect of blocking heroin treatment produces a body bereft of healing. Accounts invoke methadone's potency through its mechanism of acting on the body, wherein methadone becomes entangled with the user's body.

Participants' narratives emphasize how the very material of one's body fuses together with the substance, becoming one:

> First, it all builds up inside, right, and the heart suffers, and the liver, and urine, and everything, basically it's the living dead, what's the sense?
>
> *[Aigul']*

Methadone becomes a sort of entrapment. Longer-term users, unable to look back or quit, describe methadone as the building block of their bodies and bones:

> I told them...I've been on methadone for 15 years, my bones are already made of methadone, I won't be able to quit, it's okay, you'll quit, he said, others in worse positions quit.
>
> *[Timur]*

Interview accounts constitute methadone as *seeping* through body, to the point that it is filled up with it. For example, Alim notes that:

> When a person begins taking methadone, he gets a high. He's high from it, right, until his body is filled with methadone. It even has the property of filling up, right, methadone fills you up. He gets high, and the larger the dose, the more, basically, the better he feels. And then they don't understand themselves, i.e. they themselves don't notice how they end up, right? Drinking 300 grams, while he weighs 40 kilograms, 50 max. What's that? He can barely walk, and he's drinking 300 there. Basically, I know, I'm not stupid, I've read online what this drug is made of, and that people, if they abuse it, methadone, it really degenerates, they degenerate right before your eyes. They don't read, they don't develop, they, well, in general, they are aberrations.

Methadone is described as "taking over" the body, transforming the healthy body into a *methadone-body*. The body becomes made of methadone.

But the interaction between the heroin and methadone and the effects they produce are not the only significant relations in the drug assemblage. Methadone is often taken together with another substance, an antihistamine called Dimedrol that is available in pill form. In what follows, I explore the constitution and effects of methadone through its interaction with Dimedrol. Although emerging from accounts as the most significant player in the drug assemblage, Dimedrol use has only recently been explored in research (Meyer, 2020). Below, we explore how methadone is produced in particular ways through its relations with Dimedrol.

The methadone-Dimedrol object

A faint trace of "solitary" Dimedrol

Today, Dimedrol in Kyrgyz prisons is commonly used in combination with methadone to achieve a high. Some time after drinking methadone (about 20 minutes), Sergey explains how the pills are "crushed, shaken with water, drawn up [into a syringe]. Let's say, five tablets in five mL, and so you shoot up these five mL." He continues to explain how shooting up Dimedrol, rather than oral consumption, produces a much stronger high. While there are accounts of Dimedrol use predating the introduction of methadone into Kyrgyzstan, our interviewees narrated how Dimedrol at this time was used sparingly and mostly to reduce nausea associated with heroin use.

Present Dimedrol use is, however, a phenomenon that is perceived to go hand in hand with methadone. A cheaper alternative to heroin, it is precisely the *reaction* between the two that is the sought-after euphoria. This connection is so strong that Dimedrol only registers as a substance in participants' accounts in concert with the introduction of methadone:

> Especially now that they've introduced methadone there. Now there's methadone and Dimedrol, it's such a mess with everything.
>
> *[Taalaibek]*

> Basically, Dimedrol was available before, but it wasn't the same consistency as now. Starting in 2010, when the methadone program was set up, the way methadone and Dimedrol interact, and this reaction created a miracle, it proved to be better than heroin.
>
> *[Salamat]*

> It's new, it's methadone and Dimedrol. I haven't noticed this before. Before there was just *khanka* [home-made injection opioid from poppy straw] and heroin, as far as I remember in all prisons, now there's this methadone. People are simply dying, after a while they pass away. I was offered to join methadone, no, I didn't agree to it and I won't.
>
> *[Esenbek]*

Some accounts go as far as to say that Dimedrol was ushered in by methadone. These accounts create a narrative that prior to methadone, Dimedrol barely existed. A separable Dimedrol is a faint memory, currently non-existent, and exerting no effect on the body.

Dimedrol: a way to re-enact the heroin experience

This high stands above the high afforded by other substances. As Maksim stated, "How can I explain it? Heroin has this tinge, this flavor, when the wave is about to start. It's our kind of high [*prikhod po nashemu*]. You can taste it. It's a completely different high, just completely different." And Kyrgyzstan is the country with the best quality: "In the whole world, again, we have the best opium, again, we have the best marijuana. We have it here in Kyrgyzstan." But heroin is not regularly and readily available for all. Dimedrol becomes the surest path to this "sober" high "[with Dimedrol] the brain starts to work faster. This feeling of reality, you get a crisper image. And then it ends, and you're not high anymore."

So unlike methadone's implementations elsewhere, and in contrast to its portrayals in policy as a solution to the problem of HIV, we found that methadone in Kyrgyz prisons often is used in combination with Dimedrol. This is done to turn methadone, normally a substance described as providing no euphoria when chronically used for treatment, as a gateway to euphoria, not unlike a heroin high, as Sultan says:

> Methadone without Dimedrol doesn't get you high. It just takes away the withdrawal, stops you from being sick. But with Dimedrol, there's some kind of reaction that takes place. … It's like heroin, as though you've injected heroin.
>
> *[Sultan]*

Methadone without Dimedrol is understood as constituting a dull "robotic" existence. Adding Dimedrol re-ignites life:

> I drink methadone, I'm going down a tunnel, I see nothing… I get Dimedrol, I shoot it up and I see a white light, birds chirping. It turns out I'm alive.
>
> *[Kalmurat]*

Methadone is enacted, in terms of the high it affords, in relation to both heroin and Dimedrol. Indeed, these substances interact. Methadone blocks heroin, eliminating the high. Dimedrol, however, provides an alternative pathway to the heroin experience by activating the high that methadone makes absent:

> It seems the brain remembers that heroin trip, and Dimedrol gives this trip. But not for long. That's why the Dimedrol dose keeps growing.
>
> *[Semen]*

> Yes, and this [Dimedrol and methadone] is better than heroin, the high is stronger… You get this wave all over your body, that's twice as good as heroin. You drink methadone and you go and shake five pills, shoot them up, and there you go, the same as heroin.
>
> *[Salamat]*

Dimedrol, in a sense, works to restore the heroin high that methadone erases.

The entanglement of methadone and Dimedrol

By following "what is said" in participants' accounts, we see that the practices of substance use contaminate the relative "purity" of methadone by Dimedrol. Dimedrol is a banned substance, according to the informal rules guiding life within prison, which is even "worse" than methadone in relation to the casting of moral position and administrative and bodily power. Methadone's entanglement with Dimedrol disrupts the notion of "methadone as treatment" as proffered by global health, making it a drug. The narrative that cuts across participants' accounts is that of methadone's inextricability from Dimedrol. Daniiar, a participant on methadone, recognizing the problem with Dimedrol, states that "the only way to get rid of Dimedrol is to get rid of methadone." This flips the traditional public health response to the problem on its head: instead of decoupling Dimedrol from methadone to preserve the purity of the latter, only with the full erasure of methadone can Dimedrol disappear.

Before turning to the bodily materializations of Dimedrol and methadone, let us first pause for a closer look at how these terms are used. Accounts oscillate between referring to the substances as going hand in hand. For example, Ali says, "if there wasn't methadone, he wouldn't be looking for Dimedrol." Other accounts, such as those of Kamal and Kairat, respectively, attribute the same effects to both substances:

> People die, right? I don't know, as far as I understand it's from methadone. But they also take Dimedrol. Those methadone-dimedrolers, it's just horrible!

As Kairat explains, "Dimedrol or methadone, it's the same thing. This is the reason why I don't want to go on this methadone, because I know what happens… A person begins to transform from a human into an animal." The two substances are so intertwined in our participants' narratives that the words "methadone" and "Dimedrol" can be used interchangeably to refer to the same thing, disrupting any clear demarcation between the two. Methadone, through its incorporations, becomes multiple things and has multiple effects. Below, I look at the practices of methadone-Dimedrol to outline how these materializes. Through its practices of use, as accounted by participants, the effects of engaging with this methadone-Dimedrol complex are dehumanizing: the self transforms into an animal.

Methadone-Dimedrol practices

The interaction between methadone and Dimedrol is inordinately powerful, described as both a "miracle" and a "poison," and evidenced by its practices of administration, the high, and the body of its users. Let's take a look at each of these practices, in turn.

First, instances of Dimedrol's use constitute a toxic drug of addiction—an intoxication. Dimedrol tablets are banned but available illicitly (much like heroin was previously). They are crushed, dissolved in water, and injected around the time of drinking methadone; this injection process is repeated several times throughout the day. The procedure of Dimedrol use is repeatedly emphasized as unimaginable. As Kalmurat states, "Can you imagine? Six pills at once into the vein, into the bloodstream." Bakyi further explains this process, "You inject 40 pills a day. Can you imagine?" Barat seconds this, "They take Dimedrol by the sheets So from 9 a.m. to 5 p.m., it's 50 tablets, can you imagine what was happening? I don't even know how I'm alive still." This excessive dosing denotes an unnaturalness; such large quantities are not conducive to "natural" human life. Those continuing to live while injecting are an abhorrent marvel.

Dimedrol promises a euphoria stronger than heroin: "Experience has shown that it's even better than heroin. It's a very strong high" [Nikolai]. But this Dimedrol high has a flip side much like that of heroin: addiction: "first it's euphoria, then it's some kind of addiction to

Dimedrol, too" [Zheenbek]. Addiction, here, is evidenced by an ever-increasing need for Dimedrol: "Because they also get addicted. Later, a tablet, two, it's too little, they start taking five tablets" [Mirlan]. Like with the high, the addiction is described as being even stronger than in the case of heroin. The overwhelming nature of Dimedrol addiction is repeatedly emphasized by users. When I asked Salamat what can be done to change the practice of combining Dimedrol with methadone, he responded with the following scenario:

> Well you'll have to say that it's the end of the world in an hour, maybe then something might happen [laughter]. Otherwise, they don't care, they wouldn't even care if it's the end of the world. I've seen a person who was on methadone, he was taking a large dose and decided one fine day to quit everything, on the spot in one day. I just saw his reaction, what started happening to him...He began losing his mind right away. Afterwards he was caught in the prohibited zone and was killed, that's that...Perhaps it's withdrawal, or something else, that a person begins losing his mind, he begins pouring soup on himself and so on, begins talking in a non-human tongue, well if, well I don't know what to make of it.

The force of methadone appears to seem beyond reason by some. The extreme practices of its use and effects have equally extreme consequences: loss of control, humanity, and eventually death.

To understand prisoners' decisions surrounding methadone, it is important to consider how the practices of methadone's use produce methadone-using subjects. In the next section, we explore the production of the dehumanized methadone-Dimedrol subject, focusing particularly on how practices of methadone-Dimedrol use make evidence about this particular subject.

The dehumanized methadone mind

At the same time as offering a "way out" of the banality of the methadone routine via a rerouted heroin experience, accounts equate Dimedrol to a complete loss of moral decency. We can glimpse this in the unpredictability related to the methadone subjects who are made up through the accounts of prisoners with varying methadone experiences:

> It's like a monkey house. People are already not normal... It [Dimedrol] causes hallucinations, it closes up a person, he becomes crazy, delusions, hallucinations, talks to himself, doing things, this noise, that's it, he is lost.
>
> *[Bakhtiiar, some methadone experience]*

> They [methadone clients] would not answer your questions. Sometimes they would talk nonsense and gibberish. Their eyes are crazy. I heard someone say they would start going through garbage, or even put their hands in the toilet bowls. In a nutshell, people just become awful.
>
> *[Sultan, no methadone experience]*

These accounts of the psychology of the methadone subject work to constitute him as Other, residing on the margins of what is socially acceptable. No longer in tune with the "normal" practices of daily prison life, the subject loses touch with reality. Defining this Other in terms of an alternate reality, characterized by hallucinations and delusions, renders him unknowable. He occupies a different psychosocial space, and this space is grotesque.

But the effects of the methadone-Dimedrol object extend beyond the mind to affect the body. To further explore how subjects are governed through methadone's subjectification effects, let us reflect on how methadone with Dimedrol constitutes the body as a particular kind of body (Bacchi and Goodwin, 2016: 69).

The dehumanized methadone body

The extraordinary procedures of Dimedrol use and its psychological effects extend to its bodily material manifestations, which participants' accounts emphasize as equally "unnatural" and "inhuman." The user's body, having been "filled up" with methadone, undergoes a transformation. Users of this substance complain of blisters; wounds; abscesses; bad teeth, lungs, and livers; an addiction worse than heroin; and unprecedented drug withdrawals. As Kalmurat notes, methadone users "degenerate right before your eyes." He continues:

> They disappear, the veins vanish. They're aware. They know that their veins are burning. They know about their liver. Their hearts grow weaker. They know and consciously do it. He gave up on himself. He just gets high. He needs nothing else.

Again, the substance of methadone-Dimedrol is experienced to be powerful enough to take the will of the user hostage. The substance supersedes the body, leading to a loss of self and a loss of body. And when it overtakes the body, methadone-Dimedrol degrades. The bodies of these users are literally experienced to deteriorate and disappear:

> I see them, those people who use 100 pills at a time. It's scary even looking at this person… Their legs are like my arm.
>
> *[Alim]*

> What person in his right mind, when he sees these zombies, excuse my language, all these people with abscesses. What person in his right mind would support this program? When doctors do autopsies on these methadone users, they say they are all meat-jelly [*kholodets*] inside, they're like monsters.
>
> *[Alibek]*

These descriptions invoke the decay surrounding this methadone object—a new substance incorporating Dimedrol—which works to infect and break apart the body. While prison staff pointed to the negative effect that Dimedrol—not methadone—has on the body, within the practices of prisoners' daily lives, these two substances became interchangeable.

If methadone causes the body to deteriorate, the logical end is that the body turns to nothing. Stepan commented, "there is nothing but bones left in me." The methadone body may end in "actual death," which is sometimes presented as rationale for resisting the introduction of methadone from the outside:

> Nothing will change for the better if I start taking methadone. That is the same drug [as heroin] but is killing people much faster than heroin.
>
> *[Bashir]*

> People die, right. Well, I already know many guys who used to take methadone, my acquaintances, die. Their livers give up, lungs… As far as I understand, it's from methadone.
>
> *[Barat]*

> We clearly realize that this is the killing of drug addicts, the methadone program... During [its] nine years, half of the population died. In nine years, half of them died... It's a slow death by methadone.
>
> *[Sergei]*

The association of methadone with death, especially when aligned with Dimedrol, is so strong that some of the participants even see it as a conspiracy to kill prisoners, who use drugs. A point emphasized by Talgat who says it is "a legal way to kill people." Salamat explains further:

> The goal is just to exterminate the druggies, the thieves, and the killers. Many countries have said no to methadone. It's just our Kyrgyzstan that continues it. We have a lot of druggies. And I just see it, I see what's happening with this program, they're starting to die. At first, all's OK, he's blooming. And then one fine day, that's it, and he's a corpse... My bones started breaking, the joints were giving in, and I said, "No, that's it." I'm still young, I have a life ahead of me.

Accounts such as Salamat's often present Kyrgyzstan as an exception to the rule of banning methadone. There is a sense that while all "civilized" countries do not allow methadone, Kyrgyzstan's legislation of the methadone program is a function of the country's backwardness. Participants even recounted rumors that Americans invented Dimedrol in order to combine it with methadone to kill the drug using population.

The methadone body, especially in light of its incorporations with Dimedrol, is enacted as a *less-than-human* body. The terms used to describe methadone users ("zombies," "monsters," "animals") render them inhuman. The ill health brought about by methadone is evidenced in the visible physical degradation. This degradation is present in the personal narratives of users. Maksim says, "I lost my teeth to methadone...I drank it and half an hour later it all comes back out." Leonid, who did not take methadone, observes, "They [the methadone users] have sores and blisters... they have wounds." In both cases, bodily ailments are directly attributed to methadone, and the knowledge-making instances are those that are witnessed first-hand:

> And so this methadone. Just look at what's happening with those on methadone. You can't...just now a guy came in, it's sad looking at him. It's all because of your methadone. He's already shaking.
>
> *[Nikolai]*

> Well, I don't know, just looking at them [methadone clients], how they're killing themselves, I don't feel like it, I still feel like living.
>
> *[Kamal']*

> Well, you can tell that by just looking at the person. I tell you, it's enough to take two to three tablets and one can already see it in your eyes.
>
> *[Nurlan]*

Methadone's bodily incorporations are made real through witnessing. It is the instances of seeing methadone user's bodily transformations that makes methadone into a substance that harms. Daniiar, who was enrolled in the methadone program, is a particularly striking case. During our interview, he pointed to his body, outlining the sores with his finger, and said: "these spots right here are ripping apart, the skin. I'm beginning to dry out from these chemicals. I've lost my health. I'm already dying." Health is something finite and the methadone-Dimedrol complex, agentic, eats away at it until it disappears. By bringing me into seeing the inscriptions of methadone on the body, Daniiar was creating knowledge about methadone. *Seeing* the devastating effects of the drug—whether on one's own body or the bodies of others—is a prime agent in creating methadone as toxic.

Conclusion

At the root of an intoxicant's becoming are the knowledge-making practices of its use. That is, substances, rather than possessing solid or stable effects, are made within social practices (Dennis, 2016, Duff, 2013, Gomart, 2002). We have demonstrated that methadone's material manifestations, such as withdrawal symptoms, physical dependency, and drug embodiments, produce evidence about the substance. Pushing aside health-enabling enactments of methadone, the methadone enacted in prisoners' accounts is a toxic drug.

Locally enacted methadones, including this toxic methadone, are negotiated in relation to a drug assemblage. The relations between methadone and heroin, and methadone and Dimedrol, are key to understanding methadone's toxicity. Through its folding into health-destroying Dimedrol and away from health-producing heroin, methadone becomes a poison rather than a treatment. Methadone is intertwined with Dimedrol in complex ways to produce a methadone-Dimedrol complex and affect a sickly "methadone-body." The effects afforded by methadone take on, and then become indistinguishable from, those of Dimedrol, a substance constituted as particularly messy in the bodily damage it causes. While global health narratives treat methadone as a discrete and stable object, participants' accounts work to blur the boundaries of these substances, making it impossible to cleanly tease them apart. Not as clearly visible but, existing within the margins, a health-producing methadone also comes into view—a testament to the possibility of alternative enactments within this actor-network. Showing how a harm-producing methadone is made provides hope that, given a change in the set of implementation practices, a health-producing methadone can also be made.

In this chapter, however, we have worked with the idea of the "methadone body" to explore the material effects of methadone-Dimedrol at the level of the individual subject. We saw that a rotting methadone-Dimedrol body is enacted through the material relations of drugs with other drugs as well as drug use practices. This form of analysis illuminates the shifting bodies produced through interactions with methadone, which, while remaining unaccounted for by public health, are essential for a competent intervention implementation in the Kyrgyz prison space and beyond.

The significant implication of this theoretical shift is that, unlike within much of the public health literature, there was no methadone "out there" that could be uncovered by the removal of "barriers" to its translation. Context is, rather, an active participant in the making of local methadone and its effects. Given a different context, then, the methadone performed would also be different. This has implications for how intervention implementers think about substances and their intoxication effects. We call for a departure from the imagined stable substances articulated by much public health writing to challenge the very notion that a substance, translated to a different place, should, given ideal circumstances, produce the same health outcomes. We urge public health practitioners to consider the way interventions are made multiple times within their practices of use.

Note

1 "Sampling" is not the most appropriate term, given that this study focused more on process rather than attaining a specified end result, including the number of participants.

References

Acker, C. 2004a. Portrait of an addicted family: dynamics of opiate addiction in the early twentieth century. *In:* Tracey, S. & Acker, C. (eds.) *Altering American Consciousness: the History of Alcohol and Drug Use in the United States, 1800–2000* (pp. 165–81). Amherst: University of Massachusetts Press.

Alaimo, S. & Hekman, S. J. 2008. *Material Feminisms.* Bloomington: Indiana University Press.

Altice, F. L. 2015. *Prison-Related Research Intervention Development and Evaluation.* National Institute on Drug Abuse. Bethesda, Maryland.

Altice, F. L., Azbel, L., Stone, J., Brooks-Pollock, E., Smyrnov, P., Dvoriak, S., Taxman, F. S., El-Bassel, N., Martin, N. K., Booth, R., Stover, H., Dolan, K. & Vickerman, P. 2016. The perfect storm: incarceration and the high-risk environment perpetuating transmission of HIV, hepatitis C virus, and tuberculosis in Eastern Europe and Central Asia. *Lancet,* 388, 1228–1248.

Ancker, S. & Rechel, B. 2015. HIV/AIDS policy-making in Kyrgyzstan: A stakeholder analysis. *Health Policy Plan,* 30, 8–18.

Azbel, L., Grishaev, Y., Wickersham, J. A., Chernova, O., Dvoryak, S., Polonsky, M. & Altice, F. L. 2016a. Trials and tribulations of conducting bio-behavioral surveys in prisons: implementation science and lessons from Ukraine. *International Journal of Prisoner Health,* 12, 78–87.

Azbel, L., Polonsky, M., Wegman, M., Shumskaya, N., Kurmanalieva, A., Asanov, A., Wickersham, J. A., Dvoriak, S. & Altice, F. L. 2016b. Intersecting epidemics of HIV, HCV, and syphilis among soon-to-be released prisoners in Kyrgyzstan: Implications for prevention and treatment. *International Journal of Drug Policy,* 37, 9–20.

Azbel, L., Wegman, M., Polonsky, M., Bachireddy, C., Meyer, J. P., Sumskaya, N., Kurmanalieva, A., Dvoriak, S. & Altice, F. 2018. Drug injection within prison in Kyrgyzstan: Elevated HIV risk and implications for scaling up opioid agonist treatments. *International Journal of Prisoner Health,* 14(3), 175–187.

Azbel, L. 2020. Methadone as indiscipline: The making of the virtuous subject in Kyrgyz prisons. PhD thesis, London School of Hygiene & Tropical Medicine. DOI: https://doi.org/10.17037/PUBS.04657358

Bacchi, C. & Goodwin, S. 2016. Making and unmaking "subjects". *Post-structural Policy Analysis: A Guide to Practice.* New York: Palgrave Macmillan.

Bacchi, C. 2017. Drug problematizations and politics: Deploying a post-structural analytic strategy. *Contemporary Drug Problems,* 45, 3–14.

Bennett, J. 2010. *Vibrant Matter: A Political Ecology of Things.* Durham, NC: Duke University Press.

Berridge, V. 2012. The rise, fall, and revival of recovery in drug policy. *Lancet,* 379, 22–23.

Bielen, R., Stumo, S. R., Halford, R., Werling, K., Reic, T., Stover, H., Robaeys, G. & Lazarus, J. V. 2018. Harm reduction and viral hepatitis C in European prisons: a cross-sectional survey of 25 countries. *Harm Reduction Journal,* 15, 25.

Bonham, J., Bacchi, C. & Wanner, T. 2015. Gender and cycling: Gendering cycling subjects and forming bikes, practices and spaces as gendered objects. *In:* Bonham, J. & Johnson, M. (eds.) *Cycling Futures* (pp. 179–201). Adelaide: University of Adelaide Press.

Bojko, M. J., Mazhnaya, A., Marcus, R., Makarenko, I., Islam, Z., Filippovych, S., Dvoriak, S. & Altice, F. L. 2016. The future of opioid agonist therapies in Ukraine: A qualitative assessment of multilevel barriers and ways forward to promote retention in treatment. *Journal of Substance Abuse Treatment,* 66, 37–47.

Borisova, T. 2018. Tekushchaia situatsia v oblasti predostavleniia uslug podderzhivaiushchei terpaii metadonom v Kyrgyzskoi Respublike i plany na blishaishee budushchee. *Kruglyi stol, Rezul'taty kachestvennoi otsenki po opredeleniu sushchestvuiushchikh barierov k PTM dlia LUIN v Kyrgyzskoi Respublike: obsuzhdenie i planirovanie otvetnykh mer.* Bishkek: Kyrgyz Republic.

Boucher, R. 2003. The case for methadone maintenance treatment in prisons. *Vermont Law Review,* 27, 453–482.

Bourgois, P. 2000. Disciplining addictions: The bio-politics of methadone and heroin in the United States. *Cult Med Psychiatry,* 24, 165–195.

Carroll, J. J. 2016. For lack of wanting: Discourses of desire in Ukrainian opiate substitution therapy programs. *Transcult Psychiatry,* 53, 198–216.
Charmaz, K. 2006. *Constructing Grounded Theory.* London; Thousand Oaks, CA: Sage Publications.
Corbin, J. M. & Strauss, A. C. 1998. *Basics of Qualitative Research: Techniques and Procedures for Developing Grounded Theory.* London: Sage Publications.
Delanda, M. 2006. *A New Philosophy of Society: Assemblage Theory and Social Complexity.* London: A&C Black.
Deleuze, G. & Guattari, F. 1987. *A Thousand Plateaus.* Minnesota: Minnesota University Press.
Dennis, F. 2016. *In(tra)jecting Bodies: A Relational Approach to Injecting Drug Use, Pleasure and Harm.* PhD, London School of Hygiene & Tropical Medicine.
Duff, C. 2013. The social life of drugs. *International Journal of Drug Policy,* 24, 167–172.
Foucault, M. 1991. *The Foucault effect: Studies in Governmentality.* Chicago, IL: University of Chicago Press.
Fraser, S. & valentine, K. 2008. *Substance and Substitution: Methadone Subjects in Liberal Societies.* London: Palgrave Macmillan.
Gomart, E. 2002. Methadone: Six effects in search of a substance. *Social Studies of Science,* 32, 93–135.
Keane, H. 2013. Categorising methadone: Addiction and analgesia. *International Journal of Drug Policy,* 24, e18–e24.
Keane, H. 2018. The object in hand: Social science of the syringe. *International Journal of Drug Policy,* 61, 66–68.
Kinlock, T. W., Gordon, M. S., Schwartz, R. P., Fitzgerald, T. T. & O'Grady, K. E. 2009. A randomized clinical trial of methadone maintenance for prisoners: results at 12 months post-release. *Journal of Substance Abuse Treatment,* 37, 277–285.
Kinlock, T. W., Gordon, M. S., Schwartz, R. P., O'Grady, K., Fitzgerald, T. T. & Wilson, M. 2007. A randomized clinical trial of methadone maintenance for prisoners: Results at 1-month post-release. *Drug Alcohol Depend,* 91, 220–227.
LaMonaca, K., Dumchev, K., Dvoriak, S., Azbel, L., Morozova, O. & Altice, F. L. (2019). HIV, drug injection, and harm reduction trends in Eastern Europe and Central Asia: Implications for international and domestic policy. *Current Psychiatry Reports, 21*(7), 47. https://doi.org/10.1007/s11920-019-1038-8
Lancaster, K., Seear, K. & Ritter, A. 2017. Making medicine; producing pleasure: A critical examination of medicinal cannabis policy and law in Victoria, Australia. *International Journal of Drug Policy,* 49, 117–125.
Larney, S., Peacock, A., Leung, J., Colledge, S., Hickman, M., Vickerman, P., Grebely, J., Dumchev, K. V., Griffiths, P., Hines, L., Cunningham, E. B., Mattick, R. P., Lynskey, M., Marsden, J., Strang, J. & Degenhardt, L. 2017. Global, regional, and country-level coverage of interventions to prevent and manage HIV and hepatitis C among people who inject drugs: A systematic review. *Lancet Glob Health,* 5, e1208–e1220.
Latour, B. 2005. *Reassembling the Social: An Introduction to Actor-Network-Theory.* Oxford; New York: Oxford University Press.
Latypov, A. B. 2011. The Soviet doctor and the treatment of drug addiction: "A difficult and most ungracious task". *Harm Reduction Journal,* 8, 32.
Law, J. & Hassard, J. 1999. *Actor Network Theory and After.* Oxford; Malden, MA: Blackwell/Sociological Review.
MacArthur, G. J., Minozzi, S., Martin, N., Vickerman, P., Deren, S., Bruneau, J., Degenhardt, L. & Hickman, M. 2012. Opiate substitution treatment and HIV transmission in people who inject drugs: Systematic review and meta-analysis. *BMJ,* 345, e5945.
Marcus, R., Bojko, M. J., Mazhnaya, A., Makarenko, I., Filippovych, S., Dvoriak, S., Altice, F. L. & Springer, S. A. 2018. A qualitative assessment of attitudes about and preferences for extended-release naltrexone, a new pharmacotherapy to treat opioid use disorders in Ukraine. *Journal of Substance Abuse Treatment,* 86, 86–93.
Mazhnaya, A., Bojko, M. J., Marcus, R., Filippovych, S., Islam, Z., Dvoriak, S. & Altice, F. L. 2016. In their own voices: Breaking the vicious cycle of addiction, treatment and criminal justice among people who inject drugs in Ukraine. *Drugs (Abingdon England),* 23, 163–175.
Meyer, J. P., Culbert, G. J., Azbel, L., Bachireddy, C., Kurmanalieva, A., Rhodes, T., Altice, F. L. 2020. A qualitative study of diphenhydramine injection in Kyrgyz prisons and implications for harm reduction. *Harm Reduct J,* 17(1), 86.

Mol, A. 2002. *The Body Multiple: Ontology in Medical Practice*. Durham, NC: Duke University Press.

Moore, D. 2018. Making alcohol and other drug realities: Introduction to a special issue *Contemporary Drug Problems,* 45, 183–187.

Platt, L., Minozzi, S., Reed, J., Vickerman, P., Hagan, H., French, C., Jordan, A., Degenhardt, L., Hope, V., Hutchinson, S., Maher, L., Palmateer, N., Taylor, A., Bruneau, J. & Hickman, M. 2017. Needle syringe programmes and opioid substitution therapy for preventing hepatitis C transmission in people who inject drugs. *Cochrane Database of Systematic Reviews,* 9, CD012021.

Polonsky, M., Azbel, L., Wickersham, J. A., Marcus, R., Doltu, S., Grishaev, E., Dvoryak, S. & Altice, F. L. 2016. Accessing methadone within Moldovan prisons: Prejudice and myths amplified by peers. *International Journal of Drug Policy, 29,* 91–95. https://doi.org/10.1016/j.drugpo.2015.12.016

Polonsky, M., Azbel, L., Wickersham, J. A., Taxman, F. S., Grishaev, E., Dvoryak, S. & Altice, F. L. 2015. Challenges to implementing opioid substitution therapy in Ukrainian prisons: Personnel attitudes toward addiction, treatment, and people with HIV/AIDS. *Drug Alcohol Depend, 148,* 47–55. https://doi.org/10.1016/j.drugalcdep.2014.12.008

Polonsky, M., Rozanova, J., Azbel, L., Bachireddy, C., Izenberg, J., Kiriazova, T., Dvoryak, S. & Altice, F. L. 2016. Attitudes toward addiction, methadone treatment, and recovery among HIV-infected Ukrainian prisoners who inject drugs: Incarceration effects and exploration of mediators. *AIDS and Behavior, 20*(12), 2950–2960. https://doi.org/10.1007/s10461-016-1375-0

Rhodes, T. & Abdool, R. 2016. Drug harms and drug policies in Sub-Saharan Africa: Implementation science and HIV epidemics. *International Journal of Drug Policy,* 30, 1–6.

Rhodes, T. 2018. The becoming of methadone in Kenya: How an intervention's implementation constitutes recovery potential. *Social Science & Medicine,* 201, 71–79.

Veyne, P. 1997. Foucault revolutionizes history. In A.I. Davidson (Ed.), Foucault and his Interlocutors, Porter, C. (trans.), Chicago, IL: University of Chicago Press.

World Health Organization. 2012. WHO, UNODC, UNAIDS technical guide for countries to set targets for universal access to HIV prevention, treatment and care for injecting drug users. *In*: Organization, W. H. (ed.). Geneva.

14

TRADE-OFFS BETWEEN INTOXICATION, SAFETY, AND SOCIABILITY WITHIN A DRUG-CONSUMPTION FACILITY

Esben Houborg and Siv Schjøll Berge

Introduction

In this chapter, we present a study of how people who use a drug consumption room (DCR) in Copenhagen, Denmark think about using drugs in that setting compared with other settings, and which trade-offs they consider when deciding where to use drugs. Such considerations could involve a trade-off between minimizing the risk of an overdose and the best possible experience of getting intoxicated, or a trade-off between enjoying the company of others when using drugs, or getting more 'bang for the buck' by using alone. As part of this investigation, we are also interested in how different 'modes of use' – such as self-medication of physical or mental problems, alleviating withdrawal symptoms, solitary experience of particular forms of intoxication, drug use as a social activity, etc. – can be associated with using drugs in different settings. In doing this study, we follow previous qualitative research on how people experience using DCRs and how they consider using drugs in a DCR or in other settings (Clua-García, 2020; Duncan, Duff, Sebar, & Lee, 2017a; Duncan, Sebar, Lee, & Duff, 2019, 2020; Small, Moore, Shoveller, Wood, & Kerr, 2012; Small et al., 2011). Our contribution to this literature is that we show how users negotiate drug use in different settings, rather than mainly focusing on what happens inside the DCR. We also show the variety of different considerations that can be involved, rather than mainly focusing on risk and risk management. We emphasize the importance of considering how to regulate the boundaries between the institutional space inside a DCR and the drug scene outside a DCR when designing and managing a DCR.

Background

DCRs are intended to provide a safe and hygienic space to use drugs to prevent drug-related harm. It is a harm-reduction service that many studies have shown to be effective in reducing fatal overdoses and infections from blood-borne infectious diseases (HIV and Hepatitis B and C), increasing drug users' access to social and health benefits, and improving public order (Folch et al., 2018; Hedrich, Kerr, & Dubois-Arber, 2010; Potier, Laprévote, Dubois-Arber, Cottencin, & Rolland, 2014).

DOI: 10.4324/9780429058141-18

In 2012, the Danish Parliament made an amendment to the drug legislation that made it possible for municipalities to establish DCRs. The municipality of Copenhagen, having wanted to establish a DCR since the early 2000s, was quick to set up first one and then an additional facility. The second facility, which has been in use since 2016, is the object of our study here. Before the public DCRs were established, a private organization had already established a mobile injection facility, which the municipality took over when it became legally possible.

Much of the literature on DCRs as 'safer environment interventions' (McNeil & Small, 2014) articulates a risk-oriented public health perspective, which means a focus on risk factors that increase the likelihood of drug-related harm. There is increasingly, however, a literature that seeks to create a more varied understanding of how DCRs function by taking their point of departure in users' perspectives. This includes users' conceptions of risk (Small et al., 2012), how DCRs can change social relations among people who use drugs (McNeil & Small, 2014), DCRs as a setting for care (Duncan et al., 2019, 2020; McNeil & Small, 2014; Small et al., 2012) and for enjoying drugs (Duncan et al., 2017a), and how users negotiate using drugs in DCRs and other settings (Clua-García, 2020; Small et al., 2012).

Qualitative research on users' perspectives on DCRs has documented that reduction of health risks is only part of the benefit that DCRs can provide for marginalized people who use drugs. Apart from minimizing the risks of fatal overdoses and getting infected with, for example, HIV or Hepatitis C, DCRs can also serve to minimize some of the everyday risks, including violence, robbery, or losing drugs, that are associated with the life of a marginalized person who uses drugs (Clua-García, 2020; Fairbairn, Small, Shannon, Wood, & Kerr, 2008; Small et al., 2012). To understand this dimension of DCRs it's important to have an understanding of the social, cultural, and structural contexts within which a DCR is situated, including the characteristics of the drug scene, other available health and social services, or drug legislation and its enforcement. It has also been shown that the design of DCRs, and which alternative settings for drug use exist, can influence the extent to which DCRs are used, by whom they are used, and how they are used (Clua-García, 2020; Small et al., 2011). Some research also includes other issues, particularly how DCRs can influence the social dynamics of drug use and experiences of using drugs, including how pleasurable they are. For example, a study from Barcelona, Spain has studied reasons why people decide to use drugs in DCRs, public spaces, and private settings, and while the main topic concerns risk perceptions and risk management, the study also touches upon how different settings affect the intoxicating experiences of using drugs, and how this informs decisions about where to use drugs (Clua-García, 2020). While some people decide to use DCRs because they reduce the risks or provide a good setting for enjoying drugs, other people decide to use drugs in public spaces or private settings, because they are experienced as better settings for enjoying drugs or because it is more convenient to use drugs in these settings. This research provides insights into how users negotiate different settings to use drugs. Negotiations can include considerations of different positive and negative aspects of using drugs in a particular setting. This can, for example, involve the risk of drug-related harm, getting your high ruined by noisy people, getting disturbed or hustled by people who want a share of your drugs, or having to wait a while before you can consume your drugs. A study of people who use a DCR in Vancouver make similar observations about reasons and rationales for using or not using a DCR (Small et al., 2011, 2012). The Vancouver study also mainly focuses on users' perceptions and management of risks, but the study does touch a little on how the DCR is, for some people or in some situations, not an attractive place to use drugs. Studies like these show the complexities of DCRs as harm-reduction measures and places to use drugs but, as indicated, the primary and explicit focus is on risk and risk-reduction. It is rarer that it is the drug-using experience, and particularly the issue of intoxication, that is at the centre of research on DCRs. This is, however, the case in a study of a DCR in Frankfurt, Germany conducted by Duncan et al. (2017a). In an article appropriately titled 'Enjoying the Kick' Duncan et al., (2017a), they provide a detailed analysis of how the social, material, and atmospheric setting of the DCR influences the pleasures of using drugs. In this way, the authors highlight perhaps the most important reason why people use drugs, to get an enjoyable experience of the intoxication that drugs can provide, and which should therefore be central to evaluating DCRs. However, the literature on DCRs has only been concerned with this issue to a limited extent. It has reflected a more general trait in social drug research, although in recent years more attention has been given to the issue of the pleasurable experiences of using drugs in general (Duff, 2008; Dwyer, 2008; Holt & Treloar, 2008; Houborg, 2010; Hunt & Evans, 2008; Moore, 2008; O'Malley & Valverde, 2004; Race, 2009). The Frankfurt study also focuses on the DCR as a socio-material setting that influences the atmosphere of the service and how it creates opportunities for engagement between staff and clients that, among other things, involve care (Duncan et al., 2019). The authors seek to show the importance of an accommodating setting and atmosphere in order to provide harm reduction, which they call 'atmospheric harm reduction' (Duncan et al., 2020). By broadening the dimensions of the functioning of DCRs and how users experience such services, the research by Duncan and his colleagues makes a valuable contribution to the harm-reduction literature in general and the literature on DCRs in particular. It can also be seen as part of a trend in social drug research to pay more attention to the pleasures that can be involved in using drugs. One important contribution to this research is acknowledging that people who are dependent on drugs also enjoy them and that all use is not dependent use or self-medication. Rather, just like others, people who are dependent on drugs can engage in different 'modes of use' (Gomart, 2002; Lowenstein, Gourarier, Coppel, Lebeau, & Hefez, 1995), including dependent use, self-medication, and recreational use. DCRs and other places where drugs are used may provide settings that facilitate different modes of use and different drug-use experiences, and this may affect where and how drugs are used (Clua García, 2018, 2020). To neglect the roles intoxication and pleasure play for drug users would, as mentioned, mean ignoring much of what makes the things that drug users do meaningful to them.

This chapter should be seen as a contribution to the line of research presented above that seeks to broaden the perspectives on how DCRs function, by taking user's experiences as the point of departure. More specifically, we are interested in exploring the considerations that are involved when users decide to use or not use a DCR. While this has been touched upon in previous research, it has not to our knowledge been the centre of attention except in the study by Clua-Garcia of Barcelona (Clua-García, 2018, 2020). We will use the term 'trade-off' to investigate how the users negotiate when and where to use drugs (Kloster et al., 2021). We use this term to show how considerations of different dimensions of using drugs in different settings can be involved when deciding where to consume drugs. While this may involve cost-benefit calculations, we use the term in a wider meaning to show that it is not always straightforward and obvious for people who use drugs to do so inside a DCR. In this way, we seek to contribute to the literature that presents the varied users' perspectives of DCRs in the hope that such perspectives are taken into account when DCRs are designed and managed. Of particular concern here is how different considerations concerning intoxication and the enjoyment of using drugs can be involved when users consider to use or not to use a DCR.

Drugs can have many functions, be used in different ways, and have different effects dependent on context (Becker, 1953; Duff, 2007, 2017; Houborg, 2012; Zinberg, 1984). It would be a mistake to let a deficit model (O'Malley & Mugford, 1991) govern our way of thinking about drug use among people who, in one way or another, are dependent on drugs, that is, to think that their physical or psychological dependency is the only thing that makes them use drugs. Rather, in order to get a nuanced understanding of drug use, it would be more useful to study how different people can have different 'modes of use' in different situations and different contexts (Gomart, 2004). In our study of users' experiences with drugs in different settings, we have therefore tried to identify how different settings can be associated with different modes of use. This means that for some people, a DCR may be a good setting for some modes of use, and not for others. An important question is therefore which modes of use can the design and functioning of different DCRs accommodate? How much variability in terms of modes of use do they allow?

Study context

The DCR that is the topic of this chapter is located in the neighbourhood of Vesterbro in Copenhagen, Denmark. Vesterbro is the location of the largest open drug scene in the Nordic countries and has for decades been associated with a highly visible trade and use of heroin, cocaine, crack, methadone, and prescription drugs. Until the turn of the century, the main drug was heroin, but for the past 10–15 years, cocaine (including crack) has become the dominant drug. This does not mean that heroin has disappeared, and many of the people who participate at the drug scene are poly-drug users. The change from heroin to cocaine as the dominant drug has influenced how the drug scene manifests itself. It has become more unruly, hectic, and loud. It is estimated that between 600 and 800 people participate in the drug scene on a daily basis (Mændenes Hjem, no date). Since 2012, the municipality of Copenhagen has financed DCRs in the area (Houborg & Frank, 2014). Today, two DCRs, Skyen and H17, exist in the area with a total capacity for 28 smokers and 17 injectors at one time. The DCRs complement each other in delivering a 24-hour service, and together, H17 and Skyen have between 500 and 1,000 drug intakes per day (Mændenes Hjem, no date). One can use the facilities anonymously, and people from the rest of Denmark, Sweden, Norway, and other countries use them. When establishing the DCRs, a zone was created around them where the users are allowed to be in possession of illicit substances for personal consumption without criminal prosecution, and hence exempts the users from Denmark's zero-tolerance policy on possession of drugs. The decriminalized zone encompasses the whole area of 'Inner Vesterbro' where the drug scene is situated (Houborg, Frank, & Bjerge, 2014). The area of Vesterbro is a mixed residential and business area dominated by high- and middle-income housing (Larsen & Hansen, 2008) and restaurants, bars, cafés, and hotels due to the proximity of the main railway station. Several low-threshold and harm-reduction services exist in this gentrified area in addition to the two DCRs. In this chapter, we focus on the DCR H17.

H17 is a 1,000 square metre converted slaughterhouse of yellow brick located a short distance from Copenhagen's central station, on the edge of Copenhagen's historic red-light district, next to the old Meatpacking District and just opposite the local police station. The name H17 refers to the address, Halmtorvet 17. The staff consists of nurses and social workers. Originally, H17 was meant to offer a recreational place with a lounge and a café area for the users, but this has not been fully implemented. H17 runs an almost 24-hour service and only closes for a couple of hours a day for cleaning. However, keeping H17 open for business has proved to be difficult because of staff shortages and closures due to fights and violence inside the facility.

To access H17, one passes 'the ramp', which runs along most of the façade of H17. On the ramp, benches are bolted to the ground, and trashcans and sharps containers are mounted on the walls. As an expected consequence of the opening of H17, much of the drug trade has become centred on and nearby the ramp. Weather conditions, time of the day, and day of the month influence how many people are on the ramp and the drug scene in general. The ramp constitutes a complex place with several different functions: entrance area, waiting area for those who want to get into H17 to consume their drugs, hang-out area, sleeping area, drug-using area, and drug-trading area. The gathering of different groups of people and the diverse functions sometimes cause a restless and unruly atmosphere. From the ramp, there are three doors leading into H17 an additional entry beneath the ramp for the staff only. Users are not let into the building until there is a vacant drug-using place, unless they need to use some of the other facilities in H17, such as the toilets.

A polka-dotted automated sliding door leads to a tiny blue-painted hallway inside H17. From there, one enters a reception area, also decorated in blue shades to create a calm atmosphere. The reception area is about 12 metres long with high ceilings and skylights. The reception is a rectangular counter in the middle of the room, where the staff register the guests (anonymously, e.g., nick-names) and the drugs they plan to consume. On the reception counter, there are jugs of free juice and stacks of disposable cups for guests. In front of it, there is a trolley with injecting equipment, tin foil, and other material for those who will smoke their drugs. Behind the counter, a long frosted-glass wall separates the reception from the smoking area, and opposite doors lead to restrooms, a deposit, and the injection room.

The smoking area contains eight smoking cabins with two seats mounted in each, with glass walls and doors to close, because of the ventilation system. A maximum of 20 users are allowed in the area at the same time, and often they gather in the cabins where the drugs are; that is, all 20 could easily gather in two booths or in the passageway in front of the rooms. Because of health regulations, the staff are not allowed to enter the smoking rooms or the passageway. The time slot for smokers is 30 minutes in the case of a queue developing. If there is a queue to enter on the ramp and a big shift has to be made, people are asked to leave through the chill-out area, passing the injection rooms to avoid a traffic jam at the main entrance.

A door separates the reception area and the injection room that is located on the opposite side of the reception to the smoking area. In the injection room, steel tables are placed in a row along the wall. A frosted glass screen separates each of the eight seats available. Each table is provided with a simple chair and a hole in the table top to get rid of spent equipment. Behind the row of injection tables is a passage that is also a space for clients to walk back and forth in or to hang out with friends in, besides being the route to the individual stalls. There is always staff present in the injection room in case of an overdose. The staff can also guide the user through sanitary injection practice and help to find veins that work. The time slot for the injection stalls is 45 minutes if there is a queue. If there is no queue, one can stay longer.

H17 has five basic rules: (1) users must register and agree (by signature) to abide by the house rules, (2) minors are prohibited from entry, (3) violence and threats are not allowed, (4) no drug dealing is allowed, and (5) one must follow the instructions of the staff and comply with the time slot assigned for the intake of substances (Mændenes Hjem, no date).

Enforcement measures range from a temporary ban, usually for an hour or the rest of the day, but a severe sanction can sometimes be for longer periods. The staff are not allowed to intervene in conflicts between users and are to call the police if conflicts need to be handled. The police have special units that patrol the area, officers who know the drug scene and usually seek to resolve conflicts without the use of force (Houborg, Frank, & Bjerge, 2014).

Methods and data

The data for this chapter comes from two different studies. The first was conducted in 2017 and involved fieldwork in the area where the open drug scene is located and involved interviews with drug users, social workers and police officers. The second and primary data source comes from an evaluation of H17 conducted in 2018. Forty-one users of DCR answered a survey interviews with questions about their sociodemographic background, drug use, and the experience of using H17. They were also asked if they had any ideas for changes or improvements to the facility. The survey interviews were recorded, and the respondents were encouraged to elaborate answers when they found it relevant to do so. The recordings of the interviews were transcribed and coded in Nvivo using a codebook built around questions about drawbacks and benefits in relation to different dimensions of using drugs in H17 and other places, including at home, in public space, and the other DCR in the area. Of the participants, 68% (28) were male, and 32% (13) were female. The mean age was 40.5 (38.6 for men and 44.5 for women), ranging from 24 to 60. Danish citizens accounted for 78%; of whom 32% said that they were currently in drug treatment. Cocaine was the most frequently used drug among the respondents; 83% said that they had used cocaine inside H17 during the past week; 58% had used heroin; 41% had used methadone. Sixty-one per cent of the respondents said that they used the smoking rooms inside H17, and 64% said that they used the injection room; 27% said that they used a booth smoking room and injection room. Fifty-one per cent said that they had used H17 two times a day or more during the past week.

When we conducted a survey among users of H17 in 2018 (n = 41), we asked them why they used the DCR, and we found that the DCR served different functions for the users, not just as a safe place to use drugs, indicating how the DCRs have become part of the drug scene. Thirty-nine per cent said that it provided a sense of security because the staff could help in case of an overdose, while 66% said that the facility provided a hygienic setting for using drugs. Fifty-six per cent said that they frequented H17 to socialize with other drug users, and 61% said that they came to trade drugs inside or in the vicinity of H17. The respondents were also asked about their experiences of using the DCR. Of the ones who used the injection room, 65% said that it was a good experience to use the room compared with using drugs in other settings, and 52% of the respondents who used the smoking rooms said that it was a good place to use drugs compared with other places (Houborg, Holt, & Bancroft, 2018). These answers indicate that even though many of the respondents were satisfied with the DCR as a setting for using drugs, there were also many that seemed to have reservations. We will consider some of these reservations in the sections below. Most of the respondents (93%) agreed or partly agreed that the staff treated them well and 73% agreed or partly agreed that the staff were able to uphold the rules and keep a calm and orderly atmosphere inside the DCR. Sixty-one per cent said that they agreed or partly agreed that the staff were able to provide care for the users. The most important reasons for not using the DCR were having to wait too long (74%), preferring to use the other DCR (63%), too much noise inside the DCR (54%), not a good experience to use drugs inside the DCR (53%), and that the DCR was closed (53%).

In the following sections, we will look at some of the considerations that users mentioned, when we talked with them about using drugs in the DCR and other settings. It is thus important to have in mind that our main focus is on those participants who considered trade-offs involved in using drugs in different settings.

The DCR as a safe and legitimate place to use drugs

Our research at the open drug scene in Copenhagen has shown that the two DCRs have become an integrated part of the drug scene, and that particularly the large DCR H17 has become a central hub for drug users in the area (Houborg & Holt, 2018).

In our study, we asked users about whether H17 had affected their sense of security, and half of the respondents said that it had. One respondent said that it had him feel more safe in the area by minimizing the everyday risks associated with the drug scene.

> The scene is different today (...) there is a bit more control over the situation, there are less knifings, assaults – that is the crime has been reduced quite a bit, (...). People are not nodding off in the streets. It has become much better, also after H17 has opened, definitely.
>
> *(Isam)*

However, 76% said that they had felt a lack of security at the ramp outside the DCR.

When looking at responses about security inside H17, 56% said that it was a safe place for women, 66% said that it was a safe place for men, and 54% said that it was a safe place for transgender persons (Houborg, Bancroft, & Holdt, 2018). In the interviews, several of the respondents expressed a sense of lack of security inside the DCR when it came to protection against theft. For example, some respondents said that in the injection area, they were afraid of getting their belongings stolen when they were sitting in the injection booths and/or were intoxicated. While some of the respondents describe other users that steal drugs inside the DCR, this user freely admits that he does the stealing himself.

> Well, a lot of people get their coke taken over there because they are stoning or something like that, and their wallet and ... Well I have to admit that I have done it myself. When people have been nodding off that I have just walked past and taken his cup with coke or something.
>
> *(Fred)*

In a jurisdiction like Denmark where possession of illicit drugs is a criminal offence, a DCR creates a space where users will not be prosecuted for this offence and hence it provides a legal place to use drugs. Furthermore, a DCR makes it possible to avoid using drugs in public or semi-public settings where it can be observed by other people who pass by. In this way, the DCR provides a non-stigmatizing and legitimate place to use drugs (Duncan et al., 2017a; Small et al., 2012, 2011). Many of the participants in our study reported that H17 provides a setting for alleviation of shame, as drugs can be taken sheltered from public view, especially that of children. Particularly the wish to shield children occurs across several studies (Clua-García, 2020; Duncan et al., 2017a). About using H17, Kamas explained:

> You hide. Before, we sat outside, which was unpleasant because children passing by and such embarrassed you. Now there's a sort of freedom.
>
> *(Kamas, 50)*

The experience of shame and stigma can make public space a very stressful setting to use drugs, and a DCR can relieve such stress and, in this way, prevent the harm this could cause.

In the quote below, the user, Henrik, who injects drugs, explained how the stress of using drugs in public space makes it difficult to inject.

> I could never use drugs out here (in public). If someone comes around the corner and you sit there. To see another person do that [inject drugs]. I don't like that. It makes me far too stressed and then I can't do it. [...] Because you get stressed, so you can't hit anything [a vein], so might as well not try to do it, you waste 30 needles and get pricked all over, like a sieve. That is stupid. You only do that a couple of times.
>
> *(Henrik, 39)*

It is thus not just the opportunity to use drugs in a safer environment that makes people use a DCR, but also the fact that it provides a legitimate place to use illegal drugs. While this is clearly an improvement for many marginalized people who use drugs, for whom the alternative to using in a DCR is to use in public space, research from Vancouver has found that when such a legitimate place to use drugs is constructed, some may see it as a moral obligation to use drugs in such a setting. This may result in labelling people who do not use the DCR as immoral, irresponsible, and/or irrational, hence developing a new kind of stigmatization (Small et al., 2012). Instead of this, it is perhaps more meaningful to ask why people do not use a DCR, because they may have good reasons and it may not be irrational for them. It is precisely one of the reasons why it is important to study how people negotiate the different aspects and trade-offs involved in using drugs in a DCR and other settings.

A new social setting for using drugs: H17

DCRs are constructed as a social and material space where an illegal activity is allowed in order to minimize risk. They create a space for activities that previously would take place as part of drug scenes outside DCRs. Thus, a DCR can be seen as a hybrid space where particular aspects of the drug scene are allowed in an institutional setting. One of the important dimensions in the design and management of DCRs is how to regulate the boundaries between the institutional space inside the DCR and the drug scene outside the DCR. The rules and regulations that govern DCRs play an important role in defining this hybrid space and the boundaries between drug scene and institution. As such, they are also an important part of creating a new setting for drug use that influences the social relations and social interaction that are involved in drug-using activities (Duncan et al., 2017a, 2020; Small et al., 2012). For example, rules that do not allow the sharing or splitting of drugs interfere directly with an important practice among many marginalized drug users that can both help to secure a supply of drugs and can contribute to the formation of social relations and moral commitments (Bourgois, 1998).

The legislation on DCRs in Denmark prohibits drug dealing inside DCRs and this is also specified in the local agreement on DCRs in Copenhagen, between the Copenhagen police department and the municipality of Copenhagen. This does not, however, mean that drug sharing and drug dealing do not take place. A staff member explained how difficult it can be to stop exchanges of drugs inside the DCR.

> Drug use of course not legal, just as it isn't anywhere else in the world or society. But what we say is that you should not profit on other peoples' misery. And this means that

exchange of balls [small packages of drugs] and sharing and things like that. We know that happens and we do not clamp down on it. We clamp down when we see more organized drug dealing.

(Staff member at DCR

This means that a particular interpretation of the rules allows sharing and the exchanging of drugs among users, opposite to the information described in the Vancouver study (Small et al., 2011, 2012). This means that aspects of the social relations and the social interactions that are related to drug use outside the facility also occur inside the facility in Copenhagen, which highlights a further difference between the DCR in Copenhagen and the one in Vancouver. In Copenhagen, a key issue is how to maintain the line between drug sharing and more commercial drug dealing and related activities such as debt collection, punishment for late payments. It can be difficult to stop such activities, particularly if the material design and the functioning of the DCR makes it possible.

As described, the smoking area of H17 is separated from the rest of the DCR by a glass wall and there is a corridor from which you can access five smoking cabins designed for two users. Often, users will be gathered in the corridor or in two or three of the cabins. Because the staff does not enter this area, because of the health regulations, it becomes a place inside the DCR where activities, social relations, and social interactions that exist in the outside drug scene become possible inside the DCR, even though they are not allowed. This creates a social environment that, from time to time, creates an atmosphere that affects how some users experience using drugs at the DCR, which, in turn, influences their decisions about whether or not to use the DCR.

Søren, for example, told us that he would have used drugs somewhere else on the day we interviewed him, if he had known there would be a hectic atmosphere inside H17. He expressed frustration that the staff do not enforce the rules, because it makes using drugs inside a bad experience, and he fears that too much drug dealing will threaten the existence of the DCR.

> There are no consequences: They sit and trade inside the smoker [smoking room] with the scales out, and customers just run in or stand with pliers (...) and say 'I need so and so much'. (...) And then I told one [from the staff], 'Listen, I don't get why you don't just call the cops when you see so much of this [drug dealing] going on.' Because otherwise the place [H17] will be closed. And then we will be back to fixing on...[the streets]. If I had known there had been so much tension in there today, I had never gone inside to fix. (...). Then I hadn't done it ever. I also make sure to put away all of my stuff [not to get robbed].
>
> *(Søren, 42)*

It was not only drug dealing, or exchange and sharing of drugs that users mentioned as activities that are common outside but also occurred inside, and which could disturb the drug-using experience. Another disturbance was created by allowing people, who did not bring their own drugs to consume to come inside the DCR. They would sometimes try to buy or 'hustle' drugs inside, which could disturb other users. Nina, for example, explained how other users disturb her by trying to hustle her.

> You don't have the time to ... well, you could enjoy it, if you didn't get all those disturbances once in a while. People come and ask you, 'Can I get your cotton?', 'Can you spare a line?' all that stuff you know?
>
> *(Nina, 51)*

For several of the users we interviewed, when they got disturbed by other users or there was a noisy atmosphere, the DCR provided less than optimal conditions to 'enjoy the kick' (Duncan, Duff, Sebar, & Lee, 2017b). This could lead some of them to go somewhere else to use drugs, as mentioned by Søren above. However, it is not just push factors like disturbances from other users that can make users go somewhere else to use drugs; there can also be a combination of push and pull factors. Flemming, for example, likes to enjoy his cocaine in the sun, just like other people may like to enjoy a beer.

> Otherwise I go outside. Just not when the weather is like it is today. But when the weather is sunny I much more prefer sit outside and take a hit of coke and enjoy it in the sun. Just be by myself instead of having people shouting all the time 'hey ma', and people coming up 'hey can I have your cotton?' [cotton used to filter the drug] [...] while you are enjoying your trip, or something. Then you get angry, because then it ruins your high. So that's why I go out in the sun.
>
> *(Flemming)*

Søren from above also explained how he sometimes prefers to find a quiet spot in one of the narrow niches and allies in the old Meatpacking District outside the DCR to optimize the effect of the drug.

I: *And you don't need health workers to be present?*
S: *No. It gives ... somehow it would be best ... but if I have to choose between that and all those troubles [inside the DCR], then I would rather do without. Then I have to take the chance. (Søren, 42)*

In both cases, there is a trade-off that involves the enjoyment of drugs and, prompted by the question by the interviewer, we find out that for Søren, the enjoyment of drugs' effects balances out the risks associated with using drugs outside. In the research on drug use in different settings in Barcelona by Clua-Garcia (2020), we see similar considerations about which settings provide the best conditions for an intoxicating experience, and his research also shows that a public setting may sometimes be preferred instead of a DCR. The research by Small and colleagues also indicates similar considerations. They discovered that users would prefer the DCR precisely because they were not disturbed and hustled by other users. This was an effect of the rule that users were not allowed to share drugs.

Another trade-off relates to the financial aspects of using illicit drugs. Niels offered the reason that using drugs at H17 was too expensive for him, because he had to increase the quantity of drugs he took to compensate for the noisy atmosphere.

> I have started to do it at home instead because I get more out of it at home than I do in here. In here, there is so much noise that I don't get anything out of smoking cocaine. When I want peace and quiet, then many times I just go in here to get the drugs and then go home again... because a 200 kr. bag will last three to four hours at home and 20 minutes in here. So, it is logical that I come and go.
>
> *(Niels, 40)*

But later in the interview he told us that sometimes he would choose to use drugs at the DCR even though it was expensive, because for him drug use was not just about a particular way of getting intoxicated; it was also a social activity.

So, while the functioning of the DCR sometimes may make it difficult to engage in a mode of use that involves solitary intoxication without disturbance, it did afford the opportunity for more social modes of using drugs.

For many people, drug use is a social activity and the DCR is a new context for this activity. The literature on DCRs has touched upon this aspect more or less directly. Small et al. (2012) discuss how a Vancouver DCR severs, or at least severely curtails, social relations between users by prohibiting sharing and splitting of drugs. The same kind of individualization of drug use can be inferred from descriptions of other DCRs (Duncan et al., 2017a; Small et al., 2011) and by looking at their designs, particularly the construction of separated booths for injecting drug use. While this makes sense from a clinical perspective, it may not make sense for people for whom drug use (sometimes) is a social activity and not just a matter of (the most hygienic) injection of drugs. As mentioned above, this was the case for Niels. He describes how sometimes he would go home to consume his drugs, because the quieter setting of his home would maximize the intoxicating experience of his drugs, but sometimes he also wanted the company of others when he used drugs, and then he would stay at the DCR. Niels continued:

> But, sometimes, you are stupid enough to sit in here to have a good time and things like that. But then it is just more expensive.
>
> *(Niels, 40)*

For Niels and others like him, using H17 is not so much a negotiation or trade-off between enjoying drugs and harm reduction as it is between different ways of enjoying drugs and how this is affected by different drug-using settings. To maximize the drug effects, Niles would either choose to go home to use drugs or to enjoy the company of others, he would go to H17.

For some users, drugs are not even the primary reason why they visit the drug scene and use the DCRs. For these users, it is just as important that the drug scene is a place – for some, the only place – where they can interact with other people without experiencing stigmatization (Houborg & Holt, 2018). Drug-related activities, including drug use, is, of course, central to the social interaction between people at the drug scene, and for this reason, the fact that the DCR provides a place to meet around drug use outside the gaze of the public is important. A user explained how the setting creates a particular kind of sociability that is a rush for him.

> It could be, for example, that I feel like talking to that woman over there. That can be a rush for me. It is a kind of dependency, right. I can easily stay an hour and get some emotions up running with her, right. Then I get tired of that, and then I try to find somebody who also needs something [drugs], and I try to find somebody who has something I can be in on.
>
> *(Rami, 37)*

One could say that the DCR and the drug scene around it can mediate practices that allow marginalized drug users to be part of recreational activities equivalent to 'party users' in clubs and bars (see Duff, 2007). The examples illustrate how this particular mode of recreational use can facilitate pleasures, for these users, that would not occur in other contexts.

Negotiating time

The freedom to arrange the drug using situation the way you want to, without having to adhere to various rules and regulations, has been mentioned in the research literature as a reason for people not to use DCRs (Clua-García, 2020). While none of the users we interviewed explicitly mentioned the freedom to use drugs the way they wanted to, some of the reservations that users mentioned about using drugs in H17 can be interpreted as having to do with lack of freedom. One aspect of this concerns time: the time users want to consume and enjoy drugs and the period of time they are allowed to take up a seat inside the DCR.

Managing a DCR can involve this balance between 'drug time' and 'bureaucratic time'. On the one hand, the DCR has to manage the demand for using the service, which is done by giving users time slots during which they can consume their drugs. On the other hand, these time slots may not be enough or may be cut short for various reasons. Furthermore, users may have to queue, which sometimes can be difficult if they are experiencing withdrawal symptoms. If there is too much of a discrepancy, users may choose to use drugs outside the DCR (Small et al., 2012). Regulating time is one of the important tasks of the staff, and keeping time and getting time is one of the issues that can cause controversy in everyday life in the facility.

Nichole, who always uses drugs with her boyfriend, Chris, told us how the staff sometimes interrupt their drug-use session before their time slot is over and how, for her, this spoils the pleasant experience of using cocaine. She commented that she and her boyfriend spend a significant amount of money to buy the drugs and indicated that the money is lost if they are interrupted. We asked her if the time she is allotted inside H17 is enough, and she said that mostly it is, but that when many people are queuing up, the staff may cut their time short.

> Yes, in most cases, but sometimes when the pressure is high [many users wanting to use the facility], even though they say 45 minutes right, then they come in before time. You have just had time to inject. And that's not cool, when you have been sitting for like 5, 10 minutes and then they enter and slap that in your face.

She continues to explain that she and her boyfriend have a particular way of arranging themselves to enjoy cocaine for a short time and how the staff accommodates them.

> Like I said, we may have used like 800 kr. on coke. Because coke does not last for long, we've found out that we can chill out for maybe half an hour in here. They know that we always lie down to enjoy it afterwards. And then we signal to them that we are all right. We've been coming here for many years, so they know us. So that is…that is really nice, yes.
>
> *(Nichole, 42)*

Nicole explained how she and her boyfriend have a mode of use that involves particular expectations and rituals when they use cocaine and that H17, for the most part, is a setting that allows them to have this mode of use. However, she also told us that this precarious setup can be disturbed, for example, when the staff cut their 'time' short to increase the flow of users through the facility.

Other users explained in a similar way how they do not get the effect of the drugs they want if they are interrupted by the staff shortly after injecting. Nina, for example, explained how inside H17, '*there is time on everything, right, and that is so stressful*'. Her friend, Nina O, emphasized this when she said, '*Yeah, when we sit and smoke, then many times we only get to make it [the rock] ready, and then we have to leave, and that's why we like better to take it home, where it is much snugglier*'. At home, she can arrange the drug using setting the way she wants, and do things at her own pace and avoid the distress of being on a schedule.

Many users waiting to get in, particularly during the cold season and when the weather is bad, can put pressure on the staff to increase the flow of users through the facility, both to avoid too much unruliness and to allow as many as possible to benefit from the DCR. This means that the staff need to consider trade-offs between harm reduction and recreational time. The dilemma is that a reduction of recreational time can also increase harm because some users will choose to go somewhere else where they have more time to enjoy the drugs, or will need drugs again within a short period. However, too long a waiting time can also make users go somewhere else to use drugs (Clua-García, 2020; Small et al., 2012, 2011). But for some users, an interaction can occur between time, the ways they ingest drugs, and the weather and this interaction can sometimes be very stressful and painful. For example, for Halim, who smokes heroin, it is important to get inside H17 to use his drugs because the wind and the weather can influence how much effect he gets from the drugs. This can, however, involve a long and painful waiting time because he gets withdrawal symptoms: '*Because it was windy and raining, and I didn't have much money, so I had to wait and wait and wait, and I got pain all over my body*' *(Halim, 58)*. For a user like Halim, the DCR is an attractive place to smoke his drugs, because it provides shelter. For him, the trade-off is between experiencing withdrawal symptoms and losing the effects of the drugs because of the weather. This dilemma is, of course, even more pertinent for people who do not have alternatives to public space and a DCR. A final dimension of time that we want to mention involves users who need more time than the rules allow, because they have difficulties finding useable veins and hence get less (too little) time to enjoy the drugs when they have consumed them. When there is no queue, users are allowed to stay longer inside the DCR.

Framing modes of use

The design of H17 – and other DCRs described in the literature – creates conditions for particular modes of use, often as a consequence of safety considerations (Duncan et al., 2020; Small et al., 2011). It is thus clear that a difference is constructed between smokers and injectors and their modes of use. In the injection area of H17, there is only one room where two injectors sit behind a closed door and consume drugs. In the rest of the injection area, the users sit one by one in separate stalls with no door to close behind them. This means that injection use is mainly framed as an individual activity, not a social activity, and framed in a way that leaves little room for privacy. The rationale for this design is to make injection drug use safer. However, smoking occurs in booths where you can be in the company of others and with the possibility to close a door behind you. Smoking thus seems to be framed as a more sociable and private activity than injection. The material design and the types of social interactions and social relations it allows makes some modes of use possible, while other modes of use are made more difficult to achieve.

Several of the injection users mentioned that they would like separate rooms where they could close the door, just like the smokers. For this reason, some injection users said that they prefer to use drugs somewhere else, because they like privacy and/or enjoy the company of others when they use drugs. The user below suggested that injecting drug use is, for him, sometimes a social activity which the physical setting only allows to a limited extent. He added that a separate room would also provide better isolation from the noises coming from the smoking area of the facility

I: *Is the layout of the injection rooms alright?*
U: *No.*
I: *What's the problem?*
U: *I thought they would make booths for all.*
I: *Private booths?*
U: *Yes, with glass doors, and then make them two-and-two.*
I: *Oh, so you could sit two persons together?*
S: *Yes, [now] they have one room with two chairs and two tables, which is closed by a door. It should also be like that with the rest. Because then you can avoid all that noise and shouting and those people at the other end [the smokers]. That was what I told them when they built it. [...] And then what happens? The smokers get it. [...]. One person from the staff said to me it has to do with ODs—ODs, man! Shut up—put in some glass doors, so you can see when people slide down. (Søren, 52)*

For some users, injecting cocaine evokes a sense of togetherness, which calls for a setting with the possibility for intimacy. Nina and her friend, mentioned above, told us that when they use drugs together, they sometimes like to lie next to each other, but the design of the injection room does not include the possibility of lying down comfortably. So for them the physical setting does not always provide a satisfactory setting for some modes of use. Instead, they go home and arrange themselves a 'snuggly' setting for using drugs, as mentioned earlier. This experience could be interpreted as an experience of lack of freedom to engage in your own practices and rituals when using drugs and the possibility to arrange the drug-using setting in accordance with your own preferences. In his research, Clua-Gardia (2020) found that some users would prefer to use drugs at home or in public spaces, because it allows them more freedom. One thing that users in Clua-Garcia's study mentioned, that was not mentioned by users in our research, was that they did not like to be observed when using drugs. But perhaps the request for more privacy from some users could be interpreted as involving this dimension.

Different settings and different modes of use

In some of the interviews, respondents talked about how they had different modes of use that were associated with different situations and different settings, as well as different feelings, attitudes, and identities. This was indicated by Niels above, who used drugs at home to get the best intoxicating experience and used drugs at the DCR to get a recreational experience. However, he also mentioned that sometimes he engaged in another more social mode of use that involved the company of others inside the DCR. This implies that Niels has different modes of use depending on what he expects from using the drugs in a specific situation and this, in turn, influences his decisions about whether to use the DCR or not. Ali also has different modes of use that he associated with different settings. He mainly smokes heroin but also uses cocaine, and, in addition, takes prescribed methadone. Depending on his finances, he consumes drugs 5–15 times a day. When we talked with Ali, he told us that one of his biggest concerns was not being able to fulfil his role as a parent, son, brother, and friend. During the interview, Ali expressed guilt, shame, a bad conscience, embarrassment, and loneliness associated with distancing himself from his family and non-using friends. His drug use is thus connected with negative and demoralized feelings, which make it difficult for him to find a setting where he can enjoy drugs. The DCR was a legitimate place for him to use drugs.

I: *Yes. It is because you want to take the drugs inside the rooms [DCR]?*
A: *Exactly!*
I: *Because you don't want to take it alone?*
A: *Well, I do want to take it alone. It's just that there are no places where you can take it...well, I can go home to my own place. But I don't want...my boys also come to visit...I don't want it to smell and stuff like that, right. So that's it. Sometimes I smoke at home, but that is very rare. (Ali, 52)*

Ali's main concern is not minimizing drug-related risks, but having a place to use drugs that is less emotionally and mentally stressful and stigmatizing. But sometimes Ali would use drugs at home. Not in order to enjoy the intoxicating experience of the drugs, but to relieve withdrawal symptoms. In this way, drug use at home was associated with a medical mode of use.

> But then, of course, sometimes I smoke at home. For example, in the mornings, if I have something left from the day before and if I am sick [withdrawals], then when I get up, I smoke it, of course.
>
> *(Ali, 52)*

In other words, Ali has different modes of use in different settings where drug use has different functions and meanings and involves different practices. Other users also talked about what we call different modes of use. Most often, this involved a distinction between 'medical' and 'recreational' use, that is, using to relieve withdrawal symptoms and using to 'get high'. One participant, who has 15 years of drug-use experience, said, '*I've only used H17 to sleep in or if I had to take the methadone tablet, but that is just medicine, so...*' (Inuk). Inuk does not get prescribed methadone, but buys it on the illegal market, but still perceives it as medicine and not a recreational drug. One could say that to Inuk that H17 has a very different, almost opposite, connotation than it has to Ali. H17 does not provide a recreational setting for Inuk as '*there is always so much noise and disturbance, and when I want to enjoy my drug, then it should rather be peaceful*' (Inuk). The recreational mode of use happens outside the DCR and Inuk did not have an issue with using drugs in public or semi-public spaces like underground parking lots.

Conclusion

DCRs are harm-reduction services that can minimize drug-related harm like fatal overdoses, and the transfer of blood-borne diseases such as HIV and HCV. These risk-minimizing functions are an important reason why people use DCRs. It would, however, be a mistake to think that people use DCRs just to minimize the risks of drug use. Our own, as well as other research, has shown that there can be other reasons to use DCRs, including reduction of everyday risks associated with life as a marginalized person who uses drugs (McNeil & Small, 2014; Rhodes et al., 2006; Small et al., 2012). But risk should not be the only term by which to understand the function of DCRs for people who use drugs. A DCR can function as a setting for enjoying drugs (Duncan et al., 2017a) and receiving care (Duncan et al., 2019) and to socialize with other people who use drugs.

Our study has contributed to the literature on DCRs that try to provide a broader understanding of DCRs than just being harm-reduction services, by building on previous research and adding new perspectives. Like Clua-Garcia (Clua-García, 2020), we have been interested in understanding how a DCR can be one of several settings where people can use drugs and, like Clua-Garcia and the research from Vancouver by Small et al. (2011, 2012), we have also been interested in things that can both make DCRs attractive or less attractive as places to use drugs. Although the previous research has touched upon different dimensions that make DCRs attractive or unattractive, like the role that rules and regulations, noise, and other things play, the main focus of this research is on risk, particularly the way users themselves perceive risks and manage risks. We have wanted to extend the focus from primarily being concerned with risk. In order to contribute to the understanding of how people consider using drugs in different settings, we introduced the two heuristic ideas of 'trade-offs' and 'modes of use'. The former provides a concept for considerations expressed by users when they considered things that were attractive and less attractive when deciding to use drugs in different settings. The latter was inspired by research done by Gomart (2004) to provide a concept for different ways of using drugs that can have different functions and be associated with different expectations and rituals by the users. By using these tools, we sought to grasp the variability that can be involved when using drugs and how this variability is related to different settings. We found that for some users, the DCR provided a suitable setting for particular modes of use, for example, for a mode of use where drug use was a social activity that involved the company of other drug users. However, some users did not see the DCR as an appropriate setting for a solitary mode of use where the main objective was to have a particular intoxicating experience. We found that the design and the management of the DCR seem to be more accommodating for some modes of use than others. Private injection use in the company of another person was difficult, because only one separate room was available for injection users, while others would have to use open stalls. We also found that some users found it difficult to make the room accommodate their particular rituals and practices when using drugs (lying together on the floor).

We have been interested in the negotiations that are involved in using and not using the DCR and the different trade-offs involved. On this basis, we were able to see how different people use the DCR in different ways and have different considerations about whether and how to use it. We identified several trade-offs, including negotiations between harm reduction and pleasure, between drug effects and sociability. However, most of the trade-offs involved different aspects of pleasure and enjoyment in relation to drug use, including enjoying drug use as a social activity with other people and how this is influenced by the drug, and the setting of the users. While using drugs is a recreational social activity that many of the users enjoy doing with other people, it is clear from our findings that one of the main challenges for H17, and we suspect for DCRs in general, is to accommodate various modes of use. For example, our findings show that it can be a major challenge to have crack and opioid users in the same setting if they are not properly separated. Similarly, our findings show that it is important to pay close attention to which aspects of the drug scene outside of the DCR should be allowed inside it. If too many or the 'wrong' aspects of the drug scene are allowed inside, it can reduce the number of different modes of use that are possible in the facility, and some people will choose to use drugs in other places because using the DCR does not involve a positive trade-off.

Our research indicates that when designing and managing DCRs, attention should be paid to how they can accommodate different modes of use. But sometimes it may be just too difficult to make a DCR compete with other settings for particular modes of use, such as a recreationally relaxed mode of use on a nice sunny day.

References

Becker, H. S. (1953). Becoming a marihuana user. *The American Journal of Sociology, 59*(3), 235–242.

Bourgois, P. (1998). The moral economies of homeless heroin addicts: confronting ethnography, HIV risk, and everyday violence in San Francisco shooting encampments. *Substance Use & Misuse, 33*(11), 2323–2351.

Clua García, R. (2018). Estilos de vida de los usuarios de las salas de consumo higiénico de Barcelona. *Salud y drogas, 18*(2), 79–89. doi:10.21134/haaj.v18i2.369

Clua-García, R. (2020). Managing pleasures and harms: An ethnographic study of drug consumption in public spaces, homes and drug consumption rooms. *Salud colectiva, 16*, e2481. doi:10.18294/sc.2020.2481.

Duff, C. (2007). Towards a theory of drug use contexts: Space, embodiment and practice. *Addiction Research and Theory, 15*(5), 503–519.

Duff, C. (2008). The pleasure in context. *International Journal of Drug Policy, 19*(5), 384–392.

Duff, C. (2017). Natures, cultures and bodies of cannabis. In T. Kolind, B. Thom, & G. Hunt (Eds.), *The SAGE Handbook of Drug and Alcohol Studies* (pp. 679–693). London: Sage.

Duncan, T., Duff, C., Sebar, B., & Lee, J. (2017a). 'Enjoying the kick': Locating pleasure within the drug consumption room. *International Journal of Drug Policy, 49*, 92–101.

Duncan, T., Duff, C., Sebar, B., & Lee, J. (2017b). 'Enjoying the kick': Locating pleasure within the drug consumption room. *The International Journal of Drug Policy, 49*, 92–101. doi:10.1016/j.drugpo.2017.07.005

Duncan, T., Sebar, B., Lee, J., & Duff, C. (2019). Mapping the spatial and affective composition of care in a drug consumption room in Germany. *Social & Cultural Geography, 22*(5), 1–20.

Duncan, T., Sebar, B., Lee, J., & Duff, C. (2020). Atmospheres of engagement within a German drug consumption room. *Social Science & Medicine, 253*, 112922.

Dwyer, R. (2008). Privileging pleasure: Temazepam injection in a heroin marketplace. *International Journal of Drug Policy, 19*(5f), 367–374.

Fairbairn, N., Small, W., Shannon, K., Wood, E., & Kerr, T. (2008). Seeking refuge from violence in street-based drug scenes: Women's experiences in North America's first supervised injection facility. *Social Science & Medicine, 67*(5), 817–823.

Folch, C., Lorente, N., Majó, X., Parés-Badell, O., Roca, X., Brugal, T., … Casabona, J. (2018). Drug consumption rooms in Catalonia: A comprehensive evaluation of social, health and harm reduction benefits. *The International Journal of Drug Policy, 62*, 24–29. doi:10.1016/j.drugpo.2018.09.008

Gomart, E. (2002). Towards generous constraint: Freedom and coercion in a French addiction treatment. *Sociology of Health and Illness, 24*(5), 517–549.

Gomart, E. (2004). Surprised by methadone: In praise of drug substitution treatment in a French clinic. *Body & Society, 10*(2–3), 85–110.

Hedrich, D., Kerr, T., & Dubois-Arber, F. (2010). Drug consumption facilities in Europe and beyond. In EMCDDA (Ed.), *Harm Reduction: Evidence, Impacts and Challenges* (10th ed.). Lisbon: EMCDDA, 305–331.

Holt, M., & Treloar, C. (2008). Pleasure and drugs. *International Journal of Drug Policy, 19*(5), 349–352.

Houborg, E. (2010). Regulating intoxication and disciplining pleasure. In T. Decorte & J. Fountain (Eds.), *Pleasure, Pain and Profit. European Perspectives on Drugs* (pp. 83–100). Lengerich: Pabst Science Publishers.

Houborg, E. (2012). The political pharmacology of methadone and heroin in Danish drug policy. *Contemporary Drug Problems, 39*(Spring), 155–192.

Houborg, E., Bancroft, M., & Holdt, J. W. (2018). *Brugerundersøgelse af stofindtagelsesrummet H17*. Retrieved from København. https://blivhoert.kk.dk/sites/blivhoert.kk.dk/files/uploaded-files/bilag_3_brugerundersoegelse_h17.pdf

Houborg, E., & Frank, V. A. (2014). Drug consumption rooms and the role of politics and governance in policy processes. *International Journal of Drug Policy, 25*(5), 972–977.

Houborg, E., Frank, V. A., & Bjerge, B. (2014). From zero-tolerance to non-enforcement: Creating a new space for drug policing in Copenhagen, Denmark. *Contemporary Drug Problems, 41*(Summer), 261–291.

Houborg, E., & Holt, J. W. (2018). *Stofmiljø og hverdagsliv på Indre Vesterbro*. Retrieved from København: https://www.justitsministeriet.dk/sites/default/files/media/Arbejdsomraader/Forskning/Forskningspuljen/2018/stofmiljoe_og_hverdagsliv_paa_indre_vesterbro.pdf

Hunt, G. P., & Evans, K. (2008). 'The great unmentionable': Exploring the pleasures and benefits of ecstasy from the perspectives of drug users. *Drugs: Education, Prevention and Policy, 15*(4), 329–349.

Kloster, M., Jacobsen, J., Christensen, L., Kappel, N., Kronbæk, M., Fahnøe, K., … Houborg, E. (2021). Trade-offs in substitution treatment: A qualitative study of an opioid substitution therapy clinic as an enabling and a risk-environment *Contemporary Drug Problems, Forthcoming.*

Larsen, H. G., & A. L. Hansen (2008). Gentrification—gentle or traumatic? Urban renewal policies and socioeconomic transformations in Copenhagen. *Urban Studies, 45*(12): 2429–2448.

Lowenstein, W., Gourarier, L., Coppel, A., Lebeau, B., & Hefez, S. (1995). *La methadone et les traitements de substitution.* Paris: Doin Éditeurs.

McNeil, R., & Small, W. (2014). 'Safer environment interventions': A qualitative synthesis of the experiences and perceptions of people who inject drugs. *Social Science & Medicine, 106*, 151–158.

Mændenes Hjem. (u/å). *Stofindtagelsesrum.* Retrieved from https://maendeneshjem.dk/stofindtagelsesrum/

Moore, D. (2008). Erasing pleasure from public discourse on illicit drugs: On the creation and reproduction of an absence. *International Journal of Drug Policy, 19*(5), 353–558.

O'Malley, P., & Mugford, S. (1991). The demand for intoxicating commodities. Implications for the war on drugs. *Social Justice, 18*(4), 49–75.

O'Malley, P., & Valverde, M. (2004). Pleasure, freedom and drugs: The uses of 'Pleasure' in liberal governance of drug and alcohol consumption. *Sociology, 38*(1), 25–42.

Potier, C., Laprévote, V., Dubois-Arber, F., Cottencin, O., & Rolland, B. (2014). Supervised injection services: What has been demonstrated? A systematic literature review. *Drug and Alcohol Dependence, 145*, 48–68. doi:10.1016/j.drugalcdep.2014.10.012

Race, k. (2009). *Pleasure, Consuming, Medicine. The Queer Politics of Drugs.* Durham: Duke University Press.

Rhodes, T., Kimber, J., Small, W., Fitzgerald, J., Kerr, T., Hickman, M., & Holloway, G. (2006). Public injecting and the need for 'safer environment interventions' in the reduction of drug-related harm. *Addiction, 101*(10), 1384–1393.

Small, W., Moore, D., Shoveller, J., Wood, E., & Kerr, T. (2012). Perceptions of risk and safety within injection settings: Injection drug users' reasons for attending a supervised injecting facility in Vancouver, Canada. *Health, Risk & Society, 14*(4), 307–324.

Small, W., Shoveller, J., Moore, D., Tyndall, M., Wood, E., & Kerr, T. (2011). Injection drug users' access to a supervised injection facility in Vancouver, Canada: The influence of operating policies and local drug culture. *Qualitative Health Research, 21*(6), 743–756.

Zinberg, N. E. (1984). *Drug, Set and Setting. The Basis for Controlled Intoxicant Use.* New Haven, CT: Yale University Press.

15
INTOXICANTS IN WARFARE

Łukasz Kamieński

The conflation of "drugs" and "war" is usually associated with the "war on drugs". This, however, is not only the most recent appearance of the age-old synergy between intoxicants and warfare, but is also somewhat paradoxical, because historically force has been employed for the very opposite reason: not to suppress illicit substances but to secure drug markets. Armed conflicts were thus at times waged "for drugs", of which the mid-nineteenth-century Opium Wars are the primary example. Over the centuries, with mind-altering substances gaining in potency and with warfare becoming increasingly "drugged", the intoxicants-war relationship has expanded and become intertwined, from the medicinal use of psychoactive substances to their supervised administration for the enhancement of combat performance, the funding of war-making with tax revenues and illicit drug production and trafficking to the attempted weaponization of intoxicants, and from soldiers' unauthorized recreational drug-taking to veterans' struggles with addictions and the changing patterns of post-bellum substance manufacture, consumption, and regulation. This chapter aims to crack the code of two of these types: the use of drugs by soldiers (both self-prescribed and authorized by the military) and the employment of psychotoxic substances as chemical non-lethal weapons (NLWs). To this end, it seeks to briefly outline some aspects of the multifaceted psychopharmacological landscape of warfare across compounds, use patterns, continents, and time, with the main focus on the twentieth and twenty-first centuries.

Two recent examples prove that intoxicants continue to play a role in military affairs. First, in February 2019, Major Emre Albayrak, a US Marine Corps officer, put forward a bold proposition. He argued for the microdosing personnel with psychedelics to enhance intelligence operations, and perhaps also combat performance. Microdosing 10–20 micrograms of lysergic acid diethylamide (LSD) is sub-perceptual, i.e., insufficient to produce any hallucinogenic or harmful effects, but sufficient to provide noticeable cognitive augmentation. Albayrak's advice, given this, was that supplying soldiers with minute quantities of LSD should be considered (Albayrak 2019).

The second case is this: in March 2017, the US Patent and Trademark Office granted the Californian company Saint Brand Cannabis a patent for a "Cannabinoid formulation for the incapacitation of a human or animal" designed for "rendering a subject intoxicated, incapacitated, and/or immobilized" (*Cannabinoid* 2017, 1). The inventor touted a marijuana-based NLW as perfect for riot control and urban warfare, notwithstanding the fact that the use

DOI: 10.4324/9780429058141-19

of incapacitating agents in armed conflict is outlawed under the 1993 Chemical Weapons Convention (CWC 1993, article II.2).

Stories about intoxicants in military contexts are usually perceived as sensational, but the fact is that combatants have self-medicated with a variety of drugs throughout most of history. The practice, even if officially not permitted, was usually overlooked insofar as it did not undermine combat effectiveness and troop morale. Equally unexceptional was the approved employment of drugs either to improve the performance of an army's own units or to impair the fighting capacity of the enemy. Therefore, neither military pharmacological enhancement nor the concept of psychochemical armaments are new phenomena. If examples like the two aforementioned propositions – for personnel augmentation with microdoses of LSD and a cannabinoid weapon – generate public astonishment, it is because such practices, although well-established, have not hitherto been widely known.

The taboo: intoxicants, war, and historiography

While the "war on drugs" has been studied extensively (for a recent take on the subject, see, i.e., Crandall 2020), the use of mind-altering substances in contexts of armed conflict has been generally neglected in scholarship. Until recently, intoxication was not seen as an appealing subject for the discourse on war, and the topic was given greater attention by the historians of drug use and control policies (Courtwright 2001; Davenport-Hines 2004; Rasmussen 2008), yet with little influence on military historians. Five reasons as to why the relationship between intoxication and war was for so long an untold story can be identified (Kamieński 2016a, 293, 2016b).

First, because until the mid-twentieth century the therapeutic use of drugs (such as alcohol, opium, morphine, heroin, cocaine, and amphetamine) was commonplace, it was generally not at issue. Substances that today are controlled for being harmful were formerly legal and vital medicines. As a consequence, there was also little debate about dependence among soldiers and returned veterans, who developed their addictions through treatment or self-medication. The military use of psychopharmaceuticals as such also received scant attention, often leading to a situation in which the line between therapy and enhancement was blurred.

Second, the employment of intoxicants by armed forces was, overall, kept covert. Secrecy was crucial when the goal was to improve combat efficiency and thereby gain or maintain tactical edge. Clandestineness was even more important when psychoactive compounds were used, or being attempted to be used, as a weapon, either to subvert the enemy or its civilian population (by supplying drugs to undermine their fighting power and resilience) or to incapacitate them (through militarized psychochemical agents).

Third, since the early twentieth century, secrecy has been further fostered by the ambiguity of the practice of drugging the ranks. The development of proscriptive and prohibitionist policies, beginning in the 1910s with the Hague International Opium Convention of 1912 and the US Harrison Act of 1914, made the approved use of intoxicants among militaries increasingly taboo (Kamieński 2016a, 293). A government that penalizes mind-altering substances would want to keep covert their authorized distribution to servicemen. This double standard has been obscured by a veil of secrecy, which has also encompassed the field of scholarship.

Fourth, the research on combat motivation overlooks the pharmacological factor because it is unsettling for the authorities to acknowledge that such powerful forces as patriotism or nationalism may not suffice to commit citizens to battle. British military historian John Keegan gave a concise answer to the question of "why soldiers fight": it is because of inducement, coercion, and narcosis (Keegan 1997). The first incentive, a positive motivation, is achieved through socialization into military life, bonding, ideology, good leadership, and rewards. The second reason, a negative motivation, comprises training, discipline, obedience, and sanctions. However to inspire courage and help them endure the hardships of the battlefield, soldiers would often need a psychoactive stimulus.

Finally, many scholars have simply seen intoxicants and intoxication as irrelevant in explaining war. This view located drugs outside mainstream military history, next to such niche topics as contagious disease, climate, or sex. But as the field of military history has expanded beyond its formerly narrow boundaries, what was previously neglected is now considered a proper subject of study, be it epidemiology, environment, or sexuality. Similarly, the growing body of literature on the war-related functions of intoxicants is a harbinger of a long overdue "pharmacological turn" in war studies (Andreas 2020; Bergen-Cico 2012; Kamieński 2016a; Kan 2009; Ohler 2017; Pugh 2018).

Calling for a cultural history of alcohol in France, Thomas Brennan argued that "we can learn a great deal about society through the prism of a wine glass" (Brennan 1989, 85). Likewise, it has eventually become acknowledged that a great deal can be learned about war and the military through the prism of intoxicants. The recognition of the roles that psychopharmacology has played in armed conflicts provides an alternative and complementary perspective. It offers to shed new light on the three levels of analysis which Paul Kennedy calls "war from *below*" (the individual experience of fighting), "war from *the middle*" (how things got done and who did them at the tactical and operational levels), and "war from *above*" (the strategic and diplomatic conduct of a conflict) (Kennedy 2010, 38). The main focus of this chapter is the second one; it will also consider, to a lesser extent, the first level.

An overview of drug use by combatants

Men have fought while intoxicated on plentiful occasions for much of history. It is, therefore, imperative to identify the main motivating factors for and patterning of the use of intoxicants in military settings. Medical treatment apart, these can be grouped into five central categories discussed in this section: (1) soothing nerves and raising fighting spirits, (2) improving stamina, endurance, and performance, (3) limiting or mitigating the mental cost of combat, (4) fostering group cohesion and boosting morale, and (5) killing the monotony and banality of daily soldierly life. These are examined in detail through the historical examples of particular wars, military operations, and their effects on warfighters; more detailed contextual information is provided by the literature referred to throughout the chapter.

Inspiring courage

In *The Anatomy of Courage*, Lord Moran, Prime Minister Winston Churchill's physician, argues that every soldier has a certain supply of courage: it is "his capital and he is always spending" (2007, XXII). While no one has unlimited reserves, it is possible to recharge them. Invoking Moran's metaphor, intoxicants, like alcohol and opium (which, although they are typical depressants, both can work as mild stimulants when taken in small doses), cocaine, and amphetamines, may serve as replenishers of courage. The problem, however, is that these supplementary chemical supplies cannot be saved for later use, and the repeatability of dosing-for-recharging involves the risk of habit-formation. Thus, the double-edge: intoxicants have lifted soldiers' morale and bravery but also quite often impaired their combat capability and created the problem of addiction.

The most favorite pharmacological motivator is alcohol, the provider of the proverbial "Dutch courage". This expression, common in English since the seventeenth century, derives from the insult used by the English soldiers deployed in the Netherlands during the English-Dutch wars toward their Dutch counterparts, who they saw as unable to fight unless drunk, usually with gin (Purdy 2015). Liquid courage, however, dates back longer, to pre-modern times. Victor Davis Hanson, a prominent scholar of the Greek way of war, contends that a Greek hoplite marched into battle drunk and probably fought slightly inebriated. Wine could "stanch his fear, dull his sensitivity to physical injury and mental anguish, and make the awful task of facing an enemy phalanx that much easier" (2000, 121). Over the centuries, nations developed and adapted their specific drinks of choice. The Romans, just like later their Italian descendants, preferred wine. So did the modern French, though a standard wine provision replaced a small daily ration of distilled alcohol only early in the twentieth century. The Germans commonly issued beer, but also schnapps and wine. The Russians relied on a vodka allowance known as *charka* (125 milliliters), which was institutionalized in the eighteenth century. For their part, the Americans initially doled out rum, but switched to whiskey after the Civil War of 1861–1865 (Andreas 2020, 24–36; Dunbar-Miller 1984; Herlihy 2002, 56; Kamieński 2016a, 5–14, 19–21).

Perhaps best-known in the modern experience of war are the British rum rations during WWI. In the eighteenth century, rum replaced the earlier customary provisions of wine, beer, and brandy, but the practice was discontinued in the 1890s. However, when in September 1914 the British forces arrived at the Western Front, the regular allowance was reintroduced, justified exclusively on medical grounds as a remedy for fatigue, stress, and the hardships of arduous campaigning. The standard ration of thick, 80% proof "fatigue rum" was 2.5 ounces (about 70 milliliters), issued daily in the trenches. To give heart to men before they went over the top, a double portion was dispensed (Dunbar-Miller 1984; Holmes 2004, 329; Kamieński 2016a, 18–19, 2019).

Overall, wars have rarely been fought sober. For most of history, it was beyond question that soldiers must be routinely provided with "liquid courage". In 1777, at the height of the revolutionary struggle against Britain, general George Washington captured this common belief well: "the benefits arising from the moderate use of strong liquor have been experienced in all Armies and are not to be disputed" (in Gately 2008, 196). But soon they were challenged, for while moderately consumed alcohol can provide courage, when abused it might threaten to seriously ruin discipline and fighting power, as soldiers come to be "more interested in bottle than in battle" (Andreas 2020, 41). In fact, alcohol has caused problems to the military since antiquity and at times inopportune drinking led to defeats (Chafetz 1965, 20–23, 159). In modern times, armies increasingly struggled with drunkenness among the ranks, which already in the eighteenth century became a serious issue, for example, in the British armed forces. It was, however, in Russia that the consequences of heavy drinking were particularly devastating; following the 1917 revolution, the Bolsheviks launched an anti-alcohol crusade, deeming drunkenness counter-revolutionary. Yet, this temperance campaign was not a great success, and in late 1941 daily vodka allowances were reintroduced to hearten the Soviet troops to face the Wehrmacht (Kamieński 2016a, 15–16, 23).

WWII marked the beginning of the end of standard provisions of alcohol in soldiers' rations, though the US units deployed to fight in both Korea and Vietnam continued to receive their everyday allowance of beer (Andreas 2020, 63). Although modern militaries have sobered up, and although contemporary institutional military culture prohibits drinking, alcohol remains a popular, albeit no longer authorized, means of relieving the fear and stress of combat. Drinking for courage has been largely taken over by drinking to become desensitized to the realities of combat, a pattern of motivation which involves a higher risk of abuse. For instance, it was misuse and abuse of alcohol that posed a greater challenge to discipline in the US ranks deployed to Vietnam than the widely publicized heroin or marijuana taking (Kuzmarov 2009, 35).

Moving on to non-alcoholic examples of lubricants of courage, the African Zulus owed their reputation as fearless warriors not only to their inborn belligerence. When conquering the Zululand in 1879, the British Army encountered an enemy who supported themselves with a wide spectrum of psychoactive alkaloids. These energized the warriors' bodies but also affected their minds, rendering the Zulus amazingly brave. Shamans provided them with herbs, such as *intelezi* (a traditional plant taken in purifying rites to boost group morale), medicated beer, *dagga* (the South African variety of cannabis which, initially after being taken, has a stimulating rather than sedative effect), and probably also the toadstool known as *Amanita muscaria* or "fly agaric" (Bryant 1949, 222; Kamieński 2016a, 84–88; Kan 2009, 47).

The mushroom was certainly for a long time in circulation among the warriors of the Siberian tribes of Chukchi, Kamchadals, Koryaks, Yakuts, and Yukaghirs. A raw *Amanita muscaria* has mild psychoactive effects, but when dried it develops potent neurotoxic properties (during the decarboxylation process one of its compounds, ibotenic acid, is converted into the muscimol alkaloid, which is a sedative-hypnotic agonist of the GABAA receptors in the brain's award system). The effects are both hallucinogenic and stimulating: the fungus boosts the brain, triggers the thirst for action (in particular provoking motor hyperactivity), and alters perception by generating the feeling of omnipotence (due to the effect known as micropsy, which makes the surroundings appear as diminished). Because the urine of the *Amanita* eater retains strong psychoactive properties, having had harmful toxins filtered out of it, urine drinking was very popular among the Siberian tribes and their warriors (Mann 2000, 221). Narratives say that the mycophilic tribes of *muscaria* lovers produced fierce, muscimol-triggered warriors. Similar effects were also documented in modern accounts. During the war between Sweden and Norway in 1814, some Swedish soldiers got high on *Amanita* and fought in "a raging madness, foaming at the mouth" (Wasson and Wasson 1957, 192). In 1945, a group of Soviet soldiers, presumably from Siberia, was reported as performing fearlessly while under the influence of "fly agaric" at the battle of Székesfehérvár in Hungary (Kamieński 2016a, 38–40; Rudgley 1993, 40–41).

If prior-to-battle pharmacopoeia has assisted in preparing soldiers for combat by relieving fear and fostering a fighting mood, it has also helped in empowering them and keeping them in line when the actual fighting starts.

Enhancing performance

The less prone to fatigue and collapse troops are, the greater their edge vis-à-vis the adversary. In pursuit of superior strength, fighting endurance, vigilance, and resilience, combatants have every now and then been reinforced with stimulants which reduce tiredness and the need to sleep, promote alertness, build up stamina and self-confidence, and suppress hunger. Uppers can not only maintain but also expand fighting effectiveness. Diverse substances have been used in this way to make for more efficient warriors, such as alcohol (in small amounts), caffeine, tobacco, coca and cocaine, cola nuts, khat, amphetamines and amphetamine-like stimulants (ATS) and nootropics.

In the nineteenth century, European militaries began to embrace what traditionally had been practiced by the Andean peoples and armies: chewing coca leaves for improved endurance. Then, in 1883, a Bavarian army physician, Theodore Aschenbrandt, carried out the first experiments on soldiers with cocaine. He speculated that its appetite-inhibiting properties could help cut army food supplies by as much as 20% (Streatfeild 2002, 67). In the early twentieth century, mass-produced and in widespread use, cocaine found its way to the battlefield. It was not, however, its already common therapeutic application as a local anesthetic that proved most beneficial during WWI. Cocaine was both issued and taken unsupervised for enhancement, although the scale of this consumption remains impossible to estimate due to the lack of official records. Limited and often circumstantial evidence suggests that, blended with food rations, a powdery compound was dispensed by some of the belligerent armies to keep their units soldiering by improving their spirits and helping them stay awake and focused (Kamieński 2019).

Cocaine "fortified" early German and French pilots, who took it on long-distance sorties (Woods 1931, 42). The British Army made use of "Forced March", a mix of cocaine and cola nut extract. The medicine, part of the Tabloid brand products by Burroughs Wellcome & Co., was advertised to "allay hunger and prolong the power of endurance". One tablet "every hour when undergoing continued mental strain or physical exertion" was recommended (in Kamieński 2016a, 97). Having known that at the beginning of the twentieth century, "Forced March" had proven beneficial during polar expeditions, assisting Roald Amundsen and other explorers of Antarctica, the Army's command decided to made use of the product too. Thus, the British troops "imbibed these convenient pills, perhaps helping them endure the rigors of trench warfare" (Bourke 2010, 1817).

Early in WWI, the German Army Command intended to issue every soldier daily rations of cocaine to suppress their appetite and increase resilience, but the project was abandoned due to a limited stock of the drug (Hobhouse 2003, 230). However, when at the outset of WWII, a similar idea was devised, the military was well-equipped with a much more potent stimulant: methylamphetamine. Manufactured as Pervitin by the Berlin-based Temmler-Werke company and available in the market from 1938, it became a very popular supplement in German society. This early version of meth, which produced high- and long-lasting alertness, found its way also to the military (Ohler 2017, 34–48). Between April and December 1939, Temmler supplied the Wehrmacht with 29 million 3 mg Pervitin "assault" pills (Kemper 2002, 128). Large amounts were distributed to medical officers during the invasion of Poland in September 1939 to be tested to combat fatigue (Steinkamp 2007, 63). The Polish campaign turned out to be not only a dry run for the lightening offensive maneuver war of Blitzkrieg but also a battlefield experiment in the use of stimulants. The results were encouraging: Pervitin proved useful in keeping men alert and proficient (Beevor 2017; Ohler 2017, 62–66; Snelders and Pieters, 2011). Consequently, during the conquest of the Netherlands, Belgium, Luxemburg, and France in the spring of 1940, German troops were issued some 35 million tablets (Rasmussen 2008, 54). With its great speed and scope, the Blitzkrieg was "powered by amphetamines as much as it was powered by machine", with some soldiers taking up to four Pervitin pills a day for weeks on end (Rasmussen 2008, 54). Soon, however, meth's side-effects – such as hangover, nervousness and aggressiveness, addictiveness, and higher accident and suicide rates – were discovered. Its use was therefore limited and in December 1940, consumption dropped tenfold to 1.2 million pills a month (Nöldecke 2002; Ohler 2017, 143–148). Yet, the harsh winter conditions of the war against Russia in 1941 again brought increasing demands for the stimulant. Overall, based on the available data on average monthly supplies and use, it can be estimated that during the war the German military consumed some 200 million stimulant pills.

As in Nazi Germany, methamphetamine was the drug of choice in Japan, the country in which the compound was first synthesized in 1919. The most popular brand was Philopon (*hiropon*), produced by the Dai-Nippon Seiyaku Corporation. Coined from the Greek words *philo* ("love") and *ponos* ("work"), it was trademarked in 1941 for its ability to arouse the urge to work. In fact, stimulants were issued not only to soldiers but also to civilians employed in war-related fields. The Emperor's Army distributed *senryoku zōkyōzai*, tablets which increased the fighting spirits and helped people stay awake. Believed to improve night-vision, they were known as *nekomejo* or "cat-eye pills". Kamikaze pilots received special "storming tablets" named *tokkojo*, which consisted of meth blended with green tea powder and stamped with the emperor's crest (Edström 2015, 522; Kan 2016, 156; Satō 2008, 720; Vaughn, Huang, and Ramirez 1995).

Britain and the United States also followed suit, employing amphetamine (*speed*): 5 mg Benzedrine tablets manufactured by the US Company Smith, Kline & French (SKF). In September 1941, the Royal Navy authorized its use, followed in November 1942 by the Royal Air Force and later also by the Army (Pugh 2017). The main consumers of Benzedrine were pilots, who took it to prevent performance degradation and ward off fatigue and drowsiness, especially during long nocturnal operations (thus the popular nickname: *wakey-wakey* pills). The British military used, in total, some 72 million speed tablets (Pugh 2018, 756; Rasmussen 2008, 71).

By 1942, Benzedrine (known in the United States as *benny*) was placed in emergency kits for American bomber crews, and in 1943 also for the infantry. Although doctors could not conclusively prove that amphetamine enhanced combat performance, servicemen found it beneficial in prolonging alertness, boosting confidence, and improving a sense of well-being. Rasmussen explains that "The drug was simply too useful for the military to do without, regardless of what science had to say" (Rasmussen 2008, 71). About 15% of US soldiers took *bennies* regularly. Research carried out at the end of the war in an American military hospital revealed that 25% of the patients abused amphetamine and 89% had taken it on a regular basis during their tour of duty (Bayer 1973). In the course of the war, American armed forces used between 250 and 500 million Benzedrine sulfate tablets. Estimating the precise number would depend on the government procurement price, which is unknown (Rasmussen 2008, 84).

WWII marked the beginning of the large-scale use of synthetic stimulants. As the American military continued to use speed, during the Korean War (1950–1953), the regular prescription of dextroamphetamine (Dexedrine) for combat was introduced and its administration became almost commonplace (Rasmussen 2008, 193). The scale of the military employment of amphetamine in the 1950s was astonishing, but it should be seen in the general context of the pervasive consumption of speed across American society, which caused Charles Jackson to call the United States the "amphetamine democracy" (1975). Speed-popping within the ranks persisted as the norm in the Vietnam War (1965–1973), when pep pills were distributed not only to men leaving for long-range reconnaissance missions and ambushes but more or less routinely in general. The extent of the state-sanctioned use of amphetamines was massive. In 1971, a report by the House Selected Committee on Crime revealed that in 1966–1969 the US forces in Vietnam used 225 million 5 mg Dexedrine pills (or statistically 30–40 tablets per fighting man per year) (Iversen 2008, 72; Kuzmarov 2009, 17; Rasmussen 2008, 190–191).

The practice of enhancing performance with amphetamines persisted, and during Operation Desert Storm in the Gulf War (1990–1991), 58% of American pilots enjoyed dextroamphetamine support, while 17% flew regularly on *go pills*, as the crews nicknamed their legal uppers (Kamieński 2016a, 269). Amphetamines continued to be employed among the US pilots for "fatigue management". Under a strict control regimen and specific procedures, Dexedrine was allowed for crews to keep them alert on lengthy missions. Jet and bomber pilots embarking on sorties longer than 8 hours (for single-pilot flights) or exceeding 12 hours (for two-person crews) could be prescribed 10 mg Dexedrine pills each time (*Performance*

2000). The use of the stimulant was voluntary; those crewmembers who opted for it were upon their return to base entitled to receive sedative, sleep-inducing *no-go pills* (e.g., Ambien or Restoril). In 2003, amphetamines began to be supplemented and then in 2017 replaced by modafinil (Provigil), the eugoric psychostimulant and a common lifestyle smart drug discovered in the late 1970s in France. It promotes a natural-seeming sense of wakefulness and mental acuity by selectively arousing the central nervous system and comes with the relatively small risks typically associated with amphetamines. The maximum allowed daily dose for the US pilots is 400 milligrams of modafinil (Baranski et al. 1998; Caldwell et al. 2004; Caldwell, Caldwell, and Schmidt 2008; Kamieński 2016a, 276–280; Pigeau et al. 1995). The US military today is, it seems, the only one that officially authorizes psychostimulants for fatigue management. However, in 2011 the Chinese military unveiled its own novel anti-sleep drug called "Night Eagle", reportedly enabling men to stay awake for up to 72 hours (Moreno 2012; Ye-seul 2011).

While regular armies have mostly abandoned prescribing intoxicants to build up combat performance, the irregulars have increasingly relied on them. Following Operation Iraqi Freedom in 2003, in which the US-led coalition forces overthrew Saddam Hussein's regime, some insurgents fighting the US forces were reported to be doped up on amphetamines and cocaine (Perry 2005). The terrorists of Lashar-e-Taiba, the anti-Indian jihadist militant group based in Pakistan, who perpetrated the November 2008 attacks in Mumbai, enhanced their effectiveness with cocaine and steroids, which enabled them to withstand the Indian special forces for nearly 60 hours (McElroy 2008). For their part, the Islamic State's fighters and terrorist suicide bombers have also been reported to boost themselves with drugs. The ISIS fighters in Syria took cocaine, meth, heroin, hashish, and opioid painkillers. Yet, the main battlefield catalyst for them was Captagon (fenethylline), a synthetic ATS invented in 1961 which is metabolized in the body to form two compounds: amphetamine and theophylline (El Khoury 2020; Kamieński 2016a, 233–238, 241; Kan 2016; Keefe 2016). The jihadists also drugged children to turn them into hardened and loyal fighters. This was not, however, a unique practice as intoxication is almost intrinsic to the child-soldiering phenomenon. Since the 1990s, from Sierra Leone to Afghanistan, Somalia to Iraq, and Liberia to Mexico, young soldiers have been given drugs (especially amphetamine, cocaine, and heroin) for various purposes, including to increase their risk-taking behavior and improve performance (Kamieński 2016a, 243–262).

Recently, advances in brain science and neurotechnologies offer new prospects that could supplement or even replace psychostimulants in combat. For example, magnetic, electrical, or focused ultrasound transcranial brain stimulation allow for various forms of enhancement, including greater alertness, concentration, and learning skills. Already in 2016, the US Navy Special Warfare Development Group (Seal Team 6) began testing a brain-stimulating headset device developed for athletes by the Halo Neuroscience Company. The trials proved promising, as personnel could train faster with the same results, or at the same pace but for much better outcomes, be it operating weapons, movement-based combat skills, or decision making (Brown 2017; Seck 2017; Halo Neuroscience).

To sum up, throughout history, stimulants have served as a means for expanding fighters' physiological and cognitive abilities and thwarting fatigue.

Mitigating the mental burden of combat

The long-term effects of battle experience can have severe effects on the mental health of service members, including post-traumatic stress disorder (PTSD). Traditional methods for avoiding reactions to combat anxiety and preventing mental breakdowns, such as the psychological screening of candidates, tough training, psychiatric services on the frontline, and deployment rotation, have been supplemented with drugs. Depressants have been particularly popular in helping combatants cope with the psychological burden of soldiering. To this end, in the aftermath of battle, alcohol was often issued and troops additionally rewarded themselves with the stocks they had looted. Soldiers and veterans suffering from psychiatric disturbances have often self-medicated. Intoxication to relieve the pain of combat has a very long history. In the *Odyssey*, Homer describes how the grief and sorrow felt for companions who died in the Trojan War were drowned in *nepenthe*, most likely the tincture of opium and wine (Gahlinger 2004, 19; Homer 2002, 4.219–227, 12). In the nineteenth century, and especially during the American Civil War and the Franco-Prussian War (1870–1871), opium and morphine were dispensed liberally for their soothing effects not only on the body (as palliatives) but also on the psyche (as depressants). The psychological costs of fighting expanded with the growing scale, intensity, and mechanization of the modern battlefield. During the Vietnam War, the routine prescription of potent antipsychotic drugs (sedatives and neuroleptics, including an antipsychotic chlorpromazine) was supplemented by widespread self-intoxication by the servicemen, most commonly with alcohol, marijuana, and smokable heroin. As many as 37% of US soldiers in Vietnam who took drugs reported doing so to forget the killing and relieve the mental strain (Kuzmarov 2009, 22). Alcohol apart, the most popular self-prescribed drugs were marijuana, heroin, opium, sedatives, hallucinogens (mainly LSD), and (meth)amphetamine. Heroin, in particular, became a severe and widespread problem: in 1971, it was estimated that as many as 15% of the troops were addicted to this narcotic (Booth 1998, 272; Kamieński 2016a, 195).

In the early twenty-first century, the asymmetrical character of the wars in Afghanistan and Iraq burdened soldiers with severe stress. Insurgency and urban warfare, as well as the traumatic experience of death and injuries caused by irregular forces resulted in a significant increase in the number of US servicemen suffering from serious mental disorders (on average 11% of those returning from Afghanistan and 17% of those serving in Iraq) (Hoge et al. 2004, 13). In April 2008, there were approximately 303,000 Afghanistan and Iraq veterans diagnosed with PTSD or other severe disorders (Tanielian and Jaycox 2008, XXI). Soldiers with psychic problems on the frontline were routinely administered psychotropic drugs to quickly restore them to combat readiness. The increase in prescription medications issued to personnel was extensive. Steve Robinson, an intelligence analyst at the Department of Defense under President Bill Clinton's administration, reported that soldiers he talked to "were receiving bags of antidepressants and sleeping meds in Iraq, but not the trauma care they needed" (in Allen 2006). In 2009, some 106,000 ground force servicemen were prescribed psychotropic antidepressants or analgesics (McKinley 2010). A black market for prescription medications also emerged with Valium (diazepam) being particularly popular among troops in Iraq (Allen 2006).

The psychological costs of these conflicts also triggered new research on pharmaceuticals that could alleviate or even prevent combat-induced anxieties and PTSD. Propranolol, a popular beta-blocker used for heart and circulatory conditions, has been intensively investigated for this purpose. Results have been promising, as blocking beta-adrenergic receptors in the brain can suppress the creation of bad emotional memories and subsequently avert anxiety disorders (Kamieński 2013). So far, however, these drugs have not been recommended for the pharmaco-prevention of combat stress and anxiety disorders.

To conclude, both prescribed and self-administered psychoactive substances have assisted combatants in coping with the stress of battle and lessening the psychological experience of fighting, killing, and the presence of death.

Facilitating camaraderie and relieving boredom

The major motivational factor in terms of understanding why soldiers fight is not grand ideas or sentiments like patriotism or nationalism, but their companions (McClure and Broughton 2000, 482–483; Wong et al. 2003). Thus, primary group bonds, close relations within a small military unit, usually at the platoon level, are crucial for morale and fighting spirit. One of the activities that can foster social bonds is the collective taking of drugs. A shared experience of intoxication might be meaningful, and enhance group cohesion. Alcohol is the most common ice breaker. By increasing forthrightness between soldiers, it can facilitate camaraderie. One observer commented on the American War of Independence of 1775–1783 that "without New England rum, a New England army could not be kept together" (in Gately 2008, 195). Group drinking strengthens ties and builds trust, which is vital for the operation of a unit. This socialization function has also been performed by other intoxicants. For instance, before going into battle, the Zulus performed preparation rituals intended to fortify them. Shamans gave warriors psychoactive plants, one of which induced communal vomiting expected not only to purify men but also to bring them together "as a strong fighting force" (Kamieński 2016a, 85). Another example is the newcomer American GIs in Vietnam, for whom drug-taking was often a mandatory part of their initiation and socialization, so that smoking marijuana and heroin frequently took on the form of a ritual, being more of a group than a private experience (Kamieński 2016a, 201).

While fostering social bonding through shared intoxication can ultimately promote better combat performance, it also helps pass the time in periods of military inactivity. For over 300 years, one of the most popular antidotes to boredom has been tobacco, which is also very useful for both relaxing and stimulating the smoker (Andreas 2020, 68–100). The consequences of acute boredom, inherent in the very experience of war, can be debilitating (Mæland and Brunstad 2009) and were particularly vivid in Vietnam. In his memoir of this war, *A Rumor of War*, Philip Caputo recalls: "nine-tenths of war is waiting around for the remaining one-tenth to happen" (1996, 43). During the Soviet Afghan War (1979–1989), the Red Army soldiers also extensively reached out for intoxicants to relieve boredom. Alcohol was expensive and difficult to obtain, so hashish (locally known as *plant*), marihuana (*anasha*), and opium (*khan/chars*) were popular. Heroin and cocaine were also taken. Additionally, soldiers sampled local brands, including partly refined opium (used to produce heroin), *koknar* (a brew of boiled poppy heads), and *cheffir* (very strong tea) (Kamieński 2016a, 220–227; Reese 2000, 173). Overall, being a remedy for utter monotony, the recreational use of drugs has helped combatants remain sane.

The search for psychoactive weapons

Mind-altering substances have been employed to make soldiers stronger, faster, more resilient, and desensitized. If drugs can make humans more machine-like, then maybe intoxicants themselves can be weaponized into chemical tools of war. Disorientation, indecisiveness, hallucinations, sluggishness, seizures, and other similar intoxication-induced effects offer, potentially, highly desirable military capacity. Thus since pre-modern times, there have been attempts to use toxic plants and psychoactive ingredients (such as atropine, opium, and cannabis) as weapons, albeit non-lethal ones – that is, aimed not to kill but to confuse, disrupt, and immobilize an enemy, or overpower the populations in which they are nested. It is important to realize that weaponization entails more than technical capability, as it is closely entwined with the assignment of a coercive intentionality to an object (a psychoactive substance). Conceptually and practically, the making of a psychotropic NLW demands a twofold reconfiguration of both chemical weapons (their de-lethalization) and non-lethality (expanding the realm of mind control). Thus, militarization provides a new, violent deconstruction by instilling a different logic of functionality which, in the case of intoxicating compounds, encompasses their utility and effects as well as perception and meaning.

From cannabis to atropine to opium

2,500 years ago, the Chaldeans would set heaps of Indian cannabis on fire, thereby trying to strip their opponent of fighting power with incapacitating smoke. This method, however, was sometimes counterproductive; when the wind boomeranged, the smoke impaired the functioning of the Chaldeans themselves (Kamieński 2016a, 169). Atropine contained in *Solanaceae* plants was another substance employed to subdue the enemy without fighting. Its intoxication induces mental and behavioral impairment, including sensory inebriation, disorientation, confusion, loss of time-space relationships, illusions, and hallucinations. In 1962, Ephraim Goodman, a US Army Chemical Corps employee, penned a review of both the accidental and deliberate use of atropine and its derivates for military purposes (2010). Based on extensive library research, his manuscript was to substantiate the Corps' Cold War search for psychochemical weapons. Goodman provided a handful of examples. Around 200 BC, the Carthaginian commander Maharbal, knowing of a rebellious African tribe's fondness for wine, authorized the mixing of it with mandrake (a perennial containing atropine) and had it left in a deserted camp. When the Africans returned and drank the toxic beverage, they became disabled by atropine-induced psychedelic psychosis and were defeated by Maharbal's lurking men (Goodman 2010, 53–54; Ketchum 2006, 14). Similarly, "a standard Roman military stratagem" was to inebriate barbaric foes before ruthlessly defeating them (Andreas 2020, 18–19; Gately 2008, 38). Very few documented instances of the use of atropine for military purposes can be found in the Middle Ages. A huge historical gap in evidence follows until the seventeenth century. In 1667, during the Bacon Rebellion of Virginia settlers against the colonial governor, the British soldiers sent to crush the uprising in Williamsburg unwittingly poisoned themselves with the local plant known as James-Town Weed or jimsonweed (*Datura stramonium*). They were rendered ineffective, spending 11 days in altered states of mind (Beverley 1705, 24). An early attempt to disseminate aerosolized belladonna dates back to July 1672 and the assault on the city of Gröningen by the troops of the Bishop of Münster, Bernhard von Galen, who used crude grenades filled with the incapacitating alkaloid. The technique proved ineffective as "the heat of combustion probably destroyed active principles of vegetable poisons employed in shells" (Goodman 2010, 59). As for more modern examples, in 1881 a French unit traveling through the desert from Sudan to Algeria was poisoned with atropine by the Touareg warriors, so that the troops were debilitated by hallucinogenic delirium (Goodman 2010, 55–57). Then in 1908, 200 French troops were poisoned in Hanoi in French Indo-China by plotting Chinese reformers: "One of the intoxicated soldiers saw ants on his bed, a second fled to a tree to escape from an hallucinated tiger, and a third took aim at birds in the sky" (Goodman 2010, 57).

Moving on to WWI, and from atropine to opium, prior to an attack in the third battle of Gaza, in October–November 1917, the British General Edmund Allenby authorized the airdrop of cigarettes laced with opium on Turkish positions in Palestine. This subversive ploy was reported to "render the Turkish troops immobile" (Meinertzhagen 1960, 223–224). They probably resembled the Chinese soldiers of the mid-nineteenth century who were made unfit for duty by their pervasive opium-smoking. Many infantrymen fighting in the

Opium Wars (1839–1842 and 1856–1860) to defend the country against the flood of the smuggled drug supplied by the British East India Company were themselves heavy addicts. In fact, one explanation for the success of the Taiping Rebellion, which took power in southern China in 1851, is the epidemic addiction rates of up to 90% that afflicted the ranks of the Emperor's Army. The rampant use of opium caused general weakness, apathy, and broken discipline (Hanes and Sanello 2002, 171; Zheng 2005, 88–96). The question that intrigued some militaries in the second half of the twentieth century was whether similar effects could be achieved by the deliberate use of militarized intoxicants.

The Cold War quest for psychotoxic arsenals

After WWII, the US intelligence warned that the communists were investigating the utility of intoxicants, allegedly in preparation for psychochemical warfare. In 1951, it stated that the Soviets were experimenting with an unidentified psychotropic drug referred to as "ketjubung" (Ketchum 2006, 245–246). They were reportedly also collecting large stocks of ergot (*Claviceps purpurea*), the fungus which is parasitic in grains (mostly rye) and can be synthesized into LSD (Albarelli 2011, 375). However, these concerns over the communist military's psychoactive capabilities proved as unsubstantiated as the parallel alarmist intel that they had mastered narcotic-induced brainwashing methods, and already used them on American prisoners of the Korean War. Although imaginary, the problem triggered the United States to embark on a psychopharmacological arms race and research on weaponizing intoxicating compounds (Carruthers 2009, 174–216; Streatfeild 2007, 1–28). Other nations, including the British, Soviets, and Czechoslovakians, also joined in and experimented with hallucinogens for military applications.

In 1949, in a document entitled *Psychochemical Warfare: A New Concept of War*, Luther Wilson Greene, the technical director of the laboratories at Edgewood Arsenal, the US Army Chemical Corps' facility in Maryland, called for a doctrine of "bloodless warfare". Exposing the enemy to the effects of incapacitating agents, Greene argued, would knock them back with attacks of delusion, panic, or hysteria and thereby weaken their will to resist (Khatchadourian 2012). This prospect was taken further in the mid-1950s by the head of the Corps, Major General William Creasy. Overwhelmed by the idea of hallucinogenic weapons, he advanced the concept of "war without casualties", in which an impairing cloud dispersed over the enemy paralyzes but does not kill even the most elite units (1959, 74 f).

Although in the 1950s no effective offensive neurochemical capability existed, the idea of psychotoxic munition was not utterly fantastic because history had shown that intoxication could impede combat performance. For example, during the Egyptian campaign (1798–1801), Napoleon Bonaparte's forces developed a habit of using hashish, locally a highly popular extract from the resin of the cannabis plant. The effects of hashish-eating for the fighting efficiency of the French soldiers were so devastating, with men wasted by laziness and sluggishness, that the French authorities decided to introduce a total ban on the drug in Egypt (Kamieński 2016a, 53–54; Guba 2020, 49–82).

On other occasions, however, claims that a narcotic problem had destroyed combat readiness were mere allegations. During WWI, cocaine use was prevalent in both France and Britain; yet, they both blamed Germany of smuggling it into their cities and trenches to subvert their war effort. In 1916, a French deputy fulminated: "It seems that the Germans can't beat us with their fire or their asphyxiating gas, so now (…) they're using cocaine and morphine to wear us down" (in Padwa 2005, 340). It was, however, in Britain that this Germanophobic psychosis erupted into a nationwide drug scare. The overblown problem was presented as a deadly threat to the Empire. Allegedly, the drug-crazed soldiers on the front had become unpredictable and insubordinate. Turned into a cliché as part of a wartime conspiracy theory, cocaine became associated with hostile subversion, fostering the false myth of German drug sabotage (Berridge 1984; Kamieński 2019; Kohn 1999). Still, the deliberate circulation of drugs among an opponent's forces and population could weaken their capabilities and morale, which, in fact, made for an actual US tactic in the 1980s, when a network of dealers distributed narcotics, confiscated in the United States by law enforcement agencies, among the Soviet soldiers deployed in Afghanistan. Turning them into addicts was supposed to erode their operational capacity (Cooley 2000, 128–129). Another telling example of a narcotic myth is the Vietnam War. Because marijuana was the most common non-alcoholic drug ordinarily self-prescribed by the US soldiers, the media blamed it for the failure to win the war. Cannabis was described as a plague tormenting American troops, but the story was made up as no compelling evidence existed that marijuana smoking presented a serious obstacle to effective combat (Kuzmarov 2009).

If substance use and abuse was, sometimes falsely, believed to deteriorate military performance, an intentional deployment of hallucinogenic intoxicants could perhaps offer an immense offensive capability. The US Chemical Corps could have reasonably assumed, then, that the weaponization of psychoactive agents might prove an effective means for impairing the faculties of an adversary. Thus began the search for compounds that could feasibly enable combat through mind control, a quest for ingredients which could be dispersed over hostile forces, added to their food, or dissolved in water to deprive them of elementary fighting abilities. In its attempt to unlock the military potentials of psychotoxins, from 1955 to 1975, the Corps conducted experiments on humans. They were mainly carried out in Edgewood but also at other army bases and in army-commissioned hospitals, penitentiaries, and universities, including Baylor University, the University of Pennsylvania, Tulane University, Johns Hopkins University, and universities in Indiana, Utah, and Washington (Hornblum 1998, 131). The staff at Edgewood had no problems with recruiting volunteers, the majority of whom were drawn from among the soldiery. Many enrolled several times, encouraged by incentives such as extra pay, free three-day weekends, or relocation closer to home (Ketchum 2006, 51, 253).

The participants underwent medical screening and completed the Minnesota Multiphase Personality Inventory psychological test to reveal any mental problems. Before signing a mandatory informed consent form, each participant was required to be notified of the character and aims of the experiment (Ketchum 2006, 25, 32–33, 58). However, the staff were often not fully aware of effects of the substances to be tested, particularly when these were samples of "rejects" from the pharmaceutical industry, i.e., the compounds deemed unfit for medical commercialization. This was the case, for example, with benzilate: created in 1951 by Hoffmann-La Roche during its search for the treatment for ulcers, the compound was rejected as unsuitable due to its strongly hallucinogenic effects (Kamieński 2016a, 178). Furthermore, most of the psychoactive agents that underwent trials on humans had no name and the pharmacological terms or codenames associated with the rest meant nothing to the subjects. Hence, it was often assumed that providing participants with specific information was redundant. Dr. Gerald Klee, one of the psychiatrists involved in the program, explained that most of the volunteers "were not highly educated, and even if they had been told exactly what they were to be given, they wouldn't have understood it" (in Bowart 1978, 91). These circumstances raised concerns regarding the subjects' awareness of what they were exposed to and provoked questions as to whether they were not, to some extent, "guinea pigs". The huge battery of substances that was tested on humans under the Corp's scheme included amphetamines, atropine, 3-quinuclidinyl benzilate (BZ), LSD, mescaline, morphine, and psilocybin (Moreno 2001, 251). Marijuana, LSD, and BZ seemed particularly promising.

Experiments with liquid concentrate cannabis had already been conducted in 1943 on Manhattan Project officials (Moreno 2001, 191). Then in the late 1950s, the Corps ran human trials with a super-concentrated hash "red oil", a substance codenamed EA1476. Studies demonstrated that it could induce strong intoxication and deprive smirking soldiers of their combat skills. In 1961, a series of studies with a synthetic, pure, and undiluted analog of tetrahydrocannabinol (THC), the principal psychoactive constituent of cannabis, were carried out. Codenamed EA2233, this new cannabinoid compound was a mixture of eight stereoisomers (different spatial orientations of atoms of the same molecule) of THC. Compared with "red oil", its intoxicating effect was much stronger and longer-lasting. When in 1965 individual isomers of EA2233 became available, another series of trials was conducted with the improved version of the THC analog. The knockdown effect left subjects almost unable to move. Further experiments were thus suspended due to the health hazards. So, as the full potential of cannabinoid isomers was never investigated, a window of opportunity may still be open. As James Ketchum, the first and leading psychiatrist in the research program at Edgewood, later recalled: "This hypotensive (blood-pressure-reducing) property, in an otherwise non-lethal compound, might be an ideal way to produce a temporary inability to fight, or do much else, without toxicological danger to life" (in Lee 2008).

Another candidate for weaponization to be exploited was LSD, codenamed EA1729. The Army program of testing it on human subjects commenced in 1955 and was conducted on military and civilian personnel recruited from Army areas, mostly Edgewood (Ablard 1975). The research involved administering the drug to the servicemen orally, diluted in a liquid, prior to routine training. The general psychoactive effect on the subjects was that of being so overpowered by uncontrollable giggling and cackling that they ceased to be able to carry out even the most basic tasks (Bowart, 1978; Ketchum 2006, 99). Should this happen to an enemy, it could literally be defeated by laughter. Hence, the Army was interested in mastering effective dispersal methods that would allow it to throw "acid rain" down on enemy units and civilian populations. But the search for weaponized LSD was seriously hampered by the technical obstacles in the way of finding a suitable form, the proper dosage (in a gaseous form, LSD is three times weaker than when administered orally), and accurate means of delivery. Beginning in 1963, experiments with LSD in gaseous form aimed at designing effective methods for its aerosol dispersal were carried out. Edgewood's personnel conducted field trials at locations such as Fort Bragg (North Carolina, 1958), Fort Benning (Georgia, 1960), Fort McClellan (Alabama, 1959–1960), and Aberdeen Proving Ground (Utah 1959) (Ablard 1975, 12). Overall, about 90% of the LSD trials were conducted before 1961.

Later, around 1966, the Corps became more interested in BZ (or "Agent Buzz", codenamed EA2277) (Ketchum 2006, 244, 327). While the incapacitating effect of LSD lasts for up to 12 hours, for BZ it can be up to 80 hours (Ketchum 2006, 24, 43–47, 52). The compound induces delirium that can knock a person down, so it was an ideal candidate for weaponization. Between 1959 and 1975, BZ was tested in clinical trials on 2,800 soldiers both at Edgewood and in field experiments. In 1964, one such trial was conducted on a desert range in Utah, which entailed the spraying of Agent Buzz from a distance of 500 and 1,000 yards from the volunteer soldiers (Lee and Shlain 1992, 41). One of the aims of the whole research project at Edgewood was to find antidotes for the incapacitating agents and build defensive measures against hostile psychopharmacological attacks. Surprisingly, it was discovered that when in the correct dose, atropine, which throughout the centuries was used in military settings as an offensive debilitating substance, can be an effective antidote to Agent

BZ (Ketchum 2006, 109–116). In 1961–1962, benzilate was standardized as an incapacitating chemical weapon into an assortment of clustered munitions for aerosol delivery via grenades, mortars, cluster bombs, and rocket warheads, and adopted by the US Army. Never used in combat, in 1977, it was declared obsolete (Kirby 2006, 2007, 43).

On the whole, the pursuit of mind-breaking, intoxicating ammunition has failed. The plans for spraying an enemy with "deranging gas" or polluting their supplies with "psychotoxic water" remained largely confined to the realm of visions. Still, the notion of soft psychoactive violence continues to inspire research, as revealed by the idea for the non-lethal cannabinoid formula patented in 2017.

Conclusion

Throughout history, and particularly in the twentieth century, the matrix of psychoactive pharmacopeia and warfare was shaped by two overarching themes. The first is the disobedience as regards social norms revealed by illegitimate self-medication. The second is, by contrast, the compliance with the institutional rules and/or informal sanctions epitomized in the purposeful administration of intoxicants. These state-approved and reinforced military drug practices have been an exceptional thread in the general history of intoxicants and intoxication. Substance use, when synchronized with military/state goals, has been constructed not in terms of deviant behaviors but in a context of permissiveness. Hence, from a sociological perspective, the relationship between the individual (combatant), social group (the military), and behavior (the use of drugs) has been structured along the lines of normality. Above all, the social construction of intoxicants/intoxication and war has been shaped by the power interests of state institutions. By dispensing psychoactive substances to combatants, the authorities have managed their bodies (so as to optimize and increase performative and productive capacities) and exploited them (by conducting experiments on humans to weaponize psychochemicals). Thus, drugs in warfare might be seen as a specific politico-military antropotechnology, or "technology of the body". Likewise, anti-drug policies, control mechanisms, and penalization can be analyzed in terms of "technologies for disciplining the body". Therefore, it is instrumentality, the logic of the means-end relationship, that has marked the predominant socio-contextual meaning of intoxicants in military affairs.

References

Ablard, Charles D. 1975. *Statements before the Investigations Subcommittee House Armed Services*, 8 September, approved for release 29 April, 2004.

Albarelli, Hank P., Jr. 2011. *A Terrible Mistake: The Murder of Frank Olson and the CIA's Secret Cold War Experiments*, Walterville, OR: Trine Day.

Albayrak, Emre. 2019. "Microdosing", *Marine Corps Gazette*, February: WE1–WE5.

Allen, Terry J. 2006. "The Iraq War – On Drugs", *In These Times*, May 31, https://inthesetimes.com/article/2670/the_iraq_war_on_drugs (accessed June 10, 2020).

Andreas, Peter. 2020. *Killer High: A History of War in Six Drugs*, New York: Oxford University Press.

Baranski, Joseph, Corinne Cian, Dominique Esquivié, Ross Pigeau, and Christian Raphel. 1998. "Modafinil during 64 Hours of Sleep Deprivation: Dose-Related Effects on Fatigue, Alertness, and Cognitive Performance", *Military Psychology*, 10(3): 173–193.

Bayer, Istvan. 1973. "The Abuse of Psychotropic Drugs", *Bulletin on Narcotics*, January, https://www.unodc.org/unodc/en/data-and-analysis/bulletin/bulletin_1973-01-01_3_page003.html (accessed June 10, 2021).

Beevor, Antony. 2017. "The Very Drugged Nazis", *The New York Review*, 9 March, https://www.nybooks.com/articles/2017/03/09/blitzed-very-drugged-nazis (accessed 25 May, 2021).

Bergen-Cico, Dessa K. 2012. *War and Drugs. The Role of Military Conflict in the Development of Substance Abuse*, Boulder: Paradigm Publishers.

Berridge, Virginia. 1984. "Drugs and Social Policy. The Establishment of Drug Control in Britain 1900–1930", *British Journal of Addiction*, 79(1): 17–29.

Beverley, Robert Jr. 1705. *The History and Present State of Virginia in Four Parts*, London: Printed for R. Parker, available at Internet Archive: https://archive.org/details/historypresentst00beve (accessed 10 June, 2021).

Booth, Martin. 1998. *Opium. A History*, New York: St. Martin's Press.

Bourke, Joanna. 2010. "Enjoying the High Life. Drugs in History and Culture", *Lancet*, 376(9755): 1817.

Bowart, Walter. 1978. *Operation Mind Control*, New York: Dell.

Brennan, Thomas. 1989. "Towards the Cultural History of Alcohol in France", *Journal of Social History*, 23(1): 71–92.

Brown, Jennings. 2017. "U.S. Navy Is Zapping SEALs Brains to Make Them Super Soldiers", *Vocativ*, 4 April, http://www.vocativ.com/417576/navy-seals-neuro-stimulation (accessed June 9, 2021).

Bryant, Alfred T. 1949. *The Zulu People as They Were Before the White Man Came*, Vol. 1, Pietermaritzburg: Shuter and Shooter.

Caldwell, John, Lynn Caldwell, and Regina Schmidt. 2008. "Alertness Management Strategies for Operational Contexts", *Sleep Medicine Reviews*, 12(4): 257–273.

Caldwell, John, Lynn Caldwell, Jennifer Smith, and David Brown. 2004. "Modafinil's Effects on Simulator Performance and Mood in Pilots during 37 Hours without Sleep", *Aviation, Space, and Environmental Medicine*, 75(9): 777–784.

Cannabinoid Formulation for the Sedation of a Human or Animal. 2017. US Patent and Trademark Office. Patent No. US 9585867B2, 7 March.

Caputo, Philip. 1996. *A Rumor of War*, New York: Henry Holt and Company.

Carruthers, Susan L. 2009. *Cold War Captives: Imprisonment, Escape, and Brainwashing*, Berkeley: University of California Press.

Chafetz, Morris E. 1965. *Liquor: The Servant of Man*, Boston, MA: Little, Brown.

Cooley, John K. 2000. *Unholy Wars: Afghanistan, America and International Terrorism*, London: Pluto Press.

Courtwright, David T. 2001. *Forces of Habit: Drugs and the Making of the Modern World*, Cambridge, MA: Harvard University Press.

Crandall, Russell. 2020. *Drugs and Thugs. The History and Future of America's War on Drugs*, New Heaven: Yale University Press.

Creasy, William M. 1959. "Can We Have War Without Death?", *Reader's Digest*, September: 74 ff.

CWC. 1993. *Convention on the Prohibition of the Development, Production, Stockpiling and Use of Chemical Weapons and on Their Destruction*, Geneva: United Nations Treaty Collection.

Davenport-Hines, Richard. 2004. *The Pursuit of Oblivion. A Global History of Narcotics*, London: W.W. Norton.

Dunbar-Miller, R. A. 1984. "Alcohol and the Fighting Man – An Historical Review", *Journal of the Royal Army Medical Corps*, 130(2): 12–15.

Edström, Bert. 2015. "The Forgotten Success Story: Japan and the Methamphetamine Problem", *Japan Forum*, 27(4): 519–543.

El Khoury, Joseph. 2020. "The Use of Stimulants in the Ranks of Islamic State: Myth or Reality of the Syrian Conflict", *Studies in Conflict and Terrorism*, 43(8): 679–687.

Gahlinger, Paul. 2004. *Illegal Drugs. A Complete Guide to Their History, Chemistry, Use, and Abuse*, New York: Plume.

Gately, Iain. 2008. *Drink: A Cultural History of Alcohol*, New York: Gotham Books.

Goodman, Ephraim. 2010 (1962). *Historical Contributions to the Human Toxicology of Atropine. Behavioral Effects of High Doses of Atropine and Military Uses of Atropine to Produce Intoxication*, ed. by James S. Ketchum and Reid Kirby, Wentzville, MO: Eximdyne.

Guba, David A. 2020. *Taming Cannabis: Drugs and Empire in Nineteenth-Century France*, Montreal: McGill-Queen's University Press.

Halo Neuroscience, "Maximize Operational Readiness", https://www.haloneuro.com/pages/military (accessed 9 June, 2021).

Hanes, W. Travis III and Frank Sanello. 2002. *The Opium Wars: The Addiction of One Empire and the Corruption of Another*, Naperville: Source Books.

Hanson, Victor Davis. 2000. *The Western Way of War: Infantry Battle in Classical Greece*, Berkeley: University of California Press.
Herlihy, Patricia. 2002. *Alcoholic Empire: Vodka and Politics in Late Imperial Russia*, New York: Oxford University Press.
Hobhouse, Henry. 2003. *Seeds of Wealth. Four Plants That Made Men Rich*, Washington: Shoemaker & Hoard.
Hoge, Charles W., Carl A. Castro, Stephen C. Messer, Dennis McGurk, Dave I. Cotting, and Robert L. Koffman. 2004. "Combat Duty in Iraq and Afghanistan, Mental Health Problems, and Barriers to Care", *The New England Journal of Medicine*, 351(1): 13–22.
Holmes, Richard. 2004. *Tommy. The British Soldier on the Western Front, 1914–1918*, London: Marshall Pickering.
Homer. 2002. *The Odyssey*, trans. Rodney Merrill, Ann Arbor: University of Michigan Press.
Hornblum, Allen M. 1998. *Acres of Skin. Human Experiments at Holmesburg Prison*, New York: Routledge.
Iversen, Leslie. 2008. *Speed, Ecstasy, Ritalin: The Science of Amphetamines*, Oxford: Oxford University Press.
Jackson, Charles O. 1975. "The Amphetamine Democracy: Medicinal Abuse in the Popular Culture", *Southern Atlantic Quarterly*, 74(3): 308–323.
Kamieński, Łukasz. 2013. "Helping the Post-Modern Ajax. Is Managing Combat Trauma Through Pharmacology a Faustian Bargain?", *Armed Forces and Society*, 39(3): 395–414.
Kamieński, Łukasz. 2016a. *Shooting Up: A Short History of Drugs and War*, New York: Oxford University Press.
Kamieński, Łukasz. 2016b. "Why Have Military Historians Ignored Drug Use in the Military?", *History News Network*, 5 May, http://historynewsnetwork.org/article/162453 (accessed 9 June, 2021).
Kamieński, Łukasz. 2019. "Drugs", in *1914–1918-online. International Encyclopedia of the First World War*, ed. by Ute Daniel, Peter Gatrell, Oliver Janz, Heather Jones, Jennifer Keene, Alan Kramer, and Bill Nasson, Berlin: Freie Universität Berlin, https://encyclopedia.1914-1918-online.net/article/drugs (accessed June 11, 2021).
Kan, Paul Rexton. 2009. *Drugs and Contemporary Warfare*, Washington, DC: Potomac Books.
Kan, Paul Rexton. 2016. "This Is Your Jihad on Drugs", *War On the Rocks*, 7 March, https://warontherocks.com/2016/03/this-is-your-jihad-on-drugs (accessed June 10, 2021).
Keefe, Patrick Radden. 2016. "The Drugs of War – Captagon and the Islamic State", New York: The Century Foundation, https://tcf.org/content/report/the-drugs-of-war (accessed June 11, 2021).
Keegan, John. 1997. "Towards a Theory of Combat Motivation", in *Time To Kill: The Soldier's Experience of War in the West, 1939–1945*, ed. by Paul Addison and Angus Calder, London: Pimlico: 3–11.
Kemper, Wolf-R. 2002. "Pervitin – die Endsieg-Droge?", in *Nazis on Speed: Drogen im 3. Reich*, ed. by Werner Pieper, Lohrbach: Grüne Kraft: 122–133.
Kennedy, Paul. 2010. "History from the Middle: The Case of the Second World War", *The Journal of Military History*, 74(1): 35–51.
Ketchum, James S. 2006. *Chemical Warfare Secrets Almost Forgotten*, Santa Rosa, CA: ChemBooks.
Khatchadourian, Raffi. 2012. "Operation Delirium", *The New Yorker*, 10 December, https://www.newyorker.com/magazine/2012/12/17/operation-delirium (accessed June 1, 2021).
Kirby, Reid. 2006. "Paradise Lost: The Psycho Agents", *The CBW Conventions Bulletin*, 71: 1–5.
Kirby, Reid. 2007. "Quantifying Chemical Biological Threats", *Army Chemical Review*, Winter: 41–44.
Kohn, Marek. 1999. "Cocaine Girls. Sex, Drugs, and Modernity in London During and After the First World War", in *Cocaine. Global Histories*, ed. by Paul Gootenberg, London: Routledge: 105–122.
Kuzmarov, Jeremy. 2009. *The Myth of the Addicted Army. Vietnam and the Modern War on Drugs*, Amherst, MA: University of Massachusetts Press.
Lee, Martin A. 2008. "Synthetic Pot as a Military Weapon? Meet the Man Who Ran the Secret Program", *AlterNet*, https://www.alternet.org/2008/07/synthetic_pot_as_a_military_weapon_meet_the_man_who_ran_the_secret_program (accessed June 11, 2021).
Lee, Martin A. and Bruce Shlain. 1992. *Acid Dreams. The Complete Social History of LSD: The CIA, The Sixties, and Beyond*, New York: Grove Weidenfeld.
Mæland, Bård and Paul Otto Brunstad. 2009. *Enduring Military Boredom. From 1750 to the Present*, Basingstoke: Palgrave Macmillan.
Mann, John. 2000. *Murder, Magic, and Medicine*, Oxford: Oxford University Press.
McElroy, Damien. 2008. "Mumbai Attacks: Terrorists Took Cocaine To Stay Awake During Assault", *Telegraph*, 2 December, https://www.telegraph.co.uk/news/worldnews/asia/india/3540964/Mumbai-attacks-Terrorists-took-cocaine-to-stay-awake-during-assault.html (accessed 8 June, 2021).

McKinley, James C., Jr. 2010. "Despite Army Efforts, Soldier Suicides Continue", *New York Times*, 11 October: A11.

Meinertzhagen, Richard. 1960. *Army Diary (1899–1926)*, Edinburgh: Oliver and Boyd.

Moran, Lord. 2007 (1959). *The Anatomy of Courage. The Classic WWI Account of the Psychological Effects of War*, New York: Carroll & Graff Publishers.

Moreno, Jonathan D. 2001. *Undue Risk: Secret State Experiments on Humans*. New York: Routledge.

Moreno, Jonathan. 2012. "Stay Awake, Comrades", *Psychology Today*, 12 April, https://www.psychologytoday.com/us/blog/impromptu-man/201204/stay-awake-comrades (accessed June 11, 2021).

Nöldecke, Hartmut. 2002. "Einsatz von leistungssteigernden Medikamenten bei Heer un Kriegsmarine", in *Nazis on Speed: Drogen im 3. Reich*, ed. by Werner Pieper, Lohrbach: Grüne Kraft: 134–142.

Ohler, Norman. 2017. *Blitzed: Drugs in Nazi Germany*, Boston: Houghton Mifflin Harcourt.

Padwa, Howard. 2005. "National Security and Narcotics Control in France, 1907–1920", *Journal of the Western Society for French History*, 33: 340–351.

Performance Maintenance during Continuous Flight Operations: A Guide for Flight Surgeons. 2000. NAVMED P-6410, Fallon, NV: Naval Strike and Air Warfare Center, https://archive.org/details/NAVMEDP6410 (accessed June 10, 2021).

Perry, Tony. 2005. "Fallouja Insurgents Fought under Influence of Drugs, Marines Say", *Los Angeles Times*, 13 January, https://www.latimes.com/archives/la-xpm-2005-jan-13-fg-iraqdrugs13-story.html (accessed 9 June, 2021).

Pigeau, Ross, Paul Naitoh, Alain Buguet, Carol McCann, Joseph Baranski, Matthew Taylor, Megan Thompson, and I. Mack. 1995. "Modafinil, D-amphetamine and Placebo During 64 Hours of Sustained Mental Work. I. Effects on Mood, Fatigue, Cognitive Performance and Body Temperature", *Journal of Sleep Research*, 4(4): 212–228.

Pugh, James. 2017. "'Not… Like a Rum-Ration': Amphetamine Sulphate, the Royal Navy and the Evolution of Policy and Medical Research during the Second World War", *War in History*, 24(4): 498–519.

Pugh, James. 2018. "The Royal Air Force, Bomber Command and the Use of Benzedrine Sulphate: An Examination of Policy and Practice during the Second World War", *Journal of Contemporary History*, 53(4): 740–761.

Purdy, Elizabeth Rholetter. 2015. "Dutch Courage", in *The SAGE Encyclopedia of Alcohol. Social, Cultural, and Historical Perspectives*, ed. by Scott C. Martin, Thousand Oaks, CA: SAGE, Vol. 1: 511–512.

Rasmussen, Nicolas. 2008. *On Speed: The Many Lives of Amphetamine*, New York: New York University Press.

Reese, Roger R. 2000. *Soviet Military Experience: A History of the Soviet Army, 1917–1991*, London: Routledge.

Rudgley, Richard. 1993. *The Alchemy of Culture: Intoxicants in Society*, London: British Museum Press.

Satō, Akihiko. 2008. "Methamphetamine Use in Japan after the Second World War: Transformation of Narratives", *Contemporary Drug Problems*, 35(4): 717–746.

Seck, Hope Hodge. 2017. "Super SEALs: Elite Units Pursue Brain-Stimulating Technologies", Military.com, 2 April, http://www.military.com/daily-news/2017/04/02/super-seals-elite-units-pursue-brain-stimulating-technologies.html (accessed May 21, 2021).

Snelders, Stephen and Toine Pieters. 2011. "Speed in the Third Reich: Metamphetamine (Pervitin) Use and a Drug History From Below", *Social History of Medicine*, 24(3): 686–699.

Steinkamp, Peter. 2007. "Pervitin (Metamphetamine) Tests, Use and Misuse in the German Wehrmacht", in *Man, Medicine, and the State: The Human Body as an Object of Government Sponsored Medical Research in the Twentieth Century*, ed. by Wolfgang U. Eckart, Stuttgart: Franz Steiner Verlag: 61–71.

Streatfeild, Dominic. 2002. *Cocaine*, London: Virgin.

Streatfeild, Dominic. 2007. *Brainwash: The Secret History of Mind Control*, New York: Thomas Dunne Books.

Tanielian, Terri and Lisa H. Jaycox (eds.). 2008. *Invisible Wounds of War: Psychological and Cognitive Injuries, Their Consequences, and Services to Assist Recovery*, Santa Monica, CA: RAND Corporation, http://www.rand.org/pubs/monographs/2008/RAND_MG720.pdf (accessed May 21, 2021).

Vaughn, Michael S., Frank F.Y. Huang, and Christine Rose Ramirez. 1995. "Drug Abuse and Anti-Drug Policy in Japan. Past History and Future Directions", *British Journal of Criminology*, 35(4): 491–524.

Wasson, Valentina Pavlovna and R. Gordon Wasson. 1957. *Mushrooms, Russia and History*, New York: Pantheon Books, Vol. 1.

Wong Leonard, Thomas Kolditz, Raymond Millen, and Terrence Potter. 2003. *Why They Fight: Combat Motivation in the Iraq War*, Carlisle, PA: Strategic Studies Institute, U.S. Army War College.

Woods, Arthur. 1931. *Dangerous Drugs. The World Fight against Illicit Traffic in Narcotics*, New Haven, CT: Yale University Press.

Ye-seul, Yoon. 2011. "Medicine Developed for Chinese Army to Fight Sleep", *The Korea Times*, October, http://www.koreatimes.co.kr/www/news/nation/2011/10/182_96829.html (accessed 19 May, 2021).

Zheng, Yangwen. 2005. *The Social Life of Opium in China*, Cambridge: Cambridge University Press.

PART IV

Intoxication Practices

16

ENGAGING WITH DRUG, SET, AND SETTING TO UNDERSTAND NICOTINE USE EXPERIENCES AND PRACTICES

Julia McQuoid

Introduction

Zinberg's drug, set, and setting analytic framework (Zinberg 1984) has contributed to understanding a variety of drug use experiences and effects (Duff 2012, Moore 1993). This includes work on MDMA (Shewan, Dalgarno and Reith 2000), prescription drug misuse (Mui, Sales and Murphy 2014), cocaine (Decorte 2001), heroin (Fitzgerald et al. 2004), psychedelic drugs (Carhart-Harris et al. 2018), cannabis (Hammersley and Leon 2006), and alcohol (Shaffer and Hall 2002). The framework proposes that understanding drug use initiation, how it manifests as a recurring practice, and the effects of the drug on the individual requires an integrated analysis of three elements: 'drug (the pharmacologic action of the substance itself), set (the attitude of the person at the time of use, including his [sic] personality structure), and setting (the influence of the physical and social setting within which the use occurs)' (Zinberg 1984, 5). Largely absent from scholarship that explicitly draws on this analytic framework are nicotine use practices. A notable exception is Kolte and Schmidt-Semisch's (2002) application of the framework to consider how different patterns of intensity and frequency of smoking are maintained by different individuals (i.e., 'tobacco chippers' versus 'heavy smokers'). They emphasize the importance of social context in understanding smoking practices and the nature of addiction, a factor which has only recently and very gradually become recognized as a relevant area of scholarship in tobacco research (Poland et al. 2006).

Zinberg's approach to understanding drug use might now be viewed as rather static and simplistic alongside more contemporary drug use theories (e.g., materialist, assemblage, and post-human), given his conception of drug use as a product of preexisting, separate components (see, for example, Duff 2007). Nevertheless, I suggest that thinking broadly across 'drug, set, and setting' can serve as a useful framing device for taking stock of scholarly advances and blind spots in researching nicotine use, and may yield richer understandings of nicotine use practices and experiences. While the empirical focus of Zinberg's work was on highly intoxicating drugs, like heroin, one could argue that it is precisely the subtle psychoactive effects of nicotine and its capacity to integrate into the contexts, functions, and experiences of everyday life (Keane 2002) that should compel researchers to attend to all three elements of Zinberg's framework when examining nicotine use practices and experiences.

DOI: 10.4324/9780429058141-21

The relevance of the 'drug' element to current tobacco scholarship in contexts like the United States is clear considering how the material, aesthetic, and pharmacological properties of nicotine-containing products have rapidly evolved with the introduction and marketing of 'novel' products like diverse electronic nicotine delivery systems (ENDS) (e.g., 'pod vapes'), flavored cigarillos, snus, dissolvable tobacco products, and 'heat-not-burn' devices (Agaku et al. 2013, Auer et al. 2017, Osibogun et al. 2018). Research focusing on the mammal pharmacology of nicotine and nicotine-containing products abounds within the biomedical literature (Benowitz 2010). This body of inquiry into the material properties and effects of nicotine and nicotine-containing products does not often take into account the social contexts (setting) or the uniqueness of different individuals' motivations and expectations of use (set). Conversely, most social science research on drug use practices and experiences, including nicotine use, seems reluctant to engage with the chemical capacities of drugs to act on, with, and through human bodies (Marković 2019a).

Research focusing solely on the properties of tobacco products and the industry and regulatory forces that shape access to them provides an incomplete picture of the diversity of influences that shape use practices and experiences. As Zinberg noted: 'Availability is always intertwined with the social and psychological factors that create demand for an intoxicant' (1984, 13). Indeed, the diversity of 'sets', or psychosocial attributes and expectations of individuals engaging in nicotine use practices must also be accounted for. For example, while decades of aggressive anti-tobacco public health campaigns in places like California have vastly reduced cigarette smoking among the middle and upper classes and non-minority groups, cigarette smoking has become increasingly concentrated among groups who are more likely to lack resources, have social minority identities, experience mental health disorders, and live in socio-economically disadvantaged places (Barnett et al. 2017, Pearce, Barnett and Moon 2012, Poland 1998, Poland et al. 2006, Thompson, Pearce and Barnett 2007). Each of these groups (e.g., racial, ethnic, sexual, and/ or gender minorities) have their own collective histories and structural conditions that may influence their motivations and experiences of nicotine use (e.g., trauma-informed coping strategies). A large body of literature has documented individual characteristics and 'risk factors' for nicotine use in isolation from the pharmacological/material and contextual influences on nicotine use practices (Drope et al. 2018, Lee, Griffin and Melvin 2009).

The 'settings', or social and physical contexts, within which individuals are immersed must also be accounted for to understand if, how, and to what effect different individuals will use available nicotine-containing products. For the purposes of informing tobacco regulatory policy, strong scholarly emphasis has been placed on examining the physical tobacco retail environment, which varies in density of tobacco retail outlets and in tobacco product availability, pricing, and advertising between neighborhoods, municipalities, and states (Coxe et al. 2014, Lee et al. 2015, Luke et al. 2016). The relevance of the social dimensions of context to tobacco use has received less attention. Despite strong evidence that socio-structural inequities shape nicotine use practices, such as structural discrimination that varies geographically (Hatzenbuehler et al. 2013, Moon, Pearce and Barnett 2012), these factors rarely enter into public health discourses as intervention targets that can reduce tobacco-related disparities and harms (Frohlich et al. 2012, Graham 2012).

Tobacco scholarship will continue to lack a nuanced understanding of the drivers, motivations, experiences, and practices of nicotine use for different groups of people if it does not engage with the interwoven nature of drug, set, and setting. This is important, not only because of the knowledge gap it leaves, but because of the social distance that exists between most tobacco researchers, interventionists, and regulators and the individuals who use nicotine (Haines-Saah 2013). Many public health professionals who desire to reduce health inequities related to tobacco and nicotine are constrained in their ability to relate to the motivations and experiences of people who use them. This is likely due to lack of first-hand experiences with the drug, and, because, compared to the populations they wish to understand and engage, public health professionals are usually more socially privileged and differ in their experiences relating to everyday social contexts (e.g., being personally naïve to experiences of social minority stress). If public health as a field fails to understand and acknowledge the nicotine use experiences, motivations, and practices of different groups of people, it will continue to struggle to engage these populations in health equity interventions.

Given this need for understanding and engagement of 'hard-to-reach' populations who use nicotine, it is surprising that research documenting lived experiences of nicotine use is sparse when compared to the large body of literature examining trends in prevalence of and 'risk factors' for tobacco use (Wellman et al. 2016). This relatively small body of mostly qualitative work has begun to document the lived experiences of nicotine use for different groups. For example, sexual and gender minority individuals have reported that smoking enhances their ability to experience a sense of belonging to community (Bennett, Ricks and Howell 2014, McQuoid et al. 2019), to express resistance against oppression by rejecting dominant anti-smoking societal norms (Sanders et al. 2019), and to cope with ongoing daily stressors associated with social minority discrimination and stigma (Antin, Hunt and Sanders 2018, Matthews et al. 2017). Nicotine users have described the pleasures of using nicotine, including its meditative and therapeutic qualities as a practice (McQuoid, Keamy-Minor and Ling 2020, Tan 2013b). Nicotine can pleasurably enhance or moderate the effects of other drugs, such as alcohol and cannabis (Akre et al. 2009, Gubner et al. 2017). In a final example, the value of nicotine use practices in being able to positively alter experiences of time and space and stabilize the space-time organization of everyday routines (Graham 1993, Keane 2002, McQuoid et al. 2018a, Tan 2013b) is likely heightened within the hectic coordination of schedules and scarce down-time that characterizes much of contemporary work, family, and study life in Western countries (Southerton 2009). In short, there is evidence that nicotine use practices and experiences are diverse, nuanced, and vary between people, between situations, and across space and time, and that nicotine use can play a capacity-enhancing role in the lived experiences of different groups of people.

This chapter considers the potential for greater engagement with the interwoven elements of drug, set, and setting to enhance researcher and practitioner understandings of nicotine use practices and experiences and engage 'hard-to-reach' groups in health equity-focused efforts. The following section highlights some recent approaches in tobacco scholarship published in English that have engaged with the interplay of the drug, set, and setting elements of nicotine use practices, although not explicitly drawing from Zinberg's analytic framework.

Engagement with drug, set, and setting in tobacco scholarship

In the past two decades, or so, scholars have begun to excavate the experiences and practices of nicotine use that have been buried under more biomedically- and regulatory-focused research agendas. This work has drawn primarily from de-centered or 'more-than-human' theories, social practice theory, and theories of place, power, and performativity to engage in different ways with the drug, set, and setting elements of nicotine use.

More-than-human accounts of nicotine use

A few cultural geographers, anthropologists, and sociologists have drawn from more-than-human theories to analytically de-center humans when examining nicotine use practices and experiences. Marković (2019a) engaged Lefebvre's *rhythmanalysis* (Lefebvre 2004) and more-than-human theories (Whatmore 2002) to account for nicotine's chemical affordances (i.e., the 'drug') in their analysis of smokers' experiences in the workplace. They described the circadian rhythms of nicotine with the timing of cigarette smoking as the configuration of an eurythmia that, once established, avoids nicotine withdrawal. This rhythmic relationship was then put into analytic dialogue with the abundance of other rhythms circulating within smokers' everyday contexts. Markovic examined workers' experiences of the arrhythmias created by spatial restrictions on smoking and intensive employer demands on workers to account for their time and productivity. This analytic approach allowed for an acknowledgement of the agency and affordances of non-humans ('drug') as well as humans ('set') within everyday contexts ('setting'), bypassing the risk of framing smokers as passive victims of addiction.

Markovic drew from Deleuze and Guattari's assemblage thinking to explore vaping as a 'skeuomorphic assemblage' that converges between technology, the body, and everyday physical and social contexts (Marković 2019b). The author considered the spatio-temporal, sensorial, and embodied differences between cigarette smoking and vaping to delineate ways in which vaping produces distinct experiences of place. For example, the discrete and flexible material affordances of vaping devices make them easier to use in places where cigarettes cannot be used and give the individual more access to space and time while using nicotine, but do not offer the experience of a set apart space and time that is afforded by the material constraints of cigarettes (see also McQuoid et al. 2018a).

Thompson, Pearce, and Barnett (2009) utilized Foucauldian (Foucault 1994) and Deleuzo-Guattarian (Deleuze and Guattari 1988) frameworks to understand the unstable, or 'nomadic', social identities associated with ex-, secret, and social smoking practices. For example, they examined occasional, or 'social', smoking identities. These identities are negotiated within social contexts that are dominated by public health discourses that emphasize the addictive powers of nicotine and perpetuate a binary conceptualization of nicotine use practices: non-smokers (which comprised ex-smokers and never-smokers) and current smokers. The authors trace how occasional, or 'social', smoker identities assemble fleetingly within a particular set of materialities and conditions (temporality, space, person, cigarette) and then disassemble to produce a non-smoker identity (Thompson et al. 2009, 575).

Tan has productively employed the concept of affect from non-representational theory (Anderson and Harrison 2010, Duff 2010) to provide sensual, spatial, and agentic accounts of smokers and smoking practices (Tan 2012, 2013a, 2016b, 2016a, 2013b). The interplay of the drug, set, and setting elements in nicotine use practices and experiences is clearly registered in Tan's work. For example, Tan examines how smoking spaces both enhance and diminish smokers' capacities to engender a sense of well-being for themselves (Tan 2013b). The material properties of the 'drug' (cigarettes) produce smoke, which is socially imbued with stigma and shame as it travels between bodies, polluting spaces of encounter between smoking and non-smoking bodies (setting). This forces smokers into sanctioned or hidden smoking places, where they avoid or reduce social criticism of their smoking practice (Poland 2000) and manage their 'spoiled identities' (Goffman 1963) as smokers. In this sense, smoking spaces are largely disabling for smokers. However, Tan also recovers the agency of smokers and the enabling qualities of smoking spaces by highlighting how smoking practices can create liminal spaces within routines, spice up monotonous spaces and times, and provide a way to stabilize after crisis or disruption: 'Hence, smoking spaces are set apart from, but simultaneously enrolled in the space-times of banality' (p. 178). Tan also highlights how smoking spaces can be meditatively and therapeutically solitary, as well as highly social, as the segregation of smoking spaces heightens the social connection potential for smokers within these spaces.

Other work has focused, in particular, on rematerializing the often neglected 'drug' element within social science research on nicotine use practices, drawing from new materialist approaches (Dennis 2018) and actor network theory (ANT) (Keane 2013). Keane examined nicotine replacement therapy (NRT) as a non-human agent that is enrolled in a therapeutic network. Through this network, nicotine becomes an agent of health that is mobilized to transform the nicotine user's identity from 'smoker' to 'non-smoker': '[NRT] gives life to a model of health in which an addictive drug performs as a resource in the construction of a free subject: the non-smoker' (Keane 2013, 194). Dennis used a new materialist approach to consider the particular fleeting and momentary pleasures of smoking that arise from relations between air, smoke, and an unbounded body that may be experienced, not only as extended into space through exhaled smoke suspended in air, but also as yielding; 'an exit into infinity, into air' (Dennis 2018).

Place-embedded social practices of nicotine use

Another recent approach that has been employed in tobacco scholarship and implicitly engages with drug, set, and setting is social practice theory (Cohn 2014, Maller 2015, Reckwitz 2002, Shove, Trentmann and Wilk 2009). This work prioritizes the patterned, routine, and habitual ways in which people live their lives to understand nicotine use (Blue et al. 2016). Rather than focusing on 'risk factors' of individuals to engage in potentially health-harming or -enhancing behaviors, it understands social practices, including nicotine use, as having lives of their own in competing for, winning, and losing practitioners who reproduce, transform, or abandon social practices over time and across space. Considered this way, the evolution of nicotine use practices can be traced, and ways in which these practices compete for or lose practitioners can be observed. Blue et al. (2016) proposed social practice theory as a way to move 'beyond behavior' by understanding how nicotine use practices depend upon the ongoing integration of '(1) materials (objects, consumer goods, and infrastructures), (2) competence (including understandings of the situation, practical know-how), and (3) meanings (including embodied understandings of the social significance of the practice and past experiences of participation)' (Blue et al. 2016, 42).

Keane et al. (2017) drew on social practice theory to interpret written survey responses from Australian vapers, delineating ways in which the materials, competence, and meanings of vaping practices are distinct from those of cigarette smoking. My colleagues and I built on this by using social practice theory to understand the regular use of multiple nicotine-containing products by relatively large numbers of young Americans (McQuoid et al. 2018a). Drawing on accounts of the everyday routine activities and contexts of young adults who regularly use at least two nicotine-containing products, we traced distinctions between the materials, competences, and meanings of cigarette smoking, vaping, and smokeless tobacco use ('dip' and 'chew') practices, finding that each nicotine use practice has a distinct and complementary role to play within young adults' everyday contexts and routines. My colleagues and I also considered how smoking practices are mobilized in everyday routines by young Americans with non-binary sexual orientations (e.g., bisexual, pansexual, and queer) to help navigate everyday contexts within the dominant binary sexual landscape. We did this by integrating the methodological emphasis on everyday routines and mobility found in social practice theory and space-time geography (McQuoid, Thrul and Ling 2018b) with Foucault's analysis of sexuality and power (Foucault 1978, 1988).

Frohlich et al. (2002) drew from social practice theorists, especially Anthony Giddens, to emphasize social structure, social practices, and agency in understanding 'collective lifestyles' of smoking in different neighborhoods in Quebec, Canada. Their framework emphasizes the importance of the physical, material, and psycho-social features of neighborhoods, as well as the social meanings ascribed to people's actions and their local neighborhoods, to understand local practices of smoking. Closely related to this is Pearce et al.'s (2012) emphasis on place-based 'practices' and place-based 'regulation' in understanding pathways linking place with health-related behaviors like smoking. Glenn et al. (2017) applied the collective lifestyles framework to understand place-based social inequalities in smoking across different neighborhoods of Montreal, Canada. They used focus groups to elicit discussion regarding the social norms, practices, and agency related to smoking, and grouped neighborhoods by socio-economic status for analysis. Haines-Saah et al. (2013) also drew from the collective lifestyles framework, leveraging focus groups and young adults' photographs about smoking and smoking cessation in Vancouver, Canada to understand the interplay between cessation and the presence of a local collective lifestyle that emphasizes healthy living and outdoor physical activity.

Spatial politics, identity, and performativity of nicotine use

Foucauldian concepts of 'governmentality', Goffman's work on stigma, and Bourdieu's formulation of 'habitus' have had the longest-standing employment in research on lived experiences of nicotine and tobacco use. This body of work has largely focused on smokers' experiences of and responses to spatial smoking restrictions and anti-smoking public health campaigns (Bell 2013a, Bell et al. 2010, Collins and Procter 2011, Dennis 2011, Ritchie, Amos and Martin 2010, Tan 2013a). There is, perhaps, a slightly stronger emphasis on the interactions of 'set' with 'setting' than on the 'drug' element of nicotine use in this work. Poland's earlier analysis of the 'purification of public space' (Poland 1998, 2000) has been highly influential in this regard. Poland explored the (in)formal enforcement of spatial smoking bans as an illustration of class-based conflict over control of public space. Barnett et al. (2017) discussed the unintended consequences of smoking bans and smoking denormalization on society's least advantaged groups, exploring these processes of denormalization as 'an ongoing dance of power (Foucault), stigmatization (Goffman) and taste and class (Bourdieu)' (Barnett et al. 2017, 129).

While much of this work has focused on cigarette smoking practices within the context of tobacco denormalization, Lucherini et al. explored the uptake of ENDS, or 'vapes', through the lens of performativity – the accumulation of meaning of habits over time and space (Lucherini, Rooke and Amos 2018). In-depth interviews with young adults in Scotland revealed how embodied and spatial practices of cigarette smoking and vaping were in some ways similar and in some ways different, meaning that the performativity of vaping had yet to settle into a shared set of social norms in step with cigarette smoking performativity, which has become almost universally stigmatized as a practice.

The intersections of gender and sexual orientation identities, social context, and smoking stigma have also been examined through a focus on power, identity, and performativity (Antin et al. 2017, 2018, McCready, Glenn and Frohlich 2019, Sanders et al. 2019). Sanders, Antin,

Hunt, and Young (Antin et al. 2018, Sanders et al. 2019) explored the meanings of smoking for sexual and gender minority youth and adults in California, United States, through in-depth interviews. They examined the meanings of smoking for sexual and gender minority people within the context of aggressive tobacco denormalization and structural inequities (e.g., racism, sexism, classism, homophobia, and transphobia). Within this social context, the meanings of smoking for sexual and gender minority participants included serving as an act of resistance to social oppression, as a tool for self-care, and as a way of exerting control over day-to-day circumstances. In a more explicit engagement with place, McCready et al. (2019) used Goffman's theory of stigmatization to understand the relationship between neighborhood-level deprivation and young women's experiences of smoking stigma.

Conclusion

The three areas of engagement with the drug, set, and setting dimensions of nicotine use that I sketched above represent important progress in providing more nuanced accounts of nicotine use practices and experiences. The in-depth understanding of nicotine use that these types of accounts provide could serve as a bridge between public health practitioners and the populations they wish to engage. However, these approaches are still very much in the minority within the tobacco research field. Reluctance to fund and do this kind of work may be linked to a fear on the part of public health that acknowledging what tobacco does that is 'useful' or 'desirable' for people may undermine dominant tobacco control discourses (Bell 2013b). These discourses emphasize the addictive power of nicotine to explain use motivations and emphasize the negative health effects of tobacco in order to denormalize it as a practice (Kolte and Schmidt-Semisch 2002). As with other drugs (Zinberg 1984), it is likely feared that acknowledging the positive experiential dimensions of nicotine use, and the way that it manifests in a diversity of ways as a practice, could be perceived as condoning its use and have the effect of rolling back tobacco denormalization efforts.

Ironically, I would suggest that it is by analytically engaging with all three elements of nicotine use (drug, set, and setting) in tobacco research, and by exploring nicotine use practices and experiences in depth, that public health can find a way out of this bind. One path forward is offered by critical drug scholars who have invited researchers to consider drug use experiences as emerging dynamically and relationally from the interplay of space, embodiment, and practice. Rather than conceiving of the 'smoking experience', or other nicotine use practices like 'dipping' or 'vaping', as an isolated relationship between the individual and a tobacco product, nicotine use practices, experiences, and motivations are better understood as emerging dynamically within particular situations or contexts. In other words, the act of using nicotine is but one element in a broader assemblage. Duff characterizes the drug use context as 'an assemblage of relations drawing together diverse experiences of space and spatialisation; embodiment and becoming; conduct and social practices' (Duff 2007, 504). Malins (2017) employs Deleuze and Guattari's concept of flows of desire to understand the many experiences, practices, and motivations of drug use that emerge within different drug use contexts. People seek out and 'plug into' flows of desire by forming assemblages with the world around them and we register these connections to desire flows as emotionally charged experiences, such as pleasure, excitement, transgression, agitation, and belonging.

In this way, nicotine use practices can be understood as part of the assemblages that people form with the world around them as they seek to plug into (or out of) different registers of desire flows. Shifting public health's focus from warning against the potential harms of nicotine-containing products to emphasizing alternative ways of plugging into the capacity-enhancing experiences that different groups of people seek within nicotine use assemblages may offer a way of engaging and supporting these groups, rather than alienating them by continuing to perpetuate experiences of the 'stigmatized smoker' (Frohlich et al. 2012, Poland 1998, 2000) or framing them as victims of targeted tobacco marketing (Barnett et al. 2017). As Malins suggests, this would:

> … shift the focus away from stopping people taking drugs, to instead connecting them to new assemblages, such that they might continue to plug into desire flows, albeit through assemblages that might be healthier for them.
>
> *(Malins 2017, 131)*

As an example, this approach could be used to engage with young smokers who are increasingly adopting the practice of 'social smoking', which is characterized by light and intermittent smoking that often occurs in nightlife social settings that include alcohol (Thrul, Bühler and Ferguson 2014). While the usual public health approach would be to focus on 'educating' young people by presenting them with the health risks associated with this pattern of smoking (Schane, Glantz and Ling 2009, U.S. Department of Health and Human Services 2014), research has shown that the potential threat of future health effects of smoking does not motivate behavior change for people in earlier stages of life (Gough et al. 2009). Rather, social smoking interventions could focus on promoting the capacity-enhancing experiences that many young people seek to plug into when engaging with nightlife assemblages where social smoking often takes place, while shifting social smoking out of these assemblages (McQuoid, Keane and Ling 2021). To conclude, it may be by engaging with drug, set, and setting to dive deeper into the complexity, richness, diversity, and often contradictory nature of nicotine use experiences and practices of different groups of people in different places that public health researchers and practitioners may find bridges between their health preservation and promotion priorities and the lived experiences of the people they wish to benefit.

References

Agaku, I. T., O. A. Ayo-Yusuf, C. I. Vardavas, H. R. Alpert & G. N. Connolly (2013) Use of conventional and novel smokeless tobacco products among US adolescents. *Pediatrics,* 132, e578–e586.

Akre, C., P.-A. Michaud, A. Berchtold & J.-C. Suris (2009) Cannabis and tobacco use: Where are the boundaries? A qualitative study on cannabis consumption modes among adolescents. *Health Education Research,* 25, 74–82.

Anderson, B. & P. Harrison (2010) The promise of non-representational theories. In *Taking-place non-representational theories and geography,* eds. B. Anderson & P. Harrison, 1–34. Burlington, VT: Ashgate.

Antin, T. M. J., R. Annechino, G. Hunt, S. Lipperman-Kreda & M. Young (2017) The gendered experience of smoking stigma: Implications for tobacco control. *Critical Public Health,* 27, 443–454.

Antin, T. M. J., G. Hunt & E. Sanders (2018) The "here and now" of youth: The meanings of smoking for sexual and gender minority youth. *Harm Reduction Journal,* 15, 30.

Auer, R., N. Concha-Lozano, I. Jacot-Sadowski, J. Cornuz & A. Berthet (2017) Heat-not-burn tobacco cigarettes: Smoke by any other name. *JAMA Internal Medicine,* 177, 1050–1052.

Barnett, R., G. Moon, J. Pearce, L. Thompson & L. Twigg. 2017. Chapter 6: Smoking, denormalisation and the messy terrain of unintended consequences. In *Smoking geographies: Space, place and tobacco,* eds. R. Barnett, G. Moon, J. Pearce, L. Thompson & L. Twigg, 128–146. Chichester, West Sussex: John Wiley & Sons.

Bell, K. (2013a) Where there's smoke there's fire: Outdoor smoking bans and claims to public space. *Contemporary Drug Problems,* 40, 99–128.

———. (2013b) Whither tobacco studies? *Sociology Compass,* 7, 34–44.

Bell, K., L. McCullough, A. Salmon & J. Bell (2010) 'Every space is claimed': Smokers' experiences of tobacco denormalisation. *Sociology of Health & Illness,* 32, 914–929.
Bennett, K., J. M. Ricks & B. M. Howell (2014) "It's just a way of fitting in": Tobacco use and the lived experience of lesbian, gay, and bisexual Appalachians. *Journal of Health Care for the Poor and Underserved,* 25, 1646–1666.
Benowitz, N. L. (2010) Nicotine addiction. *New England Journal of Medicine,* 362, 2295–2303.
Blue, S., E. Shove, C. Carmona & M. P. Kelly (2016) Theories of practice and public health: Understanding (un) healthy practices. *Critical Public Health,* 26, 36–50.
Carhart-Harris, R. L., L. Roseman, E. Haijen, D. Erritzoe, R. Watts, I. Branchi & M. Kaelen (2018) Psychedelics and the essential importance of context. *Journal of Psychopharmacology,* 32, 725–731.
Cohn, S. (2014) From health behaviours to health practices: An introduction. *Sociology of Health & Illness,* 36, 157–162.
Collins, D. & A. Procter (2011) Smoking's shrinking geographies. *Geography Compass,* 5, 918–931.
Coxe, N., W. Webber, J. Burkhart, B. Broderick, K. Yeager, L. Jones & M. Fenstersheib (2014) Use of tobacco retail permitting to reduce youth access and exposure to tobacco in Santa Clara County, California. *Preventive Medicine,* 67, S46–S50.
Decorte, T. (2001) Drug users' perceptions of 'controlled' and 'uncontrolled' use. *International Journal of Drug Policy,* 12, 297–320.
Deleuze, G. & F. Guattari. 1988. *A Thousand Plateaus.* Minneapolis: University of Minnesota Press.
Dennis, S. (2011) Smoking causes creative responses: On state antismoking policy and resilient habits. *Critical Public Health,* 21, 25–35.
———. (2018) Becoming enwinded: A new materialist take on smoking pleasure. *International Journal of Drug Policy,* 51, 69–74.
Drope, J., A. C. Liber, Z. Cahn, M. Stoklosa, R. Kennedy, C. E. Douglas, R. Henson & J. Drope (2018) Who's still smoking? Disparities in adult cigarette smoking prevalence in the United States. *CA: A Cancer Journal for Clinicians,* 68, 106–115.
Duff, C. (2007) Towards a theory of drug use contexts: Space, embodiment and practice. *Addiction Research & Theory,* 15, 503–519.
Duff, C. (2010) On the role of affect and practice in the production of place. *Environment and Planning D: Society and Space,* 28, 881–895.
———. (2012) Accounting for context: Exploring the role of objects and spaces in the consumption of alcohol and other drugs. *Social & Cultural Geography,* 13, 145–159.
Fitzgerald, J., K. Dovey, P. Dietze & G. Rumbold (2004) Health outcomes and quasi-supervised settings for street injecting drug use. *International Journal of Drug Policy,* 15, 247–257.
Foucault, M. (1978) *History of sexuality.* New York: Random House, Inc.
———. (1988) Technologies of the self. In *Technologies of the self: A seminar with Michel Foucault,* ed. H. G. L. H. Martin, and P. H. Hutton, 16–49. Amherst: The University of Massechusetts Press.
———. (1994) The politics of health in the nineteenth century. In *Michel Foucault: Power—The essential works,* ed. J. Faubion, 90–105. London: Allen Lane.
Frohlich, K. L., E. Mykhalovskiy, B. D. Poland, R. Haines-Saah & J. Johnson (2012) Creating the socially marginalised youth smoker: The role of tobacco control. *Sociology of Health & Illness,* 34, 978–993.
Frohlich, K. L., L. Potvin, P. Chabot & E. Corin (2002) A theoretical and empirical analysis of context: Neighbourhoods, smoking and youth. *Social Science & Medicine,* 54, 1401–1417.
Glenn, N. M., J. Lapalme, G. McCready & K. L. Frohlich (2017) Young adults' experiences of neighbourhood smoking-related norms and practices: A qualitative study exploring place-based social inequalities in smoking. *Social Science & Medicine,* 189, 17–24.
Goffman, E. 1963. *Stigma: Notes on the management of spoiled identity.* Englewood Cliffs: Prentice-Hall.
Gough, B., G. Fry, S. Grogan & M. Conner (2009) Why do young adult smokers continue to smoke despite the health risks? A focus group study. *Psychology & Health,* 24, 203–220.
Graham, H. (1993) *When life's a drag: Women, smoking and disadvantage.* London: HMSO.
Graham, H. (2012) Smoking, stigma and social class. *Journal of Social Policy,* 41, 83–99.
Gubner, N. R., J. Thrul, O. A. Kelly & D. E. Ramo (2017) Young adults report increased pleasure from smoking cigarettes when drinking alcohol but not when using marijuana. *Addiction Research & Theory,* 2018; 26(1): 71–76.
Haines-Saah, R. J. (2013) After the smoke has cleared: Reflections from a former smoker and tobacco researcher. *Contemporary Drug Problems, 40*(1), 129–153. doi:10.1177/009145091304000107

Haines-Saah, R. J., J. L. Oliffe, C. F. White & J. L. Bottorff (2013) "It is just not part of the culture here": Young adults' photo-narratives about smoking, quitting, and healthy lifestyles in Vancouver, Canada. *Health & Place,* 22, 19–28.

Hammersley, R. & V. Leon (2006) Patterns of cannabis use and positive and negative experiences of use amongst university students. *Addiction Research & Theory,* 14, 189–205.

Hatzenbuehler, M. L., H.-J. Jun, H. L. Corliss & S. B. Austin (2013) Structural stigma and cigarette smoking in a prospective cohort study of sexual minority and heterosexual youth. *Annals of Behavioral Medicine,* 47, 48–56.

Keane, H. (2002) Smoking, addiction, and the making of time. In *High anxieties: Cultural studies in addiction*, eds. J. F. Brodie & M. Redfield, 119–133. Berkeley: University of California Press.

Keane, H. (2013) Making smokers different with nicotine: NRT and quitting. *International Journal of Drug Policy,* 24, 189–195.

Keane, H., M. Weier, D. Fraser & C. Gartner (2017) 'Anytime, anywhere': Vaping as social practice. *Critical Public Health,* 27, 465–476.

Kolte, B. & H. Schmidt-Semisch (2002) Controlled smoking: Implications for research on tobacco use. *Journal of Drug Issues,* 32, 647–666.

Lee, J. G. L., G. K. Griffin & C. L. Melvin (2009) Tobacco use among sexual minorities in the USA, 1987 to May 2007: A systematic review. *Tobacco Control,* 18, 275–282.

Lee, J. G. L., L. Henriksen, S. W. Rose, S. Moreland-Russell & K. M. Ribisl (2015) A systematic review of neighborhood disparities in point-of-sale tobacco marketing. *American Journal of Public Health,* 105, e8–e18.

Lefebvre, H. (2004) *Rhythmanalysis.* London: Continuum.

Lucherini, M., C. Rooke & A. Amos (2018) E-cigarettes, vaping and performativity in the context of tobacco denormalisation. *Sociology of Health & Illness,* 40, 1037–1052.

Luke, D. A., A. A. Sorg, T. Combs, C. B. Robichaux, S. Moreland-Russell, K. M. Ribisl & L. Henriksen (2016) Tobacco retail policy landscape: a longitudinal survey of US states. *Tobacco Control,* 25, i44–i51.

Malins, P. (2017) Desiring assemblages: A case for desire over pleasure in critical drug studies. *International Journal of Drug Policy,* 49, 126–132.

Maller, C. J. (2015) Understanding health through social practices: Performance and materiality in everyday life. *Sociology of Health & Illness,* 37, 52–66.

Marković, I. (2019a) Out of place, out of time: Towards a more-than-human rhythmanalysis of smoking. *Cultural Geographies,* 26, 487–503.

———. (2019b) Vaping like a chimney; skeuomorphic assemblages and post-smoking geographies. *Social & Cultural Geography*, 2021; 22(3): 376-402.

Matthews, A. K., J. Cesario, R. Ruiz, N. Ross & A. King (2017) A qualitative study of the barriers to and facilitators of smoking cessation among lesbian, gay, bisexual, and transgender smokers who are interested in quitting. *LGBT Health*, 4, 24–33.

McCready, G., N. M. Glenn & K. L. Frohlich (2019) "Don't smoke in public, you look like trash": An exploratory study about women's experiences of smoking-related stigmatisation and the connection to neighbourhood-level deprivation. *Health & Place,* 58, 102142.

McQuoid, J., E. Keamy-Minor & P. M. Ling (2020) A practice theory approach to understanding poly-tobacco use in the United States. *Critical Public Health*, 30(2): 204–219. doi:10.1080/09581596.2018.1541226

McQuoid, J., H. Keane & P. M. Ling (2021) Purposeful play and nightlife assemblages of (non-)smoking: Exploring a bar-based, anti-tobacco intervention for young adults. *Drugs: Education, Prevention and Policy*. doi:10.1080/09687637.2021.1932753

McQuoid, J., J. Thrul & P. Ling (2018b) A geographically explicit ecological momentary assessment (GEMA) mixed method for understanding substance use. *Social Science & Medicine,* 202, 89–98. doi:10.1016/j.socscimed.2018.02.014

McQuoid, J., J. Thrul, E. Ozer, D. Ramo & P. M. Ling (2019) Tobacco use in the sexual borderlands: The smoking contexts and practices of bisexual young adults. *Health & Place,* 58, 1–10. doi:10.1016/j.healthplace.2018.12.010

Moon, G., J. Pearce & R. Barnett (2012) Smoking, ethnic residential segregation, and ethnic diversity: A spatio-temporal analysis. *Annals of the Association of American Geographers,* 102, 912–921.

Moore, D. (1993) Beyond Zinberg's 'social setting': A processural view of illicit drug use. *Drug and Alcohol Review,* 12, 413–421.

Mui, H. Z., P. Sales & S. Murphy (2014) Everybody's doing it: Initiation to prescription drug misuse. *Journal of Drug Issues,* 44, 236–253.

Osibogun, O., Z. B. Taleb, R. Bahelah, R. G. Salloum & W. Maziak (2018) Correlates of poly-tobacco use among youth and young adults: Findings from the population assessment of tobacco and health study, 2013–2014. *Drug and Alcohol Dependence,* 187, 160–164.

Pearce, J., R. Barnett & G. Moon (2012) Sociospatial inequalities in health-related behaviours: Pathways linking place and smoking. *Progress in Human Geography,* 36, 3–24.

Poland, B. (1998) Smoking, stigma, and the purification of public space. In *Putting health into place: Landscape, identity, and well-being,* eds. R. A. Kearns & W. M. Gesler, 208–225. Syracuse, NY: Syracuse University Press.

Poland, B. D., K. Frohlich, R. J. Haines, E. Mykhalovskiy, M. Rock & R. Sparks (2006) The social context of smoking: The next frontier in tobacco control? *Tobacco Control,* 15, 59–63.

Poland, B. D. (2000) The 'considerate' smoker in public space: The micro-politics and political economy of 'doing the right thing'. *Health & Place,* 6, 1–14.

Reckwitz, A. (2002) Toward a theory of social practices: A development in culturalist theorizing. *European Journal of Social Theory,* 5, 243–263.

Ritchie, D., A. Amos & C. Martin (2010) "But it just has that sort of feel about it, a leper"—Stigma, smoke-free legislation and public health. *Nicotine & Tobacco Research,* 2010; 12(6): 622–629.

Sanders, E., T. Antin, G. Hunt & M. Young (2019) Is smoking queer? Implications of California tobacco denormalization strategies for queer current and former smokers. *Deviant Behavior,* 2020; 41(4): 497–511.

Schane, R. E., S. A. Glantz & P. M. Ling (2009) Social smoking: Implications for public health, clinical practice, and intervention research. *American Journal of Preventive Medicine,* 37, 124–131.

Shaffer, H. J. & M. N. Hall (2002) The natural history of gambling and drinking problems among Casino employees. *The Journal of Social Psychology,* 142, 405–424.

Shewan, D., P. Dalgarno & G. Reith (2000) Perceived risk and risk reduction among ecstasy users: The role of drug, set, and setting. *International Journal of Drug Policy,* 10, 431–453.

Shove, E., F. Trentmann & R. Wilk (2009) *Time, consumption and everyday life: Practice, materiality and culture.* Oxford and New York: Berg Publishers.

Southerton, D. (2009) Re-ordering temporal rhythms: Coordinating daily practices in the UK in 1937 and 2000. In *Time, consumption and everyday life: Practice, materiality and culture,* eds. E. Shove, F. Trentmann & R. Wilk, 49–66. Oxford: Berg Publishers.

Tan, Q. H. (2012) Towards an affective smoking geography. *Geography Compass,* 6, 533–545.

———. (2013a) Smell in the city: Smoking and olfactory politics. *Urban Studies,* 50, 55–71.

———. (2013b) Smoking spaces as enabling spaces of wellbeing. *Health & Place,* 24, 173–182.

———. (2016a) Feeling/filling closet smoking spaces: Negotiating public–private spheres, traversing emotional terrains. *Asian Geographer,* 33, 1–21.

———. (2016b) Scent-orship and Scent-iments on the Scent-ual: The relational geographies of smoke/smell between smokers and non-smokers in Singapore. *The Senses and Society,* 11, 177–198.

Thompson, L., J. Pearce & J. R. Barnett (2007) Moralising geographies: Stigma, smoking islands and responsible subjects. *Area,* 39, 508–517.

Thompson, L., J. Pearce & J. R. Barnett (2009) Nomadic identities and socio-spatial competence: Making sense of post-smoking selves. *Social & Cultural Geography,* 10, 565–581.

Thrul, J., A. Bühler & S. G. Ferguson (2014) Situational and mood factors associated with smoking in young adult light and heavy smokers. *Drug and Alcohol Review,* 33, 420–427.

U.S. Department of Health and Human Services. The Health Consequences of Smoking: 50 Years of Progress. A Report of the Surgeon General. Atlanta, GA: U.S. Department of Health and Human Services, Centers for Disease Control and Prevention, National Center for Chronic Disease Prevention and Health Promotion, Office on Smoking and Health, 2014. Printed with corrections, January 2014.

Wellman, R. J., E. N. Dugas, H. Dutczak, E. K. O'Loughlin, G. D. Datta, B. Lauzon & J. O'Loughlin (2016) Predictors of the onset of cigarette smoking: A systematic review of longitudinal population-based studies in youth. *American Journal of Preventive Medicine,* 51, 767–778.

Whatmore, S. (2002) *Hybrid geographies: Natures, cultures, spaces.* London: Sage.

Zinberg, N. E. (1984) *Drug, set, and setting.* New Haven, CT: Yale University Press.

17

'UNINHIBITED PLAY'

The political and pragmatic dimensions of intoxication within queer cultures

Kane Race, Kiran Pienaar, Dean Murphy and Toby Lea

Introduction

Could intoxication be understood as a politically significant activity among sexual and gender minorities? The question is likely to meet with some resistance. But approaching intoxication as an activity that grapples with the political organisation of society is not the same as recommending it as a promising strategy. We usually think of intoxication as a state of the individual body, or else a set of social or cultural or psychologically driven practices that put bodies into such a state. Since the conventional aim of these practices is to alter, manage or change the self in the world (Partanen 1981), the self emerges as the most pertinent locus of action and this produces the practice as personal in nature, relevance and consequence. To frame intoxication as a *political tactic* is to refuse this personalising effect by situating it historically and exploring the kind of practical response to certain problem-situations it might embody. The question becomes, 'how has intoxication emerged as a practical strategy that enables certain, more or less effective, navigations of social norms around sexuality and gender?', remembering that those norms are part of the political ordering of society.

The higher rates of drug and alcohol use found among LGBTQ+ people compared to broader population samples are mainly attributed to 'minority stress' by the researchers concerned (Dentato et al. 2013, Goldbach et al. 2014, Lehavot & Simoni 2011). Intoxication emerges as a form of self-medication here: a way of coping with the negative effects produced by lived experiences and expectations of stigma, discrimination and victimisation. This focus has been criticised for 'overlooking the meaningful ways in which … consumption intersects with identity, sociability, place, space and community formation for queer youth' (Hunt et al. 2019, p. 382). Indeed, when the hypothesis of minority stress fails to line up statistically significant correlations, some studies concede that gay socialising 'often occurs in bars, where alcohol is served and other drugs may be available' (Rosario et al. 2004, p. 1630), usually before recommending alternative, drug-free social spaces for minority individuals. Alcohol and other drug (AOD) use is typically approached within this literature as a problem *in and of itself*, that is symptomatic, in turn, of another social problem ('minority stress'). Little wonder there are calls for greater attention to meanings, contexts and experiences of pleasure from a growing cohort of researchers in the fields of critical drug and sexuality studies (Dennis & Farrugia 2017, Holt & Treloar 2008, Paasonen 2018, Pienaar et al. 2020a, Race 2009).

 DOI: 10.4324/9780429058141-22

Without wishing to deny the realities these different approaches configure, the binary choice they create between the competing figures of problematic self-medication and untroubled social or recreational consumption is hardly satisfying. It is not simply that recreational intoxication can lead to problems or that self-medication can bring pleasure; we are left wondering about the relevance of intoxication within the practical situations commonly confronted by those stigmatised on the basis of their sexual orientation and/or gender expression. Minority stress is conventionally defined as exposure to victimisation and discrimination, expectations of rejection and hostility, internalisation of negative attitudes about homosexuality and concerns about disclosure of identity (Meyer 2003). There is nothing very sexy about this definition, it must be said. If the injuries of social minoritisation were enough to explain disproportionate substance use within a particular population, one might expect it to hold true for other stigmatised minority groups that routinely suffer from discrimination and victimisation (ethnic and racial minorities, for example) but this is not borne out by the research evidence in any consistent way (Gillmore et al. 1990, Shih et al. 2010, Carter et al. 2017). In the 'minority stress' account of LGBTQ substance use, moreover, the individual is produced as the primary locus of injury: stigma becomes a condition of the self. The identities of sexual and gender minorities are ontologised, with intoxication produced as a means of palliating the injuries these damaged identities have incurred. But for Goffman (1963), stigma is embedded in relational dynamics; it creates problem-situations that social actors variously navigate. What if intoxication were transposed from its current makeshift status as a plaster for the wound of sexual stigmatisation and reconfigured as a pragmatic means of carrying out certain discredited activities?

In this chapter, we aim to develop such a pragmatic, performative account of the meanings, uses and effects of intoxication among gays, lesbians, bisexuals, transfolk and other assorted queers. Rather than intoxication standing as a toxic means of palliating damaged, static identities, we approach it as a practical – even creative – strategy that, for all its risks and toxicities, can enable individuals and groups to circumnavigate and disrupt prevailing gender and sexual norms. We do not deny that stigma, discrimination, social exclusion and sexual normalisation act as structuring constraints within the life-worlds and practical repertoires of LGBTQ+ groups and individuals: rather, our aim is to switch gears and translocate accounts of LGBTQ+ substance use away from the ontological register of pathological self-medication and towards the more performative and pragmatic key of tactical responsiveness to the sociomaterial situations that stigma, discrimination and normalisation create or make manifest.[1] We seek a more dynamic account of queer intoxication, in other words, that turns attention towards the practical question of what intoxication *does* for those who subject themselves with it. Intoxication is what some people *do* to allow certain things to happen – not simply a confirmation of injured being. As Judith Butler has maintained, gender and sexuality should not be mistaken for stable identities or inner truths. Rather, we might attend to 'the mundane way in which bodily gestures, movements, and enactments of various kinds constitute the illusion of an abiding gendered self' (Butler 1988, p. 519). In this chapter, we seek to engage this performative register of self-practices. For certain social subjects, certain bodily movements and enactments matter, such as drinking, getting high, getting out of it or getting wasted. But how, and why should this be the case?

In what follows, we explore the value of disinhibition as an alternative explanation for the complex relations between sexual and gender minoritisation and queer investments in intoxication. Frequent reference was made to notions of disinhibition in the 42 qualitative interviews we conducted with LGBTQ+ Australians as part of the *Chemical Practices: Enhancement and Experimentation* study in which we asked our participants about the contexts and motivations of their drug and alcohol practices. This made us want to find out more about scientific and everyday discourses of inhibition and disinhibition, their histories and how they operate. In fact, the concept of disinhibition already has considerable traction in scientific research into gay and bisexual men's substance use: in HIV behavioural research, it is liberally and often reductively used to explain HIV risk-taking and naturalise its purported connection to substance use (for critiques of this tendency, see Race 2009, pp. 164–179; Reinerman & Leigh 1987; Rhodes 1996, Worth & Rawstorne 2005). While substance use emerges simplistically as the cause or explanation of continued HIV risk-taking in much of this discourse, some psychological research in the area offers a more nuanced theorisation of the conditions that motivate some gay and bisexual men to use drugs to cognitively 'escape' awareness of HIV risk (McKirnan et al. 1996). If drugs and alcohol can be understood to be disinhibiting, this work is provocative for making this attribute a factor that informs people's motivations for use, rather than the more common and less plausible move of making sexual risk-taking the unwitting effect of consuming intoxicating substances. Drawing on a notion of disinhibition, McKirnan and colleagues maintain that 'sexual risk does not stem from a lack of community norms or personal standards, but from a desire to escape cognitive awareness of very rigorous norms and standards' (1996, p. 665). Here, drug use is said to facilitate a process of cognitive disengagement from such norms that allows people to act on their desires. Insofar as they subscribe to a notion of drugs and alcohol as disinhibiting agents, these psychological perspectives align with the cruder assertions found in the behavioural/ epidemiological HIV literature. They take the important step of interrogating the normative conditions and moral climate in which disinhibition 'makes sense' for certain subjects in certain contexts.

This chapter elaborates the concept of dis/inhibition in relation to queer identities and cultures organised around drug and alcohol use, focusing on the generative effects of intoxication for sexual and gender minorities. While associations have been established between gay male sex and the disinhibiting qualities of drug consumption, we are not aware of any research that identifies this script in the discourse of other sexual and gender minorities, including queer women, non-binary and trans people, as our research does. The first part of the chapter presents a genealogy of dis/inhibition and draws out its connections to the regime of sexuality whose contours of emergence from the late nineteenth century are famously traced by Foucault (1976). We then consider how disinhibition has been conceived and handled by symbolic interactionists in social research on intoxicated sex. The final section explores how notions of disinhibition and 'uninhibited play' are valued and mobilised more broadly in the discourses of LGBTQ+ people who use drugs and alcohol in Australia today. We explore how drugs and alcohol are said to participate in the construction of social and intimate assemblages that expand the possibilities of agency, identification, self-experimentation and connection for minoritised subjects in subcultural practices and everyday life. Read together, the genealogy of dis/ inhibition and our empirical accounts of LGBTQ+ drug and alcohol use suggest that dis/inhibition and intoxication have been animating forces in historic practices of queer and trans world-making.

A full description of the research and recruitment methods we employed for the chemical practices study appears elsewhere (Pienaar et al. 2020a). The study received ethics approval from the University of Sydney Human Research Ethics Committee (Approval number 2017/735). We asked study participants to specify their gender pronouns, sexual and gender identities, and the pseudonyms we use to refer to them in this and other publications.

Dis/inhibition: a history

Using disinhibition to account for practices of intoxication among subjects problematised on the basis of their sex is a useful starting point for our intervention. Minority stress is not the only theoretical inheritance that one might cite to work within and against the disciplinary formation that concerns us. But while disinhibition promises an alternative account of the significance of intoxication for sexual and gender minorities, it is nonetheless necessary to subject this concept to critical-historical scrutiny. Inhibition can be situated as part of nineteenth-century efforts to consolidate neurophysiology as a hard science that incorporated moralistic attitudes about human conduct into the depths of human physiology. As Roger Smith has demonstrated, the emergence of inhibition over the nineteenth century entailed a gradual reformulation of religious, moral and political powers of control in terms of the brain's control over the nervous system in a move that transformed understandings of moral regulation into natural phenomena (1992). Massive shifts in Western epistemes of power/knowledge over this period brought the human life sciences into focus as categorical sources of knowledge about the proper functioning of bodies, subjectivities and populations on the basis of the specialised access they claimed to the laws of nature (Foucault 1976). The concept of inhibition emerged as part of attempts to understand how orderly conduct could be achieved at the level of bodies: how the mind controls the body or the brain controls the operations of the nervous system. Drawing on reified concepts of the will, bound up with prevalent beliefs about morality of character, the fields of psychology, medicine and physiology came to conceive inhibition as a regulatory mechanism that enacts a hierarchical relation between the brain (the mind) and the body's nervous system and physiological functioning. Concerns about social order and the proper functioning of society were thus transposed into a biological register and treated as natural phenomena. This made disorderly, uninhibited subjects notionally available to scientific diagnosis, analysis, adjudication and correction.

One of the key sites for the elaboration and articulation of these theories were studies of intoxication. In his 1865 treatise *Stimulants and Narcotics*, the English physician Francis Anstie claimed the effects of alcohol and hashish 'ought not to be called a stimulant at all … they are, in fact, the results of a partial and highly peculiar kind of paralysis of the brain'. Invoking emerging formulations of inhibition, he wrote, 'the apparent exaltation of certain faculties should be ascribed to the removal of controlling influences, [rather] than to the positive stimulation of the faculties themselves' (1865, pp. 80–81). As this explanation indicates, the concept of inhibition enfolded prevailing conceptions of moral order and social control into a theory of nervous action that hinged on the hierarchical organisation of internal faculties and functions, implanting historically specific expectations about orderly human conduct into the bodies and brains of persons.

Parsed in this way – as a historical process that over the course of the nineteenth century individualised and biologised moralistic attitudes about personal control and socio-sexual order – the concept of inhibition can be recognised as a palmary instance of precisely the same scientific-political and epistemic shifts that produced the homosexual as 'a type of life, a life form, and a morphology, with an indiscreet anatomy and possibly a mysterious physiology' (Foucault 1976, p. 43). While Foucault's account of the perverse implantation specifies the homosexual in this passage, these historical developments are just as pertinent for the formation of trans and gender-diverse subjectivities and identities. Indeed, as David Valentine observes, 'the implicit pathology of homosexuality was seen to be evident in what contemporary social theorists would deem visibly physical and behavioural markers of non-normative *gender* expression' (2007, pp. 40–41, italics in original). We find it fitting, at any rate, that the biopolitical production of psychologised genders and sexualities finds its counterpoint in an equally biologising and biologised series of counter-strategies or counter-corporealisations over the course of the ensuing century: the individual and collective consumption of psychoactive substances within sexual and gender minority subcultures with the precise, if variously materialised, aim of effecting *disinhibitions*.

Inhibition conceived the social regulation of persons in terms of a natural process of rational self-control, reconfirming prevailing conceptions of the 'ordered life' that had hitherto held currency while re-inserting them into the neurophysiological bodies of the future. At issue in seemingly diverse behaviours such as drinking, masturbation, non-reproductive sexuality and insanity was loss of self-control, or some failure in the body and brain's inhibitory mechanisms: this is what made them cohere as conditions. Through this apparatus of bodily production, social norms and collective values were internalised as controls in and of the human organism, while the social, sexual and economic mores of the Victorians were implanted directly into the bodies of those constituted as 'moderns'. In his history of sexuality, Foucault argues that sex made it possible to group together 'anatomical elements, biological functions, conducts, sensations and pleasures and make use of this fictitious unity as a causal principle' (Foucault 1976, p. 154). The history of inhibition demonstrates how the efficient reproduction of the social and corporeal order was taken to rely on the self-regulating activity of subjects, especially in matters sexual. The appropriate exercise of inhibition was taken to ensure the proper organisation of the body politic as well as the individual *bios* of citizens, the entire developmental life of productive bodies. Failures in inhibition allowed the lower and baser faculties of the body to impose themselves on the social order with unnatural, antisocial and destabilising tendencies. They were thus psychiatrised and rendered biologically legible.

Licencing licentious conduct

If, as noted above, the psychiatrisation of homosexuality and 'sexual inversion' in the late nineteenth century invested 'unnatural' sexualities with an 'indiscreet anatomy and possibly a mysterious physiology' (Foucault 1976, p. 43) – part of what Foucault called 'the perverse implantation' – then it makes a perverse kind of sense that the subjects thus constituted should turn to the consumption of intoxicating substances professionally attributed with the power to paralyse the equally mysterious physiological mechanism of inhibition to counter their lived sense of oppression. But there is a twist here. Certainly, Anstie's (1865) assertion that intoxicating substances do their damage by inducing a 'peculiar kind of paralysis of the brain' still finds ample expression over a century later in the medical apothegm that the effects of intoxication are produced 'not by "stepping on the gas" but by paralyzing the brakes' (Muehlberger 1956, p. 40). But despite its likelihood of passing the 'pub test'[2] and the apparent sedimentation of this theory into the murky terrain of common sense, scientific attempts to locate the 'brakes' supposed to be physiologically responsible for inhibition have little to show for their efforts.[3] Indeed, a review of physiological research in the area concludes that it is not possible to understand disinhibited *behaviours* in terms of underlying neuronal activity and recommends instead a focus on cognitive expectancies; those culturally emergent scripts that variously serve to organise experiences of drinking and taking drugs (Woods & Mansfield, cited in Reinerman & Leigh 1987, p. 442).

These scripts are nothing if not heterogenous and manifold, as historical and anthropological research on 'drunken comportment' has roundly demonstrated. Indeed, the cultural and historical examples of drunken comportment that MacAndrew and Edgerton amassed in their wide-ranging study of the topic led them to conclude that intoxicated behaviour is less the product of 'alcohol's toxic assault on the seat of moral judgment, conscience, or the like [than] the particular meaning(s) attached to drunkenness in a given culture' (MacAndrew & Edgerton 1969, p. 165; see Reinerman & Leigh 1987 for an overview). Drinking can make people excitable or morose, aggressive or sociable, horny or withdrawn, violent or thoughtful depending on the cultural conventions and network of meanings that organise and invest its use in particular contexts and in conjunction with particular activities. Drinking does not always or even often induce the loss of control that Anglo-Christian modernity would have us believe. How ironic, then, that the most likely determinant of uninhibited behaviour is the cultural association between intoxication and the projected failure to control the 'baser instincts' that medicine and neurophysiology have reiterated, invested with white-coated authority and remain ever so keen to substantiate. It turns out that association is parochial and hardly the only way of organising bodies (MacAndrew & Edgerton 1969, Rhodes 1996).

If the script of disinhibition is a cultural resource that a few life sciences have essentialised, it has also become a motherload of cultural expectancies that give shape to intoxicated behaviour. But there is a further twist in this story of biological investiture that redoubles the practical utility of intoxication-as-disinhibition. Barbara Critchlow puts it plainly in her 1983 discussion of drinking and responsibility: 'When people see substances as disinhibitors due to their pharmacological properties, they accept that intoxicated people may do things they would not normally do' (1983, p. 452). That is to say, the popularity of the scientific theory of disinhibition as part of 'common sense' makes it possible to mobilise what some sociologists have called 'deviance disavowal' (Davis 1961). 'By deviance it is meant: a violation of a norm; by disavowal it is meant that a person denies his or her deviant status i.e. denies that an expectation has been violated' (Wilmot 1981, p. 14). Tim Rhodes conveys the practical appeal of this meaning-arrangement for stigmatised sexual subjects:

> Because they are commonly believed to be 'disinhibitive' [alcohol and stimulant drugs] may provide socially acceptable excuses for engaging in sexual behaviours in which people may want to engage but perhaps know they should not
>
> *(Rhodes 1996, p. 756)*

On this rendition, intoxication acquires further value by accumulating the capacity to provide a cultural alibi for disapproved sexual and social activities.

As a countertactic, this practice was clearly familiar within North American gay culture at the cusp of the modern gay movement. It even finds its way into the groundbreaking 1968 play *The Boys in the Band* (Crowley 1968), renowned for its early portrayal of modern gay life, when the characters laugh about the 'Christ-was-I-drunk-last-night syndrome' that evidently operated as a way of dodging moral reprobation around homosexual activity among this peer group of gay men.

> You see, in the Christ-was-I-drunk-last-night syndrome, you really are drunk. That part of it is true. It's just that you also do remember everything. [General laughter]. Oh God, I used to have to get loaded to go in a gay bar!
>
> *(Crowley 1969, p. 42)*

For sexually discreditable subjects, then, one of the uses of intoxication is the simple pragmatic opportunity it affords to engage the mechanism of 'deviance disavowal' to account for 'unnatural' behaviour when challenged. Proud gay advocacy has its time and its place, but perhaps liquor is quicker, after all? Disinhibition permits a practice of 'normative substantiation' (Race 2009): a counter-strategic manoeuvre that works by attributing deviations from sexual and gender norms to the anatomy of a substance whose toxicity is said to interfere substantially with the physiological balancing act that is inhibition: you are made to lose control of yourself.

Sexual drifting

Deviance disavowal is a good device to have up your sleeve when the simple acts entailed in 'you doing you' come up against the risk of punishment, moral opprobrium and violence. But deviance disavowal can only serve as a partial explanation for intoxication's appeal among abjected sexualities and genders. Surely, there is more to it than that. How does 'disinhibition' feel for sexually unacceptable subjects? What does it make possible beyond the convenience of a provisional licence? In his 2009 work on cultures of 'exceptional sex' in gay life, Race found that disinhibition – and in particular 'uninhibited sex' – was highly valued among gay male participants in hookup circles (2009, p. 176). How else to explain the scores of hookup app users that consider 'uninhibited play' a preference worth explicitly specifying on their thumbnail profiles? Whether this phrase is meant euphemistically to denote sex without condoms or 'chemsex' in a given instance is a moot point for present purposes (on chemsex, see Bourne et al. 2015, Race 2017): far from being bound up in a structure of apology or disavowal, uninhibited sex is valued here precisely as a qualitatively superior experience of sex. It evokes a kind of sex that escapes the moral rigidity of antiquated proprieties and other prudish hang-ups, the sort of sex that breaks itself free from the straightjacket of normative decorum that is imposed to restrain us from having or even entertaining the idea of having nasty, dirty, piggy, carefree sex (to borrow some terms from gay men's sexual vernacular; see Florêncio 2020); the normative/biological impulse to slam down the breaks when the slightest indication is given that mild will run to wild at any rate. Free from such encumberments, uninhibited sex has the status of a select commodity in today's gay sexual marketplace – widely asserted, highly coveted and more or less enthusiastically encountered.

In a 1981 article on sexual drinking, Richard Wilmot provides one handle on the process of valuation that turns disinhibition from an excuse for bad behaviour or apologetic source of embarrassment into a desired and desirable property:

> Sexual encounters in America are conditioned by the puritan ethos, which is to say, that they are conditioned by inhibition. When sexual encounters are so conditioned, they quite naturally lend themselves to the 'ceremonial' use of an intoxicant which has come to be culturally defined as a sexual disinhibitor.
>
> *(p. 6)*

If the sexual setting is one of inhibition, Wilmot argues, the intoxicant emerges as a cultural antidote because it 'causes one to relax in situations that have been culturally defined as rigid' (1981, p. 10). Wilmot is concerned with the interactional dynamics that lead sexual drinking to result in sexual anomie among some of his (markedly heterosexual) informants. The sexual scenario is cast as 'complicated to begin with and it grows increasingly more so with the inclusion of alcohol' (p. 7). Sex requires us to throw ourselves into a 'situation of company' in which status is sought and sounded out, and in which rebuttal and rejection are anticipated as ever-present, potentially painful and demoralising possibilities.

> If 'status anxiety' involves such poignant questions as: Does this person find me sexually masculine or sexually feminine? And/or, does this person really love me or are they being insincere? The anticipation of a rebuff provokes the anxiety. This provocation of 'status anxiety' can produce the physical manifestations of embarrassment and timidity that lead in turn to more anxiety.
>
> *(p. 8)*

For Wilmot, 'drinking alcohol as related to sex becomes meaningful only in relation to the intention to reduce inhibitions' (p. 11). In company in which sexual drinking is anticipated and/or encouraged, participants 'acknowledge that a systematic alteration is involved, one which radically reconstitutes what it is for them that is going on' (p. 11). In this sense, drinking serves to frame the situation *as* sexual, though not unproblematically or unambiguously, as it turns out. One way 'status anxiety' is dissipated is through the use of intoxicants to frame and reframe, navigate and disavow, excuse and enable the taking of risks that such high-stake games are felt to necessitate.

Alcohol reduces the tensions that inhere in status anxiety and on this basis is claimed to disinhibit. 'But the release of inhibitions does not follow any clear-cut guidelines', Wilmot perceptively observes. 'It is something that must be negotiated between the parties concerned' (p. 10). The task is made all the more vexing and complicated because of the 'interactional drifting' that alcohol affords:

> The negotiation of interactional limits is the game of sexual drinking. Persons drift about on an interactional level when they become intoxicated because it is expected that they do so. Interactional expectations are set-up … during alcoholic intoxication that can be (and usually are) non-specific, ambiguously defined, and easily broken.
>
> *(p. 12)*

Motivations become ambiguous, intentions misconstrued, jokes are taken seriously, intimate appeals ignored. *Bon courage!*

The problem, as Wilmot sees it, is that intoxication frames the sexual – or is that social? – encounter in ambiguous ways. Frustration, demoralisation and anomie result from the perceived clash between the playful, theatrical, make-believe key in which intoxicated sexual interactions occur and the sexual intentions underlying the encounter, which he describes as 'very serious concerns' (p. 11).

> Sexual drinking keys the encounter as a form of play – more specifically as a form of erotic make believe. Freedom from inhibition during times of drinking allows for the non-utilitarian… for idle enjoyment and play. Things are not to be taken seriously. It is a time for relaxation and sociability. This is how alcohol intoxication is keyed in our society – a release from the serious practical business of 'getting on in life'. Yet, when this symbolic interpretation of what alcohol is supposed to do is superimposed over the very serious subject of sex, the scenario becomes miskeyed.
>
> *(p. 11)*

A very heteromasculine discord.[4]

Wilmot's analysis is refreshingly explicit about the materialisation of sex as a generally problematic object, freighted with all kinds of status anxiety, personal vulnerabilities, moral ambiguities and cultural rigidities. Imagine how compounded these pressures become when one's sexuality and/or gender expression is deemed not only to be perverse and problematic, but 'everywhere present in [you], at the root of all [your] actions because it was their insidious and indefinitely active principle, written on [your] face and body because it was a secret that always gave itself away' (Foucault 1976, p. 43). If heterosexual couples turn to the drink to make sex easier to negotiate, queers can hardly be blamed for ordering something stronger.

Little wonder Foucault was in favour of jettisoning the false binary of repression and liberation and replacing it with something altogether different. In place of inhibition/de-repression, he promoted playful experiments with bodies, pleasures, knowledges, relations and even drugs to unlock their multiplicity and inventive possibilities (for a discussion, see Race 2017, pp. 3–7). If the notion of disinhibition installs an unwinnable battle between inhibition and desire into the physiological constitution of the docile subject, a critical-historical genealogy of dis/inhibition is useful 'because it indicates that being intoxicated commonly involves a transition between social roles, or a modification of social status' (Bancroft 2009, p. 52). And, one might add, the creation of entirely new roles, relations, affective capacities, bodily volatilities and dynamics.

For Wilmot (1981), intoxication in sexual scenarios enables 'interactional drift', a 'loosening' within which the status anxieties and other tensions inherent in the sexual encounter are accommodated, allowing the interaction to take on new moods and modalities. But where Wilmot makes the tension he perceives between seriousness and playfulness a source of demoralisation, thwarting and frustration, queer partiers help us appreciate the possibility of transforming sexual drifting from a problem into an artform. As it happens, play turns out to be one of the key modalities that gays, other queers and trans people have engaged to make sex and gender expression more expansive and enjoyable in contemporary queer settings and cultures (Race 2015, 2017). On gay hookup apps such as Grindr, for example, 'looking to play?' is one of the most common opening lines, serving to frame the encounter in advance as fun, casual and obligation-free. From queer and trans play parties to gay male party 'n' play scenes, from pup-play to role-play, from kikis to kink, play has come to connote an experimental relation to sex, bodies and their manifold potentialities that is worlds away from the 'profoundly serious, potentially romantic' hues with which some commentators persist in painting the modular sexual encounter (Reinarman & Leigh 1987, p. 451, Wilmot 1981).

Constituting sex as play makes it possible to 'highlight improvisation driven by curiosity, desire for variation and openness towards surprise' as 'things that greatly matter in sexual lives and scholarly attentions', Susanna Paasonen proposes (2018, p. 3). As sexual bodies 'move towards different scenes, fantasies, bodies and objects, and become attached to them', she writes, 'the forms, identities and subjectivities of participants are reorganised' (p. 3). For Paasonen playfulness 'intermeshes and overlaps with those of improvisation, exploration, curiosity and experimentation, yet it also stands apart from them in foregrounding pleasure and bodily intensity as key motivations for sexual activity' (p. 2). Paasonen's evocative rendition of the playful, dynamic, open-ended and performative dimensions of sexual pleasure puts a new, more positive spin on the unexpected detours, perplexing blockages, alternate routes and partial connections of sexual drifting, constituting its complicated trajectories, unpredicted deviations and wasteful expenditures as possible sources of pleasure, exploration and intensity. In order to bring out the resonances that chime across this framing of sex as play and queer and gender-diverse practices of intoxicated pleasure, sexual sociability and uninhibited sex, we devote the remainder of this chapter to our analysis of in-depth, semi-structured interviews with LGBTQ+ people who use drugs.

Uninhibited play

Unsurprisingly, the disinhibition script is widely evident in queer and gender-diverse people's accounts of negotiating their gender and sexual identities and exploring sex. For example, Fuego credits alcohol with helping them explore sex outside of heteronormative expectations in the context of their conservative upbringing:

> In terms of like sexuality and sex, I guess alcohol originally was sort of bound up in my exploration of my sexuality. Like, you know, making out with boys and that sort of thing. Well, it wasn't necessarily dependent on alcohol, but yeah, that took away my inhibitions because I went to a Catholic high school and grew up in the country, and I don't know if I would say it was frowned upon but that's the way it felt anyway in school. So, like, it wasn't really easy for us to sort of pursue, you know, things that sort of deviated from the norm.
>
> *Fuego (23, pansexual, gender diverse)*

Similarly, Nico suggests that AODs were helpful for suspending the material effects of shame and connecting with their partner in the context of early sexual experiences:

> So one of my girlfriends, when we first started being intimate [...] alcohol was hugely beneficial for me because there was so much shame, like internalised queer-phobia around [...] my feelings of desire for her. I just felt deeply ashamed and [...] when we were intimate, I would completely get out of my body and into my head [...] and that was such a disconnected experience it wasn't enjoyable for either of us. But when I was under the influence of drugs, I felt that shame melt away, I could just be in my body and experience it as the sensual, pleasurable experience that it was. Like without having any of those stories in my head about who we supposedly were and what we were doing, and it just felt good.
>
> *Nico (40, queer, non-binary)*

In Nico's account, the affirmative intensities of pleasure effectively override the trappings of constitutive shame, enabling them to 'be in [their] body and experience it as the sensual, pleasurable experience that it was'. The capacity of 'disinhibiting' substances to help consumers overcome status and performances anxieties in addition to other hesitations around queer sex such as constitutive shame was also valued in chemsex practices. For example, Dalston, a 44-year-old cisgender gay man, explains:

> I [inject crystal methamphetamine] mainly [for] the rush, you know, and the fact that it strips you bare. So all these preconceptions or worries or ruminations that you might be having about, 'What if?' or [...] 'Am I doing this right?' they tend to be replaced by an instant carnal, fleshy craving. It knocks out all the big worry [and] enables me to focus very, very sharply on what I'm doing and just get in a zone, you know. I guess it's like a flow-state, where you're not self-conscious, you're just cock-in-mouth, that's it. You're present, you're focused [...] It's a transformation.
>
> *Dalston (44, gay cis man)*

The Christian legacy of a moral and existential battle between the spirit and the flesh, which informed early conceptions of inhibition, is clearly evident in Dalston's description of 'the rush' producing 'an instant carnal, fleshy craving'. But this is regarded less as an existential failing than a pragmatic affordance of the practice that makes the realisation of sexual opportunities less awkward. Other participants spoke of the value of disinhibition not just for realising sexual possibilities but also for developing a more expansive, daring, social sense of queer personhood. For example, Dane suggests:

> I love taking these drugs. I think they clarify a lot of things. I think they illuminate a lot of things. I have learnt that I am a lot freer than I have been led to believe I am. I have a lot more agency over my own body and my experiences and my feelings. I have learnt that I have a lot more agency over my sexual experiences. I have become a lot more confident sexually taking these drugs. They have allowed me to let go of certain hang-ups and translate those over into non-high drug experiences. They have allowed me to push the limits of gender with my friends and feeling uninhibited to kind of play with that.
>
> *Dane (30, gay cis man)*

Dane's experience with drugs has, on his account, been 'clarifying', 'illuminating', and provided a greater sense of agency over his body, experiences, feelings and self that he has translated over into non-drug contexts. His comments demonstrate how the frame of 'uninhibited play' enables a process of interactional drifting that connects sex with other socio-sexual activities such as experimenting with different gendered performances together with friends.

As we have mentioned, the framing of sex as 'play' and fun contrasts with how sex is invested with 'profoundly serious' ends in some heterosexual discourse. This playful framing was very common among our study participants and it enabled them to consider the different ways in which different drugs enhanced sexual experiences, producing new bodily intensities:

> I've had some extraordinary, wonderful experiences with wonderful people on these drugs [crystal meth and GHB] that I've thoroughly enjoyed. And [I've] had really great experiences with people on a regular basis with no expectation, just a lot of fun and a lot of sex, great sex.
>
> *Drew (46, gay cis man)*

> GHB makes the experience of sexual things like getting fucked or giving someone head or something a lot more intensely sexual. It's like amping the sexualness of it up. It's also a lot more arousing. Just makes you more aroused I think, like the touch or getting touched. I like it, I like taking it especially in combination with the other [drugs].
>
> *Dane (30, gay cis man)*

For Rhianna, a 42-year-old queer woman, smoking crystal enables her to connect with her partner and enter into a more experimental space with her. In a passage that recalls Dalston's 'flow-state' above, she presents her experience in the following way:

> So the positive for me [of smoking crystal] is feeling like I've really connected with that person again, [the person] that I have chosen to be with and love. And on an intimate level for me, I think why I get really excited about [smoking crystal] is sexually for me I feel like I actually get really connected with my partner after smoking [crystal...] I get experimental in the moment with this person. So, I feel connected with her in that moment and I feel open.
>
> *Rhianna (42, queer, cis woman)*

For Ursula, a 25-year-old cisgender lesbian, the use of stimulants similarly enhances sex by multiplying possibilities of connection:

> Sex on drugs [...] just makes sex better. It has made sexual experiences [better] And emotional experiences where I'll be naked with someone, and not necessarily had sex with them. It gives it a different level of how well you can connect with that other person, even if you are just talking shit on a mattress for six hours.
>
> *Ursula (25, lesbian cis woman)*

By including 'talking shit on a mattress for six hours' in her account of better sex, Ursula recalls the kinds of interactional and sexual drift associated with sexual intoxication in the literature (Wilmot 1981, Reinarman & Leigh 1987). But for Ursula this is not a source of disappointment or a problem: it enhances her enjoyment and the intimacy of the erotic encounter. For Dane, who enthuses about the use of drugs such as GHB to enhance sex (above), these modes of interactional and sexual drifting can help constitute joyous occasions of social play and gender experimentation with his friends:

> We are constantly using [drugs] to like entertain one another and like perform for one another and kind of be silly with one another. We will, for instance, maybe have some crystal, take some [MDMA] caps and go dancing and just kind of have the best time like doing a show for one another, playing dress-ups for one another, trying on things. Most of us are putting on drag. I think we are all willing to push the boundaries of what is socially acceptable with one another and I think that's what brings us together as friends as we kind of reject ideas of how we are meant to be. You also get a kind of escape from the reality that we all have to live in and [we get to] kind of exist together in a different place. And these [drugs] definitely are a big part of that.
>
> *Dane (30, gay cis man)*

The 'different place', or heterotopia (Foucault 1971), that Dane invokes here could well be taken to stand for, and sociologically characterise, the vibrant practices of queer partying – pleasure, dancing and sexual sociability – that take place in queer subcultural spaces and cultural events, which characteristically involve the prolific use of various stimulants (Race 2017). Dane's account demonstrates how scripts of sexual disinhibition have a wider purchase than simply making the realisation of 'deviant' sex possible: they are involved in queer world-making, in making the places, spaces and sociabilities entailed in queer community-formation enjoyable, possible, appealing and meaningful for many LGBTQ+ people, as spaces in which the boundaries of what is socially acceptable can be pushed.

Michael Warner (2002) has proposed the concept of queer counterpublics to convey the sense in which queer world-making depends upon assembling collective horizons of activity for queer self-experimentation. He writes, 'a culture is developing in which intimate relations and the sexual body can in fact be understood as projects for transformation among strangers' (p. 122). We are suggesting that drug use plays an active part in making at least some of these collective, interactive settings possible: dance parties, clubs, bars, drag scenes and partying with friends have queer counterpublic effects. As Avery, a cisgender gay man of similar age to Dane, ventures:

> I would say MDMA has helped shaped the way I feel about gender. I probably see a lot more gender expression and therefore feel more confident in being a bit more

> explorative in my gender. I started doing drag about three years ago and I don't ever perform on any drugs, but instances of being on MDMA before that have helped me get there in terms of the community that I experience generally with MDMA. I would say that the community that I meet in a space where I tend to take MDMA has opened my eyes to a broader spectrum of gender and broader options for experimentation and playfulness with gender than the outside world, outside of the pink bubble of the queer night club. I think I've been on a bit of a journey with my own gender and I have experimented with more feminine manifestations in the real world because of the way that I've felt in these spaces.
>
> *Avery (31, gay cis man)*

These accounts of drag and gender experimentation in the context of stimulant use might serve as a riposte to analyses of chemsex and party 'n' play cultures that reduce these scenes and practices to normative instantiations of gay masculinity. But they also indicate the relevance of the cultural script of disinhibition for the elaboration and cultivation of a wide range of gender-non-conforming identities and practices.[5] For example, Nico, a 40-year-old non-binary participant, recounted:

> I had started questioning my gender and then I was so scared of what was coming up for me and then I went out with a friend one night. We did ecstasy and I was dancing and I had this extremely vivid, like visual and felt sense of myself (even though I mean I'm nonbinary, but I'm definitely sort of trans-masculine) and I saw myself as this man [...] just all of the physical characteristics. And it felt so real and it was such a profoundly affirming experience for me. In that moment I was like, 'I haven't been making all this stuff up, this is what's really happening for me'. It just sort of crystallised all of those questions that I'd been asking myself.
>
> *Nico (40, non-binary)*

Mira, a 25-year-old transwoman, told us, 'LSD has been really good [...] for me unpacking a lot of things in terms of my gender and sexuality'. She spoke of the value of MDMA for removing and reconfiguring feelings of anxiety about her body during sex:

> I've had sex on both MDMA and LSD wildly [...] I like both for different reasons actually because MDMA is amazing at removing a lot of gender dysphoria. I have a very complicated relationship with my genitals especially with their functionality because a lot of time [my gender] doesn't match with that. But with MDMA it just feels great because you know, you don't have that same anxiety. You don't have that same internal narrative. It allows you to connect to your physical form and your sexuality a lot easier. It's just like MD is good for accepting the equipment that I have now. And universally it has been a deeply emotional experience. There's a lot of crying usually, because just like overwhelming happiness. It's just like, 'Oh my god, something like this feels so good and so right'. So often, you can feel like that you're mismatched wires and just for a little while to feel like everything just works, that is an amazingly fun experience and good emotionally.
>
> *Mira (25, queer, trans woman)*

If MDMA is good for reducing dysphoria and making the body feel right, LSD is also sexually productive for Mira, though in a way that suggests transcending certain dimensions of the gendered body:

> LSD is good because the times I've had sex on LSD, I have lost a certain level of spatial awareness. So, I kind of forget I have a body, which is a very interesting experience. But I've also had like hallucinatory experiences on LSD, mimicking like a mental perception of, you know, like PIV [penis-in-vagina] penetrative sex, which is something that obviously really appeals to me. And that has been a very interesting experience and again that ties back into the like using [drugs to reduce] gender dysphoria and like coming to terms with things.
>
> *Mira (25, queer trans woman)*

This role of intoxicants in affirming and experiencing an alternative and desirable sense of gendered self was also apparent in Nico's account:

> There was another time where I was smoking weed and just walking down the street and I again had a very clear visual and felt sense of myself as a man and as a man primarily attracted to other queer men, and I looked, and felt, at ease, and like I knew myself, who I was, and that everything was okay.
>
> *Nico (40, non-binary)*

Meanwhile, Maddox comments on how MDMA can facilitate a sense of bodily ease, elevation, self-affirmation and smoothness in social and party settings:

> [MDMA] lifts all of me up and I am able to be like, 'Okay, this is my body and I feel good in it' like I forget my main issues with my body and I think about the good things. And sometimes I will get really vain. Like I will take a bunch of selfies or something. I go, 'Oh, I look so good' [...] like the way that I feel in [my body] like the smoothness, like the freedom. If I am high in some way it really affects like how I look at [my body] and how I experience it, and it will make me feel better.
>
> *Maddox (19, non-binary, queer)*

Interestingly, it was not only trans and non-binary participants who emphasised the constitutive role of drug use in affirmative gender expression. A number of cisgender participants also commented on this relation, illustrating how struggles with gendered norms can play a formative role in the elaboration of a range of queer sexual and social identities. Julian, a 33-year-old queer cisgender man, conveys something of this when he confides:

> I haven't always been as comfortable with the more feminine side of me. But now I guess I understand that my more feminine qualities are actually just part of my masculinity. Like being the sissy boy or being the effeminate boy growing up and not liking things that boys liked or were supposed to like, like sports and that kind of stuff. Maybe in some ways, my drug use was about coming to terms [and finding] self-acceptance [...] of how my gender is expressed [in terms of things like being] emotional, soft, [...] having like a gay voice, liking to bottom, the enjoyment of the arts.
>
> *Julian (33, queer, cis man)*

Reading these self-accounts through the lens of intoxication/disinhibition provides a particular vantage point from which to appreciate how the struggle with norms around gender *and* sexuality is real and pertinent for a much wider range of sexual and gender-diverse subjects than is sometimes asserted, even while the particular ways these norms are countered, embodied, reconfigured, rejected or resolved in the form of specific gender and sexual identities may differ substantially, with different social implications and consequences (see Halberstam 2017, Valentine 2007). Moreover, if practices of intoxication set sexual interaction and corporeal expressivity to the key of play and playfulness, as Wilmot proposes and many of our study participants' accounts suggest, we can see how these interactive scenes of 'uninhibited play' become significant in the performative experimentation with, and elaboration of, diverse sexual and gender identities and practices. As Susanna Paasonen writes:

> playful sexuality and sexual play are not antithetical to the felt gravity of sexual selves or identities but means of trying and acting them out, as well as for opening them up to variation and change. A focus on playfulness allows for conceptualising sexual selves as being in constant, more or less subtle, transformation.
>
> *(2018, p. 3)*

Queer spaces and practices of intoxication might be understood, then, as richly differentiated gatherings of sociocultural and material possibilities and self-enactments that some sexual and gender-diverse people work with to style themselves and try new things; to find out who they are and who they might be. Participation in queer counterpublics 'does not simply reflect identities formed elsewhere'; as Warner suggests, 'it is one of the ways by which its members' identities are formed and transformed' (2002, p. 121).

Conclusion

This chapter has argued that disinhibition offers a more promising conceptual framework to account for LGBTQ substance use than theories of minority stress alone because it opens up the question of what people do with drugs and how these doings help to transform the material pressures that sex and gender norms pose. This moves the scene of LGBTQ intoxication away from a model of palliative consumption and directs our attention to the constitutive effects of queer practices of intoxication – the sense in which these practices participate in the convocation of interactional modes and social pleasures that bear material significance for the elaboration of new identities. The concept of disinhibition recognises the enduring subordination of queer desires and gender-non-conformity to heteronormative, cis-normative imperatives but – unlike the theory of minority stress – casts intoxication as a practical strategy that grapples with this situation in multiple ways. More than practices whose transformative affects are confined to the self, our research demonstrates the significance of 'uninhibited play' for queer and trans world-making and identity-formation, for expanding the possibilities of corporeal self-expression, and for the transformations that queer counterpublics make possible (Warner 2002). Centring disinhibition enables a better appreciation of the constitutive effects of drug and alcohol use, directing attention to what practices of intoxication allow subjects collectively to *achieve*. Considering the impacts of queer and gender-diverse subcultures on popular culture more generally and historically, we can see how these forms of playful experimentation have contributed to the multiplication of sex and gender possibilities and a concomitant expansion of frames of sex and gender intelligibility (see Butler 2004 on grids of gender intelligibility).

Contrary to the theses of the life sciences, disinhibition does not represent some triumph of the body's baser instincts over the neurophysiological seat of moral adjudication, but could be regarded as a complex social loophole, a more or less accepted perforation in the disciplinary conventions of sexual and gendered propriety. Sexual and gender minorities have become adept at taking advantage of such loopholes to explore corporeal inclinations and facets of the self whose expression would normally be regarded or experienced as unacceptable.

In the process, they have learnt not simply to act on pre-existing desires, but also about the great multiplicity of social, sexual and corporeal pleasures and identifications, their creative potential. This multiplicity is evident, not only in the wide range of things that queer and trans people do with drugs, but in their responses to the terminology of 'intoxication', which a number of our participants regarded as reductive (see Pienaar et al. 2020b):

> I guess the word 'intoxicated' to me just doesn't describe the experience. And the person who uses the word, 'intoxicated' is either pretending or has no experience of actually being under the influence of some sort of drug [...] Just trying to sort of box it off [...] I think it's just 'state change' and there are so many different ways of changing one's state, whether it's through the influence of some sort of chemical or you know like meditation or breath work or dreaming or whatever. Like they're all just, it's all just, state change. It's all just part of that spectrum of consciousness.
>
> *Nico (40, queer, non-binary)*

The notion of 'state-change' Nico proposes here conveys how a queer theory of disinhibitions offers a more capacious angle of view onto LGBTQ+ drug use, not merely as a form of self-medication (understood as the attempt to return the body to a prior state of mental and/or physical health) but rather as a future-oriented strategy of 'counter-corporealisation', a form of queer world-making in which drugs are deployed as catalysts in experiments with the horizons of the body, gender, sexuality and subjectivity more broadly. On our reading, queer disinhibitions are more than a means of 'deviance disavowal', and they cannot be reduced to the crude binary of repression/liberation; they are a creative artform that, through playful and interactive experimentations, makes the places, spaces, sociabilities, connections and performances entailed in queer counterpublic activity enjoyable, appealing and meaningful for many LGBTQ+ people. Something to look forward to. Something that has given rise to new possibilities of existence – hence their political significance.

Acknowledgements

The research reported in this paper was funded by an Australian Research Council Discovery grant (DP170101373) awarded to Kane Race, Toby Lea and Kiran Pienaar. It was conducted by researchers from the University of Sydney, Monash University and the University of New South Wales' Centre for Social Research in Health (CSRH). CSRH is supported by a grant from the Australian Department of Health. The interviews were conducted by Dean Murphy, David Vakalis, Kiran Pienaar and Kane Race.

The authors would like to thank the study participants for sharing their experiences so generously and expansively. We also thank the project advisory panel for their insights and expertise; the Australian LGBTQ organisations that kindly assisted with recruitment; the editors of this Handbook for their encouragement and for being so patient with us; and the feedback on an earlier version of this paper we received from two anonymous reviewers, whose readings, suggestions and insights we drew on to improve the chapter.

Notes

1 On the performativity of stigma in the context of addiction, see Fraser et al. (2017).
2 The 'pub test' is an Australian term often used in media and political discourse to describe the general opinion of 'everyday Australians'. Often used as a proxy for 'public opinion', the term

suggestively connects public sphere theory to practices of social drinking in this setting. We use the term advisedly: who, after all, is the everyday Australian?

3 Alcohol has been shown to elevate cortisol – a hormone implicated in arousal – but the search for a physiologically discernable regulatory mechanism that selectively disinhibits certain behaviours has not been successful (see Reinarman & Leigh 1987).

4 The researcher's observations were made in the context of a study of (hetero)sexual drinking (his informants were six heterosexual couples). But we also take them to be indicative of a certain teleological approach to sex that prioritises pre-defined objectives (sexual conquest, penetration, orgasm) while bracketing other pleasures – the enjoyment, significance and possibilities of which have been elaborated by queers and feminists – as frustrating distractions from such 'serious' ends. (See generally Paasonen 2018, Jagose 2013 and Chapter 1.)

5 There are of course important differences between many trans identities and drag. It is nonetheless interesting that drug use was variously associated with gender experimentation, transformation and affirmation by participants who nominated transgender, non-binary and cisgender identities for themselves, respectively.

References

Anstie, F. E. (1865). *Stimulants and Narcotics, Their Mutual Relations.* Philadelphia: Lindsay and Blakiston.

Bancroft, A. (2009). *Drugs, Intoxication and Society.* Cambridge: Polity.

Bourne, A., Reid, D., Hickson, F., Torres-Rueda, S., Steinberg, P., & Weatherburn, P. (2015). "Chemsex" and harm reduction need among gay men in South London. *International Journal of Drug Policy, 26*, 1171–1176.

Butler, J. (1988). Performative acts and gender constitution: An essay in phenomenology and feminist theory. *Theatre Journal, 40*(4), 519–531.

Butler, J. (2004). *Undoing Gender.* New York/London: Routledge.

Carter, R. T., Lau, M. Y., Johnson, V., & Kirkinis, K. (2017). Racial discrimination and health outcomes among racial/ethnic minorities: A meta-analytic review. *Journal of Multicultural Counselling and Development, 45*(4), 232–259.

Critchlow, B. (1983). Blaming the booze: The attribution of responsibility for drunken behavior. *Personality and Social Psychology Bulletin, 9*(3), 451–473.

Crowley, M. (1968). *The Boys in the Band.* Great Britain: Secker and Warburg.

Davis, F. (1961). Deviance disavowal: The management of strained interaction by the visibly handicapped. *Social Problems, 9*(2), 120–132.

Dennis, F., & Farrugia, A. (2017). Drugged pleasures. *International Journal of Drug Policy, 49*, 1–172.

Dentato, M. P., Halkitis, P. N., & Orwat, J. (2013). Minority stress theory: An examination of factors surrounding sexual risk behavior among gay and bisexual men who use club drugs. *Journal of Gay & Lesbian Social Services, 25*(4), 509–525.

Florêncio, J. (2020). *Bareback Porn, Porous Masculinities, Queer Futures: The Ethics of Becoming-Pig.* London: Routledge.

Foucault, M. (1971). *The Order of Things.* New York: Vintage.

Foucault, M. (1976). *The History of Sexuality.* Vol. 1. Trans. Robert Hurley. London: Penguin.

Fraser, S, et al. (2017). Addiction stigma and the biopolitics of liberal modernity: A qualitative analysis. *International Journal of Drug Policy, 44*, 192–201.

Gillmore, M. R., Catalano, R. F., Morrison, D. M., Wells, E. A., Iritani, B., & Hawkins, J. D. (1990). Racial differences in acceptability and availability of drugs and early initiation of substance use. *The American Journal of Drug and Alcohol Abuse, 16*(3–4), 185–206.

Goffman, E. (1963). *Stigma: Notes on the Management of Spoiled Identity.* New York: Simon and Schuster.

Goldbach, J. T., Tanner-Smith, E. E., Bagwell, M., & Dunlap, S. (2014). Minority stress and substance use in sexual minority adolescents: A meta-analysis. *Prevention Science, 15*(3), 350–363.

Halberstam, J. (2017). *Trans*: A Quick and Quirky Account of Gender Variability.* Oakland: University of California Press.

Holt, M., & Treloar, C. (2008). Pleasure and drugs. *International Journal of Drug Policy, 19*(5), 349–352.

Hunt, G., Antin, T., Sanders, E., & Sisneros, M. (2019). Queer youth, intoxication and queer drinking spaces. *Journal of Youth Studies, 22*(3), 380–400.

Jagose, A. (2013). *Orgasmology.* Durham: Duke University Press.

Lehavot, K., & Simoni, J. M. (2011). The impact of minority stress on mental health and substance use among sexual minority women. *Journal of Consulting and Clinical Psychology, 79*(2), 159.
MacAndrew, C., & Edgerton, R. B. (1969). *Drunken Comportment: A Social Explanation*. Chicago: Aldine Publishing Company.
McKirnan, D. J., Ostrow, D. G., & Hope, B. (1996). Sex, drugs and escape: A psychological model of HIV-risk sexual behaviours. *AIDS Care, 8*(6), 655–670.
Meyer, I. H. (2003). Prejudice, social stress, and mental health in lesbian, gay, and bisexual populations: conceptual issues and research evidence. *Psychological Bulletin, 129*(5), 674.
Muehlberger, C. W. (1956). Medicolegal aspects of alcohol intoxication. *Michigan State Bar Journal, 35*, 38–42.
Partanen, J. (1981). Toward a theory of intoxication. In Room, R., & Colin, G. (eds.), *Alcohol and Disinhibition: Nature and Meaning of the Link* (pp. 27–41). Rockville: US Department of Health and Human Services.
Paasonen, S. (2018). *Many Splendored Things: Thinking Sex and Play*. London: Goldsmiths Press.
Pienaar, K., Murphy, D. A., Race, K., & Lea, T. (2020a). Drugs as technologies of the self: Enhancement and transformation in LGBTQ cultures. *International Journal of Drug Policy, 78*, 102673.
Pienaar, K., Murphy, D., Race, K., & Lea, T. (2020b). 'To be intoxicated is to still be me, just a little blurry' – Drugs, enhancement and transformation in lesbian, gay, bisexual, transgender and queer cultures. In Fiona Hutton (eds.), *Cultures of Intoxication: Key Issues and Debates* (pp. 139–164). Cham: Springer.
Race, K. (2009). *Pleasure Consuming Medicine: The Queer Politics of Drugs*. Durham: Duke University Press.
Race, K. (2015). 'Party and play': Online hook-up devices and the emergence of PNP practices among gay men. *Sexualities, 18*(3), 253–275.
Race, K. (2017). *The Gay Science: Intimate Experiments with the Problem of HIV*. London/New York: Routledge.
Reinarman, C., & Leigh, B. C. (1987). Culture, cognition, and disinhibition: Notes on sexuality and alcohol in the age of AIDS. *Contemporary Drug Problems, 14*, 435.
Rhodes, T. (1996). Culture, drugs and unsafe sex: Confusion about causation. *Addiction, 91*(6), 753–758.
Rosario, M., Schrimshaw, E. W., & Hunter, J. (2004). Predictors of substance use over time among gay, lesbian, and bisexual youths: An examination of three hypotheses. *Addictive Behaviors, 29*(8), 1623–1631.
Shih, R. A., Miles, J. N., Tucker, J. S., Zhou, A. J., & D'Amico, E. J. (2010). Racial/ethnic differences in adolescent substance use: Mediation by individual, family, and school factors. *Journal of Studies on Alcohol and Drugs, 71*(5), 640–651.
Smith, R. (1992). *Inhibition: History and Meaning in the Sciences of Mind and Brain*. Oakland: University of California Press.
Valentine, D. (2007). *Imagining Transgender*. Durham: Duke University Press.
Warner, M. (2002). *Publics and Counterpublics*. New York: Zone Books.
Wilmot, R. (1981). Sexual drinking and drift. *Journal of Drug Issues, 11*(1), 1–16.
Worth, H., & Rawstorne, P. (2005). Crystallizing the HIV epidemic: Methamphetamine, unsafe sex, and gay diseases of the will. *Archives of Sexual Behavior, 34*(5), 483.

18

RITUAL TO REFLEXIVITY – FROM PROMOTION AND PROBLEMATISATION OF INTOXICATION TO PROPORTIONALITY

John O'Brien

Introduction

This chapter offers a social theoretical examination of 'excess' and its regulation by drinkers in drinking occasions. Social theory attempts to offer an integrative account of social change and is oriented in particular to the question of the meaning and effect of modernisation. This is of value in alcohol studies, as research on drinking and drunkenness tends to present them in a fragmentary and negative manner, being highly specialised and focused on problems, obscuring the wider role and shaping of drinking, excess and their social context. Modernisation could also be argued to be the single greatest influence on drinking culture, profoundly effecting availability and the mode of consumption. The chapter thus examines one of the major dimensions of modernisation: deritualisation, which is a central theme in so much social theory from Durkheim, to Weber, to Foucault to Bauman. It presents an ideal-type distinction between the strongly ritualised drinking of smaller-scale, less complex societies and the destructuring of the drinking ritual in complex, modern societies. The ritualisation of drinking has a moderating effect on acute and chronic harms resulting from it, as well as producing culturally constructive outcomes. But ritual is conservative, and due to its scripted nature, is not 'creative'. Modernisation also does not see the disappearance of ritual. Drinking rituals continue, but in an altered form, with major significance for the type of drinking and degree of excess.

Promotion and Problematisation, or Proportion?

Drinking is deeply entwined within social life and is clearly a normal aspect of human culture at large, as all human groups have used some form of psychoactive substance, and nearly all have used alcohol (Sherratt, 1995b: 34). Discourse on alcohol intoxication as a whole however has a schizoid quality. Alcohol use is promoted on the one hand through several of the axiomatic 'goods' of modernity, such as freedom, choice, equality and participation in the public sphere. These values have their corresponding expressions in drinking: in liberalisation of alcohol markets and drinking culture, alcohol as a feature of consumer culture, the

DOI: 10.4324/9780429058141-23

right to drink to 'excess' indicating social and political participation, and a utilitarian argument that private 'vice' is a public good in reference to how it generates jobs and revenues.

However, there is a powerful 'problem perspective'. The focus of scholarship on drinking has tended to be on problems associated with alcohol as an intoxicant. Drinking is the subject of 'problematisation', whereby alcohol use and intoxication become something to be known, an object of discourse and something to be governed (see Bacchi, 2015). Concepts and movements such as paternalistic regulation, temperance, abstinence, prohibition, the disease model, alcohol problems model and public health, which frame alcohol negatively as an inherent danger, are products of processes that are constitutive of Western modernity, such as Protestantism and 'civility' and their culture of individualism, self-control and responsibility (Levine, 1992; Valverde, 1998). Problematisations are a product of exploitative national tax systems and state alcohol or opium monopolies and the political tactic of denigrating dominated groups as inherently associated with uncontrolled intoxication also, which produced anti-alcohol and drug movements (O'Brien, 2018). In the contemporary era, alcohol has become the target of public health policy due to its strong implication in morbidity and mortality (Babor, 2010). Public health policy, under the guidance of the WHO, has developed a goal of reducing alcohol consumption to the lowest possible level, using the rationale that all consumption involves risk, with no safe level of consumption, and most importantly due to the finding that the overall level of consumption increases the risks stemming from consumption for the cohort of problem users (Butler et al. 2017: 14–16). The current public health consensus is part of the long-debate about how alcohol should be controlled, which has gone through phases of free-market permissiveness, paternalism, prohibition and the AA two-population addiction model. Discourse on intoxication is thus largely either individualistic, narrow or politicised.

Intoxication itself is a compromised term, as it has considerable roots in nineteenth-century medical science, criminology and the moralisation and politicisation of drunkenness in temperance movements. The term contains a sense of danger and biological reductionism, as it literally denotes poison. It's etymological provenance in the late sixteenth century points to an association with spirits which were prominent in the nascent consumer culture, and with 'peculiar substances' – novel psychoactive substances – from the emerging European system of global trade, both of which were linked with a paranoia over threats to the established order by the dynamic society these substances were a part of. Even the term alcohol, describing a chemically distilled substance rather than a beverage, signifies a pharmacological understanding that fragments the substance into something shorn from its context.

Redefining the question of 'intoxication' as a question of 'proportion' – what is considered proportionate and what is considered disproportionate – would provide a more holistic viewpoint on the question. 'Drink', 'glass' or other native terms better capture alcohol as a culturally embedded social practice, and 'drunk' better denotes the cultural definition that a socially sanctioned measure or definition of what is proportionate has been passed. Latin languages, deriving the word for intoxication from ēbrius, even more directly refer to what is 'out of measure'. The Platonic notion of the golden mean is relevant here, as is Aristotle's (2009) idea that virtue is the middle road between vicious extremes – an ethos that native terms for 'intoxication' implicitly contain. Philosophy embedded in language is furthermore expressed in social practice, as the Mediterranean region appears to have a Hellenic cultural inheritance that emphasises the ritualisation of consumption, which has salutary effects. Virtue ethics did not spring from a philosopher's head, but from a way of life, part of which was the ritualisation of drinking and a strong value placed on drinking proportionately in these contexts – and a problematisation of hubris – which drunkenness was emblematic of

(Nelson, 2005; Rinella, 2010; MacLachlan, 2014). Proportion could thus be seen to be the result of a social learning process that inculcates a pragmatically useful form of conduct, in that it provides the schemes for dealing with recurrent action problems, which have emerged through trial and error, with pragmatic solutions crystallising into rituals, habits and institutions, which ultimately gain objectivity and power over individual people while also acting as a resource for them (Bateson, 2000: 273; Berger & Luckmann, 2007: 43–44, 46, 48). Such an action problem is the question of how to drink proportionately,[1] which is a feature of every drinking culture.

Learning to Measure Drinks: Culture and Ritual

Drinkers learn to drink proportionately. Constructive drinking could be described as involving a learned sense of proportion of what is in due measure, with use protected from what is culturally defined as excess, so that 'goods' are achieved through it. These goods are drinking that is supportive of circles of recognition that are supportive of identities, the capacity to modulate pleasure and risk, and minimise harm.

An alignment of *drug, set* and *setting* establishes the practices, cognitive frames and behavioural scripts that allow the regulation of consumption and the controlling of the experience (Zinberg, 1984). Indeed, most alcohol use is non-problematic as people have learned how to produce safe and positive outcomes through an appropriate tuning of the elements of drug, set and setting, with the majority of consumption used to facilitate pleasurable sociability (Peele & Grant, 1999). 'Drugs' are an aspect of the material culture of a group, which present particular spectrum of possible experiences. 'Set' is the mental frame, intention and expectation that the user brings to their use. From a developmental perspective, what is culturally acceptable drinking behaviour is learned in every society. People learn the rules of the game for when, where, with whom, and how to consume, and what is excess. Every culture has various definitions of types of excess and ideal forms of 'drunken comportment'. Users will have a learned sense of proportion also, meaning a set of internal controls that dictates the right way, the right time and the right place to consume.

Becker (1963) showed how users have to learn how to consume psychoactive substances properly, with this often requiring a considerable amount of skill, and how to interpret the feelings that a substance provokes. They learn what to expect from using a substance, with the 'expectancy effect' crucial in framing the nature of the experience, making it a cultural process rather than simple drug-administration of a particular concentration of alcohol in the blood (McAndrew & Edgerton, 1969; Room, 2001). As McAndrew and Edgerton (1969: 88, italics in original) famously stated: '*[o]ver the course of socialization, people learn about drunkenness what their society "knows" about drunkenness; and accepting and acting upon the understandings thus imparted to them, they become the living confirmation of their society's teachings*'.

'Setting' refers to the context of use, meaning both the immediate environment of use and the broader cultural environment. Alcohol itself plays an important role in constituting this broader cultural environment. Culture is a meaningful web of symbols that guides conduct (Geertz, 1973), and drinkers have an ear for what they are drinking as well as taste, as drinks are part of the symbolic web of social life. It is an important metaphor in culture, as with the vine, grapes, wine, its ritual consumption and drunkenness in the Abrahamic tradition representing the favour and disfavour of God. Alcohol like other psychoactive substances is also an important element of non-verbal symbolic communication (Gusfield, 1987: 75–76; Sherratt, 1995b: 11). Drinks and the manner in which they are used is a code that communicates messages about the meaning of events, values, attitudes towards the world, social status, affiliation to various communities, gender identity and so on. Ritual is an important aspect of setting, institutionalising stylised and rule-bound modes of consumption. The emotions that underpin ritual action and the prescriptions and proscriptions involved are unusual for the strength with which they are held (Heath, 1988: 397), tending to be linked with the 'strong evaluations' of a culture.

However, when the constellation of drug, set and setting becomes disrupted and undermined (which we will turn to in a subsequent section), rather than a cosmic order that produces constructive drinking, the outcome can be problematic for users, either through the development of dependency or through chaotic experiences of drunkenness. This can be due to problems with the *setting* due to stigmatisation, lack of informal social controls or consumption happening in aversive environments; *set* due to inexperience, mental health problems or trauma; and *drug* due to the potency, adulteration or inability to know the dose taken (Hartogsohn, 2017).

Ritual Drinking

Rituals are special occasions, requiring some collective preparation and rehearsal, have hence a dramatic function, are particularly meaningful and bound by rules and a strong sense of what is proportional and equally what is proscribed. They can be extraordinary – as with fiesta drinking, or banal – as where wine is incorporated as a foodstuff in meals, where despite the quotidian character it retains a special character as a focus of a daily ritual. Alongside the small number of abstinent societies, which have rituals focused on psychoactive substances other than alcohol, there are various ritualisations of drinking across and within societies. There is constrained ritual drinking, such as that of Orthodox Jews. There is banal drinking where alcohol is a food as in certain Mediterranean wine-drinking societies. There is communal fiesta drunkenness characteristic of medieval European and certain developing societies (Room & Mäkelä, 2000). There is the everyday drinking of 'wet' and occasional binges of 'dry' societies (Levine, 1992), and heroic and modern drinking (Partanen, 1991). There is also considerable diversity within a culture based on the social field of alcohol consumption (Lunnay et al. 2011).

Ritual is a fundamental character of drinking in all of these types of culture nonetheless. It possesses consistent elements. It is a specified place, time and manner of consumption, and with drinking nested within other activities and goals. They are usually pleasurable and exciting – involving a modulation of risk and pleasure (for example, with drinking games), are directed at action (as in a festival marking the start of the university year and the work and sacrifices that must be made), marking transitions (such as New Year or gaining adult status), transmit implicit values (with drinks often expressing gender, regional, national and class identities), conjure or reinforce bonds (with drinking inducing a shared 'flow' state, making the same steps and sharing – as in the rounds system), and articulate status and exclusions (as with the gendered nature of very many drinking rituals).

The Ritual Process

A more elaborated ideal type of ritual drinking can be given through the concept of *the ritual process*. The discussion that follows will necessarily be brief and will suffer from some diachronic and synchronic fuzziness in the description of drinking patterns, as it is a broad overview, but the hope is that the points will stand. The concept was developed by the cultural anthropologist Victor Turner in the 1960s, and since then it has been endlessly used to conceptualise how alcohol and other psychoactive substances are used. It describes a process through which there is a separation from normal social roles, an entering into a special constellation of greater freedom, possibility and equality, which is nonetheless strictly regulated, which comes to an end with participants finally returning to the social order. The middle, in-between phase, which he labelled 'liminality', is the critical one, denoting the moment of fraternity, sorority and liberty which the consumption of alcohol facilitates and symbolises.

The ritual process provides social control over consumption. Goody (2002) has argued that small-scale societies, in which the ritual process plays a significantly larger role than in complex modern societies, can be characterised by high levels of self and social restraint and consideration to others, expressed in moderate drinking occasions. This is because the ritualisation of drinking occasions and the complex web of obligations that are dramatised within them impose limits on behaviour. Alcohol use is tied up in the suspension of the social order, and through this refreshes it. Drawing on Victor Turner (1969), and his work on *rites de passage*, it is evident that the use of psychoactive substances is dramatic, and a means of symbolically keying a periodic shift of society into liminality (or in more prosaic language, a 'time-out') where the roles and hierarchies of the social structure are temporarily suspended, and people enter an in-between phase of reflection, creativity and less regulated action. In its classic form, the ritual process is a significant event in the life of a community, but it has similarities in more prosaic drinking rituals, as with Mediterranean drinking, where an aperitif marks the entrance in a somewhat liminal moment of greater freedom and equality which a glass of wine symbolises, and a coffee signalling the return to social structural roles. A movement from structure to anti-structure is frequently associated with such use of psychoactive substances (Gusfield, 1987; Pedersen, 1994; Heath, 2000).

It is the argument of Victor Turner (1969) that the ritual process is a cultural universal. Anthropological and cultural sociological scholarship tends to emphasise relativism and social constructionism, noting the wide variety of drinking patterns, historical contingency and social change, serving as evidence of the constructed nature of drinking occasions. However, as Heath (2000: 160) notes, 'it is striking that drinking often seems to serve similar purposes in very different cultures and contexts'. The reason for this underlying sameness can be explained by the fact that drinking occasions tend to take the shape of grand and mundane rituals, that conform to Turner's (1969) model of the ritual process. Drinking occasions, as forms of the ritual process, mark and structure temporal and life-course transitions, which offer a time-out from the normal roles and routine of mundane social hierarchies, where, accompanying the 'liminality' where fellowship and freedom are experienced, there is a dramatisation of sharing, which alcohol plays a central role in.

Transition

As noted above, the ritual process structures transition, and accordingly rituals cluster around the major life transitions of birth, coming of age, marriage and death, along with the range of other transitions marking changes in status, rank, role or the lifestyles, where individuals or groups step into a new identity. Rituals involving alcohol, other psychoactive substances and sanctioned excess are cross-culturally associated with transitions and initiations (see Douglas, 1987: 4; Heath, 2000: 125, 168, 196; Bancroft, 2009: 59; Babor et al. 2010: 15–16). For example, the birth of a child is often marked by a drinking occasion, as is the entry of the child into the community (Heath, 2000: 24, 82). A ritual marking one's right to drink often accompanies the acquisition of adult status. Courtship and marriage tend to be wrapped up and marked by rituals involving alcohol. Initiation into a group, or clique, or institution such as a university or army also is expressed by a particular grand drinking ritual and cycle of petty rituals. Drinking occasions often mark a change in the circumstances of the wider community, such as the accession to the throne of a new ruler, or in commemorations of a victory or defeat symbolically marked with toasts (Heath, 2000: 30).

As a psychoactive substance, alcohol plays a useful role in structuring time, by subjectively breaking up its flow, through commencing a new type of time with distinct qualities. Alongside the high points of ritual, the cycle and rhythm of cultivation of the inputs and the process of production also structured time, for instance, in how the stages in the production of wine structured the year in Southern Europe and the Near East. Alcohol rituals play a keying role, indicating the move to a new form of time, patterning movements between structure and anti-structure (Gusfield, 1987: 84), which varies between occasional crescendos of rare but highly significant events, to the more mundane regular peaks of everyday life, such as how coffee, cigarettes, aperitifs, post-work drinks and night caps mark the passage through different phases of the day. Ritual modes of drinking have long structured weeks, through marking the weekend or Sabbath, which includes wine in its central rite. Transitions in the year are marked by alcohol rituals, such as saturnalia, harvest (including specific rituals marking the harvest of ingredients for alcohol, or the maturation of drinks, such as wine harvest, Oktoberfest and the Dionysia) and carnival preceding the fasting of Lent (Heath, 2000: 20). This function of alcohol rituals in structuring time was of course much more important historically before clock time whose ascendance is a response to social complexity (see Netting, 1964), though of course it lives on in a secondary role.

Controlled Decontrolling

In the phase of liminality, there is 'anti-structure', where greater freedom from limits is allowed, with such decontrolling occasionally going so far as to become 'carnivalesque', involving an inversion of hierarchies and a reversal of the normal structures of social life (Bakhtin, 1984: 123). McAndrew and Edgerton (1969) conceptualised drinking rituals that involved sanctioned excess as 'time outs', in which there was 'cultural remission', where people could step outside of the normal responsibilities of social roles, with the rules of social conduct simplified. These are however not based on a pharmacologically driven disinhibition but rather on the symbolic cue it provides for a loosening of strictures (McAndrew & Edgerton, 1969). Thus, rather than 'intoxication, what takes place is controlled decontrolling, where norms that are bent are done so in a socially acceptable way, and in a way that has an established social role' (Bancroft, 2009: 52).

This is expressed in greater informality, transcendence of mundane roles, looser limits, a greater freedom for people to express themselves and greater emotional and affective freedom, with the possibility of ribaldry and vulgarity, at times more sexual freedom, foolishness, horseplay, aggressiveness and assertiveness (Gusfield, 1987: 79, 83; Gefou-Madianou, 1992: 12). There is often heightened competitiveness in these moments where consumption runs alongside contests such as drinking games, games of skill such as cards, games of taste, competitive displays of waste, debating or slagging. There may not merely be licence for this, but in some cultures, there is even an expectation that drinking will lead to such conduct, with consumption symbolically framing and delimiting such behaviour in social life. It is not simply that alcohol promotes relaxation through its physiological effects, but also that its presence and use symbolically frame situations as having this meaning (Heath, 2000). Rituals involving alcohol consumption are also moments where normal cognitive restraints are lowered. In the phase of liminality, participants are encouraged to think about the basic assumptions of their culture, and what lies behind the obvious and the taken for granted (Turner, 1969). Drinking rituals are of course moments for more free discussion and debate, as well as greater playfulness with morality. Furthermore, in the liminal phase, an object is often used as a vehicle for reflection, which in an abstract way symbolises deep cultural values and community. Many cultures use psychoactive substances as such an object (Sherratt, 1995a: 6). For example, for the Kofyar, beer acts as a 'locus of value', serving as a metaphor for the state of social relationships, and as a way of articulating the good life (Netting, 1964: 378). Similarly, wine plays the same role in Christianity, or in much of the pre-Islamic poetry of the Middle East, and in Islam and various Protestant sects, Mormons, and among Alcoholics Anonymous, alcohol is important alternately, in a negative way, as a way of symbolising the threat to good order in social relationships.

Decontrolling is controlled by how rituals are delimited and enclosed. Drinking rituals take place in a 'recognised social context' (Douglas, 1987: 4) that is enclosed in space and time (Heath, 2000: 137). Drinking occasions are bound by temporal divisions, which dictate when consumption can and should occur, involving what types of drink, alongside what types of behaviour and with what types of other people. As well as time, there are particular spaces where these should occur, which are often set apart from everyday life, or specially constructed and laid out for the purpose. The word 'liminality' stems from the Latin 'limen', meaning 'threshold', which is stepped over to enter into the out-of-the-ordinary (Turner, 1969: 94). 'Leisure' stems from *licere*, meaning 'to be allowed', which shares the same root as 'licence', thereby indicating that freedom and control are different aspects of the same concept. Indeed, decontrolling is intimately connected to self-control, as greater freedom goes alongside a demonstration that one can stay within limits, as in the moment of loosening there is a demonstration that the person is a competent actor. As Turner (1969) explained, liminality is a type of destructuring that is prestructured, as the ritual process organises the experience of decontrolling in an ordered and planned manner, with people experiencing a freedom that is simultaneously acted out according to a script. Drinking rituals thus contain a 'within-limits clause' (McAndrew & Edgerton, 1969), which 'implies culturally shared expectations and permissiveness, not a generalized pharmokinetic disinhibition' (Heath, 2000: 197). A crucial final limit is the presence of masters of ceremony, who play the role of maintaining order and directing the action, ensuring that the disordering remains orderly. These figures are representatives of tradition and community. Some contemporary drinking rituals continue to have masters of ceremonies of sorts, in the shape of publicans, hosts and toastmasters, though these are residual figures compared to elders in traditional rituals or the symposiarchs who orchestrated symposia.

Communitas

'Communitas' is one of the characteristics of the liminal, middle phase of rituals, which involves a strong feeling of equality and fellowship with others, due to how the liminal personae have been stripped of the markers of their social structural identities of rank, status, property and so on, and are levelled, even becoming structurally indefinable, playing with fundamental categories of identity (Turner, 1969: 95, 102, 104, 106). Drinking occasions can of course be opportunities for displaying status, but they have been very often interpreted as moments where factionalism and individualism are restrained, with the emphasis shifting to oneness, equality and fraternity. The reason most often given for drinking is indeed the experience of 'communitas', though through the common language terms of sociability, bonding, solidarity and the pleasure that flows from this (Gusfield, 1987: 79, 82;

Gefou-Madianou, 1992: 1, 11; Heath, 2000: 196; Hunt et al. 2005: 239). For this reason, it has a long history as an icon of associational life in guilds, fraternities, clubs, professional associations, political factions and machines and so on.

One of the main ways that communitas is produced is through *gift-giving*, which is dramatised in these rituals, which establishes an asymmetry and obligation between the parties, setting in train a process of reciprocity that a relationship is built on (see Mauss, 1992, Tutorsky, 2016 for an application to alcohol), with what is exchanged symbolising a recognition of the other's identity. Though this could be seen as a mere pleasantry, historically it was in fact the centre of social life before a legal order and markets come to underpin the social order, seen, for instance, in the drink exchanges among the elites of early civilisations, through which allegiances and peace were maintained (Enright, 1996). Gift giving in rituals involving alcohol is produced through a number of techniques, to establish a communion. Alcohol is typically given as a gift in some way, and it is reciprocally exchanged then. Hospitality is given as a gift, of which alcohol is an almost universal symbol. Drinking frequently takes place in the context of a meal, which is paradigmatic context of sharing. The etiquette that surrounds consumption is a means of giving and receiving respect, in turn, for instance through serving the other and observing the niceties of the ritual. Toasting is a near-universal feature of drinking rituals, where words are given to articulate the personal linkages between participants. There is a giving of oneself over to the ritual and the enthusiasm of the group, becoming fully involved in collective practices that go alongside drinking, such as singing, chanting, dancing, stories and games. Part of this is the incorporation of the same substance into one's body as others. Finally, there is frequently gift giving of alcohol or something in the context of the drinking ritual, to the ancestors, spirits and gods (Heath, 2000: 176).

Beneficial Rituals?

Psychoactive substances are frequently not associated with harmful health and social outcomes because of how they are intertwined into a cosmic order of ritual, myth, systems of reciprocal exchange, nested in an overall sense of proportion. Strong drinking rituals can result in culturally constructive outcomes of moderation and meaning-making. Partanen (1991: 213), for example, has noted that 'the ritualization of drinking, its ceremonial uses, do, in fact, exert a dampening effect on more extreme forms of drunken comportment'. Even where such ritual drinking could be considered extreme, as in Heath's (1958) example of the Bolivian Camba, or Beccaria's (2010) study of the Alpini, there can be a remarkable lack of problems considering the intensity, scale and duration of such events. Even among heroin users, widely considered to be the most powerless of psychoactive substance users in the face of their addiction to an intoxicant, it has been shown that use takes place in social rituals which are the frameworks that self-regulation and harm reduction strategies occur within (Grund, 1993). Indeed, Zinberg et al. (1975) have argued that '[c]enturies of experience with intoxicants point clearly to social control, not prohibition as the only humane and reasonably successful means of managing their use', whereby use is permitted within ritual contexts and customs.

A startling though contested finding of anthropological research on small-scale societies, whose cultures have not yet been fatally disrupted by being incorporated into the orbit of a metropolitan power, is that drinking and psychoactive substance use at large tend not to have pernicious social and health outcomes due to the way they are intertwined into a cosmic order, or an ordered totality, composed of ritual and associated myth and systems of reciprocal exchange (see Heath, 1958; Room, 1984; Tutorsky, 2016; Hartogsohn, 2017). Heath (1988: 398) explains that 'the idea that drinking is associated with problems is absent in many cultures, and the idea that it might be a major factor in the aetiology of a debilitating disease is highly unusual'. The argument goes, in brief, that alcohol use is normative, linked with beneficial outcomes rather than harms, due to its consumption in a ritually bound context involving considerable social control, with the substance seen as sacred rather than a permanently available mundane item, and is linked with the reaffirmation of social bonds and hierarchies.

Such an argument is likely to be contested through the observation that modernity has simply created a conflict between the rewards that psychoactive substances have provided in human evolution and the contemporary environment, through the enormous increase in availability of potent substances in the form of refined, purified and synthetic drugs and distilled spirits and modern beers, in the same way that obesity and diabetes are the result of the conflict between evolved tastes and the availability of fats and sugars (Nesse & Berridge, 1997). However, humans have always lived in substance-rich environments, with technological means for allowing the administration of more potent doses developed early, and moreover, despite this, all groups entirely foregoing certain forms of intoxication, though they are technically freely available.

The ritualisation of alcohol consumption has been offered as an explanation for the almost universal consumption of alcohol by Orthodox Jews and the very low levels of 'alcoholism' (Bales, 1944; Snyder, 1958). The higher level of consumption of secular Jews is linked with their removal from the constraints of tradition and ritual participation. Ritualisation has though continued despite the secularisation of Jews through the cultural legacy of a strong presence of elders to teach moderate consumption patterns, strong norms about who can drink and how, strong sanctions to enforce these norms, enacted in recognised ritual settings (Glassner & Berg, 1980). In Western, contemporary societies, something similar has been found. Alcohol problems are more likely the more consumption is distant from community and family life, with problems tending to 'occur in inverse proportion to the "communal orientation" of different groups' (Heath, 2000). Where drinking primarily occurs in the context of a meal, and where young people drink in orbit of adults, problems are less common (Brodsky & Peele 1999: 196). The link is not absolute of course, for example, with the traditionally very high levels of consumption in France linked with chronic diseases such as cirrhosis.

Groups experiencing cultural breakdown have the most severe alcohol problems. In American alcoholism research, Irish Americans have been the other to Orthodox Jews. The explanation offered is the deritualisation of drinking. This occurred through the cultural trauma of the Great Famine which devastated the peasantry, followed with an aggressive civilising offensive led by the Catholic Church that attacked popular ritual. Subsequently, the Irish were stigmatised as an outsider group in the USA compounding the ethnic stigmatisation of them in the UK that labelled them as drunkards, triggering an ambivalence towards alcohol alongside a self-fulfilling prophecy of living up to deviant labels. Finally, the aforementioned lack of established rituals made 'drunkenness' more likely (Stivers, 2000). The considerable difficulties of other groups can be found in the destruction of cultural frameworks and the ritual context of consumption through colonisation, internal colonisation and deculturation, such as communities previously isolated from the state and markets that become quickly dominated by metropoles (Tutorsky, 2016). The experience of many Native American groups and other indigenous people who have suffered cultural trauma has been even more extreme, while re-construction of traditional practices, spirituality and culture has been associated with more positive outcomes in alcohol use (Stone et al. 2006: 237). The enormous increase in alcohol-related morbidity and mortality in Russia following the collapse of Communism was linked with rapid cultural change, the undermining of a way of life and consequent fracturing of rituals (Cutler et al. 2006: 98).

Ritual and Conservatism

Much of the literature on the ritualisation of alcohol in cultural anthropology has an implicit message about its beneficial effects as a moderating and regulating force. However, a normative question is: to whom are these rituals beneficial? More recent scholarship has examined drinking rituals as an expression of power dynamics, which was underplayed in earlier scholarship (such as many of the studies referred to above), which have a functionalist bent (Dietler, 2006). Victor Turner's analysis of ritual equally is functionalist to a degree, emphasising order more than power. Drinking rituals however are about articulating status as well as equality, as inclusion implies exclusion, and the experience of equality and sameness implies difference from those outside the circle. Ritual often concentrates people in coordinated action for the recognition of rank based on age, gender, kinship, status, class, status group or party. Indeed historically, there have been prominent outsider groups with respect to rituals involving drinking: children, women, slaves and other outsider groups, who cross-culturally have been partially or fully excluded (Gefou-Madianou, 1992: 7).

Furthermore, women (to choose just one of the outsiders to ritual) are often in supporting, subordinate positions (Beccaria, 2010). This is sometimes presented as relatively benign due to it amounting to the expression of different systems of honour for the genders, rather than absolute social exclusion – for example, with women dominant in the domestic sphere, and men dominant in the public sphere, including its drinking rituals (Gefou-Madianou, 1992). Although this runs counter to the strong norm of mass culture, equality and autonomy in modern society, this feature could also be read as a way of dampening status competition between drinkers and reducing costs and anxiety related to this, through the separation of gender spheres. In pre-capitalist societies, women are often the producers and suppliers of the drink men consume from which they derive some status (Dietler, 2006). Women have played prominent roles as 'keepers of men' in drinking rituals. Women have historically played a large role as mistresses of ceremonies in drinking rituals (such as ladies in royal courts, inn keepers, geishas or shebeen queens), acting as hostesses who prepare and serve drink, acting as a moderating influence by coordinating the action and checking excesses through their power as an insider-outsider (Gefou-Madianou, 1992).

The ritual process in its ideal-type, classical form does not exist in complex, pluralistic societies, and is instead replaced by ritual-like forms, as we will see in the following section. Indeed, ritual is associated with features that modern reform movements have problematised – hierarchy, authority, exclusion and social policing of taboos. This is not merely a normative point. Mary Douglas (1987), who coined the term 'constructive drinking' to describe the culturally constructive nature of ritualised drinking studied by anthropologists, elsewhere (1996: 106–125) noted an unwarranted tendency to romanticise 'traditional societies'. The reality is that when people are presented with the choice to leave traditional societies, they invariably do so in order to engage in an agentic construction of personal identity. As alcohol becomes a commodity with the marketisation of societies, the hold of the right to drink as a patriarchal and gerontacratic privilege tends to lessen, and a cash economy allows historically outsider groups such as women the ability to participate in drinking occasions that were previously closed to them, frequently sparking resistance and outrage from the formerly privileged insiders (Suggs, 1996). There has also been a criticism of research focusing on the integrative and constructive role of drinking as ignoring political economy, ignoring the role of class and the capitalism also (Singer, 1986). While this is an important observation, it is equally important to note that for the greater part of human existence, psychoactive substance use was shaped more by local practices, with capitalism a historically recent social form, that has undermined ritual by increasingly replacing ritual with market-based relations.

The Liminoid. Ritual in Modernity

Deritualisation?

Any quick search of the terms 'alcohol' and 'liminality' will show hundreds of results, serving as evidence for the power of this concept. However, the concept is frequently used out of the context of Turner's (1969) own theory, as his interpretation was that ritual and liminality did not exist in the form he described from his anthropological fieldwork in modern societies. It is odd then how frequently 'liminality' is used to describe contemporary drinking. On a superficial level, this model can apply to grand community rituals, the festive cycle of communities and religious traditions, 'binges' typical of friends partying at home or in the night-time economy, self-created rituals of get-togethers and mealtime customs, the skid-row drinker who finds belonging and relief in the reciprocity, hustle and consumption of alcohol, and the solitary compulsive drinker in a rut of returning again and again to alcohol as a symbol of escape and attachment. The superficiality of lumping so many disparate types of drinking together is an indication of the loose manner in which the concept has been used.

The rituals involving drinking of traditional and conservative societies do not exist *per se* in complex pluralistic societies. This is the source of some of the problematic application of the concept of liminality for understanding excess. The grand rituals that once structured lives and communities are in rapid decline, replaced by the evanescent transitory and choice-based arrangements of liquid modernity, meaning that this age-old basis of informal social control plays a role in regulating consumption less and less it would seem. The traction of cultural traditions in general appears to be decreasing, seen in the rise of a globalised form of consumption focused on hedonism, in contrast to the myriad drinking worlds of the past (Gordon et al. 2012). But the role of ritual in structuring drinking and drunkenness changes rather than disappears.

The previous overview of the way that the ritual process provides social control to drinking occasions, combined with prominent anthropologists claims that this results in a moderation of harm in the contexts where this constellation exists, raises the question about what is going on in modern societies? A quick explanation would be the classic argument in Durkheimian social theory that the traditional mechanisms of social integration and regulation have been undermined in modern societies. An ideal-type distinction between 'small-scale' and 'complex societies' is, of course, just that – an abstraction that is conceptually useful, as of course in reality all societies sit on a messy continuum, and societies labelled as complex have features of simple societies and vice versa. However, Berreman (1978: 226–228, 234) does note that the terms are on balance useful. In the same way that Durkheim (2002) showed that certain groups and demographics had a cultural immunity to suicide, certain groups possess a cultural immunity to alcohol problems. Mediterranean societies have possessed such a relative immunity historically because of the way alcohol was woven into the 'matrix of the personal, social, and religious lives of the people of these societies' (Gefou-Madianou, 1992: 22).

A Durkheimian reading, emphasising the controlled nature of consumption in simple societies, and the anomic nature of consumption in complex societies is a staple of alcohol studies. Bacon (1962) explained the more problematic nature of consumption in complex societies because of their more secular and individualistic nature which provided weaker social controls. In addition, complexity and the demand for controlled conduct due to the complexity, discipline and the pressures of coordination make alcohol incompatible with many spheres of life, thus acquiring a sense of deviance, while also being pervasively available, and a technique of catharsis for dealing with the emotional strains of a highly rationalised society. Shilling and Mellor (2011: 17, 27–28, 33) more recently have argued that the 'embodied intoxication' of effervescent assemblies that characterise small-scale societies, which is often facilitated by psychoactive substance use, are problematised by the modern emphasis on autonomous individualism. In turn, psychoactive substances that promote individual self-control and provide energy and focus, such as tobacco, coffee and sugar, which are moderate in their effects but harmful over the long-term, become socially acceptable, while drug-experiences that lower the boundaries between people and undermine individualism become the focus of restrictions. Thus, substances such as alcohol became prohibited initially from defined areas of social life, later becoming more generally proscribed. Parallel to this process, social differentiation created specialised arenas for different aspects of life, such as work, family and leisure, resulting in collective intoxication being restricted to domains with little substantive connection to wider social life (albeit networking continues to be important), and with specialised agencies such as courts, public health and professions replacing communal authorities in the role of regulators of collective intoxication, making control both abstract and something that ceases to be the absolute authority of members of a community. Consumption, hence, no longer in a direct sense connects a person to wider society and is at risk of being unregulated and disordered (Shilling & Mellor, 2011: 31–32).

The Transformation of Ritual?

Rituals are pragmatic, evolving, not set in stone, can be disrupted and lost, and equally can be invented. To paraphrase Joseph Campbell: when society does not provide rituals to structure transitions, people will invent their own. Humans are animals oriented to and in need of ritual (Rappaport, 1999). The organic invention and adaption of rituals is indeed crucial for articulating what is proportionate and mitigating harms associated with excess. Within contemporary societies, cultural responses to symbolise and ritualise consumption are associated with a reduction of risk, where users themselves 'invent' their own social controls through ritualising use, creating stylised and patterned occasion for consumption surrounded by respected actions and behaviours that are proscribed and taboo (Moore, 1993). There seems to be a strong preference for an established ritual context for use, regardless of the consumers, substance used and how honoured, stigmatised or dangerous it is considered, or how chaotic the context of use could be considered. For example, in skid-row drinking, there is the 'bottle gang' where solidarity and reciprocity are enacted, which involves strong norms of how drink should be taken and how others should be treated – with most of the harms stemming from drinking experienced not a result of the ritual but the effects of the marginalisation and stigmatisation of such individuals (Spradley, 1999: 118). In these rituals, there is a stigma for individualistic intoxication – breaking the 'norm' of the sanctioned degree of decontrolling. It could be argued in fact that the ritual makes the best of such bad circumstances that the universal behaviour of seeking psychoactive experience takes place in. The influence of anthropology, ethnography and sensitivity to the 'drug, set and setting' model has also resulted in creative ritualisations of use through the invention of new masters of ceremony in the guise of harm reduction workers, who, for example, assist revellers to modulate pleasure and risk, drink and use other psychoactive substances in a manner that supports identity and circles of recognition, rather than threaten negative outcomes. An example of this is the work of volunteers in the night-time economy and clubs who offer advice, assistance and care when it is needed (Carmo Carvalho et al. 2014).

Nonetheless, rituals have difficulty in 'bedding down' in modern societies. While Victor Turner argued that the ritual process was a cultural universal, he also noted that it was expressed quite differently in modern societies, and that the ritual life that structured societies in the past no longer exists for the majority in the true sense. As discussed above, one of the major ritual occasions involving alcohol and intoxication is the initiation of the young as full members of the adult community. It is illustrative of the change in the nature of ritual to examine how drinking is involved in initiation rituals in contemporary cultures, to demonstrate the reduction in informal social control that runs in parallel with the diminished function of the ritual process. To capture the process of fragmentation and banalisation of ritual, Turner (1974) developed the concepts of the 'liminal' and the 'liminoid'. The liminoid is different from the liminal as the length of time spent in an in-between state is greatly extended, communities have less control over proceedings and those involved do so less as pure participants and more as semi-attached spectators, with their involvement not compulsory but based on choice. The in-betweenness is more of an individual than a collective passage also, which is quite detached from the major institutions of society rather than being fundamental to the process of joining them, and they involve more of a critical stance towards the establishment. Thus, when contemporary researchers speak about the liminality of drinking occasions (see Hobbs et al. 2000; Gerard, 2004; Hayward & Hobbs, 2007), such as in night-time economies, it would be more appropriate to label the conduct as liminoid, rather than liminal.

The grand rituals that marked the transition from one identity or state to another are decreasing in importance (Pedersen, 1994), as the coordination of social life takes place largely through the abstract mechanisms of clock time, abstract markets and a legal-bureaucratic order. For example, the right to drink is no longer on the basis of the admission of a group of young people into a heretofore closed aspect of the collective life of a group but is rather based on the abstract limit of chronological age. As a result, the role of alcohol in marking transitions has been banalised, as it becomes a way of 'keying' a shift into moments of scheduled hedonism that are weakly related to concrete communities (Demant & Stergaard, 2007: 519–520). Nonetheless, drinking rituals among the young go on, but in the format of the liminoid. The rites of passage as described by Turner took place over a defined and short period of time. In contemporary society, the entirety of adolescence, young adulthood and beyond can be seen as a betwixt and between phase. Thus, the phase of social drinking occasions becomes greatly extended, before the acquiring of social structural roles of career and family lead people to disengage from youth drinking culture, despite the social capital that they had previously accumulated there and the profound experiences they may have had in this milieu (Northcote, 2006).

Rituals involving alcohol have also become increasingly individualised and democratic, losing their association with kin, Church, political community, the cycle of religious holidays or community festivities linked with natural cycles of the seasons, or with the initiation into a concrete institution such as university or the army. Very old rituals and practices associated with them can live on, but in a residual form, that is little understood by those who partake in them (Beccaria & Sande, 2003; 99, 101). This is because 'a distinct rite de passage towards adulthood is no longer dominant' involving traditional rituals that drinking is an aspect of, because traditional forms of encompassing communities that a young person could be initiated into largely no longer exist (Demant & Stergaard, 2007: 519). Indeed, rituals involving drinking increasingly do not refer to even the family, with drinking occasions largely organised by young people themselves, on the basis of an education-based peer group, whose horizon is global youth culture, devising and managing their own gatherings, with a more experimental use of alcohol, away from social structural figures such as teachers, parents and other establishment figures (Beccaria & Sande, 2003: 112). Thus, they lack one of the key features of liminal rituals: masters of ceremony, with peer groups of the young enacting their own drinking rituals. Masters of ceremony that do exist are highly abstract, such as the socially engineered night-time economy venues that encourage particular behaviours, or the vague cultural notion of the 'uni-experience', as well as the internalisation of what has been learned in the family and concern over what they would think. In the absence of traditional types of masters of ceremony, these 'shadow rituals' created by the young themselves (Henriksen et al. 2011), there are fears that these will have reckless and abusive features (Johnson, 2011).

Involvement in this type of ritual is based more on choice than obligation, with them existing for the purpose of reaffirming fluid bonds. Consuming alcohol and intoxication plays a role of symbolising commitment to the fragile group. Demant and Stergaard (2007: 533) explain that 'These fragile friendships can be seen as a fluid sociality which constantly demands attention and reassurance. Partying, then, is also a way to reaffirm friendship and is therefore an integrated part of adolescents' everyday life' (517). Turner (1974: 87) himself noted the functionality of alcohol in the context of the liminoid in achieving 'flow', through its ability to narrow, focus and limit attention. The production of collective experiences is one way to anchor such protean groups, with alcohol quite useful due to its ability to 'make things happen' (Measham, 2004; Banister & Piacentini, 2008), to force the action, and create striking events, which are somehow embarrassing and shocking, that a sense of a 'legendary night' is based on (Banister & Piacentini, 2008: 314–316; Haydock, 2015). The emphasis on conjuring extraordinary experiences makes drinking occasions more associated with transgression and activities normally forbidden (Lalander, 1997: 35). Many researchers have seen in contemporary youth drinking a calculated and intense loss of control, at times to the extent of there being 'complete and utter disorder' (see Lalander, 1997: 34; Haydock, 2015). This represents a significant change in drinking culture, as while a loss of control has been taboo in Mediterranean drinking culture, even in Anglo-Saxon culture it has been normative to combine heavy drinking with a determination to not manifest visible signs of intoxication (see Beccaria & Sande, 2003, Haydock, 2015: 4). Thus, as the ritual process has been diminished, the power of informal social control has been diminished also.

Conclusion: From Ritual to Reflexivity

More recent scholarship on drinking has emphasised a 'strategic/agentive analytical framework' over a functionalist framework (Dietler, 2006). This is not merely a matter of changing theoretical fashion, as it reflects how social change has diminished the role of ritual in drinking culture and has destructured it, literally leaving people as agents faced with greater choice, in contrast to the constraining nature of traditionalist societies. While the ritual process is a social process that clearly involves a degree of agency as it must be enacted and performed, it is also socially determined to a considerable extent due to its role in reproducing the social structure. Behavioural control, in the context of deritualisation, comes less from *ritual* as an aspect of the social structure and more from *reflexivity*, involving a more individualised navigating of risk. Reflexive practices of the self increasingly are what shapes consumption, in the form of 'art of existence' (Duff, 2004) in the shape of the art and ethics of moderation and pleasure, a conscious modulation of the balance between risk and excitement, aesthetic and cultivated attitudes with respect to choices made, and using drinking to perform one's ethical orientation to the world. This connection can be seen in the profound link between drinking and self-expression and creative scenes in modernity, but also in a weakening of the ritual framework that moderated drinking in traditional and conservative societies.

Bibliography

Aristotle (2009) *Nicomachean Ethics*, Oxford: Oxford University Press.

Babor, T. (2010) *Alcohol: No Ordinary Commodity: Research and Policy*, Oxford: Oxford University Press.

Bacchi, C. (2015) 'Problematizations in Alcohol Policy: WHO's "Alcohol Problems"', *Contemporary Drug Problems*, 42(2), 130–147.

Bacon, S.D. (1962) 'Alcohol and Complex Society', in D.J. Pittman and C.R. Snyder (eds) *Society, Culture, and Drinking Patterns*, New York: John Wiley & Sons, Inc, 78–94.

Bales, R.F. (1944) 'The "Fixation Factor" in Alcohol Addiction', Ph.D. dissertation, Department of Sociology, Harvard University.

Bakhtin, M. (1984) *Rabelais and His World*, Bloomington: Indiana University Press.

Bancroft, A. (2009) *Drugs Intoxication and Society*, Cambridge: Polity Press.

Banister, E.N. and Piacentini, M.G. (2008) 'Drunk and (Dis)Orderly: The Role of Alcohol in Supporting Liminality', in A.Y. Lee and D. Soman (eds) *NA – Advances in Consumer Research*, Duluth, MN: Association for Consumer Research, 311–318.

Bateson, G. (2000) 'Double Bind', in G. Bateson, *Steps to an Ecology of Mind*, Chicago, IL: Chicago University Press, 271–278.

Beccaria, F. (2010) 'Ritual Drinking During the Annual Alpini Event in Italy', *Nordic Studies on Alcohol and Drugs*, 27(4), 357–368.

Beccaria, F. and Sande, A. (2003) 'Drinking Games and Rite of Life Projects: A Social Comparison of the Meaning and Functions of Young People's Use of Alcohol During the Rite of Passage to Adulthood in Italy and Norway', *Young*, 11(2), 99–119.

Becker, H. (1963) *Outsiders: Studies in the Sociology of Deviance*, New York: The Free Press.

Berger, P.L. and Luckmann, T. (2007) 'The Social Construction of Reality', in C. Calhoun, J. Gertis, J. Moody, S. Pfaff and I. Virk (eds) *Contemporary Sociological Theory*, Oxford: Blackwell, 43–51.

Berreman, G.D. (1978) 'Scale and Social Relations', *Current Anthropology*, 19(2), 225–245.

Brodsky, A. and Peele, S. (1999) 'Psychosocial Benefits of Moderate Alcohol Consumption: Alcohol's Role in a Broader Conception of Health and Well-Being', in S. Peele (ed) *Alcohol and Pleasure: A Health Perspective*, Philadelphia, PA: Brunner/Mazel, 187–207.

Butler, S., Elmeland, K., Nicholls J. and Thom, B. (2017) *Alcohol, Power and Public Health*, London: Routledge.

Carmo Carvalho, M., Pinto de Sousa, M., Frango, P., Dias, P., Carvalho, J., Rodrigues, M. and Rodrigues, T. (2014): 'Crisis Intervention Related to the Use of Psychoactive Substances in Recreational Settings-Evaluating the Kosmicare Project at Boom Festival', *Current Drug Abuse Reviews*, 7(2), 81–100.

Cutler, D., Deaton, A. and Lleras-Muney, A. (2006) 'The Determinants of Mortality', *Journal of Economic Perspectives*, 20(3), 97–120.

Demant, J. and Stergaard, J. (2007) 'Partying as Everyday Life: Investigations of Teenagers' Leisure Life', *Journal of Youth Studies*, 10(5), 517–537.

Dietler, M. (2006) 'Alcohol: Anthropological/Archaeological Perspectives', *Annual Review of Anthropology*, 35, 229–249.

Douglas, M. (1996) *Thought Styles: Critical Essays on Good Taste*, London: Sage.

Douglas, M. (1987) *Constructive Drinking*, Cambridge: Cambridge University Press.

Duff, C. (2004) 'Drug Use as a "Practice of the Self": Is There any Place for an "Ethics of Moderation" in Contemporary Drug Policy?', *International Journal of Drug Policy, 15*(5–6), 385–393.

Durkheim, E. (2002) *Suicide*, London: Routledge & Kegan Paul.
Enright, M. (1996) *Lady with a Mead Cup*, Dublin: Four Courts Press.
Geertz, C. (1973) *The Interpretation of Cultures*, New York: Basic Books.
Gefou-Madianou, D. (1992) *Alcohol, Gender and Culture*, London: Routledge.
Gerard, M. (2004) 'Selecting Ritual: DJs, Dancers and Liminality in Underground Dance Music', in G. St John (ed) *Rave Culture and Religion*, London: Routledge, 167–184.
Glassner, B. and Berg, B. (1980) 'How Jews Avoid Alcohol Problems', *American Sociological Review*, 45(4), 647–664.
Goody, J. (2002) 'Elias and the Anthropological Tradition', *Anthropological Theory*, 2(4), 401–412.
Gordon, R., Heim, D. and MacAskill, S. (2012) 'Rethinking Drinking Cultures: A Review of Drinking Cultures and a Reconstructed Dimensional Approach', *Public Health*, 126(1), 3–11.
Grund, J.-P.C. (1993) 'Drug Use as a Social Ritual', PhD Dissertation, Erasmus University Rotterdam.
Gusfield, J. (1987) 'Passages to Play: Rituals of Drinking Time in American Society', in M. Douglas (ed) *Constructive Drinking*, Cambridge: Cambridge University Press, 73–90.
Hartogsohn, I. (2017) 'Constructing Drug Effects: A History of Set and Setting', *Drug Science, Policy and Law*, *3*(0), 1–17.
Haydock, W. (2015) 'The Consumption, Production and Regulation of Alcohol in the UK: The Relevance of the Ambivalence of the Carnivalesque', *Sociology*, 50(6), 1056–1071.
Hayward, K. and Hobbs, D. (2007) 'Beyond the Binge in "Booze Britain": Market-Led Liminalization and the Spectacle of Binge Drinking', *The British Journal of Sociology*, *58*(3), 437–456.
Heath, D. B. (2000) *Drinking Occasions*, Philadelphia, PA: Brunner/Mazel.
Heath, D.B. (1988) 'Emerging Anthropological Theory and Models of Alcohol Use and Alcoholism', in C.D. Chaudron and D.A. Wilkinson (eds) *Theories on Alcoholism*, Toronto: Addiction Research Foundation, 353–410.
Heath, D. B. (1958) 'Drinking patterns of the Bolivian Camba', *Quarterly Journal of Studies on Alcohol*, 19(3), 491–508.
Henriksen, Ø., Sande, A. and Alkoholtisdkrift, N. (2011) 'Shadow Life in the Limelight. A Social Anthropological Perspective on Youth, Local Community, Rites of Passage and Drunkenness', *Nordic Alcohol Studies*, 11(4), 200–211.
Hobbs, D., Lister, S., Hadfield, P., Winlow, S. and Hall, S. (2000) 'Receiving Shadows: Governance and Liminality in the Night-Time Economy', *The British Journal of Sociology*, 51(4), 701–717.
Hunt, G.P., MacKenzie, K. and Joe-Laider, K. (2005) 'Alcohol and Masculinity: The Case of Ethnic Youth Gangs', in T.M. Wilson (ed) *Drinking Cultures*, Oxford: Berg, 225–254.
Johnson, J. (2011) 'Through the Liminal: A Comparative Analysis of Communitas and Rites of Passage in Sport Hazing and Initiations', *Canadian Journal of Sociology*, 36(3), 199.
Lalander, P. (1997) 'Beyond Everyday Order; Breaking Away with Alcohol', *Nordic Studies on Alcohol and Drugs*, 14(1), 33–42.
Levine, H.G. (1992) 'Temperance Cultures', in M. Lader, G. Edwards and C. Drummond (eds) *The Nature of Alcohol and Drug Related Problems*, Oxford: Oxford University Press, 16–36.
Lunnay, B., Ward, P. and Borlagdan, J. (2011) 'The Practise and Practice of Bourdieu: The Application of Social Theory to Youth Alcohol Research', *International Journal of Drug Policy*, 22(6), 428–436.
MacLachlan, B. (2014) *The Age of Grace: Charis in Early Greek Poetry*, Princeton, NJ: Princeton University Press.
Mauss, Marcel (1992) *The Gift*, London: Routledge.
McAndrew, C. and Edgerton, R.B. (1969) *Drunken Comportment*, Chicago, IL: Aldine.
Measham, F. (2004) 'The Decline of Ecstasy, the Rise of "Binge" Drinking and the Persistence of Pleasure', *Probation Journal*, 51(4), 309–326.
Moore, D. (1993) 'Social Controls, Harm Minimisation and Interactive Outreach: The Public Health Implications of an Ethnography of Drug Use', *Australian Journal of Public Health*, 17(1), 58–67.
Nelson, M. (2005) *The Barbarian's Beverage: A History of Beer in Ancient Europe*, London: Routledge.
Nesse, R.M. and Berridge, K.C. (1997) 'Psychoactive Drug Use in Evolutionary Perspective', *Science*, 278(3), 63–66.
Netting, R.M. (1964) 'Beer as a Locus of Value among the West African Kofyar', *American Anthropologist*, *66*, 375–384.
Northcote, J. (2006) 'Nightclubbing and the Search for Identity: Making the Transition from Childhood to Adulthood in an Urban Milieu', *Journal of Youth Studies*, 9(1), 1–16.
O'Brien, J. (2018) *States of Intoxication*, London: Routledge.

Partanen, J. (1991) *Sociability and Intoxication: Alcohol and Drinking in Kenya, Africa and the Modern World*, Helsinki: Finnish Foundation for Alcohol Studies.

Pedersen, W. (1994) 'Rites of Passage in High Modernity', *Young*, 2(1), 21–32.

Peele, S. and Marcus G. (1999) *Alcohol and Pleasure: A Health Perspective*, Philadelphia, PA: Brunner/Mazel.

Rappaport, R.A. (1999) *Ritual and Religion in the Making of Humanity*, Cambridge: Cambridge University Press.

Rinella, M.A. (2010) *Pharmakon: Plato, Drug Culture, and Identity in Ancient Athens*, Plymouth: Lexington Books.

Room, R. (1984) 'Alcohol and Ethnography: A Case of Problem Deflation?', *Current Anthropology*, 25, 169–78.

Room, R. (2001) 'Intoxication and Bad Behaviour: Understanding Cultural Differences in the Link', *Social Science and Medicine*, 53, 189–198.

Room, R. and Mäkelä, K. (2000) 'Typologies of the Cultural Position of Drinking', *Journal of Studies on Alcohol*, 61(3), 475–483.

Sherratt, A. (1995a) 'Introduction: Peculiar Substances', in J. Goodman, P.E. Lovejoy and A. Sherratt (eds) *Consuming Habits: Drugs in History and Anthropology*, London: Routledge, 1–10.

Sherratt, Andrew (1995b) 'Alcohol and its Alternatives: Symbolism and Substance in Pre-Industrial Cultures', in J. Goodman, P.E. Lovejoy and A. Sherratt (eds) *Consuming Habits: Drugs in History and Anthropology*, London: Routledge, 11–45.

Shilling, C. and Mellor, P.A. (2011) 'Retheorising Emile Durkheim on Society and Religion: Embodiment, Intoxication and Collective Life', *The Sociological Review*, 59(1), 17–41.

Singer, M. (1986) 'Toward a Political Economy of Alcoholism: The Missing Link in the Anthropology of Drinking', *Social Science and Medicine*, 23(2), 113–130.

Snyder, C. (1958) *Alcohol and the Jews*, New Haven, CT: Yale University Press.

Spradley, J.P. (1999) *You Owe Yourself a Drunk: An Ethnography of Urban Nomads*, Long Grove, IL: Waveland Press.

Stivers, R. (2000) *Hair of the Dog: Irish Drinking and its American Stereotype*, New York: Continuum.

Suggs D.N. (1996) 'Mosadi Tshwene: The Construction of Gender and the Consumption of Alcohol in Botswana', *American Ethnologist*, 23, 597–610.

Stone, R.A.T., Whitbeck, L.B., Chen, X., Johnson, K. and Olson, D.M. (2006) 'Traditional Practices, Traditional Spirituality, and Alcohol Cessation among American Indians', *Journal of Studies on Alcohol*, 67(2), 236–244.

Turner, V. (1974) 'Liminal to Liminoid, in Play, Flow, and Ritual: An Essay in Comparative Symbology', *Rice Institute Pamphlet-Rice University Studies*, 60(3), 53–92.

Turner, V. (1969) *The Ritual Process: Structure and Anti-Structure*, New York: Aldine De Gruyter.

Tutorsky, A.V. (2016) 'Drinking in the North of European Russia: From Traditional to Totalising Liminality', *Journal of Ethnology and Folkloristics*, 10(2), 7–18.

Valverde, M. (1998) *Diseases of the Will: Alcohol and the Dilemmas of Freedom*, Cambridge: Cambridge University Press.

Zinberg N.E. (1984) *Drug, Set, and Setting: The Basis for Controlled Intoxicant Use*, New Haven, CT: Yale University Press.

Zinberg, N.E., Jacobson, R.C. and Harding, W.M. (1975) 'Social Sanctions and Rituals as a Basis for Drug Abuse Prevention', *The American Journal of Drug and Alcohol Abuse*, 2(2), 165–182.

PART V

Alternative Approaches for Studying Intoxication

19

INTOXICATION MADE VISIBLE

The sober sciences of intoxication, euphoria, and overdose in the laboratory

Nancy D. Campbell

"[A] silent spring of intoxicants ... flows through our lives and our bodies."

—*Ronald K. Siegel, Preface to the second edition of* Intoxication: The Universal Drive for Mind-Altering Substances*: The Universal Drive for Mind-Altering Substances (2005)*

Flows of intoxicants bubble forth from the "silent spring" of which clinical pharmacologist Ronald K. Siegel wrote, shaping the modern world and continuing to do so (Courtwright 2002, 2019; Ghiabi 2018; Herlinghaus 2013). Rendering the so-called universal drive for intoxication visible for the sake of laboratory science requires pharmacologists to navigate the specifics of dangerous proximities between acute toxicity, therapeutic dose, chronic administration or "addiction," overdose, and lethal dose. This chapter explores how experimental, clinical, and behavioral scientists made intoxication tractable to laboratory sciences wherein routine observation and experimentation with human and animal subjects can be reliably reproduced.[1] Experimental infrastructures designed to produce knowledge about intoxication evolved as sober scientists grappled with objects, subjects, and effects that are ambiguous, difficult to verbalize or quantify, but sometimes lethal. This chapter begins with experiments at the world's first laboratory dedicated to producing knowledge about intoxication and addiction, the US Public Health Service Addiction Research Center (ARC) in Lexington, Kentucky. I focus on an exemplary single-subject study of intoxication conducted by Abraham Wikler (1952) and a handful of studies on barbiturate intoxication by that laboratory's research director, Harris Isbell, in the years immediately following World War II (Fraser, Shaver, Maxwell and Isbell 1953; Fraser, Wikler, Belleville, Essig and Hill 1956; Hill, Belleville, Wikler 1957; Isbell, Altschul, Kornetsky, Eisenman, Flanary and Fraser 1950). The chapter traces the emergence of behavioral pharmacology and its absorption by addiction neuroscience, concluding with recent clinical studies in an "overdose laboratory" directed by John Strang, who anchors the National Addiction Centre in the United Kingdom. The chapter showcases how laboratories operationalized concepts of intoxication, euphoria, addiction, and overdose; how conceptual practices are conserved even as established research practices, methods, and protocols are supplanted by new techniques and technologies; and implications of these research dynamics and lexical shifts for today's more integrated knowledge of intricately biosocial processes such as intoxication and addiction.

DOI: 10.4324/9780429058141-25

We begin with UCLA psychopharmacologist Ronald K. Siegel's naturalization of intoxication as a fourth "universal" drive joining hunger, thirst, and sex through seemingly "natural" experimental designs that defy categorization. He arranged encounters between plants, humans, and nonhumans, observing both intentional and accidental intoxication events, such as dizziness (Siegel 1989, 1984, 1979-1980, 1979a, 1979b, 1976, 1973, 1971; Siegel and Brodie 1984, Siegel and Jarvik 1980a, 1980b, 1975). He portrayed plants as producing elaborate chemical defenses against being eaten, animals as adopting "safe feeding strategies" to circumvent botanical guile (Hagen and Sullivan 2018, 104; Siegel 1989, 14). Crediting plant-animal interactions with "turning poisons into intoxicants and forming the new chemical bond we call addiction," Siegel depicted human taste for intoxicants as a natural evolutionary passion, fondness, even craving or habit (1989, 14, 51) and addiction as an "unnatural" pathology borne of "stubborn preoccupation" (Siegel 1989, 53). Humans evolved social norms to limit consumption and make intoxication episodic rather than chronic. Siegel's was a science in which periodicity and place reflected "drive intensity":

> Captive primates will show a remarkable drive to intoxicate themselves even in a roomy laboratory cage. Whether for reasons of exploration, curiosity, stimulation, tranquilization, dispelling boredom, or depression laboratory primates have willingly pursued such a vast array of intoxicants ... [that] they appear to medicate mental needs ...
>
> *(Siegel 1989, 99; Siegel and Jarvik 1980a, 1980b)*

Experimental accounts of animal self-medication extended capacity for intentional intoxication to rodents, dogs, and nonhuman primates, particularly rhesus macaques. The latter pervaded the twentieth-century laboratories within which pharmacological researchers evolved techniques to discern effects of chronic administration, the buildup of tolerance, the behaviors and effects associated with abrupt and gradual withdrawal. It was difficult to get nonhuman primates to self-administer or "self-medicate." Animal subjects seemed to lack that "universal drive" to such a degree that laboratory workers had to invent techniques for getting laboratory animals to ingest the drugs that humans use and abuse (Campbell 2007).

Rendering intoxication visible and discernible to instruments and observers was no easy task. Few laboratories were equipped to study neurophysiological and behavioral phenomena associated with intoxicated states. Intoxicating events are experienced within social contexts that structure them—even when they occur in laboratories. Social, political, and economic processes and situations produce and modulate intoxicating events to the point that "bodily experiences themselves differ depending on the social ritual in which those experiences are enacted" (Collins 2004, 304). Altered states of consciousness are inflected with meanings ranging from the comforts of satiety to the energetic pleasures of "collective effervescence" (Durkheim 1912; Room 2013). An auto-antonym, "addiction" contains both active and passive dichotomies of obligation, compulsion, and choice (Rosenthal and Faris 2019). Although derived from Greek (*toxikos*), "pertaining to arrows or archery," the term migrated into European vernaculars through Latin (*toxicare*) "to smear with poison" (Shrank 2012). Invoking a targeted lethality, intoxication acquired associations with drunkenness, fantastical dream-states, and fugue-states (Withington 2010, 2014). English renders intoxication and addiction negative as regards self-governance. When the sciences of addiction and intoxication were translated into instruments, methods, and scales designed to make intoxication tractable to modern pharmacological reason, the meaning of intoxication tilted away from pleasure, and towards toxicity, abuse liability, and lethality. Experimental situations were inventively engineered to measure "liking" for a drug using a conditioned place preference paradigm (Prus, James and Rosecrans 2009). Socially contextualized setting remains at the margins of laboratory science, requiring different modes of attention attuned to social relations, language, custom, ritual, and consumption practices.

Critical social studies of addiction have recently taken on the challenge of evolving a processual, material, and relational approach to behavioral and substance-based "addictions." Postpositivist approaches pressure not only the epistemological underpinnings, but the conceptual practices and material relations through which addictions have been investigated as matters-of-fact (Dennis 2019; Dennis and Farrugia 2017; Fraser and Moore 2011; Fraser, Moore, and Keane 2014; Fraser and valentine 2008; Gomart 2002, 2004; Latour 2004; Mol 1999, 2002; Rhodes and Lancaster 2019). Conjoining this critical project are postpositivist histories designed to show how laboratory-based sciences of addiction and intoxication, in concert with studies situated in drug users' social worlds, make evidence (Rhodes and Lancaster 2019). This chapter extends insights of this evidence-in-the-making conversation to laboratory-based sciences of intoxication in an effort to improve integration of social worlds with laboratory-based knowledge production.

The disappearance of desire from addiction research

Intoxication fit poorly into early twentieth-century psychoanalytic frameworks. Lawrence Kolb, author of the first diagnostic system for addiction, argued against facile associations between addiction, intoxication, and criminality. Propensity to addiction was defined in terms of degrees of psychopathology (Acker 2002; Kolb 1925a, 1925b, 1925c). Kolb pioneered animal models of addiction at the National Hygienic Laboratory in Washington, DC (forerunner of the National Institutes of Health; Harden 1986). When he became the Chief Medical Officer of the US Narcotic Farm in 1935, Kolb hired clinical researcher Clifton K. Himmelsbach to direct a small laboratory that Congress had mandated to find a cure for opiate addiction (Campbell 2007). Himmelsbach plotted the regularities of "withdrawal," which he and Kolb dubbed the Morphine Abstinence Syndrome (Himmelsbach 1941; Kolb and Himmelsbach 1938). Studies were coordinated by the Committee on Drug Addiction and Narcotics (CDAN), charged with preventing addictive pharmaceuticals from going in the U.S. market (Acker 2002; Campbell 2007; Eddy 1973; Herzberg 2020; May and Jacobson 1989).

Scientists at the US Narcotic Farm had access to "postaddicts," human subjects who were seasoned users of smoking opium, and oral, sniffed, or injected morphine or heroin, and who willingly volunteered to subject themselves to these substances for the sake of science. Officially named the Addiction Research Center (ARC) in 1948, the laboratory joined the National Institute of Mental Health (NIMH). Newly established in 1948, the World Health Organization (WHO) released an ARC-influenced report in 1950, defining addiction as an "overpowering desire and need (compulsion) to continue taking the drug and to obtain it by any means."[2] Following Himmelsbach's method and Kolb's criteria, investigator Abraham Wikler conducted a single-subject study at the ARC from fall 1947 to spring 1948. "A Psychodynamic Study of a Patient During Experimental Self-regulated Re-addiction to Morphine" followed the progress of "re-addiction" in a healthy volunteer who had previously failed at cure and stated his intent not to abstain from morphine or heroin use after discharge. The study raised questions such as why "addicts" (the term used) preferred morphine to alcohol; why they used morphine "when, presumably, the 'euphoric' effects can no longer be experienced"; whether "actively addicted" persons could lead "socially productive" lives;

and even "What does the addict mean by 'normal'?" Given "the addict's oft-repeated statement that 'morphine makes me feel normal'," Wikler's subject gradually rebuilt tolerance to very high dosage and did not voluntarily taper off morphine when the end of the study was in sight.

One of few qualitative studies ever produced at the ARC, such a study would not pass ethics review today.[3] The timing presaged the Committee's 1950 authoritative redefinition of "addiction" as "drug dependence,"[4] defined as a "state of periodic or chronic intoxication, detrimental to the individual and to society, produced by repeated administration of a drug." Skirting the pejorative "addiction," the Committee renamed itself the Committee on Problems of Drug Dependence in 1965, advancing the new definition within the WHO Expert Committee structure (1957, 1964). Wikler's single-subject study coincided with Isbell's studies of chronic barbiturate intoxication (discussed below). Wikler's article included far more psychodynamic detail than other ARC publications. His subject was a 44-year-old orthodox Jew from Detroit who started smoking opium at age 19, became "addicted" at age 22, and commenced injecting at age 33. Gambling and "bootlegging" landed him in both federal narcotics farms. When at Lexington, he had previously participated in morphine experiments. Interviewed more than 30 times during the two-month study, he shared memories, dreams, sexual experiences, fantasies, and arrests, recorded in detail. His motive for participating was revelatory: "Why not—if I can get even with the government and cheat them out of some time?"

Along with monitoring vital signs, regular EEGs, and detailed tracking of total dosage and frequency of morphine consumed during experimental re-addiction, the prose of the paper was so evocative that the reader can practically smell the cigarette smoke of the day room in the research ward. The subject's response to his first shot reads like a thick description of intoxication: "his skin was flushed, he rubbed his nose and appeared very happy. The flush subsided in a few seconds. On interrogation, he said the sensation was comparable to sexual orgasm."[5] He became "loquacious," speaking spontaneously with "pep," which Wikler interpreted to mean "freedom from anxiety about doing what he wants to do." Dreams were dutifully recorded in an almost psychoanalytic register. At the time, Wikler was himself enrolled in psychoanalytic training with Erwin Straus (Chessick 1999). Hospitalized at NIH in Bethesda for nearly a year soon after the study ended, Wikler's research trajectory shifted course towards a more neurobiological framework called "adaptational psychodynamics" (Rado 1969).

When working within the psychoanalytic framework, Wikler interpreted his subject's need for euphoria as resulting from "oral narcissistic cravings" (1952, 20). "Euphoria" presented a problem for a scientist of Wikler's ilk—not only was it difficult to operationalize, it was entirely too subjective, too interior, too "diffuse and nonspecific" (CDAN 11, 380). While chronic opiate intoxication affected "primary motivations such as fear of pain, sexual conflicts, probably hunger and some other things" (CDAN 11, 380), it could also gratify primary needs. The problem, as all persons living with addictions know and as Wikler found, was that tolerance diminished euphoria to small "thrill[s] (orgasm[s])" just after injection. Although "artificially-induced" cravings offered new gratifications that displaced "other 'natural' primary needs," they did not displace "'pharmacogenic' need," a term Wikler adopted from Sandor Rado,[6] the eminent post-Freudian psychoanalyst who founded the Center for Psychoanalytic Training and Research at Columbia University.

Adaptational psychodynamics was Rado's attempt to make psychoanalysis palatable to American scientific appetites. He located the root of addiction in abnormally intense desires for "narcotic elation" (*Adaptational Psychodynamics*, 1969, 263). He saw compulsive drug use as the manifest effect of a repetition compulsion, an "impulse neurosis" (Fenichel 1950, 368) or form of "narcotic bondage" (Rado 1957, 1963). The physiological changes associated with the "superpleasure" of intoxication were said to bypass the brain's adaptive processes, silence danger signs, and displace "ordinary pursuits and rewards of healthy life," allowing grandiose delusions and infantile impulses to uproot "reason, foresight, and judgment" (Rado 1969, 264–265). For Rado, intoxication and addiction were symptoms of immaturity, signs of arrested development.

Once returning to Kentucky, Wikler steered hard into the animal research that occupied his later career. Human craving and desire went underground in the behavioral research that dominated the late twentieth century, resurfacing when neuroscientists started studying anticipatory "priming" effects. ARC publications migrated toward neuropharmacology and physiology. But assumptions that intoxication was an artificial and immature route to gratification that displaced more "natural" and "mature" routes still flower in the twenty-first century. Wikler provided a foundational plank for framing addiction as an artificial route to satisfying naturalized needs, arguing that "individual personality, the specific effects of single and repeated doses of morphine, and the cultural attitudes towards opiate addiction, contribute to the etiology of narcotic addiction" (1952, 22). Behaviors were modulated by the psychodynamic substrate of primary and secondary needs. Those with adequate "neurotic defenses" could handle morphine and were "not apt to become narcotic addicts, nor are socially-acceptable, mature individuals" (1952, 22). Wikler did not see himself as studying "culture," "society," or "personality," but instead showed as clearly as he could the "specific effects of single and repeated doses of morphine."

ARC protocols mandated that no experimental drug be administered within six months of release. Although Wikler turned his back on the study of personality dynamics, the single subject impressed him because the subject could have calculated when the experiment would end and tapered off high-dose, pharmaceutical grade morphine so as to avoid withdrawal. But he didn't. On the study's announced final day, he had eight injections totaling 1,000 mg of morphine. His "post-reduction period" was abrupt, miserable, and accompanied by constant drug-seeking as he exited the experimental situation and moved back into the general population of a carceral institution, his anonymous mark on the sciences of intoxication intact. Open-ended experiments, in which a laboratory-housed human subject could "choose" dosage and frequency, became next to impossible due to the historical circumstances governing human research in the postwar period.

Chronic barbiturate intoxication

Consulted far too late in the process of a mysterious drug-related death, Dr. Harris Isbell could do little but watch as a fellow physician admitted to the U.S. Public Health Service Narcotic Hospital in Lexington, Kentucky,

> died during withdrawal because he failed to tell the physician in charge of his case that he had been maintaining a constant state of intoxication with Nembutal taken orally, the quantity later being estimated by his wife as about fifty capsules a day.[7]

By the late 1940s, well before the U.S. Food and Drug Administration required clinical trials, Nembutal numbered among a vast array of barbiturates. Clinical reports gave rise to the question of whether death resulted from barbiturate overdose, abrupt withdrawal, or both. The serious nature of this acute intoxication motivated Isbell to publish the first

English-language studies on chronic barbiturate intoxication and withdrawal in human beings (Isbell, Altschul, Kornetsky, Eisenman, Flanary and Fraser 1950). A steady stream of publications issued from the ARC documenting the dangers of barbiturates and recommending policy changes (Fraser 1954, 1957; Fraser, Eisenman, Wikler and Pescor 1954; Fraser, Wikler, Belleville, Essig and Hill 1956; Hill, Belleville and Wikler 1957).

At the time of the fatal incident, ARC researchers were documenting a clinical protocol for reversing opiate overdose; they hoped to extend that work to develop an "antidote" for barbiturate poisoning (Campbell 2007, 2020). Chronic use of barbiturates was not then considered "addiction," a view promoted to physicians by drug manufacturers (Rasmussen 2012, 27). By the late 1940s, some 672,000 pounds of barbiturates—or 24 doses for each person in the United States—were manufactured and consumed annually, an amount far in excess of that required to meet the nation's therapeutic needs.[8] Concerned that barbiturates were being indiscriminately prescribed, the ARC embarked—with a "great deal of trepidation," according to Isbell (1978, 35)—on a landmark series of studies on the clinical pharmacology of chronic barbiturate intoxication and withdrawal. They ensured that none of those who volunteered for the study were epileptic or psychotic. To safeguard against a death on the research ward, participants were observed round-the-clock while recording data on neurophysiological and "subjective" effects correlated with "objective" measures. Scientists first, ARC researchers viewed most physicians as dangerously under-educated about dependence potential and withdrawal. Their studies confirmed that "chronic barbiturate intoxication" produced a severe and at times deadly withdrawal syndrome—one that could result in seizures or temporary psychosis (Rasmussen 2012, 38).

Barbiturates were involved in roughly one quarter of all acute poisonings in the U.S. general hospitals by 1950. Having determined that *delirium tremens* were signs of withdrawal from alcohol (Isbell, Fraser, Wikler, Belleville, and Eisenman, 1955), Isbell and colleagues saw themselves as guardians of public health in the midst of a "synthetic flood" (Isbell 1978, 32). Integral to the international drug control community anchored by the United Nations and WHO, ARC scientists presented data to the WHO Narcotics Expert Committee in January 1952. They recommended stricter controls on "addicting non-opiate sedatives," as they called them. Despite not being derived from opium, they argued, barbiturates possessed the "power to addict individuals that use them regularly in quantities larger than would be prescribed medically" (Maurer and Vogel 1954, 102). Two pieces of evidence were adduced to show that non-medical use of barbiturates resulted in physical dependence: the degree of intoxication, often said to mimic severe alcoholism, and the severity of "withdrawal illness." Because barbiturates were often used by individuals deemed "respectable" such as healthcare professionals and patients with legitimate illnesses, they eluded the label of an "addicting" or "dependence producing" drug (Herzberg 2009, 2020). They retained their hold in the marketplace until the psychopharmacological revolution of the mid-to-late 1950s yielded the so-called happy pills—the minor tranquilizers and benzodiazepines that were the first blockbuster prescription drugs (Herzberg 2009; Tone 2009). Physicians and patients migrated away from the barbiturates as "cure-of-almost-all" drugs as their lethality became clear and their use less respectable. By the late 1950s, those using barbiturates for non-medical purposes were considered a new type of drug addict who maintained "constant state of intoxication in which they escape reality" (Maurer and Vogel 1954, 21–22). Nothing cemented these understandings so clearly as ARC studies documenting a dangerous withdrawal syndrome, and showing cross-tolerance between alcohol and barbiturates in animals as well as humans.

Problems of euphoria: mood changes in the mid-twentieth-century drug sciences

The US cities experienced a postwar spike in heroin injection as opiates and technologies to administer them became widespread. CDAN ("the Committee") convened pharmaceutical industry representatives from companies innovating in the analgesic arena; government bureaucrats, including the notorious director of the Federal Bureau of Narcotics, Harry J. Anslinger; contract researchers such as Henry K. Beecher of the Harvard Anesthesiology Lab at Massachusetts General Hospital; and intramural researchers such as Isbell and Wikler. When the ARC hosted the 11th postwar CDAN meeting at the US Narcotic Farm in Lexington, Kentucky, on January 9–10, 1953, participants discussed how to set "euphoria" on scientific footing. Wikler mused:

> By an odd coincidence we have been concerned with the problem of euphoria for many years. Our first definite conclusion is that the term 'euphoria' means very different things to different people, to the same person at different times, and also to groups of individuals after administration of different drugs ... To interpret what euphoria means is no easy task but we feel we can interpret what the individual means by euphoria by observing how he behaves verbally and non-verbally, by recording his statements and his behavior in a given setting
>
> *(CDAN 11, 378)*

Behaviors were predictable but "only if the situation is clearly delineated" because "feelings of unusual well-being" differed from one another (CDAN 11, 378–380). Whether euphoria could be "captured" in the neurophysiological sense depended on how the experimental situation was structured.

The ARC research ward was structured to control and capture all aspects of the setting that might impinge upon subjects' "moods"—except, curiously to our eyes and ears, cigarette smoking and window bars. Observers were understood to affect subjects' "mood" and experience of drug effects. For instance, Isbell recalled administering 30 mg of morphine to a post-addict who was not yet tolerant. He turned

> pale, gags, and heaves; but ask him how he feels and he is fine, wonderful. You ask him, 'You are vomiting and all this, but you are fine?' and he replies, 'Yes, it's such a good sick.' Now is that euphoria, or isn't it?
>
> *(CDAN 11, 382)*

If experimental situations could alter drug effects, then investigators had to ask, "Under what conditions are these [drugs] administered, to whom, and what for?" (CDAN 11, 379). Even anticipatory anxiety about potential pain attenuated morphine's effects to the point that Wikler urged recognition of "the fact that the action of a drug depends upon the particular experimental condition under which it is studied" (CDAN 11, 379). A proponent of setting-differentiated effects due to observing wounded soldiers as requiring less morphine by contrast to postoperative patients in hospital wards, Beecher considered "postaddicts"—especially "chronic volunteers"—to be "pharmacological sophisticates" in a "long-standing and complex drug-person relationship that does not exist in non-addicts" (Beecher 1959, 339). Some "hint of a difference," Beecher implied, led institutionalized post-addicts to *always* experience the euphoria of intoxication, whereas non-addicts rarely did (CDAN 11,

381). Post-addicts persisted in experiencing intoxication even when they were "addicted" and thus tolerant to some opiate effects.

Mid-twentieth-century laboratory studies of intoxication wrangled "euphoria" and "dysphoria" into "mood" and "mood changes." Investigators of intoxication attempted to minimize observer effects. By "manipulating the situation," investigators realized that they could block or intensify drug effects: "there is no better way to antidote the effects of analgesic drugs, subjective and objective, than to make measurements and ask questions at stated intervals" (CDAN 11, 381). Although intoxication was not simply a matter of mood—dosage "in the addict range," route of administration, and social environments that "triggered" injection events could accentuate drug effects—mood was actively explored by American investigators in the 1950s. In 1955, Beecher, Louis Lasagna and John von Felsinger published "Drug-induced Mood Changes in Man" in the prestigious *Journal of the American Medical Association (JAMA)*, a landmark study conducted at the ARC and Massachusetts General Hospital in Boston and partially funded by the Committee.

"Mood Changes" was a crucial consolidation of statistical methodologies underlying clinical trials. Emerging technologies, study designs, and sophisticated vocabularies and methodologies enabled differentiation between neurophysiological markers of intoxication. Desires for intoxication—so central to psychopathological, psychoanalytic, and pharmacodynamic accounts produced by Kolb, Rado, and the early Wikler—were swamped by a new focus on behavioral consequences of disease. The US-based scientific community persuaded the WHO to retire "addiction," in favor of the more neutral and scientific sounding "drug dependence" in the mid-1960s.[9] This period marked a migration of scientific study of intoxication away from culture, desire, and personality, and toward behavioral approaches that dominated the next decades.

Scientific succession: behavioral pharmacology comes of age

Behavioral pharmacology constituted itself as efficiently positivistic in the 1960s, dealing with knowable behavior patterns and displacing conceptual kernels and practices from older lexicons such as psychopathology or adaptational psychodynamics (Campbell 2007). Working with human and nonhuman subjects, behavioral pharmacology was premised on the concept that drugs reinforce behavior, positively or negatively:

> Ultimately ... we've got to explain the behavior of the intact, integrated organism. The behavior is always right. It is ultimately the job of the biologist to be able to predict that behavior because the behavior is the reality.[10]

The precise language of reinforcement was not assumed coextensively with "euphoria," as this would yield an inaccurate and

> almost hedonistic kind of conception of drug abuse ... Yes, in fact drugs do produce positive mood changes in humans. However, individuals continue to take [drugs] under circumstances and at times when there is absolutely no evidence of positive mood changes. It is highly likely that the bulk of the times when addicts take drugs are not associated with 'let the good times roll.' This preoccupation with talking about euphoria and positive reinforcement as if they're synonymous is sloppy thinking.[11]

Getting nonhumans to self-administer drugs that humans do was no small feat, according to the US clinical and behavioral pharmacologists who accomplished it.[12] My interviewees emphasized how animals were housed, fed, and drugged, and how they created apparatus and equipment to modify laboratory spaces prior to the commercialization of such. George Bigelow described a group housing method in which the animal-participants had individual "apartments":

> They could leave the apartment and go down to the social area and then come back through what was called the "entry chamber" and cue in their personal ID that would unlock their apartment door, and go back to the individual chamber. That experience was the beginning of my real behavior analysis scientific experience and interest. I had a little bit of exposure to some experiments in which Jack Findley had trained large primates to stick their arm out through a little hole to receive injections.[13]

Techniques evolved for managing a morphine-dependent monkey colony at the University of Michigan, as well as tinkering with methods, layout of physical space, and apparatus designed to measure schedules of drug self-administration in terms of frequency, intensity, or "motivation"—all were lively sources of human and nonhuman iteration, invention, and interaction inside and outside laboratories (Campbell 2007).

Behavioral pharmacology was a conceptual methodology based on a paradigm called "drug self-administration." This investigatory mode was developed for purposes of drug abuse liability testing and comparative pharmacology. While it resembled Pavlovian and Skinnerian approaches called "classical" and "operant" conditioning, drug abuse liability testing was used to innovate pharmaceutical analgesics and to determine whether or not they might be liable to abuse (Campbell 2007). Never mentioning "intoxication," behavioral pharmacologists traced interactions between acute and chronic effects, pharmacokinetics and dynamics such as dosage, the human or nonhuman organism being studied, and setting (Goldberg and Schuster, 1967; Schuster and Woods, 1968; Wikler and Pescor 1967).

Drug studies aimed to maintain the lives of their nonhuman subjects, but also determine at what dosage a compound would be lethal. Social context or setting matters in terms of whether or not acute effects will be lethal or not (Hartogsohn 2020). Siegel described an experiment in which rats were given a single "lethal dose" (LD) of heroin (1989, 144). Only one-third of morphine-dependent rats (i.e. "addicted" rats) died if dosed in their "home cage." In unfamiliar territory, the dose proved lethal for two-thirds. Behavioral pharmacologists manipulated multiple experimental conditions to render human and nonhuman drug and alcohol use discernible within the learning paradigms of the late 1960s—drug self-administration and conditioned place preference remain in use today. Despite the invasiveness of drug self-administration, which required animals to be caged, catheterized, or clothed in special vests which they often customized by chewing, results were understood to have concordance with human studies. Yet, problems of variation remained—individuals clearly adapted to drug exposure differently.

Beyond tolerant subjects: minding the thin line between intoxication and overdose

Tolerance is a form of neuroadaptation that does not protect against effects of chronic intoxication and overdose. Depicted as a too-muchness of intoxication, opioid overdose brings lethal risks difficult to render tractable to clinical investigation outside of anesthesiology. Researching what happens in socially situated overdose first took place through epidemiological or statistical methods, only recently migrating to clinical settings. The intractability of overdose stems partly from opioid pharmacology—a thin line threads between intoxication, therapeutic effect, and lethality, or in the suggestive vernacular of the UK, between "gouching," "going over," and dying. Overdose varies by individual levels of tolerance, risk profile, and protective factors, and because overdose events are typically but unpredictably prolonged, those seeking to intervene must be trained to recognize its signs and symptoms.

Overdose is now understood not simply as an acute lethal event or form of excess death, but as a reversible process. Behavioral or neuroscientific methods have little utility for studying overdose because they are designed to keep participants alive, managing contingencies in complex task environments. Overdose was first studied in autopsied tissue (Darke and Duflou 2016; Hubbard 2019). Clinical researchers have had difficulty creating the conditions within which to study the physiology of acute opioid intoxication. Breathing itself is refracted through place; gender, racial-ethnic, and social class formation; occupation; and metabolism (Braun 2014; Kenner 2018). "Individual and situational variability of respiratory depression caused by intravenous heroin is poorly understood" (Jolley, Bell, Rafferty, Moxham and Strang 2015). Intoxicated subjects make poor interviewees and are imprecise navigators of tasks; they present legal liabilities and raise suspicion that investigators are plying human subjects with illicit drugs. Not until experiments in heroin-assisted treatment in Europe and the UK offered opportunities for studying acute effects of opioids immediately after injection did research capacity expand.

During the 1990s, John Strang, Director of the National Addiction Centre and Head of the Addictions Department at King's College London, realized that there were moments of more acute vulnerability to overdose death into which interventions could be put. In "Death Matters," Strang (2015) parsed available data showing that risk of overdose mortality increased at three key moments: after prison release, before commencing methadone maintenance, and after it.

> There was something else striking about the data: there was localization in time and context which had surprisingly been overlooked by the big data-capturing machines. In the transit zone between time in prison and post-release return to the community, there was a horrific concentration of deaths.
>
> *(Strang 2015, 28)*

The Kings' College group undertook "socio-psychological autopsy of the overdose situation" (Strang 2015, 28). They set out to

> identify specific dangerous patterns of drug use, specific times and locations of increased risk and interventions which could potentially prevent the fatal outcomes. For the time being these remain, all too often, uncharted territories which are yet to be investigated. However, unless progress is made, the large excess mortality will continue unchecked. As intervention-interested researchers we can make a real difference, and it is our scientific and public responsibility to do so.
>
> *(Strang 2015, 33)*

Remodeling himself as an "amateur pharmacologist," Strang and colleagues designed and built an "overdose laboratory," the human subjects of which were among the forty or so British heroin maintenance patients from a clinic operating from 2008 to 2016 (Strang 2010). Far from the first such experiment (Hartnoll, Mitcheson, Battersby, Brown, Ellis, Fleming and Hedley, 1980; Perneger, Giner, del Rio and Mino 1998), European heroin maintenance has confirmed the efficacy of agonist maintenance with methadone or heroin, now a widely adopted standard of care and subject of a Cochrane review (Ferri, Davoli and Perucci 2011; Oviedo-Joekes, Brissette, Marsh, Lauzon, Guh, Anis and Schechter 2009; Fischer, Oviedo-Joekes, Blanken, Haasen, Rehm, Schechter, Strang, and van den Brink 2007; March, Oviedo-Joekes, Perea-Milla and Carrasco 2006; van den Brink, Hendriks, Blanken, Koeter, van Zwieten and van Ree 2003; van den Brink, Hendriks, Blanken and van Ree 2002). According to the author's interview with John Strang,

> Ours had about 15–20 people in it and the others were even smaller. It was incredibly intensive and incredibly interesting. This new treatment looked very encouraging as a way of turning around people who looked untreatable … [I]t also meant that we had an extraordinary research opportunity, quite apart from the heroin treatment, because it also meant that we could study what happens when an intravenous heroin injector injects pure diamorphine intravenously or intramuscularly, with no contaminants or anything else. It allowed us to study what actually happens physiologically … [W]e were able to capture what happens to their oxygen levels, showing plummeting oxygen levels in the first five minutes after injection and then coming back up. So we were able to study what were in essence small degrees of acute overdose – and we presume that the phenomena we were able to observe were the same as overdoses which lead to death except that, in our study sessions the extent of overdose was much less severe. These individuals were taking a dose of heroin which had been individually titrated and was deemed clinically to be their appropriate regular maintenance dose.
>
> *(2017, 16–18)*

Once answering basic respiratory physiology questions, the group undertook research that could not have been posed in an unsafe environment. Strang compared the overdose laboratory to an Intensive Care Unit (ICU) dedicated to experimental work and elaborated upon the questions that could be asked and answered:

> We have more work of this kind now. We have ethics approval where we're going to look at taking that same population and saying what if you increase the dose of heroin in that experimental fashion by ten percent? Or by twenty percent? How much more does that change? How much further is the oxygen drop? Or does dose not really make that much difference? The studies don't answer the questions completely, but they do tell you how critical the precise dose is (this is termed the Therapeutic Index which tells you how much safety margin there is between a dose that is effective and a dose that is lethal).
>
> *(17–18)*

Overdose studies designed to meet the highest evidentiary standards of randomized, controlled clinical trials (Blanken, Hendriks, Koeter, van Ree and van den Brink 2005; Haasen, Verthein, Degkwitz, Berger, Krausz, and Naber 2007; Strang, Metrebian, Lintzeris, Potts, Carnwath, Mayet, Williams, Zador, Evers, Groshkova, Charles, Martin and Forzisi 2010; Strang, Groshkova, Uchtenhagen, van den Brink, Haasen, Schechter, Lintzeris, Bell, Pirona, Oviedo-Joekes, Simon and Metrebian 2015) enrolled pulmonary specialist Caroline Jolley to continuously monitor respiration.). enrolled pulmonary specialist Caroline Jolley to study the biological mechanisms of the lungs with continuous respiratory monitoring.

> It remains unanswered, both within the field of addiction or in general medical settings, whether more intensive respiratory monitoring can reduce the risk of significant

> opioid-associated respiratory depression. The findings of our study highlight the need for careful physiological studies of the mechanisms of overdose in heroin addiction."
>
> *(Jolley, Bell, Rafferty, Moxham and Strang 2015)*

Not since the ARC could intoxication be studied in a clinical research ward designed from ground up. Studying overdose required scientific ingenuity. "Unprecedented natural laboratories" sprouted in Australia, Canada, Germany, Spain, Switzerland, and The Netherlands. Social, material, and legal circumstances of the NAC allowed ethical investigation of overdose in ways once foreclosed by political, technical, and ethical constraints, or inhibited by lack of scientific interest. Human subjects enrolled were fully consenting, opioid-tolerant individuals who were not acutely intoxicated or undergoing withdrawal. Not unlike Wikler's single subject, each had "failed" multiple attempts at conventional treatment. Neurophysiological measures included pupil size measurements, pulse oximetry, capnography (used to measure CO2, airflow, and metabolic changes in ventilation during anesthesia), and electrical methods such as "parasternal intercostal muscle electromyogram recordings (EMGpara) to detect acute reductions in neural respiratory drive (NRD) to determine the added value of advanced physiological monitoring over pulse oximetry alone." What would have been unfamiliar to Himmelsbach or Wikler was "breathing science," and precision instruments resulting from "the quantifying spirit" in Braun's history of the spirometer.[14]

Subjects at the ARC would have been disqualified if known to suffer illness or disease such as diabetes or COPD. By contrast, nine out of ten subjects in the 2015 London study had COPD and were on a variety of drugs besides heroin. Researchers could not identify enough subjects enrolled in prescription heroin trials who were *not* carrying a COPD diagnosis (9). Subjects enrolled at least in part because of the prospect of subjective effects of intoxication; they "await[ed] their scheduled injection of diamorphine" in such an "aroused state" that researchers feared they might hyperventilate. Some found it impossible to sit quietly. Recreating overdose in the laboratory requires subjects already well-adapted to maintenance, as non-tolerant subjects could not handle such doses and the vital mechanisms of tolerance, a complex adaptation to a respiratory depressant, remain incompletely known. Although patient-subjects experienced subjective "highs," acute respiratory depression was identified even in tolerant subjects undergoing acute intoxication. It remained unanswered whether intensive monitoring could reduce risks associated with respiratory depression. Overdose and intoxication remain elusive in laboratory and clinic, even as they are commonly enacted beyond the artificial spaces in which the sciences of intoxication are made.

Conclusion: the limits of positivism for the sciences of intoxication

Pleasure and desire stubbornly reside within intoxication, exerting a pull that exceeds the sense-making capacities of sober positivism. Scientists who pursue intoxication tread so carefully that even after decades of research, the seemingly simple mechanisms of overdose and intoxication remain unknown and under-studied. Multiplicities abound, and with them arise the need for less sober sciences—nonreductive sciences that can take into account both the social complexities of overdose and the puzzles of individual variation. Experimental situations may be organized to produce interpretive flexibility and qualitative accounts that enlarge scientific knowledge of pleasure, in addition to pain, toxicity, abuse liability, aversion, and lethality. Setting and social context organize the experience not only of intoxication but of craving, euphoria, tolerance, withdrawal, dysphoria, and lethality.

From the 1990s Decade of the Brain came the public-facing notion that intoxication "hijacks" the brain-reward system by substituting artificial compulsions or "addictions" for natural pleasures. Addiction neuroscience narrated this displacement as catalyzed by the

> activation of the reward pathways (positive reinforcement) [that] transfer information of previously neutral stimuli (reward-stimulus associations; conditioned reinforcement), loss of executive functions (hypofrontality), and a compromised reward system (hyperactivity of the anti-reward circuits; negative reinforcement) to converge in the drug addict to produce compulsive behavior.
>
> *(Koob and LeMoal 2006, 451)*

By routing behavior away from natural rewards and tilting it toward more pleasure than human brains were built to handle, individuals become "tolerant" or used to intoxicated states. Tolerance was framed as a form of neuroadaptation. Addiction neuroscientist George Koob explained this in layperson's terms on a late 1990s Bill Moyers' television special, "Close to Home: The Hijacked Brain, Part 2." Gesturing toward his orchard, Koob spoke of the finite nature of "natural" pleasure governed by regulatory processes in the brain, explaining that "our brains are built to experience a certain amount of pleasure." Acute intoxication—"artificial pleasure created by drugs"—led the brain to expect things that "differ from natural pleasures." This crucial displacement presumes that addiction's displeasures set in with tolerance, a desensitized state that inures the brain to once pleasurable effects.

Incorporating techniques and tasks developed by behavioral pharmacologists, which, in turn, built upon open-ended explorations of human intoxication like those produced at the ARC, addiction neuroscience conserved some conceptual kernels from older lexicons. Current investigators are rarely aware of continuities between notions that chronic intoxication displaces natural pleasures by artificial rewards. In the language of neuroscience, compulsive appetitive behaviors arise from "activation of the reward pathways" and a "powerful drive from the 'dark side', a negative motivational state (dysphoria, anxiety, distress, guilt, etc.)" strengthened by "environmental associations and dysregulated executive functions" (Koob and LeMoal 2006, 451). Neurobiological states of dysregulation are typically described as normally functional mechanisms "gone awry" (Volkow and Li 2004). Both the pleasures and dangers of the silent spring of intoxicants have been rendered tractable. However, social context remains less accessible to laboratory science. What remains needed is deeper comprehension of the conversations among postpositivist researchers (Dennis 2019; Dennis and Farrugia 2017; Fraser, Keane, and Moore 2014; Fraser and Moore 2011; Fraser and valentine 2008), who disrupt the dubious claims and unities through which intoxication events have been subjected to the neurobehavioral sciences. These works emphasize pleasure and positive affect, countering overemphasis on risk, harm, and vulnerability that obscures the full meaning of intoxication, euphoria, dysphoria, and overdose.

Finally, the ethics of the research summarized in this chapter remain to be discussed. The bioethical regime put into place in the US and the UK after World War II foreclosed studies of the kind performed at the ARC. As requirements for clinical trials were put into place in the early 1960s, new "technologies of respect" configured new human subjects (Reubi 2013) and thus installed new relations between the researcher and those researched (Stark forthcoming; Stark and Campbell 2018; Campbell 2007). Such technologies instilled greater social distance between researchers and subjects—helping to shift clinical researchers to preclinical projects and foreclosing consideration of craving and desire. Pharmacology, after all, is a science that radically expanded in the face of industrial demands for experimental systems involving nonhuman subjects as a strictly necessary prelude to trials involving human subjects after the early 1960s. Multiple sciences now contribute to knowledge about human and nonhuman intoxicant uses, to which this volume attests. No longer a silent spring, the sciences of intoxication now present opportunities for integration between social and scientific pursuits.

Notes

1 On scientific legitimacy, respectability, and sobriety, see Danielle Giffort, *Acid Revival: The Psychedelic Renaissance and the Quest for Medical Legitimacy* (Minneapolis: University of Minnesota Press, 2020).

2 On contentions over definition, see WHO Technical Report Series, No. 21, 1950, 6 and O'Brien, Volkow, and Li (2006).

3 The ARC practiced a precocious version of informed consent, as documented in oral history interviews with Himmelsbach (who believed that subjects should be "dealt into" experiments in which they participated). See Campbell (2007); Himmelsbach (1972, 1994).

4 WHO Technical Report Series, No. 21, 1950, 6 and O'Brien, Volkow and Li (2006).

5 Psychodynamic psychoanalyst Sandor Rado called the psychic effects of the intoxicants "pharmacothymia" or the "pharmacogenic orgasm" (1926, 1933). Referred to in the vernacular as "getting high" or "the rush," this effect is the primary indicator that a phenomenological, subjective state of opioid intoxication has been reached.

6 Similarities to neuroscientific theories from the 1990s and 2000s abound; see Koob and Bloom (1998); Koob and LeMoal (2006, 2005, 2001).

7 David W. Maurer and Victor H. Vogel, *Narcotics and Narcotic Addiction*, 3rd edition (Springfield, IL: Charles C. Thomas, 1954), 108. The case report appeared in Fraser, Shaver, Maxwell, and Isbell (1953, 1319). Investigators emphasized that there had been no previous report in English documenting the sole cause of death as abrupt abstinence from barbiturates; of the three cases published in German, two were complicated by acute organic disease in ways that made it impossible for barbiturate withdrawal to be regarded as the sole cause of death.

8 The U.S. Tariff Commission figures were used by Isbell and co-authors to contextualize their 1950 article. There were similar issues in the United Kingdom and several European countries.

9 For an unsuccessful attempt, see the seventh report of the WHO Expert Committee on Addiction-producing Drugs in 1957, followed by adoption of "drug dependence" in the fifteenth report, *WHO Technical Reports Series* 273 (1964). This shift was promoted by the US scientific addiction research community, which advocated destigmatization in the form of more precise scientific nomenclature.

10 Author's interview with C. Robert Schuster, June 16, 2004, San Juan, Puerto Rico, 49.

11 Author's interview with C. Robert Schuster, June 16, 2004, San Juan, Puerto Rico, 51.

12 Author's interviews with George Bigelow (June 2004), Joseph V. Brady (June 2007), Roland Griffiths (June 2004), Louis Harris (June 2003, January 2007), Chrys-Ellen Johanson (June 2004), Travis Thompson (February 2016), C. Robert Schuster (June 2004), and James Woods (June 2004), among others central to the making of modern behavioral pharmacology.

13 Author's interview with George Bigelow (2004, 2).

14 London was historically the site for manufacture of precision instruments and institutionalization of statistical analysis, anatomy, and physiology.

References

Acker, Caroline J. *Creating the American Junkie: Addiction Research in the Classic Era of Narcotic Control*. Baltimore, MD: Johns Hopkins University Press, 2002.

Beecher, Henry K. *Measurement of Subjective Responses: Quantitative Effects of Drugs*. New York: Oxford University Press, 1959.

Beecher, Henry K., Louis Lasagna, and John von Felsinger. "Drug-induced Mood Changes in Man." *JAMA* 157 (March 19, 1955): 1006–1020.

Blanken, Peter, Vincent M. Hendriks, Maarten W. Koeter, Jan M. van Ree, and Wim van den Brink. "Matching of Treatment-Resistant Heroin-Dependent Patients to Medical Prescription of Heroin or Oral Methadone Treatment: Results from Two Randomized Controlled Trials." *Addiction* 100, no. 1 (2005): 89–95.

Braun, Lundy. *Breathing Race into the Machine: The Surprising Career of the Spirometer from Plantation to Genetics*. Minneapolis: University of Minnesota Press, 2014.

Campbell, Nancy D. *OD: Naloxone and the Politics of Overdose*. Cambridge, MA: MIT Press, 2020.

———. *Discovering Addiction: The Science and Politics of Substance Abuse Research*. Ann Arbor: University of Michigan Press, 2007.

Chessick, Richard D. "Erwin Straus: The Phenomenology of Erwin Straus and the Epistemology of Psychoanalysis." *American Journal of Psychotherapy* 53, no. 1 (1999): 82–95.

Collins, Randall. *Interaction Ritual Chains*. Princeton: Princeton University Press, 2004.

Committee on Drug Addiction and Narcotics (CDAN). "Transcripts of the Discussion of Euphoria: A Study of Drug Induced Mood Changes in Man." 11th Meeting, Lexington, Kentucky, on January 9–10, 1953.

Courtwright, David T. *The Age of Addiction: How Bad Habits Became Big Business*. Cambridge, MA: Harvard University Press, 2019.

———. *Forces of Habit: Drugs and the Making of the Modern World*. Cambridge, MA: Harvard University Press, 2002.

Darke, Shane and Johan Duflou. "The toxicology of heroin-related death: estimating survival times." *Addiction* 111, no. 9 (2016): 1607-13.

Dennis, Fay. 2019. *Injecting Bodies in More-Than-Human Worlds*. New York: Routledge.

——— and Adrian Farrugia."Materialising Drugged Pleasures: Practice, Politics, Care." *International Journal of Drug Policy* 49 (2017): 86–91.

Durkheim, Emile. *The Elementary Forms of the Religious Life*. Trans. Joseph Swain. London: George Allen & Unwin, 1912.

Eddy, Nathan B. *The National Research Council Involvement in the Opiate Problem, 1928–1971*. Washington, DC: National Academies Press, 1973.

Fenichel, Otto. *The Psychoanalytic Theory of Neuroses*. New York: Norton, 1950.

Ferri, Marica, Marina Davoli, and Carlo A. Perucci. "Heroin maintenance for chronic heroin-dependent individuals." *Cochrane Database of Systematic Reviews*, Issue 12 (2011). Art. No.: CD003410. DOI: 10.1002/14651858.CD003410.pub4

Fischer, Benedikt, Eugenia Oviedo-Joekes, Peter Blanken, Christian Haasen, Jürgen Rehm, Martin T. Schechter, John Strang, and Wim van den Brink. "Heroin-Assisted Treatment (HAT) a Decade Later: A Brief Update on Science and Politics." *Journal of Urban Health* 84, no. 4 (2007): 552–562.

Fraser, H. Franklin, "Tolerance to and Physical Dependence on Opiates, Barbiturates, and Alcohol." *Annual Review of Medicine*, vol. 8 (1957): 427-440.

———. "Chronic Barbiturate Intoxication: Further Studies." *Archives of Internal Medicine* 94 (1954): 34–41.

Fraser, H. Franklin, Anna J. Eisenman, Abraham Wikler and Frank T. Pescor, "Chronic Barbiturate Intoxication: Further Studies." *Archives of Neurology and Psychiatry* 94 (1954): 34–41.

Fraser, H. Franklin, M. R. Shaver, E. S. Maxwell, and Harris Isbell, "Death Due to Withdrawal of Barbiturates." *Annals of Internal Medicine* 38 (1953,): 1319–1325, on p. 1319.

Fraser, H. Franklin, Abraham Wikler, Richard E. Belleville, Carl Essig and Harris E. Hill, "Minimum Dose of Barbiturates Required to Produce Physical Dependence." *Federation Proceedings* 15 (1956): 1.

Fraser, Suzanne, Helen Keane, and David Moore. *Habits: Re-making Addiction*. London: Palgrave-Macmillan, 2014.

——— and David Moore. *The Drug Effect: Health, Crime and Society*. Cambridge, UK: Cambridge University Press, 2011.

Fraser, Suzanne and kylie valentine. *Substance and Substitution: Methadone Subjects in Liberal Societies*. London: Palgrave-Macmillan, 2008.

Ghiabi, Maziyar, ed., *Power and Illicit Drugs in the Global South*. London: Routledge, 2018.

Giffort, Danielle. *Acid Redux: The Impure Scientist and the Remaking of Psychedelic Expertise*. Minneapolis: University of Minnesota Press, 2020.

Goldberg, Steven R., and C. Robert Schuster. "Conditioned Suppression by a Stimulus Associated with Nalorphine in Morphine-Dependent Monkeys." *Journal of the Experimental Analysis of Behavior* 10 (1967): 235–242.

Gomart, Emilie. "Surprised by Methadone: In Praise of Drug Substitution Treatment in a French Clinic." *Body & Society* 10, nos. 2–3 (2004): 85–110.

———. "Methadone: Six Effects in Search of a Substance." *Social Studies of Science* 32, no. 1 (2002): 93–135.

Haasen, Christian, Uwe Verthein, Peter Degkwitz, Juergen Berger, Michael Krausz, and Dieter Naber. "Heroin-Assisted Treatment for Opioid Dependence: Randomised Controlled Trial." *British Journal of Psychiatry* 191 (2007): 55–62.

Hagen, Edward H. and Roger J. Sullivan, "The Evolutionary Significance of Drug Toxicity over Reward." In *The Routledge Handbook of Philosophy and Science of Addiction*. Eds. Hanna Pickard and Serge H. Ahmed New York: Routledge, 2018, pp. 102–119.

Harden, Victoria Angela. *Inventing the NIH: Federal Biomedical Research Policy, 1887–1937*. Baltimore, MD: The Johns Hopkins University Press, 1986.

Hartnoll, Richard L., Martin C. Mitcheson, Alan Battersby, Geoffrey Brown, Margaret Ellis, Philip Fleming, and Nicholas Hedley. "Evaluation of Heroin Maintenance in Controlled Trial." *Archives of General Psychiatry* 37, no. 8 (1980): 877–884.

Hartogsohn, Ido. *American Trip: Set, Setting, and the Psychedelic Experience in the Twentieth Century*. Cambridge, MA: MIT Press, 2020.

Herlinghaus, Hermann. *Narcoepics: A Global Aesthetics of Sobriety*. London: Bloomsbury Academic, 2013.

Herzberg, David. *White Market Drugs: Big Pharma and the Hidden History of Addiction in America*. Chicago: University of Chicago Press, 2020.

———. *Happy Pills in America: From Miltown to Prozac*. Baltimore, MD: Johns Hopkins University Press, 2009.

Hill, Harris E., Richard E. Belleville, and Abraham Wikler, "Motivational Determinants in Modification of Behavior by Morphine and Pentobarbital." *AMA Archives of Neurology and Psychiatry* 77 (1957): 28.

Himmelsbach, Clifton K. Interview by Jon M. Harkness and Gail Savitt, Advisory Committee for Human Radiation Experiments. November 2, 1994.

———. Interview by Wyndham D. Miles, Oral History Interviews, Accession 613, History of Medicine Division, National Library of Medicine. May 4, 1972.

———. "The Morphine Abstinence Syndrome, Its Nature and Treatment." *Annals of Internal Medicine* 15 (1941): 829–830.

Hubbard, Justin Wade. "'You Can't Fool the P Test': American Science, the Department of Defense, and the Unlikely Invention of the War on Drugs, 1945–1980." PhD diss., Vanderbilt University, 2019.

Isbell, Harris. "Clinical Research, 1944–63." In William R. Martin and Harris Isbell, *Drug Addiction and the U. S. Public Health Service: Proceedings of a Symposium Commemorating the 40th Anniversary of the Addiction Research Center at Lexington, Ky*. Rockville, MD: U.S. Department of Health, Education and Welfare, 1978, pp. 27–41.

Isbell, Harris, Sol Altschul, Conan Kornetsky, Anna J. Eisenman, Harold G. Flanary, and H. Frank Fraser, "Chronic Barbiturate Intoxication: An Experimental Study." *Archives of Neurology and Psychiatry* 64 (1950):1–28.

Isbell, Harris, H. Franklin Fraser, Abraham Wikler, Richard E. Belleville, and Anna J. Eisenman, "An Experimental Study of the Etiology of 'Rum Fits' and Delirium Tremens." *Quarterly Journal of Studies on Alcohol*, 16 (1955): 1–33.

Jolley, Caroline J., James Bell, Gerrard F. Rafferty, John Moxham, and John Strang. "Understanding Heroin Overdose: A Study of the Acute Respiratory Depressant Effects of Injected Pharmaceutical Heroin." *PLoS One* 10, no. 10 (2015):.DOI:10.1371/journal.pone.01409

Kenner, Alison. *Breathtaking: Asthma Care in a Time of Climate Change*. Minneapolis: University of Minnesota Press, 2018.

Kolb, Lawrence, Sr. "Drug Addiction in Its Relation to Crime." *Mental Hygiene* 9 (1925a): 74–89.

———. "Types and Characteristics of Drug Addicts." *Mental Hygiene* 9 (1925b): 300–313.

———. "Pleasure and Deterioration from Narcotic Addiction." *Mental Hygiene* 9 (1925c): 699–724.

——— and Clifton K. Himmelsbach, "Clinical Studies of Drug Addiction: III. A Critical Review of the Withdrawal Treatments with Method of Evaluating Abstinence Syndromes." *American Journal of Psychiatry* 94 (1938): 759–797.

Koob, George F. and LeMoal, *Neurobiology of Addiction*, New York: Elsevier, 2006.

———. "Plasticity of Reward Neurocircuitry and the 'Dark Side' of Drug Addiction." *Nature Neuroscience* 11, no. 8 (2005): 1442–1444.

———. "Drug addiction, Dysregulation of Reward, and Allostasis." *Neuropharmacology* 24, no. 1 (2001): 97–129.

Koob, George F., and Floyd E. Bloom. "Neuroscience of Addiction." *Neuron* 21 (September 1998): 467–476.

Latour, Bruno. "Why Has Critique Run out of Steam? From Matters of Fact to Matters of Concern." *Critical Inquiry* 30, no. 2 (2004): 225–248.

March, John C., Eugenia Oviedo-Joekes, Emilio Perea-Milla, and Fracisco Carrasco. "Controlled Trial of Prescribed Heroin in the Treatment of Opioid Addiction." *Journal of Substance Abuse Treatment* 31, no. 2 (2006): 203–211.

Maurer, David W., and Victor H. Vogel, *Narcotics and Narcotic Addiction*, 3rd edition. Springfield: Charles C. Thomas, 1954.

May, Everette L., and Arthur E. Jacobson. "The Committee on Problems of Drug Dependence: A Legacy of the National Academy of Sciences, An Historical Account." *Drug and Alcohol Dependence* 23 (1989): 183–218.

Mol, Annemarie. *The Body Multiple: Ontology in Medical Practice*. Durham: Duke University Press, 2002.

———. "Ontological Politics. A Word and Some Questions." The Sociological Review 47, no. 1_suppl (May 1999): 74–89.

O'Brien, Charles P., Nora Volkow, and T-K Li. "What's in a Word? Addiction Versus Dependence in DSM-V." *American Journal of Psychiatry* 163, no. 5 (2006): 764–765.

Oviedo-Joekes, Eugenia, Suzanne Brissette, David C. Marsh, Pierre Lauzon, Daphne Guh, Aslam Anis, and Martin T. Schechter. "Diacetylmorphine versus Methadone for the Treatment of Opioid Addiction." *New England Journal of Medicine* 361, no. 8 (2009): 777–786.

Perneger, Thomas V., Francisco Giner, Miguel del Rio, and Annie Mino. "Randomised Trial of Heroin Maintenance Programme for Addicts Who Fail in Conventional Drug Treatments." *British Medical Journal* 317, no. 7150 (1998): 13–18.

Prus, Adam J., John R. James, and John A. Rosecrans. "Conditioned Place Preference." In *Frontiers in Neuroscience. Methods of Behavioral Analysis in Neuroscience*, Ed. J. J. Buccafusco, pp. 59–76. CRC Press/Routledge/Taylor & Francis Group, 2009.

Rado, Sandor. *Adaptational Psychodynamics: Motivation and Control*. Eds. Jean Jameson and Henriette Klein. New York: Science House, 1969.

———. "Fighting Narcotic Bondage." *Comprehensive Psychiatry* 4, no. 3 (1963): 160–167.

———. "'Narcotic Bondage': A General Theory of the Dependence on Narcotic Drugs." *American Journal of Psychiatry* 114, no. 2 (1957): 165–170.

———. "The Psychoanalysis of Pharmacothymia (Drug Addiction)," Trans. B. D. Lewin. *The Psychoanalytic Quarterly*, 2 (1933): 1–23.

———. "The Psychic Effects of Intoxicants." *International Journal of Psychoanalysis* 7 (1926): 396–413.

Rasmussen, Nicholas. "'Goofball Panic': Barbiturates, 'Dangerous' and Addictive Drugs, and the Regulation of Medicine in Postwar America." In *Prescribed: Writing, Filling, Using, and Abusing the Prescription in Modern America*, Eds. Jeremy A. Greene, and Elizabeth Siegal Watkins. Baltimore: The Johns Hopkins University Press, 2012, pp. 23–45, on p. 27.

Reubi, David. "Re-Moralising Medicine: The Bioethical Thought Collective and the Regulation of the Body in British Medical Research." *Social Theory and Health* 11, no. 2 (2013): 215–235.

Rhodes, Tim, and Kari Lancaster. "Evidence-Making Interventions in Health: A Conceptual Framing." *Social Science in Medicine* 238 (2019): 112488. doi: 10.1016/j.socscimed.2019.112488.

Room, Robin. "Spirituality, Intoxication, and Addiction: Six Forms of Relationship," *Substance Use and Misuse* 48 (2013): 1109–1113.

Rosenthal, Richard J., and Suzanne B. Faris, "The Etymology and Early History of 'Addiction'." *Addiction Research & Theory* 27, no. 5 (2019): 437–449.

Schuster, C. Robert, and James H. Woods. "The Conditioned Reinforcing Effects of Stimuli Associated with Morphine Reinforcement." *International Journal of the Addictions* 3 (1968): 223–230.

Shrank, Cathy, "Beastly Metamorphoses: Losing Control in Early Modern Literary Culture." In *Intoxication and Society: Problematic Pleasures of Drugs and Alcohol*, Eds. Jonathan Herring, Ciara Regan, Darin Weinberg, and Phil Withington. Basingstoke, UK: Palgrave Macmillan, 2012.

Siegel, Ronald K. *Intoxication: The Universal Drive for Mind-Altering Substances*. New York: E. P. Dutton, 1989, 2005.

———. "LSD_Induced Effects in Elephants: Comparisons with Musth Behavior." *Bulletin of the Psychonomic Society* 22 (1984): 53–56.

———. "Dizziness as an Altered State of Consciousness." *Journal of Altered States of Consciousness* 5 (1979–1980): 87–107.

———. "Ginseng Abuse Syndrome: Problems with the Panacea." *JAMA* 241 (1979): 1614–1615.

———. "Natural Animal Addictions: An Ethological Perspective." In *Psychopathology in Animals: Research and Clinical Implications*, Ed. J. D. Keehn. New York: Academic Press, 1979.

———. "Herbal Intoxication: Psychoactive Effects from Herbal Cigarettes, Tea, and Capsules." *JAMA* 236 (1976): 473–476.

———. "An Ethologic Search for Self-Administration of Hallucinogens." *International Journal of the Addictions* 8 (1973): 373–393.

———. "Studies of Hallucinogens in Fish, Birds, Mice and Men: The Behavior of 'Psychedelic' Populations." In *Advances in Neuro-Psychopharmacology*, Eds. O. Vinar, Z. Votava, and P. B. Bradley. Amsterdam: North-Holland Publishing, 1971, pp. 311–318.

Siegel, Ronald K., and Mark Brodie. "Alcohol Self-Administration by Elephants." *Bulletin of the Psychonomic Society* 22 (1984): 49–52.

Siegel, Ronald K., and Murray E. Jarvik. "DMT Self-Administration in Monkeys in Isolation." *Bulletin of the Psychonomic Society* 16 (1980b): 117–120.

———. "Self-Regulation of Coca-Chewing and Cocaine Smoking by Monkeys." In *Cocaine 1980*, Ed. F. R. Jeri. Lima, Peru: Pacific Press, 1980a, pp. 1–10.

———. "Drug-Induced Hallucinations in Animals and Man." In *Hallucinations: Behavior, Experience, and Theory*, Eds. Ronald K. Siegel, and L. J. West. New York: John Wiley, 1975.

Stark, Laura. *The Normals: A People's History*. Chicago: University of Chicago Press, forthcoming.

——— and Nancy D. Campbell. "The Ineffable: A Framework for the Study of Methods through the Case of Mid-Century Mind-Brain Sciences." *Social Studies of Science* 48, no. 6 (2018): 789–820.

Strang, John. *Interview by Nancy D. Campbell*. London, United Kingdom, March 7, 2017.

———. "Death matters: understanding heroin/opiate overdose risk and testing potential to prevent death." Addiction 110, S2 (2015): 27–35.

Strang, John, Teodora Groshkova, Ambros Uchtenhagen, Wim van den Brink, Christian Haasen, Martin T. Schechter, Nick Lintzeris, James Bell, Alessandro Pirona, Eugenia Oviedo-Joekes, Roland Simon, and Nicola Metrebian. "Heroin on Trial: Systematic Review and Meta-Analysis of Randomised Trials of Diamorphine-Prescribing as Treatment for Refractory Heroin Addiction." *British Journal of Psychiatry* 207, no. 1 (2015): 5–14.

Strang, John, Nicola Metrebian, Nicholas Lintzeris, Laura Potts, Tom Carnwath, Soraya Mayet, Hugh Williams, Deborah Zador, Richard Evers, Teodora Groshkova, Vikki Charles, Anthea Martin, and Luciana Forzisi. "Supervised Injectable Heroin or Injectable Methadone versus Optimised Oral Methadone as Treatment for Chronic Heroin Addicts in England after Persistent Failure in Orthodox Treatment (RIOTT): A Randomised Trial." *Lancet* 375, no. 9729 (2010): 1885–1895.

Tone, Andrea. *The Age of Anxiety: A History of America's Turbulent Affair with Tranquilizers*. New York: Basic Books, 2009.

van den Brink, Wim, V. M. Hendriks, Peter Blanken, M. W. Koeter, Barbara J. van Zwieten, and J. M. van Ree. "Medical Prescription of Heroin to Treatment Resistant Heroin Addicts: Two Randomised Controlled Trials." *British Medical Journal* 327, no. 7410 (2003): 310.

van den Brink, Wim, V. M. Hendriks, Peter Blanken, and J. M. Van Ree, "Beneficial Effect of Heroin in Heroin Addicts." *European Neuropsychopharmacology* 12, no. 2 (2002): S120.

Volkow, Nora D., and T-K Li, "Drug Addiction: The Neurobiology of Behaviour Gone Awry." *Nature Reviews Neuroscience* 5, no. 12 (2004): 963–970.

Wikler, Abraham. "Conditioning Factors in Opiate Addiction and Relapse." In *Narcotics*, Eds. D.M. Wilner, and G.G. Kassebaum. New York: McGraw-Hill, 1965, pp. 85–100.

———. "A Psychodynamic Study of a Patient during Experimental Self-regulated Readdiction to Morphine." *Psychiatric Quarterly* 26 (1952): 279–293.

Wikler, Abraham, and Frank T. Pescor, "Classical Conditioning of a Morphine Abstinence Phenomenon, Reinforcement of Opioid-Drinking Behavior and "Relapse" in Morphine-Addicted Rats." *Psychopharmacologia* 10 (1967): 255–284.

Withington, Phil. "Introduction: Cultures of Intoxication," *Past & Present* 222, no. Supp. 9 (2014): 9–33.

———. *Society in Early Modern England: The Vernacular Origins of Some Powerful Ideas*. Cambridge: Polity Press, 2010.

World Health Organization. "Expert Committee on Addiction-Producing Drugs. Fifteenth Report." *WHO Technical Reports Series* 273 (1964).

———. "Expert Committee on Addiction-Producing drugs. Seventh Report." *WHO Technical Reports Series* 116 (1957).

———. "Expert Committee on Drugs Liable to Produce Addiction. Report on the Second Session." *WHO Technical Reports Series* 21 (1950).

20

TRIP REPORTS

Exploring the experience of psychedelic intoxication

Jonas Bååth and Johan Nordgren

Introduction

While it is sometimes said that the truth is told by children and drunkards, popular belief has it that an intoxicated person lacks trustworthiness. This belief implies a methodological problem for the study of intoxication in human experience. Experiences of intoxication can only be produced while 'under the influence', implying the combination of the 'inner', subjective experience of intoxication and the social and material contexts of that experience. Clinical scientists use standardized surveys to analyze the research subjects' individual experiences (see e.g. Barrett, Johnson, and Griffiths 2015), and seek to define the mechanics of psychedelic experiences and possible therapeutic outcomes (dos Santos and Hallak 2020; Majić, Schmidt, and Gallinat 2015). However, Angus Bancroft exemplifies the problem of capturing experiences of intoxication with conventional scientific methods; 'It is fundamentally an experience of the individual, and although mechanisms of this experience can be described through pharmacology and neurology they cannot capture what it is, only why it is' (Bancroft 2009:73; see also Langlitz 2012:257).

In this chapter, we show how experiences of intoxication may be studied by analyzing trip reports – written and oral accounts of intoxication – from online drug information forums and libraries. We focus on trip reports of psychedelic drugs, including lysergic acid diethylamide (LSD), dimethyltryptamine (DMT) and psilocybin. These drugs, when ingested in high doses, 'have the potential to alter consciousness and to evoke phenomena such as hallucinations' (Blom 2010:249). We will analyze these trip reports as ethnographic texts, focusing on subjective *experiences of intoxication* induced from psychedelic drugs. By studying trip reports, we thus analyze experiences of intoxication as emic knowledge, i.e., placing the psychedelic drug user's knowledge and experiences at the forefront (Atkinson and Morriss 2017; Barratt and Maddox 2016).

In general, trip reports can be seen as a specific genre of drug writing containing personal written and oral reports of the experiences of drug use. Psychedelic drug users and authors of trip reports are often referred to as 'psychonauts' (cf. Blom 2010). Some of the most famous psychedelic trip reports are Aldous Huxley's *The doors of perception* (1954/2010), reporting on his experience of mescaline, Gordon Wasson's 1957 report on Mazatec 'magic mushrooms' (see Ceraso 2008) and Albert Hofmann's original report on LSD (2013). However, while white, Western and academically educated men have

 DOI: 10.4324/9780429058141-26

authored the most well-known trip reports (Jay 2019:19), psychonauts include people of diverse genders, ethnicities, classes and faiths (Knight 2013; Palmer and Horowitz 2000). Today, psychonauts share trip reports in online forums and repositories where one of several possible aims is to assist other users to experience safe and informed trips (Barratt 2017; Kjellgren and Soussan 2011; Soussan and Kjellgren 2014). The act of sharing integrates the psychonaut within a community of experienced recreational drug users, distancing themselves from 'the reckless and uninformed manner in which inexperienced users take drugs' (Söderberg 2016:301).

In the chapter, we will argue that intoxication is best analyzed as *structured experiences* (see also Kjellgren and Soussan 2011; Preller and Vollenweider 2018), in other words that intoxication experiences are not random, but instead follow observable *patterns*. We emphasize two aspects of intoxication experiences that illustrate these patterns: the *context* of intoxication and the *inner experience* of intoxication. Regarding the context of intoxication, our point of departure is based on Zinberg's conceptual triad 'drug, set and setting' (1984). He argued that the context of drug use is imperative for understanding why and how someone uses a drug, and that the experienced effects of drugs do not solely arise from 'the pharmacologic action of the substance itself' (Zinberg 1984:5). Instead, it is the combination of drug(s) and the mindset of the drug user, or 'the attitude of the person at the time of use, including personality structure' (Zinberg 1984:5), which fosters the experiences. To understand experiences of intoxication, we thus need to take the social and material contexts into account, the drug user's mindset, including personality, expectations, attitudes and knowledge of the drug, as well as the drug of choice. By applying the 'drug, set and setting' perspective to trip reports, we will show how it is possible to identify specific patterns of intoxication experiences. The other aspect we focus on is the *inner experience* of intoxication, which includes thoughts, emotions and perceptions (Majić et al. 2015; Preller and Vollenweider 2018). Inner experiences of psychedelic drugs, such as LSD and psilocybin, have been studied in clinical settings by using the 'Mystical Experience Questionnaire' (MEQ). The MEQ evaluates what religious, or 'mystical', experiences the respondents recognize while intoxicated (Barrett et al. 2015; see also Majić et al. 2015). While MEQ certainly has its uses, we will show that drugs might foster inner experiences of intoxication which do not lend themselves solely to a religious or mystic vocabulary when analyzing trip reports from online sources. The following section outlines our methodological considerations for studying trip reports.

Methodological considerations

Our data for this chapter stems from voluntarily supplied trip reports from publicly accessible online sources. This kind of material can be studied as ethnographic text (see Atkinson and Coffey 2010; Barratt and Maddox 2016; Page and Singer 2010) and lends itself to ethnographic text analysis. In ethnographic text analysis, the researcher uses 'native' texts to study the participants' constructions, conventions and practices in a given (sub)culture (Hammersley and Atkinson 2007:121–141). In our case, psychonauts are local experts who produce texts as documentary constructions of reality. These constructions, in turn, produce facts, records, diagnoses, decisions and rules that are crucial for social activities (Atkinson and Coffey 2010; cf. Atkinson and Morriss 2017; for studies of other cultures, see e.g. Gamst 1980; Gunnarsson and Elam 2012). Using an ethnographic text analysis approach, we consider the trip reports' language and content in relation to the texts' uses and functions in 'psychonaut culture', placing narratives within a cultural context while also scrutinizing their construction (Atkinson and Delamont 2006).

Empirical material

The trip reports used in this chapter come from three different drug information libraries and forums: Bluelight, Erowid and Shroomery. We chose these three libraries because they offer a vast number of trip reports gathered for different and distinct purposes. Bluelight is 'an international, online, harm reduction community committed to reducing the harms associated with drug use' (Bluelight.org 2019), and hosts a forum that covers topics related to drug use, including a sub-forum called 'Trip Reports' with over 10,000 threads (see also Barratt 2017). While only members can post, the discussions are accessible to the public without being a registered member. Erowid.org, or 'The vaults of Erowid' as its title suggests, is an online library hosted by Erowid, 'a member-supported organization providing access to reliable, non-judgmental information about psychoactive plants, chemicals, and related issues' (Erowid 2017). Erowid.org is a vast website, supplying resources on everything from cultural and religious practices to a library of published works on psychedelics. In this chapter, we refer to Erowid's 'Experience Vaults', which is the organization's library of experiences, including but not limited to trip reports (Erowid 2019). The trip reports in this vault are publicly accessible and contain information on how to cite them in journalistic or scientific works. Finally, Shroomery is an initiative to 'help spread accurate information about magic mushrooms so [that] people can make informed decisions about what they put in their bodies' (Shroomery 2019a). One of Shroomery's sub-forums is dedicated to 'trip reports', categorized according to the quantity or potency of the ingested mushroom, starting at micro dosing followed by levels 1–5, where 5 is the most potent dosage (Shroomery 2019b).

In general, drug information libraries are an important part of internet drug culture (Andersson and Kjellgren 2017; Barratt 2017; Bogenschutz 2000). In their posts, the library users both challenge and reproduce conventional narratives of drug use (Kataja et al. 2018), and the data that trip reports consist of can be called 'naturally occurring', i.e., unsolicited data supplied for intra-cultural communication (Enghoff and Aldridge 2019). They are 'naturally occurring' because first, the subject was not part of a scientifically designed study, and second, because the report was written with the aim of giving a personal account of the experience (Enghoff and Aldridge 2019). We selected individual trip reports by focusing on two criteria: first, reports of the 'classic hallucinogens', i.e., the most archetypical serotoninergic psychedelics: LSD, DMT and psilocybin (dos Santos and Hallak 2020); and second, rich and detailed descriptions and narratives of the trip. Using these criteria, we identified and studied approximately 100 reports from the three libraries. After reviewing these reports, we concluded that the sample had reached saturation due to recurring patterns and narratives of intoxication. While there are many more reports of this kind, this study sought to explore the reports as a means of studying intoxication experiences. A conclusive analysis of all available reports would thus be premature because the large quantity of data would demand a systematized framework, which is yet to be developed. This chapter might be regarded as a first step in that direction. To highlight the value of ethnographic text analysis for understanding intoxication, we focus on nine reports: four reports from Bluelight, three from Erowid and two from Shroomery. We selected these nine reports because they display an internal variety of intoxication experience while supplying clear, rich and useful examples for our thematization and analysis.

Trip reports generally share information about types of drug used, dosage and means of administration. On Erowid, several users have uploaded a table as part of their trip report accounts that includes substance(s) and dosage, but often also timing, mode of administration (e.g. smoke or liquid) and the psychonaut's body weight, that can help new psychonauts to administer their trip (see, for example, trip reports from Chris 2006; Lucy 2018; Reverse Pingpong 2017). Supplying information in this manner is common in psychonaut culture, where psychonauts often compare different drugs, dosages and means of consumption (Andersson and Kjellgren 2017; Duxbury 2018). In the following, we will quote the original trip reports and explain specific expressions or metaphors after the quotations if needed. Some quotes include parentheses which are part of the original quotes.

Ethical implications of studying online trip reports

When studying online trip reports, we also considered the following ethical issues. Online drug libraries and online forums are particularly well-suited sources of data for ethnographic text analyses since they offer first-hand accounts of intoxication. Such accounts reduce the risk of (re)producing dominant scholarly (or popular) narratives, and highlight those 'native' to the studied intoxication culture (cf. Barratt and Maddox 2016; Duxbury 2018). Since the reports are public and freely contributed, we chose to quote them in a rich and liberal manner, thus highlighting the authorship and contribution of the informants. Moreover, we followed the 'fair use' clauses on the respective online library or forum's homepage to ensure the ethical reproduction of trip report quotations. Such clauses offer important ethical guidelines since online, public posts by anonymous users often fall within a gray zone of academic ethics' guidelines. Moreover, the individual report's sensitivity and the potential risks that quoting it poses for the author might deviate drastically between different cases (Roberts 2015). We therefore sought to quote excerpts which lent themselves to anonymization without losing their analytical value, and excerpts which included little to no incriminating details beyond psychedelics use.

The experience of psychedelic intoxication

The language used in trip reports is both filled with metaphors and with particular expressions well known within the psychonaut culture. For example, when a Bluelight user writes: '*…I find my self* [sic] *with two hits of 225 ug SpongeBob blotter*' (User145667),[1] it means that s/he holds 2 × 225 micrograms of LSD infused into a small, stamp-like piece of paper, a 'blotter', with a picture of the children's cartoon character 'SpongeBob SquarePants' printed on it. As well as 'LSD', psychonauts may refer to this substance as 'acid'. 'Blotter' is the specific mode of administration. While blotter is the conventional mode of administration, LSD can be distributed as a liquid, either dropped directly on the tongue using a pipette or mixed into a beverage and drunk. When another Bluelight user writes: 'Yesterday I gave myself a fair good wallop in the head with 4HO-DMT, at 30 mg' (PippUK), s/he refers to experiencing a metaphorical sudden and surreal blow to the head following the use of 30 mg of a synthesized drug similar to psilocybin, indicated by the expression '4HO-DMT'. Psychonauts generally refer to (naturally occurring) psilocybin from a mushroom or the peyote cactus in terms of these modes of administration. In the following sections, we first explore the psychonauts' context of intoxication and then turn to the inner experience of intoxication.

Context of psychedelic intoxication

As argued above, contexts of intoxication can help us to understand observable patterns of intoxication. In the following, we will examine how trip reports reveal psychonauts' experience of intoxication and how it is shaped by and related to the psychonauts' *setting*:

psychosocial factors, including personality, attitudes, expectations and knowledge (Zinberg 1984). We will explore two important contextual factors that are discussed in the trip reports: planning a trip and the role of the setting.

Planning the trip

The importance of organized preparations before 'embarking' on a trip is widely discussed in the trip reports. Caution and preparation are integral to a proper trip, often contrasted with amateurish 'party' intoxication, and well known within a Western psychonaut culture (Söderberg 2016; see also Power 2014). Trip reports discuss the psychonaut's knowledge of different drugs' intoxication-effects – individually and in concert – as instrumental for achieving the best possible experience.

Two examples will highlight how previous experiences of a certain drug (or lack thereof) influence the psychonaut's knowledge and expectations of intoxication.

If the trip report outlines a psychonaut's first experience of a substance, it is often emphasized in the report's headline, such as 'My first DMT – can I have passed out?' (Bluelight user 3). In this example, before going into the details of the trip, Bluelight user 3 describes the psychosocial context as: 'This night, I was extremely tired. Before 12 hours of work, I only got four hours of sleep'. This context contrasts with the psychonaut's plan, namely to try DMT when 'rested and fed, on a relaxed day'. This psychonaut deviates from these plans due to his or her high expectations of DMT, '… the substance I've been obsessed with and investigated since I saw the documentary *DMT: The Spirit Molecule*. So, I decided to take the DMT right then and there around midnight' (Bluelight user 3). However, while deviating from the plan, Bluelight user 3 shows the dedication and planning that goes into embarking on a first experience of a hallucinogenic drug. Similarly, Erowid user Reverse Pingpong reports:

> I had been planning this for a long time. About six years to be precise. Actually it was the time that I first got the idea of trying psychedelics. As the moment passed I never got around to it until years later, when I happened to read a book by Albert Hoffman [sic], the father of LSD. Instantly hooked again I started looking for LSD in order to experiment with it. I've never been a drug user. A few hits of cannabis is [sic] the most I've ever done. I'm a fairly heavy drinker though, so I certainly don't patronize myself on that front. /…/ I spent a lot of time reading other peoples [sic] trip reports and gathering information about the drug I was about to take.
>
> *(Reverse Pingpong 2017)*

Both Reverse Pingpong and Bluelight user 3 show that they prepared themselves for a long time with a definitive goal in mind: to experience a drug-induced hallucination. These preparations are, to an extent, part of their 'set', meaning that the psychonaut seeks to acquire a certain mindset or mood to appreciate the trip. Moreover, Reverse Pingpong details his or her experiences of other intoxicating substances and moral disposition toward intoxication in general. Both of these psychonauts show that they do not seek to be surprised by the experience of intoxication, but rather to mimic others' experiences of psychedelic drugs as portrayed in popular media, such as the documentary mentioned. However, at the end of Bluelight user 3's report, s/he ponders whether the lack of the desired mental state could have caused the seemingly negative experience of passing out: 'I mean, I wonder if sleep deprivation, and the sudden and intense experience took me off guard, might have knocked me out?' (Bluelight user 3).

The seemingly more experienced psychonaut 'PippUK' outlines considerable practical preparations for his trip on the psilocybin-like hallucinogen 4HO-DMT. First, he had 'a light breakfast of cereal so that the little packet [4HO-DMT] would not open on an empty stomach' and prepared additional drugs to counteract eventual negative effects of the hallucinogen, such as 'a lightbulb vaporizer containing about 50mg of spice [synthetic cannabinoid]'. However, he did not prepare the 'set' in the same minute manner:

> ...in retrospect I hadn't really prepared emotionally so well. I knew that the trip was intended as a bit of DIY [Do It Yourself] therapy, because this is what I had been considering for my trip during my week off. However, that morning I had set everything up for the session but had not had the useful quiet time of contemplation about what might transpire, and I ploughed in rather hurriedly.
>
> *(PippUK)*

These trip reports suggest a belief that mental preparations are key to achieving the sought-after experience from hallucinogenic drugs, and that bad experiences might be the result of poor preparation. The reports do however deviate in one significant way. Bluelight user 3 is a novice psychonaut and thus asks the Bluelight community if the negative experience could have been caused by bad mental preparation. PippUK, however, concludes from experience that the negative experience must have been caused by bad mental or emotional preparation. Nevertheless, these psychonauts describe planned uses of psychedelics, including explicit considerations of the psychosocial context. In this way, both the reports engage with the community of psychonauts by, respectively, asking for and giving advice on the procedure of preparing one's set (cf. Andersson and Kjellgren 2017; Duxbury 2018).

The role of the setting

Beyond the drug and the set, Zinberg (1984) distinguishes the importance of *setting* for experiences of intoxication, referring to the psychonaut's material environment and, occasionally, also his/her social environment (i.e., other people, social positions and relational structures). In the following example, Bluelight user 4 reports on the setting in which s/he took 'two hits of Albert 3000 (some nice potent acid)' and remarks on the importance of the setting for the trip experience:

> I was staying in a friend's beach house together with X. Her friend Y was also there. The place is enormous (well, big for me anyway) with long hallways and a great many rooms. It was obviously built and decorated during the 1960s and was unchanged since. The floors have a fluffy bright red carpet and the curtains are bright purple. To me, the house has very 1960s furniture in matching colours /.../ The interior shows that the owners have travelled a lot, and artifacts from their travels are placed in interesting ways throughout the house. One room even has big black and white tiles.
>
> *(Bluelight user 4)*

In this report, Bluelight user 4 intersperses the experience of intoxication with a description of the setting. Both the material and social settings are described: the interior of the house, and the user's relationship with the people present and those who own and who have decorated the house. Moreover, s/he emphasizes that the setting is important for the reader to understand the experience of intoxication. The material environment is important in psychedelic culture, and some psychonauts alter the interior to control and enhance their experiences (Parley 2016). The social environment becomes especially vivid when Bluelight user 4 comments on his or her own social position; the house is described as lavish and foreign, and the label 'beach house' suggests that the owners have multiple properties. Moreover, the psychonaut's impression is that 'the owners have travelled a lot'. This example shows that the social environment influences his/her experience of intoxication. The social environment shows in the experienced distance between the psychonaut's social position (i.e., class) and the position s/he finds that the property owners inhabit, provoking thoughts about differences of socioeconomic status.

An important aspect of the social environment can also be people 'sitting' with the user, for example, a trusted companion who aids the psychonaut in different practices, which has been developed specifically within the psychedelic culture as a way of minimizing unwanted experiences, such as bad trips. Trusted companions have assisted users both in clinical and non-clinical settings (Parley 2016; Pollan 2018). Other people, close to the psychonauts, can also be important for the experience of intoxication. The following quote from Shroomery user 1 exemplifies the role of other people during the trip, here the psychonaut's wife ('wifey'), who has also ingested a psychoactive substance (thus is not functioning as a sitter):

> Then I kept coming out somewhat clear and thinking 'Oh, this must be the end of the trip' but it wasn't. I had these little 'awakenings' over and over again. I looked at my wife in bed next to me, and I saw her hair looked like a wave for [sic] ocean flowing off of her head and out into space … I did find myself a little too preoccupied with her comfort though. I must have asked her 200 times if she was ok. Next time, I'll write it on paper 'wifey is just fine, focus on yourself.'
>
> *(Shroomery user 1 2019)*

The report indicates a relationship of trust and affection, strongly related to positive experiences and the ability to experience the trip in a positive manner. The social environment, encompassing both the immediate, personal relations of the reporting subject, and his or her position in society, is thus explicitly framed as an important influence on this psychonaut's experience of intoxication. The social environment thus becomes an integral part of the intoxication experience. So far, we have focused on the context of experiences of intoxication in trip reports; in the following section, we focus on the inner experience of intoxication and how psychonauts report on these inner experiences.

Inner experiences of intoxication

'We were somewhere around Barstow on the edge of the desert when the drugs began to take hold' (Thompson 1971/2014:3). So began Hunter S. Thompson's *Fear and Loathing in Las Vegas*. By 'taking hold', the sentence implies what we seek to capture with the notion 'inner' experiences of intoxication: the arguably psychologically internal reactions and experiences of intoxicating effects taking hold, and how the reporting psychonaut understands and addresses them. In the following sections, we discuss the inner experience as a series of different stages. However, it should be noted that not all psychonauts necessarily experience all these stages in every trip.

Initial inner experiences

Examining how psychonauts report their inner experiences means analyzing how they narrate the sensations caused by the drug, along with the psychonauts' expectations of and assumptions about such trips, often using a metaphor-heavy language. We begin by exploring how psychonauts experience the initial effects of psychedelics. The following excerpt exemplifies how Erowid user Lucy narrates her initial reactions to LSD.

> When the effects started [to] kick in, my boyfriend was playing video games and I was internet surfing. Gradually I started noticing some changes in the lights, it was as if someone had been messing with the the [sic] brightness, turning it up higher. My head felt warm, as if I was sick (I wasn't) and my heart was racing. I also felt very nauseous, but I didn't throw up. Then, I got up from the sofa and started browsing around the house. [My body] … felt heavy and visually I could see light trails, but no distance or size distortion, as in, objects did not seem further, longer etc. from what I originally perceived them to be.
>
> *(Lucy 2018)*

Lucy's initial reaction to LSD is clearly framed in terms of sensory experiences: changing and trailing lights, heat, heart racing and nausea. She thus relies on a specific set of sensations to narrate her intoxication: perception-based cues which Lucy assumes the LSD has caused. These sensations tie the inner experience of intoxication to the context in which she experiences it, emphasizing how her perceptions and inner experiences change in tandem with her activities. However, Lucy also relates the intoxication experience to her expectations of LSD, pointing out that she did not experience any of the expected 'distance or size distortion'. Instead, the experience of intoxication from LSD is presented as primarily affecting her perceptions of the setting:

> Colours seemed more vibrant, and looking outside the world had an 'electric' feel to it, sometimes my vision would get blurry by all the objects' trails, but in general everything was visually crisper, like my vision jumped to high definition.
>
> *(Lucy 2018)*

In this quote, Lucy's narrative changes from the previous one in which she used perception-based sensations to evaluate whether or not she had begun to experience intoxication. In contrast to the previous quote, she has moved beyond evaluation and describes the experience of intoxication itself. At this point, she allows for a more metaphorical framing. Using metaphors like '"electric" feel' and 'like my vision jumped into high definition', she implies that it becomes harder to give concrete accounts of the intoxication and thus she relies on metaphors.

As hitherto exemplified, we find that when the psychonaut's experience of intoxication is established, the reports focus on the contents of the experience, and how the psychonaut engages with it. Lucy's report of an LSD experience suggests, moreover, that psychedelic intoxication demands active management of emotions and sensory interpretation:

> The first hours of the trip weren't all that great, nothing 'interesting' was happening and the visuals were just mild; also, I had a constant feeling of uneasiness and fear. I was having illogical thoughts, mainly that my trip would go bad like all the other times and that

> my neighbours could hear everything I was doing/saying. But as I was moving closer toward the peak of the experience, I tried to calm myself and abolish such thoughts by using reasoning, although that last thought that everyone inside a certain km radius could hear us sadly accompanied me all throughout the trip.
>
> *(Lucy 2018)*

In this quote, Lucy gives a general account of the experience in an almost dramaturgical manner, indicating that the experience of intoxication is an ongoing process, in which she explicitly seeks to manage her psychosocial context. Similar to the earlier examples of failed psychosocial preparations, Lucy posits that negative and illogical thoughts threaten the experience of intoxication. Moreover, Lucy points out that she was 'moving closer to the peak of the experience'. Taken together, Lucy's reports suggest that she is an experienced psychonaut, at least in using LSD. Moreover, she suggests that there is a pattern to the intoxication, approaching a 'peak experience', while negative thoughts might jeopardize that pattern (cf. Majić et al. 2015; Preller and Vollenweider 2018). In the next section, we examine how the movement toward the peak reaches its goal: peak experience.

Peaking in psychedelic experiences

The peak of the psychedelic experience is a recurring part of trip reports. The 'peak' refers to 'a highly intense component of the [psychedelic] experience which only occurs on occasion', that scholars have compared to mystical experiences (Majić et al. 2015, quote on p. 243). Shroomery user 2 details this kind of experience, accounting for a 'Level 5' trip, i.e., the most potent kind:

> I died. My ego dissolved and was washed away quickly. My physical body was contorting uncontrollably on my bed. I died and then I awoke again as pure energy/ consciousness/ God. I began speaking out loud, uncontrollably. In fact I think for the duration of this section of the trip I was speaking out loud continuously and without control. At first I just kept chanting and declaring 'I have awoken. I have awoken. I am awake.' It felt as if pure energy was speaking through me. I had no control over this. I began changing 'I AM I AM I AM I AM I AM' over and over again. My physical body was striking and holding poses. Some times [sic] my body was uncomfortably twisted and contorted on my bed.
>
> *(Shroomery user 2 2019)*

In this quote, the psychonaut refers to the notion 'ego death', which is a common way of describing the peak experience of a potent psychedelic intoxication (Jansen 2004; Preller and Vollenweider 2018:226). The psychonaut reports that the ego death is not only an inner experience, but also a corporeal one: taking on uncomfortable bodily poses (cf. Kjellgren and Soussan 2011). As is implied in the previous quote, this experience is reported by some as overwhelming and thus intensely negative. However, psychonauts occasionally re-interpret ego death as a positive experience on a later occasion, which might foster continued psychedelics use despite previous negative experiences (Gashi, Sandberg, and Pedersen 2021). Taken together, the reports of reaching the peak of intoxication suggest two things: first, that trip reports frame intoxication as a narrative process, with a dramatic peak, rather than a homogenous state of intoxication. Second, that intoxication is not a passive experience but that the psychonaut actively engages with it both bodily and psychosocially.

Experiences of subsiding intoxication

As the peak experience begins to wane, some psychonauts report different after effects. Erowid user Chris reflects upon her LSD trip which contained elements that she describes as 'hard hitting', including the thought that she was dead (not necessarily equated with 'ego death'):

> By now, 6 months after the trip, I have experienced a few 'flashback'-like states, where I experienced the extreme paranoia and terror that I had sometimes experienced while on LSD. I am sure they were from the experience, because I had never experienced this sort of thing before. I had always been relatively mentally healthy, if a little bit depressed at times. Despite this, I think my experience changed me for the better. I don't know what it is, but reality seems slightly different. I have learned to be more accommodating of other people, friendlier, and more accepting to different viewpoints.
>
> *(Chris 2006)*

Reflections such as these suggest that the user seeks to cope with a profound personal experience derived from the intoxication, which might be both positive and negative. Similarly, early research on the potential therapeutic effects of psychedelic drugs noted a period of 'afterglow' following relatively high dosing, which refers to a highly positive emotional and psychological state (Majić et al. 2015). Having now explored both the context of and inner experience of intoxication, we will draw the paper to a close by discussing the findings and their implications.

Discussion and conclusion: toward understanding experiences of psychedelic intoxication

This chapter set out to explore trip reports as ethnographic texts. We have examined trip reports of LSD, DMT and psilocybin as a means of understanding psychedelic intoxication as structured experiences. That is, experiences which follow observable, non-random patterns. These patterns, we have shown, emerge both in the context of intoxication – the drug, set and setting – and in the psychonauts' inner experiences of intoxication – initial, peak and subsiding effects. We have thus analyzed how trip reports bear witness not only to the direct changes in the initial experiences that drugs provoke. We have also shown how preparations, and social and material settings influence the experience and become an integral part of it. Moreover, we find that the trip reports suggest that psychedelic intoxication is a structured process with a beginning, a peak and an end, and that the psychonaut actively engages with this process (rather than merely passively experiencing it). Our analysis shows how the psychonaut experiencing such psychedelic intoxication actively influences the experience both by preparing the context of intoxication and by actively engaging with their thoughts, emotions and bodily reactions during the experience. In line with Zinberg's argument (1984), the trip reports discussed in this chapter highlight the importance of organizing the contextual aspects of intoxication to control the experience, but also that controlled intoxication includes active bodily and psychological engagement with the inner experience itself (cf. Kjellgren and Soussan 2011). These findings are certainly exploratory. Moreover, they are limited as psychonauts who author trip reports may not be representative of, or have the same experiences, as those who do not. Nevertheless, they illustrate the ways in which psychedelic intoxication can be analyzed as a structured experience.

Our analysis is consistent with earlier studies of psychonauts' online trip reporting (Duxbury 2018; Söderberg 2016; Soussan and Kjellgren 2014). Overall, trip reports can be understood as a contribution to a community of psychonauts who share particular experiences and knowledge about psychedelic trips. In line with existing studies, we find that online psychonaut culture is a form of 'citizen science', and the trip reports partly mimic scientific reports, which may aid other psychonauts in planning their intoxication experiences (Andersson and Kjellgren 2017; Duxbury 2018; Söderberg 2016; Soussan and Kjellgren 2014). In addition, the trip reports also show the problems and mistakes of psychonauts, which both inform others of the different types of risks and seek to identify causes of imperfect trips (Andersson and Kjellgren 2017; Soussan and Kjellgren 2014).

Analyzing trip reports as ethnographic texts, we question the validity of analyzing psychedelic intoxication (i.e., hallucinations) as a solely mystical, religious or existential experience, as in the case of MEQs (cf. Barrett et al. 2015; Majić et al. 2015). Our analysis shows that the inner experiences of intoxication might involve existential aspects, such as ego death, but that psychonauts do not necessarily interpret such experiences in mystic, religious or existential terms. They are rather described as their own type or category of experience. We thus argue that trip reports offer a means of studying intoxication on its own terms (see e.g. Preller and Vollenweider 2018), before assuming any similarity to other types of experiences, such as a religious experience.

In concluding this chapter, we propose that focusing on the psychedelic experiences themselves offers new and relevant methodologies for studying the recent 'psychedelic renaissance'. Unlike religious or recreational psychedelic intoxication, this renaissance is fostered by groups of psychonauts and researchers who seek to establish 'psychoactive substances as a legitimate field of research', not only for therapeutic uses but also for uses which have both therapeutic and recreational functions, including experiences of intoxication (Söderberg 2016:303). Another issue, for which trip reports offer important insights, is that popular constructions of psychedelic drugs paint them as highly unpredictable, perception-altering and controlling of the psychonaut, which fosters stigma and fear that obstruct an impartial approach to such drugs (Barratt and Maddox 2016; Langlitz 2013). Beyond challenging the stigma of psychedelic intoxication, the trip reports analyzed here give detailed information about how psychonauts use drugs, and what kinds of usage are considered wise or reckless (see also Young 1971). Consequently, we agree with Enghoff and Aldridge (2019) that trip reports authored by psychonauts for a psychonaut community offer important insights for the development of drug policy (contrasting with those authored as part of a scientific study). Mapping out and analyzing the psychonauts' reported practical strategies suggest new paths for efficient harm reduction, including advice for safe usage and the debunking of myths (see also Bilgrei 2016; Soussan and Kjellgren 2014).

Acknowledgments

We wish to thank the psychonauts whose trip reports contributed to this study. This study is partially based on data sets obtained from Bluelight.org. Bluelight.org is a non-profit online community dedicated to reducing drug-related harm. This work was conducted with authorization from Bluelight.org. The content is solely the responsibility of the authors and does not necessarily represent the official views of Bluelight.org.

Note

1 Due to different fair use clauses, the names and attributions of authorship for trip reports differ between the sources used. In line with Bluelight's attribution policy, we asked the quoted Bluelight users if they approved our use of their trip reports in this chapter. PippUK and User145667 replied affirmatively and preferred that we use their Bluelight.org usernames, while Bluelight users 3 and 4 did not reply. We have thus included the latter two trip reports, but have altered the quotations in order to ensure their anonymity while keeping the important parts for the analysis. Moreover, we have cited the trip reports from Erowid and Shroomery as references, according to the demands of their respective fair use clauses.

References

Andersson, Martin, and Anette Kjellgren. 2017. 'The Slippery Slope of Flubromazolam: Experiences of a Novel Psychoactive Benzodiazepine as Discussed on a Swedish Online Forum'. *Nordic Studies on Alcohol and Drugs* 34(3):217–229. doi: 10.1177/1455072517706304.

Atkinson, Paul, and Amanda Coffey. 2010. 'Analyzing Documentary Realities'. pp. 77–91 in *Qualitative Research*, edited by D. Silverman. London: Sage.

Atkinson, Paul, and Sara Delamont. 2006. 'Rescuing Narrative from Qualitative Research'. *Narrative Inquiry* 16(1):164–172. doi: 10.1075/ni.16.1.21atk.

Atkinson, Paul, and Lisa Morriss. 2017. 'On Ethnographic Knowledge'. *Qualitative Inquiry* 23(5):323–331. doi: 10.1177/1077800416655825.

Bancroft, Angus. 2009. *Drugs, Intoxication and Society*. Cambridge: Polity Press.

Barratt, Monica J. 2017. 'Bluelight.Org: A Harm-Reduction Community That Supports Public Health Research'. *Journal of Substance Use* 22(1):1–2. doi: 10.1080/14659891.2016.1208779.

Barratt, Monica J., and Alexia Maddox. 2016. 'Active Engagement with Stigmatised Communities through Digital Ethnography'. *Qualitative Research*. doi: 10.1177/1468794116648766.

Barrett, Frederick S., Matthew W. Johnson, and Roland R. Griffiths. 2015. 'Validation of the Revised Mystical Experience Questionnaire in Experimental Sessions with Psilocybin'. *Journal of Psychopharmacology* 29(11):1182–1190. doi: 10.1177/0269881115609019.

Bilgrei, Ola Røed. 2016. 'From "Herbal Highs" to the "Heroin of Cannabis": Exploring the Evolving Discourse on Synthetic Cannabinoid Use in a Norwegian Internet Drug Forum'. *International Journal of Drug Policy* 29:1–8. doi: 10.1016/j.drugpo.2016.01.011.

Blom, Jan Dirk. 2010. *Dictionary of Hallucinations*. New York: Springer.

Bluelight.org. 2019. 'Mission Statement'. *Bluelight.Org*. Retrieved 14 October 2019 (https://www.bluelight.org/xf/pages/Mission_Statement/).

Bogenschutz, Michael P. 2000. 'Drug Information Libraries on the Internet'. *Journal of Psychoactive Drugs* 32(3):249–258. doi: 10.1080/02791072.2000.10400447.

Ceraso, Antonin. 2008. 'Entheogens and the Public Mystery: The Rhetoric of R. Gordon Wasson'. *Configurations* 16(2):215–243.

Chris. 2006. 'Didn't Know What I Was Getting into, Hit Hard: An Experience with LSD (Exp56437)'. *Erowid.Org*. Retrieved 14 October 2019 (https://erowid.org/experiences/exp.php?ID=56437).

dos Santos, Rafael Guimarães, and Jaime Eduardo Cecilio Hallak. 2020. 'Therapeutic Use of Serotoninergic Hallucinogens: A Review of the Evidence and of the Biological and Psychological Mechanisms'. *Neuroscience & Biobehavioral Reviews* 108:423–434. doi: 10.1016/j.neubiorev.2019.12.001.

Duxbury, Scott William. 2018. 'Information Creation on Online Drug Forums: How Drug Use Becomes Moral on the Margins of Science'. *Current Sociology* 66(3):431–448. doi: 10.1177/0011392115596055.

Enghoff, Oskar, and Judith Aldridge. 2019. 'The Value of Unsolicited Online Data in Drug Policy Research'. *International Journal of Drug Policy* 73:210–218. doi: 10.1016/j.drugpo.2019.01.023.

Erowid. 2017. 'Erowid : About Us'. Retrieved 14 October 2019 (https://erowid.org/general/about/about.shtml).

Erowid. 2019. 'About the Experience Vaults : Erowid Experience Vaults'. Retrieved 14 October 2019 (https://erowid.org/experiences/exp_about.cgi).

Gamst, Frederick C. 1980. *The Hoghead: An Industrial Ethnology of the Locomotive Engineer*. First Edition. New York: Holt, Rinehart and Winston.

Gashi, Liridona, Sveinung Sandberg, and Willy Pedersen. 2021. 'Making "Bad Trips" Good: How Users of Psychedelics Narratively Transform Challenging Trips into Valuable Experiences'. *International Journal of Drug Policy* 87:102997. doi: 10.1016/j.drugpo.2020.102997.

Gunnarsson, Andreas, and Mark Elam. 2012. 'Food Fight! The Swedish Low-Carb/High Fat (LCHF) Movement and the Turning of Science Popularisation against the Scientists'. *Science as Culture* 21(3):315–334.

Hammersley, Martyn, and Paul Atkinson. 2007. *Ethnography: Principles in Practice*. London & New York: Routledge.

Hofmann, Albert. 2013. *LSD, My Problem Child, and Insights/Outlooks*,. Oxford: Oxford University Press.

Huxley, Aldous. 1954/2010. *The Doors of Perception: And Heaven and Hell*. Vol. Ho. London: Vintage Books.

Jansen, Karl. 2004. *Ketamine: Dreams and Realities*. Santa Cruz: MAPS.

Jay, Mike. 2019. *Mescaline: A Global History of the First Psychedelic*. New Haven: Yale University Press.

Kataja, Kati, Pekka Hakkarainen, Petteri Koivula, and Sanna Hautala. 2018. 'Sharing Risk Experiences of Polydrug Use on YouTube'. *Drugs and Alcohol Today*. doi: 10.1108/DAT-03–2018-0013.

Kjellgren, Anette, and Christophe Soussan. 2011. 'Heaven and Hell–A Phenomenological Study of Recreational Use of 4-HO-MET in Sweden'. *Journal of Psychoactive Drugs* 43(3):211–219. doi: 10.1080/02791072.2011.605699.

Knight, Michael. 2013. *Tripping with Allah: Islam, Drugs, and Writing*. New York, NY: Soft Skull Press.

Langlitz, Nicolas. 2012. 'Delirious Brain Chemistry and Controlled Culture: Exploring the Contextual Mediation of Drug Effects'. pp. 253–262 in *Critical Neuroscience: A Handbook of the Social and Cultural Contexts of Neuroscience*, edited by S. Choudhury and J. Slaby. John Wiley & Sons.

Langlitz, Nicolas. 2013. *Neuropsychedelia: The Revival of Hallucinogen Research Since the Decade of the Brain*. Berkeley: University of California Press.

Lucy. 2018. 'LSD – Erowid Exp – "An Unexpectedly Blissful Trip"'. *Erowid.Org*. Retrieved 13 November 2020 (https://erowid.org/experiences/exp.php?ID=111678).

Majić, Tomislav, Timo T. Schmidt, and Jürgen Gallinat. 2015. 'Peak Experiences and the Afterglow Phenomenon: When and How Do Therapeutic Effects of Hallucinogens Depend on Psychedelic Experiences?' *Journal of Psychopharmacology (Oxford, England)* 29(3):241–253. doi: 10.1177/0269881114568040.

Page, J. Bryan, and Merrill Singer. 2010. *Comprehending Drug Use: Ethnographic Research at the Social Margins*. None edition. New Brunswick: Rutgers University Press.

Palmer, Cynthia, and Michael Horowitz. 2000. *Sisters of the Extreme: Women Writing on the Drug Experience: Charlotte Brontë, Louisa May Alcott, Anaïs Nin, Maya Angelou, Billie Holiday, Nina Hagen, Diane Di Prima, Carrie Fisher, and Many Others*. Rochester, VT: Inner Traditions/Bear & Co.

Parley, Kay. 2016. *Inside the Mental: Silence, Stigma, Psychiatry, and LSD*. Regina: University of Regina Press.

Pollan, Michael. 2018. *How to Change Your Mind: What the New Science of Psychedelics Teaches Us About Consciousness, Dying, Addiction, Depression, and Transcendence*. New York, NY: Penguin.

Power, Mike. 2014. *Drugs Unlimited: The Web Revolution That's Changing How the World Gets High*. New York: St. Martin's Press.

Preller, Katrin H., and Franz X. Vollenweider. 2018. 'Phenomenology, Structure, and Dynamic of Psychedelic States'. pp. 221–256 in *Behavioral Neurobiology of Psychedelic Drugs, Current Topics in Behavioral Neurosciences*, edited by A. L. Halberstadt, F. X. Vollenweider, and D. E. Nichols. Berlin: Heidelberg: Springer.

Reverse Pingpong. 2017. 'Furthest Away From Home I've Ever Been: An Experience with LSD & Cannabis (Exp97676)'. *Erowid.Org*. Retrieved 9 October 2019 (https://erowid.org/experiences/exp.php?ID=97676).

Roberts, Lyanne. 2015. 'Ethical Issues in Conducting Qualitative Research in Online Communities'. *Qualitative Research in Psychology* 12(3):314–325.

Shroomery. 2019a. 'Shroomery – Magic Mushrooms (Shrooms) Demystified'. Retrieved 14 October 2019 (https://www.shroomery.org/).

Shroomery. 2019b. 'Shroomery – Trip Reports'. Retrieved 24 September 2019 (https://www.shroomery.org/6255/Trip-Reports).

Shroomery user 1. 2019. 'Level 3. My First Trip Was Just Amazing!' *Shroomery.Org*. Retrieved 13 November 2020 (https://www.shroomery.org/14468/My-first-trip-was-just-amazing).

Shroomery user 2. 2019. 'Level 5. 5grams. Insane'. *Shroomery.Org*. Retrieved 14 October 2019 (https://www.shroomery.org/14224/Level-5-5grams-Insane).

Söderberg, Johan. 2016. 'DIY Research in the Psychonaut Subculture. A Case of Unwanted User Innovation'. pp. 297–324. In *The New Production of Users: Changing Innovation Collectives and Involvement Strategies*, edited by S. Hyysalo, T. E. Jensen, and N. Oudshoorn. New York: Routledge.

Soussan, Christophe, and Anette Kjellgren. 2014. 'Harm Reduction and Knowledge Exchange—A Qualitative Analysis of Drug-Related Internet Discussion Forums'. *Harm Reduction Journal* 11(1):25. doi: 10.1186/1477-7517-11-25.

Thompson, Hunter S. 2014. *Fear and Loathing in Las Vegas (Harper Perennial Modern Classics)*. Glasgow: HarperCollins.

Waldman, Ayelet. 2017. *A Really Good Day: How Microdosing Made a Mega Difference in My Mood, My Marriage, and My Life*. New York, NY.

Young, Jock. 1971. *The Drugtakers: The Social Meaning of Drug Use*. Paladin.

Zinberg, Norman. 1984. *Drug, Set, and Setting: The Basis for Controlled Intoxicant Use*. New Haven, London: Yale University Press.

21

PASSION, REASON AND THE POLITICS OF INTOXICATION

Ontopolitically-oriented approaches to alcohol and other drug intoxication

Suzanne Fraser, David Moore, Adrian Farrugia and Renae Fomiatti

Introduction

'Intoxication' is a multivalent term that invokes a range of experiences – from joy and pleasure to chaos and impairment – and applies differently across different drugs and different settings of drug consumption. More broadly, it operates culturally as both elevating (the aria was 'intoxicating') and harmful (he collapsed while 'intoxicated'). When conceived in conventional neo-liberal terms (that is, the privileging of market forces, cost/benefit rationality and the self-managing individual (Petersen, 1997), intoxication sets up binaries between reason and emotion, sense and irrationality, legitimacy and illegitimacy, chaos and order (Ayres and Taylor, 2020). As such, its application can carry highly variable political implications and effects, entailing varying governance measures and practices. Directly modified by questions of class and cultural capital, it is also freighted with differentially raced and gendered meanings. In this chapter, we examine some of the political implications and effects of the notion of intoxication using two large-scale qualitative Australian research projects as case studies. In one project, the place of intoxication is examined in accounts of accidental opioid overdose and the use of the opioid antagonist naloxone; in the other, it is examined in accounts of the use of performance and image-enhancing drugs (PIEDs). In relation to naloxone, intoxication often figures as perilous: it is a liminal state adjacent to death, seductively dangerous, in need of direct biomedical intervention. While the naloxone distribution programmes created in line with this approach are an undoubted good, they tend to downplay the contexts of overdose in which risky intoxication is for many an effect of legal conditions that render drug strength opaque and dosage unmanageable. They also raise questions about what counts as intoxication and why. In relation to PIEDs, intoxication can be understood less as an immediate effect of drug consumption and more as the product of carefully managed treatment regimes, such as in the case of steroids, where men describe an intensely heightened sense of confidence, energy, power, resilience and competitiveness. Here, intoxication complicates the neo-liberal demands for productivity visible in some engagements with PIEDs, as well as the traditional polarisation of drug use and discipline and order.

In conducting our analysis, we adopt what has elsewhere been called an 'ontopolitically-oriented' approach to research (Fraser, 2020) in which bodies, corporeal changes and other

 DOI: 10.4324/9780429058141-27

material phenomena are understood to be the effect of complex processes, including meaning making and social practices. Based on science and technology studies (STS) and new materialism, this approach sees realities, including the realities of drug consumption, as emergent rather than predictable and guaranteed by biochemistry or prior states. As we will argue, this allows recognition of the ways in which different contexts and discourses of intoxication (including those operating in research itself) co-produce culturally and politically specific intoxication experiences and effects. In turn, we raise new questions about the conditions of intoxication, the assumptions made about drug effects, the meaning of intoxication and how best to respond to it. As the chapter will show, intoxication is a political designation reliant on a range of assumptions about drug-consuming subjects and practices. In making this case, the chapter will set out theoretical resources for new approaches to researching politically multiple concepts such as intoxication.

Literature review

The social science literature on intoxication is extensive. It covers broad discussions of intoxication as it relates to a range of practices and issues, including emotions, physical sensations, religious perceptions, responses to the arts and of course drugs. Researchers have sought to identify different kinds of intoxication, different ways of accounting for it, different social and cultural purposes it fulfils, and different global political dynamics and histories relating to it.

In relation to alcohol and other drugs, intoxication has often been positioned as necessarily harmful and self-evidently problematic: it threatens health and the moral order, and needs to be managed and reduced (Bancroft, 2009; Homel, Tomsen and Thommeny, 1992; McClelland and Teplin, 2001; McCreanor et al., 2008; Orcutt, 1978; Room, 2001). Anthropological and sociological research suggests however that, like alcohol and other drug consumption more generally, experiences and meanings of intoxication are shaped by cultural practices, social relations and power dynamics (Herbert and McCreanor, 2020; MacAndrew and Edgerton, 1969; Sande, 2002). Researchers have also pointed to the ways the perceived individual and social harms associated with specific forms of intoxication lead to stigmatisation and criminalisation (Yardley, 2012), and have noted that the pursuit of intoxication must be understood in the context of contemporary injunctions to rationality and moderation (Zajdow, 2010). Experiences of and responses to intoxication have further been identified as gendered (Bogren, 2008; Hunt and Antin, 2019; Moore, 2020; Moore et al., 2017). Other work has renewed attention to Durkheim's nascent theory of intoxication (Shilling and Mellor, 2011) and drawn on Plato's 'ironic intoxication' as a philosophical method (Bonner, 2013). Recent edited collections on intoxication (Hutton, 2020; Withington, 2014) emphasise two key points: (1) forms of intoxication have been part of many different human societies for millennia, and (2) practices of intoxication and their implications require social, political and cultural analyses.

Within this burgeoning literature, several key works on intoxication published over the last two decades draw specifically on the advances in alcohol and other drug studies provided by STS and its emphasis on ontological politics. The attention STS pays to the role of research in constituting, rather than merely measuring or reflecting, realities has fostered fruitful reflection on research methods, but has also offered new ways of looking at reality itself, offering a particular framework through which to understand reality: as multiple and emergent rather than singular and anterior to research or other kinds of observation. This approach has been of value to the field of drug social sciences because it helps theorise the lack of coherence and consistency long noted in drug effects, such as intoxication, and the political opportunities afforded by recognition of this inconsistency. This work is not alone in raising questions about the stability and predictability of drug effects, of course. As we noted above, anthropology, a significant contributor to STS, has long argued that drugs perform different functions in different societies, carry different meanings and even have different subjective effects, such as those relating to intoxication. MacAndrew and Edgerton's classic work, *Drunken comportment* (1969), for example, argued that, 'The way people comport themselves when they are drunk is determined [...] by what their society makes of and imparts to them concerning the state of drunkenness' (p. 165). Contrary to received wisdom, they observed, alcohol does not produce the same effects cross-culturally, and intoxication (or 'drunkenness') too varies by culture. This framing was consistent with other contemporary anthropological, sociological and historical accounts of alcohol intoxication as shaped by the historical, social and political contexts of consumption (Douglas, 1987; Gefou-Madianou, 1992; Heath, 1958; Levine, 1978; Mandelbaum, 1965; Marshall, 1979a, 1979b; Orcutt, 1978; Room, 2001), and with work on other drugs (Zinberg, 1984). While MacAndrew and Edgerton's analysis, and that of related work, is amenable in some ways to the ontological politics animating our analysis here (more on which below), it does not necessarily conform to its account of reality. It bases its analysis on the idea that all drunkenness causes 'clumsiness', but that the meanings attached to this clumsiness are not fixed. In this way, the differences it identifies could be interpreted as the result of a superstructure of meaning laid over a stable biological reality. Overall, these works do not ask direct questions about the ontological nature of drunkenness, and by extension all drug intoxication, although their social constructionist orientations (articulated in different ways) undoubtedly paved the way for later work that takes a more searching approach to the nature of reality as it pertains to drugs and their effects.

Among the earliest work to bring explicitly ontological questions and approaches to bear on issues of drug use and intoxication is Gomart and Hennion's 1999 article on agency and subjectivity, explored through a discussion of 'passionate attachment' and STS, in particular actor-network theory. The authors explore two passions – drug consumption and classical music – usually considered very distinct in terms of the status of their effects. In doing so, they argue that engagement with either is a means of constituting the self, and that such a process of constitution is an effect of a *dispositif* (an assemblage or apparatus composed of a complex range of ideas and practices (Deleuze, 1992)), rather than the achievement of an individual agent or the direct causal effect of the drug or music itself. In making their argument, their aim is to 'offer an alternative account of the ways in which subjects may be seized, impassioned and swept away' (1999, p. 221), one that avoids ascribing causal force to either the subject (such as the music connoisseur) or the object (such as a drug). As they go on to explain, 'This version of actor-network theory switches focus from the (albeit decentred) subject to what one might think of as the socio-technical "dispositifs" of passion' (1999, p. 221).

While Gomart and Hennion do not use the word 'intoxication' in their article, they do say this about music and drugs:

> Both have to do with entering into a world of strong sensations; of accepting that 'external' forces take possession of the self; of being 'under the influence' of something else; of bracketing away one's own control and will in order to be expelled or rendered 'beside oneself'.
>
> *(1999, p. 221)*

It is via this interest in processes by which the self is taken over by external forces, rendered beside itself, that their work speaks to issues of intoxication. To make their argument, they illuminate the points of commonality between intoxication through music and through drugs despite their cultural and political differences, raising questions that are otherwise invisible in considering one or the other in isolation. In this chapter, we too bring together two distinct areas of practice to illuminate notions of intoxication in new ways, to consider the possibility that the constraint of intoxication is not only limiting but productive and to think about the political implications of this reading.

Also working in STS, Sulkunen (2002) draws on its ontological concerns to discuss the attempts made to generate cultural theories of intoxication. Using the work of Latour, he argues that, '[i]ntoxication is a proto-semiotic fact between culture and nature, not being completely meaningful but not possible without meaning either' (2002, p. 253). Pointing to the need to consider the social and symbolic dimensions of intoxication as well as chemical effects, he tries to offer an approach that exceeds commonplace dualistic models of intoxication as either the straightforward result of the drug or of socially produced meaning. His closing observation that 'the cultural study of intoxication as a signifier therefore always reaches toward other realities beyond drug use itself' (Sulkunen, 2002, p. 272) is directly relevant to the analysis to be conducted here, in its location of intoxication as indivisible from the broader realities with which it is made and understood.

A recent addition to this body of literature is Pienaar et al.'s (2020) analysis of intoxication in LGBTQ communities. Drawing on two mainstays of approaches that attend to ontological politics – Karen Barad and Judith Butler – the authors remind us of the instability of drug effects and their emergence within social contexts, to argue that drug use and intoxication should be seen as productive, not just as risky and harmful. In making their argument, they also point out 'the proximity of pleasure, risk, care and intimate experimentation as prominent concerns within LGBTQ cultures offer new ways of thinking about the place of drugs and intoxication in social life' (Pienaar et al., 2020, p. 157). In this latter point can be found connections with other work written from one of the studies analysed here – Farrugia et al.'s (2019) article on the politics of care, which elucidates the intimacies produced and relied upon in couples who consume opioids together and must manage the possibility of overdose.

In sum, the literature informed by STS and related ontological theorisations of drug use and drug effects remind us of several key points for our analysis to follow:

- Drug effects such as intoxication are not determined by the pharmacological properties of substances but are made in social practices;
- In this instability, we can see that intoxication is not reifiable as a state but is better understood as a shift in relations with the self and the world;
- As such, intoxication can refer to any number of practices, including practices axiomatically positioned as antithetical to it, such as work on the self, agency and reason;
- Once intoxication is understood in this way, the political implications of labelling some phenomena 'intoxication' and declining to do so for others can be considered more clearly.

Approach

Our theoretical approach in this chapter begins with some observations made in a recent book chapter by leading social scientist of drug issues, Helen Keane (2020). In this piece, she analyses intoxication and nicotine by drawing on the work of Bancroft (2009) and Hunt and

Frank (2017). Keane sets out to depathologise intoxication and, at the same time, to offer a more subtle understanding of it that allows recognition of experiences and effects not usually recognised within definitions of intoxication. As she (Keane, 2020, p. 47) observes:

> Drunkenness is the iconic state of pathological intoxication, marked by disinhibition, mood lability, impaired judgement, inappropriate behaviour and other signs of diminished physical or mental control (American Psychiatric Association, 2013, pp. 485, 497).

Keane's aim is to consider intoxication through the substance of nicotine, identifying ways in which it invites an expansion in the meaning of intoxication, and raises questions about our tendency to treat intoxication as pathological, that is, as evidence of a diseased mind, body or lifestyle. In this context, she argues for 'a broader understanding of intoxication which incorporates less florid changes in consciousness than drunkenness' (Keane, 2020, p. 47). She quotes Bancroft on the topic, who notes that, 'Whether smoking cigarettes, drinking alcohol and coffee, or taking illicit drugs, for the majority of society's members, some kind of intoxication is a regular, often daily practice' (Bancroft, 2009, p. 5, cited in Keane, 2020, p. 47). Why does Keane seek to incorporate the effects of nicotine into accounts of intoxication? As she explains, in describing Bancroft's contribution:

> By expanding the category to include substance-induced changes in the relationship between the self and the world, whatever their intensity, Bancroft (2009) normalises the experience of and the desire for intoxication, broadening out the concept of intoxication as something that can be more subtle than ostentatious and visible alcohol and other drug intoxication.
>
> *(2020, p. 47)*

Keane draws on practice theory (which focuses specifically on the role of practices in making events and other phenomena) to conduct her analysis, identifying its ability to resist 'explanations based on universal drug properties and individual psychology' (2020, p. 50).

A related expansive definition of intoxication found in the literature and relevant to our analytical approach is simply the use of substances to alter consciousness (Hunt and Frank, 2017, p. 323). Keane is explicitly interested in this definition, arguing that it can encompass relatively mild changes in perception, such as daydreaming. Returning to nicotine, she explains that:

> The notion of a 'slight' euphoria seems oxymoronic at first glance, but it captures the particular capacity of cigarettes to create a brief opening in the smoker's day which is a minor but sustaining enhancement of routine.

More broadly, Keane's aim is to draw our attention to the ways in which 'intoxication' can be seen as a 'shift in one's relationship to the world, with no fixed meaning or inevitable consequences, either negative or positive' (2020, p. 51), and in this way, not necessarily other to the normal.

In taking up Keane's suggestion that intoxication be redefined, we are able to recognise in our data experiences of intoxication that would otherwise be neglected in research and public discourse. Doing so helps depathologise intoxication, allowing us to ask new questions about it and about the politics that shape its meaning and status. In particular, it helps identify the proximity of intoxication to the attributes and practices usually positioned as its opposite: reason, productivity and agency.

In Keane's piece and the orientation she takes to the effects of drugs and the status of intoxication, we can see connections with STS approaches that refuse conventional assumptions about the anteriority of reality and the stability of drug effects. Indeed, in setting off from her piece, we also draw on an approach that has recently been termed 'ontopolitically-oriented research' (Fraser, 2020). In an article aiming to bring together key aspects of this approach, Fraser outlines five features, also noting that further features may remain to be identified:

1. *The methodological performativity of naming*

   Fraser refers here to the terminology of 'addiction', considering its role in shaping research recruitment and analysis for a project about regular heavy drug consumption, but the same issues apply to the language of 'intoxication'. When we call something intoxication, that is, we must decide what it means and recognise that particular uses of the label have particular political effects. In this chapter, we draw on Keane, Bancroft and Hunt and Frank to consider where a more expansive definition of intoxication might take us.
2. *The ontological politics of data generation*

   Fraser also notes the ways in which specific approaches to collecting data in research shape the realities it materialises. As she observes, convenience recruitment has historically dominated drugs research, thereby foregrounding the experiences and circumstances of the most marginalised and disadvantaged. In turn, this approach materialises a reality of drug use as fundamentally about marginalisation, vulnerability and deprivation. By taking a different approach to recruitment, our projects reached participants rarely included in research, illuminating the nuances of intoxication and its relationship to apparently anomalous facilities such as titration, reason and balance.
3. *The liabilities and limits of representation*

   Also important for our analysis is Fraser's third point, which relates to the role of 'representation'. The data we use in this chapter are not to be treated as a simple window onto true events. In attending to the accounts of drug effects (such as overdose or euphoria and so on) evident in the interviews we analyse, it is necessary to recognise the discursive constitution of these experiences and terms, and equally, to try to notice relevant dynamics and effects that might be obscured or erased by the discursive conventions of intoxication.
4. *The contingency of units of study*

   As Fraser notes in her outline of ontopolitically-oriented research, the unit of study on which we base any analysis warrants scrutiny as a choice. Our analysis sees intoxication as a collective effect of a network or *dispositif*, and therefore as unstable and emergent. Seen this way, intoxication cannot be taken for granted as an effect of certain patterns of drug consumption, or of the 'behaviour' of individuals and their individual 'agency', nor assumed to be absent from other such patterns. This approach necessarily shifts focus from the individual as origin and embodiment of action to the network or *dispositif*, and therefore to dispersed and various actions and contributing agencies.
5. *Researching partial worlds*

   In Fraser's approach, and in our mobilisation of it here, there are only partial, contingent worlds, only unstable emergent subjects and objects whose perspectives and priorities cannot be taken for granted. This chapter forms part of a body of work, in other words, that seeks to illuminate a partial world of intoxication, raising questions as it does so about which partial worlds we wish to materialise.

Methods

This chapter draws on two Australian qualitative research projects: (1) an investigation into the meanings and experiences of take-home naloxone for opioid consumers and health professionals, and (2) an exploration of PIED injecting among men, with a particular emphasis on hepatitis C transmission.[1] The methodological design of both projects was informed by the ontopolitically-oriented research approach described above. Both projects were framed by new materialist theory, which emphasises the mutually constitutive relationship between knowledge practices, material objects, subjectivity and social relations. In what follows, we briefly describe some of the ontopolitical considerations that informed our research, the projects' methods and their implementation.

Commenced in 2017, the first project on impediments to scaling up take-home naloxone provision aimed to look beyond questions of whether take-home naloxone 'worked' by drawing attention to the social and political dimensions of naloxone (Farrugia, Fraser and Dwyer, 2017). The project used a purposive recruitment strategy to reach a wide variety of participants with different experiences with take-home naloxone, as well as differences in gender, age, ethnicity, socioeconomic background and types of opioid consumed. As such, a recruitment flyer with intentionally broad language ('Would you like to share your views on opioid overdose and naloxone?') was circulated through drug health services, drug consumer organisations, chronic pain peak bodies and support groups, and generalist social media. Using this approach, we recruited 28 people who consume illicit drugs and 18 who consume prescribed opioids for health issues such as chronic pain (most of the latter were not engaged in alcohol and other drug services and had hitherto rarely been included or addressed in research on take-home naloxone). In this way, the recruitment method contributed to an ontopolitical intervention that broadened understandings of the problem of overdose, and therefore the subjects of take-home naloxone, beyond people who inject drugs. The project team conducted in-depth, semi-structured interviews exploring experiences of opioid consumption and overdose; awareness of, and experiences with, take-home naloxone; access to take-home naloxone; experiences with, and perspectives on, overdose response and take-home naloxone training; and preferred modes of administering take-home naloxone. This approach elicited detailed accounts of opioid consumption, overdose events, stigma and take-home naloxone administration. Importantly, the concept of 'overdose' was broadened too. Usually positioned as a pharmacological phenomenon caused by drug consumption, our interview schedule and data analysis took a social approach to drug effects. In this way, we were able to draw out how media representations of overdose deaths, stigma and material inequalities shaped the politics of overdose and take-home naloxone responses (Fraser, Farrugia and Dwyer 2017; Farrugia, Fraser and Dwyer, 2017; Fomiatti et al. 2022). The generation of such rich detail is uncommon in research on take-home naloxone, as it is ordinarily focused on straightforwardly conceived questions of effectiveness and utility. Our interests in the social dimensions and capacities of take-home naloxone, and in re-imagining the enhancement of take-home naloxone uptake, were integral to data collection and the generation of the dataset.

The project on PIED consumption and hepatitis C transmission was funded at the same time as the take-home naloxone project, and adopted a similar ontopolitically-oriented qualitative approach. When the research team began developing research tools, such as the interview schedule, we actively sought to elaborate difference, variation and complexity within the phenomenon of PIED injecting, trying to avoid simplistic generalisations and binary comparisons with psychoactive drug injecting. With this in mind, we avoided importing taken-for-granted concepts from research into psychoactive drug consumption and eating disorders (see Fraser's (2020) remarks on the methodological performativity of 'naming'), such as dependence, addiction, body image concerns and body dysmorphia. Instead, we asked open-ended question about recent experiences and social settings of injecting, the feelings and concerns associated with injecting PIEDs, perceptions of hepatitis C, and embodiment and physical training practices, to generate accounts rich in detail and diversity and to illuminate novel matters of concern.

Connected with these issues of language, power and knowledge, the research team paid close attention to the ontopolitics of participant recruitment. As with the previous project, this project aimed to generate a wide range of experiences on the basis of location, age, ethnicity, occupational background and socioeconomic status. This meant recruiting participants (n = 60) from varied sources, including harm reduction services, primary health services, sexual health services, bars and clubs, supplement stores and sex-on-premises venues, as well as various social media platforms, such as Facebook, Twitter, Gumtree, Craig's List and Scruff, steroid and bodybuilding online forums, and *Men's Health* magazine. By working hard to recruit consumers from sites other than needle and syringe programmes, we were able to recruit men with a wide range of perspectives and experiences, some of whom were not readily visible in conventional research approaches.

In these ways, and in others we do not have the space to address here, these projects actively sought to suspend the pathologising narratives that render the complex phenomena of opioid and PIED consumption in singular and narrow ways, for example, as issues of addiction and disorder. In analysing the data from these two projects together for the first time, we aimed to allow new insights to emerge.

Analysis

Our analysis begins by exploring data collected for our project on overdose and the use of take-home naloxone. It examines the experiences recounted in the interviews to consider the role of intoxication in making sense of these experiences, and to ask which aspects of these experiences could be reconsidered in light of the politics of intoxication noted at the outset. The analysis then examines intoxication in a very different context, PIED consumption, one in which the effects of drugs are generally considered less pronounced than those relating to opioids and overdose, but may also be considered intoxication depending on our purposes. In both cases, we find a range of intoxication experiences, including familiar changes in bodily sensations, mood and consciousness, often in ways that indicate their indivisibility, as well as less familiar instances and sources of intoxication.

Overdose, revival and intoxication

Opioid overdose and the use of naloxone to prevent death would seem to map neatly onto both intoxication and its putative opposite: the rational application of a life-saving drug. Yet, as we will see below, it is possible to identify the ways in which the pursuit and experience of intoxication are not so readily dismissible as excessive, chaotic and intemperate, as the effect of questionable individual agency or behaviour. Equally, the use of naloxone is not so simply understood as the erasure of intoxication and the imposition of order and coherence.

We begin with Valentina's account of opioid overdose. As she explains:

R: We went just off to school one day, scored, had a shot in my car and we both passed out. She [Valentina's friend] woke up first and I was still out, and so she moved me over, got into the driver's seat and drove me to hospital, and I got a Narcan [naloxone] and I just came to.

I: Okay, so yeah.

R: Yeah, and then that was pretty good of her, pretty impressive of her.

I: Yeah, yeah, to get it together to get someone to hospital.

R: Yeah, totally ruined her buzz, I'm sure.

In Valentina's account of overdose, the story begins with a familiar series of events: drugs are bought illicitly, injected in a relatively isolated location, and overdose occurs, leading to unconsciousness. Here, intoxication is this loss of consciousness: the absence of conscious thought and rational action. However, immediately following these events, we are told, a series of other events occurs. Valentina's companion wakes up, identifies Valentina's overdose risk, moves her in the vehicle and then drives the vehicle to hospital. While this course of action could no doubt be criticised in that it may have involved driving while under the influence of a drug (the timeframe for the events is not available in the account, and it is worth noting that the events described occurred before the popularisation of mobile phones), it is also a strikingly organised and decisive one. Not only does Valentina's account present a (young) companion possibly saving her life, the companion seems to show a significant amount of competence and resourcefulness. In this account, we see intoxication not as the opposite of sense, order, coherence and agency, but adjacent it, afforded by other elements such as the action of stigma in shaping injecting location, and the availability of a car for transportation purposes. We are also able to identify in the overdose *dispositif* a key element often ignored in overdose accounts and official responses: the legal status of drugs and the role of prohibition in governing the location of consumption and constraining knowledge of dose.

While Valentina and her companion did not have access to naloxone while injecting, the medication emerges in other accounts of overdose and revival. Jamie describes, for example, an experience in which she was injected with naloxone by a close friend, and the administration resulted in a less intense opioid experience but one that would nevertheless qualify as intoxication:

I: I wanted to ask you a bit about the effects of the naloxone: what it felt like after it had been administered and how long the effects lasted.

R: It was good, I still felt a bit smashed but yeah.

[...]

I: So physically it didn't feel too bad, but you still felt a bit ...

R: Yeah, I still felt a bit stoned.

I: Which maybe is good, I guess.

R: Yeah it is, because you don't want to completely miss out.

While this account is rather less dramatic than that offered by Valentina, it nevertheless includes similar elements not usually associated with intoxication: moderation and sense. For Jamie, the naloxone was 'good' because it was effective, possibly saving her life, but was also not so intense as to eradicate the experience of intoxication altogether, perhaps due to thoughtful and cautious administration. In both Valentina and Jamie's accounts, Keane's call to depathologise intoxication resonates clearly, reminding us that it can coexist with, rather than simply contradict, reason, control, agency and sense.

Ghassan's account of intoxication and naloxone administration is significantly different from Jamie's. Instead of a relatively benign experience in which a degree of intoxication is preserved, Ghassan experiences a significant wrench on revival, including cold shakes, diarrhoea and vomiting. It was, he says, 'ugly':

R: So I was locked up [in gaol] for a period of time and then I got out and I never knew about tolerance levels and stuff. So I went out and used the exact same amount that I was using prior to being locked up and I was at a friend's place luckily, and his sister was there and she was an addict too, yeah, so I've had it [naloxone], and then the next thing I know, I'm waking up in [...] hospital throwing up all over, like the instant withdrawal and all that kind of stuff. Just didn't know how I got there. That was the first time.

[...]

I: Yeah, and how did you like, I guess, what view of Narcan did it give you sort of, having that experience?

R: It was ugly. It was the feeling, but it saved my life at the same time, so like I'm not the type to start jumping up and going, 'Oh yeah'. No, they did save my life [but] I didn't like it, it didn't feel good because of the instant, you know, like the vomiting and the cold shakes and the diarrhoea and all that kind of stuff.

Here, Ghassan wakes up in a hospital – a relatively controlled environment – yet, it seems that the naloxone had been administered in such a way as to induce serious negative physical effects. The impact of naloxone, and the thought and agency entailed in it, differ markedly here from descriptions in the previous examples. Rather than imposing order and coherence, the naloxone in Ghassan's account substitutes one kind of intoxication with another. Conventionally, experiences of this kind have been framed as examples of 'over-antagonism' in which too much naloxone is administered, leading to acute withdrawal symptoms or 'opioid withdrawal syndrome' (see, for example, Kim and Nelson, 2015; Neale and Strang, 2015; for a discussion of influence on post-revival actions, see Elliot, Bennett and Wolfson-Stofko, 2019). Importantly, the notion of over-antagonism suggests that there is a specific dose of naloxone that returns the recipient to 'normality'. This point goes to our interest in definitions of intoxication and their political valencies: while the symptoms induced by high doses of naloxone are rarely if ever labelled intoxication (given the implications of excess, impulsiveness and disorder the term implies), it is difficult to avoid the conclusion that the biomedically induced sensations Ghassan describes are indeed ones of (highly unpleasurable – and avoidable) intoxication. The volume of naloxone used in producing such effects might, further, be considered excessive and even intemperate. Interestingly, the concept of over-antagonism medicalises the effects of naloxone, apparently precluding the designation of intoxication, an effect primarily attributed to non-medically sanctioned drug consumption. At the same time, as Ghassan woke, he says, he recognised the logic in the use of naloxone, and despite new and unpleasant symptoms of intoxication, responded in a reasoned way. Looked at closely, then, an account like Ghassan's does much to disrupt standard understandings of intoxication, which tend to foreground poor consumer choices and conduct and the polarisation of intoxication and reason.

Other work conducted by the authors of this chapter also bears on the issues raised here. In an article stemming from the same project, we analysed the role of take-home naloxone in a caring relationship between a couple, Gabrielle (whom we interviewed) and Jeremy (her partner) (Farrugia et al., 2019). As we described, Gabrielle explains that Jeremy is terminally ill with cancer, and the intoxicating effects of his heroin consumption and risk of overdose are especially acute. Importantly, Jeremy continues to enjoy heroin consumption and Gabrielle actively supports this practice. Unlike her use of naloxone in other contexts, she does not use it to revive Jeremy from overdose. By agreement with Jeremy, Gabrielle monitors him and administers only small amounts of naloxone when she feels he is close to overdosing or appears to be 'forgetting to breathe'. This is because she wants to 'take the edge off' rather than counter his intoxication altogether. In this way, Gabrielle uses naloxone to help Jeremy maintain a pleasurable and safe experience of intoxication. Importantly for this chapter, this account also disrupts assumptions that reason and intoxication are contradictory. Such assumptions constitute two states: overdose (intoxicated) and revival (unintoxicated). Instead, Gabrielle describes modulating intoxication in ways that allow for the considered mediation of intoxicating and analgesic effects (Farrugia et al., 2019, pp. 435–436).

In summary, the project from which these accounts have been drawn identified many complexities that disrupt common assumptions about intoxication, how it happens, what it means and who is culpable. In the next section, we consider another research project in which the results also invite us to rethink received wisdom about intoxication.

PIEDs and intoxication

In this project, the role ascribable to intoxication differs significantly from that in the opioid overdose project described above. Here, we again turn to Keane's observations about the importance of including less intense effects in definitions of intoxication and unfamiliar substances (hers is nicotine) to allow us to see it at work in our participants' accounts. As we will show, the effects of PIED consumption are rarely as extreme as those described above, and are, to our knowledge, never described as intoxication in the literature, yet they nevertheless constitute important changes in bodily sensations, mood and perception, and in relations with the self. They are both positive and negative, and, as in the material presented above, can be seen to trouble the standard binaries usually applied to intoxication discourse: impulse and reason, risky illicit consumption and safe, biomedical moderation. Indeed, as has been noted elsewhere (Fraser, Fomiatti, Moore, Seear and Aitken, 2020), the PIED use in the project discussed here raises particularly stark issues for the conventional binary drawn between biomedical reason and illicit irrationality in that health professionals, especially doctors, are commonly described by participants as responding in unhelpful ways, lacking knowledge and giving inaccurate advice.

In many of the interviews we conducted, the effects of PIEDs, especially steroids, were often described in ways that linked them to anger and aggression. As Reece, for example, explains:

> When I'm on [PIEDs], like, I can be sitting there, like even now I feel like my chest is tight because I'm just … I've got high test[osterone]. But I can just be sitting there and I'll just get angry for no reason. Like, the smallest thing will set me off and the next person who says something – I could hit someone, and then you kind of can't control it, I just click, and then after you look at yourself and say, like, 'You're an idiot', like, 'Why'd you do that'?

Explaining his experience further, Reece goes on to give an example:

> We [were] in class, because I'm doing training, [and] a guy said something [while] I was, like, trying to listen to the teacher, and he kept talking, and then I turned around and I swore at him. And I was like 'Just shut the you know up, I am trying to listen' you know […] But he had only been interrupting the teacher once or twice in that instance, and I

just clicked. Everyone was like 'Ooohh, a bit angry' and everyone is staring at you and then you start shaking and stuff.

In his interview, Tibor also described important changes in perception and in relations with the self in the form of increased sensations of rising anger and impulsiveness. Importantly, however, he also talked about positive experiences that we might consider as forms of mild intoxication related to his PIED consumption:

I: And were there any other feelings or effects aside from anger that came up?
R: I was way more confident.
I: Can you give me an example?
R: Just in general, so like every day when I stand in front of the mirror I looked better and every day I felt better and this gave [me] a very good feeling, that if you are not using steroids you're not going to have, because you are not going to see any change even if you train for like two month[s]. And in this two months' time, I achieved way more and better things than what I did any time before, and my strength was like way better, so I had much more power, I could lift much more weights, I was getting bigger much faster, so it was like, yeah ... so this is why I was more confident and I felt good from it.

In Tibor's account, the consumption of a substance or group of substances elicits new and different emotions, creating a new relation with the self, even if temporarily. Tibor combines labour, planning and discipline with drugs to create 'a very good feeling'.

Henry's comments about the changes in emotions and in relations with the self connected with PIED consumption echo Tibor's, except that in the intensity he describes they are more akin to conventional formulations of intoxication. When asked about whether consuming PIEDs affected his emotions, he says:

R: Yeah, absolutely. The intensity and the rate at which emotion can rise, or the frequency within which you are in a high emotion, increases sometimes, and part of that's desirable because really it helps you getting into [a gym] workout, you know. Sometimes you hit it and sometimes you don't without gear [PIEDs], but with the right stuff, it's like you've got your finger on the fucking switch.
I: So that feeling of being emotionally heightened...
R: Energised, engaged.
I: That can help you push your training session. What else?
R: Just intensity, that intensity, and the ability to access that intensity.

Henry's words communicate a particular kind of intoxication here: there is a 'switch' at hand that may be flipped – usually in the presence of PIEDs but also occasionally without. What happens in this moment? He experiences significant emotional changes and related physical effects such that his relation with himself becomes characterised by energy, engagement and the ability to 'access' 'intensity'.

Like Henry, Ryan refers to heightened physical and emotional sensations, returning to issues of aggression and edginess:

[PIEDs] were augmenting my levels of testosterone and giving me more testosterone, so therefore it's just making me more...it's taking me away from, I guess in my language, it's taking me away from the present moment and from being myself and like pushing

> me into somewhere else, like into the future. You know, you're more aggressive, you're more edgy, you're more, I don't know, you're more vigilant about stuff, like all those different things, it's like you become more of a soldier than a peaceful human being, so to speak, you know.

Here, Ryan describes an extremely significant change in perspective from 'peaceful human being' to 'soldier'. In his account, the extra testosterone in his system is associated with changes in his relation with himself: it takes him away from the present moment and from 'being myself', pushing him 'into the future'. Ryan's highly vivid account of intoxication in his subjective experience of PIED consumption is striking. This group of substances and context are rarely if ever associated with intoxication, yet these remarks indicate that for some (including others quoted above as well), intoxication is undoubtedly involved.[2]

Alongside these accounts of anger, edginess and aggression are many of excitement and euphoria, where the effects of PIED consumption are rendered in far more positive terms. For Grant, Nathan and Alex, for example, life on PIEDs (steroids or human growth hormone) creates an enormous positive change in subjective experience of confidence, strength and power:

> So there would be ... your muscles look fuller, you look bigger. It's more of a ... what's the best way to put it, you feel supernatural basically. [...] Like you can basically conquer the world.
>
> *(Grant)*

> You know, you feel amazing, you feel confident, you feel like you can take on the world. You feel like nothing can hurt you, you know.
>
> *(Nathan)*

> And just a phenomenal feeling in the body, like I just felt unstoppable, and I was training twice a day. I just felt really good because in general I suffer from pretty major anxiety and when I was on that stuff, I had no anxiety, no fear at all.
>
> *(Alex)*

In all these descriptions, very vividly articulated experiences of intoxication emerge. Some participants could be described as intoxicated with their own growing powers of confidence, discipline, strength and agency. They are supernatural, unstoppable and invulnerable. Others are intoxicated with aggression, anger and vigilance. Effects are strikingly aligned with widely promulgated clichés of masculine agency and efficacy, indicating the ways in which, as past researchers have argued, these effects are socially and culturally constituted (Fomiatti et al., 2019). Importantly, these accounts also remind us of the ways in which intoxication, historically aligned with alcohol and with loss of consciousness, or at best compromised consciousness, may also be linked to heightened consciousness and awareness of changes in relations with the self. Of course, the euphoria conventionally associated with stimulant consumption could also be described in these terms, yet a significant difference remains in the accounts we have examined above. Here, intoxication, confidence and euphoria align with self-discipline, labour and self-improvement. Elsewhere, we have argued that PIED consumers indicate a strong desire to have informed, reasoned interactions with health professionals about their consumption and about ways of managing risks and avoiding ill-effects (Fraser et al., 2020).

In these ways too, we can see the alignment of some kinds of intoxication, experienced in certain conditions and induced through particular practices, with their putative opposites: rationality, moderation, control and productivity.

Conclusion

The two research projects analysed in this chapter offer a great deal for new understandings of intoxication, especially when considered together. As explained at the outset, our analysis was informed by Keane's (2020) expanded definition of intoxication – as a 'shift in one's relationship to the world, with no fixed meaning or inevitable consequences, either negative or positive' – and by Fraser's ontopolitically-oriented research approach. This work allowed us to recognise experiences of intoxication that would otherwise be neglected in research and public discourse. The accounts of opioid overdose and revival with naloxone showed how intoxication may coexist with, rather than simply contradict, reason, control, agency and sense; and conversely, that actions to restore sobriety may themselves induce or align with notions of intoxication. The accounts of the heightened emotion and changed relations with the self associated with PIED use highlighted the alignment of some kinds of intoxication with their putative neo-liberal opposites: rationality, moderation, control and productivity.

Taken together, the case studies demonstrate that common assumptions about intoxication, how it happens, what it means and who is culpable are thoroughly political. When conceived conventionally, intoxication sets up unhelpful binaries between reason and emotion, sense and irrationality, legitimacy and illegitimacy, chaos and order. As our analysis suggests, these distinctions do not hold up to scrutiny. Illicit drug consumers, possibly while still intoxicated themselves, can and do act decisively and save lives. The administration of naloxone can itself cause negative intoxication experiences, even in hospitals (Neale and Strang, 2015). In short, illicit drugs are as legible through notions of moderation as through notions of excess, and naloxone is as legible through excess as moderation. PIED consumers can feel angry or phenomenal, use legal and illegal drugs to do so, and incorporate labour, discipline, knowledge and care into their consumption (disrupting the conventional polarisation of drug use and productivity and discipline).

This chapter and the projects on which it is based have attended carefully to language and naming, collected stories from a wide range of participants, noticed relevant experiences, dynamics and effects that might be obscured or erased by the discursive conventions of 'intoxication', and shifted the unit of analysis so bodies, corporeal changes and other material phenomena are understood to emerge from complex processes. It has done so as an exercise in ontopolitically-oriented research, one that allows us to begin to identify other partial worlds that disrupt conventions about intoxication, moderation, reason and the self. Contrary to widely held assumptions, drug consumers work hard to calibrate intoxication carefully for a variety of reasons. Responses that ignore or dismiss such work (perhaps because of lingering neo-liberal suspicions about intoxication) are likely to impede attempts to support health and well-being, or miss opportunities to do so. Furthermore, following Keane, if we understand intoxication as a practice or relationship with the self, rather than as a state, we also need to recognise that it cannot be eradicated with simplistic measures, such as policies that ignore the contexts of overdose in which risky intoxication is often an effect of legal conditions that render drug strength opaque and dosage unmanageable (see also Fomiatti et al., 2020), or medical responses that offer PIED consumers inaccurate or unhelpful information (Fraser et al., 2020). Future research and responses need to acknowledge the many ways and degrees of being 'beside oneself' (Gomart and Hennion, 1999), the potential for measures considered antithetical to intoxication to overlap with it, as well as the productive relationship with the self sometimes afforded by intoxication.

Notes

1 Full details of the methods used in these studies – including analytical approach, coding and transcription processes, deidentification procedures and ethics approval – are available in other publications (for the take-home naloxone study, see Farrugia et al. (2020); for the PIED study, see Fomiatti et al. (2020)).
2 Also of note is the direct association Ryan draws between testosterone and clichés of male aggression. In a 2019 article (Fomiatti et al., 2019) also written from this project, this linking of masculinity and testosterone is examined, pointing to ways in which context and discourse shape subjective experiences of drug use and intoxication.

References

Ayres, T. and Taylor, S. (2020). Media and intoxication: Media representations of the intoxicated. In F. Hutton (ed.), *Cultures of intoxication: Key issues and debates*. Basingstoke: Palgrave, pp. 239–261.
Bancroft, A. (2009). *Drugs, intoxication and society*. Cambridge: Polity.
Bogren, A. (2008). Women's intoxication as 'dual licentiousness': An exploration of gendered images of drinking and intoxication in Sweden. *Addiction Research and Theory,* 16(1), 95–106.
Bonner, K. (2013). Eros and ironic intoxication: Profound longing, madness and discipleship in Plato's *Symposium* and in modern life. *History of the Human Sciences,* 26(5), 114–131.
Deleuze, G. (1992). What is a dispositif? In T.J. Armstrong (ed.), *Michel Foucault: Philosopher*. Hemel Hempstead: Harvester Wheatsheaf, pp. 159–168.
Douglas, M. (ed.) (1987). *Constructive drinking: Perspectives on drink from anthropology*. Cambridge: Cambridge University Press.
Elliot, L., Bennett, A. and Wolfson-Stofko, B. (2019). Life after opioid-involved overdose: Survivor narratives and their implications for ER/ED interventions. *Addiction,* 114, 1379–1386. DOI: 10.1111/add.14608.
Farrugia, A., Fraser, S. and Dwyer, R. (2017). Assembling the social and political dimensions of take-home naloxone. *Contemporary Drug Problems,* 44(3), 163–175.
Farrugia, A., Fraser, S., Dwyer, R., Fomiatti, R., Neale, J., Dietze, P. and Strang, J. (2019). Take-home naloxone and the politics of care. *Sociology of Health and Illness*, 41(2), 427–443.
Farrugia, A., Neale, J., Dwyer, R., Fomiatti, R., Fraser, S., Strang, J. and Dietze, P. (2020). Conflict and communication: Managing the multiple affordances of take-home naloxone administration events in Australia. *Addiction Research and Theory,* 28(1), 29–37. DOI: 10.1080/16066359.2019.1571193.
Fomiatti, R., Farrugia, A., Fraser, S., Dwyer, R., Neale, J. and Strang, J. (2022). Addiction stigma and the production of impediments to take-home naloxone uptake. *Health*, 26(2), 139–161. DOI: 10.1177/1363459320925863.
Fomiatti, R., Latham, J.R., Fraser, S., Moore, D., Seear, K. and Aitken, C. (2019). A 'messenger of sex'? Making testosterone matter in motivations for anabolic-androgenic steroid injecting. *Health Sociology Review,* 28(3), 323–338.
Fomiatti, R., Lenton, E., Latham, J.R., Fraser, S., Moore, D., Seear, K. and Aitken, C. (2020). Maintaining the healthy body: Blood management and hepatitis C prevention among men who inject performance and image-enhancing drugs. *International Journal of Drug Policy,* 75: 102592. DOI: 10.1016/j.drugpo.2019.10.016.
Fraser, S. (2020). Doing ontopolitically-oriented research: Synthesising concepts from the ontological turn for alcohol and other drug research and other social sciences. *International Journal of Drug Policy,* 82: 102610. DOI: 10.1016/j.drugpo.2019.102610.
Fraser, S., Farrugia, A. and Dwyer, R. (2017). Grievable lives? Death by opioid overdose in Australian newspaper coverage. *International Journal of Drug Policy,* 59, 28–35.
Fraser, S., Fomiatti, R., Moore, D., Seear, K. and Aitken, C. (2020). Is another relationship possible? Connoisseurship and the doctor–patient relationship for men who consume performance and image-enhancing drugs. *Social Science and Medicine*, 246, 112720.
Gefou-Madianou, D. (ed.) (1992). *Alcohol, gender and culture*. London: Routledge.

Gomart, E. and Hennion, A. (1999). A sociology of attachment: Music amateurs, drug users. In J. Law (ed.), *Actor network theory and after*. London: Blackwell, pp. 218–247.

Heath, D.B. (1958). Drinking patterns of the Bolivian Camba. *Quarterly Journal of Studies on Alcohol*, 19(3), 491–508.

Herbert, S. and McCreanor, T. (2020). Ethnicities and intoxication. In F. Hutton (ed.), *Cultures of intoxication: Key issues and debates*. Cham: Palgrave, pp. 165–185.

Homel, R., Tomsen, S. and Thommeny, J. (1992). Public drinking and violence: Not just an alcohol problem. *Journal of Drug Issues*, 22(3), 679–697.

Hunt, G. and Antin, T. (2019). Gender and intoxication: From masculinity to intersectionality. *Drugs: Education, Prevention and Policy*, 26(1), 70–78.

Hunt, G. and Frank, V. A. (2017). Reflecting on intoxication. In T. Kolind, B. Thom and G. Hunt (eds), *The Sage handbook of drug and alcohol studies: Social science approaches*. Los Angeles, CA: Sage, pp. 322–336.

Hutton, F. (ed.) (2020). *Cultures of intoxication: Key issues and debates*. Cham: Palgrave.

Keane, H. (2020). Smoking and intoxication: From control to the buzz. In F. Hutton (ed.), *Cultures of intoxication: Key issues and debates*. Cham: Palgrave, pp. 45–66.

Kim, H. and Nelson, L. (2015). Reducing the harm of opioid overdose with the safe use of naloxone: A pharmacologic review. *Expert Opinion on Drug Safety*, 14(7), 1137–1146.

Levine, L.W. (1978). *Black culture and black consciousness: Afro-American folk thought from slavery to freedom* (Vol. 530). New York: Oxford University Press.

MacAndrew, C. and Edgerton, R.B. (1969). *Drunken comportment: A social explanation*. London: Nelson.

Mandelbaum, D.G. (1965). Alcohol and culture. *Current Anthropology*, 6(3), 281–293.

Marshall, M. (1979a). *Weekend warriors: Alcohol in a Micronesian culture*. Palo Alto, CA: Mayfield.

Marshall, M. (1979b). Introduction. In M. Marshall (ed.), *Beliefs, behaviors, and alcoholic beverages: A cross-cultural survey*. Ann Arbor: University of Michigan Press, pp. 1–11.

McCreanor, T., Moewaka Barnes, H., Kaiwai, H., Borell, S. and Gregory, A. (2008). Creating intoxigenic environments: Marketing alcohol to young people in Aotearoa New Zealand. *Social Science and Medicine*, 67 (6), 938–946.

McClelland, G. and Teplin, L. (2001). Alcohol intoxication and violent crime: Implications for public health policy. *American Journal of Addictions*, 10(1), 70–85.

Moore, D. (2020). Masculinities and intoxication: Notes towards a co-constitutive approach. In F. Hutton (ed.), *Cultures of intoxication: Key issues and debates*. Cham: Palgrave, pp. 211–235.

Moore, D., Fraser, S., Keane, H., Seear, K. and Valentine, K. (2017). Missing masculinities: Gendering practices in Australian alcohol research and policy. *Australian Feminist Studies*, 32(93), 309–324.

Neale, J. and Strang, J. (2015) Naloxone – Does over-antagonism matter? Evidence of iatrogenic harm after emergency treatment of heroin/opioid overdose. *Addiction*, 110, 1644–1652.

Orcutt, J. (1978). Normative definitions of intoxicated states: A test of several sociological theories. *Social Problems*, 25(4), 385–396.

Petersen, A. (1997). Risk, governance and the new public health. In A. Petersen and R. Bunton (eds), *Foucault, health and medicine*. London and New York: Routledge, pp. 188–206.

Pienaar, K., Murphy, D., Race, K. and Lea, T. (2020). 'To be intoxicated is to still be me, just a little blurry': Drugs, enhancement and transformation in LGBTQ cultures. In F. Hutton (ed.), *Cultures of intoxication*. London: Palgrave Macmillan, pp. 139–163.

Room, R. (2001). Intoxication and bad behaviour: Understanding cultural differences in the link. *Social Science and Medicine*, 53(2), 189–198.

Sande, A. (2002). Intoxication and rite of passage to adulthood in Norway. *Contemporary Drug Problems*, 29(2), 277–303.

Shilling, C. and Mellor, P. (2011). Retheorising Emile Durkheim on society and religion: Embodiment, intoxication and collective life. *The Sociological Review*, 59(1), 17–41.

Sulkunen, P. (2002). Between culture and nature: Intoxication in cultural studies of alcohol and drug use. *Contemporary Drug Problems*, 29 (2), 253–276.

Withington, P. (2014). Introduction: Cultures of intoxication. *Past and Present*, 222(9), 9–33.

Yardley, T. (2012). *Why we take drugs*. London: Routledge.

Zajdow, G. (2010). 'It blasted me into space': Intoxication and an ethics of pleasure. *Health Sociology Review*, 19(2), 218–229.

Zinberg, N. (1984). *Drug, set, and setting*. New Haven, CT: Yale University Press.

PART VI

Scapegoated Substances

22

ALCOHOL, SLAVERY AND RACE IN BRAZIL DURING THE LONG NINETEENTH CENTURY

Lucas Brunozi Avelar and Deborah Toner

In the 1830s, shortly after achieving independence as a nation, Brazilian authorities launched a series of measures to tackle drunkenness, which they considered to be a major social problem. In this chapter, we examine how and why drunkenness emerged as a significant concern for the Brazilian state in the first half of the nineteenth century, focusing on the longer-term process of racializing drinking behaviors from colonial Brazil to the twentieth century. We argue that the stigmatization of certain types of drinks, drinking places and drinking practices has been a central component of the history of racial discrimination in Brazil. In the early nineteenth century, the expansion of the slave trade led to increasingly restrictive and violent measures to control the enslaved population. For the enslaved themselves, alcohol was integrated into their culture and consumed for a variety of reasons, including as a means of resisting slavery. For slave owners, alcohol had been used as a form of currency and to increase labor productivity, but its use was also considered a threat to their control. The escalation in anti-drunkenness legislation in the early nineteenth century contributed to political and social efforts to justify and prolong the slave system as well as to build the Brazilian state. When slavery was abolished in 1888 and a republic established in 1889, the political and economic elite put forward new plans to change drinking practices that continued to racialize drinking behaviors but in different ways. Distilled spirits were described as causing alcoholism and racial degeneration, while beer was promoted as part of efforts to modernize, de-Africanize and ultimately "whiten" Brazil as it moved into the twentieth century.

Alcohol in Colonial Brazil

Alcohol was central to the development of colonial Brazil and particularly its system of slavery. Cachaça (Brazilian rum), as a major by-product of the sugar plantations that fueled the Portuguese trans-Atlantic slave trade in the late sixteenth and seventeenth centuries, helped to expand the colonial economy. Belief in the dietary and medicinal benefits of alcohol consumption was widespread, although colonial officials were concerned about its potential role in causing social disorder and unrest, especially among the growing enslaved population, during the eighteenth century. The gold mining and coffee industries continued to stimulate Brazil's importation of African slaves in the run-up to and aftermath of its independence from Portugal in 1822, and the drinking habits of enslaved people became subject

DOI: 10.4324/9780429058141-29

to increasing scrutiny and coercive control. While racialized justifications for such discriminatory controls were made more explicit during the nineteenth century, their origins lay in the interplay of colonial directives to maximize profit while controlling the people who produced it.

The large-scale production and export of sugar formed the bedrock of the early colonial economy in Brazil, with agricultural plantations concentrated in the northeastern coastal Captaincies of Bahia and Pernambuco. Captaincies were the main administrative units of the Portuguese colonial system in Brazil, initially led by private individuals with the means to establish colonies, and later taken under Crown control. Most plantation labor was conducted by Indigenous slaves until the late sixteenth century, when the Portuguese expanded the trans-Atlantic slave trade. As many as 15,000 enslaved Africans were transported to work in Brazil's sugar, tobacco and other plantations every year by 1600 (Bakewell 1997: 310). After a series of gold mine discoveries in the southeastern region around São Paulo – today Brazil's most populous city – the Portuguese Crown established a new administrative unit of São Paulo and Minas do Ouro (Gold Mines) in 1709, before dividing this in 1720 to give the gold mines region its own administrative status as Minas Gerais (General Mines). Later in the eighteenth century, gold deposits were discovered in the interior Brazilian regions of Goiás and Mato Grosso. The distribution of Brazil's population into southern and interior regions that the mining industry spurred was further solidified in the first half of the nineteenth century, with the rise of coffee plantations and cattle ranching. Throughout this time, the transportation of enslaved Africans to Brazil expanded enormously: of the approximately 5.8 million slaves that were transported to Brazil from 1501 to 1878, roughly 2.4 million arrived between 1800 and 1850 (SlaveVoyages 2019a) (Figure 22.1).

Historically, cachaça was a distilled spirit made from either fermented sugarcane juice or molasses (a by-product from the process of refining sugar), and was the main drug traded and consumed in colonial Brazil (Mintz 1985). In his study of alcohol and slavery in Brazil, José Curto described the period from 1700 to 1830 as the "século da geribita" – the "century of geribita", another historical term for cachaça (2002: 151–199). It was produced by slave labor on sugar plantations and used as a currency in the American inland and by slave traders at the African shore, so that this form of alcohol spread on both sides of the Atlantic. Tobacco produced in the northeastern Brazilian plantations of Bahia and Pernambuco was also included in the slave trade. Together, cachaça and tobacco were used to pay for 48% of the slaves who were brought to Brazil between 1701 and 1810 (Alencastro 2000: 324). Cachaça and tobacco to Africa, enslaved Africans to Brazil, sugar to Europe: the colonial economy depended on these drugs (Azevedo Fernandes 2014; Carneiro 2021).

The historical lexicon of Brazilian cachaça shows how deeply intertwined with slavery this commodity was. Between the seventeenth and nineteenth centuries, the most commonly used names for sugarcane spirit in Brazil were *malungo*, *cachaça* and *geribita*, as well as *aguardente de cana*. Malungo, as well as describing the drink, was used to name central aspects of the experience of bondage. Malungo (sometimes spelled mulunga or malongo) was the name given to the iron chains in which Africans were bound, and the name for the relationship formed between slaves who crossed the Atlantic Ocean in the same slave ship, or who belonged to the same slave owner or plantation (Alencastro 2000: 313–314). Cachaça, geribita and aguardente de cana were less symbolically loaded terms, referring to differences in production of the spirit. Cachaça meant "honey spirit, or molasses dregs", describing the thick scum that comes out from the first boiling of the sugarcane juice (Moraes Silva & Bluteau 1789: 315; Pinto 1832: 178), whereas gerebita meant "sugarcane made from sugar dregs" (Moraes Silva & Bluteau 1789: 896; Pinto 1832: 555). Aguardente (literally, burning water)

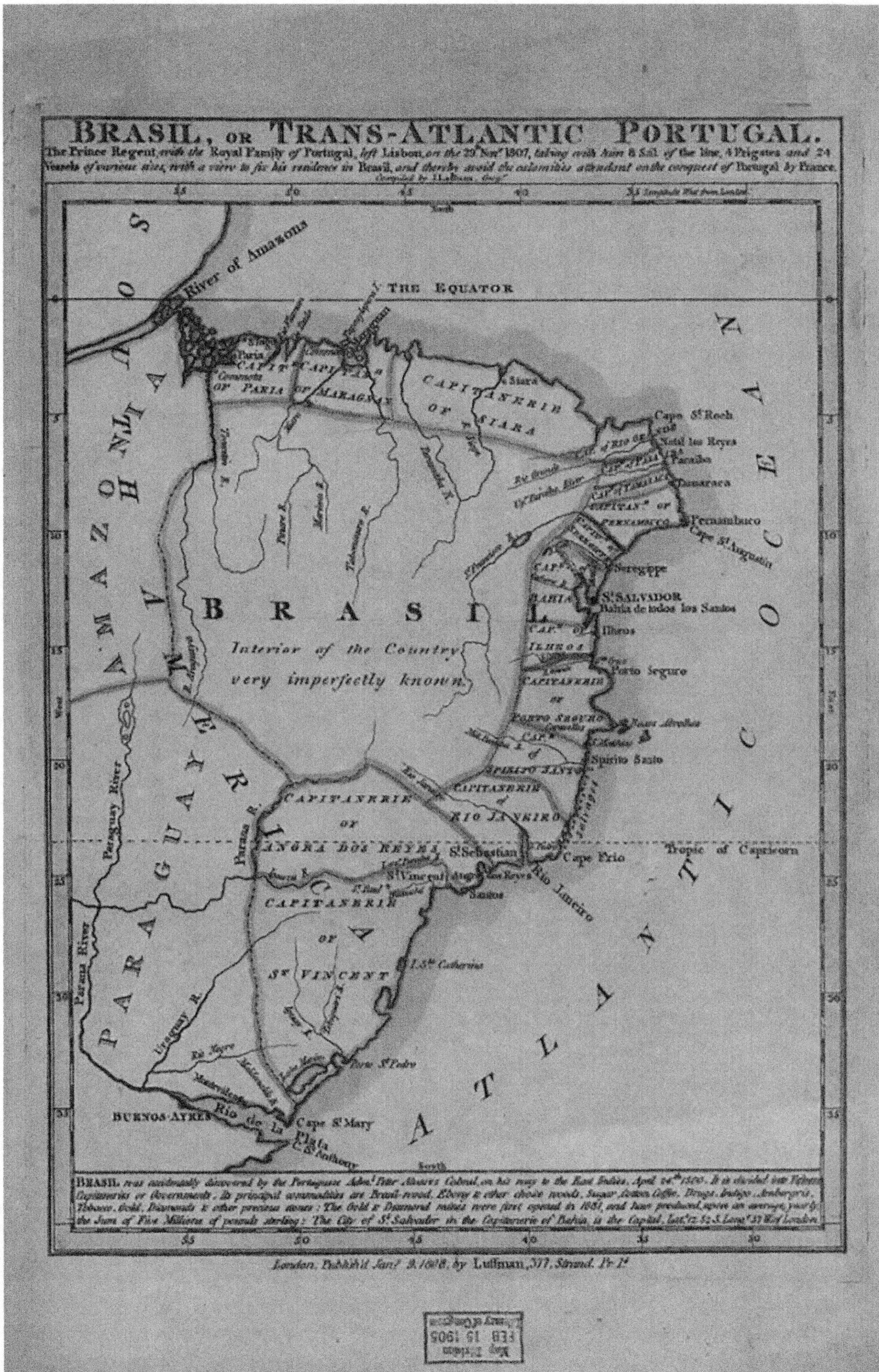

Figure 22.1 Carte du Brésil

was a generic Portuguese word for distilled spirits, and meant distilled "from sugarcane" when "de cana" was added. While the denomination of origin legislation that applies to cachaça today distinguishes it from rum – cachaça can only be made from fermented sugarcane juice, whereas rum can also be made from molasses, or a combination or both – this distinction was not observed historically (Azevedo Fernandes 2014: 46–47).

Across the colonial period, cachaça had important social roles and in many respects was understood to provide the same kinds of benefits as other "drugs". According to Antônio de Moraes da Silva's dictionary of 1813, the term drug (*droga* in Portuguese) had an expansive definition, encompassing all "exotic resources, luxury products destined to consumption, to medical use, and also as food supplies" (642). The definition included, therefore, an infinity of plants, vegetables, dyes, oils, roots, wool and/or silk goods. Consumption of these "drugs", none more so than cachaça, marked special occasions in enslaved people's lives, like parties and weddings, but also more routine daily activities. In the sugarcane mill, on hot summer days, the cachaça, served by the plantation owner, was mixed with water, sugar and lemon or orange. This mixture was the foundation of what we know today as "caipirinha", a famous Brazilian cocktail. Among Bahia's African people, cachaça was also exchanged for beans and potatoes. In the northern interior state of Pará, Indigenous laborers who worked on ginger plantations received payment in cocoa, which was the current currency in Amazonia. Mixed with tobacco and urine, it was used against fevers. It was also used to wash smallpox pustules, and along with flowers, leaves, resins and seeds, cachaça served for magical, medical, religious and empirical purposes (Priore 2005: 67).

However, alcohol was simultaneously considered problematic for both economic and social reasons. In the middle of the seventeenth century, the Portuguese Crown issued laws forbidding the production and sale of cachaça. The goal was to avoid economic competition with Portuguese wine in the Atlantic trade. But because an illegal market soon developed and cachaça production became more crucial to the profitability of sugar plantations in the face of increased competition from Caribbean sugar producers, the law was overturned in 1695, so that the colonial authorities could retrieve tax income from the legalized trade (Azevedo Fernandes 2014: 49–52; Ricardo 2014).

Colonial approaches to regulating alcohol were also shaped by social concerns about the drinking behaviors of Indigenous and Black people, both enslaved and free. As in other parts of colonial Latin America and North America, missionaries and colonial officials in Brazil frequently wrote in alarmed tones about Indigenous consumption of distilled spirits. Despite the trade and exchange of alcohol often being vital to the establishment and maintenance of Indigenous-colonial relationships, Indigenous practices of ritual intoxication and drunkenness were regarded with fear, suspicion, misunderstanding and even disgust, and became part of wider set of categories employed in colonial discourse to construct Indigenous people as "other" to the European colonizers. The so-called "drunken Indian" stereotype which developed in different ways across the Americas became an "essential element in the formation of this colonial narrative" of Indigenous inferiority and barbarism (Azevedo Fernandes 2014: 58; see also Mancall 1995; Quintero 2001; Earle 2008; Earle 2014; Córdova 2015).

More than elsewhere, likely due to Brazil's greater and longer-lasting use of the trans-Atlantic slave trade, such racialized ideas about drinking behaviors were also extended to the Black population during the colonial period. During the eighteenth century, the Portuguese Crown vacillated between accepting or prohibiting alcohol use by the Black population. On the one hand, there was a belief that cachaça stimulated enslaved Africans to work harder both on agricultural plantations and in the mines. This was consistent with broader understanding of drugs as both medicine and food at the time. On the other hand, slave owners and colonial officials feared that the cachaça trade and consumption allowed enslaved Africans to conduct secret gatherings, and exchange goods and information which could lead to social unrest or even rebellions. In the southeastern Captaincy of Minas Gerais, enslaved people forced to work in the gold mines were caught and punished for hiding gold under their fingernails in order to buy cachaça sold by "Negras de tabuleiro" (selling women). Likewise, the Portuguese Crown was concerned about cachaça production and consumption because they worried that it distracted enslaved people from their work and that the drinking and drunkenness of enslaved people threatened the "public tranquility". But in the last decades of the eighteenth century, when gold mining declined, opinions about cachaça changed to a more tolerant posture (Figueiredo & Venâncio 2005: 36–41).

Racial ideas underpinned some of these concerns. According to Jorge Benci, an Italian Jesuit who lived in Brazil from 1683 to 1700 and developed a set of precepts to regulate relations between slave owners and slaves, drunkenness was a sin to which Africans were inclined because they were considered the "sons of Ham". This refers to a biblical episode involving drunkenness in which a curse of perpetual servitude was placed on one line of Ham's descendants, and some Christian thinkers used this "curse" to explain why Africans had dark skin and to justify their enslavement, as well as depicting them as inclined to drunkenness. Some slave owners agreed that enslaved Africans should be made to work even on Holy Days because it was a way to prevent them from indulging in wine and dances or fights (Benci 1977: 192–193). Benci considered Black people to be "more skillful for all kinds of evils" and given over to impudence (Lotierzo 2011: 79).

Therefore, in the colonial period, both positive and negative ideas circulated about alcohol. On the one hand, alcohol was recognized as bringing medical, dietary and economic benefits, including tax income and improved productivity. On the other hand, particularly regarding the enslaved populations' drinking, there were concerns about alcohol consumption leading to social unrest and/or resistance. Some slaves did use alcohol in ways suspected by slave owners, and there existed some punishments for slave drunkenness. But the temporary prohibition against the production of cachaça was driven mainly by economic concerns – protecting Portuguese-produced wines in trade – rather than social concerns. Ultimately, the interests of the slave trade and slave economy were too strong to maintain the prohibition of alcohol. However, in the wake of Brazilian independence in 1822, and the establishment of an "imperial" constitution in 1824, alcohol and concerns about drunkenness became entangled in Brazilian elites' attempts to square the contradictions inherent in promoting liberal ideology in an expanding slave society. While liberalism was strongly contested in nineteenth-century Brazil, as it was elsewhere in Latin America, it was very influential in shaping the political culture of Rio de Janeiro, the capital city of the Brazilian Empire after independence from Portugal in 1822. Yet by the mid-nineteenth century, Rio de Janeiro was also the city with the largest number of slaves in the world. The increasingly explicit racialization of the problem of drunkenness, and the increasing concentration of criminal punishments for public drunkenness on the bodies of enslaved people, was connected to attempts to reconcile liberalism and slavery.

Alcohol and the Paradoxes of Liberalism in Post-Independence Brazil

The city of Rio de Janeiro underwent profound changes in the early nineteenth century, which led to attacks on established drinking practices. Napoleon's invasion of the Iberian Peninsula in 1808 sparked political transformations across the Spanish and Portuguese empires in the Americas. The Portuguese Court moved to Rio de Janeiro to escape Napoleon, stimulating growth of the urban population and deepening changes in the political culture of the city. In 1822, Brazilian independence was achieved. The expanded white population of the capital, influenced by Enlightenment ideas, political ideologies of liberalism, secularization and constitutionalism, sought to remake the city into an exemplar of a "civilized" society, and its population into rational, moral citizens for the success of the new nation. At the same time, the enslaved population of Brazil and of Rio de Janeiro expanded greatly. Among the 2.4 million Africans estimated to have been transported to Brazil as slaves between 1801 and 1850, at least 880,447 are known to have disembarked at Rio de Janeiro (SlaveVoyages 2019b). Consequently, by 1849, Rio was the city with the highest number of enslaved people in the modern world (Karasch 2000; Chalhoub 2012; Marquese & Salles 2016).

Liberalism meant free trade and political rights, but not for the enslaved and the ever-expanding slave system. Land and property rights – including the right to own slaves – were protected to maximize the economic opportunities involved in ending the colonial monopoly on trade with the Portuguese metropolis (Bosi 1992; Franco 1993; Parron 2009: 28–87; Marquese & Parron 2011). These circumstances produced a clash of forces that led to new justifications for slavery based on ideas of African racial inferiority and to the criminalization of public drunkenness, developments that were intertwined. Ideals of liberal citizenship within the new constitutional monarchy promoted sobriety and social order for the whole population.

The Viscount of Cairu, José da Silva Lisboa (1756–1835), a Brazilian politician and economic advisor to D. João, prince regent of Brazil from 1816 to 1822, published a moral manual in 1824 that denounced intoxication as inimical to the proper behavior of responsible, productive citizens in the new nation and empire. His *Moral Constitution and Obligation of the Citizens* proclaimed that:

> this law condemns drunkenness, as the most vile and pernicious vice. The drunkard, depriving himself of the right use of the senses, and of the reason that God has given him, desecrates the benefit of the Godhead; he is reduced to the condition of the brutes; is unable to guide his steps; falls as an epileptic; his weakness makes him an object of derision and contempt of all around him: if in this state he contracts, he ruins and loses his business: being out of himself, he says injurious words, provokes enemies, and cause regrets: he fills his home with disturbances and displeasures, and ends his life by an untimely death or a sickly old age.
>
> *(Lisboa 1824: 92)*

For the Viscount, alcohol intoxication, a "pernicious vice", would block appropriate social and economic behavior for a citizen of the Brazilian Empire: the drunkard disrespects God, has mental and physical health problems – including self-destructive behaviors – he is frowned upon and even socially ridiculed; he acts in a uneconomical way; breaks social peace; compromises family life and dies early or ages poorly. Drunkenness was thus an obstacle to fulfilling the ideals of family, religion, work, social order and a healthy body. In the liberal view, drunkenness was irrational, immoral, unhealthy, anti-social and unproductive: anathema to good citizenship.

Since impoverished, non-white and enslaved sectors of the population were already considered less well-equipped for the responsibilities of liberal citizenship, their drinking behaviors became entangled in elite rationalizations that excluded them from the rights of citizenship. In the case of enslaved and free Africans and Afro-Brazilians, their use and perceived abuse of alcohol were increasingly understood in racialized terms, as something to which they were innately inclined. Ernst Ebel, a German traveler visiting Rio de Janeiro in

1824, registered in his diary that cachaça was a "harmful drink" consumed only by the poor and especially the Black population. For the Black population, Ebel wrote that such was their lack of self-control in the use of alcohol that such control would need to be strictly imposed:

> With regard to the nature of the negro in general, opinion is one: it is useless to treat it well. We must keep it under severe control: the men are too inclined to drink, to steal, and to laziness; the women [...] it is so difficult to moderate their instinct, that they practice their acts with greater shamelessness
>
> *(Ebel 1972: 45)*

The use of words such as "nature" and "instinct" to describe Black men as drunken, lazy thieves and Black women as sexually uncontrollable suggests that these characteristics were innate, contributing to the development of a racial stereotype. This discourse, recorded by Ebel, was widespread, not only in the works of foreign observers but also among Brazilian authors. According to this racist ideology, the lack of self-control possessed by Black people meant that stricter regulations around alcohol were needed to control their behavior.

Consequently, while governing authorities identified urban taverns – public drinking places – as potential sites of popular dissent and unrest, the measures they applied to the whole population during periods of socio-political crisis were retained to control enslaved people for a much longer time. During the struggles for separation from Portugal in 1822, for instance, the State Council proposed a series of measures for the country's security, which included controls on the operation of taverns and surveillance of tavern-goers' activities. These proposals sought to put spies in the taverns and gambling houses of Rio de Janeiro where people "usually speak with more freedom" (Atas 1822: 87–93; see also Bretas and Rosemberg 2013). These general measures did not outlast the political crisis of the early 1820s; however, legal proscriptions forbidding the "gathering of slaves" in drinking houses lasted throughout the nineteenth century (Santana 2020: 13. See also Avelar 2021).

Similarly, punishments for violating the new 1830 law against public drunkenness were more severe and violent for the enslaved. Article 60 of the 1830 Criminal Code, which remained in effect until the end of the Imperial State in 1889, provided for torture to be used against enslaved people who violated this and other laws:

> If the defendant is a slave... he will be condemned in the case of lashes and after suffering them, will be delivered to his master, who will be obligated to bring him with an iron for the time and the period established by the judge, the lashes will be fixed in the sentence, and the slave shall not receive more than fifty lashes per day
>
> *(Alencastro 2007: np)*

In addition to whipping, slave owners were entitled to punish enslaved people for drunkenness by imposing physical restraints such as the tinplate mask (see Figure 22.2). Imprisonment was another common punishment for the crime of public drunkenness. Rio de Janeiro's municipal government published the Posture Code in 1830, laws designed to "modernize" daily life in the capital city and to restrain cultural practices deemed "backward". This included provision for Justices of the Peace to temporarily confine "all those who are found on the street in a state of drunkenness" to protect them from being injured or killed in accidents such as being run over or stepped on by horses. The law applied to all residents of the city, but was overwhelmingly used against Africans, both enslaved and free. The Posture Code also introduced regulations for street cleanliness, dress and behavioral comportment, and the

Figure 22.2 HARRO-HARING, Paul. Scene at a tavern: sailors trade with black women. Tropical sketches of Brazil, 1840. Available in: Paul Harro-Harring - Instituto Moreira Salles (ims.com.br)

operation of commercial establishments, including taverns, that amounted to a crackdown, even criminalization, of African culture. The 1830 Code was the first to prohibit the sale and use of the "pito do pango" (marijuana joints, also known as maconha), the consumption of which was particularly associated with the enslaved and free Black population. Paragraph 7° of Title 2 in the 1830 Code provided that

> the sale and use of the pango pito is prohibited, as well as the conservation of it in public houses. The offenders will be fined, namely: the seller in 20$000, and the slaves and more people, who use it, in three days in jail.
>
> *(Código de Posturas 1830, Title 2, § 7°)*

Gatherings of the enslaved to drink, sing and dance were also defined as obstructions to public space that promoted disorders (Santana 2020: 13).

In 1838, another Posture Code transferred the responsibility of dealing with public drunkenness to the *Policía da Corte* (Court Police), marking an escalation of the repression against drunkenness (Rodrigues 1981; Lopes 2004). To the existing prohibition of marijuana consumption, the 1838 Code added prohibitions against other components of enslaved people's cultural practice in Rio de Janeiro, including *entrudo* (a religious dance) and the *casa de zungu*, popular eating places for a type of soup. These measures were part of an effort to achieve what Gilberto Freyre called the "desafricanization" of Brazil (2003: 458). As Sidney Chalhoub has highlighted, daily life in Rio de Janeiro continued to defy the de-Africanization ideology of the Posture Codes, not least through the resistance of the enslaved, for whom taverns and public houses were important spaces for sociability and clandestine activities, including the consumption of alcohol and marijuana (Chalhoub 1990). In 1854, the Posture Code was republished and the article sustained:

> it is prohibited in drinking houses, taverns or other public places, gatherings of people with tocatas, dances or voices: the house owner will be fined 30$000 rs; and being a public place, each of the offenders will be fined in 6$000 rs and put in prison until the fine is paid; those who don't have the money, pay with 4 days in jail.
>
> *(Código de Posturas 1854: 55–56)*[1]

For comparison, an enslaved craftsman aged 20–29 years was valued at an average of 324 réis in the first half of the nineteenth century.

In rural areas, paternalistic slave owners portrayed slavery as a way of protecting the enslaved from their alleged impulses toward drunkenness. As part of the measures to control consumption of alcohol on plantations, a handbook for slave owners recommended providing a piece of land for the enslaved to produce their own food such as coffee, corn, beans and bananas. To prevent enslaved people from going to roadside taverns to sell or exchange their surplus, as had been customary, they were prohibited from exchanging these goods off the plantation. Slave owners were, moreover, exhorted to pay a "reasonable price" for these products to reduce the incentive for the enslaved to risk breaking the rules anyway. Taverns were places where Africans went to exchange products for alcohol, tobacco and tools with tavern-keepers. Small but regular allowances of tobacco and cachaça were distributed as part of this paternalistic effort for maintaining "peace in *senzalas*" (the slave quarters), but there were also violent punishments for drunkenness or excess in consumption. In cases of intoxication, the enslaved were punished by flogging of "20 to 50 lashes" (Werneck 1847: 24–25).

The recommendations of slave owners about alcohol and taverns didn't change substantially after 1850 when the transatlantic slave trade was prohibited and interrupted in Brazil. In 1861, a group of landowners described taverns as their "greatest enemies", due to the clandestine trade of coffee, which enslaved laborers produced and took from the plantations for sale within taverns (Stein 1990: 208). Despite prohibitions against and punishments for such actions, it is clear that the enslaved continued to resist the system of slavery through conducting such commerce in taverns. In 1878, only ten years before the abolition of slavery, plantation owners complained that it seemed taverns' "exclusive purpose is to trade with slaves during the night, [the slaves are] incited by thieves to steal from their masters, who are thus obliged to inflict punishments on them" (Congresso Agrícola 1878: 32). The authors of this 1878 report finished by arguing that "there are so many evils, losses and disturbances that these small establishments of illicit trade bring to farmers, they can rightly be considered the greatest scourge of farming" (Congresso Agrícola 1878: 32).

Frequenting taverns to sell produce raised on their own land allocations or taken from the plantation's main crop was only one way in which alcohol featured in enslaved people's resistance to slavery. In the first half of the nineteenth century in Rio de Janeiro, historian Mary Karasch argues that "to alleviate the burden of slavery, many slaves indulged in drink and smoking diamba (maconha, marijuana)". While, from "the landlord's view, drink, after laziness and robbery, was the great defect of the Black population", from the perspective of the enslaved, drug consumption was part of their "nonviolent resistance" to slavery. Acts of resistance included conducting spiritual rituals to cast spells over slave owners, harming plantation productivity by working deliberately slowly and feigning illness, and engaging in self-harm. Within these experiences, the use of alcoholic beverages was common among enslaved women and men for different reasons: cachaça was cheap and it was essential to their diet; it featured in religious rituals; and, importantly "drinking was also an important part of the social life of the slaves" (Karasch 2000: 437).

Alcohol and tavern-going also became embedded within cultural expressions, such as folklore, religion and dance, of West Central African peoples in the Brazilian Empire's slave system. These cultural expressions contested the racial stereotype of Black drunkenness constructed as part of the liberal rationalization of slavery. *Jongo*, for instance, was (and is) a group dance formed by a large circular group of men and women singing together, clapping hands at the same time, shaking their bodies without moving place, and in the center one or two dancers demonstrate the steps. The singer improvises stanzas, the group answers back and to the side musicians play instruments loudly. The ritual goes on day and night once cachaça circulates. Alcohol had a strong spiritual and communal component in these meetings, which were part of enslaved people's culture in nineteenth-century Brazil (Gallet 1934: 62; see also Dias 2001; Agostini 2007; Slenes 2007).

The following stanzas from *jongo* expressions and folklore illustrate how alcohol and tavern-going could offer space for the resistance and critique of slavery, as well as highlight the hypocrisy of racist discourse that attributed inequality and oppression to Black people's alleged tendency toward drunkenness.

> Quando Baranco vai na venda|Logo dizi tá sequentario,|Nosso preto vai na venda,|Acha copo ta viraro [When white man goes to tavern | it is because he is restless | our black man goes to tavern|look for alcohol because he is furious].
>
> *(Lopes 1988: 171)*

> Branco dize quando more|Jesucrisso que o levou,|E o pretinho quando more,|Foi cachaça que o matou [When white man dies|Jesus Christ took him|and when black man dies|it was cachaça (rum) that killed him].
>
> *(Goulart 1971: 71)*

Operating within these stanzas is what Michael Pollak has described as "underground memory" as opposed to "official memory". Underground memory is transmitted inside family, associations and networks of social and/or political sociability, "forbidden, unspeakable or shameful memories that are jealously guarded into structures of informal communications and go unnoticed by encompassing society" (Pollak 1989: 3–15). The majority of Africans who were forcibly transported to Brazil and the Caribbean as slaves shared beliefs about the spiritual importance of alcohol that were incorporated and adapted into slave culture. For many West Central African peoples, alcohol was especially important to ceremonial occasions in which ancestors were honored, and in funerary rites, both to help the passage of the deceased to the spiritual world and to keep channels of communication open between the deceased, the living and the wider community of ancestors (Smith 2005: 101–102). In the context of slavery, such rituals were adapted to deal with transitions and dislocations in general (not just funerals and deaths), as a means of bringing a sense of order, continuity and social cohesion to the inherently traumatizing and destabilizing experience of slavery. The consciousness of racialized double standards in the "official memory" of drinking practices expressed in the *jongo* stanzas above, together with their palpable anger, simultaneously exposes the exploitation to which enslaved peoples were subject and lay claim to tavern-going and drinking as legitimate means of dealing with trauma that political and economic elites sought to deny them in the nineteenth century.

The criminalization of public drunkenness in the 1830s was driven by the growing concerns of Brazilian elites to control and suppress marginalized groups, especially the enslaved, who were seen as troublesome or socially disruptive. This was justified by an ideology in which drunkenness, already understood as a sin associated with Africans because of their supposed biblical descent from Ham, was viewed as an immoral, irrational behavioral vice to which Africans and Afro-Brazilians were innately susceptible. Paternalistic measures on slave plantations and legal punishments for public drunkenness in cities like Rio de Janeiro were designed to increase control over the enslaved population by minimizing their opportunities for resistance through cultural expressions, solidarity-building sociability and access to clandestine gatherings and trade in taverns. In the following decades, as the abolition of slavery was increasingly debated, especially after the closure of the transatlantic slave trade in 1851, the Black population's relationship with alcohol was used to justify the perpetuation of slavery. After the abolition of slavery in 1888 and the establishment of a republican political system in 1889, new pseudo-scientific racial theories and medicalized understandings of alcohol abuse were added to this longer-term racial discourse about drunkenness to justify and rationalize racial inequality in republican Brazil.

In 1837, a slave owner somewhat sympathetic to the cause of abolition expressed concerns that freeing the enslaved Black population could lead to the further spread of the vice of drunkenness throughout the population. Frederico Leopoldo Cezar Burlamarqui, in his *Analytic Memory about the Slave Trade*, stated that while the system of slavery worked to "demoralize the customs" of the country, abolition posed two major problems. First, the lack of a substantial alternative workforce to substitute for the labor of the enslaved and, second, the behavioral influence of a large unemployed Black population on the rest of society. His position was predicated on the view that without the compelling force of slavery, Black people would not work productively because "they vegetate in a state closest to the most brutal" and, being given over to the "vice of drunkenness", the formerly enslaved would spread this vice throughout the lower classes and even "going to classes 'higher'". Indeed, he argued that the vice of drunkenness had already "been communicated to them [the lower classes] by the slaves". But, because he viewed drunkenness as an inclination innate only to the enslaved, abolition would accelerate the transmission of the vice throughout society by increasing social contact between the formerly enslaved and the rest of the population (Burlamarqui 1837: vi, 43, 134).

More than a decade after the closure of the trans-Atlantic slave trade made the abolition of Brazil's slave system an increasing inevitability, the stereotype of Black drunkenness was used to decry proposals for immediate, rather than gradual abolition. In 1866, the magistrate Luiz Francisco da Câmara Leal described the proposal for immediate abolition as

> an inexcusable political imprudence to put thousands of men exalted by drunkenness, real or deriving from delirious imagination, the acquisition of the ever aspired and never forgotten gift of freedom - without the slightest corrective, without giving them proper occupation, without directing them to the love of order, respect for institutions, recognition of the rights of all, social freedom, which is born of observance of the laws, and obedience to their enforcers.
>
> *(Leal 1866: 32)*

Expressing many of the same fears as Burlamarqui had, about the limited capacity of the enslaved to live as productive, orderly liberal citizens after emancipation, he suggested that the proposal for immediate abolition was the result of a real or imagined drunkenness on the part of those fighting for freedom. In other words, for Leal, the demand for an immediate end to slavery was a mere nonsense of drunks, to be disregarded as totally irrational. Instead, he argued that a more gradual emancipation would not only allow for the payment of compensation to slave owners for their lost property, but also to prepare the enslaved for the rights and responsibilities of their freedom (Leal 1866: 17–29).

By the 1880s, when steps toward abolition had been taken – most notably, the Law of the Free Womb in 1871, which meant that enslaved women's children would be born free – the idea that without the controlling force of slavery, Black Brazilians would languish in drunken ruin that had become widespread, even among some of those who supported abolition. Such ideas helped to perpetuate stark economic and political inequalities in post-emancipation Brazil by providing a rationalization for the continued economic exploitation and political disenfranchisement of Black people. Louis Couty, a French physiologist and Professor at the National Museum in Rio de Janeiro, argued that while the abolition of slavery was necessary, the newly emancipated Black person "becomes for some time useless or less useful" (Couty 1881: 7). He suggested that enslaved Black people in Brazil's cities were good porters, carpenters or masons, but when "they are set free and, shortly thereafter, having become drunkards or lazy, they only work when compelled by very limited needs" (Couty 1881: 29).

Beliefs in the redemptive virtues of slavery had already appeared in the early nineteenth century, and they remained powerful even among those who agreed that abolition was necessary. Couty, for instance, believed that Brazil needed to abolish slavery so that the country could exploit all its natural potential, populate the territory and make savings: "It is therefore necessary to suppress this work, not because it is harmful to a class of men, but because it is detrimental to an entire social evolution" (Couty 1881: 42). The combination of economic liberalism and racism allowed Couty to defend the use of violence in dealing with the enslaved population:

> It is quite true that if a serious misconduct, such as theft, complete drunkenness, or prolonged absence – and these faults are far from rare – is incurred, the black is liable to corporal punishment. But after taking fifty lashes, the unfortunate will not be changed, and his force of inertia will remain unchanged.
>
> *(Couty 1881: 45)*

Couty's pessimism that even violent punishment would not deter the enslaved from drunkenness was informed by the premise that Black people were unsuited to driving efficiencies and improvements in coffee production, one of Brazil's largest export industries by the late nineteenth century. He described the "social characteristics" of "negros" as lazy and child-like, making them vulnerable to the "low" attractions of alcohol consumption:

> Most black adults have many of the characteristics of children in our civilized societies. Like children, they have relatively developed lower senses, especially taste and hearing. The black man likes tobacco, rice, and well roasted corn, loves sweets, *rapadura*, but, above all, he likes cachaça or impure sugarcane brandy made in the country. During the night, and by sacrificing himself more for this passion than for freedom itself, he may even work on Sundays. In this way a slave whose particular field is cultivated can simply be a more determined drunkard. Despite all the vigilance, all the prohibitions, all the punishments, you often see drunken slaves on the farms, and according to general consensus, drunkenness is their greatest defect.
>
> *(Couty 1881: 77)*[2]

Couty concluded his racist yet anti-slavery book stressing that even "the best treated slave can be, like others, thieves and drunkards" and, when freed, "they will become disobedient, arrogant, drunks and drunkards, and it will be necessary to get rid of them". While he viewed slavery as incompatible with Brazil's economic modernization, the institution had, he argued, protected the enslaved and, in the absence of such protection, he was convinced that "because of their laziness or drunkenness" emancipated slaves would be "unable to support themselves" (Couty 1881: 97). This dilemma was, for elites like Couty, the Brazilian white man's burden. According to Frantz Fanon, "it is not possible to subjugate man without logically making them inferior from one side to another. And racism is nothing more than the affective, emotional and sometimes intellectual explanation of this inferiorization" (Fanon 2014; see also Avelar 2020). The long-term process of racializing the drinking practices of enslaved and free Black people in Brazil had developed in tandem with colonialism and the institution of slavery. After the abolition of slavery in 1888, the creation of republican Brazil in 1889 and the promotion of European immigration to "whiten" and "modernize" Brazil in the following decades, new intellectual dimensions were added to the longer-term racial discourse about drunkenness to explain ongoing racial inequalities in Brazilian society.

Modernity and the Racialization of Drinking Behaviors in Post-Abolition Brazil

Brazil's new republican government responded to the abolition of slavery by encouraging mass immigration from Europe, with policies that were envisioned as effecting economic modernization and national progress. The new federal republic was dominated by the economic powerhouse states of São Paulo and Minas Gerais, in a largely oligarchical system that was nicknamed the "café com leite" (coffee with milk) alliance because these states were dominated by coffee production and cattle ranching, respectively. These political and economic elites exerted strong influence on Brazil's immigration policies, which were predicated on racist assumptions about the greater industriousness of European workers, compared to newly emancipated slaves and the Black population in general, and were animated by the goal of "whitening" Brazilian society demographically, socially and culturally (Skidmore 1999: 69–79; see also Meade 1997). Coffee producers set up recruitment agencies in European port cities, the state subsidized transportation fares for European migrants and other incentives were offered to encourage the migration of whole families, as a means of promoting a moral social order based on family stability and as a means of keeping wages low. At the same time, with Decree Law 528, Brazil prohibited the migration of Asians and Africans (Lesser 2013: 69–73).

Scientific racism formed part of the intellectual and ideological justification of this immigration policy and other aspects of the modernizing agenda of Brazilian elites in this era. As in other parts of Latin America, scientific racism, especially in the form of degeneration theory, shaped medical, psychiatric and criminological studies of alcoholism, marking a new stage in the racialization of drinking behaviors in Brazil. Degeneration theory, emerging from the influential work of French psychiatrists Valentin Magnan and Benedict Morel, provided a hereditary framework for interpreting social problems such as poverty, mental illness and crime as advancing progressively from one generation to the next. Within this framework, alcoholism was "thought to be both a major cause and consequence of this process of degeneration, with implications for public health, national productivity, and social order" (Toner 2021: 181). While these ideas were influential in many national contexts during the late nineteenth and early twentieth centuries, they were used to pathologize the drinking behaviors of different demographic groups in different places. In France, Spain and Chile, for instance, where the majority of the population was considered ethnically white, fears about degeneration were concentrated on the urban working classes (Bynam 1984: 69–70; Sournia 1990: 98–108; Rebolledo 2013: 145–162). In Latin American nations where the "drunken Indian" stereotype had taken powerful hold as part of colonial discourse that "othered" and "inferiorized" Indigenous peoples – such as Mexico, Guatemala and Bolivia – alcoholic degeneration combined concerns about race and social class, in connection with their largely Indigenous and mestizo (mixed Hispanic-Indigenous heritage) lower classes (Toner 2015: 212–216). In Brazil, such discourse was concentrated on Africans, Afro-Brazilians and their descendants.

In 1894, Nina Rodrigues, a Brazilian doctor (1862–1906) influenced by social Darwinists like Cesare Lombroso, Herbert Spencer and Francis Galton, published "As raças humanas" (The human races), on criminal psychology in Brazil. Rodrigues argued for a differentiated criminal treatment of Afro-Brazilians, Indigenous and mixed-race groups, all of whom he described as "inferior races". He asserted that the causes of racial degeneration were miscegenation, alcoholism and "miasmatical emanations" (Rodrigues 1894: 151). In line with the racial hygienists and social Darwinists he cited, Rodrigues viewed alcoholism as one of the "abnormalities" that threatened national progress and social disorder because of its degenerating effects on subsequent generations, especially among the Afro-Brazilian population. He stated that

> the black creole [a term meaning born in Brazil] kept the brutal instincts of the African alive: he is bitter, violent in his sexual impulses, much given to drunkenness and this background of character impresses his stamp on the current colonial criminality.
>
> *(Rodrigues 1894: 124)*

The author therefore believed that drunkenness was a "brutal instinct" of Afro-Brazilians inherited, in turn, from Africans, and that tendencies to alcohol abuse, sexual aggression and criminality were hereditary characteristics that these groups transmitted to their descendants.

The republican government tried to lower alcohol consumption with laws and campaigns based on ideas of racial hygiene that connected alcoholism to problems of mental illness, crime and disease. The Penal Code in its twelfth chapter, "of beggars and drunks", made both habitual drunkenness and public drunkenness crimes punishable by 15 days imprisonment (article 396), and the same penalty applied to anyone who would "provide to someone, in a public space, drinks to get him drunk, or to increase drunkenness" (article 397). Article 238, moreover, stipulated that public employees would lose their jobs for habitual drunkenness, with no possibility of getting another job until they could demonstrate their reformed ways. Citizenship rights, already extremely restricted in republican Brazil, were also removed for offenses related to drunkenness (Santos 2018: 330). The great majority of patients admitted to the National Hospice for the Insane in Rio de Janeiro in the early 1900s were classified as alcoholics with "toxic psychoses" (Moreira 2015: 54). In 1912, a total of 19,950 people in Rio de Janeiro were recorded as having been arrested or prosecuted, as having died from tuberculosis or by suicide, or as registered patients of the Hospice (asylum). Of this total 14,750 were deemed to be alcoholics (Souza 2004: 68).

Distilled spirits, especially cachaça consumption which had long been associated with Afro-Brazilians, were linked to this medicalized framework of alcoholism and degeneration. A biographer of a slave owner commented that "the cachaça was the first and most important freedom which the freed slaves used and abused" and cachaça "ruined the poor people who still continue to wander without knowing how to enjoy the freedom that was so much touted" (Viotti 1992: 510). The memoirs of Luis Edmundo, an influential journalist, poet and historian, praised the efforts to modernize and de-Africanize Rio de Janeiro around the turn of the twentieth century, and identified taverns as particular sites of African sociability and culture that tarnished the city. Edmundo described taverns as dirty, inhospitable and abject, frequented by drunken Black women and men, who play African instruments, dance, drink and laugh while the "cachaça drips" (Edmundo 2003, vol. I: 76). For Edmundo, such spaces meant that "the city was still a village of Africans", and the customs of mainly Black tavern-goers harmed the image of the capital city Brazilian elites wanted to project as modern and civilized (Edmundo 2003, vol. 1: 120).

While distilled spirits, and especially cachaça, were associated with Afro-Brazilian sociability, backwardness, disease, mental illness and crime, at the same time beer drinking was actively promoted as modern and healthy and featured significantly in plans to Europeanize – and thereby "civilize" – the capital city Rio de Janeiro. Fluminense Park, established in 1902, was emblematic of this process. In addition to its elegant gardens, carousel, theater, orchestral performances, film projection and electric lighting, all "symbols of modernity", Fluminense Park had a "huge space for beer consumption, especially draft beer and Bock Ale from Brahma". The Park quickly became an important leisure center and "the best beer advertising center, greatly helping the increase of beer consumption" (Marques 2014: 307). Urban modernization reforms were both helped by international investment and designed to attract more foreign capital and to support the efforts to attract European migration. Beer advertisements alluded to its medieval European origins of production (see Figure 22.3), as well as its nutritional, even medicinal, value (see Figure 22.4), to shape new consumption habits in the city.

By centering elegantly dressed white women as domestic consumers (Figure 22.4), advertisements dissociated beer from the wider medical and social concerns about alcohol that targeted Afro-Brazilian consumption habits by focusing on distilled spirits such as cachaça and the space of the tavern. Beer halls, such as the one in Fluminense Park, were promoted as mixed-gender and socially elite spaces (see Figures 22.5 and 22.6), alluding to romance, refinement and modern forms of recreation (Marques 2014: 307). These advertisements, published in magazines like *Fon Fon* that set out to publicize "symbols of modernity", contributed to an idealized whitening of Brazil's drinking culture and society as a whole.

Figure 22.3 Brahma Bull-Bock Advertisement

Figure 22.4 Brahma-Porter Advertisement

Figure 22.5 Companhia Cervejaria Brahma Advertisement

Figure 22.6 Bock-Ale Teutonia Advertisement

Beer became a symbol of modernity in other parts of Latin America at the same time, in opposition to traditional drinks associated with Indigeneity, such as pulque in Mexico and chicha in Colombia, while wine served a similar symbolic function in attracting European migrants to Argentina (Hibino 1992; Bunker 1997: 231–233; Hanway 2014: 91; Stein 2014: 210–215). Beer consumption in Brazil fluctuated in the subsequent decades, but steadily became the most widely consumed alcoholic drink from about the middle of the twentieth century up to the present day (Flacso 2021: 81).

Conclusion

The promotion of beer drinking as modern, healthy, civilized and, ultimately, "white", stood in stark contrast to the public campaigns against distilled spirits and the laws against drunkenness dating back to the early nineteenth century. These alcohol regulations were framed by racial assumptions and fears about the drinking behaviors of non-white people, especially enslaved and free Africans, that had been formed under colonialism. Distilled spirits, especially cachaça, were the main alcoholic drinks consumed by Africans and non-Africans alike on a wide range of occasions in colonial life. But the drinking practices of enslaved groups were increasingly associated with religious and social disorders and resistance to slavery by the end of the colonial period and afterward. In the early nineteenth century, the newly independent Imperial State used legislation and police powers to control drinking practices. In the countryside, slave owners tried to prevent slaves from tavern-going and drunkenness by providing pieces of land, permitting dances and music on plantations, providing rations of alcohol and tobacco, and threatening and exercising violent punishments. Despite these measures, enslaved and free Africans continued to engage in alcohol consumption and tavern-going, shaping both rural and urban forms and spaces of sociability. After abolition in the late nineteenth century, ideas about the racial degeneration of the Black population and non-whites as a whole became influential, and alcoholism was considered evidence of their inferiority. This contributed to the broader modernization agenda of the political and economic elite in republican Brazil, under the motto "order and progress", where order meant urbane beer consumption instead of cachaça-based drunkenness and progress meant de-Africanization of society and culture.

Notes

1 The quotation mentions "rs" referring to "réis" that was the currency of that period.
2 *Rapadura* is a sweet and solid bar made from molasses of sugarcane.

References

Agostini, Camilla (2007). 'As artes de Ngoma no Brasil: o jongo/caxambu e as comunidades escravas no sudeste oitocentista,' *Anais do I Seminário de Pós-Graduandos do CEO/PRONEX*. Rio de Janeiro, 23–24 August.

Alencastro, Luiz Felipe de (2007). Punir sem encarcerar. *Revista Piauí, 5* (February). Available in: Punir sem encarcerar (uol.com.br).

Alencastro, Luiz Felipe de (2000). *O trato dos viventes: formação do Brasil no Atlântico Sul*. São Paulo: Companhia das Letras.

Atas do Conselho de Estado (1822). *Representação do Procurador Estevão Ribeiro Rezende propondo medidas para a segurança do país. Sessão de 10 de setembro de 1822, Vol. I. 87–93.* Rio de Janeiro: Senado Federal & Arquivo Nacional.

Avelar, Lucas Brunozi (2020). Estigma e experiência do malungo: a cultura etílica da venda. *Revista Ingesta, 2*(1), 7–30.

Avelar, Lucas Brunozi (2021). 'A cultura de taverna da escravidão,' Comunicação apresentada no 10° Encontro Escravidão e Liberdade no Brasil Meridional, 11–13 May, 2021. Available in: lucas_avelar.pdf (escravidaoeliberdade.com.br).

Azevedo Fernandes, João (2014). Liquid Fire: Alcohol, Identity and Social Hierarchy in Colonial Brazil. In Aurea TOXQUI and Gretchen PIERCE, eds. *Alcohol in Latin America: A Social and Cultural History*, pp. 46–66. Tucson: University of Arizona Press.

Bakewell, Peter (1997). *A History of Latin America: Empires and Sequels, 1450–1930*. Malden: Blackwell Publishers.

Benci, Jorge (1977). *Economia Cristã dos Senhores no Governo dos Escravos*. São Paulo: Grijalbo.

Bretas, Marcos Luiz and Rosemberg, André (2013). A história da polícia no Brasil: balanços e perspectivas. *Revista Topoi, Rio de Janeiro, 14*(26), 162–173.

Bosi, Alfredo (1992). *Dialética da Colonização*. São Paulo: Companhia das Letras.

Bunker, Steven (1997). 'Consumers of Good Taste': Marketing Modernity in Northern Mexico, 1890–1910. *Mexican Studies/Estudios Mexicanos, 13*(2), 227–269.

Burlamarqui, Frederico Leopoldo C. (1837). *Memória analítica acerca do comércio de escravos*. Rio de Janeiro: Typographia Commercial Fluminense.

Bynum, W.F. (1984). Alcoholism and Degeneration in Nineteenth-Century European Medicine and Psychiatry. *British Journal of Addiction, 79*, 59–70.

Carneiro, Henrique (2021). Alcohol and Drugs in Brazil. *Oxford Research Encyclopedia of Latin American History*. Oxford: Oxford University Press. https://oxfordre.com/latinamericanhistory/view/10.1093/acrefore/9780199366439.001.0001/acrefore-9780199366439-e-945.

Chalhoub, Sidney (1990). *Visões da liberdade: uma história das últimas décadas da escravidão na corte*. São Paulo: Companhia das Letras.

Chalhoub, Sidney (2012). *A força da escravidão: ilegalidade e costume no Brasil Oitocentista*. São Paulo: Companhia das Letras.

Código de Posturas da Ilustríssima Câmara Municipal do Rio de Janeiro (1854). Rio de Janeiro: Typografia Dous de Dezembro.

Código de Posturas Municipais (1830 e 1838) – Typografia Imperial Nacional, Arquivo Geral da Cidade do Rio de Janeiro.

Congresso Agrícola do Rio de Janeiro (1878). *Colleção de documentos*. Rio de Janeiro: Typographia nacional.

Córdova, James M. (2015). Drinking the Fifth Cup: Notes on the Drunken Indian Image in Colonial Mexico. *Word & Image, 31*(1), 1–18.

Couty, Louis (1881). *L'Esclavage au Brésil*. Paris: Garnier.

Curto, José (2002). *Álcool e escravos*. Lisboa: Editora Vulgata.

Dias, Paulo (2001). A outra festa negra. In István JANCSÓ and Iris KANTOR, eds. *Festa: cultura e sociabilidade festiva na América Portuguesa*. São Paulo: Hucitec.

Earle, Rebecca (2008). Algunos pensamientos sobre 'El indio borracho' en el imaginario criollo. *Revista de Estudios Sociales* (Colombia), *29*, 18–27.

Earle, Rebecca (2014). Indians and Drunkenness in Spanish America. *Past and Present, 222*, Supplement 9, 81–99.

Ebel, Ernst (1972). *Rio de Janeiro e seus arredores em 1824*. São Paulo: Companhia Editora Naciona, Translated and notes from Joaquim de Souza Leão Filho.

Edmundo, Luis (2003). *O Rio de Janeiro do meu tempo*. Brasília: Senado Federal, Vol 1.

Fanon, Frantz (2014). Racismo e cultura. *Portal Geledés*, 24 May.

Figueiredo, Luciano & Venâncio, Renato P. (2005). Águas ardentes: o nascimento da cachaça. In Luciano FIGUEIREDO et al., eds. *Cachaça: alquimia brasileira*. Rio de Janeiro: 19 Design.

Flacso (2012). *Consumo de bebidas alcoólicas no Brasil*, Relatório de Pesquisa. Rio de Janeiro: FLACSO.

Franco, Maria Sylvia Carvalho (1993). "All the world was America": John Locke, liberalismo e propriedade como conceito antropológico. *Revista USP, 17*, 30–53.

Freyre, Gilberto (2003). *Casa grande & Senzala*. São Paulo: Global.

Gallet, Luciano (1934). *Estudos do Folclore*. Rio de Janeiro: Editores Brasil.

Goulart, José Alípio (1971). *Da palmatório ao patíbulo (castigo de escravos no Brasil)*. Rio de janeiro: Conquista.

Hanway, Nancy (2014). Wine Country: The Vineyard as National Space in Nineteenth-Century Argentina. In Gretchen Pierce and Áurea Toxqui, eds. *Alcohol in Latin America: A Social and Cultural History*, pp. 89–103. Tucson: University of Arizona Press.

Hibino, Barbara (1992). Cervecería Cuauhtémoc: A Case Study of Technological and Industrial Development in Mexico. *Mexican Studies/Estudios Mexicanos, 8*(1), 23–43.

Karasch, Mary (2000). *A vida dos escravos no Rio de Janeiro, 1808–1850*. São Paulo: Cia das Letras.

Leal, Luiz Francisco da Câmara (1866). *Considerações de projeto de lei para a emancipação dos escravos*. Rio de Janeiro: Typographia de Pinheiro & Companhia.

Lesser, Jeffrey (2013). *Immigration, Ethnicity and National Identity in Brazil, 1808 to the Present*. Cambridge: Cambridge University Press.

Lisboa, José da Silva (1824). *Constituição moral e deveres do cidadão*. Rio de Janeiro: Typographia Nacional.

Lopes, Emilio Carlos Rodriguez (2004). *Festas públicas, memória e representação: um estudo sobre manifestações políticas na Corte do Rio de Janeiro, 1808–1822*. São Paulo: Humanitas.

Lopes, Nei (1988). *Bantos, males e identidade negra*. Rio de Janeiro: Forense Universitaria.

Lotierzo, Tatiana H. P. (2011). *Contornos do (in)visível: A redenção de Cam, racismo e estética na pintura brasileira do último Oitocentos*. Dissertação de Mestrado em Antropologia Social. Universidad de São Paulo.

Mancall, Peter (1995). *Indians and Alcohol in Early America*. Ithaca: Cornell University Press.
Marques, Teresa Cristina (2014). *A cerveja e a cidade do Rio de Janeiro: de 1888 ao início dos anos 1930*. Jundiaí: Paco Editorial.
Marquese, Rafael de Bivar and Parron, Tâmis (2011). Internacional escravista: a política da Segunda Escravidão. *Revista Topoi* (Rio de Janeiro), *12*(23), 97–117.
Marquese, Rafael de Bivar and SALLES, Ricardo (2016). *Escravidão e Capitalismo histórico no século XIX: Cuba, Brasil, Estados Unidos*. Rio de Janeiro: Civilização Brasileira.
Meade, Teresa A. (1997). *Civilising Rio: Reform and Resistance in a Brazilian City, 1889–1930*. University Park: Pennsylvania State Press.
Mintz, Sidney (1985) *Sweetness and power: The Place of Sugar in Modern History*. New York: Viking.
Moraes Silva, A. de (1813). *Diccionario da Lingua Portugueza*. 2. ed. Lisboa: Typographia Lacérdina.
Moraes Silva, Antonio de & Bluteau, Rafael (1789). *Diccionario da lingua portuguesa*. Lisboa: Simão Tadeu Ferreira.
Moreira, Thamires Sarti Ribeiro (2015). *Maratonas e rambles: repressão aos tóxicos no início do século XX*. Mestrado em História Social. Universidade Estadual de Campinas.
Parron, Tâmis (2009). *A política da escravidão no Império do Brasil, 1826–1865*. Dissertação de Mestrado em Histórial. Universidad de São Paulo.
Pinto, Luís Maria da (1832). *Dicionario da Lingua Portuguesa*. Ouro Preto: Typographia de Silva.
Pollak, Michael (1989). Memória, Esquecimento, Silêncio. *Estudos Históricos, Rio de Janeiro, 2*(3), 3–15.
Priore, Mary Del (2005). Do copo ao corpo. E do corpo à alma: cachaça, cultura e festa. In Luciano FIGUEIREDO et al. *Cachaça: alquimia brasileira*. Rio de Janeiro: 19 Design.
Quintero, Gilbert (2001). Making the Indian: Colonial Knowledge, Alcohol, and Native Americans. *American Indian Culture and Research Journal, 25*(4), 57–71.
Rebolledo, Mauricio Becerra (2013). *Ruina, degeneración y contagio: Toxicomanía y peligrosidad social en Chile. Sociedad Hoy, 25*, 145–162.
Ricardo, Raphael Martins (2014). *A cachaça nos dois lados do Atlântico: produção, comércio e proibição (1640–1695)*. Dissertação (mestrado). Universidade Estadual Paulista.
Rodrigues, Antonio Martins et al. (1981) *A Guarda Nacional no Rio de Janeiro (1831–1918)*. Rio de Janeiro: Pontifícia Universidade Católica.
Rodrigues, Nina (1894). *As raças humanas e a responsabilidade penal no Brazil*. Rio de Janeiro: Guanabara.
Santana, Kátia Lucilene de Oliveira Silva (2020). Ajuntamentos e política na Corte Regencial (1831–1833). *Revista Ágora, 31*(1), 1–23.
Santos, Eduardo Ribeiro dos (2018). A proibição de entorpecentes na República: notas sobre eugenia, urbanização e o racismo científico brasileiro. In Marisa Feffermann et al, eds. *Interfaces do genocídio no Brasil: raça, gênero e classe*, pp. 327–343. Sáu Paulo: Instituto de Saúde.
Slavevoyages (2019a). Estimates. https://slavevoyages.org/assessment/estimates (accessed June 20, 2021).
Slavevoyages (2019b). The Trans-Atlantic Slave Trade Database. https://slavevoyages.org/voyage/database#tables (accessed June 20, 2021).
Slenes, Robert (2007). Eu venho de muito longe, eu venho cavando: jongueiros cumba na senzala centro-africana. In Silvia Hunold LARA and Gustavo PACHECO, eds. *Memória do jongo: as gravações históricas de Stanley J. Stein, Vassouras, 1949*, pp. 109–156. Rio de Janeiro/Campinas: Folha Seca/Cecult.
Skidmore, Thomas E. (1999). *Brazil: Five Centuries of Change*. Oxford: Oxford University Press.
Smith, Frederick (2005). *The Caribbean Rum: A Social and Economic History*. Gainesville: University Press of Florida.
Sournia, Jean-Charles (1990). *A History of Alcoholism*, trans. by Nick Hinndley and Gareth Stanton. Intro. by Roy Porter. Oxford: Blackwell.
Souza, R. L. (2004). Cachaça, vinho, cerveja: da Colônia ao século XX. *Revista Estudos Históricos*, Rio de Janeiro, 1(33), 56–75. Available in: http://bibliotecadigital.fgv.br/ojs/index.php/reh/article/view/2211 (Acesso em 3 dez. 2019).
Stein, Stanley J. (1990). *Vassouras: um município brasileiro do café, 1850–1900*. Rio de Janeiro: Nova Fronteira.
Stein, Steve (2014). Essence and Identity: Transformation in Argentine Wine, 1880–1920. In Gretchen Pierce and Áurea Toxqui, eds. *Alcohol in Latin America: A Social and Cultural History*, pp. 210–241. Tucson: University of Arizona Press.

Toner, Deborah (2015). *Alcohol and Nationhood in Nineteenth-Century Mexico*. Lincoln and London: University of Nebraska Press.
Toner, Deborah (2021). Cultural Representations. In Deborah Toner, ed. *Alcohol in the Age of Industry, Empire and War*, pp. 175–193. London: Bloomsbury Academic.
Viotti, Emilia (1992). *Da senzala à colônia*. São Paulo: Unesp.
Werneck, Francisco Lacerda (1847). *Memórias sobre a fundação de uma fazenda*. Rio de Janeiro: Typographia Universal de Laemmert.

23

STREET-LEVEL POLICING, STRUCTURAL VIOLENCE AND HABITUS

Accounts of street-involved cannabis users in Nigeria

Ediomo-Ubong E. Nelson

Introduction

Consumption of cannabis among street-involved youths has been fairly well documented in the existing literature (Adlaf, Zdanowicz & Smart, 1996; Thompson, Barczyk, Gomez et al., 2010; Bender, Thompson, Ferguson et al., 2012; Bozinoff, Small, Long et al., 2017), but few studies have explored their experiences of policing in relation to cannabis use (Ti, Wood, Shannon et al., 2013; Nelson, 2018; 2021b). There is a dearth of studies that explore the direct perspectives of street-involved youths on cannabis use and street policing, which involves surveillance, street patrols, crackdowns and arrests. The possession and use of cannabis are legally prohibited under the 1961 United Nations Single Convention on Narcotic Drugs. Influenced by this convention, national drug laws (including Nigeria's) have mainly focused on strengthening law enforcement, including policing of drug markets and arrest of dealers and users. A disproportionate burden of drug policing is borne by the most visible and vulnerable populations, including young people who use drugs, live on the streets and experience social exclusion (Werb, Kerr, Li et al., 2008; Ti, Wood, Shannon et al., 2013; Nelson, 2018; 2021b). In this study, I explore the accounts of street-involved youths on cannabis use and street-level policing; highlighting the negative effects it has on their health and well-being. The study is based on primary data collected through qualitative interviews with street-involved youths in the city of Uyo, Akwa Ibom State in Nigeria. Apart from providing information on a relatively under-researched subject, the study seeks to echo voices from the streets on the harms of zero-tolerance policies in order to challenge dominant narratives used to justify the continuation of a "war on drugs" at a time when this approach is losing support in other countries of the world (Csete & Sanchez, 2013; Nelson & Obot, 2020). Specifically, I pose three key questions: What is the broader social and structural context in which cannabis use by street youths takes place? What are their encounters with the police and what effects do these have on their health and well-being? How do they respond to policing and how do such responses contribute to their structural vulnerability (i.e. reinforces their subordinated positions in society's power hierarchy)? Answers are expected to broaden understanding of

 DOI: 10.4324/9780429058141-30

the social and structural context of drug-related harms as well as support the development and implementation of public health-centered and human rights-based policies.

Cannabis, drug laws and enforcement practices in Nigeria

Cannabis is the most commonly used illicit drug in Nigeria. A nation-wide survey of drug use conducted in 2018 indicated that an estimated 10.8% of persons aged 15–65 years (10.6 million people) had used cannabis in the past year, which is far more than the proportion of opioids users (4.7% or 4.6 million people) in the same population (United Nations Office on Drugs and Crime [UNODC], 2019 Cannabis accounts for 47.9% of people seeking treatment for substance abuse in Nigeria (Economic Community of West African States [ECOWAS], 2018). Although cannabis has been cultivated and distributed along the West African coast since the 1920s (Akyeampong, 2005), it is reported that trade and consumption of the drug did not grow significantly until after World War II when soldiers returning from the middle east and elsewhere brought the plant to Nigeria and other West African countries (Asuni, 1964). The plant found a habitat and grew easily in Nigeria's tropical climate so that large-scale cultivation and exportation to Western markets were reported by the 1960s (Obot, 2004).

Until the late 1950s, cannabis smoking was regarded as the fringe habit of a small group of urban laborers, ex-soldiers and seamen, who consumed it mostly to enable them to undertake physical labor (Klantschnig, 2014). Beginning from the 1960s, with media reports of a "hemp boom" in Lagos, increased seizures of cannabis and discovery of farms were recorded. Increased cultivation of cannabis has been attributed to decline in the market price of cocoa and the lucrativeness of cannabis when compared with other cash crops (Klantschnig, 2014). Similarly, the low cost of cannabis spurred local consumption so that by the late 1960s, "cannabis spread from the fringe habits of ex-soldiers and port workers...to other social classes who used it for diverse reasons, including recreation, as a marker of modernity and social identities" (Klantschnig, 2014, p. 75). Cannabis use has entered the cultural mainstream. It is consumed by diverse groups, including transport workers, students and bar patrons. Street-involved youths (homeless, out-of-school young people, who live on the streets, engage in street-based income-generating activities and experience social exclusion) are the most visible group of cannabis consumers in Nigeria (Klein, 1999; Nelson, 2018; Dirisu, Shickle, & Elsey, 2019; Nelson, 2021a).

Cannabis use, though increasingly common, remains highly moralized and users are stigmatized and marginalized by other members of the community (Dirisu, Shickle, & Elsey, 2019; Nelson, 2021c). Media portrayals that associate cannabis use with mental illness and criminality (Nelson & Obot, 2020) reinforce stigma and social discrimination of cannabis users, particularly street-involved users who consume cannabis in hotspots (places where young people hang out to sell and consume cannabis) and other semi-pubic settings (Nelson, 2018; 2021b). As Sandberg (2012) argued, the discrepancy between young people's interest in cannabis and (proscriptive) social norms leads to the development of subcultures as figurative representations of use and shared identity. Cannabis is often used by street-involved youths as a way of coping with the traumatic effects of social exclusion (Klein, 1999; Dirisu, Shickle, & Elsey, 2019; Nelson, 2021a, 2021b), but the risk of dependence and adverse health and psychological effects increases when it is consumed over a long period of time (Hall & Pacula, 2003). Punitive drug policies, including police harassments, incarceration and other criminal sanctions for cannabis use, however, cause more harms to these youths than those caused by the drug.

Concerns about the over-publicized health and social harms of cannabis use (e.g. crime and mental illness) have reinforced preference for punitive drug laws, which may be traced back to the earliest drug ordinances introduced by the colonial government in Nigeria (Obot, 2004; Nelson & Pates, 2017). Cannabis is classified as a dangerous drug along with cocaine and heroin in domestic drug laws, which are applicable in all states of the Nigerian federation (Klein, 2001). Cannabis is the main focus of domestic drug laws, which is driven by concern over state power rather than findings from scientific research (Klantschnig, 2016). Klantschnig (2009) has shown that Nigeria's drug control system operates on the basis of a discourse that emphasizes "crises, correction and success". In this discourse, illicit drug trafficking and consumption are portrayed as a social crisis affecting social order and inviting a military-style campaign of social correction. Law enforcement outcomes, particularly seizure and arrest (see information in Table 23.1), are displayed as measures of performance, which reinforces the notion of a drug crisis as well as a targeted and successful response.

Nigeria's drug laws have contained some of the most punitive sanctions imposed on cannabis trafficking and use (Obot, 2004). The current drug law has been described as almost a verbatim duplication of the 1988 UN Convention, covering every aspect of drug trafficking and related offenses (Kavanagh, 2013). One of the aims of the law is to "eliminate" cannabis production, trafficking and consumption. The Indian Hemp Decree of 1966 included death penalty or 21 years imprisonment for the cultivation of cannabis, 10 years imprisonment for trafficking in cannabis and another 10 years for possession and/or smoking of cannabis. The Indian Hemp Act of 1975 removed the death penalty and reduced sanction for cannabis smoking to six months and/or a fine. The Special Tribunal (Miscellaneous Offences) Decree of 1984 reinstated death penalty for the use of cannabis, which was later replaced with life imprisonment in the amended Decree of 1986.

Decree 48 of 1989, which is now an act of parliament CAP N30 Laws of the Federation of Nigeria, established the National Drug Law Enforcement Agency (NDLEA) to coordinate drug control activities in the country. The NDLEA combines supply and demand reduction activities, which were previously discharged by different agencies. The agency has been criticized for targeting cannabis users and retail-level dealers, while traffickers who accumulate millions of dollars in profit from drug trade operate with impunity (Williams, 2014). Most arrests for drug-related offenses are on charges of cannabis peddling and use, resulting in many "casualties, including hundreds of people convicted on several years' sentences for smoking cannabis inside a joint" (Klein, 1999, p. 68). A review of arrest data for 2006, for

Table 23.1 Cannabis seizure and arrest of traffickers by the NDLEA (2010–2015)

Year	*Seizure*	*Arrest*
2010	174,661.59	6,788
2011	191,847.91	8,639
2012	228,794.13	8,052
2013	205,373	8,843
2014	53,878,194.52	8,826
2015	871,480.32	8,778
2016	187,394	8,257
2017	191,084.2	10,009

Source: NDLEA, 2016/ECOWAS, 2018.

instance, indicated that over 80% of those detained for drug-related offenses were cannabis users and retailers (Gyong, 2009).

The NDLEA, which operates as a specialized police agency, enforces drug laws in conjunction with the Nigerian Police Force (NPF). Law enforcement is aimed at drug interdiction and crime prevention (Nelson, 2018). Common law enforcement practices include surveillance and street patrols, crackdowns on drug markets as well as arrest and prosecution of offenders (e.g. dealers and users). Extra-legal practices such as planting of evidence, extortion of money from drug users, sexual harassment, physical violence, threats and other human rights abuses are telling features of everyday street-level drug policing (Nelson & Brown, 2019; Nelson, 2018; 2021c). Physical violence contravenes prohibition of the use of excessive force under the Nigeria Police Force Order No. 237 (Lawyers Committee for Human Rights, 1992), while extortion violates Article 324 of the Police Act, which requires that a police officer "offer prompt obedience to lawful order" and "be determined and incorruptible in the exercise of his duties" (Omotola, 2007, p. 627).

Poor remuneration and widespread impoverishment among police personnel fuel corruption and extra-legal practices. Extortion is a common means through which lower cadre officers attempt to supplement their meager incomes (Ibeanu, 2007). As Klein (1999) argued, the policing of cannabis users is governed by the revenue imperative of the under-paid police personnel who needs to make up for unrealistic wages. Poor and socially disadvantaged populations bear the brunt of police abuses, which suggests a social class bias in police corruption (Agbiboa, 2015). Street-involved youths who use cannabis are the most affected group (Klein, 1999; Dirisu, Shickle, & Elsey, 2019; Nelson, 2018; 2021b). Their inability to afford bail fee or legal representation exacerbates their vulnerability to predation by police officers, resulting in untold suffering and harms, including dispossession, imprisonment, health harms and loss of employment prospects (Nelson, 2018).

Structural violence and habitus – theoretical framing

Drawing on conceptual tools such as "risk environment" (Rhodes, 2002), "structural violence" (Farmer, 1996), "structural vulnerability" (Quesada, Hart, & Bourgois, 2011) and "everyday violence" (Scheper-Hughes & Bourgois, 2004), drug use researchers have gone beyond individual/micro-level explanations and emphasized the wider structural and inter-personal contexts in which drug use and harms occur. This development reflects the recognition that drug harms are "virtually meaningless outside their socio-cultural as well as political economic contexts" (Bourgeois, 2003, p. 32), and that drug use is "a symptom – and a vivid symbol – of deeper dynamics of social marginalization and alienation" (Bourgeois, 1995, p. 2). These concepts capture the different ways vulnerability to drug-related harms are shaped by structural and systemic factors. The structural production of harms is mediated by "enforcement-based policies that disproportionately affect those using drugs as well as those already suffering intense and systematic discrimination" (Rhodes, Wagner, Strathdee et al., 2012, p. 4).

Structural violence and vulnerability

In an attempt to "resocialize" drug-related harms by showing its social-structural and political economic antecedents, researchers have used the concept of "structural violence" to show how these harms are reproduced within wider social relations of structural inequality. Structural violence describes social arrangements that contribute to inequality in a manner that constrains human agency and increases harm for vulnerable populations (Farmer, 1996; Kleinman, 2000). It references large-scale forces such as poverty and gender inequality that structure unequal access to goods and services and create conditions that reproduce the risk of drug-related harms. Put simply, structural violence shows how social institutions (e.g. criminal justice system) may harm people by preventing them from meeting basic needs. The concept of "structural vulnerability" sharpens understanding of structural violence by accounting for how mutually reinforcing economic, political, cultural and psychodynamic insults that dispose individuals and groups toward harms are embodied (Quesada, Hart, & Bourgois, 2011). It emphasizes how individuals and groups internalize their depreciated status in ways that shape behavior and self-concept (Holmes, 2011). An individual is structurally vulnerable when the acceptance of her or his location in society's hierarchy prevents him from attaining optimum well-being. The institutionalization and everyday internalization of structural violence through punitive policing practices render it invisible as a feature of lived experience (Rhodes, Wagner, Stradthee et al., 2012). This has both "symbolic" and "embodied" effects. Symbolic violence describes a process whereby social practices legitimate the existing hierarchies so that those who are dominated accept and contribute to their structural subordination (Bourdieu & Wacquant, 1992). However, structural violence is embodied as "oppression illness", which is the chronic effects of social mistreatment and discrimination (Singer, 2004). Drug use, particularly high-risk drug use, may be seen as a response to "oppression illness" and social stress in high-risk environments (Gee, Delva & Takeuchi, 2007).

Habitus

The disadvantage of macro-structural perspectives on drug-related harms is that they tend to be "over-deterministic", and do not account for the role of agency, subjectification and non-material forces in the dynamic and mutually constitutive relationship between individuals and society (Rhodes, Wagner, Strathdee et al., 2012). In response, researchers have explored drug users' creativity and inventiveness in relation to macro-structural forces. Some have found the concept of "habitus" (Bourdieu, 1990) useful in analyzing the reciprocity of structure and agency in the field of illicit drug use. Defined as "systems of dispositions that are shaped by the experiences of actors in particular positions in social structure" (Calhoun, Gerteis, Moody et al., 2007, p. 261), habitus draws attention to how individuals internalize, and take for granted specific ways of acting and being which correspond with social structures. In simple terms, habitus refers to the set of beliefs, attitudes and practices, acquired by reason of an individual's social location, which shapes how she or he responds to the environment. It is not an ensemble of relatively fixed and unaltered dispositions, but is flexible and capable of improvisation and adaptation to different situations. Habitus is acquired through repetition as individuals interact within specific "fields" or domains of social life. Grundetjern and Sandberg (2012) have used the concept of habitus to analyze women's survival strategies in a gendered drug economy that favors men. Haritavorn (2014) has explored how gendered habitus enabled women to position themselves in relation to structural and gendered violence, and the choices and strategies they adopted to lessen the effects of social discrimination and inter-personal violence. In this study, I use "structural violence" and "habitus" to explain the interplay of structural inequality, social discrimination and punitive policing in the production of drug-related harms among street-involved youths who use cannabis, and to highlight the situated strategies they adopt in response to street-level policing, which suggests internalized social practices that resist, just as they reinforce, social structures.

Data and methods

The study was conducted in Uyo, Akwa Ibom State in Nigeria. The city's population is estimated at 1,143,689 people, including migrants from other ethnic groups. Basic social amenities such as healthcare, housing, electricity, water and transportation are inadequate. Commerce, services and a variety of low-level office, administrative or salaried positions in the civil service are the foci of the economy. An estimated 51% of the population lives in absolute poverty (National Bureau Statistics, 2010). Most earn a precarious living toiling in a poorly regulated informal sector, where the boundary between what is legal and illegal is blurred. There is a significant level of illicit drug use in the city, and cannabis is the most commonly used drug (United Nations Office on Drugs and Crime [UNODC], 2019). Ninety-seven (n = 97) street-involved young persons who use cannabis were recruited for the study through venue-based sampling from eleven (11) "hotspots" (popularly known as "bunks") identified through ethnographic mapping. Cannabis hotspots are informal socio-spatial contexts where young people hang out to sell and/or consume cannabis. Examples are nightlife environments, abandoned buildings, market stalls, school compounds (used during non-school hours) and abattoirs.

For the purpose of this study, a "street-involved youth" is a young person (21–35 years) who engages in street-based income-generating activities and spends most of her/his time among street-involved peers. The inclusion criteria were being a current cannabis user, defined as having used cannabis in the last 30 days, and having experienced police crackdown on a cannabis hotspot. Participants were mostly males (78/80%). They were between the age of 21 and 34 years. The highest level of education attained by any participant was secondary education; the majority had only primary education. They were from poor households and earned a precarious living from informal income-generating activities such as commercial transportation, manual labor, touting, hair weaving, and food vending and (casual) sex work. Some participants were homeless or unstably housed, alienated from relations, orphaned or had a single parent whose earnings could not meet the basic needs of the household (e.g. accommodation and feeding) (Table 23.2).

Data were collected through in-depth, individual interviews facilitated by a topic guide, which was revised in the course of data collection and analysis. Interviews were conducted by trained male and female field assistants, who were recovering cannabis users trained on how to build rapport with participants and conduct interviews on sensitive subjects without causing tension. The use of peers as interviewers fostered trust, enhanced co-operation and facilitated elicitation of sensitive information that would evade conventional self-report interviews (Elliot, Watson, & Harris, 2002). Interviews took place at office spaces leased for the purpose of interviews, which provided privacy and safety for the participants. Interview questions of focal interest concerned factors influencing cannabis use, preferred physical settings for using cannabis and reasons for preferring these settings, perceptions of street-level policing, experience of police crackdowns on cannabis hotspots, effects of crackdowns and strategies adopted to detect and evade police arrest. Interview questions were worded in ways that would enable the discovery of key themes relevant for exploring cannabis use and experiences of street-level policing among the study population. Interviews generally lasted between 45 minutes and 1 hour, and were tape-recorded with the (verbal) consent of each participant. Recorded interviews were transcribed verbatim and checked for accuracy. A thematic approach was adopted in the analysis to identify patterns of meaning in the data (for details of the data analysis process, see Nelson, 2018). Selected verbatim comments (identified by interviewee's sex) are used to illustrate important analytic themes. Participants received two bars of toilet soap in appreciation of their participation. The study was approved by the Institutional Review Board of the University of Uyo, Nigeria.

Table 23.2 Socio-demographic characteristics of the participants (n = 97)

	Number of participants (#)	*Percentages (%)*
Sex		
Male	78	80
Female	19	20
Age	31	32
21–25	38	39
26–30	28	29
31–34	57	59
Educational attainment	40	41
Primary	24	25
Secondary	73	75
Relationship status	37	38
Regular	18	19
Others	21	22
Housing	21	22
Living with parent/relation		
Living with partner		
Living with friend		
Homeless		

Source: Data collection.

Social exclusion and cannabis use among street-involved youths

The participants' accounts emphasized how the realities of marginalization and social inequality contributed to initiation of cannabis use. Although differing on many points, the key themes in the accounts were constraints on opportunities for gainful employment owing to a lack of formal education leading to "hustling on the streets" (i.e. engaging in street-based income-generating activities). This, in turn, facilitated contact with other street-involved youths who used cannabis leading to acceptance and adoption of cannabis use. This trajectory is captured in the following comment:

> I started smoking because things were very tough. Then I used to hang around with some friends and they encouraged me to try it (cannabis). They told me that I should take it that it will help me forget some of my worries.
>
> *(Male participant)*

For most participants (74/76%), a social learning process which involved continuous interactions with peers within cannabis subcultures undermined social control on behaviors (Becker, 1968). This led to cannabis being seen as "normal" within these subcultures, while being stigmatized in the wider community. For example, a male participant commented:

> There is nothing to worry about… Before I used to fear that people will judge me for smoking weed, but now I am not afraid anymore. I see my guys taking it all the times… now I know that there is nothing wrong with it. It is just a plant.

Most female participants (13/68%) were introduced to cannabis use by their male sexual partners (Nelson, 2021c). As Klein (2001) observed almost two decades ago among cannabis users in southwest Nigeria, many women are introduced to the drug by their boyfriends and cannabis smoking may accompany the first sexual experience of young women. A female participant noted:

> I didn't use to smoke weed. I use to take only alcohol in parties. It was my former boyfriend who made me take it. He used to bring it home to smoke in the house we were living together. I started smoking weed when we were together.

Most participants denied the adverse effects of cannabis on their health ("They say weed has made you sick, but I don't believe"; "I know Igbo can cause problems for people, but not someone like me"), but extolled the positive effects of consumption (Hathaway, 2004). Beliefs about the positive effects of cannabis consumption are an important part of youth subcultures, and are important for understanding initiation and maintenance of cannabis use (Holm, Sandberg, Kolind et al., 2014). While other illicit drugs were available and consumed in the hotspots, cannabis was lauded for fostering a sense of belonging and community for street-involved youths (81/83%) ("Weed is not like other drugs... It makes people feel like family, you know").

Cannabis consumption offered most street-involved youths (79/81%) a means of coping with the traumatizing effects of social exclusion. "Forget all the worries", "freeing my mind" and "helps me get through the day" were common reasons given for smoking cannabis. This supports the view that cannabis is valued by youths because it eases anxiety and enables daily functioning (Dirisu, Shickle, & Elsey, 2019). The anxiety-easing effect of cannabis needs little elaboration in Nigeria where living conditions are so precarious that any substance that alleviates anxiety could be seen as serving a social function (Klein, 2001; 2009). Ironically, the intoxicating properties of cannabis, which is positively valued by users for easing anxiety, account for the moralization of the substance and stigmatization of its users (Room, 2005).

Cannabis hotspots provided most male participants (69/71%) a social context to develop "street masculinity", which is characterized by public consumption of cannabis and a propensity for violence. A similar association between cannabis smoking and violent masculinity was reported by Klein, where a participant noted that "some people take it (cannabis) and start fighting to let people know they are hard..." (2001, p. 115). A participant in the present study stated:

> People will take it just to show that they are tough, that they can make trouble... If you can smoke many wraps and still "hold your side" (maintain comportment), others will hail you.
>
> *(Male participant)*

Most participants (77/79%) used cannabis in "hotspots", which provided a space where users could "socialize" (i.e. meet with friends). Hotspots also provided a social context for social recognition achieved by conveying the latest news in local politics, sports and entertainment, and bragging about one's sexual adventures. While consuming cannabis in hotspots signified that participants belonged to street subcultures, it also amplified their exclusion from mainstream society and fostered stigma and marginalization (see Hammersley, Jenkins, & Reid, 2001; Room, 2005).

Consumption of cannabis reproduced negative social categorizations and "stigmatizing conflicts" with community and the police (Hathaway, 2004). Accounts emphasized the labeling of cannabis users as criminals regardless of their actual criminal status ("People call us criminals because we smoke weed"). Societal perceptions associating cannabis use with mental illness also contributed to the view that cannabis users are unstable and potentially dangerous. Hotspots were seen as nuisances and law enforcement activities targeting cannabis hotspots enjoyed community support ("Nobody wants to see people smoking weed around... They will call police").

Cannabis use, social deviance and policing

Cannabis is an illegal substance, and its trade and use are subject to sanctions by the state (Room, 2005). Law enforcement, as an expression of state sanction for cannabis use, was a recurrent theme in the participants' accounts. For example, participants emphasized that cannabis hotspots were the target of frequent crackdowns by police patrol teams and this made visiting hotspots a risky venture. Cannabis is the primary target of street-level policing in Nigeria (Klein, 1994; Klantschnig, 2014). Most participants (67/69%) had experienced multiple police crackdowns on cannabis hotspots, which they variously described as a "terrible experience" and a "nightmare" (see Erickson, van der Maas, & Hathaway, 2013). A male participant narrated:

> One day I went to the spot and bought some weed. Before I could even light the stuff, I heard people shouting "police" and everybody started running. I threw it away and ran. I've had that experience several times.

According to the participants, the key reason for the policing of cannabis hotspots is the illegal status of the drug. Cannabis consumption, therefore, becomes "primary deviance", and its disapproval leads to the marginalization of its users (Knuttila, 2002). Since most users are from socially marginalized households, street-level policing may be seen as exacerbating their marginality (Nelson, 2018). Policing also contributed to the normalization of violence in the day-to-day life of street cannabis users. According to a female participant:

> Police arrests people who use drugs because they have committed a crime. Cannabis is an illegal drug. Those who smoke cannabis are treated like criminals. When you are caught taking it, you will be taken to police cell.

Cannabis hotspots were also targeted because of the widespread view that cannabis users are criminals, regardless of their actual criminal status. Hotspots were, therefore, seen as hideouts of criminals and crackdowns are considered part of the crime prevention mandate of the police. Some participants (47/48%) acknowledged that some cannabis users engage in criminal activities such as cultism, armed robbery, shoplifting, pick-pocketing and swindling. They, however, felt that characterizing all cannabis users as criminals was an unfounded generalization[1] (Dirisu, Shickle, & Elsey, 2019). Such generalization reflects a negative categorization of cannabis users, which contributed to stigma and discrimination. A female participant explained:

> People think that those who smoke weed are criminals, and that hotspots are places where cultists and criminals hide. If you smoke weed people will see you as a criminal, and they will suspect you. It is very bad.

Societal stigma related to cannabis use tended to drive the behavior underground and facilitated the development of subcultures of cannabis use situated in hotspots ("I don't want trouble with anybody. I smoke at the bunk with people who can understand"). This corroborates Sandberg's (2012) view that subcultural use of cannabis is usually the result of negative societal attitudes that force young people to hide their use to avoid the effect of stigma. Participants also hide to use cannabis for fear of police harassment and extortion, as seen in the following comment:

> Police come to the hotspots frequently. They behave as if they have nothing else to do than to harass people. When they come, they arrest many people in order to make money. Police is our major problem.
>
> *(Male participant)*

Street-level policing did not deter cannabis consumption. Participants (64/66%) attributed their persistent use of cannabis, even in the face of repressive policing, to dependence on the substance as well as its usefulness for daily functioning and for coping with personal and social problems (see also Dirisu, Shickle, & Elsey, 2019; Nelson, 2021b, 2021c). The discrepancy between young people's motivations for cannabis use and the legal assumptions underlying criminalization partly accounts for the failure of zero-tolerance policies to deter young people from using cannabis (Klantschnig, 2014).

Policing, structural violence and well-being

Policing practices targeting street-involved cannabis users show how state sanctions for substance use could include deprivation of liberty (Room, 2005). The "coercive authority" of the police (Terrill, Paoline, & Manning, 2003) may translate into brutality, including threatened and enacted physical violence. Physical violence meted to people who use drugs by police officers is common (Sarang, Rhodes, Sheon et al., 2010). Most participants (61/63%) narrated being beaten by police officers. They explained that beatings violate their human rights, and portend negative consequences for their health and well-being. A male participant stated:

> The police can be very brutal and heartless. I have experienced it. I was once caught by the police when I went to buy some weed. They pointed a gun at me. I was so scared that I almost fainted. They punched me and threw me into the van… They treated me as if I am not a human being like them.

Street-level policing generated fear among participants ("You are afraid all the time because of the police"). Fear of police beatings, arrest and extortion was so palpable that the majority of participants (64/66%) were willing to do anything within their powers to escape from the police. The internalization of structural violence through fear had negative health effects ("It (fear) can drive you crazy… You just get sick"). A female participant (7/37%) described maltreatment of female cannabis users by police officers:

> Police officers will not say because you are a woman we will not beat you. Of course, they will not treat women the way they treat men. They will be less violent with women. But they will still push you around.

Arrested cannabis users (43/44%) could be extorted by police officers. Dealer-users who are arrested could have their drugs impounded along with financial proceeds. Accounts indicated that confiscated items were usually not submitted at the police station, but were appropriated by the police officers. This was seen as theft perpetrated by officers ("They treat us as criminals but they are the ones who steal from us"). Extortion and other corrupt practices by police officers are forms of structural violence that negatively impacted the well-being of street-involved youths.

Incarceration was seen as a severe form of structural violence toward street-involved youths. Accounts highlighted a pervasive fear of incarceration among participants due to the significant financial cost of obtaining bail. Nigerian anti-drug laws deny bail for persons arrested for drug-related offenses, including personal drug use (Klein, 1999). Apart from the inherent injustice, this practice encourages extortion of offenders by police officers. Police officers easily escape the adverse consequences of their misdeeds since cannabis users deem it more expedient to offer money than to be arrested and charged for drug-related offenses ("Once they tell you that you cannot be bailed, you will offer anything to be free"). A male participant explained:

> Nobody wants to be locked up in police cell. They will not release you unless you pay a huge sum of money. Those who are arrested because of drugs cannot be bailed. Police will use this to collect so much money from you.

Social marginality and estrangement from family and other sources of social support mean that some cannabis users cannot afford bail and may therefore languish in detention. Incarceration combines with poverty and lack of social support to further marginalize street-involved youths. Incarcerated users experience dehumanizing prison conditions, which includes overcrowding, poor sanitation and health risks (Osasona & Koleoso, 2015). A male participant stated:

> The cell is a terrible place. I have spent four days in the police cell before so I know what I am talking about. It is very dirty and stinking. The odour can kill you. You can't sleep or eat in that place. I felt sick inside the cell.

Incarceration also confers a criminal record, which further compromises the life-chances of street-involved youth. Accounts showed how a criminal record creates barriers to employment and other opportunities for street-involved youths. Crucially, a criminal record fostered stigma and hampered employment prospects for participants who had served prison terms (39/40%) ("You cannot get good job to do because you have been in prison… you are like a criminal"). Unemployment, in turn, creates risk for involvement in criminal activities as a means of survival, and this constitutes "secondary deviance" (Room, 2005). Criminalization does not reduce the use of cannabis; it may even foster it by exacerbating the conditions that made young people initiate cannabis use in the first place.

Street habitus and responses to policing

Street-involved youths are not passive victims of structural violence in the forms of repressive policing practices. They adopt different safety strategies based on their understanding of police tactics and the street environments ("street habitus") to avoid police detection and arrest. Street habitus has been described by Sandberg and Fleetwood (2016) as the "internalization of social marginalization and structural violence entrenched through experience and socialization". For street-involved youths, habitus involved heightened vigilance to detect police presence at the hotspot and to escape from the scene. As an expression of "group habitus", or shared internalized dispositions (Bourdieu, 1990), some users would alert others about the police so that everyone could escape. Accounts indicated that it is a "street code" to run when others are running. A male participant commented:

> Once police officers enter the place you will see everybody running. It is only a fool that will not run. It is better to be caught trying to escape than to be picked up like a piece of wood.

Running is a key escape strategy for street cannabis users. Accounts emphasized that this was so common that it was said to be used by some users as a ruse to fool the others ("They will start running and when you join, they will laugh at you"). This did not stop people from running when they saw others doing so. A male participant stated:

> If you don't run because you feel someone is trying to fool you, you may find that police men were actually around and you are caught. It is better to run than to be caught. So, you just run, whether it is true or not.

Most participants (54/55%) threw away the wraps of cannabis in their possession as they took off for safety. This was a common practice because in the event of being caught, it is the possession of drugs and related paraphernalia that justifies arrest. Accounts indicated that some cannabis users (21/22%) would swallow wraps of cannabis so that no incriminating evidence could be found on them. A female participant commented:

> Police officers must not see you holding weed. You have to put it away. You may have to swallow your weed so they don't see it on you. If police find weed on you, you are in big trouble.

Accounts showed how street-involved youths were selectively targeted by police officers during crackdowns. Those who fit the "junkie" stereotype (looking unkempt) are often apprehended by police officers. Street habitus therefore meant beating the junkie stereotype through "impression management" (Goffman, 1959). Improving personal appearance to avoid police detection and arrest was a common escape strategy. A male participant stated:

> The police are looking for a young man who has not had a bath for many days. One who is dressed in a dirty jean and torn T-shirt, and whose lips are burnt by cannabis smoke. Then you walk pass well dressed, with your smart phone in your hand. You don't look at them. They will not suspect that you are a user.

As cannabis users engaged with street policing, they adopted new attitudes and practices, which overtime became part of street habitus. This habitus is often demonstrated in situations where policing did not follow familiar patterns. For example, police officers occasionally stopped all "suspects" for search regardless of their appearance. This involves frisking and stripping suspects, and ransacking purses, wallets and pockets (Dixon & Maher, 2002), which could be seen as sexual harassment of female users by mostly male police officers. Participants generally counted on "luck" in such circumstances. A male participant commented:

> Everything depends on your luck. You escape because you are lucky. That's all. Sometimes you can pretend that you are not a drug user and go free. But other times the officers will stop everybody for search, even if you don't look like a drug user.

Others articulated a more empirically based understanding of changing street policing strategies, suggesting that street habitus may be updated the hard way, including through witnessing or experiencing arrest. A male participant narrated:

> One time police came to the hotspot and we took off, not knowing that there were police officers running with us. They pretended to be "customers" (i.e. cannabis users). Before we knew it they turned and arrested people... I learnt a lesson that day... You have to watch your back when you escape. Know who is with you.

Accounts indicated that arrested cannabis users could beg for pardon or offer money to police officers to be freed on-the-spot. Bribing police officers was seen as a smart thing to do since suspects on drug charges have no right to bail (Klein, 1999).

Discussion

The findings show that limited opportunities for gainful employment in the formal sector, owing to low educational attainment, and street involvement facilitated contact with street youths who use cannabis and influenced initiation of cannabis use by participants. At the inter-personal level, contact with other street-involved youths who use cannabis normalized the behavior and made it possible for participants to start using. This shows that cannabis use initiation is not solely the consequence of an individual's decision or action, but is also influenced by negotiated actions between individuals (Holland, Ramazanoglu, Sharope et al., 1992) and macro-structural factors (Rhodes, Wagner, Shannon et al., 2012). Structural antecedents of cannabis use included poor educational attainment and lack of employment opportunities. However, inter-personal relationships and shared beliefs about the positive effects of cannabis undermined social control mechanisms and facilitated the development of cannabis subcultures (Becker, 1968; Holm, Sandberg, Kolind et al., 2014).

Conventional explanations of drug use behavior view it as the outcome of individual decisions and actions. The data presented in this study shows that cannabis use by street-involved youths is influenced by social and structural factors, not only individual decisions. Following Buchanan, Khoshnood, Stopka et al. (2002, p. 40), I emphasize that drug use behaviors are "largely symptom(s) of deeper social structural inequalities and... efforts to eliminate illegal narcotics use are, and will continue to be, futile until (the) society address(es) these fundamental antecedent political-economic problems". Drug use and related harms are "features of the political economy of social suffering" (Rhodes, 2009, p. 196). For marginalized street-involved youths, cannabis use serves as self-medication for "oppression illness", which is the "product of the impact of suffering from 'social mistreatment'; a type of stress disorder where the source of the stress is being the object of widespread and enduring discrimination, degradation, structural violence and abusive derision" (Singer, 2004, p. 17). Against this background, social policies that seek to improve access to social services, including education, healthcare, housing and employment, for street youths may do more to reduce drug-related harms than enforcement-based policies that often exacerbate these problems.

In Nigeria, studies have consistently associated cannabis use among young people with lived experiences of structural inequality (Klein, 1999; 2001; Nelson, 2018; Dirisu,

Shickle, & Elsey, 2019, Nelson, 2021a, 2021b, 2021c). Cannabis use provides street-involved young people with the benefits they are excluded from, including coping with personal and social problems, relieving anxiety and stress, access to income-generating opportunities and social bonds. However, inclusion and exclusion go hand in hand (Dixon & Maher, 2002). Cannabis is an illicit drug and its use is subject to state sanction. Although it fosters social bonds among users, it also attracts stigma and discrimination which reinforce their exclusion from mainstream society (Hammersley, Jenkins, & Reid, 2001; Room, 2005). Stigma is not only attached to cannabis use, but also to the physical environment where it is used so that these environments become the material symbolism of social marginalization and exclusion or a form of symbolic violence against these youths (Bourdieu & Wacquant, 1992).

As the participants' accounts highlighted, street-involved youths lived day to day in a context of violence and fear. They were subjected to beatings and harassments by police officers. They were frisked, stripped and searched for "incriminating evidence" and extorted in ways that they saw as unfair, inhumane and violating fundamental human rights. Accounts also revealed unlawful practices by police, including sexual harassments, confiscation and dispossession of drugs, money and other valuables. The zenith was incarceration for possession of cannabis for personal use, which exposed these young people to health risks in prison environments. I found that violence was ubiquitous in the lives of street-involved youths, and there was an inevitability of emotional and psychological harms alongside the physical ones. Violence, exercised through police authority, was internalized and embodied as inhuman conditions of life that dehumanizes, depersonalizes and discredits (Shotter, 1993).

I argue that punitive policing that facilitates dispossession and impoverishment, health risks, stigma and criminal record in the absence of social services can amplify drug-related harms for an already marginalized population. As Elliot, Golub and Dunlap (2012, p. 218) pointed out, punitive policing "establishes a context in which the risks of deleterious forms of psychosocial exposure may trump those involved with the actual marijuana use". Apart from a restrictive deterrence, including modifications of cannabis use practices to avoid detection and sanction, street-level policing did not reduce cannabis use but displaced it to neighborhoods where it was previously unknown (see Nelson, 2018). Similarly, street-level policing, partly implemented as a crime control measure, may unintentionally increase crime as street youths released from police detention without means of livelihoods turn to criminal activities to generate income for survival.

The findings document different situational strategies adopted by street-involved youths to detect and evade police arrest, which indicates that these youths are not passive toward structural violence mediated by punitive policing practices. Social theorists have emphasized the capacity of human agents for invention and creativity. In drug use research, "habitus" (Bourdieu, 1990) is widely used as a conceptual tool to explore internalized capacity for resistance and inventiveness in relation to structural constraints among people who use drugs (Grundetjern & Sandberg, 2012; Haritavorn, 2014; Sandberg & Fleetwood, 2016). I argue that the balance between agency and structure in the field of illicit drug use is itself determined by structural forces. The strategies used by street-involved youths did not always enable them to avoid police arrest or mitigate the disempowering effects of structural forces. In some cases, it led to more harms and suffering, reproducing a vicious cycle in which those who are oppressed are unconsciously complicit in their structural subordination (Bourdieu, 2000). This proves that Kleinman, Das and Lock (1997, p. ix) were right in arguing that, "social suffering results from what political, economic and institutional power does to people, and reciprocally, from how these forms of power themselves influence responses to social problems".

My findings support the case for structural interventions to reduce drug-related harms for street-involved youths. Importantly, they highlight the need for a public health approach to street-level policing, which involves the exercise of discretion by law enforcement officers in order to balance different interests, including crime control, health and human rights (Moore, 1992; Maher & Dixon, 1999). Government should prioritize and invest in treatment services for people who use drugs, particularly for street-involved youths who use in potentially harmful ways (Mallet, Rosenthal, & Keys, 2005; Nelson & Francis, 2021d) and face significant barriers to healthcare services (Barker, Kerr, Nguyen et al., 2015). The Nigerian state should follow the example of other countries who have found decriminalization of drug possession for personal use effective in reducing consumption and facilitating access to treatment for dependent users. Decriminalization of personal drug use is also an essential measure for curbing drug-related corruption in the police and safeguarding the rights and dignity of people who use drugs.

Conclusion

Despite the large investments that have gone into government efforts to curb cannabis use through enforcement-based approaches, such efforts have not delivered their expected impacts. Instead, they have served as structural and systemic mechanisms that mediate violence and suffering in the day-to-day lives of street-involved youths, reinforcing the very conditions that facilitated their use of drugs in the first place. This is so because current policies do not consider the social-structural and political economic forces that influence drug use behaviors. A distorted view of drug use that blames individuals and exonerates the system contributes to ineffective policies that are based on misguided priorities (e.g. investment in policing while neglecting treatment and social services for young people who use drugs). I argue that street cannabis use (and retail trade) will persist as long as young people are structurally excluded from basic social and economic benefits through the failure of the Nigerian "petro-state" to redistribute oil revenue and redress fundamental structural inequality. The development of social policies that promote equity and inclusion and improve access to basic social services for the vast majority of young people offers scope for the reduction of drug consumption and related harms in Nigeria.

Note

1 None of the participants admitted being involved in criminal activities, but attributed such activities to anonymous others.

References

Adlaf, E. M., Zdanowicz, Y. M., & Smart, R. G. (1996). Alcohol and other drug use among street-involved youths in Toronto. *Addiction Research*, 4(1), 11–24.

Agbiboa, D. E. (2015). Policing is not work; it is stealing by force: corrupt policing and related abuses in everyday Nigeria. *Africa Today*, 62(2), 95–126.

Akyeampong, E. (2005). Diaspora and drug trafficking in West Africa: a case of Ghana. *African Affairs*, 104(416), 429–447.

Asuni, T. (1964). Socio-psychiatric problems of cannabis in Nigeria. *Bulletin on Narcotics*, 16(2), 17.

Barker, B., Kerr, T., Nguyen, P., Wood, E., & DeBeck, K. (2015). Barriers to health and social services for street-involved youth in a Canadian setting. *Journal of Public Health Policy*, 36(3), 350–363.

Becker, H. S. (1968). *Outsiders: studies in the sociology of deviance*. New York: Free Press.

Bender, K., Thompson, S. J., Ferguson, K., Komlo, C., Taylor, C. & Yoder, J. (2012). Substance use and victimization: street-involved youth's perspectives and service implications. *Children & Youth Services,* 34, 2392–2399.

Bourdieu, P. (1990). *The logic of practice.* Stanford, CA: Stanford University Press.

Bourdieu, P. (2000). *Pascalian meditations.* Stanford, CA: Stanford University Press.

Bourgeois, P. (1995). *In search of respect: selling crack in El Barrio.* Cambridge: Cambridge University Press.

Bourgeois, P. (2003). Crack and the political economy of suffering. *Addiction Research & Theory,* 11, 31–37.

Bourdieu, P., & Wacquant, L. (1992). *An invitation to reflexive sociology.* Chicago, IL: University of Chicago Press.

Bozinoff, N., Small, W., Long, C., DeBeck, K., & Fast, D. (2017). Still "at risk": an examination of how street-involved young people understand, experience and engage with "harm reduction" in Vancouver's inner city. *International Journal of Drug Policy,* 45, 33–39.

Buchanan, D., Khoshnood, K., Stopka, T., Shaw, S., Santelices, C., & Singer, M. (2002). Ethical dilemmas created by the criminalization of status behaviour: cases examples from ethnographic field research with injection drug users. *Health Education & Behaviour,* 29(1), 30–42.

Calhoun, C., Gerteis, J., Moody, J., Pfaff, S., & Virk, I. (2007). *Contemporary sociological theory.* Oxford: Blackwell Publishing.

Csete, J., & Constanza, J. (2013). *Telling the story of drugs in West Africa: the newest front in a losing war?* Policy Brief 1. Global Drug Policy Observatory/Swansea University.

Dixon, D., & Maher, L. (2002). Anh Hai: policing, culture and social exclusion in a street heroin market. *Policing & Society,* 12(2), 93–110.

Dirisu, O., Shickle, D., & Elsey, H. (2019). Perspectives of young cannabis users within the Nigerian policy context: the paradox of criminalization as a deterrence strategy. *Journal of Substance Use,* 24(1), 73–78.

Economic Community of West African States (ECOWAS) (2018). *West Africa drug report: statistics and trends on illicit drug use and supply (2014–2017).* Addis Ababa: ECOWAS.

Elliot, E., Watson, A. J., & Harris, U. (2002). Harnessing expertise: involving peer interviewers in qualitative research with hard-to-reach populations. *Health Expectations,* 5, 172–178.

Elliot, L., Golub, A., & Dunlap, E. (2012). Off the street and into "the cut": deterrence and displacement in NYC's quality of life marijuana policing. *International Journal Drug Policy,* 23, 210–219.

Erickson, P., van der Maas, M., & Hathaway, A. (2013). Revisiting deterrence: legal knowledge, use context and arrest perception for cannabis. *Sociologicky Casopis,* 49(3), 427–448.

Farmer, P. (1996). On suffering and structural violence: a view from below. *Daedalus,* 125(1), 261–283.

Gee, G. C., Delva, J., & Takeuchi, D. T. (2007). Relationships between self-reported unfair treatment and prescription medication use, illicit drug use and alcohol dependence among Filipino Americans. *American Journal of Public Health,* 97, 291–305.

Goffman, E. (1959). *The presentation of self in everyday life.* New York: Anchor Books.

Grundetjern, H., & Sandberg, S. (2012). Dealing with a gendered economy: female drug dealers and street capital. *European Journal of Criminology,* 9(6), 621–635.

Gyong, J. E. (2009). A sociological assessment of the national drug law enforcement agency's (NDLEA) strategies of arrest and detention in Nigeria. *Current Research Journal of Social Sciences,* 2(3), 127–132.

Hall, W. D., & Pacula, R. L. (2003). *Cannabis use and dependence: public health and public policy.* Cambridge: Cambridge University Press.

Hammersley, R., Jenkins, R., & Reid, M. (2001). Cannabis use and social identity. *Addiction Research & Theory,* 9(2), 133–150.

Haritavorn, N. (2014). Surviving in two worlds: social and structural violence of Thai female injecting drug users. *International Journal of Drug Policy,* 25, 116–123.

Hathaway, A. D. (2004). Cannabis users' informal rules of managing stigma and risk. *Deviant Behaviour,* 25, 559–577.

Holland, J, Ramazanoglu, C., Sharope, S., & Thompson, R. (1992). Pressured pleasure: young women and the negotiation of sexual boundaries. *Sociological Review,* 40, 645–674.

Holmes, S. M. (2011). Structural vulnerability and hierarchies of ethnicity and citizenship on the farm. *Medical Anthropology,* 30(4), 425–449.

Holm, S., Sandberg, S., Kolind, T., & Hesse, M. (2014). The importance of cannabis culture in young adult cannabis use. *Journal of Substance Use,* 19(3), 251–256.

Ibeanu, O. (2007). Criminal justice reform: policing service delivery. In: Otteh, J. (ed.) *Reforming for justice: a review of justice sector reforms in Nigeria, 1999–2007.* Lagos: Access to Justice.

Kavanagh, C. (ed.) (2013). *Harmonizing drug legislation in West Africa – A call for minimum standards.* Background Paper #9, West African Commission on Drugs/Kofi Annan Foundation.

Klantschnig, G. (2009). The politics of law enforcement in Nigeria: lessons from the war on drugs. *Journal of Modern African Studies,* 47(4), 529–549.

Klantschnig, G. (2014). Histories of cannabis use and control in Nigeria, 1927–1967. In Klantschnig, G., N. Carrier, and C. Ambler (eds.) *Drugs in Africa: histories and ethnographies of use, trade and control.* New York: Palgrave Macmillan, pp. 69–88.

Klantschnig, G. (2016). The politics of drug control in Nigeria: exclusion, repression and obstacles to policy change. *International Journal Drug Policy,* 30, 132–139.

Klein, A. (1994). Trapped in traffic: growing problems of drug consumption on Lagos. *Journal of Modern African Studies,* 32(4), 657–677.

Klein, A. (1999). Nigeria and the drugs war. *Review of African Political Economy,* 26(79), 51–73.

Klein, A. (2001). "Have a piss, drink ogogoro, smoke igbo, but don't take gbana"-hard and soft drugs in Nigeria: a critical comparison of official policies and the view on the street. *Journal of Psychoactive Drugs, 33*(2), 111–119.

Klein, A. (2009), Mules or couriers: the role of Nigerian drug couriers in the international drug trade. In Childs, M. D. and T. Falola (eds.) *The changing worlds of Atlantic Africa: essays in honor of Robin Law.* Durham, NC: Carolina Academic Press, pp. 411–429.

Kleinman, A. (2000). The violences of everyday life. In Ramphele, M., A. Kleinman, P. Reynolds, & V. Das (eds.) *Violence and subjectivity.* Berkeley: University of California Press, pp. 226–241.

Kleinman, A., Das, V., & Lock, M. (eds.) (1997). *Social suffering.* Berkeley: University California Press.

Knuttila, M. (2002). *Introducing sociology: a critical perspective* (Second edition). Ontario: Oxford University Press.

Lawyers Committee for Human Rights (1992). *The Nigerian police force: a culture of impunity.* New York.

Maher, L., & Dixon, D. (1999). Policing and public health: law enforcement and harm minimization in a street-level drug market. *British Journal of Criminology,* 39(4), 488–512.

Mallet, S., Rosenthal, D., & Keys, D. (2005). Young people, drug use and family conflict: pathways into homelessness. *Journal of Adolescence,* 28, 185–199.

Moore, M. H. (1992). Problem solving and community policing. In Tonry, M. & N. Morris (eds.) *Modern policing.* Chicago, IL: University of Chicago Press, pp. 99–158.

National Bureau of Statistics (2010). *National poverty rates for Nigeria: 2003–2004 (Revised) and 2009–2010.* Abuja: NBS.

Nelson, E. E. (2018). Police crackdowns, structural violence and impact on the well-being of street cannabis users in a Nigerian city. *International Journal of Drug Policy,* 54, 114–122.

Nelson, E. E. (2021a). 'I take it to relax... and chill': perspectives on cannabis use from marginalized Nigerian young adults. *Addiction Research & Theory.* doi: 10.1080/16066359.2021.1895125.

Nelson, E. E. (2021b). 'I cannot stop taking weed cos it makes me survive': cannabis use, criminal sanctions and users' experiences in Nigeria. *Drugs: Education, Prevention and Policy.* doi: 10.1080/09687637.2021.1972936.

Nelson, E. E. (2021c). Intersectional analysis of cannabis use, stigma and health among marginalized Nigerian women. *Sociology of Health & Illness,* 43(3), 660–677.

Nelson, E. E., & Brown, A. S. (2019). Extra-legal policing strategies and HIV risk environment: accounts of people who inject drugs in Nigeria. *Drugs: Education, Prevention and Policy,* 27(4), 312–319.

Nelson, E. E., & Essien, N. F. (2021d). Redefining recovery: accounts of treatment experiences of dependent cannabis users in Nigeria. *Journal of Substance Abuse Treatment, 125,* 1–7.

Nelson, E. E., & Obot, I. S. (2020). Beyond prohibition: responses to illicit drugs in West Africa in an evolving policy context. *Drugs and Alcohol Today,* 20(2), 123–133.

Nelson, E. E., & Pates, R. (2017). Supply control, demand reduction or harm reduction? Developments and directions for drug policy in Nigeria. *Addiction Research and Theory,* 26(6), 465–469.

Obot, I. S. (2004). Assessing Nigeria's drug control policy, 1994–2000. *International Journal of Drug Policy,* 15, 17–26.

Omotola, S. (2007). The police and the challenges of sustainable democracy in Nigeria: contributions and constraints. *Pakistan Journal of Social Science,* 4, 620–631.

Osasona, S. O., & Koleoso, O. N. (2015). Prevalence and correlates of depression and anxiety disorder in a sample of inmates in a Nigerian prison. *International Journal of Psychiatry in Medicine,* 50(2), 203–218.

Quesada, J., Hart, L. K., & Bourgois, P. (2011). Structural vulnerability and health: Latino migrant laborers in the United States. *Medical Anthropology,* 30(4), 339–362.

Rhodes, T. (2002). The risk environment: a framework for understanding and reducing drug-related harm. *International Journal of Drug Policy,* 13, 85–94.

Rhodes, T. (2009). Risk environments and drug harms: a social science for harm reduction approach. *International Journal Drug Policy,* 20, 193–201.

Rhodes, T., Wagner, K., Strathdee, S. A., Shannon, K., Davidson, P., & Bourgois, P. (2012). Structural violence and structural vulnerability within the risk environment: theoretical and methodological perspectives for a social epidemiology of HIV risk among injection drug users and sex workers. In O'Campo, P., and & J. R. Dunn (eds.) *Rethinking social epidemiology: towards a science of change.* Dordrecht: Springer, pp. 205–230.

Room, R. (2005). Stigma, social inequality and alcohol and drug use. *Drug & Alcohol Review,* 24, 143–155.

Sandberg, S. (2012). Cannabis culture: a stable subculture in a changing world. *Criminology & Criminal Justice,* 13(1), 63–79.

Sandberg, S., & Fleetwood, J. (2016). Street talk and Bourdieusian criminology: bringing narrative to field theory. *Criminology & Criminal Justice,* 17(4), 1–17.

Sarang, A., Rhodes, T., Sheon, N., & Page, K. (2010). Policing drug users in Russia: risk, fear and structural violence. *Substance Use & Misuse,* 45, 813–864.

Scheper-Hughes, N., & Bourgois, P. (2004). Introduction: making sense of violence. In Scheper-Hughes, N. & P. Bourgois (eds.) *Violence in war and peace: an anthology.* Oxford: Blackwell Publishing, pp. 1–27.

Shotter, J. (1993). Psychology and citizenship: identity and belonging. In Turner, B. S. (ed.) *Citizenship and social theory.* London: SAGE.

Singer, M. (2004). The social origins and expressions of illness. *British Medical Bulletin,* 69, 9–19.

Terrill, W., Paoline, E., & Manning, P. (2003). Police culture and coercion. *Criminology,* 41(4), 1003–1034.

Thompson, S. J., Barczyk, A., Gomez, R., Dreyer, L., & Pompham, A. (2010). Homeless, street-involved emerging adults: attitudes towards substance use. *Journal of Adolescent Research,* 2(25), 231–257.

Ti, L., Wood, E., Shannon, K., Feng, C., & Kerr, T. (2013). Police confrontations among street involved youths in a Canadian setting. *International Journal of Drug Policy,* 24, 46–51.

United Nations Office on Drugs and Crime (UNODC) (2019). *Drug use in Nigeria 2018.* Vienna: UNODC.

Werb, D., Kerr, T., Li, K., Montaner, J., & Wood, E. (2008). Risks surrounding drug trade involvement among street-involved youth. *American Journal of Drug and Alcohol Abuse,* 34, 810–820.

Williams, P. (2014). Nigeria criminal organizations. In Paoli, L. (ed.) *The oxford handbook of organized crime.* Oxford: Oxford University Press, pp. 254–269.

24

ETHNIFIED INTOXICATION – KHAT USE AND THE SOMALI COMMUNITY IN SWEDEN

Johan Nordgren

Introduction

Khat is a plant that is grown and used for its stimulant effects in several nations on the Arabian Peninsula and in East Africa. The ways in which khat is used vary between settings, but its use is generally a male pastime, where the recently harvested leaves and stems of the plant are chewed and stored in the cheek (Carrier 2007). Specifically, this chapter focuses on khat use and its association with a Somali community in Sweden.

In places where khat is a legal commodity, the consumption often takes place in special khat cafés, known as a *mafrish* in Somali, where users meet to socialize, gossip, give advice, support each other or watch the news or sports (Carrier 2007). The pleasurable effects of khat use are referred to as *mirqaan* in Somali (Carrier & Klantschnig 2012: 29) and entail a stimulation of the central nervous system which facilitates social interaction. Khat users often spend a few hours of pleasurable socialization and conversation with friends or acquaintances, which could be comparable to the "Western" habit of after-work beer drinking. This aspect of khat use as a somewhat socially accepted pastime is common in countries where khat is a legal commodity, for example, in Somalia. Consequently, migrating to countries where khat is classified as an illicit substance changes the context for use (Anderson et al. 2007; Carrier 2007).

Khat is currently an illicit substance in most European countries, with Norway and Sweden as the first to criminalize khat in 1989, followed by Denmark and Finland in 1993. The Norwegian and Swedish bans on khat were primarily based on customs interceptions of khat at airports, and since the plant material contained cathinone and cathine, two substances banned both in Sweden and internationally, khat as a plant material was rather quickly classified as an illicit drug. In the late 1980s, khat was not extensively used in Sweden, and the decision to ban khat was based on the pharmacological classifications of the UN drug conventions (Nordgren 2017).

The use of khat has subsequently been controversial in Europe. Carrier and Klantschnig note that: "Perceptions of [khat] are polarized: some see it as a noxious drug destroying health and the social fabric, while others extol its virtues as a mild stimulant whose consumption binds people together" (Carrier & Klantschnig 2012: 29). This division in attitudes toward khat is notable in production countries, but has also been seen in diaspora contexts in

 DOI: 10.4324/9780429058141-31

Europe. Klein has summarized some of the negative effects ascribed to khat use: "Khat, it is claimed, diverts active Somali men from the workplace, drains state-benefit-dependent household budgets, puts a strain on family relationships, and prevents the integration of Somalis into the UK mainstream" (Klein 2007: 57). This type of discourse about khat has shaped discussions about the criminalization of khat in the Netherlands and in the UK. Khat was classified as a "soft drug" in the Netherlands at the beginning of 2013 and as an illicit class C drug (least capacity for harm) in the UK in the summer of 2014 (Nabben & Korf 2017). As khat was criminalized in the Netherlands and in the UK, there has been a shift in the type of khat used in the diaspora, from newly harvested khat to dried khat in the form of leaves or a green powder, referred to as *grabo*. Dried khat is significantly less potent than fresh khat but is easier for users to access through international parcel shipments (Kassim et al. 2015).

In the early 2000s, khat use began to be described in media reports as explicitly of concern to Somali immigrants and their culture, not only in Sweden, but also in other Scandinavian countries. The use was claimed to cause unemployment, divorce, violence, psychoses and other mental health issues, as well as lack of integration, family financial issues and various social problems (Osman & Söderbäck 2011; Nordgren 2017). The public debate about khat in Sweden focused exclusively on khat use as a significant problem among the Somali community. Khat was an issue that mobilized different actors in the Somali diaspora over several years in Sweden. Anti-khat campaigns were initiated by Somali ethno-national organizations, and voices calling for increased police focus on khat use and smuggling appeared, and the various physical and social harms of khat use and abuse were reported in daily newspapers. Local social services, medical institutions and Somali ethnic organizations were engaged in stopping khat use and offering help and care to those who used khat in problematic ways. These initiatives were often deployed at the local municipal level in cooperative projects initiated by local Somali organizations. The notion of "cultural competence" was frequently employed in khat projects as a tool to get Somalis to quit using khat, for example, by recruiting Somalis of high standing in the community to inform about the potential harms of using khat (Nordgren 2017).

Taken together, these developments have made the use of khat an example of what I call *ethnified intoxication*. This concept denotes the process by which a psychoactive substance and its use is "made ethnic" in social discourses and practices (Nordgren 2017). For example, by the time specific municipal projects against khat use were initiated in the second half of the 2000s, khat had become thoroughly associated with Somali immigrants, as seen in the projects' tendencies to target the Somali ethnic minority as a whole. This was a general development in the Scandinavian countries, judging by the synchronicity of similar projects in Denmark and Norway at that time (Nordgren 2017).

Public discourses and societal interventions about Somalis and khat use in Sweden combine into an interesting case in which a criminalized drug becomes associated with a particular ethnic group. Ethnicity is a notoriously slippery concept that is used in different ways across scientific disciplines, theoretical schools of thought and in everyday language (Baumann 1996; 1999; Jenkins 2008; Eriksen & Jakoubek 2019). My perspective on ethnicity follows scholars such as Richard Jenkins and Gerd Baumann and is processual and constructionist, which means that ethnicity is something that is continually socially constructed through everyday interactions and through societal discourses. This view makes it difficult and to some extent futile to pinpoint what ethnicity *is*. Instead, the focus lies on how ethnicity is *made*, what *changes occur* over time and how it is *understood* in different social settings (Jenkins 2008).

Overall, this chapter is about interrelationships between intoxicants and ethnicity. Taking a point of departure in qualitative interviews with ethno-national civil society organization representatives in the Somali community in Malmö, Sweden, it examines how khat use and Somalis as an ethnic minority in Sweden have become entangled in public discourse.

My analysis is another example of a long tradition within social sciences to research how ethnicity and intoxicants or illegal drugs have become entangled (Musto 1973/1999; Helmer 1975; Reinarman 1979; Bourgois 1996/2003; Manderson 1997; Jenkins 1999; Bucerius 2014). An important theme in research about drug use and ethnic minorities is constructions and associations between ethnic or racial minorities and how these have influenced drug policy and attempts to control the use of drugs in society. Common threads in existing research are that moral panics regarding drugs and ethnicity occur because of racism, stereotypes, systematic discrimination and socioeconomic class relations between social groups. The entanglement of ethnicity and drugs is a sensitive issue, considering that drug use is a criminal offense and is associated with a strong social stigma, particularly if one is physically dependent or engages in problematic drug use (Singer & Page 2014). In Sweden, khat use is ethnified as a kind of illicit drug use engaged in by members of the Somali community.

In the following, I will first briefly present some methodological considerations about my fieldwork at Somali ethnic organizations in Sweden and the interviews I conducted with community representatives. I will then present the main findings from the study, with a focus on how the Somali organization representatives engaged with the issue of khat use. Finally, I will discuss my findings by drawing attention to how ethnicity and intoxication can be understood through different "construction sites of ethnicity" – arenas where ethnicity comes into play and becomes important.

Methods and data

During a period of fieldwork from 2014 to 2016, I conducted 16 qualitative semi-structured interviews with persons who were active in Somali ethno-national organizations (see Nordgren 2017 for the original study). In total, 11 different organizations are represented in the empirical material. The site of the fieldwork was Malmö, Sweden, a city of around 300,000 inhabitants in the south of the country. Several Somali organizations in the city offer a range of activities, help and resources to persons who identify as ethnic Somalis. To some extent, these organizations, which often have locales situated in socioeconomically marginalized areas of the city, act as "integration centers", as members and visitors are offered practical help, for example, with their contacts with various governmental bodies. The organizations also offer integration projects, youth activities and study circles.

I contacted the chairpersons in several Somali organizations, who I interviewed and who referred me to other interviewees they felt had valuable knowledge about khat use in Sweden. The interviews concerned the interviewee's personal background in relation to engagement in a Somali organization, his or her views on khat and khat use, an assessment of the extent of khat use in Malmö, views of khat in relation to Somali ethnicity, and the potential for stigmatization of the Somali ethnic minority while discussing khat use as a Somali problem, and also covered methods of helping those who use khat in problematic ways.

Five of the interviewees were women, reflecting the fact that there were few women in general having elected positions in the organizations. The organizations are similar to those studied by sociologist Nauja Kleist's in her study of Danish-Somali ethno-national organizations. Kleist found those to be male-gendered spaces of recognition within a diaspora context, where "high-status Somali men use associational and community involvement to create alternative social spaces of recognition", where social esteem and respectability can be acknowledged (Kleist 2010).

The interviews took place face to face, in the locales of the organizations, in cafés or at my office at the university, and each interview took around one hour to conduct. I asked to record all of the interviews, but four of the interviewees did not want to be recorded. In those cases, I took detailed notes during the interview and expanded these notes as soon as possible after the interview. Three of the interviewees were not comfortable conducting the interview in Swedish, so these interviews were carried out in English. I have made minor grammatical changes to the quotations, while trying to retain the colloquial nature of everyday speech. I have anonymized the interviewees and their organizations. Although I felt I achieved empirical saturation during the fieldwork, 16 interviews is a somewhat limited sample and I use the interview material to theorize about ethnicity and intoxicants, not to generalize about Somali ethnic organizations or their representatives.

In the work on this chapter, I have revisited the empirical material from the original study in order to draw up some further research findings about ethnified intoxication. My analytical approach when returning to the transcribed interviews has been abductive (Charmaz 2014) in the way I have let the analysis be guided by both my thematic coding of the empirical material and by theoretical literature concerning intoxicants and ethnicity.

Results

In the following, I will discuss how the Somali organization representatives understood and discussed the issue of khat use and how they navigated between different discourses about ethnicity and intoxicants.

The Somali representatives who I interviewed were keen to discuss public discourses about both the Somali group in Sweden and perceptions about khat use. The Somali community has become more visible as increasing numbers of people from Somalia have migrated to Sweden since the 1990s. This migration pattern is associated mostly with the Somali civil war, which has created a Somali diaspora in the West (Pérouse de Montclos 2003). In Scandinavia, the Somalis, as a group, are constructed as a particularly vulnerable and at-risk population, often described in discourses about the integration of all ethnic minorities as being the specific group "most difficult to integrate" (Fangen 2007). Somali minority members have been stereotyped as engaging in khat use, female genital mutilation, criminality and Islamic radicalism. Stigmatizing public discourses about the Somali community meant that the interviewees discussed the public image of Somalis in Sweden. One of the Somali organization representatives discussed his view on how Somalis are portrayed in Sweden:

> The problem [with the image] is that you have a whole lot of people who don't have any problems. People of Somali background who work, do research, play football, and so on. That never shows in the media. /.../ What you hear about Somalis often concerns khat or war or terror or pirates. /.../ When these are the only things discussed it gets really problematic. /.../ I claim that this contributes to creating a [negative] image of the Somali group in Sweden. /.../ It's khat, female genital mutilation, pirates, and so on.
> *(Caadil)*

Caadil and other interviewees resisted this construction and stereotyping of the Somali minority as a homogenous problematic ethnic collective. Khat use was one piece of this stigmatizing puzzle, and the interviewees expressed great concern about this unwanted association between a criminalized intoxicant and their ethnic minority group. They actively resisted this association because they argued that it created stigma toward the Somali ethnic minority as a whole. One organization representative said:

> You stigmatize a whole group for something that maybe one or two percent of that group does. So I think that it's no problem to focus on the khat issue, but you have to bring up this issue in a way that does not stigmatize a whole group.
>
> *(Mursal)*

A common view held among the representatives was that projects specifically targeting the Somali ethnic minority in relation to khat did not represent the best way forward. Instead, initiatives focusing on structural issues such as making it easier for Somalis to get employment and enroll in education were proposed. Some of the interviewees argued that it was "unfair" that Somalis were targeted exclusively, since they could identify other ethnic categories of people that, in their view, were prone to using khat. This was a way to resist the meaning ascribed to khat use as relating to Somali ethnicity, by claiming that khat use was not exclusive to Somalis:

> It is not only Somalis who chew. /.../ Alright, it is the largest group that chews. But also the Ethiopians chew. People from Yemen chew.
>
> *(Shamso)*

Similarly, Mursal engaged in ethnic boundary-making (Eriksen & Jakoubek 2019), situating khat use mainly within Yemeni culture:

> Khat grows in Ethiopia and Kenya. If it were part of our society, then it would have grown also with us [Somalia and Somaliland are dependent on khat importation from neighboring countries]. And also, when people say that it is our culture, I mean, it originally came from Yemen.
>
> *(Mursal)*

By attempting to include a larger population, those from other East African nations and from the Arabian Peninsula, the interviewees aimed to reduce the ethnic targeting of Somalis in general in relation to khat in the Swedish setting.

In public discourse, khat use has often been discussed as an important reason for socioeconomic marginalization among men of Somali background (Anderson et al. 2007). Most of the interviewees, however, tended to describe khat use as a way of navigating and handling a situation of marginalization and discrimination in Swedish society, turning the dominant discourse of cause-and-effect on its head. This was related to a symptom perspective held by several of the interviewees, a view that explains individual drug use as a way of handling difficult structural socioeconomic circumstances. In a way, what the interviewees were saying was that khat use is a social problem that has been put in an ethnic disguise (cf. Ålund 2002; Eliassi 2013). The interviewees nuanced the image of khat use as a problem of Somali ethnicity or culture, by bringing up complexities regarding socioeconomic marginalization and gender issues in the Somali diaspora setting. Bilan recounted a story which represents an example of the gendering of khat use:

> One husband who chewed too much khat always came home late after chewing and by then everyone in the family had gone to bed. This man then always slept throughout the

> day and when he woke up the wife had gone to work and the children to school. One day the husband saw a small child in the apartment and asked his wife whose child that was. The wife told him that it was their child, whereupon the husband replied: "When did we get that?"
>
> *(Bilan)*

In Bilan's narrative, the husband is lacking in his care of the family and he is depicted as a weak figure in comparison to his responsible wife, who is active and works, and their children, who go to school. The husband is unemployed and spends as much time as he can socializing with his friends away from the family, employing the functions of khat use, a pleasure only he can partake in. The husband is so irresponsible that he even forgets who his own children are. Bilan's narrative can be put in relation to what has become known as "getting the black sack", described by Kleist as "women, tired of their unemployed, good-for-nothing husbands chewing *khat* instead of helping out with the daily chores, kick them out with their belongings in a big black rubbish bag" (Kleist 2007: 141, italics in original). This narrative highlights gendered socioeconomic problems in a diaspora setting, rather than explaining khat use as explicitly ethnic.

The interviewees also framed the issue of khat use through more nuanced lenses than the perspectives represented in public discourse. The interviewees frequently described khat use as a serious social problem, but also spoke about the functions associated with khat use, which include being social, engaging in building strong social relationships and efforts in understanding and helping each other. This was seen as important to those who use khat regularly, since those users experienced social exclusion and marginalization. However, this exclusion was also seen as a consequence of the users spending too much time engaging in khat use with their friends or acquaintances. Mursal and several others pointed out the positive social functions of khat use, a function that nevertheless could become problematic:

> So all these problems mean that people start or continue to chew khat. And then that turns into a social club. They chew together, it's a club. They share experiences, they speak about their problems, and no one else in the society understands them better than they themselves can understand each other. So each person is dependent on the other, on the active listening of the other. And when you have lots of problems then you want someone who listens. And the more you chew together, the more you listen to each other. And this has become some sort of therapy for the Somalis.
>
> *(Mursal)*

Although the use of khat in Sweden is extensively explained in ethnic terms, the representatives of Somali organizations framed the issue of khat use as a social problem, specifically by drawing on discourses pertaining to what are generally referred to as "drug and alcohol problems". They argued that it is possible to use khat in a controlled manner, but that some people become addicted or use khat too frequently. Those who use khat too much were referred to as being *muqayil*. "That means that that person chews a lot /.../ [Somalis] don't really have a word for [drug] abuse... [khat is seen] as eating food, nothing dangerous. But *muqayil* means that this person doesn't do anything else besides chewing" (Caadil). This kind of person represents the stereotypical khat chewer, a male person who is unemployed and who spends day and night chewing khat to the detriment of his familial responsibilities.

The notion of muqayil hints at a division between the use and abuse of khat. Ayax argued that:

> There are users and abusers. Right now there are no users anymore, only abusers, because the users cannot get hold of khat when they want. A user might have a day off on Friday, but [the khat shipment] doesn't come on Friday but on Monday
>
> *(Ayax)*

Since the khat market is criminalized, the users have a hard time planning their use, being at the mercy of when and where new shipments of khat enter the country. In Ayax's argument, this means that it is difficult to use khat in a non-problematic way, since the irregularities of the illicit market mean that one would have to forsake regular activities such as work or education. Extending this argument, Ayax said that the khat *user* can use khat when he wants to or feels a need to do it, but the khat *abuser*: "He might take *grabo* or fresh khat, he doesn't work. Because he only waits and waits [for khat], he's an abuser. He has nothing to lose because he has lost his life" (Ayax).

Descriptions of being *muqayil* were similar to the ways "drunkards" and "drug addicts" have been described in alcoholism and drug addiction discourses (cf. Singer & Page, 2014), and these descriptions draw not on ethnicity, but relate to "drug problems". The interviewees thus made a clear distinction between use and abuse of khat and offered a more nuanced view of khat that distinguished problematic khat use from recreational khat use.

Considering the way cultural competence has been framed as the solution to the problem of khat use in both Sweden and Scandinavia broadly, it is interesting to note that the representatives from the Somali organizations instead proposed interventions more in line with how drug abuse prevention and treatment are generally organized in Sweden. They focused on regular substance abuse treatment options and prevention work in the form of readily available information, but no one suggested that these interventions would be tailor-made for the Somali ethnic group in particular. Those who rejected specific projects and interventions concerning khat instead argued for broad structural developments that would allow more Somalis to gain employment or education. In their statements, the interviewees more commonly suggested that problematic khat use would be resolved by a focus on enabling Somalis to acquire employment or education. Mustafe's statement is an example of a common view among the interviewees:

> Those who are in some form of dependency situation, it's difficult for them. Perhaps they need professional treatment methods. But those who only chew khat, and who are still young, it's very easy to turn their behavior around through vocational training, work and school. There must be other things put in place that show them a better future.
>
> *(Mustafe)*

This conceptualization was common, meaning that drug treatment was suggested for those who had a problematic use of khat, while most *users* would be able to stop using if only they were able to find employment or enroll in education. Mursal elaborated on this position:

> What you need to do is to identify these individuals and create jobs for them. People I know who used before stopped because they got a job or began to study. Then they got into another [social] sphere, they changed friends. So [khat use] is more a thing of peer-pressure and a social thing. /.../ It's a habit, you get habituated to a vicious cycle /.../ It's not that you miss [khat] so much that your body shakes and so on. But if that person can get into a situation where he can see happiness and feel that the situation is positive, then he will be able to stop.
>
> *(Mursal)*

However, this solution was often understood as problematic because of discrimination toward the Somali ethnic category in Sweden, which makes it difficult to get a job. Mursal insisted strongly on the need to create work opportunities for the Somali group. That was a common theme in the interviews, and several of the interviewees spontaneously spoke at length about the difficult situation within the Somali community in relation to work and possibilities to gain work experience. The suggestion of employment opportunities instead of treatment is interesting since it implies a view of khat use as more of a negative habit, rather than as an "addictive behavior" or a "khat use disorder", as suggested by medical research (Duresso et al. 2016). Although khat use might sometimes be used in problematic ways, the interviewees constructed the *solutions* to problematic khat use less in relation to the drug itself or to ethnicity and culture, and more to the socioeconomic situations of the users.

Discussion

As seen in the interviewees' statements, khat use is a complex phenomenon that can be explained in a wide range of ways. Although ethnic explanations loom large in prevalent understandings of khat use, all of the ethnic explanations have non-ethnic counter arguments brought up by the Somali community representatives. How can we make sense of this?

A useful tool when disentangling processes relating to ethnicity is Richard Jenkins' notion of *contexts of ethnic categorization*. Jenkins (2008) discusses several "construction sites" of ethnic categorization that range from formal to informal, including classifications of ethnicities made by governments, organized politics and everyday social interactions. For example, organized politics is a "construction site" of ethnicity where social problems might become constructed as identified with ethnic groups and categories. Politicians, public officials, news media journalists and commentators may shape and promote moral panics concerning ethnically constructed social issues (Jenkins 2008: 71). Khat use is one such social problem which in Sweden has tended toward becoming a drug scare, although not a full-blown one (Nordgren 2017). Musto (1973/1999) analyzes how some drug use in the U.S. has been ascribed to ethnic minorities, permitting more punitive measures to be taken against minorities when blamed for what are essentially "domestic evils" integral to American society (Musto 1973/1999: 298). As Jenkins argues, politics has historically provided a platform where ethnic chauvinism and moral panics about ethnic problems are expressed, thus furthering inter-ethnic conflicts in society (Jenkins 2008).

Jenkins also highlights the way ethnicity is constructed by ethnic organizations that aim to represent ethnic minorities in society (Jenkins 2008: 68). For example, the Somali civil society ethnic organizations in Sweden claim to represent Swedish-Somalis and constitute an arena of ethnic construction, both internally to the group and externally to the Swedish ethnic majority society. Contexts of ethnic classification and construction are not hierarchical however; they "overlap systematically in complex and interesting ways" (Jenkins 2008: 73). This overlapping between different social contexts contributes to the resilience of certain constructions of ethnicity. For example, if ethnicity becomes significant in many different settings, ethnic explanations become robust and resistant to change (Jenkins 2008).

How can the organization representatives engaged with the issue of khat use be understood by reference to these construction sites of ethnicity? In the *Results* section, we could see that the representatives had identified several settings where the notions of Somali ethnicity overlapped. In most cases, the ethnic identification was negative and stigmatizing, and so the representatives resisted becoming caged by involuntary chains of associations, particularly associations between "Somaliness" and illicit drug use, but also other stigmatized activities.

When Somali organizations in Malmö initiated projects against khat use they reached out to members of the Somali community and tried to influence those who used khat to quit using. As such, the project activities were aimed internally at the ethnic group, but also externally at the ethnic majority society by way of signaling that khat use is a Somali ethnic problem that the community is taking seriously. In public discourse and in societal interventions such as projects aiming to stop khat use in Sweden, khat use has been strongly defined as a "Somali problem" (Nordgren 2017). Drugs such as alcohol, amphetamine or cannabis in Sweden are not seen as ethnic, and thus there is no specific ethnic community that is singled out to take responsibility for reducing their use. Use of these "non-ethnic" intoxicants is rather a problem for the state, municipalities, the police and health care system to respond to. Regarding khat use, a range of national and local municipal actors implied that there was a responsibility of the Somali community to stop khat use. This notion has been identified by Goddard (2012) as a "responsibilization of communities", meaning that ethnic minority communities or organizations are sometimes pressured to reduce or solve social problems that are constructed as "their own". An interesting overlap here is that the organizations wanted to stop khat use in the setting of everyday interactions, but also wanted to consider the political arena and how Somalis and khat use are discussed in the media.

One informal ethnic construction site is public interactions with others, such as "verbal and non-verbal cues which are used to allocate unknown others to an ethnic category" (Jenkins 2008: 66). Studies by, for example, Bourgois (1996/2003) or Bucerius (2014) offer micro-sociological analyses of the way ethnicity, race and social marginalization interact in the daily lives of people. For most of the interviewees, it was not problematic to say that some Somalis use khat; this was a kind of ethnic construction of khat in the everyday setting. But they were generally very sensitive to the fact that defining khat use as something Somali on the political arena might have more far-reaching implications. This is because everyday constructions of social problems that are sanctioned by public discourse and national and local institutions can acquire a privileged status (Jenkins 2008). As noted before, the interviewees were very concerned with the predominantly negative public image of Somalis in Sweden, and one way of deflecting this was to engage in ethnic boundary-making by stating that other ethnic groups also use khat. In Sweden today, being identified as Somali is more often negative and pejorative than not, and for the organization representatives, khat use is one reason for that. Thus, the Somali organizations acted to balance the need to help and support community members who use khat in problematic ways, with the risk of increasing the stigma of assumed propensity for khat use to be transferred to people of Somali background living in Sweden in general.

Another formal "construction site" is, as mentioned, the official classification of ethnicity, when governments conduct population censuses or surveys, or scientists study drug use prevalence within different ethnic groups. These classifications of people are an often used knowledge base influencing how policy formulation, targeted resources and social control measures through institutional and governmental ascription of ethnicity are enacted (Gutmann 1999; Jenkins 2008). Official classification of ethnicity is common within epidemiological approaches to intoxicant use where respondents are asked to self-identify by choosing from a list of "ethnicities" or "races". These categories are then compared to each other in relation to prevalence of self-reported drug use (De Kock et al. 2017). Such official classifications of ethnicity aim to reduce the complexity of everyday ethnic identification into manageable variables. The classifications are often used by social welfare actors in order to provide services to specific groups that might be categorized as marginalized. In the UK, for example, "black and minority ethnic" populations have been in focus for health care and social welfare interventions (Beddoes et al. 2010). The interviewees seldom suggested solutions and help based on ethnicity or cultural behaviors, although such interventions are prevalent in social work and public health projects related to khat use in Scandinavia (Nordgren 2017). This is not very surprising, given the way the interviewees often resisted the association between Somalis and khat use. In their statements, the interviewees more commonly suggested that problematic khat use would be resolved by focusing on enabling Somalis to acquire employment or education.

The case of khat as an ethnified intoxicant is thus an example of how the entanglement of ethnicity and drugs encompasses different sites of ethnic construction. The results of the study show that in a setting where a specific kind of illicit intoxicant use is defined as inherently ethnic, the interviewees could offer other viable explanations for the use. The over-determination of ethnic explanations (Jenkins 2008) is problematic since other structural issues such as unemployment, poverty, marginalization, gender relations and social exclusion tend to disappear from view. Approaches to understanding intoxicant use that do not reflect critically about definitions and uses of ethnic explanations thus inadvertently mask structures of inequality and can obscure other social causal forces impacting on groups and individuals (Bourgois & Schonberg 2009).

More broadly, drug use among migrant minorities has become a social and political issue in most "Western" countries (see, for example, Bucerius 2014; Lalander 2017). In Sweden and Scandinavia, persons with a migrant background who use intoxicants have been described in public discourses centered around social work as "vulnerable immigrants" rather than "threatening immigrants" since the late 1980s (Nordgren 2017). Having been a refugee, experiences of forced migration before arriving in Sweden and the psychologically distressing situation of waiting for permits and staying in refugee centers were all defined as important reasons for immigrants starting to use drugs in Sweden. The so-called "drug abusing immigrants" have been viewed by government institutions as a population at risk and in need of targeted initiatives in order to make treatment attractive to them (Nordgren 2017). As early as the 1990s, the Swedish National Board of Health and Welfare wanted to enroll migrants into treatment, and asked: "What can we do to ensure that drug abusers with an immigrant background get access to our drug addiction treatment?" (quoted in Nordgren 2017). Treatment itself is often presented as crucial, amounting to a form of *treatmentality*, where treatment is posited as a self-evident solution to address problematic drug use and, by extension, a way of exercising social control and producing normalization (Jöhncke 2009). Through historical case studies of ethnified intoxicant use and both repressive political rhetoric and ethnic conflicts as a backdrop, we can see that in the case of Sweden's extensive welfare state focus, khat is ethnified, but with the aim of including ethnified drug users rather than excluding them. While Chinese Canadians during the 1920s opium drug scare were defined and targeted as a threatening and risky population that should be deported (Carstairs 1999), Somalis in Sweden are instead defined and targeted as a population at risk, a specific group seen as burdened by khat use and thus entitled to social welfare interventions (Nordgren 2017).

Within social welfare provisions, once a social problem has been ethnified, it is difficult to take a step back and ponder other explanatory models that could be used to understand the problem at hand. It is also possible that a social problem is not really a problem, which is an issue that has been extensively discussed in social problems theory (Goode 1990) but which is beyond the scope of this chapter. In cases where the use of an intoxicant has become entangled with ethnicity, my suggestion is to ask the following critical questions: Why has this particular intoxicant become associated with an ethnic group? Who is making and proposing the association? Are there underlying or unexpected motives or intentions behind the associations made (such as offering help and care, normalization, or racism and discrimination)? What are the potential and plausible effects of the entanglement? What other, non-ethnic, explanatory aspects might be of use in order to understand the problem? I think that these questions can be important in furthering our understanding of ethnified intoxicants in a way that does not lean too much on ethno-cultural explanations and that promotes critical and nuanced analyses of intoxicant use in society.

References

Anderson, D., Beckerleg, S., Hailu, D., & Klein, A. (2007) *The khat controversy: Stimulating the debate on drugs*. Oxford: Berg.

Ålund, A. (2002) 'Sociala problem i kulturell förklädnad' [Social problems in cultural disguise], in Meeuwisse, A. & Swärd, H. (Eds.) *Perspektiv på sociala problem* [Perspectives on social problems], pp. 293–312. Stockholm: Natur och Kultur.

Baumann, G. (1996) *Contesting culture. Discourses of identity in multi-ethnic London*. Cambridge: Cambridge University Press.

Baumann, G. (1999) *The multicultural riddle. Rethinking national, ethnic, and religious identities*. New York: Routledge.

Beddoes, D., Sheikh, S., Khanna, M., & Francis, R. (2010) *The impact of drugs on different minority groups: A review of the UK literature*. London: The UK Drug Policy Commission (UKDPC).

Bourgois, P. (1996/2003) *In search of respect: Selling crack in El Barrio*, Second edition. Cambridge: Cambridge University Press.

Bourgois, P.I., & Schonberg, J. (2009). *Righteous dopefiend*. Berkeley: University of California Press.

Bucerius, S.M. (2014) *Unwanted – Muslim immigrants, dignity and drug dealing*. New York: Oxford University Press.

Carrier, N.C. (2007) *Kenyan khat: The social life of a stimulant*, African Social Studies Series. Leiden: Brill.

Carrier, N.C., & Klantschnig, G. (2012) *Africa and the war on drugs*. London: Zed Books Ltd.

Carstairs, C. (1999) 'Deporting "Ah Sin" to save the White race: Moral panic, racialization, and the extension of Canadian drug laws in the 1920s', *Canadian Bulletin of Medical History*, vol. 16, pp. 65–88.

Charmaz, K. (2014) *Constructing grounded theory*. Thousand Oaks: Sage Publications.

De Kock, C., Decorte, T., Vanderplasschen, W., Derluyn, I., & Sacco, M. (2017) 'Studying ethnicity, problem substance use and treatment: From epidemiology to social change', *Drugs: Education, Prevention and Policy*, vol. 24(3), pp. 230–239.

Duresso, S.W., Matthews, A.J., Ferguson, S.G., & Bruno, R. (2016) 'Is khat use disorder a valid diagnostic entity?', *Addiction*, vol. 111(9), pp. 1666–1676.

Eliassi, B. (2013) 'Orientalist social work: Cultural otherization of Muslim Immigrants in Sweden', *Critical Social Work*, vol. 14(1), pp. 33–47.

Eriksen, T.H., & Jakoubek, M. (Eds.) (2019). *Ethnic groups and boundaries today: A legacy of fifty years*. Abingdon, Oxon: Routledge.

Fangen, K. (2007) 'Citizenship among young adult Somalis in Norway', *Young*, vol. 15(4), pp. 413–434.

Goddard, T. (2012) 'Post-welfarist risk managers? Risk, crime prevention and the responsibilization of community-based organizations', *Theoretical Criminology*, vol. 16(3), pp. 347–363.

Goode, E. (1990) 'The American Drug Panic of the 1980s: Social construction or objective threat?', *International Journal of the Addictions*, vol. 25(9), pp. 1083–1098.

Gutmann, M.C. (1999) 'Ethnicity, alcohol, and acculturation', *Social Science & Medicine*, vol. 48, pp. 173–184.

Helmer, J. (1975) *Drugs and minority oppression*. New York: The Seabury Press.

Jenkins, P. (1999) *Synthetic Panics – The symbolic politics of designer drugs*. New York: New York University Press.

Jenkins, R. (2008) *Rethinking ethnicity. Arguments and explorations*, Second edition. London: Sage Publications.

Jöhncke, S. (2009) 'Treatmentality and the governing of drug use', *Drugs and Alcohol Today*, vol. 9, pp. 14–17.
Kassim, S., Dalsania, A., Nordgren, J., Klein, A., & Hulbert, J. (2015) 'Before the ban – An exploratory study of a local khat market in East London, U.K', *Harm Reduction Journal*, vol. 12(19), pp. 1–9.
Klein, A. (2007) 'Khat and the creation of tradition in the Somali diaspora', in Fountain, J. & Korf, D.J. (Eds.) *Drugs in society – European perspectives*, pp. 51–61. Abingdon: Radcliffe Publishing Ltd.
Kleist, N. (2007) *Spaces of recognition – An analysis of Somali-Danish associational engagement and diasporic mobilization*, PhD thesis, Copenhagen: Sociologisk Institut, University of Copenhagen.
Kleist, N. (2010) 'Negotiating respectable masculinity: Gender and recognition in the Somali Diaspora', *African Diaspora*, vol. 3, pp. 185–206.
Lalander, P. (2017) 'Illegal street economies and drugs: Getting involved, skilled and trying to quit', in Kolind, T., Thom, B. & Hunt, G. (Eds.) *The SAGE handbook of drug and alcohol studies. Social science approaches*, pp. 644–660, London: Sage.
Manderson, D. (1997) 'Substances as symbols: Race rhetoric and the tropes of Australian drug policy', *Social & Legal Studies*, vol. 6(3), pp. 383–400.
Musto, D.F. (1973/1999) *The American disease – Origins of narcotics control*, 3rd edition. Oxford: Oxford University Press.
Nabben, T., & Korf, D.J. (2017) 'Consequences of criminalisation: The Dutch khat market before and after the ban', *Drugs: Education, Prevention and Policy*, vol. 24(4), pp. 332–339.
Nordgren, J. (2017) *Making drugs ethnic – Khat and minority drug use in Sweden*, PhD thesis, Malmö: Malmö University.
Osman, F., & Söderbäck, M. (2011) 'Perceptions of the use of khat among Somali immigrants living in Swedish society', *Scandinavian Journal of Public Health*, vol. 39, pp. 212–219.
Pérouse de Montclos, M-A. (2003) 'A refugee diaspora – When the Somali Go West', in Koser, K. (Ed.) *New African Diasporas*, pp. 37–55. London: Routledge.
Reinarman, C. (1979) 'Moral entrepreneurs and political economy: Historical and ethnographic notes on the construction of the cocaine menace', *Contemporary Crises*, vol. 3, pp. 225–254.
Singer, M., & Page, B.J. (2014) *The social value of drug addicts: Uses of the useless*. Walnut Creek, CA: Left Coast Press.

25

SYMBOLIC MEANING OF THE AMPHETAMINE-TYPE STIMULANT PROBLEM THROUGHOUT THE RESTORATION OF JAPANESE SOCIETY AFTER WWII

Drug control and the construction of the other

Akihiko Sato

Introduction

Amphetamine and methamphetamine are categorized as amphetamine-type stimulants (ATS hereafter). Japan is one of the first countries to establish a law to control ATS. The Stimulant Control Law in Japan was passed in 1951 and has been amended more than 20 times since. Although ATS was almost eradicated in the 1950s by strict control, it returned, with people abusing the drugs and becoming addicted in the 1970s and 1980s. Japanese society has officially experienced an ATS epidemic several times since the end of WWII.

Considering the history of the ATS problem and its control in Japan, many current Japanese scholars believe in a narrative, supported by official documents, that "the Stimulant Control Law was established because ATS caused addiction and psychosis after losing WWII". However, it is argued that this narrative may be a retrospectively constructed invention. This chapter will give an alternative account of the ATS problem and its control in Japan. In so doing, it will be shown that ATS in post-war Japan is not just a drug that has affected the health of Japanese people but has functioned as a symbolic device with which Japanese society has drawn its political, economic, and social boundaries. Furthermore, ATS as a symbolic device has been used to maintain social order throughout the restoration period of post-war Japanese society. Such a process is vital in understanding Japanese drug policy.

In the following, this chapter will begin by describing the process in which the Stimulant Control Law was established and amended in the 1950s, presenting a legitimate story of the law. This explanation of the process draws on a condensed description of the author's previous studies on ATS, followed by further consideration of the conversion of medical knowledge on ATS (Sato 2006, 2009a, 2020). Second, the chapter will show that

 DOI: 10.4324/9780429058141-32

ATS control, both in the 1970s and in the 1980s, was, respectively, organized based on each stage of the process of restoration of Japanese society, which yielded a newer symbolic meaning for ATS.

Material and methods

In order to discuss the processes and the mechanism of ATS control, contemporary documents of the period on ATS have been used, including newspaper reports, news magazine reports, the minutes of the Japanese National Diet (equivalent to the parliament), and academic articles in medical journals. All news items related to ATS in three major newspapers in Japan after WWII until the end of the 1980s have been examined: Asahi Shinbun (hereafter Asahi), Mainichi Shinbun (hereafter Mainichi), and Yomiuri Shinbun (hereafter Yomiuri). When referring to a report, the name of the newspaper source and its date of publication will be displayed in the text. All minutes of the Japanese National Diet (hereafter ND) discussions in reference to ATS during the same period have also been examined. However, only the minutes referred to in the chapter are listed in the references. These materials were used to describe the historical process on ATS-related matters. The chapter draws on a sociological method of the historical description that Gusfield used in his studies of the Temperance Movement in the United States (1968). As he pointed out, the purpose of the sociological description of a historical process is to interpret and generalize the properties of the process (Gusfield 1968). For example, he analyzed the discourse and the rhetoric of the Woman's Christian Temperance Union using a wide variety of printed materials. He revealed that the function of Temperance was to maintain, and even improve, the status of the declining old middle class in the new and mobilizing circumstances of American society early in the twentieth century. Although the present study's phenomenon takes place in a different time, Gusfield's method is still applicable in analyzing movements for the control of ATS in Japanese society. Following his study and method, the chapter focuses on discussing functions of the movement to control ATS in its original context using the abovementioned material.

Additionally, all the medical papers related to ATS which were published in Japan, since the first detailing the discovery of methamphetamine (Nagai 1893), until the end of the 1980s, were examined and analyzed with the perspective of discourse analysis. Discourse analysis is a method for analyzing talk and texts as social practices and describes the resources that are utilized to make those practices possible, drawing on ethnomethodology, speech act theory, and semiology (Potter and Wetherell 1987; Potter 1996). As used in many textbooks on qualitative research methods in sociology and social psychology (Richardson 1996, Silverman 2021), discourse analysis is seen as being one of the effectual qualitative methods for analyzing discourse in sociological investigation. In Discursive Constructionism (Potter and Hepburn 2008), a perspective of discourse analysis, talk, and text are treated in their own right, "not" to show any reality that is assumed to lie behind such talk and texts. Rather, talk and texts are analyzed as constructing work, in which some available discursive resources are used to construct a reality relevant to the context of such talk and texts (Potter and Hepburn 2008). By using discourse analysis, medical papers on ATS have been analyzed in terms of what functions those papers – and the medical knowledge produced – perform in the given context. This discourse analytic approach, along with Gusfield's method, enables the robust analysis necessary to show how medical knowledge both established and sustained the foundation of the crucial processes in problematizing ATS and institutionalizing ATS control. In the following sections, the symbolic process of ATS will be discussed in detail.

The beginning of the ATS problem after the war

Dominant story on ATS control

The ATS problem has quantitatively been the most prioritized drug problem in Japan (see Figure 25.1). Compared to other countries, it is one of the most unique features of the Japanese drug scene. In other words, in order to investigate the Japanese drug scene and drug policy, it is vital to discuss how ATS and its control in Japan are problematized. Legislative control of ATS began with the Stimulant Control Law of 1951.

Official documents on the establishment of the Stimulant Control Law often referred to a narrative as follows: Japan had a recognizable methamphetamine problem soon after WWII, because many people were using stimulants as a means to relieve their mental stress, after losing the war. The prevalence of ATS addiction and psychosis consequently led to the establishment of the law (Tadokoro 1998). Statistical data on the number of arrests for violation of the Stimulant Control Law illustrates the increase (Figure 25.1).[1] In the 1970s when the second wave of a Stimulant Abuse Epidemic hit Japanese society, the same story was again referenced, in order to legitimize contemporary measures.

However, as previously discussed, this narrative was constructed retrospectively, that can be labeled "the post-1954 framing", and is, therefore, an invention (Sato 2020). The post-1954 framing was constructed during the movement for the eradication of ATS in 1954, and consequently rationalized the strict control over ATS by re-writing the earlier history of the ATS problem. An alternative account of the narrative, supported by the contemporary documents analyzed for this chapter, will be discussed.

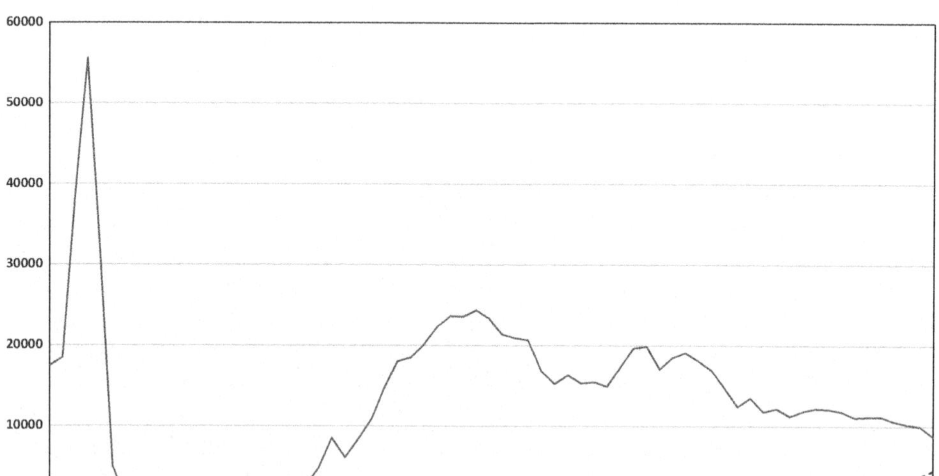

Figure 25.1 Number of arrests for violation of drug laws in Japan 1951–2019

Beginning of ATS control and the condemnation of some groups in the late 1940s

Methamphetamine was discovered in Japan in 1888 (Nagai 1893). However, it sank into oblivion in Japan until the 1940s, when several researchers began to argue for its medical application (Horimi et al. 1940; Ariyama 1941; Miura 1941). ATS was then made available for commercial use in Japan as various patented medicines (Sato 2009a: 721). Philopon (i.e., methamphetamine) was one of the most popular ATS and its name was synonymous with ATS until the 1970s. ATS was used even by the Imperial Japanese Armed Forces during wartime.

Some contemporary documents suggested that many people after the war recognized that ATS was useful for enhancing their productivity of work.[2] One such record was found in the minutes of the ND, with one representative of the ND calling into question the administrative measures for ATS in November 1949 after Philopon was designated as a powerful drug to prevent abuse. The representative complained about a limited allocation of production to control the amount of ATS,[3] claiming,

> I have some questions about the Philopon problem. The Ministry of Health and Welfare, in the name of the permanent undersecretary, asked every pharmaceutical company to stop producing or reduce the amount of production of Philopon and other stimulants. However, the general working public and the industry have been suffering from such measures. According to medical and pharmaceutical points of view, the stimulants represented by Philopon are excellent drugs.
>
> *(ND 1949, November 24: 1116)*

He added that the problems associated with Philopon were confined to small groups of users and that it would be better to enforce strict control over them, rather than controlling ATS use by the entire population.

As shown above, ATS had already drawn people's attention by its abuse. However, it also indicates that people in the late 1940s still talked about the positive effects of ATS, even after it was claimed to be problematic. The problems associated with ATS were not attributed to the drug itself but to specific groups such as novelists, performers, and students, who were thought to be responsible for the ATS abuse problem (Asahi 1949, March 29). In other words, the ATS problem was not interpreted as an "ATS induced problem" but a "specific groups induced problem" (Sato 2006: 242). The discourse of the representative of the ND constructed and defined the current problem as related to ATS, as the situation was caused not by the *effect* of ATS but by the *specific group* of people. The "general working public" also used the same drug, but with no blame. This was the beginning of the symbolic process of ATS in Japan.

Moral judgment and medical knowledge

One of the reasons behind adopting two measures on ATS by the Ministry in 1949, i.e., the designation of being a powerful drug and the guidelines for ATS production, was prior to their adoption. It is traced to the two conspicuous deaths of celebrities: the death of a popular comedienne, Miss Wakana (Kikuno Kawamoto, 1910–1946), in October 1946 and of a famous novelist, Sakunosuke Oda (1913–1948), in January 1948. Both were well known for using Philopon and their deaths were attributed to it (Sato 2009a: 723).

The demand for ATS control by medical doctors

After Miss Wakana's death, the first medical paper claiming an ATS problem in Japan was presented at a conference on internal medicine in 1947. The paper mentioned just one case related to the acute intoxication of methamphetamine (Nakazaki and Mori 1947). However, attendees of the conference were quick to respond to the case and vehemently insisted upon the need for control of ATS by medical doctors, referring to Miss Wakana's death and also to ATS abuse by other performers.

It can be argued that those comments at the conference demonstrate that a conversion of discourses in ATS studies had begun. The contents of these comments had explicitly converted from those of the ATS studies published before Miss Wakana's death. For example, Taro Horimi commented on the 1947 medical paper, arguing that his research experience had indicated the need for controlling ATS by medical doctors (Horimi 1947). However, in his paper of 1940, which was the very first paper on ATS, he discussed the possibility of medical applications of ATS with no mention of such problems as discussed at the conference (Horimi et al. 1940). A significant gap existed between the existing medical studies of ATS at that time and the discussion of the ATS researchers at the conference. This suggests that ATS studies were converted in the days before the ND's debate on the establishment of law to control ATS. The following section argues how such a conversion happened and how it functioned.

The condemnation of specific people

At the 1947 conference, Miss Wakana and other performers' ATS use was specifically problematized. However, the use of ATS by healthy and busy workers was not seen as a problem by the medical community. Following the conference presentation, medical doctors discussed that ATS should be controlled by medical doctors and that *specific groups* were to be held responsible for causing the problem. Shigeo Iwata of Osaka Medical College, who worked at the same laboratory as the two abovementioned presenters (Nakazaki and Mori), referenced the death of Miss Wakana and claimed that medical doctors should have been aware of the fact that some performers used ATS carelessly. He argued that methamphetamine needed to be controlled by medical doctors, insisting that the medicine was inhumane because it was based on the "unscrupulous studies" (Iwata 1947: 99), in which people of less competence were forcibly stimulated to do *menial* work at night during wartime (Iwata 1947). He added that ATS was "suitable for the workers who make irresponsible remarks" (Iwata 1947: 99) such as performers and novelists, but unsuitable for the workers who do *proper* work, such as healthy office workers. "Inhumane and irresponsible", these are the reasons why ATS should be controlled by medical doctors. Iwata's comments show *two functions* of a new medical discourse on the ATS problem. *The first function* is a justification of the conversion of medical knowledge on ATS, because those existing studies were conducted in "inhumanely". Iwata's account on the inhumanity of the existing studies gave rise to a new context for Nakazaki and Mori's presentation and as a rationalization of their presentation. *The second* is an exertion of a moral judgment on the performers and other ATS users from the medical perspective. The comments suggested that many users like performers were working irresponsibly and that their conscience was numbed. Iwata's view was not unique, with similar discourses being found in the following years (Suzuki 1949).

Other contemporary discourses outside of the medical field help us to understand the reasons why, for example, novelists were accused of abusing the use of ATS. Novelists, known to use ATS, had been categorized as being of the "après-guerre" (post-war) generation like Sakunosuke Oda mentioned earlier. They were often censured as being immoral, partly for their decadent literary style, but also partly for their use of ATS. Some critics suggested that their ATS use reflected the wartime darkness because ATS use was associated with the Imperial Japanese Armed Forces that forced young people to engage in Kamikaze attacks (Hirano 1949).

These discourses on the AST problem insisted upon the relationship between ATS abuse and immoral groups like performers and novelists, whereas healthy workers were not accused of ATS use. One representative review article on ATS in 1950, written at the request of the Japanese Medical Association, suggested that healthy office workers could use it without becoming addicted. The reason for their drug use was formulated as not being due to any internal craving but as an insignificance, in which they had to finish heavy work schedules (Kasamatsu and Kurino 1950).

These two opposing discourses clearly demonstrate that moral judgment and medical evaluation worked together to set a boundary between ATS use by ordinary people and ATS abuse by immoral people like performers and novelists. Immoral people were also often interpreted as being psychopaths in medical articles, and such diagnosis functioned as the reason for addiction (Kasamatsu and Kurino 1950). Papers even evaluated the content of theater scripts from a medical perspective. For example, one study discussed a comedy actor, who abused ATS and was hospitalized. It analyzed his script and concluded that the cause of the problem existed in the actor himself; "his association of ideas was superficial, but he was deluded that he enhanced his ability while using drugs. That is because he could entertain a *lowbrow* audience with such scripts" (Motoyoshi 1949: 9). Medical analysis judged the value of the scripts, treating them as evidence for his psychological problem. Consequently, *lowbrow* entertainment was interpreted as being a symptom of such problems. In contrast, the same medical perspective insisted that ATS use by healthy and busy workers was not problematic. These descriptions reveal that medical knowledge of ATS began to function as the agency which delineated the boundary between "use" and "abuse". This case evidences a transformation of the medical knowledge on ATS after the war. In the following section, I will elaborate on the transformation, because it indicates a crucial basis for the establishment of ATS control.

Conversion of medical research on ATS

After ATS became problematized, the scientific properties of ATS became fixed to legitimize the problem narrative of ATS. These fixed properties, in turn, became the criteria for appraisal. Appraisal discourse is the basis for establishment of laws and other means of control of ATS.

The initial studies on ATS

In order to illustrate the conversion of medical knowledge and its function in post-war Japan, the initial ATS studies in the early 1940s need to be examined. Until the problematization of specific ATS users, all medical studies on ATS "inquiry" (i.e., examining the properties of ATS) are based on several types of experiments. The description of the initial studies is formulated as follows. They began with a consideration of the properties, based on the structural formula of ATS, followed by several hypothetical features verified with experiments. Most of the experiments consisted of observations of the behaviors under the influence of

ATS and the reports by trial subjects on the physiological and psychological influences. The trial subjects consisted of several categories of people, including patients suffering from depression. The discussion and considerations pointed out both positive and negative effects of using ATS. Positive effects included feeling great, confident, aggressive, focused, etc. Negative effects included sleeplessness, lack of appetite, sudation, etc. (Horimi et al. 1940; Ariyama 1941; Miura 1941).

After these initial studies were published, many subsequent ATS studies followed and began to adopt more objective methods of measurement of the effects, such as measuring the strength of back muscles and speed of free association. Various studies emerged from pharmacology, neurology, internal medicine, and biochemistry that constituted a whole body of ATS research. All of them adopted similar types of descriptive sequences as the initial studies to inquire the properties of ATS. The method of these studies should be interpreted as the typical and standard way of scientific investigation. The method adopted a standard procedural sequence of verifying the hypothesis based on the features of the material deduced from the structural formula of ATS and other existing studies (Uchimaru 1942; Tanaka 1943; Oota and Egami 1944; Yoshino 1943). This type of medical discourse is called "inquiry discourse" (Sato 2006: 223–227).

Using a discourse analytic perspective (Potter & Wetherell 1987), we now look at how those descriptions are formulated to achieve certain functions rhetorically. What all these early studies on ATS reveal are constructed elements. Those studies did not merely report the scientific facts of ATS. What they achieved in those texts was that the studies constructed elements of *what ATS does* in a given context (see Potter & Wetherell 1987). They proposed and constructed particular features of ATS, which were subsequently used to associate all of the results of the separate experiments. In other words, the features of ATS derived from the structural formula, and the verified results function as the connecting plugs, by which all the experiments on ATS connect together, even if those experiments were undertaken by separate people in separate situations. For example, Ariyama (1941) grouped a total of 156 students for an experiment of ATS use and asked them to report on several effects they felt when taking 10 mg (43 cases), 20 mg (56 cases), and 40 mg (57 cases) of the drug. Among the results, for example, "liveliness" was reported by 19% of 10 mg users, 25% of 20 mg users, and 53% of 40 mg users. "Liveliness" was designated as one of the features of ATS use. Following the discourse analytic perspective, referring to "liveliness" acquires a discursive function that serves to connect every case of the experiment drawing on this ATS study. All described features function as such in the ATS studies (Sato 2006). Scientific practice on ATS was realized with "inquiry discourse" that made any general reference to the features of ATS possible by going beyond every local study situation. It means that inquiry discourse is the discourse discussing the properties of ATS, making it possible for the description of the ATS studies to connect one to another. Referring to the features of ATS is performative, which gives rise to the connection of local experiments, thus establishes a category of "ATS studies".

From inquiry to appraisal discourse

A gradual conversion occurred after the problematization of ATS users involves two ways of change. The first conversation is observed in the way in which the contents of the studies are organized. For example, newer studies always began by referring to the contemporary situation of ATS, e.g., a claim that the ATS user caused problems in society, instead of referring to a hypothesis derived from the structural formula of ATS and the results of the existing studies. The explicit reference to the problems in the society functions as the basic assumption to "appraise" the properties of ATS. The reason why and/or to what extent ATS caused the problem became the principal purpose of study instead of searching for and discovering any new features of ATS. Therefore, the feature of ATS is constructed as being already fixed, that is, something bad which will cause problems. This is then formulated as a basic assumption of newer ATS studies. Clinical observations became one of the most important sources for the appraisal and discussion as mentioned above (Motoyoshi 1949).

Another change took place in the structure of the ATS research field. In the early days of research on ATS, various types of studies were carried out with their own research questions, shaped by varying disciplines. However, newer studies posed common questions related to "the reason and the extent of the ATS problem" and consequently, gave rise to a unifying structure in the field. The aforementioned review article typically exemplified such conversion (see 2 pages before in this chapter for Kasamatsu and Kurino 1950). It collected many existing ATS studies from various disciplines and reviewed and re-organized them in order to answer the question regarding the ATS problem, including intoxication. However, no experimental study gave any satisfactory answer to the question, nor evidenced any factor to support their claim of these fixed features. Only psychopathological studies with clinical observations provided the answer. For example, pharmacological studies were reviewed by referring to some aspects of ATS features related to the pharmacological effects like the physiological changes of the body such as a rise in blood pressure. In short, the review only suggested the scarcity and high value of ATS as an adrenergic derivative, without any reference to the cause of the problems. Psychological studies were also reviewed, suggesting that there were numerous reports on both positive and negative psychological effects. However, when summarizing the effects in psychological studies, Kasamatsu and Kurino devalued those positive effects as being false and imagined. Indeed, their own psychopathological observations gave some satisfactory descriptions to address the cause of the problems. The authors found a difference in the ATS effects between healthy office workers and those people with a weak will, flippant personality, or with mood problems (Kasamatsu and Kurino 1950: 96–98). Here, a categorization by them is evident. The former people (i.e., healthy office workers) who used ATS were not problematized, while the latter were formulated as being abusers of ATS. They were categorized as psychopaths in the texts, and even suggested that they were the cause of the problems, attributing to the personality of the psychopath or drawing a link between the drug and the personality.

Furthermore, the study concluded the need to control sales of ATS, but this recommendation was based solely on their own psychopathological study. This had profound implications because the psychopathological study became the key to unifying the ATS field by providing a primary frame to interpret the features of ATS and its problems. The psychopathological framework became the default framework in the field. As such, the psychopathological study by Seijun Tatetsu and his colleagues in 1956 (Tatetsu et al. 1956) has been referred to as "the classic" ATS study even today (Yanagida and Itsumi 1993). ATS studies with the psychopathological framework continued to stand in the frontline of the ATS field, which will be discussed further in the penultimate section on the 1980s.

The type of medical discourse discussed above is called "appraisal discourse" (Sato 2006: 225–229) in contrast to the "inquiry discourse" of the initial studies. What all these newer studies on ATS *did* and *achieved* in their texts is that they constructed and substantiated a specific value by which the results of the experiments and observations were "judged and appraised" (Sato 2006: 226). The features of ATS had already been fixed as something bad, causing problems. As Canguilhem discussed in his book titled *The Normal and the Pathological*

(1989), physiological pathology fundamentally needs a basic value based on which objective observation and analysis can be developed. Such a value intrinsically derives from the subjective experience of a patient, suffering from any difficulty. Psychopathological thought, in contrast to physiology, was constructed and based not on the subjective value of patients, but on a moralistic value. Such a moralistic value was repeatedly invoked and accomplished as "appraisal discourse" (e.g., Saito 1952). What "appraisal discourse" achieved is that the descriptions of searching for and even discovering the factors gave account of the fixed features of ATS. "Appraisal discourse" subsequently accomplished the realization of the specific value on which such searching and discovering were premised. Clinical observations, being formulated as the successful description of discovering the factors with a psychopathological frame, achieved a moralist value, based on which the psychopathological framework was organized as the moral judgment.

There still existed a few studies which are organized around "inquiry discourse" (e.g., Tanaka 1948). Later, some of the contents of those studies were then converted to resources to answer a new question. For example, Mitsuru Higo discussed ATS in terms of "respiration of brain", which is categorized as an "inquiry discourse" (Higo 1949). Hiroshi Tai and his colleagues a while later tried to verify the cause and process of ATS intoxication with Higo's study (Tai et al. 1955); yet, they failed to do so. As such, ATS studies as "inquiry discourse" were located at the fringe of the research field. The results of those studies were to be utilized as a resource for "appraisal discourse", as in the abovementioned review. This phenomenon is called the conversion "from inquiry discourse to appraise discourse" in ATS studies (Sato 2006). Notably, the conversion from inquiry discourse to appraise discourse seems to have taken place gradually.

This conversion is highly significant in the process of problematization of ATS and the establishment of its control, because it substantiated the activities which drew the boundary between the normal and the pathological, instead of the moral and the immoral. In other words, newer medical discourse, "appraise discourse", helped to distinguish between the moral and immoral without a moralist vocabulary. The distinction was justified only with medical or psychopathological vocabulary. For example, two medical doctors were invited to the Diet as witnesses to testify on the cause and the extent of ATS problems in the discussion of the Stimulant Control Law in 1951 (ND 1951, February 15: 1–10). "Appraise discourse" produced by them worked well in drawing the boundary between the morals of ordinary people and the immoral, namely *rowdies*, *gamblers*, and other delinquents such as psychopaths with *weak wills*, who can be categorized using a medical vocabulary. Testimony using medical vocabulary therefore substantiated the need for a legitimate control of production and sale of ATS and constructed a substructure to establish the Stimulant Control Law, which will be discussed in the following section.

Youth problem and the reason for ATS control

In this section, the movement leading to the establishment of the Stimulant Control Law will be discussed in detail. Let me now return to the main route and discuss my alternative story on the establishment of ATS control. In the late 1940s, when the aforementioned conversion of medical knowledge was gradually proceeding, ATS problems outside of the medical field were still being attributed to the *specific groups* of users, whereas busy and healthy office workers, who did make use of ATS, were not accused. In order for a movement to establish strict control, such as total prohibition, other crucial factors that were supposed to be influential across society were required. What are considered here are those factors concerned with the responsibility for the causes of youth delinquency. Unlike today's treatment of youth, young people were not accused during that period; they were treated as victims.

Youth as victim of ATS problem

During 1949 and 1950, ATS began to be associated with a problem related to street children. Many of them were war orphans and the population was huge. Official statistics for 1948 showed that the number of orphans was 123,511 with only 12,202 of them (9.8%) being housed (Findings of the national research on orphans in February 1948 by the Ministry of Health and Welfare). Their problems were often attributed to ATS use (ND 1949, October 24). However, street children were not so much blamed for their ATS use but were rather seen as victims of adult hoodlums. For example, street children were exploited by those adults who offered them ATS in exchange for stealing things (Asahi 1949, November 22). The children could not purchase ATS themselves as it was controlled as a powerful drug.

The National Council of Youth Problems, made up of representatives from all prefectures and Ministries, sat on December 9 and 10, 1950 in order to discuss youth problems. One division of the Council discussed several causes of the problems, such as smoking, drinking, and ATS abuse. They insisted that education was needed to prevent young people from delinquency and that the smugglers who distributed ATS to the youth had to be controlled (NCYP 1951). The conference delegates demanded legal measures to control the production and distribution of ATS to help solve youth delinquency and related problems.

During the Council's discussion, the National Police Headquarters finally revealed that ATS produced by Toyama Chemical, a pharmaceutical company, had caused a "mass sexual assault incident" in Saitama Prefecture. One hundred young people were arrested over the incident and almost all of them had used ATS.[4] The National Police added that the company produced over 10 million ampoules of ATS quarterly, whereas its production quota by the Ministry was set at only 51,000 ampoules. However, the quota limit was just an administrative guideline and had no legal basis. As a result, Toyama Chemical was fined only a small amount of money. This was subsequently labeled as the Toyama Chemical Incident. Because of it, the Police Headquarters strongly stressed the need to pass legislative control of ATS production, including its distribution and sale, to prevent young people from committing delinquent acts (NCYP 1951: 98).

The Stimulant Control Law of 1951 and the prohibition of possession

Researchers in the 1980s insisted that the Stimulant Control Law of 1951 was established because of the problematizing of ATS effects that were highlighted when the abovementioned "mass sexual assault incident" was reported (Tamura 1982). The reason why the mass sexual assault incident later resurfaced will be discussed further below. However, as the discussion in the previous section shows, the cause of youth problems was not attributed to the effects of ATS, but to its production, distribution, and sale. In the discussion to establish the Law in the Diet, some psychopathologists testified that it was immoral people, i.e., psychopaths, who were likely to become addicted to ATS, and therefore it needed to control the distribution of ATS. The Stimulant Control Law was intended to control production and distribution in order to prevent people from using ATS and becoming addicted.

One significant aspect of the new law was the provision to prohibit the possession of ATS. If the main problem was thought to lie in the psychopathological effect of ATS, as misinterpreted today (Tamura 1982), the possession by users should also have been strictly controlled.

The law, however, was intended to maintain strict control over smugglers. A government official clarified the issue of possession in the Diet:

> Clause number fourteen prohibits possession. One of the most difficult matters that official control bodies are faced with is the lack of a legal basis for controlling possession. They cannot prosecute those who possess stimulant to sell in the town like Ueno.
>
> *(ND 1951, May 23:14–15)*

The Stimulant Control Law was passed in June 1951. It prohibited smugglers from possessing ATS, so that they, not the users, were arrested. However, ATS users also became the target of enforcement after 1954 (Sato 2020). After the Stimulant Control Law was established in 1951, with its sole purpose being to control production and distribution, ordinary people stopped using ATS and the majority of users shifted from being busy workers to *delinquent* youths, who had access to underground markets. This might be one of the reasons why the connection between youth problems and ATS use was often given so much attention, even after the law was established (Sato 2020).

Political factors and ATS in the 1950s

Just after the Stimulant Control Law came into force in July 1951, almost all newspaper reports on ATS dealt with issues of smuggling and of illegal production. Those reports on the enforcements reflected the very purpose of the new law. They also suggested that there still remained the youth problem of ATS use. However, by the middle of 1952, a new discourse related to ATS emerged. The new elements were, surprisingly, Koreans living in Japan and communists. A Korean village was reported to be the site for smuggling ATS and interestingly, one of the arrests made was revealed to be an ex-member of the Communist Party (Asahi 1952, August 25). The reason why the news at this time suddenly referred to "Korean village" and "communist" was because the relationship of these words had become significant in post-war Japanese society.[5] In the following, the political context of Japan in the 1940s and 1950s will be explained in detail, in order to fully understand the peculiar reference made to those terms suddenly emerging in ATS-related reports and media articles.

Context of the new words "Korean" and "communist"

After losing the war in 1945, Japan had been occupied by the General Headquarters/Supreme Commander for the Allied Powers (GHQ/SCAP) under the leadership of General Douglas MacArthur. During the period of occupation, armed forces of the Communist Party of China gained superiority over the forces of the Chinese Nationalist Party on the Chinese Mainland next to Japan. The People's Republic of China was founded by the Communist Party in 1949. General MacArthur demanded that the Japanese Communist Party should be designated illegal. Therefore, the Japanese Cabinet decided to purge all communists from official positions. As a result, over 10,000 people lost their jobs. In addition, the Korean War broke out in June 1950 and the menace of communism began to be talked about even in the Diet.[6] This trend continued further in 1952 when large anti-government demonstrations were organized on May Day in several big cities. The government officially announced that "foreign communist countries" were to blame for such disturbances (ND 1952, July 1). This was the context in which new terms such as "Korean village" and "communist" began to appear in ATS-related news around 1952 (Sato 2006: 339–341). The illegal production and smuggling of ATS began to be interpreted as being connected with the communists through the Korean villages.

Ill-founded connection and a missing discourse on ATS production

In the years following, ATS discourse containing the words "Korean" and/or "communist" was often found in texts that discussed matters related to ATS (Yomiuri, 1953, July 3). However, the connection between the menace of communism and the illegal activities related to ATS was still unclear and almost always ill-founded. The head of the crime prevention department of the Metropolitan Police insisted in the Diet in October 1953 that 71% of the arrests were Koreans and that the police forces were raiding Korean villages as their utmost priority (ND 1953, October 30). However, this might be seen as a self-fulfilling prophecy, because prioritized investigations in the Korean villages realized a high rate of arrests, with 38,514 being made in 1953. This accounted for the upward curve in the number of arrests for violations of the Stimulant Control Law in the 1950s (see Figure 25.1). The trend continued until 1954, when the connection between communism and ATS was more explicitly made, despite there being no evidence (see the next section for further elaboration).

It is noteworthy, though, that there was a discourse, which should have received more attention, to understand the reason why the Korean people illegally produced ATS. ATS production had become a way for Korean people to make a living during this period which was marked by disorganization and destitution after losing war. However, this discourse did not appear except in a few newspaper articles. One of them reported that ATS had been distributed to rural areas and that illegal manufacturers were mostly occupied by Korean workers as follows:

> The Metropolitan Police thought that because Korean people could no longer expect dealing with second-hand clothes, unrefined *sake*, and tobacco as the ways for making a living, they shifted to manufacturing Philopon, because it is relatively easy to produce it in a small space.
>
> *(Asahi 1953, August 17)*

Although the article finally used this situation of poverty as the reason for the implicit communist intervention, it is a very rare discourse in which the production of ATS is represented as a way of making a living.

While the ATS problems related to "production and distribution" were thought to be responsible for the Korean people during this period, the problem related to "use" was still connected to Japanese young people. However, the people responsible for the problem moved from street children to delinquent youths, who had access to underground markets. The problem therefore became viewed as being a family problem of delinquent youth. Newspapers sometimes reported that the criminal behavior of young sons was often caused because they could not afford to purchase ATS. For example, there was a report of a mother, who complained that her son never worked and spent all his parents' money on ATS (Yomiuri 1953, March 7). The lazy and violent life of a youth, who craved ATS, was also reported in a feature article, stating that the father could no longer stand his son's violence, and had killed him (Yomiuri 1953, April 12). These issues and anti-ATS movements against the Koreans merged into one social movement to "protect" young people from the harm of ATS, caused by the Koreans and communists (Sato 2020).

A new discourse on the ATS problem and a campaign to eradicate it

The year 1954 can be considered a milestone in the history of ATS control in Japan. As discussed above, while the Stimulant Control Law of 1951 was established to control illegal production and smuggling, ATS use was not its primary target. However, the Kyoko Incident in 1954, described below, and its subsequent interpretation, began to alter the meaning of ATS use.

Kyoko Incident 1954

In April 1954, an 11-year-old schoolgirl, Kyoko, was sexually assaulted and murdered in the restroom of a primary school in Tokyo. After the arrest of a suspect, the cause of the incident was finally interpreted as being his abnormal psychological and behavioral problems. Philopon was believed to be responsible, a view based on the psychopathologists' account of the incident. Contemporary newspaper articles began to denounce Philopon and stressed the importance of eradicating ATS, advocating that the drug made young people lose their minds and commit crimes (Asahi 1954, May 7).

Merger of the discourses on ATS and the campaign to eradicate it

The denunciation of Philopon indicated that the two discourses on ATS merged at this time – one that ATS caused psychopathic problems and the other that ATS was a substance used for a possible communist invasion. In June 1954, the Stimulant Control Law was amended, in part to impose heavier punishment for violations of the law. The amendment was not meant, at that time, to secure the eradication of addicts and users but instead smuggling and illegal production. In the discussion in the Diet, responding to a representative of the Diet who had argued that addicts should be arrested and treated as criminals, the chief of the Metropolitan Police replied that addicts should be treated as patients unless they committed crimes (ND 1954, May 20). However, the question asked by the representative nevertheless highlights that people had begun to think that addicts should be treated as criminals.

The objective of the amendment in 1954 was meant to be a fight against the Koreans and communists. In a Diet debate regarding this amendment, the law was also discussed in terms of revising the Immigration Law, including the enforced repatriation of Korean people (ND 1954, May 25). This reflected the public perception that Korean people living in Japan were smuggling ATS and that many of them were communists or communist sympathizers.

In October 1954, the government launched a campaign for the total eradication of ATS, which resulted in 55,664 people being arrested, as shown in Figure 25.1. It is still the largest number of arrests in the history of the Stimulant Control Law. The campaign was directed against assumed hostile forces, i.e., the Koreans. When it was launched, the head of the crime prevention department of the Metropolitan Police commented that the police would tighten control over the smugglers, even if the Koreans tried to interfere in their work (Asahi 1954, October 15).

Nationalist discourse on the ATS problem

The Metropolitan Police published their report of the campaign with a nationalistic tone in the following year: "In order to maintain the purity of Japanese ethnicity and, especially to attempt to raise young people ensuring our future generations, now is the time when we have to pluck up our courage to eradicate stimulants" (Metropolitan Police Headquarters 1955: 1). The latter part of the report referred explicitly to the Koreans:

> 70 percent of these smugglers, illegal producers and bootleggers consist of Korean people and they gnaw at the bodies and spirits of approximately one million and five hundred thousand of our fellow countrymen. At its most extreme we seem to be living with a large crowd of people going insane and becoming brutal offenders... Our fellow countrymen, especially young people, are the victims of Korean people pursuing their own interests...
>
> *(Metropolitan Police Headquarters 1955: 19–20)*

As these remarks show, the amendment and the resulting movements were undertaken to tighten control over smuggling and the illegal production of ATS that were interpreted as a way for the Koreans to profit. Interestingly, the police stopped referring to communism because they could not find any evidence of communist invasion. There were also numerous campaigns in many cities for the parents of young addicts. Young addicts were interpreted as the victims of the Koreans' misdeed (Sato forthcoming). Finally, the success resulted in a maximum number of arrests in 1954 and 1955 (Figure 25.1).

In the course of the campaign, the arrest of people who used ATS was interpreted as a means of finding the smugglers and producers. Many parents even wished that their children be arrested, saying that they had become violent and spent their money only on drugs. At the same time, the need for hospitalization and treatment of users began to be discussed publicly. This led to the amendment of the Mental Health Law in the following year, 1955, making it possible to hospitalize users.

After the 1954 campaign

After the campaign, the Stimulant Control Law was again amended in 1955 to impose a heavier punishment for possession and to control the raw materials of ATS. In the discussion for this amendment, North Koreans, instead of mere "Koreans", were especially mentioned as being responsible for the ATS problem in Japan (ND 1955, July 12) referring to its communist background.

The White Paper on Crime of 1960 summarized the ATS problem in the latter half of the 1950s. As it shows, the rate of prosecution dropped dramatically from 63.5% in 1955 to 37.1% in 1958, which meant that those cases viewed as in need of punishment had decreased sharply (Table 25.1). The White Paper also revealed that the proportion of categories of violation of

Table 25.1 Rate of prosecution (The White Paper on Crime 1960: 110)

Year	*Number of newly registered suspects*	*Rate of prosecution (%)*
1953	34,944	53.6
1954	53,352	63.6
1955	32,099	63.5
1956	6,645	58.0
1957	1,823	41.7
1958	609	37.1

the Stimulant Control Law had changed. In 1959, illegal ATS production led to only 1% of all arrests for violation of the law (The White Paper on Crime 1960: 111).

As discussed above, ATS problems in the 1950s were mainly argued as being a political problem in the post-war Japanese society. There were several discourses that gave rise to various meanings of the ATS problem; "ATS was a means to promote invasion by Koreans and communists", "ATS causes crime", "ATS makes young people commit crimes", "ATS makes people go insane", etc. Although these different discourses were used depending upon the specific situation, the discourse on invasion by the Koreans and communism often acted as the dominant story in constructing the view that ATS was a problem. Consequently, the ATS problem in the 1950s had begun to function as a political symbol operating to create boundaries between Japanese people and others.

The second wave of epidemic and crime syndicates

At the start of the 1960s, ATS was given little attention as a dangerous drug, compared to other narcotics, such as heroin. Narcotic addicts were reported to be observed in port cities such as Yokohama, and violent syndicates, called *Boryokudan*, were believed to be responsible for the prevalence of use. However, the number of narcotic-related arrests decreased around the middle of the 1960s as shown in Figure 25.1, because of the tightening control over narcotics based on an amendment of the Narcotics Control Law in 1963. Given this decline, ATS problems began to be reported again. An important distinction exists between small-scale violent syndicates and large-scale ones. The former was labeled a "violent syndicate", an independent organization within its local territory, whereas the latter was called a "crime syndicate", a united organization of multiple "violent syndicates" exerting its power over wide areas. Both types of syndicates were crucial to any investigation of ATS problems in the 1970s.

Until around the middle of the 1960s, ATS-related illegal activities were still mainly discussed within a discourse which associated their use with the notion of a Korean invasion (Asahi 1962, July 10). However, by the late 1960s, the role of violent syndicates began to be viewed as responsible for the ATS problems. This relationship became one of the key issues in ATS control. In order to understand the reason why this relationship began to appear, it is important to examine the process of democratization of Japanese society.

Japanese society and the "feudalistic" way

The violent syndicate and its problem had been debated in the ND since 1947 (ND 1947, July 4). The debate had continued for an unexpectedly extended period and finally ended in 1991 when a law to control the syndicates, the Act on Prevention of Unjust Acts by Organized Crime Group Members 1991, was established. The reason why the debate began just after the end of the war was because of the transformation of the Japanese social and political systems that occurred in the post-war period. Japanese society had been forced to change from a "feudal" type of society to a more democratic type because traditional Japanese ways of operating were viewed as the cause of the war.[7] Violent syndicates were perceived as symbols of the "feudalistic" society. For example, an editorial of Asahi Shinbun in July 1947 insisted that "feudalistic" violent groups were a menace to civil society and the reason for social disorder; "It is needless to say that the boss of violent syndicate is the typical example" of feudalism (Asahi 1947, July 1). Violent syndicates increased dramatically after the war because they amassed huge profits from underground markets that flourished because of shortages of food and daily goods. While the National Police Force exercised strict control over them from 1947 onward, and their numbers declined, nevertheless they regained their strength after 1952 with the repeal of the Regulations of Organizations Act, the end of the GHQ occupation, and the beginning of Japanese sovereignty.

In spite of police crackdowns, the syndicates gradually united to organize and transform their activities from profit-making using threats and violence to more subtle types of activities, including right-wing political campaigns to collect donations and/or fixing dissenting voices at stockholders' meetings. A number of companies made use of crime syndicates in labor disputes, such as that of the Mitsui Mi'ike Coal Mine in 1960, one of the most famous labor disputes in post-war Japan (Asahi 1960, March 30). In the course of such transformation, some of the syndicates began to use narcotic smuggling as a source of revenue.

The rise of crime syndicates and ATS smuggling: from the 1960s to the 1970s

Because of the strict enforcement of the law, the number of violent syndicates and their membership had gradually decreased, however crime syndicates were increasing in number (see Table 25.2). The percentage of members of crime syndicates rose from 25.9% in 1963 to 55.7% by 1972. The corresponding percentage of crime syndicates themselves also rose from 22.2% in 1963 to 71.1% by 1972. Crime syndicates developed widely, occupying the place that local violent syndicates had previously occupied.

Concerning the enforcement at that time, police forces adopted two methods. One was to intervene in the relationship between the boss and the henchman. To protect such a relationship was always thought to be a feudalistic duty for the henchman. "It was a very Japanese way of thinking" (Asahi 1965, March 2), and it was almost impossible to intervene. The second way was attempted to interrupt the flow of funds. This was successful, but also led to the rise and development of "wide-area" crime syndicates, who found profitable ways of smuggling illicit but top-selling items like guns and drugs. As such, smuggling ATS became an appealing business for crime syndicates.

ATS as a symbol of the outlaw economy

Control over crime syndicates and ATS were separately discussed at an official level during the 1950s. For example, the Metropolitan Police set up a countermeasure headquarters for violent syndicates and, separately, for ATS in November 1954 (Asahi 1954, November 10). However, the connection between them became more widely acknowledged in the 1970s. Crime syndicates had begun to manufacture ATS in the 1970s – thereby acquiring a source

Table 25.2 Number of violent and crime syndicates 1963–1972 (made by the author based on The White Paper on Police 1973)

Year		*1963*	*1964*	*1965*	*1966*	*1967*	*1968*	*1969*	*1970*	*1971*	*1972*
All violent and crime syndicates	groups	5216	4573	3944	3790	3752	3603	3500	3781	3214	2957
	members	184019	177035	156393	147171	142660	138288	139089	138056	129432	123044
Wide-area crime syndicates	groups	1158	1242	1157	1367	1364	2285	2251	2296	2214	2102
	%	22.2%	27.2%	29.3%	36.1%	36.4%	63.4%	64.3%	60.7%	68.9%	71.1%
	members	47604	49609	46732	52514	51631	69575	73161	74909	71884	68523
	%	25.9%	28.0%	29.9%	35.7%	36.2%	50.3%	52.6%	54.3%	55.5%	55.7%

of funding, while other sources were cut off from them by the police forces. The notion that "ATS was a source of funding for crime syndicates" only emerged in the early 1970s.

Interestingly though, the actual process of smuggling ATS was not occupied by the crime syndicates. People other than syndicate members were reported as smuggling ATS in the 1970s. A typical example was one of the most famous and largest smugglers of the 1970s, named Tamamoto. He was often referred to during this period (Asahi, 1973, January 19), even in the Diet (ND 1973, July 17). He was known as the general manager of the largest smuggling project in Japan. Although some crime syndicates cooperated with his distribution, he himself was not a member of the syndicates but an ex-CEO of a ballast digger company. Therefore, people other than syndicate members were reported on for smuggling and distributing ATS. Almost all of them confessed to their motivation to acquire funds for their business.

According to newspaper articles, ATS smuggling was not just a problem concerning crime syndicates but also encompassed ordinary people pursuing profits by illegal measures in the first half of the 1970s. Rather, illicit traffic by the crime syndicates was interpreted as just one kind of various illegal economic activities:

> One of the non-negligible aspects of the cases is that this type of illicit traffic has sometimes been treated as an object of investment or speculation by ordinary companies.
>
> *(Asahi 1973, January 24)*

Later, smuggling ATS became the principal fund-raising activity for crime syndicates. "Sixty-three percent of crime syndicate' funds come from ATS" (Asahi 1978, September 8). It has been suggested that eradicating ATS in the 1970s functioned as a way of excluding people from the illegal economy, and, as a result, such an illegal economy became more concentrated in the hands of the crime syndicates.

Here, there is a significant shift in the symbolic meaning of ATS. As the eradication of crime syndicates funds typically shows, ATS problems in the 1970s were always focused on and discussed as the illegal economic activities. On the contrary, ATS was the symbol of politics in the 1950s as mentioned earlier. Even the violent syndicates were problematized because of their symbolic meaning of "feudalism". However, as the post-war era ended, the symbolic meaning of the syndicates shifted from the political to the economic. ATS also became a commodity of illicit traffic outside the boundaries of respectable Japanese society. Therefore, the strict law enforcement against ATS-related activities can be interpreted as a symbolic effort to mark the boundaries of society, especially during the period of economic growth in the 1960s and the 1970s. Japan experienced a remarkable high economic growth from the late 1950s until the middle of the 1970s, also known as the "Japanese Miracle" (Johnson 1982). Thus, ATS became a symbol of the outlaw economy of Japanese society.

So far, the conversion of the symbolic meaning of ATS, from being a political tool in the 1950s to an economic tool in the 1970s, has been discussed. The following section will show another symbolic conversion, the change to the psychological.

Psychopathological features of ATS and their symbolic meaning

"After-effects" and "Stop using stimulant otherwise give up being human"

In this section, "after-effects" discourse is important in the conversion process of the symbolic meaning of ATS. As the crackdown on crime syndicates continued, a brutal incident occurred in June 1981, known as the Fukagawa Random Street Murder Incident. Four people were killed and two people injured on a street in the Fukagawa area in Tokyo. After the arrest, the offender confessed that he murdered people after he became frustrated when his job application for a sushi restaurant was rejected. However, almost all newspapers reported that the murders were caused by the effect of ATS, and linked to his career of using ATS. This soon became interpreted as the "after-effects" syndrome of ATS.

The "after-effects" discourse was originally developed by psychopathologists, but its application to ATS addiction was sometimes questioned, even by them (Kato 1981). After this incident, the media started to use the discourse when reporting on accounts of brutal crimes caused by ATS users, or even ex-users, regardless of whether the drug itself had been taken at the time of the incident. "After-effects" became a very convenient concept for any ATS problem. Similar ATS-related incidents were reported on during 1981 and 1982 that use of the drug always caused psychopathological crimes, i.e., unusual and abnormal crimes.

The Fukagawa incident attracted people's attention so much that it was even referred to in the Diet, which discussed an order that a person, when being deemed a threat to society, could be taken into custody even if he or she had not yet committed a crime (ND 1981, Oct 14). The order was called "*Foan shobun*" and the ATS addict was discussed as a typical case. ATS began to be treated as an evil substance, capable of provoking anyone, even those who did not have abnormal characters, to commit psychopathological and unusual crimes. The symbolic meaning of ATS had gone beyond the political symbol of the 1950s. Most significantly, this new formulation of ATS became linked to one of the most famous slogans against the drug in Japan: "Stop using stimulants otherwise give up being human".

Boundary of the society and ATS use

The very discourse of "ATS always causes psychopathological and unusual crimes" – which is underpinned by the "after-effects" concept – has been the key to understanding the control of ATS in Japan since the Fukagawa Random Street Murder. The slogan was repeatedly stated and, by the 1980s, had become common knowledge.[8]

Furthermore, legal action changed, based on a psychopathological idea. If ATS caused a psychopathological crime, the offender should be treated as a patient, not a criminal. The offender should be interpreted as losing control of oneself. However, a new category of ATS mental disorder, named "Anxiety-situational reaction type", was invented by the psychopathologist Akira Fukushima (1977). From the mid-1980s onward, it became a dominant pronouncement in ATS cases when judging criminal responsibility (Aoki 1996).[9] The invention of the new category consequently changed the interpretation of the criminals' capacity, to being located between taking full responsibility and temporary insanity. Thus, when ATS caused a psychopathological crime, the offender began to be treated as a criminal, not a patient.

However, several psychiatrists and law researchers began to criticize this diagnosis for two reasons (Aoki 1996; Nakatani 1999). One was because "Anxiety-situational reaction type" was just an idea, and therefore it was difficult to isolate it from other disorders within clinical experiences. A second is because Fukushima went beyond the role of a psychiatric examiner. As he insisted, this category was introduced on the assumption that the general public had been unconvinced if an ATS addict had received immunity from responsibility. He manifestly introduced moral judgment into the psychiatric test of ATS, and therefore, the category has been criticized as being against the psychiatrist's ethic.

Whether valid or not, this new category has frequently been adopted in psychiatric testing in ATS cases. It has introduced the moral judgment, that "ATS addicts should be punished", into medical or psychopathological discourse on ATS. With the slogan "Stop using stimulant, otherwise give up being human", ATS use draws the psychological and social boundary of society.

Conclusion: symbolic meaning of ATS and the reconstruction of Japanese society

This chapter has illustrated how the symbolic meaning of ATS has changed throughout different time-periods in post-war Japan. In the 1950s, ATS became a political symbol to create both political and ethnic boundaries. However, in the 1970s, when the Second Wave of ATS Epidemic hit, it became an economic symbol, marking the boundaries of sound and immaculate economic activities. During the 1980s, it was reformulated again, with a new symbolic meaning emerging, that established the psychological and behavioral boundaries between citizens and outsiders. Such boundaries were often rationalized using the newly introduced medical interpretation and its popularized notion. The dominant story and discourse of each period led to the construction of each framework in which ATS, and related activities, acquired their symbolic meanings. The frame therefore reflects each period.

Consequently, ATS cannot be viewed solely as a psychoactive substance, but instead must also be viewed as a symbolic device constructing different boundaries within Japanese society. Several discourses that constituted symbol and symbolic acts organized people's perceptions and feelings concerning drug use and drug-related problems. Medical knowledge often functions as a discursive device to support such activities. These are the keys to understanding Japanese drug policy. As Gusfield and other researchers discussed in their work (Reinarman and Levine 1995), rhetoric and other discursive devices always exert great influence in the process of constructing drug policies. Furthermore, this chapter has discussed that it is important for researchers to scrutinize the performative features of discourses on matters related to intoxicating substances. It is also noteworthy that scientific knowledge can sometimes play a key role in these processes.

Finally, we are left with one simple question: Why did Japanese society need those activities to create such boundaries? As the moralist and nationalist discourse typically suggests, Japanese society needed "others" to draw the contour of "ourselves". After losing WWII and the subsequent destruction of social order, Japanese society persevered in its effort to reconstruct itself and to restore its precious and respectful political, economic, and social order. In this process, ATS legislated as an illicit drug operated as a symbolic device, helping in different ways to construct boundaries around a notion of "otherness".

Notes

1 Figure 25.1 displays official statistics from the White Papers, published by the Ministry of Justice in Japan. It suggests that there are limitations in representing the prevalence of those drugs in terms of a "dark figure". National and school surveys based on representative, probabilistic samples with self-reported data on present and past drug use should be the ideal, but there is no such survey within Japan. The best option therefore is to use the official statistics of drug law violation.

2 Besides the contemporary documents, the author interviewed elderly veterans on post-war methamphetamine use and was informed that once the war was over, they took home with them methamphetamine which had been stockpiled in the Armed Forces and used the drug to remain awake while studying or working through the night. They claimed that ATS was a very useful medicine and did not cause any harm (Sato 2006, 2009a).

3 In March 1949, the Ministry of Health and Welfare announced that it had already designated ATS as a powerful drug, meaning that it could not be purchased by people under 14 years of age, nor could it be bought without a prescription. In the autumn of 1949, the Ministry also issued administrative guidelines (i.e., order without legal basis) and regulations to every pharmaceutical company to refrain from the production of ATS.

4 The "mass sexual assault incident" was reported in October 1951. Approximately 100 young people in Tsuchiai village in Saitama Prefecture were arrested on charges of rape, robbery, and other crimes (Sato 2009a, footnote 12). The incident was also discussed as a typical post-war delinquency in the National Diet (ND 1950, November 29).

5 It is important to note the reasons why many Korean people had been living in Japan. The most influential reason was that the Korean Empire was annexed to the Empire of Japan. Korea became a protectorate of Japan by the Japan-Korea Treaty of 1905, following the Japanese victory over the Russian Empire in the Russo-Japanese War (1904–1905). Following this treaty, Japan formally annexed Korea with the Japan-Korea Treaty of 1910. The annexation continued for 35 years, until September 1945, when the Governor-General of Korea surrendered to the Allied Powers. Under the rule of Japan, many Korean people migrated to work in Japan, resulting in the formation of Korean communities, especially in the large cities. Korean people were also commandeered to work on the Japanese mainland after the National Mobilization Law was established in 1938. The population of Korean people living in Japan in 1940 was approximately one million, two hundred and forty thousand (National census of 1940).

6 The Korean War was a war between a socialist state, North Korea, supported by China and the Soviet Union and a capitalist state, South Korea, supported by the United Nations, principally organized by the United States.

7 The meaning of the word "feudalistic ('*houkenteki*' in Japanese)" which was often used just after the WWII can be interpreted as "authoritarian paternalism supported by pseudo-familial relationship". Such a relationship had been typically observable between the Japanese Emperor and his Japanese people since the Meiji Restoration (1868). The Meiji Restoration is always referred to as the beginning of the age of modernization in Japan. Interestingly, Japanese modernization progressed based on the reestablished anti-modern relationship.

8 The pragmatic meaning and implication of the slogan "give up being human ('*Ningen yame masuka*' in Japanese)" in Japanese society might be different from its literal translation in English. The slogan actually means "stop using ATS otherwise you will become an abnormal existence and be excluded from our society". In Japanese society, there is a great deal of pressure to fit in with everybody else. If one is excluded from society, this would mean a sort of social death. The slogan precisely captures the Japanese attitude toward ATS and its users in the 1980s, insisting that they should not be hospitalized as patients, but excluded from the society. Consequently, they were treated as something similar to "internal others". A self-help institution called the DARC (Drug Addiction Rehabilitation Center) in Tokyo was established for "recovery" from ATS and other drug addiction in the middle of the 1980s against such social circumstances (Sato 2009b).

9 "Anxiety-situational reaction type" was a condition incorporating paranoid illusion. However, as Fukushima insisted (1977), such illusion can be comprehensible with the information about the situation in which the patient lives and the carrier of the patient, whereas the illusion of paranoid schizophrenia cannot be comprehensible. Such comprehensibility was interpreted as evidence that there still remained a reason.

References

Aoki, Norihiro, 1996, "Methamphetamine Dependence and Criminal Responsibility", *Kyoto Sangyo University Essays. Social Science Series*, 13, 107–144.

Ariyama, Noboru, 1941, "New Stimulant β-Phenylisopropylamin", *Psychiatria et Neulogia Japonica*, 45, 730–745.

Canguilhem, Georges, 1989, *The Normal and the Pathological*. New York: Zone Books.

Fukushima, Akira, 1977, *Studies in Criminal Psychology I*. Tokyo: Kongo Shuppan.

Gusfield, Joseph R., 1986, *Symbolic Crusade: Status Politics and the American Temperance Movement*, 2nd Edition. Champaign: University of Illinois Press.

Higo, Mitsuru, 1949, "Effects of awaking amine and histamine on respiration of brain", *Folia Pharmacologica Japonica*, 45, 94–95.

Hirano, Imao (1949) "Philopon Disaster: Modes of lives of postwar novelists", *Sekai Hyoron*, December 1949, 68–71.

Horimi, Taro (1947) "Additional Comment", *The Journal of the Japanese Society of Internal Medicine*, 36(5/6/7), 99.

Horimi, Taro, Yokota, Akira, Inoue, Ken, Soya, Kunio, and Egawa, Shoichi, 1940, "On the act of Hospitan on mental conditions", *Osaka Medical Journal*, 39, 827–837.

Iwata, Shigeo (1947) "Precaution for Continues Use of Philopon", *The Journal of the Japanese Society of Internal Medicine*, 36(5/6/7), 98–99.

Japan Medical Association (1950) "Editorial: Where does Philopon go", *The Journal of Japan Medical Association*, 24(2), 141.

Johnson, Chalmers, A., 1982, *MITI and the Japanese Miracle: The Growth of Industrial Policy, 1925–1975*, Stanford University Press.

Kasamatsu, Akira and Kurino, Ryu (1950) "Intoxication of Analeptic Amin", *The Journal of Japan Medical Association*, 24(2), 92–101.

Kato, Nobukatsu, 1981, "Flashback of Stimulant addict", *Japanese Journal of Clinical Psychiatry*, 10(10), 1203–1208.

Metropolitan Police Headquarters (1955) *The Harm and evil of Stimulants (Philopon) and the Measures to Cope with it*. Tokyo: Metropolitan Police Headquarters.

Miura, Kinnosuke, 1941, "On a stimulant made of ephedra to remove weariness", *Jikken Ihou*, 28, 7–12.

Motoyoshi, Isao (1949) "On the hallucinosis of Philopon", *Japan Medical Journal*, 1337,8–10.

Nagai, Nagayoshi (1893) "Results of the Research on the Contents of Chinese Medicine Maou", *Journal of the Pharmaceutical Society of Japan*, 139, 901–933.

Nakatani, Yoji, 1999, "Mental disorder related to drugs and alcohol and criminal responsibility", in Matsuishita, Masaaki ed., *Encyclopedia of Clinical Psychiatry vol.8*, 387–400.

Nakazaki, Toshizo and Mori, Hironobu (1947) "One Case of Acute Intoxication of Philopon", *The Journal of the Japanese Society of Internal Medicine*, 36(5/6/7), 98.

Oota, Yukito and Egami Fujio, 1944, "Studies in amine oxidases in the brain tissue", *Kagaku*, 14, 202–203.

Potter, Jonathan, 1996, "Discourse analysis and constructionist approaches: theoretical background", in Richardson, 1996, 125–140.

Potter, Jonathan, and Alexa Hepburn, 2008, "Discursive Constructionism", in James A. Holstein and Jaber F. Gubrium, eds., *Handbook of Constructionist Research*. New York: The Guilford Press, 275–293.

Potter, Jonathan, and Margaret Wetherell, 1987, *Discourse and Social Psychology: Beyond Attitudes and Behaviour*. London: SAGE.

Reinarman, Craig and Levine, Harry G., 1995, "The Crack attack: America's latest drug scare, 1986–1992", in Best, Joel, ed., *Images of Issues: Typifying Contemporary Social Problems*, Second Edition. New York: Aldine de Gruyter, 147–186.

Richardson, John T.E., ed., 1996, *Handbook of Qualitative Research Methods for Psychology and the Social Sciences*. Leicester: The British Psychological Society.

Saito, Masao, 1952, "Awaking amine and social significance of it (Review)", *Kyoto Medical Journal*, 3, 30–34.

Sato, Akihiko (2006) *Drug and Discourse: Methamphetamine in Japan*. Tokyo: Toshindo.

Sato, Akihiko (2009a) "Methamphetamine use in Japan after the Second World War: Transformation of narratives", *Contemporary Drug Problems*, 35 Winter/2008, 717–746.

Sato, Akihiko (2009b) "Japan's long association with amphetamines: What can we learn from their experiences?", in Pates, R. and Riley, D. eds. *Interventions for Amphetamine Misuse*. Oxford: Wiley-Blackwell, 147–158.

Sato, Akihiko (2020) "Methamphetamine users and the process of condemnation in Japan: Framing and influence" in Susanne MacGregor and Betsy Thom eds., *Risk and Substance Use*. Abingdon: Routledge.

Sato, Akihiko (forthcoming) "Family and Japanese drug policy", *The proceedings for "International Conference of 'Family Support Service for Adult Drug Addicts'" in Soochow University*, Taiwan, September 23 and 24, 2021.

Silverman, David, 2021, *Qualitative research 5th edition*. London: SAGE.

Suzuki, Sanzo, 1949, "Performers and Philopon", *The Journal of Japan Medical Association*, 23(7), 474.

Tadokoro, Sakutaro, 1998, *Narcotics and Stimulant: Various aspects of drug abuse*. Tokyo: Seiwa Shoten Publishers.

Tai, Hiroshi, Ezoe Tsutomu, Sato, Nobukatsu, 1955, "Biochemical studies in stimulant intoxication (1)(2)", *Psychiatria et Neulogia Japonica*, 57(3), 115–124, 124–130.

Tamura, Masayuki (1982) "Methamphetamine epidemic and law enforcement", *Japanese Journal of Sociological Criminology*, 7, 4–32.

Tanaka, Kiyoshi, 1943, "The influences of the awakening amine on the efficiency of mental and physical works", *Fukuoka Medical Journal*, 36(9), 840–849.

Tanaka, Kiyoshi, 1948, "Studies in individual difference of drug reaction: Awaking amine case", *Folia Pharmacologica Japonica*, 44(1), 85.

Tatetsu, Seijun, Goto, Akio and Fujiwara, Tsuyoshi, 1956, *Stimulant Intoxication*. Tokyo: Igaku Shoin.

The National Council of Youth Problem (NCYP) (1951) *Minutes of the National Council of Youth Problem*, December 9th and 10th, 1950.

Uchimaru, Tadahiko, 1942, "A biochemical experiment of Philopon", *Jikken Ihou*, 28, 873–876.

Yanagida, Tomoji and Itsumi, Tekmitsu, 1993, *Stimulant Addiction*. Tokyo: Chugai Igakusha.

Yoshino, Shigeru, 1943, "On Tachyphylaxie and vascular action of an awaking amine", *Folia Pharmacologica Japonica*, 38(2), 54.

The Minutes of the National Diet (ND)

1947, Plenary Session no.11, the 1st Lower House, July 4

1949, Committee of Health and Welfare no.7, the 5th Upper House, October 24

1949, Plenary Session no.18, the 6th Upper House, November 24

1950, Plenary Session no. 5, the 9th Upper House, November 29

1951, Committee of Health and Welfare no.6, the 10th Upper House, February 15

1951, Committee of Health and Welfare no.29, the 10th Upper House, May 23

1952, Plenary Session no.59, the 13th Lower House, July 1

1953, Committee of Health and Welfare no.1, the 17th Upper House, October 30

1954, Committee of Health and Welfare no.48, the 19th Lower House, May 20

1954, Committee of Health and Welfare no.49, the 19th Upper House, May 25

1955, Committee of Social Affairs and Labor no. 39, the 22nd Lower House, July 12

1973, Committee of Local Administration no.34, the 71st Lower House, June 22

1981, Committee of Law no.1, the 95th Lower House, October 14

Newspapers

Asahi Shinbun 1947, July 1, "Social justice and eradication of violent syndicate".

1949, March 29, "Philopon, designated as a powerful drug".

1949, November 22, "Fearful Philopon disaster".

1952, August 25, "Illicit manufacturing a hundred thousand of Philopon".

1954, May 7, "There still exists another Sakamaki".

1954, October 15, "To eradicate Philopon problems".

1954, November 10, "Metropolitan Police assume to perpetuate".

1960, March 30, "A crash between the external organization and the picket".

1962, July 10, "Members of an illicit manufacturing group were arrested en masse".

1965, March 2, "New stage to unearth violent syndicates".

1973, January 19, "An arrest warrant against Tamamoto".

1973, January 24, "Need to enforce stricter control on stimulants and narcotics".

1978, September 9, "Stimulant ruin the citizens".

Yomiuri Shinbun 1953, March 7, "Philopon-addicted son".

1953, April 12, "Father beat his Philopon-addicted son to death".

1953, July 3, "Crack down 6 illicit manufacturing sites of Philopon".

PART VII

Discourses shaping intoxication and people who use intoxicants

26

RISK, INTOXICATION AND DEATH

Contemporary media framing of drug-related deaths

Susanne MacGregor and Betsy Thom

Introduction

Concern about the issue of intoxication and death from substance use has moved through various phases and, associated with this, perceptions of problems and solutions have also changed. In the UK in the 1970s, deaths from barbiturate use and multiple drug misuse were identified as a problem; in the 1980s, heroin overdose became more prominent. In the 1990s, the focus was on ecstasy deaths then, in the early twenty-first century, binge drinking became a key issue with worries about 'out of control' intoxication, especially among young people in city centres, and early death due to liver cirrhosis. In the past two decades, rising attention has been given to drug-related deaths (DRDs) with prescribed opioids and then illicit fentanyl being identified as major concerns.

Debate has focused on the risks associated with the consumption of psychoactive substances, with overdose and death being the ultimate risk. Intoxicating substances are linked with a number of dimensions of danger, including overdose, psychological dependence, unintended injury, violence, acute or chronic mental or physical illness, and death from chronic illness. These dimensions of danger are related, in turn, to mode, pattern and context of use and who is using (including one's developmental stage, physical and mental health) (Room and Lubman, 2010).

Intoxication as a form of danger can be acute or chronic. Acute intoxication tends to be the headline event but chronic intoxication also contributes to outcomes. Yet another effect of intoxication is the pleasurable effect of altered consciousness, which, indeed, is one of the purposes of using alcohol and drugs. The perceived positive effects of intoxication can also influence body functioning, for example, producing increased concentration or relaxation, or sexual pleasure (Hunt et al., 2007; Milhet et al., 2019; Teodorini et al., 2020).

Underlying these discussions are different understandings of the concept of 'risk'. However, how risk is understood in the public domain generally draws on people's fears (Reinarman, 1994). The 'rational choice' neo-liberal ideology underlying the 'risk society' approach to public health in contemporary Western societies assumes that each individual citizen will be able to assess their own risk, alter their behaviour accordingly and take responsibility for the outcomes of their decisions and actions (Beck, 1986; Lupton, 1993) – a view which

DOI: 10.4324/9780429058141-34

carries the implication that those who cannot operate in this way are non-citizens to be excluded or controlled. In practice, much public health advice involves addressing people's fears and focuses on the avoidance of risk.

The media provide a key means through which understanding of risk, the links between risk and behaviour and the adoption of 'appropriate' responses are reflected and disseminated. The differential attention given to selected deaths can present a distorted image of risk, hampering individuals' awareness and ability to calculate their own risk. In addition, risk is not evenly shared and is not solely under individual control. Social or collective behaviour also matters. And while public health debates tend to focus on 'evidence', in the field of policy, values are as important. Perspectives on DRDs are underpinned by implicit assumptions and values, such as what constitutes acceptable behaviour, who is a 'worthy' person, the nature of responsibility and blame for negative consequences.

Based on the recent phenomena of steeply rising numbers of drug-related and overdose deaths, this chapter analyses how these have been accompanied by various competing explanations. Drawing on the literature and our own research, we consider how DRDs have been framed in the media and how such media framing has impacted on public perceptions and policy responses. Explanations reviewed below in this chapter generally define the issue as a crisis and propose solutions. An overriding argument is of policy failure, with the number of deaths being seen as a key indicator. One set of explanations focuses on 'bad actors' such as drug dealers and organised crime, Big Pharma and associates such as lax-prescribing doctors and chemists, and new substances, especially illicitly produced fentanyl. Another set focuses on the characteristics of victims, such as an ageing cohort of entrenched illicit drug users left over from earlier heroin epidemics, and social responses to them, singling out the operation of stigma and social marginalisation, exclusion and isolation. Lack of services for this group is also seen as a contributory factor, linked to inadequate funding due to policy choices such as fiscal austerity or generally weak welfare regimes, and to ideological features deriving from prohibitionist policies which act against harm reduction measures such as access to naloxone or Safe Injecting Facilities. Other explanations identify more long-term social determinants, such as educational and income inequality, and spatial inequalities linked to the decline of employment opportunities in post-industrial societies – phenomena captured as 'diseases of despair' (Case and Deaton, 2015).

These varied explanations emerge clearly in research examining rises in DRDs in the USA, Canada, Australia, Sweden, Scotland and elsewhere, (for example Man et al., 2019, National-Academies-of-Sciences-Engineering-and-Medicine, 2019).

To contextualise our analysis of different explanations, we begin by presenting brief details of rising trends in DRDs in a range of countries. We then provide an overview of key themes relevant to our topic drawn from the literature, noting especially analyses of the media as a key player in shaping public and official perspectives and its role as a political platform. Finally, we present the findings of a small study of national and local print media coverage of DRDs in the UK.

Throughout the chapter, apart from where we quote directly from other sources, we use the term 'drug-related deaths' (DRDs). It is important to note, however, that across the literature and in media sources, a number of different terms are used to describe deaths where drugs were directly or indirectly associated with death. These terms include death from 'drug overdose' or 'opioid overdose', 'drug-related suicide', 'fatal drug-related poisoning', 'intentional' and 'unintentional' drug-related death. The differences between the terms are important, indicating the type of substance involved and intentionality, differences which are likely to affect how the death is framed by doctors, relatives or the media.

The issue of rising numbers of drug-related deaths

Rates of DRDs vary widely both across and within countries. Table 26.1 provides some examples of national estimates. Keeping in mind that the sources of information for these estimates may differ in many respects regarding how DRDs are defined and recorded, the date data were collected, how the information is gathered and how complete the data are, and cultural and policy differences, nevertheless, they provide a good indication of why the issue of DRDs may provoke greater concern in one country compared to another.

Rising rates of DRDs and perceptions of reasons why this is happening can be illustrated by looking at the USA, Canada and Europe, regions where there has been increasing concern and discussion on the topic.

In the USA, between May 2019 and May 2020, 81,230 Americans died of drug overdoses – the highest number of drug deaths ever recorded in a 12-month span (Centers-for-Disease-Control-and-Prevention, 2021). In Canada, there were at least 15,393 opioid-related deaths between January 2016 and December 2019 with the highest number of deaths occurring in 2018 (Canadian-Centre-on-Substance-Use-and-Addiction, 2020). In Europe, more than 7,000 DRDs are reported every year, equivalent to a mortality of circa 18 deaths per million population aged 15–64 years (Millar and McAuley, 2017, p. 2). However, there is considerable variation in the extent of DRDs within European countries: for instance, the rates reported in many of the northernmost European countries exceed 40 per million population, whereas in many southern European countries, there are fewer than ten DRDs per million per annum. Scotland now has the highest rate of drug deaths in Europe (National-Records-of-Scotland, 2020); 1,264 DRDs were registered in Scotland in 2019, 6% more than in 2018. This was the largest number ever recorded and more than double that of ten years earlier (545 in 2009).

Table 26.1 Examples of estimated DRDs by country and date

Country	*Date*	*National estimate per 1 million population age 15–64*
Portugal	2017	6.5
Italy	2018	8.6
Luxembourg	2018	9.4
Slovakia	2018	17.7
Germany	2018	23.6
Estonia	2018	46.0
Kenya	2016	48.9
Iran	2017	53.6
Russian Federation	2018	54.2
UK	2017	82.9
Finland	2017	83.9
N. Zealand	2016	88.5
Sweden	2017	92.8
Australia	2017	102.6
Canada	2018	179.8
USA	2017	314.5

Source: DATAUNODC https://dataunodc.un.org/data/drugs/Mortality accessed March 15th, 2021.

Among the factors proposed as contributing to the rise in DRDs, four stand out. First, increases or changing use of different substances – increases in opioid use, including prescription opioids and fentanyl (Gomes et al. 2018; Felbab-Brown et al., 2020), and a rise in cocaine-related deaths (Hedegaard et al., 2019; Hamilton and Eastwood, 2020, Hedegaard et al., 2020). Second, the role of social actors, in particular the activities of the pharmaceutical industry, and over-prescribing by doctors (Felbab-Brown et al., 2020). Third, it has been reported that, in some countries at least, an ageing, opiate-using cohort currently dominates demand for substance misuse services and this will continue into the future (ACMD, 2019, p. 8). Finally, the impact of social environmental conditions – specifically deprivation – has been reported as a key factor in relation to inter-country DRD rates (House-of-Commons-Scottish-Affairs-Committee, 2019; Peters et al., 2019; Allik et al., 2020; Hamilton and Eastwood, 2020). In some cases, several of these factors are seen to combine to increase the likelihood of DRDs. Peters et al. (2019), analysing data from the USA, identified that there is *not a single opioid overdose epidemic, rather multiple and overlapping ones*: a prescription opioid epidemic, a synthetic-prescription mixture epidemic, a heroin epidemic and an opioid overdose syndemic (consisting of all three of the above). Their study found that, in the USA, the *prescription-related epidemic* counties could be described as 'left behind' the rest of the nation. These communities were less populated, more remote, older and mostly white, with a history of drug abuse and were former farm or factory areas that had been in decline since the 1990s (Peters et al., 2019, pp. 28–29). By contrast, high heroin and opioid syndemic counties tended to be more urban, connected, diverse and in general more economically secure. So, they argue, it is primarily the prescription epidemic counties that exemplify the 'deaths of despair' narrative (Case and Deaton, 2015; Copeland et al., 2020). Similarly, analysing trends in DRDs between 2001 and 2018 in Scotland, Allik et al. (2020) commented that:

> High rates of mortality from alcohol, suicides and drugs, especially in the more deprived areas, can be better explained by theories emphasising marginalisation – lack of power (political and economic) opportunities and social support structures to overcome adverse life events. They speak of despair, of self-destructive behaviours that can have a direct effect on mortality through suicide or an indirect impact through substance abuse.
>
> *(Allik et al., 2020, p. 7 of 10)*

These explanatory themes emerge again when we look at how DRDs are framed in different social discourses.

Framing the problem and proposing solutions: competing paradigms

Adopting the approach found in the work of Carol Bacchi (Bacchi, 2012), we now consider how deaths from drugs are problematised. Expert accounts and common sense perceptions merge together in policy discussions and often utilise ideas of danger (MacGregor and Thom, 2020). Both approaches in contemporary societies build on assessments of risk profiles (Moore, 2018). A shared ambition is to reduce overdose risk. Ways of framing (Goffman, 1974) the issue of drug deaths are set within broader competing paradigms of 'prohibition' versus 'regulation' and of 'abstinence' versus 'harm reduction'.

Prohibitionist/abstinence arguments and related policies

Prohibitionist arguments and policies focus on views of the risk properties of substances. The schedules at both international and national levels are supposed to arrange drugs in a single hierarchy of dangerousness.

> There is a long history of psychoactive substances being regarded as dangerous and subsequently being banned or forbidden. Often the bans were introduced on substances new and unfamiliar to a society, which were viewed as more dangerous than substances which were well known and enculturated.
>
> *(Room and Lubman, 2010, p. 97)*

The recent dominant policy response to rising DRDs has concentrated on opioids and focused on controlling supply by reducing diversion of prescribed opioids and promoting appropriate opioid prescribing, as well as on improving the care of people with opioid use disorders, with, for example, new guidelines for clinical practice being issued in both the USA and Canada in 2016 and 2017, respectively (Gomes et al., 2018; Ballreich et al., 2020; John-Hopkins-Bloomberg-School-of-Public-Health, 2020). Since 2012, the perception has been that the illicit opioid market has become more toxic, especially due to the emergence of clandestinely manufactured fentanyl, leading to a sharp increase in opioid-related fatalities (Gomes et al., 2018). In this view, bad actors, illicit suppliers and dangerous substances are highlighted, especially illicit fentanyl, along with alcohol, cocaine and benzodiazepine.

Similarly, in the UK, the Conservative government – prior to the coronavirus pandemic – aimed to launch a new initiative to drive down DRDs and tackle addiction. New measures would be taken to tackle over-prescribing of opioids. The policies were based on the perception that substance misuse/addiction is a key driver of crime, can fuel mental health crises, prompt homelessness and lead to an early death (Conservative-Party, 2019).

Regulation/harm reduction arguments and related policies

Harm reduction approaches focus on risk profiles and aim to reduce the risks of use (Release, 2019). Attention is also paid to characteristics of the environment within which use takes place, the aim being to manage risk, especially to avoid death (Houborg and Asmussen, 2014). One aim of engagement and treatment is, over time, to discourage intoxication and replace this with stable or moderate substance use. Harms are seen as arising from policy itself, especially the illegal status of certain substances which leads to variations in the form and content of substances. Because of a lack of testing, users do not know what they are taking. Because of the need to avoid scrutiny, use is covert: such hiding away makes it difficult for others to intervene in the event of overdose.

An alternative set of perceptions and policy proposals have developed in parts of USA (Oregon) and Canada (Vancouver): responding to the crisis, Vancouver in 2020 voted to decriminalise street drugs (Winter, 2020). This would potentially put them in conflict with the federal government. The aim would be to remove the threat of criminal sanctions for possessing small amounts of street drugs for personal use within the city.

Arguments for harm reduction approaches are made by campaigning organisations like *Release* and *Scottish Drug Forum* in the UK. Noting that there have been local agreements between police and local agencies to allow front of house drug checking at festivals and clubs, Release argues that Drug Consumption Rooms (DCRs) are also a proven harm reduction response. So, Release concludes, 'The only reason they would not extend the same thinking to DCRs is likely because of the profile of those who would use this facility, namely poor, marginalised groups who have little access to support from anywhere else' (Eastwood, 2019).

Competing frames

Both of these competing frames utilise a concept of 'vulnerability' with risks being linked to polydrug use and social marginalisation, and overdose receiving particular attention. Distinctions are made between drug users, with some being seen as more worthy or deserving than others. These frames are conveyed into the public arena in multiple ways, especially through political statements and policy documents, organisational practices and research publications. The media is one important player and the following section focuses on the role of the media in framing and explaining DRDs.

The media as the key player and political platform

The shape of policy is the outcome of competition between alliances of actors – like experts, advocacy organisations, politicians – upholding or challenging established sets of arrangements (MacGregor, 2017). The main sites of struggle are within the institutions of the state itself and associated groups, like political parties, parliaments, civil service, and pressure groups and the mass media. The latter are an important set of players in their own right and they also provide the forums within which competing ideas and interests argue their case. Press, television and radio, along with social media, have influence at national and local levels. In this chapter, particular attention will be given to the role of the media in influencing the framing of the problem of drug deaths.

In a recent UK parliamentary report, Sharon Brand, an individual with lived experience of problem drug use who is now in recovery, is quoted as saying:

> The media have a huge part to play, with the language they use and how they portray people who use drugs. [...] The language and the images the media sometimes use are horrendous. They dehumanise people. They do not treat people as human beings; they treat them as less than that. That has been the case for a long time—since the war on drugs, I think.
>
> *(House-of-Commons-Scottish-Affairs-Committee, 2019, p. 52)*

There is currently a moral panic around DRDs. Stan Cohen introduced the concept of 'moral panic' to explain what happens when a condition or group of persons becomes defined as a threat to societal values and interests (Cohen, 1973, p. 9). When this happens, the issue is presented in a stereotypical fashion by the mass media, politicians comment on related moral principles and experts pronounce their diagnoses and solutions. Sometimes, nothing changes in spite of this flurry of concern but at other times perceptions are altered and policy change ensues (Cohen, 1973).

Much analysis of the media focuses on the way in which conventional hostile views of drugs and drug use have framed policy debates. Opinions stated in the press are taken as expressions of public opinion by politicians and, in turn, influence public opinion. Nick Davies commented, for example, that the *Daily Mail* (a key right-wing newspaper in the UK) is not so much a defender of the establishment as concerned principally to respond to and shape its readers' views (Davies, 2009). Malcolm Dean, like Davies, a respected investigative journalist, has commented that ministers adjust their policies on drugs and law and order to fit with what the tabloids want (Dean, 2012).

Studies of the role of the media have charted the media's role in framing and reframing the issues of drugs and DRDs in recent years. Observers have noted a turn towards a limited acceptance of harm reduction approaches.

The fear of drug deaths and a 'war on drugs' mind-set

David Altheida has analysed the role of the news media in promoting a public discourse of fear and shown how the mass media and public perceptions of social problems are inexorably linked: the mass media play a large role in shaping public agendas by influencing what people think about (Altheide, 1997). Altheida analysed the media forms and frames guiding the selection and presentation of reports emphasising fear (such as crime, drugs and violence) and observed that bad news always wins out over good news stories. He says:

> Frames are the focus, a parameter or boundary, for discussing a particular event. Frames focus on what will be discussed, how it will be discussed, and above all, *how it will not be discussed* … An example is treating illegal drug use as a 'public health issue' as opposed to a 'criminal justice issue'.
>
> *(Altheide, 1997, p. 651) (our italics)*

The mass media are part of a problem-generating machine geared to entertainment, voyeurism and the quick fix. The problem frame 'promotes a discourse of fear that may be defined as the pervasive communication, symbolic awareness and expectation that danger and risk are a central feature of the effective environment' (Altheide, 1997) p.648). In media culture, he argues, there is an absence of the ordinary (Altheide, 1997, p. 652) and the discourse involves attributing blame. The target of fear is socially constructed. Often, the persons used to inspire fear are members of the despised and powerless groups in society (Altheide, 1997, p. 663). In the USA from the 1980s onwards, fear merged with drugs, especially linking to crime and violence in 1994. Gangs and drugs were highlighted. Fear provides politicians with agendas, dramatic scripts and news media pronouncements of remedies to 'make us safe' (Altheide, 1997, p. 665).

In another study, Forsyth examined the representativeness of newspaper reports of deaths attributed to illegal drug use. He found that some drugs were more likely to be mentioned in newspaper stories concerning drug deaths than others. Atypical drug fatalities such as those involving teenage females or recreational drugs, especially ecstasy, received a disproportionate amount of press attention. He argued that it is the very unusual nature of some illegal drug deaths that renders them newsworthy. By focusing on certain drugs or certain types of deaths, the media oversimplify complicated issues (Forsyth, 2001).

Forsyth's account focused on Scotland and pointed out that in the late 1980s, fewer than ten deaths per annum were recorded as being as a result of drug dependence. This situation changed dramatically during the 1990s (Forsyth, 2001, p. 436). Forsyth observes that crucially a context of more drug deaths means more selective press reporting. His study looked at official data for the whole of the 1990s, identifying 2,255 toxicologically confirmed drug deaths and compared these data with a sample of newspaper reports. Seven-hundred fifty news reports concerned fatalities, 546 of which were all directly attributed to illicit drug use. His study found that a large proportion of these newspaper cases carried very little supplementary information about the circumstances of death, such as which drugs were involved (Forsyth, 2001, p. 440).

Scientific explanation of drug deaths highlights a complex pattern of poly-substance use. Forsyth's study found however that in news reports there was a stereotypical ecstasy death at first time use of only one pure MDMA pill – this type of occurrence was in fact very rare (Forsyth, 2001, p. 443). Forsyth concluded that there 'seems to be little correspondence between individual drug deaths reported in the newspapers and those recorded by the Registrar General for Scotland' (Forsyth, 2001, p. 444). Reporting of deaths in the news focused on events which were newsworthy. Forsyth concluded that there was 'a tendency for the press to devote more column inches of newsprint to deaths characterised by teenage, female, ecstasy use rather than to those of older, opioid/benzodiazepine using males which predominate in the toxicological statistics' (Forsyth 2001, p. 446).

The 2000s saw a proliferation of media reporting about an opioid epidemic in North America. Webster and colleagues conducted a qualitative thematic analysis of 826 articles in Canadian popular news media between 2000 and 2017 (Webster et al., 2020). These reports described an array of opioid-related harms, such as addiction, overdose and overdose mortality. The study found that patients tended to be dichotomised as either innocently following physicians' prescriptions or involved in drug-seeking as an aspect of lives characterised by addiction and street crime. Thus, they argue, the social construction of the opioid epidemic polarised individuals as good or bad. Stigmatising references were made to so-called addicts. Many articles used dramatic and sensational language. Efforts were made to identify which individuals or groups to blame, with criminality being a key theme. In the early period of the epidemic, explanations focused on the naivety of users and physicians. By 2012, media coverage clearly conveyed a sense of danger around prescription opioids. Later, concern was expressed about fentanyl. In these media accounts, very little light was shone on the associations between opioid use, mental illness, alcohol use and poverty. Members of higher status groups who became addicted, such as those who were white and middle class, were more often portrayed as innocent victims. This study supports the analysis made by Mendoza and colleagues, who contrasted the attention given to a surge in opioid overdose deaths among suburban and rural whites in the USA with the war on drugs of the 1980s and 1990s, when DRDs were framed as largely affecting urban Black and Latinx populations. They claim that community groups and policy makers have been much more sympathetic to the white and middle-class victims of this new epidemic (Mendoza et al., 2019).

The racial dimension in narratives has also been explored. Daniels and colleagues observed how discussions in mainstream news media altered during the opioid epidemic (Daniels et al. (2018). Their work focuses on depictions in television shows in the USA. They note that American drug policy has been driven by racism, evidenced by the fact that about half of people in the US federal prisons are there for drug offences. They too comment on the recent turn towards more sympathetic views on drug users, which concentrate less on racist notions of (Black) drug fiends, and more on seeing the white women – who are often now the focus of concern – as victims, based on assumptions about their supposed innocence. Conventionally, they say, 'active drugs users are routinely portrayed as risk-taking outsiders who should be actively excluded from society' (Daniels et al., 2018, p. 332). However, where white drug use is concerned in the US narratives, it is more often portrayed as a medical rather than a criminal problem.

Fraser and colleagues carried out research on newspaper coverage of drugs in Australia, focusing on accounts of the deaths of non-celebrities (Fraser et al., 2018). They found that the metaphors mobilised presented overdose as the natural result of the dangers of drugs and of the personal problems and characters of those affected. They found an absence of detail about the lives of those who had died from opioid overdose. The accounts supported common sense notions of overdose as fundamentally the effect of drug consumption, addiction and the criminality of consumers. Drugs fuel overdose but those affected somehow have within them the seeds of their own destruction.

The logic presented ran as follows: drugs are dangerous; they can lead to death, especially among those imperfect souls touched by mental illness, trauma or deprivation (Fraser et al. 2018, p. 32). This analysis of newspaper coverage of accidental death by overdose showed that it tends to anonymise victims and treat their deaths as part and parcel of their flawed, half-lived lives. Where death occurred, its significance was in the pain it caused to immediate family (Fraser et al., 2018, p. 34). They conclude that newspaper coverage supports existing discourses of addiction, which overwhelmingly present lives affected by it in singular terms as pathological, disorganised, harmful and tainted. They argue that 'until the lives of opioid consumers come to be considered grievable, the measures known to reduce overdose deaths may struggle to find public support' (Fraser et al., 2018, p. 18).

From an analysis of 1,735 articles published between 1990 and 2017, Jauffret-Roustide and Cailbault conclude that the public conversation leaves little room for drug users (Jauffret-Roustide and Cailbault, 2018). Their study focused on the issue of DCRs. Various studies have shown that DCRs diminish the rate of overdoses. Jauffret-Roustide and Cailbault looked at the context in which DCRs were debated in France; that is how the issue was framed. They looked at the relation between the local and the national levels and highlighted how current actions and discourses borrow from past controversies. For some time, DCRs were invisible in the media. Events then propelled the issue to the national stage. At the local level, opposition to DCRs focused on the threat perceived to local residents' well-being and quality of life: there was fear of attracting marginalised populations to their neighbourhood. The voices of drug users themselves were barely present in these debates. Drug users were discounted as they were assumed to be irrational, irresponsible and untrustworthy.

In the prohibitionist/war on drugs paradigm, chronic or hard drug users are seen as unable to operate rationally and thus for their own and the general public good should be subjected to controls through the criminal justice and public health systems. In the harm reduction approach, drug users are granted agency and seen as able to act together to protect themselves if placed in supportive conditions (Stimson, 1989, Rhodes, 2002). Adverse events (leading to DRD) are as much a result of social exclusion as of the toxicity of substances.

The turn to support for harm reduction and a regulation paradigm

The issue of DCRs also figured in Scottish debate (Atkinson et al., 2019). Atkinson and colleagues reviewed 174 articles, noting a rhetoric of abstinence and recovery underpinning arguments against DCRs. They conclude that attempts to introduce and gain public and political support for harm reduction responses through the news media face challenges within the context of prohibitionist UK drugs policy.

However, in their study, Atkinson et al. found also that while politically right-leaning and Scottish sources were more likely to portray proposals for DCRs negatively, a proportion of reports were supportive of the proposals.

Overall, they found that at this time a discourse of public health dominated over that of criminalisation, with proposals for a DCR being set within what was seen as a public health emergency. The focus was however very narrowly on the injecting event itself, with a lack of attention to the need for provision in housing, employment and welfare support. A discourse of urgency emphasised the need for policy change. The concept of vulnerability was again also employed, for example, with reference to the issue of an ageing population of people who used heroin.

So, it was the acute crisis of rising DRDs and overdoses which seemed to have allowed a turn towards increased acceptance of a harm reduction approach (increasingly referred to as a 'public health' approach in places like Scotland, Canada and the USA though one quite narrow in focusing on safe injecting alone). There had arisen, it seemed, a consensus that the problem was one of public injecting, drug use, HIV infections and DRDs among a specific group of individuals in the city centre of Glasgow. Around this, the old debates between harm reduction and abstinence revolved. Different actors drew on different statistics in differing ways to support their arguments. However, the voices and experiences of people who use drugs were absent and silenced, relative to the voices of experts, professionals and politicians. There was a lack of attention to the individual lives of the people who were using drugs. 'The news media and actors chose to draw on and prioritise statistical evidence and ignore individual stories and experiences' (Atkinson et al., 2019, p. 72).

A study of 54 English language Canadian newspapers found that the volume of coverage doubled in 2008 and quadrupled in 2016, linked to critical changes in Canadian drug problems and policies (Wild et al., 2019). Supervised drug consumption accounted for almost half of all newspaper coverage. These authors conclude that Canadian newspapers independently shaped public discourse, frequently characterising harm reduction positively and from a health perspective. However, while progressive, this move was limited as the debate was distorted by over concentration on supervised consumption which crowded out discussion of other harm reduction interventions and tools.

Similarly, Quan and colleagues explored how Canadians' perceptions of the opioid crisis developed over time, influenced by one newspaper's reporting over an 18-year period (Quan et al., 2020). Six-hundred fifty relevant articles were reviewed with peaks noted in 2009, 2012 and 2016. Responsibility for the epidemic was attributed to pharmaceutical companies, physicians and foreign countries. Of the 650 articles reviewed, 22.3% referred to general statements of risk as evidence to support their claims. The factors mentioned included the potency of fentanyl and other drugs mixed with opioids when sold illegally. Articles warned about the risk of overdose and mentioned ways to mitigate overdose deaths such as naloxone kits. The study found that over time from 2009 to 2018, the use of stigmatising language such as 'junkies' or 'addicts' declined with, especially from 2016 onwards, more use of terms like 'people who use drugs' or 'people who suffer from addiction'. 'The shift towards less stigmatizing use of language was closely interlinked with the framing of the opioid crisis as a public health rather than criminal issue' (Quan et al., 2020, page 5 of 11). However, there remained an emphasis on fear-based campaigns. Only 11.4% of all articles discussed secondary causes of the opioid crisis such as gaps in the healthcare system. The root causes of high-risk drug use such as social inequity, socio-economic disparities and unresolved trauma were mentioned even less often.

Collins et al. have also shown how conventional moralistic messaging around drug use stigmatises people who use drugs (Collins et al., 2018). In the context of the recent unprecedented North American opioid overdose crisis, they argue that it is important to shift moralistic messaging to its alternative of evidence-based harm reduction because of the impact of discourse on reinforcing stigma and the need to shift the discourse to allow alternative solutions to the problem of overdose deaths. Solutions favoured include the low threshold 'supervised injection facilities' termed 'overdose prevention sites' in British Columbia. The term 'overdose prevention sites' focuses attention on prevention in the context of a public health emergency and is deliberately preferred to the terms 'supervised injection facilities' or 'drug consumption rooms' – terminology which risks evoking moralistic interpretations. Related interventions which can also be promoted within this frame of 'overdose prevention' include syringe exchange schemes, naloxone distribution and opioid agonist therapy. Words matter when in the midst of a public health emergency.

A comparison of national and local news coverage in the UK

Influenced by the findings of prior research, we carried out a small study of media coverage of DRDs over a 12-month period in the UK. The aim was to compare national and local coverage of the issue to explore any differences between national and local levels.

It was decided to focus primarily on print media: for this analysis, we took a 12-month period, November 2018 to November 2019, and accessed newspapers analysable via *Factiva* at the British Library. We selected to focus on *Daily Mail*, *The Times* and *Sunday Times*, *The Bolton News*, *Manchester Evening News*, *Paisley Daily Express*, *Birmingham Mail* and *Birmingham Post*. The selection aimed at geographical spread and inclusion of local, regional and national newspapers. Choice of the *Daily Mail* and *Times* newspapers was deliberately to focus on those most likely to influence the current Westminster Conservative government, in power since 2010 (omitting the more liberal papers such as *The Guardian* and *Independent*). In addition, we looked in a preliminary way at *BBC online*, *STV online*, *HuffPost* (Huffington Post) and *The Irish News* online. Search terms were drugs/substance use/abuse/deaths.

A number of official reports were frequently cited from national bodies like Public Health England (PHE), Office for National Statistics (ONS), National Health Service (NHS) and Scottish government and from local government bodies as well as from think tanks like the Centre for Social Justice (CSJ) and issue-specific parliamentary groups like All Party Parliamentary Groups (APPGs) (Table 26.2).

National coverage of drug-related deaths

At national level, most coverage was analytic – detached and at a high level of abstraction. Coverage focused on issues and policy remedies, prompted by reports from reputable or influential bodies like ONS, PHE, CSJ or APPGs, demonstrating the role of experts and evidence in providing material for national coverage. Reports on individual deaths were rare. Where they were reported, they were of celebrities or the children of celebrities. Detailed stories about individuals were restricted to the unusual or exceptional.

Responsibility for the problem included blaming those affected but there were few profiles of the individuals involved: for example, no detail was provided on deaths in prisons, where it was said that prisoners were 'dropping like flies' (although it was pointed out that most had underlying health issues). The individuals who died were often seen as naïve, unhealthy or flawed, perhaps as the result of early trauma. Even so, chaotic users were seen as responsible – 'knowing the risks she still took it'. Danger was also seen to lie with 'dangerous substances', such as spice, Xanax or fentanyl, or with 'dangerous groups and people', especially illegal sellers and sources. Particular attention was paid to the 'new' – new drugs or the new dangerous space of the internet (Table 26.3)

Table 26.2 Themes and evidence sources in UK newspapers

Newspaper	*Number of items*	*Themes*	*Illustrative items*	*Evidence sources*
Daily Mail	176	Party policies Policy debate Role models Opioid Britain Addiction can affect people in all classes and ages Ease of access to drugs	*28.8.2019* Britain's drug disgrace – drug capital of Europe *12.9.2019* 'this was an individual who took drugs voluntarily and has succumbed to the side effects of those drugs accidentally' *12.11.2019* Role of prescriptions	PHE report APPG report Individual stories from elite or celebrity families Inquest reports CSJ reports
The Times and *Sunday Times*	463	Drug crisis Fear of US style epidemic Variety of substances and sources – online/festivals/dial up; cocaine, opioids, tranquillisers, skunk Policy debate in UK and in Scotland Who to blame – SNP? Purdue Pharma? Inequality? Deprivation? GP prescribing? Innovations – SIF? Medical cannabis? Drug testing? Variety of people affected – celebrities and families; MPs and families; musicians; rugby players; ordinary Scots teens	*30.12.2018* 'call for shooting galleries as fatalities rise' *24.2.2019* In depth story on hostel for homeless *7.4.2019* Since 2007 the annual number of opioids prescribed by GPs has risen by 10 million *20.4.2019* Four prisoners die after taking bad batch of spice *25.6.2019* 'Safe' rooms as response to substance abuse deaths *14.8.2019* Generation X most likely to die from drug overdose *4.10.2019* Rugby players die in Sri Lanka – 'innocent about narcotics' *17.10.2019* No progress in Drug Crisis after 550 more deaths	Investigative reports – Sunday Times Opioid Crisis series analysed a decade's worth of data NHS reports Obituaries Official statistics Inquest reports ONS reports PHE reports Expert opinions
The Bolton News and *Manchester Evening News*	103	Policy and practice role of local drug teams Easy access to drugs Effects and dangers of drugs Homelessness Toxic substances: Mixing cocaine and alcohol Fentanyl; painkillers Middle aged drug problem Role of black market	*5.1.2019* drug tragedy of bright and intelligent man *7.9.2019* tragic life and death of loving mum hooked on drugs from age 11 *11.12.2019* beaten stabbed and humiliated – the reality of life on the streets of Bolton *11.1.2019* tragedy of mother addicted to painkillers for 28 years *25.6.2019* tragedy of beautiful mum with painkiller addiction	Inquest reports PHE reports and local data ONS

Paisley Daily Express	51	Numbers of dead Rising rates SCF Characteristics of dead Key drugs Decriminalisation Homelessness Recovery	*17.1.2019* tragic case/recovery *19.9.2019* fresh moves to end drug-related deaths	Report to Health and Social Care Board Court cases
Birmingham Mail and *Birmingham Post*	96	Poverty MPs/policy rethink Policy reform -heroin prescribing Causes of death Deaths caused by irresponsible substance users Recovery Main substances Homelessness	*28.9.19* Driver high on drugs *23.10.19* Cocaine death/spiked drugs *2.5.19* Heroin and homeless death *17.10.19* Addict left girl friend to die in crash	Inquest reports Criminal cases Local data on drug deaths

Table 26.3 Illustrations of coverage in national newspapers

Newspaper	*Evidence*	*Policy references/ explanations*	*References to individuals*
Daily Mail	UK one in three of Europe's overdose deaths	cuts to treatment budgets by local authorities	
The Times	23 people a week die in Scotland from suspected overdose	Illicit online pharmacies Illegal unregulated purchases Adulterated substances 'Super strength' drugs Bad batch of spice Very inexperienced user	Two British rugby players – innocent about narcotics' – died in Sri Lanka after taking 'brown sugar' A young father overdosed on Valium he bought on the web; age 32 he had a successful career as a product manager. His addiction was fuelled from illicit online pharmacies
Sunday Times	Extensive investigation into Britain's opioid crisis	Tramadol and codeine obtained free from GPs Crack cocaine bought with money from sex work Value or not of naloxone – a hostel staff member has revived 15 people with naloxone and CPR	Sarah gang raped as a child in foster care – later became a sex worker – had 11 children – all taken into care at birth – found dead aged 30 in her hostel room as a result of an overdose of fentanyl and heroin

Local coverage of drugs issues and drug-related deaths

As at national level, local reports were often based on publications from ONS or PHE, which then prompted coverage of the issues and provided local data. Again, as at national level, the opioid crisis in the USA provided a template for a discussion of the drugs issue with commentaries on whether or not this epidemic could happen in the UK. The relatively extensive coverage of issues relating to substance use leads us to conclude that drug use and drug problems have become *normalised* in media discourse. Particularly notable was an assumption of *the normality of cocaine use,* with references to 'recreational cocaine use' even by officials and in court reports.

Along with the ordinariness of drug use – and thus it not being counted as newsworthy – was the theme of *unpredictability* which was deserving of comment. Unpredictability was seen to arise because of the context of illegality but also because of the inherent uncertainties in the drug market and the phenomenon of varied individual reactions – what kills one person might not have killed another. The theme of an ordinary person put into extraordinary circumstances because of drug use also figured where drug use could produce paranoia and extreme behaviour. So, at local level in the accounts, *unpredictability* and *fate and bad luck* were themes, along with occasional undertones of *unfairness.*

Special attention to the new is a notable feature at local level, as at national, with new dangers including that of combining substances (such as cocaine, alcohol, codeine, antidepressants and painkillers) – the mixing of legal and illegal substances was highlighted. There was a prominent discussion of *new* substances (such as fentanyl). There was also some attention to a *new* age group – the 'middle aged drug problem'.

Explanations at local level also pointed to naïve innocent users, for example, in the 'tragedy of beautiful mum with painkiller addiction' who had been prescribed tablets for a bad back and pains in her legs. This was an *unlucky and inexplicable* event: this combination of drugs might kill one person but not another – we 'can't say exactly why she died – she took an excess and combination of drugs'.

Inquest reports selected for coverage focused on the strange and sensational but also showed the complexity of the circumstances surrounding a drug death. Cause of death was rarely simply an overdose, though this did figure such as high levels of heroin 'well over the level which would prove fatal to even a repeat drug user' or combinations of substances – a 'fatal cocktail'. Other events and factors were also shown to have played their part, such as hanging, blood poisoning or sepsis.

The question underlying the local reports, as at national level, was how to account for these deaths and who to blame: and as at national level, the drug, the user and the seller all figured in these accounts. Risk-taking individuals who died were seen as ultimately responsible – they knew what they were doing but perhaps could not control themselves. So, these deaths were of flawed individuals. But, after death, some attempt would be made to recover a sense of them as individual human beings – for their sake but perhaps more so for the family. In Coroners' summings-up, there seemed to be an ethical concern to *respect* the living relatives and respect the dead: 'he was a person and it is important to recognise that there were times when he was successful'; 'it is clear to me that Tracy was a lovely lady'.

At local level, there was also some discussion of what services had done or not done: had drug services done enough to refer people to appropriate services or had emergency services, like police or fire, responded appropriately? The notion of trying to learn lessons from these sad cases featured.

There were also examples of 'recovery' stories where people had been able to 'turn their life around' (Table 26.4).

Table 26.4 Illustrations of coverage in local newspapers

Newspaper location	*Evidence*	*Policy references/explanations*	*References to individuals*
Bolton	Inquest reports	fluctuating strength and purity of heroin purchased illicitly Poly substance use Variety of substances – crack cocaine, diazepam, pregabalin, methadone Chronic drug use; long histories of drug use Criticism of local drug teams	ordinary people living at home with their families Woman addicted from a young age, had used intravenously previously, smoked 20 cigarettes a day, drank heavily, had chronic liver disease, COPD and Hep C *walking a tight rope every time she took drugs*
Manchester	Inquest reports Police reports	Mental illness – perhaps induced by drug-taking Physical effects of substances vary in different people	George, a devoted daddy, a family man, a true friend, age 25, working as a sales assistant – lived with his partner and baby. Death due to a heart attack or seizure – the level of cocaine taken – said the toxicologist – *was only what might normally be taken recreationally* A young mother died after drinking and taking drugs on a *rare night out* – death due to acute cardiac failure, partly caused by cocaine use. The toxicologist said her alcohol level was low and *her cocaine level recreational*
Birmingham	Official reports – number of people dying from drug use in the West Midlands at highest level since records began in 1993. 521 deaths in West Midlands in a three-year period. Inquest reports	Links to poverty MPs call for rethink on policy Local crime commissioner calls for heroin prescribing Homelessness	32 year old father of two children, died of a heart attack after taking cocaine with friends – the cocaine in his system was at an amount well below levels normally associated with fatalities – pathologist – he had pre-existing heart disease and this combined with a chest infection and cocaine use led to the heart attack – mother said – I think the cocaine was spiked and that killed him. Homeless man was 'a loving and caring man' whose life had simply spun *out of control*

Online and TV coverage of local events and action

Online articles are not as restricted in length as print media are. They respond to events quickly and immediately. For example, there were reports on seven suspected drug deaths in ten days in Belfast in November 2019. *BBC online* covered this story: a 'shocking cluster of deaths' is newsworthy.

Similarly, *The Irish News* covered this event, describing what was known about those who had died and linking to warnings issued by public health agencies. They also quoted political leaders who called for changes in policy and practice – more early intervention, easier access to harm reduction support, detox treatment and crisis response – and one who said, 'Behind those who have died are mothers, fathers, sons and daughters and we can no longer sit back and allow this to continue'.

In December 2019, *STV News* reported on a candlelight vigil being held in Glasgow for all those who died in DRDs in the past year. Around 800 wooden crosses had been planted in the garden of Springburn Parish Church to represent those who had died after taking narcotics since April. The church minister said that drug addiction must be treated as a public health emergency as he revealed that around a third of the 500 funerals he had conducted over the last five years were drugs-related. Campaigners aimed to break the stigma surrounding drug use, accept that deaths are happening, start a public conversation and see the links to homelessness.

The radical campaigning platform *HuffPost* reported on 'This Is How Austerity Is Exacerbating Dundee's Drugs Crisis' in November 2019. This was a collaboration between HuffPost UK and investigative journalism platform *The Ferret* and looked at the impact of the government's austerity policy in Scotland. The article reported on the death of a woman whose post-mortem revealed that she had taken etizolam, pregabalin and methadone. She left behind a seven-year-old daughter. She also became another one of the 400 DRDs in Dundee over the past decade.

The article quoted Ewan Gurr, a former drug user who established the city's first food bank and said that there are a myriad of reasons why people use crack and heroin, but it's widely acknowledged that deprivation is linked to drug use. This online article quoted from a report by the Dundee Drugs Commission, which said that poverty was one of the root causes of the city's drug crisis. The article also quoted from a former heroin user, co-founder of Recovery Dundee who said that:

> there's now three generations of families that have been unemployed. So you've got three generations of people that have been addicted, and then their grandchildren and children are now becoming addicted. I think that the impact of what happened 30 years ago is now showing and manifesting in so many different ways in communities like mine especially.

In summary

The type of reporting of drug deaths varies with the level of the targeted readership, that is, whether it is local to a town or city, regional or national. The degree of abstraction increases with distance. At local level, there is more detail on individual lives, often drawing on reports from Coroners Courts. Apart from discussions based on the detail of individual deaths, other coverage may consider policy proposals and build around reports from expert bodies.

Extensive in-depth reporting and use of quotations from people with living experience of drugs is rare in newsprint though found in television reporting. Online reports are willing to make links to austerity, poverty and deprivation and structural and cultural influences, whereas print media more often confine themselves to focusing on immediate behavioural choices.

Conclusion

In recent years, in parts of North America and Europe, debate on drug overdose and DRDs has become more nuanced and better informed. This has been brought about to a large extent by attention to a crisis of DRDs, informed by reports from public health bodies and expert commissions as well as by the sophisticated building of alliances between reformist pressure groups and health journalists and the use of committees and commissions to mobilise evidence and opinion. The role of relatives and friends of those who have died has also been influential in reducing stigma and revealing the 'grievable' human lives which lie behind bare statistics. This turn has been played out in the space of media coverage.

A constellation of players has come together to focus on the issue of drug deaths and in places these actions are bringing about a shift in perceptions and policies. A key role has been played by the accumulation of compelling evidence in reports by experts (Collins et al., 2018; Tsai et al., 2019; AMA OPIOID-TASK-FORCE, 2020; Lippold and Ali 2020; Institute-for-Clinical-and-Economic-Review, 2021) which is then mobilised in alliance with pressure groups of advocates, drug users and family members (Smith, 2021).

Change is evident in places such as Vancouver and Scotland. The Scottish government has established a Drugs Deaths Taskforce and the First Minister has become directly involved in the debate. A former drug user turned activist, Peter Krykant, raised the profile of the issue of Safe Consumption Rooms in Glasgow by taking the initiative to provide these himself with a mobile van. He parked his white van in the streets of Glasgow to give people a safe place to inject illegal drugs.

Through this direct action, media attention has focused on the issue and raised it higher on the political agenda. These actions combined with pressure from advocacy groups like *Anyone's Child* have added a different kind of expert evidence to the debate – derived from people with direct experience of drugs and drug deaths.

Policy and the law respond to people's fears. At the same time, fears are socially constructed, including through press reports. Societies are selective about what fears to focus on. Insofar as death occurs among the poorer and marginalised, they cause few ripples on public life and do not influence debate or lead to policy changes. These are, as Fraser et al. (2018) call them, 'ungrievable lives' with little significance for powerful decision makers. The issues which prompt attention are being at the top of international league tables or alarming rises in the number of deaths. A turn towards acceptance of a harm reduction approach seems to be emerging, with important support coming from police, with coverage of the issue in the media encouraging politicians to respond. However, the understandings of harm reduction are thin. The search seems often to be for a simple solution such as providing an overdose prevention site/SIF with much less attention to underlying longer-term causes of poor health or addressing the gaping holes in social and health support services.

References

ACMD 2019. *Ageing Cohort of Drug Users*. London: ACMD.

Allik, M., Brown, D., Dundas, R. & Leyland, A. H. 2020. Deaths of despair: case-specific mortality and socioeconomic inequalities among young men in Scotland. *International Journal of Equity in Health*, 19, 10.

Altheide, D. L. 1997. The news media, the problem frame and the production of fear. *The Sociological Quarterly,* 38, 647–668.

Atkinson, A. M., Mcauley, A., Trayner, K. M. A. & Sumnall, H. R. 2019. 'We are still obsessed by this idea of abstinence': A critical analysis of UK news media representations of proposals to introduce drug consumption rooms in Glasgow UK. *International Journal of Drug Policy,* 68, 62–74.

Bacchi, C. 2012`. Introducing the 'What's the Problem Represented to be?' approach. *In:* Bletsas, A. & Beasley, C. (eds.) *Engaging with Carol Bacchi,* pp. 21–24. Adelaide: University of Adelaide Press.

Ballreich, J., Mansour, O., Hu, E., Chingcuanco, F., Pollack, H., Dowdy, D. & Alexander, C. 2020. Modelling mitigation strategies to reduce opioid-related morbidity and mortality in the US. *JAMA Network Open,* 3(11), 14.

Beck, U. 1986. *Risk Society: Towards a New Modernity.* London: Sage.

Canadian-Centre-on-Substance-Use-and-Addiction 2020. Canadian Drug Summary. *Prescription Opioids.*

Case, A. & Deaton, A. 2015. Rising morbidity and mortality in midlife among white non-Hispanic Americans in the 21st century. *PNAS,* 112, 15078–15083.

Centers-For-Disease-Control-and-Prevention. 2021 February 22. Overdose deaths accelerating COVID-19: expanded prevention efforts needed. Melissa Watts (press release).

Cohen, S. 1973. *Folk Devils and Moral Panics.* St Albans: Paladin.

Collins, A. B., Bluthenthal, R. N., Boyd, J. & Mcneil, R. 2018. Harnessing the language of overdose prevention to advance evidence-based responses to the opioid crisis. *International Journal of Drug Policy,* 55, 77–79.

Conservative-Party 2019. Conservatives to launch new plan to tackle addiction. November 28 (press release).

Copeland, W. E., Gaydosh, L., Hill, S. N., Godwin, J., Harris, K. M., Costello, J. & Shannahan, L. 2020. Associations of despair with suicidality and substance misuse among young adults. *JAMA Network Open,* 12.

Daniels, J., Netherland, J. C. & Lyons, A. P. 2018. White women, US popular culture, and narratives of addiction. *Contemporary Drug Problems,* 45, 329–346.

Davies, N. 2009. *Flat Earth News.* London: Vintage Books.

Dean, M. 2012. *Democracy Under Attack: How the Media Distort Policy and Politics.* Bristol: Policy Press.

Eastwood, N. 2019. Drug related deaths – Playing politics while people die. *BMJ Opinion Online* [Online]. Accessed November 4.

Felbab-Brown, V., Caulkins, J. P., Graham, C., Humphreys, K., Pacula, R. L., Pardo, B., Reuter, P., Stein, B. D. & Wise, P. H. 2020. The opioid crisis in America: Domestic and international dimensions. *Foreign Policy and Global Economy & Development programs.* Washington, DC: Brookings.

Forsyth, A. J. M. 2001. Distorted? A quantitative exploration of drug fatality reports in the popular press. *International Journal of Drug Policy,* 12, 435–453.

Lippold, K. and Ali, B. 2020. Racial/ethnic differences in opioid – involved overdose deaths across metropolitan and non-metropolitan areas in the United States *Drugs and Alcohol Dependence,* Vol 212, July, 108059.

Fraser, S., Farrugia, A. & Dwyer, R. 2018. Grievable lives? Death by opioid overdose in Australian newspaper coverage *International Journal of Drug Policy,* 59, 28–35.

Goffman, E. 1974. *Frame Analysis: An Essay on the Organisation of Experience.* Cambridge, MA: Harvard University Press.

Gomes, T., Khuu, W., Martins, D., Tadrous, M., Mamdani, M. M., Paterson, J. M. & Juurlink, D. N. 2018. Contributions of prescribed and non-prescribed opioids to opioid related deaths: Population-based cohort study in Ontario, Canada. *BMJ,* 362, 29 August, 362k3207.

Hamilton, I. & Eastwood, N. 2020. Drug deaths in England and Wales rise for eighth consecutive year. *The Conversation UK* [Online]. Accessed October 14 2020.

Hedegaard, H., Bastian, B. A., Trinidad, J. P., Spencer, M. R. & Warner, M. 2019. Regional differences in the drugs most frequently involved in drug overdose deaths: United States, 2017. *National Vital Statistics Reports.* Washington, DC: U.S. Department of Health and Human Services.

Hedegaard, H., Miniño, A. M. & Warner, M. 2020. *Drug Overdose Deaths in the United States, 1999–2019.* Atlanta Georgia: Centers for Disease Control and Prevention.

Houborg, E. & Asmussen, F. 2014. Drug consumption rooms and the role of politics and governance in policy processes. *International Journal of Drug Policy,* 25, 972–977.

House-of-Commons-Scottish-Affairs-Committee 2019. *Problem Drug Use in Scotland*. London: HC 44 (4 November) House of Commons.
Hunt, G. P., Evans, K. & Kares, F. 2007. Drug use and meanings of risk and pleasure. *Journal of Youth Studies*, 10, 73–96.
Institute-for-Clinical-and-Economic-Review 2021. *Supervised Injection Facilities and Other Supervised Consumption Sites: Effectiveness and Value, Final Report*. New England: New England Comparative Effectiveness Public Advisory Council.
Jauffret-Roustide, M. & Cailbault, I. 2018. Drug consumptions rooms: Comparing times, spaces and actors in issues of social acceptability in French public debate. *International Journal of Drug Policy*, 56, 208–217.
John-Hopkins-Bloomberg-School-of-Public-Health 2020. *Saving Lives from Overdose during a Pandemic*. Bloomberg School of Public Health Baltimore.
Lupton, D. 1993. Risk as moral danger: The social and political functions of risk discourse in public health. *International Journal of Health Services*, 23, 425–435.
MacGregor, S. 2017. *The Politics of Drugs: Perceptions, Power and Politics*. London: Palgrave Macmillan.
MacGregor, S. & Thom, B. (eds) 2020. *Risk and Substance Use: Framing Dangerous People and Dangerous Places*. London and New York: Routledge.
Man, N., Chrzanowska, A., Dobbins, T., Degenhardt, L. & Peacock, A. 2019. *Trends in Drug Induced Deaths in Australia 1997–2018*. Sydney: National Drug and Alcohol Research Centre.
Mendoza, S., Rivera, A. S. & Hanson, H. B. 2019. Re-racialisation of addiction and the redistribution of blame in the white opioid epidemic. *Medical Anthropology Quarterly*, 33(2), 242–262.
Milhet, M., Shah, J., Madesclaire, T. & Gaissad, L. 2019. Chemsex experiences: narratives of pleasure. *Drugs and Alcohol Today*, 19, 11–22.
Millar, T. & McAuley, A. 2017. *EMCDDA Assessment of Drug-Induced Death Data and Contextual Information in Selected Countries Contract Number CT.15.IBS.0137.1.0*. Lisbon: EMCDDA.
Moore, D. 2018. Making alcohol and other drug realities: Introduction to a special issue. *Contemporary Drug Problems*, 45, 183–187.
National-Academies-of-Sciences-Engineering-and-Medicine 2019. *An Approach to Evaluate the Effects of Concomitant Prescribing of Opioids and Benzodiazepines on Veteran Deaths and Suicides*. Washington, DC: The National Academies Press.
National-Records-of-Scotland 2020. *Drug-Related deaths in Scotland in 2019*. Edinburgh: Scottish Government.
Opioid-Task-Force 2020. *Progress Report: Physicians' Progress toward Ending the Nation's Drug Overdose and Death Epidemic* (p. 7). Chicago: American Medical Association.
Peters, D. J., Monnat, S. M., Hochstetler, A. L. & Berg, M. T. 2019. The Opioid hydra: Understanding overdose mortality epidemics and syndemics across the Rural-Urban continuum. *Rural Sociology*, 0, 1–34.
Quan, A. M. L., Wilson, L. A., Mithani, S. S., Zhu, D. T., Bota, A. B. & Wilson, K. 2020. Reporting on the opioid crisis (2000–2018): Role of The Globe and Mail, a Canadian English-language newspaper in influencing public opinion. *Harm Reduction Journal*, 17, 11.
Reinarman, C. 1994. The social construction of drug scares. *In:* Adler P A & Adler P. (eds.) *Constructions of Deviance: Social Power, Context, and Interaction* (Chapter 15, pp. 155–165). Boston, MA: Wadsworth Publishing.
Release 2019. *Saving Lives: Best Practice Guidance on the Provision of Naloxone for People Who Might Experience or Witness an Opioid Overdose*. London: Release.
Rhodes, T. 2002. The 'risk environment': A framework for understanding and reducing drug-related harm. *International Journal of Drug Policy*, 13, 85–94.
Room, R. & Lubman, D. I. 2010. Politics and science in classifying the dangers of drugs. *Evidence Based Mental Health*, 13, 97–99.
Smith, A. 2021. 'A Slow Train Comin' – Changing attitudes on drug-related deaths. Available from: http://www.sdf.org.uk/a-slow-train-comin-changing-attitudes-on-drug-related-deaths/.
Stimson, G. V. 1989. Syringe-exchange programmes for injecting drug users. *AIDS*, 3, 253–260.
Teodorini, R. D., Rycroft, N. & Smith-Spark, J. H. 2020. The off-prescription use of Modafinil: An online survey of perceived risks and benefits. *PLoS ONE*, 15(2), e0227818.
Tsai, A. C., Kiang, M. V., Barnett, M. L., Beletsky, L., Keyes, K. M., Mcginty, E. E., Smith, L. R., Strathdee, S. A., Wakeman, S. E. & Venkataramani, A. S. 2019. Stigma as a fundamental hindrance to the United States opioid overdose crisis response. *PLoS Med*, 16, e1002969.

Webster, F., Rice, K. & Sud, A. 2020. A critical content analysis of media reporting on opioids: The social construction of an epidemic. *Social Science and Medicine,* 244, 9.
Wild, T. C., Koziel, J., Anderson-Baron, J., Hathaway, J., Mccurdy, A., Xu, X., Asbridge, M., Belle-Isle, L., Hathaway, A., Macpherson, D. & Hyshka, E. 2019. Media coverage of harm reduction 2000–2016: A content analysis of tone, topics and interventions in Canadian print news. *Drug and Alcohol Dependence,* 205, 10599–107599.
Winter, J. 2020. Vancouver plan to decriminalize street drugs sets up battle with Ottawa. *The Guardian,* 3 December 2020.

27

CLEARING THE AIR

Toxic healthism and cigarette(s) (smoke) as (in)toxicant(s)

Qian Hui Tan

'Toxic' as a new buzz word: geographies of toxicity

In the last few years, the word 'toxic' has been mobilised quite ubiquitously to denote an unsavoury mode of power dynamics in both academic and popular discourses. Such 'toxic' machinations of power operate on a variety of scales (on a macro scale, e.g. to critique settler-colonialism and on a meso/micro scale, e.g. toxic sexism/masculinities; see Cielemęcka and Asberg 2019). Taking this flurry of interest in the politics of 'toxicity' as a point of departure, I attempt to complicate bio-medicalist interpretations of (second-hand) smoking as necessarily toxic or intoxicating. In teasing out some of the key points I have gleaned from the literature on toxic and smoking geographies, I make a bold case for the ways in which healthism as a discursive and material practice is ultimately a toxic one.

As a human geographer by training, I suggest that it may be instructive to review a resurgence of research emphasis on toxic spaces within the discipline. I suggest that the burgeoning scholarship on the environmental geographies of toxicity and other closely associated ideas such as contagion and pollution are ostensibly relevant to a more specific phenomenon pertaining to the geographies of smoke and smoking intoxication. Consequently, I hope to synthesise these two discrete bodies of work in order to better inform a more robust conceptualisation of toxicity/intoxication vis-a-vis a healthist rhetoric on cigarette smoking. A geo-environmentalist perspective on the spatiality of toxicities does not entail intoxication per se. Nevertheless, I demonstrate that the key takeaways from this body of work are highly applicable to (second-hand) smoking, which is plugged into a 'new age of toxicity' (Walker 2011; i.e. 'the ubiquitous condition of chemically altered living-being'; Murphy 2017: 497).

Overall, I identify two general but pertinent points in the literature on toxic geographies. First, the dissipation of toxicants is highly uneven across space, which, in turn, perpetuates the asymmetrical power relations between different social groups. In modern toxicology, a scientific-technocratic definition of toxicity (and toxic risk) is based on specific quantities of allowable pollution, thereby determining the extent to which a substance might endanger living organisms. However, this is a deceptively simplistic view not just because it is often difficult to quantify toxic exposure but also because it may be difficult for the body to register it qualitatively (see later discussion on sensory perplexity). Moreover, the fetishisation of the wayward particle as the inherent (micro-)locus of toxicity would occlude the 'contours

DOI: 10.4324/9780429058141-35

of position and power' that shape who or what gets deemed as toxic on a much larger scale (Calvillo 2018; Fiske 2018: 394; Liboiron et al. 2018).

Unsurprising, (infra)structures have been put in place to 'neutralise' toxic bodies/entities and to shield the 'pure' and privileged from toxic exposure (Murphy 2004). Aside from calls to espouse environmental justice, Cielemęcka and Asberg (2019: 105) propound that everyone therefore is complicit in the material/discursive (re)production of toxicity within a consumerist/capitalist system. Correspondingly, an attunement to politics toxicity can illuminate the kinds of power relations that enable non-toxic lifestyles while extinguishing toxic ones (Liboiron et al. 2018).

Despite the installation of such (infra)structures, more individuals have come to realise that toxic pollutants/contaminants/waste cannot be bound in space. For Litvintseva (2019), there is therefore no spatial 'outside' for externalising toxic materials. If this is the case, then no entity can fully protect itself from being vulnerable to, neither can it be absolved from being responsible for toxic exposure. However, Cielemęcka and Asberg (2019: 105) have alluded to the conundrum that societies are in, that a colonialist-medicalist impulse to detox or purify every single sphere of one's existence in a bid to return to some idealised pristine state is also equally unviable.

Second, (feminist) environmental geographers and other social scientists have highlighted the importance of fixing the analytical gaze on the 'geography closest in'—that of embodiment. Scholars have insisted that the biochemical materiality of corporeality matters vis-a-vis a somatic-sensory awareness that is responsible for rendering toxins perceptible (or not, even) after a protracted period of exposure (Cielemęcka and Asberg 2019; Davies 2019; Mah and Wang 2019). For this reason, toxic effects and affects are mutually imbricated (e.g. with toxic smoke being smelled and felt), along with the corporeal as both a 'mechanism of toxic worlding and a toxic world unto itself' (Nading 2020: 211).

Notably, Senanayake's (2020: 1555) conceptualisation of 'sensuous perplexity' offers an invaluable insight into how bodily responses to toxicity can sometimes perpetuate 'uncertainty about what harms and what heals' while living in polluted locales. Accordingly, 'embodied witnessing' can be so much more ambivalent than what scientists and policy makers make it up to be. As a corollary, confusions about the health and ecological risks from toxic exposure are multiplied rather than mitigated through diverse and conflicted versions of somatic knowing (Senanayake 2020). Sensory perplexity therefore complicates a reductionist apprehension of toxicity by modern scientific knowledge. Having outlined the academic context whereby studies on toxic geographies are situated, the rest of this chapter proceeds to zoom in on the (in)toxic(ating) geographies of cigarette smoke/smoking.

The '(not-so-)toxic' geographies of smoking/smoke

Intoxication has been pathologised by bio-medicalist and public health institutions. After all, a subscription to a physiologically injurious act must be logically flawed and morally reprehensible (Hunt and Frank 2016). Just as how a bio-scientific model of toxicology strips environmental pollution of its complexity, a dominant public health approach bent on eradicating toxic-induced harm similarly fails to recognise other ways of theorising (in)toxication (see Bancroft 2009; Hutton 2020). Such a bio-medicalisation of cigarette smoking usually implies identifying and isolating its (psycho)active ingredient, i.e. nicotine. Nicotine is not exactly the most toxic component in cigarettes (compared to e.g. tar and carbon monoxide) but it is 'addictive' (i.e. connoting physical dependency) and is therefore intoxicating.

Besides the long-term smoking of regular cigarettes, other forms of nicotine self-poisoning include an excessive inhalation of the nicotine solution loaded in e-cigarette vaporisers (Hughes and Hendrickson 2019) or the copious use of nicotine replacement therapy patches (Woolf et al. 1996). Crucially, the construction of the smoker as a nicotine 'addict' reduces them into a Pavlovian automation lacking in volition (see Berridge 2003).

But what is perhaps most unique to this phenomenon (including cigars and weed which lie outside the ambit of this chapter) is that smokers are arguably not just (in)toxicating themselves. Rather, in spewing out noxious fumes, they are also jeopardising the health of other non-smokers who are reluctantly made to inhale second-hand smoke. Major health organisations have reported that there is 'no safe level of exposure to tobacco smoke' and there is a general scientific consensus that second-hand smoke can cause respiratory tract infections in non-smokers (Öberg et al. 2011; Barnett et al. 2016). Couching smoking/smoke in the language of risk/threat thereby justifies the draconian regulation of cigarette sale (packaging with gory pictures and no logo), purchase (minimum age for smoking) and consumption (public smoking bans).

I have previously argued (Tan 2013a; 2017) that smoking introduces an invasive sensory assault on non-consenting passive smokers akin to that of respiratory rape. Regardless of whether the sensory effluent generated by smokers is chock-full of carcinogens, the foul odour of second-hand smoke is all it takes to invoke a visceral response enough to 'subjectively justify the expulsion of the source' (Dennis 2016: 132). Simultaneously, Fiske (2018) reminds us that such embodied responses of revulsion do not necessarily provide evidentiary claims of a substance's toxicity. Yet, the smoker who carelessly leaves behind malodorous smoke/smell and cigarette butts in their wake is a 'quintessential polluter of space' (Marković 2019: 488) and a vector of toxicity (Tan 2013a; 2016d; 2017). In this case, the medicalisation of smoking works in tandem with a culturally inflected sensory citizenship to reify the smoker as a toxic(ating) presence overspilling their corporeal boundaries. Consequently, bio-medicalist and public health institutions might benefit from a more holistic appreciation of the 'cultural algorithms' (Bancroft 2020: 69) and sensual relations that smoking is caught up in it.

As mentioned earlier, the odorous and odiously toxic nature of second-hand smoke has shaped interventionist public health policies and spurred urban design projects at arresting its proliferation (Tan 2013a). Smoking bans in both indoor and outdoor public spaces have been progressively extended across many cities, such that smokers are increasingly only allowed to light up in designated smoking areas. For instance, a pilot project launched in 2013 touted Yishun as the first completely smoke-free residential neighbourhood/constituency in Singapore (where my research on smoking spaces was based; *The Straits Times* 2013a; 2013b). This entailed that smokers in Yishun would have to refrain from lighting up even in open air areas (selectively permitted elsewhere). Instead, they could only do so in about 50 dedicated smoking 'pavilions' dotted all over the neighbourhood (*The Straits Times* 2017; Figures 27.1–27.3).

Such sheltered 'pavilions' were three by three metres in size, partitioned on three sides and furnished with benches as well as a cigarette butt disposal bin (*The Straits Times* 2014a; 2014b). Consonant with the intention to enhance air quality (by eliminating aero-contagion/toxicity, Tan 2017) and curb the littering of butts, these smoking points were placed strategically at grass patches, away from housing units and thorough fare. This purportedly ground-up initiative was shored up by volunteer smoke-free ambassadors, private sponsors (for the construction of the smoking huts) as well as a collaboration with Health Promotion Board and National Environmental Agency.

Figures 27.1 Interior of a designated smoking point in Yishun, Singapore
Source: Author's own.

Smoking's shrinking geographies (see Collins and Procter 2011; i.e. a more censorious socio-spatial climate for smoking/smokers) may seem like a reasonable or rational development on first glance. Despite the existence of an ever-expanding public smoking ban (and the recent raise in the minimum age limit for smoking to 21), members of the public in Singapore are still calling for more stringent and punitive means to 'stub out' the '(in) toxic(ating)' habit (*The Straits Times* 2021a). After all, *The Straits Times* (2021a) has reported in an almost alarmist tone that '300 non-smokers die each year because of exposure to second-hand smoke', with 383 such deaths in 2016 (*The Straits Times* 2021d; without the proper citation of sources).

On closer inspection, however, socio-legal regulatory regimes that purport to 'protect' innocent non-smokers from toxic exposure to second-hand smoke are problematic on at least two fronts. First, such regimes are profoundly political and by extension, possibly steeped in toxic violence. Public health institutions and state agencies exercise what Foucault (1982) calls pastoral power, which gains its legitimacy from attending to 'the wellbeing and moral propriety of both individuals and communities' (Martin and Waring 2018: 1293). This justifies the (toxic) infantalisation of both smokers (as passive victims of Big Tobacco) *and non-smokers* (as passive victims incapable of moving away from second-hand smoke and hence, necessitating pastoral care). Additionally, pastoral power underscores an affectively charged pre-emptive governmentality that is bent on preventing future smoking-related mortality/morbidity in the present (Tan 2016b; 2016c).

Second, some of these regulatory policies are thoughtless at worst and ridden with discursive contradictions at best. The porous boundaries between the public and private domains

Figure 27.2 A designated smoking point in Yishun, Singapore
Source: Author's own.

imply that urban planners, policy makers and public health experts will have to consider how (a) traditional methods of spatially managing toxic smoke/smell via separation or distanciation, and/or containment are highly ineffective (see Tan 2017); and that (b) smoking prohibitions in one location merely divert the practice somewhere else. For Liboiron et al. (2018: 332), such traditional 'hallmarks of 20th-century pollution control' are anachronistic because they are erroneously premised on the possibility of 'material purity' or a non-toxic reality.

It is by now an acknowledged reality that comprehensive public smoking bans displace smokers into the domestic realm, thereby exposing vulnerable segments of the population, such as children, pregnant women and individuals with respiratory problems to second-hand smoke (Ho et al. 2010). Nonetheless, the impact of the recent COVID-19 restrictions on smoking practices in public and private places has been less commonly discussed. During a pandemic-induced 'circuit-breaker' (or lock-down) in Singapore, smokers were not permitted to leave their residential units just for a puff because smoking was classified as a non-essential activity. Smoking corners at outdoor eateries such as coffee shops and hawker centres

Figure 27.3 Inside a designated smoking point in Yishun, Singapore
Source: Author's own.

were closed (following a no dining-in policy), and all designated smoking points along Orchard Road (a retail belt downtown) were not in operation either (ibid). The scarcity of public smoking areas and work-from-home arrangements entailed that more were smoking within the confines of the home (as opposed to at the workplace). Correspondingly, complaints of incoming second-hand smoke from smoking neighbours rose during that time. Because of how cigarette smoke and smell disrespect spatial boundaries, shutting one's windows was not very helpful in keeping them out (Tan 2013a; *The Straits Times* 2020b).

Smoking at home is lawful; yet, smokers have been constantly advised by authority figures to smoke away from their windows, balconies and doors (*The Straits Times* 2020b). Contestations over clean (non-toxic) air space between smokers and non-smokers escalated during the last two years, to the extent that a formal ban on smoking at home near open windows was broached in Parliament (*The Straits Times* 2020d). A combination of soft (e.g. moral suasion) and hard (e.g. 'the big stick of enforcement') methods (*The Straits Times* 2020a) was mobilised by the state and other stakeholders to incite in smokers a sense of sensory civic responsibility/response-ability (Tan 2016d; Liboiron et al. 2018). While the proposed home smoking ban conceded to infringing on an individual's right to smoke in one's personal space, it had conveniently omitted the fact that that would invariably be subjecting the smoker's family members to the toxic sensory effluent instead. Discussions within popular and academic discourses that multiply agency/action among smokers and non-smokers are urgently needed. Set against the backdrop of a 'permanently polluted world' (Liboiron et al. 2018: 332), such discussions are also required to foreground the untenability of smoking away from non-smokers (indoors/outdoors) in a high-rise, densely built urban environment like Singapore. Following many other critical geographers working in the field of toxicity, I call for new 'ethical grammars' to be developed in the technical and aesthetic responses to living in a toxic world (Graeter 2020; Nading 2020, see also Liboiron et al. 2018).

While I have expounded on the perception of smokers as an intoxicated source of toxicity, there is still room for reappraising smoking as a not-so-(in)toxic(ating) lifestyle. This is especially the case since critical intoxication studies have begun to problematise the notion of (smoking) 'addiction' and 'intoxication'. The scope of 'intoxication' has been extended substantially to encompass less florid shifts in consciousness compared to, for instance, a more conspicuous manifestation of drunkenness from alcohol. Critical scholars have contended that there is a range of altered/intoxicated states of consciousness (Hunt and Frank 2016), some of which may even be integral to maintaining a semblance of normalcy. Bancroft terms this mode of maintenance 'functional intoxication' (2009: 147) vis-a-vis the judicious pharmacological use of intoxicants.

Keane (2020) has observed that smokers perform the persona of the 'addict' only in selected situations. For the most part, their rationally driven 'controlled loss of control' (Measham 2004) is designed to assist them with getting through the work day. Far from being enslaved to or debilitated by their nicotine 'addiction', such a calibrated mode of intoxication (Hunt and Frank 2016) serves as a means of self-actualisation. Self-actualisation is accomplished by an assertion of one's 'rights to pleasure, hedonism or escapism' (Riley et al. 2010: 37). Accordingly, on top of unpacking smoking's socio-cultural significance, scholars are paying more attention to the embodied, sensorial and affective registers that smoking (intoxication) can conjure up (see Tan 2012; Hunt and Frank 2016). The term 'chemosocialities', for instance, addresses the intersections between the social and the sensory-affective, with intoxication facilitating nonbiological modes of belonging (Shapiro and Kirksey 2017).

On another note, the rituals of cigarette smoking have evolved over the years, from hand-rolled, machine-rolled, to electronic cigarettes. This novel mode of '*smoking*' e-cigarettes/vaporisers, also known as vaping, has stirred up much debate on whether they are less (in)toxic(ating) for the self and other as compared to traditional cigarettes (see Marković 2021). Bell and Keane (2012) have put forth some incisive points on how the advent of e-cigarettes muddies the medical-discursive binary between 'good' and 'bad' nicotine as well as toxic and not-so-toxic fumes (vape is not entirely free from toxic aerosols, but it is supposedly an odourless mist). On the one hand, e-cigarettes have been perceived as a slightly safer alternative to combusting/smoking tobacco. They are supposedly safer because they rehabilitate the 'bad' nicotine in traditional cigarettes with 'good' therapeutic doses (sans some of the toxic chemicals in traditional cigarettes), not unlike those present in nicotine replacement patches and *Nicorette* chewing gum. On the other hand, e-cigarettes have been cast as the 'latest incarnation of the tobacco menace' (Bell and Keane 2014: 49).

Despite eliminating the production of carcinogenic acrid fumes and, in turn, a likely reduction of second-hand smoke-related diseases, the sale, purchase, possession and use of e-cigarettes (and their accessories) remain illegal in Singapore (since 2018, for various reasons, with one of them being a pre-emptive strike against a gateway to traditional smoking, see Bell and Keane 2014; *Today* 2019; *The Straits Times* 2021a; 2021b). The prohibition of e-cigarettes/e-smoking has not mitigated its upward trend, especially among youths. Rather, it has merely led to an illicit trade of e-cigarettes (even with regular hauls and seizures by the Health Sciences Authority, *The Straits Times* 2021d) and stealth vaping (*The Straits Times* 2021c; see also Marković 2019). In other words, the prohibition of e-cigarettes contributes minimally to a reduction in toxic exposure among non-smokers while exacerbating the marginalisation of e-smokers (e.g. driving them underground and branding them as criminals).

Detoxifying healthist discourses on intoxication?

I wish to clarify that I am by no means denying the voluminous epidemiological evidence pointing towards the slew of toxicants packed in cigarette smoke and how it undermines both the smoker and the passive smoker's physical well-being. However, in view of the salient points that I have teased out on the geographies of toxicity, I propound that healthism perpetuates the notion of health as an individualised moral imperative, and is hence a somewhat toxic enterprise, on both epistemological and empirical grounds. Health as an imperative is often inextricable from an overarching biopolitical governmentality that incites a neoliberal responsibilisation of the self. The performance of such a normative responsibility hinges on one's competency at being clean (i.e. detoxed) and healthful which, in turn, maintains the purity of one's surrounding air spaces. Healthism as a genre of toxic harm therefore operates by delineating the addicted abject smoking body as the symbolic other or constitutive outside of the rationally regulated non-smoker. Put another way, toxic healthism disrupts some practices (i.e. smoking) in order to reinforce others (i.e. the denormalisation of smoking; see also Liboiron et al. 2018: 335).

Additionally, the 'toxic' properties in healthism are derived from what Nixon (2011: 2) calls 'slow violence' in which 'delayed destruction' is dissipated across time and space such that it is occluded and 'typically not viewed as violence at all'. The subjugation of alternative cultural narratives of intoxication/intoxicants (usually because they are deemed as unscientific) reinforces the epistemic authority of biomedical and public health claims while inflicting epistemic violence on others.

Toxic violence can be unpacked via its two interrelated constituents, i.e. the intention to be brutal as well as the evidence of brutality (see Mukherjee et al. 2011). Smoking denormalisation programmes deliberately manufacture health/olfactory stigma against smokers so as to 'scare them straight' into quitting via gory images of bodies ravaged by carcinogens plastered on cigarette boxes (Thompson et al. 2009; Bell et al. 2010). Nevertheless, the questionable ethical implications of establishing smoking as a site of moral approbation in the name of public health tend to be swept under the carpet. Consequently, the emotional geographies of slow healthist violence, such as self-condemnation and guilt, are 'literally hidden into the tissues of subaltern [smoking] bodies' (Nixon 2011; Armiero and Fava 2016: 79; see also Mahtani 2014). Meanwhile, the brutality wielded at smokers is evident in apartheid-like urban architectures, from zoning (very few smoking areas relegated to the periphery of compounds or in secluded areas) to cloistering (closet like smoking enclosures or rooms; Tan 2016a). The marginalisation of smokers spatially reminds them of their social marginalisation, that they are a public health menace or liability to society, even as they are learning to be more considerate to non-smokers (Tan 2016d; 2017). The pervasiveness of healthist discourses has made it challenging to even extend a sympathetic critique of the smoker's plight (e.g. their socio-spatial exclusion and denigration) without stirring up a furore—of either speaking in favour of Big Tobacco or subverting commonsensical public health knowledge (see Bell and Dennis 2013)—because how could anyone be against health and detoxification?

Concluding thoughts

In this last subsection, I advocate for a diversification of not-so-toxic or not-so-healthist discourses on smoking. I am most inspired Berlant's (2007) ruminations on 'self-medication' (see also Valverde 1998 as a means of 'getting by'. I posit that this not-so-toxic slant acknowledges the sensorial perplexities if not the pleasures that are precipitated by a state of moderate intoxication. For example, this implies not glossing over the not-so-(in)toxic(ating) kinds of affective-sensuous smoking embodiment and spatialities that may be life-enhancing even as they are detrimental to one's physical health (Tan 2013b; see also Klein 1993).

Cigarette smoking is an example of a neoliberal consumerist practice that contradicts the neoliberalisation of self-responsibilisation. If a smoking 'epidemic' was conceived as a 'sickness of sovereignty' (Berlant 2007: 12), a 'disease of the will' (Valverde 1998) or a 'crisis of antiwill' (with antiwill gesturing towards a collective defined by its compulsions Williams 1991: 219), then healthist institutions may have been wilfully blind to how smoking is merely an understandable reaction to a stressful existence. Moreover, Berlant's (2007) 'slow death' points towards a modern capitalist condition whereby one is already gradually dying from work-related debility/dis-ease, rather than simply from first/second-hand smoke. Smoking, along with other 'spreading-out activities' or 'scandals of the appetite' like sex and eating are the only 'few spaces of controllable, reliable pleasure [that] people' have left (Berlant 2007: 757). Smoke breaks help with mindful exhalations that punctuate time, thereby getting one through an exhaustingly toxic work day/environment. A way forward in multiplying healthist discourses might be to not impute into smokers too much will or too little will. More often than not, smokers who are trying to 'get by' in life are not resisting the moral imperative of health (or non-toxicity). Neither are they cultural dupes lining the pockets of tobacco companies and/or heartless, intentional purveyors of toxic second-hand smoke.

As much as a politics of toxicity reproduces the (e.g. healthist and purist) status quo, it can also reconfigure some of these political relations in ways that contribute to better liveability. Liboiron et al. (2018) call the process of affecting and being affected in a permanently polluted world 'toxic worlding' (see also Langwick 2017; Nading 2020). In it, I imagine a space where (second-hand) smoke/smoking holds the potential for spurring ethical socio-spatial-sensual engagements among smokers and healthist institutions/non-smokers. These engagements would be less preoccupied with detoxifying/purifying/correcting institutions/individuals/ environments and more concerned with creative rearrangements or modifications that would lend themselves to a more harmonious co-existence between stakeholders or social groups. Meanwhile, a more humane and less toxic public health approach could begin with making space for more smoking options, such as e-cigarettes, having more designated smoking areas that are more spacious and accessible, among other more accommodative strategies.

References

Armiero, M. and Fava, A. (2016). Of humans, sheep, and dioxin: A history of contamination and transformation in Acerra, Italy. *Capitalism Nature Socialism*, *27*(2), 67–82.

Bancroft, A. (2009). *Drugs, intoxication and society*. Polity: London.

Bancroft, A. (2020). Illicit drugs and intoxication. In F. Hutton (ed.) *Cultures of intoxication*. Palgrave Macmillan: London, pp. 67–86.

Barnett, R. et al. (2016). *Smoking geographies: Space, place and tobacco*. John Wiley & Sons: London.

Bell, K. and Keane, H. (2012). Nicotine control: E-cigarettes, smoking and addiction. *International Journal of Drug Policy*, *23*(3), 242–247.

Bell, K. and Dennis, S. (2013). Towards a critical anthropology of smoking: Exploring the consequences of tobacco control. *Contemporary Drug Problems*, 40(1), 3–19.

Bell, K. and Keane, H. (2014). All gates lead to smoking: The 'gateway theory', e-cigarettes and the remaking of nicotine. *Social Science & Medicine*, *119*, 45–52.

Bell, K. et al. (2010). Smoking, stigma and tobacco 'denormalization': Further reflections on the use of stigma as a public health tool. *Social Science & Medicine*, *70*(6), 795–799.

Berlant, L. (2007). Slow death (sovereignty, obesity, lateral agency). *Critical Inquiry*, *33*(4), 754–780.

Berridge, V. (2003). Post-war smoking policy in the UK and the redefinition of public health. *Twentieth Century British History*, *14*(1), 61–82.

Calvillo, N. (2018). Political airs: From monitoring to attuned sensing air pollution. *Social Studies of Science*, *48*(3), 372–388.

Cielemecka, O. and Åsberg, C. (2019). Toxic embodiment and feminist environmental humanities introduction. *Environmental Humanities*, *11*(1), 101–107.

Collins, D. and Procter, A. (2011). Smoking's shrinking geographies. *Geography Compass*, *5*(12), 918–931.

Davies, T. (2019). Slow violence and toxic geographies: 'Out of sight' to whom? *Environment and Planning C: Politics and Space*, np.

Dennis, S. (2016). Forcing things together that are normally kept apart: Public health knowledge and smoking practice. *Social Analysis*, *60*(2), 116–132.

Fiske, A. (2018). Dirty hands: The toxic politics of denunciation. *Social Studies of Science*, *48*(3), 389–413.

Foucault, M. (1982). The subject and power. *Critical Inquiry*, *8*, 777–795.

Graeter, S. (2020). Infrastructural Incorporations: Toxic storage, corporate indemnity, and ethical deferral in Peru's neoextractive era. *American Anthropologist*, *122*(1), 21–36.

Ho, S. Y. et al. (2010). Comprehensive smoke-free legislation and displacement of smoking into the homes of young children in Hong Kong. *Tobacco Control*, *19*(2), 129–133.

Hughes, A. and Hendrickson, R. (2019). An epidemiologic and clinical description of e-cigarette toxicity. *Clinical toxicology*, *57*(4), 287–293.

Hunt, G. and Frank, V. (2016). Reflecting on intoxication. In T. Kolind, et al. (eds.) *The SAGE handbook of drug and alcohol studies*. SAGE: London, pp. 322–336.

Hutton, F. (2020). Cultures of intoxication: 'New' psychoactive substances. In F. Hutton (ed.) *Cultures of intoxication: Key issues and debates*. Palgrave Macmillan: London, pp. 87–110.

Keane, H. (2020). Smoking and intoxication: From control to the buzz. In F. Hutton (ed.) *Cultures of intoxication*, pp. 45–66. London: Palgrave Macmillan.

Klein, R. (1993). *Cigarettes are sublime*. Duke University Press: Durham.

Langwick S. (2017). A politics of habitability: plants, healing, and sovereignty in a toxic world. *Cultural Anthropology*, *33*(3), 415–443.

Liboiron, M. et al. (2018). Toxic politics: Acting in a permanently polluted world. *Social Studies of Science*, *48*(3), 331–349.

Litvintseva, S. (2019). Asbestos: Inside and outside, toxic and haptic. *Environmental Humanities*, *11*(1), 152–173.

Mah, A. and Wang, X. (2019). Accumulated injuries of environmental injustice: Living and working with petrochemical pollution in Nanjing, China. *Annals of the American Association of Geographers*, *109*(6), 1961–1977.

Mahtani, M. (2014). Toxic geographies: Absences in critical race thought and practice in social and cultural geography. *Social & Cultural Geography*, *15*(4), 359–367.

Marković, I. (2019). Out of place, out of time: towards a more-than-human rhythmanalysis of smoking. *Cultural Geographies*, *26*(4), 487–503.

Marković, I. (2021). Vaping like a chimney; skeuomorphic assemblages and post-smoking geographies. *Social & Cultural Geography*, *22*(3), 376–402.

Martin, G. and Waring, J. (2018). Realising governmentality: Pastoral power, governmental discourse and the (re) constitution of subjectivities. *The Sociological Review*, *66*(6), 1292–1308.

Measham, F. (2004). Play space: Historical and socio-cultural reflections on drugs, licensed leisure locations, commercialisation and control. *International Journal of Drug Policy*, *15*(5-6), 337–345.

Mukherjee, J. et al. (2011). Structural violence: A barrier to achieving the millennium development goals for women. *Journal of Women's Health*, *20*(4), 593–597.

Murphy, M. (2004). Uncertain exposures and the privilege of imperception: Activist scientists and race at the US Environmental Protection Agency. *Osiris*, *19*, 266–282.

Murphy, M. (2017). Alterlife and decolonial chemical relations. *Cultural Anthropology*, *32*(4): 494–503.

Nading, A. (2020). Living in a toxic world. *Annual Review of Anthropology*, *49*, 209–224.

Nixon, R. (2011). *Slow Violence and the environmentalism of the poor*. Harvard University Press: Cambridge.

Öberg, M. et al. (2011). Worldwide burden of disease from exposure to second-hand smoke: A retrospective analysis of data from 192 countries. *The Lancet*, *377*(9760), 139–146.

Riley, S. et al. (2010). The 'pleasure citizen' Analyzing partying as a form of social and political participation. *Young*, *18*(1), 33–54.

Senanayake, N. (2020). Tasting toxicity: Bodies, perplexity, and the fraught witnessing of environmental risk in Sri Lanka's dry zone. *Gender, Place & Culture*, *27*(11), 1555–1579.

Shapiro, N. and Kirksey, E. (2017). Chemo-ethnography: An introduction. *Cultural Anthropology*, *32*(4), 481–493.
Tan, Q. H. (2012). Towards an affective smoking geography. *Geography Compass*, *6*(9), 533–545.
Tan, Q. H. (2013a). Smell in the city: Smoking and olfactory politics. *Urban Studies*, *50*(1), 55–71.
Tan, Q. H. (2013b). Smoking spaces as enabling spaces of wellbeing. *Health & Place*, *24*, 173–182.
Tan, Q. H. (2016a). Feeling/filling closet smoking spaces: negotiating public–private spheres, traversing emotional terrains. *Asian Geographer*, *33*(1), 1–21.
Tan, Q. H. (2016b). Governing futures and saving young lives: Willful smoking temporalities and subjectivities. In B. Evans and J. Horton (eds.) *Play and recreation, health and wellbeing*. Springer Reference: Singapore, pp. 509–522.
Tan, Q. H. (2016c). Living fast and dangerously? Spatio-temporalities of happy and healthful smoking futures. *Singapore Journal of Tropical Geography*, *37*(1), 94–109.
Tan, Q. H. (2016d). Scent-orship and Scent-iments on the Scent-ual: The relational geographies of smoke/smell between smokers and non-smokers in Singapore. *The Senses and Society*, *11*(2), 177–198.
Tan, Q. H. (2017). Atmospheric affinities: Olfactory accounts of aero-pollution between smokers and non-smokers in Singapore. In K. Low and D. Kalekin-Fishman (eds.) *Senses in cities: Experiences of Urban settings*. Routledge: London, np.
The Straits Times (2013a). No smoking in Nee Soon South except at designated areas, 11 Jul.
The Straits Times (2013b). Clearing the air nationwide, 28 Jul.
The Straits Times (2014a). Launch of first community-led smoke-free zone at Nee Soon South, 5 Jan.
The Straits Times (2014b). Nee Soon South's smoke-free zone slow to catch on, Smokers puff away outside designated smoking areas, 8 Jan.
The Straits Times (2017). Nee Soon South estate to get 50 designated smoking points by end-2017.
The Straits Times (2020a). Second-hand smoke complaints in residential areas rise as more work from home due to Covid-19, 29 Aug.
The Straits Times (2020b). More complaints about noise and cigarette smoke during circuit breaker, 30 May.
The Straits Times (2020c). Getting riled up by neighbours' cigarette smoke, noise and litter during circuit breaker, 31 May.
The Straits Times (2020d). Parliament: Ban smoking near windows and on balconies in homes, says Louis Ng, 5 Oct.
The Straits Times (2021a). Time to do more to stub out smoking in Singapore, 3 Jan.
The Straits Times (2021b). Rise in vaping trend worrying, 28 Feb.
The Straits Times (2021c). Vaping on the rise in Singapore: Harder to thwart illicit trade as e-vaporisers are easier to hide, 28 Feb.
The Straits Times (2021d). HSA seizes biggest haul of over $2m worth of e-vaporisers, related components in Boon Lay, 25 Oct.
Today (2019). Why Singapore bans e-cigarettes, 31 Jan.
Thompson, L. et al. (2009). Scared straight? Fear-appeal anti-smoking campaigns, risk, self-efficacy and addiction. *Health, Risk & Society*, *11*(2), 181–196.
Valverde, M. (1998). *Diseases of the will: Alcohol and the dilemmas of freedom*. Cambridge University Press: Cambridge.
Walker, B. (2011). *Toxic archipelago: A history of industrial disease in Japan*. University of Washington Press: Seattle.
Williams, P. (1991). *The alchemy of race and rights*. Harvard University Press: Cambridge.
Woolf, A. et al. (1996). Self-poisoning among adults using multiple transdermal nicotine patches. *Journal of Toxicology: Clinical Toxicology*, *34*(6), 691–698.

28

FIGHTING INTOXICATION AND ADDICTION

International drug control as a self-perpetuating social system

Axel Klein

Faith-based agitation against "drugs" has been and continues to be a major contributor to the doctrine-like quality of control policies such as the indifference to poor efficacy or unintended consequence. At its core lies an obsession with a pathologised notion of the *drug* as a moralised inhuman agent (Weinberg, 2011) that is intoxicating, addictive, fluid and ubiquitous, and posing a global threat: the "world drug problem" (UNGASS). The measures taken in response comprise sets of practices and routine activities that have acquired some of the qualities of a "social system" (Luhmann, 2006). That means an interlocking set of UN Commissions and international treaties that require national governments to pursue control measures that are monitored by international agencies with technical assistance functions. There is a lively exchange of information inside the system, and a stringent policing of boundaries, as, for instance, with alcohol and tobacco, two intoxicating substances outside of the purview of the drug control agencies, but subject to very different forms of control regimes (i.e., they are legal) even though often consumed in conjunction. Finally, there are feedback loops, where the actual effect of the control measures is to exacerbate the risks that they were supposed to reduce.

In its current form, the system provides operating principles and a cover for the distribution of material and symbolic benefits and costs. The interlocking support of privileged beneficiaries, I argue, is exacerbating social harm-producing practices that have long de-coupled from the ostensible goals they claim to be striving for, such as public health, morality or safety. Run as a social system, the primary concern is not resolving the *world drug problem*, but to perpetuate itself, that is the drug control system. Solutions, be they reducing harms or redefining the problem by rescheduling a substance as medicine, need to be developed by "heretics" outside of the system.

The divine warning to prohibitionists

The Athenian playwright Euripides tells in *The Bacchae* how king Pentheus, having refused to welcome Dionysus into the city of Thebes, disguises himself in wig and skirts and steals into the woods after dark, to spy on the revelries of the wine god's drunken followers. From a lookout high in the branches of a tree, he watches the maenads lose themselves in ecstatic

 DOI: 10.4324/9780429058141-36

revelry. Suddenly discovered, he tries to flee, but a horde of women, including his wife and mother, run him down and in a frenzy, tear him limb from limb. Wine has the power of turning mild-mannered ladies of the court into raging amazons. Dizzying and dangerous, the sensations it produces are so compelling that night after night, the women defy law and propriety to drink and dance again (Euripides, 2003/410 BC).

Later, kings learn to be more accommodating and build a temple to Dionysus inside the city walls. Thus placated, the god, now all grace and benevolence, instructs them to mix their wine with water, and counsels moderation. Another poet has him caution: "Three *bowls do I mix for the temperate: one to health, which they empty first; the second to love and pleasure; the third to sleep. When this bowl is drunk up, wise guests go home*"[1] (Ebulus, 340 BC/2004). Protected by rituals and a refined culture of consumption, the Greeks came to value wine as the elixir that eases suffering, brings joy and lubricates social life. Policy makers today appear bent on repeating Pentheus' follies. Instead of building temples where the new intoxicants can be regulated and tamed, they have driven them into the criminal underworld that is haunted by the hungry ghosts of the addicted (Mate, 2018).

Drugs policy, I argue, is an anomaly that requires explanation. Its idealist premise of a "drug free world" has long been discredited as unachievable as illicit drug use persists even in tightly controlled authoritarian countries, the collateral damage is exacting with burgeoning populations of incarcerated drug offenders and violent drug trafficking groups, and policy alternatives are readily available. For decades, the Netherlands have demonstrated how the distribution of cannabis can be organised without suffering either rampant consumption increases or a mental health crisis.

The persistence of prohibition defies the assumption that policy formation in modern democracies tends to adjust to emerging empirical evidence and shifting social attitudes. For instance, the legal restrictions imposed on the basis of religion or race, prohibitions on divorce, abortion, extra-marital sexual relations or homosexuality have all been lifted over the past century in many parts of the world. Contrarily, the drug policy at the global level, in spite of some advances, remains by and large mired in a set of measures that were designed and imposed over a century ago. To explain such imperviousness to change, I suggest considering the mechanisms that have been established in pursuit of drug control as a *social system* that is dedicated to the simple overarching objective of self-preservation and expansion.

For our purposes, two aspects of systems theory are salient in understanding drug control. First, the observation of a difference as a common, defining feature of everything that is inside to determine what is system and what is environment. Second, there is the function of the feedback loop, which in mechanical or biological systems performs a self-corrective function to ensure stability or homeostasis (Bateson: 1971: 315). Herein lies the paradox, because the resolution of the problem would lead to the termination of the system established in response to it. An end to the "drug scourge" would also end drug control.

The ostensible goal of a "drug free world" as advertised by the United Nations Office of Drugs is instead harnessed to legitimate a series of activities by the state and often involving violence such as the arrest of drug "offenders", the seizure of goods and the eradication of crops, through the use of the enforcement capacity of the state (Keen & Andersson, 2018). Here, the over-reliance on policing measures within drug control, and lamented as a "dislocation" (UNODC, 2008) by senior system insiders, results in a dual paradox. The powers of law enforcement are overwhelmingly negative "Using violence, depriving people of their freedom" (Kotsko, 2012) and whatever the level of investment, cannot rebuild a community (Simon, 2007). Hence, other activities are required, with different players and investments, including school "education", the establishment of wards for addicts in mental hospitals and so on. Before long, the objective of achieving a drug-free world is replaced by a preoccupation with managing these operations.

In the meantime, drug market participants are adapting to these interventions. Rising violence and greater health risks are used to call for further expansion of the system. The erstwhile concern to procure the health and well-being of all mankind, as stated in the preamble of the 1961 Single Convention on Narcotic Drugs is replaced with a crusade against the consumers, distributors and makers of *drugs* that has no end point or final objective (Gregory, 2011).

The mobilisation of state-violence against designated sections of the citizenry leads inadvertently to the amplification of the very risks that early advocates for drug control first warned about. The substances themselves, now illicit drugs that are being produced clandestinely, without quality control or consumer protection are more dangerous. Just as significant is the impact on product strength as the "iron law of prohibition" leads to the displacement of low potency/value products (beer, opium) by high potency/value products (whisky, heroin) (Ciccarone, 2017).

And counterintuitively, interdictions assist the spread of consumption habits as drug suppliers open up new routes for their cargo, what is known in law enforcement as the "balloon effect". Along the new supply routes, drug traffickers pay local collaborators in kind, creating markets in places where none were before, something known as "spill-over" (Naranjo, 2010). Far from containing and reducing the drug problem, these ostensible displays of "control" have the effect of accelerating the spread and making the drug problem truly global.

Set up in the aftermath of the First World War, the global drug control system established a system of economic planning. It replaced market dynamics with committees of technical experts to determine the quantities of controlled drugs that national governments needed. Having survived the neo-liberal turn in the 1980s and 1990s, the drugs field remains an anomalous pocket of economic planning, and has been called a failure "because it is a socialist enterprise" (Friedmann, 1992).

State-led intervention in the function of drug markets has produced another transformative effect. The value of minor agricultural commodities (cannabis, coca, opium poppy) has been so inflated that they now comprise a significant portion of global trade. This artifice has helped in lifting the economic and policy significance of the entire field. Since all production and distribution are sub-contracted to criminal organisations, this *drugs* economy erodes the administrative and governance functions of a corruptible state and dislocates communities with unprecedented levels of violence. Since they are outside of the law and unable to resort to rational arbitration, all *drug* businesses, whether South American Cartels, or London street gangs, are left to settle their differences, increase their market share and protect themselves from law enforcement by using violence (Reuter, 2009; Thoumi, 2009). Once established, illicit drug economies also attract violent actors, organised crime or insurgent groups as security providers and regulators (Felbab-Brown, 2017).

As the consequences reverberate across society, the impact varies significantly between different communities. Vulnerable, voiceless minorities and marginal groups bear the brunt in terms of social deprivation, political repression and adverse public health. On the other side are the material benefits, social and political advantages accruing to small groups of professionals, policy makers and organised criminals. They have succeeded in constructing the "drug problem" as a "backlash issue" where the identify politics around race, class and gender intertwine and manifest in policy shifts around criminal sentencing, welfare reform and the war on drugs (Courtwright, 2010). In the US, advocates of the targeted repression of drug violations have managed to appeal to electoral majorities when combined with the systematic manipulation of the electoral system (Alexander 2010; McCoy 2019).[2]

In Europe, early opium adopters and heavy alcohol users such as Charles Baudelaire or Thomas de Quincey borrowed images from biblical sources when depicting passage from intoxication to addiction. (Jay, 2011). First the temptation of the pleasure promised by the drug lures the users into an intoxicated euphoria, from where he falls into the pit of dependence, a pharmacological take on the fall of man, while the cycle of recovery and relapse forms a kind of purgatory. For many problematic alcohol users, the attraction of Alcoholics Anonymous lay, inter alia, in the appeal to a Higher Power, which resonated strongly with a latent Christian experience. The recovering alcoholic in admitting the total "loss of control" makes "a decision to turn our will and our lives over to the care of God as we understood him" (Schneider, 2015). Central concepts of temptation, damnation and redemption have been excised from their religious context and given new currency in a secular setting. At its foundation lies the most powerful mythical construct of all, the drug, as the quasi-personified evil through that dual function of intoxication and addiction.

This moral dimension to the understanding of the problem is captured in the preamble to the Single Convention on Narcotic Drugs, the foundational treaty of the post-war control system which states that "addiction to narcotic drugs constitutes a serious evil for the individual and is fraught with social and economic danger to mankind" (INCB, 1972: 13).

The function of the UN drug control treaties has been compared to religious texts in their promulgation of abstinence from certain drugs in the way others forbid certain foods and activities (Cohen, 2003). Official communications by the International Narcotics Control Board (INCB), the Commission on Narcotic Drugs or the United Nations Office on Drugs and Crime, regularly affirm the main articles of faith – those drugs pose a threat to humanity, and that they can only be contained with international cooperation. With regular invocations of the *World Drug Problem*, these are rituals attempting to "create and maintain a particular culture, a particular set of assumptions by which experience is controlled" (Douglas, 1966: 143) and which belongs to the domain of the sacred.

From Christian condemnation to psychiatric evaluation

If religious heritage has been important in lending legitimacy and a cultural register of symbols, narratives and tropes, many religious organisations have long been calling for tougher controls. Arguably, these demands can be traced to the conflicted relationship that Christian churches have had with wine. It is the sacrament in Holy Communion and its cultivation was for long the economic mainstay of monastic orders. Yet, every wedding in Canaan where wine is a metaphor for the bounty of life is matched by condemnations of bibulous excess and licentious living.

No such ambiguity surrounds attitudes towards other psychoactive substances. Achieving altered states was a major component in the herbal remedies employed by traditional healers in medieval Europe, often women. Out of body experiences, shapeshifting and the sense of flying were attributed to the craft of witches and investigated by the Holy Office of the Inquisition. Opening offices in New Spain in 1571, the organisation saw to the systematic persecution of people consuming of coca, peyote, ayahuasca and San Pedro cactus, hallucinogens and stimulants that were embedded in the cultural and spiritual practice of newly subjugated indigenous populations (Escohotado, 2010).

Catholicism then does recognise how these substances can effectively open alternate realities. In pre-Hispanic American cultures, such experiences that are inadequately described by "intoxication", were employed for self-discovery or vision quest. Under the guidance of shamans, the transporting effect of mind-altering plants was conventionally used for healing the sick or resolving social tensions. Church leaders understood this as a rival source of spiritual authority and cosmic wisdom. Claiming a monopoly over all matters spiritual, the clerics integrated the substances of the New World into their binary moral prism. In the graphic and irrefutable language of biblical certainty, these plants are attributed to the devil, and the altered state they produce as an encounter with pure evil.[3]

In North America around that time, Evangelical Protestants found a different object to crusade against spiritous liquors (a technological development on wine). The clergyman and medical doctor, Benjamin Rush, who has been credited with the *discovery* of addiction (Levine, 1978) was one of many activists campaigning for the prohibition of all alcohol. An ever more sophisticated political movement with a focus on a single objective struck tactical alliances with suffragettes and racial supremacists to achieve electoral majorities (Okrent, 2010). Similar initiatives were taken up in Britain among "clergymen and upper-class reformers", before extending to other classes. Over time the position of the campaigners hardened from "temperance" to "tee-totalism" (Berridge, 2013) and the goal of moderation was abandoned as illusory.

The trend emerging at the turn of the nineteenth/twentieth century across North America and Europe displayed several common features. Addiction, a psycho-medical condition that had a causal agent, became an explanatory paradigm that could satisfy popular curiosity about problematic behaviours, while simultaneously engendering a scientific discourse. Experts from different fields began formulating a technical vocabulary (disease, alcoholism, dependence), devising therapeutic remedies (abstinence, psycho-social therapies, isolation) and staking out a new professional terrain (addiction science/therapy) that legitimised interventions and held promise of a cure (Jellinek, 1961).

Further in their efforts at restricting and directing the behaviour of individuals, movement leaders augmented their appeals from pulpit and broadsheet with the coercive powers of the state. In North America and Scandinavia, temperance activists took control of legislative assemblies to impose tough restrictions on alcohol sales at municipal, state and eventually national level (Okrent, 2010). Initially at least they were floated with popular support, as a policy from below. But very quickly, they became absorbed into the administrative practice of the fast-expanding modern state. Counterintuitively, it is in the US where the most wide-ranging governmental powers were appropriated, the most elaborate control agencies established and an ideology of selective abstinence is formulated. Incubated in the hothouse of American industrial modernity, the model has been vigorously exported and, a 100 years on, remains the model for global approaches to controlling drugs.

Alcohol prohibition, America's Great Experiment, so intimately interwoven with salient features of contemporary life like income taxes, organised crime and cocktails, is a rupture in the relationship between citizen and society at the dawn of the contemporary state. But it also marks a moment in the continual re-ordering of cultural values. At the core of prohibition lies the repudiation of any lingering notion that "intoxication", or what in antiquity was referred to as "divine madness", holds spiritual or cultural benefit. The desecration of intoxication resonates in the framing of contemporary medical discourse about alcohol that revolves almost exclusively around costs and risks (Babor et al., 2010). When benefits do find mention, they are *hedonic*, that is, unquantifiable, frivolous and morally suspect (Coveney & Bunton, 2003).

In accounting for regular drug use, experts shifted from a religious to a medical frame of reference. During the eighteenth century, the colonial authorities in Latin America were denouncing habitual coca use as a demonic practice. In the early twentieth century, cocainism, by contrast, is diagnosed as a "disease of the will" (O'Malley & Valverde, 2004) that requires correction by medical professionals from the emerging domains of psychiatry and psychotherapy.

From the 1920s onwards, the American Psychiatric Association has been providing guidance in identifying criteria and symptoms of different mental health conditions. The 1934 edition of the Standard Classified Nomenclature of Diseases for the first time mentions Drug Addiction. Refined over its subsequent iterations it has most recently been listed as "Substance Use Disorder", in edition IV of the Diagnostic and Statistical Manual of Mental Disorders of the American Psychiatric Association.[4]

A further notable shift occurs in the social response. Where nineteenth-century clerics prayed for the sinner's soul, today's medical practitioners are healing the patient's mind. Since the focus of medical professionals is the individual, the contributions of other professions are needed to suppress the illicit manufacture and distribution that make these substances available in the first place.

Cultural values and secular control in the modern state

The addict is not only self-destructive but, it is feared, also poses a risk to wider society. When riding the "high" (i.e., being intoxicated) his behaviour is unpredictable and potentially dangerous. Though expedient before battle, when alcohol and amphetamines are issued to make soldiers brave with "Dutch courage" (Kamienski, 2016), this poses a grave risk to public order, particularly where people work in industrial settings or have access to firearms and motor cars (Dingwall, 2006). Further, in his quest for drugs, the addict is no longer constrained by manners, morals or law. Drugs, then, pose as a paired risk: intoxication is believed to lower the threshold of violent behaviour, while the compulsive urge of addiction impairs rational control.

If the first sets a challenge to the most traditional functions of the state as monopolist of violence, the second poses an affront to civilisational values around liberty and the autonomy of the self.

The ideal on which contemporary democracies are built is that citizens enjoy a panoply of inalienable rights in return for which they comply with the law. Public order is no longer upheld today by terror and ignorance, but discipline and self-control exercised by the rational, self-governing individual over his/her self. A substance that clouds the faculty of reason or clarity of thought, therefore, threatens to subvert the social contract and comes to the attention of the authorities.

The first manifestations of drug control occurred in colonial settings where the laissez faire of the nineteenth century gives way to the uncompromising dirigisme of the modern state. In the appropriated lands of the American West and the overseas colonies the US acquired after the 1895 war of conquest with Spain, drug control for the first time intersects with political oppression, economic exploitation and cultural eradication. Restrictions on the sale of alcohol were imposed in the European colonies and coordinated by the Brussels Conference Act of 1890 simultaneously, addressing the fears of white settlers while lending a paternalistic appearance to naked imperial aggression unleashed by the "scramble of Africa" (Ambler, 1990). Since the governance structures of the colonial states were weak (McCoy, 2019), opportunities arose for clergymen to play dominant roles. They could combine secular functions with self-appointed custodianship for the moral well-being of the colonial subjects, including a check on "native" indulgences, be these the smoking of opium in the Philippines or ingesting peyote mushrooms among the Comanchees (Courtwright, 1982; Jay, 2019).

Colonial administration provided a platform for political agitation at intergovernmental level, ostensibly on behalf of the un-represented colonial peoples who by the consensus of the occupiers had not reached the political maturity to arrange their own affairs. Activists, many, perhaps most, with religious affiliations, took it upon themselves to protect the health and well-being of native populations. This required international cooperation eventuating in the 1912 International Opium Convention, where contracting states undertook to voluntarily scale back production and trade in opium and cocaine products. Initially, the newly formed bureaucratic agencies, such as the Permanent Central Opium Board (PCOB), were staffed by a fair quota of church men and women. Yet, after realising its objective and creating a global set of repressive controls, the force of religious activism was spent as temperance crusaders found their fervour being tempered by the tepid routines of secular bureaucracies (McAllister, 2000). Quite soon, moral exhortations and prayer were pushed aside by a new regime of criminal sanctions.

In parallel with the growth of an ostensibly rational administration, prohibition agents, police and customs officers became more aggressive and punitive (UNODC, 2008a). The evolving international regime not only prevented Dionysus from spreading the gospel of moderation, but it also blinded kings and rulers to seeing that it was their actions that were exacerbating the problems that they had set out to contain.

International drug control as a social system

Today's kings and their subjects, socialised by "education and prevention", luggage and body searches, sniffer dogs and dawn raids, television adverts and urine tests, are unaware of how surreptitiously drug control arrived in the early twentieth century. In the preceding era, government interest in the trade of tobacco, alcohol or coffee had focused solely on revenue generation. When governments first gathered to discuss the trade in opium at the behest of a Chinese state whose leaders worried about the drain on foreign exchange and the intrusion of foreign powers, they agreed to the strictures emanating from the 1913 Opium Convention on the assumption that these were voluntary (Pietschmann, 2007).

It is important to recall the different regulatory landscape at the time when across Europe heroin was sold openly as an analgesic, cocaine until 1903 added to the most famous of cordials, while saccharine was only available on prescription to protect sugar revenues and the clandestine merchandise of extensive and violent trafficking networks (Merki, 1998).

Tougher regulations restricting access to intoxicating substances when introduced during the First World War, in the UK, for example, by the Defence of the Realm Act, were motivated by concern over the war effort, not public health.[5] Yet by the mid-1920s, all opium and coca products were controlled in all the major countries, with a dedicated agency established under the United Nations predecessor, the League of Nations, to monitor compliance. The agreements were preceded neither by scientific evaluation nor parliamentary debate in any democratic nation. Instead, the requirement to "enact the necessary legislation without delay" to "accept and deposit", the ratifications of the Opium Convention were slipped into Article 295 of the Treaty of Versailles at the behest of the American delegation (Bewley-Taylor, 2001). For powers wishing to sign the treaty and formally put an end to the hostilities there was no negotiation. Virtually at the stroke of a pen, the first International Opium Convention gained near-universal adherence (UNODC, 2008b).

A fitting description for this transformation is autopoiesis, a notion borrowed from biochemical theory to capture the sudden arrival and circular self-production of the social system around the operational communication of information (Luhmann, 2006). Once created, the core function of the PCOB that was located within the newly established League of Nations was the gathering of data: on the quantity of drugs that are required for medical purposes, have been manufactured, imported/exported, seized and impounded.

Part of the process involves the medical authorities of signatory states to report their annual requirements of controlled medicines. The successor agency to the PCOB is the INCB, which scrutinises these and often requests clarifications or alterations, before granting authorisation. Significantly, the process is run solely to the reference criteria internally generated by operating procedures and takes no heed of the requirements that are external to the system. The system therefore is solely preoccupied with the potential diversion of controlled medicines from medical settings into recreational markets (for the so-called *abuse*) and has no concern for the needs of patients in Low and Middle Income Countries with no access to pain medication because of these control measures (Klein et al., 2020).

For drug control, the internal communication of reports is far more important than any consideration of the impact the reported actions are having on the external environment, including, with regard to access to controlled medicine, the criteria of patient care. Hence, the launch of annual reports by INCB and its sister agency the United Nations on Drugs and Crime (UNODC) are highlights of the ceremonial gathering by the Commission on Narcotic Drugs, a UN body with a membership of 54 member states. What the very name signifies is how the system establishes itself through the pivotal *observation* of a *difference* that distinguishes the system from the environment. Once that distinction has been made, the system continually reviews and evaluates all information to then determine what is inside the system and what isn't (Gershon, 2005). In our case, the crucial observation is the discovery, definition and problematisation of *drugs*.

The drug fetish at the core of the system

There have been suggestions that the term drug is an invented regulatory construct, and that in order to move forward in drug policy, it may have to be abandoned altogether (Seddon, 2016). It is worth recalling that until the late Victorian era, the word *drug* stood for substances and compounds that had therapeutic applications. Whether they were medicine or poison was a question of dosage (Porter, 1996). In contemporary discourse, the terms *drugs* and *problem* are almost synonymous. For the champions of the control system, the central question is not what a drug is, but what it allows the system to do.

The system has grown well beyond counting of drug events and extends its tentacles into a dazzling array of fields. A foundational text like the UNGASS 2016 Outcome Document provides guidance on activities ranging from curriculum development for primary schools to the pharmacological analysis of precursor chemicals to planning crop substitution for poppy farmers. What lends coherence to the activities of schoolteachers, pharmacists and agriculturists is that they are all directed *against* what in UN parlance is the *World Drug Problem*. The wide range of activities, the resources they require and, most spectacularly, the powers that have been appropriated by the state in order to pursue them depend upon a shared understanding of that menace.

It consists of two peculiar types of effect: it is psychoactive and physically overpowering (Sherrat, 1995), two more positive interpretations of the state of intoxications. And because this is perceived at least in parts, as pleasurable, consumption becomes habit forming. Often, they cause considerable physical discomfort, particularly, but by no means only, in the initial stages of use. Partly because of the gratification and pleasure received, if only momentarily, people continue using even in the face of adverse consequences. Consumption can spread so quickly in spite of efforts by the authorities, that it is often referred to, and paradoxically, as an epidemic. At both population levels as well as in the case of individual consumers, the relationship between user and drug has modified conventional subject/object relations. Drugs, then, have the quality of a non-human agent or *actant* (Gomart, 2002; Weinberg, 2011) a connection reaching back into the demonology and possession cults of a different era (Room, 2003).

Important aspects of the control system as it stands today were constructed in the Great Experiment of US alcohol prohibition, 1920–1933. Once the precedent had been set, alcoholism defined as a disease, and legislation and bureaucracies established, alcohol itself was no longer required. Instead, the class of *drugs* is continually expanded to more manageable substances, where there is no pushback by powerful industries. Today, alcohol does not form part of the *World Drug Problem*, associated health issues are under the mandate of the World Health Organization not the UNODC, and wine is served in the cafeteria of the UN Secretariat in Vienna.

More serious from the system perspective is the current tussle over the status of cannabis. Legal reforms in different countries in recognition of the plants' medicinal qualities, suggest that classification under the control system is provisional, until the evidence base changes. Reasonable as this proposition may appear, it underestimates the moral certitude that has been adopted by the system in justifying the draconian measures taken by governments against drug offenders – from capital punishment for traffickers to mass incarceration. Moreover, with hundreds of millions of aficionados on a fast-rising upward trend, cannabis constitutes the global drug that requires global cooperation through the drug control bureaucracies (Bewley-Taylor & Jelsma, 2014).

A redefinition of cannabis as medicine would reveal as inaccurate the position that has been held by key agencies over many decades. That would expose the system as fallible and subject to error. Moreover, integrating cannabis into the spectrum of freely available substances threatens to dissolve altogether the very difference on which the system is based. Developing good manufacturing standards, setting limits on THC content, refining licencing laws, age restrictions for the protection of minors, traffic guidance, etc., threaten to normalise the substance and to undermine the peculiarity on which the class is based.

Alongside the normalisation of cannabis are discussions that challenge the notion of intoxication and anti-social behaviour by distinguishing between the effects of different substances. In many cases, it is alcohol the non-drug that is most often associated with violence, while cannabis, MDMA and opiates render their consumers peaceful, harmonious and placid. It is equally apparent that addiction is no logical outcome of consumption, but of a complex set of variables. For many problematic users, using the drug is a symptom of other inter-connected challenges, including health problems that cannot be cured by conventional medicine (Klein & Potter, 2018). Further, extending the term "addiction" to a range of behaviours from exercise to internet gaming has further loosened its definitive power.

These discussions are avoided because drug control has used the ontological basis of *drugs as evil* to fend off mounting criticisms over the consequences of prohibition. The reaction is self-referential, pointing back to the erstwhile agreements to control and the purported need to protect the young and vulnerable. But this sidesteps the single most significant characteristic of the social system in action: the feedback loop, the way that resources are taken from the environment, transformed and send back to make significant changes in the environment.

Making drugs dangerous via the drug control feedback loop

To recall, in Europe the consumption levels of the principal substances under control were risible at the end of the First World War when the international system was formed. They were just as low in 1961, when the control functions were transferred to the United Nations and a new set of treaties came into force. Irrespective of official prohibitions and the accompanying legal sanctions, levels of consumption have been rising steadily across Western countries since, to the point where illicit drug consumption has become a rite of passage for emerging adults and has stabilised as a culturally normalised form of consumer behaviour for a significant subset of the population. The system, and with few exceptions the governments that form a core part thereof ignore the charge of policy failure and simply repeat the claim that drug use is dangerous and illegal.

There is far more truth to those claims today than there was nearly a century ago. The psychoactive potency of each of the three principal product categories – opiates, coca products and cannabis – is far higher than it was in the 1920s. Drug market actors respond to illegalisation by transforming the weight/value calculus of their product. Since value is ultimately measured in the strength, traders introduce products with maximum potency and minimum weight.

Softer, lighter products like opium, beer, low THC cannabis vanish from the market, to be replaced by heroin, spirits and "skunk", i.e., cannabis with high levels of THC. One of the first consequences of imposing systemic controls on drug markets and suppressing cultural rituals and events of drug use is therefore to amplify the toxicity of the product. First, there is the upward drive-in potency; second, there is increased adulteration; third, opacity over content and quality leads consumers to sometimes lethal misjudgements of product potency.

As the product alterations are noted by drug control agencies, they feed back into the policy discourse on penalties and increased controls. More dangerous drugs lead to tougher punishments. Markets respond with changes in the risk/reward calculus, including the greater adulteration of drug products, intensified violence against informers and the distribution of ever more potent substances (Miron, 1999). All the while, demand continues to expand, partly driven by a hard core of dependent users who fund their habits by introducing neophytes, often highly vulnerable individuals, to these secret delights. As enforcement keeps prices artificially high, a growing number of dependent users resort to committing property crimes in order to supply their needs (Preble & Casey, 1969).

The drug control system, then, changes the environment from which it distinguishes itself, not by resolving but amplifying the problem to which it owes its existence.

After the system has become operational the drugs circulating in the illicit market bear little resemblance to the products that once were used in integrated cultural settings or medical practice. Now they have high potency, are made with cheap, often toxic ingredients and adulterated with harmful substances. To avoid brutalisation or arrest by law enforcement, consumers retreat to remote often hazardous, unsanitary places like the so-called shooting galleries, crack houses or public toilets (Bourgois, 1998; Briggs, 2010). The self-fulfilling prophesy of the drug control system has been to make drugs and their use more dangerous.

But the biggest transformation in the environment is achieved by a qualitative change. The genius of the drug control system was to move the focus of policy makers and public to distribution and production. With rising property crime and spiralling violence further up the supply chain, drug control is now seen as a necessary policy and tool for fighting crime. According to one former UNODC Secretary, this constitutes a policy displacement, where public health has been pushed into the background "public security is now frequently perceived as the primary, or at least the most effective, way of solving the drug problem" (UNODC, 2008a).

Astute, though this observation may be in tracking government priorities, it is inaccurate in suggesting that this is a recent development. In fact, prohibition was always conceived of as mobilising the repressive power of the state under the pretext of public health, or to use the notion of illness for social control (Szasz, 1970). Second, many policy makers are more interested in mobilising security forces against rivals or to keep the population on its toes. Third, it is now a well-established belief that public security and fighting the drug barons *is* the very purpose of drug control, illustrating how the two distinct concepts of drugs and crime have been merged through continuous association.[6]

The web of criminality through which drugs traverse from production to consumption is the most original and magnificent achievement of the system. It follows a simple logic, where market participants at every stage along the commodity chain respond to enforcement by employing violence to secure their operations. What exacerbates this trend is the disproportionate value of the drugs, itself a consequence of artificially produced scarcity, in the remote production areas, along transit corridors, or in retail markets in immiserated communities. Drug economies overshadow the economic alternatives and afford the means for dealing in extreme violence.

Participation in the drug trade becomes a precondition for holding power in parts of Myanmar, Afghanistan, Colombia or Mexico (McCoy, 2019). At the level of local drug markets, disputes and rivalries between market participants are outside the law or the remit of local government planning.

What the drug control system has engineered through a system of prohibitions and market distortions is to make drugs and drug dealers exponentially more dangerous. Shifting focus onto the criminality has added a further twist to the spiral, as the drug control system itself becomes the object of the protective measures. The third significant international treaty post-Second World War, the 1988 United Nations Convention Against Illicit Traffic in Narcotic Drugs and Psychotropic Substances, is designed entirely to increase state powers to investigate and heavily punish their drug offending citizens.[7] Having criminalised drug consumption, the responsibility for the now pervasive and multi-faceted problems has been attached to the drug consumers, and the focus of the authorities shifted to their suppliers. These two groups bear the brunt of the interventions, but the costs are spread across society.

They include the powers of the state in performing invasive luggage and body searches, mass screening in the form of urine and blood testing, and the reversal of the legal principle by requiring drug offenders to prove their innocence and many more.[8] Less attention is paid to the way the appropriation of powers and resources has benefited key professional groups whose support is crucial to upholding the system.

Beneficiaries – power holders and professions

If the system sustains itself by exponentially amplifying actual and collateral damage, exemplified by the so-called US opioid crises (Beletsky & Davis, 2017; Ciccarone et al., 2017; Kolodny et al., 2015) and the massacres of alleged "drug dealers" in the Philippines (Bo Jensen & Hapal, 2018), its perpetuation is only possible with the active support of key interest groups. While the breadth of the system provides openings, for a wide range of players, think of the virtue signalling by royal and other sponsors of drug education charities, it is the interlocking support of three particular interest groups that uphold the system in its splendour.

First are the health professionals who have risen from the margins of medical science to establish a thriving industry in the delivery of (drug) addiction treatment. As in many other domains, the actual methods are contested between competing schools, but none have as yet established the aetiology of addiction. Since it is not known what causes addiction, there are also no cures, a fact acknowledged by the anodyne description of a bio-psycho-social condition. In spite of poor outcomes, a fact underlined by the inclusion of "relapse" into treatment models, the industry continues to flourish, while lending legitimacy and a human face to a repressive system. Plus, they link back to the ostensible purpose of the drug control conventions as being to promote "The health and well-being of mankind".

Drug treatment in many countries is mandatory, as elaborated by the resource intense inter-agency hybrid system known in the US as drug courts. In effect, the initial diagnosis of *drug abuse* is made by legal fiat in declaring non-medical consumption illegal. Drug consumers/abusers are therefore directed into treatment by courts and families to address a "drug abuse disorder" that has become detached from the status of addiction.

The main response to the drug problem, however, is punitive, even in places where this is moderated by the either so-called harm reduction measures or low-level corruption. Drug control is constructed upon a presumption that the state has the right to punish, which explains the dominant role of law enforcement in the system. Owing to the system-changing impact of the feedback loop, a drug control strategy conceived for the protection of public health is now led by the criminal justice system. In many ways, this has been a godsend, as society transferred significant resources to newly created agencies and departments, lavishly equipped and furnished with powers that were not deemed possible before (body searches, urine tests, home invasion by law enforcement, telephone tapping).[9]

Further resources are continually transferred from drug market participants in the form of bribes and pay-offs. Corruption has plagued law enforcement in every country, and often inflicting system damage, be this in engendering a property seizure oriented "policing for profit" as in many US states, to the co-option of specially trained military units like the Mexican Flechas.[10]

At a more mundane level policing offenders is mostly harmless and simple because the presence of the drug establishes guilt and obviates the need for time-consuming detective work. Because drug consumption is culturally so deeply embedded, police officers can generate a steady flow of arrests to demonstrate productivity. In conclusion, whether as gamekeepers or poachers, law enforcement agencies and their representative organisations constitute a vociferous lobby for, as well as the biggest material beneficiary of, drug control.[11]

In the US, trade unions representing police and prison officers as well as the professional associations for state attorneys have been outspoken opponents of both medical cannabis and proposals for reducing penalties for non-violent drug offences (Boettke et al., 2013).[12] There are also international networks connecting senior police officers, drug control agencies and policy makers, such as Heads of National Drug Law Enforcement Agencies (HONLEA), or police organisations like Ameripol that are dedicated to expanding drug control. Indeed, Europol was founded as an informal forum for exchanging police information on drug trafficking and presents an in-house analysis of organised crime threats to advance its own institutional interests (Carrapiço & Trauner, 2013).

Involving law enforcement in deliberations about the status of drugs and appropriate responses, itself indicative of the systemic shift away from protecting public health, provides an irreproachable foundation for decision making. By citing the ostensibly disinterested advice from medical and law enforcement representatives, policy makers have built campaigns on the promise to be tough on drugs. It has allowed them to appear active in addressing social ills without taking on powerful interests, to create electoral majorities against a common enemy and most ingeniously, a mechanism of blaming the poor for their own predicament. Not surprisingly, the drug control Conventions and the control system that has been erected around them continue to enjoy vigorous support from many national governments around the world. From Cairo to Beijing, recalcitrant citizens can be stopped and searched, arrested and beaten, incarcerated and tortured, in the name of drug control, with the tacit support of international agencies.

Conclusion – the system needs to be defunded, deconstructed and dismantled

Drug control in its current form remains a startling anomaly. It was inspired by the crusading zeal of nineteenth century evangelists, who saw in the control of first alcohol then other *drugs* social issues that could lend relevance to their declining institutions. By insinuating themselves into the sinews of colonial empire building and the emerging twenty-first century state, they helped create a bureaucratic assemblage that has defied all expectations and challenges. The current system with its UN Commissions, agencies and treaties has carved out a socialist niche economy in the domain of "controlled medication", where resources are allocated by technical committee and the market has been suspended. The predictable consequences have been an explosion of criminality, corruption at all levels of the state and the tangled growth of bureaucratic entities. Their core interests are self-preservation and the allocation of resources to different interest groups, chief among these criminal justice players and different health officials, whose main role is to give their public health blessings to an essentially repressive system.

The unfolding debacles from the erosion of governance across weak states, the financing of civil was from Colombia to Afghanistan, to the US synthetic opioid crises or the collapse of palliative care in Lower and Middle Income Countries (Knaul et al., 2018), have all been cycled back into further expanding the system. Reform has therefore to come from the outside as in the decade long campaign to redefine cannabis from *drug of abuse* to medicine. It has been resolutely resisted by the system agencies, exemplified by the US Drug Enforcement Administrations' consistent attempts to prevent any systematic assessment of the medical benefit and/or risk of marijuana.

In the beginning of the twentieth century, however, the system was erected without the globally most widely used intoxicating, habit forming substance being included. Eventually efforts to repress alcohol consumption petered out even in the US, but by then the system had already been established around a string of other substances and the powers amassed by control bureaucracies and enforcement agencies. Equally, the system will take the gradual *normalisation* of cannabis in its stride, and perhaps compensate by including tobacco. System continuity, just as its original creation or autopoiesis, was contingent on the convergence of political and professional interests. No single substance is important in themselves, but the cultural presentation of altered states as intoxication and (some of) the agents that produce it as *drugs*. In re-framing and managing the risks associated with consumption as we move forward, the defunding of repressive machineries has to be accompanied by a revision of terminology. There is already a long discussion about the stigmatising power of pseudo-medical language such as the term abuse (Scholten et al., 2017). It is just as important to destigmatise the items of consumption and the mind-altering plant products that have for millennia accompanied the human journey and stop using the term drugs.

Notes

1 The text continues to warn of the consequence of excess:

> The fourth bowl is ours no longer, but belongs to violence; the fifth to uproar, the sixth to drunken revelry the seventh to black eyes. The eighth is the policeman's, the ninth belongs to biliousness, and the tenth to madness and hurling the furniture. Too much wine, poured into one little vessel, easily knocks the legs from under the drinkers.

2 Through inter alia (i) voter suppression as in demanding identification at ballot stations or by disenfranchising convicted felons, including drug offenders, (ii) through the partisan rezoning of constituency boundaries and the (ii) rural bias that is inherent in the electoral college system used for the US presidential election.

3 Pragmatism won out over zealousness in the decision on coca which though despised by the authorities was tolerated because labourers in mines and farms found it invaluable (Escohotado, 2010).

4 As is apparent from the sheer proliferation of diagnostic labels and the difficulty found in getting consistency among psychiatrists, the text is key for unlocking health insurance funding. In recent years, the US National Institute for Drug Abuse (NIDA) has reinforced the biological foundation by defining addiction as a brain disease.

5 The UK Act limited the opening times of public houses to prevent alcohol induced absenteeism among munitions workers. It stayed in place after the end of hostilities, essentially unchanged until the 1990s.

6 Note the history of attributing criminality to intoxicating substances, and the appeal to crime reduction as a legitimation of repression. At the beginning of Prohibition, the Reverend Billy Sunday stirred audiences with this optimistic prediction: the reign of tears is over. The slums will soon be a memory. We will turn our prisons into factories and our jails into storehouses and corncribs. Men will walk upright now; women will smile, and children will laugh. Hell will be forever for rent (Okrent, 2010:2).

7 Article 3 of the 1988 Convention enjoins the parties to "take into account the grave nature" of "production, manufacture, extraction; preparation, …, transport, importation or exportation of any narcotic drug or any psychotropic substance" and make it liable to sanctions like "imprisonment or other forms of deprivation of liberty, pecuniary sanctions and confiscation". They are further urged to employ "discretionary legal powers under their domestic law … to maximize the effectiveness of law enforcement", to discourage early parole and establish a long statute of limitations.

8 Less visible because they happen in remote regions of Low- and Middle-Income Countries is the indiscriminate use of toxic substances to destroy drug crops, the subjection of civilian populations to military actions and killings by government "security" forces and the break-down of public order lawlessness in many drug-producing countries (Keen & Andersson, 2018).

9 Before the global war on terror created a new set of internal enemies the most extensive appropriations of police power were pioneered in combating drug trafficking.

10 An elite formation formed for the specific purpose of combating drug traffickers which then established itself as one of the most powerful cartels.

11 One notable exception is the organisation Law Enforcement Against Prohibition (LEAP), an advocacy group comprising former law enforcement officers who are campaigning for drug policy reform.

12 According to Boettke et al., "Among the groups supporting continuation of drug prohibition, perhaps the most influential have been police and prison guard unions. … In 2008, for example, the National Fraternal Order of Police (FOP) lobbied Congress to increase the penalties for offenses involving particular types of narcotics, to create a registry and public database for persons convicted of certain drug offenses and to establish increased penalties and mandatory sentences."

References

Ambler, C. (1990). Alcohol, Racial Segregation and Popular Politics in Northern Rhodesia. *The Journal of African History*, 31(2), 295–313.

Babor, T. F., Caetano, R., Casswell, S., Edwards, G., Giesbrecht, N., Graham, K., Grube, J. W., Hill, L., Holder, H., Homel, R., Livingston, M., österberg, E., Rehm, J., Room, R., & Rossow, I. (2010). Alcohol: No Ordinary Commodity: Research and Public Policy. In *Alcohol: No Ordinary Commodity: Research and Public Policy*. https://doi.org/10.1093/acprof:oso/9780199551149.001.0001

Beletsky, L., & Davis, C. S. (2017). Today's Fentanyl Crisis: Prohibition's Iron Law, Revisited. *International Journal of Drug Policy, 46*, 156–159. https://doi.org/10.1016/j.drugpo.2017.05.050

Berridge, V. (2013). *Demons: Our Changing Attitudes to Alcohol, Tobacco, and Drugs.* Oxford: Oxford University Press.

Bewley-Taylor, D., Jelsma, M. T. B. (2014). *The Rise and Decline of Cannabis Prohibition.* Transnational Institute.

Bo Jensen, S., & Hapal, K. (2018). Police Violence and Corruption in the Philippines: Violent Exchange and the War on Drugs. *Journal of Current Southeast Asian Affairs.* https://doi.org/10.1177/186810341803700202

Boettke, P., Coyne, C., & Hall, A. (2013). *Keep Off the Grass: The Economics of Prohibition and U.S. Drug Policy.* Oregon Law Review, 91, 1069–1096.

Bourgois, P. (1998). Just Another Night in a Shooting Gallery. *Theory, Culture & Society.* https://doi.org/10.1177/026327698015002002

Briggs, D. (2010). Crack Houses in the UK: Some Observations on Their Operations. In *Drugs and Alcohol Today.* https://doi.org/10.5042/daat.2010.0726

Carrapiço, H., & Trauner, F. (2013). Europol and Its Influence on EU Policy-Making on Organized Crime: Analyzing Governance Dynamics and Opportunities. *Perspectives on European Politics and Society.* https://doi.org/10.1080/15705854.2013.817804

Ciccarone, D. (2017). Editorial for "US Heroin in Transition: Supply Changes, Fentanyl Adulteration and Consequences" IJDP Special Section. *International Journal of Drug Policy.* https://doi.org/10.1016/j.drugpo.2017.06.010

Ciccarone, D., Ondocsin, J., & Mars, S. G. (2017). Heroin Uncertainties: Exploring Users' Perceptions of Fentanyl-Adulterated and -Substituted 'Heroin.' *International Journal of Drug Policy, 46.* https://doi.org/10.1016/j.drugpo.2017.06.004

Cohen, P. (2003). The drug prohibition church and the adventure of reformation. In *International Journal of Drug Policy.* https://doi.org/10.1016/S0955-3959(03)00012-4

Courtwright, D. T. (1982) *Dark Paradise: Opiate Addiction in America Before 1940.* Cambridge, MA: Harvard University Press

Courtwright, D. T. (2010). The NIDA Brain Disease Paradigm: History, Resistance and Spinoffs. *BioSocieties, 5*(1), 137–147. https://doi.org/10.1057/biosoc.2009.3

Coveney, J., & Bunton, R. (2003). In Pursuit of the Study of Pleasure: Implications for Health Research and Practice. *Health.* https://doi.org/10.1177/1363459303007002873

Douglas, M. (1966). *Douglas, Mary.* London: Routledge.

Escohotado, A. (2010). *The General History of Drugs*, Vol. 1. Valpariaso, Chile: Graffiti Militante Press.

Felbab-Brown, V. (2017). Organized Crime, Illicit Economies, Civil Violence & International Order: More Complex than You Think. *Daedalus.* https://doi.org/10.1162/DAED_a_00462

Friedman, M (1992). The Drug Was as a Socialist Enterprise. In Friedman, M. and Szasz, T. (eds.), *Liberty and Drugs.* New York: The Drug Policy Foundation. http://druglibrary.org/special/friedman/socialist.htm accessed 19/08/2020

Gershon, I. (2005). Seeing Like a System: Luhmann for Anthropologists Ilana Gershon Emerson College. *Anthropological Theory*, 5, 99–116.

Gomart, E. (2002). Towards generous constraint: Freedom and coercion in a French addiction treatment. *Sociology of Health and Illness.* https://doi.org/10.1111/1467-9566.00307

Gregory, D. (2011). The everywhere war. *Geographical Journal.* https://doi.org/10.1111/j.1475-4959.2011.00426.x

Jay, M. (2019). *Mescaline: A Global History of the First Psychedelic.* Yale, MI: Yale University Press.

Jellinek, E. (1961). *The Disease Concept of Alcoholism.* New Haven, CT: Hillhouse Press, 1960. 246 pp. In *Social Work.* https://doi.org/10.1093/sw/6.3.128

Keen, D., & Andersson, R. (2018). Double Games: Success, Failure and the Relocation of Risk in Fighting Terror, Drugs and Migration. *Political Geography.* https://doi.org/10.1016/j.polgeo.2018.09.008

Klein, A., Patwardhan, S., & Loglo, M. G. A. (2020). Divergences and Commonalities between the US Opioid Crisis and Prescription Medicine Mis/Use in West Africa. *International Journal of Drug Policy, 76.* https://doi.org/10.1016/j.drugpo.2019.102640

Klein, A., & Potter, G. R. (2018). The Three Betrayals of the Medical Cannabis Growing Activist: From Multiple Victimhood to Reconstruction, Redemption and Activism. *International Journal of Drug Policy.* https://doi.org/10.1016/j.drugpo.2017.12.004

Knaul, F. M., Farmer, P. E., Krakauer, E. L., De Lima, L., Bhadelia, A., Jiang Kwete, X., Arreola-Ornelas, H., Gómez-Dantés, O., Rodriguez, N. M., Alleyne, G. A. O., Connor, S. R., Hunter, D. J., Lohman, D., Radbruch, L., del Rocío Sáenz Madrigal, M., Atun, R., Foley, K. M., Frenk, J., Jamison, D. T., ... Zimmerman, C. (2018). Alleviating the Access Abyss in Palliative Care and Pain Relief—An Imperative of Universal Health Coverage: The Lancet Commission report. *The Lancet*, *391*(10128), 1391–1454. https://doi.org/10.1016/S0140-6736(17)32513-8

Kolodny, A., Courtwright, D. T., Hwang, C. S., Kreiner, P., Eadie, J. L., Clark, T. W., & Alexander, G. C. (2015). The Prescription Opioid and Heroin Crisis: A Public Health Approach to an Epidemic of Addiction. *Annual Review of Public Health*, *36*(1), 559–574. https://doi.org/10.1146/annurev-publhealth-031914-122957

Levine, H. (1978). The Discovery of Addiction: Changing Conceptions of Habitual Drunkenness in America. *Journal of Studies on Alcohol*, *39*, 143–174.

Luhmann, N. (2006). System as Difference Organization, *Organisation*, 13(1), 37–57.

Mate, G. (2018). *In the Realm of Hungry Ghosts*. London: Penguin.

McCoy, A. (2019). *In the Shadow of the American Century: The Rise and Decline of U.S. Global Power*. Chicago, IL: Haymarket Books.

Miron, J. (1999). Violence and the U.S. Prohibitions of Drugs and Alcohol. *American Law and Economics Review*. https://doi.org/10.1093/aler/1.1.78

Naranjo, A. J. (2010). Spillover Effects of Domestic Law Enforcement Policies. *International Review of Law and Economics*. https://doi.org/10.1016/j.irle.2010.07.001

O'Malley, P., & Valverde, M. (2004). Pleasure, Freedom and Drugs. *Sociology*. https://doi.org/10.1177/0038038504039359

Okrent, D. (2010). *Last Call: The Rise and Fall of Prohibition*. New York: Scribner. https://doi.org/10.1017/s1931436100000985

Pietschmann, T. (2007). A Century of International Drug Control. *Bulletin on Narcotics*. https://doi.org/10.18356/0c4846f3-en

Porter, R. (1996). The History of the "Drugs" Problem. *Criminal Justice Matters*, *24*, 3–5.

Preble, E., & Casey, J. J. (1969). Taking Care of Business – The Heroin User's Life on the Street. *Substance Use and Misuse*. https://doi.org/10.3109/10826086909061998

Reuter, P. (2009). Systemic Violence in Drug Markets. *Crime, Law and Social Change*. https://doi.org/10.1007/s10611-009-9197-x

Room, R. (2003). The Culture Framing of Addiction. *Janus Head*, 6(2), 221–234.

Seddon, T. (2016). Inventing Drugs: A Genealogy of a Regulatory Concept. *Journal of Law and Society*. https://doi.org/10.1111/j.1467-6478.2016.00760.x

Szasz, T. S. (1970). *The Manufacture of Madness. A Comparative Study of the Inquisition and the Mental Health Movements*. New York City: Harper and Row.

Thoumi, F. E. (2009). Políticas antidrogas y la necesidad de enfrentar las vulnerabilidades de Colombia. *Analisis Politico*, 22(67), 60–82.

UNODC. (2008a). Making Drug Control Fit for Purpose: Building on the UNGASS Decade. *UN Doc No E/CN.7/2008/CRP.17, March 7.*

UNODC. (2008b). *World Drug Report*. United Nations, Vienna, Austria

Weinberg, D. (2011). Sociological Perspectives on Addiction. *Sociology Compass*, *5*(4), 298–310. https://doi.org/10.1111/j.1751-9020.2011.00363.x

29

HANDLING COMPLEXITY

Constituting the relationship between intoxication and violence in Australian alcohol policy discourse

David Moore, Helen Keane, Duane Duncan and Emily Lenton

Introduction

Anthropological, sociological and historical research has long argued that drug use and intoxication are shaped by the cultural, social and political-economic contexts of consumption (Becker, 1953; Douglas, 1987; Gefou-Madianou, 1992; Heath, 1958; Levine, 1978; Lindesmith, 1947; MacAndrew & Edgerton, 1969; Mandelbaum, 1965; Marshall, 1979; Nicholls, 2003). In this framing, drug effects and experiences, including intoxication, arise from the interactions between 'drug' (pharmacological properties), 'set' (individual characteristics) and 'setting' (sociocultural context) (Zinberg, 1984). Criminological research has also taken a keen interest in the relationship between intoxication and aggression (Fagan, 1990; Felson & Staff, 2010; Miles, 2012; Tomsen, 2005), youth research in the emerging cultures and practices of intoxication among young people (Blackman, 2017; Measham & Brain, 2005; Measham & Moore, 2008), cultural studies in the relationship between intoxication and modernity (Alexander & Roberts, 2003; Nancy, 2016; Reith, 2005), and recent sociological research in the gendering of intoxication (Hutton, 2020; Moore, 2020), media representations of intoxication (Ayres & Taylor, 2020; Ruddock, 2020), 'less florid' forms of intoxication (Keane, 2020), and intoxication and sexualities (Pienaar et al., 2020a; 2020b).

Intoxication and its effects also feature centrally in alcohol and other drug policy, but in this context, intoxication is generally presented as a universal and singular state. Crucially, it is constituted as a threat to health and social order, both a harm in itself and a source of other harms. The exclusion of the multiplicity of intoxication in policy – multiple contexts, multiple practices, multiple meanings and multiple effects – enables networks of harm to be identified and linked, and strategies to reduce this harm to be recommended and justified. Intoxication is both problematised and prioritised; thus, preventing intoxication is equated with preventing harm, and other elements related to alcohol consumption tend to be relegated to the background (Keane, 2009; Manton & Moore, 2016).

However, the style of explanation and rationales found in alcohol policy documents do not exhaust the forms taken in policy discourse. In this chapter, we examine the accounts generated during in-depth interviews with Australian alcohol policy stakeholders, in particular their reflections on the relationship between intoxication and violence. As key actors in

 DOI: 10.4324/9780429058141-37

the policy process, they mobilise a range of assumptions and concepts in policy development and implementation. We find that the stakeholder accounts provide an instructive contrast with the certainties evident in policy documents. Drawing on Mol and Law's (2002) discussion of the handling of complexity in knowledge practices, we identify various modes of explanation in these accounts, which include engaging with multiplicity as well as returns to simplification.

In our exploration of the policy expert interviews, we have been inspired by Fraser's (2016) analysis of the way in which Australian and Canadian alcohol and other drug professionals articulate concepts of addiction. In the accounts generated by her interviews, Fraser (2016, p. 6) argues that two simultaneous trajectories are evident:

> one moving towards difference in participants' insistence on the multitude and diversity of factors that make up addiction problems and solutions, and the other towards unity in their tendency to return to narrow disease models of addiction in uncomfortable, sometimes dissonant, strategic choices.

Drawing on the work of Bruno Latour, Fraser argues that the interviewed professionals operate in two modes treated as distinct by Latour: when 'articulating the multiplicity and diversity of addiction, they grope towards a vision of a "multiverse of habits"' – that is, they seek to acknowledge the complex practices making up 'addiction'. However, when they discuss possible responses to such complex behaviour, they tend to simplify: 'in turning to reifying disease labels of addiction they take for granted, and work within, a "universe of essences"', that is, 'the kind of universe made up of stable matters of fact' (Fraser, 2016, p. 8).

Our interviews also demonstrated two modes and trajectories, but in our case the simplification was not that of essences, but rather an emphasis on evidence and the prioritisation of public health benefits. In what follows, we outline our theoretical approach and our method, before providing a brief account of how intoxication and violence are addressed in selected policy documents. We then move to our main discussion of the handling of complexity by policy practitioners.

Approach

In their discussion of the handling of complexity in knowledge production, Mol and Law (2002, p. 1) pose the following questions, which are relevant to our analysis of alcohol policy:

> No one would deny that the world is complex, that it escapes simplicities. But what is complexity, and how might it be attended to? How might complexity be handled in knowledge practices, nonreductively, but without at the same time generating ever more complexities until we submerge in chaos?

Mol and Law consider standard forms of scientific enquiry, in which a single order organises the simplification of complex phenomena and becomes the 'basis for action' (2002, p. 3) (e.g., clinical trials in medicine). When multiple orders are gathered together, the dichotomy between 'simple' and 'complex' begins to dissolve. This is because the various 'orderings' of a specific object or topic – such as the relationship between intoxication and forms of acute harm such as violence – render 'reality' in different ways and do not always produce and reinforce the same kinds of simplification. Furthermore:

> If there are different modes of ordering that coexist, what is reduced or effaced in one may be crucial in another so that the question no longer is, Do we simplify or do we accept complexity? It becomes instead a matter of determining *which* simplification or simplifications we will attend to and create and, as we do this, of attending to what they foreground and draw our attention to, as well as what they relegate to the background.
>
> *(Mol & Law, 2002, p. 11)*

On the basis of this work, we can make two observations relevant to our analysis: that knowledge production (including our own) inevitably shapes phenomena as it observes and responds to them, and that forms of simplification are an inevitable part of any knowledge enterprise. Because different policy knowledges produce different realities, the process by which particular versions, and the simplifications they attend to and create, come to be taken as legitimate is contested and therefore open to change. Such a framework allows us to ask several important questions about the politics of alcohol policy: Which simplifications are created to handle complexity and what do they foreground and relegate? What effects result from these framings? Are there alternative ways of constituting intoxication, causation and harm, and alternative forms of simplification, that might result in different framings and therefore different effects?

Method

Our analysis is based on research conducted for an Australian Research Council-funded project on the comparative treatment of gender in research and policy on alcohol and violence in Australia, Canada and Sweden. In this chapter, the main dataset we use comprises in-depth, semi-structured interviews with Australian health or related policy stakeholders whose work includes a major focus on alcohol policy issues. The interview dataset (n = 16, 12 female participants) was generated by first identifying relevant national, state and local government departments, non-government alcohol and other drug sector organisations, and health and related agencies with a major interest in alcohol policy. Potential participants within these organisations were invited to take part on the basis of their professional role and/or reputation in the alcohol policy field, and were sent individual emails with information about the project. Participants included policy managers and policy staff from national, state or local government health, social welfare and liquor licencing departments, and national or state non-government health, sector and related organisations delivering public health advocacy or alcohol policy advice.

Interviews were conducted in person when possible and convenient, as well as by Skype or telephone. For this type of professional interviewee, data gained via different interview formats (i.e., face-to-face, telephone and Skype) are of equal quality (Hanna, 2012). The interviews sought to map stakeholders' training in gender issues, chart diverse views on gender and alcohol-related problems among young people, trace the development of complex ideas and perspectives, and understand how gendered concepts and practices are conceived and developed in policy. In addition to general questions about the aims of alcohol policy and the uses of research, specific questions asked about the causes of violence in the night-time economy, whether alcohol 'affects' men and women differently, and the role of gender in violent events. The semi-structured interview schedule also included questions about the extent to which gender and the relationship between men and violence are addressed in alcohol policy. We note that in asking about the causes of violence, we were ourselves prompting forms of simplification. The interviews provided opportunities to explore the range of gender concepts used by participants in their policy-related work, and the complexities of relating these concepts to policy development and implementation.

Interviews were digitally recorded, professionally transcribed and coded thematically using NVivo. Analysis used the respected inductive constant comparison method (Seale, 1999). Initial analysis was carried out and notes made on emergent data categories. The identified categories were discussed by the research team and a coding frame developed (e.g., the relationship between alcohol and violence, alcohol's effects on men and women, and barriers to addressing violence). Several interviews were double-coded to ensure coding consistency, and the codes relating to intoxication were then analysed. The research received approval from human research ethics committees at Curtin University (HRE2018-0103), The Australian National University (2018/819) and La Trobe University (HEC19340).

In addition to the interviews, we also collected a set of 23 publically accessible Australian national, state and territory government alcohol policies, strategies or related supporting documents, which we have analysed elsewhere (Duncan et al., 2020, 2022). In this chapter, we focus on two documents produced by state governments that focus specifically on violence in the night-time economy: *Fact sheet: Strategies to reduce alcohol-related assault in entertainment precincts* (New South Wales Department of Justice & Australian Institute of Criminology, 2012) and the *Safe Night Out Strategy* (Queensland Government, 2014). The two datasets – transcripts of interviews with policy stakeholders and alcohol policy documents – allowed us to compare the forms of policy discourse circulating in each. We begin with an analysis of the policy texts.

Analysis

Policy texts

Contemporary Australian alcohol policy discourse and practice needs to be understood in the historical, institutional and political contexts of a long period of liberalisation in alcohol regulation, which began in the 1990s under the influence of national competition policy. The broad trend has been towards increased alcohol availability, through growth in the number and types of outlet, the range of products, and the days and hours of sale, although there has been some reversal in recent years (Wilkinson et al., 2016). The notion of the night-time economy, understood in terms of revitalised urban leisure zones producing both economic value and public amenity, was key to the governmental programme of regulatory relaxation. As Shaw (2014) has argued, the night-time economy construct identifies bars, clubs and alcohol consumption as the core of the night-time city and of night life itself. The implication of the night-time economy in exacerbating and intensifying violence in the city has produced a sustained policy debate about 'alcohol-fuelled violence', including federal and state enquiries (e.g., Legal and Constitutional Affairs References Committee, 2016) and a review of the impact of liquor law reforms in New South Wales (Callinan, 2016). The highlighting of intoxication and violence expressed in the policy documents we studied reflects and reproduces this political and institutional context. The solutions presented in the documents also show the influence of the 'total consumption model' in public health, based on the idea that drinking problems are most effectively addressed through managing the rates and patterns of drinking in the population as a whole (Room & Livingston, 2017).

Alcohol policy documents, especially those attached to a national strategy, have certain characteristic and generic features related to the communication of objectivity and neutrality. As Fraser and Moore observe in relation to illicit drug policy, these texts must

'must establish and sustain their authority and legitimacy' (2011, p. 500). Authorship by a committee or other organisational entity rather than individual named authors implies that the documents are the product of a 'balanced, broad-based, disinterested committee acting responsibly and beyond the corrupting influence of the personal' (Fraser & Moore, 2011, p. 501). In addition, authorship by an organisational entity 'generates authority by linking the contents to experts and other specialist stakeholders chosen as possessing a privileged relationship to the area of policy development' and ensures that 'accountability for the text is distributed and sequestered'.

In general, although the policy documents we studied rarely made directly causal claims about alcohol intoxication and violence, the relationship between intoxication and harm is strongly framed in terms of the effects of alcohol on the individual. Other socio-material forces and elements that might bear on this relationship are much less visible. It is 'intoxication', understood simply as the universal result of excess alcohol consumption, that works as the primary hub around which forms of acute alcohol-related harm are clustered. In addition, references to alcohol-related violence tend to be sited within coverage of a wider range of acute and chronic forms of harm associated with intoxication.

Two of the analysed policy texts deal specifically with alcohol-related violence in the night-time economy. The first – *Fact sheet: Strategies to reduce alcohol-related assault in entertainment precincts* (New South Wales Department of Justice & Australian Institute of Criminology, 2012) – describes a wide range of measures for addressing 'intoxicated and aggressive patrons'. These measures include new rules, regulations and training for venue staff and management, community mobilisation, media campaigns, the introduction of lock-outs, stricter enforcement of licencing laws, increased public transport and so on. By listing these multiple elements, which include transport and training as well as the regulation of drinking, the document makes room for complexity. However, the multiplicity of measures is corralled in service of a common aim:

> to prevent or discourage potentially aggressive patrons from being able to purchase and consume alcohol to the point of intoxication, which can impair their decision-making ability and increase their risk of becoming involved in an alcohol-related incident.
>
> *(New South Wales Department of Justice & Australian Institute of Criminology, 2012, p. 4)*

Although complexity is implied in the range of suggested measures, the reduction of intoxication is singled out as the target of intervention. Furthermore, intoxication *per se* is presented as a self-evident form of harm: 'There is evidence [...] that certain licensed premises are engaged in operating practices that are encouraging *patron intoxication and other problems* associated with alcohol consumption' (New South Wales Department of Justice & Australian Institute of Criminology, 2012, p. 3, emphasis added). The many factors shaping intoxicated behaviour – chiefly gender but also age, social class, ethnicity, experience, tolerance, drinking setting and so on – disappear from view.

The second policy document that deals specifically with alcohol-related violence in the night-time economy – the *Safe Night Out Strategy* (Queensland Government, 2014) – aims to 'restore responsible behaviour and respect, stamp out alcohol and drug-related violence and ensure Queensland's nightlife is safe for all' (p. 2). The document has this to say about alcohol (and other drug) intoxication and violence:

> Everyone wants to enjoy a good night out, but too often in Queensland the occasion is ruined by the bad behaviour of those who become unduly intoxicated through alcohol

> and drugs. Sometimes this irresponsible conduct involves indiscriminate aggression and violence that, sadly, can lead to tragic consequences.
>
> *(Queensland Government, 2014, p. 2)*

> A culture of reckless intoxication and aggressive behaviour is a problem in many parts of Queensland, and it's time to take action to stop the violence.
>
> *(Queensland Government, 2014, p. 3)*

Although a number of concepts are mobilised in the two quotations – bad behaviour, undue intoxication, irresponsible conduct and a culture of reckless intoxication – which, if unpacked or elaborated, might be used to handle complexity, the simplification is clear: intoxication (even though qualified by the adverb 'unduly') leads to bad behaviour, including violence. Again, as we saw in the New South Wales example, other forces and elements implicated in both intoxication and violence are made absent. In addition, the first quotation further simplifies by dividing the population into two opposing categories, on the basis of a correct relationship with intoxication. On the one hand, there is the law-abiding public, addressed as 'everyone', those who seek and have a right to fun and relaxation (including moderate drinking) in the night-time economy; on the other, there is the excessively intoxicated minority whose bad behaviour places them outside the limits of enjoyment.

In the two policy documents focusing on alcohol and violence, a simplified emphasis on intoxication relegates from view the many other socio-material forces and elements that bear on this relationship, and which might provide the basis for alternative ways of handling complexity. However, the style of explanation and rationales found in alcohol policy documents do not exhaust the forms that policy discourse takes. We turn next to the accounts of Australian alcohol policy stakeholders, and in particular to their reflections on the relationship between intoxication and violence.

Policy stakeholder accounts

Unsurprisingly, the policy stakeholder accounts, gathered mostly by face-to-face interviews, provide reflexive and nuanced styles of explanation very different from the concise certainties of the collectively authored policy texts. The semi-structured interview format, carried out by an attentive interlocutor, encourages participants to provide elaborated accounts in which their knowledge and expertise is entangled with the construction of identity and the presentation of self. There is thus more space for complexity and questioning, although, as we will see, simplifications are also created in order to justify policy responses and communicate commitment to the public health enterprise. Although the interviews we conducted with policy stakeholders covered a wide range of forms of alcohol-related harm, we focus here mainly on the relationship between intoxication and a specific acute harm: violence.

Like Fraser (2016), we identified two general trajectories in the accounts of the relationship between alcohol intoxication and violence offered by policy stakeholders: the first acknowledging complexity in the relationship between intoxication and violence, and the second returning to the key role of alcohol in violence. Both themes are visible in some participant accounts whereas in others only the first theme is emphasised. For example, Sue offers an account of night-time economy violence that emphasises complexity. As we see in the extract below, she references venue density, the congregation of people in night-time economy precincts (particularly men), temperament, masculinity, (possibly) multiculturalism, alcohol intoxication (with the latter especially relevant to late-night violence) and extended licenced-venue trading hours:

> I would say it would be kind of the growth and clustering of lots of licenced outlets. I think population movement into central districts, I think groups of men predominantly, yeah, I mean, I suppose there is a whole science around temperament and all that which is not my area. [...]. I think it comes down to that, I mean even gender equality plays into that, that kind of expectation of what it means to be a man, those sorts of things about, you know, male aggression or expectations when you are with groups of mates. I don't know if multiculturalism has something to do with, I am not sure, it's not my area of expertise, but I think alcohol has a pretty central role in, if you are talking about entertainment precinct late-night violence, alcohol, it's absolutely part of it, you can't say it's got nothing to do with alcohol, it's just to do with the types of people and you know, we know what the data says around proliferation of [...] on-premises liquor and the late trading hours definitely, we have seen experiments in Newcastle and other places which really show quite substantial reductions if you can tweak the alcohol [availability].

In Sue's reflection above, many different elements are assembled to paint a picture of multiple forces and relations that come together in violent events. One problem she identifies in relation to this heterogeneity is expertise. In policy practice, as in many areas of knowledge production, the ability to speak about and address issues with legitimacy is circumscribed by expertise based on specific training and experience. Therefore, Sue recognises the importance of psychology (temperament) and culture (multiculturalism) but in both cases, she demonstrates restraint in incorporating these features into her explanation for violence because it would take her outside her area of expertise.

Consistent with her attentiveness to multiplicity, Sue complicates the idea of causation in relation to alcohol and violence later in her interview, preferring the more limited claims made by the language of contribution:

> We often use the term 'alcohol-fuelled violence' because we're not saying alcohol is causing the violence as such [...] but it fuels, it kind of exacerbates, it's like that severity and frequency thing that if you've got a group of people who are looking for some biffo [physical or verbal conflict] and they happen to be drunk as well, it's probably going to be worse than if they weren't drunk. But not every incident is necessarily alcohol-related either. Some of those king hits, like I think there has been some where a person wasn't necessarily intoxicated, so that's why you've got to be really careful [...]. That's why I just don't even use the word 'causation', that's why we try to say, 'let's just forget about causation because we're never going to come to a resolution'. It's actually 'how is alcohol contributing part of the mix?'

Sue folds the term 'alcohol-fuelled violence', which is widely used in media reports, policy and research, into her reflective account, interpreting 'fuelling' to mean exacerbation rather than causation. Her reading of the phrase contrasts with critical criminological and sociological analyses of the term, which regard it as a device that frames the relationship between alcohol and violence as directly causal (Flynn et al., 2016; Moore et al., 2017). Flynn et al., for example, argue that the repetition of this term restricts discussion of the personal, relational, situational and sociocultural dimensions of alcohol use (2016, p. 186). Viewed from this critical sociological perspective, Sue's statement remains consistent with the simplifying discourse of alcohol policy, exemplified in the term 'alcohol-fuelled violence', while also attempting to open it up to complexity.

Stuart's interview provides another illustration of the co-existence of the two trajectories – of complexity and simplification – within the same account. He includes a wide range of issues – intoxication, preloading, masculinities, individual personalities, price, the culture and characteristics of venues, and liquor licencing enforcement – in the following reply to a question about the causes of violence in the night-time economy:

> Well okay, that's a big one. There are obviously intersecting causes. So I've got to kick-off with intoxication by people and so there're issues there around the time people spend drinking in the [licensed] venues, but that's now complicated by the preloading that's taking place. We've also got to talk about men and their attitudes to drinking [...]: there's undoubtedly a group or a sector of the male population [...] who see aggression as being a part of their maleness. So there's an intersecting number of factors there in terms of individual personalities, some people are more aggressive than others. There's a sense of ... a certain type of male for whom that is particularly true, but there's also the impact of the price of alcohol that can encourage more drinking. There's a type of venue too that encourages or is tolerant of violence and that can be a cultural issue for that venue, but it can also be exacerbated, or some venues can ... almost encourage violence, through their design. You know [...] over-crowding, furniture, the layout of the furniture and so on, there's a whole lot of factors in there and also I suppose ... I also want to mention the enforcement of liquor licencing, you know, by law enforcement, by the regulators, which I would argue is often very lax.

Stuart's response to the 'big' question of the causes of violence takes the form of a list of factors. As Mol and Law argue, a list is a form of ordering that does not claim completeness: 'If someone comes along with something to add to the list, something that emerges as important, this may indeed be added to it' (2002, p. 14). Although this is not to say that Stuart's list of factors is open to the inclusion of elements regarded as important to others but outside the alcohol policy field, the possibility is there in the potentiality of its open-ended form. In addition, Stuart explicitly identifies the relationship between the items he lists as intersectional. The relationship between factors such as men's attitudes to drinking, overcrowding and time spent drinking is not simply additional; they intersect to produce variable situations of violence. Later in his interview, Stuart explicitly addresses the issue of intoxication and causation in a way that echoes his references to complexity. His formulation is similar to that offered by Sue, although it retains the use of 'causation' and 'cause':

> The way that I read the research, alcohol has been described as a contributing cause [of violence]. I know causation is discussed with this issue, there are various perspectives on it and whether alcohol causes violence or whether it contributes to it, I know that's a vexed issue, but [...] I like the notion that it's a contributing cause. So clearly [...] violence is not a necessary response to alcohol and [alcohol's] not sufficient [for violence] because not everyone who drinks gets violent or not everyone who gets intoxicated becomes violent. But I think for some people in some circumstances, alcohol does incite violence.

In this excerpt (and in other sections of his interview), Stuart recognises not only the complexity of causation, but also the existence of different perspectives that make the issue of alcohol and violence a 'vexed' rather than simple matter. Rather than expressing his knowledge as factual, he talks about his beliefs and the explanations that he prefers. However, elsewhere in his account, the public health approach to alcohol, with its focus on population-level consumption, is presented as the effective solution to harm. His deployment of the terminology of acute harms and chronic harms also has a classificatory effect, gathering a range of negative effects into the single category of harm:

> I think the [public health] approach is that the best way of reducing alcohol-related harm across the population is to reduce the drinking, the general per capita drinking levels of a population and therefore, that will have an impact on the acute harms and chronic harms. Obviously, the acute harms [such as violence] are coming from intoxication on single episodes of drinking and chronic harm [is] emanating from regular high level or even regular drinking over many years.

For Stuart, it appears that the public health approach is distinguished from the other perspectives he mentions because of its grounding in authoritative scientific evidence. For example, strategies to reduce alcohol availability are supported by quantitative research:

> The research indicates that there's [...] a very strong correlation between the length of time that venues are operating late at night and the level of intoxication, the level of violence and the problems that are consequent ... you know, drink driving, aggression, inside and outside the venues, so yeah, we see [measures such as reduced trading hours] as positives.

The focus on regulatory changes was also a feature of Natalie's account (e.g., earlier closing times, lock-out laws, bans on particular type of drinks being served after specific times and so on). She explained her support for these strategies with reference to the 'alcohol lobby', which is:

> very firmly embedded in the political process and very articulate about treating alcohol problems as individual issues: that, you know, individuals need to either be punished by law enforcement or treated by the health system, but it's not alcohol that's the problem, it's the individual characteristics that made it a problem.

A 'key' strategy articulated by Natalie for countering the alcohol lobby is to make use of the 'current research evidence that's relevant to the policy debate'. As in Stuart's account, the categories of 'research evidence', 'relevance' and 'policy' serve to stabilise knowledge and exclude complexity so that identifiable measures that are within the realm of current public health orthodoxy can be put in place.

Natalie's referencing of evidence as the basis for effective action was particularly noteworthy because it contrasted with another section of her interview, in which she was eloquent about what she called the 'dickhead problem':

> The more academic way of describing it might be 'hyper-masculinity' I suppose, so, you know, there's a cohort of men who are ill equipped to resolve emotional problems with words and who have not been kind of raised to understand that it's not okay to just spray your anger everywhere over everybody. Maybe sometimes, you know, you should learn to tolerate disappointment. Yeah, I don't know that I have a lot more to say about it, other than it seems to be a particularly male problem, a particular type of male problem.

Unlike alcohol availability and the evidence-based policies that can be trusted to produce beneficial changes in behaviour, Natalie states that the dickhead problem of hyper-masculinity will 'always be a problem … I don't think we can regulate […] against that'. For Natalie then, while men's conduct and emotional responses are a key part of the alcohol-violence nexus, they are appropriately excluded from policy responses because they are the wrong sort of problem, both too deep-seated and too broad to respond to feasible strategies of government and control.

There is also the risk that a focus on men might divert attention from the actions and responsibilities of the alcohol industry. As Stuart suggests, 'there's a really strong sense of, well I think a belief or even a fear, that if we were to focus on a group [i.e., men], then it would take the heat off the industry and I think that's a really strong sense in the [alcohol policy] field'. He also thought that most policy makers would implicitly see population-level strategies as targeting men without excusing the industry. Thus, a reading of wider political and strategic issues also frames the investment of some policy stakeholders in simplified accounts of alcohol intoxication and violence, despite their awareness of complexity.

Compared to Sue, Stuart and Natalie, there were several policy experts who were much more unequivocal about alcohol's causal role in violence and willing to give this factor primacy, thereby simplifying the relationship between intoxication and violence. For example, in answering the question, 'What causes violence', Richard replied, 'I think it is over-consumption of alcohol'. Steven also emphasises what he calls the 'pretty simple equation' of alcohol intoxication with violence:

> Well there's clearly a connection [… between injury and assault and] the amount of alcohol that is consumed in night-time economy destinations. There's a very significant body of evidence that shows the greater availability of alcohol [… is linked to] higher rates of harm, particularly violence and injury as you know, indicated by arrests, emergency department presentations, hospitalisations and an enormous research base that shows that availability is about the trading hours and the levels of consumption of alcohol and studies that show high levels of intoxication in these night-time entertainment precincts. It's a pretty simple equation.

Later in his interview, Steven is even more unequivocal:

I: What are the causes of violence in the night time economy?
S: Booze. […] It's pretty simple. It increases the risks. You know people's behaviour changes when they are affected by alcohol.
I: You would see alcohol as causal?
S: Absolutely and that's what the evidence shows. An enormous body of evidence.

However, even in the strongly simplifying accounts of Richard and Steven, complexity is brought back in, often in discussions of gender and its relationship to intoxication. For instance, Steven modifies his earlier statement about booze simply causing violence, with a reference to its differential effects on men and women (which he also supports with a reference to evidence):

> I think there's a growing body of evidence that shows that alcohol makes … that men as a consequence of consuming alcohol tend to become more aggressive. I think that's probably the kind of key take-out from what we know about men … the difference between men and women and their behaviours.

Steven goes on to say that:

> Those sort of characteristics that lead to kind of group behaviour, the kind of urging one another on in drinking sessions and then the way that all too frequently gets out of hand and I suppose there's issues like that sense of entitlement that appears when people are intoxicated or seemingly appears when people are intoxicated and that might affect how that impacts on young women, for instance, and the sexual assaults or unwanted behaviour from men.

Richard also brings gender into his account of alcohol effects in terms of a differential of harm for men and women: 'intoxicated women are probably more at risk than intoxicated men of being the victim of others' unwanted behaviour'. Here Richard explicitly identifies women's vulnerability to sexual and physical violence but leaves 'unwanted behaviour' ungendered. Thus while gender complicates Steven and Richard's accounts of the causal link between intoxication and violence, they both envisage gender through what Sophie Yates calls the 'big G' model (2018). This is gender as a category, an individual attribute that usually maps onto sex. What is not brought into play is what Yates refers to as the 'small g' model, which conceives of gender as a process and emphasises hierarchical relations between gendered categories. The small g model would enable attention to gendered patterns of intoxication, including encounters among men or women as well as between men and women.

In a different way from Natalie, Richard constitutes gender as a difficult space for intervention. In response to a question about whether he thought men's violence is being addressed in current alcohol policy measures, he reflects on measures explicitly targeting a specific category versus the general strategy of harm reduction:

> Given the reliance on things like banning notices on individuals, I suspect they are far more used to target men than women. So, I would say yes, that would be true. In terms of other measures, I'm not … I mean I've seen obviously some advertising-type education material that targets men, but because of the measures to reduce harm appear so limited, I'm less clear about stuff that's being done at all in that space. I mean I think, you know, obviously the regulator is trying to enforce the existing regulation, but enforcing regulation around serving people who are intoxicated appears very difficult, and I'm trying to think why else venues get sanctioned for irresponsible advertising, but again that's not related specifically to addressing men's behaviour.

While recognising the potential value and logic of targeted measures, Richard identifies the harms of intoxication as pervasive and unpredictable. Therefore the promotion of public health as a common good requires measures that apply to and shape drinking environments as a whole.

Conclusion

In this chapter, we have drawn on Mol and Law's (2002) framework to analyse the handling of complexity in Australian alcohol policy discourse: specifically, the handling of the relationship between alcohol and violence. In doing so, we acknowledge that our own analysis, like all knowledge production, is contingent on the ways in which we have chosen to handle the complexity of our data. In the two policy documents that focus on alcohol and violence, we saw how a simplified emphasis on intoxication relegated from view the many other factors shaping intoxicated behaviour, which might form the basis for alternative ways of handling complexity. In the accounts offered by alcohol policy stakeholders, a more complicated dynamic is at work. The contrasting trajectories identified by Fraser (2016) are evident in our data: policy stakeholders acknowledge complexity in the relationship between alcohol intoxication and violence but, for a range of reasons, also render it in more straightforward terms when considering responses. Notably, the simplifications we identify all work in much the same direction: policy responses need to reduce alcohol availability (and therefore intoxication) in order to reduce violence. Stakeholders also commonly invoke a specific form of research 'evidence' – usually quantitative – to support this simplification. In considering this tension, we need to bear in mind that, as we noted earlier, contemporary alcohol policy is, in many ways, a reaction to the liberalisation that occurred in the 1990s, and that the nature of policy work means that the policy levers available in a specific area may be limited. It is also possible to see in the interview accounts general support for the well-established public health principle that a direct relationship exists between per capita alcohol consumption and harm, and a belief that this offers the strongest strategic ground for achieving the desired changes in alcohol policy. Such framing tends to reinforce the allocation of causal responsibility to alcohol, authorises blanket measures that pay little attention to the range of forces and elements co-constituting violence, and unnecessarily limits the choices for those unlikely to contribute to violence. It also sidelines approaches to intoxication, and to alcohol more generally, that mobilise alternative ways of handling complexity. This situation is beginning to change, however, with policy discourses attending to the social and cultural aspects of drinking being developed in the Australian Drug Foundation's Good Sports Program (https://adf.org.au/programs/good-sports/) and the Victorian Health Promotion Foundation's Alcohol Cultures Framework (VicHealth, 2019).

In offering this analysis, our aim is not to argue that alcohol should not be the focus of government policies and discourse but to call attention to the simplifications evident in them and to their effects. As we have argued, the simplifications evident in the analysed policy discourse foreground, for the most part, the pharmacology of alcohol and the reduction of alcohol availability. What if alcohol policy relied on different forms of research that emphasised the gendering of alcohol-related violence (Carrington et al., 2010; Lindsay, 2012; Tomsen, 1997, 2005) or took a more critical view of the methods, assumptions and practices of the research it currently relies on (Buss, 2015; Moore et al., 2017, 2020, 2021; Walby & Towers, 2017)? What different effects might result if the simplification was of a different order: for example, if men's drinking was identified as the main issue of policy concern with respect to violence? As an authoritative discourse that plays a key performative role in the constitution of realities, the allocation of government resources and the governance of health, alcohol policy deserves close scrutiny for what it can tell us about the contemporary problematisation of intoxication.

Acknowledgements

The research was conducted with the support of an Australian Research Council Discovery Grant (DP18010036). Chief investigators on the project are David Moore and Helen Keane. Partner investigators are Kathryn Graham and Mats Ekendahl. Research staff working on the project are Duane Duncan and Emily Lenton. The project has been based in two institutions over time: the National Drug Research Institute, Curtin University, and the Australian Research Centre in Sex, Health and Society, La Trobe University. The National Drug Research Institute is supported by core funding from the Australian Government under the

Drug and Alcohol Program and also receives significant funding from Curtin University. We extend our sincere thanks to the interview participants who gave their valuable time to take part in our research.

References

Alexander, A. & Roberts, M.S. (eds) (2003). *High culture: Reflections on addiction and modernity*. New York: SUNY Press.

Ayres, T. & Taylor, S. (2020). Media and intoxication: Media representations of the intoxicated. In Hutton, F. (ed.), *Cultures of intoxication: Key issues and debates*. Cham: Palgrave Macmillan, pp. 239–261.

Becker, H.S. (1953). Becoming a marihuana user. *American Journal of Sociology*, 59(3), 235–242.

Blackman, S. (2017). Young people and intoxication: Illegal drugs, alcohol and legal highs. In Furlong, A. (ed.), *Routledge handbook of youth and young adulthood* (2nd edition). Abingdon: Routledge, pp. 258–265.

Buss, D. (2015). Measurement imperatives and gender politics: An introduction. *Social Politics*, 22(3), 381–389.

Callinan, I.D.F. (2016). *Review of amendments to the Liquor Act 2007 (NSW)*. Sydney: New South Wales Department of Justice. URL (consulted 12 January 2021): https://www.liquorandgaming.nsw.gov.au/documents/public-consultations/independent-liquor-law-review/Liquor-Law-Review-Report.pdf

Carrington, K., McIntosh, A. & Scott, J. (2010). Globalization, frontier masculinities and violence: Booze, blokes and brawls. *British Journal of Criminology*, 50, 393–413.

Douglas, M. (ed.) (1987). *Constructive drinking: Perspectives on drink from anthropology*. Cambridge: Cambridge University Press.

Duncan, D., Keane, H., Moore, D., Ekendahl, M. & Graham, K. (2022). Making gender along the way: Women, men and harm in Australian alcohol policy. *Critical Policy Studies*, 16(1), 1–18.

Duncan, D., Moore, D., Keane, H. & Ekendahl, M. (2020). Obscuring gendered difference: The treatment of alcohol and violence in Australian government policy. *Social Politics*, https://doi.org/10.1093/sp/jxaa038.

Fagan, J. (1990). Intoxication and aggression. *Crime and Justice*, 13, 241–320.

Felson, R.B. & Staff, J. (2010). The effects of alcohol intoxication on violent versus other offending. *Criminal Justice and Behavior*, 37(12), 1343–1360.

Flynn, A., Halsey, M. & Lee, M. (2016). Emblematic violence and aetiological cul-de-sacs: On the discourse of 'one-punch' (non) fatalities. *British Journal of Criminology*, 56, 179–195.

Fraser, S. (2016). Articulating addiction in alcohol and other drug policy: A multiverse of habits. *International Journal of Drug Policy*, 31, 6–14.

Fraser, S. & Moore, D. (2011). Governing through problems: The formulation of policy on amphetamine-type stimulants (ATS) in Australia. *International Journal of Drug Policy*, 22, 498–506.

Gefou-Madianou, D. (ed.) (1992). *Alcohol, gender, and culture*. London: Routledge.

Hanna, P. (2012). Using internet technologies (such as Skype) as a research medium. *Qualitative Research*, 12, 239–242.

Heath, D.B. (1958). Drinking patterns of the Bolivian Camba. *Quarterly Journal of Studies on Alcohol*, 19(3), 491–508.

Hutton, F. (2020). Femininities and intoxication. In Hutton, F. (ed.), *Cultures of intoxication: Key issues and debates*. Cham: Palgrave Macmillan, pp. 187–210.

Keane, H. (2009). Intoxication, harm and pleasure: An analysis of the Australian National Alcohol Strategy. *Critical Public Health*, 19(2), 135–142.

Keane, H. (2020). Smoking and intoxication: From control to the buzz. In Hutton, F. (ed.), *Cultures of intoxication: Key issues and debates*. Cham: Palgrave Macmillan, pp. 45–66.

Legal and Constitutional Affairs References Committee. (2016). *Need for a nationally-consistent approach to alcohol-fuelled violence: Interim report*. Canberra: Commonwealth of Australia.

Levine, H.G. (1978). The discovery of addiction: Changing conceptions of habitual drunkenness in America. *Journal of Studies on Alcohol*, 39(1), 143–174.

Lindesmith, A.E. (1947). *Opiate addiction*. Bloomington: Principia Press.

Lindsay, J. (2012). The gendered trouble with alcohol: Young people managing alcohol related violence. *International Journal of Drug Policy*, 23, 236–241.

MacAndrew, C. & Edgerton, R. (1969). *Drunken comportment: A social explanation.* London: Nelson.
Mandelbaum, D.G. (1965). Alcohol and culture. *Current Anthropology*, 6(3), 281–288.
Manton, E. & Moore, D. (2016). Gender, intoxication and the developing brain: Problematisations of drinking among young adults in Australian alcohol policy. *International Journal of Drug Policy*, 31, 153–162.
Marshall, M. (1979). *Weekend warriors: Alcohol in a Micronesian culture.* Palo Alto: Mayfield.
Measham, F. & Brain, K. (2005). 'Binge' drinking, British alcohol policy and the new culture of intoxication. *Crime, Media, Culture*, 1(3), 262–263.
Measham, F. & Moore, K. (2008). The criminalisation of intoxication. In Squires, P. (ed.), *ASBO nation: The criminalisation of nuisance.* Bristol: Policy Press, pp. 273–288.
Miles, C. (2012) Intoxication and homicide: A context-specific approach. *British Journal of Criminology*, 52(5), 870–888.
Mol, A. & Law, J. (2002). Complexities: An introduction. In Law, J. & Mol, A. (eds.), *Complexities: Social studies of knowledge practices.* Durham: Duke University Press, pp. 1–22.
Moore, D. (2020). Masculinities and intoxication: Notes towards a co-constitutive approach. In Hutton, F. (ed.), *Cultures of intoxication: Key issues and debates.* Cham: Palgrave Macmillan, pp. 211–235.
Moore, D., Duncan, D., Keane, H. & Ekendahl, M. (2021). Displacements of gender: Research on alcohol, violence and the night-time economy. *Journal of Sociology*, 57(4), 860–876.
Moore, D., Fraser, S., Keane, H., Seear, K. & Valentine, K. (2017). Missing masculinities: Gendering practices in Australian alcohol research and policy. *Australian Feminist Studies*, 32, 309–324.
Moore, D., Keane, H. & Duncan, D. (2020). Enacting alcohol realities: Gendering practices in Australian studies on 'alcohol-related presentations' to emergency departments. *Sociology of Health and Illness*, 42, 3–19.
Nancy, J-L. (2016). *Intoxication* (trans. by Philip Armstrong). New York: Fordham University Press.
New South Wales Department of Justice & Australian Institute of Criminology. (2012). *Fact sheet: Strategies to reduce alcohol-related assault in entertainment precincts.* URL (consulted 12 January 2021): http://www.crimeprevention.nsw.gov.au/Documents/Councils-Factsheets/alcohol-related_assault_factsheet.pdf
Nicholls, J. (2003). Gin Lane revisited: Intoxication and society in the gin epidemic. *Journal for Cultural Research*, 7(2), 125–146.
Pienaar, K. Murphy, D., Race, K. & Lea, T. (2020a). Sexualities and intoxication: 'To be intoxicated is to still be me, just a little blurry' – Drugs, enhancement and transformation in lesbian, gay, bisexual, transgender and queer cultures. In Hutton, F. (ed.), *Cultures of intoxication: Key issues and debates.* Cham: Palgrave Macmillan, pp. 139–163.
Pienaar, K. Murphy, D., Race, K. & Lea, T. (2020b). Drugs as technologies of the self: Enhancement and transformation in LGBTQ cultures. *International Journal of Drug Policy*, 78: 102673.
Queensland Government. (2014). *Safe night out strategy.* URL (consulted 12 January 2021): https://cabinet.qld.gov.au/documents/2014/Jun/SafeNightOutBill/Attachments/Strategy.pdf
Reith, G. (2005). On the edge: Drugs and the consumption of risk in late modernity. In Lyng, S. (ed.), *Edgework: The sociology of risk taking.* New York: Routledge, pp. 227–246.
Room, R. & Livingston, M. (2017). The distribution of customary behavior in a population: The total consumption model and alcohol policy. *Sociological Perspectives*, 60(1), 10–22.
Ruddock, A. (2020). Social media and intoxication: 'Tweaker Nation': Celebrating drug use on Tumblr. In Hutton, F. (ed.), *Cultures of intoxication: Key issues and debates.* Cham: Palgrave Macmillan, pp. 263–282.
Seale, C. (1999). *The quality of qualitative research.* London: Sage.
Shaw, R. (2014). Beyond night-time economy: Affective atmospheres of the urban night. *Geoforum*, 51(1), 87–95.
Tomsen, S. (1997). A TOP NIGHT: Social protest, masculinity and the culture of drinking violence. *British Journal of Criminology*, 37, 90–102.
Tomsen, S. (2005). 'Boozers and bouncers': Masculine conflict, disengagement and the contemporary governance of drinking-related violence and disorder. *Australian & New Zealand Journal of Criminology*, 38(3), 283–297.
VicHealth. (2019). *Alcohol cultures framework: A framework to guide public health action on risky drinking cultures.* Melbourne: VicHealth.
Walby, S. & Towers, J. (2017). Measuring violence to end violence: Mainstreaming gender. *Journal of Gender-Based Violence*, 1, 11–31.

Wilkinson, C., Livingston, M. & Room, R. (2016). Impacts of changes to trading hours of liquor licences on alcohol-related harm: A systematic review 2005–2015. *Public Health Research & Practice*, 26(4), e2641644.

Yates, S. (2018). Power, process, plumbing: Big G and small g gender in Victoria's family violence policy subsystem. *Australian Journal of Public Administration*, 77(4), 568–582.

Zinberg, N.E. (1984). *Drug, set, and setting*. New Haven: Yale University Press.

PART VIII

Notions of Excess

30

ALTERED STATES

Changing conditions of excess in European drinking cultures[1]

Dorota Dias-Lewandowska, Laura Fenton, Sam Goodman and Beat Kümin

Introduction

Drawing on four distinct, yet complementary, cases, this chapter provides a historically and culturally comparative perspective on the socially contested boundary between excess and moderation in relation to alcohol. Beginning with late medieval and early modern Western Europe and sixteenth- to nineteenth-century Poland, and then turning to twentieth-century and contemporary Britain, the chapter explores how various religious, state and cultural authorities have sought to define excessive and moderate drinking, and how a diverse set of actors has negotiated their drinking in relation to these textual and visual discourses. As such, the chapter considers the continual interplay between the definition, regulation and practice of excess in a range of contexts, identifying how definitions, regulations and practices of excess exist in a state of changing reciprocation, and reinscription over time; the case studies illustrate how the perception of excess drives regulation, and how these regulatory efforts themselves can serve to produce and invite excess. Further, the authors argue that contradictions and double standards abound in authorities' efforts to construct the boundary between excess and moderation in each instance under study, suggesting that one of the consistent contentions over the definition of excess is this inconsistency.

The chapter starts with an examination of a fundamental transformation process in the sixteenth century. In the Age of the Reformations, medieval Christendom fragmented into rivalling confessions. Being a Catholic or Protestant provided one of the main sources of personal identities and a source of fierce tensions right up to military conflict within and between groups. Often in close collaboration with the emerging states, the various Churches sought to form theologically uniform and socially disciplined bodies of believers, demarcating themselves not just against non-Christian minorities of Jews and Muslims but also each other. Excessive drinking became a prominent target of their campaigns. Seen as a waste of divine resources and a pathway into sin, inebriation attracted particular censure. However, the sale of alcoholic beverages generated income for clergy and parish communities alike, while conviviality played a key part in social bonding among the laity. The first case study of this chapter thus traces the negotiation of these contrasting impulses, finding both confessional and contextual differences in the definition of excess.

DOI: 10.4324/9780429058141-39

As explored in the chapter's second case study, excessive drinking among Polish nobles in the early modern period was seen as a social norm and a part of national identity. Thus, clergy criticising drunkenness among the elites were more focussed on the economic consequences of buying expensive foreign wines, leaving the moral aspects of sinful behaviour in the background. At that time, Polish peasants forced by propination laws (a set of entitlements that increased alcohol-related revenues for land-owning elites) to consume and buy vodka produced by the distilleries of landowners were absent in the general debate on excess. Starting from the second half of the eighteenth century, when the first approaches to change the drinking culture to a more moderate culture began, debate over excess reached a turning point. The social norm of excessive drinking became a national problem. With the loss of independence and an inefficient economy based on grain production, the mass consumption of alcohol at the end of the eighteenth century in the lower classes became a serious issue. At this point, the main actor to blame for such national misery was vodka. In the national debate on drunkenness conducted by the Church, scientists, temperance movements and social activists, the idea that spirits were harmful was so strong that almost until the end of the nineteenth century, it was considered less dangerous to actively promote the consumption of beer, wine and cider.

The governance of excess shifted considerably over the course of the twentieth century in Britain, with a diverse range of actors involved in constituting the boundary between excess and moderation. In relation to overall consumption, the first half of the century was in general terms a time of moderation and sobriety. In the 1950s and 1960s, 'binge drinking' referred to a form of overindulgence that could last several days and which was connected to clinical understandings of alcoholism (Berridge, Herring and Thom 2009). By the century's closing decade, the term was synonymous with a routinised weekly ritual (ibid). Against the backdrop of these changes, the chapter's third case study explores how excess was governed in British society over the course of the century. As the fourth and final case study on contemporary British drinking cultures illustrates, modern breweries such as BrewDog no longer associate excess with problematic drinking and thus attempt to disassociate themselves from it, but rather have sought to make the extreme a central part of their ethos and branding. Such an approach is at odds with the advice from the UK Chief Medical officer, who has advocated ever-decreasing limits on alcohol intake, and indeed states that there is no safe amount of alcohol consumption (Press Association 2016). The result is a disjunction in which the average drinker is caught between the encouragement towards the pursuit of the exceptional in relation to flavour, strength and style, and the knowledge of the need for moderation and caution when it comes to volume. Excess thus becomes a fluid concept, and moves away from the measurement of amounts alone to the character, space and intent of the consumption too.

The chapter is thus the product of an interdisciplinary approach that seeks to bring together the conversant disciplines of history, sociology, anthropology and communications studies. This interdisciplinarity is itself reflective of the discussions and specialisms of the Drinking Studies Network Excess Cluster, out of which the chapter developed. Though broad in its temporal and cultural focus, the chapter benefits from a considerable degree of productive thematic and analytical overlap as a consequence of its collaborative origins, offering insight into a heterogeneous field of study. As the chapter makes clear, there is no singular definition of what constitutes 'excess', nor is there a form of regulation consistent across the temporal span and cultural contexts that it covers; instead, as Rod Phillips argues, 'excess' and 'moderation' are mutable terms set and defined in relation to established norms of behaviour in cultures and societies that are themselves fluid over time (2014: 23). Given that a full survey of the multiplicities of excess would thus greatly exceed the scope of a single chapter, the advantage of a case study approach is that it enables the identification and analysis of common, recurrent themes across these differing periods, and supporting its thesis with regard to the role of various agents (particularly Church and state authorities, social/scientific elites and the individual), the concern over differing types of alcohols consumed (chiefly ale/beer, wine and spirits), and the shifting means of regulation used to meet them. This juxtaposition makes it possible to observe how the perception, regulation and consumption of alcohol, all of which are subject to continuous change over the centuries, consistently influence the way drinking limits are created, crossed and redefined.

Each case study draws on key texts from the relevant period and secondary literature to identify a set of concerns that have influenced and conditioned how excess is negotiated; these concerns are in varying degrees specific to the context of the case, while also illuminating shared tensions across the cases as a whole.

Its long-term approach, furthermore, allows the chapter to trace the cultural history of excessive drinking from a period without a concept of 'alcoholism' via a phase when heavy drinking became subject to medicalisation right through to modernity, where excess and frequency of drinking are factors referring directly to the definition and diagnosis of addiction. Taken together, the cases illustrate the often contradictory and multi-faceted nature of attempts to define and regulate excess and moderation across this temporal span, and present a picture of the trans-historical and cross-cultural significance of intoxication and intoxicants to rituals of hospitality and conviviality in European societies. Last but not least, the examples also show the recurrent importance of the type of alcoholic beverage in the discourse on drinking limits. This can be observed not only at the level of strength, taste or nature of the drink, but also in the context of viewing the beverage as national, local or 'one's own', as compared to imported, foreign drinks. In the final analysis, what becomes apparent in these studies is the semantic fluidity of the notion of excess, which may turn from a social norm into undesirable behaviour, with the simultaneous evolution of the very concept of excess itself.

Case study 1: Navigating boundaries of excess in Europe's long Reformation

Building on classical tradition, medieval Europeans understood heavy drinking as disrupting the specific mixture between the four 'humours' (blood, yellow bile, black bile and phlegm) which shaped human character and physiology. Given that the Greek physician Galen had classed 'cold' and 'wet' female bodies as inherently weak, prone to greater destabilisation by beverages with 'hot' and 'fiery' attributes, men – particularly those of a sanguine disposition – could be allowed larger volumes than women. Humoral theory thus justified gender- and temperament-specific boundaries of consumption, typically defined as the points after which individuals started to lose control over their bodily fluids (Tlusty 2001: Chs. 3, 7). Straightaway, this signals the importance of directions coming from authorities. Alongside 'scientific' voices, however, there were numerous other influences on demarcations between acceptable and unacceptable intake. Among them, we find local and central governments as well as period notions of personal honour, which associated masculinity with the ability to hold copious amount of drink, join in witty alehouse exchanges and pay one's fair share of the tap; in short, to excel at 'good fellowship' (Hailwood 2014). Similar ideas circulated right across the social scale including the most distinguished companies and environments, as documented in Archduke Ferdinand II's record of convivial occasions at his Tyrolean base of Ambras Castle (a Drinking Book started in 1567: Igály 2010).

The chief arbitrator of norms in pre-modern Europe, however, was the Christian Church and its focus lay on the salvation of souls. According to Catholic doctrine, admission to heaven involved a consideration of merit, commensurate with the extent to which humans observed God's commandments, performed works of mercy (e.g. giving drink to the thirsty) and stayed clear of the seven deadly sins (among which gluttony, i.e. culinary overindulgence, loomed large [Duffy 2005: pt. I]). The *Mireour du Monde*, a fourteenth-century French moral treatise, contrasted churches as sites for divine worship with taverns as strongholds of the devil, while priests disseminated comparable messages during annual Easter confessions or when admonishing congregations from the pulpit (Chavannes 1847). One of the most notable German preachers, Johann Geiler von Kaisersberg, deplored the sin of drunkenness, seen to be indicative of a string of other human failures and follies, in a published sermon of 1498 (Strauss 1971: 211–215). Yet at the same time, parish operations relied on convivial occasions like 'church ales', distant ancestors of modern fêtes. Dedicated officials sold what local women had brewed for the purpose, with the proceeds supporting the administration and enhancement of religious activities. In the English South-West, churchwardens easily derived over two thirds of their revenues from this source (Kümin 1996: 116). Alongside, monastic orders produced their own beer for internal as well as external consumption. At Freising in Bavaria, a present-day brewery boasts licencing records going back to 1040 (Weihenstephan: https://www.weihenstephaner.de/en/our-brewery/history/)! In viticulture areas, furthermore, ecclesiastical institutions claimed around 10% of the vintners' output under the title of tithes. This was way more than priests could use up on their own, prompting the retailing of fermented beverages on sacred premises. At the Imperial Diet of Worms in 1521, the German estates complained that 'many clerics have turned to tavern keeping ..., put[ting] up tables for dice, bowls, or cards and invite people to play' (Strauss 1971: 61).

The various strands of (Counter-)Reformations prompted some of Europe's longest and most fundamental transformation processes, starting with Hussite/Humanist critiques of church abuses in the fifteenth century and concluding with the consolidation of rivalling confessions by the late seventeenth (Rublack 2016). An important catalyst was Martin Luther's insistence that the Bible should be the sole guide in spiritual matters. With regard to our chapter's emphasis on the significance of specific drinks, this opened fresh tensions between positive scriptural references to wine as a gift of God (for example, at the wedding of Cana [John 2: 1–10]) and Protestant ideals of a more ascetic lifestyle (prompting clamp-downs on popular culture which scholars have labelled as a 'Triumph of Lent' [Burke 2009: pt 3]). Luther himself very much enjoyed the odd drink, particularly beer given that he lived outside the main wine-producing zones, classing it as a 'little elevation' and a social lubricator, especially when entertaining at his Wittenberg home, where his wife (a former nun) Katharina von Bora engaged in domestic brewing. Many famous, at times notorious, quotations derive from slightly inebriated table talks recorded for posterity by pupils and guests (Luther 1967). However, as a pastor, he was acutely aware of the – physical as well as spiritual – dangers of excessive consumption. A 1539 sermon on 'Soberness ... against Gluttony and Drunkenness' set out to square the circle. Luther's proposed solution centred on the fundamental notion of 'moderation', specifically understood as staying on the right side of the divide between acceptable 'human' and reprehensible 'animal' behaviour:

> God does not forbid you to drink, as do the Turks; he permits you to drink wine and beer; he does not make a law of it. But do not make a pig of yourself; remain a human being. If you are a human being, then keep your human self-control. Even though we

> do not have a command of God, we should nevertheless be ashamed that we are thus spit upon by other peoples. ... If you have been a pig, then stop being one.
>
> *(Luther 1539)*

Apart from clerical expectations, the passage also tells us something about demarcations from non-Christian religions: explicitly Ottoman Turks, expected to abstain altogether, and implicitly Jews, whom derogatory propaganda often depicted alongside a sow and thus linked to beastly behaviour (even though their attitudes towards alcohol were equally differentiated). While pragmatic, Luther's advice remained rather general, leaving case-by-case decisions of what exactly constituted too much to the imbibers. Period evidence underlines the difficulty of holding the line, with many throwing themselves quite literally to the dogs (Figure 30.1). In an attempt to separate themselves from such reprobates bound for damnation, radical Anabaptists first floated the idea of abstinence in Christian Europe (Schleitheim Confession 1527: Art. 4) but theirs remained an isolated voice until the temperance movements of the nineteenth century.

At the risk of oversimplification, Lutheranism constituted a 'half-way house' between Catholicism – whose followers participated in an extensive festive culture revolving around saints' feasts, church dedication days and pilgrimages (while benefitting from periodic absolution of their sins through the sacrament of confession) – and the more austere Swiss Reformation led by Huldrych Zwingli in Zurich and subsequently John Calvin in Geneva. In the Bernese countryside, an area which had adopted the former's teachings in 1528, ministers embarked on concerted social disciplining. The outcome was mixed: while some doctrinal and organisational measures met with grassroots support, parishioners resented the

Figure 30.1 Extract from Barthel Beham, 'Country Fair' (woodcut, *c.* 1530)
Source: public domain

clampdown on conviviality (Schmidt 1995). At Neuenegg, a village adjacent to Catholic Fribourg, young men and women regularly crossed the confessional divide to partake in seasonal dances held just across the border, a pastime officially banned in their own territory. The threat of punishment by the parochial authorities, charged with the enforcement of Zwinglian standards (recorded by the court e.g. on 30 July 1654, 29 July 1666, 7 May 1671), failed to discourage them, nor did patrons of the local Bear inn always live up to godly expectations. On 10 April 1659, for example, the pastor and elders reprimanded a married woman who, instead of going to church, had headed straight for the public house, where she overindulged to such an extent that she threw up on the way back. Similarly, on 28 October 1680, local official Peter Freiburghaus was cited for getting so 'full' of drink that he could no longer sit down or walk home, while wasting divine gifts by throwing wine all around him (Consistory Court Protocols 1650–; Kümin 2007: 71, 182, Pl. VI).

Much the same story of lay-clerical and elite-popular negotiation could be told for Calvinist regions like Scotland, the Huguenot 'crescent' stretching across southern France, and parts of Eastern Europe. A classic example is post-Reformation England. Here, the moderate Elizabethan settlement came under fire from 'hotter sorts' of Protestants who sought to bring the established Church closer in line with Geneva (Durston and Eales 1996). Once again, drinking played an important and ambivalent role. As in other Reformed areas, while communion wine was no longer believed to transubstantiate into the blood of Christ (as in Catholicism), its relevance to the laity arguably increased through the administration of the Eucharist in both kinds. Many parishes provided cheap claret for the common folk but superior sweet malmsey and muscadine for the better sorts (Craig 1993: 376); recent scholarship has noted parallels between this 'sacred' ritual and the pledging of healths in the tavern (McShane 2014). At the same time, the so-called 'Puritans' fought a sustained battle against the allegedly corrosive role of the alehouse, a cultural offensive with a similarly polarising effect, in the sense that communities tended to split into a select godly elite and a majority attached to convivial forms of popular culture (Wrightson 1981), i.e. along lines of 'class'. In the long run, the traditions of 'Merry England' eroded, with a nadir under the nonconformist Interregnum of the 1650s, until the restoration of the Stuart dynasty and Church of England redressed the balance in the later seventeenth century (Hutton 2001). During the Enlightenment of the 1700s, attacks on drinking then prioritised utilitarian over religious concerns; it was also the time when 'alcoholism' first gained recognition as an illness rather than a moral failure, marking the gradual rise of medical at the expense of religious authority (Porter 1985).

Looking back over the period, Catholics and Reformed both faced conflicts of interests between religious doctrines and moral teachings on the one hand and pastoral considerations and financial incentives on the other. Boundaries of excess thus varied, in terms of occasion, social status, gender as well as confessional orientation, with the bulk of the population – and indeed many clergymen – firmly opposed to any notion of incompatibility between Christian identity and 'moderate' drinking.

Case study 2: 'Drunk as a Pole': from a social norm to a national problem[2]

Stories of spectacular feasts, toasts and nobles drinking until they fell over and forcing their companions to make toasts with glasses filled with the best Tokay wines played a major part in the debate concerning drinking in early modern Poland. Thus, 'to drink like a Pole' became a phrase defining an excessive, theatrical and oppressive consumption of enormous amounts of alcohol but at a given time and place.

The words 'drunk as a Pole' supposedly derived from Napoleon, who wanted to express his appreciation not only for the courage and morale of Polish forces, but also for their strong heads (Moskalewicz and Zieliński 1995: 224). But already in the seventeenth century, John Worlidge wrote:

> In Poland, he is most accounted of that will drink most healths; and held to be the bravest fellow, that carries his liquor best; being of opinion, that there is as much valour to be found in drinking as in fighting
>
> *(Worlidge 1678)*

Thus, for contemporaries, the notion of moderation related not to consumption volumes, but to the right timing of drinking and maintaining abstinence when necessary.

Historically, excessive consumption of alcohol was an obvious, necessary and desirable behaviour within a culture of hospitality linked to the ideology of Sarmatism, based on the historical legend about the descent of the Polish nobility from the ancient Sarmatians. An ideal citizen combined strict morality with noble kindness and the attitude of a defender of the Catholic faith and homeland. This idealisation of rural life and tranquillity was interrupted from time to time by the arrival of guests who provided occasions for numerous drinking rituals (Figure 30.2).

Although at the time Europeans viewed Poles as beer-drinking barbarians (Flandrin and Flandrin 1999: 307–317), wine posed a rather more serious problem for native preachers and moralists. The nobility justified their love for wine with medical recommendations. Claiming that the native beer was too cold for the local climate, they claimed that they had to warm their stomachs with foreign, mainly Hungarian, wines (de Tende 1686: 268).

Figure 30.2 Aleksander Orłowski, 'Uczta u Radziwiłłów', first half of the nineteenth century

Source: National Museum in Warsaw, photograph by Krzysztof Wilczyński

Wine consumption had already been stigmatised by the preacher Piotr Skarga in the second half of the sixteenth century. He described it as an unnecessary luxury replacing the drinking of good old beer (Rychcicki 1850: 253). Almost a 100 years later, Szymon Starowolski expressed similar grumblings in his sermons on the renewal of the Republic of Poland. These promulgated a rhetoric of doom and gloom for his homeland, the main reason being luxury and excess, especially withdrawal from the 'old Polish life' and replacing beer with wine (Starowolski 1656: 39). Such religious voices continuously warned against the consequences of drunkenness, yet above all the consumption of expensive imported alcohols and the conflict between tradition and modernity (Dias-Lewandowska 2014: 33–37).

The reign of the Wettin dynasty (1697–1763) marked the end of the ideology of Sarmatism and the point from which Sarmatian noblemen dressed in kontush and toasting with Hungarian wine became synonymous with backwardness and ignorance (Dias-Lewandowska 2015). During the reign of the last king of Poland, Stanisław August Poniatowski (1763–1795), occasional excessive drinking was no longer perceived as a social norm, but rather as the cause of the country's demise (Wybicki 1777–1778: 122). His diaries record a personal pledge not to abuse strong beverages and the king considered greater sobriety among the Polish aristocracy to be instrumental for the decrease of drunkenness in the realm at large (Poniatowski 1870: 10). In progressive circles, moderate intake of – mostly French – wine became the new standard to aspire to, a sobering cultural reorientation credited with a large part in 'superstitions and drunkenness disappearing' (Ney 1844: 382). The most conservative members of the nobility remained faithful to Hungarian wine. Despite many reforms, however, it proved impossible to save the country from the partitions and eventual loss of independence.

At this point, the first serious treaties on alcohol and drunkenness began to appear. In his *Dzieło o pijaństwie* ('Works on Drunkenness') of 1818, Jakub Szymkiewicz contrasted the decrease in alcohol consumption in the upper classes with its rise among the common people and workers. He called for the creation of a ladder of restraint, with the elite, nobility and aristocracy – who were to set an example of moderation – providing leadership at the top; the clergy – who should heed their own calls for moderation – playing an important part one step below; and women – whose drunkenness apparently boosted high child mortality and domestic strive – laying social foundations at the bottom (Szymkiewicz 1818: 19–20, 278–279). The presumed increase in consumption among the lowest groups was related to an inefficient feudal economy based mainly on grain production. Propination laws (a set of privileges boosting alcohol-related revenues for landowners), the obligation of peasants to purchase certain amounts of vodka from inns owned by the nobility and the practice of paying for work with alcohol also played crucial roles (Burszta 1950; Levin 2003). Combined with technological advances in distilling and the rise of cheap vodka from potatoes, the problem of drunkenness among peasants became ever more pressing (Figure 30.3).

From the middle of the nineteenth century, the focus of European debate on drunkenness shifted from overindulgent imbibers to contextual factors and the effects of specific beverages (Lucas 2004: 71). According to the foreign occupants of Polish lands, addiction resulted from habitual drinking linked to social misery rather than occasional consumption for pleasure, as it should be. Germans, allegedly, went through seven times as much vodka, but without becoming drunkards (Herman 1845). In Poland, the stigmatisation of this particular beverage began earlier still. It became a public enemy, which even other alcohols were enlisted to fight against. The idea of lesser evil – in the shape of wine, beer or cider consumption – is particularly evident in folk literature (Zschokke 1845: 4–5).

Figure 30.3 Aleksander Orłowski, 'Zabawa w karczmie', 1800
Source: National Museum in Krakow

In the discourse on excessive drinking, the blame for widespread drunkenness was attributed not only to the liquor itself, but also to the actors involved in the production, distribution and use of alcohol as a means of oppression. Especially frowned upon were the Jewish inns. The Jews who ran them, however, because of the specific legal and customary conditions at the time, had few other career paths available to them. Even though the main profits from this activity, owing to propination laws, were obtained by the nobility, it was the Jews who, because of their direct contact with peasants, became the scape goats held responsible for the problem of excessive drinking (Moskalewicz, Zieliński 1995; Dynner 2014). The nobility however, especially in the nineteenth century, were also seen as guilty by omission since they failed to promote sobriety and still took advantage of propination laws. The third main culprit were the invaders, who effectively prevented the establishment of temperance societies, thus spreading drunkenness, in what was perceived as an attempt to prevent the Poles from taking up the fight for their independence (Chociszewski 1891).

In highly moralised tales, the main characters were often priests with the authority to disseminate scientific knowledge and to educate peasants on the dangers of specific beverages (Z.N. 1846: 25–26). Some anti-alcohol discourses also targeted the kind of moderate consumption previously supported by doctors (Perzyna 1793: 261), leading to debates on whether restraint should be total. Some groups within the temperance movement recommended coffee and tea (while acknowledging the need for lower prices: Celichowski 1890), the *Promieniści* society [Friends of Useful Entertainment] advocated the use of milk in celebrations (Krasińska 2013: 247) while others promoted domestic cider as a healthier and cheaper alternative to vodka and wine (Gwiazdka 1865: 212). Eventually, even the apparent nutritional value of wine or beer came under attack:

> While looking at vodka as a scapegoat, on which one could blame the fatal consequences of drunkenness [...] in beer and wine, which were opposed to vodka, one tried to find nutrients in order to use them as an excuse and justify the consumption of these beverages
>
> *(Flaum 1894: 102)*

In conclusion, therefore, Polish discourses on excessive drinking gradually moved from the elite to the lower classes. In spite of the cultural changes of the late eighteenth century, perceptions of incidental, ritualised and almost forced alcohol consumption among nobles persisted for a long time. As late as 1882, during the Geneva Sanitary Congress, Dr Lubesski, sought to counter 'drunk as a Pole' stereotypes with statistics showing lower consumption levels than in many other European countries (The Lancet 1882: 634). In the nineteenth century, however, the main emphasis came to be placed on the type of alcohol, the context and the social group that consumed it. As a kind of compromise between moderation and total abstinence, many voices condemned the strongest spirits while recommending the consumption of weaker beverages.

Case study 3: Governing excess in twentieth-century Britain

The boundary between excess and moderation was a recurring site of contestation in twentieth-century Britain. While much of the historiography has until recently positioned debates over alcohol as a 'binary conflict between advocates and opponents of the liberal distribution of drink' (Yokoe 2019: 267), this representation misses the intricate patterns giving rise to both excess itself and to how authorities have attempted to govern it. Though in decline as an organised movement for social reform, some scholars have argued that the moral concerns of the Victorian-era temperance movement continued to influence public health discourses on excess (Yokoe, 2019; Yeomans, 2014). A diffuse 'cast of characters' was involved in governing excess in twentieth-century Britain, including but not limited to central and local government, breweries, scientists, the medical profession and public health campaigners. Their respective levels of power and influence in constituting the boundary between excess and moderation shifted over the course of the century. Britain in the twentieth century thus offers an interesting case study of a period of relatively intense change in how excess was governed, in terms of the authorities and institutional arrangements involved, and in particular the relative significance of the state, the alcohol industry, and the scientific and medical professions in this process. These institutions were also in a situation of flux, which has, in turn, affected how excess has been understood and governed.

In the Edwardian period (1901–1910), the decline in levels of alcohol consumption that began in the late nineteenth century was still in play (Jennings 2016). However, a high proportion of drinking environments, in particular pubs, was designed for 'vertical drinking' (that is, drinking while standing up) and thus encouraged the rapid consumption of alcohol (Gutzke 2014: 218). Public displays of drunkenness were by no means uncommon in many towns and cities. The construction of a central licencing regime, the Central Control Board (CCB) in 1915, to limit the impact of excessive drinking on the country's ability to succeed in the First World War resulted in tighter restrictions on when alcohol could be purchased, as well as resulted in increased duties. The CCB was regarded as effective in reducing public drunkenness (Duncan 2013: 3; Yokoe 2019: 268), and within a few years of its inception had come to be regarded by its chairman, Lord D'Abernon (1857–1941), among others, less as a wartime measure and more as means for addressing the causes of intemperance in a rational, scientific manner (Greenaway 2003). Licencing has been a chief means by which the state has at different junctures enacted and retracted its powers over the sale of alcohol, and by extension its management of levels of consumption.[3] As taxes on alcohol constitute an important source of revenue for the treasury, licencing is a mechanism that allows for a measure of control over public drunkenness while sustaining income. However, the central state is neither unified nor a sole player in the governance of excess. As Jennings (2016) argues, systems of regulation are enacted in practice at the local level, involving licencing magistrates, as well as publicans, police officers and others who influence how drunkenness is managed in local communities.

Breweries and the wider alcohol industry have also played a key role in creating conditions for excess and moderation. In the interwar period (1918–1939), many Edwardian public houses were redesigned to encourage more moderate, slower drinking and to create calmer, more convivial atmospheres by measures such as providing food, installing better lighting and building more spacious interiors (Gutzke 2014). This paved the way for women in particular to drink in licenced premises in higher numbers than previously (ibid), a pattern that Langhamer (2003) argues was propelled further by conditions on the Homefront during the Second World War. Langhamer contends that women's reports to Mass Observation and other sources from the time 'paint a picture of wartime as a period during which women made significant recourse to the public house as an arena for leisure and during which their alcohol consumption increased markedly' (2003: 424). While it has been argued that the immediate post-war years were characterised by many women's retreat from public drinking spaces (Gutzke 2014), young people – including young women – began drinking in licenced premises in increased numbers in the decades that shortly followed. Indeed, the second half of the twentieth century was characterised by both a diversification in the age and gender of drinkers, a multiplication in the types of places where drink could be sold and, in the main, increasingly liberal licencing laws (Jennings 2016). Of particular concern to health campaigners in the late twentieth and early twenty-first centuries has been the rise in off-sales. Low-cost alcohol sold in supermarkets was identified as a leading contributor to rising rates of liver disease from the 1990s onwards. Price was identified by campaigners as a key site for intervention. From 2006, Scottish Health Action on Alcohol Problems, a partnership of the Medical Royal Colleges, led a campaign for the introduction of 'minimum unit pricing' in Scotland, which eventually became law in 2018.

Moving beyond the state and industry, medical and scientific expertise has been central to the constitution of the boundary between excess and moderation in twentieth-century Britain. The medical understandings of excess that circulated in the twentieth century have their roots in the second half of the previous century, when 'an embryonic group of doctors with a clear interest in inebriety/addiction' emerged (Berridge 2013: 70). However, medical interest was not simply in forms of excess, like addiction and drunkenness, but also in how to quantify moderation. In the 1860s, the physician Francis Edmund Anstie (1833–1874) devised 'Anstie's limit', a measure of moderate alcohol consumption that Kneale and French argue is a key precursor to the notion of the 'unit' used in late twentieth-century and early twenty-first-century public health guidelines (Kneale and French 2015: 111). Like the 'unit', Anstie's limit was a measure of pure alcohol (ibid: 111).

The middle decades of the twentieth century are notable for the prominence of psychiatry in popularising a disease model of alcoholism. In the Victorian period (1837–1901), campaigners involved in the temperance movement positioned excess as a moral matter signalling drinkers' inability to control their desire for drink, whereas in the twentieth century, the rising prominence of 'alcoholism' positioned regular drunkenness as a condition that called for medical intervention, particularly in the form of psychiatric treatment (Thom 1999). Published in 1960, E.M. Jellinek's *Disease Concept of Alcoholism* was particularly significant in advancing the understanding of alcoholism as a condition that was confined to a small proportion of drinkers and that could be addressed through psychiatric treatment (Thom 1999: 209; Jennings 2016: 169).

From the mid-1970s onwards, a public health approach emerged as a key and later dominant player in the construction of excess. Originally a movement aimed at improving housing and sanitary conditions in cities undergoing rapid growth in the nineteenth century, the version of public health that became increasingly dominant in alcohol policy circles in the closing decades of the twentieth century was principally focussed on the individual and his or her health-related choices (Berridge 2013: 165–169; Jennings 2016: 169); this version of public health has its origins in the epidemiological transition which followed the Second World War, including increased interest in the causes and treatment of chronic (as opposed to infectious) diseases as a result of longer life spans. The rise of a public health approach to alcohol witnessed a 'redefinition of the problem in epidemiological…terms as arising from levels of alcohol consumption in the population as a whole and, at an individual level, as a result of lifestyle and "risk behaviour"' (Berridge, Herring and Thom 2009: 599). The language of 'prevention' and 'risk' came to overtake the focus on 'treatment' in how excess was understood and regulated (ibid: 598–599). 'Problem' drinking became an issue for the population as a whole: something everyone was at risk of, and no longer the reserve of those with the disease of alcoholism. Any amount of drinking could damage one's health, though those who drank above amounts cited in public health guidelines were especially placing themselves in harm's way. Nevertheless, one set of expert discourses does not entirely replace its predecessor (ibid), and the figure of 'the alcoholic' remains a powerful cultural trope.

For a variety of reasons, including rising levels of disposable income (Jennings 2016: 24), per capita consumption started to rise from the 1950s onwards (Smith and Foxcroft 2009: 10). In the closing decades of the century, changes in licencing laws and local authority regulations lead to the transformation of the night-time economy in city and town centres, and to what criminologists, sociologists and others have called a 'culture of intoxication' among young adults (Measham and Brain 2005). This culture is argued to be characterised by 'determined drunkenness' (ibid), that is, by an instrumentalist orientation towards intoxication as part of a hedonistic pursuit of pleasure. Intoxication through drinking 'alcopops' and other flavoured alcoholic drinks became widely understood by young adults as another means of reaching the 'altered state' that had been previously sought through club drugs, like ecstasy (Collin and Godfrey 1997; Measham 2004). The industry's efforts to engage younger consumers were largely successful, as evidenced by the increased consumption of alcopops and the corresponding halt in the upward trend of illicit drug use between 1995 and 2003 (Measham and Ostergaard 2009). Hayward and Hobbs (2007: 438) point to the 'aesthetic processes aimed at encouraging alcohol-related excitement and excess', such as in marketing and wider forms of cultural production, which sit uncomfortably alongside voices condemning excess, like the 'late night morality plays' of television programmes like *Booze Britain*. Such programmes were part of what the authors called a 'dual narrative': a simultaneous celebration and condemnation of excess (ibid: 438). The tension between a cultural celebration of excess and a set of conflicting normative concerns about the damage caused by drunkenness was also at the heart of policy making. The New Labour government, in power from 1997 until 2010, oversaw legal changes that allowed for alcohol to be sold 24 hours a day, a far cry from the CCB's imposed last orders of 9pm. As Jennings (2016: 4) notes, the

2003 Licensing Act ended '450 years of magistrates' control of licensing' when it came into force in 2005.

Adopting a long-term historical frame, consumption rates are characterised by recurring, cyclical increases, which temporarily reverse a longer-term pattern of decline (Chartres 2004: 39). The most recent of these periods of increased consumption was the second half of the twentieth century (ibid). During these decades, public health and other discourses encouraging moderation existed alongside the increased liberalisation of licencing laws, which from the 1961 Licensing Act onward initially saw growth in the types of businesses which could sell alcohol (until supermarkets later came to dominate off-trade sales), a relaxing of restrictions on the times of day when alcohol could be sold and a gradual weakening and the eventual removal of magistrates' authority in licencing matters (Jennings 2016). In 2001, overall responsibility for licencing was transferred from the Home Office to the Department for Culture, Media and Sport, a telling move that underscored the growing link between licencing and the alcohol and leisure industries (ibid: 202). From the point of view of successive UK governments, governing excess meant performing a balancing act between the desire to generate revenue and foster conditions for the creation of profit on the one hand, and the requirement to maintain public order on the other hand, with a public health approach having more success in the devolved administrations, principally Scotland, where, as mentioned, Minimum Uni Pricing became law in 2018. It is to one increasingly prominent part of the alcohol industry in the twenty-first century – the craft brewer, BrewDog – and its construction of excess that we now turn.

Case study 4: BrewDog, Craft Beer and twenty-first-century excess

Readers opening up BBC News on 22 July 2010 would have been forgiven for thinking their eyes were deceiving them, or that perhaps they had had a little too much to drink the night before. However, what lay before them really was a beer bottle protruding from a stuffed grey squirrel. Pictured was one of just 12 bottles of 'The End of History', a Belgian blonde ale produced by then up-and-coming UK brewer BrewDog. Aside from its limited edition, everything else about this beer was calculated with excess in mind; a bottle ranged between £500 and £700, depending on the size and type of the animal in which it came encased, and the ABV was a deliberately tabloid-baiting 55% (*BBC News Online* 2010). It was, for a time, the strongest beer in the world, and succeeded in putting BrewDog in all of the major British newspapers; tabloids all dutifully ran stories expressing fears over the kind of irresponsible drinking that such products would doubtless encourage.[4] However, viewed in context of BrewDog's development over the past decade, 'The End of History' was less the gimmick that BrewDog's detractors labelled it at the time, and instead part of a pattern for a brewery for whom excess has always been a commonplace, and, as time has shown since, a deliberate part of their business model and brand.

'The End of History' was the culmination of BrewDog's early ambitions towards notoriety. As Jon Henley has observed, super-strength beers and a range of publicity stunts, including driving a tank through streets of north London, helped cement their self-declared reputation as 'a post-punk, apocalyptic, motherfucker of a craft brewery' (2016). Henley notes too that these activities have won BrewDog as many critics as they have supporters among the public and beer writers. Jessica Boak and Ray Bailey provide a dispassionate overview of BrewDog's early history, noting that while their effect on the UK beer market and culture is palpable, their style is not unique, and rather follows a pattern set by the California-based Stone Brewing's 'Arrogant Bastard' ale first brewed in 1996, over a decade before BrewDog existed (2014: 209). Such similarities suggest that what BrewDog reveal about contemporary drinking cultures is that ideas of excess need not simply be understood as the amount of alcohol consumed, but rather a pervasive ethos of their brand identity and of the US-influenced British craft scene in general. Differing distinctly from the Campaign for Real Ale (CAMRA), which began as a traditionalist movement in Britain in the 1970s, the modern UK craft beer community is modelled on a US-style tendency towards invention and extremes of flavour, as Pete Brown and other commentators have noted (Brown 2009). While there is a shared point of common ground between CAMRA and craft beer in their response to the homogenisation of brewing as a result of nineteenth- and twentieth-century industrialisation, the manner in which this opposition is manifest is vastly different. The notion of excess seems entirely alien to CAMRA, which seeks a continuation of typically much lighter and milder beers brewed with established methods; for craft beer, innovation and the pushing of boundaries are key. In light of this influence, and their own behaviours, this case study argues that instead of viewing BrewDog's stunts in isolation, they must be recognised as the bedrock of the brewery's corporate identity and market identity, as well as indicative of the kinds of rhetorical and practical hyperbole engaged in by elements of the UK craft brewing industry, influencing aspects of contemporary drinking culture from style, flavour, price and promotion.

British beer culture has been often characterised by excess. While the physiological effect and social position of beer itself is quite different from spirits such as vodka, or those drinks with more apparent class-based connotations such as wine, there was a consistent concern in the nineteenth and twentieth centuries that the working classes would be unable to moderate their behaviour without regulatory pressure from the state. In the late twentieth century, however, that responsibility began to shift, eventually coming to rest on the shoulders of the neoliberal individual by the time that craft beer culture emerged. Shifting class boundaries and upward social mobility in the twentieth century meant that well-known drinking subcultures such as the 'Lager Louts' of the 1980s or the 'Ladettes' of the 1990s prompted the association of excessive behaviour largely in relation to or as a result of quantity of alcohol consumed by individuals (Marsh and Fox-Kibby 1992), and the resultant social disorder that arose as a consequence.[5] In the modern craft scene though, excess exists on a range of levels beyond that of simply ABV, quantity consumed and binge drinking. BrewDog and its products exemplify a kind of consciously performed excess associated with craft beer, from the exaggerated post-industrial aesthetic of their bars, the provocative names of their mainly high-strength and highly hopped beers, the extent of their merchandising, as well as their sense of self-importance, evinced in their website's declaration of how they 'bleed craft beer' (2019).

Alongside the breathless tone of founder James Watt's book *Business for Punks* (2015), BrewDog's website affirms their tendency towards self-aggrandisement. The description for their 7.4% ABV Jackhammer IPA is as follows:

> 'PRESS THE BUTTON. IT'S IRRESISTIBLY SITTING THERE, WAITING. DON'T HESITATE. HAMMER IT.
>
> Start with a colossal grapefruit aroma. Pile on bitterness after thumping bitterness, and ride the anarchy wherever it takes you. The caramel razor is sharp, but the resinous bite drills straight through your taste buds. For blitzing the mediocre, raising hell and revelling in the aftermath, Jack Hammer is the end of the line. The hopped-up, pucker-mouthed terminal extreme of craft brewing. This beer is bitter. Very bitter. If you push that button, don't say we didn't warn you...
>
> *(BrewDog 2018)*

In its adoption of such excessive rhetoric and tone, BrewDog's declarative marketing, and indeed, their 'manifesto' evokes those of movements such as F.T. Marinetti's Futurists, with a similar use of diction that interweaves the violent and the sensuous in pursuit of an ultimate gratification (Somigli 2003). This, and their apparent preoccupation with all things terminal, from the acknowledgement of Francis Fukuyama in 'The End of History' through to the 'end of the line' and Trumpian talk of button-pushing, lends their copy the competing qualities of an all-caps over-excitability alongside that of postmodern nihilism (Gambino 2018).

'Jackhammer' is indicative of BrewDog's penchant for combining the excessively overblown, and often demonstrably untrue, claim alongside a sense of existential dread. Watt writes in *Business for Punks* that it is not enough to simply start a business; instead, an 'encapsulating mission' is required, and that 'business punks' must be willing to 'put it all on the line' and face down challenges before they become 'a fully-loaded AK47 pointed at your neck' (2014: 4–6). It appears that it in all elements of their business BrewDog must always operate with an exceptional intensity, which serves to normalise their prior excesses and require ever further extremes; such an approach, it is implied, must then must be adopted in the tastes of their consumers, further shifting craft beer towards excess.[6] As Helana Darwin has noted, such behaviour affirms the acutely masculine nature of craft beer, expressed in connoisseurship as opposed to quantity consumed (Chapman 2017).[7] BrewDog's much-publicised 'punk' persona can similarly be read as part of this deliberate adoption of excess, and hyperbole within their marketing and advertising rhetoric. From its inception, punk has been associated with a deliberately excessive aesthetic, designed to push the boundaries of acceptable dress, behaviour, taste and the creative arts (Hebdige 1991; Wilkinson, 2016). BrewDog offers a postmodern reworking of this punk persona in which the associations of anarchic, excessive tendencies remain, however, the subversive meaning of punk is lost amidst their efforts to dominate the market.

Indeed, it is arguable that everything about BrewDog is framed in relation to excess, except, possibly, the actual drinking. For while BrewDog's prices might not seem excessive compared to other craft breweries (most beers cost £4–6 in their own bars, depending on ABV) such prices are nonetheless prohibitively high for some, limiting the amount they will consume in a visit (Worley 2017), or tacitly pricing out some demographics altogether. Similarly, in thinking about how much craft beer drinkers consume on a regular basis, it is apparent that BrewDog bars are marketed not the kinds of drinking places that are to be visited every day, and are instead 'destination' bars as opposed to what Paul Jennings (2011) would argue constitutes a 'local'. Concurrently, BrewDog have benefited from long-standing distribution deals with ubiquitous and nationwide UK pub chain J.D. Wetherspoon and in most major UK supermarkets, where its flagship 'Punk IPA' will sell for between £1.29 and 1.99 over the bar, and in six packs of 330 ml cans for £6, respectively.[8] Such cheapness, especially in supermarkets, recalls the contemporary concern over the ease of excessive drinking at home (Seth and Randall 2011; Foster and Ferguson 2012). Indeed, one or two of BrewDog's stronger beers such as 'Jackhammer' (even Punk IPA is a fairly potent 5.6%) will easily surpass the recommended daily unit allowance as outlined by the UK's Chief Medical Officer in August 2016 (BrewDog 2019).

In conclusion, in spite of their detractors BrewDog remain one of the most widely recognised UK craft beer brands. They continue to make inroads into the North American market, as well as the UK, as evinced by the fact that their television channel, DrinkTV, is now a fixture of British Airways in-flight entertainment, accompanied by 'Speedbird 100', a commemorative centenary session IPA brewed exclusively for BA and their 'Equity Punks' shareholders (BrewDog 2019). The veracity of their 'punk' persona has always been questionable, but as the brewery grows ever larger and more corporate in their affiliations, it will remain to be seen whether they continue to generate outrage in pursuit of their next publicity coup or tabloid headline, or whether it is indeed possible to teach an old dog new tricks. Whatever happens, it appears that stuffed squirrels were not the end of BrewDog's history of excess, but rather just the end of its beginning.

Discussion and conclusion

As the historian and sociologist Joseph Gusfield (1996) has argued, the ways in which drinking has been constructed as a problem that requires intervention have varied historically. Drinking and drunkenness have been understood and acted on in ways that invite cross-cultural and historical comparison. Accordingly, our chapter has zoomed in on four distinct but complementary case studies. Looking over the different historical, geographical and cultural contexts examined above throws into relief the complex negotiation of the boundaries of excess between authorities and drinkers. The cases discussed in this chapter share several thematic and substantive concerns. First, the cases of Reformation Europe, Poland and twentieth-century Britain all point to tensions and contradictions in official responses to drunkenness and the resulting attempts at regulation, while the case of BrewDog illustrates the power of marketing discourses that exceed the logic of state regulation.

In medieval and early modern Europe, the Christian Church was a key source of moral guidance and social norms. Yet in their pronouncements on excess, both Catholics and Protestants sent mixed messages: on the one hand, overindulgence wasted precious resources and set imbibers on a pathway to sin, but on the other hand wine was a gift of God – in fact an indispensable component of the most revered sacrament of the Eucharist – and the sale of fermented drinks a major source of revenues for pastors as well as parishioners. Some clerics ran their own taverns and an iconic reformer like Martin Luther had no objection to the occasional 'elevation'. Alcohol, furthermore, helped to differentiate Christians from the religious 'other', specifically Muslims and Jews.

In early modern Poland the nobility's culture was based on extremes. Until the end of the seventeenth century, the *Ieiunium Polonicum* was one of the strictest fasts in Europe, with the number of fasting days reaching more than 200. The Polish nobility of the Baroque era demonstrated opposite characteristics: the strict fasts and zealous Catholicism were accompanied by flamboyance, sumptuousness and disregard for the clergy's admonitions concerning moderation. Despite scrupulous observance of fasts, the aristocratic tables were weighed down with expensive wines and sophisticated fish dishes, which Poland was well known for at that time. In the nineteenth century, the discussion about excess and moderation changed its character. Previously known for their festive lifestyle, land-owning and other elites expressed concern over the excessive drinking of the peasantry and working classes, while simultaneously sustaining a socio-economic order that created the conditions giving rise to drunkenness in the first place. Nevertheless, the new social, economic and political circumstances forced the discussions about excessive alcohol consumption. The concern for sobriety was also linked to the struggle for independence which would not have been achieved without the cooperation of all social classes.

Similarly, tensions and contradictions underpinned the British central state's approach to the governance of excess in the twentieth century. As with the early modern Church, alcohol sales provided vital tax revenue while at the same time drunkenness raised issues of public order. During the First World War, these tensions came to a head, leading to the creation of the CCB. While this experiment in centralised control was short-lived, the tensions underpinning its construction persist. In the closing decades of the twentieth century, local authorities had to balance their ambitions for economic revitalisation via the expansion of the 'night time economy' with the pressures on policing and health services that public drunkenness brought with it.

The contemporary UK craft beer scene embodies its own set of contradictions. On the one hand, excess is integral to BrewDog's brand identity, with 'excess' being redefined from the amount of alcohol consumed to an ethos, central to the brand, their corporate marketing communications and the implied behaviour it expects from its consumers. On the other hand, pricing, high ABV and the fact their beer is served predominantly in 'destination' pubs pose practical constraints on how much is consumed. Likewise, despite various confrontations with alcohol trade body the Portman Group over their alleged support of excessive drinking, BrewDog nevertheless observes UK licencing requirements around alcohol by including the standard health-warnings, and unit counts on the labelling of their products. BrewDog's relationship to excessive drinking can, therefore, be read in a neoliberal light in so much as while the company recognises that it sells a harmful product, the responsibility for managing the consumption of it falls on the individual consumer.

A further overarching chapter insight is the interplay of different constellations of agents. With the influence of the twentieth-century authorities of Church and State either declining in the case of the former, or becoming more remote and disinterested in the case of the latter, and without the social hegemony of a nobility as found in other European countries, the neoliberal individual is left to moderate their drinking behaviour as dictated by their lifestyle, habits and financial means. In another indication of changing cultural frameworks, warnings about alcohol's harmful effects by the UK Chief Medical Officers and Public Health England replace the moral authorities of previous contexts and periods; however, their efforts are advisory rather than prescriptive, and agency remains with the drinker themselves. BrewDog's apparent advocacy of excess as an ethos may appear provocative and distasteful to some, but it remains legal, and in its legality permits the brewery to absolve itself from any culpability around excessive drinking.

A third shared theme is that efforts to construct boundaries between excess and moderation are protean in nature; they can weave together long-standing religious and cultural beliefs with more recent, emerging forms of thought and practice. Agendas, priorities and concerns beyond the immediate scope of alcohol regulation – such as projects of nation building and the realignment of the respective responsibilities of states and citizens – can become interwoven with attempts to govern drunkenness. Moral concerns are not simply replaced by medical, 'scientific' ones, or vice versa. Drunken bodies emerge as a site of comment and intervention from a range of perspectives, echoing disparate sets of interests and concerns.

Prior to the scientific advances in the early modern period, heavy drinking was understood to threaten the balance of the body's four 'humours', with men's constitutions seen as (on the whole) better suited to the intake of fiery beverages than those of women. While Church doctrine centred on the salvation of souls, bodies remained key to how contemporaries understood excess. In early modern Poland, religious voices warning against the consequences of excessive drinking were particularly opposed to the consumption of *imported* alcoholic drinks. The boundary between excess and moderation was, in this sense, being carved out in tandem with the boundaries of the nation and national identity. In the nineteenth century, the focus shifted to the type of alcohol being consumed by the peasantry and working classes, with strong spirits, principally vodka, seen as particularly troublesome for the health and well-being of these social groups. The rhetoric condemning strong spirits, accompanied by the development of abstinence societies, was, however, faced with a continued obligatory propination, which was not abolished or limited in most of Poland's annexed territories until the end of the nineteenth century.

In late twentieth-century British society, the version of public health to be adopted into alcohol guidelines was not an approach that consistently emphasised the influence of environments and other external factors on health, but rather one that firmly placed individuals' decision-making capacities centre stage. The 2003 Licensing Act and related earlier changes repositioned the state's role: not that of guardian of shared norms and standards, but instead as a facilitator of market expansion with a background role in preserving public order. In contemporary craft beer culture, there has been a shift away from concerns over the potential for violent social disorder arising as a result of excessive alcohol consumption, as characterised by the 'Lager Lout' of the 1980s, and, instead, a growing concern for the health implications of middle-class drinking habits has arisen in its place (Knight 2018). Beer, so often viewed as a 'healthier' (or at least more benign) alternative alcoholic drink to the much stronger spirits or fortified wines available until relatively late in the twentieth century, has likewise begun to shift into an area of health concern as the average ABV percentage of popular supermarket and draught beers increases to between 5% and 6% ABV. Similarly, the fashion for double IPAs and imperial stouts, though served in smaller amounts of 1–2/3rds of a pint, nonetheless normalises the presence of excessively strong beers within the mainstream of the British beer-drinking subculture, whereas previously, those beers (typically lagers) of 8% ABV and above that were generally available in the UK market, such as Carlsberg Special Brew and Tennent's Super, were thought to signify a very different, and far more problematic, kind of excess linked to an association with lower class, and therefore socially aberrant, drinking habits and consequent social disorder. It remains to be seen whether this taste for stronger craft beers inculcates a more 'continental' style of consumption based on appreciation of flavour, style and ingredients, or whether the sheer economics of drinking such products acts as a self-limiting force on the behaviours of the craft drinker, curtailing consumption, and making cost a further form of excess to be associated with modern beer. Alternately, given the typical transatlantic influence of US craft beer on the UK scene, as well as growing health concerns over home drinking, the developing trend for alcohol-free or table beers of 2%–4% ABV may yet become a popular option in Britain too. If so, BrewDog are again at the forefront of such moves, with two beers, 'Nanny State' and 'Punk AF' (both 0.5% ABV), offering drinkers a lighter alternative to the heavier beers that dominate elsewhere in craft culture.

Lastly, efforts to govern excess and promote moderation must contend with the enduring place of intoxication in wider culture, particularly in relation to festive and everyday rituals of conviviality and hospitality. From the church ales of late medieval villages to the craft beer outlets of the present, drinkers frequently flaunt or ignore attempts to reduce their access to alcohol, appreciating it as a social lubricant and a tool for social bonding. In mid to late twentieth-century Britain, young people and women increasingly participated in drinking rituals. Public health discourses emerging from the mid-1970s that presented the 'risks' of drinking as an issue for everyone, and not just 'alcoholics', did not reverse rising levels of overall consumption, though they had other effects. Within the craft beer subculture, the formation of community groups whether digital, regional, local or national is facilitated by, if not entirely dependent on, the appreciation and consumption of alcohol.

Alongside many continuities, however, the preceding contributions also point to change over time: in line with the long-term process of state formation, regional and central authorities took an ever more active role in regulation and taxation. While never totally suppressed, the moral and spiritual power of the Christian Churches in Europe faced increasing challenges by arguments based on 'reason', economic motives and public health considerations; in the present, such health concerns have become the responsibility of governments, charities and even the British tabloids, who use their platform and position to regularly decry the binge drinking habits observed in city centres, or the creeping dangers of home drinking. From the predominantly oral appeals of medieval Europe via the first mass medium of print to the digital resources of the present, furthermore, drinkers have become exposed to an ever more differentiated and often discordant plurality of voices vying to influence their behaviour. Stakeholders now range from teetotallers to global beverage brands, technological tools stretch to personalised advertising algorithms on social media platforms and official yardsticks involve ever-shifting 'expert' advice on safe drinking limits. Moreover, the picture has been made all the more complex by the upheaval caused by the COVID-19 global pandemic, and its effects on drinking habits across the world. These too show signs of extreme variation, from moves towards much greater state-mandated restriction and regulation such as in South Africa, or concern over a dramatic increase in 'problem' drinking observed in the UK as a result of social isolation or as a result of young people continuing to socialise regularly in pubs and bars. Given the ongoing nature of the pandemic, as well as the shifting impact that the various measures to contain it have on our lives, it is unlikely that boundaries of excess will become clearer and less contentious anytime soon.

Notes

1 This chapter is the result of a collaboration among members of the Drinking Studies Network's 'Understanding Excess' cluster. The introduction and conclusion are co-productions (hence our names appear in alphabetical order) but each of the case studies was written by a single author: the first on boundaries of excess in Europe's Reformation by Beat Kümin; the second on constructions of excess in sixteenth- to nineteenth-century Poland by Dorota Dias-Lewandowska; the third on the governance of excess in twentieth-century British society by Laura Fenton and the fourth on constructions of excess by the contemporary craft brewer BrewDog by Sam Goodman.

2 The case study was written as part of research financed by the National Science Centre, application no 2016/20/S/HS3/00107.

3 Licening is a key topic in the history of the governance of alcohol. See, as examples, the many studies cited by Yokoe (2019).

4 The title was soon reclaimed by German brewery Schorschbräu, and latterly by Keith Brewery's 67.5% 'Snake Venom' (Drink Supermarket 2019) [Accessed 22/6/19].

5 'Ladette' gained recognition later, entering the Oxford English Dictionary in 2001 (*BBC News*, 12 July 2001). [Accessed 22/6/19].

6 For example, Double IPAs (IPAs of 8% ABV or above) were once a rarity however, breweries such as Verdant, from Cornwall UK, include 21 DIPAs and 3 imperial stouts out of 88 beers listed on their Untappd profile, representing over a quarter of their production to date. Likewise, Pete Brown relates that at a US craft beer expo in 2008 Dogfish brewery ran their draught beers through tubes of raw hops in pursuit of more flavour (2009: 19).

7 Darwin's work recalls Thorstein Veblen's remarks on the specialisation of consumption among the discriminating individual (2009).

8 Prices correct as of June 2019.

References

BBC News Online. 12 July 2001. 'Ladettes enter dictionary'. Available from: http://news.bbc.co.uk/1/hi/uk/1434906.stm. [Accessed 22/6/19].

BBC News Online. 22 July 2010. 'Dead animal beer bottles at £500 each "perverse"'. Available from: http://www.bbc.co.uk/news/mobile/uk-scotland-north-east-orkney-shetland-10725024. Accessed [22/6/19].

Berridge, V. (2013). *Demons: Our Changing Attitudes to Alcohol, Tobacco, and Drugs*. Oxford: Oxford University Press.

Berridge, V., Herring, R., and Thom, B. (2009). 'Binge drinking: A confused concept and its contemporary history'. *Social History of Medicine*, 22, 3, 597–607.

Boak, J. and Bailey, R. (2014) *Brew Britannia: The Strange Rebirth of British Beer*. London: Aurum.

Brewdog. 2019. 'Jackhammer'. Available from: https://www.BrewDog.com/usa/jack-hammer-usa. [Accessed 23/6/19].

Brewdog. 2019. 'Our Charter'. Available from: https://www.BrewDog.com/community/culture/our-charter. [Accessed 23/6/19].

Brewdog. 2019. 'Speedbird 100'. Available from: https://www.BrewDog.com/speedbird-100. [Accessed 23/6/19].

Brown, P. (2009). *Hops & Glory: One Man's Search for the Beer that Built the British Empire*. London: Pan.

Burke, P. (2009). *Popular Culture in Early Modern Europe*. 3rd edn. Farnham: Ashgate Publishing.

Burszta, J. (1950). *Wieś i karczma. Rola karczmy w życiu wsi pańszczyźnianej*. Warszawa: Ludowa Spółdzielnia Wydawnicza.

Celichowski, Z. (1890). *Kawiarnie ludowe*. Poznań: Towarzystwo Szerzenia Wstrzemięźliwości.

Chapman, N. G. (2017). *Untapped: Exploring the Cultural Dimensions of Craft Beer*. Morganstown: West Virginia University Press, 222–236.

Chartres, J. A. (2004). 'Spirits in the North-East? Gin and other vices in the long eighteenth century'. In Berry, H., Gregory, J. (eds.) *Creating and Consuming Culture in North-East England, 1660–1830*. Aldershot: Ashgate, 37–56.

Chavannes, F., ed. (1847). *Le mireour du monde: Manuscrit du quatorzième siècle*. Genève: [n.p.].

Chociszewski, J. (1891). *Słówko o ruchu wstrzemięźliwości w ziemiach polskich*. Poznań.

Collin, M. and Godfrey, J. (1997). *Altered State: The Story of Ecstasy Culture and Acid House*. London: Serpent's Tail.

Consistory Court Protocols (1650–). 'Neuenegg, Gemeindearchiv'. *Chorgerichts-Manuale*, vols 1–3.

Craig, J. S. (1993). 'Cooperation and initiatives: Elizabethan churchwardens and the parish accounts of Mildenhall'. *Social History*, XVIII, 357–380.

Dias-Lewandowska, D. (2014). *Historia kulturowa wina francuskiego w Polsce od połowy XVII do początku XVIII wieku*. Warszawa: Muzeum Pałacu Króla Jana III w Wilanowie.

Dias-Lewandowska, D. (2015). 'Traditional and Polish Tokay vs. Modern Foreign Champagne: Wine and identity in Poland from the late seventeenth to the early nineteenth century'. In Toner, D., Hailwood, M. (eds.) *Biographies of drink: A case study approach to our historical relationship with alcohol*. Newcastle upon Tyne: Cambridge Scholars Publishing, 138–157.

Drink Supermarket. (2019). 'Keith Brewery'. Available from: https://www.drinksupermarket.com/brands/keith-brewery. [Accessed 22/6/19].

Duncan, R. (2013). *Pubs and Patriots: The Drink Crisis in Britain during World War One*. Liverpool: Liverpool University Press.

Duffy, E. (2005). *The Stripping of the Altars: Traditional Religion in England c.1400–c.1580*. 2nd edn. New Haven: Yale University Press.

Durston, C. and Eales, J. eds, (1996). *The Culture of English Puritanism 1560–1700*. Basingstoke: Macmillan.

Dynner G. (2014). *Yankel's Tavern: Jews, Liquor, and Life in the Kingdom of Poland*. Oxford University Press.

Flandrin, J.-L. and Flandrin, M. (1999). 'Regards occidentaux sur les banquets de Pologne aux XVIIe et XVIIIe siècles'. In Kuklo C. (ed.) *Między polityką a kulturą*. Warszawa: Wydawnictwo Naukowe PWN, 307–317.

Flaum, M. (1894). 'Alkohol i alkoholizm'. In *Biblioteka Warszawska vol. 1*, Warszawa: Drukarnia Gazety Codziennej, 74–126.

Foster, J. H. and Ferguson, C. S. (2012). 'Home Drinking in the UK: Trends and Causes'. *Alcohol and Alcoholism*, 47, 3, 355–358. Available from: https://doi.org/10.1093/alcalc/ags020. [Accessed 23/6/19].

Gambino, L. (2018). 'Donald Trump boasts that his nuclear button is bigger than Kim Jong-un's'. *The Guardian*, Available from: https://www.theguardian.com/us-news/2018/jan/03/donald-trump-boasts-nuclear-button-bigger-kim-jong-un. [Accessed 23/6/19].

Greennaway, J. (2003). *Drink and British Politics since 1830: A Study in Policy-Making*. London: Palgrave MacMillan.

Gusfield, J. R. (1996). *Contested Meanings: The Construction of Alcohol Problems*. Madison: University of Wisconsin Press.

Gutzke, D. W. (2014). *Women Drinking Out in Britain since the Early Twentieth Century*. Manchester: Manchester University Press.

Gwiazdka, C. (1865) 'Gospodarka i przemysł'. *Gwiazdka Cieszyńska*, 27, 211–213.

Hailwood, M. (2014). *Alehouses and Good Fellowship in Early Modern England*. Woodbridge: Boydell & Brewer.

Hayward, K. and Hobbs, D. (2007). 'Beyond the binge in "booze Britain": Market-led liminalization and the spectacle of binge drinking'. *British Journal of Sociology*, 58, 3, 437–456.

Hebdige, D. (1991). *Subculture: The Meaning of Style*. London: Routledge.

Henley, J. (2016). 'The aggressive, outrageous, infuriating (and ingenious) rise of BrewDog'. *The Guardian*. Available from: https://www.theguardian.com/lifeandstyle/2016/mar/24/the-aggressive-outrageous-infuriating-and-ingenious-rise-of-BrewDog. [Accessed: 22/6/19].

Herman, J.N. (1854) *Myśl o uregulowaniu handlu okowitą za pomocą spółki akcyjnej*. Warszawa: Drukarnia Juliana Kaczanowskiego.

Hutton, R. (2001). *The Rise and Fall of Merry England: The Ritual Year 1400–1700*. New edn. Oxford: Oxford University Press.

Igály, Ludwig Igálffy von (2010), *Die Ambraser Trinkbücher Erzherzog Ferdinands II. von Tirol*, vol. 1, Vienna: Kunsthistorisches Museum.

Jellinek, E.M. (1960). *The Disease Concept of Alcoholism*. New Haven: College and University of Press.

Jennings, P. (2011). *The Local: A History of the English Pub*. London: The History Press.

Jennings, P. (2016). *A History of Drink and the English, 1500–2000*. Abingdon: Routledge.

Kaisersberg in Strauss ed. 1971:211–215.

Kneale, J. and French, S. (2015). 'Moderate drinking before the unit: Medicine and life assurance in the Britain and the US, c. 1860–1930'. *Drugs: Education, Prevention and Policy*, 22, 111–117.

Knight, K. (2018). 'Why are women judged for liking a tipple or two?: KATHRYN KNIGHT reveals why she doesn't feel bad about her daily drink'. *Daily Mail*. Available from: https://www.dailymail.co.uk/femail/article-6236997/Why-women-judged-liking-tipple-two.html?ns_mchannel=rss&ito=1490&ns_campaign=1490. [Accessed 18/9/19].

Krasińska, I. (2013). 'Ruch abstynencki w Wielkopolsce w latach 1840–1902'. *Folia Historica Cracoviensia*, 19, 247–278.

Kümin, B. (1996). *The Shaping of a Community: The Rise & Reformation of the English Parish c. 1400–1560*. Aldershot: Scholar Press.

Kümin, B. (2007). *Drinking Matters: Public Houses and Social Exchange in Early Modern Central Europe*. Basingstoke: Palgrave Macmillan.

Langhamer, C. (2003). '"A public house is for all classes, men and women alike": Gender, leisure, and drink in second world war England'. *Women's History Review*, 12, 3, 423–443.

Levine H. (2003) 'Alcohol monopoly to protect the non-commercial sector of eighteenth-century Poland'. In Douglas M. Mary Douglas collected works, vol. X, *Constructive Drinking, Perspectives on Drink from Anthropology*. London, New York: Routledge, 250–269.

Lucas, B. (2004) 'Reducing discursive complexity – The case of alcohol policies in Europe (1850–2000)'. In Müller, R. and Klingemann, H. (eds.) *From Science to Action? 100 Years Later – Alcohol Policies Revisited*. New York, Boston, Dordrecht, London, Moscow: Kluwer Academic Publishers, 71–100.

Luther, M. (1539). *Sermon on Soberness and Moderation*. Available from https://www.prca.org/standard_bearer/volume79/2002oct15.html (accessed 10/9/2019).

Luther, M. (1967). *Table Talk*, ed. T. G. Tappert (Luther's Works, vol. 54). Minneapolis: Fortress Press.

McShane, A., (2014). 'Material culture and "political" drinking in seventeenth-century England'. *Past & Present*, 222, issue supplement 9, 247–276.

Measham, F. (2004). 'The decline of ecstasy, the rise of "binge" drinking and the persistence of pleasure'. *Probation Journal*, 5, 309–326.

Measham, F. and Brain, K. (2005). '"Binge" drinking, British alcohol policy and the new culture of intoxication'. *Crime, Media, Culture: An International Journal*, 1, 3, 262–283.

Measham, F. and Østergaard, J. (2009). 'The public face of binge drinking: British and Danish young women, recent trends in alcohol consumption and the European binge drinking debate'. *Probation Journal*, 56, 415–434.

Moskalewicz, J. and Zieliński, A. (1995). 'Poland'. In Heath D.B. (ed.) *International Handbook on Alcohol and Culture*. Westport: Greenwood Press, 224–236.

Ney, K. (1844). *Zbiór nauk dla młodzieży szkół katolickich*. Leszno, Gniezno: Ernest Günther.

Perzyna, L. (1793). *Lekarz dla włościan czyli rada dla pospólstwa*. Kalisz: Drukarnia J.O. Xcia Jmci prymasa arcy-biskupa gnieźnieńskiego.

Phillips, R. (2014). *Alcohol: A History.* Chapel Hill. North Carolina University Press.

Poniatowski, S.A. (1870). *Pamiętniki króla Stanisława Augusta Poniatowskiego*, B. Zalewski (ed.). Drezno: J.I. Kraszewski.

Porter, R. (1985). 'The drinking man's disease: The "pre-history" of alcoholism in Georgian Britain'. *British Journal of Addiction*, 80, 385–396.

Press Association. (2016). 'No safe alcohol limit, new guidelines to say'. *The Guardian*. Available from: https://www.theguardian.com/society/2016/jan/01/no-safe-alcohol-limit-new-guidelines-to-say. [Accessed 18/9/19].

Rublack, U. ed. (2016). *The Oxford Handbook of the Protestant Reformations.* Oxford: Oxford University Press.

Rychcicki, M.J.A. (1850). *Piotr Skarga i jego wiek, t. 2.* Kraków: Zakład Wydawnictwa Dzieł Katolickich.

Schleitheim Confession of the Swiss Brethren (1527). Available from: https://www.anabaptists.org/history/the-schleitheim-confession.html (accessed 10/9/2019).

Schmidt, H.R. (1995). *Dorf und Religion: Reformierte Sittenzucht in Berner Landgemeinden der Frühen Neuzeit.* Stuttgart: Gustav Fischer Verlag.

Seth, A. and Randall, G. (2011). *The Grocers: The Rise and Rise of Supermarket Chains.* London: Kogan Page.

Smith, L. and Foxcroft, D. (2009). Drinking in the UK An exploration of trends. York: Joseph Rowntree Foundation. Available from: https://www.jrf.org.uk/sites/default/files/jrf/migrated/files/UK-alcohol-trends-FULL.pdf (accessed 11/9/2022).

Somigli, L. (2003). *Legitimizing the Artist: Manifesto Writing and European Modernism, 1885–1915.* Toronto: University of Toronto Press.

Starowolski, S. (1656). *Reformacja obyczajów Polski.* Kraków: Franciszek Cezary.

Strauss, G. ed. (1971). *Manifestations of Discontent in Germany on the Eve of the Reformation.* Bloomington: Indiana University Press.

Szmigin, I., Griffin, C., Mistral, W., Bengry-Howell, A., Weale, L., and Hackley, C. (2008). 'Re-framing "binge" drinking as calculated hedonism: Empirical evidence from the UK. *International Journal of Drug Policy*, 19, 5, 359–366.

Szymkiewicz, J. (1818). *Dzieło o pijaństwie.* Wilno: Drukarnia XX Pijarów.

Tende, G. de (1686). *Relation Historique de la Pologne.* Paris: Nicolas le Gras.

The Lancet (1882). 'International debate on alcoholism'. *The Lancet*, 120, 3085, 633–634.

Thom, B. (1999). *Dealing with Drink: Alcohol and Social Policy: From Treatment to Management.* London: Free Association Books.

Tlusty, B.A. (2001). *Bacchus and Civic Order: The Culture of Drink in Early Modern Germany.* Charlottesville: University of Virginia Press.

Veblen, T. (2009). *The Theory of the Leisure Class.* Waiheke Island: The Floating Press.

Watt, J. (2015). *Business for Punks: Break All the Rules The BrewDog Way.* London: Penguin.

Weihenstephan Brewery. 'History'. Available from https://www.weihenstephaner.de/en/our-brewery/history/ (accessed 10 September 2019).

Wilkinson, D. (2016). *Post-Punk, Politics and Pleasure in Britain.* London: Palgrave Macmillan.

Worley, W. (27 August 2017). 'London Pub criticised for Pint costing £13.40'. *The Independent.* Available from: https://www.independent.co.uk/news/uk/home-news/london-pub-criticised-pint-costing-1340-craft-beer-cloudwater-double-ipa-borough-market-a7915096.html. [Accessed 23/6/19].

Worlidge, J. (1678). *Vinetum Britannicum: Ora Treatise of Cider and Other Wines and Drinks.* London: Dring.

Wrightson, K. (1981). 'Alehouses, order and reformation in rural England 1590–1660'. In Yeo, S. and E. eds. *Popular Culture and Class Conflict 1590–1914: Explorations in the History of Labour and Leisure.* Brighton: Harvester, 1–27.

Wybicki, J. (1777–1778). *Listy patriotyczne do Jaśnie Wielmożnego eks-kanclerza Zamoyskiego, prawa układającego, pisane, t.1–2.* Warszawa: Michał Gröll.

Yeomans, H. (2014). *Alcohol and Moral Regulation: Public Attitudes, Spirited Measures and Victorian Hangovers.* Bristol: Bristol University Press.

Yokoe, R. (2019). 'Alcohol and politics in twentieth-century Britain'. *The Historical Journal*, 62, 1, 267–287.

Zschokke, H. (1845). *Zaraza gorzałkowa.* Lwów: Franciszek Piller i spółka.

Z. N. (1846). *Domowy krzyż czyli: co trzymać i sądzić o piciu gorzałki.* Leszno: Ernest Günther.

31

FROM 'PLEDGE' TO 'PUBLIC HEALTH'

Medical Responses to Ireland's Drinking Culture, c. 1890–2018

Alice Mauger

Few nationalities rival the Irish for the sustained attention their drinking customs have received. The impression of Irishness as somehow synonymous with drunken joviality has been bolstered by the global dominance of drink exports like Guinness and Jameson, the international popularity of Irish-themed bars and, of course, the proliferation of alcohol-fuelled festivities around the world every St Patrick's Day. Given these deep-rooted cultural associations, it is unsurprising that Ireland's 'drinking culture' and attempts to change it have long been identified as subjects worthy of extensive scholarly investigation. For generations, researchers have presented drink in Ireland as posing a distinctive case study, not least because of its socio-cultural and political prominence at several historical junctures. Topics of special interest have included the rise and fall of influential temperance movements (Ferriter 1999; Kerrigan 1992; Malcolm 1980, 1986; Townsend 2002) and socio-cultural explanations for the alleged heavy drinking customs of the Irish, both at home and abroad (Bales 1962, 1980; Cassidy 1996; Fitzpatrick 1971; O'Connor 1975, 1978; Stivers 1976). More recently, policy and healthcare responses to what is now termed alcohol-related harm have come under the spotlight (Butler 2002, 2010, 2015; Malcolm 2012; Mauger 2019, 2021; Reidy 2014).

Since the 1890s, medico-scientific, voluntary and state responses have converged in three distinct phases. The first occurred at the turn of the twentieth century, when medical acceptance of a 'disease concept' of inebriety internationally coincided with the establishment of inebriate reformatories, the founding of a new major temperance association and attempts to restrict public house opening hours, all against a backdrop of increased Irish nationalism. The second phase began in the 1960s, when the re-emergence of medico-scientific interest in alcoholism overlapped with heightened political awareness and activity in the sphere. Notably, the renewed significance of alcoholism in this era intersected with attempts to reinvent Ireland's international profile as a modern and open nation with much to offer for potential foreign investors. The final instance is Ireland's relatively recent adoption of a public health approach to alcohol. The Public Health (Alcohol) Act, 2018, which has been overwhelmingly supported by Irish medical bodies, is currently being rolled out in stages. This Act is set to introduce *inter alia* minimum unit pricing, health warning labels on alcohol products and rigorous restrictions on marketing and advertising. These measures are purportedly aimed

DOI: 10.4324/9780429058141-40

at changing Ireland's drinking culture, with politicians and medical experts now framing alcohol as a serious public health problem.

Combining a historiographical survey of existing works with the author's own research on medico-scientific and state responses to inebriety and later, alcoholism, this chapter will explore shifting representations of Ireland's 'drinking culture' during these three phases and assess how competing discourses have influenced attempts to change it. By drawing together these often distinct strands of scholarship, it is intended to present a more rounded picture of the Irish experience than has hitherto existed. While much of this trajectory mirrors the international picture, especially contemporary developments in Britain and the United States, this chapter will argue that Ireland makes for an interesting example of national interests with a long historical lineage. In turn, it hopes to provide a useful comparative framework for those examining similar concerns in other countries.

In his introduction to *Drinking Cultures: Alcohol and Identity*, the anthropologist Thomas M. Wilson has underscored the importance of alcohol consumption to the 'production and reproduction of ethnic, national, class, gender and local community identities' both past and present (2). For Wilson:

> drinking is itself cultural; it is not so much an example of national and other cultural practices, in the sense that it is a performance of something that runs deeper in the national or ethnic makeup, as much as it is itself a bedrock of national and ethnic culture. As such it is an integral social, political and economic practice, a manifestation of the institutions, actions and values of culture.
>
> *(2–3)*

Drawing on Wilson's definition, this chapter employs the term 'drinking culture' to embrace various aspects of drinking practices in Ireland, including who was drinking, how much, when and where. Such perspectives are essential to deepening our understanding of intoxication in the Irish context.[1] By concentrating on the evolution of medical responses, the chapter will consider how experts interpreted and attempted to shape specific forms of social behaviour, customs and beliefs around intoxication – in this case via alcohol. As will be shown, these responses have involved engagement with temperance activity, legislative reform, psychiatry and public health. While this chapter refers in places to external commentary on Ireland's drinking culture, it does not attempt to evaluate such research as this would be beyond the scope of the present analysis. Instead, the focus is on examining *Irish* medical responses to what was often portrayed as a national problem. Importantly, and in contrast to many European countries, for much of the period examined, a majority of drinking in Ireland took place in public houses and without meals. Moreover, and as will be discussed, until the 1970s, these public houses were largely 'male spaces' with women either completely excluded or confined to separate areas such as snugs (Malcolm 1998: 51).

'Ireland Sober, Ireland Free'?

Representations of specific drinking cultures, especially ones emphasising excessive or harmful levels of alcohol consumption, tend to reflect broader socio-cultural and/or political conditions. From this vantage point, both drink and drinking practices can assume multiple and often metaphoric meanings. These forces are found to operate time and again in colonial portrayals of the hard drinking practices of indigenous peoples, usually to justify the suppression of existing customs as part of a civilising mission. This impulse formed part of the rationale for English writers' critical commentary on Irish drinking practices since the sixteenth century. While such accounts are undoubtedly prejudiced, Elizabeth Malcolm warns against downgrading them to mere validations for imperialism, noting their potential to impart valuable evidence about the place of alcohol in Irish society (1986: 3). Likewise, while acknowledging racial bias in nineteenth-century observations of the heavy drinking and consequent violence of the Irish people, Diarmaid Ferriter accepts such interpretations as indicators of the degree alcohol could permeate Irish life, especially at wakes and funerals (1999: 6). Nevertheless, there is little doubt that colonial depictions of allegedly heavy drinking cultures may be exaggerated and therefore at least partially unreliable.

That is not to say that national representations are untouched by broader societal developments and aspirations. Wilson, cited above, has suggested that where alcohol and drinking are considered problematic, both morally and from a health perspective, they may also form part of social and political integration and order, where culture and identity can play roles in both the acceptance and avoidance of drinking (2005: 21). Building on this idea, in her exemplary study of alcohol and nationhood in nineteenth-century Mexico, Deborah Toner has underlined the historical importance of discourses about alcohol consumption. These debates, she observes:

> offer profound insights into the ways in which a society understands its cultural sense of self, diagnoses its problems and celebrates its achievements, and constructs both internal and external "others" against which its own identity can be defined.
>
> *(2015: 38)*

This reasoning certainly applies to Ireland in the late nineteenth century as drinking became imbued with new meaning.

Beginning in the 1870s, Irish representatives in Westminster campaigned to secure a devolved government for Ireland, a movement known popularly as Home Rule.[2] At the same time, steeply rising alcohol consumption and high numbers of arrests for drunkenness were generating public alarm, as well as growing concern among doctors about the health implications of heavy drinking. Although consumption levels and arrests declined in the 1880s and 1890s, a widespread belief lingered among many that the Irish were disgracing themselves morally, politically and culturally through their heavy drinking (Ferriter 2015: 4; Malcolm 2012: 110–111). Irish nationalist opinion was divided as to the true extent of the problem, let alone how to tackle it. For some, sobriety held the key to political independence from Britain, a notion frequently repeated in the popular slogan, 'Ireland sober, Ireland free'. But for others, draft legislation aimed at restricting weekend opening hours for public houses symbolised the British parliament's veiled and patronising attacks on longstanding Irish customs (Malcolm 1980: 94–98, 1986: 271). The centrality of public houses in these debates is unsurprising, given their importance as social, economic and political centres in both rural and urban Ireland. While irregular, heavy drinking at fairs, wakes or weddings was still common in the nineteenth century, from 1850, public houses were the principal Irish recreational venues, albeit for men (Malcolm 1998: 51–53, 72; see also Kearns 1996).

These competing nationalist and imperialist discourses infused medico-scientific debates about alcohol and problem drinking in Ireland. Internationally, by the 1890s, medical thought had come to redefine inebriety as a disease rather than a vice (Berridge 1990, 2013; Levine 1978; Valverde 1998). As historians of alcohol have compelling shown, the disease concept gained authority in Britain, Europe and the United States at this time not due to any scientific breakthrough but rather, in response to a discrete set of social factors, including the influence of evangelical temperance interests and the increasing status of psychiatry and the medical profession more generally (Berridge 1990: 999; Nicholls 2009: 67; Porter 1985: 393). Similar forces were at work in Ireland, where the medical community broadly subscribed to this understanding of addiction. Like their British colleagues, some Irish doctors were heavily swayed by temperance ideology. But beyond adhering to international frameworks, cultural and political idiosyncrasies clearly inflected their opinions as to the place of alcohol within Irish society (Mauger 2019: 17–29).

In an especially blatant assertion of the value of sobriety to the struggle for Irish national self-governance, one contributor to the *Dublin Journal of Medical Science* in 1904 proclaimed:

> One of the heaviest blows which a patriotic Ireland could possibly inflict on its neighbouring British rulers would be given by taking the pledge all round – old and young – and keeping it! Why, we often say to ourselves, do not patriotic politicians utilise this fact?
>
> *(The Medical Temperance Review 1904: 139)*

This proposal alluded to the abstinence pledge, such as that taken by members of the Pioneer Total Abstinence Association formed in 1898 by the Catholic priest, Fr James Cullen. Notably, while the Pioneer Association quickly became associated with the nationalist cause, this was not the exclusive political ideology underpinning temperance in Ireland. From the late 1820s, a Protestant anti-spirits movement emerged in Ireland, particularly in Dublin and Ulster, largely in response to the drunken violence of the 1798 rebellion, intensifying campaigns for Catholic Emancipation and high levels of spirit consumption (Malcolm 1986: 55–56). According to Malcolm, following the demise of Fr Theobald Mathew's Catholic temperance 'crusade' in the 1840s, the growth of teetotalism became synonymous with 'middle-class, pro-British Protestants who used it to bolster their own position' while 'denigrating the customs and habits of their Catholic social inferiors' (Malcolm 1980: 113). Yet by the early twentieth century, some increasingly militant Irish nationalists were finding much in common with teetotalism, under the vanguard of Cullen's Pioneer Association, particularly the renewed belief that sobriety would invigorate the independence struggle. Mirroring these broader societal tendencies, by the turn of the twentieth century, several prominent Irish medical practitioners, regardless of religion or political leaning, were openly promoting and engaging in these movements (Mauger 2019: 28–29).

Chief among this group was Dr Ephraim MacDowel Cosgrave, physician to several Dublin hospitals and president of the Irish branch of the British Medical Temperance Association (Woods 2009: 13). Cosgrave published energetically on alcohol and temperance and was an ardent advocate for establishing inebriate homes in Ireland (Cosgrave 1982, 1897, 1901). The origins of these institutions are widely attributed to the temperance-based Washingtonian movement in the United States which, during the first half of the nineteenth century, created small private homes providing moral treatment for voluntary patients (Berridge 2004: 5). Dedicated retreats for inebriates then began to spring up, first in Boston, New York and San Francisco in the 1850s, and later in Chicago, Philadelphia and parts of Canada in the 1860s and 1870s (MacLeod 1967: 218, 2012: 110). By now, medical practitioners in England were successfully working to promote comparable institutions, coming into being by stages under a series of Habitual Drunkards (later Inebriates) Acts (MacLeod 1967). Medical support was reinforced by the Society for the Study and Cure of Inebriety, which under the leadership of Dr Norman Kerr campaigned for a state-funded inebriate reformatory system (Berridge 1990).

In Ireland, Cosgrave's stance echoed renewed calls from the wider medical community and popular press for institutions for 'chronic drunkards'. In keeping with the disease concept, inebriate reformatories were presented as a sympathetic alternative to criminalising drunkards and confining them in prisons. Proponents hoped these new institutions would offer a chance to treat and even cure inebriety (Berridge 1990: 991, 2004: 4). The rise of eugenics as a science also influenced this campaign, reflecting a deep-rooted belief that alcohol was a major cause of degeneration (Malcolm 2012: 111; Cox 2012: 61). In several European contexts, this was linked to rising fears about the impact of women's drinking on the future of the nation (Berridge 2013: 89; Dunbar 2018; Prestwich 2003). Medical opinion highlighted the greater biological risks alcohol posed to women, both personally and to their unborn children. These views found their way into temperance rhetoric as well as the functioning of the inebriate reformatory system. Both Ferriter and Malcolm have pointed to the idea that drunkenness in women was viewed as a greater evil, while at the same time, it was felt that virtuous women might lead their families along a righteous path to sobriety (Ferriter 1999: 71–73; Malcolm 1980: 67–68). Perhaps moved by these arguments, Cullen initially intended the Pioneer Association to serve female members only (Ferriter 1999: 20–21).

Of particular concern in many quarters was the practice of clandestine drinking by women at the notorious spirits-grocers, a form of mixed trading outlet carrying a range of household commodities and licenced to sell alcohol. Official reports abounded in the late nineteenth century of women leaving these venues at best mildly intoxicated with some barely able to walk (Kearns 1996: 16). In 1894, Brigade-Surgeon F.E. McFarland, a retired Consultant Physician to the Ulster Hospital for Women and Children, singled out this phenomenon warning that:

> The grocer's spirit licence has done much harm, especially to women. It has already made of them inebriates; women especially, should not be exposed to temptation. There are times of physical weakness which render them an easy prey to drink when once the habit is formed. Women who formerly would not be seen in a public-house cannot now buy their necessaries without being exposed to temptation. The downfall with them is very rapid, and the outlook for the children very bad. This law should be repealed.
>
> *(McFarland 1894: 488)*

While the spirits-grocers were no longer granted licences from 1910, fears about women's drinking persisted, especially during the First World War. These included anxieties around female shebeen keepers and soldiers' wives who reportedly squandered their separation allowance on drink (Dunbar 2018).

It was within this intellectual climate that the state-funded reformatories were eventually sanctioned by new legislation, introduced in 1898 (Inebriates Act 1898). Rather than responding to medical appeals, however, it was at the repeated requests of the Unionist MP, William Johnston, that this Bill was applied to Ireland ('Inebriates Bill' 1898; 'Habitual Inebriates Bill' 1898).[3] George Bretherton has contended that Irish support came from diverse groups, ranging from temperance advocates to local government bodies to clerical and medical professionals and penologists (1986: 474). Yet as Beverly A. Smith has shown, the Bill was extended to Ireland in its later stages almost as an afterthought (1989: 58). The resulting Act sanctioned the committal of inebriates to state or charitable-funded reformatories if they were tried and convicted of drunkenness at least four times in one year. In Ireland, this led to the creation of four institutions. But of these four, only the Lodge Retreat in Belfast (est. 1902) accepted voluntary inmates and limited admissions to fee-paying, Protestant women.

The remaining three could only be accessed by those committed through the courts. These were the State Inebriate Reformatory in Ennis (est. 1899), and St Patrick's (est. 1906) and St Brigid's (est. 1908) certified inebriate homes for Catholic men and women, respectively. Given the fears around women's drinking in this period, it is unsurprising that research on both prisons and inebriate reformatories has suggested that the legal courts were often less sympathetic towards the women brought before them for drink-related crimes and appeared to be quicker to send women to institutions for drunkenness than men. In fact, both the Ennis State Reformatory and the certified reformatories contained more women than men (Malcolm 2012: 114).

In spite of strong medical backing prior to their establishment, the inebriate homes were short-lived and, as in Britain, had all but wound down by the end of the First World War. A key issue was that what medical reformers (both in Britain and Ireland) had campaigned for, that is, compulsory powers to detain non-criminal inebriates, never became law. Moreover, the four Irish institutions served only a very small cohort. By 1917, St Patrick's had admitted only 148 men since opening and St Brigid's, 151 women. The Inebriate Retreat at Belfast, meanwhile, had treated 209 patients and the State Inebriate Reformatory at Ennis, 274 (*Fourteenth Report of IIIA* 1918: 4; *Fortieth Report of GPBI* 1917–1918: xii; Malcolm 2012: 120; see also Reidy 2014). In her comprehensive analysis of Irish inebriate reformatories, Malcolm has concluded that a vital reason for their decline was the generally permissive public attitude towards drunkenness, although this essentially applied to men rather than women. Once established, this tolerant outlook fostered scepticism and at times hostility among local councils, nationalist politicians, the courts, the churches and crucially the medical profession, as to the value of inebriate reformatories (Malcolm 2012: 115–116). Even within the anti-drink ranks, Bretherton has outlined clear divisions by the turn of the century between:

> on the one side, the old elite, increasingly tied to the Unionist party, arguing that the drunkard should be locked up; [and] on the other side, a militantly nationalist group, some of them teetotallers, taking their stand with voluntarism and Catholicism, while claiming that drunkenness would no longer exist if the British were out of Ireland.
>
> *(1986: 479)*

Political disharmony was similarly self-evident in discussions about the proposed introduction of restricted weekend opening hours for public houses. This was at least partly a testament to the political clout of both Irish publicans and brewing and distilling companies in this period and beyond. In the late nineteenth and early twentieth centuries, publicans achieved a high degree of social, economic and political prominence, especially in nationalist politics. Brewing and distillation, meanwhile, remained politically important well into the twentieth century due to the high levels of employment they provided as well as the revenue their products yielded (Kadel 2015). Echoing the sentiments of the Home Rule Party, in 1895 a review article in the *Dublin Journal of Medical Science* denounced the 'grandmotherly legislation and coercion':

> The liberty of the subject is sufficiently restricted already, and the patience with which millions of law-respecting citizens tolerate the curtailment of their personal liberty lest a weak brother should offend is a marvellous testimony to our inborn respect for law. Restrictions and pledges cannot create an Utopia.
>
> *('Review of Norman Kerr,* Inebriety*' 1895: 50)*

At this stage, the licencing laws governing Ireland remained scattered across 25 Acts of Parliament, a fact which likely motivated the House of Lords' 1898 Commission on Intoxicating Liquor. A testament to the lack of political sway the medical community held at this juncture, only a handful of the 259 witnesses examined were medical men and those who did give evidence were queried on their legal rather than medical knowledge (*Minutes of Evidence taken before the Royal Commission on Liquor Licensing Laws* 1898: 527).

No doubt stimulated by the lacklustre performance of the inebriate homes, Ireland's ever-expanding lunatic asylums remained primary sites of care for the intemperate. In fact, alcohol-related admissions became so common that by 1900, one in ten were attributed to drink (Finnane 1981: 146). Paradoxically, given their medical character, few doctors in Ireland or internationally favoured asylums for the treatment of inebriety (Mauger 2019; Prestwich 1994). This professional apathy was heightened in the early twentieth century as the causal connection between intemperance and insanity became contested and alcohol was increasingly seen as a 'stumbling block' for the already 'unstable brain' (Cox 2012: 61–62; Pick 1989: 201–202). Likewise, the perceived links between heredity and inebriety began to disintegrate, influenced by the growing popularity of the Freudian movement as well as research by University College London scientists that found no marked evidence connecting parental alcoholism to mental defects in children, and therefore shifted the emphasis away from concerns about women's drinking (Berridge 2013: 91). It is also conceivable that the demise of the inebriate homes undermined medical authority, given the very public support many prominent doctors had pledged for this initiative in the outset.

By the end of the First World War, medical interest in inebriety had waned and political barometers swung sharply towards limiting drinking rather than treating diseases attributed to drunkenness. Among the most infamous of these tactics was the United States' prohibition experiment, resulting in a nationwide ban on drinking from 1920 until 1933. Following the Irish War of Independence (1919–1921) and the partition of the island into two separate states (1920–1922), the newly formed Irish Free State government responded swiftly to the 'drink question'.[4] In the first decade of independence, the state initiated an intoxicating liquor commission, restricted pub opening hours and decreased the number of pub licences (Butler 2010: 24–28, Ferriter 2015: 5–6). That medical involvement in these developments remained minimal signifies both declining international interest in inebriety during the interwar years and anxieties about persistently high infant mortality rates and infectious diseases, which remained a priority for the Irish medical community. There was also a marked decrease in alcohol consumption and reported deaths from liver cirrhosis, following general trends in the United Kingdom (Berridge 2013: 165; Ferriter 2015: 9).

The Disease View and the 'Drunken Irish'

The repeal of Prohibition signalled shifting attitudes towards alcohol and a new 'disease view' of addiction began to take root. Earlier interpretations framing drink as an inherently addictive substance were now gradually supplanted by this new concept that rendered alcohol harmless for most but with the potential to cause disease in a minority of vulnerable or 'defective' individuals (Levine 1978: 494; see also Yokoe 2019). The disease view was championed by the prominent epidemiologist and leader of the World Health Organization's (WHO) alcohol research programme, E.M. Jellinek, through whom it filtered into the United Kingdom. The spread of Alcoholics Anonymous from the United States to Europe by the 1950s also propelled its popularity (Thom 1999: 72; see also Yokoe 2019).

This new concept of alcoholism was comparatively slow to take hold in Ireland, in spite of some medical activity in the addiction arena. In the 1940s, the Irish Medical Association lobbied for provision to treat 'addicts' in a new Mental Treatment Bill ('Mental Treatment Bill, 1944' 1945: 7–8). Introduced in 1945, the resulting Act reflected the Association's input. The statute stipulated that any individual who had, due to addiction, been medically certified as dangerous to others, incapable of managing their affairs or at risk of developing a mental disorder could be detained in a mental hospital against their will for up to six months or two years in certain cases (Mental Treatment Act 1945: s.2, s.189). Though it is tempting to decipher this development as a proof of the acceptance of alcoholism as a disease in need of treatment, Shane Butler has convincingly demonstrated the lack of state support for this measure (2002: 23–24, 2010: 29–30). Moreover, as will be discussed, it was not until the 1960s that psychiatrists in Ireland began openly supporting the disease theory (see also Mauger 2021). Therefore in many ways, this development merely emulated the recommendations of medical temperance advocates like Kerr and Cosgrave, half a century earlier, for compulsory powers to institutionalise non-criminal inebriates. Rather than separate, specialist institutions, however, the Act cemented the role of psychiatric hospitals in the treatment of addiction.

Another plausible explanation for the lacklustre medical enthusiasm for the alcoholism model in Ireland lies in the strong influence of the Catholic Church both in the realms of healthcare and education and on the development of psychiatry in these decades. As David Healy has persuasively illustrated, church intervention in the politics of social welfare, combined with an alliance with Irish medicine, dictated the evolution of health services in Ireland (Healy 1996: 275; see also Barrington 1987). Increasingly, most Irish doctors were themselves Catholics, often deeply committed ones, and this likely informed their practice. Other examples where this has occurred include Catholic disapproval of psychoanalysis or behaviourism; opposition by the Irish Medical Association to the proposed provision of free health services for mothers and children under the age of five in the 1950s; and a sustained denial of the occurrence of syphilis in Ireland into the 1980s (Healy 1996). Contemporary church teaching, which was primarily concerned with temperance, as well a general culture of toleration around drunkenness for many groups, may therefore have contributed to the Irish medical profession's delay in embracing the disease view of alcoholism.

While continuing to attract little attention in Irish medical circles, psychiatrists working in Britain and the United States frequently documented disproportionate numbers of Irish alcohol-related admissions to mental hospitals in these regions (Malzberg 1930, 1940; Meyer 1933; Sullivan and Glatt 1956). Alongside these studies, sociologists and anthropologists reinforced the impression that Irish drinking behaviour was somehow distinctive (see Mauger 2021; Stivers 1976: 5–14). Perhaps the best-known example is the work of the Harvard researcher, Robert Bales, whose 1944 doctoral dissertation contrasted Jewish and Irish social norms and attitudes towards drink (see Bales 1980).[5] In 1962, Bales published his findings on the assorted roles alcohol performed in Irish culture. These included drinking for medicinal purposes, to prevent damp and cold, as a substitute for food during famine or religious fasts, to relieve sexual tension in young rural men facing lifelong celibacy due to inheritance practices and as an 'overt and active and persistent aggression against the English'. Alcohol tended not to be condemned, Bales found, and the practice of 'treating' or buying rounds only served to exacerbate Ireland's heavy drinking culture, with alcohol omnipresent at christenings, funerals and wakes (1962).

In fashioning his treatise on Ireland's drinking culture, Bales had borrowed heavily from the work of two Harvard anthropologists, Conrad M. Arensberg and Solon T. Kimball, who observed and recorded their findings on the lives, relationships and economy of the small farmer class and the people of Ennis town in County Clare in the rural West of Ireland in the 1930s (1940; see also 3rd ed., 2001). Arensberg and Kimball's resultant book, *Family and Community in Ireland*, contributed greatly to the durable premise that heavy drinking among rural males was an important 'safety valve in the release of sexual tension'. It also supported the image of the mother-dominated Irish family which, as will be seen, came to influence Irish medical discourses in later decades (Arensberg and Kimball, 3rd ed., 2001: 56–58). It should be noted, however, that Arensberg and Kimball argued that both mothers *and* fathers played a dominant and even controlling role in their sons' lives, with the son largely subordinated by both parents but especially his father (Arensberg and Kimball, 3rd ed., 2001: 52). Aside from relying on Arensberg and Kimball's appraisal, Bales' depiction of Irish social life was mostly based on texts dating from the sixteenth to nineteenth centuries, and tended to both illustrate and strengthen popular explanations for excessive drinking in the Irish. While the tendency in these decades was to frame alcoholism as a male problem, Bales' emphasis on Irish bachelors was later contradicted by research demonstrating that at the turn of the twentieth century, both single and married Irish men *and* women showed higher rates of 'alcoholism' than their equivalents in other ethnic groups (Room 1968).[6] As several scholars have stressed, studies of this type were also undermined due to an assumption that heavy drinking in Irish migrants was characteristic of drinking behaviour in Ireland (Cassidy 1996; Lynn and Hampson 1970; Malcolm 1986; O'Connor 1975).

Concerns about Ireland's drinking culture took on a renewed political urgency in the 1950s, as it became linked to declining population and increasing levels of emigration, especially by women. In 1954, a report from the Commission on Emigration and Population Problems partly blamed the exodus on the 'relative loneliness, dullness and generally unattractive nature of life in many parts of rural Ireland', calling for increased diversity in venues for entertainment, recreation, education and culture, as opposed to simply pubs (173–174). In the same year, a collection of essays edited by Fr John A. O'Brien entitled *The Vanishing Irish* (1954) went further in citing rural male Irish drinking practices as a key reason for declining marriage rates. For example, Edmund J. Murray contended that 'ninety-five per cent of Ireland's eligible women would marry tomorrow were the eligible men of the nation to transfer their affections from horses and dogs and football matches and "pubs" to the nobler activities of courtship and marriage' (1954: 72). Likewise, Mary Frances Keating, in the same collection wrote of 'Marriage-shy Irishmen', while complaining that even for those who failed to evade matrimony:

> [...] he indulges in some form of escapism after recovering from his first panic. The favourite forms of escape are drinking, gambling, politics and sport. He is not a good husband or a good father, and the blame for the fact that the Irish are a vanishing race must be laid squarely and solely on his shoulders.
>
> *(Keating 1954: 166)*

While these claims colourfully depict the perceived links between drinking practices and population decline, it was not until the following decade that political awareness of *alcoholism* was perceptible.

By the 1960s, Irish politicians were becoming increasingly conscious of the claims circulating abroad about an Irish predisposition to alcoholism. Critically, this recognition occurred at a time when the country's Taoiseach (head of government) Seán Lemass was seeking membership of the European Economic Community. In 1962, Lemass complained of 'persistent and irritating falsehoods' about the 'drunken Irish', made worse, he claimed, by the BBC's tendency to constantly reproduce this caricature (Viney 1964: 8). This frustration at the racial stereotyping of the Irish echoed that of nationalist politicians in the late nineteenth century and was, perhaps, understandable, given robust attempts in the 1960s to transition Ireland from a rather conservative and insular nation to one that could be proudly modern and open. As one journalist succinctly put it:

> Few Irishmen would disagree that the image of the "drunken Paddy" whether fictionally presented on British television screens or factually endorsed in the magistrates' courts of West London, is humiliating to the Irish at home. And if Mr Lemass is also concerned lest foreign industries are put off coming to Ireland through fears of drunken labour and absenteeism, this too is understandable.
>
> *(Viney 1964: 8)*

Possibly adding to Lemass' irritation were recent reports that the Irish were drinking less alcohol than the British. In 1958 the Central Statistics Office registered Ireland's annual per capita consumption as 64.3 litres of beer and 1.2 litres of spirits compared to Britain's annual consumption of 79.1 and 1.1 litres, respectively. The previous year, a Commission on Intoxicating Liquor had complacently announced that drink was no longer a serious problem in Ireland (Ferriter 1999: 190–191). Yet, these findings failed to take account of the very high numbers of total abstainers. The Pioneer Total Abstinence Association had gone from strength to strength during the first half of the twentieth century and by 1959, claimed nearly 500,000 members – in a population of approximately 2.8 million. Irish attitudes towards alcohol in this period could therefore be described as ambivalent, or as Ferriter has phrased it, Ireland was a 'nation of extremes'. Overall, however, Ferriter has described the drinking culture in this era as one of 'toleration', in which excessive consumption was mostly viewed as both gregarious and entirely respectable. Importantly, though, this culture of toleration applied to men, while women were more likely to be targeted by the Pioneers and to be abstainers (1999: 2, 168, 191). Nonetheless, there is evidence that some women were drinking heavily, and even undergoing treatment for alcoholism. For example, in St Patrick's Hospital in Dublin, there was a steady increase in the admission rate of 'alcoholic patients' from 230 in 1958 to 735 in 1968, during which time the number of women treated for alcoholism rose from 50 to 150 (Cooney 1970: 220). As in earlier periods, there was an emphasis on the clandestine nature of Irish women's drinking, with the physician to St Patrick's Hospital reporting in 1962 that excess drinking, especially in women, was often so well concealed that diagnosis was made 'on the clinical features alone' (Martin 1962: 120).

While Ireland was not the highest annual per capita consumer of alcohol, the problem of alcoholism, both at home and abroad, drew increasing attention. In 1958 alone, some 561 patients (5%) admitted to Irish mental hospitals had been diagnosed with 'alcoholism' and a further 92 (0.7%) with 'alcoholic psychosis' (*Report of IMH* 1960: 15). In response, psychiatrists began advocating for state support for a national council on alcoholism, eventually formed in 1966. The establishment of this voluntary organisation was chiefly credited to experts at two private psychiatric institutions in Dublin, the St John of God Hospital and St Patrick's Hospital. Both had developed specialist alcoholic treatment facilities in this decade and were widely held to be leaders in the addiction field. In the same year, the Commissioners of Inquiry on Mental Illness reported that they could find no detailed survey of the number of alcoholics in Ireland but were aware of research in the United States and Britain highlighting disproportionate rates among the Irish there. While contesting that such findings signified the extent of alcoholism in Ireland, the Commissioners declared that based on the experience of practising Irish psychiatrists, the problem was serious and deserved immediate attention, including extensive research activity (*Report of CIMI* 1966: 79–80). In fact, it was later reported that admissions for alcoholism were continuing to rise from 1,638 (10.6%) in 1965 to 2,874 in 1969 (14.6%) (O'Hare and Walsh 1970: 13). While this surge may partially indicate that diagnosis was increasing in step with heightening medical interest, it is clear that by now alcoholism treatment had come firmly under the purview of psychiatry.

The 1960s also saw much broader endorsement of the disease view in Ireland. Dr John G. Cooney, a consultant psychiatrist at St Patrick's Hospital, was an especially avid supporter (Cooney 1963). Cooney was responsible for setting up a specialist treatment programme for alcohol-related disorders at St Patrick's and published and presented extensively on the disease view. This concept was also widely promoted by the Irish National Council on Alcoholism (INCA), whose main objective was to educate the public on the signs, causes and effects of the disease of alcoholism, as well as available treatments. INCA, as Butler has observed, was given clear and unequivocal public policy acceptance by the 1966 Commissioners (2002: 38–39). Yet in spite of growing support in some circles, others pointed to social and cultural factors in their research on alcoholism.

Among the most prominent was Dr Dermot Walsh, a practising psychiatrist who became the Director of the Mental Health Section of the Irish Medico-Social Research Board (later Health Research Board) in 1969. In 1962, Walsh had written of Ireland's peculiar cultural environment, including, he claimed, persistent ancient folk customs, superstitions and magical beliefs; centuries of war and hardship, the lasting consequences of the Great Famine of the 1840s; and the 'deeply ambivalent and conflict-laden relationship' between Irish mothers and their sons. Within this setting, Walsh premised, the Irish were:

> in a general sense freer in their use of alcohol than most nationalities. There seems little doubt that drinking plays a large part in dealing with many deeper frustrations and conflicts … Alcohol, too, has in high degree the effect of inducing and enhancing the fantasy life which is so inherently a part of Irish cultural heritage.
>
> *(1962: 65–66)*

At the Medico-Social Research Board, he went on to conduct studies into the prevalence of alcoholism in Ireland and in 1969, pronounced psychiatric admissions for alcoholism much higher than in Britain or the United States (Walsh 1969). This assertion did not sit well with other workers. In 1970, researchers at the Irish Economic and Social Research Institute (ESRI) refuted Walsh's findings, underlining Ireland's lower annual per capita drink consumption, lower death rates from alcoholism and liver cirrhosis and lower conviction rates for drunkenness compared to the United Kingdom, Europe and the United States (Lynn and Hampson 1970). The debate continued, with Walsh attributing Ireland's lower annual per capita consumption to high levels of total abstinence. Walsh also contended that alcoholism was not necessarily a fatal disease, that links with liver cirrhosis remained uncertain and that lower conviction rates might merely reflect more lenient societal attitudes towards drunkenness. 'For the Irish', he concluded, 'wherever they may be, alcoholism is a serious problem' (1970: 205).

Continuing resistance to Walsh's findings is evidence of the sustained professional disagreement relating to alcoholism in Ireland. At the source of this dispute, the central tenet of the disease view proved troublesome for some commentators. For them, the suggestion that alcoholism indicated some inherent defect in certain individuals was difficult to accept in a country with rising psychiatric admissions for that disorder (Mauger 2021). It follows that claims of an Irish predisposition due to some biological, ethnic trait might have been perceived as posing a threat to Irish identity. Perhaps partially in reaction to this, an emphasis on Ireland's drinking culture, and broader cultural influences on Irish drinking behaviour, remained popular into the 1970s. In a submission to INCA, the Director of the Irish Medico-Social Research Board, Dr Geoffrey Dean, emphasised the predominance of 'cultural factors' in determining drinking behaviour. Among them, Dean listed the 'rather extreme attitude' of the Catholic Church in its condemnation of sins involving sex; the 'authoritarian' Irish education system, pressures to conform to cultural norms; and loneliness caused by segregating the sexes both in school and in social activities (Dean 1973). In spite of his initial championing of the disease concept, even Cooney was not opposed to this alternative framework. According to him, modernisation was responsible for a range of new influences on Irish drinking habits which were leading to an increase in alcoholism. These included greater social mobility and disposable income, the shift from dimly lit, all-male pubs to brightly lit bars and singing lounges catering to young men and women; expense account drinking in the cities; and the supremacy of alcohol both in business deals and on all social occasions. By now, Cooney was espousing a 'multifactorial theory', suggesting that exposure to a critical amount of alcohol in a favourable setting would predispose certain individuals by reasons of metabolic and/or personality factors, to develop the disease (1971: 53).

Such concerns about the growing popularity of drinking were informed by altering attitudes to alcohol consumption and addiction across many countries in the 1970s. This change was driven by epidemiological findings linking rising annual per capita intake with a concurrent growth in alcohol-related harm, including deaths from liver cirrhosis and convictions for drunkenness and drink-driving. As discussed, this approach was favoured by researchers at the ESRI. Put simply, drink was now presented as a problem for 'total populations' rather than a predisposed minority. This new theory, which became known as the public health perspective, gradually replaced the disease concept (Thom 1999; Yokoe 2018). With a shift away from biological or psychological understandings of alcoholism, the culture around drinking was therefore firmly under the spotlight. A marked adherence to this new focus was evident in INCA's report to the Minister for Health in 1973. By now, the Council's members were divided between those who still supported the disease view, usually psychiatrists, and other researchers, especially epidemiologists, who promoted the public health perspective (Butler 2002: 53–55). Probably by way of compromise, the report recommended the prevention of both alcoholism and excessive drinking by altering social and cultural attitudes to drink (INCA 1973: 10).

Changing Ireland's Drinking Culture

In spite of a growing emphasis on the potentially harmful aspects of Ireland's drinking culture, ideological clashes between proponents of the disease view and the public health perspective persisted in the decades following 1970. Internationally, the WHO increasingly endorsed a preventive or health promotion model (see Thom 1999). In England, during the 1970s and 1980s, well-funded campaigns developed to promote 'sensible drinking', reflecting a shifting focus away from 'alcoholics' and heavy drinkers (Mold 2020). Yet as Butler has comprehensively outlined, in Ireland, there was a continued reluctance to implement public health alcohol policies. Among the reasons he has presented are a sustained general cultural tolerance of alcohol alongside a lack of political commitment borne of the realisation that measures aimed at controlling and restricting drinking behaviour were electorally unpopular. While INCA had begun to show some signs of supporting public health principles, it remained a divided and largely dormant operation throughout its lifetime and was eventually wound down in 1988. Moreover, the expansion of institutional care for alcoholism, both within the existing public healthcare framework and outside of it, signalled an enduring reliance on treatment rather than preventive models. In 1978, the first of several private rehabilitation in-patient units, the Rutland Centre, was founded by a Catholic priest, Fr Raphael Short and enjoyed substantive state support (Butler 2002: 44–72). Meanwhile, there is evidence that the disease model 'both flourished and remained embedded within the alcohol treatment system' into the twenty-first century (Cullen 2011: 251–261).

Perhaps as a result of the treatment model's persistence, psychiatric admissions for alcoholism continued to increase and by the mid-1970s made up one-half of male admissions and one-third of all admissions (Walsh 1987: 748). These rates remained high into the 1980s and 1990s, accounting for between one quarter and one fifth of all total admissions up until 1995 (Butler 2002: 46). Simultaneously, alcohol consumption continued to climb. Between 1948 and 1970, annual intake per person had risen by 60% from 3.2 litres to 5.1 litres (Ferriter 1999: 203). In 1970, it stood at 7.0 litres of pure alcohol per adult increasing to 10.1 litres by 1986 and to 14.1 litres by 2001 (Ferriter 2015: 17). Yet, these rising rates apparently caused little concern at government level. In 1996, the Health Promotion Unit within the Department of Health (est. 1988) published its *National Alcohol Policy – Ireland* report. The document's tone suggested that neither the public health approach, nor fears about Ireland's drinking culture, had yet entered the official lexicon:

> There is evidence that the description of the Irish as a particularly alcohol-prone race is a myth. Indeed it is doubtful whether Ireland ever occupied a prominent role with regard to alcohol use or misuse.
>
> *(National Alcohol Policy – Ireland 1996: 11, cited in Ferriter 205: 706)*

It could be argued that such a tack was predictable, given the neo-liberal policy climate which characterised the 'Celtic Tiger' era, the popular name for Ireland's economic boom of the mid-1990s to late 2000s. Within this environment, the state was broadly opposed to intervening in the alcohol market via taxation or by restricting advertising (Butler 2009: 343). However, as was the case in England, this period saw the arrival of a policy community committed to implementing such measures to reduce alcohol-related harm. This group boasted strong medical participation, including from physicians, public health doctors and psychiatrists (Thom 1999: 110–120). In Ireland, the policy community was formalised by the establishment of the charity, Alcohol Action Ireland in 2003. Meanwhile, the Minister for Health established a Strategic Task Force on Alcohol, a committee dominated by public health advocates, which published several reports beginning in 2002.

The early 2000s also saw the emergence of new concerns around Ireland's drinking culture as European-wide research studies began to examine binge drinking. While this concept was not a new one, its meaning had now shifted from heavy drinking over several days to a single drinking session leading to intoxication. Internationally, binge drinking became an important social, political and media concern, especially with regard to young people and more often young women (Berridge, Herring and Thom 2009). But the Irish, it seemed, were particularly prone. According to one study of 35 European countries in 2004, Irish teenagers displayed the highest level of binge drinking and were almost twice as likely to smoke marijuana or hashish than the European average (Downes 2004: 6). Such findings once again pointed towards something anomalous in Irish drinking behaviour. From the twentieth-century emphasis on the quantities the Irish drank, there now came a growing focus on the manner in which they consumed alcohol. For many, this offered an explanation for the age-old conundrum of disproportionate psychiatric admissions and alcohol-related problems in Irish populations.

While by now most medical commentators tended to agree that alcohol should be targeted as a major public health problem, the influence of the drinks industry was regarded as one of the 'biggest barriers to change' (Ferriter 2015: 21). The balance of power began to shift, however, in 2009, when the Department of Health established a steering group to formulate a national alcohol policy to be integrated into the existing National Drugs Strategy. This Steering Group was chaired by the public health doctor and Chief Medical Officer, Dr Tony Holohan, and its members included representatives of the College of Psychiatrists of Ireland, the Royal College of Physicians of Ireland (RCPI), the Irish College of General Practitioners and Alcohol Action Ireland. Its report, published in 2012, stated that the average Irish adult in 2010 drank 11.9 litres of pure alcohol annually and that given 19% of the adult population were abstainers, the actual amount consumed was considerably more. Moreover, the report stated, adults in 2010 were still drinking more than twice the annual average of those in 1960. The report also drew attention to both binge drinking in adults and drinking in young people. While some emphasis was placed on the need to improve access to interventions, treatment and rehabilitation services for alcohol use disorders, the strategy's central aim was 'the promotion of healthier lifestyle choices throughout society in relation to alcohol'. The report therefore recommended the introduction of a legislative basis for minimum unit pricing, restrictions on alcohol marketing and advertising and a phasing out of drinks industry sponsorship of sport and other large public events (*Steering Group Report* 2012: 7, 11, 14, 22–23, 24, 35). The following year, the Irish government announced its intention to incorporate several of the Steering Group's recommendations to reduce alcohol-related harm into new public health legislation and in December 2015, approved the Public Health (Alcohol) Bill. A staunch supporter of the Bill, the Minister for Health, Leo Varadkar, who worked as a hospital doctor and general practitioner prior to his political career, described it as 'the most far-reaching proposed by any Irish government, with alcohol being addressed for the first time as a public health measure'. Echoing the concerns expressed by the Steering Group and policy advocates, Varadkar drew attention to the fact that Ireland now ranked fifth out of 28 European Union member states for alcohol consumption and second across Europe for binge drinking (O'Halloran 2015: 8).

Medical support for the Bill was consolidated under the newly formed Alcohol Health Alliance Ireland, a joint venture between the RCPI and Alcohol Action Ireland. Similar in makeup to the United Kingdom's Alcohol Alliance, its membership included medical experts, public health campaigners, NGOs, the Health Service Executive, the College of Psychiatrists of Ireland and the Irish Heart Foundation (Berridge 2013: 226). The alliance was chaired by Prof Frank Murray, a liver specialist at Beaumont Hospital, Dublin and former president of the RCPI. Murray has been an especially avid proponent of the public health approach, publishing widely in the media and in medical periodicals. While giving evidence at a Dáil (lower house of Irish parliament) reading of the Bill in March 2015, Murray appealed to a lingering national sensitivity towards the 'drunken Irish' stereotype:

> There is plenty of public discourse about alcohol and unease about our image as a nation of heavy drinkers. This is not something of which we are generally proud. I believe the time is right to implement radical solutions to address the awful problem of alcohol in Ireland.
>
> *('General Scheme of Public Health (Alcohol) Bill' 2015)*

This concern was doubtfully the driving force behind the Bill, which could be attributed to several factors, including the critical state of the healthcare system and the successful implementation of the 2004 ban on smoking in all enclosed places of work, including pubs and restaurants. Yet, it is noteworthy that this viewpoint has persisted into the present century. Speaking in the Dáil in October 2018 as the Bill passed its final stage, the new Minister for Health, Simon Harris, explicitly highlighted both the government's embrace of a public health approach and a strong desire to change Ireland's drinking culture:

> For the very first time in our history, we are legislating for alcohol as it affects our health and it is right and proper that we do so. We know that we have a relationship with alcohol in this country that is not good, damages our health, harms our communities and harms many families. The measures in this Bill will make a real difference to changing the culture of drinking in Ireland over a period of time.
>
> *('Public Health (Alcohol) Bill' 2018)*

The Public Health (Alcohol) Act was signed into law by the President of Ireland on 17 October 2018. At the time of writing, and in the context of a global pandemic, only time will tell the extent to which Harris' aspiration will be realised.

Conclusion

As demonstrated by several significant studies on other regions, anxieties about intoxication, particularly those linked to addiction and alcohol-related harm, are by no means unique to Ireland (see, e.g., Berridge 2013; Nicholls 2009; Prestwich 1988, 1994; Savelli 2011; Schrad 2014; Toner 2015; White 1996). While many of the developments outlined here largely mirrored those taking place internationally and especially in the United Kingdom, this chapter has highlighted how the specific cultural meanings attached to excessive drinking in a nation internationally renowned for this problem mapped onto these shifting frameworks, informing Irish medical perceptions and responses. In the decades leading up to independence, political divisions and a strong temperance tradition were markedly visible in medical discourses around inebriety. By the 1960s, persistent claims about an alleged Irish susceptibility to alcoholism seemingly diluted support for the disease view at a time when it was seen as damaging to Ireland's international profile. Instead, cultural explanations were sought and increasingly promoted. Recent campaigns for the introduction of public health alcohol legislation have revealed unprecedented unity among medical responses to problem drinking as indicated by the Alcohol Health Alliance Ireland's diverse membership. While the reasons for this cooperation are complex, it is clear that misgivings about Ireland's drinking culture have endured. In conclusion, one might argue that the Irish experience is at once both distinctive and commonplace, making for a nuanced example of the ways in which political aspirations, social-cultural environment and medico-scientific discourses coalesce to influence our understanding of intoxication.

Acknowledgements

I would like to say an especially warm 'thank you' to the anonymous peer reviewer for their thought-provoking and valuable feedback which has helped to shape this chapter. I would also like to thank Professor Geoffrey Hunt and Dr Richard McElligott for their insightful conversations. The research was kindly funded by a Wellcome Trust postdoctoral fellowship (Ref: 205455/Z/14/Z) and I am indebted to the Trust for their support.

Notes

1 For an excellent discussion on the cultural and historical significance of intoxication, see Phil Withington, 'Introduction: Cultures of Intoxication', *Past and Present* Supplement 9 (2014), pp. 9–33.
2 Under the 1800 Act of Union, Ireland's parliament was abolished and the country came under the direct control of the British parliament in London. Elected Irish representatives sat in the British parliament at Westminster.
3 As a Unionist and prominent Orangeman, Johnston was an opponent of Irish Home Rule.
4 Given space constraints, the six counties which formed the separate state of Northern Ireland will not be included in the analysis in subsequent sections of this chapter.
5 This dissertation was published in 1980.
6 Later anthropological works further emphasised the persistence of a heavy drinking culture among middle-aged and elderly bachelor small farmers, which was characterised by high rates of mental illness and in particular schizophrenia. See, for example, Brody 1973 and Scheper-Hughes 1979.

References

Arensberg, Conrad M. and Solon T. Kimball. *Family and Community in Ireland* (Cambridge: Harvard University Press, 1940).

Arensberg, Conrad M. and Solon T. Kimball. *Family and Community in Ireland* (3rd ed.) (Ennis: Clasp Press, 2001).

Bales, Robert F. 'Attitudes towards Drinking in Irish Culture', in David J. Pittman and Charles R. Snyder (eds), *Society, Culture and Drinking Patterns* (London and New York: John Wiley & Sons, 1962), pp 157–187.

Bales, Robert F. *The "Fixation Factor" in Alcohol Addiction: An Hypothesis Derived from a Comparative Study of Irish and Jewish Social Norms* (New York: Arno Press, 1980).

Barrington, Ruth. *Health, Medicine & Politics in Ireland, 1900–1970* (Dublin: Institute of Public Administration, 1987).

Berridge, Virginia. 'The Origins and Early Years of the Society 1884–1899', *British Journal of Addiction* 85 (1990), pp 991–1003.

Berridge, Virginia. 'Punishment or Treatment? Inebriety, Drink, and Drugs, 1860–2004', *Lancet* 364 (2004), pp 4–5.

Berridge, Virginia. *Demons: Our Changing Attitudes to Alcohol, Tobacco & Drugs* (Oxford: Oxford University Press, 2013).

Berridge, Virginia, Rachel Herring and Betsy Thom. 'Second Opinions: Binge Drinking: A Confused Concept and its Contemporary History', *Social History of Medicine* 22, no. 3 (2009), pp 597–607.

Bretherton, George. 'Irish Inebriate Reformatories, 1899–1920: A Small Experiment in Coercion', *Contemporary Drug Problems* 13, no. 3 (1986), pp 473–502.

Brody, Hugh. *Inniskillane: Change and Decline in the West of Ireland* (London: Allen Lane, 1973).

Butler, Shane. *Alcohol, Drugs and Health Promotion in Modern Ireland* (Dublin: Institute of Public Administration, 2002).

Butler, Shane. 'Obstacles to the Implementation of an Integrated National Alcohol Policy in Ireland: Nannies, Neo-Liberals and Joined-Up Government', *Journal of Social Policy* 38, no. 2 (2009), 343–359.

Butler, Shane. *Benign Anarchy: Alcoholics Anonymous in Ireland* (Dublin: Irish Academic Press, 2010).

Butler, Shane. 'Ireland's Public Health (Alcohol) Bill: Policy Window or Political Sop?', *Contemporary Drug Problems* 42, no. 2 (2015), pp 106–117.

Cassidy, Tanya M. 'Irish Drinking Worlds: A Socio-Cultural Reinterpretation of Ambivalence', *International Journal of Sociology and Social Policy* 16, no. 5 (1996), pp 5–25.

'Commission on Emigration and Other Population Problems 1948–54', *Majority Report* (1954).

Cooney, John G. 'Alcoholism and Addiction in General Practice', *Journal of the Irish Medical Association* 53, no. 314 (1963), pp 54–57.

Cooney, John G. 'Rehabilitation of the Alcoholic', *Journal of the Irish Medical Association* 63, no. 396 (1970), pp 219–222.

Cooney, John G. 'Alcohol and the Irish', *Journal of the Irish Colleges of Physicians and Surgeons* 1, no. 2 (1971), pp 50–70.

Cosgrave, Ephraim MacDowel. 'The Control of Inebriates', *Dublin Journal of Medical Science* 93 (1892), pp 178–185.
Cosgrave, Ephraim MacDowel. *Brief History of the Society* (Dublin: Corrigan & Wilson, 1897).
Cosgrave, Ephraim MacDowel. *Experimental Proofs of the Role of Alcohol* (London: Ideal Publishing Union, 1901).
Cox, Catherine. *Negotiating Insanity in the Southeast of Ireland, 1820–1900* (Manchester: Manchester University Press, 2012).
Cullen, Barry. 'Treating Alcohol-Related Problems within the Irish Healthcare System, 1986–2007: An Embedded Disease Model of Treatment?', *Drugs: Education, Prevention and Policy* 18, no. 4 (2011), pp 251–260.
Dean, Geoffrey. 'A Need for a Philosophy in our Approach to Alcohol', in Irish National Council on Alcoholism, *Alcoholism – Report to the Minister for Health* (Dublin: Three Candles Ltd, 1973), Appendix M.
Downes, John. 'Scale of Teen Binge Drinking Problem Revealed', *Irish Times*, 15 Dec. 2004.
Dunbar, Holly. 'Women and Alcohol during the First World War in Ireland', *Women's History Review* 27, no. 3 (2018), pp 379–396.
Ferriter, Diarmaid. *A Nation of Extremes: The Pioneers in Twentieth-Century Ireland* (Dublin: Irish Academic Press, 1999).
Ferriter, Diarmaid. *The Transformation of Ireland 1900–2000* (London: Profile Books, 2005).
Ferriter, Diarmaid. 'Drink and Society in Twentieth-Century Ireland', *Proceedings of the Royal Irish Academy* 115c (2015), pp 1–21.
Finnane, Mark. *Insanity and the Insane in Post-Famine Ireland* (London: Croom Helm, 1981).
Fitzpatrick, Joyce. 'Drinking and Young People', *Alcohol and Alcoholism* 6, no. 3 (1971), pp 90–94.
Fortieth Report of the General Prisons Board, Ireland [GPBI] 1917–1918, xii, Cmd. 42, HC 1918 x.845.
Fourteenth Report of the Inspector for Ireland under the Inebriates Acts [IIIA], 1879 to 1900, being for the year 1917, 4, Cd. 9114, HC 1918 x.669.
'General Scheme of Public Health (Alcohol) Bill 2015: Royal College of Physicians of Ireland', *Dáil Éireann Debate*, 10 March 2015.
'Habitual Inebriates Bill', *House of Commons Debate*, 18 July 1898 vol. 62, cc 223–225.
Healy, David. 'Irish Psychiatry in the Twentieth Century', in Hugh Freeman and German E. Berrios (eds), *150 Years of British Psychiatry, Volume II: The Aftermath* (London & Atlantic Highlands: The Athlone Press, 1996).
Inebriates Act 1898 (61 & 62 Vict.) c. 60.
'Inebriates Bill', House of Commons Debate 25 April 1898 vol. 56, c 977.
Irish National Council on Alcoholism [INCA], *Alcoholism – Report to the Minister for Health* (Dublin: Three Candles Ltd, 1973).
Kadel, Bradley. *Drink and Culture in Nineteenth-Century Ireland: The Alcohol Trade and the Politics of the Irish Public House* (London and New York: I.B. Tauris, 2015).
Kearns, Kevin C. *Dublin Life and Lore: An Oral History* (Dublin: Gill & Macmillan, 1996).
Keating, Mary Frances. 'Marriage-shy Irishmen', in John A. O'Brien (ed.), *The Vanishing Irish: The Enigma of the Modern World* (London: W.H. Allen, 1954), pp 164–176.
Kelly, Brendan D. 'Irish Medical Organisation Doolin Memorial Lecture 2019: Rhetoric and Reality in Mental Health – Ireland and the World', *Irish Journal of Medical Science* 189 (2020), pp 1127–1134.
Kerrigan, Colm. *Father Mathew and the Irish Temperance Movement 1838–1849* (Cork: Cork University Press, 1992).
Kielhorn, Friedrich-Wilhelm. 'The History of Alcoholism: Brühl-Cramer's Concepts and Observations', *Addiction* 91, no. 1 (1996), pp 121–128.
Levine, Harry G. 'The Discovery of Addiction: Changing Conception of Habitual Drunkenness in America', *Journal of Studies on Alcohol* 15 (1978), pp 493–506.
Lynn, Richard and Susan Hampson. 'Alcoholism and Alcohol Consumption in Ireland', *Journal of the Irish Medical Association* 63, no. 392 (1970), pp 39–42.
MacLeod, Roy M. 'The Edge of Hope: Social Policy and Chronic Alcoholism 1870–1900', *Journal of the History of Medicine and Allied Sciences* 22, no. 3 (1967), pp 215–245.
Malcolm, Elizabeth. 'Temperance and Irish Nationalism', in F.S.L. Lyons and R.A.J. Hawkins (eds), *Ireland under the Union: Varieties of Tension (Essays in Honour of T.W. Moody)* (Oxford: Clarendon Press, 1980), pp 69–114.

Malcolm, Elizabeth. *'Ireland Sober, Ireland Free': Drink and Temperance in Nineteenth-Century Ireland* (New York: Syracuse University Press, 1986).

Malcolm, Elizabeth. 'The Rise of the Pub: A Study in the Disciplining of Popular Culture', in James S. Donnelly Jr. and Kerby A. Miller (eds), *Irish Popular Culture 1650–1850* (Dublin and Portland: Irish Academic Press, 1998), pp 50–77.

Malcolm, Elizabeth. 'Between Habitual Drunkards and Alcoholics: Inebriate Women and Reformatories in Ireland, 1899–1919', in Margaret H. Preston and Margaret Ó hÓgartaigh (eds), *Gender and Medicine in Ireland 1700–1950* (New York: Syracuse University Press, 2012), pp 108–122.

Malzberg, Benjamin. 'Mental Disease and "the Melting Pot"', *Journal of Nervous and Mental Disease*, 72, 4 (1930), pp 379–395.

Malzberg, Benjamin. *Social and Biological Aspects of Mental Disease* (Utica, NY: State Hospitals Press, 1940).

Martin, Edward. 'Organic Disease as the Cause of Admission to a Psychiatric Hospital', *Journal of the Irish Medical Association* 50, no. 299 (May 1962), pp 117–122.

Mauger, Alice. *The Cost of Insanity in Nineteenth-Century Ireland: Public, Voluntary and Private Asylum Care* (Basingstoke: Palgrave MacMillan, 2018).

Mauger, Alice. '"The Holy War Against Alcohol": Alcoholism, Medicine and Psychiatry in Ireland, c. 1890–1921', in Steven J. Taylor and Alice Brumby (eds), *Healthy Minds in the Twentieth Century: In and Beyond the Asylum* (Basingstoke: Palgrave Macmillan, 2019), pp 17–52.

Mauger, Alice. '"A Great Race of Drinkers": Irish Interpretations of Alcoholism and Drinking Stereotypes, 1945–1975', *Medical History* 65, no. 1 (January 2021), pp 70–89.

McFarland, F.E. 'The Effects of Alcohol on our Military and Civil Population at Home and Abroad', *Dublin Journal of Medical Science* 98 (1894), p. 488.

Mental Treatment Act (1945 no. 19) (22 May 1945).

'Mental Treatment Bill, 1944', *Journal of the Medical Association of Éire* vol. 16 (Jan-Jun 1945), 7–8.

Meyer, Adolph. 'Alcohol as a Psychiatric Problem', in Haven Emerson (ed.), *Alcohol and Man* (New York: Macmillan, 1933), pp 296–297.

Minutes of Evidence Taken before the Royal Commission on Liquor Licensing Laws [C 8980], H.C. 1898, vol. xxxviii, 527.

Mold, Alex. 'From the Alcoholic to the Sensible Drinker: Alcohol Health Education Campaigns in England', in Mark Jackson and Martin D. Moore (eds), *Balancing the Self: Medicine, Politics and the Regulation of Health in the Twentieth Century* (Manchester: Manchester University Press, 2020), pp 64–94.

Murray, Edmund J. 'The Key to the Problem', in John A. O'Brien (ed.), *The Vanishing Irish: The Enigma of the Modern World* (London: W.H. Allen, 1954), pp 65–77.

Murray, Frank. 'Ireland's Public Health Bill: Crucial to Reduce Alcohol Harm', *Lancet* 390 (2017), pp 2222–2223.

National Alcohol Policy – Ireland (Dublin: Stationery Office, 1996).

Nicholls, James. *The Politics of Alcohol: A History of the Drink Question in England* (Manchester: Manchester University Press, 2009).

O'Connor, Joyce. 'Cultural Influences and Drinking Behaviour: Drinking in Ireland and England: A Tri-Ethnic Study of Drinking Among Young People and their Parents', *Alcohol and Alcoholism* 10, no. 3 (1975), pp 94–121.

O'Connor, Joyce. *The Young Drinkers: A Cross National Study of Social Cultural Influence* (London: Tavistock, 1978).

O'Halloran, Marie. 'Varadkar Bill to Tackle Alcohol as "Public Health Measure"', *Irish Times*, 12 May 2015.

O'Hare, Aileen and Dermot Walsh. *Activities of Irish Psychiatric Hospitals and Units 1965–1969* (Dublin: Medico-Social Research Board, 1970).

Pick, Daniel. *Faces of Degeneracy. A European Disorder, c.1848–c.1918* (Cambridge: Cambridge University Press, 1989).

Porter, Roy. 'The Drinking Man's Disease: The "Pre-History" of Alcoholism in Georgian Britain', *British Journal of Addiction* 80 (1985), pp 385–396.

Prestwich, Patricia E. *Drink and the Politics of Social Reform: Antialcoholism in France since 1870* (Palo Alto, California: The Society for the Promotion of Science and Scholarship, 1988).

Prestwich, Patricia E. 'Drinkers, Drunkards and Degenerates: The Alcoholic Population of a Parisian Asylum, 1867–1914', *Histoire Sociale/Social History* 27, no. 54 (1994), pp 321–335.

Prestwich, Patricia E. 'Paul-Maurice Legrain (1860–1939)', *Addiction* 92, no. 10 (1997), pp 1255–1263.

Prestwich, Patricia E. 'Female Alcoholism in Paris, 1870–1920: The Response of Psychiatrists and of Families', *History of Psychiatry* 14, no. 3 (2003), pp 321–336.

'Public Health (Alcohol) Bill 2015: Report Stage (Resumed) and Final Stage', *Dáil Éireann Debate*, 3 Oct. 2018, 972, no. 8.

Reidy, Conor. *Criminal Irish Drunkards: The Inebriate Reformatory System 1900–1920* (Dublin: The History Press Ireland, 2014).

Report of the Commission of Inquiry on Mental Illness [CIMI] (Dublin: Stationary Office, 1966).

Report of the Inspector of Mental Hospitals [IMH] for the Year 1958 (Dublin: Stationery Office, 1960).

'Review of Norman Kerr, *Inebriety: Its Etiology, Pathology, Treatment, and Jurisprudence, 3rd edition*', *Dublin Journal of Medical Science* 99 (1895), p 50.

Roberts, Bertham H. and Jerome K. Myers. 'Religion, National Origin, Immigration and Mental Illness', *American Journal of Psychiatry* 110, no. 10 (1954), pp 759–764.

Room, Robin. 'Cultural Contingencies of Alcoholism: Variations Between and Within Nineteenth-Century Urban Ethnic Groups in Alcohol-Related Death Rates', *Journal of Health and Social Behaviour* 9, no. 2 (1968), pp 99–113.

Savelli, Mat. 'Diseased, Depraved or just Drunk?: The Psychiatric Panic over Alcoholism in Communist Yugoslavia', *Social History of Medicine* 25, no. 2 (2011), pp 462–480.

Scheper-Hughes, Nancy. *Saints, Scholars and Schizophrenics: Mental Illness in Rural Ireland* (London, Berkeley: University of California Press, 1979).

Schrad, Mark Lawrence. *Vodka Politics: Alcohol, Autocracy, and the Secret History of the Russian State* (Oxford: Oxford University Press, 2014).

Smith, Beverly A. 'Ireland's Ennis Inebriates' Reformatory: A Nineteenth-Century Example of Failed Institutional Reform', *Federal Probation* 53 no. 1 (1989), pp 53–64.

Steering Group Report on a National Substance Misuse Strategy (Dublin: Department of Health, 2012).

Stivers, Richard. *A Hair of the Dog: Irish Drinking and American Stereotype* (University Park: The Pennsylvania State University Press, 1976).

Sullivan, J.D. and Glatt, Max Meier. 'Irish Alcoholics in an English Mental Hospital', *Journal of the Irish Medical Association*, 39, 223 (1956), 146–149.

'The Medical Temperance Review', *Dublin Journal of Medical Science* 118 (1904), p 139.

Thom, Betsy. *Dealing with Drink: Alcohol and Social Policy from Treatment to Management* (London: Free Association, 1999).

Toner, Deborah. *Alcohol and Nationhood in Nineteenth-Century Mexico* (Lincoln: University of Nebraska Press, 2015).

Townsend, Paul A. *Father Mathew, Temperance and Irish Identity* (Dublin: Irish Academic Press, 2002).

Valverde, Mariana. '"Slavery from Within": The Invention of Alcoholism and the Question of Free Will', *Social History*22, no. 3 (1997), pp 251–268.

Valverde, Mariana. *Diseases of the Will: Alcohol and the Dilemmas of Freedom* (Cambridge: Cambridge University Press, 1998).

Viney, Michael. 'Alcoholism in Ireland I: The Irish and the Bottle', *Irish Times*, 6 Apr. 1964.

Walsh, Dermot. 'Cultural Influences in Psychiatric Illnesses in the Irish', *Journal of the Irish Medical Association*, 50, 297 (March 1962), pp 62–68.

Walsh, Dermot. 'Alcoholism in Dublin', *Journal of Irish Medical Association* 61, no. 371 (1968), pp 153–156.

Walsh, Dermot. 'Alcoholism in the Republic of Ireland', *British Journal of Psychiatry* 115 (1969), pp 1021–1025.

Walsh, Dermot. 'Letters to the Editor – Alcohol Consumption in Ireland', *Journal of the Irish Medical Association* 63, no. 395 (1970), p. 205.

Walsh, Dermot. 'Alcoholism and the Irish', *Alcohol and Alcoholism* 7, no. 2 (1972), pp 40–47.

Walsh, Dermot. 'Alcohol and Alcohol Problems Research Ireland', *British Journal of Addiction* 82 (1987), pp 747–751.

White, Stephen. *Russia Goes Dry: Alcohol, State and Society* (Cambridge: Cambridge University Press, 1996).

Wilson, Thomas M. 'Drinking Cultures: Sites and Practices in the Production and Expression of Identity', in Thomas M. Wilson (ed.), *Drinking Cultures: Alcohol and Identity* (Oxford and New York: Berg, 2005), pp 1–24.

Woods, C.J. 'Cosgrave, Ephraim MacDowel', in James McGuire and James Quinn (eds), *Dictionary of Irish Biography* vol. 2 (Cambridge: Cambridge University Press, 2009), p 13.

Yokoe, Ryosuke. 'Alcohol and Politics in Twentieth-Century Britain', *The Historical Journal* 62, no. 1 (2019), pp 267–287.

32

'DRINKING HIMSELF TO DEATH'

The Chronic Drunkard in British Mid-Victorian Fiction and Culture

Pam Lock

Introduction

> Drink and the devil had done for the rest—
> Yo-ho-ho, and a bottle of rum!

The pirate song invented by Robert Louis Stevenson for his popular adventure novel, *Treasure Island* (1881–1882) affirms the association between drunkenness, immorality, and mortality in the public imagination by the end of the nineteenth century (Stevenson, *Treasure Island,* p. 233). The delivery of these lines—the shanty feel of the verses and the boisterous singing of the pirates in many of its iterations—reminds the reader of the reasons for alcohol's continuing popularity: its role in social gatherings as a key part of the relief and conviviality of the group and the individual. Stevenson carefully differentiates between the moderate drinkers (predominantly the heroes of the novel) and the drunkards (the pirate crew with the notable exception of the amoral and often soberly merciless Long John Silver). Although it is not Stevenson's style to be didactic, he is interested in exploring cause and effect. His characters understand and accept the physical and psychological consequences of their actions. The pirates in *Treasure Island* know that drinking to excess turns them into 'beasts' and does long-term damage to their bodies and minds. These are not the jolly drunkards of earlier centuries. Like many later Victorian drunkards in fiction, Stevenson's pirates use alcohol to help them manage the difficult and physically demanding work their 'trade' requires and helps them deal with the resulting distress by offering an oblivion in which they can forget.

The British fascination with the drunkard evident in Victorian fiction was not new to literature. The sustained popularity of bawdy tales in Britain in the Middle Ages featuring habitual or regular drunkenness demonstrates that the drunkard has long been a favourite figure in the British imagination. The revelry and drunken acts in *Sir Gawain and the Green Knight* and *The Canterbury Tales* often prompt key plot points or revelations. Shakespeare's Falstaff appears in multiple plays (a repetition that is extremely unusual in the author's work) making him one of the most famous drunkards in the world. Falstaff's recurrence and his 'strong appeal to our sympathies' is therefore important to the wider public perception of the British drunkard in his mixture of brutish corruption and comic charisma (Tolman, p. 82). The late seventeenth and early eighteenth centuries saw a slow increase of doctors speaking

DOI: 10.4324/9780429058141-41

out against drunkenness. In the mid-eighteenth century, public opinion on drinking and drunkenness was influenced by accounts of the so-called 'gin craze', informed and influenced by Hogarth's famous pictures, 'Gin Lane' and 'Beer Street' and the related writings of Henry Fielding on the links between crime and drink. These representations focused on working-class drinkers, making them grotesque and dangerous to themselves and others. Towards the end of the eighteenth century, the characters of Falstaff and John Bull were simultaneously conflated and opposed in satirical works. Satirical caricatures of John Bull designed to 'critique [...] political power' counted on Bull's reputation for excessive drinking to support a variety of positions as he became 'accessible to a wide range of political groups and interests' (Taylor, 'John Bull...', pp. 108, 106). In these representations, beer is both the healthful drink of the vigorous, sturdy John Bulls depicted in anti-French reform prints, and the downfall of the misled John Bull in anti-Whig propaganda. As the nineteenth century progressed, the ambiguity of concepts of drunkenness increased and fictional drunkards were progressively darker and more dangerous, a warning to readers and a reminder of the fragility of the human body and mind. As Kathleen McCormack argues, 'Victorian novels usually punish [drunkards] severely with sickness, death, or poverty', or at least chronic drunkards (McCormack, p. 138). Yet, these representations enacted more than a 'punishment'. New medical developments in understandings of the effects of alcohol on the body and mind led to greater attention to detail and nuance in the depiction of fictional drunkards. I have therefore specified the 'chronic' drunkard as the focus for this chapter, what we might now colloquially call the 'alcoholic'.[1] This, combined with the rise of realism, made fiction a key player in the increasingly diverse public discourses on drinking and drunkenness.[2]

The first half of the nineteenth century marked a significant surge of developments in medical interest in alcohol and my first section will focus on the place of fiction in public discussions on habitual drunkenness and other effects of alcohol during this period. As David Clemis outlined in his chapter on 'Medical Expertise and the Understandings of Intoxication in Britain, 1660–1830', the shift in public understandings of alcohol's effects on the body and mind was partly prompted by popular publications on new medical theories about drinking and drunkenness. Although physicians such as Stephen Hales were writing about the dangers of drink in the early eighteenth century, the popularity of the works by Erasmus Darwin, Thomas Trotter, and the imported writings of American physician, Benjamin Rush, at the end of the eighteenth century spread word of new developments in medical approaches to the consumption of alcohol and the treatment of drunkards in Britain.[3] These new medical descriptions of the damaging effects of prolonged heavy drinking further problematised notions of innocently 'merry' England and gave scientific foundation to developing ideas about drinking and drunkenness. The development of medical understandings of the effect of alcohol had two key centres: the body and the mind. Physiological experiments demonstrated in significantly improved detail the short-term effects of alcohol on the body such as circulation, organ function, and brain function. Closer attention in asylums to the relation between different forms of madness and the consumption of alcohol, and written accounts of the observations of physicians working in asylums, improved medical and, in the longer term, public understandings of the damaging effects of regular heavy alcohol consumption on the brain.[4] The study of alcohol-related diseases such as 'delirium tremens' also increased the focus on physiological and psychological complaints that were thought to be entirely caused by the consumption of alcohol.[5] This new medical and public interest in the consumption of alcohol, combined with the rise of realism in the 1840s, inspired a wide range of authors to write an unprecedented number of detailed and complex 'alcoholic' characters during this period.

Some doctors also challenged the doctrine held by many Christian denominations that drunkenness was a sin that could and should be 'treated' only by the church and its officers (and was therefore not the business of doctors). In his introduction, Trotter states that

> The habit of inebriation [...] has seldom been the object of medical admonition and practice. The priesthood hath poured forth its anathemas from the pulpit; and the moralist, no less severe, hath declaimed against it as a vice degrading our nature. Both have meant well; and becomingly opposed religious and moral arguments to the sinful indulgence of animal appetite. But the physical influence of custom, confirmed into habit, interwoven into the action of our sentient system, and reacting on our mental part, have been entirely forgotten.
>
> *(Trotter, p. 13)*

However, habitual drunkenness was still generally seen as a vice in Britain, or a mixture between vice and disease. Public discourses and popular publications commonly mixed moral and medical approaches to maximise the impact of each. The tension between what are commonly known in alcohol studies as the vice and disease models was one of the powerful drivers of fictional interest in the habitual drunkard. The Brontë sisters' characterisations of Huntingdon and Hindley depict habitual drunkenness both as a moral lapse or sin and as a disease to be treated by doctors. The title of George Eliot's short fiction featuring a female alcoholic, 'Janet's Repentance', demonstrates Eliot's focus on the moral perspective despite the medical accuracy of the portrayal. The choice of the religious concept of repentance demonstrates an understanding of drunkenness as a sin.[6] The rise and popularity of realism from the 1840s gave authors the opportunity to move away from simplistic representations of the drunkard as simply comic or tragic.

The rapid rise of temperance (anti-drink) campaigns during the first half of the nineteenth century also contributed to the dissemination of medical and religious understandings of drinking and drunkenness. The work of temperance campaigners strongly influenced changes to the portrayal of the drunkard in the nineteenth century as authors of popular and temperance fiction entered into discourses using their fiction to support, complicate, and challenge anti-drinking messages. Although disparate in their aims and organisation, temperance groups were usually collectively known as 'the temperance movement'. One key distinction that appeared in the mid-century was the distinction between those groups advocating moderation in various ways (which were predominantly middle-class) and those promoting total abstinence from alcohol, often known as teetotalist groups (which were predominantly working-class in leadership and had strong links to the labour movement). The temperance movement's role in the improved public understanding of the potential harm of regular drunkenness was not only through lobbying of parliamentary and medical representatives but, more widely, through their publications and public events (lectures, plays, parades, festivals, etc.). Temperance campaigners made extensive use of the potential of the decreasing costs associated with press and publications facilitated by cheaper printing processes and the increasing proportion of literacy across the population which also promised greater incomes and audiences.[7] The boom of the temperance press led to the creation of 'temperance fiction'; poems, short stories, and novels designed to demonstrate the dangers of drink and the advantages of sobriety. These fictions frequently accompanied the articles, reports, and drunkard's confessions that made up the bulk of the content of temperance newspapers and magazines. In the early days, this new genre was quite crude and often overlapped with other moral guidance and conduct fiction. Reliant on simple moral stories, early temperance fiction was designed to horrify its middle-class audience to reassure them of their choice of sobriety, or set an example to its working-class targets to encourage reform and sobriety.[8] According to Brian Harrison, much of the temperance movements' effort was 'wasted':

> Mayhew saw a man who had vigorously praised Cruikshank's *Bottle* drunk three hours afterwards, and Kohl observed that a quarter of the audience watching a temperance drama were drunk; while such spectacles might have been popular, they probably had little effect on daily conduct.
>
> *(Harrison, p. 356)*

Annemarie McAllister challenges Harrison's over-generalisation of this example. Her recent research demonstrates that the social and celebratory elements of temperance gatherings were extremely popular, offering attendees (mostly 'converted' temperance supporters) an enjoyable alternative to the social life of the pub and the bottle, and not simply a stopping point between pubs.[9] However, popular writers such as Charles Dickens, George Eliot, Anthony Trollope, and Wilkie Collins challenged teetotal campaigners. Although they acknowledged and wrote about the dangers of regular or chronic drunkenness, they defended the right of the majority to drink moderately. By the 1850s and 1860s, the temperance movement had responded to this challenge in two key ways. The development of a more sophisticated approach to fiction, bolstered by relatively lucrative temperance fiction prizes to attract higher quality works, and the advocation of temperance principles by well-respected physicians, encouraged by essay prizes and support for popular and well-circulated monographs. Temperance fiction became a route for new authors, particularly female authors like Clara Lucas Balfour and Hesba Stretton, to get published and to earn a living from their writing. Ellen Wood (author of one of the triumvirate of popular sensation novels, *East Lynne* (1860)) published her first novel, *Danesbury House* (1860), via a temperance prize awarded by the Scottish Temperance League which went on to become one of the most popular temperance novels of the century, and persuaded her reluctant publisher to finally take her first popular novel. Hesba Stretton's children's story, *Jessica's First Prayer* (1866), outsold Alice in Wonderland.

The didactic purposes of characterisations of the drunkard in these various types of fiction were also influenced by the increased availability of printed publications and the increase in literacy which led to larger readerships from a wider social spread. The increase in the number of periodicals led to opportunities for specialisation so that these didactic messages could truly be targeted at specific audiences. In temperance fiction, for example, some stories were specifically aimed at potential members, to aid their conversion, such as 'A Word in Season, or, the Sailor's Widow', which appeared in one of temperance campaigner, Joseph Livesey's early temperance magazines as an inspirational story for both father's considering abstinence for the sake of their children, and children encouraged to promote temperance in their parents, while other fictions were written with the aim of maintaining the temperance convictions of existing members such as Wood's *Danesbury House* which included aspirational encouragements for the Scottish Temperance League's predominantly middle-class readership.

This chapter is divided into two sections to flesh out the history of the figure of the habitual drunkard from two essential approaches. The first section focuses on fiction's place in the public discourses on new medical understandings of the drunkard in the first half of the nineteenth century. The second section focuses on gender and class, particularly the increase in social mobility to address the function of the figure of the habitual drunkard in exploring new theories around identity. Having examined descriptions of predominantly male drunkards in the first two sections, I will pay particular attention to the fictionalisation of female drunkenness in this section. Although I will address class first and gender second, the intersectional nature of these categories means that there will be considerable overlap between the two discussions. The combination of these two sections aims to give an overview of the fictional drunkard as a nexus for anxieties about class, gender, and change while at the same time standing as a cautionary figure with a didactic purpose.

Vice or Disease? Fictional Interactions With and Challenges to New Medical Developments on Habitual Drunkenness

In the first half of the nineteenth century, new terms were coined or appropriated by physicians such as 'habitual drunkenness', 'chronic drunkenness', and 'delirium tremens'. These came into prevalent use to identify regular heavy drinkers in medical terms. The common modern term 'alcoholism' was not coined until 1849 by the Swedish physician Magnus Huss and it took several decades to become popular, only gaining its current dominance in the twentieth century. As such, I will avoid using this modern term unless justified by the context.

Following the first popular medical treatises on drinking and drunkenness by Erasmus Darwin, Thomas Trotter, and Benjamin Rush, popular monographs and articles by physicians and physiologists on the effects of alcohol and the treatment of habitual drunkenness became increasingly common. Key players in the first half of the century included surgeon and phrenologist Robert MacNish (1802–1837), the physiologist and temperance activist, W. B. Carpenter (1813–1885), and physician James Miller (1812–1864). Their writing continued to be influential throughout the century, particularly because of their promulgation by temperance campaigners. This section will focus on this first surge of change, between the beginning of the nineteenth century and about 1860. Articles were published on the benefits and dangers of alcohol as a medicine, a food, and a poison by national medical journals such as *The Lancet* and the *BMJ*. Temperance-specific journals were established such as the early and short-lived *Temperance Lancet* (1841–1842), the National Temperance League's *The Medical Temperance Journal* (1869–1892), and the British Medical Temperance Association's *The Medical Pioneer* (1892–1897).[10] The common use of alcohol as a medicine, and as a mixing agent in the popular opiate laudanum, complicated these discourses.[11] As a result, as Lilian Shiman notes, '[t]he medical profession was a target for much temperance propaganda [in the hope that they] would be persuaded to desist from recommending spirits as medicine except where absolutely necessary' (Shiman, p. 12). Debates on the dangers of habitual drunkenness entered the popular sphere through newspapers and periodicals of all persuasions. From the mid-1840s, articles detailing the autopsies carried out on 'drunkards' were common in local and national newspapers as well as temperance-specific publications. These gruesomely described the drunkard's 'fatty' and 'enormous' livers, their 'unhealthy' intestines, and 'inflammation' of the brain resulting from their habitual use of alcohol.[12] I argue that fiction was the other key publication that captured, translated, and engaged with debates about the advantages and dangers of drinking and drunkenness. The following gives an overview of the key authors involved in these debates and the extant literary and historical research that links these to the wider cultural discourse.

Early Medical Approaches to the Chronic Drunkard: The Brontës, Eliot, Dickens, and Collins

The Brontë sisters were at the vanguard of the development of the figure of the drunkard in mainstream fiction. Their particular educational and personal backgrounds led them to create some of the earliest psychologically complex characterisations of chronic drunkards in the nineteenth century. There was, of course, a parallel continuity of the traditional tragi-comic male drunkard. William Thackeray's *Vanity Fair* (1848) published in the same year as Anne Bronte's *The Tenant of Wildfell Hall* (1848) includes the famous comedic account of Josh Sedgley's disastrous hangover, which prevents him from proposing to Becky Sharp. Likewise, Charles Dickens provided his readers with a rich array of happy drunkards throughout his writing career. The drinkers in sacrosanct pubs like the 'Maypole Inn' in *Barnaby Rudge* (1841) and the 'Three Jolly Fellowship Porters' in *Our Mutual Friend* (1864–1865) are not dangerous drunkards but convivial companions enjoying a regular but usually moderate serving of beer and shared punch. Dickens's dangerous drunkards are always victims of their circumstances, usually working class, sometimes violent but always out of their own control and a part of a minority to be pitied. These differed from the careful physiological and psychological depictions that entered usefully into medical debates on drunkenness of authors such as the Brontë sisters. In Dickens's case, they were about the socio-economics of debates about drinking and drunkenness and a deliberate part of his regular attacks on the temperance movement.

The Brontë sisters' novels marked a significant milestone in the depiction of the drunkard. They had an unusually good understanding of the scientific, medical, and religious implications of drunkenness because of the emphasis on Natural Theology in their home schooling by their father, Patrick Brontë (1777–1861). Paul Jennings notes that Patrick was an early promoter of temperance. As early as 1827, Patrick chaired a public meeting in the vestry calling for the 'Suppression of Whisht Shops' and by the 1830s he was president of the Haworth Temperance Society (Jennings, p. 139). As a result, the sisters would have been very familiar with the development of anti-drink teachings and fiction through the pamphlets commonly used by temperance campaigners. We know from the family diaries and letters that parishioners suffering from the effects of personal or family drinking sometimes visited the house for aid from the curate and that these conversations were often witnessed by the sisters. The children's juvenilia show an interest in the links between drink and trauma.[13] As the sisters began writing their first novels for publication in the mid-1840s, their brother Branwell's damaging relationship with intoxicants (especially alcohol and opium) was peaking so their experience of chronic drunkenness was not only personal but raw. Anne euphemistically mentions in her diary paper of 31 July 1845 that Branwell had had 'much tribulation and ill health' and that 'we hope he will be better and do better in future' (Barker, p. 132). She mixes the medical with the moral by the loaded comparative adjective, 'better'. Anne's combination of this conventionally moral phrasing with her reference to his tribulation and ill health complicates the implied meaning of 'do better' and 'be better' revealing her mixed feelings about his illness. In other words, she associates his problems with both ill health and lack of moral effort.

The sisters took differing approaches to habitual drunkenness in their work. Excepting the brief characterisation of John Reed in *Jane Eyre* (1847) and the 'mob led by drunken working-class Methodists' in *Shirley*, Charlotte tended to give most attention to female drunkenness in minor characters (usually nurses but including the famous 'madwoman in the attic' Bertha Mason); Anne and Emily wrote two of the most famous drunkards in Victorian literature. Anne's Arthur Huntingdon in *The Tenant of Wildfell Hall* (1848) and Emily's Hindley Earnshaw in *Wuthering Heights* demonstrate the overlap between contemporary religious and medical theories about the 'cause' of chronic drunkenness complicating the vice:disease binary (McCormack, pp. 137–148, p. 144). They represent a challenge to notions of the innocence of youthful excess in men and the possibility of a 'cure' for the chronic drinker. Anne demonstrates her understanding of recent nature-nurture debates in the press in Helen's fears that Huntingdon's drinking is inherited. Helen removes their son (illegally) from the family home and works to develop an aversion to alcohol in him while they are away in an attempt to protect little Arthur from the influence of his father. Anne also challenges physicians like Robert Macnish and J. C. Lettsom who advised that drunkards should slowly reduce their drinking, rather than stop suddenly. Macnish compares the urge to drink as 'more insatiable than the longings of a pregnant woman' and describes sudden cessation as 'dangerous' and less 'likely to be lasting' (Macnish, pp. 157, 162). In *Tenant*, Lord Lowborough tries to quit drinking by slow steps and moderation, but is always tempted back into excess. Only when he swears immediate and total abstinence does he successfully stop. When Arthur is unable and unwilling to reduce or stop his drinking, Helen comes to the dramatic realisation that she cannot fulfil the 'saviour' role expected of her as wife. She becomes a very early and insightful example of a representation of what we would now commonly describe as 'co-dependence'.[14]

Further, Emily and Anne's characterisations of Huntingdon and Hindley challenged notions of 'cure' in both medical treatises and temperance guides. Grotesquely physical in their nature, the deaths of the two characters demonstrate the sisters' understanding of the links between heavy drinking, delirium tremens, and apoplexy. Huntingdon and Hindley's deaths are attributed to an irrepressible urge to drink. Anne declares in the Preface to the Second Edition that her novel is deliberately didactic to 'reveal the snares and pitfalls of life to the young and thoughtless traveller' (Brontë, 'Preface', *Tenant*, p. 39). Huntingdon describes a physical urge to quench 'an infernal fire in [his] veins' (Brontë, *Tenant*, p. 227). Sadly, the action is ironic for, instead of quenching the fire, he is feeding it. Roy Porter notes that Carl von Brühl-Cramer described excessive drinking as analogous to 'the power of fevers to create unslakable thirsts' in his influential 1819 disease model of habitual drunkenness.[15] The association of chronic drunkenness with an infernal fire persists through the nineteenth century. Charles Lamb describes the 'first steps' to sobriety as 'not like climbing a mountain but going through a fire' (Lamb, p. 3). John B. Gough's confessional account of his struggle with an 'appetite' for alcohol describes a 'dreadful burning sensation' in his stomach 'as if the fires of the pit had been kindled there' (Gough, pp. 249–250). The metaphor and this selection of contemporary religious, moral, and medical examples demonstrate the common mixing of the medical and moral in descriptions of habitual drunkenness. In contrast, Hindley's drinking is one of a range of suicide attempts following the death of his beloved wife. His suicidal urge to 'drink[...] himself to death deliberately' is reminiscent of suicidologist Karl Menninger's (1893–1990) work on alcohol and suicide (Brontë, *Wuthering Heights*, p. 190). Menninger refers to this as a wish for 'suicidal comfort' in reaction to 'great anxiety' (Menninger, p. 146).[16] Emily's realistic and detailed descriptions of Hindley's death of apoplexy following a series of extended periods of heavy drinking demonstrate the popular understanding of this possibility. I argue that these deaths demonstrate the sisters' pessimism for the fate of their brother.

As described in more detail in the next section, there was a surge in representations of fictional female drunkards in the 1850s. These constituted two types: the drunken wife as a drain on her husband and community such as Dickens's unnamed drunken wife in *Hard Times* (1854), Collins's Rebecca Murdoch in 'The Ostler' (1855), and the pitiful, damaged woman drinking to escape such as Aunt Esther in Elizabeth Gaskell's *Mary Barton* (1848) and George Eliot's Janet Dempster in 'Janet's Repentance' (1857). Although the former type sometimes demonstrates the developing understanding of links between physical and mental deterioration and heavy drinking of this period, the latter type is more interesting in medical terms. Although Eliot's Janet's Repentance occasionally falls into temperance tropes such as the confessional sequences with the preacher, Mr. Tryan, as Steven Earnshaw argues, it is 'the first serious treatment of a habitual female drunkard' (Earnshaw, p. 148). Janet is the victim of domestic abuse at the hands of her drunken and violent husband, the lawyer Robert Dempster. Janet's compulsive drinking and the typical external triggers such as her 'cruel' husband are complicated by her own shame and self-hatred. As Steven Earnshaw points out, the temperance narrative's 'encounter with hell' is 'usually done to show that drinking is bad and will more or less *literally* lead straight to hell, [however] it is not the same as the religious-philosophical self-despair Eliot identifies with Janet' (Earnshaw, p. 150). By making it clear that Robert Dempster's behaviour is the direct cause of Janet's drinking, Eliot complicates the addiction narratives of doctors and temperance advocates. Janet's urge to drink is prompted by the desperation of her circumstances. Although she struggles to start with, Janet stops drinking as soon as her husband's power over her is diminished by his illness and then removed by his death. There is not a distinct physical need as described by Macnish and Carpenter. This is unsurprising, given that her partner, the writer G. H. Lewes, was in a public battle with famous physiologist, W. B. Carpenter, in the mid-1850s after Lewes wrote a blistering attack on Carpenter's medical temperance treatise, *The Physiology of Temperance and Total Abstinence* (1853). In the following decade, temperance fiction was to become increasingly sophisticated and influential on other, more popular genres.

Temperance Fiction and Sensation Fiction

In 1859–1860, the spectacular sales of Collins's *The Woman in White* (1860) and accompanying press commotion launched in the public imagination the new genre which would come to be known as 'Sensation Fiction'.[17] As Pamela Gilbert observes, 'The new genre [Sensation Fiction] was distinctively transgressive in that it was thought to appeal directly to the 'nerves', eliciting a physical sensation with its surprises, plot twists, and startling revelations' and was to become 'one of the most distrusted—and most popular—forms of the period' (Gilbert, p. 2). In the same year, a slightly more modest but nonetheless popular temperance novel was published by the Scottish Temperance League, Ellen Wood's *Danesbury House* (1860). Wood, ever sensitive to the tastes of contemporary readers, brought the thrills of the emergent sensation novel to the melodrama inherent in temperance fiction to create the bestselling temperance work of the nineteenth century. This novel falls into a sub-genre of its own that I term 'temperance sensation'. Wood's characters die dramatically in their droves as a result of their own or others' drinking. The novel represents a study of inheritance and upbringing in its account of the (mis)adventures of the Danesbury family and their friends, relations, and workers. Mr. Danesbury's children are 'divided' between two vastly contrasting mothers. The first Mrs. Danesbury, a water drinker and temperance advocate is tragically killed in a carriage accident (symbolically caused by a drunken gatekeeper) on her way to save her baby, accidentally given laudanum by his tippling nurse, but not before instilling her strong morals in her elder children. The second Mrs. Danesbury is an impatient, careless mother who drinks regularly for relief and pseudo-medical reasons, whose bad influence leads her children to drink from an early age. The older children flourish and grow up to become a good influence on their families and communities; the younger children fall into dissolute ways, ruin their father financially and emotionally, and die gruesomely as a result of their habitual drunkenness. The first Mrs. Danesbury's baby, William, strengthens and complicates this educational divide. Born to the first Mrs. Danesbury but predominantly raised by the second, he almost shares the sad end of his younger brothers but is saved (at the eleventh hour of course) by the aid of his older siblings. Thus, Wood demonstrates the intricate relationship between nature and nurture that many physicians of this period were exploring in their own writing. James Miller, whose *Alcohol: Its Place and Power* was published a couple of years before *Danesbury House* by the same temperance association, bemoans the dangers of this association of drunkenness in parents and the habits of their children in terms of generation:

> And the worst of it is, that the disease so induced does not terminate with him or her who produced it. If, unhappily, children be born, they will inherit the evil of their progenitors: studented in body, and often in mind.
>
> (Miller, p. 122)

Although 'popular' sensation fiction authors such as Wilkie Collins and Mary Elizabeth Braddon tended to support moderation rather than temperance or total abstinence, they also recognised the dangers of habitual drunkenness. In *The Woman in White* (1860), Sir Percival's downfall is escalated by his increasingly erratic drinking. Likewise in Braddon's *Lady Audley's Secret* (1862), another villain, Luke Marks, suffers his slow death from the injuries he sustains in the pub fire set by Lady Audley partly as a result of his tendency to drunkenness. He is comatose and only rescued from the flames by the moderate and therefore alert Robert. In both cases, this again echoes Miller's medical writings on the 'effects of alcohol' (Miller, p. 163). He describes 'subdivisions' of behaviour according to increased doses of alcohol, larger doses resulting in 'anger and contention; rioting and revenge; assaults and housebreakings' and still larger doses making the drinker 'ripe for sudden bloodshed, murder, rape' (Miller, p. 163). *Alcohol: Its Place and Power* was owned by Collins and although I am not suggesting that he or Braddon shared Miller's advocation of abstinence (their work encourages the use of alcohol and other stimulants for reflection and cogitation), they were similarly concerned about the effects of regular heavy drinking and used new medical understandings about its effects on mood and mental control to accentuate their villains' malevolent characteristics.

These authors exemplify the important place of fiction in topical discourses on drinking and drunkenness in their interaction with contemporary medical and popular writers. The focus on individual characterisation in a work of fiction powerfully demonstrates the issues with generalisation in the conclusions of some medical and temperance writers. Their characters enact the interplay of the moral and medical and demonstrate the individuality of a condition like habitual drunkenness which complexly arises from and affects the body and mind. Most importantly, at a time when there was pressure to 'fix' the drunkard, they question the possibility of a 'cure' when faced with the multiplicity of 'cause'.

Gender and Class

Until Anne Brontë's *Tenant,* little was written on drunkenness among the landed and middle classes. The assumption was that drunkenness was only a problem for the working and under classes. That is, although there was no question that the more 'respectable' classes did drink and sometimes heavily, many writers argued that this was acceptable because they were able to control themselves, unlike the lower classes.[18] Developing from the madness of the 'gin craze' in the eighteenth century, the rhetoric about the dangers of working and underclass drinking to society and order was a key driver of representations of the drunkard in the nineteenth century.[19] As Jean Charles Sournia comments, the concern in the eighteenth century was

> rather surprisingly [...] based on social rather than medical grounds: drunkenness was upsetting social order in that the lower classes, thought to be the sole indulgers in

> alcoholic excess, were becoming unruly. Drink was seen as a primary cause of poverty, crime, immorality, and violence; lower class drinkers were frequently described as irresponsible and ignorant.
>
> *(Sournia, p. 20)*

As James Nicholls observes, "Defoe complained that 'now so far are the common people infatuated with *Geneva* [gin], that half the work is not done as formerly'" (Nicholls, p. 37). The class-centric 'moral panic' whipped up by such commentators in the eighteenth century gave a strong foundation to the controlling patriarchal messages of such writings in the nineteenth century. This was partly prompted by increases in social mobility which threatened traditional hierarchies and associated power dynamics. Some sections of the temperance movement used this rhetoric as a warning for middle-class members to encourage them to be abstinent for fear of losing their social position to drink.[20] Other temperance groups, particularly those with working-class roots and a focus on total abstinence (teetotalism), took advantage of this widespread rhetoric to promote their campaigning against drink as a way for working-class members to secure respectability and thereby climb the social ladder.[21]

Class Matters

The working and under classes were the most likely to be portrayed as drunkards in Victorian fiction.[22] It is clear from her preface to *The Tenant of Wildfell Hall* that Anne Brontë's decision to depict upper class drunkards was deliberate because she saw a gap that needed to be filled for the sake of truth and to warn young men and women about the dangers of drink. She describes Huntingdon as an 'extreme' example but affirms that 'I know that such characters do exist' (Brontë, 'Preface', *Tenant,* p. 40). George Eliot's Janet Dempster retains her respectability because of her class and her husband's wealth. They do not need to scrimp and save for drink and she is not left in debt after his death. Where the drunkard's impact on the family and the community was clearest in fiction (and in contemporary newspaper reports such as sanitary and crime statistics) was when the cost of 'the bottle' in time and money could be considered deadly, and when poverty speeded up the physiological effects of heavy drinking. In his lecture 'Drunkenness as an Indirect Cause of Crime', John Taylor makes the direct link between poverty and the 'sum spent by the working classes upon intoxicating liquors', quoting Porter's description of this as 'voluntary taxation' and without which he suggests that 'abundant means would be at their disposal' (Taylor, 'Drunkenness...' pp. 9–10).

Popular illustrator and caricaturist, George Cruikshank's gradual conversion to temperance in the 1840s was partly inspired by his father's death from delirium tremens and partly by his worries about his own increasingly extreme drinking bouts. This led him to produce one of the most influential anti-drink stories of the century, *The Bottle* (1847). A few years later, he signed the pledge. Told in a series of illustrated prints with dramatic accompanying descriptions, *The Bottle* charts the short and disastrous history of a family after the husband introduces his wife to 'the bottle' for the first time and encourages her 'just to take a drop' (Plate 1). Initially merry, the story quickly takes a darker turn. The husband loses his job, their clothes and furniture are sold to 'supply the bottle' (Plate II), and the family are forced to resort to begging. Their youngest child dies of starvation and the husband kills his wife with the bottle that is the source of their misery (naturally) after which he is left 'a hopeless maniac' (Plate VIII). *The Bottle* was swiftly followed by a sensational sequel: *The Drunkard's Children* (1848). This second series chronicles the downfall of the remaining children into vice, crime, and premature death. Cruickshank's publications were so popular that, by

October of the same year, *The Bottle* had been turned into a play by T. P. Taylor and a variety of theatrical versions were performed as temperance entertainments for the rest of the century. Although his fame as Charles Dickens's illustrator no doubt added to the success of the series, Cruikshank's conversion disgusted his friend and caused them to permanently part ways. In particular, Cruikshank's temperance versions of classic fairy tales in *George Cruikshank's Fairy Library* (1853), prompted Dickens to publish a public objection titled 'Fraud on the Fairies' (1853) in his own popular periodical, *Household Words* (1850–1859). Dickens opposed teetotalism because of his basic objection to universal abstinence (i.e. the idea that everyone should stop drinking alcohol). He saw drinking as an important source of relief and conviviality for the majority of the population, particularly the working and middle classes. In one of several vitriolic anti-temperance articles, he argues: 'Because Bill Brute, the robber in Newgate, and Mr. Brallaghan of Killalloo, resident down the next court, make wild beasts of themselves under the influence of strong liquor, therefore Jones, the decent and industrious mechanic, going to Hampton Court for a summer day with his wife and family is not to have his pint of beer and his glass of gin and water' (Dickens, 'Demoralisation...', p. 1). The fleeting characterisation of these working-class men—'Bill Brute' representing the criminal classes and 'Jones' the 'industrious' skilled worker—is a direct response to the equally extreme caricatures of Cruikshank and other temperance writers' in their focus on the drinking of the working classes.

However, Dickens was equally concerned about the dangers of chronic drunkenness. The gruesome description of the life of a drunkard and his ruined family in 'The Drunkard's Death' in *Sketches by Boz* (1836) bears a striking similarity to Cruikshank's approach in *The Bottle* and *The Drunkard's Children*. A man falls to the temptation of drink and becomes a burden on his wife and children. Unable to earn a good living between them, his wife dies of starvation and disease, his sons turn to crime and end in death or custody. At first, his daughter attempts to support him but, after he drunkenly betrays his son to the authorities, she disappears and he is left to support himself. At the end, he throws himself in the river and then symbolically changes his mind after he enters the water and tries to return to land but is swept away by the rushing waters of the Thames. The difference between these two fictions is subtle but key to the difference between representations of pro-moderation and pro-abstinence rhetoric. While Cruikshank's tale focuses on the titular 'bottle', implying that its introduction to any household leads inevitably to the downfall of the family, Dickens's tale suggests that some drunkards are impelled by 'misfortune and misery' and 'by far the greater part have wilfully, and with open eyes, plunged into the gulf from which the man who once enters it never rises more, but into which he sinks deeper and deeper down, until recovery is hopeless', placing the onus on the circumstances of the individual rather than the intoxicant per se (Dickens, 'Drunkard's Death', p. 555). This focus on the individual continued to manifest itself in his fiction for the rest of his life. Sarah Gamp in *Martin Chuzzlewit* (1842–1844) follows the traditional stereotype of the drunken and careless nurse. Most famously, the grotesque Krook in *Bleak House* (1852–1853) whose drinking ends with his spectacular death from spontaneous combustion was carefully researched by Dickens as outlined by Gordon S. Haight and Brooke D. Taylor.[23] Finally, Jenny Wren's drunken parent, Mr. Dolls, named by her as 'the bad child' is kept by her earnings as a dolls' dressmaker in his last complete novel, *Our Mutual Friend* (1864–1865). Dolls, unable to see the long-term repercussions because of his immediate need for drink, betrays his daughter's confidence for 'sixty three pennyworths of rum' (Dickens, *Our Mutual Friend*, pp. 696–697). Dickens's conclusions that habitual drunkenness was a symptom of, rather than a cause of, poverty corresponded with other socio-political observers of the time such as Friedrich Engels. However, his single-minded attack lacked the gradation of fellow social commentator Henry Mayhew's accounts which both agreed that habitual drunkenness was a symptom of poor living conditions and, at the same time, acknowledged that drink contributed to the misery of the lower classes by re-directing time and money away from necessities and personal improvement. Dickens's prominent and influential voice in the 1840s and 1850s maintained the focus on the drunkenness of the lower classes while at the same time safeguarding his aim to make the members of the temperance movement ridiculous.

The impact of the realities of increasing social mobility on the individual also troubled both conservative and liberal writers. To generalise, the conservatives worried that it demonstrated the perils of rejecting the place ordained for a person by God; the liberals regarded the vulnerability of those attempting to better themselves as a failing of society and government. Anthony Trollope reflects on this in his *An Autobiography,* outlining his inner conflict between his belief in the God-given rights of the upper classes to their social position and his feeling of 'injustice' at the 'misery' of the working classes (Trollope, *Autobiography,* p. 292). His characterisation of industrialist, Roger Scatcherd in *Dr. Thorne* (1858) exemplifies another trope of the second half of the nineteenth century, the socially mobile drunkard. Stimulated by drink and ambition, stonemason Scatcherd makes his name and his fortune in the new railway boom, as a leading engineer.[24] Initially, he effectively uses alcohol as a stimulant to allow him to work the long hours required for his success (and is admired by his peers for his capacity for both) but the effects of regular heavy drinking on his body and mind combined with his feelings of alienation brought on by his new social status, lead to a tragic decline. On his deathbed, as Dr. Thorne begs him to stop drinking to save his life, Scatcherd proclaims his feelings of isolation and despair: 'What gratification can I have except the brandy bottle?' (Trollope, *Dr. Thorne,* p. 124). Scatcherd leaves a legacy of both the railways he has built and an inheritance which allows his niece, Mary Thorne, to marry into the Squire's almost bankrupt family (although she marries for love). Trollope thus allays his conservative conscience by enabling Mary's marriage and returning the money and lands that the Squire has sold to Scatcherd to his son. At the same time, his sympathetic portrayal of Scatcherd reminds the reader of the vulnerability of men moving across class boundaries. Trollope continued to muse on the relationship between alcohol and social mobility in his later fiction. The suicides of Julius Mackenzie in 'The Spotted Dog' (1870) and Augustus Melmotte in *The Way We Live Now* (1875) are both attributed to alcohol and a change in social class. Mackenzie is a scholar, brought low by his own drinking and that of his drunken wife; Melmotte takes his own life fearing arrest after a disastrous 36-hour drinking binge. Unlike Scatcherd, Melmotte (a fraudster) and MacKenzie (who destroys the book he is supposed to be editing) leave destruction and distress behind them. It is not clear, however, whether Trollope was simply working through a series of possible conclusions or developing his ideas on this subject with time. His return to this sort of character, and his different approaches in these writings, demonstrates how much of an interesting enigma the 'social mobile drunkard' was to him.

I finish this section on class with Hardy's portrayal of the ultimate fictional Victorian drunkard, Michael Henchard in *The Mayor of Casterbridge* (1886). Hardy's depiction follows a surprisingly similar line to Trollope's drunkards, though in a more Hardian manner. Henchard, a haytrusser and regular heavy drinker, becomes intoxicated at a country fair on smuggled rum concealed in furmity (a traditional wholesome spiced wheat and milk drink) and auctions his wife and child to a sailor for five pounds.[25] When Henchard awakes the morning after the drunken auction, he is unable to find his family and swears a 21-year pledge to abstain from alcohol. The drunken and morally questionable transaction which catalyses Henchard's transition from husband and father to businessman forms a foundation for the making and re-making of non-biological family ties, a process that Henchard repeats in the novel.[26] Unlike his fellow socially mobile characters in the texts mentioned above, it is this period of sobriety that spurs him on to success. Henchard moves to Casterbridge to become a successful grain merchant and Mayor of the town. However, on the very day that marks the expiration of his pledge, he returns to drinking and, precipitated by a series of drinking bouts, quickly declines in status and health until he is once again a haytrusser, working the very land that was once his own. I consider this to be a deliberate return to his original character, in part reflecting his discomfort in his new position and in part Hardy's fatalistic philosophical approach. Henchard dies, filled with regret and seeking anonymity as set out in his famous will, reversing his long search for reputation and wealth.

The Female Drunkard

In fiction, male drunkards are the majority. Like the common rhetoric on class, male drunkenness was also frequently represented as a cause of poverty, crime, and violence (rather than a result of poverty as Engels and Dickens argued, for example); the time and money spent in the pub deprived their wives and children of money and care. In *Danesbury House*, when the 'Danesbury Operatives' are introduced, the narrator describes the contrast between the cottages of the men who pass their wages to their wives to allow them to create 'pleasant dwellings' and those who 'drank their wages away' and so 'huddled with their wives and families into the downstairs rooms' (in order to let the 'two upper rooms') (Wood, p. 65). This sort of rhetoric demonstrates the intersections between anxieties about the lower classes detailed above and gender dynamics. The female drunkard is different from the male drunkard; her gender matters and a drunken woman continues to be regarded as somehow 'worse' than a man in the same condition. Her drunkenness is the most despicable and irresponsible of all and the least curable. However, class is also key. Depictions of the female drunkard are predominantly confined to the lower and under classes. Middle- and upper-class female drunkards are rare and generally more respectable or forgivable.

The female drunkard is a fleeting and shadowy character, even at her most outrageous. She is usually depicted as a comparison with another character (such as Dickens's juxtapositioning of the drunken unnamed wife and the saintly Rachael in *Hard Times*) or described by others in the story (such as the mothers in Sarah Stickney Ellis's *Family Secrets* (1842) and Hesba Stretton's *Jessica's First Prayer* (1866)). However, she is key to understanding the gendered social norms of Victorian Britain and the women who challenged them. Women bore the ultimate responsibility for drinking and drunkenness in the family. Engels argued that '[i]t is morally and physically inevitable that, under such circumstances, a very large number of working-men should fall into intemperance' given the 'comfortless' home and working conditions in the newly industrialised towns (Engels, pp. 102–103). The comfort of the home was considered a female responsibility, so Engels's comment implicates women as well as employers in male drunkenness. Lady Bell describes the consequences of a drunken and careless wife in her reflections on her philanthropic work with factory hands in *At the Works* (1907). She gives an example of a newly married couple:

> The wife, a fretful, delicate, rather silly woman, had begun drinking very soon after their marriage. The husband, a respectable, upright, domestic sort of man, a good citizen and a good workman, gradually found that the money was being frittered away and his home neglected. Finally, depressed and wretched, he took to going out of his

> uncomfortable home and remaining at the public-house, and began drinking himself. He said he did not care for it, but he liked 'forgetting about things,' and he took absolutely the only course open to him which gave him at once change of scene and material warmth and comfort.
>
> *(Bell, p. 248)*

Bell places the blame for the husband's drinking squarely with the 'silly' wife in the exhausted and pitiful 'finally'. His lack of pleasure in alcohol and the contrast between his 'uncomfortable' home and the 'warmth and comfort' of the pub emphasises the wife's responsibility for him taking up drinking to 'forget[...] about things'. Drunken mothers also feature heavily in melodramatic accounts of working-class living conditions. Harriet Beecher Stowe, writing about her experiences in Manchester in *Sunny Memories,* describes driving past gin shops and seeing 'Mothers go there with babies in their arms, and take what turns the mother's milk to poison' (Beecher Stowe, p. 134). Temperance campaigner and speaker, Mary Bayly, dramatically wrote 'the effects of this vice [drunkenness] upon herself, her husband, and her family, are terrible in the extreme. No tongue can express what the child of a drunken mother suffers' (Bayly, p. 136). Temperance articles and tracts encouraged young women to join the cause arguing that, in the words of the 'Young Woman's Tract': 'The abstinence cause is calculated, when espoused by young women, to dignify the female character' ('Young Woman's Tract', p. 7). However, as I shall describe later in this section, this notional female responsibility for personal and familial sobriety was challenged by some influential authors. Anne Brontë's Helen Huntingdon writes in capitals in her diary: 'he may drink himself dead, but it is NOT my fault' (Brontë, *Tenant,* p. 279).

Fictional depictions of the dangers of female drinking to the sanctity of the home were exemplified by Sarah Stickney Ellis's writings on a woman's role in the family and society. The popularity of her early works, *The Women of England* series (1839–1843), boosted sales of her later collection of more specifically temperance-related tales, *Family Secrets* (1842). Like much temperance fiction of this period, the families featured are predominantly working class. These stories dramatically featured grotesque drunken mothers stealing money and clothes from their children to feed their mortifying habit and greedy drunken husbands, depriving their families of their money and time (usually represented as food, clothes, care, and instruction) and shaming them morally. In 'The Favourite Child', the main character, Maria, describes her mother's descent into drinking:

> [H]er husband was a hard man, and stinted her of many things she had been used to. I believe he meant well, but they got to harsh words one against another, and so my mother took to drinking to drive away her grief, and then he left her.
>
> *(Stickney Ellis, p. 270)*

Maria's mother's drinking worsens due to her husband's treatment (implied domestic violence) and then he leaves as a result of her drinking. Their resulting poverty and her need for drink leads Maria's mother to steal from her sick and starving daughter to pay for her habit. The chain of blame created demonstrates a symbiotic relationship between alcohol and domestic violence with the child as the ultimate victim.

However, other authors used drinking to demonstrate the vulnerability of women in Victorian society. Elizabeth Gaskell's Aunt Esther in *Mary Barton* (1848), although she is abandoned by her soldier-lover when he is sent to Ireland, only turns to drink *after* losing her child. When her child becomes ill, she is unable to run her shop and the doctor's bills rapidly reduce her savings to nothing. Although she becomes a prostitute to support herself and her new habit in the end, Gaskell makes it clear that she had worked hard to try to save herself from financial and moral ruin. As such, she is represented as pitiful rather than disgusting:

> Such as live like me could not bear life if they did not drink. It's the only thing to keep us from suicide. If we did not drink, we could not stand the memory of what we have been, and the thought of what we are, for a day.
>
> *(Gaskell, p. 145)*

For her, drinking is an escape from her reality, her grief, and her memories but she defends her love for her soldier and her little girl.

In the 1850s, there was a significant increase in representations of the fictional female drunkard in popular mainstream novels. This coincided with a surge in the development of the women's rights movement and agitation for changes to the Married Women's Property Act and the related divorce laws. In 1854, Charles Dickens contrasted the sober and decent weaver Stephen Blackpool in *Hard Times* with his beastly and unnamed drunken wife. Written to support Lord Cranworth's bill to amend the divorce laws, Dicken's portrayal of Blackpool's wife is deliberately disgusting and chief among her bad habits is drunkenness.[27] As Dayton Haskin notes, Dickens and his allies in this campaign 'did not envisage a remedy for the plight of women [...] The reformers' concern was the prohibitive expense of divorce for men' (Haskin, p. 211). Dickens outlines his primary purpose for 'No. 2' of *Hard Times* (Chapters 9–15; published 29 April 1854) in his 'Working Memoranda':

> **Chapter X**
>
> open Law of divorce. Stephen Blackpool and Rachael
> (Wolverhampton black ladder)
> Finds his bad wife at home 'Come awa' from th' bed! 'Tis
> mine! Drunk agen? Ah! why not'[28]

The heading, 'open Law of Divorce', specifies that he plans to 'open' the topic in Chapter 10.[29] Dickens's first description of Blackpool's wife in his notes is simply that she is 'bad', but when he creates a mnemonic by outlining a brief conversation between Stephen and his wife, Dickens demonstrates what he means by 'bad' in two examples: Stephen's attempt to ban her from the marital bed (to which she is no longer entitled or welcome): 'Come awa' from th' bed! 'Tis mine!'; and her defiant drunkenness: 'Drunk agen? Ah! why not!'. This conversation, slightly amended and developed, appears in the final text. This is the reader's first introduction to his wife and he discovers her symbolically lying on the hearth in his cottage, extremely drunk:

> 'Heaven's mercy, woman!' he cried, falling farther off from the figure. 'Hast thou come back again!'
>
> [...] After an impatient oath or two, and some stupid clawing of herself with the hand not necessary to her support, she got her hair away from her eyes sufficiently to obtain a sight of him. Then she sat swaying her body to and fro, and making gestures with her unnerved arm, which seemed intended as the accompaniment to a fit of laughter, though her face was stolid and drowsy.

[...] 'Back agen?' she screeched, after some minutes, as if he had that moment said it. 'Yes! And back agen. Back agen ever and ever so often. Back? Yes, back. Why not?'

[...] 'I'll sell thee off again, and I'll sell thee off again, and I'll sell thee off a score of times!' she cried, with something between a furious menace and an effort at a defiant dance. 'Come awa' from th' bed!' He was sitting on the side of it, with his face hidden in his hands. 'Come awa! from 't. 'Tis mine, and I've a right to t'!'

As she staggered to it, he avoided her with a shudder, and passed—his face still hidden—to the opposite end of the room. She threw herself upon the bed heavily, and soon was snoring hard. He sunk into a chair, and moved but once all that night. It was to throw a covering over her; as if his hands were not enough to hide her, even in the darkness.

(Dickens, Hard Times, p. 70)

Dickens develops on his original mnemonic, elaborately describing the 'bad wife['s]' inhuman, physical repulsiveness, her disconcerting emotional instability, and her threateningly disjointed speech. Dickens is carefully emphasising the cost to Blackpool of being inextricably bonded to his wife, emotionally and financially, as part of the book's role in agitation for changes to the divorce laws. Dickens's attention to these 'costs' demonstrates his focus on the demonisation of the 'bad wife' to serve the androcentric purposes of his ongoing campaigns for freer access to divorce for men.

The following year, Dickens published a short story by Wilkie Collins which explored a more dangerous version of the drunken woman in the Christmas edition of *Household Words, The Holly-Tree Inn*. Ostensibly, a sort of ghost or supernatural story, 'The Ostler' (1855), is a warning against associating with strange women from out of town. The protagonist, Isaac, has a dream about a woman threatening him with a knife. A few years later, he rescues and marries a psychologically disturbed female stranger, Rebecca Murdoch, who is about to commit suicide with laudanum.[30] Soon after their marriage, the wife withdraws to 'seek the deadly self-oblivion of drink' (Collins, p. 15). Despite his famous promotion of the precepts of polygamy, the key objections to Rebecca's drinking are sexual accusing her of making 'acquaintances of the most dangerous kind' and keeping 'company with drunkards' (Collins, p. 15). The link between family respectability and female drunkenness is confirmed when she arrives for his mother's funeral 'inflamed and shameless with drink' (Collins, p. 17). The embodied implications of 'inflamed' suggests a parallel between passion and drunkenness. The combination with the mention of shamelessness, emphasises the immoral implications of her intoxication. The introduction of a new knife to the house, resembling the one from the dream, is decidedly phallic and he becomes 'afraid [...] to sleep in the same room with her', instead, walking about at night, dozing in the parlour or sitting up with his sick mother. After escaping their home, he is haunted by her in his dreams, demonstrating the long-term damage a drunken wife can cause to a sensitive husband like Isaac.

In 1857, George Eliot wrote against these androcentric stereotypes by creating Janet Dempster, the heroine of 'Janet's Repentance', a 'scene' from her first collection of fiction, *Scenes of Clerical Life*. Also written in support of agitation for changes to the divorce laws, Eliot supported Barbara Leigh Smith's appeals to better protect wives against domestic abuse and to enable wives separated from their husbands to earn and retain their own money and property (inspired by the work of Caroline Norton, whose writings detailed the injustices suffered by her at the hands of a drunken husband she could not legally escape). The eponymous Janet, driven to drink by her drunken and abusive husband, is nonetheless beautiful, graceful, and intelligent, spending much of her free time doing good works in the community. Only her husband's abuse leads her to drink, in an attempt to 'arm herself in leaden stupor' (Eliot, p. 333). She escapes him after he casts her from the house. After her husband's death from delirium tremens, Janet is finally released from his control and increases her charitable works demonstrating the positive possibilities of divorce for women trapped in unhappy or brutal marriages. Janet can repent without fearing long-term shame because she is intelligent, beautiful, and kind but most of all, she is middle-class. In her depiction of Janet, Eliot shows an awareness of the tropes of fictions about female drunkards and challenges the generalisation of depictions such as Collins and Dickens. Janet bears some similarities to Aunt Esther in *Mary Barton,* in that her drinking is justified by traumatic family circumstances. However, instead of Esther's stereotypical release through an early 'merciful' death, Janet is helped to achieve a 'cure' through the support of her community and religion, represented by her friend Mrs. Pettifer and the Rechabite curate, Mr. Tryan and the release from her abusive husband through his early death.

Nonetheless, temperance fiction continued to push the notion of female responsibility for the sobriety and good morals of the family and wider community. This is exemplified by Ellen Wood's 1860 *Danesbury House* (as discussed above in Temperance Fiction and Sensation Fiction above). By prioritising upbringing as the pivotal impact on these children via their two different mothers, Wood continues to confirm the importance of the female role in the family in the fight against habitual drunkenness, contradicting Anne Brontë and George Eliot's challenges. Published a few years later, Hesba Stretton's equally popular, *Jessica's First Prayer,* begins with a description of Jessica refusing new clothes from a potential benefactor because '[i]f you was to give me fine clothes like your little girls, mother 'ud only pawn them for gin' (Stretton, p. 85). The precious child's straight forward attitude to her inability to accept desperately needed help because of her mother makes her plight all the more pitiable and the mother all the more monstrous.

Towards the end of the century, more melancholy and pitiable fictional female drunkards appear. Inspired by Zola's novels and George Gissing's own tragic relationship with his first wife, Nell Harrison, whose damaging drinking destroyed their relationship and her life, Gissing published *The Nether World* (1889) and *The Odd Women* (1893). In *The Nether World* (1889), Mrs. Candy's body is 'vitiated by the drugs' from Mrs. Green's beer-shop, and, by the end of the novel, she cares 'only for beer' despite her collection of temperance pledges over the fireplace (Gissing, p. 76). In *The Odd Women,* the female protagonist's sister, Virginia, becomes a secret drinker, slipping into railway cafes and grocers for a tipple while running errands and becoming increasingly strange and ill as the story progresses.[31] Gissing's tippling women demonstrate his anxiety for women making themselves vulnerable while seeking or managing unsought independence. His odd women, unable to find a husband because of the unequal gender split of the population in the final decades of the century, seek solace in drink to replace the families they were denied.

A Final Reflection

The elements of the fictional drunkard exemplified in these sections are, of course, interdependent. Class, gender, religion, and new medical developments intersect in fiction, and it is the resulting points of tension that make the most interesting and innovative characterisations of the drunkard. Just as Trotter, Macnish, and Miller wrote specifically about the different impact of drunkenness on women and men and of their concerns for the morals as well as the health of the working and underclasses, so certain types of authors wrote at these points of intersection. The study of the figure of the habitual drunkard in fiction is essential to our understanding of mid-Victorian anxieties for the individual, the family, the community, and the nation. This precarious figure, sometimes comic, usually tragic, is always extreme and therefore useful to exemplify social issues, both highlighting problems (in the case of Dickens's *Hard Times*) and portraying possible ideals (in the case of *Danesbury House*). For some, the habitual drunkard is a warning to defend tradition and enforce social norms and boundaries. For others, it is a nexus of imaginative experiments with the possibilities offered by increased opportunities to transgress such boundaries and assert individuality. Either way, the fictional chronic drunkard not only warns us to drink 'well' or not at all, but also reminds us of the fragility and value of human life.

Notes

1 As Steven Earnshaw points out, this is not the only proper approach to the habitual drinker and for more information on the notion of different approaches to identity and drunkenness, I recommend his book, *The Existential Drinker* (Manchester: Manchester University Press, 2019).

2 The Penguin Dictionary of Literary Terms and Literary Theory describes the aims of realism as a literary movement as 'The portrayal of life with fidelity'. This relatively new imperative to portray 'real' life led to shift of focus away from the aristocracy, or at least encompassing other socio-economic groups. J. A. Cuddon (ed.), *Dictionary of Literary Terms and Literary Theory* (London: Penguin 2014), p. 590.

3 Erasmus Darwin, *Zoonomia* (Cambridge: Cambridge University Press, 2011); Thomas Trotter, *An Essay, Medical, Philosophical, and Chemical on Drunkenness and Its Effects on the Human Body* (Philadelphia: Anthony Finley, 1813); Benjamin Rush, 'Inquiry into the Effects of Ardent Spirits on the Human Body and Mind', reprinted in *Quarterly Journal of Studies on Alcohol*, 4 (1944), 324–341.

4 See, for example, Benjamin Collins Brodie, *Psychological Inquiries: In a Series of Essays* (London: Longman, Brown, Green, and Longmans, 1854) and James Miller, *Alcohol: Its Place and Power* (Glasgow: Scottish Temperance League, 1859).

5 For a useful account of the medicalisation of the treatment of habitual drunkenness, see Clemis (cited above) and Iain Smith, 'Doctoring in a Whisky-Injured Nation: The Medical Response to the "Alcohol Question" in Scotland, 1855–1925', unpublished thesis, University of Glasgow, 2018.

6 As discussed with Steven Earnshaw, verbal communication, June 2015.

7 Indeed, the very 'weight' of this publication has necessitated that I be very selective with the amount of temperance fiction included in this chapter. To do justice to the representation of the drunkard in temperance fiction would require a separate chapter or a larger work.

8 For example, an early example from one of Joseph Livesey's periodicals, 'A Word in Season, or the Sailor's Widow', tells the story of a tippling man instantly converted to abstinence by the tears of his 'beautiful child' after hearing a servant tell of the drunken death of her son, Jemmy, stating, 'We none of us can tell how much we all owe you for making us acquainted with the story of poor Jemmy: and I shall not fail to comply with your request to drink no more brandy'. Anon., 'A Word in Season, or, the Sailor's Widow', *Livesey's Moral Reformer*, 23 (Feb. 1839), pp. 217, 219–220.

9 See, for example, Annemarie McAllister, 'The Alternative World of the Proud Non-Drinker: Nineteenth-century public displays of temperance', *The Social History of Alcohol and Drugs*, 28:2 (Summer 2014) 161–189.

10 For more information on temperance periodicals, see Annemarie McAllister, 'Temperance Periodicals', in *The Routledge Handbook to Nineteenth-century Periodicals and Newspapers* (London: Routledge, 2016), pp. 342–354.

11 Lilian Shiman notes that the 'popular belief in the need for alcohol in maintaining good health is not surprising when we find that the medical profession itself held similar views. Nineteenth-century doctors were dependent on alcoholic beverages for many of their cures. Lilian Lewis Shiman, *Crusade against Drink in Victorian England* (New York: Palgrave Macmillan, 1988), p. 35. An extreme example of this can be found in James Kneale, 'Dr Granville's Thunderbolt: Drink and the Public in the Life of One Nineteenth Century Doctor', *Social History of Alcohol and Drugs*, 28:2 (2014), 120–141.

12 Anon., 'Fatal Affray in the Dark', *Morning Post* (30 Mar 1847), p. 7; Anon., 'Manslaughter at St. James's Back', *Bristol Mercury* (9 Mar 1850), p. 6.

13 For more details, see Emma Butcher, 'War Trauma and Alcoholism in the Early Writings of Charlotte and Branwell Brontë', *Journal of Victorian Culture*, 22.4 (2017), 465–481.

14 For more on this, see Pam Lock, 'Death and the Alcoholic: Public Discourses in Anne Brontë's *The Tenant of Wildfell Hall*', *Social History of Alcohol and Drugs* (2015), 29–47.

15 Roy Porter, 'Introduction', pp. xii–xiii. Porter refers to *Ueber die trunksucht und eine rationelle Heilmethode derselben* (1819). Thomas Trotter, *An Essay, Medical, Philosophical, and Chemical on Drunkenness and Its Effects on the Human Body*, ed. by Roy Porter (London: Routledge, 2013).

16 See also Pam Lock, 'Hindley's "Reckless Dissipation": Making Drunkenness Public in Emily Brontë's *Wuthering Heights*', *Brontë Studies*, 44:1 (2019), 68–81.

17 Although, as Annemarie Beller's research on 'instances of emergent sensationalism' reveals, this boom did not come out of nowhere. Anne-Marie Beller, 'Sensation fiction in the 1850s', *The Cambridge Companion to Sensation Fiction*, ed. by Andrew Mangham (Cambridge: Cambridge University Press, 2013), pp. 18; 8.

18 See, for example, G. H. Lewes's attack on total abstinence in which he states:

> So long as the Temperance advocates confine themselves to effecting a reform among the poorer classes, [...] they are doing righteous work, and may be pardoned their outbreaks of zeal, their passionate foolishness, their bitter animosity, and all the "wild and whirling words" with which they rival Methodists and Emancipationists.

He specifies that 'very few of [his middle-class readers] are likely to be among the intemperate; to them the Teetotal arguments are impertinent'. G. H. Lewes, 'The Physiological Errors of Teetotalism', *Westminster Review* (1852), 96–97.

19 For more information, see James Nicholls, 'A new kind of drunkenness: the gin craze', *The Politics of Alcohol* (Manchester: Manchester University Press, 2009).

20 For example, the popular Scottish Temperance League were led by middle-class members, and published their 'moral suasian' for the moral improvement and entertainment of a specifically middle-class audience, with the aim of changing parliamentary law to discourage and encouraging a ban on the consumption of alcohol.

21 As Annemarie McAllister has observed, there was a notable, though permeable, class divide between these groups as teetotallers tended to have a greater working-class leadership and membership, whereas moderate groups tended towards the middle classes. See Annemarie McAllister, *Demon Drink? Temperance and the Working Class*, Chapter 7 (e-book).

22 Patrick Colquhoun's 1814 'Map of English Society' defines the under classes as 'paupers, vagrants, gypsies, idle persons supported by criminal activity'. Patrick Colquhoun 'Map of English Society in 1814', *A Treatise on the Wealth, Power, and Resources of the British Empire* (London: Joseph Mawman, 1814).

23 See Brooke D. Taylor, 'Spontaneous Combustion: When "Fact" Confirms Feeling in *Bleak House*', *Dickens Quarterly*, 27:3 (2010); Gordon S. Haight, 'Dickens and Lewes on Spontaneous Combustion', *Nineteenth-Century Fiction,* 10:1 (1955), 53–63.

24 This character capitalises on the 'railway mania' that started in 1845. In the second half of the nineteenth century, £3 billion were spend on building railways in Britain creating 16,000 miles of track. Figures taken from the national archives: https://www.nationalarchives.gov.uk/education/resources/victorian-railways/.

25 The wife-selling scenario that begins the novel may seem unlikely to a modern audience but, as Norman Page notes, it was not unusual during the time in which the novel is set, before changes to the divorce laws in the 1850s, and not unknown in the 1880s when Hardy was writing. Norman Page, *Wilkie Collins: The Critical Heritage* (London: Routledge, 1995).

26 As Tess O'Toole argues, it is 'an attempt to reconfigure family relations that sets its plot in motion; the opening episode of the novel [...] portrays a dramatic dissolution of family structure, a willed unmaking of the marital and paternal ties forged by law and by biological procreation'. Tess O'Toole, *Geneaology and Fiction in Hardy: Family Lineage and Narrative Lines* (Basingstoke: Palgrave Macmillan, 1997), p. 19.

27 Lord Cranworth unsuccessfully submitted bills to change the divorce laws in 1854 and 1856. The Matrimonial Causes Bill was introduced for second reading in the House of Lords, which received royal assent on 28 August 1857.

28 Charles Dickens, *Hard Times [manuscript]. Planning Notes*, Victoria and Albert Museum, MSL/1876/Forster/163.

29 This formula is repeated in the notes, indicating the first appearance (or opening) of a central subject or theme.
30 Laudanum is usually a mixture of opiates and alcohol.
31 For more information on women's secret drinking during this period, see Jen Wallis, 'A Home or a Gaol? Scandal, Secrecy, and the St. James's Inebriate Home for Women', *Social History of Medicine,* 31:4 (2018), 774–795 and David Beckingham, 'Private Spirits, Public Lives: Sober Citizenship, Shame and Secret Drinking in Victorian Britain', *Journal of Victorian Culture*, XX:XX, 1–16.

References

Alfano, Christine Lynn, 'Under the Influence: Drink, Discourse, and Narrative in Victorian Britain', unpublished dissertation, Stanford University, (1996).
Anon., 'The Young Woman's Tract: Or, the Temperance question commended to the attention of Females', *Ipswich Tracts*, No. 55.
Anon., 'Fatal Affray in the Dark', *Morning Post* (30 Mar 1847).
Anon., 'Manslaughter at St. James's Back', *Bristol Mercury* (9 Mar 1850).
Anon., 'A Word in Season, or, the Sailor's Widow', *Livesey's Moral Reformer*, 23 (Feb. 1839), pp. 219–220.
Barker, Juliet, *The Brontës: A Life in Letters* (London: Viking, 1997).
Bayly, Mrs, *Ragged Homes and How to Mend Them* (London: James Nisbet and co., 1855).
Beckingham, David, 'Private Spirits, Public Lives: Sober Citizenship, Shame and Secret Drinking in Victorian Britain', *Journal of Victorian Culture,* XX:XX (2021), 1–16.
Beecher Stowe, Harriet, *Sunny Memories of Foreign Lands: Volume I* (Scotts Valley, CA: CreateSpace Independent Publishing Platform, 2015).
Bell, Lady, *At the Works. A study of a Manufacturing Town* (London: Edward Arnold, 1907).
Beller, Anne-Marie, 'Sensation fiction in the 1850s', *The Cambridge Companion to Sensation Fiction*, ed. by Andrew Mangham (Cambridge: Cambridge University Press, 2013), pp. 7–20.
Brodie, Benjamin Collins, *Psychological Inquiries: In a Series of Essays* (London: Longman, Brown, Green, and Longmans, 1854).
Brontë, Anne, *The Tenant of Wildfell Hall*, ed. by Lee A. Talley (Plymouth: Broadview Editions, 2009).
Brontë, Emily, *Wuthering Heights*, ed. by Beth Newman (Plymouth: Broadview Editions, 2007).
Butcher, Emma, 'War Trauma and Alcoholism in the Early Writings of Charlotte and Branwell Brontë', *Journal of Victorian Culture*, 22:4 (2017), 465–481.
Clemis, David, Medical Expertise and the Understandings of Intoxication in Britain, 1660 to 1830', in *Intoxication and Society. Problematic Pleasures of Drugs and Alcohol*, ed. by Jonathan Herring, Ciaran Regan, Darin Weinberg and Phil Withington (Basingstoke: Palgrave Macmillan, 2013), pp. 33–51.
Colquhoun, Patrick 'Map of English Society in 1814', *A Treatise on the Wealth, Power, and Resources of the British Empire* (London: Joseph Mawman, 1814).
Collins, Wilkie, 'The Ostler', *Household Words*, XII (1855), 581–590.
Cruikshank, George, *The Bottle and The Drunkard's Children* (London: Cowan & Gray, Ltd, 1906).
———, *The Cruikshank Fairy-Book* (London: G. P. Punam's Sons, 1911).
Cuddon, J. A. (ed.), *Dictionary of Literary Terms and Literary Theory* (London: Penguin 2014).
Darwin, Erasmus, *Zoonomia* (Cambridge: Cambridge University Press, 2011).
Dickens, Charles, 'Demoralisation and Total Abstinence', *The Examiner* (27 Oct 1849).
———, 'The Drunkard's Death', *Sketches by Boz,* ed. by Dennis Walder (London: Penguin, 1995).
———, *Our Mutual Friend*, ed. by Adrian Poole (London: Penguin, 1997).
———, *Hard Times [manuscript]. Planning Notes*, Victoria and Albert Museum, MSL/1876/Forster/163.
———, *Hard Times,* ed. by Kate Flint (London: Penguin Books, 2003).
Earnshaw, Steven, 'Drink and Metaphysics, Four case studies from the Victorian Period', *The Social History of Alcohol and Drugs*, 28:2 (Summer 2014), 143–160.
———, *The Existential Drinker* (Manchester: Manchester University Press, 2019).
———, *The Pub in Literature: England's Altered State* (Manchester: Manchester University Press, 2000).
Eliot, George, *Scenes of Clerical Life*, ed. by David Lodge (London: Penguin Books, 1980).
Engels, Frederick, *The Condition of the Working-Class in England in 1844* (Cambridge: Cambridge University Press, 2010).
Gaskell, Elizabeth, *Mary Barton* (London: W. W. Norton & Company, 2008).
Gilbert, Pamela K. (ed.), *A Companion to Sensation Fiction* (Oxford: Wiley-Blackwell, 2011).

Gissing, George, *The Nether World* (London: J. M. Dent and Son, 1973).
Gough, John B., 'John B. Gough. Concluding Part', *The Abstainer's Journal* (November 1853).
Haight, Gordon S., 'Dickens and Lewes on Spontaneous Combustion', *Nineteenth-Century Fiction,* 10:1 (June 1955) 53–63.
Harrison, Brian, *Drink and the Victorians. The Temperance Question in England 1815–1872* (London: Faber & Faber, 1971).
Haskin, Dayton, 'George Eliot as a "Miltonist": Marriage and Milton in Middlemarch', in *Milton and Gender,* ed. by Catherine Gimelli Martin (Cambridge: Cambridge University Press, 2004), pp. 207–222.
Jennings, Paul, *The Local* (Stroud: Tempus, 2007).
Kneale, James, 'Dr Granville's Thunderbolt: Drink and the Public in the Life of One Nineteenth Century Doctor, *Social History of Alcohol and Drugs*, 28:2 (2014) 120–141.
Kneale, James, and Sean French, '"The Relations of Inebriety to Insurance": Geographies of Medicine, Insurance and Alcohol in Britain, 1840–1911', in *Intoxication and Society. Problematic Pleasures of Drugs and Alcohol*, ed. by Jonathan Herring, Ciaran Regan, Darin Weinberg and Phil Withington (Basingstoke: Palgrave Macmillan, 2013), pp. 87–109.
Lamb, Charles, *Confessions of a Drunkard* (Adelaide: The University of Adelaide Library, 2019).
Lewes, G. H., 'The Physiological Errors of Teetotalism', *Westminster Review* (Jan. 1852), 96–97.
Lock, Pam, 'Death and the Alcoholic: Public Discourses in Anne Brontë's *The Tenant of Wildfell Hall', Social History of Alcohol and Drugs* (2015) 29–47.
———, 'Hindley's "reckless dissipation": Making Drunkenness Public in Emily Brontë's *Wuthering Heights*', *Brontë Studies*, 44:1 (2019) 68–81.
Macnish, Robert, *The Anatomy of Drunkenness* (Philadelphia, PA: Carey, Lea and Carey, 1828).
Makras, Kostas, 'Dickensian Intemperance: The Representation of the Drunkard in 'The Drunkard's Death' and *The Pickwick Papers' 19: Interdisciplinary Studies in the Long Nineteenth Century,* 0(10).
McAllister, Annemarie, *Demon Drink? Temperance and the Working Class* (e-book).
———, 'Temperance Periodicals', in King et al. (eds), *The Routledge Handbook to Nineteenth-Century Periodicals and Newspapers* (London: Routledge, 2016).
———, 'The Alternative World of the Proud Non-Drinker: Nineteenth-Century public displays of temperance', *The Social History of Alcohol and Drugs*, 28:2 (Summer 2014).
McCormack, Kathleen, 'Intoxication and the Victorian Novel', in William Baker and Kenneth Womack, *A Companion to the Victorian Novel* (London: Greenwood Press, 2002), pp. 137–148.
Menninger, Karl, *Man Against Himself* (London: Harcourt Brace Jovanovich, 1985).
Miller, James, *Alcohol: Its Place and Power* (Glasgow: Scottish Temperance League, 1859).
Nicholls, James, *The Politics of Alcohol* (Manchester: Manchester University Press, 2009).
O'Toole, Tess, *Geneaology and Fiction in Hardy: Family Lineage and Narrative Lines* (Basingstoke: Palgrave Macmillan, 1997).
Page, Norman, *Wilkie Collins: The Critical Heritage* (London: Routledge, 1995).
Rush, Benjamin, 'Inquiry into the Effects of Ardent Spirits on the Human Body and Mind', Reprinted in *Quarterly Journal of Studies on Alcohol*, 4 (1944), 324–341.
Shiman, Lilian Lewis, *Crusade against Drink in Victorian England* (New York: Palgrave Macmillan, 1988).
Smith, Iain, 'Doctoring in a Whisky-Injured Nation: The Medical Response to the "Alcohol Question" in Scotland, 1855–1925', unpublished thesis, University of Glasgow, 2018.
Sournia, Jean-Charles, *A History of Alcoholism*, trans. by Nick Hindley and Gareth Stanton (Oxford: Basil Blackwell Ltd, 1990).
Stevenson, Robert Louis, *Treasure Island* (Plymouth: Broadview editions, 2011).
Stickney Ellis, Sarah, *Family Secrets or Hints to Those Who Would Make Home Happy* (London: Fisher, Son & Co., 1842).
Stretton, Hesba, *Jessica's First Prayer* (London: The Religious Tract Society, n.d.).
Taylor, Brooke D., 'Spontaneous Combustion: When "Fact" Confirms Feeling in *Bleak House*', *Dickens Quarterly* 27:3 (Sept. 2010), 171–184.
Taylor, John, *Drunkenness as an Indirect Cause of Crime. A Paper Read before the National Association for the Promotion of Social Science. Bradford, 1859* (Location unknown: National Temperance League, 1859).
Taylor, Miles, 'John Bull and the Iconography of Public Opinion in England c. 1712–1929', *Past & Present,* 134 (Feb. 1992), 93–128.

Tolman, Albert H., 'Shakespeare Studies: Part IV. Drunkenness in Shakespeare', *Modern Languages Notes*, 34:2 (Feb. 1919), 82–88.
Tomalin, Claire, *Charles Dickens. A Life* (London: Penguin, 2011).
Trollope, Anthony, *Dr Thorne* (London: Penguin Books, 1991).
———, *An Autobiography* (Oxford: Oxford University Press, 2008).
Trotter, Thomas, *An Essay, Medical, Philosophical, and Chemical on Drunkenness and Its Effects on the Human Body* (Philadelphia, PA: Anthony Finley, 1813).
———, *An Essay, Medical, Philosophical, and Chemical on Drunkenness and Its Effects on the Human Body*, ed. by Roy Porter (London: Routledge, 2013).
Wallis, Jen, 'A Home or a Gaol? Scandal, Secrecy, and the St. James's Inebriate Home for Women', *Social History of Medicine*, 31:4 (2018) 774–795.
Wood, Ellen, *Danesbury House*, ed. by Curt Herr (Alfred, NY: Whitlock Publishing, 2009).

33

TEA, ADDICTION AND LATE VICTORIAN NARRATIVES OF DEGENERATION, C. 1860–1900

Ian Miller

In August 1895, Theresa Galleway, age 41, collapsed on the floor of her Dudley home suffering from a fit. Theresa's daughter, Alice, discovered her but decided not to send for a doctor as her mother appeared to recover. Later that evening, Alice left her mother alone in bed but, upon returning an hour later, found her dead. It was the task of the Deputy Coroner, Mr Child, and local doctor, J.D. Price, to establish what might have caused Theresa's untimely death. Investigations revealed that Theresa had suffered regularly from 'fainting fits' seemingly worsened by consuming excessive amounts of tea. Upon finding the brain healthy, the medical men began to doubt the evidence about fits. Instead, they decided to examine Theresa's heart, which they found to be grossly enlarged, and her stomach, which was distended with fluid, probably tea. Child and Price concluded that the stomach's condition had interfered with the action of the heart, causing death. A bemused member of the jury enquired: 'Do you wish us to understand that death was due to tea drinking?', to which Mr Child affirmed: 'Any fluid might have caused the distension of the stomach, but in this case, it appeared to be tea' (*Berrow's Worcester Journal*, 1895).

The seventeenth century saw the beginning of a long-term shift towards British domination of the global tea trade, accelerated by the formation of the British East India Company. Tea became increasingly useful to state revenue (Rappaport, 2017). Throughout the nineteenth century, tea production was a key British colonial venture, the temperance movement advocated the less intoxicating drink as a welcome alternative to alcohol, and middle-class tea parties became fashionable. Tearooms opened across most British towns and cities. The British developed a profitable tea industry, creating fierce competition between Chinese and Indian traders (Forrest, 1973; Moxham, 2003; Ketabgian, 2007; Rose, 2010; Sharma, 2011; Rappaport, 2017; see also, among others, Pettigrew, 2001; MacFarlane & MacFarlane, 2003; Griffiths, 2007; Hair & Hohm 2009; Saberi, 2010; Ellis, Coulton & Mauger, 2015). Competition ultimately lowered the costs of tea in countries such as Britain and Ireland (Liu, 2020). Yet, the circumstances surrounding Theresa Galleway's death suggests that tea could be considered deeply problematic for health, addiction and well-being. This essay explores how and why, in the closing decades of the late nineteenth century, the consequences of excessive tea drinking caused anxiety and debate.

In the nineteenth century, new nutritional sciences emerged, transforming how scientists, physicians and the public understood food and drink consumption. Early modern dietetic

DOI: 10.4324/9780429058141-42

theories had typically viewed a person's bodily responses to food as dependent upon their individual constitution, and as variable from person to person. In contrast, Victorian nutritional chemistry offered new, empirical understandings of diet and moved towards establishing standardised nutritional rules that, ideally, most people should follow (Kamminga & Cunningham, 1995). Meanwhile, Western society rapidly urbanised and more efficient global trading systems developed. Westerners now had access to all manner of new foods from around the globe. However, this did not necessarily mean good health. Urbanisation dislocated consumers from the rural sources of food production areas, creating new consumer cultures. Particularly in Britain, jingoistic popular culture often celebrated free trade as having brought innovations such as cheap tea while at the same time scorning alien cultures of consumption (Trentmann & Flemming, 2006). Set against this backdrop, concern mounted about the nutritional well-being of the poorer classes who, it seemed, could not be trusted to purchase the foods which nutritional scientists considered healthy. By the end of the century, working-class urban life was associated with dyspepsia, nervousness and under-nutrition (Miller, 2011).

The essay demonstrates that concerns about tea addiction became central to late Victorian debates on working-class nutrition and consumption. It focuses on Britain, Ireland and America, countries where excessive tea drinking came to be seen as a significant problem. In Britain and America, discussion focused primarily on the bodily implications of urbanisation and industrialisation. In contrast, Irish debates were pre-occupied with the rapid process of dietary change that had followed the devastating Great Famine (c. 1845–1851) and discouraged peasants from over-depending on potatoes as a dietary staple (Miller, 2014). In America, tea was less popular than coffee, partly due to the country's proximity to Caribbean and Latin American coffee plantations. Nonetheless, alarm about tea addiction briefly emerged in the 1890s. Accordingly, the chapter focuses primarily on Britain and Ireland, with some cross-Atlantic cross-comparison due to the ties of language, lineage and, especially in the Irish case, high levels of post-Famine emigration.

In an era when modern understandings of food, diet and nutrition were at a relatively formative stage, the late Victorians asked: Which foodstuffs were safe? Which were addictive? What were the potential consequences of excessive consumption for physical and mental health? Which substances were suitable for consumption and which should be classified as for medicinal use only? While alcohol was quite clearly addictive, socially disruptive and morally ruinous, tea occupied a more ambiguous space in the late Victorian dietetic imagination. Tea did not cause as many social problems as alcohol. Nor was it as obviously associated with vices such as violence and prostitution. But, when consumed in particular ways, it emerged as a potentially threatening substance.

Despite this pronounced historical concern about tea addiction, tea has not featured heavily in the literature on addiction, having been overshadowed by coffee, alcohol and illicit drugs (Courtwright, 2001). Erika Rappaport's monumental study of tea and empire focuses relatively briefly on the perceived health problems associated with drinking too much tea (Rappaport, 2017). An otherwise thorough study of caffeine states (inaccurately) that 'tea has rarely, if ever, appeared on anyone's list as a substance that ought to be put beyond the pale of law or morality' (Weinberg & Bealer, 2001). Historians who have discussed the relationship between tea and health typically focus on mid-century adulteration debates rather than the inherent addictive properties within tea itself or contemporary perceptions of its toxic, socially perilous nature (Rappaport, 2017). Most historians have instead explored the civilised middle-class tea party and the symbolic uses of tea drinking as a marker of middle-class social civility and polite society (Fromer, 2008).

However, middle-class tea drinking ideals differed profoundly from the realities of working-class consumption. Rather than daintily sipping tea from small tea-cups in polite company, the less affluent preferred stewing cheap, unhealthy concoctions of tea all day long on their stoves, often consuming little else but a few slices of processed white bread. Hence, while navigating questions about the potentially addictive, dangerous nature of tea, the late Victorians were forced to find ways to continue upholding tea as a healthy, civilised drink – indeed, one with significant economic value – while at the same time condemning its misuse among certain groups. As with many other aspects of Victorian life, the key message that emerged was to demonstrate moderation and avoid excess. The chapter makes clear that tea drinking was a morally, physically and emotionally ambiguous past-time. Yet, excessive tea drinking also served as a metaphor for social relations, an example of excess and reckless passions among the poorer classes, a problem feared by the middle classes for its revolutionary potential. Reformers presented excessive tea drinking as the first step on a slippery slope towards more serious problems such as chronic alcoholism, whether drunk to excess or precociously administered to babies. But this interpretation, with its emphasis on personal blame, concealed pressing social issues such as inadequate wages to buy sufficient and wholesome food such as milk, oatmeal, potatoes and perhaps even meat.

Tea, Nerves and Degeneration

In the early nineteenth century, occasional comments were made about the lack of proper nourishment in a cup of tea. However, most commentators happily described tea drinking as one of life's pleasure (Cottager's Monthly Visitor, 1830). The tone of discussion changed dramatically later in the century as tea became more widely available to a broader range of consumers. Throughout the nineteenth century, the quantity of tea purchased in the United Kingdom rose from around 24,000 lb per year to 225,000 lb. The introduction of lower duties in the 1850s contributed to tea's ever cheapening cost. In Ireland, per capita consumption of tea rose from 0.5 pounds to 2.2 pounds between the late 1830s and early 1860s and continued to rise throughout the remainder of the century (Burnett, 1999). As mentioned above, coffee was more popular in America, although tea's popularity nonetheless increased towards the end of the century (Courtwright, 2001).

In the 1860s, dietary surveys undertaken across Britain and Ireland revealed a notable rise in tea consumption across all social classes, but especially among the poor who had previously not been able to afford tea. In his well-received surveys, Medical Officer for the Privy Council, Edward Smith, warned that tea contained little nutritive material and could not compensate for proper nourishment (Sixth Report of the Medical Officer of the Privy Council, 1863). It was in this decade that warnings about excessive tea drinking began to be voiced. Annual health reports submitted to the British government warned that working-class communities, especially those in the north, were in a state of physical degeneration, partly in consequence of over-depending on tea as a dietary staple. A key clue was that people seemed much shorter in height than the previous generation (Third Report of the Medical Officer of the Privy Council, 1865). The public greeted these messages with mixed responses. After all, this was a time when the temperance movement was at its height and when respectable middle-class tea parties were in vogue.

In 1872, pioneer of occupational medicine, John Thomas Arlidge, then employed as a pottery inspector in Staffordshire, warned that tea injured the nerves, potentially creating hereditary problems likely to be passed down to the next generation. Aldridge was particularly scornful of working-class women relying on tea as a principal dietary staple with only a few slices of bread and butter. He conceded that some women had been driven to this diet through poverty and desperation, but still thought that housewives could advantageously improve their budgeting skills and replace tea with nutritious food. The British conservative newspaper, the *Spectator*, immediately voiced its displeasure by asserting that it did not believe a word of Aldridge's scaremongering comments. Tea drinking, the *Spectator* argued, only injured a few people, often those with particular constitutions, the sedentary, those with 'hysteric tendencies' and women 'worn out with other excitements'. 'There is no proof that it is injurious to the mass of the people', insisted the *Spectator*, 'who take very little in actual quantity...whose nerves are strengthened by labour and who are constantly in the open air' (Manchester Times, 1872).

Aldridge's arguments are worth reflecting on momentarily as they reveal much about how physicians viewed the relationship between food intake, bodily health and also social well-being. Evidently, Aldridge preferred to blame women for the resultant health problems of consuming too much tea. The gendering of tea consumption is notable. Women were generally, but not exclusively, blamed for the excessive tea drinking problem. This fitted in with the trend of blaming mothers for faulty child-rearing and perceiving women as a less rational, more impulsive sex inherently prone to compulsive disorders (Appignanesi, 2019). Of course, such perspectives ignored the fact that many women chose to provide male and younger family members with nutritious food as part of a family economy that made sense in the context of poverty and resourcefulness. Simultaneously, these narratives blamed individual housewives instead of fully considering the harmful socio-economic environments that encouraged high dependence on unsuitable foodstuffs.

In addition, Aldridge's emphasis on nerves reflects late Victorian tendencies to concentrate on the physiological symptoms of addiction, rather than their behavioural precursors and effects (Foxcroft, 2007). Aldridge viewed morbid conditions of the nervous system as a direct cause of personal and social degeneration. In the 1820s, M.P. William Cobbett had argued that tea 'has badness in it', disrupting sleep and weakening nerves, adding that tea drinking among the poorer classes caused laziness and encouraged girls to gossip rather than work (Cobbett, 1833). But in the late nineteenth century, nerve damage was considered far more insipid and threatening. By then, evolutionary theory had begun to dominate medical, scientific and social thought. It now seemed plausible that entire species, even humans, could degenerate to become the weakest, rather than fittest, in the battle for survival. Neurologists and psychiatrists came to believe that pathological heredity could pass from one generation to the next. It was this notion of change over time that marked the crucial difference between old and new hereditarian concerns over tea. As Janet Oppenheim argues, in the early nineteenth century, a nervous *temperament* was just passed on. However, late century nervous *degeneration* was more frightening and disgraceful. Once set in motion, it seemed to be an irreversible process, dragging entire families into an inexorable downward spiral of declining physical and mental powers. Collectively, nervous pathology could bring entire societies and civilisations down (Oppenheim, 1991; see also Pick, 1989).

This feeds into broader arguments on addiction made by Susan Zieger who suggests that addiction appeared so ominous in the late nineteenth century as it was a dangerously individualised form of self-medication completely beyond the control of physicians. Addiction rested somewhere between immorality and disease. It was not illness *per se*, but could easily transmute into physical, mental and moral decay. Despite its non-disease status, late Victorian physicians nonetheless presented addiction as a pathological illness which only they should set out to remedy. Moreover, throughout the nineteenth century, the standard terminology changed from inebriety to addiction while the immorality of the addict was increasingly framed as racial defect in the influential discourses of degeneration and, slightly later, eugenics. Rather than being just an unwelcome personal habit, addiction was now demarcated as a sign of inherited biological defect. Particularly in the 1890s, Zieger argues, both medical and mainstream discourses represented inebriates and other addicts as social parasites, unproductively sapping life from the social body. Addiction was a problem for both national and physical bodies and could rarely be separated from other social ills (Zieger, 2008). Those addicted to specific substances seemed so overwhelmingly involved that they had transformed into different people, alien to their own society and their own previous identities. Initially applied to alcoholism, the stigma of addiction did not remain confined to them for long (Alexander, 2008).

In relation to tea, blame was placed firmly on the working classes for their new-found habits, who found themselves accused of carelessness and recklessness. One key allegation was that the poor over-consumed tea not out of necessity, but for its mentally exciting and exhilarating effects. Doctors feared that such decadent behaviour had a potentially shattering effect on the nerves and, as Edwin Brown argued in 1863 to the Midland Scientific Association, risked 'lowering the vital energies of the nation'. Brown made the relation between personal and national behaviour clear when informing his audience that the Chinese were now 'degenerate representations of their ancestors who, prior to their being a tea-drinking nation, carried fire and sword over large portions of Europe and Asia' (Derby Mercury, 1863). At a time of Empire-building and rising global influence, the argument was resonant: Britain itself was under threat from reckless forms of tea consumption.

As degeneration narratives infiltrated the *fin de siècle*, physicians and the public take warnings about excessive tea consumption more seriously. In October 1883, the Dean of Bangor, Henry Edwards, spoke at a meeting on establishing cookery classes in elementary schools. Controversially, the Dean announced that, if he had his own way, there would be much less tea drinking. The Dean believed that oatmeal and milk had once produced 'strong, hearty, good-tempered men and women'. However, excessive tea drinking had now 'created a generation of nervous, discontented people who were forever complaining of the existing order of the universe, scolding their neighbours and sighing after the impossible'. The Dean insisted that good cooking would much improve this situation. Moreover, he argued that 'over much tea drinking, by destroying the calmness of the nerves, was acting as a dangerous, revolutionary force among us'. For the Dean, tea addiction was the first step towards gin addiction. The root of the problem was 'an ignorant wife'; the end result was 'ruin, intemperance and disease' (Berrow's Worcester Journal, 1883).

Like Aldridge before him, the Dean framed excessive tea drinking as both a personal and national problem, one in which women were especially complicit. Even if a man had succumbed to excessive tea drinking, blame was still placed on his wife's insufficient housewifery skills. The Dean invoked contemporary themes of physical and national decay while cautioning that the extent of the problem posed a national threat. The personality changes seemingly induced by tea addiction affected social and political outlooks. Indeed, the Dean's statement attracted so much attention due to its invoking of revolution. It pinpointed tea as the very cause of inflamed personal passions that could too easily mutate into political revolutionary zeal. All of this stemmed from deliberately induced nervous exhilaration.

The Dean received significant national publicity. He responded to a flood of angry letters sent to the *Daily Telegraph* (many penned by tea retailers) by stating:

> I have been amused by the criticism which my protest against the above excess has provoked. Angry tea traders have sent me earnest remonstrances. Your own article

> of the 10th inst. is severe, but hardly fair, as it attributes to me sentiments that I never uttered. I claim the right of explaining…I have never denounced good tea or moderate tea drinking. I said in my condemned speech, 'Tea and bread and butter are very good in their proper place and proportion'. I did protest against the bad housewifery which is undermining the physique of many Welsh workmen.

The Dean reiterated that his concern was with *bad housewifery*, not tea drinking as such, and concluded with 'let me add, I have no objection to any moderate tea drinking' (Western Mail, 1883).

The *Pall Mall Gazette* also published a number of letters on the Dean's speech, including one by Berkshire reverend, Charles W. Stubbs, who believed that

> as much superfluous money is expended on tea and sugar as would maintain four million subjects in bread. If it is considered what a fatal enemy excessive tea drinking is to the human body, how much it impairs the vigour of the constitution and debilitates the mind, the pernicious influence of it will be more apparent.

Stubbs described tea as a 'pernicious commodity that tends to our very ruin'. Stubbs was particularly contemptuous of recent calls to lower tea duties (Pall Mall Gazette, 1883).

Evidently, the Dean was forced to navigate the business interests of tea traders, naturally inclined to condemn commercially damaging publicity, as well as the responsible, usually middle-class, tea drinkers considered unlikely to fall prey to over-consumption and nervous disorder. Discussion of the problem was undoubtedly class-fuelled. In many ways, excessive tea drinking served as a metaphor for ideas about the civilised middle and upper classes, and the passion-fuelled, reckless lower classes whom degeneration theory warned might out-reproduce the more civilised, 'advanced' members of British society. As the root of the problem was the careless working-class housewife in need of domestic education as a remedy.

This is not to say that all critics placed blame on the individual or familial level. When providing evidence to an 1894 government enquiry into the Merioneth slate quarries, Winifred Ellis made a point of commenting on the 'incessant tea drinking' and neglect of traditional foods such as porridge which she believed destroyed stamina, caused indigestion and enfeebled both body and mind. As she explained,

> tea has such a charm for some people that they are sensitive about putting away the cups and saucers when they are not actually in use. Tea often serves as breakfast, dinner and supper, the only accompaniment being bread and butter and sometimes tinned meat.
>
> *(Birmingham Daily Post, 1894)*

It is notable, however, that Ellis, unlike many of her contemporaries, refrained from providing moral judgement on the miners. Her argument insisted that locals worked in dense, foggy and unwholesome atmospheres that caused thirst, weak appetite and enfeebled digestion. In her words,

> it is not fair to attribute to quarrymen the fact of being possessed of an unnatural and excessive craving for tea drinking. Tea allays thirst. It is a necessary stimulant, though not much more, but it helps the assimilation of nourishing food.
>
> *(Departmental Committee on Merionethshire Slate Mines, 1895)*

Evidently, Ellis was more sympathetic to the occupational and structural problems that encouraged many workers to depend heavily upon tea as a dietary staple. Ellis rejected ideas that excessive tea drinking stemmed from some innate, internal immoral desire for exhilaration. Nonetheless, Ellis still perceived excessive tea drinking, whatever its causes, as injurious to the nerves, as an addictive social practice with portentous implications for future generations.

Tea, Minds and Bodies

During the 1880s and 1890s, the *British Medical Journal* contributed considerably to debates on excessive tea drinking, posing various questions. Was tea really evil? Was concern over its excessive consumption just a medical fashion? Were the nerves really as aggravated by tea as claimed? Was excessive tea drinking itself the real problem or the absence of nutritious foods to accompany tea? Was 'tea drunkenness' as physically and morally dangerous as alcoholism? (British Medical journal, 1886). In 1883, the *BMJ* was quick to report on the Dean's speech and, like many contemporaries, predicted 'little less than our general physical and moral decadence as a people and nation if we persevere in our addiction to the pleasures of the tea pot' (British Medical Journal, 1883). Five years later, the journal stated, 'the habit of tea drinking is becoming more and more thoroughly national in the British islands' for rich and poor alike. The journal argued that these problems were less common in middle-class 'real society' which enjoyed civilised afternoon teas. However, the working classes consumed their tea too hot, over-stimulating their hearts (British Medical Journal, 1888).

Of particular concern was the destruction of tea's flavour during the process of infusing tea in boiling water. Many physicians believed that this left high proportions of dyspepsia-causing tannin in the drink. According to the *BMJ*, 'indigestion is unknown among tea drinkers in the East and it is, in all probability, only the result of our defective use of the leaf' (British Medical Journal, 1892). Tannin was the issue which physicians typically worried about, although theine (or caffeine) was often mentioned. In 1908, prominent physician Sir Lauder Brunton, in a discussion of the effects of tannin, described the tell-tale signs of tea-induced mental degeneration – diminished self-restraint, nervousness, undue sensitiveness, timidity, uncontrollable emotions – accompanied by physical symptoms, including giddiness, headache, ringing in the ears, severe neuralgia and tremulousness (Observer, 1908). Further debate was sparked by Surgeon Major W.T. Black in 1888 when the *BMJ* published his letter on the masses of poor teeth which he had regrettably encountered at recruiting stations. Black blamed this on excessive tea consumption (British Medical Journal, 1888). His somewhat speculative letter received a lukewarm response. The *New York Times* ridiculed the debate. It consulted six eminent New York doctors who all expressed astonishment that such a 'ridiculous and untenable' theory was being taken seriously (New York Times, 1888).

Excessive tea drinking was considered of such importance that it featured regularly in turn-of-the-century government enquiries. Vanessa Heggie has argued that the Inter-Departmental Committee on Physical Deterioration, established in 1904, was primarily concerned with diet, exercise and alcohol (Heggie, 2008). Certainly, witnesses at the Committee were very much concerned with tea's impact on national health. Dr R.J. Collie, Medical Inspector for the London School Board, claimed that children lucky enough to reach adulthood if raised on tea were pale, anaemic, prone to disease and had a half-starved appearance. Most of those raised on tea, he argued, could be found from the age of three onwards in children's wards suffering from tuberculosis. He described one group as 'open-mouthed, stupid-looking children, the result of adenoid overgrowth brought about by insufficient feeding' (Inter-Departmental Committee on Physical Deterioration, 1904). Mrs Bostock, Health Visitor for the Manchester and Salford Ladies Health Society, observed that many working-class mothers started feeding tea to their babies as early as five months old, entirely undiluted with milk (Inter-Departmental Committee on Physical Deterioration, 1904). Dr Alexander Haig warned that the poorer classes were essentially swallowing large quantities of uric acid (Inter-Departmental Committee on Physical Deterioration, 1904). Of course, there was a distinct difference between over-depending on tea and being addicted to its tannic properties. However, contemporaries often presented the weaning of the young on tea as the first step towards a lifetime of addiction and nervous degeneration, inevitable consequences of poor nutritional feeding at the start of life. It seems evident that most British debates shied away from discussing the broader political and socio-economic determinants that encouraged poverty, presenting the root of under-nutrition as resting in personal domestic behaviour. The solution was to encourage behavioural change in working-class families.

In Ireland, too, excessive tea drinking was blamed for a spectrum of social problems. Nineteenth-century journalists and physicians were fixated with the amount of tea that the Irish poor could consume. In 1900, Michael McDonagh, writing for the British monthly literary periodical *Nineteenth Century*, reported one encounter with a Kilkenny peasant during which he was:

> Invited by a peasant to a cup of tea, the liquor being black and strong through lengthy stewing, and giving the writer a sensation of dizziness in the head, although the peasant seemed to relish it highly. 'If I do but get the cup o'tay', said he, 'I'm content. It rises the heart in me when I'm poorly'. M'Donagh asked, 'Do you drink much of it?'. The reply was 'I be at it mornin', noon and night. Oh, it's mighty refreshin', and he smacked his lips after drinking the second cup.
>
> *(Reprinted in The Star, 1900)*

In the 1880s, the Irish press debated the Dean of Bangor's speech, not least because parallel concerns about the nature and extent of tea drinking were coming to the fore in Ireland. The *Irish Times* newspaper wrote that the Dean's outburst carried important warnings for Ireland. Tea, so the newspaper's readers were informed, was an unsuitable principal food of adults and was physically harmful to children subsisting upon nothing else but the substance, as was suspected to be the case among Ireland's lower classes. 'Tea-making to excess among this class is a form of laziness which produces – there can be no doubt about it – mischievous results', explained the newspaper, continuing by lamenting that 'it takes too much the place of solid food' (Irish Times, 1883). Reports emerged of washerwomen, kitchen girls and mothers filling the out-patient departments of Belfast's hospitals complaining of headache, nausea, loss of appetite, physical distress after eating and chronic dizziness (Belfast Newsletter, 1887).

A key difference in Ireland was the tendency to link national decay and excessive tea drinking to post-Famine dietary change (Miller, 2014). In the decades after the Famine, the Irish poor enjoyed an increasingly diverse diet facilitated by a burgeoning consumer culture. However, by the 1890s, the Irish poor seemed far less healthy than they had been while subsisting on potatoes. Labourers themselves noticed this decline, suggesting that the poor could be sometimes active agents in these debates. At the Royal Commission on Labour (1893–1894), Mr Lynch, a labourer from Delvin, Co. Westmeath, insisted that 'the children are spoilt in their youth from not having milk. The people are killing themselves with tea. The men don't work so well in consequence. Stirabout and milk used to be a grand thing for them' (Royal commission on Labour, 1893–1894). Similarly, a farmer named Mr Ramage maintained that, 'I think the modern food is deteriorating the men's strength' (Royal Commission on Labour, 1893–1894). Mr L. Ward, a ploughman, stated that, 'They were stronger men in the old days. Now they are more prone to heart disease and other ills which I believe is owing to the modern diet' (Royal Commission on Labour, 1893–1894). It seemed to some that nutritional health had been compromised due to the diminishing popularity of the potato. The post-Famine Irish body was characterised by weak physical calibre. As in Britain, fears emerged that the Irish poor nonetheless threatened to perpetually reproduce, tarnishing the physical vitality of future generations.

Concern peaked in the 1890s when official investigations were pursued into a nationwide rise in asylum admissions. An official enquiry directly linked the problem to the inability of the poorer classes to purchase nutritious food, heightened levels of vexation and worry caused by economic depression and a consequent derangement of physical and mental functions (Townend, 2002). However, most asylum owners blamed rising admissions first and foremost on the widespread reliance on poor-quality Indian tea, stewed rather than infused. This, it seemed, was creating peculiar forms of dyspepsia that was debilitating nervous systems nationwide. Diet, they suggested, had unquestionably contributed to increasing insanity levels, and that large numbers of asylum patients now bore the scars of scant, improper food: 'the insanity of malnutrition' (Alleged Increasing Prevalence of Insanity in Ireland, 1894).

In 1894, Thomas Drapes, resident medical superintendent at Enniscorthy District Asylum, published an article on the matter in *Journal of Mental Science*. Drapes observed that what was most puzzling, and worrying, about the alleged increase of insanity was that admissions were rising at a time when the population level was rapidly declining due to emigration. Drapes confirmed that nearly all of the superintendents of Irish asylums thought that tea had impacted indirectly on Irish mental well-being when consumed as a substitute for more nutritious food. He warned that 'we see its effects in the number of pale-faced children, who are brought up on it instead of the old time-honoured, but now nearly abandoned, porridge and milk' (Drapes, 1894). Little surprise that in 1905, the Bishop of Ross described the tea-addicted body as a 'jerry-built house that tumbles down at the first shock. Hence, the decayed teeth, poor blood, weak hearts, delicate lungs that give way under any severe strain' (Irish Independent, 1905). Notably, Scottish lunacy inspectors also viewed excessive tea drinking as a major cause of rising insanity cases, stating that decoctions of tea had 'an unsettling effect on subjects mentally unstable from birth, at adolescence or at the climacteric' (Observer, 1908). As outlined above, Arlidge had depicted the problem of excessive tea drinking in terms of race. Since at least the Famine period, Irish emigrants to Britain had been associated with excess and unruliness (see, among others, Swift & Gilley, 1989). Despite being white and European, the nineteenth-century Irish were often portrayed as a 'Celtic' race, set apart from the British 'race', and defined heavily by excitability, effeminacy, irrationality and, as Joanna Bourke suggests, heightened levels of mental health issues and psychological excitability. Debates on tea drinking often confirmed stereotypical and racialised views of Irishness (Bourke, 2000). (See also Curtis, 1997 [1971]).

In America, coffee was more popular than tea (Pendergrast, 2010). However, from the 1880s, the 'English fashion' increased in popularity. One Chicago newspaper reported in 1887 that:

> I foresee from tea drinking a harvest for physicians. The ladies will acquire a taste for it from the adoption of a silly fashion which is the outgrowth of this absurd spring of English manners. They will eventually use it extensively at all hours of the day.
>
> *(Sedalia Weekly Bazoo, 1887)*

Of particular interest was the peculiar case of Peter Phelan, reported internationally. In 1899, Phelan was admitted into Bellevue Hospital, New York, in a critical condition, drifting in-between mentally clarity and delirium. It transpired that Phelan had been known to drink up to 30 strong cups of tea each day. When interviewed, local doctor, George F. Shrady, stated:

> The case is a very unusual one. It may be, however, that Phelan's condition may be due not so much to the tea itself as to the fact that he tried to substitute it for food. His case should not, however, deter anyone from drinking tea in moderation. Properly made and taken in moderation, tea is not only harmless, but positively beneficial.
>
> (Evening Times, *1899)*

Phelan was a 40-year-old assistant stage carpenter at New York's Broadway Theatre until he suffered a nervous collapse. Reportedly, he had developed cravings for tea as fierce as the alcoholic's craving for alcohol. Phelan had mostly replaced food with strong tea. However, one day he found himself unable to leave his bed. He tried to cure himself by drinking even more tea but found this frustratingly difficult to digest. Upon hearing that Peter was ill, his mother transported him to her home where physicians attended him. However, they were at a loss for a diagnosis. At this point, Peter was transferred to Bellevue Hospital where doctors diagnosed him as a 'tea drunkard' (*Evening Times*, 1899). They learnt that he had become fond of tea as a child and been allowed to drink as much of it as he liked. As a young man, he became accustomed to drinking six to eight cups a day. Gradually, this increased until the age of 40 to 30 cups a day. He reported that he was receiving good attention but complained that he convince the staff to offer him a cup of tea (*Evening Times*, 1899).

Tea Drunkards?

The invoking of 'tea drunkenness' in journalistic coverage of Phelan raises questions about precisely how toxic, addictive and exhilarating the Victorians thought tea could potentially be. For more conservative elements of society, the 'sin' of seeking gratification of the desire for artificial stimulation was the same, regardless of whether it was sought in tea, alcohol or drugs (Health Reformer, 1875). But the majority of doctors framed excessive tea drinking as a health or moral problem rather than sin, albeit a problem with significant moral implications. Some were in no doubt that tea was an insidious poison. Slow poisoning was an important Victorian concern, as demonstrated in debates about arsenic (either deliberately slipped in meals or workplace exposure) and other prominent poisoning controversies (Watson, 2003; Burney, 2006; Whorton, 2010; Stratmann, 2016). Could it have been that tea was yet another substance working its toxic way through unsuspecting bodies? In 1899, a London coroner concluded that furniture dealer, C.H. Holmes, had died from a dyspepsia-induced fit brought on by excessive tea drinking. Holmes believed that tea had slowly destroyed the nervous system, eventually causing heart disease (Guardian, 1899). However, associating tea with poison implied that people such as Holmes were unwitting victims of their appetites for tea.

As mentioned above, most physicians insisted that excessive tea consumers knowingly and deliberately consumed excessive quantities for its decadent, exhilarating effects. They likened tea to alcohol and framed excessive tea drinking in terms of addiction. The newfound association of tea with nervous pathology was particularly problematic for temperance advocates. Indeed, their very success had rested largely upon upholding tea as a suitable alternative to alcohol (Rappaport, 2017). When an inquest was held on a London man, John Charles Fairman, in 1862, the coroner was pleased to hear that Fairman had been a temperate man but regretted discovering that he had habitually consumed at least three quarts of tea per day, against the advice of his wife. The coroner, upon finding Fairman's heart to be twice the size as it should have been, concluded that 'excessive tea or cocoa drinking is as dangerous as intoxicants' (New York Times, 1902). Perhaps the most extreme argument on this matter was made in 1903, one Chicago Professor announced that whiskey for breakfast was far less injurious than tea or coffee, although his colleagues swiftly announced their intentions to continue drinking non-alcoholic beverages for breakfast (Turner County Herald, 1903).

Meanwhile, in Philadelphia, eminent surgeon, Charles D. Green, warned in 1877 that:

> While we have been turning our eyes up on the more obvious and vulgar evils attendant upon the free use of alcohol, we have been blind, have been overlooking the sneaking, insidious action of a bland peaceful seducing liquid, which has been sapping the foundation of manhood and honesty. Alcohol sends a few to the jail or to the madhouse, but tea acts through the nervous system on the conscience and turns us into a nation of sneaks and thieves. Look at the Chinese, the Japanese! Nations of sneaks and thieves!
>
> *(Daily Gazette, 1877)*

For Green, tea had far more deep-rooted consequences than alcohol. Being drunk might lead to short-term problems such as violence and crime. Yet, for him, the influence of tea reached far more insidiously and permanently into the body, causing entire races to take on degenerative qualities. The implication was clear: it wouldn't be too long before the American race went the same way as the Asiatic races had supposedly done.

The *BMJ* similarly portrayed excessive tea drinking in terms of addiction, a substance which needed to be replaced with an alternative product if the working classes were to wean themselves off (British Medical Journal, 1887). In 1906, one American doctor advised women to take up smoking instead (New York Times, 1906). Nineteenth-century Britain had a number of retreats for alcoholics, most of which limited the amount of tea provided. Staff reported that the cravings for tea could be just as fierce as for alcohol. Occasionally, they admitted patients suffering only from tea addiction. One staff member at St. Veronica's Retreat reported of a tea-addicted patient: 'She would go into a state of coma. She would lie about just like any woman who was drunk, would do no work, neglect her house, her children, her husband, everything' (*Report of the Departmental Committee on Treatment of Inebriates*, 1893–1894). Similar arguments were made in Ireland, particularly in relation to the most impoverished areas such as Connemara where, in 1910, one School Inspector reported that 'the use of tea is now carried to such dangerous excess that it ranks before alcohol as an enemy of the public health'. As an alternative, the inspector recommended consuming soup (Irish Independent, 1910).

The framing of excessive tea drinking as dangerous addiction raised questions about whether tea drinking should be banned outright, or at least regulated. Controversially, in 1872, Arlidge argued that the reforming zeal of the temperance movement should also be directed towards repressing 'tea-tippling'. 'Bitter and strong is the agitation at the present period against beer and other intoxicating liquors as the root of all evils', insisted Arlidge,

> but in my opinion there is room for agitation against tea drinking, as carried on in the way spoken of, for I am convinced that a deterioration of health among the working classes, and a lowered vitality in the rising generation are consequences of the abuse of the beverage in question.

Arlidge viewed tea as potentially dangerous and addictive as alcohol. If anything, the temperance movement had created a vacuum in which new liquid beverages had been sought. As tea ruined digestion and enfeebled the heart, Arlidge firmly believed that tea ought to be classified as a narcotic poison (Medical Times and Gazette, 1872).

By the end of the century, some social reformers were going further. In 1895, Dr J.E. Cooney wrote in the *Windsor Magazine* that both alcoholic drinks and tea were abused, and could be safely abolished as beverages, being made available for medicinal uses only. Cooney believed that tea was a 'useless, expensive and noxious drink' which spoiled nature's beverage – water (Reprinted in Yorkshire Herald, 1895). Evidently, this formed part of a process of determining which substances were safe and which were far from and formed part of a broader process of deciding whether or not certain substances should be banned. The Victorians saw alcohol as a grave threat. Historians have argued that anti-alcohol campaigns were a form of moral regulation (Yeomans, 2014). In the late nineteenth century, the 'spectre of the drunkard' also became entangled with a discussion about degeneration. Moral and medical concerns about alcohol abounded; yet, this clashed with, and fitted uneasily into, a capitalist system geared up to cater to an expanding consumer market. Put more bluntly, alcohol made too much tax revenue to ever be banned or classified as for medicinal use only (Berridge, 2013; Hands, 2019). A similar argument could be made for tea. In the face of trade interests, themselves entangled with political and economic interests, physicians could only issue grave warnings and encourage moderation. In this context, health advice focused intently on drinking moderately and, for the most part, veered away from the idea of banning tea outright.

Those concerned about tea consumption developed the idea that tea caused its own type of drunkenness. 'Tea drunkenness' was characterised by exhilaration which impacted gravely on the nervous system. Like alcohol, tea needed to be consumed in moderation and with due care paid to quality (Aberdeen Weekly Journal, 1895). In 1895, a group of New York doctors announced that at least 10% of the patients at the city's main dispensary were suffering from the effects of 'tea drunkenness', which they believed to be 'almost more distressing than that of alcoholic indulgence'. One Brooklyn doctor, James Wood, announced that 10% of patients applying for treatment at New York's chief dispensary were 'tea drunkards' suffering from headache, vertigo, insomnia, heart palpitations, mental confusions, nightmares, nausea, hallucinations, morbid depression of spirits and even suicidal impulses. Wood described excessive tea drinking as 'almost more distressing than that of alcoholic indulgence'. These patients typically drank up to 15 pints of tea each day and were predominantly of Irish origin (Southern Star, 1895; Newcastle Weekly Courant, 1895).

Phelan's aforementioned case provides particular insight into how physicians perceived the effects of extreme tea drunkenness. The doctors described his condition as follows:

> His face and body were saffron hued and his lips, gums and eyelids white. He was scarcely able to move and when he did his respiration was like that of one who had run up a steep hill. The lifting of his hand made his breath come fast.

The *Evening Times* described Phelan as looking like a 'wax manikin'. It was only after several days of hospitalisation that Peter was able to provide the doctors with his health history (*Evening Times*, 1899). Phelan's case was problematic as it coincided with the United States' Church Army's opening of its first tea saloon in New York (*Evening Times*, 1899). The Army sought to convert New Yorkers from liquor and beer to tea. Its saloon sold fine tea at a cheaper cost than beer. Reportedly, over 200 people patronised the new saloon in its first three hours of operation (*Evening Times*, 1899).

Regardless of whether tea drinkers were 'drunk' or not, many doctors undoubtedly feared that excessive tea drinking was a first step on the path to full-blown alcoholism. Once the nervous stimulus provided by tea started to wane, alcohol was the next obvious place in which it might be found, that is, if the dyspeptic pains caused by tea had not already driven sufferers to alcohol for pain relief (British Medical Journal, 1889). In that sense, addictive liquids were placed on a spectrum of addiction. If the key goal was to achieve nervous exhilaration, then it seemed logical to presume that over-use of tea might eventually lead to misuse of alcohol, a far more potent substance. Both excessive tea and alcohol consumption symbolised to Victorians a lack of restraint, especially among the poorer classes, and an unwillingness to shy away from activities feared to be impacting collectively upon the nervous system, creating a 'nervous society' destined to degenerate.

Remedying the Problem

Bad publicity inevitably disgruntled the tea trade. As part of its marketing campaign, Mazawattee tea advertising portrayed Ceylon as the source of healthy tea. The Mazawattee Tea Company was founded in 1887 by the Densham family and was one of the most advertised tea firms. The company became famous for its adverts showing an aged, bespectacled and toothless grandmother drinking her favourite brand of tea. It specialised in selling tea from Ceylon rather than China (Rappaport, 2017). One of its advertisements, distributed widely in the early 1890s, featured an imaginary conversation between an interviewer and a doctor. The doctor discussed 'a mania of late years for low price tea' with the result being that Britain had 'been so flooded with rubbish that many of you don't even know what the taste of good tea is'. The doctor blamed the public for attempting to obtain fine tea at cheap prices. For the fictional doctor, drinking tea was not so much the problem, but the consumption of the wrong types of tea, for this was causing health to deteriorate across Britain. In this account, Chinese tea, not tea itself, was the problem.

The company insisted to readers that cultivating tea in Ceylon was an important initiative as it promised to alleviate the health problems currently rampant across working-class communities. 'China tea has greatly deteriorated', explained the doctor, but 'on the other hand, there is a large proportion of soft, mellow tea sent from India that is far more palatable and contains no more tannin than the China growths'. The doctor continued by making much of Mazawattee's trained team of tasters who checked the quality of tea coming into the British market. He concluded that, 'our great aim and ambition is to elevate the public taste for tea' and to 'be the indirect means of changing a frown into a smile at many a British tea table' (Church Times, 1892).

Of course, the advertisement needs to be situated within its context of building trade within the British Empire and of helping fend off long-standing competition with China. It provided an image of British Empire plantations helping produce a pure, healthy, civilised and perhaps British brew. This process was also boosted by developments in transport which had increased the speed of exchanges around the world (Rappaport, 2017). However, at the same time it somewhat cynically played upon contemporary socio-cultural anxieties and completely refused to acknowledge any problems in advertising that was causing issues of dependence and ill-health among the impoverished. According to the fictional doctors, consumers themselves were at fault for choosing to buy the wrong tea, even if the 'correct' tea was more costly (even more cynically, advertisements for Charles Forde's Bile Beans for biliousness presented their products as the only cure for excessive tea drinking, a means of helping unfortunate women wean themselves off their habits) (Derby Mercury, 1900).

Some innovators attempted to produce products that would remove the tannic acid. One of these, distributed in powder form, was named Nu-Tea. It claimed to treat tea leaves at a high heat to eliminate the tannin (Hampshire Advertiser, 1891). In 1892, one aspiring entrepreneur developed an 'anti-tannic teapot'. However, the *BMJ*, while admiring the objectives, ridiculed the pot for being 'based upon fanciful belief rather than real scientific principles'. The teapot heated the leaves before boiling water was poured on them. On this occasion, the *BMJ* added that 'no tea drinker who respects his stomach or understands the flavour of tea would ever drink tea mixed with milk and sugar, which is merely a sort of tannin broth'. As an alternative, the *BMJ* advised using a Japanese teapot containing a porcelain strainer (British Medical Journal, 1892). In America, one physician produced a new cereal-based drink – nervine coffee – replete with advertisements warning that tea and coffee were just as addictive, destructive and dangerous as alcohol (Western Kansas World, 1898). And, of course, the introduction of the tea bag in the early twentieth century encouraged tea to be consumed in moderation, going some way towards allaying Victorian fears of the physical, emotional and moral dangers of excessive consumption.

Conclusion

In the late nineteenth century, tea was prominent in broader discussion of addiction, degeneration and class difference. The late Victorians were forced to consider the potentially addictive, health-threatening nature of tea while navigating the interests of tea traders, government interests in taxation and the status of tea as an emblem of status and civility in middle-class life. Discourses of degeneration framed working-class tea consumption as a dangerous pursuit, one which threatened the vitality of the nation as a whole. Excessive tea drinking was a metaphor for the perceived recklessness and fervour of the working classes which they so feared. Yet alarm about excessive tea drinking also had non-metaphorical aspects. The poorer industrial classes were indeed under-fed and under-nourished. Their conditions of poverty undoubtedly encouraged many to forego nutrition, particularly self-sacrificing women prone to providing other family members with more nutritious food items. Debates on excessive tea drinking mostly faded away after the start of the twentieth century. Potential reasons might include new technologies such as tea bags which helped ration the strength of consumed tea, improved awareness of nutrition among working-class communities due to the prevalence of health advice aimed at mothers from the voluntary sector and, potentially, stronger interest in other forms of addiction among doctors.

References

Aberdeen Weekly Journal. (31 January 1895), 4.

Alexander, B.K. (2008). *The Globalisation of Addiction: A Study in the Poverty of Sprit*. Oxford: Oxford University Press.

Alleged Increasing Prevalence of Insanity in Ireland: Special Report from the Inspectors of Lunatics to the Chief Secretary, Reports of Commissioners, House of Commons, 1894, C.7331, vol. xliii.647, 4–5.

Appignanesi, L. (2009). *Mad, Bad and Sad: A History of Women and the Mind Doctors from 1800 to the Present*. London: Virago.

Belfast Newsletter, (27 September 1887), 6.

Berridge, V. (2013). *Demons: Our Changing Attitudes to Alcohol, Tobacco and Drugs*. Oxford: Oxford University Press.

Berrow's Worcester Journal, (13 October 1883), 7.

Berrow's Worcester Journal, (31 August 1895), 3.

Birmingham Daily Post, (10 April 1894), 3.

Bourke, J. (2000). 'Effeminacy, ethnicity and the end of trauma: The sufferings of 'shell-shocked' men in Great Britain and Ireland, 1914–1939'. *Journal of Contemporary History, 35*, 57–69.
British Medical Journal, (10 December 1887), 1294.
British Medical Journal, (10 September 1892), 580–581.
British Medical Journal, (12 March 1892), 567.
British Medical Journal, (14 April 1888), 812.
British Medical Journal, (14 December 1889), 1353–1354.
British Medical Journal, (20 October 1883), 786.
British Medical Journal, (24 July 1886), 170–171.
British Medical Journal, (5 May 1888), 985.
Burnett, J. (1999). *Liquid Pleasures: A Social History of Drinks in Modern Britain*. London: Routledge.
Burney, I. (2006). *Poison and the Victorian Imagination*. Manchester: Manchester University Press.
Church Times, (26 February 1892), 204.
Clarkson, L.A. & Crawford, E.M. (2001). *Feast and Famine: A History of Food and Nutrition in Ireland, 1500–1920*. Oxford: Oxford University Press.
Cobbett, W. (1833). *Cottage Economy*. New York: John Doyle.
Cottager's Monthly Visitor, (September 1830), 402–404.
Courtwright, D.T. (2001). *Forces of Habit: Drugs and the Making of the Modern World*. Cambridge, M.A.: Harvard University Press.
Curtis, L.P. (1997 [1971]). *Apes and Angels: The Irishman in Victorian Caricature*. London: Smithsonian Institution Press.
Daily Gazette, (17 April 1877), 1.
Departmental Committee on Merionethshire Slate Mines, House of Commons, Reports of Commissioners, C.7692, 1895, 134–135.
Derby Mercury, (1 August 1900), 3.
Derby Mercury, (22 April 1863), 2.
Drapes, T. (1894). 'On the alleged increase of insanity in Ireland'. *Journal of Mental Science, 40*, 519–548.
Ellis, M., Coulton, R. and Mauger, M. (2015). *Empire of Tea: The Asian Leaf that Conquered the World*. London: Reaktion Books.
Evening Times, (25 May 1899), 5.
Evening Times, (26 May 1899), 5.
Evening Times, (9 June 1899), 2.
Forrest, D.M. (1973). *Tea for the British: The Social and Economic History of a Famous Trade*. London: Chatto and Windus.
Foxcroft, L. (2007). *The Making of Addiction: The 'Use and Abuse' of Opium in Nineteenth-Century Britain*. Aldershot: Ashgate.
Fromer, J.E. (2008). *A Necessary Luxury: Tea in Victorian England*. Athens, O.H.: Ohio University Press.
Griffiths, J. (2007). *Tea: The Drink that Changed the World*. London: Andre Deutsch.
Guardian, (20 May 1899), 4.
Hair, V.M. & Hoh, E. (2009). *The True History of Tea*. London: Thames and Hudson.
Hampshire Advertiser, (25 November 1891), 4.
Hands, T. (2019). *Drinking in Victorian and Edwardian Britain: Beyond the Spectre of the Drunkard*. Basingstoke: Palgrave Macmillan.
Health Reformer, (May 1875), 155–159.
Heggie, V. (2008). 'Lies, damn lies and Manchester's recruiting statistics: Degeneration as an 'urban legend' in Victorian and Edwardian Britain'. *Journal of the History of Medicine and Allied Sciences, 63*, 178–216.
Inter-Departmental Committee on Physical Deterioration: Minutes of Evidence Vol II, Reports of Commissioners, House of Commons, 1094, cd.2210, p. 167.
Irish Independent, (11 September 1905), 4.
Irish Independent, (14 April 1910), 4.
Irish Times, (20 October 1883), 3.
Kamminga, H. & Cunningham, A. (eds). (1995). *The Science and Culture of Nutrition, 1840–1940*. Amsterdam: Rodopi.
Ketabgian, T., Foreign Tastes and Manchester Tea Parties: Eating and Drinking with the Victorian Lower Orders. In Wagner, T.S. and Hassan, N. (eds). (2007). *Consuming Culture in the Long Nineteenth Century: Narratives of Consumption, 1700–1900*. Lanham: Lexington.

Liu, A.B. (2020). *Tea War: A History of Capitalism in China and India.* New Haven: Yale University Press.

MacFarlane, A. & MacFarlane, I. (2003). *The Empire of Tea: The Remarkable History of a Plant that Took Over the World.* New York, N.Y.: Harry N. Abrams.

Manchester Times, (15 June 1872), 6.

Medical Times and Gazette, (25 May 1872), 603.

Miller, I. (2013). "A Dangerous Revolutionary Force Amongst Us': Conceptualising Tea Drinking in the British Isles'. *Cultural and Social History, 10*, 419–438.

Miller, I. (2011). *A Modern History of the Stomach: Gastric Illness, Medicine and British Society, 1800–1950* Pickering and Chatto.

Miller, I. (2014). *Reforming Food in Post-Famine Ireland: Medicine, Science and Improvement, 1845–1922.* Manchester: Manchester University Press.

Moxham, R. (2003). *Tea: Addiction, Exploitation and Empire.* London: Robinson.

New York Times, (20 May 1888), 13.

New York Times, (27 August 1906), 1.

New York Times, (6 July 1902), 16.

Newcastle Weekly Courant, (12 January 1895), 2.

Observer, (26 July 1908), 12.

Observer, (26 July 1908), 12.

Oppenheim, J. (1991). *Shattered Nerves: Doctors, Patients and Depression in Victorian England.* Oxford: Oxford University Press.

Pall Mall Gazette, (13 October 1883), 3–4.

Pendergrast, M. (2010). *Uncommon Grounds: The History of Coffee and How it Transformed the World.* New York, N.Y.: Basic Books.

Pettigrew, J. (2001). *A Social History of Tea.* London: Benjamin Press.

Pick, D. (1989). *Faces of Degeneration: A European Disorder, c.1848–1918.* Cambridge: Cambridge University Press.

Rappaport, E. (2017). *A Thirst for Empire: How Tea Shaped the Modern World.* Princeton, N.J.: Princeton University Press.

Report of the Departmental Committee on Treatment of Inebriates, Reports of Commissioners, House of Commons, 1893–1894, C.7008, p. 34.

Rose, S. (2010). *For all the Tea in China: Espionage, Empire and the Secret Formula for the World's Favourite Drink.* London: Arrow.

Royal Commission on Labour. The Agricultural Labourer, Vol. IV, Ireland Part III, Reports of Commissioners, House of Commons, 1893–1894, C.6894-xxi, vol. xxxvii Pt.1.341, p. 126

Saberi, H. (2010). *Tea.* London: Reaktion Books.

Sedalia Weekly Bazoo, (8 February 1887), 7.

Sharma, J. (2011). *Empire's Garden: Assam and the Making of India.* Durham, N.C.: Duke University Press.

Sixth Report of the Medical Officer of the Privy Council, House of Commons, 1863 [3416], vol. 28.

Smith, E. (1861). *On the Uses of Tea in the Healthy System.* Unknown Publisher.

Southern Star (5 January 1895), p. 2.

Stratmann, L. (2016). *The Secret Poisoner: The Victorian Age of Poisoning.* New York, N.Y.: New York University Press.

Swift, R. & Gilley, S. (eds). (1989). *The Irish in Britain, 1815–1939.* London: Pinter.

The Star, (12 July 1900), 4.

Third Report of the Medical Officer of the Privy Council, [3484] 1865, vol. 26, p. 481.

Townend, P.A. (2002). *Father Mathew, Temperance and Irish Identity.* Dublin: Irish Academic Press.

Trentmann, F. & Flemming, J. (eds). (2006). *Food and Conflict in Europe in the Age of the Two World Wars.* Basingstoke: Palgrave Macmillan.

Turner County Herald, (14 May 1903), 1.

Watson, K. (2003). *Poisoned Lives: English Poisoners and their Victims.* London: Hambledon Continuum.

Weinberg, B.A. & Bealer, B.K. (2001). *The World of Caffeine: The Science and Culture of the World's Most Popular Drug.* London: Routledge.

Western Kansas World, (2 April 1898), 3.

Western Mail, (16 October 1883), 4.

Whorton, J. (2010). *The Arsenic Century: How Victorian Britain was Poisoned at Home, Work and Play.* Oxford: Oxford University Press.

Yeomans, H. (2014). *Alcohol and Moral Regulations: Public Attitudes, Spirited Measures and Victorian Hangovers*. Bristol: Policy Press.
Yorkshire Herald, (6 August 1895), 6.
Zieger, S. (2008). *Inventing the Addict: Drugs, Race and Sexuality in Nineteenth-Century British and American Literature*. Amherst: University of Massachusetts Press.

34

CONCEIVING ADDICTION

Historical constructions of chronic intoxicant use

David Clemis

Addiction as a Historical Problem

From the earliest reflections on their use, the power of intoxicants to alter cognition, emotional states, and comportment has been both celebrated and a cause of anxiety. There has been much less ambivalence expressed in the nearly equally long-standing concern that some people seem incapable of discontinuing the use of intoxicants even while acknowledging the harms arising from their consumption. Concerns about the problems of excessive, chronic use of intoxicants are present throughout history and across the societies in which they have been widely consumed. Despite the persistence and ubiquity of those concerns, however, historians have not been inclined to speak of the history of addiction as they might speak of the histories of famine, disease, violence, or other perennial afflictions. Although the essential psychoactive properties of alcohol have not changed and its metabolisation and general effects on the human body have not substantially altered over time, addiction has not been conceived as a discrete, historically constant phenomenon. Indeed, as modern debates about its nature, causes, and meaning attest, while there is much shared concern about consequences of excessive, chronic, harmful intoxicant consumption, there is no consensus on what constitutes "excess," "chronic" use, or "harm." For the historian, then, the history of intoxicant addiction is not simply a story of the evolving responses to a particular, fixed aspect of the human condition, but rather it is the history of conceptions or constructions of human responses to intoxicant use. As various scholars have observed, addiction has been examined through several distinct lenses, and the range of problems associated with it have been connected or distinguished in a variety of ways.[1] Moreover, intoxicant addiction is not a singular problem, but rather a cluster of variously connected problems whose causes, nature, and imagined solutions are informed by other diverse historically shifting social, cultural, political, and economic factors.

This selective survey of conceptions of addiction across a considerable range of historical periods seeks to reveal something of both the range of factors and interests that have informed various historical conceptions of addiction, while at the same time identifying the persistence or reoccurrence of key ideas or forms of thinking on this matter. The framing of this historical survey is informed by and engages with recent debates amongst modern clinicians, theorists, and researchers about the nature and construction of addiction. Several

DOI: 10.4324/9780429058141-43

scholars have offered typologies of modern conceptions of addiction variously framed by medical/scientific essentialism; social constructionist and cultural studies perspectives; or, more recently, science and technology studies and posthumanism.[2] Elements of these various recent perspectives, along with their values, and logics, can be identified in earlier medical, legal, and moral thinking about chronic, excessive consumption of alcohol. But this historical examination and reflection upon this subject is not simply an exercise in locating analogues and antecedents of current concepts in addiction studies. Rather, it is hoped that a genuinely historical approach may be stimulating and lend critical perspectives to contemporary debates. Questions about moral agency or self-control, the nature of harm, the meaning of dependence, together with cultural, scientific, epistemological, political, and economic framings of addiction, all feature largely in modern debates over the nature and meaning of addiction. In reflecting on these matters, it may be useful to consider various historical understandings of chronic intoxicant use in relation to conceptions of the soul and body, the nature of personal identity, and the problem of free will.

This chapter references selected instances in the history of conceptions of chronic intoxication to provide some sense of the range and possibilities of such thinking. In societies where there is widespread use of intoxicants, thinking about their excessive, chronic use is pervasive but often multifaceted because of the range of the economic, political, medical, moral, and legal dimensions to the problems associated with chronic intoxicant use. Accordingly, various conceptions of addiction within a given society may be diverse and sometimes in tension. Distinct social interests or identities, as well as particular professional authorities, generate differing perspectives on the matter. Thus, broad societal understandings of addiction are informed by, and are composites of, various ideas and values emanating from these distinct perspectives whose interaction and mutual responses often inform one another. Charting the formation and interaction of such thinking is an important but vast task but beyond the scope of this paper. Since the aim here is to historicise conceptions of addiction in order to give some sense the range, possibilities, connections, and differences of those conceptions, this paper is principally concerned with understandings of the idea of addiction as it appears principally in medical and legal discourses across time. The focus here is on the examination of conceptions of intoxicant addiction over the broad course of Western history, with some reference to other regions. The principal focus is on alcohol consumption, given the rich documentation of its ubiquity and very long history of continuous use.

Much recent scholarship on the history of addiction has been concerned with medical, institutional, and public health policy responses in the nineteenth and twentieth centuries.[3] Jose Cree and Rebecca Lemon have each recently produced studies of the usage of the term *addiction* in the early modern period, when it is shown to have first gained currency in English. These scholars explore how religious and literary texts articulate early modern conceptions of addiction in terms of conceptions of the self and the relations between the individual and others (especially God or the Devil, but also lovers, friends, etc.). In this context, addiction is a notion of wide but also subtle application.[4] Jessica Warner has suggested that something like the modern idea of addiction emerged in English religious discourse in the seventeenth century.[5] Warner acknowledges that there is much ambiguity in the various early modern uses of the term "addicted." Indeed, the use of the terms "addicted" and "disease" was richer and less clinically restricted than is the case today, and their use was in many instances rather metaphorical. Peter Frenetzy has noted that chronic drinking was often listed amongst a variety of faults that were clearly not thought of as diseases in any modern sense.[6] These were not naturally occurring disorders of the mind or body, but volitional acts.

The Ancient West

Across the range of Abrahamic, Greek, Roman, and other ancient texts, the loss of self-control is a central feature in references to the heavy consumption of intoxicants. Certainly, there are occasional *Biblical* references to wine's capacity to "gladden the heart" and injunctions to "give strong drink unto him that is ready to perish, and wine unto those that be of heavy hearts. Let him drink, and forget his poverty, and remember his misery no more."[7] Overwhelmingly, however, the concern in *Scripture* is over the consequences of excessive drinking. Both the *Old* and *New Testaments* offer repeated warnings: "Wine is a mocker and beer a brawler; whoever is led astray by them is not wise"; and, "Do not get drunk on wine, which leads to debauchery. Instead, be filled with the [Holy] Spirit."[8] To the modern reader, these might appear to be cautions about the loss of self-control, but they are better understood as calls to resist the inevitable temptation to sin. The difference has something to do with what might be called the agency of the substance. In this ancient view, alcohol does not displace or impair the self—there is no hijacking of cognitive processes here—rather, intoxication simply weakens the capacity of the individual to resist the inevitable pull of sin. It is important to recognise that abstinence or moderate consumption of intoxicants is itself part of the righteous path which one ought to follow. In this context, intoxication is seen through a moral, or rather, spiritual lens. Chronic drinking is persistent sinning rather than some modern notion of addiction. In the sense that Lemon and Cree have identified in the early modern period, for the ancient Jews and early Christians too, chronic drinkers may be *addicted* to drink, but they were not addicts so much as ardent sinners. In this view, the integrity of the self is not diminished by intoxication such that moral agency could no longer be ascribed to the drunkard.

Amongst Greek and Roman writers of the classical era, discussions of chronic drinking were largely concerned with its evils and deleterious health and moral effects. There was not, however, much consideration of the causes of chronic drinking, nor was there a sense that the chronic drinker had a unique kind of problem. Dionysus and the rituals of bacchanalian cults provided powerful images of the intoxicated person as wholly given over to a wilful embracing of the irrational and various ecstatic pleasures.[9] The god of wine's hold on an individual might be irresistibly strong and dramatically transformative, compelling the drinker to uncharacteristic and extraordinary behaviour, but this was not behaviour they regretted nor sought to end. Further, as J. D. Rolleston observed nearly a century ago, in ancient Greek and Roman writings, drunkenness was not generally seen as impairing cognition such that moral agency was undermined. Indeed, Rolleston cites the proverbial claims *in vino veritas* and "wine is the touchstone of character," together with various episodes in classical literature, all in support of the notion of "wine being the mirror of the soul."[10] This suggests that although the drunken person's comportment might betray a high level of intoxication, their essential self remains intact. Thus, although excessive drinking might produce some serious problems, the drunkard's incapacity to give up persistent drinking in the face of acknowledged harm was not amongst them, nor was their continuing cognitive impairment seen to be such that they were "no longer themselves" and ought be absolved of culpability for the harm they might do.[11]

Early Modern Galenism

This general sense of the character of intoxication and the nature of chronic, excessive drinking is most richly developed in what might be called the Hippocratic/Galenic medical paradigm prevalent in Europe and its colonies of settlement from third century BC to the later seventeenth century. The elements of this paradigm did not constitute a systematic, unified, or entirely coherent body of medical thought, and it evolved enormously over the course of that period. What is referred to here as "Galenic medicine" encompasses thinking originating in the writings ascribed to Hippocrates and Galen but upon which there was much commentary and elaboration by subsequent pagan, Islamic, and Christian writers.[12] Across this sprawling, manifold corpus on the human mind and body, conceptions of intoxication and addiction were remarkably consistent. Central to these views was the understanding of how psychoactive substances were understood to have their effects, and how those effects were thought to bear on consciousness, personal identity or the self, and the moral agency and culpability of intoxicated persons. As in the ancient literary sources noted above, ancient, medieval, and early modern Galenic medical understandings of intoxication were not such that individuals were subject to an enduring loss of self-control of the kind that would become central to some modern notions of addiction. To understand how this was so, it is important to recognise that the Galenic conception of the self and its engagement with the mind/body problem is quite unlike that which would emerge in post-Cartesian medicine in the seventeenth century.

Galenic medical writings from the ancient to the early modern periods asserted a unified sense of the self through a kind of ecological interaction of the mind or soul, the body, and its external environment. At the heart of this scheme were the four humours: blood, yellow bile, black bile, and phlegm. The character of each humour derived from its unique combination of two of the essential elements: earth; air; fire; and water. The humours, along with the body's key organs (the liver, heart, and brain), and the animal spirits, which animated the body, were collectively known as "the naturals." The temperament or complexion of an individual arose from the particular balance of their humours. One's mental and physical health, indeed the constitution of one's self, was a function of, or arose within, the complex interaction of the naturals and their responses to six additional factors known as the "non-naturals": the physical environment; sleep; food and drink; exercise; and emotional states.[13] While the distinctions between mind and body were clearly recognised, they were understood as two intimately bound aspects of the self. As the seat of consciousness and conscience, the mind or soul might be deemed the more complex, interesting aspect of the self, but the mutual interdependence of the mind and body meant that, normally, the understanding of mental states entailed an awareness of the condition of the body. As Robert Burton wrote in *The Anatomy of Melancholy:*

> For as the distraction of the mind, amongst other outward causes and perturbations, alters the temperature of the body, so the distraction and distemper of the body will cause a distemperature of the soul, and 'tis hard to decide which of the these two do more harm to the other.[14]

This view is evident in early modern medical writers' discussions of intoxication and the medicinal use of alcohol. Normally, the interaction of the soul and body was facilitated through the movement of animal spirits, the finest grade of matter, whose "natural heat" conveyed the "power of the soul."[15] The composition of the spirits is very important; if they are impure or "mingled with any strange or forraigne quality," the "tanquillity of minde" is disturbed. Francis Bacon, amongst others, observed that alcohol, or "spirits of wine," displaced the natural animal spirits, thereby disrupting that tranquility of mind. The resulting "swift and unquiet motion of the spirits" also distorted vision, diminished motor control, and produced other features of drunken comportment.[16] But the effects of alcohol consumption on a person's mental states could also be positive. Wine was widely prescribed as a remedy for melancholy because it would strengthen the disturbed person's "natural heat" and rebalance the excessive black bile thought to be the cause of their depressive mental state. Wine might also be used to relieve the unhappy and disconsolate as its "mild fumes and vapours so irrigate the braine, that it may procure them quiet and comfortable sleepe...."[17] Their connection meant that the mind and body were consonant across a range of an individual's physical, affective, and moral conditions. As the German physician, Simeon Partlicius (*fl.* 1620–1624), wrote: "... the body and soul are knit together by a certain Sympathy or Consent, and derive vertue and vice from one another, and if there be such a Harmony between them, the one must needs require help as well as the other...."[18] Intoxication and chronic drinking were encompassed in this vision. Such vices impacted and were expressed through the mind and body together. In the mid-seventeenth century, the noted physician Humphrey Brooke wrote:

> Tis observable, that there is a mutual influence from the Body upon the Mind, and from the Mind upon the Body:...That therefore thou mayest be Vertuous, keep they self in good Health; that thou mayst be in good health, keep thy self Vertuous, and Regulate thy Passions.[19]

Drunkenness was a vice that both arose and was experienced in both mind and body. Alcohol was understood to be a material substance that substantially affected the body producing intoxication which had mental effects: impaired cognition and distorted, extraordinary emotional states and comportment.

Understanding the effects of alcohol and the nature of drunkenness in this way might be thought to be problematic, given medieval and early modern Christians' belief in the immortal, immaterial nature of the soul, which was held to be the seat of consciousness and conscience. This would ascribe an agency to alcohol that was neither technically explicable nor theologically and morally acceptable. But the technical problem of how a material substance such as alcohol could affect the immaterial soul, and the doctrinally unpalatable assertion that mental states might simply be the results of particular physiological conditions were not engaged by early modern Galenic physicians' thinking about intoxication and chronic drinking. Such concerns would not arise and become problematic until the seventeenth century's post-Cartesian understanding of the dualistic self with its distinct elements of mind and body, and when viewed through the lens of the period's emerging empirically oriented science. For Galenists such as Humphrey Brooke, Robert Burton, or Simeon Partlicius, the self was not understood through the disaggregation and distinction of its component parts; rather, theirs was an attempt to understand the individual as a union of mind and body and in relation to the wider world. Human behaviour, then, was seen as rising in the context of a kind of network of connections between the naturals (the elements of the body), non-naturals (behaviours and bodily processes), and contra-naturals (diseases or causes of illness), which together in the microcosm of the individual were connected to the macrocosm of the universe.[20] In several late Medieval texts, Philippa Maddern has seen the "indissoluble bond between soul and body that alone constituted individual identity."[21] This conception of a braided self intwining mental, moral, and physiological strands owed much to Medieval Aristotelianism. Rejecting the Platonic detachment of the soul from the body, Thomas Aquinas asserted that the soul was the form of the body, thus establishing the integral connection of body and soul. Through this lens, the soul was seen as the formal cause of the body, which together constituted the self.[22]

This framing of the matter helped shaped medieval and early modern Galenistic accounts of intoxication and chronic drinking as epistemological projects. The Galenist's aim was to explain the condition of patient's body, mind, and environment as they constituted the whole self. The effects of alcohol on the body, mind, and behaviour of an individual were not understood essentially in causal mechanical and chemical terms (although there is something of that) but rather as different manifestations of an essential moral quality of the individual. Thus, alcohol was not seen as interfering with the brain and causing faulty reasoning—as might be the case in later, more modern accounts of intoxication.[23] Rather, for the Galenist, the state of the drunken body, the malfunctions of cognition and perception, the distortions of emotions, and strained social relations were all distinguishable aspects of a singular disturbed condition in a given drunken individual. Certainly, the language of causation appears in Galenist medical writing—alcohol dislodges the animal spirits resulting in slurred speech and misperceptions—but in terms that might bear on the moral culpability of the drunken person, or in which we might say that chronic intoxication undermines moral agency, the Galenist would see these less as causes of cognitive failure, but rather as coincident with it. The various causes and manifestations of drunkenness are all simultaneously related to who the person fundamentally is. Drunkenness arose in the course of the interaction of the naturals and non-naturals that are constitutive of an individual's condition and identity. It is not as if there is an essential, normal, core self (a post-Cartesian idea of the self) that has been interfered with by alcohol. It is not the case that one could be said to have lost self-control *because* of intoxication; rather, the self arises from the interaction of the naturals, non-naturals, and contra-naturals in the context of the individual's complexion. When the consumption of alcohol, a non-natural, gives rise to intoxication, that is who an individual is; and that self is culpable for what it does. In this view, drunkenness is less something that happens *to* the body and the mind, than it *is* a simultaneously interwoven moral, social, as well as physiological condition, and state of cognitive impairment.[24]

The key elements of modern conceptions of addiction are not readily apparent in these late medieval and early modern notions of the self, intoxication, and chronic drinking. There are some interesting parallels between Galenic ideas about chronic drinking and some aspects of recent neuroscience/brain disease and multifactorial accounts of addiction, especially in terms of the interaction of physiology, social environments, and behaviours.[25] Nevertheless, as discussed above, the Galenists did not conceive of the self in such a way that substantially accords with modern notions of *loss of self-control*. The drunkards' "enslavement" to their vice and sins arose from, or was an expression of, their essential selves; it was not simply the unintended consequence of succumbing to the psychochemical effects of alcohol. The physiological, spiritual, social, and moral harm of chronic drinking does feature largely in medical and moralistic tracts of the sixteenth and seventeenth centuries. Yet, while there is regret for sinfulness, there is nothing akin to a key element in modern conceptions of addiction: an acknowledgement of the harmfulness of chronic drinking together with an expressed desire to stop, which is, nevertheless, frustrated by some experience of dependence, compulsion, or failure of volition owing to the agency of an intoxicating substance.

Before composition of the Christian Galenist texts, the *materia medica* of Islamic physicians in the medieval and early modern periods included alcohol. Indeed, especially in cases of mental health problems, Christian medical writers cited the Persian physician Avicenna (Ibn Sīnā, 480–1073 AD) and his recommendation that occasional drunkenness might ease the effects of melancholy.[26] But the general proscription against intoxication and even the consumption of alcohol meant that, for the most part, intoxication and chronic drinking were thought to be moral and religious failings. Hence, amongst most Islamic physicians, the agency of the chronic drinker was implied.[27]

In ancient and medieval China, views of intoxication and chronic drinking were essentially similar to those in the Galenic West. Chinese literary texts occasionally celebrated intoxication as a means to lift spirits, and so drunkenness itself was not thought to be necessarily a bad thing.[28] Indeed, perhaps most famously, the poet Li Bai observed in the eighth century:

> To drown the ancient sorrows,
> we drank a hundred jugs of wine
> there in the beautiful night.[29]

Also in the eighth century, the Japanese poet Ōtomo Tabito found a more bitter sweet relief in a perhaps more authentic, if intoxicated, frame of mind:

> Rather than be wise
> Churning out words,
> Better drink your saké,
> And weep drunken tears.[30]

In the early fourteenth century, Yoshida Kendō decried the vulgarity and loathsomeness of the drunkard; yet, he could not help acknowledging that "a drinker is amusing, and his offence is pardonable."[31] Still, both Chinese and Japanese medieval writers show the same concern about chronic excess as the Galenist writers in the European and Islamic worlds. In the late sixteenth century, Lo Yü-jen wrote scathingly of the drunkenness of the Wan-li Emperor and his addiction to vice.[32] Translators' use of the English word "addiction" in poetic and literary descriptions of chronic drinking in ancient and medieval Chinese texts seems apt, given the sense of the word in European texts of the period. This is not a modern notion of addiction in which a kind of agency is ascribed to intoxicating substances which impairs self-control. Rather, in all of these societies, the key to addiction or chronic intoxication is the moral weakness of the drinker. Amongst his many reflections on the effects of drinking, Li Bai observes that, "Wine does not delude people, they delude themselves."[33]

Seventeenth-Century Empiricism and Eighteenth-Century Neurology

In the Western world, over the course of the seventeenth century, Galenic medicine gave way to new "iatrochemical" and "iatromechanical" approaches that gradually changed the theory, methods, and practice of medicine, but they did not precipitate modern addiction theory. Nevertheless, the "medical revolution of the seventeenth century" did significantly change the character of medical approaches and conceptions of chronic drinking.[34] The epistemological frame of the new medicine was strongly empirical and bore the influence of Cartesian dualism in its separation of mind and body. Herman Boerhaave (1668–1738), for example, maintained that, although the mind and body constituted an interactive unity, they nevertheless were of completely distinct, different natures. Moreover, despite mind-body interaction, Boerhaave believed that the physician could know nothing about either the particular workings of the mind nor the nature of its connection to the body. The doctor's sphere, then, was clear:

> … the great Business of a Physician is to be acquainted with the Means of restoring lost Health, and no cure can be effected by him, but through some Change in the human

> Body by the Application of others, therefore this Search after the Connexion between the Body and the Mind not appertaining to a Physician is to be rejected....The Physician, who cures the Diseases of the body, is not sollicitous about those of the Mind; for when the first is set to rights, the latter will quickly return to its Office.[35]

Because physicians could neither explain the physiological basis of the compulsion to drink, nor reliably and consistently treat that condition, such effectively dualist iatromechanical views had the practical consequence of assigning the physiological consequences of habitual drinking to physicians, while leaving the causes to moralists. This comfortably accorded with theologians' views that the immaterial soul, the seat of consciousness and conscience could not be affected by a material substance such as alcohol. As a consequence, the sin/vice understanding of chronic drinking became yet more firmly entrenched.

In the early eighteenth century, moralists and physicians, who essentially wrote as moralists, strongly affirmed the drunkard's self-control. Certainly, drink was tempting, but it was the path of sin and personal destruction. Nevertheless, it was believed that individuals had the power to resist such temptation, as a 1712 tract put the matter:

> Therefore the only way to avoid being Drunk is to exercise your intellects, and the Faculties of your Mind, especially your Memory; to remind you of the Filithy Discourses, and Sights, which you have heard, seen or read of Drunkenness, as also of the Madness and Follies, committed [by] Lewd and Debauch'd Persons, in their Excesses of Drinking, and by Drunkards, the Ruin and Destruction of their Bodies, Goods, and Estates, and the Danger of their Souls Emanently pursuing.[36]

As Roy Porter has observed, across the eighteenth century, many elements of modern disease conceptions of addiction appear in the writings of various physicians and moralists. But it is important to note that while there are occasional assertions of the loss of self-control, substance dependence, agency of substance, acknowledged harm, and descriptions of chronic drinking as a disease, there is often ambivalence and sometimes stark contradiction in eighteenth-century thinking on chronic drinking. Stephen Hales' 1733 pamphlet, *A friendly admonition to the drinkers of brandy, and other distilled spirituous liquors*, clearly illustrates the tensions in the thought of this period. Hales describes the drunkard as enslaved and addicted, although the drunkard's moral agency is emphasised:

> Then how much more should those who have been addicted to Drunkenness, bridle their Appetite, and abstain from Intemperance, notwithstanding they have thereby brought upon themselves such an unnatural depraved Thirst, as gives them great Uneasiness to forbear drinking...[37]
>
> No Habit, however long in contracting, is impossible to be removed; it may be done, though with some Difficulty. There is no one so far gone in the Disease of Drunkenness, or any other Sin whatever, but there is room for a Cure...[38]

And yet, so powerful is the hold of alcohol that the chronic drinker is without volition:

> To recover him from this Condition, he must be, as it were, forced into his Liberty, and rescued, in some measure, from his own depraved Desires; he must be dealt with like a Madman, and be bound down, to keep him from destroying himself.[39]

> Hence we see what little Hopes there is of reclaiming, by any Arguments whatever, these miserable Wretches, who are thus inslaved. For these Reasons, Men ought to be extremely cautious, how on any Pretence whatsoever they indulge the Beginnings of so pernicious a Custom...[40]

In the first half of the eighteenth century, the era of the "Gin Craze," it may be that the perception of a spectacular increase in the consumption of higher alcohol by volume distilled spirits destabilised the notion that chronic drinking was simply a matter of bad moral choices and that the qualities of alcohol were seen by some as a factor in the problem.[41] Yet, in the absence of a compelling medical explanation of the mechanism or process of dependence, the drunkard's ultimate moral agency was still widely and strongly asserted.

Most historians generally accept that it was not until the end of the eighteenth century, with the work of Benjamin Rush and Thomas Trotter, together with the beginnings of the temperance movement and the emergence of the psychiatric profession, that a recognisably modern disease concept of chronic drinking began to gain purchase.[42] It did so because over the course of the eighteenth century, there developed a new neurological aspect of medicine that was able to overcome the empirical, epistemological barriers and mind/body dualism that had prevented iatromechanical medicine from seeing chronic drinking as a disease. There had long been much discussion of the nerves and their bearing on mental health. But from the mid-eighteenth century, medical writers professionally appropriated neurological discourse as they became particularly concerned with the nervous system.[43] With respect to thinking about intoxication, these developments began in 1749 with David Hartley's *Observations on Man,* which proposed that mental states and behaviour could be explained through the processes of the body's neurological system. Influenced by Newtonian physics and Lockean concepts of sensation, perception, ideas, and association, Hartley held that the vibration and conveyance of minute particles were the means by which perception, cognition, and the sensations of pleasure and pain were generated. He believed that alcohol intoxication had a particular effect on the body and mind: "[t]he common and immediate effect of wine is to dispose to joy, i.e., to introduce such kinds and degrees of vibrations into the whole nervous system or into separate parts thereof as are attended with moderate continued pleasure."[44]

This general conception of the nervous system and its particular understanding of intoxication were elaborated in subsequent discussions of intoxication and chronic drinking. In the 1790s, Erasmus Darwin and John Coakley Lettsom asserted that, while alcohol produced pleasure, it so damaged the nerves that the exercise of volition was undermined.[45] William Cullen was not directly concerned with intoxication; yet, his work constituted an important step towards seeing that defective patterns of perception and cognition were the consequence of neurological damage. It came to be held that physicians did not need to physically observe such neurological damage and repair it in order to aid patients. It was thought that it might be enough to understand patients' patterns of perception and cognition to treat psychological afflictions.[46] It was this general scheme that allowed Thomas Trotter, Benjamin Rush, and those who followed them, to see chronic drinking as a disease. As Trotter observed: "[t]he habit of drunkenness is a disease of the mind. The soul itself has received impressions that are incompatible with its reasoning powers."[47] Rush observed that although the chronic drinker initiated their affliction through the free exercise of choice, the habit of drinking transformed intoxication into a necessity.[48]

The Nineteenth Century: Disease and Alcoholism

This disease conception of chronic drinking did not preclude the language of vice in the writings of either physicians or more popularly oriented moralists. The decision to persistently consume alcohol to the point of intoxication was, of course, thought to be a great moral fault, and the nineteenth-century temperance movements devoted themselves to dissuading people from choosing to start down that path. But with the wider acceptance and elaboration of Trotter's and Rush's disease concept, the sense of drunkenness as a vice shifted. While the habit of chronic, heavy drinking was understood to be freely made, and so was morally condemned, the neurological damage it inflicted was seen as resulting in a loss of self-control. In 1832, Robert Macnish observed that

> moral lectures do not come within the scope of a medical treatise, and seem to be of little use at any time in terrifying drunkards from the continuance in their destructive vice....Drunkenness debases and brutifies the intellect so much, that neither moral nor religious considerations have any great effect upon it.[49]

As William Bynum has observed, Carl von Brühl-Cramer's influential *Ueber die Trunksucht und eine rationelle Heilmethode derselben* (1819) even more strongly eschewed moral or spiritual considerations in characterising the chronic drinker asserting: "since moderate drinking is not considered immoral, the disease cannot be immoral."[50] Brühl-Cramer conceived of "dipsomania" (*Trunksucht*) entirely as a disease manifest as "an involuntary desire for the use of ardent spirits."[51] It was seen as arising from a predisposition and had to be treated through medicines and dietary management.[52]

Although the language of disease had long been part of physicians and moralists' accounts of addiction, in the work of Rush, Trotter, and their successors, the formulation of the idea of addiction as a disease was importantly different in two ways. First, it did not invariably reference sin. Sin and disease had long rhetorical and conceptual associations, but these did not carry on into the new medial discourse of chronic drinking in the nineteenth century. Certainly, vice was spoken of, but vice did not have the inevitability or universality of sin. Drunkenness, as a vice could be avoided, and while some might succumb to it, others did not. Second, this disease conception of chronic drinking was invoked because disease could be treated. Such physicians believed that they could "cure" chronic drinking, and so throughout much of the nineteenth century, there were a variety of therapeutic approaches and experiments in search of successful treatments for chronic drinking.

Habit was critical in the conception of the diseased will, and it became central in its cure. Rush held that the habit "may be easily broken" through substitution of other drinks such as coffee, "simple water," and wine (the disease of chronic drinking was thought to arise from distilled spirits).[53] Most medical writers in the nineteenth century, however, acknowledged how difficult it was to repair the will and enable the chronic drinker to give up the habit. Trotter observed: "the cravings of appetite for the poisonous draft are to the intemperate drinkers as much the inclinations of nature for a time, as a draught of cold water to a traveller panting with thirst in a desart."[54] Accepting that the volition of the chronic drunkard was damaged and hard to repair, Macnish sought to provide an account of the physical and mental suffering caused by excessive consumption in hopes of discouraging it in the first place.[55]

As the nineteenth century progressed, various experts proposed regimes for the refashioning or reviving of the drunkard's will. In 1812, Benjamin Rush proposed that both as an act of charity and in the public interest, drunkards should be confined to a hospital "for the exclusive reception of hard drinkers." He reasoned that the harm drunkards inflicted upon their families and society warranted confinement in the same way the incarceration of thieves did. Having been committed to such a "sober house" by a court of physicians and magistrates, the drunkard, under the direction of a physician, would abstain from ardent spirits, have their food regulated, work for their own or the public benefit, and be subject to "all the religious, moral, and physical remedies" that Rush believed to be helpful.[56] This notion was adopted and championed by J. Edward Turner, who endorsed and developed the inebriate asylum concept in a paper in 1854.[57] Four years later, Turner founded the New York State Inebriate Asylum, which took its first patients in 1864. Turner articulated an influential vision of inebriety as a disease. Against critics of that view, he argued that although drunkenness entailed moral degradation, it was nevertheless a disease with an "independent pathology and morbid anatomy, which is as well marked and defined as the morbid anatomy of any disease that the human family is heir to."[58]

Perhaps inevitably, this new disease conception shifted focus from the moral qualities of the drunkard to the agency of the substance alcohol. The very rich historiography of temperance movements and alcohol regulation tells the story of the perceived threat of alcohol in the nineteenth and twentieth centuries.[59] This understanding of the power of alcohol to destroy the will prompted many physicians to proclaim the importance of their profession in dealing with what came to be seen as a major social problem. The disease concept and the public health threat of chronic drinking were influentially brought together in Mangus Huss' *Alcoholismus chronicus* (*Chronic Alcohol Disorder*) (1849–1851), which coined the potent and enduring term "alcoholism." The public health effects of drinking led many physicians to first express concern about the misuse of alcohol and eventually to join in calls for temperance.[60] These concerns resulted in the foundation of the American Association of the Study and Cure of Inebriety in 1870 and its British counterpart in 1884.

As Mariana Valverde has shown, physicians' formulation of the disease concept of chronic drinking became enmeshed in the various interests and agendas of moral reformers, physicians, jurists, and legislators. Inevitably, wider social and cultural tensions exposed the concept's limitations and saw it wrenched in different directions by the period's ideological conflicts and competing social visions. The notion of a disease of the will, the remedy of which required an exercise of the will, left a rather indeterminate role for the physician and left open the intervention of non-medical agents. More significantly, this paradox made legislation on the institutional commitment of inebriates impractical, thus exposing the incoherence of this framing of the disease concept.[61] It is evident that before the First World War, the disease concept originating with Rush and Trotter but most fully articulated by J. Edward Turner and Norman Kerr was no longer influential. The legislation and institutions it had inspired proved impractical and, failing to realise its vision, were eventually abandoned. The American Association of Inebriety dissolved in 1912 and Britain's Society for the Study of Inebriety became a much diminished force.[62]

The Twentieth Century: The Meanings of Disease

While the decline of these institutions signalled the collapse of this iteration of the disease model, a general notion of chronic drinking as a disease persisted in the discourse of philanthropic organisations such as the Salvation Army and Alcoholics Anonymous (AA). But it did so largely to the extent that it was congenial to the aims of reducing the stigma attached to chronic drinkers and conveying a sense of the powerful the grip of alcohol upon them. Harry Levine has suggested that after prohibition, the essence of the problem of alcoholism was relocated to the body of the individual; it is only some people who, "for reasons unknown, become addicted to alcohol."[63] Thus, while the notion of disease is present in the AA approach, it is reframed in acknowledgement of the particularity of every individual. In this view, the paradox of chronic drinking as a disease of the will that can only be overcome by acts of the will is not found troubling, but rather is embraced. In this view, alcoholism is a condition of ongoing personal crisis whose resolution will only come by the recovery of the self through personal, spiritual development.[64]

It was not until the 1940s that physicians again engaged in substantial new thinking about the causes and treatment of chronic drinking. Initially, through the work of E.M. Jellinek, the basis of the disease conception shifted.[65] Turner, Kerr, or Brühl-Cramer believed chronic alcohol drinking to be a disease in which the substance destroyed bodily tissues producing a range of deleterious physiological and psychological conditions leading to various moral and social harms. Jellinek redefined the disease in terms of the drinker's loss of control and the harms that arose therefrom. His influential five categories of problem drinking patterns arranged conceptions of loss of control and harm together with their severity and duration in a typology that spanned a range of drinking behaviours and their consequences. In only two of these categories was the loss of control deemed sufficient to constitute a disease. This model retained some of the virtues of the old disease concept—attempting to reduce stigmatisation and conveying a sense of the affliction's strong grip—and it better accorded with common understandings of the experience of chronic drinking. That it did so was the inevitable consequence of Jellinek's principal research subjects: members of AA.[66] Effectively, the new model used a scheme of harms and markers of loss of control as diagnostic signs, which became the symptoms and defining characteristics of the disease. Scholars and researchers have subsequently found the evidentiary basis for Jellinek's model wanting, but its influence has been enormous. It was embraced by AA, and institutionally entrenched at the Yale Centre for Studies in Alcohol (1935), the National Council of Alcoholism (1950), and the World Health Organization, where Jellinek was active in the 1950s.[67] Yet while the post-Jellinek framing of harm and loss of control within a disease framework became the basis of much medical and expert discourse on alcohol problems, the vision of a disease characterised by a clearly delineated aetiology and discrete set of symptoms slipped from view. As Valverde has shown, Jellinek's approach was eclectic and influential but the lines of influence were various and divergent.[68] In the later twentieth century, the term "disease" became less widely used, but the notions of harm, loss of control, and the sense of the condition as an affliction all featured very largely in expert discourse and conceptions of drug and alcohol problems. They were entrenched in the successive diagnostic schemes of the W.H.O.'s *ICD* and the American Psychiatric Association's *DSM*. Notions of harm and loss of control then became key elements in the conceptualisation of addiction and deeply informed subsequent research, as well as attracted considerable scholarly commentary.[69]

This research is often seen as dividing into either sociological or biomedical accounts of addiction. Darin Weinberg has observed that contemporary social science understandings of addiction are largely derived through social interactions (between clinicians and patients) in which the object of study is the nature of the patient's wider social interactions in the course of their lives.[70] Jellinek's typology and the diagnostic criteria of successive editions of *ICD* and *DSM* have drawn much scholarly commentary for their construction and use of social interactions. What constitutes harm must invariably be cast, in large measure, in terms of local social contexts that may vary considerably across and between societies and over time. Note, for example, two of the *DSM's criteria:*

> 6. Continued alcohol use despite having persistent or recurrent social or interpersonal problems caused or exacerbated by the effects of alcohol.
> 7. Important social, occupational, or recreational activities are given up or reduced because of alcohol use.[71]

The conception of these problems and activities, their significance, and the manner and extent to which they are affected by the chronic drinker's alcohol consumption all admit to considerable variability. Various sectional or community identities, as well as shifting cultural norms, undermine the coherence and stability of these criteria in the construal chronic drinkers' experience. While this may not undermine practitioners' confidence in the criteria's local clinical utility, it does mean that they do not readily yield a technically coherent, consistent, universal concept of addiction. Furthermore, the identified harms that constitute the criteria of alcohol use disorder are difficult to disaggregate from other causes of social, psychological, and physiological harm. Poverty, various forms of social exclusion, and/or mental health problems make the distinct conception of alcohol use disorder difficult to establish. Other cultural factors, too, have made this conception of alcohol use disorder problematic. This model relies on the chronic drinker's self-reporting of their desires, experiences, and cognitive and affective states. Thus, it relies on an understanding of the self rooted in modern conceptions of subjectivity and personal identity which are increasingly contentious. Similarly, the notion of loss of self-control, as diagnostic criteria, depends on contentious historically contingent values and measures pertaining to conception of the self and self-regulation within changing patterns of economic, social, and cultural relations.[72]

Recent neuroscience-based accounts of addiction as a brain disease have become preeminent. The increasing influence of this approach owes much to its empirical grounding and its reinforcement of the loss of self-control element of the disease model.[73] Explanations of addiction, and especially relapses into harmful substance use in terms of a "hijacking" of the "neural reward system," have provided an empirical, medical explanation that appears to preserve a place, initially at least, for the substance user's agency. As NIDA director, Nora Volkow, has put the matter:

> ...most drugs of abuse exert their initial reinforcing effects by activating reward circuits in the brain and that, while initial drug experimentation is largely a voluntary behaviour, continued drug use impairs brain function by interfering with the capacity to exert self-control over drug-taking behaviours and rendering the brain more sensitive to stress and negative moods.[74]

Various scholars have been critical of inferences or speculations about the nature of addiction that extend beyond existing biomedical evidence. It has been suggested that the hijacked neural reward system model is not yet sufficiently detailed to define the limits of addiction. Its extension into "process addictions," including such as activities as sex, gambling, and digital gaming, suggests that anything producing pleasure and stimulating dopamine is, in principle, potentially disease-addictive.[75] Weinberg has argued that such biomedical accounts of addiction fail to embrace how "cultural learning and social context shape whether and how drug use becomes pleasurable or compelling."[76] In the face of the differences amongst people's pleasure in drug taking, and the fact that their experiences of intoxication can be circumstantially contingent, Weinberg questions biomedical accounts' claims that "the ingestion of certain chemicals *invariably* produces pleasurable experiences."[77] Although its proponents suggest that "neuroscience identified addiction" should be understood "as a chronic brain disease with strong genetic, neurodevelopmental, and sociocultural components,"[78] Helen Keane has observed, those sociocultural components are "relegated to the vague background realm of 'environmental influences' or refigured as effects of disordered brain chemistry."[79] Indeed, it is difficult to see how, in the current construction of biomedical accounts, it could be otherwise. It is not presently possible to map the sociocultural experience of the chronic substance user into the neuroscientific understandings of mental states. The key to the notion of the loss of control must lie in the conception of the nature of the self as a conscious agent, which is apparently enmeshed, or perhaps, constructed, within an ecology of social, cultural, and physical conditions. Weinberg asserts that "it is absolutely indispensable for addiction research to include clear concepts of what the self actually is such that we find it capable of moving into and out of control of human actions in the first place."[80] This may well be, but it engages the enormous philosophical and psychological questions of what the self is, what it controls, and what it means to say that the self does or does not have control. These are matters going to the heart of what constitute the parameters of the self, and what are the contexts, inputs, and conditions of its agency.

Conclusions: The Intoxicated Self through History

It is tempting to assert that the history of Western medicine's various attempts to understand chronic drinking are crudely reducible to shifting conceptions of the self. A richer grasp of the matter will acknowledge that conceptions of the self and the idea of addiction have been subject to the social, moral, and political climates, as well as the epistemological frames through which they have been constructed. In the general Galenic understanding of chronic drinking, personal identity is preserved, and however extraordinary or problematic the drunkard's behaviour, their essential self-control and moral culpability is retained. In this construction of the self through the interaction of the mind, body, and environment, chronic drunkenness is, in effect, a kind of expression of the self. As the new epistemological frame of the seventeenth-century medical revolution prompted a more empirically driven conception of what constitutes medical understanding and knowledge generation, the self was cast within a Cartesian dualistic framework. The empirical inability to account for the formation of mental states meant that drunkards were held to be ensnared by their own vice. Over the course of the eighteenth century, with the waning of theological demands that the soul be conceived as the immaterial seat of consciousness and conscience, intoxication and drunkenness came to be understood as arising from alcohol-induced neurological damage. It then became possible for something of a modern disease concept to emerge in which loss of self-control can be alleged—this is an idea of the displaced or impaired self. Certainly, neither within the field of medicine nor more broadly across society was this paradigm universally accepted. Nevertheless, despite its considerable reconfiguration from the time of Rush and Trotter to Turner and Kerr, the disease concept of chronic drinking exerted great influence. Jellinek and the second iteration of the disease concept proved to be so influential because it was rooted in the categorisation of behaviours rather than particular strong conception of the self. This enabled researchers to elaborate on Jellinek's basic model in a variety of different ways. It thus informed or set the parameters for both much biomedical and sociocultural research. The synthesis that is proposed in the conception of addiction "as a chronic brain disease with strong genetic, neurodevelopmental, and sociocultural components,"[81] however problematic contemporary scholars may find it, interestingly bears some similarity to the Galenic view in its eclectic, cross-disciplinary aspirations. Both are constructed beyond the dichotomous sin/vice versus disease/medicalised delineation of conceptions of addiction that inevitably arose out of seventeenth-century medicine's embracing of a mind/body dualism and the virtual detachment of mental states from physiological conditions. Neuroscience findings, particularly relating to neuro-plasticity, as well as work in the social sciences, have led some addiction experts to emphasise that choice is seen as not necessarily rational, and that the complex interaction of physiological conditions with cognitive acts problematises the notion of self-control.[82] Such addiction theorists posit a complexity of mind/body interaction which effectively transcends the old mind/body dualism and dissolves the free choice versus disease dichotomy.

However, it is important to note that early modern Galenists seldom engaged the problem of how material and immaterial substances interact. For them, it was simply not the key problem, and its resolution was not necessary within their epistemological framework. Theirs was as a kind of Aristotelean understanding of the soul as the animator of life in which psychological and biological explanations were not completely distinct, discrete aspects of one's being.[83] Moreover, the primary aim of their accounts was to understand the person as an integrated whole. Thus, the qualities and character of intoxication, which are now commonly understood within various distinct social, moral, physiological, and psychological categories, were, for the early modern Galenist, much more likely to be woven together within a more comprehensive conception of intoxication. In this way of thinking, the effects of alcohol on the body (a non-natural effect on the natural self), its impairment of cognition, and the social context and consequences of drinking were all seen as of a piece. The moral agency of the drunkard could not be denied because their inclination to drink, the character of their drunken comportment, together with the personal and social impacts of their drinking, all simultaneously arose from, and were constitutive of, their *self*. In the twenty-first century, there is no consensus on anything like such an integrative, expansive conception of the self; nor is it at all clear what such an idea would entail. It may be that in its absence, the marrying of biomedical and sociocultural conceptions of addiction will remain a challenge.

Notes

1 Robin Room, "The Cultural Framing of Addiction," *Janus Head* 6, no. 2 (2003): 221–234; Helen Keane, "Addiction: Critical Reflections on a Debated Concept," in *The Sage Handbook of Drug & Alcohol Studies*, edited by Betsy Thom, Geoffrey Hunt, and Torsten Kolind (Thousand Oaks: Sage Publications, 2016), 367–381; Griffith Edwards, "The Trouble with Drink: Why Ideas Matter," *Addiction* 105, no. 5 (2010): 797–804; Craig Reinarman, "Addiction as Accomplishment: The Discursive Construction of Disease," *Addiction Research & Theory* 13, no. 4 (2005): 307–320.

2 Suzanne Fraser, David Moore, and Helen Keane, *Habits: Remaking Addiction* (London: Palgrave Macmillan 2014); Helen Keane, "Addiction: Critical Reflections"; Darin Weinberg, "Post-Humanism, Addiction and the Loss of Self-Control: Reflections on the Missing Core in Addiction Science," *International Journal of Drug Policy* 24, no. 3 (2013): 173–181.

3 Jean-Charles Sournia, *A History of Alcoholism* (Oxford, New York: B. Blackwell, 1990); Mariana Valverde, *Diseases of the Will: Alcohol and the Dilemmas of Freedom* (Cambridge; New York: Cambridge University Press, 1998); Berridge, *Demons: Our Changing Attitudes to Alcohol, Tobacco, & Drugs* (Oxford: Oxford University Press, 2013); Virginia Berridge and Alex Mold, "Special Issue on Concepts of Addiction in Europe, 1860s-1930s," *Social History of Alcohol & Drugs: An Interdisciplinary Journal* 28, no. 1 (2014); Virginia Berridge, Jennifer Walke, and Alex Mold, "From Inebriety to Addiction: Terminology and Concepts in the UK, 1860–1930," *Social History of Alcohol & Drugs: An Interdisciplinary Journal* 28, no. 1 (Winter 2014): 88–106; Dan Malleck, "The Meaning of Addiction in the Rubbing Alcohol Habit: The Rise and Fall of the Rubby," *Social History of Alcohol & Drugs: An Interdisciplinary Journal* 25, no. 1/2 (Fall 2011): 130–147; David T. Courtwright, *The Age of Addiction: How Bad Habits Became Big Business* (Cambridge: Harvard University Press, 2019).

4 Jose Murgatroyd Cree, "Protestant Evangelicals and Addiction in Early Modern English," *Renaissance Studies* 32, no. 3: 446–462; Jose Murgatroyd Cree, "The Invention of Addiction in Early Modern England" Ph. D., University of Sheffield, 2018; and Rebecca Lemon, *Addiction and Devotion in Early Modern England* (Philadelphia: University of Pennsylvania Press, 2018).

5 Jessica Warner, "'Resolv'd to drink no more'; Addiction as a preindustrial construct," *Journal of Studies on Alcohol*; 55–56 (1994), 685, 689; and Jessica Warner, "Before There Was 'Alcoholism': Lessons from the Medieval Experience with Alcohol," *Contemporary Drug Problems* 19, no. 3 (1992): 409–429.

6 Peter Ferentzy, "From Sin to Disease: Differences and Similarities between Past and Current Conceptions of Drunkenness", *Contemporary Drug Problems* 28 (2001): 363–390.

7 *Psalms* 104:15; and *Proverbs* 31:6–7 (King James Version).

8 *Proverbs* 20:1; and *Ephesians* 5:18.

9 Sournia, *A History of Alcoholism*, 5–6; and Andrew Dalby, *The Story of Bacchus* (London: British Museum Press, 2005).

10 J. D. Rolleston, "Alcoholism in Classical Antiquity," *The British Journal of Inebriety* XXIV, no. 3 (1927): 104–105.

11 Rolleston, "Alcoholism in Classical Antiquity," 101–120.

12 Owsei Temkin, *Galenism: Rise and Decline of a Medical Philosophy* (Ithaca: Cornell University Press, 1973), 103.

13 The humoral system during the Renaissance is described in Mary Lindemann, *Medicine and Society in Early Modern Europe,* 2nd ed. (Cambridge: Cambridge University Press, 2010), 14, 88; Valentin, Groebner, "Complexio/Complexion: Categorising Individual Natures, 1250–1600," in *The Moral Authority of Nature,* edited by Lorraine Daston and Fernando Vidal (Chicago: University of Chicago Press, 2010), 361–383. Fernando Vidal, *The Sciences of the Soul: The Early Modern Origins of Psychology* (Chicago, Ill: University of Chicago Press, 2011) 34–35; and Harold J. Cook, "Medicine and the New Philosophy in Seventeenth-Century England," in *Reappraisals of the Scientific Revolution,* edited by David C. Lindberg and Robert S. Westman (Cambridge: Cambridge University Press, 1990), 397–436.

14 Robert Burton and Holbrook Jackson, *The Anatomy of Melancholy* (New York: New York Review of Books, 2001), I: 374.

15 Thomas Sydenham, *Dissertatio Epistolaris ad Gulielmum Cole, M.D. de Observationibus nuperis circa curationem variolarum confluentium Nec non de Affectione Hysterica Per Tho. Sydenham, M.D.* (London: Walteri Kettilby, 1682), 103, 105, 119, 121f, 123, & 126; Levinus Lemnius, *The Touchstone of Complexions…* (London, 1633), 11; see also Hansruedi Isler, *Thomas Willis, 1621–1675: Doctor and Scientist* (New York: Hafner Publishing, 1968), 135–137; and, Richard Sugg, *Smoke of the Soul: Medicine, Physiology and Religion in Early Modern England* (London: Palgrave Macmillan, 2013), 3–4.

16 Francis Bacon, *Sylva Sylvarum: Or a Naturall Historie. In Ten Centuries… Published after the Authors Death. By William Rawley* (London, 1627), 187; and Levinus Lemnius, *The Touchstone of Complexions…* (London, 1633), 11–13, 24, 78–79, 237–281.

17 James Hart, *ΚΛΙΝΙΚΗ* [Klinike] *or the Diet of the Diseased* (London: J. Beale for R. Allot, 1633), 123.

18 Simeon Partlicius, *A New Method of Physick: Or, a Short View of Paracelsus and Galen's Practice…*; (London: Peter Cole, 1654), 45.

19 Brooke, Humphrey, *Ugieine or a Conservatory of Health….* (London: G. Whittington, 1650), 224–225.

20 Jacques Bos, "The Rise and Decline of Character: Humoral Psychology in Ancient and Modern Medical Theory," *History of the Human Sciences* 22, no. 3 (2009): 29–50.

21 Philippa Maddern, "Murdering Souls and Killing Bodies: Understanding Spiritual and Physical Sin in Late-Medieval English Devotional Works," in *Conjunctions of Mind, Soul, and Body from Plato to the Enlightenment,* edited by Danijela Kambasković (Dordrecht: Springer, 2014), 29–30.

22 Thomas Aquinas, *Summa Theologica,* I.75.4, trans. Fathers of the Dominican Province, revised by Daniel J. Sullivan, *Great Books of the Western World,* edited by Robert Maynard Hutchins, vol. 19 (Chicago: University of Chicago Press, 1954), 381; and, E. Ruth Harvey, *The Inward Wits: Psychological Theory in the Middle Ages and the Renaissance* (London: Warburg Institute, 1975), 54–56; Anthony Kenny, *New History of Western Philosophy* (Oxford: The Clarendon Press, 2010), 191–193; and Fernando Vidal, *The Sciences of the Soul: The Early Modern Origins of Psychology* (Chicago, 2011), 31–32.

23 David Clemis, "Medical Expertise and Understandings of Intoxication in Britain, 1660–1830," in *Intoxication and Society. Problematic Pleasures of Drugs and Alcohol*, eds. Jonathan Herring, Ciaran Regan, Darin Weinberg, and Phil Withington (Basingstoke, 2013), 42–47.

24 David Clemis, "Great Annoyance to Their Mindes": the Humours, Intoxication, and Addiction in English Medical and Moral Discourses, 1550–1730", in *Humorality in Early Modern Art, Material Culture, and Performance,* edited by Kaara L. Peterson and Amy Kenny (Basingstoke: Palgrave/Macmillan, 2021).

25 Barbara S. McCrady and Elizabeth E. Epstein, in Barbara S. McCrady and Elizabeth E. Epstein (eds.), "Introduction," in *Addictions. A Comprehensive Guidebook*, 2nd ed. (Oxford: Oxford University Press, 2013), xix–xx; Suzanne Fraser, David Moore, and Helen Keane, *Habits: Remaking Addiction* (London: Palgrave, 2014), 3; Howard I. Kushner, "Taking Biology Seriously: The Next Task for Historians of Addiction?," *Bulletin of the History of Medicine* lxx, (2006), 115–143.

26 Robert Burton, *The Anatomy of Melancholy* (New York: New York Review of Books, 2001), II: 245; Sajjad H. Rizvi, "Avicenna (Ibn Sina)" in *Internet Encyclopedia of Philosophy*, ISSN 2161–0002, *https://iep.utm.edu/avicenna/;* and, A. S. Sarrafzadeh, et al., "Ibn Sina (Avicenna)" *Neurosurgical Focus* 11, no. 2 (2001): 3.

27 Stephanie Honchell, "Islamic Law," in *The SAGE Encyclopedia of Alcohol. Social, Cultural, and Historical Perspectives,* edited by Scott C. Martin (Thousand Oaks: SAGE Publications, 2015); and, Kathryn Kueny, *The Rhetoric of Sobriety: Wine in Early Islam* (Albany: State University of New York Press, 2001).

28 Mu-Chou Poo, "The Use and Abuse of Wine in Ancient China," *Journal of the Economic and Social History of the Orient* 42, no. 2 (1999): 123–151.

29 Li Bai, "Mountain Drinking Song" https://americanliterature.com/author/li-bai/poem/mountain-drinking-song.

30 Ōtomo Tabito, "Soaking in Sake" trans. Jeffery Bownas and Anthony Thwaite in *Lampham's Quarterly, Intoxication* 6, no.1 (Winter 2013): 26.

31 Yoshida Kendō, *Essays in Idleness*, c. 1330 quoted in *Lampham's Quarterly – Intoxication,* 6 no. 1 (Winter 2013): 147.

32 *The Plum in the Golden Vase or, Chin P'ing Mei,* Vol. 4, *The Climax*, edited by David Tod Roy (Princeton University Press, 2011), 726n. 81; also see Roy, *The Plum in the Golden Vase*, Vol. 1, 464n. 4.

33 *The Plum in the Golden Vase,* Vol. 4, 722n33.

34 Andrew Wear, "Medical Practice in Late Seventeenth- and Early Eighteenth-Century England: Continuity and Change," in *The Medical Revolution of the Seventeenth Century*, edited by Roger French and Andrew Wear (Cambridge: Cambridge University Press, 1989), 294–302; Lindemann, *Medicine and Society*...97–109.

35 Herman Boerhaave, *Dr. Boerhaave's Academical Lectures on the Theory of Physic* (London: W. Innys, 1744), 1:70; also see Cook, "Medicine and the New Philosophy ...", 399.

36 Anon., *An Antidote against Drunkenness; being the Drunkards's Looking Glass*... (London, 1712), 27.

37 Stephen Hales, *A Friendly Admonition to the Drinkers of Brandy, and Other Distilled Spirituous Liquors*.... 2nd ed., (London: Joseph Downing, 1734), 21.

38 Hales, *A Friendly Admonition*, 22.

39 Hales, *A Friendly Admonition*, 8.

40 Hales, *A Friendly Admonition*, 10.

41 James Nicholls, *The Politics of Alcohol: A History of the Drink Question in England* (Manchester: Manchester University Press, 2009); Jessica Warner, *Craze: Gin and Debauchery in an Age of Reason* (New York: Four Walls Eight Windows, 2002); Patrick Dillon, *The Much-Lamented Death of Madam Geneva: The Eighteenth-Century Gin Craze* (London: Review, 2002); and, Peter Clark, "The 'Mother Gin' Controversy in the Early Eighteenth Century," *Transactions of the Royal Historical Society* 38 (1988): 63–84.

42 Benjamin Rush, *An Inquiry into the Effects of Spirituous Liquors on the Human Body* (Boston: Thomas and Andrews, 1790); Thomas Trotter, *De Ebrietate ejusque effectibus in corpus humanum* (M.D. diss. University of Edinburgh, 1788); Thomas Trotter, *An Essay, Medical, Philosophical, and Chemical, on Drunkenness.* 2d ed. (London: Longman, Hurst, Rees, and Orme, 1804); Joseph Hirsh, "Enlightened 18th-century views of the alcohol problem," *Journal of the History of Medicine and Allied Sciences*, 4 (1949): 230–236; Hirsh's work followed the seminal publication: E. M. Jellinek, "Phases in the Drinking History of Alcoholics: Analysis of a Survey Conducted by the Official Organ of

Alcoholics Anonymous," *Quarterly Journal of Studies on Alcohol*, 7 (1946): 1–88. See also E. M. Jellinek, *The Disease Concept of Alcoholism* (New Haven: Hillhouse, 1960); Harry Gene Levine, "The Discovery of Addiction: Changing Conceptions of Habitual Drunkenness in America," *Journal of Studies in Alcohol* 39 (1978): 143–174; Roy Porter, "The Drinking Man's Disease: The Pre-History of Alcoholism in Georgian Britain," *British Journal of Addiction* 80 (1985): 385–396; also see Nicholls, *The Politics of Alcohol*.

43 Heather Beatty, *Nervous Disease in Late Eighteenth-Century Britain: The Reality of a Fashionable Disorder* (London: Pickering & Chatto, 2012), 7–35.

44 David Hartley, *Observations on Man, His Frame, His Duty, and His Expectations* (London: J. Johnson, 1749), 1:393.

45 Erasmus Darwin, *Zoonomia; or, the Laws of Organic Life* (London: J. Johnson, 1796), 1:252; John Coakley Lettsom, *History of Some of the Effects of Hard Drinking* (London: W. Darton and Co., 1789, 7–8.

46 William Cullen, *First lines of the Practice of Physic...* (New-York: J. Crukshank and R. Campbell, Philadelphia, R. Hodge, S. Campbell, and T. Allen, 1793), 2:258–259, 2:273; see also Roy Porter, "Medicine," in *An Oxford Companion to the Romantic Age: British Culture, 1776–1832*, edited by Clara Tuite, Iain McCalman, and Gillian Russell (Oxford: Oxford University Press, 2001), 176.

47 Thomas Trotter, *Essay*, 172. See also Rush, *An Inquiry*; Roy Porter, *Flesh in the Age of Reason* (New York; London: W.W. Norton, 2004), 311–314, 400–401; and Clemis, "Medical Expertise," 44–47.

48 Benjamin Rush, *Medical Inquiries and Observations Upon Diseases of the Mind* (Philadelphia: Kimber & Richardson,, 1835), 261, 264.

49 Robert Macnish, *The Anatomy of Drunkenness* (Glasgow: W.R. McPhun, 1832), vii–viii.

50 William F. Bynum, "Chronic Alcoholism in the First Half of the 19th Century," *Bulletin of the History of Medicine* 42, no. 2 (1968): 171.

51 Carl von Brühl-Cramer, *Ueber die Trunksucht...* (Berlin: Nicolai, 1819), 21–22, quoted in William F. Bynum, "Chronic Alcoholism in the First Half of the 19th Century," *Bulletin of the History of Medicine* 42, no. 2 (1968): 170.

52 Bynum, "Chronic Alcoholism..." 173.

53 Rush, *Ardent Spirits...*, 20.

54 Trotter, *An Essay*, 172.

55 Macnish, *The Anatomy of Drunkenness*, vii–viii.

56 Rush, *Medical Inquiries...*, 261, 265–266.

57 J. Edward Turner, *The History and Pathology of Inebriety* (1854) cited in T. D. Crothers, *Sketch of the Late Dr. J. Edward Turner, the Founder of Inebriate Asylums* (Hartford, 1889), 7.

58 J. Edward Turner, *History of the New York Inebriate Asylum* (New York: J. Edward Turner, 1888), 27.

59 This work includes: Brian Howard Harrison, *Drink and the Victorians; the Temperance Question in England, 1815–1872* (Pittsburgh: University of Pittsburgh Press, 1971); J. Blocker, *American Temperance Movements Cycles of Reform* (Boston: Twayne, 1989); Susanna Barrows and Robin Room, *Drinking: Behavior and Belief in Modern History* (Berkeley: University of California Press, 1991); Nicholls, *The Politics of Alcohol.....*

60 Bynum, "Chronic Alcoholism..." 174; Valverde, *Diseases of the Will...*, 68–95.

61 Mariana Valverde, ""Slavery from Within': The Invention of Alcoholism and the Question of Free Will," *Social History* 22, no. 3 (1997): 267–268; Mariana Valverde, *Diseases of the Will: Alcohol and the Dilemmas of Freedom* (Cambridge; New York: Cambridge University Press, 1998), 68–94.

62 Griffith Edwards, "The Trouble with Drink: Why Ideas Matter," *Addiction*, 105 (2009): 800.

63 Levine, "The discovery of addiction," 144.

64 Keane, "Addiction: Critical Reflections," 370.

65 Research Council on Problems of Alcohol. Scientific Committee and E. M. Jellinek, *Alcohol Addiction and Chronic Alcoholism* (New Haven: Yale University Press, 1942); E. M. Jellinek, "Phases in the Drinking History of Alcoholics: Analysis of a Survey Conducted by the Official Organ of Alcoholics Anonymous," *Quarterly Journal of Studies on Alcohol* 7 (1946): 1–88.; and, E. M. Jellinek, *The Disease Concept of Alcoholism*.

66 Valverde, *Diseases of the Will*, 110–111.

67 Joseph W. Schneider, "Deviant Drinking as Disease: Alcoholism as a Social Accomplishment," *Social Problems* 25, no. 4 (1978): 365–369; Craig Reinarman, "Addiction as Accomplishment: The Discursive Construction of Disease," *Addiction Research & Theory* 13, no. 4 (2005): 313; Edwards, "The Trouble with Drink" 801.

68 Valverde, *Diseases of the Will*, 114–119.
69 "Substance-Related and Addictive Disorders," in *Diagnostic and Statistical Manual of Mental Disorders,* DSM Library: American Psychiatric Association, 2013. http://library.mtroyal.ca:3420/doi/full/10.1176/appi.books.9780890425596.dsm16#CHDIBCJD; and, "Mental and behavioural disorders due to psychoactive substance use (F10-F19)" in "Chapter V, Mental and behavioural disorders (F00-F99) in WHO, *International Statistical Classification of Diseases and Related Health Problems,* 10th Revision, 2015, http://apps.who.int/classifications/icd10/browse/2015/en#.
70 Darin Weinberg, "Praxis, Interaction and the Loss of Self-Control," in *Intoxication and Society. Problematic Pleasures of Drugs and Alcohol*, edited by Ciaran Regan Jonathan Herring, Darin Weinberg, and Phil Withington (Basingstoke: Palgrave Macmillan, 2013), 232.
71 "Substance-Related and Addictive Disorders."
72 Room, "The Cultural Framing," 224–228; and, Keane, "Addiction", 375–377.
73 Fraser, *Habits*, 27. For popular reception neuroscience brain disease accounts, see Jeffery Kluger, ed., *The Science of Addiction* (New York: Time/ Meredith Corporation, 2019); and, Fran Smith, "The Science of Addiction," *National Geographic* (September 2017): 30–55.
74 Nora D. Volkow and Marisela Morales, "The Brain on Drugs: From Reward to Addiction," *Cell* 162, no. 4 (2015): 712.
75 Keane, "Addiction," 373; and Reinarman, "Addiction as Accomplishment..." 309.
76 Weinberg, "Praxis," 234.
77 Weinberg, "Praxis," 234.
78 Volkow, "The Brain on Drugs," 712.
79 Keane, "Addiction," 372.
80 Weinberg, "Praxis," 235.
81 Volkow, "The Brain on Drugs," 712; see also McCrady and Epstein, 'Introduction,' xix–xx; Fraser, *Habits,* 3; and, Kushner, 'Taking Biology Seriously," 115–143.
82 Jeffrey Stephen Poland and George Graham, *Addiction and Responsibility* (Cambridge, Mass., 2011), 3; Marc Lewis, *The Biology of Desire: Why Addiction Is Not a Disease* (Toronto: Doubleday Canada, 2015), 11–22.
83 Katherine Parker and Eckhard Kessler, 'The Concept of Psychology', in *The Cambridge History of Renaissance Philosophy*, edited by Charles B. Schmitt and Quentin Skinner (Cambridge: Cambridge University Press, 1988), 455–463.

INDEX

Note: **Bold** page numbers refer to tables; *italic* page numbers refer to figures and page numbers followed by "n" denote endnotes.

Abdulkarim, A. 52
academic conferences, as drinking sites 181–184
'acid house' 134, 138n6
acid house party Bill 128, 134
acid rain 252
actor network theory (ANT) 205, 206, 265
acute intoxication 321
Adam *see* ecstasy
adaptational psychodynamics 312
addiction 311, 312, 347, 485; amphetamine-type stimulants 414; Cheever's evocative allegory of 74; defined 311; Dimedrol 213–214; heroin 213–214; as historical problem 581–582; methadone 205; nicotine 463; opiate 24–25; tea 564–577; theories of 587–589
Addiction Research Center (ARC) 311–314, 320, 322n3
Addictive Consumption: Capitalism, Modernity and Excess (Reith, 2018) 90
Adekeye, O.A. 52
Adler, M. 166
adulteration 109
Afghanistan 247
Africa: Brazil's importation of African slaves 361–362; drug use in 51–53; Khat in 400; Zulus 243
age 183, 299, 316–317
Agora 103, 106
agorism 109
Albayrak, E. 239
alcohol 20, 73, 161, 242; abstinence from 185; in colonial Brazil 361–365; modernity and the racialization of drinking behaviors in post-abolition Brazil 373–377; and paradoxes of liberalism in post-independence Brazil 365–373; prohibition 27; rituals 294–295; use in workplace 179–181
alcohol by volume (ABV) 169
alcohol-fuelled violence 490
Alcohol Health Alliance Ireland 536, 537
alcoholic drinks and social class 118
alcoholic psychosis 532
Alcoholics Anonymous (AA) 296, 471, 529, 591, 595n42
alcoholism 503, 530, 532, 546, 590–591
Alcoholismus chronicus 591
alcohol policy discourse 484–496
alcohol violence 496
Aldridge, J. 338
ale 21, 114, 116, 120, 121, 503
Alexander, B. 29
Allenby, E. 249
Allik, M. 440
All Party Parliamentary Groups (APPGs) 447
altered consciousness 178
Altered State (Collin, M.) 129
altered states 310, 501–519
Alternative London 136
Altheida, D. 443
American Homebrewers Association 114, 115
American Psychiatric Association 346, 473, 592
Amis, M. 70, 72
amphetamine 51, 245–246
amphetamine democracy 245
amphetamine-type stimulants (ATS) 243, 246, 412; "after-effects" discourse 428–429; psychopathological features 428–430;

smuggling 427; symbolic meaning 428–430; as symbol of outlaw economy 427–428
Amundsen, R. 244
The Anatomy of Courage (Moran, L.) 241
The Anatomy of Melancholy (Burton, R.)584
Anslinger, H.J. 24, 314
Anstie, F.E. 275, 276, 511
antidote 314
anti-khat campaign 401
Anti-Narcotic League 162
Antin, T.M.J. 266–267
anti-smoking movement 23–24
anxiety-situational reaction type 429, 431n9
Anyanwu, O.U. 52
Apperson, G.L. 170
appraisal discourse 419–420
Aquinas, T. 595n22
ARC *see* Addiction Research Center (ARC)
Arensberg, C.M. 530, 531
Aristotle 96, 291
Ariyama, N. 418
Arlidge, J.T. 566, 567, 572, 574
Armstrong, L. 22
arrhythmias 264
Asahi Shinbun 413
Asberg, C. 458
Aschenbrandt, T. 243–244
Asia 24, 204, 568
Atkinson, A.M. 445
atropine 249–250
ATS *see* amphetamine-type stimulants (ATS)
ATS control: after 1954 campaign 425–426; campaign 424–426; condemnation of groups in late 1940s 415; condemnation of specific people 416–417; conversion of medical research 417–420; demand for control by medical doctors 415; in Japan 412–431; Kyoko Incident 1954 424; nationalist discourse 424–425; political factors and ATS in 1950s 422–423; problem after WWII 414–415; Stimulant Control Law of 1951 421–422; youth problem and reason for 420–422
Australia: LGBTQ+ in 273–274; methadone treatment in 206; vapers in 34
Australian alcohol policy discourse, handling complexity in: approach 485–486; method 486–487; policy stakeholder 489–494; policy texts 487–489
Azbel, M.F. 197

The Bacchae 468
Bacchi, C. 208, 440
Bacchus 596n9
Bacon, S.D. 301
Bailey, R. 513
Bales, R. 530, 531
Balfour, C.L. 545
"balloon effect" 470
Bancroft, A. 37, 40, 97, 178, 187, 328, 345, 346, 463
Barad, K. 345
barbiturates 314
Barnaby Rudge (1841) 547
Barnett, R. 264, 266
Bassi, K. 29n1, 30n2
Bataille, G. 89
Baumann, G. 290, 401
BBC online 452
The Beatles 22
Beccaria, F. 297
Becker, H.S. 35, 54, 60, 63, 292
Beck, J. 132
Beecher, H.K. 314, 316
The Beer Academy 118
beer gardens 8
beer geek 121
Behan, B. 23
behavioral pharmacology 316–317
Bell, D. 96
Bell, E. 182
Bell, K. 463
Benci, J. 365
Benjamin, W. 30n5
Bennett, J. 169
Bentbaša, Sarajevo 147
Bentsen, L. 132
Benzedrine 245
Berger, B. 29
Berlant, L. 464, 465
Berman, D. 131
Berreman, G.D. 300
Berryman, J. 72
Biden, J. 136
Big Data 91, 95
Bigelow, G. 317
Big Food 94–95
Big Gambling 95–96
'big G' model 494
binge drinking 502
Bishop, E. 72, 74, 79
Bishop's Beer 169
Black, W.T. 570
Blitzkrieg 244
Bluelight 330, 339n1
Blue, S. 34, 265
Boak, J. 513
Boerhaave, H. 587
Boettke, P. 481n12
bootlegging 312
Booze Britain 512
Bordo, S. 98
Bosnia: coffee consumption in 143–156; coffee cultures 144
The Bottle (1847) 551

Bourdieu, P. 119
Bourgois, P. 408
Bourke, J. 572
The Boys in the Band (Crowley 1968) 277
Braddon, M.E. 550
Brain, K. 92
Braudel, F. 23
Braun, V. 55
Brazil 144; alcohol and paradoxes of liberalism in post-independence 365–373; alcohol in colonial 361–365; craft beer consumers in 120; modernity and the racialization of drinking behaviors in post-abolition 373–377
Brennan, T. 241
Bretherton, G. 527, 528
BrewDog 502, 513–516
Brewery, K. 519n4
brewpubs 115–117
Bridget Jones's Diary (Fielding, 1996) 80
Bridgman, T. 181
Britain: governing excess in twentieth-century 510–513
British Medical Journal 570
The Brontë sisters 546–549
Brooke, H. 585
Brown, E. 568
Brown, P. 122
Bruno, R. 70, 73
Brunton, L. 570
Brussels Conference Act (1890) 473
Bucerius, S.M. 408
Buchanan, D. 394
'Buddha of euphoria' 136
Bukowski, C. 77
Bulls, J. 543
Bunyan, J. 71
buprenorphine 198
Bureau of Narcotics 25
Burns, R. 72
Burroughs, W. 91, 92
Burton, R. 584, 585, 595n14, 597n26
Business for Punks (Watt, 2015) 514
Butler, J. 273, 345
Byron, L. 72

cachaça 361, 362, 364, 369, 374
cafés 143, 146, 150, 155, 160, 161, 165
caffeine 95, 161, 163, 182, 565
Cailbault, I. 445
caipirinha 364
Californian Department of Public Health 36
Calvin, J. 505
Campaign for Real Ale (CAMRA) 115, 118, 120, 121, 514
Campbell, C. 91
Campbell, J. 301
CAMRA *see* Campaign for Real Ale (CAMRA)
Canada: collective lifestyles of smoking 266; drug-related deaths in 439, 441; MDMA in 130
cannabis 24, 51, 52, 195, 249–250; hotspots 387, 389; legalisation 122; in medicines 24; in Nigeria 383–385; use among street-involved youths 382–396; in warfare 249–50
capital destruction 166
capitalism 91, 96–97
Caputo, P. 248
'carefully managed hedonism' 97
Caribelli, G. 146
Carpenter, W.B. 546, 549
Carpentier, C. 192
Carrier, N.C. 400
Carry on Jeeves (Wodehouse, 1925) 72
cat-eye pills 245
Catholicism 471, 505, 516
Center for Psychedelic and Consciousness Research 26
Central Control Board (CCB) 510
Centre for Social Justice (CSJ) 447
Chaldeans 249
champagne 118
Champion, S. 127
Chandler, R. 72
Chapman, N.G. 121
charka 242
Cheever, J. 69, 74, 75, 77, 81
cheffir 248
Chemical Weapons Convention (CWC) 240
chemosocialities 463
Child Messenger Act (1901) 171
Children's Act (1908) 171
China: Taiping Rebellion 250; tea 576; tobacco 167–168
Chinese Nationalist Party 422
chronic addiction 309
chronic barbiturate intoxication 313–314
chronic drinking 582–583, 585–592
Chronicle of Higher Education 183, 185
chronic volunteers 315
Churchill, W. 241
Cielemęcka, O. 458
cigarette smoking 458, 463, 465
citizens: as consumers 29; as workers 29
Civil War 247
clandestineness 240
Clarke, V. 55
Clemis, D. 543, 595n23
Clinton, B. 247
close-fistedness 167
Clua-García, R. 223, 230, 234, 236
Cobbett, M.P.W. 567
cocaine 52, 226, 244, 250
CODA 27–29
codeine 57

coffee: as mourning 152–155; as social stimulant 145–147; on street 150–152
coffeehouse 145, 146, 163, 164
Cohen, S. 128, 442
Cold War 22, 143, 249–253
Coleridge, S. 90
collective lifestyles framework 266
Collin, M. 129
Collins, A.B. 446
Collins, R.L. 69
Collins, W. 545–550
colonialism 28
commensal hospitality 166
Committee on Drug Addiction and Narcotics (CDAN) 311, 315
Committee on Problems of Drug Dependence 312
commodification 90–93, 105–106
commodities 7, 22, 28, 90–93, 95, 96, 99, 102, 169
communitas 296–297
Comprehensive Drug Control Act 24
Confessions of an English Opium Eater (deQuincey, T.) 90
"consciousness of induced consciousness" 29
conservatism: ritual and 299–300
constructive drinking 292, 299
contemporary imprisonment 194
Controlled Substances Act 132
Cooke, M.G. 71
Cooney, J.E. 575
Cooney, J.G. 534
COPD 320
Cope, N. 194
coping with stress 40
corporate interests 7
cortisol 288n3
Cosgrave, E.M. 526, 527, 530
counter-corporealisation 287
counterperceptions 147
counter-reformation 504
Courtwright, D. 28, 161, 169
Couty, L. 372, 373
COVID-19 461
craft beer 113
craft drinks: connoisseurship and intoxication 119–122; emergence of 113, 115; revolution 115–117; taste and status 117–119
craving and 'the bliss point' 94–95
Creasy, W. 250
Cree, J. 582, 583
Crewe, B. 193, 194, 197, 198
crime syndicate 426
Criminal Code (1830) 367
criminalization 371
Criminal Justice and Public Order Act (1994) 135
Critchlow, B. 277
Croatia 147
Cruikshank, G. 545, 551, 552
Crusoe in England (1976) 79, 80
cryptomarkets 102–104, 107–109
crystal-meth *see* methamphetamine
Csikszentmihályi, M. 96
Cullen, J. 526
Cullen, W. 589
cultural capital 8, 26, 114, 116, 183, 342
cultural competence 401, 406
cultural remission 295
culture: and ritual 292–293; of sharing 198
cultures of intoxication 128
Curry, R. 79
Curto, J. 362

Da Ali G Show 135
D'Abernon, L. 510
Dalton, S. 78
Danesbury House (Wood, 1860) 545, 549, 558
Dangerous Drugs Act (1920) 25
Daniels, J. 444
Darcy, C. 53
Darwin, E. 543, 546, 589
Darwin, H. 121, 515
Das, V. 395
Datura stramonium see James-Town Weed
David Copperfield (Dickens, 1849) 71
Davies, N. 442–443
Dayton Peace Agreement (DPA) 150, 155
DCR *see* drug consumption room (DCR)
Dean, G. 534
Defence of the Realm Act 474
degeneration theory 373
Deleuze, G. 168
delirium tremens 546, 558
Deller, J. 128
Delmestri, G. 118
Demant, J. 303
Dennis, N. 166
Dennis, S. 265
Department of Health and Human Services 33
depressants 247
depression 57
deQuincey, T. 90
deranging gas 253
de-ritualisation 300–301
Derrida, J. 89
Dertadian, G. 63
desafricanization of Brazil 368
designer drugs 92
desire 311–313
detoxification 464
deviance disavowal 277, 278
dextroamphetamine 245, 246
džezve 147, 149, *149*

dhikir/zikir 145
diamorphine 104, 320
Dickens, C. 71, 161, 167, 169, 545–549, 552, 553, 556, 557, 560n27
Dietler, M. 166, 172
Dimedrol 208, 211–217
dimethyltryptamine (DMT) 330, 332
Dionysus 468, 469, 474, 583
dipsomania 590
Dirisu, O. 52
Discursive Constructionism 413
disease 529–534, 546; and alcoholism 590–591; concept 523, 525, 527, 534, 591, 592; meanings of 591–594
Disease Concept of Alcoholism (Jellinek, 1960) 512
dis/inhibition 275–276, 286
divine madness 472
DIY (Do It Yourself) therapy 332
DMT: The Spirit Molecule (documentary) 332
The doors of perception (1954/2010) 328
Douglas, M. 105, 118, 299
Drapes, T. 572
DRDs *see* drug-related deaths (DRDs)
Dream Songs (1969) 72
drinking: banal 293; constructive 292, 299; cultures 14, 116, 290–291, 302, 502, 524; Mediterranean 294; modernity and the racialization, in post-abolition Brazil 373–377; ritual 293; vertical 510; at work 179–181
drinking places 159–160; atmosphere 170; commensality 164–165; expanded sites, mobile objects 171–172; gift of drink 166–167; hospitality 164–165; and intoxicants, 1850–1950 161–163; material culture 166; material engagements 168–170; public places and intoxication 163–164; sociability 164–165
drinking studies network 502, 519n1
drug: commodification 105–106; definition 364; distribution 101–102; intoxicating consumption 91–93; making 104–105; self-administration 317; social organisation and 196–198
drug abusing immigrants 409
Drug Addiction Rehabilitation Center (DARC) 431n8
drug consumption room (DCR): in Copenhagen, Denmark 224–225; establishment 222; H17 224–233; harm-reduction service 221; institutional space and drug scene 228; legislation 228; modes of use 233–235; risk minimization 222; as safe and legitimate place 227–228; Skyen 224; social setting for using drugs 228–231; time slots 232–233; trade-offs 221, 223, 230, 233, 236
drug consumption rooms (DCRs) 442
drug control 26–27; beneficiaries 478–480; Christian condemnation to psychiatric evaluation 471–473; cultural values and secular control 473–474; divine warning to prohibitionists 468–471; feedback loop 477–478; international 474–475
drug control system 13, 384, 468, 470, 477–478
drug dealers 101–103, 438, 478
drug dealing, in prisons 197
drug dependence 312, 322n9
drug distribution markets 7
Drug Enforcement Administration (DEA) 130, 132
drug foods 90, 92
drug free world 469
drug policy 469
drug potency 104, 106–108
drug-related crime 27, 191–192
drug-related deaths (DRDs) 437, 438; competing paradigms 440–442; local coverage of drugs issues and 450, **451**; media framing 442–447; national coverage 447, **448–449**; online and TV coverage of local events and action 452; prohibitionist/abstinence 441; regulation/harm reduction 441–442; rising rates of 439–440; vulnerability 442
Drugs Deaths Taskforce 453
drug trafficking 384
drug use: before, during and after imprisonment 191–193; by combatants 241–248; gendering of 52–53; motivations for 193–196; in Nigeria 51–53
The Drunkard (MacNeice, 1946) 83
The Drunkard's Children (1848) 551
drunk as a Pole 502–510
drunken comportment 10, 276, 292, 297, 595
drunken deportment 170
drunkenness 19, 20, 26, 90, 178, 344, 346, 366, 504, 586; chronic 546, 547; determined 92, 114
DSM's criteria 592–593
Dublin Journal of Medical Science 526
Duff, C. 170
Duis, P. 164
Duncan, T. 223
Dundee's Drugs Crisis 452
Dunlap, E. 395
DuPois, M. 99
Durkheim, E. 70, 290, 300
Duster, T. 24, 25, 29n1
dysphoria 285, 316

Earleywine, M. 69, 75
Earnshaw, S. 73, 77
East Lynne (Wood, 1860) 545
Ebel, E. 367
e-cigarettes 36, 48, 463
Economic and Social Research Institute (ESRI) 533

ecstasy 93; before the rave, 1912–1985 130–132; criminalisation 132; cultural trappings 128; and dance culture in UK, 1986–2009 132–136; emergence of 130; *see also* 3,4-methylene-dioxy-meth-amphetamine (MDMA)
Edgerton, R.B. 276, 292, 295, 344
EDM (Electronic Dance Music) 129
Edmundo, L. 375
Edwards, H. 568
The Effects Can Last Forever campaign 128, 134, 135
E is for Ecstasy 136
electronic gaming machines (EGMs) 95
electronic nicotine delivery systems (ENDS) 262
Eliot, G. 544–549, 558
Elliot, E. 395
Elster, J. 70
emotion 57
endorphins 178
Energy Flash (Reynolds, S.) 129
Engels, F. 554
Enghoff, O. 338
England: cocaine use 25; ecstasy and dance culture in 132–136; tobacco in 23
Enlightenment 29
Erowid 330, 339n1
"ethnic cleansing" campaign 152
ethnicity 4, 12, 146, 150, 401–403, 407–409
ethnified intoxication 401
euphoria 178–179, 312, 315–316
Euripides 468
Europe: beer-laden porridge 20–21; drinking cultures in 501–519; drug-related deaths 439; drug use before, during and after imprisonment 191–193; immigration 373; khat use in 400; methadone implementation in 204; smoking in 162
European Court of Human Rights 156n8
Everybody In the Place 128
excess 290–292, 481n1, 501, 581; BrewDog 513–516; craft beer 513–516; governance of 502, 510–513; navigating boundaries in Europe's long Reformation 503–506; social norm to national problem 502–510
'the experience economy' 90–91
Eyal, N. 91
Ezzell, M.B. 53

The Face (magazine) 132, 133
Facebook 92
Factotum (1975) 77
Family and Community in Ireland (Arensberg & Kimball) 531
Fanon, F. 373
Farrugia, A. 345, 356n1
fatigue rum 242
Fear and Loathing in Las Vegas 334
female drunkard 554–558
femininity 7, 52, 56, 64, 76, 81, 121
fentanyl 106, 447
Ferentzy, P. 595n6
The Ferret 452
Ferriter, D. 525, 527, 532
feudalism 426–427
Fielding, H. 80, 543
Fiesta: The Sun Also Rises (Hemingway, 1926) 79
fildžani 147, 149
Finalise Early (FE) 107
Findley, J. 317
Fiorucci Made Me Hardcore 128
Fischler, C. 165
Fitzgerald, F.S. 77, 78
Flack, W. 116
Fleetwood, J. 392
Foan shobun 429
Fogel, C. 63
food 7, 23, 90–96, 152, 172, 179, 183, 387, 565
Forced March 244
Foucault, M. 97, 274–276, 280, 290, 460
Foxx, A.J. 185
Franco-Prussian War 247
Franklin, B. 20
Frank, V.A. 346, 347
Fraser, S. 206, 347, 355, 445, 453, 485, 487, 489, 495, 595n2
Frederico Leopoldo Cezar Burlamarqui 371
French cafés 164
Frenetzy, P. 582
Freudian movement 529
Frew, E. 184
Freyre, G. 368
Frohlich, K.L. 266
Frydl, K.J. 28
Fukushima, A. 429
Fukuyama, F. 515
functional intoxication 37–41, 463

Galen 503, 584
Galenic Medical Paradigm 583–584
Galenic medicine 584, 587
Galenism 583–587
gambling 22, 95–96, 312
Gaskell, E. 555
gender and class 550–551
General Headquarters/Supreme Commander for the Allied Powers (GHQ/SCAP) 422
George Cruikshank's Fairy Library (1853) 552
Gerich, J. 75
Germany: drinking places 163; drug consumption room in 223; drug-related deaths in 439; MDMA in 130, 136
Giddens, A. 91, 266
Giffort, D. 25, 322n1

Gilbert, P. 549
Gillespie, D. 22
gin craze 543, 550, 560n19, 589
Gin Lane and Beer Street 543
Gissing, G. 558
Glenn, N.M. 266
Global North 90
glocalisation 129
Goddard, T. 408
Goffman, E. 27, 266, 273
Golub, A. 395
Gomart, E. 344
Good Beer Guide 118
Goodbye to Berlin (Isherwood, 1939) 79
Goodman, E. 249
Good Morning, Midnight (Rhys, 1939) 79
Goodwin, S. 208
Goody, J. 294
Gorski, P. 28
Gough, J.B. 162, 548
governance 96–98
governmentality 97, 207, 266
Grace, S. 195
Graham, H. 40
Great British Beer Festival 118
The Great Good Place (Oldenburg, 1989) 164
Green, C.D. 574
Greene, L.W. 250
Greenwood, R. 118
Gregg, M. 180
grey zone 180–181
Grindr 280
Grundetjern, H. 386
The Guardian (newspaper) 135
Gulf War 245
Gurr, E. 452
Gusfield, J.R. 23, 92, 430, 516
Guthman, J. 99
gutter-water 54

H17 224–233; *see also* drug consumption room (DCR)
Habermas, J. 163
Habitual Drunkards Act 526
habitual drunkenness 546
habitus 386
Habsburg 144, 146, 147
Hague International Opium Convention (1912) 240
Haig, A. 571
Haight, G.S. 552
Haines-Saah, R.J. 266
Haine, W.S. 164
Hajdarpašić, E. 146, 156n6
Hales, S. 543, 588, 595n37
Hamilton, J. 162
Hamilton, P. 76
Hammer, J. 514
Hangi, A. 147
hangovers 69–83
Hangover Square (Hamilton, 1941) 76
Hanson, V.D. 242
Hard Times (1854) 548
Hardy, T. 71
Haritavorn, N. 386
harm 9, 13, 42, 48, 103, 128, 186, 385
harm reduction approach 441–442
Harrison, B. 545
Harrison Narcotic Act (1914) 25
Harris, S. 537
Harrisson, T. 166
Hartley, D. 589
Haskin, D. 556
Hattox, R. 146
Hayward, K. 512
Heads of National Drug Law Enforcement Agencies (HONLEA) 479
healthism 464
Heath, D.B. 294, 297, 298, 530
hedonism 101–109
Heggie, V. 570
Hemingway, E. 79
Henderson, E.F. 182
Henley, J. 513
Hennion, A. 344
Henry, J. 135
hepatitis C 27, 203
heroin 104–106, 195, 208, 209, 212, 224, 247
Herring, J. 70
Herzegovina, coffee consumption in 143–156
heterotopia 283
Higo, M. 420
Hilton, M. 161
Himmelsbach, C.K. 311, 320
Hippocrates 584
historical representations 581–599
HIV/AIDS 27, 203, 274
Hobbs, D. 512
Hofmann, A. 328, 332
Hogarth 543
Holmes, C.H. 573
Home Rule 525
Home Salon 169
homosexuality 275
Horimi, T. 416
Horowitz, V. 22
hotspots 387, 389
House Selected Committee on Crime 245
How to Build Habit-Forming Products (Eyal, 2014) 91
Hromadžić, A. 150–152
Hubbard, P. 116
HuffPost 452
Hunt, G. 198, 267, 345, 347

Hussein, S. 246
Huss, M. 546, 591
Huxley, A. 25, 328
hyper consumption 91
hyper-masculinity 492, 493

Illicit Drug Anti-Proliferation Act (2003) 136
imprisonment 367; motivations for drug use 193–196; pains of 193–196; prevalence of drug use before, during and after 191–193; social organisation and drugs 196–198
impulse neurosis 312
incarceration 392
In Darkest England And The Way Out (Booth, W.) 162
Indian Hemp Act (1975) 384
Indigenous people 374
The Information (Amis, 1995) 70, 72
Ingbar, Y. 75
inquiry discourse 420
Inside Higher Education (Layton, R.) 184, 185
intellectualisation 118
Intensive Care Unit (ICU) 319
internalized moral principle 70, 73
International drug control 474–475
International Narcotics Control Board (INCB) 471, 475
International Opium Convention (1912) 474
intoxicated self 594–595
intoxicating environments 92, 95
intoxication: definition of 19–20, 178, 355; and femininity 7, 52, 56, 64, 76, 121; and masculinity 62–64; territory of 20
intoxication practices, challenging and changing 184–186
intoxigenic digital spaces 92
Iraq 247
Ireland: drinking culture 523–538; Home Rule 525, 538n3
Ireland Sober, Ireland Free 524–529
Irish Free State 529
Irish Home Rule 525, 538n3
Irish Medical Association 530
Irish National Council on Alcoholism (INCA) 533, 535
The Irish News 452
Irish Pioneer Total Abstinence Association 526, 532
ironic intoxication 343
Isbell, H. 313, 314
Isherwood, C. 79
Istanbul 137, 145, 154, 164

Jackson, C. 81, 245
Jackson, H. 595n14
Jacobs, W.W. 167
James-Town Weed 249
Jane Eyre (Reed, 1847) 547
Japan, ATS control in: ATS problem after WWII 414–415; campaign 424–426; Kyoko Incident 1954 424; medical research 417–420; methods 413; moral judgment and medical knowledge 415–417; political factors 422–423; second wave of epidemic and crime syndicates 426–428; Stimulant Control Law of 1951 421–422; symbolic meaning of ATS 428–430; youth problem and reason for 420–422
Japanese Communist Party 422
Japanese Medical Association 417
Japanese Miracle 428
Japanese National Diet 413, 415
Japan-Korea Treaty of 1905 431n5
Jarvinnen, J. 97
Jauffret-Roustide, M. 445
Jellinek, E.M. 512, 529, 592, 594
Jenkins, R. 401, 407
Jennings, P. 511, 512, 515, 547
Jessica's First Prayer (Stretton, 1866) 545
Jews 298, 509
jimsonweed *see* James-Town Weed
Joe-Laidler, K. 129, 137
John Barleycorn: Alcoholic Memoirs (London, 1913) 73
Johnson, O. 52
Jolley, C. 319
Jones, G. 132
José da Silva Lisboa 366
Journal of the American Medical Association (JAMA) 316
Juul 36, 48

kafići 150, 151
Karasch, M. 369
Kasamatsu, A. 419
Keane, H. 34, 35, 45, 48, 265, 345–347, 355, 463, 595n2, 598n64
Keating, M.F. 531
Kennedy, A.L. 81
Kennedy, P. 241
Kerr, N. 526, 530, 591, 592, 594
ketamine 129, 136, 137
"ketjubung" 250
khat: anti-khat campaign 401; association with somali community in Sweden 400–410; negative effects 401; pleasurable effects 400
khat cafés 400
Khoshnood, K. 394
'kilns' 159
Kimball, S.T. 530, 531
King, D. 182
King James 23
Klantschnig, G. 384, 400
Klee, G. 251
Klein, A. 385, 389, 401

Kleist, N. 402, 405
Klinenberg, E. 165
Koch, E.S. 120
Kofyar 296
Kohn, M. 25
koknar 248
Kolb, L. 311, 316
Kolte, B. 261
Koob, G. 321
Korean War 245, 250, 431n6
Kublai Khan (Coleridge, S.) 90
Kurino, R. 419
Kyoko Incident 1954 424
Kyrgyz prisons, methadone treatment in: analysis 208; methadone-Dimedrol 211–217; methadone in relation to heroin 208–211; methods 206–208; theoretical approach 205–206

Lady Audley's Secret (Braddon, 1862) 549–550
Laing, R.D. 133
Lamb, C. 548
Langhamer, C. 511
Larney, S. 192
Lasagna, L. 316
Lashar-e-Taiba 246
Latham, A. 165, 168, 169
Latour, B. 168, 485
Law Enforcement Against Prohibition (LEAP) 481n11
Law, J., 485, 491, 494
Layton, J. 165
Layton, R. 184
League of Nations 24
Leary, T. 25, 131
Leckey, M. 128
Lefebvre, H. 264
legal highs 92, 93, 136
Lemass, S. 531, 532
Lemon, R. 582, 583
Lennox, A. 132
lethal dose (LD) 317
Lettsom, J.C. 548, 589
Levine, H.G. 20, 28, 29, 29n1, 591–592, 598n63
LGBTQ+ 272, 273; dis/inhibition 275–276; licentious conduct 276–278; sexual drifting 278–280; uninhibited play 281–286
Li Bai 587
liberalism 365–373
Liboiron, M. 460, 465
licening 519n3
The Life and Death of Mr. Badman (Bunyan, 1680) 71
limbic capitalism 28
liminality 294–296, 300
liminoid 301–303
Lipton, B. 186
liquid courage 242
Livesey, J. 545
Lloyd, C. 192, 195, 196
Lloyd's of London 187
local coverage, of drug-related deaths 450, **451**
Lock, M. 395
London, J. 73, 74
The Lost Weekend (Chandler, 1944) 72, 81
Lowborough, L. 548
Lo Yü-jen 587
LSD *see* lysergic acid diethylamide (LSD)
Lucherini, M.C. 266
Luhmann, N. 13
lutheranism 505
Luther, M. 504, 505, 516
lysergic acid diethylamide (LSD) 25–26, 131, 239, 252, 284, 285, 330, 331, 335

MacAndrew, C. 276, 344
MacArthur, D. 422
MacNeice, L. 83
Macnish, R. 546, 548, 558, 590
mafrish 400
Magnan, V. 373
Maguire, S. 120
Maher, C. 63
Mainichi Shinbun 413
Mair, J. 184
Malcolm, E. 525–528
Malins, P. 267, 268
Malungo 362
marijuana 24, 35, 55, 251; *see also* cannabis
Marijuana Tax Act (1937) 24
market exchange 101
Markham, F. 95
Marković, I. 264
Martin Chuzzlewit (1842–1844) 552
Mary Barton (1848) 548, 555
masculinity 53, 76; construction and reinforcement 62–63
Mass Observation 166, 167, 173, 511
mass sexual assault incident 431n4
Matthee, R. 163, 164
Mauss, M. 166
The Mayor of Casterbridge (Hardy, 1886) 71, 553
McAllister, A. 545, 560n21
McAndrew, C. 292, 295
McCormack, D. 168, 169
McCormack, K. 543
McCready, G. 267
McDonagh, M. 571
McDonaldisation of beer 115
McFarland, F.E. 527
McKay, G. 135
McKirnan, D.J. 274
McQuoid, J. 34, 45

MDMA *see* 3,4-methylene-dioxy-meth-amphetamine (MDMA)
meanings of drunkenness 12, 591–594
Measham, F. 52, 92, 97
the media 12, 51, 64, 251, 403, 407, 437–453
The Medical Pioneer (1892–1897) 546
The Medical Temperance Journal (1869–1892) 546
Medico-Social Research Board 533, 534
Meier, P.S. 33
Meiji Restoration 431n7
Mellor, P.A. 301
Melville, C. 135
Melville, H. 73
Mendoza, S. 444
Menninger, K. 548
Mental Treatment Bill 530
mescaline 131
methadone: and Dimedrol 211–217; in Kyrgyz prisons 203–218; psychological effects 214–217; in relation to heroin 209–210; as taking over body 210–211; withdrawal 209
methamphetamine 57, 244, 413, 415, 430n2
methodological considerations 329–337
3,4 methylenedioxyamphetamine (MDA) 130
3,4-methylene-dioxy-meth-amphetamine (MDMA) 105, 127, 130, 137n1, 283, 284, 476
mild intoxication 184
Miller, J. 546, 558
Millier, B.C. 79–80
Mill, J.S. 96
Milloy, M.J. 192
Minas do Ouro 362
Minas Gerais 362, 365
minority stress 273, 275
Mireour du Monde 504
Misuse of Drugs Act 1971 133
Mjåland, N. 198
mlinovi 147, 149, *149*
modafinil 246
moderation 10, 13, 71, 90, 116, 120, 186, 343, 352, 355, 501–504, 516
modern consumption 91
modernisation 290
Mol, A. 485, 491, 494
mood changes 316
Moore, D. 35, 595n2
moral careers 23–26
moral panic 128, 134, 442, 550
Moran, L. 241
Morel, B. 373
more-than-human theory 264–265
Morgan, P. 131
morphine 25, 247, 311
morphine abstinence syndrome 311
Moss, S. 170, 173
Muraven, M. 69, 75
Murphy, S. 29n1
Murray, E.J. 531
Muslim 145, 146, 150, 152
Musto, D.F. 407
Mystical Experience Questionnaire (MEQ) 329, 338

naloxone 342, 349, 351, 352
Napoleon Bonaparte 250, 365
narcotic bondage 312
Narcotics Control Law 426
national coverage, of drug-related deaths 447, **448–449**
National Drug Law Enforcement Agency (NDLEA) 384, 385
National Health Service (NHS) 447
National Institute of Mental Health (NIMH) 311
National Institute on Drug Abuse (NIDA) 93, 178, 481
naturally occurring 330
"the naturals" 584
Naysmyth, P. 132, 133
Nazi 244
necropolitics 156n11
necroviolence 156n11
Neinhaus, K. 69
Nembutal 313
neoliberalism 90, 91, 99
neolocalism 116
Nestle, M. 94
Netherlands 24, 26, 27, 242, 244, 320, 401
The Nether World (Gissing, 1889) 558
networking 183, 184
neural respiratory drive (NRD) 320
neurology 418, 587–589
neuroscience 93
new prudentialism 97
new psychoactive substances (NPS) 195
newspapers 163, 401, 413, 444, 447, **448, 449, 451**
nic'd out 42, 48
nic'd up 33–49
Nicholls, J. 550, 595n41
nicotine 458; circadian rhythms 264; control and calibration 41–43; drug, set, and setting 263–267; identity 266–267; more-than-human theory 264–265; performativity 266–267; place-embedded social practices 265–266; spatial politics 266–267; vaping 33–49
nicotine replacement therapy (NRT) 265
NIDA *see* National Institute on Drug Abuse (NIDA)
'Nietzsche sickness' 73, 81
Nigeria: cannabis use, social deviance and policing 390–391; drug laws and enforcement practices in 383–385; policing, structural violence and well-being 391–392; social exclusion and cannabis use among

street-involved youths 388–390; street habitus and responses to policing 392–394
Nigerian Police Force (NPF) 385
Nigeria, recreational drug use in: constructing and reinforcing masculinity 62–63; coping with diverse negative emotions 55–58; data analysis 55; gendering, of drug use 52–53; heartbreaks management 58; participants and interviews 53–54, **54**; pleasurable sex enhancement 60; sexual arousal 61–62; smoking competition 62–63; study site 53–54; tramadol, in sex elongation 58–60; women's power in sex negotiation 61
"Night Eagle" 246
Nixon, R. 24, 464
Non-Aligned Movement 144
non-drinking academics 185
non-lethal weapons (NLWs) 239
normalisation 92
normative substantiation 278
North America 118, 127, 145, 153, 155, 277, 364, 444, 446, 472

obesity 98
O'Brien, J.A. 531
Oda, S. 415, 417
The Odd Women (Gissing, 1893) 558
Office for National Statistics (ONS) 447
Oldenburg, R. 160, 164
O'Malley, P. 97
onion hosting 102
online drug market: drug commodification 105–106; drug making 104–105; illicit drug culture 101–103; infrastructure 107–108; research 103; risk-reflexive subjectivity 106–107; supply chain effects 105–106; user subjectivity 101
ontopolitically-oriented approach 342–356
opiate use 25
opioid overdose 349–350
opioid withdrawal syndrome 351
opium 247, 249–250
Oppenheim, J. 567
oppositional valence 26
oppression illness 386
Orford, J. 78
organisational culture 181
Osborne, G.B. 63
'The Ostler' (1855) 557
Ōtomo Tabito 587, 597n30
Ottoman 144, 146, 147
Our Mutual Friend (1864–1865) 547, 552
Outing (magazine) 71
Out of It (Walton, 2003) 89
overdose 309, 317–320, 349–352

Paasonen, S. 280, 286
Pakistan 246
Papazian, C. 114
Papua New Guinea 145
Paradise (Kennedy, 2004) 81
Parker, H. 93
Partanen, J. 297
Partlicius, S. 585, 595n18
pastoral power 460
Pearce, L. 264, 266
performance and image-enhancing drugs (PIEDs) 342; hepatitis C transmission 348; and intoxication 352–355
Permanent Central Opium Board (PCOB) 474, 475
perverse implantation 275, 276
Pervitin 244
Peters, D.J. 440
pharmacogenic orgasm 322n5
Pharmacopoeia 24
pharmacothymia 322n5
pharmakon 98
Phillips, R. 502
Philopon *see* methamphetamine
The Physiology of Temperance and Total Abstinence (1853) 549
PIEDs *see* performance and image-enhancing drugs (PIEDs)
Pienaar, K. 345
The Pilgrim's Progress (Bunyan, 1678; 1684) 71, 72, 73
Pini, M. 137
Pioneer Total Abstinence Association 526, 532
PippUK 332, 339n1
"pito do pango" 368
pleasure 27–29, 35, 89, 198–199
Plester, B. 179, 180
Poland 13, 244, 261, 262, 266, 501, 508, 516
policing: social deviance and 390–391; street habitus and responses to 392–394
policy stakeholder 489–495
The politics and poetics of transgression (Stallybrass and White, 1986) 163
Pollak, M. 370
polydrug 56
Porter, R. 588
Portuguese 362
positivism, limits of 320–322
post-addicts 315, 316
post-Cold War 144
Post Office (1971) 77
Poststructural Interview Analysis 207
post-traumatic stress disorder (PTSD) 246
Posture Code (1830) 367, 368
"The Potato Eaters" 21
potency, drug 104, 106–108
prescription drugs 1, 4, 64, 182, 224, 314
Presley, E. 22
Priestley, J. 71

prisons: drug dealing in 197; intoxication in 191–199; prisoner society 196–198
problematisation 290–292
prohibition 469
promotion 290–292
proportion 290–292
propranolol 247
Protestantism 71, 291
Prozac 21
psilocybin 330
psychedelics 25, 104, 330; context of 331–334; inner experiences 334–336; methodological considerations 329–331; peaking in psychedelic experiences 336; renaissance 338; role of setting 333–334; subsiding intoxication 337; trip planning 332–333
psychoactive commodities 90, 93, 95, 96
psychoactive substances 9, 20, 22, 37, 53, 89, 92, 182, 195, 291, 293–298, 301, 401, 441
psychoactive weapons 248–249
Psychochemical Warfare: A New Concept of War 250
psychonauts 328, 329, 331
psychotoxic arsenals 250–253
psychotoxic water 253
Public Health (Alcohol) Act 523, 537
Public Health England (PHE) 447
public health policy 291
pubs 116, 159, 160, 162–164, 167, 199, 517, 531
pub test 276, 287n1

Quan, A.M.L. 446
queer cultures 272–287
3-quinuclidinyl benzilate (BZ) 252

racism 373
Rado, S. 312, 316, 322n5
Rapadura 372, 378n2
Rappaport, E. 565
rationality 106–107
re-addiction 311, 312
real ale 116, 120, 123n1
reciprocal demonization 26
recreational drug use, in Nigeria: constructing and reinforcing masculinity 62–63; coping with diverse negative emotions 55–58; data analysis 55; gendering, of drug use 52–53; heartbreaks management 58; participants and interviews 53–54, **54**; pleasurable sex enhancement 60; sexual arousal 61–62; smoking competition 62–63; study site 53–54; tramadol, in sex elongation 58–60; women's power in sex negotiation 61
red oil 252
Reducing Americans' Vulnerability to Ecstasy (RAVE) Act 136
Reed, J. 547
Reese, J.F. 116
the reformation 501
Reinarman, C. 28
Release and *Scottish Drug Forum* 441
Renaissance 29
Reverse Pingpong 332
Reynolds, S. 129, 138n3
Rhodes, T. 204, 205, 277
rhythmanalysis 264
Rio de Janeiro 365–367, 371
risk 437–453, 512
risk environment 193, 199n2
risk-reflexive subjectivity 106–107
Ritalin 21
Ritchie, J.E. 162
rituals: beneficial outcomes 297–299; of cigarette smoking 463; communitas 296–297; and conservatism 299–300; controlled decontrolling 295–296; culture and 292–293; drinking 293; gift giving in 297; in modernity 300–303; process 293297; to reflexivity 290–304; transformation 301–303; transition 294–295
Robinson, D. 120
Robinson, S. 247
Rodrigues, N. 374
Rohypnol (Ruchy) 54, 56, 63
Rolfe, A. 78
Rolleston, R.D. 583
The Romantic Ethic and the Spirit of Modern Consumerism (Campbell, 1987) 91
Room, R. 92, 595n1
Roseberry, W. 118
Rosenbaum, M. 29n1, 132
Rosenzweig, R. 26
round-buying 166
Royal Navy 245
Ruchy (Rohypnol) 54, 56, 63
A Rumor of War 248
Rush, B. 472, 543, 546, 589, 590, 595n42

Sagvaag, H. 180, 184
St Patrick's Day 523
Sala, G. 159, 160, 167, 170
Sandberg, S. 383, 386, 391
Sanders, E. 266–267
Sao Paulo 362
Sarajevo 145, 147–149
Sarmatism 508
Saturday Night and Sunday Morning (1958) 77
Sauerbronn, J.F.R. 120
Saunders, N. 136
scapegoating 11–12, 510
scaremongering approach 127
Schivelbusch, W. 163
Schmidt-Semisch, H. 261
Schnell, S.M. 116
Schüll, N.D. 95

science and technology studies (STS) 343, 345
scientific racism 373
secrecy 240
Sedgley, J. 547
Šehović, A. 145, 152, 153
self-actualisation 463
self-control 69, 75, 276
self-flagellation 74, 77
self-government 194
self-medication 194, 195, 272, 273, 310, 464
Senanayake, N. 458
sensation fiction 549–550
sensuous perplexity 458
sex negotiation, women's power in 61
sexual arousal 61–62
sexual drifting 278–280
sexual drinking 279
sexual harassment 185
Shilling, C. 301
Shiman, L. 546, 559n11
Shroomery 330, 339n1
Shulgin, A. 127, 130
side effect 105
Siegel, R.K. 132–133, 309, 310
Sierra Leone 246
Silk Road 92
Sillitoe, A. 77
Simmel, G. 165
Sinatra, F. 22
Singapore, smoking point in 459–461
Single Convention on Narcotic Drugs 470, 471
Skarbek, D. 196
Sketches by Boz (1836) 552
Slade, G. 197
Slatter, R. 172
slaves 365, 366
Small, W. 227, 230, 231, 236
smart drugs 92
Smith, B.A. 527
Smith, E. 566
Smith, R. 275
smoking 34, 160; and drinking 162; (not-so-) toxic geographies of 458–463
smoking ban 459, 460
smoking competition 62–63
smoking corners 461–462
smoking games 62
smoking points, in Yishun, Singapore 459, *460–462,* 462
social and personal control mechanism 75–83
social class 53, 115, 117–119, 318, 383, 488
social constructionism 54
social context 262–264, 317
social control 26, 27
social deviance and policing 390–391
social exclusion 388–390
Socialist Federal Republic of Yugoslavia (SFRY) 144, 155n1
social marginalization 393
social media 123, 185
social organisation and drugs 196–198
social practice theory 265, 266
social smoking 264, 268
social supply 101, 102
Somalia 246, 400, 403, 404
Somali immigrants 401
Somali problem 408
Sournia, J.-C. 550, 595n3
Sousslof, C. 29n1
Soviet Afghan War 248
Span, S. 69, 75
Spicer, A. 182
spill-over 470
Spracklen, K. 120
Starck, P. 131
Starmer, S. 135
Starowolski, S. 508
'state-change' 287
status anxiety 279
status politics 23, 92, 93
status recategorization 118
Steinbeck, J. 73, 74
Stepney, M. 184
Stergaard, J. 303
Stevens, J. 131
Stevenson, R.L. 542
stigmatization 266, 267
Stimulant Control Law (1951) 414, 420–422
Stimulants and Narcotics (Anstie, 1865) 275
Stojaković, J. 154
Stolac 150–151
Stopka, T. 394
Storming Heaven (Stevens, J.) 131
The Straits Times (2021a) 460
Strang, J. 309, 318, 319
Straus, E. 312
stress 40
Stretton, H. 545
structural violence 385–386, 391–392
structural vulnerability 385–386
Stubbs, C.W. 569
STV News 452
substance use 52
sudden sickness 78
Sue 490
Sufi mystics 145
suicidal comfort 548
Sulkunen, P. 345
The Sun (newspaper) 128, 134
supply chain 105–106
Swedish National Board of Health and Welfare 409
'The Swimmer' (Cheever, 1964) 69, 74

Sydenham, T. 595n15
Sykes, G. 193
symbolism 121, 122
synthetic cannabinoid receptor agonists (SCRAs) 195
Syria 246
Szymkiewicz, J. 508

Tai, H. 420
Taiping Rebellion 250
take-home naloxone 348
Tan, Q.H. 264, 265
Tatetsu, S. 419
Taylor, D. 552
tea: addiction 564–577; drunkenness 573–576; excessive drinking 568, 574; mind and body 570–573; nerves and degeneration 566–570
temperance fiction 549–550
temperance movement 23, 413, 544
The Tenant of Wildfell Hall (Anne, 1848) 71, 547, 551, 560n15
tetrahydrocannabinol (THC) 252, 476, 477
Thackeray, W. 547
Thaemlitz, T. 129, 137, 138n4
THC *see* tetrahydrocannabinol (THC)
thematic analysis 55
This Side of Paradise (Fitzgerald, 1920) 77
Thompson, H.S. 334
Thompson, L. 264
Thurnell-Read, T. 120, 170
tobacco 21, 23, 161, 262; British per capita consumption (1850) 161; in China 167–168; in England 23; pipe 163; scholarship 262–263; Tobacco 21 law 36
tolerance 317–318
Tompkins, C. 196, 197
Toner, D. 525
Tor 102
Tortilla Flat (Steinbeck, 1935) 73
toxic 457–458
toxicity: geographies of 457–458
traditional-punishment model 69–75, 81
tramadol 51–52, 54, 58–60
Trance and Dance in Bali (documentary film, 1952) 30n6
transgression 75
Treasure Island (Stevenson, 1881–1882) 542
Treaty of Versailles 474
Treeby, M. 70, 73
trip reports 328–339
Trocki, C. 92
Trojan War 247
Trollope, A. 545, 553
Trotter, T. 543, 544, 546, 558, 589, 590, 594, 598n47
Turkey 145
Turner, J.E. 591, 592, 594, 598n57
Turner, V. 293, 294, 296, 299, 300, 302
Twain, M. 26
Twitter 92, 123

Uchendu, E. 57
The UK: brewpubs in 115; Campaign for Real Ale (CAMRA) 115, 120; drug-related deaths 437–439; ecstasy and dance culture in 132–136; penal power in prisons 194
'The Unbeliever' (Bishop, 1946) 72, 73, 81
uninhibited play 281–286
United Nations Office of Drugs (UNOD) 469
United Nations on Drugs and Crime (UNODC) 475
United Nations Single Convention on Narcotic Drugs 382
United States Dispensatory 24
University of Sydney Human Research Ethics Committee 274
The US: alcohol prohibition 28; The Beatles in 22; cannabis, and opiates in 25; craft breweries in 114, 115; drug-related deaths in 439–440; saloons 164; status politics 23
US Chemical Corps 251
U.S. Food and Drug Administration 313
US Harrison Act (1914) 240
US Narcotic Farm 311, 315
U.S. National Institute on Drug Abuse 206
US Navy Special Warfare Development Group 246
US Patent and Trademark Office 239

Valentine, K. 206
valium (diazepam) 247
Valverde, M. 35, 591
Van de Baan, F.C. 192
Vanity Fair (Thackeray, 1848) 547
vaping 463; competences 34; control and calibration 41–43; forging social connection and community 43–47; functional intoxication 37–41; intoxicating elements 37–47, **38–39**; materials 34; meanings 34; as skeuomorphic assemblage 264; spatial flexibility 34–35
Vasilou, E. 198
Veblen, T. 160, 165, 519n7
Vermeer, J. 21
vertical drinking 510
Veyne, P. 205
vice of drunkenness 371
Vietnam War 251
violence 185
violent syndicates 426
vital materialism 169
Volkow, N. 593
Von Brühl-Cramer, C. 590, 592, 598n50

Von Felsinger, J. 316
Vrecko, S. 98
vulnerability 442, 446

Walker, B. 181
Wallace, A. 120
Walsh, D. 533
Walton, S. 89, 90
Ware, J.R. 162
warfare, intoxicants in: drug use by combatants 241–248; historiography 240–241; psychoactive weapons 248–253
Warner, J. 582, 595n5
Warner, M. 283, 286
war on drugs 24, 240, 382
Washington, G. 242
Wasson, G. 328
Watt, J. 514
The Way We Live Now (1875) 553
Weber, M. 96
Webster, F. 444
Weinberg, D. 592–594, 598n75
Weschler, L. 30n3
West, C. 52
Wetherspoon, J.D. 515
Whitaker, M. 183
WHO *see* World Health Organization (WHO)
Wikler, A. 309, 311–315, 320
Wilmot, R. 278–280, 286
Wilson, T.M. 524, 525
Wilton, R. 53
wine 23, 118, 296, 469, 583
'withdrawal-relief' recovery method 69, 74
Withington, P. 164
Wodehouse, P.G. 72
The Woman in White (Collins, 1860) 549–550
The Women of England series (1839–1843) 555
'women's alcohol' 52
Wood, E. 545, 549
Wood, J. 575
workplace, alcohol use in 179–181
World Health Organization (WHO) 20, 203, 204, 311
World War I 162, 477, 527
World War II 28, 162, 309, 383
Worlidge, J. 507
Wright, M.A. 135
Wurdz, G. 71

'X' *see* ecstasy

Yates, S. 494
Yomiuri Shinbun 413
Yoshida Kendō 587
Young, M. 95, 267
Young Woman's Tract 555
Yugoslavia 143
yuppie coffee 118

Zeff, L. 130
zero-tolerance policy 196, 224
Zieger, S. 568
Zimmerman, D.H. 52
Zinberg, N.E. 104, 193, 261, 262, 297, 329, 333, 337
Zulus 243
Zuxiang, W. 168
Zwingli, H. 505

Printed in Great Britain
by Amazon

62105431R10360